HUMAN RIGHTS AND
CRIMINAL JUSTICE

AUSTRALIA
Law Book Co.
Sydney

CANADA and USA
Carswell
Toronto

HONG KONG
Sweet & Maxwell Asia

NEW ZEALAND
Brookers
Wellington

SINGAPORE and MALAYSIA
Sweet & Maxwell Asia
Singapore and Kuala Lumpur

HUMAN RIGHTS
AND
CRIMINAL JUSTICE

Second Edition

by

Ben Emmerson Q.C.
of the Middle Temple, Barrister
and
Andrew Ashworth Q.C. (Hon.)
Vinerian Professor of English Law
University of Oxford
and
Alison Macdonald
of Matrix Chambers,
Barrister

LONDON
SWEET & MAXWELL
2007

Published in 2007 by
Sweet & Maxwell Limited of
100 Avenue Road, Swiss Cottage, London NW3 3PF
(*http://www.sweetandmaxwell.co.uk*)
Typeset by Interactive Sciences Ltd, Gloucester
Printed and bound in Great Britain by William Clowes Ltd, Beccles, Suffolk

No natural forests were destroyed to make this product;
only farmed timber was used and replanted.

ISBN 97 80421876101

A catalogue record for this book
is available from the British Library

©
Ben Emmerson Q.C., Andrew Ashworth Q.C. & Alison Macdonald
2007

PREFACE

The years since the publication of the first edition in 2001 have seen a substantial increase in human rights-related cases. It was expected that the Human Rights Act would lead to many criminal cases in the English courts being decided, in part at least, by reference to human rights—mostly cases on procedure and evidence, but also some decisions on substantive criminal law and sentencing. But the European Court of Human Rights in Strasbourg has also increased its output of judgments, some of them with the UK as the respondent state, and many—such as *Stafford, Beckley, Edwards and Lewis*, and (soon to come) *O'Halloran and Francis*—have produced significant and controversial effects in English law.

In this second edition we endeavour to bring together and to analyse the relevant parts of European human rights law and their implications for English criminal practice, drawing also on wider comparative sources. Ben Emmerson and Andrew Ashworth were and are delighted that Alison Macdonald agreed to take on the role of co-editor of this edition. Thus Andrew Ashworth and Alison Macdonald have acted as editors, with Ben Emmerson assuming a general supervisory role. Individual chapters have been up-dated by members of the team of writers named on the title page, including Alison Macdonald and Andrew Ashworth, and final revisions were carried out by the editors. The preparation of this second edition has been a demanding task, and Ben Emmerson, Andrew Ashworth and Alison Macdonald wish to record their thanks to other members of the editorial team for their contributions, and to Caroline Shaw, Lindsay Emerson and others at Sweet and Maxwell for their forbearance and support. Our aim is to state the relevant law as at January 1, 2007, though it has been possible to take account of a few subsequent developments.

B.E.
A.A.
A.M.
May 2007.

LIST OF CONTRIBUTORS

General Editors

Ben Emmerson Q.C.
Barrister, Matrix Chambers

Andrew Ashworth Q.C. (Hon.)
Vinerian Professor of English Law, University of Oxford

Alison Macdonald
Barrister, Matrix Chambers

Contributors

Andrew Ashworth Q.C. (Hon.)
Vinerian Professor of English Law, University of Oxford

Alex Bailin
Barrister, Matrix Chambers

Andrew Choo
Professor of Law, University of Warwick; Barrister, Matrix Chambers

Danny Friedman
Barrister, Matrix Chambers

Phillippa Kaufmann
Barrister, Doughty Street Chambers

Charlotte Kilroy
Barrister, Matrix Chambers

Julian Knowles
Barrister, Matrix Chambers

Helen Law
Barrister, Matrix Chambers

Alison Macdonald
Barrister, Matrix Chambers

Blinne Ní Ghrálaigh
Barrister, Matrix Chambers

Duncan Penny
Barrister, 6 King's Bench Walk

Matthew Ryder
Barrister, Matrix Chambers

Michelle Strange
Barrister, Doughty Street Chambers

CONTENTS

PART ONE

APPENDICES

INDEX

TABLE OF CASES

TABLE OF EUROPEAN AND INTERNATIONAL LEGISLATION

TABLE OF UK STATUTES AND FOREIGN NATIONAL LEGISLATION

TABLE OF CASES BEFORE THE EUROPEAN COMMISSION ON HUMAN RIGHTS

TABLE OF CASES BEFORE THE EUROPEAN COURT OF HUMAN RIGHTS

CASES BEFORE THE INTER-AMERICAN COURT OF HUMAN RIGHTS

TABLE OF EUROPEAN CASES

TABLE OF RULES

TABLE OF UK STATUTORY INSTRUMENTS

CHAPTER 1

THE EUROPEAN CONVENTION ON HUMAN RIGHTS

A. INTRODUCTION

The European Convention for the Protection of Human Rights and Fundamental **1–01**
Freedoms[1] is an international treaty adopted by the Member States of the Council
of Europe and opened for signature in November 1950. The Convention was
ratified by the United Kingdom in March 1951, and entered into force in
September 1953. A state's obligations are defined by the Convention itself, read
together with those optional Protocols which the state has chosen to ratify[2] but
subject to any reservations[3] or derogations[4] which have been notified to the
Secretary General of the Council of Europe.

Any person, non-governmental organisation or group of individuals situated **1–02**
within the jurisdiction of a contracting state has a right of individual petition to
the European Court of Human Rights under Art.34 of the Convention. This
extends to legal as well as natural persons, and is not confined to those with a
lawful right to be present in the territory of the state concerned.[5] Before submitting a petition the applicant must first exhaust any effective or potentially
effective domestic remedies.[6] The petition must be filed within six months of the
date of the violation, or the date of the final domestic remedy touching on the
subject matter of the complaint.[7]

A decision of the court is final and binding.[8] Although the court does not have **1–03**
jurisdiction to quash the decisions of a national authority, or to overturn a

---

[1] Cmnd.8969.
[2] The United Kingdom has ratified Protocol 1, containing the right to property (Art.1), the right to
education (Art.2), and the duty to hold free elections (Art.3); Protocol 6 concerning the permanent
abolition of the death penalty; and Protocol 13 concerning the abolition of the death penalty in all
circumstances. The Government has indicated its intention to sign, ratify and incorporate Protocol 7
containing safeguards relating to the expulsion of aliens (Art.1), a right of appeal in criminal cases
(Art.2), a right to compensation for miscarriages of justice (Art.3), the prohibition on double jeopardy
(Art.4), and the right to equality between spouses (Art.5).
[3] See para.1–161 below.
[4] See para.1–164 below.
[5] *D. v United Kingdom* (1997) 24 E.H.R.R. 423.
[6] Art.35(1).
[7] Art.35(1).
[8] Art.46(1).

criminal conviction, its judgments are more than merely declaratory in nature. Under Art.41 of the Convention the court has power to award "just satisfaction" to the victim of a violation in the form of compensation for pecuniary and non-pecuniary loss, and to make a full award of costs. More importantly, the contracting states are under an obligation to "abide by the decision of the court in any case to which they are parties".[9] This obligation is enforceable by the Committee of Ministers of the Council of Europe which has the task of "supervising the execution" of the court's judgments.[10]

B. ORIGINS AND INFLUENCE[11]

I. The Universal Declaration of Human Rights

1–04   In the immediate aftermath of the Second World War the international community entered a phase of intense diplomatic activity aimed at establishing inter-governmental structures which could prevent a recurrence of the atrocities of the previous decade and, at the same time, forge new political alliances for the post-war era. On June 26, 1945 the United Nations Charter was signed in San Francisco. A Human Rights Commission was established by the United Nations to begin work on proposals for an International Bill of Rights. The early results looked promising. The Universal Declaration of Human Rights was adopted by the General Assembly of the United Nations on December 10, 1948. Shortly afterwards, however, attempts to create a legally enforceable system of international human rights protection within the United Nations ran into the buffer of diplomatic procrastination. The two United Nations covenants[12] defining the rights outlined in the Universal Declaration, and establishing international machinery for their enforcement, were not concluded until December 1966 and did not come into force for a further 10 years.

II. The Council of Europe

1–05   In Europe meanwhile the movement for greater political integration was gathering momentum. Unofficial European movements sprang up in a number of western European countries.[13] In 1948 these organisations united, at the Congress

---

[9] Formerly Art.53.

[10] In the exercise of their powers under Art.46(2). See para.1–159 below; and see generally Adam Tomkins, *The Committee of Ministers; Its roles under the European Convention on Human Rights* [1995] E.H.R.L.R. 49. Note however that the Committee of Ministers' role under Art.32 of the Convention has been abolished by Protocol 11.

[11] For a comprehensive overview of the history of the Convention see Lester and Pannick (eds), *Human Rights Law and Practice* (Butterworths, 1999) Ch.1. See also Marston, *The United Kingdom's Part in the Preparation of the European Convention on Human Rights 1950* (1993) 42 I.C.L.Q. 796; Anthony Lester "Fundamental Rights: the United Kingdom Isolated?" (1984) P.L. 46; *Collected Edition of the Travaux Préparatoires of the European Convention on Human Rights*.

[12] The International Covenant on Civil and Political Rights, and the International Covenant on Economic, Social and Cultural Rights.

[13] The principal organisations were the United Europe Movement in Britain; the Economic League for European Cooperation; the French Council for United Europe; the European Union of Federalists; *Nouvelles Équipes Internationales*; and the Socialist Movement for the United States of Europe.

of Europe in the Hague, to form the European Movement which was to act as a permanent but unofficial organisation to promote European unity. The Congress passed a number of resolutions around which the Council of Europe was subsequently constructed. Its international juridical section, which included Sir David Maxwell-Fyfe,[14] set about producing a draft human rights convention which would stand as a condition of entry to the new unified Europe.

Intergovernmental action soon followed. In January 1949 the governments of the **1–06** United Kingdom, France and the three Benelux countries convened a diplomatic conference attended by 10 European countries. Germany, which had not yet regained its sovereignty, was excluded. The conference was given the task of drafting a treaty for the establishment of a Council of Europe. In so doing, the 10 governments went a long way towards carrying out the proposals made at the Hague Congress.

The Statute of the Council of Europe was signed in London on May 5, 1949. The **1–07** preamble declared that the contracting states were:

> "reaffirming their devotion to the spiritual and moral values which are the common heritage of their peoples and the true source of individual freedom, political liberty, and the rule of law, principles which form the basis of all genuine democracy". This broad aspiration was reinforced by Article 3 of the Statute which provided that every member state "must accept the principles of the rule of law and of the enjoyment by all persons within its jurisdiction of human rights and fundamental freedoms".

The organs of the Council of Europe included an executive branch, the Commit- **1–08** tee of Ministers, which was made up of the Foreign Minister of each member state or their deputy; and a Parliamentary Assembly (originally known as the Consultative Assembly) consisting of elected members of the national parliaments. One of the Council of Europe's first tasks was to draft a legally binding human rights convention. The Committee of Ministers was asked by the Parliamentary Assembly to draw up a draft convention which would, for the most part, contain more specific defintions of the rights set out in the Universal Declaration of Human Rights, and which would establish a European Court of Human Rights for the purpose of ensuring collective enforcement.

III. The European Convention on Human Rights

The European Convention on Human Rights broke new ground in international **1–09** law in three important respects. First, it adopted a principle of collective enforcement of human rights. The signatory states recognised that the most effective way to prevent human rights abuses by public officials was to require states to submit to a form of external scrutiny which encroached on their national sovereignty. The responsibility for protecting human rights was no longer to rest with each state, but was to be a shared responsibility of the international community. Whereas international conventions had hitherto been regarded as reciprocal

---

[14] Later Home Secretary and Lord Chancellor Kilmuir.

arrangements between nation states, the European Convention on Human Rights created:

"a network of mutual, bilateral undertakings, objective obligations which, in the words of the preamble, benefit from a 'collective enforcement' ".[15]

In international law, these obligations bind all three branches of government—the Executive, the Legislature and the Judiciary.[16]

1–10   The second important departure from traditional international law was the inclusion of a right of individual petition—a recognition that individuals could have rights enforceable on the international plane. The right of individual petition lies at the heart of the Convention system, and has played a decisive role in its success. It has enabled individuals to seek remedies for human rights violations against the public authorities of their own states across a wide range of issues, and irrespective of whether the violation occurred through governmental or Executive action, through decisions of the elected legislature, or through rulings of the national courts.

1–11   The third important feature of the Convention system was the establishment of supervisory machinery to interpret, apply and enforce the Convention: the European Commission of Human Rights whose function was to determine the admissibility of a complaint, to establish the facts, and to express a non-binding opinion on the merits; the European Court of Human Rights, an independent and public judicial institution with one judge from each member state, whose function was to give a final and binding judgment and, if appropriate, to award just satisfaction in favour of the complainant; and the Committee of Ministers which had the dual functions of supervising the execution of court judgments, and determining the merits of any complaint which was not considered suitable for reference to the court.

1–12   Despite these innovative features the Convention was an international treaty, and like any international treaty, it contained the maximum acceptable to the state willing to go least far. That state was the United Kingdom. British diplomats lobbied hard for the right of individual petition to be made optional, and for the jurisdiction of the Commission to be conditional upon regular renewal. Their efforts were successful and the Convention enforcement machinery was weakened as a result. We are often reminded that the United Kingdom was the first state to ratify the Convention, in March 1951. But it is perhaps equally important

---

[15] *Ireland v United Kingdom* (1979–80) 2 E.H.R.R. 25, para.239; See also *Austria v Italy* (1961) 4 Y.B. 116 at 138: "The obligations undertaken by the High Contracting Parties in the Convention are essentially of an objective character, being designed rather to protect the fundamental rights of individual human beings from infringement by any of the High Contracting Parties than to create subjective and reciprocal rights for the High Contracting Parties."

[16] The position in national law is different: The Human Rights Act 1998 does not bind the Legislature so that it will, in some instances, remain possible for an individual's Convention rights to breached by incompatible primary legislation, without an effective remedy being available in the national courts.

to remember that the British government did not accept the right of individual petition until January 1966.[17]

IV. The influence of the Convention

The Convention came into force on September 23, 1953, but the court did not begin functioning until 1959. In the first 15 years of its operation the court heard an average of one case a year. In some years, it met only once and then only because it was required to do so under the Rules of Court for its plenary administrative session.[18] Since then however, the court's caseload has grown steadily, due partly to an increasing awareness of its existence among the citizens and lawyers of the member states, and partly to the enlargement of the Council of Europe itself.
1–13

The decisions of the European Commission and Court of Human Rights have produced a body of caselaw which extends its influence far beyond the parties to the individual case. Whilst a given judgment is only binding on the state concerned, other Convention states will look to the judgment for guidance as to the compatibility of their own domestic law with the requirements of the Convention.[19] In this way, the Convention has become "a constitutional instrument of European public order in the field of human rights".[20] As the former President of the court has put it, the Convention is now "the single most important legal and political common denominator of the states of Europe in its widest geographical sense".[21]
1–14

The influence of the Convention is not however confined to European legal systems. It was used as the basis for the human rights chapters in many of the independence constitutions adopted in Commonwealth Africa and the Commonwealth Caribbean. This was partly because British lawyers had played a central role in the drafting of the Convention, and partly because the United Kingdom had extended its obligations under the Convention to its dependent territories in 1953. The Convention was therefore an obvious source of inspiration for the Commonwealth constitutions. Commonwealth courts have come to accept the importance of interpreting equivalent constitutional guarantees in the light of their history and sources and, "whererever applicable, pronouncements on provisions similar to [constitutional human rights provisions] either by
1–15

---

[17] For a fascinating account of the ministerial and diplomatic negotiations behind this process, see Lord Lester of Herne Hill Q.C., "UK Acceptance of the Strasbourg Jurisdiction: What Really Went On in Whitehall in 1966" [1998] P.L. 327.

[18] Rolv Ryssdall, "The Coming of Age of the European Convention on Human Rights" [1996] E.H.R.L.R. 18 at 20.

[19] An example is the court's judgment in *Brogan v United Kingdom* (1989) 11 E.H.R.R. 117, following which the Netherlands introduced legislation restricting the time which may elapse between a suspect's arrest and first production in court.

[20] *Chrysostomos, Papachrysostomou and Loizidou v Turkey* (1991) 68 D.R. 216 at 242.

[21] Rolv Ryssdall, "The Coming of Age of the European Convention on Human Rights" [1996] E.H.R.L.R. 18.

national courts or by international institutions".[22] Given that the text of many of these constitutional human rights guarantees is the same or very similar to the Convention, it is hardly surprising that the judgments of the European Court of Human Rights have been cited with approval by the constitutional courts of Canada, New Zealand, South Africa, Hong Kong, India, Zimbabwe and Mauritius, amongst others, and have served as a useful source of guidance for the Privy Council in exercising its constitutional jurisdiction. In 2003, the caselaw of the European Court was cited for the first time by the United States Supreme Court.[23] This cross-fertilization of jurisprudence reflects not only the close relationship of the various texts, but also the universality of the underlying concepts and values.

1–16   On the international plane, the European Convention was the model for the American Convention on Human Rights, which came into force in 1978, and served as one of the principal reference texts for those drafting the African Convention on Human and Peoples' Rights. The caselaw of the European Court of Human Rights has been extensively relied upon by the institutions established under both of these regional mechanisms. References to Convention caselaw are also to be found in the decisions of the United Nations treaty bodies, including the decisions of the Human Rights Committee on individual applications under the Optional Protocol to the International Covenant on Civil and Political Rights, and in the decisions of the International Criminal Tribunal for the Former Yugoslavia and Rwanda.

1–17   Finally, it should be recalled that the court itself has given the Convention a measure of extra-territorial effect by holding that decisions to extradite[24] or deport[25] individuals to non-Convention countries where they risk treatment in violation of their Convention rights may engage the responsibility of the expelling state; and by holding that states are obliged to refuse their co-operation in criminal matters where an individual's conviction has resulted from a flagrant denial of justice in a non-Convention state.[26]

C. PROCEDURE

I. Institutional reform

1–18   By the early 1990s the Convention system had become a victim of its own success. Between 1988 and 1994 the number of applications registered by the Commission trebled from just over 1,000 each year to a little under 3,000. In the first 15 years of its operation, the court considered an average of one case a year.

---

[22] *Pointu and Others v The Minister of Education and Anor.* (1996) S.C.J. 359, Supreme Court of Mauritius. See generally Vinod Boolel, "The Influence of the European Convention on the Constitutional Law of Mauritius" [1996] E.H.R.L.R. 159.

[23] *Lawrence v Texas* 59 US 558 (2003).

[24] *Soering v United Kingdom* (1989) 11 E.H.R.R. 439.

[25] *D v United Kingdom* (1997) 24 E.H.R.R. 423; *Hilal v United Kingdom* (2001) 33 E.H.R.R. 31.

[26] *Drozd and Janousek v France and Spain* (1992) 14 E.H.R.R. 745.

By 1995 that figure had grown to more than 60 cases a year. The court took until 1985 to deliver its first 100 judgments. In the 10 years which followed, it delivered 550.

The growing number of cases meant that it already took an average of five years **1–19** between the initial lodging of an application by the Commission, and the final determination of a case by the court or the Committee of Ministers. The two-tier procedure also gave rise to a considerable duplication of effort and expense. With the admission of new member states the position was set to worsen. By the early 1990s it was becoming clear that the machinery would break down under the strain if it was not substantially overhauled. At the same time there was an increasing recognition that the role of the Committee of Ministers, a political body, in adjudicating on certain Convention complaints was anomalous. There was now a general agreement that the system of protection under the Convention should become fully judicial.

Negotiations began for the adoption of a new Protocol to the Convention which **1–20** would have the twin objectives of simplifying the structure with a view to shortening the length of proceedings and strengthening the judicial character of the system. These negotiations reached their conclusion when Protocol 11 was opened for signature by the member states on May 11, 1994. Protocol 11 abolished the European Commission of Human Rights and provided for the establishment of a single full-time court to replace the previous two-tier system. It also abolished the role of the Committee of Ministers in adjudicating on complaints, confining its functions to the supervision of states' compliance with the judgments of the court.

Protocol 11 entered into force on November 1, 1998. The new court inherited a **1–21** backlog of 6,000 cases. With the disappearance of the Commission in November 1999, there were more than 16,000 cases awaiting determination. At the time of writing, further reform of the system is pending with the imminent coming into force of Protocol 14, which builds on the changes brought about by Protocol 11. Unlike Protocol 11, Protcol 14 leaves unchanged the structure of the court and the basic procedures for bringing a case, but introduces changes designed primarily to regulate the workload of the court, especially at admissibility stage. The changes which will be brough about by Protocol 14 are considered at 1–171 to 1–176 below. However, the fundamental system will remain that created by Protocol 11. That is examined below, after considering the system which it replaced.

II. The procedure prior to November 1998

The former procedure is of more than merely historical interest. Under s.2(1) of **1–22** the Human Rights Act 1998 a domestic court or tribunal determining any question which has arisen in connection with a Convention right is required to take into account not only judgments of the Court but also decisions of the Commission under former Art.26 and 27(2) of the Convention,[27] Commission

---

[27] Under Protocol 11 the admissibility criteria which were formerly set out in Arts 26 and 27(2) of the Convention are now embodied in Art.35(1) and (3).

opinions given in a report adopted under former Art.31, and decisions of the Committee of Ministers under Art.46.[28]

1–23   Prior to the coming into force of Protocol 11, it was for the Commission to ascertain the facts of the case, and to determine the admissibility of the application under former Arts 26 and 27. Article 26 embodied the requirement for the prior exhaustion of effective or potentially effective domestic remedies and the requirement that a complaint be introduced within six months of the date of the violation, or the conclusion of the last domestic remedy touching on the subject matter of the complaint.[29] Article 27 required the Commission to reject as inadmissible any complaint which was anonymous, which was substantially the same as a complaint previously considered by the Commission or "another procedure of international investigation or settlement", or which the Commission considered to be: (a) incompatible with the Convention; (b) manifestly ill-founded; or (c) an abuse of the right of petition.[30] Proceedings before the Commission were strictly confidential and Commission hearings took place in private.

1–24   Once a case had been declared admissible, the Commission was required to put itself at the disposal of the parties with a view to securing a friendly settlement pursuant to former Art.28(1)(b).[31] In the absence of a friendly settlement, the Commission was required to express its opinion on the merits of the complaint in a report adopted under former Art.31. Thereafter, the case could be referred to the court for a final and binding judgment, either by the Commission or by the government, but not by the applicant.[32] This had to be done within a period of three months from the adoption of the Commission's report on the case.[33] Protocol 9, which permitted individuals to refer a case from the Commission to the Court was never signed or ratified by the United Kingdom. The Court could only examine those complaints which had been declared admissible by the Commission.

1–25   If neither the Commission nor the government referred the case to the Court, it was referred for decision by the Committee of Ministers under former Art.32(1). The execution of Court judgments was supervised by the Committee of Ministers

---

[28] The references in s.2(1) are apt to confuse since s.2(1)(b) and (c) refer to the *former* Arts 26, 27(2) and 31 of the Convention relating to the functions of the Commission, whereas s.2(1)(c) refers to the function of the Committee of Ministers under Art.46 of the Convention *as amended by Protocol 11*. Note however that s.21(3) of the 1998 Act provides that for this purpose the reference to Art.46 is to be taken as including a reference to Arts 32 and 54 of the Convention immediately prior to its amendment (i.e. it includes "judicial" decisions of the Committee of Ministers under the old procedure).

[29] These requirements are now to be found in Art.35(1), see paras 1–46 to 1–70 below.

[30] These admissibility criteria are now contained in Art.35(2) and (3) and are, of course, determined by the court; see paras 1–71 to 1–96 below.

[31] This function is now performed by the court pursuant to Art.38(1)(b), see para.1–107 below.

[32] Former Arts 44 and 48.

[33] Former Art.47.

in the exercise of their powers under former Art.54.[34] Under Protocol 11, the Committee of Ministers' enforcement functions are now to be found in Art.46(2).

Accordingly, under s.2(1) of the Human Rights Act 1998 domestic courts are **1–26** required to have regard to: (i) Court judgments and (under the new procedure) Court admissibility decisions; (ii) Commission admissibility decisions; (iii) Commission decisions on the merits of a complaint; and (iv) Committee of Ministers' decisions supervising the execution of court judgments and adjudicating on the merits of a complaint which was not referred to the court.[35]

III. The procedure under Protocol 11

Protocol 11 to the Convention, which entered into force on November 1, 1998, **1–27** provides for the establishment of a single full time Court to replace the previous two-tier system. The procedure to be followed in proceedings before the Court is set out in Protocol 11 itself, and in the Rules of Court.[36] The Court has a power to issue practice directions[37] and may depart from the prescribed procedure in a particular case, after first consulting the parties.[38]

The Court sits in Committees (of three judges), in Chambers (of seven judges) **1–28** and, exceptionally, in a Grand Chamber (of 17 judges).[39] The President of the Court is currently Mr Wildhaber (Switzerland). The Court is currently divided into five sections pursuant to Art.27 of the Convention; each Committee or Chamber consists of three or seven judges drawn from the same section. At the time of writing, Mr Rozakis (Greece) is President of the First Section; Mr Costa (France) is President of the Second Section; Mr Zupančič (Slovenia) is President of the Third Section; Sir Nicolas Bratza (United Kingdom) is President of the Fourth Section; and Mr Lorenzen (Denmark) is President of the Fifth Section.[40] The national judge sits *ex officio* in any case brought against the state in respect of which he was elected,[41] but may not preside in any such case.[42]

---

[34] See para.1–159 below.

[35] s.21(3) of the Human Rights Act 1998 provides that the reference in s.2(1)(d) to Art.46 includes a reference to Arts 32 and 54 of the Convention immediately prior to its amendment by Protocol 11.

[36] At the time of writing, the current version of the Rules of Court was that dated July 2006; updates and amendments can be obtained at *www.echr.coe.int*.

[37] Rules of Court, r.32. There are currently practice directions on requests for interim measures, the institution of proceedings under Art.34, and written pleadings.

[38] r.31.

[39] Art.27(1); rr.24–27.

[40] Up to date information about the composition of the court and its work can be obtained at *www.echr.coe.int*.

[41] Art.27(2).

[42] r.13.

Institution of proceedings

1–29 An individual application must be submitted in writing and signed by the applicant or his or her representative.[43] Unless the President of the Chamber decides otherwise, an application must be made on the application form provided by the Registry.[44] The application must set out the name, date of birth, nationality, sex, occupation and address of the applicant[45]; the name, occupation and address of his or her representative, if any[46]; the name of the respondent state[47]; a succinct statement of the facts and of the alleged violation of the Convention and relevant argument[48]; a succinct statement of the applicant's compliance with the admissibility criteria[49]; and a statement of the object of the application, including any claims for just satisfaction which the applicant may wish to make under Art.41.[50] It must accompanied by copies of any relevant documents, including judgments of the domestic courts.[51]

Legal Representation and Legal Aid

1–30 There is no requirement that an applicant must be legally represented for the purposes of the initial submission of an application.[52] However, representation is mandatory for any oral hearing, and for any written proceedings which take place after a case has been declared admissible, unless the President of the Chamber decides otherwise.[53] The applicant's representative must generally be an advocate who is: (a) authorised to practice in one of the contracting states; *and* (b) resident in the territory of one of the contracting states.[54] If the applicant wishes to be represented by someone who does not fulfil these criteria then the specific approval of the President must be obtained.[55] Either way, a signed power of attorney or authority to act must be supplied to the Registry.[56] In exceptional cases, the President may direct the applicant to seek alternative representation if he considers that the circumstances or conduct of the advocate warrant this course.[57]

1–31 Legal aid is not available from the court for the initial preparation or submission of an application. Some domestic funding, under the Legal Services Commission's legal help scheme, may be available to assist in making the initial

---

[43] r.45(1).
[44] r.47(1).
[45] r.47(1)(a).
[46] r.47(1)(b).
[47] r.47(1)(c).
[48] r.47(1)(d) and (e).
[49] r.47(1)(f).
[50] r.47(1)(g).
[51] r.47(1)(h).
[52] r.36(1).
[53] r.36(3). If the President gives the applicant leave to present his or her own case, this may be made subject to a requirement that the applicant be assisted by an advocate or other approved representative.
[54] r.36(4)(a).
[55] r.36(2).
[56] r.45(3).
[57] r.36(4)(b). Such a direction may be made at any stage of the proceedings.

application. Once an application has been communicated to the respondent government, the President of the Chamber may grant Council of Europe legal aid to the applicant for all subsequent stages in the proceedings,[58] if it is necessary for the proper conduct of the case, and the applicant has insufficient means to meet all or part of the costs entailed.[59] Any case which has been communicated to the respondent government will, almost by definition, satisfy the first of these requirements. As to the second requirement, an application for legal aid must be accompanied by a form declaring the applicant's capital, income, and financial obligations, duly certified (where appropriate) by the relevant domestic authorities.[60] The relevant domestic authority in the United Kingdom is the Legal Services Commission. The court does not, however, apply the national threshold for eligibility, and may be willing to grant legal aid where the applicant's means would not qualify on domestic scales. The decision to grant or refuse legal aid is to be made by the President[61] after the government has been afforded an opportunity to submit any comments in writing.[62] The Registrar will then fix the rate of fees and expenses to be paid in accordance with the scales currently in force.[63]

Council of Europe legal aid encompasses legal fees, travel and subsistence **1–32** expenses, and any other costs or expenses necessarily incurred in pursuing the application.[64] The rates are not generous compared with the scale of fees charged by lawyers in the United Kingdom. However, the professional rules of both branches of the legal profession allow conditional fee agreements to be made in respect of litigation in Strasbourg. In the event of a finding of a violation, the court will generally award costs in favour of the applicant on an equitable basis.[65] Any sums already paid in legal aid will be deducted from the court's award of costs.[66]

Interim Measures

Under r.39[67] the Chamber or, in an urgent case, its President may indicate to the **1–33** respondent government any interim measures which it considers should be adopted in the interests of the parties or of the proper conduct of the proceedings before it.[68] Such an indication may be given either at the request of the applicant, or by the court of its own motion. The procedure is designed primarily to ensure that once the court is seized of a complaint, the respondent state does not take

---

[58] r.91.
[59] r.92.
[60] r.93.
[61] r.93(3).
[62] r.93(2).
[63] r.95.
[64] r.94(2).
[65] See para.1–147 below.
[66] This is standard procedure for all successful legally aided applications.
[67] Formerly, r.36. The Court's Practice Direction on requests for interim measures is set out at (2003) 36 E.H.R.R. CD 153 and on the court's website at *www.echr.coe.int.*
[68] r.39(1).

steps which would deprive any subsequent finding of a violation of its practical effect.

1–34   An application for interim relief must be made promptly, and must be accompanied by a statement of the facts, and an outline of the applicant's complaint under the Convention. Rule 39 may not be invoked if the applicant is still in the process of exhausting a potentially effective domestic remedy, unless the remedy is incapable of having suspensive effect. Subject to these requirements, an application can be dealt with very speedily indeed, and sometimes within a matter of hours.[69] A r.39 indication will usually be made for a limited but renewable period. If the court declines to give such an indication, it may nevertheless take urgent steps to communicate the complaint to the government concerned, and may expedite the hearing of the application.[70]

1–35   The court will only grant interim relief if it considers that there is a real risk of irreparable harm to the applicant, and there is "good reason to believe" that a violation will eventually be found.[71] Interim measures have generally been confined to expulsion cases (deportation or extradition), where it is alleged that the applicant will be killed or will suffer ill-treatment in breach of Arts 2 or 3 of the Convention. In *Soering v United Kingdom*[72] the applicant complained that his extradition to the United States to face trial for murder would expose him to prolonged detention on "death row" in breach of Art.3. The President indicated to the government that:

> "it was desirable, in the interests of the parties and the proper conduct of the proceedings, not to extradite the applicant to the United States until the Court had an opportunity to examine the application".

It is not always necessary, however for the applicant to establish a risk of intentional ill-treatment. Serious health risks may sometimes suffice. In *Poku v United Kingdom*[73] a request was made in respect the proposed deportation of a woman who was in the late stages of a difficult pregnancy and who had a history of miscarriages. Likewise, in *D v United Kingdom*[74] a request for suspension was made in respect of an applicant who was suffering from AIDS, and who alleged that he would be deprived of treatment if he were deported to St Kitts. In *Evans v United Kingdom*[75] the court granted interim relief requesting that the applicant's embryos be preserved until it determined whether the refusal of the Human Fertilisation and Embryology Authority to allow her to have IVF treatment following her partner's withdrawal of consent violated Arts 2, 8 and 14 of the Convention.[76]

---

[69] For detailed explanation of the procedure, see Simor and Emmerson (eds.), *Human Rights Practice* (Sweet & Maxwell, 2000, and twice-yearly updates), Chs 19 to 21.

[70] r.40; see para.1–43 below.

[71] *Cruz Varas v Sweden* (1992) 14 E.H.R.R. 1 at para.103.

[72] (1989) 11 E.H.R.R. 439.

[73] (1996) Application No.26985/95.

[74] (1997) 24 E.H.R.R. 243.

[75] (2006) 43 E.H.R.R. 21.

[76] The court subsequently rejected the application on the merits.

The court has generally been unwilling to grant interim relief in relation to   **1-36**
detention or fair trial issues. There are, however, exceptions. In *Llijkov v Bulgaria*[77] a request was made concerning measures to protect the health of a
prisoner on hunger strike. And in *Ocalan v Turkey*[78] the court took the unusual
course of requesting assurances that the leader of the Kurdish separatist movement (PKK) would receive adequate facilities to ensure that his trial for alleged
terrorist offences was fair.[79]

Where a r.39 indication has been given, the Chamber will notify the Committee   **1-37**
of Ministers[80] and may request information from the respondent state.[81] Such an
indication is not, however, binding on the government concerned.[82] The Court
relies on the goodwill and co-operation of the contracting states.[83] Although
states have almost invariably complied with such requests, the Court has held
that this does not give rise to an enforceable expectation of compliance. In *Cruz
Varas v Sweden*[84] the applicant was expelled to Chile, despite a r.39 indication
requesting suspension of the deportation order. The applicant argued that the
action of the Swedish authorities was an interference with the right of individual
petition, in breach of Art.34.[85] He submitted that the history of state compliance
with requests for interim measures had acquired the status of a settled practice
which affected the interpretation of the Convention. The court, by a narrow
majority, held that subsequent practice "cannot create new rights and obligations
which were not included in the Convention at the outset". Compliance with a r.39
indication lay at the discretion of the contracting state. The Court nevertheless
pointed out that a state which fails to comply with such a request "knowingly
assumes the risk of being found in breach of Article 3". Accordingly:

> "where the state has had its attention drawn in this way to the dangers of prejudicing
> the outcome of the issue . . . any such finding would have to be seen as aggravated by
> the failure to comply with the indication".[86]

---

[77] (1997) Application No.33977/96.

[78] Unreported, 1999.

[79] It was doubtless significant in this case that the applicant faced the death penalty if convicted.

[80] r.39(2).

[81] r.39(3).

[82] This is to be contrasted with the position under other international treaties: see, for example,
Art.63 of the American Convention on Human Rights. In *Thomas and Hilaire v Baptiste* [2000] 2
A.C. 1 the Privy Council held that it would be in breach of the due process clause in the Constitution
of Trinidad and Tobago to execute an individual whilst his complaint was still under consideration by
the Inter-American Commission and Court of Human Rights. This was despite the fact that the state
had repudiated the Convention after the applications had been introduced. The Inter-American Court
of Human Rights reached the same result in *Hilaire, Constantine and Benjamin et al v Trinidad and
Tobago* (2003) 10 I.H.R.R. 1068, where it held that the execution of individuals with complaints
pending before the Inter-American system violated the Inter-American Convention on Human
Rights.

[83] *Cruz Varas v Sweden* (1992) 14 E.H.R.R. 1 at para.100.

[84] (1992) 14 E.H.R.R. 1.

[85] See paras 90-104. The judgment refers to Art.25(1) which provided, in part, that "The High
Contracting Parties . . . undertake not to hinder in any way the effective exercise" of the right of
individual petition. Under the amendments effected by Protocol 11, this provision is now to be found
in Art.34.

[86] *Cruz Varas (supra)* at para.103.

1–38   There have been a number of unsuccessful attempts to create a legally enforceable system of interim relief within the Council of Europe.[87] When Protocol 11
was adopted there was considerable debate as to whether the *Cruz Varas* principle should be overturned. In the end, however, there was insufficient consensus
on the point to achieve an amendment to the Convention. However, in *Mamatku-
lov and Askarov v Turkey*[88] the applicants had been extradited from Turkey to
Uzbekistan to face terrorist charges, despite a r.39 indication, made on the basis
that they faced torture or inhuman or degrading treatment in Uzbekistan. The
Grand Chamber, upholding the decision of the Chamber,[89] held that a Contracting State in a case where a r.39 indication has been made is under an obligation
to comply with that indication and to refrain from any act or omission which
might prejudice the integrity and effectiveness of the Court's final judgment. The
Court stressed that, under Protocol 11, the right of individual petition is no longer
optional, and that Art.34 imposes an obligation not to hinder the right of petition,
including by extraditing applicants in the face of r.39 indications, thus taking
them away from contact with their lawyers.[90]

Preliminary Consideration

1–39   Once a case is registered, a judge rapporteur will be assigned to it by the relevant
Chamber[91] and will prepare a confidential report on the case summarising the
facts and issues, and making a provisional proposal on the admissibility and, if
appropriate the merits of the complaint.[92] The rapporteur may refer the case to a
Committee which may, by unanimous vote, declare a case inadmissible or strike
it off the list if it considers that further examination of the application is
unnecessary.[93] The decision of a Committee is final[94] and must be supported by
reasons,[95] although the reasons given in Committee decisions tend to be brief and
formulaic in character.

1–40   Unless the Committee is unanimous in its decision to declare a case inadmissible
or to strike it off the list, it will be referred to a full Chamber which will decide
on the admissibility and merits of the application.[96] Decisions on admissibility
and merits will be taken separately, unless the Chamber, in exceptional circumstances, decides otherwise.[97] The Chamber may, at that stage, either declare the
application inadmissible or decide to invesigate it further.[98]

---

[87] See, for example, Consultative Assembly Recommendation 623(1971) calling on the Committee
of Ministers to draft an additional protocol to the Convention providing for a power to make binding
orders for interim relief.
[88] (2005) 41 E.H.R.R. 25.
[89] 14 B.H.R.C. 149.
[90] The obligation not to hinder the right of individual petition was also emphasised by the court in
Poleshchuk v Russia (2006) 42 E.H.R.R. 35, paras 27–31 (refusal to allow imprisoned applicant to
post his application to the court, and pressure on him not to pursue his application).
[91] r.49.
[92] r.49(3) and (4).
[93] Art.28.
[94] Art.28.
[95] Art.45(1).
[96] Art.29(1).
[97] Art.29(3).
[98] r.54(2).

Written pleadings

If the Chamber does not declare an application inadmissible, it will communicate **1–41** it to the respondent state, and request the government's written observations on the admissibility and merits of the case.[99] The Chamber will generally invite the applicant to submit written observations in reply, and may invite further written pleadings from the parties, if necessary.[100] It is for the President to fix the time limit for each stage of the proceedings.[101] The time limits laid down must be strictly adhered to.[102] Any pleadings or other documents filed outside the time limit will be excluded from the case file unless the President, in the exercise of his discretion, decides otherwise.[103]

Joinder and simultaneous examination

The Chamber may, either at the request of the parties or of its own motion, order **1–42** the joinder of two or more applications.[104] Alternatively, the President may, after consulting the parties, order that applications which have been assigned to the same Chamber should be examined simultaneously.[105]

Expedition

The examination of a complaint under the Convention can take several years. In **1–43** cases of urgency, however, the President may authorise the Registrar to inform a contracting state of the introduction of an application, and a summary of its objects.[106] This procedure is available whether or not the court has made a request for interim measures pursuant to r.39.[107] Whilst cases will ordinarily be dealt with in the order in which they become ready for examination, the court has a specific power to prioritise particular applications—in effect an order for expedition.[108] In *Soering v United Kingdom*[109] the applicant's complaint concerning his proposed extradition was determined by the court in just under a year; and in *X v France*[110] a complaint made by an applicant who was dying of AIDS was resolved in 13 months. In *Pretty v United Kingdom*, a case where the applicant was terminally ill, the court gave judgment[111] exactly five months after the judgment of the House of Lords.[112]

---

[99] r.54(2)(b).

[100] r.54(2)(c).

[101] r.59(4).

[102] r.38(1). For the purpose of determining whether a time limit has been complied with, the relevant date is the date of certified dispatch. If there is no certified date of dispatch, the relevant date is the date of receipt.

[103] r.38(1).

[104] r.42(1).

[105] r.42(2).

[106] r.40.

[107] r.40 provides that the urgent notification procedure is "without prejudice to the taking of any other procedural steps".

[108] r.41.

[109] (1989) 11 E.H.R.R. 439.

[110] (1992) 14 E.H.R.R. 483.

[111] (2002) 35 E.H.R.R. 1

[112] [2002] 1 A.C. 800.

Admissibility[113]

1–44 The criteria for determining the admissibility of a complaint are set out in Art.35:

(a) Under Art.35(1) the court may only deal with an application after all domestic remedies have been exhausted, "according to the generally recognised rules of international law",[114] and within a period of six months from the date on which the final decision was taken in the national system.[115]

(b) Under Art.35(2) the court may not deal with any application which is anonymous[116] or which is substantially the same as a matter which has already been examined by the court[117] or which has already been submitted to "another procedure of international investigation or settlement".

(c) Finally, Art.35(3) requires the court to declare inadmissible any individual application which it considers to be: (a) incompatible with the provisions of the Convention[118]; (b) manifestly ill-founded[119]; or (c) an abuse of the right of petition.[120]

1–45 Before taking its decision on admissibility the Chamber may decide, either at the request of the parties or of its own motion, to hold an oral hearing. If this occurs then unless the Chamber, in exceptional circumstances, decides otherwise, the parties will be asked to address both the admissibility and the merits of the application at a single hearing.[121] Any decision to declare a complaint inadmissible (with or without a hearing) is final,[122] subject to the Court's inherent power to reopen the case in exceptional circumstances to rectify a manifest error of fact or assessment of the relevant admissibility requirements,[123] and must be supported by reasons.[124] If the respondent intends to contest admissibility, it must do so at admissibility stage: other than in exceptional circumstances, the court will not entertain a challenge to admissibility if this is made for the first time at the merits stage.[125]

---

[113] See generally Leo Zwart, *The Admissibility of Human Rights Petitions* (Martinus Nijhoff, 1994).

[114] See para.1–46 below.

[115] See para.1–65 below.

[116] See para.1–71 below.

[117] See para.1–73 below.

[118] See paras 1–74 to 1–94 below.

[119] See para.1–95 below.

[120] See para.1–98 below.

[121] r.54A. For the procedure to be followed at an oral hearing, see para.1–115 below.

[122] *Campbell and Fell v United Kingdom* (1984) 7 E.H.R.R. 165 at para.65.

[123] *Storck v Germany* (2006) 43 E.H.R.R. 6, para.67.

[124] Article 45(1) and r.56(1). If the case has been declared inadmissible by a Chamber then the decision must state whether it was taken unanimously or by a majority: r.56(1). There is, however, no provision for dissenting opinions to be appended to an inadmissibility decision. Article 45(2) and r.74(2), which make provision for dissenting opinions, apply only to a judgment on the merits of a complaint.

[125] *Prokopovich v Russia* (2006) 43 E.H.R.R. 10, paras 27–30.

Exhaustion of domestic remedies

The first admissibility requirement in Art.35(1) is that the applicant must have **1–46** exhausted all domestic remedies before pursuing a complaint in Strasbourg. The court has frequently stated that the primary responsibility for ensuring compliance with the standards laid down in the Convention lies with the national authorities.[126] In accordance with the general principles of international law, member states must have the opportunity to redress any violation of Convention rights within the domestic legal system.[127] The European Court becomes involved "only through contentious proceedings and once all domestic remedies have been exhausted".[128] The requirement to exhaust domestic remedies also enables the national courts to make any necessary findings of fact. Although such findings are not binding on the European Court of Human Rights, they will only be disturbed if the national court has drawn an unfair or arbitrary conclusion from the evidence before it.[129]

In determining whether the applicant has taken the necessary steps in the **1–47** domestic legal system, Art.35(1) must be applied with "some degree of flexibility and without excessive formalism".[130] The applicant is under an obligation to make "normal use" of those remedies which are "likely to be effective and adequate".[131] He is not required to pursue remedies which, though available in theory, would be incapable in practice of providing any effective redress for the complaint concerned.[132] An *ex post facto* remedy in damages will not necessarily be sufficient.[133] In certain situations national law must afford a means of preventing a violation if a remedy is to be regarded as effective.[134] By the same token, where national law does provide a procedure for preventing a violation, the applicant will generally be expected to make use of it.[135] The court has emphasised that the effectiveness of the remedy must take into account the objective realities of the particular case. In *AB v Netherlands* the court held that:

> "in assessing the remedy suggested by the Government, the Court must take account not only of its existence in the legal system of the Netherlands Antilles but also of the

---

[126] See, among numerous other authorities, *Akdivar v Turkey* (1997) 23 E.H.R.R. 143.

[127] *DeWilde Ooms and Versyp v Belgium* (1979–80) 1 E.H.R.R. 373 at para.50.

[128] *Handyside v United Kingdom* (1979–80) 1 E.H.R.R. 737 at para.48.

[129] *Klaas v Germany* (1994) 18 E.H.R.R. 305 at 338 paras 24–31; *Edwards v United Kingdom* (1993) 15 E.H.R.R. 417 at para.34; *Van Mechelen v Netherlands* (1998) 25 E.H.R.R. 647 at para.50; *Barbera, Messegue and Jabardo v Spain* (1989) 11 E.H.R.R. 360.

[130] *Van Oosterwijk v Belgium* (1981) 3 E.H.R.R. 557 at paras 30–41; *Guzzardi v Italy* (1981) 3 E.H.R.R. 333 para.72; *Cf. Cardot v France* (1991) 13 E.H.R.R. 583.

[131] *Donnelly v United Kingdom* (1972) 4 D.R. 4 at para.72.

[132] *Stogmuller v Austria* (1979–80) 1 E.H.R.R. 155 at para.11; *Vernillo v France* (1991) 13 E.H.R.R. 880 at para.27; *Lawless v United Kingdom* (1958) 2 Y.B. 308 at 326.

[133] *X v United Kingdom* (1977) 10 D.R. 5 (applicant complaining about conditions of detention in a mental hospital not required to bring civil action in damages); *X v France* (1988) 56 D.R. 62 (in the context of a claim of excessive detention on remand, an action for damages is not a remedy requiring exhaustion).

[134] *M v France* (1984) 41 D.R. 103 (in the context of threatened expulsion in breach of Art.3, appeal without suspensive effect cannot be regarded as effective).

[135] *Cardot v France* (1991) 13 E.H.R.R. 853 at para.34.

general legal and political context in which it operates, as well as the personal circumstances of the applicants."[136]

1–48   Difficult issues arise where the merits of any domestic remedy are dubious. The Court exerts pressure on potential applicants to make use of any national procedure which "does not clearly lack any prospect of success".[137] But in many cases, there may be room for differences of opinion as to whether an untried remedy is likely to succeed. The mere fact that there may be doubts about the prospects of success is not sufficient to absolve the applicant from the requirement to exhaust domestic remedies.[138] Where national case law is unclear, contradictory or in the process of ongoing interpretation, the domestic courts must, in general, be afforded the opportunity to clarify or develop the law.[139] The decision of the court in *D v Ireland*[140] is a striking example of this approach. The applicant became pregnant with twins, and it was discovered that one foetus had died in the womb and that the second foetus had a chromosomal abnormality which the applicant believed was fatal. She did not seek advice about the possibility of an abortion in Ireland, where the only exception to the prohibition on abortion related to a substantial risk to the life of the mother, but rather went to the UK for an abortion. She argued that the need to travel to the UK for an abortion in the case of a lethal foetal abnormality, coupled with the restrictions on information available in Ireland about abortion services abroad, violated her rights under Arts 3, 8 and 10 of the Convention. The Court emphasised the importance, in a common law system, of allowing the courts to develop the constitution by way of interpretation. The Court accepted that the applicant's case would have been a test case and that, in order to obtain the abortion which she sought, she would have to persuade the Irish Courts to extend the limited circumstances in which abortions are permitted. However, the court considered that she ought to have taken at least preliminary steps in the domestic legal system, including obtaining legal advice, issuing proceedings and obtaining an urgent hearing in the High Court to determine preliminary issues. This is a harsh decision on the facts of the case, requiring a pregnant woman to bring a test case in urgent and distressing circumstances, but is consistent with the Court's emphasis on the need to give domestic courts an opportunity to develop the law so as to protect the Convention rights.[141]

---

[136] (2003) 37 E.H.R.R. 48, para.72. See also *Conka v Belgium* (2002) 34 E.H.R.R. 54, in which the Court took account, in finding that an appeal against deportation had not been an effective remedy, the fact that the information on that remedy was handed to the applicants in the police station on a piece of paper in tiny print in a language they could not understand, that they had not had adequate access to an interpreter, and that their lawyer was only informed of their impending deportation after the time limit for filing an appeal had expired, (paras 44–45), and *Salman v Turkey* (2002) 34 E.H.R.R. 17 (paras 86–88).

[137] *DeWilde Ooms and Versyp v Belgium* (1979–80) 1 E.H.R.R. 373.

[138] *Donnelly v United Kingdom* (1972) 4 D.R. 4 at para.72.

[139] *Whiteside v United Kingdom* (1994) 76–A D.R. 80; *Spencer v United Kingdom* [1998] E.H.R.L.R. 348.

[140] App.No.26499/02, June 28, 2006.

[141] For similar reasoning, see *Upton v United Kingdom*, App.No.29800/04, 11 April 2006. The court emphasised that, where it may be possible for legislation to be read compatibly with the Convention pursuant to s.3 of the Human Rights Act 1998, domestic proceedings should be brought.

Similarly, where new legislation is introduced, it may be necessary for the applicant to test its application before the national courts before pursuing a complaint in Strasbourg.[142]

There is, however, a competing imperative to pursue any complaint within the six **1–49** month time limit. For this purpose time begins to run from the date of the violation, or from the conclusion of the last potentially effective domestic remedy, whichever is the latest. Time spent pursuing remedies which could not, on any view, have been effective, can result in an application being declared inadmissible for failure to observe the six month time limit.[143] Considerable care is therefore required in determining whether a particular remedy should be pursued. However, in *Şahin v Turkey*[144] the Court stated that:

"The Court reiterates that, under its case law, while an applicant is, as a rule, in duty bound to exercise the different domestic remedies before applying to the Convention institutions, it must be left open to the Convention institutions to accept the fact that the last stage of such remedies may be reached after the lodging of the application, as long as the remedies are exhausted before the decision on admissibility."[145]

In cases of uncertainty, the Court's approach is as follows: where previous or **1–50** subsequent litigation before the national courts has raised the same point without success, this will usually be sufficient to establish that the remedy was ineffective.[146] If the applicant can show that there is settled legal opinion to the effect that the remedy would be not succeed, there is no obligation to make use of it.[147] The Court may be willing to accept the written opinion of senior counsel that the remedy in question would be bound to fail.[148] But if the advice subsequently turns out to be wrong, the applicant will not be able to rely upon the fact of having obtained advice in order to excuse non-exhaustion. In *K, F and P v United Kingdom*[149] counsel's advice was held not to absolve the applicants from an obligation to apply for leave to appeal to the House of Lords, especially since the Court of Appeal had given leave in a similar case soon afterwards.

It is not always necessary for the applicant to have pleaded a violation of the **1–51** Convention in specific terms before the national courts.[150] In general, the court adopts a substantive rather than a formal approach. It is the *substance* of the applicant's Convention complaint which must previously have been put before the relevant national authority.[151] But where the Convention is incorporated into

---

[142] This has obvious implications for the Human Rights Act 1998, some of which are considered below.

[143] *X v Switzerland* (1980) 22 D.R. 232; *Temple v United Kingdom* (1985) 42 D.R. 171; *X v Ireland* (1981) 26 D.R. 242; *H v United Kingdom* (1983) 33 D.R. 247.

[144] (2005) 41 E.H.R.R. 8.

[145] Para.62.

[146] *Campbell v United Kingdom* 14 D.R. 186.

[147] *DeWilde Ooms and Versyp v Belgium* (1979–80) 1 E.H.R.R. 373 at para.50.

[148] *McFeely v United Kingdom* (1980) 20 D.R. 44 at 71–76; *H v United Kingdom* (1983) 33 D.R. 247.

[149] (1984) 40 D.R. 298 at 300.

[150] *Arrowsmith v United Kingdom* (1978) 8 D.R. 123.

[151] *Gasus Dossier-und Fordertechnick GmbH v Netherlands* (1995) 20 E.H.R.R. 360; *Castells v Spain* (1992) 14 E.H.R.R. 445.

national law, it may be incumbent on the applicant to go further, and to show that the relevant Convention provisions have been invoked directly in the domestic courts,[152] particularly if this is the only means by which the point can be ventilated.[153] In *Van Oosterwijk v Belgium*[154] the Court explained its approach in these terms:

> "Undoubtedly, in domestic proceedings the Convention as a general rule furnishes a supplementary ground of argument, to be prayed in aid if judged suitable for achieving an objective which is in principle rendered possible by other legal arguments ... In certain circumstances it may nonetheless happen that express reliance on the Convention before the national authorities constitutes the sole appropriate manner of raising before those authorities first, as is required by [Article 35(1)] an issue intended, if need be, to be brought subsequently before the European review bodies."[155]

1–52   The burden of proving the existence of an effective remedy lies on the state.[156] However, once the existence of such a remedy has been raised, it is for the applicant to establish why the remedy was unavailable or inadequate in the circumstances[157]; or to identify other, exceptional, considerations which are said to absolve him from the requirement to exhaust those remedies which exist. In *Henaf v France*,[158] the Court held that the fact that the applicant's civil claim for domestic redress had been struck out because of his failure to pay a deposit into court did not count as a failure to exhaust domestic remedies, in light of the fact that the applicant had been in detention at the relevant time, was in poor health, had language difficulties and was not legally represented.[159]

1–53   In determining whether a remedy was genuinely effective, the Court will require a close correlation between the applicant's complaint and the remedy relied upon by the government. In *T and V v United Kingdom*[160] two juvenile applicants complained that their trial in an adult Crown Court was in breach of Arts 3 and 6 of the Convention since they had been unable to participate effectively in the proceedings, due to their immaturity and emotional vulnerability, and the public nature of their trial. The government raised the plea of non-exhaustion, arguing that the applicants' trial lawyers had failed to apply for a stay of the criminal proceedings in the Crown Court. Although there was no authority which directly supported the existence of a jurisdiction to stay in these circumstances, the government pointed to the decision of the Privy Council in *Kunnath v The State*[161] in support of the argument that English common law required a criminal

---

[152] *Cardot v France* (1991) 13 E.H.R.R. 853.

[153] See generally Kruger, "The Practicalities of a Bill of Rights" [1997] E.H.R.L.R. 353.

[154] (1981) 3 E.H.R.R. 557 at para.33.

[155] This is a principle which is likely to arise in connection with claims which can only be brought under s.7(1)(a) of the Human Rights Act 1998.

[156] *T and V v United Kingdom* (2000) 30 E.H.R.R. 121 at para.57; *DeWilde Ooms and Versyp v Belgium* (1979–80) 1 E.H.R.R. 373 at para.60; *DeWeer v Belgium* (1979–80) 2 E.H.R.R. 439 at para.26; *Guincho v Portugal* (1982) 29 D.R. 129 at 140.

[157] *Donnelly v United Kingdom* (1972) 4 D.R. 4 at para.64; *Akdivar v Turkey* (1997) 23 E.H.R.R. 143 at para.68.

[158] (2005) 40 E.H.R.R. 44,

[159] Para.33. See also *Isayeva v Russia* (2005) 41 E.H.R.R. 38 at paras 154–161.

[160] (2000) 30 E.H.R.R. 121.

[161] [1993] 1 W.L.R. 1315.

defendant to be able to understand and participate in the proceedings. In *Kunnath*, the Privy Council had said:

"It is an essential principle of the criminal law that a trial for an indictable offence should be conducted in the presence of the defendant. The basis of this principle is not simply that there should be corporeal presence, but that the defendant, by reason of his presence, should be able to understand the proceedings and decide what witnesses he wishes to call, whether or not to give evidence and if so, upon what matters relevant to the case against him."

Kunnath, however, concerned the absence of an interpreter. In the court's view,   **1-54** the government had failed to establish that a similar principle would have been applied to an application to stay the proceedings on grounds of the defendants' immaturity and emotional disturbance. The court subjected the government's claim that the remedy would have been effective to a very close scrutiny before rejecting it[162]:

"The Court observes that in the *Kunnath* case the Privy Council was concerned with the very different situation of an accused person who was unable to participate in the criminal proceedings against him because they were conducted in a language which he did not understand. It notes the well-established rule of English criminal law that, in order to obtain a stay of proceedings, a defendant suffering from a disability such as mental illness must establish before a jury that he is 'unfit to plead', that is that he lacks the intellectual capacity to understand the plea of guilty or not guilty, to instruct his solicitors and to follow the evidence. In addition, English law attributes criminal responsibility to children between the ages of ten and fourteen, subject, at the time of the applicant's trial, to the proviso that the prosecution had to prove beyond reasonable doubt that, at the time of the alleged offence, the child understood that his behaviour was wrong as distinct from merely naughty. Finally, it is the rule that children over the age of ten accused or murder, manslaughter and other serious crimes are tried in public in the Crown Court. It is not suggested that the applicant's immaturity and level of emotional disturbance were sufficient to satisfy the test of unfitness to plead. Further, the prosecution were able to rebut the *doli incapax* presumption in respect of the applicant. However, the government have not referred the Court to any example of a case where an accused under a disability falling short of that required to establish unfitness to plead has been able to obtain a stay of criminal proceedings on the grounds that he was incapable of fully participating in them, or where a child charged with murder or another serious offence has been able to obtain a stay on the basis that the trial in public in the Crown Court would cause him detriment or suffering. In these circumstances, the Court does not consider that the government have discharged the burden upon them of proving the availability to the applicant of a remedy capable of providing redress in respect of his Convention complaints and offering reasonable prospects of success."

The applicant must be able to demonstrate that national time limits[163] and   **1-55** procedural requirements have been complied with,[164] unless they are manifestly unreasonable. In *Cardot v France*[165] the Court summarised the position in this way:

---

[162] See *T and V* (2000) 30 E.H.R.R. 121 at para.59–61.
[163] *W v Germany* (1986) 48 D.R. 102.
[164] *Cunningham v United Kingdom* 43 D.R. 171; *T v Switzerland* (1991) 72 D.R. 263.
[165] (1991) 13 E.H.R.R. 853 at para.34.

"Admittedly, Article 26 must be applied with some degree of flexibility and without excessive formalism, but it does not require merely that applications should be made to the appropriate domestic courts and that use should be made of remedies designed to challenge decisions already given. It normally requires also that the complaints intended to be made subsequently at Strasbourg have been made to those same courts, at least in substance and in compliance with the formal requirements and time limits laid down in domestic law, and, further, that any procedural means which might prevent a breach of the Convention should have been used."

1–56   In exceptional circumstances the Court will absolve an applicant from the requirement to exhaust available remedies, where there are compelling reasons for doing so. In *Akdivar v Turkey*[166] the court held that:

"One such reason may be constituted by the national authorities remaining totally passive in the face of serious allegations of misconduct or infliction of harm by state agents, for example where they have failed to undertake investigations or offer assistance. In such circumstances it can be said that the burden of proof shifts once again, so that it becomes incumbent on the respondent government to show what it has done in response to the scale and seriousness of the matters complained of."

In practice, however, it is rare for the Court to make an exception. The absence of legal aid is not generally regarded as a sufficient reason for failure to make use of remedies which are available,[167] although the position may be otherwise where the applicant could not reasonably be expected to conduct litigation without legal representation.[168] In an early case, the Commission suggested that the fact that the applicant was a patient in a psychiatric hospital did not relieve him of the responsibility to institute proceedings.[169] On the other hand, where there is more than one remedy available to an applicant it may be sufficient to show that a reasonable choice has been made.[170]

1–57   In order to be "effective", the remedy need not necessarily be judicial. The applicant must also make use of any administrative remedies available, providing they are realistically capable of affording effective redress.[171] However, the Court will scrutinise administrative remedies with particular care to determine their availability and effectiveness in practice. An administrative remedy will only be effective if the authority in question has jurisdiction to give a binding ruling on the complaint. Purely advisory powers are insufficient.[172] The fact that

---

[166] (1997) 23 E.H.R.R. 143; See also *Aksoy v Turkey* (1997) 23 E.H.R.R. 553.

[167] *Van Oosterwijk v Belgium* (1981) 3 E.H.R.R. 557.

[168] *Cf. Airey v Ireland* (1979–80) 2 E.H.R.R. 305; *Granger v United Kingdom* (1990) 12 E.H.R.R. 469.

[169] *X v United Kingdom* (1977) 10 D.R. 5.

[170] *Yagci and Sargin v Turkey* (1995) 20 E.H.R.R. 505 at paras 41–43; *Cremieux v France* (1989) 59 D.R. 67 at 80. The selection of the appropriate remedy is primarily a matter for the applicant: *Airey v Ireland* (1979–80) 2 E.H.R.R. 305 at para.23.

[171] *McFeely v United Kingdom* (1980) 20 D.R. 44 at 72.

[172] *Agee v United Kingdom* (1976) 7 D.R. 164. In *Assanidze v Georgia* (2004) 39 E.H.R.R. 32, the court held that the report of a parliamentary investigation committee into a criminal conviction was not an effective remedy, since the committee's report did not entail the conviction being set aside or reviewed. (para.128) In any event, "The Court would be extremely concerned if the legislation or practice of a State were to empower a non-judicial authority to interfere in court proceedings or to call judicial findings into question." (para.129).

an administrative remedy is discretionary will not necessarily result in it being regarded as ineffective,[173] although it is a factor pointing in that direction.[174]

The power to award an *ex gratia* payment is not an effective remedy requiring **1–58** exhaustion.[175] Neither is an applicant obliged to make use of exceptional administrative procedures which fall outside the normal legal remedies available. Thus, a criminal defendant is not obliged to petition the Criminal Cases Review Commission (CCRC) for a reference to the Court of Appeal under s.9 of the Criminal Appeal Act 1995 before pursuing a complaint in Strasbourg.[176] Once an appeal has been finally dismissed the applicant's conviction and sentence will acquire the quality of *res judicata*[177] and the ordinary appellate process is then at an end. In *Rowe and Davis v United Kingdom*[178] the CCRC referred the applicants' convictions back to the Court of Appeal after the European Commission of Human Rights had declared their complaints under Art.6 admissible, but before the case had been argued before the court. The Court nevertheless proceeded to determine the merits of the applicants' complaint before their appeal against conviction had been heard by the Court of Appeal.

Where administrative remedies are involved, the court will be astute to detect any **1–59** conflict of interest or lack of independence. In *Khan v United Kingdom*[179] the Court held that the system of police complaints established under the Police and Criminal Evidence Act 1984 did not meet the requisite standards of independence needed to constitute sufficient protection against the abuse of authority and thus provide an effective remedy. In reaching this important conclusion, the Court attached particular significance to the limited powers of the Police Complaints Authority; to the function of the Home Secretary in appointing, remunerating and dismissing members of the PCA; and to the role played by the Chief Constable of the force under investigation. A new body, the Independent Police Complaints Commission, was set up by the Police Reform Act 2002.

In *Silver v United Kingdom*[180] the Court drew a distinction between challenges **1–60** directed to the validity of a Ministerial or Departmental order or policy, and challenges directed to a specific measure of implementation. In the former case, executive remedies are unlikely to be regarded as effective since they involve an appeal to the body which adopted the policy in the first place. But where the applicant complains that a policy, acceptable in itself, has been wrongly implemented, there will be an onus on him to petition the relevant authorities for redress. In the context of the prison disciplinary rule at issue in *Silver*, the court said:

---

[173] *X v United Kingdom* (1977) 10 D.R. 5.

[174] *Byloos v Belgium* (1990) 66 D.R. 238; *X v Denmark* (1981) 27 D.R. 50.

[175] *Temple v United Kingdom* (1985) 42 D.R. 171.

[176] See, by anology, *X v Ireland* (1981) 26 D.R. 242; *X v Denmark* (1981) 27 D.R. 50; *KS and KS v Switzerland* (1994) 76–A D.R. 70.

[177] A conviction will be *res judicata* when an appeal against conviction is finally dismissed or the relevant time limit has expired. An appeal out of time will not meet the requirements of Art.35(1) unless the court has extended time, and proceeded to hear the appeal.

[178] (2000) 30 E.H.R.R. 1.

[179] (2001) 31 E.H.R.R. 45.

[180] (1983) 5 E.H.R.R. 347.

"As for the Home Secretary, if there were a complaint to him as to the validity of an Order or Instruction under which a measure of control ... had been carried out, he could not be considered to have a sufficiently independent standpoint to satisfy the requirements of Article 13. As the author of the directives in question, he would in reality be judge in his own cause. The position, however, would be otherwise if the complainant alleged that the measure of control resulted from a misapplication of one of those directives. The Court is satisfied that in such cases a petition to the Home Secretary would in general be effective to secure compliance with the directive, if the complaint was well-founded."

1–61   The Court will consider the effectiveness of domestic remedies by reference to the state of national law at the time of its admissibility decision, rather than the date of introduction of the complaint.[181] If, therefore, domestic law has developed so as to afford a remedy which was not previously available then this will provide a ground for declaring the complaint inadmissible, providing of course that the applicant's complaint remained within the national time limits when the change in the law took effect.[182]

1–62   Applying these principles to criminal cases in the United Kingdom it is possible to draw a number of conclusions. As a general rule, a criminal defendant will be expected to pursue any available avenue of appeal, and to raise the substance of any Convention arguments before the appeal court. Thus, in *Edwards v United Kingdom*,[183] the court considered that non-disclosure of relevant evidence at the time of the applicant's trial was in breach of Art.6. However, in the Court's view, the violation had been remedied by the disclosure of the evidence prior to the hearing of the appeal, since the Court of Appeal had able to assess the impact of the evidence on the safety of the conviction. Insofar as the applicant sought to challenge the non-disclosure of evidence on grounds of public interest immunity, the court considered that his failure to make an application to the Court of Appeal for production of the document was fatal to his complaint.[184]

1–64   Assuming that the criminal proceedings concluded after the Human Rights Act 1998 came into force on October 2, 2000, which is now likely to be the case, the position can be summarised as follows:

(a) If the alleged violation involves a rule of practice, or a principle of the common law, then it will almost certainly be incumbent on the applicant to invoke Convention arguments in the domestic courts. This is because under the Human Rights Act, Convention rights will take precedence over any pre-existing rule of this kind.[185]

(b) Where a provision of primary legislation is involved, the applicant will in general be expected to argue for a new construction which is compatible

---

[181] *Luberti v Italy* (1981) 27 D.R. 181.
[182] *Campbell and Fell v United Kingdom* (1985) 7 E.H.R.R. 165; *Ringeisen v Austria* (1979–80) 1 E.H.R.R. 455 at paras 89–93.
[183] (1993) 15 E.H.R.R. 417.
[184] Para.38.
[185] See Ch.3 below.

with Convention rights in accordance with s.3 of the 1998 Act.[186] This will be the case even if there is prior appellate authority on the point.[187]

(c) The most difficult problems will arise where there appears to be no "possible" construction which would be compatible with Convention rights. Is a declaration of incompatibility under ss.4 and 5 of the new Act to be regarded as an effective remedy, requiring exhaustion, despite the fact that it does not affect the validity, operation or continuing enforcement of the legislation, and despite the fact that it is not binding on the parties to the proceedings in which it is made? The safest course may be to assume that the applicant is under an obligation to seek a declaration of incompatibility since this will trigger the power to make a remedial order in s.10 and Sch.2 of the Human Rights Act. While a prospective amendment to the offending legislation would not, in itself, provide an effective remedy, Sch.2 enables the responsible Minister to make a retrospective amendment, and to grant supplementary or consequential relief to the individual.[188] However, in *Hobbs v UK*[189] the Court concluded that a declaration of incompatibility was not an effective remedy within the meaning of Art.13.

(d) Particular care is required when determining whether judicial review should be pursued:

(i) If the applicant's complaint relates to a failure to follow procedural rules, or an error of law, then judicial review is capable of providing an effective remedy. However, in *G v United Kingdom*[190] the Commission held that the possibility of applying for judicial review of a refusal of legal aid in a criminal case could not be regarded as effective on the facts. Moreover, the practical availability of judicial review as a means of challenging an error of law in the course of a criminal prosecution has been severely circumscribed by the House of Lords' decision in *R. v Director of Public Prosecutions ex parte Kebilene*.[191]

(ii) As to challenges which are directed to the merits of a decision, the court has held that judicial review is an effective remedy where the applicant alleges that a decision to extradite or deport him would involve a serious risk of treatment contrary to Arts 2 or 3.[192] This is because the domestic courts adopted a test of "anxious scrutiny" which coincides with the tests adopted by the court. However, where

---

[186] See para.3–31 below.

[187] See para.3–32 below.

[188] See paras 3–38 to 3–39 below.

[189] Application No.63684/00 (18.6.02). In *Dodds v UK* (App.59314/00 (8.4.03)) the ECtHR declined to re-visit or reverse *Hobbs* despite the UK's invitation. See also *Walker v UK*(Application No.37212/02, 16.3.04); *Pearson v UK* (Application No.8374/03, 27.4.04); *B&L v UK* (Application No.36936/02 29.6.04) and *PM v UK* (Application No.6638/02 19.7.05).

[190] (1988) 56 D.R. 199.

[191] [2000] 2 AC 326.

[192] *Soering v United Kingdom* (1989) 11 E.H.R.R. 439; *Vilvarajah v United Kingdom* (1992) 14 E.H.R.R. 248; *D v United Kingdom* (1997) 24 E.H.R.R. 423.

a violation of Art.8 was in issue[193] judicial review was held to be ineffective. In *Smith and Grady v United Kingdom*[194] the court held that the irrationality threshold applied when the court is considering a challenge to the merits of an administrative decision

" . . . was placed so high that it effectively excluded any consideration by the domestic courts of the question of whether the interference with the applicants' rights answered a pressing social need or was proportionate to the . . . aims pursued, principles which lie at the heart of the Court's analysis of complaints under Article 8 of the Convention."[195]

In the light of this decision, the Administrative Court is of course required to adopt a more intrusive threshold for a judicial review directed to the merits of a decision under the Human Rights Act. Assuming that the test applied in the domestic courts coincides with the approach of the European Court of Human Rights under Art.8, there will be a corresponding onus on the applicant to seek judicial review. The inadequacy of pre-HRA judicial review was underlined by the Grand Chamber in *Hatton v United Kingdom*,[196] where the court again held that judicial review at that time had been unable to consider whether the State's actions (in that case, the planning of night flights at Heathrow) represented a justifiable limitation on the applicants' private lives.[197]

(e) The Court has in the past been prepared to accept that appeal to the House of Lords is an exceptional remedy, available only where a case involves a point of law of general public importance. As such, an applicant has only been required to apply for leave to appeal to the House of Lords where there is a realistic prospect that leave would be granted on the facts.[198] The Human Rights Act has broadened the scope of constitutional complaints which satisfy the requirements for the grant of leave. Potential applicants would therefore be well advised to apply for leave to appeal to the House of Lords in any case where it is considered likely that an application to Strasbourg will be made.

(f) In order to minimise the risk of falling foul of the six months rule in cases where the merits are doubtful, an applicant should consider lodging a protective application to Strasbourg. There is no express provision in the rules for this procedure, but the Registry is usually prepared to open a file on a complaint whilst domestic remedies are in the process of exhaustion (providing of course that they have been exhausted by the time the court rules on admissibility). In that way, the applicant is protected both from an argument that the complaint is inadmissible for non-exhaustion, and from

---

[193] And presumably also a violation of Arts 9 to 11 and Art.14.

[194] (2000) 29 E.H.R.R. 493.

[195] This was despite the fact that the Court of Appeal had taken account of the human rights context, and had held that the more substantial the interference with human rights, the more the court would require by way of justification before it was satisfied that decision was reasonable.

[196] (2003) 37 E.H.R.R. 28.

[197] Paras 137–142.

[198] *McGonnell v United Kingdom* (2000) 30 E.H.R.R. 289 (concerning a similar right of appeal from the Royal Court of Guernsey to the Privy Council).

an argument that it was introduced outside the six month time limit. If this course is to be adopted, the applicant must submit a detailed letter of introduction, accompanied by the appropriate forms, and explaining that further remedies are being pursued in the national courts. The applicant should then maintain contact with the Registry. An application cannot be kept dormant indefinitely and may have to be re-introduced.[199]

(g) The final point relates to the rule that compliance with Art.35(1) is to be determined according to the remedies available at the time when the court makes its ruling on the admissibility of the application. Under s.22(4) of the Human Rights Act a criminal defendant is entitled to invoke Convention rights retrospectively in certain circumstances.[200] It follows that even if there was no remedy available at the time the application was introduced, this may not necessarily be the position when the Court comes to rule on the admissibility of the complaint.

The six months rule

The second limb of Art.35(1) provides that the Court may only consider an **1–65** application which has been introduced within six months "from the date on which the final decision was taken". Where there are effective or potentially effective domestic remedies for the violation, time begins to run from the day after the final decision in the process of exhaustion. If the national court or tribunal gives its ruling in public, then the date of judgment is generally taken to be the date on which the ruling is given. If the ruling is not given in public, then time runs from the date on which the applicant or his lawyer first received formal written notification.[201] Where the reasons for the national court's ruling are relevant to the application to Strasbourg, then the relevant date will be the date on which the applicant or his lawyer received the text of the court's reasoned judgment.[202]

Where the applicant has made an unsuccessful attempt to invoke a national **1–66** remedy which was obviously ineffective (either because it had no prospect of success or because it was exceptional or discretionary in character[203]) time will run from the date he should have been aware of the situation.[204]

---

[199] Reid, *A Practitioners Guide to the European Convention of Human Rights* (Sweet & Maxwell, 1998), p.20.

[200] See para.3–04 below.

[201] *X v France* (1983) 32 D.R. 266; *K, C and M v Netherlands* (1995) 80–A D.R. 87 at 88; *Cf. Aarts v Netherlands* (1991) 70 D.R. 208 (Delay by lawyer in communicating the ruling to the applicant did not suspend the time limit: The relevant date was the date upon which the lawyer was informed).

[202] *P v Switzerland* (1984) 36 D.R. 20; *Worm v Austria* (1998) 25 E.H.R.R. 454.

[203] See, for example, *X v Ireland* (1981) 26 D.R. 242, where the rejection of the applicant's petition to the Attorney General for a certificate of appeal to the Supreme Court on a point of law of exceptional public importance was held not to have extended the time limit under the Convention.

[204] *X v Switzerland* (1980) 22 D.R. 232; *Temple v United Kingdom* (1985) 42 D.R. 171; *X v Ireland* (1981) 26 D.R. 242; *H v United Kingdom* (1983) 33 D.R. 247; *Lacin v Turkey* (1995) 81–A D.R. 76 at 81. In *Dallos v Hungary* (2003) 37 E.H.R.R. 22, the court held that the remedy alleged to be ineffective by the respondent State was in fact an effective one, and that therefore the six month time limit only started to run when that remedy—which the applicant had used—was exhausted. The claim was therefore within time.

1–67   In a case in which there is no potentially effective domestic remedy available, time generally runs from the date of the act or omission in issue. There are three principal exceptions to this rule:

(a) The six month time limit will not apply where the applicant's complaint relates to a state of affairs which is continuing when the Court examines the admissibility of the application, or to a provision of domestic law which is said, by its very existence, to violate the applicant's Convention rights. In *McFeely v United Kingdom*,[205] where the applicant complained about repeated punishments for persistent refusal to obey prison rules, the Commission held that time would only start to run "after this state of affairs had ceased to exist". Similarly, in *Norris v Ireland*,[206] where the applicant complained that the offence of gross indecency, by its very existence, interfered with his rights under Art.8, there could be no question of the complaint being out of time.

(b) Where the action complained of is authorised under an administrative measure extending over a period of time, the six months period will run from the last date on which the measure caused prejudice to the applicant's Convention rights. In *Christians Against Racism and Fascism v United Kingdom*[207] the applicant organisation complained about an order under s.3 of the Public Order Act 1936, banning processions within the Metropolitan Police district for two months. Time was held to run from the date of a procession which the applicant had planned to hold, rather than from the date on which the order had been made.

(c) Where the applicant was initially unaware of the violation, time runs from the date of knowledge. In *Hilton v United Kingdom*[208] the applicant was a journalist who discovered that she may have been the subject of MI5 security vetting procedures nine years earlier, when she was rejected for an appointment at the BBC. Time was held to run from the date of this discovery.

1–68   In relation to criminal proceedings, the relevant date will usually be the conclusion of any appeal.[209] Where a criminal prosecution involves multiple charges, and the applicant's conviction for one offence is affirmed before the remaining charges have been finally determined, time runs (in relation to the first offence) from the date on which the first conviction was affirmed, rather than from the conclusion of the proceedings as a whole.[210]

1–69   The date of introduction will, as a general rule, be considered to be the date of the first communication from the applicant setting out, even summarily, the object of the application.[211] The communication relied upon must, as a minimum,

---

[205] (1980) 20 D.R. 44 at 76.
[206] (1991) 13 E.H.R.R. 186.
[207] (1980) 21 D.R. 138.
[208] (1988) 57 D.R. 108.
[209] As to the obligation to seek leave to appeal to the House of Lords, see para.1–64(e) above.
[210] *N v Germany* (1982) 31 D.R. 154.
[211] r.47(5).

identify the applicant and particularise the complaint in sufficient detail to enable the court to comprehend the violation alleged.[212] The relevant date is the date of posting or transmission shown on the documents, rather than the date of receipt.[213] Telephone communication is not sufficient,[214] save perhaps in cases of extreme urgency and importance.[215]

The Court has a discretion to direct that a different date should be treated as the   **1–70** date of introduction where there are good reasons for doing so.[216] However, it is a discretion which is rarely exercised in the applicant's favour. Neither a lack of knowledge of the applicable law,[217] nor an applicant's illness or mental incapacity[218] has been held to be sufficient justification for departing from the strict requirements of Art.35(1).

Anonymity and Confidentiality

In accordance with Art.35(2)(a), the Court may not consider an anonymous   **1–71** application.[219] All written applications submitted under Art.34 must adequately identify the applicant for the benefit of the Court and the respondent government.[220] Applicants who do not wish their identity to be disclosed *to the public* must submit a statement of the reasons which are said to justify a departure from the normal rule of public access to information in proceedings before the Court.[221] An order preserving anonymity will only be made in "exceptional and duly justified cases".[222] For an example of a criminal case in which the court has granted anonymity see *ADT v United Kingdom*.[223]

---

[212] *Khan v United Kingdom* (1995) 21 E.H.R.R. CD 67 (a letter setting out the applicant's name and the fact that his complaint related to "an immigration matter" held to be insufficient). See however, *P.M. v United Kingdom* (2004) 39 E.H.R.R. SE21, where the applicant's lawyers' initial letter to the court, summarising the complaint, was taken to be the relevant communication for the purpose of the time limit, rather than the full application, which was not filed until three months later. The court noted that "While no doubt it might have been possible for [the applicant's lawyers] to act with more speed, it may be noted that they kept the Registry apprised of their progress, ensuring that there was no appearance of the matter lying dormant. In the circumstances, the Court does not consider that the overall period discloses a lack of expedition or any abusive or unreasonable conduct on the part of the applicant's representatives." (p.261) This shows that, where delays are encountered, it is important to keep the Registry informed.

[213] It is nevertheless a sensible precaution to establish that the communication has actually been received in the Registry by the prescribed date.

[214] *Rosemary West v United Kingdom* (1997) 91–A D.R. 85.

[215] In *West, supra* n.214, the Commission was prepared to assume that there might be very exceptional circumstances in which an oral application would suffice, but held that it would require an overriding reason why it was not possible to submit an application in writing, coupled with an express and unequivocal statement on the part of the applicant and his lawyer that they were seeking formally to introduce an application by this means.

[216] r.47(5).

[217] *Bozano v Italy* (1984) 39 D.R. 147.

[218] *X v Austria* (1975) 2 D.R. 87 at 88; *K v Ireland* (1984) 38 D.R. 158 at 160.

[219] Art.35(2)(a).

[220] r.47(1)(a).

[221] r.47(3).

[222] r.47(3).

[223] (2001) 31 E.H.R.R. 33.

1–72   All pleadings and other documents deposited with the Registry, apart from those filed for the purposes of friendly settlement negotiations, are available for inspection by the public.[224] Either party may, however, apply to the President for an order that the pleadings or documents, or any part of them, should remain confidential. Such an order may be made in the interest of morals, public order or national security, where the interests of juveniles or the protection of the private life of the parties so require, or to the extent strictly necessary in the opinion of the President in special circumstances where publicity would prejudice the interests of justice.[225] Any such application must be supported by reasoned argument and must specify which of the documents or pleadings it relates to.[226] In addition, the President may make a confidentiality order of his or her own motion.[227]

Substantially the same

1–73   Article 35(2)(b) provides that the Court may not consider an application which is substantially the same as a matter that has already been examined by the Court or has already been submitted to another procedure of international investigation or settlement and which contains no relevant new information. Where an application has already been determined in Strasbourg, the Court may only reconsider it if there are fresh factual considerations. A complaint may, however, be re-submitted if it was initially rejected for non-exhaustion of domestic remedies and the applicant has since complied with the requirements of Art.35(1). Similarly, in *W v Germany*[228] the Commission held that where a previous application concerning delay in domestic proceedings had been rejected, the continuation of those proceedings constitutes a new fact allowing a re-examination of the complaint. However, new grounds of argument based on the same facts will not suffice.[229]

So far as criminal cases in the United Kingdom are concerned, there are no other relevant international procedures available.

Application incompatible with the Convention

1–74   The first limb of Art.35(3) provides that the court may not consider any application which is incompatible with the Convention. There are four grounds of incompatibility:

(a) Incompatibility *ratione temporis*. A complaint will be incompatible with the Convention if the events to which it relates occurred before the Convention came into force, or before it was ratified by the state against which the complaint is made.

---

[224] Art.40(2) and r.33(1).
[225] r.33(2).
[226] r.33(1).
[227] r.33(3).
[228] (1986) 48 D.R. 102.
[229] *X v United Kingdom* (1981) 25 D.R. 147.

(b) Incompatibility *ratione loci*. An application will be incompatible if it relates to events occurring outside the territory of the contracting state and where there is no link with any authority within the jurisdiction.[230]

(c) Incompatibility *ratione personae*. An application will be incompatible if it is directed towards a state which is not a party to the Convention; if it is a complaint against an individual or a body for which the state is not responsible[231]; or if the applicant lacks standing[232] or is unable to show that he is a victim of the violation alleged.[233]

(d) Incompatibility *ratione materiae*. An application will be declared inadmissible if it asserts a right which is not protected by the Convention, or if the complaint(s) made fall outside the scope of the particular right(s) invoked.

Territorial application

The protection afforded by the Convention extends to any person within the jurisdiction of the contracting state,[234] or of any overseas territory for whose international relations that state is responsible under Art.56. Where a state exercises *de facto* control over another state's territory,[235] or where agents of a contracting state detain an individual abroad,[236] any person affected by the action may bring a complaint against the state concerned. Moreover, authorised agents of a state, such as its diplomatic and consular authorities, and its armed forces, not only remain subject to the state's jurisdiction abroad, but bring any other persons or property over which they have authority within the state's jurisdiction.[237]   **1–75**

---

[230] See para.1–75 below.
[231] See para.1–76 below.
[232] See para.1–80 below.
[233] See para.1–84 below.
[234] Art.1.
[235] *Loizidou v Turkey* (1997) 23 E.H.R.R. 513. See also *Assanidze v Georgia* (2004) 39 E.H.R.R. 32: the fact that the Ajaran Autonomous Republic is part of the territory of Georgia gave rise to a presumption of jurisdiction, which the respondent State had not rebutted on the evidence. (paras 139–143); *Ilaşcu v Moldova and Russia* (2005) 40 E.H.R.R. 46; *Issa v Turkey* (2005) 41 E.H.R.R. 27, paras 65–82. In *Bankovic v Belgium* 11 B.H.R.C. 435, the court held that the NATO states had not exercised effective control over Serbia during its bombing campaign, and that therefore Serbia did not during that period fall within the territorial ambit of the Convention. For an analysis of the domestic and Strasbourg caselaw on Art.1, see Wilkinson S., "Focus on Article 1", [2004] *Judicial Review* 243. The English courts have grappled with the application of the Convention and the Human Rights Act 1998 to British-controlled areas of Iraq: see *R. (Al-Jedda) v Secretary of State for Defence* [2006] EWCA Civ 327, [2006] H.R.L.R. 27; and *R. (Al-Skeini) v Secretary of State for Defence* [2005] EWCA Civ 1609, [2006] 3 W.L.R. 508. The court has held that Art.1 cannot itself be the subject of a separate breach, even if invoked in conjunction with other articles of the Convention: *Doğan v Turkey* (2005) 41 E.H.R.R. 15, para.120.
[236] *Reinette v France* (1989) 63 D.R. 189.
[237] *Mrs W v Ireland* (1983) 32 D.R. 211 at para.14. Note however, that taking part in the activities of the European Union or the Council of Europe in not, in itself, sufficient: *Confederation Francais Democratique du Travail v the European Communities and their Member States* (1978) 13 D.R. 231.

State responsibility

1–76   The applicant's complaint must be directed towards a person for whom or a body for which the state is responsible. The Commission and the Court have, in the past, left open the question whether the state is responsible for certain public bodies such as the BBC,[238] British Rail,[239] and the Bar Council Professional Conduct Committee.[240] This issue is brought into sharp focus by s.6 of the Human Rights Act 1998, which provides that the legal duty to act compatibly with Convention rights applies to any "public authority", a term which is defined so as to include "any person, certain of whose functions are functions of a public nature".[241] It is important, however, to recall that the Convention can impose positive obligations on the state to protect a private individual from a violation of his Convention rights by another private individual.[242] Accordingly, the fact that the "proximate cause" of a violation was the act or omission of a private individual is not necessarily decisive.[243]

1–77   A further issue which may arise under the rubric of state responsibility is the question of vicarious liability for unauthorised acts of government servants. The Commission has explained the Convention approach as follows[244]:

> "[T]he responsibility of a state under the Convention may arise for acts of all its organs and servants. As in connection with international law generally, the acts of persons acting in an official capacity are imputed to the state. In particular, the obligations of a Contracting Party under the Convention can be violated by a person exercising an official function vested in him, even where his acts are outside or against instructions."

1–78   Thus, in *A v France*[245] the court held that the state was liable for the unauthorised acts of a police officer who had made a recording of a telephone conversation without the necessary authorisation and in breach of French law. Similarly, in *Cyprus v Turkey*[246] the Commission held the state responsible for acts of rape by Turkish soldiers on the ground that it had "not been shown that the Turkish authorities took adequate measures to prevent this happening or that they generally took any disciplinary measures following such incidents". And in *Ireland*

---

[238] *Hilton v United Kingdom* (1988) 57 D.R. 108 at 117–118.
[239] *Young, James and Webster v United Kingdom* (1982) 4 E.H.R.R. 38 at paras 48–49.
[240] *X v United Kingdom* (1978) 15 D.R. 242.
[241] See s.6(3)(b). See paras 3–22 to 3–27. Note, however, that where a private body is brought within the extended definition of a "public authority" by virtue of s.6(3)(b) the duty to act compatibly does not apply to any act or omission which is private in nature: s.6(5).
[242] See para.2–59 below.
[243] Thus, in *Young, James and Webster v United Kingdom* (1982) 4 E.H.R.R. 38 at para.49 the court held that although the "proximate cause" of the applicants' complaint was an agreement between British Rail and the railway unions, "it was the domestic law in force at the relevant time that made lawful the treatment of which the applicants complained". Accordingly the state's responsibility would be engaged for the failure to secure the applicant's rights "in the enactment of domestic legislation". It was this finding which made it unnecessary to consider whether "the state might also be responsible on the ground that it should be regarded as employer or that British Rail was under its control".
[244] *Wille v Liechtenstein* (1997) 24 E.H.R.R. CD 45.
[245] (1994) 17 E.H.R.R. 462.
[246] (1982) 4 E.H.R.R. 482.

v United Kingdom[247] the court was dismissive of the Government's argument that it could not be held liable for unlawful ill-treatment of detainees:

"It is inconceivable that the higher authorities of a state should be, or at least should be entitled to be, unaware of the existence of such a practice. Furthermore, under the Convention those authorities are strictly liable for the conduct of their subordinates; they are under a duty to impose their will on subordinates and cannot shelter behind their inability to ensure that [detainees' rights are] respected."

This approach has the potential to bring about a significant change to the principles of vicarious liability in human rights cases. Compare the cases of *Makanjuola v Metropolitan Police Commissioner*[248] with *Aydin v Turkey*.[249] In *Makanjuola* the plaintiff alleged that she had been indecently assaulted by a police officer who had first offered to suppress a report on an immigration offence in return for sex. Henry J. held that the Commissioner was not vicariously liable under s.48 of the Police Act 1964 since the officer had not been acting in the performance or purported performance of his functions. In *Aydin*, by contrast, the applicant alleged that she had been raped whilst in police custody. The court noted that "rape leaves deep psychological scars on the victim which do not respond to the passage of time as quickly as other forms of physical and mental violence",[250] and had no difficulty at all in ascribing responsibility to the state.

1–79

Standing

The court may receive applications from any legal or natural person, non-governmental organisation or group of individuals, claiming to be a victim of a violation of the Convention.[251] There is no requirement that the complainant must be a citizen of the respondent state, or of any Council of Europe member state.[252] It is sufficient if the complainant is *either* physically[253] *or* legally within the jurisdiction. An applicant need not have legal capacity under domestic law: a complaint can be introduced by a child[254] or a person who is mentally incapacitated,[255] whether or not there is a parent or competent adult willing to act on their behalf.

1–80

An individual may submit a complaint through a duly authorised representative. Parents may represent their children unless there is a conflict of interest or the

1–81

---

[247] (1979–80) 2 E.H.R.R. 25.
[248] *The Times*, August 8, 1989.
[249] (1998) 25 E.H.R.R. 251.
[250] Para.83.
[251] Art.34.
[252] See, for example, *Ahmed v Austria* (1997) 24 E.H.R.R. 278; *D v United Kingdom* (1997) 24 E.H.R.R. 423.
[253] In *D v United Kingdom* (1997) 24 E.H.R.R. at para.48 the court held that it was unnecessary for the applicant to have entered the United Kingdom "in the technical sense" (i.e. lawfully) since he was physically present.
[254] *SP, DP, and T v United Kingdom* (1996) 22 E.H.R.R. CD 148.
[255] *X and Y v Netherlands* (1986) 8 E.H.R.R. 235.

parent lacks the necessary standing to act on the child's behalf.[256] Custodial parents and legal guardians apart, the court will generally require either a signed letter of authority stating that the applicant wishes the representative to act, or some other evidence of the representative's authority.[257] Next of kin may introduce an application on behalf of an individual who has died[258]; and may continue a complaint where the applicant dies during the course of the proceedings, providing the next of kin has a sufficient interest in the case.[259]

1–82   The right of individual petition extends to corporate bodies,[260] to non-governmental organisations[261] and to groups of individuals, including political parties[262] and trade unions.[263] Complaints may not, however, be brought by local or central government bodies,[264] or by other public authorities.[265] Where a complaint is brought by an organisation with the necessary standing, it must be signed by

---

[256] See *Hokkanen v Finland* (1995) 19 E.H.R.R. 139, where the father lacked standing to represent his child under domestic law, and *Scozzari and Giunta v Italy* (2002) 35 E.H.R.R. 12, where the court observed that "in the event of a conflict over a minor's interests between a natural parent and the person appointed by the authorities to act as the child's guardian, there is a danger that some of those interests will never be brought to the court's attention and that the minor will be deprived of effective protection of his rights under the Convention. Consequently, as the Commission observed, even though the mother has been deprived of parental rights—indeed that is one of the causes of the dispute which she has referred to the court—her standing as the natural mother suffices to afford her the necessary power to apply to the court on the children's behalf, too, in order to protect their interests." (para.138)

[257] In *SP, DP, and T v United Kingdom* (1996) 22 E.H.R.R. CD 148 the children's legal representative was held sufficient, despite the inability of the children to give instructions. In *Z v United Kingdom* Application No.28945/95 the Official Solicitor, acting on behalf of children abused by their parents, was held sufficient.

[258] *McCann v United Kingdom* (1996) 21 E.H.R.R. 97; *Osman v United Kingdom* (1999) 1 F.L.R. 198. In this situation the complaint is brought in the name of the next of kin rather than that of the deceased. In

[259] *X v United Kingdom* (1982) 4 E.H.R.R. 188; *Laskey, Jaggard and Brown v United Kingdom* (1997) 24 E.H.R.R. 39; *X v France* (1992) 14 E.H.R.R. 483.

[260] *Air Canada v United Kingdom* (1995) 20 E.H.R.R. 150: *Autotronic AG v Switzerland* (1990) 12 E.H.R.R. 485; *National and Provincial Building Society v United Kingdom* (1998) 25 E.H.R.R. 127. In exceptional cases, the court may be willing to pierce the corporate veil and allow individual shareholders to bring a complaint in respect of an administrative act directed against the company: *Neves E Silva v Portugal* (1989) 13 E.H.R.R. 576; *Agrotexim and others v Greece* (1996) 21 E.H.R.R. 250.

[261] *Association X v United Kingdom* (1978) 14 D.R. 31; *Metropolitan Church of Bessarabia v Moldova* (2002) 35 E.H.R.R. 13.

[262] *Liberal Party v United Kingdom* (1980) 21 D.R. 211. The Commission held that a political party, as "a gathering of people with a common interest", can be considered as a non-governmental organisation or group of individuals. See also *Vatan v Russia* (2006) 42 E.H.R.R. 7: political party with its own legal personality entitled to bring a claim, but on the facts of the case, was not the victim of the alleged breaches.

[263] *CCSU v United Kingdom* (1987) 50 D.R. 228; *Cf. Ahmed v United Kingdom* (1995) 20 E.H.R.R. CD 72.

[264] *Rothenthurm Commune v Switzerland* (1988) 59 D.R. 251; *Ayuntamiento de M. v Spain* (1991) 68 D.R. 209.

[265] In *BBC v United Kingdom* (1996) 84A D.R. 129 the Commission left open the question whether the BBC had standing to bring a complaint under the Convention. *Cf. Hilton v United Kingdom* (1988) 57 D.R. 108 where the Commission left open the question whether the state could be held responsible for the acts of the BBC which were alleged to have breached the applicant's Convention rights.

those competent to represent the organisation.[266] If the organisation or group has no clearly defined legal structure then the application should be signed by all of those on whose behalf it is submitted.

Unincorporated bodies can act on behalf of their members providing they **1–83** identify those members who are "directly affected" by the measure in question, and establish their authority to represent them.[267] In certain circumstances an unincorporated association may itself claim to be a victim of a violation. In *Christians Against Racism and Fascism v United Kingdom*,[268] for example, the applicant association was entitled to claim victim status in respect of an order under s.3 of the Public Order Act 1936 banning a planned procession.

Victim status

In order to qualify as a "victim", within the meaning of Art.34, it is generally **1–84** necessary to establish that the applicant has been directly affected by the measure in issue. The Convention does not permit a class action.[269] Nor does it entitle an individual or organisation to claim in the abstract that a law is incompatible with the Convention.[270]

It does not necessarily follow that an applicant must have suffered a specific **1–85** detriment.[271] The court has held that in certain situations the concept of a victim may include a person who runs the risk of being directly affected by a law, even in the absence of measures applying it to him or her. In *Norris v Ireland*[272] the applicant was found to be a victim of a law criminalising consensual homosexual activity in private, although he had not been prosecuted, and the risk of prosecution was "minimal". The very existence of the law in question affected the applicant, since he was forced to choose between refraining from sexual activity on the one hand and breaking the law on the other. The same reasoning was applied by the Commission in *Sutherland v United Kingdom*,[273] in connection with a complaint that the age of consent for lawful homosexual activity was in breach of Arts 8 and 14 of the Convention. The applicant in that case was found to be a victim despite the fact that the domestic authorities had never shown any interest at all in his sexual activities. Similarly, in *Bowman v United Kingdom*[274] the applicant alleged that her prosecution for incurring unauthorised expenditure

---

[266] r.45(2). In *Credit and Industrial Bank v Czech Republic* (2004) 39 E.H.R.R. 39, the applicant bank had been placed into compulsory administration. The former President of its Board of Directors made an application to the Court. The State argued that the compulsory administrator was the only person with authority to represent the bank in such a claim. However, the Court held that, in the circumstances, to require the bank to contest the appointment of the administrator while being represented by the administrator in proceedings before the Court would render its right of access to the Court under Art.34 "theoretical and illusory" and rejected the State's argument. (paras 51–52).

[267] A failure to identify the members on whose behalf the complaint is made may result in the application being rejected as anonymous.

[268] (1980) 21 D.R. 138.

[269] *Lindsay v United Kingdom* (1997) 23 E.H.R.R. CD 199.

[270] *X v Austria* (1976) 7 D.R. 87.

[271] *Eckle v Germany* (1983) 5 E.H.R.R. 1 at para.66.

[272] (1991) 13 E.H.R.R. 186 at para.31.

[273] (1997) 24 E.H.R.R. CD 22.

[274] (1998) 26 E.H.R.R. 1.

during an election was in breach of the right to freedom of expression in Art.10. Although she had been acquitted of the charge the Court held that she was nevertheless a victim of the alleged violation. The acquittal was on technical grounds (the summons had been issued outside the statutory time limit) and the fact that she had been prosecuted was an indication that unless she modified her behaviour during future elections she was liable to prosecuted again, and possibly convicted and punished. This was sufficient to establish that she was directly affected by the very existence of the law in question.[275]

1–86   The important point to note about this group of cases is that the finding of a violation was based not on a potential future breach, but on the state of affairs existing at the time of the complaint. In each case the provisions of domestic law were alleged, by their mere existence, to have a direct effect on the applicants, and therefore to have violated their Convention rights to privacy and freedom of expression respectively.

1–87   In the context of Art.3 however the Court has been prepared to go further, and has accepted that a potential future violation may be sufficient in itself to satisfy the victim requirement. This approach was first signalled in *Campbell and Cosans v United Kingdom*,[276] a corporal punishment case, where the Court observed *obiter* that "a *mere threat* of conduct prohibited by Article 3 may itself conflict with that provision", provided the threat was sufficiently real and immediate. As an example, the Court suggested that to threaten an individual with torture might constitute "at least" inhuman treatment. This approach was taken to its logical conclusion in the landmark decision of *Soering v United Kingdom*.[277] The applicant in that case complained that the decision to extradite him to face trial in the United States would involve a breach of Art.3 of the Convention since he would, if convicted, be liable be detained under intolerable conditions on death row. Despite the inherent uncertainty in the situation—and, in particular, the possibility of an acquittal—the Court held that the applicant could claim to be a "victim" of the potential violation. In the court's view, the gravity of the harm to which he was potentially exposed justified a relaxation of the "victim" requirement[278]:

> "It is not normally for the Convention institutions to pronounce on the existence or otherwise of potential violations of the Convention. However, where an applicant complains that a decision to extradite him would, if implemented, be contrary to Article 3 by reason of its foreseeable consequences in the requesting country, a departure from

---

[275] The Court's approach in *Bowman* is consistent with *Times Newspapers Ltd v United Kingdom* (1990) 65 D.R. 307 in which the Commission observed that a publisher might be a victim of a violation of Art.10, arising from real uncertainty in the law of defamation, even though no defamation proceedings had been brought against any of its newspapers. *Cf. Leigh, Guardian Newspapers and Observer Ltd v United Kingdom* (1984) 38 D.R. 75, where the Commission held that the applicants could not claim to be victims in relation to a decision of the House of Lords establishing potential liability in contempt, simply on the basis that on some future date, in unknown circumstances, they may be prosecuted.

[276] (1982) 4 E.H.R.R. 293 at para.26.

[277] (1989) 11 E.H.R.R. 439. See also the decision of the UN Human Rights Committee in *Judge v Canada* (2005) 40 E.H.R.R. SE4.

[278] At para.90.

this principle is necessary, in view of the serious and irreparable nature of the alleged suffering risked, in order to ensure the effectiveness of the safeguard provided by that Article."

The Court established the fundamental principle that a decision to extradite a **1–88** fugitive offender will give rise to an issue under Art.3, and hence engage the responsibility of the contracting state, if there are "substantial grounds for believing" that the person concerned faces a "real risk" of being subjected to torture or inhuman or degrading treatment or punishment in the requesting country. In *D v United Kingdom*[279] the Court applied the same approach to a decision to deport a convicted drug trafficker after the expiry of his sentence.[280] However, in *GHH v Turkey*[281] the court held that since the applicants, Iranian nationals who feared breaches of Arts 2, 3 and 8 if deported from Turkey to Iran, were living in the United States by the time the court came to consider the merits, the threat of unlawful treatment was no longer in existence and accordingly the applicants were no longer "victims" within the meaning of Art.34.[282]

The Court has also given an extended meaning to the term "victim" in the **1–89** context of secret surveillance and other intelligence-gathering measures. A relaxation of the "victim" requirement is necessary in this area to ensure that the right of individual petition is effective. The applicable principles are considered in Ch.7 below.[283]

In certain circumstances an individual may claim to be an "indirect victim" for **1–90** the purposes of Art.34. This will usually arise where the applicant has suffered as a result of a violation of the Convention rights of another and the primary victim is unable to pursue a complaint. Thus, in *McCann v United Kingdom*[284] the relatives of three members of an IRA active service unit killed by British soldiers in Gibraltar were held to be indirect victims of a violation of the right to life in Art.2. Similarly, in *Osman v United Kingdom*,[285] which concerned an alleged failure by the police to prevent a homicidal attack, the court assumed that the wife of the deceased could claim to be an indirect victim. In *McGlinchey v United Kingdom*[286] the applicants were the children and mother of a woman who died in prison, and were again assumed by the court to have standing to bring the claim, while in *Jordan v United Kingdom*[287] the applicant brought proceedings on behalf of his son, who had been killed by security forces in Northern Ireland. The situation where an applicant dies while the application is pending was considered in *Jecius v Lithuania*,[288] where the Court held that:

---

[279] (1997) 24 E.H.R.R. 423.
[280] This was despite the fact that the risk of inhuman treatment identified in that case arose not from the threatened acts of the authorities in the state concerned, but from the absence of adequate medical facilities.
[281] (2003) 37 E.H.R.R. 4.
[282] Para.28.
[283] At paras 7–06 to 7–09.
[284] (1996) 21 E.H.R.R. 97.
[285] (1999) 1 F.L.R. 198.
[286] (2003) 37 E.H.R.R. 41.
[287] (2003) 37 E.H.R.R. 2.
[288] (2002) 35 E.H.R.R. 16.

"Where an applicant dies during the examination of the case concerning the unlawfulness of detention, the heirs or next of kin of an applicant may in principle pursue the application on the applicant's behalf."[289]

1–91   The Court has held, on a number of occasions, that it is not necessary for an applicant to show that the measure in question has caused specific prejudice or damage[290] (damage being relevant primarily to the assessment of just satisfaction under Art.41). Thus, in *Artico v Italy*,[291] the Court held that where a criminal defendant could establish that his legal representation failed to meet the standards imposed by Art.6(3)(c), it was unnecessary, and arguably impossible, for him to prove that effective representation would have secured his acquittal. Similarly, in *Benham v United Kingdom*[292] the Court found a violation of Art.6(3)(c) arising from the absence of legal aid for committal proceedings in the Magistrates Court, but awarded the applicant no compensation

"in view of the impossibility of speculating as to whether the magistrates would have made the order for [the applicant's] detention had he been represented at the hearing before them".

1–92   On the other hand, an individual may fail to qualify as a victim if adequate redress has been afforded in the national legal system. Thus, the Commission has held that an applicant who complains that his conviction was obtained in breach of the due process guarantees in Art.6, will cease to be a victim if he has been acquitted,[293] if his conviction has been quashed,[294] or if the procedural defect has been fully remedied on appeal.[295]

However, a decision or measure favourable to the applicant is not sufficient to deprive him of his status as a "victim" unless the national authorities have acknowledged, either expressly or in substance, and then afforded redress for, the breach of the Convention.[296]

1–93   In *Eckle v Germany*[297] the criminal proceedings against the applicants were found to have exceeded the reasonable time guarantee in Art.6(1). The domestic courts had reduced the sentence imposed on the applicants and discontinued subsequent proceedings. On the facts, this was held not to have deprived the applicants of their status as victims. However, the court went on to say that the position may be different where the national courts have acknowledged the breach of the Convention and have adequately reduced a criminal sentence with the express intention of providing appropriate redress for the violation.

---

[289] Para.41.
[290] *Eckle v Germany* (1983) 5 E.H.R.R. 1 at para.66.
[291] (1981) 3 E.H.R.R. 1 at para.35.
[292] (1996) 22 E.H.R.R. 293 at para.68; See also *Perks and Others v United Kingdom* (2000) 30 E.H.R.R. 33.
[293] *X v Austria* (1974) 1 D.R. 44 at 45.
[294] *Reed v United Kingdom* (1979) 19 D.R. 113 at 142 (quashing of an adjudication by a prison Board of Visitors).
[295] See *Edwards v United Kingdom* (1993) 15 E.H.R.R. 417. *Cf. Rowe and Davis v United Kingdom* (2000) 30 E.H.R.R. 1; *Condron and Condron v United Kingdom* [2001] 31 E.H.R.R. 1.
[296] *Posokhov v Russia* (2004) 39 E.H.R.R. 21, at para.35.
[297] (1983) 5 E.H.R.R. 1 at paras 66 to 70. See also *Dalban v Romania* (2001) 31 E.H.R.R. 39, para.44.

The question whether the domestic courts have provided adequate redress will in **1–94**
the end depend upon the nature of the violation alleged. Where, for example, the
applicant's complaint relates to the substance of the criminal law,[298] rather than
any specific measure which has been taken against him, it will often be difficult
for the prosecution to argue that an acquittal or a successful appeal has remedied
the violation.[299] As we have seen, the Court did not consider that the acquittal of
the applicant in *Bowman v United Kingdom*[300] deprived her of her status as a
victim in the context of a complaint that the existence of a particular criminal
offence violated her right to freedom of expression.

Manifestly ill-founded

The second limb of Art.35(3) requires the Court to declare inadmissible any **1–95**
application which is manifestly ill-founded. This has been interpreted as a test of
prima facie arguability. In principle it applies to cases where the evidence
submitted fails to substantiate the complaint; where the facts do not disclose an
interference with a protected right; where the interference is plainly justified; or
where the applicant has ceased to be a victim. In practice however, the Court has
used this ground of inadmissibility as a means of controlling its caseload, and has
often conducted a detailed examination of the merits of a complaint before
declaring it to be "manifestly" ill-founded.

Abuse of the right of petition

The third limb of Art.35(3) requires the Court to declare inadmissible any **1–96**
complaint which constitutes an abuse of the right of petition. It may be applied
in cases of forgery or misrepresentation; vexatious or repeated applications;
offensive or provocative language[301]; or deliberate breach of the court's rulings.
A refusal to enter into friendly settlement negotiations will not constitute an
abuse of the right of petition.[302] Nor is an application abusive merely because it
has a political motivation[303]; or because it is brought by a criminal defendant who
has absconded from custody.[304]

Estoppel

The Rules of Court specifically provide that a respondent state must raise any **1–97**
inadmissibility arguments in its written or oral observations prior to the court's

---

[298] See para.1–85 above and Ch.8 below.
[299] Unless the court in question is able under the Human Rights Act to remove the incompatibility
by construction: see para.3–34 below.
[300] (1998) 26 E.H.R.R. 1.
[301] *Stamoulakatos v United Kingdom* (1997) 23 E.H.R.R. CD 113. See also the admissibility
decision in *Norwood v United Kingdom* (2005) 40 E.H.R.R. SE11, where the court held that the
application, by a BNP member who had displayed posters which were highly offensive to Muslims,
was inadmissible as an abuse of the right of petition and incompatible *ratione materiae* with the
provisions of the Convention, pursuant to Arts 35(3) and (4).
[302] *Andronicou and Constantinou v Cyprus* (1997) 25 E.H.R.R. 491.
[303] *Akdivar v Turkey* (1997) 23 E.H.R.R. 143; *Cf. McFeely v United Kingdom* (1980) 20 D.R. 44;
McQuiston v United Kingdom (1986) 46 D.R. 182 (An application motivated by the desire for
publicity or propaganda may be abusive if it is not supported by any facts or if it is outside the scope
of the Convention).
[304] *Van der Tang v Spain* (1996) 22 E.H.R.R. 363.

decision on admissibility, unless it is impracticable to do so.[305] This reflects the long-established practice of the former court.[306] In *DeWilde, Ooms Versyp v Belgium (No.1)*[307] the respondent government was estopped from raising preliminary objections to admissibility which had not been argued before the Commission. The Court explained that:

> "It is in fact the usual practice in international and national courts that objections to admissibility should as a general rule be raised *in limine litis*. This, if not always mandatory, is at least a requirement of the proper administration of justice and of legal stability ... [I]t results clearly from the general economy of the Convention that objections to jurisdiction and admissibility must, in principle, be raised first before the Commission to the extent that their character and the circumstances permit."

Likewise, in *Artico v Italy*,[308] the Court emphasised that "the structure of the machinery of protection established by ... the Convention is designed to ensure that the course of the proceedings is logical and orderly". In the Court's view "the spirit of the Convention requires that respondent States should normally raise their preliminary objections at the stage of the initial examination of admissibility, failing which they will be estopped".

1–98   Moreover, any admissibility objection must be clearly and explicitly pleaded.[309] If an argument has been raised prior to a ruling on admissibility that the applicant is not a "victim" within the meaning of Art.34, it is not open to the government to resurrect the same argument at a later stage in the form of a plea of non-exhaustion.[310] Similarly, if the government has relied on one remedy in support of a plea of non-exhaustion at the admissibility stage, it may be estopped from invoking a different remedy thereafter.[311] In *Aydin v Turkey*,[312] a case involving an allegation of rape in custody, the government was estopped from arguing non-exhaustion and abuse of the right of individual petition since it had failed to assert these arguments clearly before the Commission. A similar conclusion was reached by the court in *Eugenia Michaelidou Developments Ltd and Tymvios v Turkey*.[313]

1–99   The Court may however declare a case inadmissible at any stage of the proceedings.[314] There are three principal situations in which the court will be prepared to consider admissibility objections at the merits stage of its deliberations. The first is where the objection was raised at the appropriate time, but was wrongly

---

[305] r.55. For an example of the application of this principle see *Baskay and Okcuoglu v Turkey* (Application Nos 23536/94 and 24408/94) Judgment of July 8, 1999, paras 68–70.

[306] *De Wilde, Ooms and Versyp v Belgium* (1979–80) 1 E.H.R.R. 373; *Artico v Italy* (1981) 3 E.H.R.R. 1; *Bozano v France* (1986) 9 E.H.R.R. 297.

[307] (1979–80) 1 E.H.R.R. 373 at paras 53–54.

[308] (1981) 3 E.H.R.R. 1 at para.27.

[309] *Foti v Italy* (1983) 5 E.H.R.R. 313 at para.47: "vague assertions" of non-exhaustion of domestic remedies found insufficient.

[310] *Pine Valley Developments v Ireland* (1992) 14 E.H.R.R. 319 at para.45.

[311] *Tomassi v France* (1993) 15 E.H.R.R. 1 at para.106.

[312] (1998) 25 E.H.R.R. 251 at para.60.

[313] (2004) 39 E.H.R.R. 36.

[314] Art.35(4).

rejected.[315] Although the existing decisions in this category concern Commission rulings on the admissibility of a complaint, there is no reason in principle why the same point could not arise under Protocol 11 (where a Chamber has rejected an admissibility objection which is then re-argued before the Grand Chamber, either on a relinquishment[316] or on a referral[317]).

The second situation is where there has been a development in national law **1–100** clarifying the existence of a domestic remedy which appeared doubtful when the admissibility of the application was initially considered. *Campbell and Fell v United Kingdom*[318] is an example. At the time of the Commission's decision on the admissibility of the applicants' complaints, there was binding Divisional Court authority excluding the possibility of judicial review.[319] This was subsequently reversed by the Court of Appeal.[320] In the court's view the government could not have been expected to raise the plea of non-exhaustion prior to the decision of the Court of Appeal, and accordingly no estoppel arose.[321]

The third situation is where the scope of the applicant's complaint has broadened **1–101** since the admissibility decision so as to generate new admissibility objections not previously open to the government. In *Bonisch v Austria*[322] the application, which alleged a breach of Art.6(1), was declared admissible by the Commission. In his memorial to the Court however, the applicant argued that in addition to the pleaded violation of Art.6(1), the complaint disclosed a breach of the presumption of innocence in Art.6(2). The Court held that it had jurisdiction to consider the new argument since it had "an evident connection" with the complaints which the applicant had raised before the Commission. However, the fresh complaint would be subject to any admissibility objections which could have been taken at the appropriate stage.[323]

Finally, it should be noted that it is not open to a contracting state to rely on an **1–102** objection to admissibility which is inconsistent with a submission made on its behalf before the national courts. Thus, for example, it is not open to a government to argue that an applicant has failed to exhaust domestic remedies when it has argued in the domestic proceedings that such remedies are unavailable.[324]

---

[315] *Van Oosterwijk v Belgium* (1981) 3 E.H.R.R. 557 paras 30–34; *Cardot v France* (1991) 13 E.H.R.R. 853 at paras 32–36; *Bahaddar v Netherlands* (1998) 26 E.H.R.R. 278.

[316] See para.1–114 below.

[317] See para.1–149 below.

[318] (1985) 7 E.H.R.R. 165.

[319] *R. v Hull Prison Board of Visitors ex parte St Germain and others* [1978] 2 All E.R. 198.

[320] [1979] Q.B. 425.

[321] In the case of the first applicant, however, the court considered that it would be unjust to reject the complaint for non-exhaustion since he had allowed the time limit for judicial review to expire in reliance in the Commission's decision: para.63.

[322] (1987) 9 E.H.R.R. 191.

[323] In the event the court did not consider it necessary to rule on the alleged violation of Art.6(2).

[324] *Pine Valley Developments v Ireland* (1992) 14 E.H.R.R. 319; *Kolompar v Belgium* (1993) 16 E.H.R.R. 197.

Post admissibility procedures

1–103   Once a case has been declared admissible the Chamber will have the functions of examining the merits of the application and placing itself at the disposal of the parties with a view to reaching a friendly settlement.[325] The Chamber may carry out fact-finding investigations anywhere in the territory of the Convention states, and may hold an oral hearing. At any point prior to the delivery of a judgment on the merits, the Chamber may decide to relinquish jurisdiction in favour of a Grand Chamber. If the Chamber decides to retain jurisdiction it will deliver a judgment on the merits of the complaint and on the applicant's claim for just satisfaction.

Factual investigations

1–104   Article 38(1)(a) provides that the Court may undertake an investigation to clarify the facts of a case, and if it does so, the respondent state must "furnish all necessary facilities". Whilst the seat of the Court is at Strasbourg, the rules expressly permit the Court to perform any of its functions elsewhere in the Council of Europe, and enable the Court to delegate its investigative functions to individual judges.[326]

1–105   The Chamber may obtain any evidence which it considers capable of providing clarification of the facts of the case. It may request the parties to furnish documents, or hear any witness, including an expert witness, whose testimony or statements seem likely to assist; it may depute an individual judge or a delegation of judges to conduct an inquiry, carry out an on the spot investigation, or take evidence in any manner; it may appoint an independent expert to assist a delegation; and it may ask any person or institution to obtain information, express an opinion or make a report on any specific point.[327]

1–106   Where a fact-finding delegation is appointed, the head of the delegation presides over any hearing and the delegation has jurisdiction to exercise any power conferred on a Chamber under the Convention or the Rules of Court.[328] The President of the Court may request the assistance of the government of any contracting state in making the necessary arrangements for on the spot investigations, or for the service of summonses to procure evidence or attendance of witnesses situated in the state's territory.[329]

Friendly settlement

1–107   Once an application has been declared admissible the Registrar will contact the parties with a view to securing a friendly settlement "on the basis of respect for human rights as defined in the Convention and its protocols".[330] The Chamber

---

[325] Arts 38 and 39.
[326] r.19(1) and (2).
[327] r.A1, Appendix to the Rules (Concerning Investigations).
[328] r.A2.
[329] rr.A2 and A5.
[330] Art.38(1)(b) and r.62(1).

may take any steps that appear appropriate to facilitate such a settlement.[331] Each party's proposals will be communicated to the opposing party and, in exceptional cases, the Registry may convene a meeting to discuss the proposals. The friendly settlement procedure is confidential.[332] Any position may be adopted by either party without prejudice to the arguments they have advanced or may advance in the proceedings.[333] Thus, no written or oral communication, or concession made in the course of friendly settlement negotiations may be referred to or relied on in the contentious proceedings.[334]

Prior to the introduction of Protocol 11 it was common for the Commission to **1–108** communicate its provisional view of the merits of a complaint to the parties in confidence, with a view to promoting a friendly settlement. The Explanatory Report to Protocol 11 appears to assume that the court will follow the same practice.[335] Such a procedure does not, however, sit comfortably with the Court's function of delivering a final and binding judgment on the merits of a case, and the court has not been enthusiastic about disclosing the state of its deliberations to the parties before it has reached a final decision.

Any settlement reached between the parties must be approved by the Chamber, **1–109** to ensure that it has been reached on the basis of "respect for human rights".[336] If the court approves a settlement then the application will be struck off the court's list.[337] The court will then issue a decision containing a brief statement of the facts and the solution reached.[338]

Most friendly settlements consist of monetary compensation together with the **1–110** payment of the applicant's reasonable legal costs.[339] Sometimes, however, a government may agree to introduce changes to rules of practice or delegated legislation as part of the settlement.[340] It is rare for states to agree to amend or introduce primary legislation since it will usually be impossible for the government to guarantee that any proposal will be approved by the legislature. Where an amendment to primary legislation is the only way to prevent further violations, the government will sometimes agree to introduce draft legislation into Parliament, and ask the Court to adjourn its consideration of the case pending the

---

[331] r.62(1).

[332] Art.38(2).

[333] r.62(2). A refusal to enter into friendly settlement negotiations cannot be characterised as an abuse of the right of petition: *Andronicou and Constantinou v Cyprus* (1998) 25 E.H.R.R. 491.

[334] r.62(2).

[335] (1994) 17 E.H.R.R. 514 at 529, para.78.

[336] r.62(3). In principle, the court may reject a settlement reached between the parties. This is only likely to occur in practice if the complaint disclosed a pattern of violations, and the government had no plans to amend the relevant provisions of domestic law.

[337] Art.39, r.62(3).

[338] Art.39.

[339] It is always preferable to include a figure for costs as part of the agreed settlement approved by the court since there is no method of taxation in the friendly settlement procedure once the case has been struck off the list.

[340] In *Faulkner v United Kingdom*, *The Times*, January 11, 2000 the government agreed, as part of the friendly settlement approved by the court, to introduce a system of civil legal aid for Guernsey.

outcome.[341] In *Broniowski v Poland*,[342] the case reached a friendly settlement at Grand Chamber stage, since Poland had enacted remedial legislation following the judgment of the Chamber.

Withdrawal

1–111   Once a complaint has been registered, it is for the Court to decide whether or not the case should proceed to a final judgment on the merits. The applicant is not free to withdraw at will. The Court may strike off its list any complaint which the applicant does not intend to pursue, or which has been resolved.[343] However, the court must continue with its examination of the case if "respect for human rights as defined in the Convention and the protocols thereto so requires".[344] This reflects the fact that many applications have implications for the public order of the Council of Europe, so that the significance of a case may not be confined to the vindication of the rights of the individual applicant.

1–112   In *Tyrer v United Kingdom*[345] the applicant had been sentenced to judicial corporal punishment on the Isle of Man following his conviction for an offence of assault. The punishment had been carried out six years earlier, when the applicant was aged 15. Whilst the complaint was being considered by the Commission, the applicant indicated that he wished to withdraw. The Commission refused to accede to his request on the ground that "the case raised questions of a general character affecting the observance of the Convention which necessitated a further examination of the issued involved". The applicant took no further part in the proceedings. When the case came before the Court, the government applied to strike it out of the list in view of the applicant's position and in view of the fact that legislation had been adopted by the Manx Parliament to abolish corporal punishment for assault. The Court held that it could only strike a case from the list if there had been "a friendly settlement, arrangement or other fact of a kind to provide a solution to the matter". In the Court's view, the applicant's request to withdraw unilaterally did not constitute a friendly settlement or a solution to the matter. Nether did the Court consider the proposal to amend the law constituted a solution:

> "There is no certainty as to whether or when the proposal will become law and, even if adopted, it cannot erase a punishment already inflicted. What is more, the proposed legislation does not go to the substance of the issue before the Court, namely whether judicial corporal punishment as inflicted on the applicant in accordance with Manx legislation is contrary to the Convention."

1–113   By contrast in *Z v United Kingdom*[346] the Commission permitted the withdrawal of an application which had been introduced by the Official Solicitor on behalf of a child. The complaint alleged that the failure of social services to protect the

---

[341] This course was adopted following the Commission's decision in *Sutherland v United Kingdom* (1997) 24 E.H.R.R. CD 22.
[342] (2006) 43 E.H.R.R. 1.
[343] Art.37(1).
[344] Art.37(1).
[345] (1979–80) 2 E.H.R.R. 1.
[346] Application No.29392/95.

child and her four siblings from parental abuse was in breach of Art.3. The child had since been adopted, and her adoptive parents had expressed an intention to withdraw. In reaching the conclusion that the child should cease to be an applicant, the Commission

> "had regard to the expressed wishes of the adoptive parents who, in the normal course of events, would be the appropriate representatives of D, and to the fact that the important Convention issues in the case would be examined in respect of the remaining applicants".[347]

Relinquishment to a Grand Chamber

Where a case raises a serious question concerning the interpretation of the Convention, or where the judgment of the Chamber may be inconsistent with a previous judgment of the court, the Chamber may, at any time before it has rendered its judgment, relinquish the case to a Grand Chamber, unless one of the parties to the case objects.[348] If the Chamber proposes to adopt this course, the Registrar will notify the parties, who will have one month within which to file a "duly reasoned" objection.[349] The Chamber need not give reasons for its decision to relinquish jurisdiction.[350] A Grand Chamber dealing with a case which has been relinquished prior to judgment by the Chamber will include the national judge elected in respect of the state against which the case has been brought,[351] the President and Vice Presidents of the Court, and the Presidents of the four Chambers.

1–114

Oral hearings

There is no absolute entitlement to an oral hearing, but the Explanatory Report to Protocol 11[352] creates a strong presumption in favour of an oral stage to the proceedings.[353] As we have seen, a Chamber may decide to hold such a hearing before declaring a case admissible. Where the Chamber has declared the case admissible on the written pleadings alone, an oral hearing can be held at the merits stage, if either party requests one or the court considers it appropriate.[354]

1–115

---

[347] Para.23.

[348] Art.30.

[349] r.72(2). Under r.72(2), an objection which is not "duly reasoned" will be considered invalid by the Chamber. There is no indication in the Convention or the Rules as to what reasons need to be advanced. This gives rise to a potential conflict between the Rules and the Explanatory Report to Protocol 11 (1994) 17 E.H.R.R. 514. Paras 46 and 79 of the Explanatory Report suggest that the reason why relinquishment has been made subject to the approval of the parties is to ensure that they are not otherwise deprived of their right to a re-hearing under Art.43. However, r.72 suggests that once the Chamber has decided to relinquish jurisdiction the parties must advance adequate reasons for their objection.

[350] r.72(1).

[351] Art.27(2). The national judge may not however preside: r.13.

[352] (1994) 17 E.H.R.R. 514.

[353] Para.44 provides that "The procedure will be written and oral, unless otherwise decided by the court after consultation with the parties". Paragraph 45 provides "The parties will present their submissions by means of a written procedure. Oral procedure will consist of a hearing at which the applicant . . . and the respondent state will have the right to speak.".

[354] r.59(3).

However the Chamber may decide to dispense with an oral hearing.[355] It will consider, under r.59(3), whether "the discharge of its functions under the Convention" requires such a hearing. Historically, oral hearings on the merits have been the norm, but the increasing workload of the court has led to hearings being dispensed with in a greater number of cases.

1–116   Where a hearing is held, the Court may ask the parties to address specific issues in their oral pleadings. The President will decide the order and duration of the parties' submissions.[356] In a typical case, the applicant will begin, and will be afforded 30 minutes to address the principal issues in the case. The government will respond for a similar period. The members of the Court may then put further questions to the parties' representatives.[357] The parties will then be given a further 15 minutes in which to answer the judges' questions and respond to the submissions of the opposing party. Exceptionally, the Court may summon witnesses to give evidence on oath,[358] who may then be examined by the judges and the parties.[359]

Evidence and burden of proof

1–117   There are no formal rules for the admissibility of evidence under the Convention. Parties may submit any relevant documentary material, whether or not it complies with the formalities of domestic law governing admissibility, and there is no restriction on the admission of hearsay evidence. Such evidence was called by the Court in *Tepe v Turkey*,[360] in order to try to establish the complex facts relating to the disappearance of the applicant's son.

1–118   At the admissibility stage, the government bears the burden of proving the existence and availability of effective remedies in the national legal system in support of plea of non-exhaustion.[361] Once the existence of such a remedy has been raised it is for the applicant to show why it was unavailable or inadequate in the circumstances.[362]

1–119   The Court does not apply formalised rules for the burden and standard of proof, when it comes to consider the merits of a complaint. Instead, it will base its assessment on an examination of "all the material before it, whether originating from the Commission, the Parties or other sources" and, if necessary, material

---

[355] The court has construed its powers to dispense with an oral hearing flexibly, enabling it to decide straightforward cases—which would previously have been referred to the Committee of Ministers—without an oral hearing at any stage.

[356] r.64(1).

[357] r.64(2).

[358] r.A1.

[359] r.A7.

[360] (2004) 39 E.H.R.R. 29. See also *Cicek v Turkey* (2003) 37 E.H.R.R. 20 and *Bilgin v Turkey* (2003) 36 E.H.R.R. 50.

[361] See para.1–52 above.

[362] *Donnelly v United Kingdom* (1972) 4 D.R. 4 at para.64; *Akdivar v Turkey* (1997) 23 E.H.R.R. 143 at para.68.

obtained by the court of its own motion.[363] The court's approach to the evidence is determined by the nature of the violation and the issues in dispute between the parties.

In general, it is for the applicant make out a *prima facie* case that there has been **1–120** an interference with a protected right,[364] and to raise at least an arguable basis for an eventual finding of a violation. In the absence of any evidence on a disputed issue of fact, the court will tend to accord the benefit of the doubt to the government, unless the nature of the breach is such as to create a presumption in the applicant's favour.[365] In *Goddi v Italy*[366] for example, the applicant complained that he had not been produced for the hearing of his appeal. He maintained that he had notified the prison authorities of the date of the hearing. The government contested this allegation, but neither party adduced any evidence in support of its position. The court held that in these circumstances it was unable to resolve the dispute, and it was not therefore prepared to find that the Italian authorities were at fault. However, where the applicant has submitted evidence in support of a complaint it is not enough for the government to express reservations about that evidence. The state is under a positive duty to provide the court with any relevant information which is in its possession, or to which it could gain access.[367]

The Court will start from an assumption that the domestic authorities have acted **1–121** impartially,[368] in good faith[369] and in accordance with domestic law.[370] It will generally rely on findings of fact which have been reached by the domestic courts, unless they have drawn arbitrary conclusions from the evidence before them.[371] This is especially true in cases which depend on the credibility of witnesses.[372] As the Commission observed in *Stewart v United Kingdom*[373] "the national judge, unlike the Commission, has had the benefit of listening to the witnesses at first hand and assessing the credibility and probative value of their testimony".

---

[363] *Ireland v United Kingdom* (1979–80) 2 E.H.R.R. 25 at para.160. The court has since held that this approach is applicable in individual applications as well as inter-state cases: *Artico v Italy* (1981) 3 E.H.R.R. 1 at para.30.

[364] *Artico v Italy* (1981) 3 E.H.R.R. 1 at para.30.

[365] See paras 1–125 and 5–36 below.

[366] (1984) 6 E.H.R.R. 457.

[367] *Artico v Italy* (1981) 3 E.H.R.R. 1 at para.30.

[368] *LeCompte, Van Leuren and DeMeyer v Belgium* (1982) 4 E.H.R.R. 1 at para.58.

[369] *Kraska v Switzerland* (1994) 18 E.H.R.R. 188.

[370] See *Esbester v United Kingdom* (1993) 18 E.H.R.R. CD 72 at 76, where the Commission found that the compilation of intelligence information about the applicant under the Security Services Act 1989 was compatible with Art.8 because of the statutory safeguards and "the absence of any evidence or indication that the system is not functioning as required by domestic law".

[371] *Klaas v Germany* (1994) 18 E.H.R.R. 305 at paras 29–31; *Edwards v United Kingdom* (1993) 15 E.H.R.R. 417 at para.34; *Van Mechelen v Netherlands* (1998) 25 E.H.R.R. 647 at para.50; *Barbera, Messegue and Jabardo v Spain* (1989) 11 E.H.R.R. 360; *Kostovski v Netherlands* (1990) 12 E.H.R.R. 434 at para.39; *Monnell and Morris v United Kingdom* (1987) 10 E.H.R.R. 205 at paras 49 and 69.

[372] *Murray and ors v United Kingdom* (1995) 19 E.H.R.R. 193 at paras 57–63; *Klaas v Germany* (1993) 18 E.H.R.R. 305 at 338 paras 30–31.

[373] (1984) 39 D.R. 162 at 168.

1–122   If an interference is established or admitted, the burden will shift to the government to advance "relevant and sufficient reasons" to justify it.[374] The government is expected to adduce evidence in support of any justification which it advances.[375] The standard of justification required depends on the nature of the violation. In *Dudgeon v United Kingdom*,[376] for example, the Court held that the government must demonstrate "particularly serious reasons" to justify an interference with a person's private sexual activity. Similarly, the Court has held that "very weighty reasons" are required to justify a difference in treatment based on gender, race or other "suspect categories" of discrimination.[377] Where an interference with the right to freedom of expression is in issue, the justification must be "convincingly established".[378]

1–123   The burden of justifying an arrest or detention always rests on the government.[379] In *Fox, Campbell and Hartley v United Kingdom*[380] the government found itself unable to discharge this burden since the evidence upon which it sought to rely involved matters of national security which it was unable to disclose. The Court was not prepared to rely on a bare assertion that the arrest was justified:

> "The Court must be enabled to ascertain whether the essence of the safeguard afforded by Article 5(1)(c) has been secured. Consequently the respondent government has to furnish at least some facts or information capable of satisfying the Court that the arrested person was reasonably suspected of having committed the alleged offence."[381]

1–124   The limited information supplied by the government did not meet the minimum standard set by Art.5(3)(c) for judging the reasonableness of a suspicion relied upon to justify the arrest of an individual. There had therefore been a violation of Art.5. However, four years later, in *Murray v United Kingdom*,[382] the Court was "prepared to attach some credence" to the government's assertion that the applicants' arrests were justified by confidential information. Whilst such an

---

[374] See, for example, *Buckley v United Kingdom* (1997) 23 E.H.R.R. 101 at para.77. In the context of alleged discrimination contrary to Art.14 the court has held that the burden is on the applicant to demonstrate a difference in treatment on grounds of "status" between himself and another person who is in a relevantly similar position: *Selcuk and Asker v Turkey* (1998) 26 E.H.R.R. 477 at para.102. If this burden is discharged then it is for the government to establish an "objective and reasonable justification" for the difference: *Darby v Sweden* (1991) 13 E.H.R.R. 774 at para.31; *Marckx v Belgium* (1979–80) 2 E.H.R.R. 330 at para.32.

[375] *Autotronic AG v Switzerland* (1990) 12 E.H.R.R. 485 at paras 60–63. See also *Smith and Grady v United Kingdom* (2000) 29 E.H.R.R. 493 at para.99, where the court referred to "the lack of concrete evidence" to substantiate the justification for excluding homosexuals from the armed forces; *Kokkinakis v Greece* (1994) 17 E.H.R.R. 397 where the court found a violation of Art.9 on the ground that the government had adduced no evidence that the applicant was guilty of attempting to convert others to his faith "by improper means".

[376] (1982) 4 E.H.R.R. 149.

[377] *Karlheinz and Schmidt v Germany* (1994) 18 E.H.R.R. 513 at para.24; *East African Asians Case* (1981) 3 E.H.R.R. 76.

[378] *Barthold v Germany* (1985) 7 E.H.R.R. 383 at para.58.

[379] *Zamir v United Kingdom* (1983) 40 D.R. 42.

[380] (1991) 13 E.H.R.R. 157.

[381] Para.34.

[382] (1995) 19 E.H.R.R. 193 at para.59.

assertion could never be sufficient in itself,[383] the Court went to considerable lengths in *Murray* to identify other objective evidence which was capable of justifying the applicants' arrests.

Where it is alleged that state agents have inflicted inhuman and degrading **1–125** treatment, the Court has observed that "heightened vigilance" is required.[384] In *Ireland v United Kingdom*[385] the Court held that a violation of Art.3 requires proof beyond reasonable doubt, but went on to say that "such proof may follow from the coexistence of sufficiently strong, clear and concordant inferences or of *similar unrebutted presumptions of fact*".[386] One such presumption of fact arises where an applicant has sustained injuries whilst in police custody.[387] Equally, the court has held in cases of lengthy disappearances at the hands of security forces that there arises a presumption that the individuals concerned have been killed, imposing a burden on the State to justify its actions.[388]

Judgment on the merits

In the absence of a friendly settlement or relinquishment, the Chamber will **1–126** deliver a judgment on the merits of the application. Whether it is sitting as a Chamber or a Grand Chamber, the Court deliberates in private and its deliberations are secret.[389] The Registrar may be present but may not take part in the deliberations.[390] The Court's judgments are expressed in the form of a single collegiate ruling, which may be accompanied by separate opinions in which individual judges express concurring or dissenting views.[391] Article 45(2) provides that

"if a judgment does not represent, in whole or in part, the unanimous opinion of the judges, any judge shall be entitled to deliver a separate opinion".[392]

This represents a compromise between the usual common law approach, under which each member of the Court is required to state his or her decision, however briefly, and the approach adopted by the European Court of Justice and some constitutional courts[393] where a single judgment is delivered with no scope for elaboration or dissent by individual judges.

---

[383] See para.60.

[384] *Ribitsch v Austria* (1996) 21 E.H.R.R. 573 at para.32.

[385] (1979–80) 2 E.H.R.R. 25.

[386] At para.161.

[387] See para.5–36 below.

[388] This approach has been taken in numerous cases against Turkey, including *Cicek v Turkey* (2003) 37 E.H.R.R. 20 and *I Bilgin v Turkey* (2002) 35 E.H.R.R. 39.

[389] r.22(1).

[390] r.22(2).

[391] Any decision of the Chamber must state whether it was taken unanimously or by a majority and must be accompanied by reasons: r.56(1).

[392] See also r.74(2) which provides that "any judge who has taken part in the consideration of a case shall be entitled to annex to the judgment either a separate opinion, concurring or dissenting from that judgment, or a bare statement of dissent".

[393] Art.34(4)(5) of the Irish Constitution, for example, expressly provides that where the Supreme Court is called upon to determine the constitutional validity of a law, the court is to nominate one of its number to give the judgment and no other opinion, dissenting or concurring, is to be delivered.

1–127 The content of the judgment is prescribed by the Convention and the Rules of Court. Art.45(1) simply requires that "reasons shall be given for judgments, as well as for decisions declaring a case admissible or inadmissible". Rule 74 is more specific. It provides that the judgment must set out the names of the judges; the date of the adoption of the judgment; a description of the parties; the names of the agents, advocates or advisers of the parties; an account of the procedure followed; the facts of the case; a summary of the submissions of the parties; the reasons in point of law; the operative provisions of the Convention; the decision, if any, in respect of costs; the number of judges constituting the majority; and, where appropriate, a statement of which language text is to be regarded as authentic.[394]

1–128 The Court's decisions are reached by voting on specific resolutions,[395] following discussion between the judges about the precise form of words to be used. Under this process of collegiate decision-making the judges adopt the formulation which the greatest number are able to agree upon. The Court's judgments rarely display the depth of judicial analysis which common lawyers are accustomed to expect. Important principles are often reduced to a set formula which is repeated, more or less verbatim, in one judgment after another.

1–129 This economy of reasoning sometimes means that major questions of interpretation can be left open. Moreover, the court has in the past been inclined to decide cases on the narrowest possible ground. If it has found a violation of one provision of the Convention, it will often decline to rule on another alleged violation arising out of the same complaint. In *Campbell and Fell v United Kingdom*,[396] for example, the Court found that the absence of a right to consult privately with a legal representative constituted a breach of Art.6. Having reached this conclusion the Court considered it unnecessary to go on to consider whether it was also in breach of Art.8. Similarly, in *Malone v United Kingdom*[397] the Court found that the absence of legal regulation for the interception of telecommunications was in breach of Art.8, and declined to consider whether the applicant had also been the victim of a violation of Art.13.

Just satisfaction

1–130 Article 41 of the Convention provides that:

> "if the Court finds that there has been a violation of the Convention ... and the internal law of the High Contracting Party concerned allows only partial reparation to be made, the Court shall, if necessary, afford just satisfaction to the injured party".[398]

---

[394] Court judgments are normally given in either English or French, but the court may direct that a particular judgment should be given in both official languages: r.57(1).

[395] r.23. The resolution must be formulated in precise terms (r.23(4)). Abstentions are not permitted (r.23(2). In the event of a tie the President has the casting vote (r.23(1)).

[396] (1985) 7 E.H.R.R. 165.

[397] (1985) 7 E.H.R.R. 14.

[398] Prior to Protocol 11, this power was set out (in identical terms) in Art.50 of the Convention.

The Court does not have jurisdiction under Art.41 to quash a criminal conviction,[399] or to issue any order requiring the national authorities to take particular steps to remedy a violation.[400] It is confined to the award of monetary compensation and costs. Moreover, the Court's powers under Art.41 are discretionary.[401] Just satisfaction cannot be claimed as of right.

Awards under Art.41 may encompass: 1–131

(a) pecuniary loss suffered as a result of the violation including, if appropriate, loss of earnings and a sum equivalent to any penalty imposed by the national courts;

(b) non-pecuniary loss, i.e. compensation for physical injury, suffering and distress caused by the violation; and

(c) legal costs and expenses incurred in attempting to forestall or secure redress for the violation, both through the domestic legal system and under the Convention.

The Court will include interest on compensation where this is necessary to avoid unfair diminution in its value.[402]

Any claim for just satisfaction must be set out in the applicant's written observations on the merits of the complaint or, if no such observations have been filed, in a special document filed no later than two months after the decision declaring the case admissible.[403] The claim should be itemised in detail, and accompanied by all relevant supporting documents.[404] The Court may include its ruling on just satisfaction in the judgment on the merits of the complaint.[405] However if the issue in not "ready for decision" the Court will reserve it, and fix the subsequent 1–132

---

[399] *Schmautzer v Austria* (1996) 21 E.H.R.R. 511 at paras 43–44. See also *Maestri v Italy* (2004) 3 E.H.R.R. 38, para.47, where the court emphasised that a finding of a violation imposes on the State a legal obligation not just to pay those concerned the sums awarded by way of just satisfaction, but also to choose, subject to supervision by the Committee of Ministers, the general and/or, is appropriate, individual legal measures to be adopted in its domestic legal order to put an end to the violation. See *Mehemi v France* (2004) 38 E.H.R.R. 16 at para.43 for observations to the same effect.

[400] See, for example, *Ireland v United Kingdom* (1979–80) 2 E.H.R.R. 25, an inter-state case in which the court rejected a request made by the Irish government that criminal prosecutions should be brought against those responsible for ill-treatment in custody, and *Credit and Industrial Bank v Czech Republic* (2004) 39 E.H.R.R. 39, where the court held that it had no jurisdiction to require the respondent State to restore the applicant bank's banking licence (para.87). In *Finucane v United Kingdom* (2003) 37 E.H.R.R. 29, the court refused to order a fresh investigation into the killing of the applicant's husband, holding that it fell to the Committee of Ministers under Art.46 to consider what practical steps may be required by way of compliance. In *Appleby v United Kingdom* (2003) 37 E.H.R.R. 38, the court emphasised that Art.13 could not be interpreted as requiring a remedy against the state of national law, as otherwise the court would be imposing on Contracting States a requirement to incorporate the Convention.

[401] *Sunday Times v United Kingdom* (Unreported) November 6, 1980.

[402] See, for example, *Stran Greek Refineries v Greece* (1994) 19 E.H.R.R. 293 at 331 paras 82–83.

[403] r.60(1).

[404] r.60(2).

[405] r.75(1).

procedure.[406] The parties may, at this stage, negotiate a settlement and, providing the Court considers the settlement to be "equitable", it will strike the case out of the list.

1-133   An award of compensation[407] may be reduced, or even refused altogether, if the applicant's own conduct has contributed to the loss suffered. In *Johnson v United Kingdom*[408] the Court reduced the compensation awarded for excessive detention in a psychiatric hospital on the ground that the applicant had adopted a "negative attitude towards his rehabilitation" and had refused to co-operate with plans to find him suitable accommodation in the community. And in *McCann, Savage and Farell v United Kingdom*[409] the Court refused to award any compensation for a violation of the right to life "having regard to the fact that the three terrorist suspects who were killed had been intending to plant a bomb on Gibraltar". On the other hand, the fact that the applicant has serious criminal convictions is not, in itself, a ground for reducing an award.[410]

Pecuniary loss

1-134   Where causation is established, the Court is generally prepared to award any pecuniary losses which the applicant is able to substantiate. In *Allenet de Ribemont v France*[411] the applicant was awarded compensation for damage to his business opportunities as a result of statements by public officials which breached the presumption of innocence in Art.6(2). In *Baggetta v Italy*[412] the Court awarded compensation for the financial repurcussions of criminal proceedings which had failed to conclude within a reasonable time. And in *Lingens v Austria*[413] the applicant was awarded a sum equivalent to the fine and costs which had been awarded against him in proceedings for criminal defamation, together with a sum to represent a loss of profits.

Non-pecuniary loss

1-135   The assessment of non-pecuniary loss is inherently uncertain. The Court rarely gives detailed reasons for its awards, usually confining itself to a statement that the assessment has been made "on an equitable basis". Whilst it is possible to identify certain general principles, the Court's application of those principles to particular cases has been inconsistent and unpredictable.

1-136   The primary purpose of any award of just satisfaction is to put the applicant into the position that he would have been in if the violation had not occurred.[414] It

---

[406] r.75(1).

[407] For a detailed examination of the court's caselaw on damages, see Scorey D., and Eicke T., *Human Rights Damages: Principles and Practice* (Sweet & Maxwell, 2001).

[408] (1999) 27 E.H.R.R. 296.

[409] (1996) 21 E.H.R.R. 97 at para.219.

[410] In *Weeks v United Kingdom* (1991) 13 E.H.R.R. 435, for example, the applicant who was serving a life sentence for armed robbery and firearms offences, was awarded a substantial sum in damages for a breach of Art.5(4) (see (1988) 10 E.H.R.R. 293).

[411] (1995) 20 E.H.R.R. 557.

[412] (1988) 10 E.H.R.R. 325.

[413] (1986) 8 E.H.R.R. 407.

[414] *Piersack v Belgium* (1984) 7 E.H.R.R. 251 at para.12; Scorey D., and Eicke T., *Human Rights Damages: Principles and Practice* (Sweet & Maxwell, 2001).

follows that exemplary damages (which are intended to punish and deter "oppressive, arbitrary and unconstitutional action by servants of the government"[415]) are not awarded under Art.41.[416]

The Court does not recognise a separate category of aggravated damages. **1–137** Nevertheless it frequently makes an award for non-pecuniary loss in respect of anxiety, distress and injury to feelings. Thus, awards have been made for feelings of "frustration and helplessness" arising from an inability to argue for early release[417]; and for "confusion and neglect" caused by ineffective legal representation.[418] When awarding compensation for injury to feelings the court does not always require specific evidence in support.

Where the applicant has suffered a specific detriment as a result of the violation, **1–138** the Court has usually been willing to make an award for non-pecuniary loss. In *Tomasi v France*[419] the applicant was awarded more than FF 700,000 in respect of assaults in police custody,[420] and delay in the conduct of criminal proceedings.[421] And in *Quinn v France*[422] the Court awarded the applicant FF10,000 for 11 hours wrongful detention with no aggravating features.

It is not always necessary to prove any tangible or physical harm. In *S v* **1–139** *Switzerland*[423] the applicant was awarded Sfr 2,500 for interference with his right to communicate with his lawyer in confidence whilst he was in detention. Other examples include *Z v Finland*[424] where an award of 200,000 FIM was made in respect of the disclosure of confidential medical information about a witness in court proceedings; *Funke v France*[425] where an award of FF 50,000 was made for an unlawful search and for subsequent infringements of the protection against

---

[415] *Rookes v Barnard* [1964] A.C. 1129.

[416] See *Campbell v United Kingdom* (1993) 15 E.H.R.R. 137 at paras 68–70 where the court rejected a claim for £3,000 advanced on the ground that such an award might "discourage the Government from interfering with prisoners' correspondence". Note, however, that in certain cases the court has made an award which comes close to an award of exemplary damages. In *Teixeiru de Castro v Portugal* (1999) 28 E.H.R.R. 101 the court awarded the applicant a significant sum under the heading of non-pecuniary loss following his prosecution for an offence of drug dealing committed as a result of police entrapment. *Cf. Fose v Minister of Safety and Security* (1997) 2 B.H.R.C. 434 at 466–468 where the South African Constitutional Court held that exemplary damages were outside the scope of "appropriate relief", as that term is used in the Interim Constitution, since they amounted to the anomalous imposition of a penalty in civil proceedings which would be paid out of public funds, and would constitute a windfall to the victim.

[417] *Weeks v United Kingdom* (1991) 13 E.H.R.R. 435.

[418] *Artico v Italy* (1981) 3 E.H.R.R. 1.

[419] (1993) 15 E.H.R.R. 1.

[420] See also *Ribitsch v Austria* (1996) 21 E.H.R.R. 573 (applicant awarded £6,287 in relation to assaults in police custody); *Aksoy v Turkey* (1997) 23 E.H.R.R. 553 (£25,040 awarded in respect of serious ill-treatment in custody over a period of 14 days); *Aydin v Turkey* (1998) 25 E.H.R.R. 251 (£25,000 for rape and assault in custody, together with failure to carry out an effective investigation).

[421] This was in addition to compensation which the applicant had received for excessive detention on remand in domestic proceedings.

[422] (1996) 21 E.H.R.R. 529.

[423] 1992) 14 E.H.R.R. 670.

[424] (1998) 25 E.H.R.R. 371.

[425] (1993) 16 E.H.R.R. 297.

self-incrimination; and *Halford v United Kingdom*[426] where the applicant was awarded £10,000 for unlawful interception of her private office telephone. If, however, the applicant's challenge relates to the very existence of law, rather than a specific measure applying it to him, the Court will often conclude that the finding of the violation is sufficient just satisfaction.[427]

1–140 The Court is generally reluctant to award compensation if there is a tenuous causal link between the violation and the loss claimed.[428] Particular problems of causation will arise where the Court has found a violation of one of the procedural provisions of Art.5 or Art.6, and the applicant claims compensation for the consequences of a conviction. The Court's approach can be illustrated by reference to three types of complaint: applications alleging a lack of independence or impartiality in the tribunal; applications involving the admission of evidence in breach of Art.6; and applications based upon the absence of effective legal representation.

1–141 Where the applicant's complaint relates to the structural independence or impartiality of a tribunal, the Court is usually unwilling to speculate as to whether the outcome of the domestic proceedings would have been different if they had conformed to the procedural requirements of Art.6.[429] Thus, in *Findlay v United Kingdom*[430] the Court declined to award compensation where the applicant had been convicted by a Court Martial which was found to be procedurally unfair in its constitution. The Court took a similar approach in *Hauschildt v Denmark*[431] (where the applicant complained that some of the judges who tried him had made previous adverse rulings at a preliminary stage of the criminal proceedings); in *Holm v Sweden*[432] (where the jury included five members who were connected with one of the parties); and in *Remli v France*[433] (where there was evidence of race bias within the jury which had not been properly investigated).

1–142 In cases concerning the admission of evidence in breach of Art.6 there is a marked inconsistency of approach. In *Delta v France*[434] the Court awarded a substantial sum where the applicant's conviction was based on hearsay evidence admitted in breach of Art.6. The Court expressly declined to speculate as to whether the applicant would have been acquitted if the evidence had been excluded, stating simply that it was "not unreasonable" to regard the applicant as having suffered a real loss of opportunity. In *Windisch v Austria*[435] the Court found a clear causal link between the admission of the evidence of anonymous witnesses in breach of Art.6, and the applicant's detention in custody as a result of his conviction. In the Court's view the applicant was entitled to compensation

---

[426] (1997) 24 E.H.R.R. 371.
[427] *Norris v Ireland* (1991) 13 E.H.R.R. 186; *Bowman v United Kingdom* (1998) 26 E.H.R.R. 1 at para.51.
[428] See, for example, *Saunders v United Kingdom* (1997) 23 E.H.R.R. 313.
[429] *Vacher v France* (1997) 24 E.H.R.R. 482; *Schmautzer v Austria* (1995) 21 E.H.R.R. 417.
[430] (1997) 24 E.H.R.R. 221.
[431] (1990) 12 E.H.R.R. 266 at paras 55–58.
[432] (1994) 18 E.H.R.R. 79 at paras 35–36.
[433] (1996) 22 E.H.R.R. 253.
[434] (1993) 16 E.H.R.R. 574.
[435] (1991) 13 E.H.R.R. 281 at para.35.

for the loss of his liberty since this was "the direct consequence of the establishment of his guilt, which was effected in a manner that did not comply with Article 6". Similarly, in *Teixeira de Castro v Portugal*[436] the applicant was awarded compensation where the Court found that evidence obtained by entrapment had been admitted in breach of Art.6.

However, in *Saunders v United Kingdom*[437] the Court refused to award com- 1–143
pensation in respect of a violation of Art.6 arising from the admission of compulsory questioning evidence. The Court was apparently concerned that such an award might be interpreted as casting doubts on the correctness of the applicant's conviction:

> "[The Court] cannot speculate as to the question whether the outcome of the trial would have been any different had use not been made of the transcripts by the prosecution and, like the Commission, underlines that the finding of a breach of the Convention is not to be taken to carry any implications as regards that question. It therefore considers that no causal connection has been established between the losses claimed by the applicant and the Court's finding of a violation."

The Court reached the same conclusion, following *Saunders*, in *Kansal v United Kingdom*.[438]

Similar inconsistencies are apparent where the procedural violation consists of 1–144
the absence of effective legal representation. In *Artico v Italy*[439] the Court accepted that it was unnecessary for an applicant to prove prejudice in order to establish a violation of Art.6(3)(c). This would, in the Court's view, be "asking the impossible" since it could never be proved conclusively that effective legal representation would have secured the applicant's acquittal. The Court went on to award the applicant a substantial sum for "confusion and neglect" caused by ineffective legal representation.[440] Similarly in *Goddi v Italy*[441] the Court awarded compensation on the ground that the applicant's domestic appeal had been dismissed in the absence of his lawyer,[442] observing that:

> "[T]he outcome might *possibly* have been different if Mr Goddi had had the benefit of a practical and effective defence. In the present case such a loss of real opportunities warrants the award of just satisfaction."[443]

In other cases, however, the Court has held that in order to receive any compensa- 1–145
tion at all an applicant must prove that legal representation would have had a decisive effect on the outcome of the domestic proceedings. In *Benham v United Kingdom*[444] the applicant was sentenced to 30 days imprisonment for failure to pay the Community Charge, under a procedure for which there was no legal aid

---

[436] (1999) 28 E.H.R.R. 101.
[437] (1997) 23 E.H.R.R. 313 at paras 83–89.
[438] (2004) 39 E.H.R.R. 31, at para.34.
[439] (1981) 3 E.H.R.R. 1 at para.35.
[440] *Artico v Italy* (1981) 3 E.H.R.R. 1.
[441] (1984) 6 E.H.R.R. 457.
[442] The applicant was also absent, although this was not central to the Court's decision.
[443] Our emphasis.
[444] (1996) 22 E.H.R.R. 293.

available. The Court found a violation of Art.6(3)(c), but declined to speculate "as to whether the magistrates would have made the order for B's detention had he been represented at the hearing before them". Accordingly, he was awarded no compensation for the breach.[445]

1–146   This ruling was challenged in *Perks and others v United Kingdom*[446] a series of linked applications raising similar issues. In the *Perks* judgment the court adopted the same general approach as in *Benham*. However one of the applicants—a man who suffered from serious mental and physical handicaps—was singled out for an award of compensation. This was primarily due to a concession by the government that a reasonably competent solicitor would have drawn the man's disabilities to the attention of the magistrates.[447]

Costs

1–147   Where the Court has found a violation of the Convention, it will generally make an award of costs in favour of the successful applicant. Such an award is made "on an equitable basis", taking account of the violations alleged and found. If the applicant has succeeded on one alleged violation but failed on another, the Court may award only part of his legal costs.[448] Moreover, the scale of fees charged by lawyers in the United Kingdom is higher than in many other parts of the Council of Europe, and the Court has, on occasions, made significant deductions from the fee claims submitted by applicants from this country. Any sums already paid in legal aid will be deducted from the Court's award of costs.[449]

1–148   The circumstances in which an award of costs can be made against an unsuccessful applicant are very limited.[450] The applicant can never be required to pay the government's legal costs or any costs associated with the preparation of the government's case. However, an unsuccessful applicant can, exceptionally, be

---

[445] This was despite an earlier High Court ruling that there was insufficient evidence to justify the magistrates' decision. In *Gabarri Moreno v Spain* (2004) 39 E.H.R.R. the court upheld the applicant's complaint under Art.7 of the Convention that he had not received the appropriate reduction in sentence to take into account the mitigating factors in his case, but held that it could not award any pecuniary damage on the basis of speculation about how long he ought in fact to have served (para.38) It did, however, award a sum for non-pecuniary damage. See also *Sigurdor Arnarsson v Iceland* (2004) 39 E.H.R.R. 20, where the court refused to speculate as to what the outcome of the domestic proceedings in question would have been if oral evidence had been taken from the applicant and certain witnesses (para.42).

[446] (2000) 30 E.H.R.R. 33.

[447] The Divisional Court had expressly found that it was "unlikely" that the magistrates would have sent the applicant to prison if they had understood the extent of his handicaps.

[448] See, for example, *Benham v United Kingdom* (1996) 22 E.H.R.R. 293; *Mats Jacobsson v Sweden* (1991) 13 E.H.R.R. 79. This is not, however, an invariable practice: see *Osman v United Kingdom* (2000) 29 E.H.R.R. 245; *Eckle v Germany* (1983) 5 E.H.R.R. 1; *Sunday Times v United Kingdom (No.2)* (1979–80) 2 E.H.R.R. 317; *Perks v United Kingdom* (2000) 30 E.H.R.R. 33.

[449] This is standard procedure for all successful legally aided applications.

[450] This corresponds with the practice adopted by the Privy Council and the Supreme Court of South Africa, where a principle has been recognised that courts should exercise special caution before making an award of costs against a party invoking the protection of the courts for his or her constitutional human rights. Judicial protection and vindication of human rights is a matter of public rather than purely individual concern and it would therefore be contrary to the public interest if substantial costs awards were to act as a deterrent to the vindication of individual rights.

required to pay the costs of securing the attendance of witnesses or obtaining evidence *which has been requested by the Court on his or her behalf.* The general rule is that the party who requested that the evidence be obtained should bear the costs, unless the Court directs otherwise.[451] If the applicant is successful then the witness costs will of course generally be recoverable from the government as part of the applicant's bill of costs. But if the applicant is unsuccessful then he may be left to pay the costs of the witness concerned. However, the Court has discretion to direct that the costs be borne by the Council of Europe.[452]

Subsequent referral to the Grand Chamber

Within three months of the judgment of a Chamber, either party can request a re-hearing before a Grand Chamber under Art.43(1). During that period, the judgment of the Chamber will not become final. Such a request will be considered by a panel of five judges appointed by the Grand Chamber. The panel will grant the request   **1–149**

> "if the case raises a serious question affecting the interpretation or application of the Convention ... or a serious issue of general importance".[453]

The request must specify the issue or issues which are said to satisfy these requirements.[454] No new evidence or argument may be put forward at this stage: the panel is confined to a consideration of the existing case file.[455] The panel is not required to give reasons for a refusal to refer a case to the Grand Chamber.[456]

If the panel grants the request for a referral, the Grand Chamber will decide the case by means of a judgment.[457] A further oral hearing is possible, but the Grand Chamber is likely, in most cases, to rely upon the verbatim record of the hearing before the Chamber. The composition of the Grand Chamber is basically the same on a referral as on a relinquishment.[458] However, the Grand Chamber may not include any judge who sat in the Chamber which rendered the judgment, apart from the President of that Chamber, and the national judge of the respondent state.[459] The Grand Chamber is able to reconsider the admissibility of parts of the application which have been declared admissible by the Chamber,[460] but is likely to do so only in exceptional circumstances. However, it is not able to   **1–150**

---

[451] r.A5(6).

[452] r.A5(6).

[453] Art.43(2).

[454] r.73(1).

[455] r.73(2).

[456] r.73(2).

[457] Art.43(3). Grand Chamber decisions involving the United Kingdom include *Ezeh and Connors v United Kingdom* (2004) 39 E.H.R.R. 1 (compatibility of prison disciplinary hearings with Art.6 of the Convention), and *Hatton v United Kingdom* (2003) 37 E.H.R.R. 28 (compatibility of night flights scheme at Heathrow with Art.8 of the Convention); *Roche v United Kingdom* (2006) 42 E.H.R.R. 30 (access of service personnel to court and to their medical records); *Hirst (No.2) v United Kingdom* (2006) 42 E.H.R.R. 42 (right of prisoners to vote).

[458] See para.1–114 above.

[459] Art.27(3).

[460] *Odievre v France* (2004) 38 E.H.R.R. 43, para.22.

declare admissible parts of the application which have been declared *inadmissible* by the Chamber.[461] Even where the parties seek a referral only on one aspect of the case, the Grand Chamber will decide the whole case afresh by means of a new judgment.[462]

1–151   The risk that this procedure will unduly complicate or prolong proceedings is offset by the power of the Chamber to relinquish jurisdiction before delivering its judgment. Although the parties have the right to submit a "duly reasoned" objection to prior relinquishment,[463] any party who has made such an objection is likely to encounter serious difficulty in obtaining a subsequent referral of the case to the Grand Chamber.

Third party interventions

1–152   Article 36(2) and r.61, together provide that the President of a Chamber may, in the interests of the proper administration of justice, invite or grant leave to any person[464] who is not a party to the proceedings to make submissions or take part in the proceedings.[465] Any request for leave to intervene must be "duly reasoned" and submitted within 12 weeks after the written procedure has been fixed.[466] Leave will generally be confined to the submission of written comments, but the President may, in exceptional cases, grant leave to take part in an oral hearing.[467] Any written submissions (known as *amicus curiae* briefs) will be communicated to the parties, who will be given an opportunity to file observations in reply.[468]

1–153   The Court will consider the expertise of the intervenor and the extent to which an *amicus* brief could provide information or evidence which would not otherwise be available to the Court. The President will usually specify the ambit of the intervention in detail, and will often prescribe its length. The grant of leave will usually be made conditional on a concise written submission which conforms to the terms set by the President.

1–154   *Amicus* interventions will typically be received from non-governmental organisations offering a perspective on the issues which supplements the arguments put forward by the parties. They are expected to be non-partisan, and to refrain from commenting on the merits of the individual application. The Court is, however,

---

[461] *Sommerfeld v Germany* (2004) 38 E.H.R.R. 35, at para.41.

[462] *Nachova v Bulgaria* (2006) E.H.R.R. 43, paras 83–86.

[463] See para.1–114 above.

[464] The Explanatory Report to Protocol 11 (1994) 17 E.H.R.R. 514 at 529, para.91 explains that this may be a legal or natural person.

[465] Where the applicant is a national of another contracting state, that state may intervene as of right. In *Soering v United Kingdom* (1989) 11 E.H.R.R. 439 the applicant was a German citizen whose extradition was sought from the United Kingdom to the United States. Germany intervened in the application arguing that it was prepared to try the applicant in Germany, where the death penalty did not apply.

[466] r.44(2)(b).

[467] r.44(2)(a). In *T and V v United Kingdom* [2001] 1 All E.R. 737 the mother and father of a child who had been murdered by the applicants was granted leave to make written and oral submissions on the role of the victim in the sentencing process.

[468] r.44(5).

generally receptive to accurate and reliable interventions on relevant national, international or comparative law, and will often receive submissions on wider factual issues which may be relevant to the Court's assessment of a case.

In *Malone v United Kingdom*,[469] the Post Office Engineering Union was granted **1–155** leave to file a memorial in connection with a complaint about telephone interception. In *Soering v United Kingdom*[470] Amnesty International was permitted to intervene to give evidence about the "death row phenomenon" in the United States. More recent examples include *Chahal v United Kingdom*[471] where Liberty and others intervened in relation to the system of adjudication of immigration appeals involving questions of national security; *Murray v United Kingdom*[472] where Amnesty International, Liberty and others intervened in a case which concerned the drawing of adverse inferences from a suspect's failure to testify; *Khan v United Kingdom*[473] where Justice and Liberty filed a joint brief setting out the comparative law position on the exclusion of unlawfully obtained evidence; *T and V v United Kingdom*[474] where the court gave leave to Justice to intervene on the international standards governing the treatment of juvenile offenders, and to the parents of a child murdered by the applicants who wished to make submissions on the role of the victim in the criminal justice system; *Sheffield and Horsham v United Kingdom*[475] where Liberty filed a comparative analysis of the legal and medical implications of transsexualism; *Senator Lines GmbH v 15 EC Member States*,[476] where the European Commission made submissions on the way in which fundamental rights are observed and applied by the Community institutions; and *Hatton v United Kingdom*,[477] where Friends of the Earth made submissions on international environmental law.

This aspect of the Court's procedure has had a significant influence on the **1–156** approach of the appellate courts in the United Kingdom where important issues are raised under the Human Rights Act. Even before the Act was passed the House of Lords had permitted a number of *amicus* interventions in criminal cases.[478] Since the Act has been in force, there have been a significant number of interventions, primarily in judicial review cases, some of which raised criminal justice issues, but also in criminal cases.[479]

---

[469] (1988) 7 E.H.R.R. 14.
[470] (1989) 11 E.H.R.R. 439.
[471] (1997) 23 E.H.R.R. 413.
[472] (1996) 22 E.H.R.R. 29.
[473] (1995) 21 E.H.R.R. CD 67.
[474] (2000) 30 E.H.R.R. 121.
[475] (1999) 27 E.H.R.R. 163.
[476] (2004) 39 E.H.R.R. SE3.
[477] (2003) 37 E.H.R.R. 28.
[478] For example in *R. v Sultan Khan* [1997] A.C. 558 Liberty was permitted to intervene; and in *R. v Secretary of State ex parte Venables and Thompson* [1998] A.C. 407 Justice was given leave. In *R. v Bow Street Stipendiary Magistrate ex parte Pinochet Ugarte* [2000] 1 A.C. 147 the House of Lords permitted Amnesty International to intervene in an extradition case with major international law implications. In *A and Others v Secretary of State for the Home Department* (2005) 2 A.C. 68, Liberty was permitted to intervene before the House of Lords in a major constitutional case.
[479] For a summary of such cases and an analysis of the role of interventions in the domestic courts, see Mona Arshi and Colm O'Cinneide, *Third-party interventions: the public interest reaffirmed*, [2004] P.L. 69; Hannett S., *Third Party Interventions: In the Public Interest?* [2003] P.L. 128; Harlow C., *Public Law and Popular Justice* (2002) 65 M.L.R. 1.

Advisory Opinions

1–157   The court has a very limited jurisdiction to give advisory opinions on legal questions concerning the interpretation of the Convention and its protocols.[480] An advisory opinion may only be given at the request of the Committee of Ministers,[481] and may not deal with "any question relating to the content or scope of the rights or freedoms defined [in the Convention]", or with any other question which the court or the Committee of Ministers might have to consider in the course of adjudicating on a Convention complaint.[482]

Interpretation, revision and rectification

1–158   Any party may, within 12 months of the delivery of the Court's judgment, apply to the Registrar, requesting an interpretation of the judgment.[483] The Court may also consider an application from either party for the revision of a judgment if a fact is discovered which could have had a decisive influence on the court's judgment, and which could not reasonably have been known to the party relying on it at the time of the judgment.[484] Any application for revision must be made within six months of the original judgment. The Court has a general discretion to rectify clerical errors and obvious mistakes in admissibility decisions or judgments, within one month of the decision in question.[485]

Execution of court judgments

1–159   Under Art.46(1) state parties undertake "to abide by the final judgment of the Court in any case to which they are parties". The judgment is to be "transmitted to the Committee of Ministers, which shall supervise its execution".[486] Thus, it is the Committee of Ministers which oversees action taken by governments in response to a finding of a violation. The primary focus of the Committee of Ministers' role is to ensure that the appropriate remedies are put into effect by the state concerned. In some cases this will mean no more than the payment of compensation and costs to the applicant by way of just satisfaction.[487] In other cases, however, the judgment may require legislative, constitutional, administrative or regulatory amendment.[488] The Committee of Ministers' functions

---

[480] Art.47.

[481] Art.47(1).

[482] Art.47(2). The procedure for obtaining an advisory opinion is set out in rr.82–90. In *Decision on the Competence of the Court to Give an Advisory Opinion* (2004) 39 E.H.R.R. SE9, the court considered a request from the Chairman of the Committee of Ministers of the Council of Europe for the court to give an advisory opinion on Recommendation 1519(2001) of the Parliamentary Assembly concerning "the co-existence of the Convention on Human Rights and Fundamental Freedoms of the Commonwealth of Independent States and the European Convention on Human Rights." The court held that it did not have jurisdiction to give the opinion sought, since it related to a question which the court might have to consider in contentious proceedings instituted under the Convention.

[483] r.79.

[484] r.80.

[485] r.81.

[486] Art.46(2).

[487] For an account of this function see Robertson and Merrils, *Human Rights in Europe* (3rd edn, 1993), pp.341–341.

[488] In a survey of 162 resolutions adopted by the Committee of Ministers up to 1992, 74 required some kind of legislative or administrative change: See Adam Tomkins, *The Committee of Ministers; Its roles under the European Convention on Human Rights* [1995] E.H.R.L.R. 49 at 58.

under Art.46 generally involve a dialogue with the government concerned as to the nature and extent of the remedy required.[489] The applicant may also make representations, if the Committee of Ministers considers this necessary.[490]

In an extreme case of non-compliance the Committee of Ministers has the power **1–160** to take enforcement action against the state concerned. Article 3 of the Statute of the Council of Europe provides that every member state:

> "must accept the principles of the rule of law and of the enjoyment by all persons within its jurisdiction of human rights and fundamental freedoms".

If the Committee of Ministers considers that a state has seriously violated this obligation it may take action under Art.8 of the Statute to suspend the state concerned and request that it withdraw from the Council of Europe.[491] In the unlikely event of a refusal to withdraw, the Committee of Ministers may expel the state concerned.[492]

D. RESERVATIONS AND DEROGATIONS

Reservations

Article 57 of the Convention provides that any state may, when signing the **1–161** Convention or when depositing its instrument of ratification, make a reservation in respect of any particular provision of the Convention, to the extent that any law then in force in its territory is not in conformity with the provision. Any reservation must relate to the law of the contracting state, rather than to actions taken by its officials.

A reservation must be specific in its terms: Art.57(1) provides that "reservations **1–162** of a general character will not be permitted". Moreover, it must contain a brief statement of the law concerned.[493] In *Gradinger v Austria*[494] the Court held that Austria's reservation to Art.4 of Protocol 7, which prohibits double jeopardy in criminal cases, was invalid. The reservation did not set out clearly the laws in respect of which it applied, and was insufficiently specific in its terms.[495] In

---

[489] In three Swiss cases, for example, the Committee of Ministers considered that it was sufficient for the government to publicise the Court's judgment to enable the relevant authorities to take account of it in similar cases in future: *Minelli v Switzerland* Resolution DH(83)10; *Zimmerman and Steiner v Switzerland* Resolution DH(83)17; *Schoenenberger v Switzerland* D.H.(89)12. In *Sejdovic v Italy* (2006) 42 E.H.R.R. 17, the Court called upon Italy, under Art.46, to take measures to remedy a structural problem in the criminal justice system, which was liable to deprive those convicted *in absentia* of a retrial and thus to lead to many applications to the court: see paras 44–47.

[490] Note to r.2(a) of the Rules adopted by the Committee of Ministers for the application of former Art.54.

[491] Greece withdrew from the Council of Europe and renounced the Convention in 1969, following proceedings by the Committee of Ministers under Art.8 of the Statute of Council of Europe. It was readmitted in 1974 following the restoration of democracy.

[492] Art.8 of the Statute of the Council of Europe.

[493] Art.57(2).

[494] Judgment October 23, 1995.

[495] See also *Chorherr v Austria*, judgment September 24, 1998 at para.20.

Weber v Switzerland[496] the Court reached a similar conclusion in relation to a Swiss reservation designed to exclude from Art.6 any criminal charges "which, in accordance with the Cantonal legislation, are heard before an administrative authority".

1–163   The United Kingdom's only reservation is in respect of Art.2 of Protocol 1 (the right to education) and is outside the scope of this work. Under the Human Rights Act 1998, this reservation, and any future reservation, must be designated by an order of the Secretary of State in order to have effect in domestic law.[497]

Derogations

1–164   Article 15(1) provides that:

> "In time of war or other public emergency threatening the life of the nation any High Contracting Party may take measures derogating from its obligations under this Convention to the extent strictly required by the exigencies of the situation, provided that such measures are not inconsistent with its other obligations under international law."

1–165   Certain rights are, however, are of such high importance that no derogation is permitted, even in times of national emergency.[498] This applies to the right to life in Art.2 (save to the extent that a death is the result of a lawful act of war); the prohibition on torture and inhuman and degrading treatment in Art.3; the prohibition on slavery and servitude in Art.4(1)[499]; and the prohibition on the retrospective application of the criminal law in Art.7. Since derogations limit the application of the Convention rights, they will be strictly interpreted against the derogating State.[500]

1–166   The United Kingdom's first derogation applied to Art.5(3). It was entered in response to the judgment in *Brogan v United Kingdom*,[501] where the Court held that detention for four days and six hours under the Prevention of Terrorism (Temporary Provisions) Act 1984 was incompatible with the requirement that a detained person should be brought promptly before a judge or judicial officer following arrest. The derogation preserved the power of the Secretary of State to extend the period of detention of persons suspected of terrorism in connection with Northern Ireland for a total of up to seven days. The Human Rights Act 1998 retains the derogation[502] but places a time limit of five years on its operation[503] subject to renewal by order of the Secretary of State.[504]

---

[496] (1990) 12 E.H.R.R. 508.

[497] s.15. Note that whilst a designated derogation must be renewed at periodic intervals (s.16), the same does not apply to reservations.

[498] Art.15(2).

[499] But not the prohibition on forced or compulsory labour in Art.4(2).

[500] See for example *Yaman v Turkey* (2005) E.H.R.R. 49, paras 65–70 (geographical limits of derogation strictly applied).

[501] (1989) 11 E.H.R.R. 117.

[502] s.14(1)(a). The text of the derogation is set out at Sch.3 Pt I.

[503] s.16.

[504] See para.3–24 below.

The compatibility of the United Kingdom derogation with the terms of Art.15   **1–167**
was tested in *Brannigan and McBride v United Kingdom*.[505] The Court held that
it falls to each contracting state, in the first instance, to determine whether there
exists a public emergency threatening the life of the nation and, if so, to decide
on the measures necessary to overcome the emergency. Despite the language of
strict necessity in Art.15(1), states were to be afforded a wide margin of
appreciation.[506] The Court held that in determining whether the state had
exceeded this margin, it had to give:

> "appropriate weight to such relevant factors as the nature of the rights affected by the
> derogation, the circumstances leading to, and the duration of, the emergency situa-
> tion".

The Court was in no doubt that there was a national emergency in the United
Kingdom at the time when the derogation was entered, this being the relevant
moment for the application of Art.15.[507] As to the extent of the measures taken
the court observed[508]:

> "Having regard to the nature of the terrorist threat in Northern Ireland, the limited scope
> of the derogation and the reasons advanced in support of it, as well as the existence of
> basic safeguards against abuse, the Court takes the view that the Government has not
> exceeded its margin of appreciation in considering that the derogation was strictly
> required by the exigencies of the situation."

On November 11, 2001, the United Kingdom passed the Human Rights Act 1998   **1–168**
(Designated Derogation) Order 2001.[509] The Order derogated from Art.5(1)(f) of
the Convention, and paved the way for the Anti-Terrorism, Crime and Security
Act 2001, s.21 of which allowed the Home Secretary to certify non-British
nationals as "suspected international terrorists" and s.23 of which allowed those
who had been so certified to be detained indefinitely without charge or trial. In
A and Others v Secretary of State for the Home Department[510] the House of
Lords ruled, by eight votes to one, that the derogation was unlawful since it was
disproportionate and discriminatory. On the proportionality issue, the Judicial
Committee ruled that ss.21 and 23 did not address the threat posed to the United
Kingdom by UK nationals, permitted foreign nationals suspected of Al-Quada
activities to pursue those abroad if there was any country to which they could go,
and permitted the certification and detention of persons who were not suspected
of presenting any threat to the security of the UK. These measures had not been
shown to be "strictly required by the exigencies of the situation" within the
meaning of Art.15(3). On the discrimination issue, the decision to detain non-
nationals but not to detain nationals who may pose an equal threat was held to be
unjustified and therefore unlawful. Lord Hoffmann also went so far as to rule that

---

[505] (1994) 17 E.H.R.R. 539.

[506] Para.43.

[507] The Court held that it was not necessary to consider whether the emergency still existed "since
a decision to withdraw a derogation is, in principle, a matter within the discretion of the State"
(para.47).

[508] Para.66.

[509] S.I. 2001/3664.

[510] (2005) 2 A.C. 68.

the Government had failed to establish the existence of a "public emergency threatening the life of the nation."

The impugned provisions were not renewed by the Government following the decision of the House of Lords. They lapsed on March 14, 2005, and on March 16, the United Kingdom notified the Council of Europe that the derogation was withdrawn.

1–169   In place of detention without trial, the Government introduced a system of "control orders" in the Prevention of Terrorism Act 2005. The Act establishes two types of control orders: "derogating" orders, which would require the UK to derogate again from Art.5 of the Convention, and "non-derogating" orders, which the Government considered could be implemented compatibly with the full range of Art.5 rights. No relevant derogation has been made to date, so the only control orders which have been made are of the "non-derogating" type. In *Re MB*,[511] the procedures for imposing such orders were challenged. Sullivan J. held that, for the purposes of Art.6 of the Convention, the proceedings were to be classed as civil, rather than criminal.[512] He went on to consider whether s.3 of the 2005 Act, which confined the claimant to arguing that the decision of the Secretary of State to impose the control order was "legally flawed", applying public law principles, complied with Art.6. He concluded that:

> "Standing back and looking at the overall picture, there can be only one conclusion. To say that the Act does not give the respondent in this case, against whom a non-derogating control order has been made by the Secretary of State, a fair hearing in the determination of his rights under Article 8 of the Convention would be an under-statement. The court would be failing in its duty under the [Human Rights Act 1998], a duty imposed upon the court by Parliament, if it did not say, loud and clear, that the procedure under the Act whereby the court merely reviews the lawfulness of the Secretary of State's decision to make the order upon the basis of the material available to him at that earlier stage are conspicuously unfair. The thin veneer of legality which is sought to be applied by s.3 of the Act cannot disguise the reality, that controlees' rights under the Convention are being determined not by an independent court in compliance with Art.6.1, but by executive decision-making, untrammelled by any prospect of effective judicial supervision."[513]

1–170   The court went on to make a declaration of incompatibility in respect of the provisions. Given the severe interference with private life which even a "non-derogating" control order can cause, and the inability of a court hearing a judicial review application to consider the merits of the imposition of the order, this result must be correct. However, on appeal by the Secretary of State, the "thin veneer of legality" supplied by the possibility of judicial review was held by the Court of Appeal to be sufficient to satisfy the requirements of Art.6(1).[514]

The second case to come before Sullivan J. under s.3(10), *Secretary of State for the Home Department v JJ and others*, concerned considerably more onerous control orders imposed on six individuals, including house curfews of 18 hours per day, geographical limitations on movements in the remaining six hours,

---

[511] [2006] EWHC 1000 (Admin); [2006] H.R.L.R. 878.
[512] Para.38.
[513] Para.102.
[514] *Secretary of State for the Home Department v MB* [2006] EWCA Civ 1140, [2006] H.R.L.R. 37.

electronic tagging, and severe restrictions in several other areas including visitors, pre-arranged meetings, use of communications equipment and bank accounts.[515]

The matter was heard in the Administrative Court before the Court of Appeal's decision in *MB*. Sullivan J. quashed all six orders, finding that they imposed conditions which were the "antithesis of liberty" as protected under Art.5 of the Convention. The Home Secretary had no power to make such orders, which could only be imposed following a designated derogation under s.14 of the Human Rights Act. The decision was upheld by the Court of Appeal.[516] At the time of writing the decisions in *JJ* and *MB* are on appeal to the House of Lords.[517]

Protocol 14

As mentioned above, the procedures set out in Protocol 11 to the Convention will **1–171** be modified by Protocol 14 when it comes into force, upon ratification by all 46 Member States. Unlike Protocol 11, which introduced fundamental structural changes to the Strasbourg institutions, Protocol 14 retains the existing system, with some modifications designed primarily to deal with the vast and increasing workload of the Court. Protocol 14 was agreed by the members of the Council of Europe on May 13, 2004, with an undertaking to take all necessary steps to bring it into force within two years. The adoption of the Protocol marked the culmination of a process intiated at the European Ministerial Conference on Human Rights, held in Rome in November 2000. Protocol 14 was signed by the UK on July 13, 2004, and laid before Parliament on November 15, 2004. On January 27, 2005, the Government notified the Council of Europe of its ratification.

The text of the Protocol was accompanied by an Explanatory Report by the **1–172** Committee of Ministers, which explains the objects and content of the reforms.[518] The Report begins by summarising the reforms brought about by Protocol 11, and setting out the continual increase in the Court's workload: there were 18,164 applications in 1998 (when Protocol 11 came into force), and 34,546

---

[515] [2006] EWHC 1623 (Admin); [2006] EWCA Civ 1141, [2006] 3 W.L.R. 866.

[516] [2006] EWCA Civ 1141; [2006] H.R.L.R. 38.

[517] At the time of going to press, there had recently been three further control orders decisions. In *Secretary of State for the Home Department v AF* [2007] EWHC 651 (Admin), Ouseley J. held that, while the case was "finely balanced", the restrictions imposed on the applicant by the control order (he was prevented from leaving his flat for more than 10 hours a day and could only visit a certain geographical area when out, had to wear an electronic tag, and required prior identification and approval for visitors to his flat) amounted to deprivation of liberty under Art.5, rendering the control order a nullity. Ouseley J. did hold, however, following *MB* in the Court of Appeal, that AF had had a fair hearing despite that fact that the case against him was, essentially, entirely undisclosed to him. The control orders at issue in *Secretary of State for the Home Department v E* [2007] EWHC 233 (Admin) and *Secretary of State for the Home Department v Abu Rideh* [2007] EWHC 804 were also quashed on the basis that they breached Art.5. Each of these three decisions also contains discussion of the Convention compliance of various aspects of the process by which control orders are made and reviewed.

[518] *Explanatory Report Adopted by the Committee of Ministers at its 114th Session on May 12, 2004*, reproduced at (2004) 39 E.H.R.R. SE8. For further discussion of the background, see Steven Greer, *Reforming the European Court of Human Rights: towards Protocol 14* P.L. 2003, 663–673.

in 2002, an increase of 90 per cent. In 2003, the Court disposed of 1,500 applications per month, significantly lower than its monthly target of 2,300. Due to accessions to the Convention, it now has 46 signatories and covers 800 million people. At the end of 2003, 65,000 applications were pending before the Court, creating a potential backlog which would threaten the Court's effectiveness and credibility.

1–173   Protocol 14 introduces changes in four main areas: the process for filtering out unmeritorious cases, the test for admissibility, procedures for dealing with repetitive cases, and the execution of judgments. In order to allow more applications to be processed, and clearly unmeritorious ones to be filtered out quickly, the Protocol introduces a single judge formation of the Court (as opposed to three judges, as at present) which can declare applications inadmissible or strike them out of the Court's list "where such a decision can be taken without further examination."[519] This decision is final. If the single judge does not declare an application inadmissible or strike it out, it will be forwarded to a committee or chamber for further examination. The single judge will not be able to consider cases where the respondent State is the state by whom they were elected as a judge. They will be assisted by non-judicial rapporteurs.[520]

1–174   The most widely-discussed provision of Protocol 14 is Art.12, which inserts a new Art.35(3)(b) into the Convention, to allow the Court to declare an application inadmissible if if considers that:

> "the applicant has not suffered a significant disadvantage, unless respect for human rights as defined in the Convention and the Protocols thereto requires an examination of the application on the merits and provided that no case may be rejected on this ground which has not been duly considered by a domestic tribunal."

For two years following the entry into force of the Protocol, only Chambers and the Grand Chamber will be allowed to apply this new criterion. The single judges will not be able to do so, in order to allow time for case-law to develop and to ensure consistent application of the test.

This change is explained by the Committee of Minsters as follows:

> "The introduction of this criterion was considered necessary in view of the ever-increasing caselaw of the Court. In particular, it is necessary to give the Court some degree of flexibility in addition to that already provided by the existing admissibility criteria, whose interpretation has become established in the case law that has developed over several decades and is therefore difficult to change. This is so because it is very likely that the numbers of individual applications to the Court will continue to increase, up to a point where the other measures set out in this protocol may well prove insufficient to prevent the Convention system from becoming totally paralysed, unable to fulfil its central mission of providing legal protection of human rights at the European level, rendering the right of individual petition illusory in practice. The new criterion may lead to certain cases being declared inadmissible which might have resulted in a

---

[519] Amended Art.27, which becomes Art.26.
[520] Amended Art.25, to be new Art.24.

judgment without it. Its main effect, however, is likely to be that it will in the longer term enable more rapid disposal of unmeritorious cases."[521]

The Joint Committee on Human Rights has reported on the provisions of **1–175** Protocol 14.[522] It has raised particular concerns about the new admissibility requirement, and has advised Parliament that:

> "the undoubted restriction on the right of individual petition which this new require-ment constitutes is acceptable only in light of the national implementation measures which are also required."[523]

This refers to the Committee of Ministers' emphasis on the principle of sub-sidiarity, first developed in the European Union, according to which the protec-tion of rights should primarily be ensured at national level. The Committee of Ministers adopted three recommendations at the same time as Protocol 14, aimed at ensuring protection of rights at national level.[524] The view of the Joint Committee on Human Rights is that much remains to be done to ensure protec-tion of rights in the United Kingdom, and that the new, more restrictive admissi-bility requirements of Protocol 14 will only be acceptable if much work is done to strengthen rights protection domestically and to prevent violations from occurring in the first place. Similar concerns have been expressed by non-governmental organisations, including Amnesty International.[525]

Turning to ways of dealing with repetitive cases—cases following a "pilot" **1–176** judgment which establishes a breach of the Convention—the Protocol introduces a new system by which three-judge committees of the Court will be able, if unanimous, to declare applications admissible and determine them on their merits. This can be done in cases where the questions raised concerning the interpretation or application of the Convention are covered by well-established case-law of the court.[526] The state concerned is able to contest the "well-established" nature of the issues, but if it agrees, then the Committee is likely to give judgment on all aspects of the case very quickly.

On the subject of execution of judgments of the Court, the Committee of Ministers is given stronger powers. Protocol 14 amends Art.46 of the Convention to empower the Committee to ask the Court to interpret a final judgment, for the purpose of facilitating the supervision of its execution. It is also given the power to bring infringement proceedings before the Court, if it considers that a State is refusing to abide by a final judgment of the Court. If the Court finds that this is

---

[521] *Explanatory Report*, paras 78–79.
[522] Joint Committee on Human Rights, First Report of Session 2004–2005.
[523] Para.39.
[524] *Recommendation on the Verification of the Convention Compatibility of Draft Laws, Existing Laws and Administrative Practice*, Rec (2004) 5, *Recommendation on the Improvement of Domestic Remedies*, Rec (2004) 6, *Recommendation on the ECHR in University Education and Professional Training*, Rec (2004) 4.
[525] *European Court of Human Rights: Imminent reforms must not obstruct individuals' redress for human rights violations*, May 11, 2004. For further discussion, see Marie-Aude Beernaert, *Protocol 14 and new Strasbourg procedures: towards greater efficiency? And at what price?*, E.H.R.L.R. 2004, 544–557.
[526] Amended Art.28.

the case, it will refer the case back to the Committee of Ministers for it to consider what measures to take.

Protocol 14 also provides that judges of the Court are to be elected for a single nine-year term,[527] and revises the system of appointment of ad hoc judges so that, instead of the respondent State choosing an ad hoc judge once a particular case has started, the judge is chosen by the President of the Court from a list submitted by the State in advance.[528] New Art.59(2) of the Convention also envisages the possible accession of the EU to the Convention.

---

[527] Amended Art.23.
[528] New Art.26(4).

CHAPTER 2

PRINCIPLES OF INTERPRETATION

A. INTRODUCTION

I. The Vienna Convention on the Law of Treaties

The interpretation of the Convention is governed by the principles enunciated in   **2–01**
Arts 31 to 33 of the Vienna Convention on the Law of Treaties (May 23, 1969).[1]
The "general rule" in Art.31 of the Vienna Convention is that a treaty:

"shall be interpreted in good faith in accordance with the ordinary meaning to be given
to the terms of the treaty in their context and in the light of its object and purpose".[2]

The context includes the preamble to the treaty and any other agreements which
the parties have entered into which may be relevant to the interpretation of the
treaty.[3] Whilst the "ordinary meaning" of words is to be adopted where this is
consistent with the object and purpose of the Convention, a "special meaning"
is to be given to a term if it established that the parties so intended.[4] Recourse
may be had to supplementary means of interpretation, including the *travaux
préparatoires*, only where the meaning is otherwise ambiguous, obscure or
absurd.[5] The English and French texts of the Convention are to be treated as

---

[1] Art.4 of the Vienna Convention provides that the Vienna Convention does not have retrospective
effect. It does not therefore strictly apply to to the European Convention on Human Rights (which
was concluded in 1950). Nevertheless, in *Golder v United Kingdom* (1979–80) 1 E.H.R.R. 525 paras
29–30 the court accepted that the Vienna Convention provided the appropriate international law
guidance for the determination of the scope and content of the European Convention. The Vienna
Convention has been described as "not so much an innovation but rather a codification of previous
practice" F. Matscher, "Methods of Interpretation of the Convention", in Macdonald R. St. J.,
Matscher F. & Petzold H., *The European System for the Protection of Human Rights* (Martinus
Nijhoff, 1993), p.65; for general discussion, see Brownlie I., *Principles of Public International Law*
(6th edn, Oxford, 2003), Ch.27. For analysis of the status of the Human Rights Act 1998 as a statute
incorporating a treaty into domestic law, see Fatima S., *Using International Law in Domestic Courts*
(Hart Publishing, 2005), Ch.7.
[2] See Art.31(1), Vienna Convention.
[3] Art.31(2) and (3).
[4] Art.31(4). This is the basis for the European Court of Human Rights adoption of an autonomous
approach to the construction of certain Convention terms: see paras 2–43 to 2–45 below.
[5] Art.32.

equally authentic[6] and are presumed to have the same meaning.[7] In cases of divergence between the English and French versions, the meaning which best reconciles the two texts, having regard to the object and purpose of the treaty, is to prevail.[8] In *Golder v United Kingdom*[9] the Court observed that:

> "In the way in which it is presented in the 'general rule' in Article 31 of the Vienna Convention, the process of interpretation is a unity, a single combined operation; this rule, closely integrated, places on the same footing the various elements enumerated in the four paragraphs of the Article".

2–02   This approach to interpretation leaves the Court a wide degree of latitude as to which of the elements of the "general rule" should be emphasised in a particular case. The Court will usually begin with a textual analysis, including (if necessary) a comparison between the English and French texts. However, the Court has sometimes been willing to interpret a provision in a way which is inconsistent with the "ordinary meaning" of the words, where this is necessary in order to give effect to the object and purpose of the Convention.[10]

II. Object and purpose

2–03   The principal object and purpose of the Convention is the protection of individual rights from infringement by the contracting states.[11] The Convention seeks to achieve this objective through the maintenance and promotion of "the ideals and values of a democratic society".[12] The Convention is "a constitutional instrument of European public order in the field of human rights".[13] It cannot therefore be interpreted merely as a reciprocal agreement between the contracting states. Rather, it creates:

> "a network of mutual, bilateral undertakings, objective obligations which, in the words of the preamble, benefit from a 'collective enforcement'."[14]

---

[6] Art.33(1). The last paragraph of the ECHR provides in terms that the French and English language versions are equally authentic.

[7] Art.33(3).

[8] Art.33(4).

[9] (1979–80) 1 E.H.R.R. 525 paras 29–30.

[10] Frequently, this technique is adopted in a manner designed to achieve more effective protection of human rights. On rare occasions, however, the court has adopted a similar approach in order to restrict Convention rights: see, for example, *Pretto v Italy* (1984) 6 E.H.R.R. 182 at para.26.

[11] *Austria v Italy* (1961) 4 Y.B. 116 at 138; *Ireland v United Kingdom* (1979–80) 2 E.H.R.R. 25 at para.239.

[12] *Kjeldsen and others v Denmark* (1979–80) 1 E.H.R.R. 711 at para.53. These principles are reflected in the preamble to the Convention which speaks in terms of the "maintenance and further realisation of human rights and fundamental freedoms" on the basis of "an effective political democracy", and the primacy of "the rule of law".

[13] *Chrysostomos, Papachrysostomou and Loizidou v Turkey* (1991) 68 D.R. 216 at 242.

[14] *Ireland v United Kingdom* (1979–80) 2 E.H.R.R. 25 at para.239; *Austria v Italy* (1961) 4 Y.B. 116 at 138; *Chrysostomos, Papachrysostomou and Loizidou v Turkey* (1991) 68 D.R. 216 at 242.

Particularly important features of a democratic society, in the context of criminal **2–04**
cases, are "pluralism, tolerance and broadmindedness"[15] and the "rule of law".[16]
The Court has emphasised that the protection of the right to life (in Art.2 of the
Convention), and the prohibition on torture and inhuman and degrading treatment (in Art.3) together enshrine "one of the basic values of the democratic
societies making up the Council of Europe".[17] Democratic values also involve a
recognition of the importance of the rights of the defence in criminal proceedings, since the right to a fair trial "holds a prominent place in a democratic
society".[18] The requirement in Art.6(1) for an "independent and impartial"
tribunal encompasses the principle of separation of powers in a democracy, and
guarantees the independence of the courts from the executive,[19] the parties,[20] and
the legislature.[21] Freedom of expression is "one of the essential foundations of a
democratic society"[22] and access by the media to the courts is of particular
importance in ensuring a fair and public trial[23] and in maintaining public
confidence in the courts.[24]

It is important to distinguish between "democratic values" and the protection of **2–05**
majority sentiment. The duty to protect inalienable rights sometimes requires the
Court to set standards, even where these do not meet with majority approval.[25]
The Convention exists, at least in part, to protect the rights of unpopular groups
and individuals. If the democratic process were always sufficient there would be
no necessity for a code of legally enforceable minimum rights. The Court has
therefore been careful to emphasise that:

> "although the interests of the individual must on occasion be subordinated to those of
> a group, democracy does not simply mean that the views of the majority must always
> prevail: a balance must be achieved which ensures the fair and proper treatment of
> minorities and avoids any abuse of a dominant position".[26]

---

[15] *Handyside v United Kingdom* (1979–80) 1 E.H.R.R. 737 at para.49; *Dudgeon v United Kingdom*
(1981) 4 E.H.R.R. 149 at para.53.

[16] *Golder v United Kingdom* (1979–80) 1 E.H.R.R. 525 at para.34; *Klass v Germany* (1979–80) 2
E.H.R.R. 214 at para.55; *Iatrides v Greece* Judgment March 25, 1999 para.62.

[17] *McCann, Savage and Farrell v United Kingdom* (1996) 21 E.H.R.R. 97 at para.147 citing
Soering v United Kingdom (1989) 11 E.H.R.R. 439 at para.88.

[18] *DeCubber v Belgium* (1985) 7 E.H.R.R. 236 at para.30; *Colozza v Italy* (1985) 7 E.H.R.R. 516
at para.32; *Soering v United Kingdom* (1989) 11 E.H.R.R. 439 at para.113; *Van Mechelen v
Netherlands* (1998) 25 E.H.R.R. 647 at para.58.

[19] *McGonnell v United Kingdom* (2000) 30 E.H.R.R. 289.

[20] *Campbell and Fell v United Kingdom* (1985) 7 E.H.R.R. 165 at para.78.

[21] *Crociani and others v Italy* (1980) 22 D.R. 147; *Demicoli v Malta* (1992) 14 E.H.R.R. 47 Op.
Comm. para.40.

[22] *Handyside v United Kingdom* (1979–80) 1 E.H.R.R. 737 at para.49; *Sunday Times v United
Kingdom (No.1)* (1979–80) 2 E.H.R.R. 245 at para.65; *Lingens v Austria* (1986) 8 E.H.R.R. 407 at
paras 41–42.

[23] *Axen v Germany* (1984) 6 E.H.R.R. 195 at para.25.

[24] *Hodgson, Woolf Productions and the NUJ v United Kingdom* (1988) 10 E.H.R.R. 503; *Worm v
Austria* (1998) 25 E.H.R.R. 454 at para.50.

[25] In *Inze v Austria* (1988) 10 E.H.R.R. 394 at para.44 the court considered that support amongst
the local population for measures discriminating against illegitimate children merely reflected "the
traditional outlook".

[26] *Young, James and Webster v United Kingdom* (1981) 4 E.H.R.R. 38 at para.63.

Thus, the Court has consistently held that degrading forms of punishment cannot be justified on the ground that they have been in use for a long time or meet with general approval.[27] In *Tyrer v United Kingdom*[28] the Court held that judicial corporal punishment was in breach of Art.3, despite the fact that a majority of the population of the Isle of Man favoured its retention. As the Court pointed out:

> "it might well be that one of the reasons why they view the penalty as an effective deterrent is precisely the element of degradation which it involves".

Similarly, in *Handyside v United Kingdom*[29] the Court held that the right to freedom of expression extends to information and ideas that "offend, shock or disturb society or a section of it"; and in *Dudgeon v United Kingdom*[30] the Court found that criminal offences prohibiting consensual homosexual activity in private were in breach of Art.8, despite the "strength of the view that it would be seriously damaging to the moral fabric of Northern Ireland" if such conduct were to be decriminalised.

2–06   References to the object and purpose of the Convention are not to be dismissed as mere statements of aspiration. Together they form the core guiding principles to the Convention's interpretation and application. In *Wemhoff v Germany*[31] the court observed that it is

> "necessary to seek the interpretation that is most appropriate in order to realise the aim and achieve the objective of the treaty, and not that which would restrict to the greatest degree possible the obligations undertaken by the parties".

Similarly, in *Golder v United Kingdom*[32] the Court said that it would be "a mistake" to see the reference to the rule of law in the Preamble to the Convention as a "merely . . . rhetorical reference, devoid of significance for those interpreting the Convention". And in *Soering v United Kingdom*[33] the Court observed that;

> "In interpreting the Convention, regard must be had to its special character as a treaty for the collective enforcement of human rights and fundamental freedoms. Thus, the object and purpose of the Convention as an instrument for the protection of individual human beings require that its provisions be interpreted and applied so as to make its safeguards practical and effective."

B. The Court's Interpretative Techniques

2–07   In order to give effect to the object and purpose of the Convention, the Court has developed a series of interpretative techniques that differ significantly from the

---

[27] *Tyrer v United Kingdom* (1978) 2 E.H.R.R. 1; *Campbell and Cosans v United Kingdom* (1988) 4 E.H.R.R. 1 at para.29.
[28] (1978) 2 E.H.R.R. 1 at para.31.
[29] (1979–80) 1 E.H.R.R. 737.
[30] (1981) 4 E.H.R.R. 149.
[31] (1979–80) 1 E.H.R.R. 55 at para.8.
[32] (1979–80) 1 E.H.R.R. 525 at para.34.
[33] (1989) 11 E.H.R.R. 439 at para.87.

common law approach to legal reasoning. The remainder of this chapter examines the principal themes that emerge from the Court's caselaw.

I. Practical and Effective Interpretation

It is a general principle governing the interpretation of a law-making treaty[34] that:

> "particular provisions are to be interpreted so as to give them their fullest weight and effect consistent with the normal sense of the words, and with other parts of the text, and in such a way that reason and a meaning can be attributed to every part of the text".[35]

2–08

Applying this principle, the Court has rejected a formalistic approach, holding that the Convention "is intended to guarantee not rights that are theoretical and illusory but rights that are practical and effective".[36]

The Convention is thus concerned with the substance of an individual's position rather than its formal classification, and Courts may need to "look behind appearances and examine the realities of the procedure in question".[37] One consequence of this approach is that compliance by the state with the letter of a Convention obligation will not necessarily be sufficient, if the protection afforded in practice has been substantially undermined. In *Artico v Italy*,[38] where the legal aid lawyer appointed to represent the applicant was shown to have been ineffective, the Court found a violation of Art.6(3)(c). Noting that this provision guaranteed legal "assistance" rather than simply the "nomination" of a lawyer, the court pointed out that:

2–09

> "[M]ere nomination does not ensure effective assistance, since the lawyer appointed may die, fall seriously ill, be prevented for a protracted period from acting, or shirk his duties. If they are notified of the situation, the authorities must either replace him or cause him to fulfil his obligations."[39]

---

[34] International law distinguishes between law-making treaties (*traités-loi*) and contractual treaties (*traités-contrats*). In a law-making treaty, such as the European Convention on Human Rights, the intention of the contracting parties is not simply to establish reciprocal undertakings, but to create objective rights with corresponding legal liabilities.

[35] Fitzmaurice G.G., *The Law and Procedure of the International Court of Justice*, (Grotius, Cambridge, 42–9 1986), p.345, cited in Merrils J.G., *The Development of International Law by the European Court of Human Rights* (2nd edn, Manchester, 1993), p.77. See also Jacobs and White, *The European Convention on Human Rights* (2nd edn, Oxford), p.35.

[36] *Marckx v Belgium* (1979–80) 2 E.H.R.R. 330 at para.31; *Airey v Ireland* (1979–80) 2 E.H.R.R. 305 at para.24; *Artico v Italy* (1981) 3 E.H.R.R. 1 at para.33; *Soering v United Kingdom* (1989) 11 E.H.R.R. 439 at para.87.

[37] See, amongst numerous other authorities, *Deweer v Belgium* (1979–80) 2 E.H.R.R. 439 at para.44; *Adolf v Austria* (1982) 4 E.H.R.R. 315 at para.30; *Welch v United Kingdom* (1995) 20 E.H.R.R. 247 at para.27.

[38] (1981) 3 E.H.R.R. 1 at para.33.

[39] See also *Goddi v Italy* (1984) 6 E.H.R.R. 457 at para.31 where the state was found in violation of Art.6(3)(c) since the lawyer appointed to represent the applicant was unable properly to represent his client, who had absconded. The court held that in order to ensure effective legal assistance, the trial should have been adjourned.

Moreover, the Court held that it was not necessary for the applicant to establish that the shortcomings in legal representation had caused actual prejudice to his case. This would be "asking the impossible" since it could never be proved that effective representation would have secured the acquittal of an accused. The Court considered that an interpretation which introduced this requirement into Art.6(3)(c) "would deprive it in large measure of its substance".[40] In *Campbell and Fell v United Kingdom*[41] the Court held that Art.6(3)(c) implied not merely effective representation at the hearing itself, but an adequate opportunity for prior consultation.

2–10 *Minelli v Switzerland*[42] provides another example of practical and effective interpretation. In that case the Court was called upon to determine whether the presumption of innocence in Art.6(2) applied to an application for an award of costs to an acquitted defendant. The government argued that the right to be presumed innocent applied only to the determination of a criminal charge, and not to proceedings subsequent to an acquittal. The court disagreed, holding that Art.6(2) "governs criminal proceedings in their entirety, irrespective of the outcome of the prosecution, and not solely the examination of the merits of the charge". The presumption of innocence would therefore be violated by a judicial pronouncement after acquittal reflecting an opinion that the accused was, in reality, guilty of the offence.

2–11 One of the most important illustrations of the effectiveness principle is the Court's recognition of the Convention's extra-territorial effect. In its landmark decision in *Soering v United Kingdom*[43] the Court held that a decision to extradite an individual to a non-Convention state where there were substantial grounds for believing that he would be exposed to inhuman or degrading treatment contrary to Art.3 would engage the responsibility of the state from which extradition was sought. The Court held that a decision to surrender an individual in such circumstances:

> "would hardly be compatible with the underlying values of the Convention, that 'common heritage of political traditions, ideals, freedom and the rule of law' to which the Preamble refers".[44]

While an obligation to refuse co-operation was "not explicitly referred to in the brief and general wording of Article 3", a decision to surrender an individual to face such treatment "would plainly be contrary to the spirit and intendment of the Article". There was therefore an "inherent obligation not to extradite".[45] This principle has since been extended to a decision to deport a convicted drug trafficker after the expiry of his sentence.[46]

---

[40] Para.35.
[41] (1985) 7 E.H.R.R. 165 at para.99.
[42] (1983) 5 E.H.R.R. 554. See also *Leutscher v Netherlands* (1996) 24 E.H.R.R. 181.
[43] (1989) 11 E.H.R.R. 439.
[44] Para.88.
[45] *Soering* at para.88.
[46] *D v United Kingdom* (1997) 24 E.H.R.R. 423.

In *Aydin v Turkey*[47] the Court held that where an individual made an allegation of torture or inhuman or degrading treatment, the state was under an obligation to carry out

2–12

> "a thorough and effective investigation capable of leading to the identification and punishment of those responsible, and including effective access for the complainant to the investigatory procedure".

The court has emphasised the same principle in the context of Art.2.[48]

II. Rights to be broadly construed/restrictions to be narrowly interpreted

The effectiveness principle has led the Court to hold that provisions of the Convention conferring rights are to be broadly and purposively construed, whilst those establishing exceptions and limitations must be restrictively interpreted. Further, Art.18 of the Convention provides that the restrictions set out in the Convention "shall not be applied for any purpose other than those for which they have been prescribed." In *Gusinsky v Russia*, the Court held that there could be a violation of Art.18 in conjunction with another article.[49] The application of the effectiveness principle is most apparent in relation to the qualified rights in Arts 8 to 11. In its interpretation of these provisions the Court has consistently maintained that a generous construction is appropriate in determining the scope of the protected right set out in the first paragraph of each article.[50] In *Niemetz v Germany*,[51] for example, the court held that the concepts of a person's home and private life in Art.8 included business premises and activities, on the ground that:

2–13

> "it would be too restrictive to limit the notion [of private life] to an 'inner circle' in which an individual may live his own personal life as he chooses".

Similarly, in *Kokkinakis v Greece*[52] the right to freedom of thought, conscience and religion in Art.9 was held to apply not only to recognised religious or ethical value systems but also to the conscientious beliefs of "atheists, agnostics, sceptics and the unconcerned".

However, when the Court turns to assess the purported justification for an interference with the protected right (under the second paragraph of each of these

2–14

---

[47] (1998) 25 E.H.R.R. 251 at para.103.

[48] See for example *Jordan v United Kingdom* (2003) 37 E.H.R.R. 2, *Caciki v Turkey* (2001) 31 E.H.R.R. 133. The principle was applied in the domestic context in *R. (Amin) v Secretary of State for the Home Department* [2004] 1 A.C. 653.

[49] (2005) 41 E.H.R.R. 17, at paras 73–78. The Court found a violation of Art.18 in conjunction with Art.5, based on the fact that the applicant's liberty had been restricted not only for the legitimate purpose of bringing him before the competent legal authority, but also in order to intimidate him. These additional, illegitimate, purposes led to the violation of Art.18.

[50] A possible exception to this is *Laskey and ors v United Kingdom* (1997) 24 E.H.R.R. 39, where the court doubted whether organised group sadomasochism was fully within the notion of private life.

[51] (1993) 16 E.H.R.R. 97 at paras 29 to 30.

[52] (1994) 17 E.H.R.R. 397.

Articles) it has generally adopted the strict approach exemplified in *Klass v Germany*[53]:

> "The cardinal issue arising under Article 8 in the present case is whether the interference . . . is justified by the terms of paragraph 2 of the Article. This paragraph, since it provides for an exception to a right guaranteed by the Convention, is to be narrowly interpreted."

Applying this approach, the Court held that powers of secret surveillance:

> "are tolerable under the Convention only insofar as strictly necessary for safeguarding the democratic institutions".

Likewise, when determining whether an inteference with freedom of expression under Art.10(1) is justified by reference to the public interests identified in Art.10(2), the Court has held that it is:

> "faced not with a choice between two conflicting principles but with the principle of freedom of expression that is subject to a number of exceptions which must be narrowly interpreted".[54]

2-15 Whilst the application of this principle is most clearly seen in relation to Arts 8 to 11, it has in fact been applied to all Convention rights.[55] Thus, the right to life in Art.2 has been held to encompass both deliberate and unintentional loss of life.[56] Its provisions must be strictly construed and any deprivation of life must be subjected to the "most careful scrutiny".[57] In the context of the right to personal liberty in Art.5, the Court has held that the exceptions set out in para.5(1)(a) to (f) provide an "exhaustive definition" of the circumstances in which a person may be deprived of his or her liberty and are to be given a narrow interpretation.[58] A wide interpretation:

> "would entail consequences incompatible with the notion of the rule of law from which the whole Convention draws its inspiration".[59]

In *Cuilla v Italy*[60] the Court applied this approach in holding that the arrest and detention of a suspect pending an order for "preventive measures" fell outside the permitted exceptions in Art.5(1), despite the acknowledged importance of the fight against organised crime in Italy.

---

[53] (1979–80) 2 E.H.R.R. 214 at para.42.
[54] *Sunday Times v United Kingdom* (1979–80) 2 E.H.R.R. 245 at para.65.
[55] The prohibition on forced or compulsory labour in Art.4(2) is a possible exception. The Court has held that the categories established in Art.4(3) are not limitations on the right in Art.4(2). Rather, they delimit the content of that right and therefore aid its interpretation: *Schmidt v Germany* (1994) 18 E.H.R.R. 513; *Van der Mussele v Belgium* (1984) 6 E.H.R.R. 163. It would seem to follow that Art.4(2) does not necessarily prohibit all forms of compulsory labour which are outside the examples set out in Art.4(3).
[56] *Stewart v United Kingdom* (1985) 7 E.H.R.R. 453; *Oneryildiz v Turkey* (2005) 41 E.H.R.R. 20.
[57] *McCann, Savage and Farrell v United Kingdom* (1996) 21 E.H.R.R. 97 at paras 147–150.
[58] *Winterwerp v Netherlands* (1979–80) 2 E.H.R.R. 387 at para.37.
[59] *Engel v Netherlands* (1979–80) 1 E.H.R.R. 647 at para.69.
[60] (1991) 13 E.H.R.R. 346 at para.41.

The right to a fair trial in Art.6 is also to be given a broad construction[61] since   **2–16**
a restrictive interpretation "would not be consonant with the object and purpose
of the provision".[62] Any restriction on the rights of the defence is to be scrutinised with special care, and departures from a truly adversarial procedure are to
be kept to the minimum possible. In the leading case of *Van Mechelin v
Netherlands*[63] the Court observed that:

> "Having regard to the place that the right to a fair administration of justice holds in a
> democratic society, any measures restricting the rights of the defence should be strictly
> necessary. If a less restrictive measure can suffice then that measure should be
> applied."

III. Permissible limitations must not impair the essence of a Convention right

Another aspect of the doctrine of practical and effective interpretation is the   **2–17**
principle that limitations and conditions imposed on the exercise of a Convention
right must not impair its very existence or deprive it of its effectiveness.[64] In *Fox,
Campbell and Hartley v United Kingdom*[65] the government argued that a power
of detention which was exercisable on the ground of "genuine suspicion" was
sufficient to meet the requirements of Art.5(1)(c) which permits arrest or detention on "*reasonable* suspicion" of the commission of an offence. The Court held
that the difficulties associated with policing terrorist crime, including the need to
protect informers:

> "cannot justify stretching the notion of 'reasonableness' to the point where the essence
> of the right secured by Article 5(1)(c) is impaired".

In *Golder v United Kingdom*[66] the government sought to argue that Art.8, which
protects (amongst other things) the right to respect for a person's correspondence, applied only to state interference with existing correspondence rights, and
did not therefore restrict the state's right to control or prohibit correspondence to
and from prisoners. Not surprisingly, the Court rejected this argument, holding
that:

> "it would be placing an undue and formalistic restriction on the concept of interference
> with correspondence not to regard it as covering the case of correspondence which has
> not yet taken place, only because the competent authority, with power to enforce its
> ruling, has ruled that it will not be allowed".

---

[61] *Moreiva de Azvedo v Portugal* (1992) 13 E.H.R.R. 731 at para.66; *Delcourt v Belgium*
(1979–80) 1 E.H.R.R. 355.
[62] *De Cubber v Belgium* (1985) 7 E.H.R.R. 236 at para.30.
[63] (1998) 25 E.H.R.R. 647 at para.59.
[64] *Mathieu-Mohin and Clerfayt v Belgium* (1988) 10 E.H.R.R. 1 at para.52; *Ashingdane v United
Kingdom* (1985) 7 E.H.R.R. 528 at para.57. *Winterwerp v Netherlands* (1979–80) 2 E.H.R.R. 387 at
para.60; *Lithgow v United Kingdom* (1986) 8 E.H.R.R. 329 at para.194; *Philis v Greece* (1991) 13
E.H.R.R. 741 at para.59.
[65] (1991) 13 E.H.R.R. 157 at para.32.
[66] (1979–80) 1 E.H.R.R. 525.

IV. Evolutive interpretation

2–18 The Convention has been described as a "living instrument which must be interpreted in the light of present day conditions".[67] It calls for an evolutive and dynamic approach to its interpretation rather than a static and historical one. The concepts used in the Convention are therefore to be understood in the context of the democratic societies of modern Europe, and not according to the conceptions of 50 years ago when the Convention was drafted.[68] As Lord Hope pointed out in *R. v Director of Public Prosecutions ex parte Kebilene*[69] "the Convention should be seen as an expression of fundamental principles rather than as a set of mere rules".

2–19 Whilst evolutive interpretation has an important role to play in ensuring that rights remain relevant, a court applying the Convention cannot, through the process of interpretation, create wholly new obligations which the contracting parties have not undertaken. Thus, in *Soering v United Kingdom*[70] the Court rejected the submission of Amnesty International that:

> "evolving standards in Western Europe regarding the death penalty required that the death penalty should now be considered as an inhuman and degrading punishment within the meaning of Article 3".

The Court observed that Art.3 could not have been intended by the drafters of the Convention to include a general prohibition on the death penalty since the death penalty was expressly permitted by Art.2. Noting that the death penalty in peacetime had in fact been abolished by all contracting states, the Court observed:

> "Subsequent practice in national penal policy, in the form of a generalised abolition of capital punishment, could be taken as establishing the agreement of the Contracting States to abrogate the exception provided for under Article 2(1) and hence remove a textual limit on the scope for evolutive interpretation of Article 3. However, Protocol No.6, as a subsequent written agreement, shows that the intention of the Contracting Parties as recently as 1983 was to adopt the normal method of amendment of the text in order to introduce a new obligation to abolish capital punishment in time of peace and, what is more, to do so by an optional instrument allowing each State to choose the moment when to undertake such an engagement. In these conditions, notwithstanding the special character of the Convention, Article 3 cannot be interpreted as generally prohibiting the death penalty."

2–20 Similarly, in *Cruz Varas v Sweden*[71] the court held that in the absence of a specific provision in the Convention enabling the court to make a legally binding order for interim relief, a failure by a state to comply with a request for interim measures could not be regarded as an interference with the right of individual

---

[67] *Tyrer v United Kingdom* (1979–80) 2 E.H.R.R. 1 at para.31; *Airey v Ireland* (1979–80) 2 E.H.R.R. 305 at para.26.

[68] It is for this reason that the *travaux préparatoires* are of only marginal relevance in the interpretation of the Convention.

[69] [1999] 3 W.L.R. 972.

[70] (1989) 11 E.H.R.R. 439.

[71] (1992) 14 E.H.R.R. 1 see paras 1–33 to 1–38 above.

petition. Despite the history of almost invariable compliance with such requests, the Court could not "create new rights and obligations which were not included in the Convention at the outset".

Evolutive interpretation thus requires the Court to strike a careful balance, which **2–21** recognises that it is not the task of the interpreter to change the content of a norm established in the Convention, whilst at the same time acknowledging that if the content of a norm "has undergone a change in social reality, the interpreter must take account of this".[72] As a former President of the Court has put it[73]:

> "Human rights treaties must be interpreted in an objective and dynamic manner, by taking into account social conditions and developments; the ideas and conditions prevailing at the time when the treaties were drafted retain hardly any continuing validity. Nevertheless, treaty interpretation must not amount to treaty revision. Interpretation must therefore respect the text of the treaty concerned."

The Court must, in the end, make a judgment as to whether a new social or legal standard has achieved sufficiently wide acceptance to affect the interpretation and application of the Convention. In making this judgment a consideration of comparative law and practice within Europe and elsewhere may be relevant, as may other international agreements which the contracting parties (or the majority of them) have concluded.

Many Convention concepts are obviously rooted in the current legal and social **2–22** standards of the contracting states. The requirements of the "protection of morals", for example, or the question of whether an interference with a Convention right is "necessary in a democratic society" can only be judged according to contemporary standards, and the court has been particularly willing to adopt an evolutive approach to such questions. Thus, in *Dudgeon v United Kingdom*[74] the Court observed that:

> "As compared with an era when [the legislation] was enacted there in now a better understanding and, in consequence, an increased tolerance of homosexual behaviour to the extent that it is no longer considered to be necessary or appropriate to treat homosexual practices [between consenting adults in private] as in themselves a matter to which the sanctions of the criminal law should be applied. The Court cannot overlook the marked changes which have occurred in this regard in the domestic law of the member states."

Dudgeon was concerned with the position of gay men over the age of 21. It took **2–23** a further 15 years before the Convention organs came to accept that the same principle should apply to those aged over 16. In *Sutherland v United Kingdom*[75] the Commission overturned its previous caselaw,[76] holding that the potential

---

[72] Sereni *Diritto Internazionale* 1 (1956), p.182 cited in Matscher F., "Methods of Interpretation of the Convention" in Macdonald R. St. J., Matscher F. and Petzold H., *The European System for the Protection of Human Rights* (Martinus Nijhoff, 1993), p.70.

[73] Bernhardt R., *The European Dimension: Studies in Honour of Gérard J. Wiarda* (Koln, 1988), p.65 at p.71.

[74] (1982) 4 E.H.R.R. 149 at para.60.

[75] (1997) 24 E.H.R.R. CD 22.

[76] *X v United Kingdom* (1980) 19 D.R. 66.

application of the offence of gross indecency to consensual sexual activity between 16 and 17 year old males was in breach of Arts 8 and 14. In coming to the conclusion that a differential age of consent for gay men could no longer be justified, the Commission referred to "major changes" which had occurred in professional opinion on the need to protect young gay men and the desirability of an equal age of consent. The Commission considered that it was:

> "opportune to reconsider its earlier case law in the light of these modern developments and, more especially, in the light of the weight of current medical opinion that to reduce the age of consent to 16 might have positively beneficial effects on the sexual health of young gay men without any corresponding harmful consequences".

In *L and V v Austria*[77] the court again drew on what it considered to be a growing European consensus in holding that the imposition of a higher age of consent for gay sex breached Art.14 when read with Art.8. In *Smith and Grady v United Kingdom*[78] the Court considered the ban on homosexuals in the army, which the Government sought to justify in part with reference to the prejudices of members of the armed forces. The Court held that such negative prejudices could not amount to a justification for the intereference with the applicants' rights.

2–24   This requirement for a dynamic interpretation is not, however, confined to the qualified rights in Arts 8 to 11. It applies generally, and governs the interpretation of all aspects of the Convention. In *Tyrer v United Kingdom*[79] the Court held that judicial birching was in breach of Art.3, saying that it:

> "could not but be influenced by the developments and commonly accepted standards in the penal policy of the member states of the Council of Europe".

In the Court's view it was the standards which were currently prevalent which were decisive of the issue, and not those which were prevalent when the Convention was adopted: Art.3 embodied the *concept* of inhuman and degrading punishment and not the particular *conception* which may have been held in 1950.

2–25   Similarly in *Winterwerp v Netherlands*[80] the Court found that the term "person of unsound mind" in Art.5(1)(e) was:

> "[A] term whose meaning is continually evolving as research in psychiatry progresses, an increasing flexibility in treatment is developing, and society's attitude to mental illness changes, in particular so that greater understanding of the problems of mental patients is becoming more widespread."

And in *Borgers v Belgium*[81] the Court held that the requirements of a fair trial in Art.6 had undergone a "considerable evolution" in the Court's caselaw, particularly as regards the importance attached to the appearance of fairness, and the increased sensitivity of the public to the fair administration of justice.

---

[77] (2003) 36 E.H.R.R. 55.
[78] (2000) 29 E.H.R.R. 493.
[79] (1979–80) 2 E.H.R.R. 1 at para.31.
[80] (1982) 4 E.H.R.R. 228.
[81] (1993) 15 E.H.R.R. 92.

The inevitable consequence of this approach is that the strict doctrine of prece- 2–26
dent does not apply to decisions of the European Court and Commission of
Human Rights. Older Convention caselaw must be approached with this principle in mind. Where there is some evidence that standards may be in transition, the
Court may be willing to reconsider its own decisions at relatively frequent
intervals, and sometimes even calls for a particular situation to be kept under
review. In *Rees v United Kingdom*,[82] for example, the court rejected a complaint
under Art.8 brought by a transsexual who had been denied the right to a change
of legal status. Nevertheless the Court said that it was "conscious of the
seriousness of the problems affecting these persons and the distress they suffer",
and continued;

> "The Convention has always to be interpreted in the light of current circumstances. The
> need for appropriate legal measures should therefore be kept under review, having
> regard particularly to the scientific and societal developments".

In the subsequent cases of *Cossey v United Kingdom*[83] and *Sheffield and Horsham v United Kingdom*[84] the Court adhered to its earlier decision in *Rees*, but
by a diminishing majority in each case. In the *Sheffield* case, the finding of no
violation was by a majority of only 11 to nine, and the court openly criticised the
United Kingdom for its failure to carry out a review of the need to maintain the
existing arrangements. Whilst voting with the majority "after much hesitation"
the British judge, Sir John Freeland, suggested that further inaction by the United
Kingdom "could well tilt the balance in the other direction". The balance finally
changed in the case of *Goodwin v United Kingdom*,[85] where the Court took note
of the continuing international trend in favour of legal recognition of the new
sexual identity of post-operative transsexuals (even though there could not yet be
said to be a European consensus on the issue) and found that the UK had
breached Art.8 by refusing to accord such legal recognition.

The Court's evolutive approach to interpretation does not, however, mean that 2–27
the parties can simply ignore a previous decision of the Court which has been
reached after hearing full argument. Whilst the strict doctrine of precedent has no
place in Strasbourg, there is, in practice, a heavy onus on an applicant seeking to
persuade the Court to depart from a recent decision. In *Wynne v United Kingdom*,[86] a case concerning the rights of a mandatory life sentence prisoner, the
Court suggested that it would require "cogent reasons" to depart from the
conclusion that it had reached on the nature of the mandatory life sentence three
years earlier in *Thynne, Wilson and Gunnell v United Kingdom*.[87] However, in
Stafford v United Kingdom[88] the Court accepted that, while it would not depart
from previous decisions "without cogent reason",[89] since:

---

[82] (1987) 9 E.H.R.R. 56.
[83] (1991) 13 E.H.R.R. 622.
[84] (1999) 27 E.H.R.R. 163.
[85] (2002) 35 E.H.R.R. 18. See also *Van Kuck v Germany* (2003) 37 E.H.R.R. 51.
[86] (1995) 19 E.H.R.R. 333 at para.36.
[87] (1991) 13 E.H.R.R. 666.
[88] (2002) 35 E.H.R.R. 32.
[89] Para.71.

"the Convention is first and foremost a system for the protection of human rights, the Court must... have regard to the changing conditions in Contracting States and respond, for example, to any emerging consensus as to the standards to be achieved."[90]

The Court considered that there had been "significant developments in the domestic sphere"[91] relating to the judicialisation of the life sentence, and concluded that:

"the finding in *Wynne* that the mandatory life sentence constituted punishment for life can no longer be regarded as reflecting the real position in the domestic criminal justice system of the mandatory life prisoner."[92]

V. Practice in other jurisdictions

2–28 The Court has observed that the main purpose of the Convention is:

"to lay down certain international standards to be observed by the Contracting States in their relations with persons under their jurisdiction".[93]

Thus, the Court has consistently held that the existence of a "generally shared approach" in other contracting states is relevant to the application of the Convention[94] although "absolute uniformity" is not required.[95] The Court has no systematic means of establishing the comparative law position on a particular issue, even within the Council of Europe. It relies on the collective experience of the judges of the Court, on the research of the parties, and on any *amicus* interventions[96] for its information.

2–29 As we have seen, the Court was heavily influenced by commonly accepted European standards in *Tyrer v United Kingdom*[97] and *Dudgeon v United Kingdom*.[98] On the other hand, when considering the length of a criminal sentence the Commission has held that "the mere fact that an offence is punished more severely in one country than in another does not suffice to establish that the punishment is inhuman or degrading".[99] And in *T and V v United Kingdom*[100] the Court referred to the absence of a European consensus on the age of criminal

---

[90] Para.68.
[91] Para.69.
[92] Para.79.
[93] *Belgian Linguistics Case (No.1)* (1979–80) 1 E.H.R.R. 241 at 250 para.[e].
[94] *Marckx v Belgium* (1979–80) 2 E.H.R.R. 330 para.41; *Tyrer v United Kingdom* (1979–80) 2 E.H.R.R. 1 para.31; *Dudgeon v United Kingdom* (1982) 4 E.H.R.R. 149 para.60; *X, Y and Z v United Kingdom* (1997) 24 E.H.R.R. 143 para.52.
[95] *Sunday Times v United Kingdom (No.1)* (1979–80) 2 E.H.R.R. 245 para.61; *Muller v Switzerland* (1991) 13 E.H.R.R. 212 para.35; *Wingrove v United Kingdom* (1996) 24 E.H.R.R. 1 para.58; *F v Switzerland* (1988) 10 E.H.R.R. 411 para.33. *Monnell and Morris v United Kingdom* (1987) 10 E.H.R.R. 205 para.47.
[96] See para.1–152 above.
[97] (1978) 2 E.H.R.R. 1.
[98] (1982) 4 E.H.R.R. 149.
[99] *C v Germany* (1986) 46 D.R. 176.
[100] (2000) 30 E.H.R.R. 121, paras 73–74.

responsibility in concluding that the prosecution of two boys for a murder committed when they were 10 was compatible with Art.3 of the Convention. In *Vo v France*[101] the court noted the lack of any European consensus on the issue of when a foetus becomes a "person" for the purposes of the right to life in Art.2 of the Convention.[102]

When called upon to determine whether an interference with freedom of expres-   **2–30**
sion is justified under the protection of morals exception in Art.10(2), the Court has often stressed that "it is not possible to find in the legal and social orders of the contracting states a uniform Europen conception of morals".[103] Thus, in *Handyside v United Kingdom*,[104] the Court attached little significance to the fact that the book to which the applicant's conviction related had been distributed elsewhere in Europe without attracting prosecution. Similarly, in *Wingrove v United Kingdom*[105] where the applicant's complaint under Art.10 related to the English offence of blasphemy, the Court observed that;

"[T]here is no uniform European conception of the requirements of 'the protection of the rights of others' in relation to attacks on their religious convictions. What is likely to cause substantial offence to persons of a particular religious persuasion will vary significantly from time to time and from place to place, especially in an era characterised by an ever growing array of faiths and denominations."

The Court's reference to comparative practice in *Monnell and Morris v United*   **2–31**
Kingdom[106] was unusual. The applicants complained that a "loss of time" order under s.29(1) of the Criminal Appeal Act 1968[107] was in violation of Art.5. In concluding that such an order was compatible with Art.5(1)(a) the Court noted that:

"[U]nder the law of many of the Convention countries detention pending a criminal appeal is treated as detention on remand and a convicted person does not start to serve his or her sentence until the conviction has become final. In such systems, the appellate court itself determines the sentence and, in some of them, exercises a discretion in deciding whether or to what extent detention pending appeal shall be deducted from the sentence."

Finally, it should be borne in mind that the Court's consideration of comparative   **2–32**
practice is not necessarily confined to European jurisdictions. In *Chahal v United Kingdom*[108] the Court relied on the practice adopted in Canada for resolving national security cases as illustrating that:

---

[101] (2005) 40 E.H.R.R. 12.
[102] Para.82.
[103] *Muller v Switzerland* (1991) 13 E.H.R.R. 212 para.35; *Handyside v United Kingdom* (1979–80) 1 E.H.R.R. 737.
[104] (1979–80) 1 E.H.R.R. 737.
[105] (1997) 24 E.H.R.R. 1 at para.58.
[106] (1988) 10 E.H.R.R. 205 at para.47.
[107] Under s.29(1) the Court of Appeal may, if it considers that an appeal is without merit, direct that time served between the imposition of the sentence and the disposal of the appeal should not count towards the accused person's sentence. As to the circumstances in which such an order may be made see *Practice Direction (Crime: Sentence: Loss of Time)* [1980] 1 W.L.R. 270.
[108] (1997) 23 E.H.R.R. 413 at para.131.

"there are techniques which can be employed which both accommodate legitimate security concerns . . . and yet afford the individual a substantial measure of procedural justice".

VI. Ordinary meaning

2–33 In interpreting a provision of the Convention, the Court will seek to ascertain the ordinary meaning of a word insofar as this accords with the context of the provision and the object and purpose of the Convention.[109] In determining the ordinary meaning of a term, regard should be had to the French and English texts of the Convention, both of which are equally authentic.[110] On occasions, the Court has resorted to dictionary definitions. In *Luedicke, Belkacem and Koc v Germany*[111] the Court was concerned with the meaning of Art.6(3)(e) of the Convention, which provides that an accused person is to be provided with "the free assistance of an interpreter". The German government argued that when viewed in its context this provision allowed for the costs of an interpreter to be reclaimed from a convicted defendant. The Court held that:

> "the ordinary meaning of the terms '*gratuiment*' and 'free' in Article 6(3)(c) of the Convention [was] not contradicted by the context of the sub-paragraph, and [was] confirmed by the object and purpose of Article 6".

These terms denoted:

> "neither a conditional remission, nor a temporary exemption, nor a suspension, but a once and for all exemption or exoneration".

2–34 In the event of a conflict between the ordinary meaning of a provision and the clear object and purpose of the Convention, the latter will generally prevail. In *Wemhoff v Germany*[112] the Court was called upon to interpret Art.5(3), which provides that an accused is "entitled to trial within a reasonable time *or* to release pending trial". As the Court observed, a "purely grammatical" construction would leave the authorities with a choice between two obligations—that of conducting the proceedings within a reasonable time, or that of releasing an accused pending trial. The Court was:

> " . . . quite certain that such an interpretation would not conform to the intention of the High Contracting Parties. It is inconceivable that they should have intended to permit their judicial authorities, at the price of release of the accused, to protract proceedings beyond a reasonable time."

As a result, Art.5(3) is to be read as if the word "or" is replaced by the word "and".

2–35 A similar approach is evident in relation to Art.6(3)(c), which provides that the accused has the right:

---

[109] *Johnson v Ireland* (1987) 9 E.H.R.R. 203 at para.51. *Luedicke, Belkacem and Koc v Germany* (1979–80) 2 E.H.R.R. 149 at para.40.
[110] *Luedicke, Belkacem and Koc v Germany* (1979–80) 2 E.H.R.R. 149 at para.40.
[111] (1979–80) 2 E.H.R.R. 149 at para.40.
[112] (1979–80) 1 E.H.R.R. 55 at paras 4–5.

"to defend himself in person *or* through legal assistance of his own choosing *or*, if he has not sufficient means to pay for legal assistance, to be given it free when the interests of justice so require".

Here again, the wording of the English text of Art.6(3)(c) suggests that the right to free legal representation is an alternative to the right of an accused person to represent himself. However, in *Pakelli v Germany*[113] the Court preferred to follow the French text, which links the rights contained in Art.6(3)(c) by the word "*et*", on the basis that this would result in a more faithful reflection of the underlying aims of Art.6. Accordingly, the Court held that Art.6(3)(c) guarantees three related but independent rights:

> "Having regard to the object and purpose of this Article, which is designed to secure effective protection of the rights of the defence . . . a person charged with a criminal offence who does not wish to defend himself in person must be able to have recourse to legal assistance of his own choosing; if he does not have sufficient means to pay for such assistance, he is entitled under the Convention to be given it free when the interests of justice so require."[114]

A second issue which arose in the *Wemhoff*[115] case was whether the period to be considered in connection with the right to "trial within a reasonable time" in Art.5(3) came to an end when the accused was first produced before the trial court, or continued until the trial court's judgment was delivered. The Court noted that the English text permitted either interpretation, but the use of the word "*jugée*" in the French text allowed for only one meaning, namely that the period to be considered continued until the judgment terminating the trial: **2–36**

> "Thus confronted with two versions of a treaty which are equally authentic but not exactly the same, the Court must, following established international law precedents, interpret them in a way that will reconcile them as far as possible. Given that it is a law-making treaty it is also necessary to seek the interpretation that is most appropriate in order to realise the aim and achieve the object of the treaty, not that which would restrict to the greatest degree possible the obligations undertaken by the Parties. It is impossible to see why the protection against unduly long detention on remand, which Article 5 seeks to ensure for persons suspected of offences, should not continue up to the delivery of judgment rather than cease at the moment the trial opens."[116]

---

[113] (1984) 6 E.H.R.R. 1.

[114] At para.31. Note, however, that in *X v Austria* (Application No.1242/61) the Commission observed that;

"While [Article 6(3)(c)] guarantees the right to an accused person that proceedings against him will not take place without an adequate representation of the case for the defence, [it] does not give an accused person the right to decide for himself in what manner his defence should be assured . . . the decision as to which of the two alternatives should be chosen, namely the applicant's right to defend himself in person or to be represented by a lawyer of his own choosing, or in certain circumstances one appointed by the court, rests with the competent authorities concerned."

[115] (1979–80) 1 E.H.R.R. 55.

[116] Note that the right to the determination of a criminal charge within a reasonable time in Art.6(1) of the Convention has been interpreted as including the time taken for the final determination of any appeal: *Neumeister v Austria (No.1)* (1979–80) 1 E.H.R.R. 91 at para.19; *Wemhoff v Germany* (1979–80) 1 E.H.R.R. 55; *Konig v Germany (No.1)* (1979–80) 2 E.H.R.R. 170 at para.98; *Eckle v Germany* (1983) 5 E.H.R.R. 1 at para.76.

2–37　A similar problem arose in *Brogan v United Kingdom*[117] in connection with the permissible interval between a person's arrest and first appearance in court. There, the court was faced with a difference between the word "promptly" in the English text of Art.5(3) and the word "*aussitot*" in the French text (which literally means immediately). The Court held that:

> "the use in the French text of the word '*aussitot*', with its constraining connotation of immediacy, confirm[ed] that the degree of flexibility attaching to the notion of 'promptness' [was] limited".

As a result, a delay of four days and six hours was found to exceed the time permitted under Art.5(3).

2–38　In the *Belgian Linguistics Case (No.2)*[118] the Court was concerned with the scope of the prohibition on discrimination in Art.14. The English text guarantees the delivery of Convention rights "without discrimination", whereas the French text uses the much stricter term "*sans distinction aucune*". The Court considered that:

> "one would reach absurd results were one to give Article 14 an interpretation as wide as that which the French version seems to imply".

2–39　A final example is provided by the case of *Jespers v Belgium*[119] where the Commission observed, in connection with Art.6(3)(c), that;

> " . . . the word 'facilities' (French 'facilités') is qualified by the adjective 'adequate' (French 'nécessaire'). Despite the slight difference in meaning between the adjective in the French text and the one in the English text it is clear that the facilities which must be granted to the accused are restricted to those which assist or may assist him in the preparation of his defence."

2–40　Where one language version uses a particular word or phrase throughout the Convention, whilst the other version includes slight differences, the likelihood is that the differences have no significance. The French text, for example, uses the term "*prévues par la loi*" throughout Arts 8 to 11, as well as in Art.1 of Protocol 1. The English text, on the other hand, uses the term "in accordance with the law" in Art.8, "prescribed by law" in Arts 9 to 11 and "provided for by law" in Art.1 of Protocol 1. The Court has attached no significance to the different versions of the English text.[120]

VII. Travaux Préparatoires

2–41　Recourse to *travaux préparatoires*[121] is classed as a supplementary means of interpretation under Art.32 of the Vienna Convention on the Law of Treaties. It

---

[117] (1989) 11 E.H.R.R. 117 at para.59.
[118] (1979–80) 1 E.H.R.R. 252 at 284, para.10.
[119] (1981) 27 D.R. 61 at para.57.
[120] *Sunday Times v United Kingdom (No.1)* (1979–80) 2 E.H.R.R. 245 at para.48. (The Court referred, in this connection, to Art.33(4) of the Vienna Convention.)
[121] See *Collected Edition of the Travaux Préparatiores of the European Convention on Human Rights*.

may be deployed only in order to confirm the meaning of a provision as established in accordance with Art.31,[122] or where the application of the principles in Art.31 leaves the meaning ambiguous, obscure or absurd. This restriction is especially appropriate to the European Convention on Human Rights, in view of the Court's evolutive approach to interpretation.[123] Whilst the *travaux préparatoires* may have a certain relevance in determining the object and purpose of the Convention, they cannot be used as a primary aid to the construction of particular provisions. Thus, in *Lawless v Ireland*[124] the Court observed that:

"Having ascertained that the text of Article 5 paragraphs (1)(c) and (3) is sufficiently clear in itself, [and] having also found that the meaning of this text is in keeping with the purpose of the Convention, the Court cannot, having regard to a generally recognised principle regarding the interpretation of international treaties, resort to the preparatory work."

The Court has sometimes referred to the *travaux préparatoires* in order to   2–42
confirm an interpretation which it had already reached by other means.[125] But it has been perfectly prepared to adopt a construction which appears to conflict with the *travaux préparatoires* if it considers this is necessary to ensure that Convention rights are given practical effect in a modern context.[126]

VIII. Autonomous terms

Many of the terms used in the Convention, and especially those concerned with   2–43
due process rights, refer directly to established concepts in domestic law. As we have seen, Art.31 of the Vienna Convention envisages the possibility of a "special meaning" being given to particular terms used in a treaty, where this is necessary to achieve the purpose of the measure in question. Under the European Convention on Human Rights, this process is known as "autonomous interpretation".

There are two principal reasons why the Court interprets Convention terms   2–44
"autonomously". First, where a particular term does not have an identical scope in the national legal systems of the contracting states, such an approach is necessary to ensure uniformity of the Convention's application.[127] More importantly, autonomous interpretation is necessary in order to prevent contracting states from evading their obligations by classifying procedures in national law so

---

[122] See para.2–01 above.

[123] See paras 2–18 to 2–27 above.

[124] (1979–80) 1 E.H.R.R. 15 at para.14.

[125] *James v United Kingdom* (1986) 8 E.H.R.R. 123; *Belgian Linguistic Case (No.2)* (1979–80) 1 E.H.R.R. 252; *Johnston v Ireland* (1987) 9 E.H.R.R. 203; *Marckx v Belgium* (1979–80) 2 E.H.R.R. 330.

[126] *Golder v United Kingdom* (1979–80) 1 E.H.R.R. 525; *Campbell and Cosans v United Kingdom* (1982) 4 E.H.R.R. 293; *Young, James and Webster v United Kingdom* (1982) 4 E.H.R.R. 38; *Sigurjonsson v Iceland* (1993) 16 E.H.R.R. 462.

[127] Jacobs and White refer to a similar approach adopted by the Court of Justice of the European Communities to the meaning of terms in both the EC Treaty and the Brussels Convention on Civil Jurisdiction and the Enforcement of Judgments: Sir Francis Jacobs and Robin White, *The European Convention on Human Rights* (2nd edn, Oxford, 1996) pp.28–29.

as to deprive an individual of his Convention rights. To take an extreme example, an autonomous approach to the term "persons of unsound mind" in Art.5(1)(e) is necessary to prevent a state from classifying dissidents as mentally unbalanced, and then relying on that classification in order to detain them in a closed institution. Thus, in its interpretation of Art.5(1)(e) the Court requires a close correlation between the legal and medical definitions of unsoundness of mind, and has held that a person may only be detained on the basis of objective medical expertise.[128]

2–45 The process of autonomous interpretation has significant implications for the criminal law. The very concept of "criminal" proceedings has been autonomously defined so as to include certain types of proceeding which would be classified as civil, disciplinary or administrative proceedings in national law.[129] An autonomous approach has also been taken to the meaning of the term "charge" in Art.6(1)[130]; to the term "witness" in Art.6(3)(d)[131]; and to the term "penalty" in Art.7.[132]

IX. Implied rights

2–46 In order to ensure that the protection afforded by the Convention is practical and effective the Court has, on occasions, been prepared to imply rights into the Convention which are absent from its text. We have already seen how, in the context of extradition, the Court has implied into Art.3 of the Convention an obligation on contracting states to refuse co-operation where a fugitive's extradition might expose him to inhuman or degrading treatment. In *Soering v United Kingdom*[133] the Court emphasised the importance of other international agreements as an aid to the interpretation of Convention rights. Referring to the United Nations Convention Against Torture and Other Cruel, Inhuman or Degrading Treatment or Punishment (1984), the Court observed[134];

> "The fact that a specialised treaty should spell out in detail a specific obligation attaching to the prohibition of torture does not mean that an essentially similar obligation is not already inherent in the general terms of Article 3 of the European Convention."

In *Aydin v Turkey*[135] the Court relied on the United Nations Torture Convention in order to imply into Art.13 of the Convention a duty on the state to carry out a prompt and impartial investigation into allegations of serious ill-treatment in custody.

---

[128] *Winterwerp v Netherlands* (1979–80) 2 E.H.R.R. 387 at paras 36–38.
[129] *Engel v Netherlands* (1979–80) 1 E.H.R.R. 647 at para.678. This subject is considered in detail in Ch.4 below.
[130] See, e.g. *Adolf v Austria* (1982) 4 E.H.R.R. 315 at para.30; *Eckle v Germany* (1983) 5 E.H.R.R. 1 at para.73; *Deweer v Belgium* (1980) 2 E.H.R.R. 439 at para.46. See Ch.4 below.
[131] See, e.g. *Kostovski v Netherlands* (1990) 12 E.H.R.R. 434. See para.15–113 below.
[132] See *Welch v United Kingdom* (1995) 20 E.H.R.R. 247 at para.27. See para.16–80 below.
[133] *Soering v United Kingdom* (1989) 11 E.H.R.R. 439.
[134] At para.87.
[135] (1998) 25 E.H.R.R. 251 at para.103.

The right to a fair trial, in Art.6, has been given a particularly open-textured 2–47 interpretation, allowing scope for a range of rights to be read into its text by implication. The Court has held that the rights accorded to criminal defendants by Art.6(2) and 6(3) are "specific aspects of the general principle stated in paragraph 1" and are therefore to be regarded as a "non-exhaustive list" of minimum rights which form "constituent elements, amongst others, of the notion of a fair trial in criminal proceedings".[136] The relationship between the right to a fair trial in Art.6(1) and the specific rights set out in Art.6(2) and (3) has been described as "that of the general to the particular".[137] As the Commission put it in *Jespers v Belgium*[138]:

> "Article 6 does not define the notion of a fair trial in criminal cases. Paragraph 3 of that Article lists certain specific rights which constitute essential elements of that general notion. The term 'minimum' [in Article 6(3)] clearly shows that the list of rights in paragraph 3 is not exhaustive and that a trial could well not fulfil the general conditions of a fair trial even if the minimum rights guaranteed by paragraph 3 were respected."

This approach has enabled the Court and Commission to imply into Art.6 a right 2–48 of access by the accused to the unused evidence in the possession of the prosecution.[139] In *Edwards v United Kingdom*[140] the Court held that:

> "it is a requirement of fairness under Article 6(1) . . . that the prosecution authorities disclose to the defence all material evidence for or against the accused".

It has also enabled the Court to develop strong protection for legal professional privilege.[141] Thus, in *S v Switzerland*[142] the Court invoked Art.8(2)(d) of the American Convention on Human Rights, and Art.93 of the Standard Minimum Rules for the Treatment of Prisoners[143] in order to imply into Art.6 the right to consult with a solicitor privately and free from state supervision.

The cases of *Funke v France*[144] and *Saunders v United Kingdom*[145] provide 2–49 further examples of this process. Article 14(2)(g) of the International Covenant on Civil and Political Rights expressly provides that an accused person has the right "not to be compelled to testify against himself or to confess guilt". That right was not however included in the text of Art.6 of the European Convention. Despite this omission, the Court in *Funke* held that a person charged with a criminal offence within the meaning of Art.6 had the right to remain silent and not to contribute to incriminating himself.[146] Three years later, in *Saunders* the Court explained its approach in more detail:

---

[136] *Deweer v Belgium* (1979–80) 2 E.H.R.R. 439 at para.56.
[137] *Jespers v Belgium* (1981) 27 D.R. 61 at para.54.
[138] (1981) 27 D.R. 61 at para.54.
[139] *Jespers v Belgium* (1981) 27 D.R. 61 at para.56.
[140] (1993) 15 E.H.R.R. 417 at para.36.
[141] As to legal professional privilege generally, see paras 14–16 to 14–26 below.
[142] (1992) 14 E.H.R.R. 670 at para.48.
[143] Annexed to Resolution (73) 5 of the Committee of Ministers.
[144] (1993) 16 E.H.R.R. 297.
[145] (1997) 23 E.H.R.R. 313.
[146] Para.44.

"The Court recalls that, although not specifically mentioned in Article 6 of the Convention, the right to silence and the right not to incriminate oneself, are generally recognised international standards which lie at the heart of the notion of a fair procedure under Article 6. Their rationale lies, *inter alia*, in the protection of the accused against improper compulsion by the authorities, thereby contributing to the avoidance of miscarriages of justice and to the fulfilment of the aims of Article 6."

2–50 Similarly, in *T and V v United Kingdom*[147] the Court relied in part on the United Nations Convention on the Rights of the Child, and the Standard Minimum Rules for the Administration of Juvenile Justice (the Beijing Rules) to conclude that the procedures for trying juveniles charged with serious crime should be adapted so as to enable the defendant to participate fully and effectively in the trial process. In that case the Court found a violation of Art.6 where two juvenile defendants charged with murder had been tried in public in an adult Crown Court, and their names and photographs had been released to the press. Here again, it was perhaps significant that Art.14(4) of the International Covenant on Civil and Political Rights specifically requires that the procedure for juvenile trial be adapted to take account of the defendant's age and the desirability of promoting rehabilitation. Far from pointing towards a deliberate omission in Art.6, the existence of relevant international instruments, which had been widely ratified, enabled the Court to conclude that a specially adapted procedure was a generally recognised international standard for the fair trial of juveniles. This, of course, is entirely in accordance with the evolutive approach to interpretation outlined above.

2–51 It does not follow that any right contained in a comparable international instrument will necessarily be implied into the Convention. As one commentator has observed, a tribunal charged with interpreting the Convention has to strike a careful balance[148]:

"Although implied terms are unavoidable if the interpretation of agreements is to produce sensible results, how far the interpreter may go in this direction is always likely to be controversial. Interpreting a treaty is one thing, rewriting it another, and if excessive caution is likely to produce decisions with no regard for the purpose of the agreement, excessive zeal turns the judge into a legislator, abusing his authority as interpreter to impose on the parties an agreement they never made."

2–52 An example of a situation in which the Commission was not prepared to read into the Convention a right expressly contained in the International Covenant is the protection of an accused against double jeopardy. Article 14(7) of the International Covenant expressly provides that:

"No one shall be liable to be tried or punished again for an offence for which he has already been finally convicted or acquitted in accordance with the law and penal procedure of each country".

In its early caselaw the Commission left open the question whether this principle could be implied into the right to a fair trial in Art.6.[149] However, in 1983, in *S*

---

[147] (2000) 30 E.H.R.R. 121.
[148] Merrils J.G., *The Development of International Law by the European Court of Human Rights* (2nd edn, Manchester, 1993), p.85.
[149] See, for example, *X v Austria* (1970) 35 CD 151.

v Germany[150] the Commission held that "the Convention system guarantees neither expressly nor by implication the principle of *ne bis in idem*". If such a principle was to be included within the Convention then it would require legislative action by the contracting states. Shortly after this decision, on November 22, 1984, Protocol 7 to the Convention was opened for signature, which made express provision for double jeopardy along lines very similar to Art.14(7) of the Covenant.

X. Positive obligations

The principal purpose of the Convention is the protection of individual rights   **2–53** from infringement by the contracting states. In general, this object is achieved by the imposition of negative obligations on the state and its officials, requiring them to refrain from interference with the rights in question. However, the Court has recognised that in order to secure truly effective protection, certain rights must be read as imposing obligations on the state to take positive action. These are known as "positive obligations", and they derive, at least in part, from the overarching duty on the contracting states in Art.1 of the Convention to "*secure* to everyone within their jurisdiction" the rights and freedoms set out in the Convention.[151]

Some positive obligations are inherent in the text of the Convention itself. Article   **2–54** 2, for example, provides that the right to life "shall be protected by law". This imposes an express obligation on the state, as a minimum, to:

> "secure the right to life by putting in place effective criminal law provisions to deter the commission of offences against the person, backed up by law enforcement machinery for the prevention, suppression and sanctioning of breaches of such provisions".[152]

Similarly, Art.6 imposes an express obligation on the state to establish courts which operate within a reasonable time,[153] interpreters[154] and legal aid in criminal proceedings.[155]

A second form of positive obligation arises where the state has some pastoral   **2–55** responsibility for the individual which has been delegated to a private body. In *Costello-Roberts v United Kingdom*,[156] for example, the Court held that the state would be liable for abusive corporal punishment, amounting to inhuman or degrading treatment, not only in state schools but also in private schools. In the Court's view, the state could not:

---

[150] (1983) 39 D.R. 43.

[151] The recognition of positive obligations is carried over into the Human Rights Act, not only by the duty to "have regard" to Convention jurisprudence in s.2 of the Act, but also by s.6(6) which expressly provides that the Act's provisions are to apply not only to positive actions by public authorities, but also to "a failure to act".

[152] *Osman v United Kingdom* (2000) 29 E.H.R.R. 245. See also *Oneryildiz v Turkey*, App. No.48939/99, November 30, 2004.

[153] Art.6(1).

[154] Art.6(3)(e).

[155] Art.6(3)(c).

[156] (1995) 19 E.H.R.R. 112 at para.27.

"absolve itself from responsibility . . . by delegating its obligations to private bodies or individuals".[157]

2–56 The principle of positive obligations, however, extends considerably further than this. The Court has become increasingly willing in recent years to imply positive obligations into Convention rights which are expressed in purely negative terms. Thus, in relation to Art.8, the Court has held that[158]:

> "[T]he object of the Article is 'essentially' that of protecting the individual against arbitary interference by public authorities. Nevertheless, it does not merely compel the state to abstain from such interference: in addition to this primarily negative undertaking, there may be positive obligations inherent in an effective 'respect'."

2–57 In determining whether or not a positive obligation exists:

> "the Court will have regard to the fair balance that has to be struck between the general interest of the community and the competing public interests of the individual, or individuals, concerned".[159]

In striking this balance, the legitimate aims set out in the second paragraphs of Arts 8 to 11 may have a "certain relevance".[160]

2–58 The Court has recognised that effective protection may require states to take legislative or administrative action to prevent one private individual from violating the Convention rights of another.[161] In *Plattform Ärtze für das Leben v Austria*[162] the court held that the right to freedom of assembly in Art.11 of the Convention imposed obligations on the police to protect a peaceful demonstration from disruption by violent counter-demonstrators:

> "Genuine, effective freedom of peaceful assembly cannot . . . be reduced to a mere duty on the part of the state not to interfere: a purely negative conception would not be compatible with the object and purpose of Article 11. Like Article 8, Article 11 sometimes requires positive measures to be taken, even in the sphere of relations between individuals."

2–59 The "positive obligations" doctrine has significant implications for the rights of victims of crime. The Court has held that the state is under a duty to adopt an adequate system of law to deter and punish individuals guilty of violating the Convention rights of others,[163] and that any available defences must not be cast

---

[157] This principle too is carried over into the Human Rights Act by s.6(3)(c) which provides that the Act's provisions bind "any person, certain of whose functions are of a public nature". See Ch.3. In *Calvelli and Ciglio v Italy*, App.No.32967/96, the court emphasised that State responsibility for ensuring that systems are in place to protect life extends to private healthcare.

[158] *Marckx v Belgium* (1979–80) 2 E.H.R.R. 330 at para.31.

[159] *McGinley and Egan v United Kingdom* (1999) 27 E.H.R.R. 1; *Rees v United Kingdom* (1987) 9 E.H.R.R. 56 para.37.

[160] *Rees v United Kingdom* (1987) 9 E.H.R.R. 56 at para.37.

[161] See generally Clapham, *Human Rights in the Private Sphere* (Clarendon, 1993).

[162] (1991) 13 E.H.R.R. 204 at para.32.

[163] *X and Y v Netherlands* (1985) 8 E.H.R.R. 235: *Osman v United Kingdom* (2000) 29 E.H.R.R. 245, para.115.

in terms so wide as to undermine the effectiveness of the criminal sanction.[164] Where the right to life and the right to be protected from inhuman and degrading treatment are concerned, the police[165] and other relevant public bodies[166] are now recognised as being under a positive operational obligation to take reasonable measures to prevent a criminal violation of an individual's rights under Arts 2 and 3; and (where such violations have occurred) to carry out an effective and independent investigation[167] which is capable of leading to the identification and prosecution of the offender.[168] Whilst the issue has not been finally resolved in Strasbourg, it seems likely that the prosecuting authorities are under a corresponding duty to prosecute in appropriate cases.[169] Where a crime involves a serious violation of the victim's Convention rights, the adoption of adequate criminal laws and their effective enforcement through investigation and prosecution must now be seen as constituent parts of the state's positive obligation to "secure" the Convention rights of victims and potential victims. These issues are considered in more detail in Ch.18 below. The positive obligations principle may also have implications for the rights of those convicted of notorious crimes. In *Venables and Thompson v News Group Newspapers and Others*[170] the President of the Family Division held that Art.2 imposed a positive obligation on the Court to grant an injunction protecting the identity of an offender who was at serious risk of life-threatening attack. The same type of injunction was granted, for the same reasons, in *Maxine Carr v News Group Newspapers and Others*.[171]

XI. Implied limitations

Just as the Court has been willing to imply rights into the text of the Convention   **2–60** where this is necessary to render its protection practical and effective so it has, on occasion, recognised that certain rights carry with them implied limitations which are not spelt out in the text. The extent of these limitations is not subject to any general formula[172] and depends very much upon the context, and especially upon the nature of the right in question. As always, the guiding principle is that limitations must not undermine the effective protection of the right concerned.

---

[164] *A v United Kingdom* (1999) 27 E.H.R.R. 611.

[165] *Mrs W v United Kingdom* (1983) 32 D.R. 190; *Mrs W v Ireland* (1983) 32 D.R. 211; *Osman v United Kingdom*, Judgment of October 28, 1998. *Z and others v United Kingdom*, Application No.29392/95 Judgment May 10, 2001 (concerning the liability of social services under Art.3 for failure to take an abused child into care).

[166] *Deweer v Belgium* (1979–80) 2 E.H.R.R. 439 at para.49: "[I]t is not the Court's function . . . to elaborate a general theory of such limitations".

[167] *McCann, Savage and Farrell v United Kingdom* (1996) 21 E.H.R.R. 97 at para.161.

[168] *Aydin v Turkey* (1998) 25 E.H.R.R. 251 at paras 103–109.

[169] *Aydin v Turkey* (1998) 25 E.H.R.R. 251 at para.103 (the investigation must be capable to leading to the "*punishment*" of the offender); *Osman v United Kingdom* (2000) 29 E.H.R.R. 245, para.115 (The state must establish effective machinery for the "*sanctioning*" of criminal violations of the right to life). See also the decision of the Inter-American Court of Human Rights in *Velaquez-Rodriguez v Honduras* (1989) 28 I.L.M. 291.

[170] January 8, 2001.

[171] [2005] EWHC 971 (Q.B.).

[172] *Deweer v Belgium* (1979–80) 2 E.H.R.R. 439 at para.49: "[I]t is not the Court's function . . . to elaborate a general theory of such limitations".

2–61 The areas in which the Court has been most willing to accept the existence of implied limitations is where the right itself has been implied by the Court into the text of the Convention, or where it involves the recognition of a positive obligation on the state. In the civil law context, for example, the Court has recognised that Art.6 includes a right of access to court for the resolution of a dispute concerning a civil right or obligation.[173] However, in *Ashingdane v United Kingdom*[174] the Court held that this right is not absolute and may be subject to limitations since by its very nature it calls for regulation by the state "which may vary in time and place according to the needs and resources of the community and of individuals". The Court went on, however, to hold that any such restrictions must not reduce the individual's access to court in such a way as to impair the essence of the right. Furthermore, the Court said:

> "a limitation will not be compatible with Article 6(1) if it does not pursue a legitimate aim, and if there is not a reasonable relationship of proportionality between the means employed and the aim sought to be achieved".[175]

2–62 A similar principle has been applied in relation to criminal proceedings. Under Art.6(1) a person charged with a criminal offence has, in principle, the right to a determination by a court. This does not, however, prevent the prosecution from withdrawing an indictment or abandoning a criminal charge without a ruling from a court, even though the consequence of such action is to deprive the accused of a formal acquittal.[176] As the court observed in *Deweer v Belgium*[177]:

> "The 'right to a court', which is a constituent element of the right to a fair trial, is no more absolute in criminal than in civil matters. It is subject to implied limitations, two examples of which are . . . [a] decision not to prosecute and [an] order for discontinuance of the proceedings".

2–63 In *Murray v United Kingdom*,[178] another case concerned with implied rights, the Court held that the right to remain silent under police questioning, and the privilege against self-incrimination were not "absolute in the sense that the exercise by the accused of the right to silence cannot under any circumstances be used against him at trial".[179] Whether the drawing of adverse inferences from an accused's silence infringed Art.6 was to be determined in the light of the conditions upon which an inference may be drawn, the weight attached to it, and the degree of compulsion inherent in the situation.[180] A similar limitation was recognised by the court in *Rowe and Davis v United Kingdom*[181] in the context of the implied right to disclosure of unused material. The Court held that while Art.6 generally requires the prosecution to disclose to the defence all material

---

[173] *Golder v United Kingdom* (1979–80) 1 E.H.R.R. 525; *Ashingdane v United Kingdom* (1985) 7 E.H.R.R. 528; *Fayed v United Kingdom* (1994) 18 E.H.R.R. 393.
[174] (1985) 7 E.H.R.R. 528 at para.57.
[175] *ibid.*
[176] *X, Y and Z v Austria* (1980) 19 D.R. 213 at 217–218.
[177] (1979–80) 2 E.H.R.R. 439 at para.49.
[178] (1996) 22 E.H.R.R. 29.
[179] At paras 46–47.
[180] At para.47. See also *Condron and Condron v United Kingdom* (2000) 31 E.H.R.R. 1.
[181] (2000) 30 E.H.R.R. 1.

evidence for or against the accused, considerations of national security or the protection of vulnerable witnesses could, in certain circumstances, justify an exception to this rule (providing there were adequate procedural safeguards in place to protect the rights of the accused). The type of safeguards required in public interest immunity hearings from which the defendant and his lawyers are excluded was considered further in *Edwards and Lewis v United Kingdom*.[182]

In *Osman v United Kingdom*[183] the Court held that Art.2 imposed a positive   **2–64** obligation on the police to take reasonable steps to prevent a foreseeable homicidal attack. The Court was, however, careful to emphasise that this obligation had to be "interpreted in a way which does not impose an impossible or disproportionate burden on the authorities".[184] Moreover, it could not be interpreted in a manner inconsistent with the rights of the suspect in view of the:

> "need to ensure that the police exercise their powers to control and prevent crime in a manner which fully respects the due process and other guarantees which legitimately place restraints on the scope of their action to investigate crime and bring offenders to justice, including the guarantees contained in Articles 5 and 8 of the Convention".

The Court has, for obvious reasons, been cautious in implying limitations into   **2–65** express Convention rights. Nevertheless, where the right concerned is framed in general terms, without detailed or exhaustive definition, the Court has held that there may be "room for implied limitations".[185] As we have seen, the right to a fair trial in criminal cases is not exhaustively defined in Art.6(1),[186] and the specific rights contained in Arts 6(2) and 6(3) are regarded as "constituent elements" of the general notion of a fair trial.[187] While this allows the Court to imply additional fair trial guarantees into Art.6(1), it also enables it to adopt a substantive rather than a formalistic approach to breaches of Arts 6(2) and (3). Thus, in *Croissant v Germany*[188] the Court held that the right of an accused to defend himself in person, which is expressly guaranteed by Art.6(3)(c) does not prevent the national authorities from imposing reasonable restrictions on the right to appear without a lawyer in a complex case; and the right to counsel of choice has been held not to apply to a defendant whose representation is funded by legal aid.[189] Similarly, the right of an accused in Art.6(3)(d) "to examine or have examined witnesses against him" does not amount to an absolute bar on the admission of documentary hearsay.[190] In keeping with its approach to the interpretation of Art.6(1) the Court will examine the importance of the disputed hearsay in the context of the prosecution case as a whole,[191] and will take account of any safeguards imposed by domestic law.[192]

---

[182] [2005] 40 E.H.R.R. 24.
[183] (2000) 29 E.H.R.R. 245.
[184] Para.116.
[185] *Mathieu-Mohin and Clerfayt v Belgium* (1988) 10 E.H.R.R. 1 at para.52.
[186] *Jespers v Belgium* (1981) 27 D.R. 61 at para.56.
[187] *Deweer v Belgium* (1979–80) 2 E.H.R.R. 439 at para.56.
[188] (1993) 16 E.H.R.R. 135.
[189] *X v United Kingdom* (1983) 5 E.H.R.R. 273.
[190] See Ch.15, below.
[191] See, for example, *Unterpertinger v Austria* (1991) 13 E.H.R.R. 175.
[192] *Trivedi v United Kingdom* (1997) 89A D.R. 136.

2–66   In *Pretto v Italy*[193] the Court took the unusual course of invoking the object and purpose of the Convention in order to restrict the rights of the accused, albeit in a matter of formality rather than substance. The Court held that the apparently unqualified requirement in Art.6(1) for a public pronouncement of judgment did not apply to a court of cassation (or, presumably, to any appellate court). It was sufficient to meet the requirement of public "pronouncement" if the judgment was lodged in the court registry where it would be available for inspection by the public. As the court observed[194]:

> "[M]any member states of the Council of Europe have a long-standing tradition of recourse to other means, besides reading out aloud, for making public the decisions of all or some of their courts, and especially of their courts of cassation, for example deposit in a registry accessible to the public. The authors of the Convention cannot have overlooked that fact . . . The Court therefore does not feel bound to adopt a literal interpretation. It considers that in each case the form of publicity to be given to the 'judgment' under the domestic law of the respondent state must be assessed in the light of the special features of the proceedings in question and by reference to the object and purpose of the Convention."

2–67   The Court's recent caselaw has accorded increasing recognition to the rights of victims and witnesses in the criminal justice system. This can, of course, bring with it corresponding limitations on the due process rights of the accused. In *Doorson v Netherlands*[195] the Court held that in appropriate cases the interests of the defence must be "balanced against those of witnesses or victims called upon to testify". Whilst noting that Art.6 does not expressly require the interests of witnesses to be taken into account, the Court pointed out that in certain situations, and especially where there is a serious risk of reprisals, the rights of the victim or witness under other provisions of the Convention[196] may be imperilled if protective measures are not taken.

2–68   There is one area in which the Court has not been prepared to countenance implied limitations, and that is where the right in question is both defined and subject to express qualification. This arises in relation to the qualified rights in Arts 8 to 11, which lay down in detail the conditions under which the state may interfere with the protected right in issue. The court has held that where the Convention itself spells out the permissible qualifications on a right, there is no justification for further implied limitations. Thus, in *Golder v United Kingdom*,[197] in the context of an alleged interference with the right to correspondence in Art.8, the Court held that:

> "The restrictive formulation used at Article 8(2) ('There shall be no interference . . . except such as . . . ') leaves no room for the concept of implied limitations. In this regard, the legal status of the right to respect for correspondence, which is defined by Article 8 with some precision, provides a clear contrast to that of the right [of access] to a court."

---

[193] (1984) 6 E.H.R.R. 182.
[194] Para.26.
[195] (1996) 23 E.H.R.R. 330 at para.70.
[196] The court referred to Arts 2, 3, 5 and 8.
[197] (1979–80) 1 E.H.R.R. 525 at para.44.

XII. Waiver of Convention rights

The Court has held that: 2–69

> "the nature of some of the rights safeguarded by the Convention is such as to exclude a waiver of the entitlement to exercise them, but the same cannot be said of certain other rights".[198]

The limits of doctrine of waiver have never been fully spelt out by the Court. The guiding principle however is that any waiver

> "must be made in an unequivocal manner, and must not run counter to an important public interest".[199]

Not surprisingly, the Court has been very reluctant to accept that a person can   2–70 waive the right to personal liberty in Art.5. Thus, in *De Wilde, Ooms and Versyp v Belgium*[200] the Court observed that;

> " . . . the right to personal liberty is too important in a 'democratic society' within the meaning of the Convention for a person to lose the benefit of the protection of the Convention for the single reason that he gives himself up to be taken into detention. Detention might violate Article 5 even although the person concerned might have agreed to it. When the matter is one which concerns the *ordre public* within the Council of Europe, a scrupulous supervision by the organs of the Convention of all measures capable of violating the rights and freedoms which it guarantees is necessary in every case."

Similarly in *Amuur v France*[201] the Court held that an asylum seeker who was detained in an airport transit area could not be taken to have waived his rights under Art.5 simply because it was possible for him voluntarily to leave the country in which he was seeking refuge.

So far as Art.6 is concerned, the position is more complex. The Court's approach   2–71 depends on the aspect of the right which is in issue. In *Pfeifer and Plankl v Austria*[202] the Court doubted whether it would ever be possible for a defendant to waive the fundamental right in Art.6(1) to a tribunal which was independent and impartial. In the Court's view "such a right is of essential importance, and its exercise cannot depend on the parties alone". Accordingly, a failure to object to two judges who had been involved in the investigation of an offence was held not to amount to a waiver.[203]

---

[198] *Albert and LeCompte v Belgium* (1983) 5 E.H.R.R. 533 at para.35.
[199] *Schuler-Zraggen v Switzerland* (1993) 16 E.H.R.R. 405 at para.58; *Hakansson and Sturesson v Sweden* (1991) 13 E.H.R.R. 1 at para.66; *Colozza v Italy* (1985) 7 E.H.R.R. 516 at para.28. In *Van der Mussele v Belgium* (1984) 6 E.H.R.R. 25 the Court held that the fact that a barrister had voluntarily entered the legal profession did not mean that he had waived his right to complain about an obligation inherent in the professional rules to perform free representation It was, however, a significant factor in assessing whether he had been required to perform forced or compulsory labour in breach of Art.4(2).
[200] (1979–80) 1 E.H.R.R. 373 at para.65.
[201] (1996) 22 E.H.R.R. 533 at para.48.
[202] (1992) 14 E.H.R.R. 692 at paras 38–39.
[203] See also *Obserchlick v Austria (No.1)* (1995) 19 E.H.R.R. 389.

2–72 The Court has held that it is open to an accused person to waive the right to a trial altogether, provided any "settlement" of criminal proceedings is express and unequivocal, and that it is freely entered into.[204] Implied waiver of the right to a hearing in one's presence is more problematic. In a number of cases the Court has stated that a defendant who fails to attend for his trial, after having been given effective notice of it, will only be taken to have forfeited the right to a hearing in his presence if the waiver is clear and unequivocal.[205] The difficulty, of course, lies in determining when a failure to appear amounts to a deliberate and unequivocal waiver. The Court has attempted to resolve this problem by holding that the state may proceed in the absence of an accused where it has acted diligently but unsuccessfully to secure his attendance, providing the accused is able to obtain "a fresh determination of the merits of the charge" when he later learns of the proceedings.[206]

2–73 The right to a hearing in public can also be waived. In *Albert and LeCompte v Belgium*[207] the Court held that this aspect of Art.6 may "yield in certain circumstances to the will of the person concerned". In the Court's view:

> "neither the letter nor the spirit of Article 6(1) would prevent [an applicant] from waiving, of his own free will and in an unequivocal manner . . . the entitlement to have his case heard in public."

The court has been prepared to accept that an implied waiver is possible in this context. In *Hakansson and Sturesson v Sweden*[208] the Court held that the failure of the applicants to apply for an oral hearing of their appeal (which was possible under Swedish legislation) amounted to an unequivocal waiver of the right to a public hearing. The position will of course be otherwise if there is no provision for such a hearing in domestic law, or if there is little prospect of securing one.[209] Equally, it is plain that an accused can waive the right to be represented by a lawyer.[210]

XIII. Convention to be read as a whole

2–74 Article 31 of the Vienna Convention on the Law of Treaties[211] requires that provisions of a treaty should be construed in their context. The Court has interpreted this to mean that:

---

[204] *Deweer v Belgium* (1979–80) 2 E.H.R.R. 439 (concerning the "settlement" of criminal proceedings). As to the implications of this decision for the reduction of a sentence following a plea of guilty, see para.16–77 below.

[205] *Colozza v Italy* (1985) 7 E.H.R.R. 516; *Brozicek v Italy* (1990) 12 E.H.R.R. 371 at paras 43–46.

[206] *Colozza v Italy* (1985) 7 E.H.R.R. 516 at para.29.

[207] (1983) 5 E.H.R.R. 533 at para.35.

[208] (1991) 13 E.H.R.R. 1 at para.67.

[209] *H v Belgium* (1988) 10 E.H.R.R. 339.

[210] *Melin v France* (1994) 17 E.H.R.R. 1 at para.25.

[211] See para.2–01 above.

"the Convention and its Protocols must be read as a whole; consequently a matter dealt with mainly by one of their provisions may also, in some of its aspects, be subject to other provisions thereof".[212]

The fact that the subject-matter of a complaint is addressed directly in an optional **2–75** protocol which the state concerned has not ratified will not necessarily be decisive, since the issue may also be covered by a provision of the Convention itself.[213] In *Guzzardi v Italy*[214] the Court held that a suspected Mafia member was deprived of his liberty within the meaning of Art.5 when he was made the subject of a compulsory residence order confining him to a small island where his movements were closely monitored by officials. This was despite the fact that freedom of movement, a more apposite right in the circumstances, was expressly guaranteed by Art.2 of Protocol 4 which Italy had not ratified.

In *Ekbatani v Sweden*[215] the government relied on the adoption of Protocol 7, to **2–76** argue that "only the fundamental guarantees of Article 6 applied in appeal proceedings" and that these did not include the right to an oral hearing on appeal. The Court noted that the Explanatory Report to Protocol 7 emphasised that "the Protocol cannot be interpreted as prejudicing the rights guaranteed by the Convention"[216] and drew attention to the provisions of Art.53 of the Convention.[217] The Court concluded that there was:

"no warrant for the view that the addition of this Protocol was intended to limit, at the appellate level, the guarantees contained in Article 6 of the Convention".[218]

It does not follow however that the existence of an unratified protocol is **2–77** irrelevant. In *Soering v United Kingdom*[219] the Court treated the adoption of Protocol 6 as determinative of the issue of whether it was possible, through the technique of evolutive interpretation, to hold that the death penalty was *per se* in breach of Art.3. The Court considered that by including an optional protocol prohibiting the death penalty, the contracting parties had signalled their intention "to adopt the normal method of amendment of the text in order to introduce a new obligation".[220] Accordingly, the virtual abolition of the death penalty throughout the Council of Europe could not justify an evolutive interpretation of Art.3, so as to amount to a prohibition on the death penalty altogether.

---

[212] *Abdulaziz, Cabales and Balkandali v United Kingdom* (1985) 7 E.H.R.R. 471 at para.60.
[213] In *Abdulaziz, Cabales and Balkandali* the court rejected the Government's argument that immigration matters were governed solely by Protocol 4 which the United Kingdom had not ratified.
[214] (1981) 3 E.H.R.R. 333.
[215] (1991) 13 E.H.R.R. 504.
[216] Explanatory Report para.43.
[217] The court in fact referred to Art.60, which was the predecessor to Art.53 prior to Protocol 11.
[218] At para.26.
[219] (1989) 11 E.H.R.R. 439. The United Kingdom has since ratified Protocol 13, which abolishes the death penalty in all circumstances.
[220] See para.2–19 above.

XIV. The lex specialis principle

2–78   The Court sometimes refers to a provision of the Convention as the *lex specialis* for a particular complaint.[221] This principle holds that if there is an article of the Convention which is specifically aimed at the subject-matter of the application, then that provision will generally be applied in preference to a more general provision, since it more closely reflects the intentions of the contracting parties.

XV. The Rule of Law

2–79   The preamble to the Convention refers to the "rule of law" as an integral part of the "common heritage" of the contracting states.[222] The Court has held that this is one of the "fundamental principles of a democratic society"[223] and should be treated as a guiding principle in the interpretation of the Convention.[224] In *Silver v United Kingdom*[225] the Court held that respect for the rule of law implied:

> "that an interference by the authorities with an individual's rights should be subject to effective control. This is especially so where . . . the law bestows on the executive wide discretionary powers."

In *Klass v Germany*,[226] the Court held that where intrusive surveillance was in issue such control should normally be assured by the judiciary, since "judicial control offer[s] the best guarantees of independence, impartiality and a proper procedure". However a review carried out by a body which is truly independent of the executive may suffice in some circumstances, even if it is not strictly judicial in character, providing the body concerned is "vested with sufficient powers and competence to exercise an effective and continuous control".[227]

XVI. The principle of legal certainty

2–80   A number of Convention rights contain an express requirement that state action must be "lawful", "prescribed by law" or "in accordance with the law". Whenever such a reference appears in the text, it is to be interpreted as a semi-autonomous concept, involving a mixed Convention and domestic law interpretation. First, the act in question must have a legal basis in national law. Statute law, secondary legislation, applicable rules of European Community law,[228]

---

[221] This principle pulls in the opposite direction to the requirement to read the Convention as a whole, and the Court has applied it selectively.

[222] The "rule of law" is also referred to in the preamble to the Statute of the Council of Europe, and in Art.3 of the Statute, which provides that "every Member of the Council of Europe must accept the principle of the rule of law . . . ".

[223] *Iatrides v Greece* Judgment March 25, 1999, para.62.

[224] *Golder v United Kingdom* (1979–80) 1 E.H.R.R. 525 at para.34.

[225] (1983) 5 E.H.R.R. 347 at para.90.

[226] (1979–80) 2 E.H.R.R. 214 at para.55.

[227] *Klass* at para.56. This qualification does not, of course, apply to Arts 5 and 6.

[228] *Groppera Radio AG v Switzerland* (1990) 12 E.H.R.R. 321.

ascertainable common law,[229] and even rules of professional bodies[230] may be sufficient. However, non-statutory guidance to the executive is unlikely to be sufficient since it will not usually have the force of law.[231]

In addition the law itself must meet certain "quality of law" requirements. It **2–81** must be *publicly accessible* so as to enable citizens to ascertain the applicable legal rules in advance; and it must be sufficiently *precise* for the individual to be able to regulate his conduct in accordance with the law. More generally, the Court has recognised that the principle of legal certainty distinguishes government based upon the rule of law from government characterised by excessive executive or judicial discretion, which carries with it the potential for arbitrary interference with individual rights.[232] A law which confers a discretion must, as a minimum, give an adequate indication of the scope of the discretion.[233]

The principle of legal certainty has been interpreted as requiring that a citizen **2–82** must be able to foresee, to a degree that is reasonable in the circumstances, the consequences that a given action may entail.[234] This does not mean that the individual must be able to predict the legal consequences of his actions with absolute certainty. As the Court has observed:

> "[E]xperience shows this to be unattainable . . . Whilst certainty is highly desireable, it may bring in its train excessive rigidity and the law must always be able to keep pace with changing circumstances. Accordingly, many laws are inevitably couched in terms which, to a greater or lesser extent, are vague and whose interpretation and application are questions of practice".[235]

In judging whether a legal rule satisfies the requirements of certainty and foreseeability, the Court will approach the question on the assumption that the applicant could have obtained appropriate legal advice.[236] The fact that a statutory provision is capable of more than one construction does not necessarily involve a breach of the principle of legal certainty.[237] Nor does the fact that a common law offence may be susceptible to change over time, providing any development is reasonably foreseeable and consistent with the essence of the offence.[238]

---

[229] *Sunday Times v United Kingdom (No.1)* (1979–80) 2 E.H.R.R. 245 at paras 46–53.

[230] *Barthold v Germany* (1985) 7 E.H.R.R. 383 at para.46.

[231] *Khan v United Kingdom* [2000] Crim.L.R. 684 (concerning Home Office guidance on intrusive surveillance).

[232] *Amuur v France* (1996) 22 E.H.R.R. 533 at para.50.

[233] *Silver v United Kingdom* (1983) 5 E.H.R.R. 347. In certain instances the requirement for legal certainty may imply the need for procedural safeguards. Thus, in *Hentrich v France* (1994) 18 E.H.R.R. 440 at para.42 the court found a violation of Art.1 of Protocol 1 where the revenue authorities operated a pre-emptive procedure where they believed there to be a sale at an undervalue. The procedure was found to be in breach because it "operated arbitrarily and selectively, and was scarcely foreseeable, *and it was not attended by basic procedural guarantees*".

[234] *Sunday Times v United Kingdom (No.1)* (1979–80) 2 E.H.R.R. 245 at para.49.

[235] *Sunday Times v United Kingdom (No.1)* (1979–80) 2 E.H.R.R. 245 at para.49.

[236] *Sunday Times v United Kingdom (No.1)* (1979–80) 2 E.H.R.R. 245 at para.49; *Cantoni v France* Judgment November 15, 1996.

[237] *Castells v Spain* (1992) 14 E.H.R.R. 445; *Vogt v Germany* (1996) 21 E.H.R.R. 205.

[238] See Ch.10.

2–83   The application of this principle in criminal cases can be illustrated by reference
to Arts 5 and 7 of the Convention and by reference to the qualified rights in Arts
8 to 11. Article 5(1), for instance, requires that any deprivation of liberty must be
"lawful" and carried out "in accordance with a procedure prescribed by law".
The court has held that the requirement embodied in these terms:

> "refers essentially to national law and lays down the obligation to conform to the
> substantive and procedural rules of national law".[239]

In addition, however, a detention must be "in keeping with the purpose of Article
5, namely to protect the individual from arbitrariness".[240] In *Amuur v France*[241]
the Court pointed out that this latter requirement reflects the principle of respect
for the rule of law which runs throughout the Convention:

> "In laying down that any deprivation of liberty must be effected 'in accordance with a
> procedure prescribed by law', Article 5(1) primarily requires any arrest or detention to
> have a legal basis in domestic law. However, these words do not merely refer back to
> domestic law; like the expressions 'in accordance with the law' and 'prescribed by law'
> in the second paragraphs of Articles 8 to 11, they also relate to the quality of the law,
> requiring it to be compatible with the rule of law, a concept inherent in all the Articles
> of the Convention. In order to ascertain whether a deprivation of liberty has complied
> with the principle of compatibility with domestic law, it therefore falls to the Court to
> assess not only the legislation in force in the field under consideration, but also the
> quality of the other legal rules applicable to the persons concerned. Quality in this sense
> implies that where a national law authorises deprivation of liberty . . . it must be
> sufficiently accessible and precise, in order to avoid all risk of arbitrariness."

2–84   In *Zamir v United Kingdom*[242] the Commission recognised that even in the
context of a deprivation of liberty, some flexibility in the law is permissible:

> "While particular decisions of the courts may be seen as unexpected within the legal
> community, it does not follow that the legal rule in question was not sufficiently
> certain . . . The Commission's approach must be to examine whether the margin of
> uncertainty that surrounds legal rules in this field of law, exceeds acceptable bounda-
> ries."

2–85   In relation to the substantive criminal law, the requirement for legal certainty is
embodied in Art.7. On its face Art.7 constitutes no more than a guarantee against
the retrospective application of the criminal law. However, consistent with its
short title in the Convention (*"no punishment without law"*) the court has held
that Art.7 is to be broadly construed. Thus, Art.7 has been held to embody the
principle that the criminal law must not be extensively construed to an accused's
disadvantage, and that criminal offences must be clearly defined in law.[243]

---

[239] *Amuur v France* (1996) 22 E.H.R.R. 533 at para.50; *Tsirilis and Koyloumpas v Greece* (1998)
25 E.H.R.R. 440 at para.42; *Benham v United Kingdom* (1996) 22 E.H.R.R. 293 at para.40; *Quinn
v France* (1996) 21 E.H.R.R. 529 at para.47; *Winterwerp v Netherlands* (1979–80) 2 E.H.R.R. 387
at para.37.
[240] *Amuur v France* (1996) 22 E.H.R.R. 533 at para.50; *Quinn v France* (1996) 21 E.H.R.R. 529
at para.47.
[241] (1996) 22 E.H.R.R. 533 at para.50.
[242] (1983) 40 D.R. 42 at para.91.
[243] *Kokkinakis v Greece* (1994) 17 E.H.R.R. 397 at para.52.

Accordingly, Art.7 prohibits the extension of a statutory or common law offence so as to encompass conduct which would not previously have been regarded as a crime.[244] However, in *SW and CR v United Kingdom*[245] the Court emphasised that this principle does not prohibit the development of the criminal law through judicial decisions.

Each of the qualified rights in Arts 8 to 11 of the Convention stipulate the **2–86** conditions on which an interference by the state with the right concerned will be permissible. The first condition which must be satisfied is that the measure taken was "prescribed by law" or "in accordance with law". There is no significance to be attached to the minor differences between the terminology employed in these provisions.[246] In each case, the Convention requires that the measure in question has "some basis in domestic law"[247] and that the domestic law must satisfy the "quality of law" requirements discussed above.

In *McLeod v United Kingdom*[248] the court was concerned with the police power **2–87** of entry without warrant into a person's home to deal with or prevent a breach of the peace. The applicant argued that the common law power of entry was insufficiently clear to meet the quality of law requirement in Art.8. The common law power had been preserved (without elaboration or clarification) by s.17(6) of the Police and Criminal Evidence Act 1984. Having reviewed the domestic authorities on the issue, the court concluded that the power was "defined with sufficient precision for the foreseeability criterion to be satisfied".

Two cases illustrate the operation of this principle in relation to the powers of the **2–88** English courts to make bindover orders. In *Steel and others v United Kingdom*[249] the applicants complained that the law governing bindovers for breach of the peace was inconsistent, and in particular that the domestic caselaw contained contradictory statements of principle. However, a number of these apparent conflicts had been resolved in a series of decisions in the Divisional Court. Having regard to these developments, the Court observed that:

> "[T]he concept of breach of the peace has been clarified by the English courts over the last two decades, to the extent that it is now sufficiently established that a breach of the peace is committed only when an individual causes harm, or appears likely to cause harm, to persons or property, or acts in a manner the natural consequence of which would be to provoke others to violence. It is also clear that a person may be arrested for causing a breach of the peace or where it is reasonably apprehended that he or she is likely to cause a breach of the peace. Accordingly, the Court considers that the relevant legal rules provided sufficient guidance and were formulated with the degree of precision required by the Convention."

---

[244] In *Harman v United Kingdom* (1984) 38 D.R. 53 the Commission declared admissible an application in which it was claimed that the domestic courts had created a wholly new category of contempt. The case eventually settled without a judgment from the court.

[245] (1996) 21 E.H.R.R. 363 at paras 36 (SW) and 34 (CR). See further discussion of this issue in Ch.10, paras 10–35 to 10–45.

[246] *Sunday Times v United Kingdom* (1979–80) 2 E.H.R.R. 245 at para.48.

[247] *Silver v United Kingdom* (1983) 5 E.H.R.R. 347 at para.86.

[248] (1998) 27 E.H.R.R. 493.

[249] (1999) 28 E.H.R.R. 603; [1998] Crim.L.R. 893.

2–89   In *Hashman and Harrup v United Kingdom*,[250] by contrast, the Court held that the power of a court to bind an individual over to be of good behaviour (that is not to act *contra bonos mores*) was insufficiently defined to enable the affected individual to identify the sort of behaviour which would be likely to breach the order. The Court reiterated the principle that "a norm cannot be regarded as a 'law' unless it is formulated with sufficient precision to enable the citizen to regulate his conduct". The level of precision required depended:

> "to a considerable extent on the content of the instrument in question, the field it is designed to cover, and the number and status of those to whom it is addressed".

The most precise definition of conduct *contra bonos mores* was that provided by Glidewell L.J. in *Hughes v Holley*,[251] namely behaviour which is "wrong rather than right in the judgment of the majority of contemporary fellow citizens". In the Court's view, conduct falling within this definition was "not described at all, but merely expressed to be 'wrong' in the opinion of the majority". This formulation lacked sufficient objectivity to amount to a legal rule. Accordingly, the exercise of the power by the Crown Court was found to be in violation of Art.10.

2–90   The distinction between these two cases lies not only in the legal defintion of the prohibited conduct, but also in the nature of the conduct proved against the applicants in each case. In *Steel* the complainants had been convicted of a breach of the peace, and so might reasonably foresee what conduct was said to be unacceptable. The complainants in *Hashman*, on the other hand, had committed no offence, and had no objective standard against which to judge whether their future conduct would be regarded as "wrong rather than right".

2–91   The term "in accordance with law" in Art.8(2) has a special meaning in the context of powers of secret surveillance.[252] In *Malone v United Kingdom*[253] the Court accepted that the requirement of foreseeability cannot mean that an individual must be able to predict with certainty whether or not the authorities are likely to intercept his communications in any given situation. However, domestic law must indicate "with reasonable clarity" the circumstances and conditions under which such surveillance can occur.[254] Domestic procedures permitting intrusive surveillance must be based on a framework of positive rules—with the force of law—for regulating the operation of the system,[255] and must include adequate and effective safeguards against abuse.[256]

XVII. Necessary in a democratic society

2–92   The second condition for any interference with the rights protected in Arts 8 to 11 is that it must be "necessary in a democratic society" in pursuit of one or more

---

[250] (2000) 30 E.H.R.R. 241.
[251] [1988] 86 Cr.App.R. 130.
[252] See Ch.7 below.
[253] (1984) 7 E.H.R.R. 14.
[254] *Malone v United Kingdom* (1984) 7 E.H.R.R. 14.
[255] *Kruslin v France* (1990) 12 E.H.R.R. 547; *Kopp v Switzerland* (1999) 27 E.H.R.R. 91.
[256] *Klass v Germany* (1979–80) 2 E.H.R.R. 214 at para.55.

of the legitimate aims prescribed in the second paragraph of each Article. These aims vary according to the right in issue, but typically include the interests of national security, public safety, or the economic well-being of the country; the prevention of disorder or crime; the protection of health or morals; and the protection of the rights and freedoms of others.

The Court has, over the years, used a number of different formulations for determining whether an interference was "necessary in a democratic society" in the sense in which that expression is used in Arts 8 to 11. In *Sunday Times v United Kingdom*[257] the Court held that: **2–93**

> "whilst the adjective 'necessary' is not synonymous with 'indispensible', neither does it have the flexibility of such expressions as 'admissible', 'ordinary', 'useful', 'reasonable' or 'desireable'; rather it implies a 'pressing social need'".

In applying the "pressing social need" test, subsequent cases have emphasised that:

> " . . . it is for the Court to make the final determination as to whether the inteference in issue corresponds to such a need, whether it is 'proportionate to the legitimate aim pursued', and whether the reasons given by the national authorities to justify it are 'relevant and sufficient' ".[258]

In recent years it has become the settled practice of the Court, when faced with an alleged violation of Arts 8 to 11, to consider the question in two distinct stages. First, the Court will inquire whether the measure in question pursued one of the stated legitimate aims. More often than not, this turns out to be uncontroversial. Secondly the Court will inquire whether there is a "reasonable relationship of proportionality" between the means employed and the aim sought to be achieved. It is on the issue of proportionality that most alleged violations of Arts 8 to 11 ultimately turn.[259] **2–94**

The concept of "necessity" has a stricter connotation where it arises elsewhere in the Convention. In the context of alleged violations of the right to life, the Court has held that the use of the term "absolutely necessary" in Art.2(2) indicates that: **2–95**

> "a stricter and more compelling test of necessity must be employed from that normally applicable when determining whether state action is 'necessary in a democratic society' under paragraph 2 of Articles 8 to 11 of the Convention".[260]

Any force used by the state "must be *strictly* proportionate to the achievement of the aims" set out in Art.2(2).[261] This approach probably owes more to the

---

[257] (1979–80) 2 E.H.R.R. 245 at para.59; see also *Handyside v United Kingdom* (1979–80) 1 E.H.R.R. 737 at para.48.

[258] *Barthold v Germany* (1985) 7 E.H.R.R. 383 at para.55. See, to similar effect, *Sunday Times v United Kingdom (No.1)* (1979–80) 2 E.H.R.R. 245 at para.59; *Olsson v Sweden* (1989) 11 E.H.R.R. 259.

[259] As to the court's approach to the concept of proportionality, see paras 2–99 to 2–112 below.

[260] *McCann and ors v United Kingdom* (1996) 21 E.H.R.R. 97 at para.149; *Andronicou and Constantinou v Cyprus* (1998) 25 E.H.R.R. 491 at para.171.

[261] *ibid.*

importance of the right at stake than to the precise terminology employed in the text of Art.2.

2-96   The Court has taken a similar approach to the prohibition on torture and inhuman or degrading treatment or punishment. The text of Art.3 makes no explicit reference to the requirement of "necessity". Nevertheless, in *Ribitsch v Austria*[262] the Court emphasised that:

> "in respect of a person deprived of his liberty, any recourse to physical force which has not been made *strictly necessary* by his own conduct diminishes human dignity and is in principle an infringement of the right set forth in Article 3 of the Convention."

2-97   Article 6(1) permits the exclusion of the press and the public:

> "to the extent *strictly necessary* in the opinion of the Court in special circumstances where publicity would prejudice the interests of justice"

—a textual restriction which does not apply to the other grounds for exclusion permitted by Art.6(1). In *Handyside v United Kingdom*,[263] the Court suggested that the language of this exception pointed to a restrictive approach. In practice, however, the Court has eschewed a mechanistic application of the text, and has applied the exception in a realistic manner which takes account of the nature of the proceedings in issue. In the context of prison disciplinary proceedings a proportionality test similar to that applicable under Arts 8 to 11 has been applied. In *Campbell and Fell v United Kingdom*[264] the Court held that a requirement to permit public access to proceedings heard inside a prison[265] "would impose a disproportionate burden on the authorities of the state". However, in *Diennet v France*,[266] where proceedings before a medical disciplinary tribunal were in issue, the Court held that the exclusion of the public was in breach of Art.6:

> "While the need to protect professional confidentiality and the private lives of patients may justify holding proceedings in camera, such an occurrence must be *strictly required* by the circumstances."

The Court will look at the practical reality of the position when deciding what is strictly required in the circumstances. In *Riepan v Austria*,[267] the Court held that the holding of a criminal trial inside a prison violated the right to a public hearing. There had been no formal restriction on attendance of the public, but the Court observed, in finding a violation of Art.6, that:

> "the holding of a trial outside a regular court room, in particular a place like a prison to which the general public on principle has no access, presents a serious obstacle to its public character. In such a case, the State is under an obligation to take compensatory

---

[262] (1996) 21 E.H.R.R. 573 at para.38.

[263] (1979–80) 1 E.H.R.R. 737 at para.48.

[264] (1985) 7 E.H.R.R. 165 at para.87.

[265] Or to require the accused to prisoner to be transported from the prison to a public court in every case.

[266] (1996) 21 E.H.R.R. 554. See also *Albert and Le Compte v Belgium* (1983) 5 E.H.R.R. 533; *H v Belgium* (1988) 10 E.H.R.R. 339.

[267] App.No.35115/97, November 14, 2000.

measures in order to ensure that the public and the media are duly informed about the place of the hearing and are granted effective access."[268]

Another application of the strict necessity principle in the context of Art.6 is to be found in the case of *Van Mechelen v Netherlands*.[269] In that case the court established the important principle that any measures which restrict the rights of the defence in a criminal case should be "strictly necessary" such that if a less restrictive measure could suffice then that measure should be adopted.

Finally it should be noted that Art.15 permits derogations in times of public   **2–98**
emergency "to the extent *strictly required* by the exigencies of the situation". Despite the wording of this provision, the court has recognised that the national authorities enjoy a margin of appreciation in assessing whether such an emergency exists and, if so, what measures are necessary to deal with it.[270]

XVIII. Proportionality

Although the principle of proportionality is not mentioned in the text of the   **2–99**
Convention itself, it has become a dominant theme in the Court's caselaw.[271] The Court has held that proportionality is "inherent in the whole of the Convention".[272] However, it arises in a number of different contexts with subtly different meanings. Proportionality, in the classic sense, is the technique by which the Court determines whether an interference with one of the qualified rights protected in Arts 8 to 11 is necessary in a democratic society.[273] But it is also central to the determination of whether there is an unjustified difference in treatment in breach of Art.14[274]; it is the Court's principal yardstick for testing the limits of implied rights, such as the right of access to court[275]; and it is the means by which the Court determines whether a positive obligation should be imposed on a contracting state in any given situation.[276]

In these contexts, proportionality involves two closely related concepts. First, it   **2–100**
implies that there must be a rational connection between the public policy objective which a particular measure pursues, and the means which the state has employed to achieve that objective.[277] Secondly, it involves the striking of a fair

---

[268] Para.29.

[269] (1998) 25 E.H.R.R. 647 at para.59.

[270] *Ireland v United Kingdom* (1979–80) 1 E.H.R.R. 15 at para.28; *Brannigan and McBride v United Kingdom* (1994) 17 E.H.R.R. 539 at para.43. See further Ch.1.

[271] See generally, Essien, "The Principle of Proportionality in the Caselaw of the European Court of Human Rights" in Macdonald R. St. J., Matscher F. and Petzold H., *The European System for the Protection of Human Rights* (Martinus Nijhoff, 1993).

[272] *Sporrong and Lonroth v Sweden* (1983) 5 E.H.R.R. 35 at para.69; *Soering v United Kingdom* (1989) 11 E.H.R.R. 439 at para.89.

[273] See para.2–94 above.

[274] *Belgian Linguistic Case (No.2)* (1979–80) 1 E.H.R.R. 252.

[275] *Ashingdane v United Kingdom* (1985) 7 E.H.R.R. 528 at para.57; and see paras 2–61 to 2–62 above.

[276] *McGinley and Egan v United Kingdom* (1999) 27 E.H.R.R. 1; *Rees v United Kingdom* (1987) 9 E.H.R.R. 56 para.37 and see para.2–53 above.

[277] *James v United Kingdom* (1986) 8 E.H.R.R. 123 at para.50.

balance between the demands of the general interest of the community, and the requirements of the protection of an individual's fundamental rights.[278] On either formulation, the Court must in the end determine whether a measure of interference which is aimed at promoting a legitimate public policy is either unacceptably broad in its application, or has imposed an excessive or unreasonable burden on certain individuals.[279] Accordingly, even where it is clear that there is a legitimate reason for restricting the exercise of a Convention right, the authorities must show that the measures actually applied to the applicant did not go beyond what was necessary to achieve that objective.

2–101 The burden of establishing proportionality lies on the government.[280] The Court will sometimes formulate the question by asking whether the state has demonstrated "relevant and sufficient" reasons for a restriction or interference. In *Jersild v Denmark*[281] the Court explained that it would;

" . . . look at the interference complained of in the light of the case as a whole and determine whether the reasons adduced by the national authorities to justify it are relevant and sufficient and whether the means employed were proportionate to the legitimate aim pursued."

Thus, in *Goodwin v United Kingdom*[282] an order for the disclosure of a journalist's source of information for a story was held to be disproportionate because it was not supported by "relevant and sufficient reasons"; and in *Dudgeon v United Kingdom*[283] the government's justification was described as relevant "but not sufficient to justify the maintenance in force of the impugned legislation".

2–102 The standard of justification required depends on a range of factors including the nature of the right in issue, the extent of the interference, the importance of the public policy justification which is relied upon, and the context in which the interference has occurred. The Court has identified certain qualified rights as deserving of special protection. Thus, the state must demonstrate "particularly serious reasons" to justify an interference with an intimate aspect of private life[284]; any justification for an interference with the right to freedom of expression must be "convincingly established"[285]; measures which obstruct correspondence with a lawyer,[286] or intrude on legal professional privilege[287] require

---

[278] *Sporrong and Lonroth v Sweden* (1983) 5 E.H.R.R. 35 at para.69; *Soering v United Kingdom* (1989) 11 E.H.R.R. 439 at para.89.

[279] See, for example, *Sporrong and Lonroth v Sweden* (1983) 5 E.H.R.R. 35 at para.73.

[280] *Smith and Grady v United Kingdom* (2000) 29 E.H.R.R. 493 at para.99; *Kokkinakis v Greece* (1994) 17 E.H.R.R. 397; *Autotronic AG v Switzerland* (1990) 12 E.H.R.R. 585 at paras 60–63; *Vereinigung Demokratisher Soldaten Osterreichs and Gubi v Austria* (1995) 20 E.H.R.R. 56; *Buckley v United Kingdom* (1997) 23 E.H.R.R. 101 at para.77.

[281] (1995) 19 E.H.R.R. 1 at para.31.

[282] (1996) 22 E.H.R.R. 123.

[283] (1982) 4 E.H.R.R. 149 at para.61.

[284] *Dudgeon v United Kingdom* (1982) 4 E.H.R.R. 149.

[285] *Barthold v Germany* (1985) 7 E.H.R.R. 383 at para.58; *Autotronic AG v Switzerland* (1990) 12 E.H.R.R. 585 at para.61.

[286] *Golder v United Kingdom* (1979–80) 1 E.H.R.R. 524 paras 41–45.

[287] *Silver v United Kingdom* (1983) 5 E.H.R.R. 347; *Campbell v United Kingdom* (1993) 15 E.H.R.R. 137.

particularly compelling justification[288]; and the Court will require "very weighty reasons" to justify a difference in treatment on grounds of sex, race or other "suspect categories".[289]

The extent of the interference will obviously be another highly material factor. A **2–103** measure which reduces or restricts a right "in such a way or to such an extent that the very essence of the right is impaired" will, almost by definition, constitute a disproportionate interference.[290] In *Smith and Grady v United Kingdom*[291] the Court referred to the "exceptionally intrusive character" of disciplinary investigations which had been carried out into the applicants' sexual orientation. In general, however, a criminal prosecution involves a more substantial interference than a measure applied in civil proceedings and will therefore require a weightier justification. Where it is alleged that criminal proceedings have interfered with one of the rights protected by Arts 8 to 11,[292] the Court will look to the combination of the prosecution, the conviction and the sentence to determine whether the measure taken was proportionate. In *Laskey v United Kingdom*[293] the Court attached importance in its assessment of proportionality to the fact that the applicants' sentences for sadomasochistic assault had been reduced by the Court of Appeal. Similarly, in *Hoare v United Kingdom*,[294] a case concerning the distribution of obscene videotapes, the Commission considered that the sole issue of proportionality was the length of the prison sentence imposed. Non-custodial measures will of course vary greatly in gravity. In *Handyside v United Kingdom*[295] an allegedly obscene book distributed by the applicant was confiscated, but could have been reprinted with the offending passages removed. In *Muller v Switzerland*,[296] on the other hand, the Court considered that an order for the forfeiture of an original oil painting raised particularly serious concerns.[297]

As a means of testing proportionality, the Court will often inquire whether the **2–104** state could have achieved the same objective by other means, less harmful to the rights of the individual. Thus, in *Campbell v United Kingdom*[298] a blanket rule permitting the opening of prisoners' mail was found to breach Art.8. The government's argument that the interference was necessary to establish that letters did not contain prohibited material was rejected on the ground that these concerns could have been met by opening correspondence in the presence of the prisoner without actually reading it. Where the state has amended its law since

---

[288] *Niemietz v Germany* (1993) 16 E.H.R.R. 97 at para.37 (search of lawyer's office).

[289] *Karlheinz and Schmidt v Germany* (1994) 18 E.H.R.R. 513 at para.24. See para.2–138 below.

[290] *Rees v United Kingdom* (1987) 9 E.H.R.R. 56 at para.50; *Golder v United Kingdom* (1979–80) 1 E.H.R.R. 525; cf. *Fox, Campbell and Hartley v United Kingdom* (1991) 13 E.H.R.R. 157 at para.32. And see para.2–99 above.

[291] (2000) 29 E.H.R.R. 493 at para.90.

[292] See generally Ch.8 below.

[293] (1997) 24 E.H.R.R. 39 at para.49.

[294] [1997] E.H.R.L.R. 678.

[295] (1979–80) 1 E.H.R.R. 737.

[296] (1991) 13 E.H.R.R. 212 at para.43.

[297] In the end, however, the court rejected the applicant's complaint on the ground that he could have applied to the Cantonal Court for the return of the painting and had failed to do so.

[298] (1993) 15 E.H.R.R. 137.

the interference occurred, in a way which provides more effective protection for Convention rights, this may be some evidence that the previous regime was disproportionate.[299]

2–105 If an interference involves the exercise of a discretionary power, the principle of proportionality may impose requirements of procedural fairness. In the context of Art.8, the Court has said:

> "Whenever discretion capable of interfering with the enjoyment of a Convention right such as the one in issue in the present case is conferred on national authorities, the procedural safeguards available to the individual will be especially material in determining whether the respondent state has, when fixing the regulatory framework, remained within its margin of appreciation. Indeed, it is settled case law that, whilst Article 8 contains no explicit procedural requirements, the decision-making process leading to measures of interference must be fair and such as to afford due respect to the interests safeguarded to the individual by Article 8."[300]

Similarly, where powers of intrusive surveillance are in issue, the Court has observed that the existence of independent safeguards against abuse is part of the "compromise between the requirements for defending democratic society and individual rights".[301]

2–106 The strength of the public policy in issue will often be decisive. In *Leander v Sweden*,[302] where national security considerations were invoked, the Court was prepared to accord the state a wide margin of appreciation. Particularly difficult issues can arise where the court is required to balance competing Convention rights. In some cases, for example, the right to freedom of expression can come into conflict with the right to a fair trial.[303] In *Worm v Austria*[304] the Court was concerned with the prosecution of a journalist for publishing an article about Hannes Androsch, the former Austrian Vice Chancellor. The article was published while Mr. Androsch was facing criminal proceedings for tax evasion and stated that he was guilty of the offence with which he was charged. The applicant was convicted of having exercised prohibited influence on criminal proceedings. In considering the proportionality of the measure, the Court observed that:

> "here is a general recognition that the courts cannot operate in a vacuum. Whilst the courts are the forum for the determination of a person's guilt or innocence on a criminal charge, this does not mean that there can be no prior or contemporaneous discussion on the subject-matter of criminal trials elsewhere, be it in specialised journals, in the general press or amongst the public at large. Provided that it does not overstep the bounds imposed in the interests of the proper administration of justice, reporting, including comment, on court proceedings contributes to their publicity and is thus perfectly consonant with the requirement under Article 6(1) of the Convention that hearings be in public . . . However, public figures are entitled to the enjoyment of the

---

[299] *Inze v Austria* (1988) 10 E.H.R.R. 394 at para.44.
[300] *Buckley v United Kingdom* (1997) 23 E.H.R.R. 101 at para.76.
[301] *Klass v Germany* (1979–80) 2 E.H.R.R. 214.
[302] (1987) 9 E.H.R.R. 433 at para.59.
[303] See, for example, *Sunday Times v United Kingdom (No.1)* (1979–80) 2 E.H.R.R. 245; *Allenet de Ribemont v France* (1995) 20 E.H.R.R. 557; *Worm v Austria* (1998) 25 E.H.R.R. 454.
[304] (1998) 25 E.H.R.R. 454 at paras 50–59.

guarantees of a fair trial set out in Article 6, which in criminal proceedings include the right to an impartial tribunal, on the same basis as every other person. This must be borne in mind by journalists when commenting on pending criminal proceedings since the limits of permissible comment may not extend to statements which are likely to prejudice, whether intentionally or not, the chances of a person receiving a fair trial or to undermine the confidence of the public in the role of the courts in the administration of criminal justice."

In *Bowman v United Kingdom*[305] the Court was concerned with a criminal **2–107** prosecution for incurring unauthorised election expenditure. The Court noted that:

"free elections and freedom of expression, particularly freedom of political debate, together form the bedrock of any democratic system".

Nonetheless, the Court observed,

"in certain circumstances the two rights may come into conflict, and it may be considered necessary, in the period preceding or during an election, to place certain restrictions, of a type which would not usually be acceptable, on freedom of expression, in order to secure the 'free expression of the opinion of the people in the choice of the legislature'."

The principle of proportionality has a more limited role to play in relation to **2–108** those rights that are unqualified on their face. The Court has used the language of proportionality in a variety of contexts, often with very different connotations. In *McCann and others v United Kingdom*,[306] for instance, the Court held that when considering whether the use of lethal force was justified under Art.2 a test of *strict* proportionality should be applied. In *Soering v United Kingdom*[307] the Court suggested that a sentence which was "wholly unjustified or grossly disproportionate" to the gravity of the crime could, in principle, amount to inhuman and degrading treatment in breach of Art.3. In *Van der Mussele v Belgium*[308] the Court held that a requirement to provide legal services free of charge, as a condition of entry to the legal profession, could only amount to forced labour (within the meaning of Art.4):

"if the service imposed a burden which was so excessive or disproportionate to the advantages attached to the future exercise of that profession that the service could not be treated as having been voluntarily accepted".

Finally, in *Deweer v Belgium*[309] the Court found a violation of Art.6 where the applicant had been offered the choice between paying a relatively modest fine by way of a "compromise" or facing extended criminal proceedings during which his business would have remained closed by administrative order. Whilst such a

---

[305] (1998) 26 E.H.R.R. 1 at para.42–43.
[306] (1996) 21 E.H.R.R. 97 at para.149; See also *Andronicou and Constantinou v Cyprus* (1998) 25 E.H.R.R. 491 at para.171.
[307] (1989) 11 E.H.R.R. 439 at para.104 (Conditions on death row in the United States found to violate Art.3).
[308] (1984) 6 E.H.R.R. 25 at para.37.
[309] (1979–80) 2 E.H.R.R. 439 at para.51.

procedure would not necessarily violate Art.6, the Court found that the applicant had been deprived of his right to a fair trial since there was a "flagrant disproportion" between the two alternatives facing him. These cases illustrate the shades of meaning which have been attached to the Convention concept of proportionality and serve as a warning against treating it as if it were a term of art.

2–109   The principle of proportionality is an important feature of constitutional review in all jurisdictions that have a Bill of Rights (although the terminology used is not always exactly the same). The common law constitutional courts have adopted a rather more analytical approach to the application of this principle than has the European Court of Human Rights. In *R. v Oakes*[310] the Canadian Supreme Court applied a two stage test for determining whether an interference with a constitutional right is "demonstrably justified in a free and democratic society".[311] First, the objective which the measure is designed to achieve must be of sufficient importance to warrant overriding a constitutionally protected right or interest. This is the equivalent of the "legitimate aim" stage of the Strasbourg analysis. Secondly, the measure chosen to achieve the objective must be "proportional". In determining this latter question, the Supreme Court established three guiding principles:

(a)   The measure adopted must be carefully designed to achieve the objective in question; it must not be arbitrary, unfair or based on irrational considerations.

(b)   The limitation or interference should impair as little as possible the right or freedom in question.

(c)   Even if an objective is of sufficient importance, and the first two elements of the proportionality test are satisfied, it is still possible that, because of the severity of the deleterious effects of a measure on individuals or groups, the measure will not be justified by the purposes it is intended to serve.[312]

The Canadian Supreme Court has also emphasised that the proportionality principle must be "applied flexibly, so as to achieve a proper balance between individual rights and community needs"[313] and that the burden of proving justification always rests squarely on the state.[314]

2–110   A very similar approach has been endorsed by the Privy Council. In *De Freitas v Permanent Secretary of Ministry of Agriculture, Fisheries, Lands and Housing*[315] Lord Clyde approved a three stage test for determining whether a measure

---

[310] [1986] 1 S.C.R. 103; (1986) 26 D.L.R. (4th) 200.
[311] Under s.1 of the Canadian Charter of Rights and Freedoms 1982.
[312] See also *RJR-MacDonald Inc v Attorney-General of Canada* [1995] 3 S.C. 199 at para.60; *R. v Edwards Books and Art Ltd* [1986] 2 S.C.R. 713.
[313] *Ross v New Brunswick School District No.15* [1996] 1 S.C.R. 825 at 872.
[314] *Andrews v Law Society of British Columbia* (1989) 56 D.L.R. (4th) 1 at 21.
[315] (1999) 1 A.C. 69.

was "arbitrary or excessive" within the meaning of the Constitution of Antigua. The court should ask itself whether;

"(i) the legislative objective is sufficiently important to justify limiting a fundamental right;
(ii) the legislative measures designed to meet the objective are rationally connected to it; and
(iii) the means used to impair the right or freedom are no more than is necessary to accomplish that objective."[316]

In *Thomas and Hilaire v Baptiste*[317] the Privy Council held that time limits imposed by Trinidad for exhausting rights of petition to the United Nations Human Rights Committee in a death penalty case were:

"disproportionate because they curtailed the prisoners rights further than was necessary to deal with the mischief created by the delays in the international appellate processes".

In *S v Makwanyane and Another*[318] the South African Constitutional Court   **2–111**
approached the issue in this way:

"The limitation of constitutional rights for a purpose that is reasonable and necessary in a democratic society involves the weighing up of competing values, and ultimately an assessment based on proportionality . . . The fact that different rights have different implications for democracy . . . means that there is no absolute standard which can be laid down for determining reasonableness and necessity. Principles can be established, but the application of those principles to particular circumstances can only be done on a case by case basis. This is inherent in the requirement of proportionality, which calls for a balancing of different interests. In the balancing process, the relevant considerations will include the nature of the right that is limited, and its importance to an open and democratic society based on freedom and equality; the purpose for which the right is limited and the importance of that purpose to such a society; the extent of the limitation, its efficacy, and particularly where the limitation has to be necessary, whether the desired ends could reasonably be achieved through other means less damaging to the right in question."

In *Coetzee v The Government of the Republic of South Africa*[319] Sachs J. put it   **2–112**
more simply;

"The more profound the interest being protected, and the graver the violation, the more stringent the scrutiny; at the end of the day, the court must decide whether, bearing in mind the nature and intensity of the interest to be protected, and the degree to which, and the manner in which it is infringed, the limitation is permissible."

---

[316] P. 80.
[317] [2000] 2 A.C.
[318] 1995 B.C.L.R. 665 (CC) at 708D–G, *per* Chaskalson P. (cited with approval in *Coetzee v The Government of the Republic of South Africa* [1995] 4 L.R.C. 220 at 239–40).
[319] [1995] 4 L.R.C. 220 at 239–40.

XIX. Subsidiarity

2–113 The concept of subsidiarity was recognised by the European Court of Human Rights many years before it assumed its present importance in the European Community law context. It has been defined as the principle that:

> "a central authority should have a subsidiary function, performing only those tasks which cannot be performed effectively at a more immediate or local level".[320]

The concept of subsidiarity reflects three basic features of the Convention system.

(a) First, the list of rights and freedoms set out in the Convention is not exhaustive, so that contracting states are free to provide better protection under their own law or by any other international agreement. This principle finds expression in Art.53 which states that nothing in the Convention

> "shall be construed as limiting or derogating from any of the human rights and fundamental freedoms which may be ensured under the laws of any High Contracting Party or under any other agreement to which it is a Party".[321]

(b) Secondly, the Convention does not impose uniform rules. It lays down standards of conduct, and leaves the choice of implementation to the contracting states. The court has held that it cannot assume the responsibility for prescribing national standards in detail since that would be to:

> " . . . lose sight of the subsidiary nature of the international machinery of collective enforcement established by the Convention. The national authorities remain free to choose between the measures which they consider appropriate in those matters governed by the Convention. Review by the Court concerns only the conformity of those measures with the requirements of the Convention."[322]

(c) Thirdly, the Court has repeatedly stressed that the national authorities are generally in a better position than the supervisory bodies in Strasbourg to strike the right balance between the competing interests of the community and the protection of the fundamental rights of the individual. This principle is reflected in Art.1 which obliges states to secure Convention rights to everyone within their jurisdiction; by Art.13, which requires an effective remedy before a national authority for any arguable breach of a Convention right; and by Art.35(1) which provides that an applicant must first exhaust any effective or potentially effective domestic remedy before introducing a complaint under the Convention.[323] It is also reflected in the so-called "fourth instance" and "margin of appreciation" doctrines.

---

[320] *New Shorter Oxford English Dictionary*, p.3123.
[321] This principle is also enshrined in the Human Rights Act 1998, s.11, see Ch.3 below.
[322] *Belgian Linguistics Case (No.2)* (1979–80) 1 E.H.R.R. 252 at para.10.
[323] See para.1–46 above.

XX. Fourth instance doctrine

The Court has held that it is not its function to substitute its own judgment for **2–114** that of the national courts, or to act as a fourth instance appeal.[324] Its role is confined to ensuring that the contracting states have complied with their obligations under the Convention. This is the source of the twin principles that the assessment of domestic law is primarily for the national courts[325]; and that the Court will not interfere with the findings of fact made by the domestic courts, unless they have drawn arbitrary conclusions from the evidence before them.[326]

XXI. Margin of appreciation

The margin of appreciation is a doctrine of restrained review at the international **2–115** level, which reflects the primary role that the national authorities, including the courts, are intended to perform in human rights protection. According to a former judge of the Court it is simply the term used to describe "the amount of latitude left to national authorities once the appropriate level of review has been decided by the Court".[327] The concept incorporates a degree of discretion into the Court's assessment, particularly where difficult issues of social, moral or economic policy are involved, on which there is no clear European consensus.[328] In *James and others v United Kingdom*[329] the Court explained that:

> "Because of their direct knowledge of their society and its needs, the national authorities are in principle better placed than the international judge to appreciate what is 'in the public interest'. Under the system of protection established by the Convention, it is thus for the national authorities to make the initial assessment both of the existence of a problem of public concern . . . and of the remedial action to be taken . . . Here, as in

---

[324] *Edwards v United Kingdom* (1992) 15 E.H.R.R. 417 at para.34.

[325] *Winterwerp v Netherlands* (1979–80) 2 E.H.R.R. 387 at para.37; *Wassink v Netherlands* (1990) Series A No.185–A at para.24; *Bozano v France* (1987) 9 E.H.R.R. 297 at para.58; *Van der Leer v Netherlands* (1990) 12 E.H.R.R. 567; *Benham v United Kingdom* (1996) 22 E.H.R.R. 293; *Loukanov v Bulgaria* (1997) 24 E.H.R.R. 121.

[326] *Klaas v Germany* (1994) 18 E.H.R.R. 305 at paras 29–31; *Edwards v United Kingdom* (1992) 15 E.H.R.R. 417 at para.34; *Van Mechelen v Netherlands* (1998) 25 E.H.R.R. 647 at para.50; *Barbera, Messegue and Jabardo v Spain* (1990) 11 E.H.R.R. 360; *Kostovski v Netherlands* (1990) 12 E.H.R.R. 434 at para.39; *Monnell and Morris v United Kingdom* (1988) 10 E.H.R.R. 205 at paras 49 and 69.

[327] See Kavanaugh K., *Policing the margins: rights protection and the European Court of Human Rights* [2006] E.H.R.L.R. 422; Shany Y, *Towards a general margin of appreciation doctrine in international law?* [2005] E.J.I.L. 907; Sweeney J, *Margins of appreciation: cultural relativity and the European Court of Human Rights in the post-Cold War era* [2005] I.C.L.Q. 459; Sales P. and Hooper B., *Proportionality and the form of law*, [2003] L.Q.R. 426; Rivers J., *Proportionality and variable intensity of review*, [2006] C.L.J. 174; Macdonald R. St. J., *Methods of Interpretation of the Convention* in MacDonald, Matscher and Petzold (eds) *The European System for the Protection of Human Rights* (Martinus Nijhoff, 1993); Paul Mahoney *Judicial Activism and Judicial Self Restraint in the European Court of Human Rights: Two Sides of the Same Coin* [1990] H.R.L.J. 57; Nicholas Lavender, "The Problem of the Margin of Appreciation" [1997] E.H.R.L.R. 380.

[328] Such as the issue of when human life begins: see *Evans v United Kingdom* (2006) 43 E.H.R.R. 21, paras 45–47.

[329] (1986) 8 E.H.R.R. 123 at para.46.

the other fields to which the safeguards of the Convention extend, the national author-ities accordingly enjoy a certain margin of appreciation."

2–116 There is no universal formula for determining when and how the margin of appreciation should be applied,[330] although the Court has given reasons for its application in particular contexts. The width of the discretion left to the contract-ing states will vary, according to such factors as the nature of the Convention right in issue, the importance of that right for the individual, the nature of the activity involved in the case,[331] the extent of the interference,[332] and the nature of the state's justification.[333] In practice this means that the intensity of the Court's review can range from extreme deference on issues such as social and economic policy,[334] and national security,[335] to hard edged review in cases involving criminal procedure,[336] intimate aspects of private life,[337] or political debate on matters of public interest.[338] Where there is a clear European consensus on a particular issue, the Court will generally be unwilling to accord the state a significant margin of appreciation.[339]

2–117 The Court has consistently emphasised that the margin of appreciation goes "hand in hand"[340] with European supervision, and that it can never supplant the Court's primary duty to assess the proportionality of a measure. Even at its widest, therefore, the margin of appreciation;

> " . . . does not mean that the [Court's] supervision is limited to ascertaining whether the respondent state has exercised its discretion reasonably, carefully and in good faith; what the Court has to do is to look at the interference complained of in the light of the case as a whole and determine whether it was 'proportionate to the legitimate aim pursued' and whether the reasons adduced by the national authorities to justify it are 'relevant and sufficient'."[341]

---

[330] Two former judges of the court have suggested that the margin of appreciation is simply incapable of definition, since it is wholly dependent on the context of a particular case: Bernhardt R., "Thoughts on the Interpretation of Human Rights Treaties", in Matscher and Petzold (eds) *Protecting Human Rights: The European Dimension* (1988); Macdonald R. St. J., "Methods of Interpretation of the Convention" in Macdonald R. St. J., Matscher F. and Petzold H., *The European Systems for the Protection of Human Rights* (Martinus Nijhoff, 1993).

[331] *Buckley v United Kingdom* (1997) 23 E.H.R.R. 101 at para.129; *Rasmussen v Denmark* (1985) 7 E.H.R.R. 352 at para.40.

[332] *Dudgeon v United Kingdom* (1982) 4 E.H.R.R. 149.

[333] *Sunday Times v United Kingdom (No.1)* (1979–80) 2 E.H.R.R. 245 at para.59.

[334] *Buckley v United Kingdom* (1997) 23 E.H.R.R. 101; *Powell and Rayner v United Kingdom* (1990) 12 E.H.R.R. 355; *James and others v United Kingdom* (1986) 8 E.H.R.R. 123 at para.46.

[335] *Leander v Sweden* (1987) 9 E.H.R.R. 433.

[336] *Borgers v Belgium* (1993) 15 E.H.R.R. 92; See also the comments in *Sunday Times (No.1) v United Kingdom* (1979–80) 2 E.H.R.R. 245 at para.59.

[337] *Dudgeon v United Kingdom* (1981) 4 E.H.R.R. 149.

[338] *Barthold v Germany* (1985) 7 E.H.R.R. 383; *Bowman v United Kingdom* (1998) 26 E.H.R.R. 1; *cf. Wingrove v United Kingdom* (1996) 24 E.H.R.R. 1.

[339] *Rasmussen v Denmark* (1985) 7 E.H.R.R. 352 at para.40; *Sunday Times v United Kingdom (No.1)* (1979–80) 2 E.H.R.R. 245 at para.59. See also para.2–28 above.

[340] *Handyside v United Kingdom* (1979–80) 1 E.H.R.R. 737 at para.49.

[341] *Vogt v Germany* (1996) 21 E.H.R.R. 205 at para.52(iii); *Sunday Times v United Kingdom (No.1)* (1979–80) 2 E.H.R.R. 245 at para.59; *Dudgeon v United Kingdom* (1982) 4 E.H.R.R. 149 at para.59.

The complex interplay between the various factors involved makes it difficult to identify hard and fast principles governing the application of the margin of appreciation to particular rights or particular grounds of interference.[342] The essence of the court's task is to assess the extent to which the proportionality balance would be more appropriately performed at the national level in any given case. This is an issue of jurisdictional policy, which ultimately depends on the nature of the issues in dispute between the parties. **2–118**

Thus, where the protection of morals exception in Art.10(2) is relied upon to restrict the right to freedom of expression, the Court has generally been inclined to allow a relatively wide margin of appreciation. In *Handyside v United Kingdom*,[343] a case concerning the distribution of allegedly obscene material, the Court explained that: **2–119**

> "[I]t is not possible to find in the domestic law of the various contracting states a uniform European conception of morals. The view taken by their respective laws of the requirements of morals varies from time to time and from place to place. By reason of their direct and continuous contact with the vital forces of their countries, state authorities are in principle in a better position than the international judge to give an opinion on the exact content of those requirements of morals as well as on the 'necessity' of a 'restriction' or 'penalty' intended to meet them . . . Nevertheless, Article 10(2) does not give contracting states an unlimited power of appreciation. The Court, which . . . is responsible for ensuring observance of those states' engagements, is empowered to give the final ruling on whether a 'restriction' or 'penalty' is reconcilable with freedom of expression as protected by Article 10. The domestic margin of appreciation thus goes hand in hand with a European supervision."

Similarly, in *Wingrove v United Kingdom*[344] the Court allowed a broad margin of appreciation in the context of restrictions on the right to freedom of expression said to be justified in order to protect the rights of others to respect for their religious convictions. The British Board of Film Classification had refused a certificate to a videotape on the ground that it was blasphemous. In finding no violation the Court observed: **2–120**

> "Whereas there is little scope under Article 10(2) of the Convention for restrictions on political speech or on debate of questions of public interest, a wider margin of appreciation is generally available to the Contracting States when regulating freedom of expression in relation to matters liable to offend intimate personal convictions within the sphere of morals or, especially, religion. Moreover, as in the field of morals, and perhaps to an even greater degree, there is no uniform European conception of the requirements of 'the protection of the rights of others' in relation to attacks on their

---

[342] The apparent lack of consistency in the court's caselaw has attracted serious criticism. Macdonald R. St. J. has identified a "disappointing lack of clarity" ("Methods of Interpretation of the Convention" in MacDonald R. St. J., Matscher F. and Petzold H., *The European System for the Protection of Human Rights* (Martinus Nijhoff, 1993). See also Lord Lester of Herne Hill Q.C.: "The concept of the 'margin of appreciation' has become as slippery and elusive as an eel. Again and again the Court now appears to use the margin of appreciation as a substitute for coherent legal analysis of the issues at stake." ("The European Convention on Human Rights in the New Architecture of Europe" in *Proceedings of the 9 International Colloquy on the European Convention on Human Rights* (Council of Europe, 1996)).
[343] (1979–80) 1 E.H.R.R. 737 at paras 48–89.
[344] (1997) 24 E.H.R.R. 1 at para.58.

religious convictions. What is likely to cause substantial offence to persons of a particular religious persuasion will vary significantly from time to time and from place to place, especially in an era characterised by an ever growing array of faiths and denominations. By reason of their direct and continuous contact with the vital forces of their countries, State authorities are in principle in a better position than the international judge to give an opinion on the exact content of these requirements with regard to the rights of others as well as on the 'necessity' of a 'restriction' intended to protect from such material those whose deepest feelings and convictions would be seriously offended."[345]

2–121   However, where the right to freedom of expression is restricted in order to maintain the authority and impartiality of the judiciary, the Court has held that the margin of appreciation should be narrower. This is because the notion of the authority of the judiciary is the subject of a broad level of agreement among the parties to the Convention, and is a more objective concept than the protection of morals or religious convictions. In *Sunday Times v United Kingdom (No.1)*[346] the Court observed that:

> "The domestic law and practice of the contracting states reveal a fairly substantial measure of common ground in this area. This is reflected in a number of provisions of the Convention, including Article 6, which have no equivalent as far as 'morals' are concerned. Accordingly, here a more extensive European supervision corresponds to a less discretionary power of appreciation."[347]

2–122   In *Dudgeon v United Kingdom*,[348] the government relied on the Court's *Handyside* judgment to argue that a wide margin of appreciation was appropriate whenever the protection of morals was in issue. But, as the Court pointed out, this was to ignore the difference in the extent of the interference between a criminal prosecution for private sexual activity on the one hand, and the public distribution of allegedly obscene material on the other. Whilst the public policy justification for a restriction was an important factor in determining the intensity of review, it was not necessarily decisive. The scope of the margin of appreciation would be determined not only by "the nature of the aim of the restriction", but also by "the nature of the activities involved".[349] Since the applicant's activities involved a "most intimate aspect of private life", the state's margin of appreciation was narrow, and the government would have to demonstrate "particularly serious reasons before interferences on the part of the public authorities can be legitimate for the purposes of Article 8(2)".[350]

2–123   Since the margin of appreciation has been developed as a means of delineating the supervisory functions of an international court, it has no direct application to cases brought under the Human Rights Act 1998. As we have seen, there are two principal strands of reasoning which underlie the Court's approach. The first is

---

[345] See also *Gündüz v Turkey* (2005) 41 E.H.R.R. 5, paras 37–41, where the court emphasised that States would be accorded a broader margin of appreciation when regulating "hate speech", even where the regulation involved criminal sanctions.

[346] (1979–80) 2 E.H.R.R. 245.

[347] Para.59; see also *Worm v Austria* (1997) 25 E.H.R.R. 454.

[348] (1982) 4 E.H.R.R. 149.

[349] Para.52.

[350] Para.52; see also *Smith and Grady v United Kingdom* (2000) 29 E.H.R.R. 493.

that the function of an international court is different from that of a national court; and the second is that in certain cases there may be a lack of European consensus on a particular point. Both rationales are inextricably bound up with the institutional position of the European Court of Human Rights. As a former President of the Court has explained, the Strasbourg margin of appreciation is a direct function of the principle of subsidiarity.[351]

At the institutional level, the margin of appreciation doctrine sets the European   **2–124** Court's standard of review and (together with the "fourth instance" doctrine) distinguishes constitutional challenge (or *cassation*) from an appeal on fact and/ or law. The European Court of Human Rights is a court of constitutional review, which depends on inter-governmental co-operation and support for its mandate. Like any reviewing court it is reluctant to substitute its own opinion for that of the body under review. It is no part of the European Court's function to set finely calibrated standards within the national legal system. That is the function of the domestic authorities.

More importantly, the Strasbourg margin of appreciation applies to the response   **2–125** of the national authorities as a whole, *including the courts*. When applied to decisions of the national courts, its rationale is that those courts are better placed to carry out the necessary assessment because they are more closely in touch with local conditions. The European Court's self-denying ordinance presupposes that the national courts will have scrutinised a case, with the benefit of local knowledge, before it is brought to Strasbourg; and that in doing so they will have made a primary, rather than a secondary, judgment of the proportionality of any interference with Convention rights. The changes to the Court's admissibility criteria, contained in Protocol 14, emphasise the importance of domestic judicial scrutiny: the new admissibility criterion, which allows a case to be declared inadmissible if the applicant:

> "has not suffered disadvantage, unless respect for human rights as defined in the Convention and the Protocols thereto requires an examination of the application on the merits",

applies *only* if the case has already been "duly considered by a domestic tribunal." The Council of Europe has emphasised, while promoting the Protocol, the importance of strengthening rights protection at the domestic level, so that the Strasbourg Court becomes a remedy of last resort.[352]

Once the different functions of the national and the international court have been   **2–126** identified, it becomes obvious that the Strasbourg margin of appreciation cannot be applied by the national court. Under s.6 of the Human Rights Act 1998 the domestic courts, as public authorities, are bound by the duty to act compatibly with Convention rights, unless they are prevented from doing so by primary

---

[351] Rolv Ryssdall, "The Coming of Age of the European Convention on Human Rights" [1996] E.H.R.L.R. 18 at 24.
[352] See further Ch.1.

legislation which cannot be interpreted compatibly with Convention rights.[353] The Strasbourg margin of appreciation only becomes relevant to this process if the decision of the national court comes to be re-examined by the European Court of Human Rights. If the national courts were to apply the Strasbourg margin of appreciation directly to decisions of the legislature or the executive, within their own legal system, an element of "double counting" would creep in, and an important part of the rationale for the European Court's approach would disappear. As Sir John Laws has pointed out:

> "The margin of appreciation doctrine, as it has been developed in Strasbourg, will necessarily be inapt to the administration of the Convention in the domestic courts for the very reason that they are domestic; they will not be subject to an objective inhibition generated by any cultural distance between themselves and the state organs whose decisions are impleaded before them".[354]

In *R. (Mahmood) v Secretary of State for the Home Department*,[355] Laws L.J. went on to state that:

> "the 'margin of appreciation' as that term is deployed in Strasbourg cases, is apt to connote a self-denying ordinance adopted by an international court precisely because it is an international court, and is based upon the conception that the national authorities are in the first instance best placed to decide how the Convention rights should be measured and distributed in their jurisdiction."

Sedley L.J. has commented that "Any decision of the Strasbourg Court that a potential breach falls within the member states' margin of appreciation belongs to its jurisprudence, not to ours."[356]

2–127 This is not, however, to say that the Court's jurisprudence on the margin of appreciation is irrelevant, to cases brought under the Human Rights Act. It could hardly be irrelevant, since it circumscribes the Court's review of the proportionality of a measure. The national courts will need to be aware of the Strasbourg caselaw on the margin of appreciation, if only to ensure that they do not adopt a less intrusive standard of scrutiny.[357] Moreover, the Act itself provides that the Court's caselaw is to be taken into account by a national court when considering

---

[353] Human Rights Act 1998, ss.3 and 6. As the Lord Chancellor pointed out during the debates on the Act: "The courts will often be faced with cases that involve factors perhaps specific to the United Kingdom which distinguish them from cases considered by [the Strasbourg Court]". January 19, 1998 484 (H.L.) 1270 at 1271.

[354] Sir John Laws, "The Limitations of Human Rights" [1998] P.L. 254 at 258.

[355] [2001] 1 W.L.R. 840, para.31. See also *R. (International Transport Roth GmbH) v Secretary of State for the Home Department* [2003] Q.B. 728, where Laws L.J. stated that "We do not apply the Strasbourg margin of appreciation, because we are a domestic, not an international, tribunal." (para.81).

[356] *Knight v McNicholls* [2004] 1 W.L.R. 1653 at para.38.

[357] It has also been suggested that 'the width of the margin of appreciation accorded . . . by the EctHR is an indication of the appropriate width of the area of discretionary judgment' with the domestic courts should accord the decision maker: *R. (Trailer and Marina (Leven) Ltd) v Secretary of State for the Environment, Food and Rural Affairs* [2004] Env. L.R. 828, *per* Ouseley J. at para.63.

any question which has arisen in connection with a Convention right.[358] In *R. v Stratford Justices ex parte Imbert* Buxton L.J. attempted the square the circle thus[359]:

"The application of the doctrine of the margin of appreciation would appear to be solely a matter for the Strasbourg Court. By appealing to the doctrine that court recognises that the detailed content of at least some Convention obligations is more appropriately determined in the light of national conditions . . . The English judge cannot therefore himself apply or have recourse to the doctrine of the margin of appreciation as implemented by the Strasbourg Court. He must, however, recognise the impact of that doctrine upon the Strasbourg Court's analysis of the meaning and implications of the broad terms of the Convention provisions: which is the obvious source of guidance as to those provisions, and a source that in any event the English court will be obliged, once section 2(1)(a) of the 1998 Act has come into force, to take into account."

How then have the national courts fixed the appropriate standard of review under   **2–128** the Human Rights Act? The Human Rights Act does not require the national courts to take the place of the primary decision-maker whenever an executive or legislative decision infringes human rights. The recognition that other public bodies are often better placed than the courts to carry out the necessary assessment is a universal feature of constitutional review, in Europe and elsewhere. At the constitutional level, the relative specialist knowledge of the body under review on the one hand, and the court on the other, will always be a relevant factor. The level of scrutiny will depend upon the court's conception of the separation of powers principle, and the respective responsibilities of the judiciary *vis-à-vis* the other two branches of government. At one end of the spectrum the court is usually the arbiter of what is procedurally fair in a criminal trial, and this points to a thorough and searching scrutiny in criminal cases.[360] At the other end of the spectrum, the legislature has not only the relevant expertise but also the necessary democratic mandate to make decisions in the field of public finance.

The Canadian Supreme Court has adopted a sliding scale of constitutional   **2–129** review, which preserves the most intrusive standard of scrutiny for criminal cases. In *RJR-MacDonald Inc v Attorney-General of Canada*[361] La Forest J. commented:

"Courts are specialists in the protection of liberty and the interpretation of legislation and are, accordingly, well placed to subject criminal justice legislation to careful scrutiny. However, courts are not specialists in the realm of policy-making, nor should they be. This is a role properly assigned to the elected representatives of the people,

---

[358] s.2. Note that the obligation on the national courts is to take the Convention caselaw into account. They are not bound to follow the Strasbourg approach in every respect.

[359] [1999] 2 Cr.App.R. 276.

[360] Even in the criminal context, however, a degree of deference to the legislature will sometimes be appropriate. The Privy Council has observed that;

"In order to maintain the balance between the individual and the society as a whole, rigid and inflexible standards should not be imposed on the legislature's attempts to resolve the difficult and intransigent problems with which society is faced when seeking to deal with serious crime. It must be remembered that questions of policy remain primarily the responsibility of the legislature." (*per* Lord Woolf in *Attorney-General of Hong Kong v Lee Kwong-kut* [1993] A.C. 951 at 975C–D.)

[361] [1995] 3 S.C.R. 199 at 279 and 331–332.

who have at their disposal the necessary institutional resources to enable them to compile and assess social science evidence, to mediate between competing social interests and to reach out and protect vulnerable groups."[362]

2-130 Similarly, in *Libman v Attorney-General of Quebec*[363] the Supreme Court pointed out that;

" . . . in the social, economic and political spheres, where the legislature must reconcile competing interests in choosing one policy among several that might be acceptable, the courts must accord great deference to the legislature's choice because it is in the best position to make such a choice. On the other hand, the courts will judge the legislature's choices more harshly in areas where the government plays the role of the 'singular antagonist of the individual'—primarily in criminal matters—owing to their expertise in these areas."

2-131 The application of this principle under the Human Rights Act does not mean "stripping" the Strasbourg margin of appreciation of its international dimension, since this would be virtually impossible to do. Rather, it requires the courts to ascertain their own scale of national constitutional review. To quote Sir John Laws again:

"[I]t is necessary to distinguish the idea of a margin of appreciation, which is apt for an international court reviewing a national decision, from the different idea of a discretion left to elected authorities on democratic grounds."[364]

It has been suggested[365] that the factors which should influence this scale include the importance of the right at stake; the seriousness of the interference with that right; the relative specialist knowledge of the body under review; the democratic mandate of that body; whether the interference aims to promote competing rights of others; whether the applicant comes from a particularly vulnerable group; and whether the context is one in which there is a discernable European standard. It has been suggested that:

"The more the legislation concerns matters of broad social policy, the less ready will be a court to intervene."[366]

---

[362] See also *Irwin Toy Ltd v Attorney-General of Quebec* [1989] 1 S.C.R. 927 at 993–994; *McKinney v University of Guelph* [1990] 3 S.C.R. 229 at 304–305; *Stoffman v Vancouver General Hospital* [1990] 3 S.C.R. 483 at 521. See also Clement J., *Introducing Canadian Rights Jurisprudence: Part I* [2004] J.R. 159, and *Introducing Canadian Rights Jurisprudence: Part II* [2004] J.R. 207.

[363] (1997) 3 B.H.R.C. 269 at 289E–F.

[364] Sir John Laws, "Wednesbury" in *The Golden Metwand and the Crooked Cord: Essays in Public Law in Honour of Sir Willliam Wade QC* (1998), p.201.

[365] Singh, Hunt and Demetriou, "Is there a Role for the Margin of Appreciation in National Law after the Human Rights Act?" [1999] E.H.R.L.R. 15. See also Clayton R., *Principles for judicial deference* [2006] J.R. 109.

[366] *Wilson v First County Trust Ltd* [2004] 1 A.C. 816, *per* Lord Nicholls at para.70. A similar view was expressed by Lord Bingham in *R. v Lichniak* [2003] 1 A.C. 903: considering the mandatory life sentence, Lord Bingham stated that the fact that that statutory provision "represents the settled will of a democratic assembly is not a conclusive reason for upholding it, but a degree of deference is due to the judgment of a democratic assembly on how a particular social problem is best tackled." (para.14)

The importance of subject matter, and the fact that the courts will be willing to find a rights violation even in areas where some latitude is due to the decision maker, was explained as follows by Lord Nicholls in *Ghaidan v Godin-Mendoza*[367]:

"The readiness of the court to depart from the views of the legislature depends upon the subject matter of the legislation and of the complaint. National housing policy is a field where the court will be less ready to intervene. Parliament has to hold a fair balance between the competing interests of tenants and landlords, taking into account broad issues of social and economic policy. But, even in such a field, where the alleged violation comprises differential treatment based on grounds such as race or sex or sexual orientation the Court will scrutinise with intensity any reasons said to constitute justification. The reasons must be cogent if such differential treatment is said to be justified."

The existence of a variable standard of constitutional review under the Human Rights Act, which is distinct from the Strasbourg margin of appreciation, was recognised by the House of Lords in *R. v Director of Public Prosecutions ex parte Kebilene and others*,[368] where Lord Hope observed that: **2–132**

"[The doctrine of the margin of appreciation] is an integral part of the supervisory jurisdiction which is exercised over state conduct by the international court. By conceding a margin of appreciation to each national system, the Court has recognised that the Convention, as a living system, does not need to be applied uniformly by all states but may vary in its application according to local needs and conditions. This technique is not available to the national courts when they are considering Convention issues within their own countries. But in the hands of the national courts also the Convention should be seen as an expression of fundamental principles rather than as a set of mere rules. The questions which the courts will have to decide in the application of these principles will involve questions of balance between competing interests and issues of proportionality. In this area difficult choices may have to be made by the executive or the legislature between the rights of the individual and the needs of society. In some circumstances it will be appropriate for the courts to recognise that there is an area of judgment within which the judiciary will defer, on democratic grounds, to the considered opinion of the elected body or person whose act or decision is said to be incompatible with the Convention . . . It will be easier for such an area of judgment to be recognised where the Convention itself requires a balance to be struck, much less so where the right is stated in terms which are unqualified. It will be easier for it to be recognised where the issues involve questions of social or economic policy, much less so where the rights are of high constitutional importance or are of a kind where the courts are especially well placed to assess the need for protection."

The difficulty of assessing the "discretionary area of judgment" to be accorded to Parliament came into sharp focus in *R. v Lambert and ors*.[369] In that case, the Court of Appeal held that the provisions of ss.5(4), 28(2) and 28(3) of the Misuse of Drugs Act 1971 (specific "knowledge" defences available on a charge of possession of drugs) were compatible with the presumption of innocence in Art.6(2). Lord Woolf C.J. held that as a matter of principle a balance must be struck between the demands of the general interest of the community and the **2–133**

[367] [2004] 2 A.C. 557, at para.19.
[368] [1999] 3 W.L.R. 972.
[369] [2002] 2 A.C. 545.

protection of the fundamental rights of the individual. He observed that the burden of proof imposed by the Act had been deliberately cast on the accused by Parliament, for policy reasons which it considered justified. Since 1971 that justification had increased. Although the method selected by the legislature had been "roundly criticised" the court did not consider that Parliament's chosen course violated Art.6. The House of Lords reached the opposite conclusion, by a majority of 4:1 holding that Parliament's true intention could be met through the imposition of a purely evidential burden of proof.[370] The Court of Appeal again emphasised the importance of deferring to the legislature in *R. v Benjafield and ors*[371] when considering the assumptions made under the confiscation provisions of the Drug Trafficking Act 1994 and the Criminal Justice Act 1988. Applying Lord Hope's formulation in *Kebilene*, the Court of Appeal considered that it was incontrovertible that the legislation addressed a serious social problem and Parliament had sought to offset the interference with the presumption of innocence by providing a number of safeguards to the defendant. Shortly after *Benjafield* was decided, the Privy Council reached the same conclusion (albeit by a slightly different route) in relation to confiscation legislation in Scotland. In *McIntosh v Lord Advocate*,[372] Lord Bingham held that the Proceeds of Crime (Scotland) Act 1995 struck a fair balance between the competing interests at stake, adding that the statutory scheme was "approved by a democratically elected Parliament and should not be at all readily rejected".

2–134   The relative expertise of the courts *via-a-vis* the legislature was invoked by the Privy Council in *Brown v Stott*[373] in holding that the provisions of s.172(2) of the Road Traffic Act 1978 were compatible with the protection against self-incrimination in Art.6(1). The Board distinguished the decision in *Saunders v United Kingdom*[374] noting that Parliament was at least as well placed as the judiciary to assess the balance between the safety of road users and the rights of the accused. Lord Steyn explained that:

> "On this aspect the legislature was in as good a position as the court to assess the gravity of the problem and the public interest in addressing it. It really then boils down to the question whether, in adopting the procedure enshrined in section 172(2), rather than a reverse burden technique, it took more drastic action than was justified. While this is ultimately a question for the court, it is not unreasonable to regard both techniques as permissible in the field of the driving of vehicles."

2–135   In *R. v Johnstone*[375] the House of Lords again expressed the view that Parliament has, within limits, a discretion as to how to define the elements of an offence. Lord Nicholls stated that: "for a reverse burden of proof to be acceptable there must normally be a compelling reason why it is fair and reasonable to deny the accused person the protection normally guaranteed to everyone by the presumption of innocence",[376] but went on to say that: "In evaluating these factors the

---

[370] *R. v Lambert* [2002] 2 A.C. 545.
[371] [2003] 1 A.C. 1099.
[372] [2003] 1 A.C. 1078.
[373] [2003] 1 A.C. 681.
[374] (1997) 23 E.H.R.R. 313.
[375] [2003] 1 W.L.R. 1736.
[376] Para.49.

court's role is one of review. Parliament, not the court, is charged with the primary responsibility for deciding, as a matter of policy, what should be the constituent elements of a criminal offence."[377] In *R. v A*,[378] however, a majority[379] of the House of Lords identified the limits to this approach when considering whether a statutory restriction on the cross-examination of a rape complainant was compatible with Art.6. The restriction had been imposed by Parliament to redress the "twin myths" that a woman who is sexually active is either promiscuous or untruthful or both. As Lord Steyn put it:

"Clearly the House must give weight to the decision of Parliament that the mischief encapsulated by the twin myths must be corrected. On the other hand, when the question arises whether in the criminal statute in question Parliament has adopted a legislative scheme which makes an excessive inroad into the right to a fair trial the court is qualified to make its own judgment and must do so".

The issue of the "discretionary area of judgment" arose in the national security context in *R. (A and others) v Secretary of State for the Home Department*.[380] A majority of the House of Lords (Lord Hoffmann dissenting) held that the courts had not erred in accepting the government's argument that there was a "public emergency threatening the life of the nation." Lord Bingham explained why he did not feel able to question that conclusion:

"The more purely political (in a broad or narrow sense) a question is, the more appropriate it will be for political resolution and the less likely it is to be an appropriate matter for judicial decision. The smaller, therefore, will be the potential role of the court. It is the function of political and not judicial bodies to resolve political questions. Conversely, the greater the legal content of any issue, the greater the potential role of the court, because under our constitution and subject to the sovereign power of Parliament is is the function of the courts and not of political bodies to resolve legal questions. The present question seems to me to be very much at the political end of the spectrum."[381]

However, as explained in Ch.1, the House of Lords went on to find (Lord Walker dissenting) that the legislation in question was unlawful, since it was disproportionate and discriminatory.

It is important to point out that even in Strasbourg, where the broader international margin of appreciation is applicable, the Court's standard of deference **2–136**

---

[377] Para.51. For another example of a reverse burden case, see *Attorney General's Reference (No.1 of 2004)* [2004] 1 W.L.R. 2111, "The assumption should be that Parliament would not have made an exception without good reason.", *per* Lord Woolf C.J. at 52(d).

[378] [2002] 1 A.C. 45.

[379] Lord Hope held that the provision in issue fell within the ambit of policy in which the courts should defer on democratic grounds to the considered opinion of the legislature: "I think that, if any doubt remains on this matter, it raises the further question whether Parliament acted within its discretionary area of judgment when it was choosing the point of balance indicated by [the relevant provision]. The area is one where Parliament was better equipped than the judges are to decide where the balance lay. The judges are well able to assess the extent to which the restrictions will inhibit questioning or the leading of evidence. But it seems to me that in this highly sensitive and carefully researched field, an assessment of the prejudice to the wider interests of the community if the restrictions were not to take that form was more appropriate for Parliament."

[380] [2005] 2 W.L.R. 87.

[381] Para.29.

allows considerably fewer "degrees of latitude"[382] to the state than the *Wednesbury*[383] standard of review. We have already seen that the Strasbourg margin of appreciation is not confined to "ascertaining whether the respondent state has exercised its discretion reasonably, carefully and in good faith".[384] More significantly, the irrationality threshold has led to the condemnation of judicial review as an ineffective remedy by the European Court of Human Rights. This was despite the fact that the Court of Appeal had recognised a heightened level of scrutiny for judicial review in human rights cases.[385] In *Smith and Grady v United Kingdom*,[386] the challenge to the Ministry of Defence ban on homosexuals serving in the armed forces, the Court observed that the *Wednesbury* threshold;

" . . . was placed so high that it effectively excluded any consideration by the domestic courts of the question of whether the interference with the applicants' rights answered a pressing social need or was proportionate to the national security and public order aims pursued, principles which lie at the heart of the Court's analysis of complaints under Article 8 of the Convention."

In *Hatton v United Kingdom*, the case concerning Heathrow night flights and whether they violated the Art.8 rights of those living nearby, the Grand Chamber again considered whether judicial review was a sufficient remedy:

" . . . it is clear, as noted by the Chamber, that the scope of review by the domestic courts was limited to the classic English public law concepts, such as irrationality, unawfulness and patent unreasonableness, and did not at the time (that is, prior to the entry into force of the Human Rights Act 1998) allow consideration of whether the claimed increase in night flights under the 1993 Scheme represented a justifiable limitation on the right to respect for the private and family lives or the homes of those who live in the vicinity of Heathrow airport."[387]

2–137 The reconciliation of these principles with the standard adopted by the Administrative Court on judicial review was considered in *R. (Mahmood) v Secretary of State for the Home Department*.[388] Lord Phillips M.R. held that under the 1998 Act, the courts should anxiously scrutinise Executive decisions which interfere with human rights. In a case concerning an alleged violation of Arts 8 to 11, this would involve asking the question whether, judged by an objective standard, the decision maker could reasonably have concluded that the interference was necessary to achieve one or more legitimate aims recognised by the Convention. As Laws L.J. put it in the same case, the 1998 Act "does not authorise the judges to stand in the shoes of Parliament's delegates, who are decision makers given their responsibilities by the democratic arm of the state". That would require the judges to "usurp those functions of government which are controlled and distributed by powers whose authority is derived from the ballot box". It followed that

---

[382] See Neill L.J. in *Rantzen v Mirror Group Newspapers (1986) Ltd* [1994] Q.B. 670.
[383] *Associated Provincial Picture Houses Ltd v Wednesbury Corporation* [1948] 1 K.B. 223.
[384] *Vogt v Germany* (1996) 21 E.H.R.R. 205 at para.52(iii), see para.2–117 above.
[385] *R. v Ministry of Defence ex parte Smith* [1996] Q.B. 517.
[386] (2000) 29 E.H.R.R. 493 at para.138.
[387] (2003) 37 E.H.R.R. 28, at para.141.
[388] [2001] 1 W.L.R. 840.

there must be "a principled distance" between the court's adjudication and the Executive's decision, which would be based on the merits of the case. *Mahmood* was considered in the House of Lords in *R. v Secretary of State for the Home Department ex parte Daly*.[389] Lord Steyn observed that the test laid down in *Mahmood* was "couched in language reminiscent of the traditional *Wednesbury* ground of review". After citing with approval the test for proportionality laid down in *de Freitas v Permanent Secretary of Ministry of Agriculture, Fisheries, Lands and Housing*[390] he continued:

"The starting point is that there is an overlap between the traditional grounds of review and the approach of proportionality. Most cases would be decided in the same way whichever approach is adopted. But the intensity of review is somewhat greater under the proportionality approach. Making due allowance for important structural differences between various convention rights, which I do not propose to discuss, a few general-isations are perhaps permissible. I would mention three concrete differences without suggesting that my statement is exhaustive. First, the doctrine of proportionality may require the reviewing court to assess the balance which the decision maker has struck, not merely whether it is within the range of rational or reasonable decisions. Secondly, the proportionality test may go further than the traditional grounds of review inasmuch as it may require attention to be directed to the relative weight accorded to interests and considerations. Thirdly, even the heightened scrutiny test developed in *R. v Ministry of Defence, ex p. Smith*[391] is not necessarily appropriate to the protection of human rights ... [T]he intensity of the review, in similar cases, is guaranteed by the twin requirements that the limitation of the right was necessary in a democratic society, in the sense of meeting a pressing social need, and the question whether the interference was really proportionate to the legitimate aim being pursued. The differences in approach between the traditional grounds of review and the proportionality approach may therefore sometimes yield different results. It is therefore important that cases involving convention rights must be analysed in the correct way. This does not mean that there has been a shift to merits review. On the contrary, as Professor Jowell[392] has pointed out the respective roles of judges and administrators are fundamentally distinct and will remain so. To this extent the general tenor of the observations in *Mahmood* are correct. And Laws L.J. rightly emphasises in *Mahmood* 'that the intensity of review in a public law case will depend on the subject matter in hand'. That is so even in cases involving Convention rights. In law context is everything."

C. SPECIFIC PROVISIONS

I. Non-discrimination

Article 14 provides that: **2–138**

"The enjoyment of the rights set forth in this Convention shall be secured without discrimination on any ground such as sex, race, colour, language, religion, political or other opinion, national or social origin, association with a national minority, property, birth or other status."

---

[389] [2001] 2 A.C. 532.
[390] [1999] 1 A.C. 69; see para.2–110 above.
[391] [1996] Q.B. 517 at 554.
[392] "Beyond the Rule of Law: Towards Constitutional Judicial Review" [2000] P.L. 671 at 681.

The Convention differs from other international instruments in that its anti-discrimination provision may only be invoked *in conjunction* with a substantive Convention right.[393] There is, however, no requirement for an applicant to show that there has been a violation of the substantive Convention right concerned. As the Court observed in the *Belgian Linguistic Case (No.2)*[394];

> "While it is true that this guarantee has no independent existence in the sense that under the terms of Article 14 it relates solely to 'rights and freedoms set forth in the Convention', a measure which in itself is in conformity with the requirements of the Article enshrining the right or freedom in question may however infringe this Article when read in conjunction with Article 14 for the reason that it is of a discriminatory nature."

Thus, providing the complaint falls within the broad ambit of a Convention right, it is sufficient that there has been a failure to afford equal treatment in the delivery of that right.[395] It is "as though Article 14 formed an integral part of each of the provisions laying down the specific rights and freedoms".[396]

2–139   Article 14 is a general prohibition on unequal treatment on grounds of "status", which guarantees equality before the law. To that extent, it affords a broader range of protection than domestic anti-discrimination legislation. The term "other status" has been held to include sexual orientation,[397] transsexuality,[398] illegitimacy,[399] professional status,[400] and even pension status.[401] However, the House of Lords held in *R. (S) v Chief Constable of South Yorkshire*[402] that the retention of DNA and fingerprint evidence from those who had previously been arrested, but not from others, did not discriminate on the ground of status since having been arrested or not "is not analogous to any of the expressed proscribed grounds such as sex, race, gender or religion."[403]

2–140   The Court's structured approach requires two questions to be posed.[404] First, the court will inquire whether there has been a difference in treatment between two

---

[393] *cf.* Art.26 of the International Covenant on Civil and Political Rights.

[394] (1979–80) 1 E.H.R.R. 252 at para.9. For domestic authorities on whether a case is "within the ambit" of a Convention right for the purposes of Art.14, see *Ghaidan v Godin-Mendoza* [2004] 2 A.C. 557, and *R. (Erskine) v Lambeth London Borough Council* [2003] EWHC 2479 (Admin).

[395] *Rasmussen v Denmark* (1985) 7 E.H.R.R. 352. This point is well illustrated by *RM v United Kingdom* (1994) 77A D.R. 98, where the Commission accepted that discrimination in sentencing could, in principle, amount to a breach of Art.5 in conjunction with Art.14. *Cf. Botta v Italy* (1998) 26 E.H.R.R. 241 (right of disabled person to access to a holiday beach did not fall within the ambit of Art.8, so Art.14 inapplicable).

[396] *RM v United Kingdom* (1994) 77A D.R. 98 at 105.

[397] *Sutherland v United Kingdom* (1997) 24 E.H.R.R. CD 22.

[398] *Sheffield and Horsham v United Kingdom* (1999) 27 E.H.R.R. 163.

[399] *Marckx v Belgium* (1979–80) 2 E.H.R.R. 330.

[400] *Van der Muselle v Belgium* (1984) 6 E.H.R.R. 163.

[401] *Szrabjer and Clarke v United Kingdom* [1998] E.H.R.L.R. 230.

[402] [2004] 1 W.L.R. 2196.

[403] Para.51, *per* Lord Steyn. The Convention meaning of "status" was discussed by Brooke L.J. at para.34 of *Michalak v London Borough of Wandsworth* [2003] 1 W.L.R. 617.

[404] *Belgian Linguistic Case (No.2)* (1979–80) 1 E.H.R.R. 252.

persons who are in a "relevantly similar"[405] position, on grounds of the victim's "status".[406] The burden of proving this lies on the applicant.[407] If this burden is discharged, the Court must go on to determine whether the difference which has been identified has an "objective and reasonable" justification.[408] Here, the burden lies on the state.[409] The Court's assessment involves the familiar process of asking whether there is a legitimate aim for the difference in treatment, and whether there is "a reasonable relationship of proportionality between the means employed and the aim sought to be realised".[410] This requires the Court to:

"strike a fair balance between the protection of the interests of the community and respect for the rights and freedoms safeguarded by the Convention".[411]

In determining whether a difference in treatment satisfies the proportionality test the court will allow the state a certain margin of appreciation, and will have regard to comparative European practice[412] and any relevant international standards.[413] This structured approach was set out, in the domestic context, by Brooke L.J. in *Michalak v London Borough of Wandsworth*[414]:

"If a court follows this model it should ask itself the four questions I set out below. If the answer to any of the four questions is 'no', then the claim is likely to fail, and it is in general unnecessary to proceed to the next question. These questions are:

(i) Do the facts fall within the ambit of one or more of the substantive Convention provisions . . . ?

---

[405] *National and Provincial Building Society v United Kingdom* (1998) 25 E.H.R.R. 127 at para.88. For domestic discussion of whether categories are "relevantly comparable", see *R. (Carson) v Secretary of State for Work and Pensions* [2006] 1 A.C. 173 (overseas pensioners not directly comparable to pensioners living in the UK); *R. (Hindawi) v Secretary of State for the Home Department* [2004] EWHC 78 (Admin) (determinate sentence prisoners liable to deportation relevantly comparable to determinate sentence prisoners not so liable.)

[406] For examples of case which failed at this hurdle, see *Stubbings and others v United Kingdom* (1997) 23 E.H.R.R. 213 where the court described the comparison between negligently and intentionally inflicted injury (for the purposes of different limitation periods) as "artificial"; and *Van der Muselle v Belgium* (1984) 6 E.H.R.R. 163 where a trainee barrister's claim that he was treated differently from trainees in other professions was rejected on the ground that there were fundamental differences between the various professions.

[407] See the court's approach in *Selcuk and Asker v Turkey* (1998) 26 E.H.R.R. 477 at para.102 and *Mentes v Turkey* (1998) 26 E.H.R.R. 595 at para.96.

[408] *Belgian Linguistic Case (No.2)* (1979–80) 1 E.H.R.R. 252 at para.9.

[409] *Darby v Sweden* (1991) 13 E.H.R.R. 774 at para.31 (where the state failed to put forward any substantive justification); *Marckx v Belgium* (1979–80) 2 E.H.R.R. 330 at para.32 (where the court rejected a generalised assertion unsupported by evidence).

[410] *Belgian Linguistic Case (No.2)* (1979–80) 1 E.H.R.R. 252 at para.10; *Darby v Sweden* (1991) 13 E.H.R.R. 774 at para.31.

[411] *Belgian Linguistic Case (No.2)* (1979–80) 1 E.H.R.R. 252 at para.9.

[412] *Rasmussen v Denmark* (1985) 7 E.H.R.R. 352.

[413] *Inze v Austria* (1988) 10 E.H.R.R. 394.

[414] [2003] 1 W.L.R. 617 at para.20. A further question was suggested by Stanley Burnton J. in *R. (Carson) v Secretary of State for Work and Pensions* [2002] 3 All E.R. 994: "in my judgment, there is a fifth question to be considered, although it may well be that Brooke LJ intended it to be encapsulated in his question (iii). That question is: is the basis for the different treatment of the complainant as against that of the chosen comparators based on 'any ground such as sex, race, colour, language . . . or other status' within the meaning of Article 14?" (para.51)

    (ii) If so, was there different treatment as respects that right between the complainant on the one hand and the other persons put forward for comparison ('the chosen comparators') on the other?

    (iii) Were the chosen comparators in an analogous situation to the complainant's situation?

    (iv) If so, did the difference in treatment have an objective and reasonable justification: in other words, did it pursue a legitimate aim and did the differential treatment bear a reasonable relationship of proportionality to the aims sought to be achieved?"

However, reservations have been expressed that these questions involve some overlap, and that "A rigidly formulaic approach is to be avoided".[415]

2–141 Certain forms of discrimination are regarded as particularly serious. Very weighty reasons would have to be advanced to justify a difference in treatment on any one of these grounds. The court has identified gender,[416] illegitimacy,[417] nationality,[418] race[419] and sexual orientation[420] as falling within these "suspect categories", and has held that in a serious case, discrimination on certain of these grounds could amount to inhuman and degrading treatment contrary to Art.3.[421] Positive discrimination will not violate Art.14 if it has an objective and reasonable justification, since "certain legal inequalities tend only to correct factual inequalities".[422]

2–142 The principle of equal treatment is enshrined in all comparable constitutional instruments,[423] and has been recognised by the Privy Council as a fundamental principle of constitutional adjudication. In *Matadeen v Pointu*[424] Lord Hoffmann observed that the requirement to treat like cases alike and unlike cases differently was a "general axiom of rational behaviour".

---

[415] *Ghaidan v Godin-Mendoza* [2004] 2 A.C. 557, *per* Baroness Hale at para.134.

[416] *Karlheinz and Schmidt v Germany* (1994) 18 E.H.R.R. 513 at para.24; *Van Raalte v Netherlands* (1997) 24 E.H.R.R. 503 at para.42; *Abdulaziz, Cabales and Balkandali v United Kingdom* (1985) 7 E.H.R.R. 471; *Burghartz v Switzerland* (1994) 18 E.H.R.R. 101; *Schuler-Zraggen v Switzerland* (1993) 16 E.H.R.R. 405.

[417] *Inze v Austria* (1988) 10 E.H.R.R. 394.

[418] *Gaygusuz v Austria* (1997) 23 E.H.R.R. 364. Nationality was the basis of the discrimination found to be unlawful in *R. (A and others) v Secretary of State for the Home Department* [2005] 2 A.C. 68, in which the House of Lords found that legislation allowing non-national suspected international terrorists to be detained without trial, but not nationals, breached Art.14 of the Convention.

[419] *East African Asians Case* (1981) 3 E.H.R.R. 76.

[420] *Sutherland v United Kingdom* (1997) 24 E.H.R.R. CD 22; *Smith and Grady v United Kingdom* (2000) 29 E.H.R.R. 493 at para.121.

[421] *East African Asians Case* (1981) 3 E.H.R.R. 76; *Smith and Grady v United Kingdom* (2000) 29 E.H.R.R. 493 at para.121.

[422] *Belgian Linguistic Case (No.2)* (1979–80) 1 E.H.R.R. 252; See also *DG and DW v United Kingdom* (1986) 49 D.R. 181—tax advantage for married women had "an objective and reasonable justification in the aim of providing positive discrimination" to encourage married women back to work. For an example of the "objective justification" test in action, see the decision of the House of Lords in *R. (A and others) v Secretary of State for the Home Department* [2005] 2 A.C. 68.

[423] See, for example, Canadian Charter of Rights and Freedoms, s.15; New Zealand Bill of Rights Act, ss.19 and 20; South African Constitution, s.8.

[424] [1998] 3 W.L.R. 18 at 26F.

II. Abuse of rights

Article 17 provides that;   **2–143**

"Nothing in this Convention may be interpreted as implying for any State, group or person any right to engage in any activity or perform any act aimed at the destruction of any of the rights and freedoms set forth herein or at their limitation to a greater extent than is provided for in the Convention."

The aim of this provision is to prevent the state, or any individual within its   **2–144** jurisdiction, from invoking a Convention right in order to perform acts which are *aimed* at undermining the Convention rights of others. It is therefore directed towards two very different situations. The first is where the state seeks to rely on a Convention right in order to justify an interference or restriction with another Convention right. In this situation, Art.17 provides that the limitations[425] contained within the articles creating substantive rights are exhaustive: the state cannot derive from one provision of the Convention a justification for implying greater restrictions into another Convention right.

Insofar as it applies to individuals, however, Art.17 has been interpreted restrictively by the Court. In particular, the Court has held that it cannot be relied upon   **2–145** to deprive those who are charged with serious crime of the due process guarantees afforded by Arts 5 to 7 of the Convention.[426] In *Lawless v Ireland (No.3)*,[427] a case involving internment for alleged terrorism, the Court observed that:

" . . . the purpose of Article 17, in so far as it refers to groups or individuals, is to make it impossible for them to derive from the Convention a right to engage in any activity, or perform any act aimed at destroying any of the rights and freedoms set forth in the Convention. Therefore no person may be able to take advantage of the provisions of the Convention to perform acts aimed at destroying the aforesaid rights and freedoms. This provision, which is negative in scope, cannot be construed *a contrario* as depriving a physical person of the fundamental individual rights guaraneed by Articles 5 and 6 of the Convention. In the present case [the applicant] has not relied on the Convention in order to justify or perform acts contrary to the rights and freedoms recognised therein but has complained of having been deprived of the guarantees granted in Articles 5 and 6 of the Convention."

The potential conflict which the court foreshadowed in *Lawless* eventually   **2–146** materialised in *SW and CR v United Kingdom*,[428] a case concerning the retrospective removal of the marital rape exemption by the House of Lords.[429] In a concurring opinion in the Commission, the Irish member argued that the House of Lords' decision would have amounted to a breach of Art.7 were it not for the fact that the applicant had violated his wife's right to respect for her physical and moral integrity, a component of the concept of private life recognised by Art.8. Relying on Art.17 she said that the applicant was:

---

[425] As to implied limitations see para.2–60 above.
[426] Neither can the gravity of an alleged offence ever justify treatment in breach of Art.3: *Ribitsch v Austria* (1995) 21 E.H.R.R. 573.
[427] (1979–80) 1 E.H.R.R. 15 at para.7.
[428] (1996) 21 E.H.R.R. 363. See further, para.10–35 below.
[429] *R. v R.* [1992] A.C. 559.

" . . . indisputably seeking to rely on Article 7 to justify the act of forcing his wife to have sexual intercourse with him . . . an act aimed at destroying her right to bodily integrity. However, Article 17 precludes him from deriving from the Convention justification for his conduct or a finding that the United Kingdom authorities infringed his fundamental rights by punishing such conduct after a fair trial."

The flaw in this reasoning is that the applicant was not in reality relying on Art.7 to assert a right to engage in criminal activity. He was asserting a right to be tried, convicted and sentenced for alleged criminal activity in accordance with the Convention's guarantees. The construction adopted by the Irish member of the Commission would mean that any defendant charged with a serious offence against the person would unable to rely on the due process guarantees of the Convention. The court rightly declined to adopt this analysis.[430]

2–147 Article 17 may nevertheless be relevant in the criminal context where the assertion of the Convention right *in itself* involves an attack on the rights of others. In *Glimmerveen and Haagenback v Netherlands*,[431] for example, the Commission relied on Art.17 to hold that speech which was intended to incite race hatred was outside the protection of Art.10 altogether, because of its potential to undermine the rights of the targeted minority. In subsequent cases, however, the Commission and the court have reached the same conclusion without reference to Art.17, holding simply that prosecutions for race hate speech are necessary in a democratic society within the meaning of Art.10(2).[432]

III. Convention not to prejudice existing rights

2–148 Article 53 provides;

"Nothing in this Convention shall be construed as limiting or derogating from any of the human rights and fundamental freedoms which may be ensured under the laws of any High Contracting Party or under any other agreement to which it is a Party."

2–149 The object of Art.53 is to make it clear that the list of rights and freedoms set out in the Convention is not exhaustive, and that states are free to provide more extensive human rights protection either in their national law, or through other international agreements. This principle is reflected in s.11 of the Human Rights Act 1998. As the Lord Chancellor explained in the course of the debates on the Act:

"Convention rights are, as it were, a floor of rights; and if there are different or superior rights or freedoms conferred by or under any law having effect in the United Kingdom, this is a Bill which only gives and does not take away."[433]

---

[430] Note, however, that the court referred to the "essentially debasing character of rape" in concluding that the decision of the House of Lords was not "at variance with the object and purpose of Article 7". In the court's view, "the abandonment of the unacceptable idea of a husband being immune against prosecution for rape of his wife was in conformity not only with a civilised concept of marriage but also, and above all, with the fundamental objectives of the Convention, the very essence of which is respect for human dignity and human freedom" (para.44/42).

[432] (1979) 18 D.R. 187.

[432] *Kuhnen v Germany* (1988) 56 D.R. 205; *Jersild v Denmark* (1995) 19 E.H.R.R. 1. See para.8–33 below.

[433] November 18, H.L. col.510.

CHAPTER 3

THE HUMAN RIGHTS ACT 1998

A. INTRODUCTION

The Human Rights Act 1998 gives "further effect"[1] in domestic law to the rights **3–01**
and freedoms guaranteed under the European Convention on Human Rights. The
White Paper *Rights Brought Home* explained that the legislation was intended to
enable people in the United Kingdom to enforce their Convention rights directly
in the British courts, without having to incur the expense and endure the delay of
taking a case to the European Court of Human Rights in Strasbourg.[2] Under the
Act it is unlawful for any public authority, including a court or tribunal at any
level, to act in a manner which is incompatible with a Convention right, unless
required to do so by the terms of primary legislation which cannot be interpreted
in a manner which is compatible with the Convention.[3] Convention rights thus
take precedence over rules of common law or equity,[4] and over most (but not all)
subordinate legislation.[5] Primary legislation must be read and given effect in a
manner which is compatible with Convention rights, "so far as it is possible to
do so".[6] If it is impossible to resolve a conflict between a Convention right and
a provision of primary legislation by construction, the higher courts may grant a

---

[1] This terminology is intended to reflect the fact that prior to the Human Rights Act 1998 the courts
of the United Kingdom already had recourse to the Convention in a variety of circumstances: HL
Debs, col.478 (November 18, 1997). For a useful summary of the pre-Act position see Beloff and
Mountfield, "Unconventional Behaviour? Judicial Uses of the European Convention in England and
Wales" [1996] E.H.R.L.R. 467. During the Committee Stage in the House of Lords, Lord Monson
suggested an amendment to add the word "additional" before "Human Rights" to avoid a "propagan-
distic title". He was concerned that "the sort of voter who reads only the tabloids and watches only
commercial television could be forgiven for being persuaded that prior to 1 May 1997 [the date of
the Labour Party won the 1997 general election] the UK was in a state of semi-tyranny compared with
the liberal paradise to be found on the Continent of Europe". Lord Williams of Mostyn, Under-
Secretary of State, Home Office, responded that "if it is an additional human rights Bill, that would
be additionally propagandist". The amendment was withdrawn. See 583 HL Official Report (5th
series) cols 1167–1169 (November 27, 1997).
[2] *Rights Brought Home*, Cmnd.3782, (1997), p.1.
[3] s.6.
[4] See para.3–55 below.
[5] See para.3–59 below.
[6] s.3(1): see para.3–58 below.

formal "declaration of incompatibility",[7] drawing the position to the attention of Parliament, and enabling the relevant Minister to amend the legislation by order if there are "compelling reasons to do so".[8] However, until such time as the incompatible legislation is amended—if at all—it remains valid, operative and enforceable.[9] In this way, the Act enables the courts to afford considerable protection to fundamental rights, while maintaining the principle of Parliamentary sovereignty.[10]

3–02   A person who claims that a public authority has acted (or proposes to act) in a manner which is incompatible with the Act may bring free-standing proceedings under the Act in an appropriate court or tribunal,[11] or may rely on a Convention right in any other legal proceedings being brought,[12] providing he is (or would be) a "victim" of the unlawful act for the purposes of Art.34 of the Convention.[13] Where a court finds that a public authority has acted (or proposes to act) in such a manner, it may grant such relief or remedy or make such order, within its powers, as it considers "just and appropriate".[14] In determining any question which arises under the Act in connection with a Convention right, all courts and tribunals must take into account any relevant judgment of the European Court of Human Rights, opinion of the European Commission of Human Rights, or decision of the Committee of Ministers of the Council of Europe.[15]

B. INTERPRETATION

3–03   Constitutional human rights legislation is "*sui generis*, calling for principles of interpretation of its own, suitable to its character".[16] Therefore, in interpreting any such legislation, the court must pay due respect to the language used and to the traditions and usages which have given meaning to the language.[17] The guiding principle is that an enactment giving effect to fundamental rights has a

---

[7] ss.4 and 5: see para.3–67 below.
[8] s.10: see para.3–71 below.
[9] s.3(2)(b).
[10] Lord Steyn in *obiter dicta* in *Jackson and others v HM Attorney-General* [2006] 1 A.C. 262 at para.102r questioned an unqualified doctrine of Parliamentary supremacy: "The classic account given by Dicey of the doctrine of the supremacy of Parliament, pure and absolute as it was, can now be seen to be out of place in the modern United Kingdom. Nevertheless, the supremacy of Parliament is still the *general* principle of our constitution. It is a construct of the common law. The judges created this principle. If that is so, it is not unthinkable that circumstances could arise where the courts may have to qualify a principle established on a different hypothesis of constitutionalism. In exceptional circumstances involving an attempt to abolish judicial review or the ordinary role of the courts, the Appellate Committee of the House of Lords or a new Supreme Court may have to consider whether this is a constitutional fundamental which even a sovereign Parliament acting at the behest of a complaisant House of Commons cannot abolish."
[11] s.7(1)(a): see para.3–75 below.
[12] s.7(1)(b): see para.3–76 below.
[13] s.7(1), 7(3) and 7(7): see para.3–77 below.
[14] s.8(1): see para.3–81 below.
[15] s.2: see para.3–36 below.
[16] *Ministry of Home Affairs v Fisher* [1980] A.C. 319 at 329C–E PC.
[17] *ibid.* at 329E–F.

"special character" which calls for a broad and purposive approach to construction.[18] It requires:

> "a generous interpretation avoiding what has been called 'the austerity of tabulated legalism', suitable to give to individuals the full measure of the fundamental rights and freedoms referred to".[19]

The court should look to "the substance and reality of what was involved and should not be over-concerned with what are no more than technicalities".[20] The moral and political values underpinning the legislation must be taken into account.[21] Where appropriate, courts should be willing to look to comparative caselaw since "[e]very system of law stands to benefit by an awareness of the answers given by other courts and tribunals to similar problems".[22] However, decisions on the interpretation of constitutional human rights provisions in other jurisdictions are of persuasive rather than binding authority.[23] That being said, the European Court has recently become increasingly receptive to the human rights jurisprudence of non-European countries,[24] as has the House of Lords.[25]

The permissible limit to which such interpretation may be taken was considered **3–04** by the Privy Council in three cases concerning the consitututionality of the mandatory death penalty in the Caribbean, namely *Boyce & Joseph v The Queen, Matthew v The State* and *Watson v The Queen*.[26] The bare majority of the nine-judge Privy Council held that the outer limits of constitutional interpretation had been reached and could not be stretched so as to render unconstitutional the mandatory imposition of the death penalty—this despite the fact that this view put Barbados, for example, in "flagrant breach of its international obligations".[27] The decisions reversed a 3 to 2 majority Privy Council Trinidad decision on precisely the same point handed down just seven months previously in *Roodal v The State*.[28]

---

[18] *Ministry of Transport v Noort* [1992] 3 N.Z.L.R. 260 at 271, 276–278; *R. v DPP ex parte Kebilene and ors* [1999] 3 W.L.R. 972 at 988 HL, *per* Lord Hope.

[19] *ibid.* at 328G–H; *Attorney-General of Gambia v Momodou Jobe* [1984] A.C. 689 at 700H (PC); *Attorney-General of Hong Kong v Lee Kwong-kut* [1993] A.C. 951 at 966B–E (PC); *Vasquez and O'Neil v R.* [1994] 1 W.L.R. 1304 at 1313B *et seq.* (PC); *Flicklinger v Crown Colony of Hong Kong* [1991] 1 N.Z.L.R. 439 at 440.

[20] *Huntley v Attorney-General for Jamaica* [1995] 2 A.C. 1 at 12G–H (PC).

[21] *Matadeen v Pointu and ors* [1999] 1 A.C. 98 *per* Lord Hoffman.

[22] *R. v Khan (Sultan)* [1997] A.C. 558, (HL) *per* Lord Nicholls at 583C. See also *Reynolds v Times Newspapers* [2001] 2 A.C. 127; *R. (Daly) v Secretary of State for the Home Department* [2001] 2 A.C. 532, HL *per* Lord Cooke at para.30 and *R. v Lambert* [2002] 2 A.C. 545, HL at para.40.

[23] *Attorney-General of Hong Kong v Lee Kwong-kut* [1993] A.C. 951 at 966G (PC); *Brown v Stott* [2003] 1 A.C. 681, PC, *per* Lord Hope at p.724.

[24] e.g. *Allan v UK* (2003) 36 E.H.R.R. 12 and *Hurst v UK (No.2)* (2004) 38 E.H.R.R. 40.

[25] See, e.g. the Canadian Supreme Court decisions considered in *R. v A (No.2)* [2002] 1 A.C. 45, para.27; *R. v Lambert* [2002] 2 A.C. 545, paras 34, 45 and 40; *R. v Johnstone* [2003] 1 W.L.R. 1736, para.49; *R. (Pretty) v Director of Public Prosecutions* [2002] 1 A.C. 800, paras 19–23 and para.55; *Reyes v R.* [2002] 2 W.L.R. 1034.

[26] [2005] 1 A.C. 400, 433, 472.

[27] *Boyce & Joseph* at [78].

[28] [2005] 1 A.C. 328. The Privy Council's willingness to re-consider and overrule such a recent decision is in sharp contrast to the approach taken by the House of Lords in *R. v Kansal (No.2)* [2002] A.C. 69.

3–05   According to Lord Hoffmann, the:

> " 'living instrument principle' has its reasons, its logic and its limitations. It is not a magic ingredient which can be stirred into a jurisprudential pot together with 'international obligations', 'generous construction' and other such phrases, sprinkled with a cherished aphorism or two and brewed up into a potion which will make the Constitution mean something which it obviously does not. If that provokes accusations of literalism, originalism and similar heresies, their Lordships must bear them as best they can . . . The Constitution does not confer upon the judges a vague and general power to modernise it."[29]

Lord Bingham, however, in a forceful dissent, emphasised the fundamental importance of the broad and liberal construction to be given to constitutional provisions and their evolving status.[30] He noted that:

> "[recently, the Privy Council] has also brought to its task of constitutional adjudication a broader vision, recognising that a legalistic and over-literal approach to interpretation may be quite inappropriate when seeking to give effect to the rights, values and standards expressed in a constitution as these evolve over time. It is such an approach which Lord Wilberforce stigmatised, in the phrase of Professor de Smith which he made famous, as 'the austerity of tabulated legalism'.[31] It is such an approach also which, in our opinion, vitiates the reasoning of the decision of the majority in this appeal.".[32]

C. Retrospective Application in Criminal Proceedings

3–06   The operative provisions of the Human Rights Act came into force on October 2, 2000.[33] The general rule is that a complainant may not commence proceedings under s.7(1)(a) of the Act,[34] or rely on Convention rights in accordance with s.7(1)(b)[35] unless the act or omission complained of occurred after October 2, 2000.[36] However, the Act has a partially retrospective application which had, in the early years of the Act's operation, some important implications for criminal proceedings. Pursuant to s.22(4), where the proceedings have been brought by or at the instigation of a public authority,[37] and the individual wishes to invoke his Convention rights as part of a defence to those proceedings, he may do so "whenever the act in question took place".

3–07   The effect of s.22(4) was first considered in *R. v DPP ex parte Kebilene and others*.[38] The case concerned a challenge to the compatibility of reverse onus

---

[29] *per* Lord Hoffmann in *Boyce & Joseph* at paras 59, 28.

[30] *Matthew* at paras 42 to 46. It is unusual for a dissenting judge to give a separate opinion in a criminal Privy Council appeal. Lord Nicholls also added an unprecedented second dissenting opinion.

[31] de Smith, *The New Commonwealth and its Constitutions* (1964), p.194; *Minister of Home Affairs v Fisher* [1980] A.C. 319, 328.

[32] *Matthew* at para.34. See further Bailin and Knowles, *Hanged By A Comma?* [2004] J.R. 4.

[33] The Human Rights Act 1998 (Commencement No.2) Order 2000 (S.I. 2000/1851).

[34] See para.3–75 below.

[35] See para.3–76 below.

[36] ss.7(1) and 22(4).

[37] It is open to doubt whether s.22(4) can apply to a private prosecution.

[38] [1999] 3 W.L.R. 175 (DC); [1999] 3 W.L.R. 972 (HL).

provisions under ss.16A and 16B of the Prevention of Terrorism (Temporary Provisions) Act 1989 with the presumption of innocence in Art.6(2) of the Convention. Relying on s.22(4), the applicants sought judicial review of the decision to prosecute,[39] arguing that any conviction in the proceedings was liable to be rendered unlawful retrospectively when the remaining provisions of the Act came into force. In the Divisional Court, Lord Bingham C.J. agreed[40]:

> "If, at the time of the appeal hearing, the central provisions of the 1998 Act had been brought into force, the applicants would on appeal be entitled to rely on sections 7(1)(b) and 22(4) of the Act and the convictions (on the hypothesis of inconsistency between section 16A and the Convention) would in all probability have to be quashed, at some not inconsiderable cost to the public purse."

Before the House of Lords, it was argued on behalf of the DPP that s.22(4) did **3–08** not apply to an appeal against conviction since proceedings in the Court of Appeal (Criminal Division) were instituted by the individual appellant and not by a public authority. The effect of this construction would have been to permit defendants to invoke Convention rights retrospectively at trial, but not on appeal. Lord Steyn rejected this submission. It was, he observed, "an argument of some technicality"[41]:

> "The language of the statute does not compel its adoption and a construction which treats the trial and the appeal as parts of one process is more in keeping with the purpose of the Convention and the Act of 1998."

On this construction, an appellant in proceedings which were initially instituted **3–09** by a public authority could rely on his Convention rights on appeal, notwithstanding that the first instance proceedings were determined prior to October 2, 2000. Thus, in *R. v Lambert and ors*[42] Lord Woolf C.J. accepted that in light of s.22(4) it was incumbent on the Court of Appeal (Criminal Division) to approach the safety of a conviction as if the Act had been in force at the time of the trial.[43] It did not, however, follow that non-compliance with the Convention before the Act came into force would be regarded as a ground for extending time for appealing.

The issue was considered in detail in *R. v Benjafield and ors*.[44] Lord Woolf **3–10** reiterated that it would not usually be appropriate to grant leave to appeal out of time where the grounds of appeal were based on post-trial changes in the law, including the enactment of the Human Rights Act. Where, however, the appeal involved a point of general public interest, it might be appropriate to depart from the normal practice.

---

[39] In giving his consent to the prosecution, the DPP had concluded that there was no incompatibility, and the applicants sought a declaration that his understanding was wrong.

[40] [1999] 3 W.L.R. 175 at 187C.

[41] [1999] 3 W.L.R. 972 at 982.

[42] [2002] Q.B. 1112.

[43] The court had "reservations as to whether Parliament coud have intended such a result" but accepted that it was the correct interpretation where an appellant alleged a breach of the right to a fair trial in Art.6.

[44] [2001] 3 W.L.R. 75. The Court of Appeal's decision was upheld by the House of Lords [2002] 1 A.C. 1099.

3–11 The implications of this approach for cases referred to the Court of Appeal by the Criminal Cases Review Commission (CCRC) under s.9 of the Criminal Appeal Act 1995 were considered in *R. v Kansal*.[45] Rose L.J. pointed out that there was no statutory time limit on a reference back. Combined with the retrospective application of the Human Rights Act, this had two consequences:

"(i) the CCRC, subject to the proper exercise of the discretion conferred by section 9 of the Criminal Appeal Act, can refer to this Court a conviction following a trial whenever it took place; (ii) this Court, once such a reference has been made, has no option, however old the case, but to declare the conviction unsafe if that is the result either of the admission of evidence obtained in breach of Article 6 or of a change in the common law, which is deemed always to have been that which it is authoritatively declared to be."

The appeal in that case was based upon the admission at trial of answers obtained as a result of compulsory questioning in a manner incompatible with the European Court's judgment in *Saunders v United Kingdom*.[46] The appellant's trial had taken place five years before the judgment in *Saunders* was delivered. The court quashed the appellant's conviction "with no enthusiasm whatever", noting that the reference back procedure effectively deprived the court of any discretion to refuse leave where an appeal is based on a subsequent change in the law:

"For over 20 years this Court has adopted a pragmatic approach, confirmed by successive Lord Chief Justices, whereby a refusal to extend time to apply for leave to appeal has filtered out those seeking to take advantage of a change in the law since they were convicted. This, in our judgment, reflects the public interest that there be finality in litigation and it is an approach which has also helped this Court to concentrate its limited resources on determining more meritorious appeals arising from more recent convictions. Subject to the outcome of further consideration of the breadth of the CCRC's discretion, it appears that Parliament, consciously or unconsciously, has completely emasculated that approach. If so, the consequential prospective workload for the CCRC and for this Court is alarming. If this is what Parliament intended, so be it. If not, the sooner the matter is addressed, by Parliament or by the House of Lords on appeal from this Court, the better."

3–12 Rose L.J.'s call for a reconsideration of these difficult issues was answered by the House of Lords in *R. v Lambert*.[47] By a 4 to 1 majority,[48] their Lordships held that neither s.22(4), nor s.6 of the Human Rights Act permitted an appellant to rely on his Convention rights on appeal in order to challenge a decision of a trial court made prior to October 2, 2000, where the judicial decision in question was

---

[45] [2001] 3 W.L.R. 751.

[46] (1997) 23 E.H.R.R. 313.

[47] [2002] 2 A.C. 545. As to the implications of these decisions for the Court of Appeal, see Ch.17.

[48] Lord Steyn dissented on this issue. In his view the House of Lords, as a public authority, was bound to act compatibly with Art.6. For an appellate court to uphold a conviction after October 2, 2000 which had been obtained in breach of Art.6 prior to that date would be to act incompatibly and therefore unlawfully. This did not involve retrospectivity. Section 6 regulated the powers of the court for the present and for the future. There was no legitimate basis for restricting the plain words of the section. The construction of the majority would frustrate the intention of the Act, and would lead to a continuing residue of non-compliant decisions of public authorities kept indefinitely in effect by their own antiquity.

lawful at the time it was made.[49] Lord Hope, however, drew a distinction between challenges directed to the act of the trial court, and challenges directed to decisions of the prosecutor. Despite concurring with the majority on this issue, he held that the Act would nevertheless operate retrospectively on appeal where the appellant relied on an alleged breach of his Convention rights by the prosecuting authority.

In *R. v Kansal (No.2)*,[50] the House of Lords reconsidered its decision in *Lambert*   **3–13** and, although the majority took the view that it had been wrongly decided on retrospectivity, held that there was no compelling reason to depart from its recent decision and accordingly allowed the Crown's appeal. The House was unwilling to overrule *Lambert*, which had been decided just four months previously, and also refused to refer the matter to a seven-judge court. According to Lord Steyn, *Lambert* was wrongly decided because:

> "First, the word 'proceedings' covers both trials and appeals. Section 7(6) does not require a different approach. Indeed section 7(6)(a) and (b) are not mutually exclusive e.g. an appeal to the Divisional Court on a case stated by the Crown falls under both. Secondly, the rationale of section 22(4) was not appreciated in *Lambert*. We now know that 'proceedings brought by or at the instigation of a public authority' in section 22(4) were singled out for special treatment in recognition of the United Kingdom's international obligations under the European Convention for the Protection of Human Rights and Fundamental Freedoms from the date of ratification by the United Kingdom in 1951 or the date of conferment of the right of petition in 1966. This rationale does not support the artificial distinction between criminal trials and appeals. Thirdly, in *Lambert* the majority was strongly influenced by the view that the contrary interpretation would lead to the challenging of old convictions. It is now clear that there is a perfectly effective filter by way of the discretion of the Court of Appeal to refuse to extend time for leave to appeal in such cases. Moreover, a similar filter is applicable to the decision of the Criminal Cases Review Commission."

The compelling reason not to depart from *Lambert* was:

> "Taking into account that we are not dealing with the entire future of the Human Rights Act 1998, but only with a transitional provision on which the House has very recently given a clear-cut decision, I am persuaded that it would be wrong now to depart from the ratio decidendi of *Lambert*."[51]

Lord Hope's dissenting view[52] that it was better to face up to the mistake in   **3–14** *Lambert* and correct it as soon as possible and that, in the wider public interest, "correction is more desirable than consistency", did not prevail. The House of

---

[49] The case concerned a reverse onus clause in the Misuse of Drugs Act 1971 which, construed according to conventional cannons of construction, was held to be incompatible with the presumption of innocence in Art.6(2). The majority of the House of Lords held that when read with the benefit of the interpretative obligation in s.3, the relevant provision should, henceforth, be construed as imposing a purely evidential burden on the accused. The appellant could not, however, take the benefit of this ruling since s.22(4) did not apply to a challenge brought on appeal to a decision of a court or tribunal (in this case, the decision to direct the jury on the appropriate burden of proof) made before ss.3 and 6 of the Act came into force.

[50] [2002] 2 A.C. 69.

[51] paras 26 to 7.

[52] At paras 51 and 53.

Lords' reluctance to overrule such a recent decision is in sharp contrast to the approach taken by the nine-judge Privy Council in *Boyce & Joseph v The Queen*; *Matthew v The State* and *Watson v The Queen*[53] overruling a 3 to 2 majority decision on exactly the same point determined by the Privy Council seven months previously: *Roodal v The State*.[54]

3–15   The position under s.22 is now finally settled: the Human Rights Act does not apply to appeals where the trial took place prior to October 2, 2000. Thus, for example, the *Saunders* defendants' convictions remained undisturbed: *R. v Lyons*.[55]

3–16   Similarly, in *Re McKerr*[56] the House of Lords held that the procedural duties under Art.2 imposed by the Human Rights Act on the State to investigate deaths did not apply when the deaths occurred before October 2, 2000. The fact that the UK was under a continuing international obligation to provide an effective investigation was immaterial. The decision is somewhat difficult to reconcile with the Strasbourg decision in *Cyprus v Turkey*.[57] In *Commissioner of Police for the Metropolis v Hurst*[58] the problem presented itself differently: although the death occurred *prior* to the coming into force of the Act, the inquest came *after*, having been adjourned pending criminal proceedings in which the killer of the claimant's son had been convicted of manslaughter. The Court of Appeal held that in deciding whether there was "sufficient cause" for the Coroner to exercise his discretion to re-open the inquest under s.16(3) of the Coroners Act 1988, firstly, the Convention rights referred to in s.3 Human Rights Act were the UK's international obligations as opposed to obligations created by s.6[59] and secondly, as a result thereof, s.16(3) had to be read and given effect in a way which was compatible with the UK's international obligations,[60] even if those obligations were not directly enforceable because of the non-retrospective effect of the Human Rights Act. That required a resumption of the inquest, which was to be endowed with all the characteristics of an effective investigation identified in *R. (Middleton) v W. Somerset Coroner*.[61] Absent the discretionary element in s.16(3) of the Coroners Act 1988, however, the outcome would have been determined by *Kansal (No.2)*.

3–16A   The decision of the Court of Appeal was reversed by the House of Lords.[62] Following *McKerr*, the House held (Baroness Hale and Lord Mance dissenting in

---

[53] [2005 1 A.C. 400, 433, 472.

[54] [2005] 1 A.C. 328. See para.3–03a *et seq.* above.

[55] [2003] 1 A.C. 976, HL (the *Lyons* defendants having intervened in *Kansal (No.2)*) and *Lyons v UK* 37 E.H.R.R. CD 183. See also *R. v Daniel* [2003] 1 Cr.App.R. 6 and *R. v Benjafield* [2002] 1 A.C. 1099.

[56] [2004] 1 W.L.R. 807 following the decision in *McKerr v UK* (2001) 34 E.H.R.R. 553 that the investigations had breached Art.2.

[57] (2002) 35 E.H.R.R. 30. As this decision was not cited in *McKerr*, it has been argued that *McKerr* is wrongly decided: Clayton et al. *Key HRA Cases in the Last 12 Months* [2004] E.H.R.L.R. 614.

[58] [2005] EWCA Civ 890.

[59] Following the approach in *Ghaidan v Godin-Mendoza* (discussed below).

[60] Reflecting the position pre-HRA: e.g. *R. v Secretary of State for the Home Department, ex p Brind* [1991] 1 A.C. 696, HL, 748A–F.

[61] [2004] 2 A.C. 182.

[62] [2007] 2 W.L.R. 726.

part) that the right to an investigation was an ancillary part of the right to life under Art.2, and therefore only arose in respect of deaths occurring after October 2, 2000. Their Lordships did not consider that the relevant provision of the Coroners Act contained a relevant ambiguity, and in any event it could not be supposed that Parliament would have wanted the *Middleton* approach to be adopted for all future inquests, regardless of the date of the death. With respect to the coroner, their Lordships considered that it was impossible to say that the unincorporated international obligation was so obviously material to his decision whether or not to resume the inquest that he was required to give effect to it.

A further aspect of non-retrospectivity of the Act is that conduct which was   **3–17** lawful at the time it took place cannot be made unlawful by the operation of the Act.[63]

D. THE CONVENTION RIGHTS

I. The rights incorporated

Section 1(1) of the Act identifies the rights to which the Act gives domestic   **3–18** effect,[64] namely the right to life (Art.2); the prohibition of torture (Art.3); the prohibition of slavery and forced labour (Art.4); the right to liberty and security (Art.5); the right to a fair trial (Art.6); the principle of no punishment without law (Art.7); the right to respect for private and family life (Art.8); the right to freedom of thought, conscience and religion (Art.9); the right to freedom of expression (Art.10); the right to freedom of assembly and association (Art.11); the right to marry and found a family (Art.12); the prohibition of discrimination (Art.14); the protection of property (Art.1 of Protocol 1); the right to education (Art.2 of Protocol 1); the right to free elections (Art.3 of Protocol 1); and the abolition of the death penalty in peacetime (Arts 1 and 2 of Protocol 6). The text of these rights is set out in Sch.1 to the Act.

II. The omission of Articles 1 and 13

Articles 1 and 13 of the Convention are not included in the list of scheduled   **3–19** rights. Article 1 enshrines the obligation on contracting states to "secure to everyone within their jurisdiction" the rights and freedoms set out in the Convention. The Government's reason for omitting Art.1 was explained by the Lord Chancellor during debates. It was, he said, unnecessary for this obligation to be specifically incorporated because the Human Rights Act itself "gives effect to

---

[63] *Wainwright v Home Office* [2002] Q.B. 1334, CA; [2004] 2 A.C. 406, HL.
[64] The rights incorporated are those set out in Sch.1: see s.1(3).

Article 1 by securing to people in the United Kingdom the rights and freedoms of the Convention".[65]

3–20   Domestic and ECHR case law makes clear that the Act does not only apply to "people in the United Kingdom" but has extra-territorial effect in some circumstances. In the most detailed domestic analysis of the principles to date, the Court of Appeal in *R. (Al-Skeini) v Secretary of State for Defence*[66] held that the Human Rights Act was in principle capable of having extra-territorial effect where a person falls within the "jurisdiction" of the UK under the Convention. It held that the Divisional Court had been wrong to limit the Convention concept of jurisdiction to "quasi-territorial" premises such as a British-run prison in Iraq. The claimants were seeking an Arts 2 and 3 compliant inquiry into civilian deaths in Iraq and the court held that "jurisdiction" could, for example, include a person under arrest at an Iraqi hotel but was not broad enough to include persons who were at liberty and not yet in the control of British forces. In *R. (Abbasi) v Secretary of State for Foreign & Commonwealth Affairs*[67] the Court of Appeal held that, where a state enjoys extra-territorial jurisdiction over an individual and acts in the exercise of that jurisdiction, that individual will be deemed to be within the jurisdiction for the purposes of Art.1. However, in *R. (Quark Fishing Ltd) v Secretary of State for Foreign & Commonwealth Affairs (No.2)*[68] the House of Lords held that s.7 Human Rights Act damages cannot lie for unlawful deprivation of a valuable fishing licence where Protocol 1 had not been formally extended (under Art.56) to the relevant British Overseas Territory. In *Ullah* and *Razgar*[69] the House of Lords applied *Soering v UK*[70] in the immigration context, holding that qualified, non-Art.3 rights can also be violated by conditions in a receiving state (outside the UK) to which a person was sent by the UK following immigration control—although causation was the guiding principle rather than extra-territoriality. In *R. (Farrakhan) v Secretary of State for the Home Department*[71] it was conceded by the Respondent that the applicant could rely on his Convention rights even though he was outside the jurisdiction at the time of his application. In *R. (B) v Secretary of State for the Foreign and Commonwealth Office*[72] the Court of Appeal held that the Human Rights Act applies to UK consulates abroad. In *In re B (A Child) (Care Proceedings: Diplomatic Immunity)*[73] Dame Butler-Sloss raised the possibility that UK jurisdiction under the Human Rights Act could overlap with the extra-territorial jurisdiction of another state over its diplomatic agents. In general, human rights law equates territory

---

[65] HL Debs, col.475 (November 18, 1998). See also Lord Lester of Herne Hill at *Hansard* HL 18 November 1997, col.466.
[66] [2006] 3 W.L.R. 508.
[67] [2003] U.K.H.R.R. 76 at para.76.
[68] [2006] 1 A.C. 529.
[69] *R. (Ullah) v Special Adjudicator; R. (Razgar) v Secretary of State (No.2)* [2004] 2 A.C. 323, 368 (respec.). See further Ward *Ullah and HRA Territoriality* [2003] J.R. 170.
[70] (1989) 11 E.H.R.R. 439 at para.91: applied in later cases such as *Cruz Varas v Sweden* (1991) 14 E.H.R.R. 1 para.69 and *Vlivarajah v UK* (1991) 14 E.H.R.R. 248 para.103 and *Tomic v UK* (Application No.17837/03 October 14, 2003).
[71] [2002] Q.B. 1391.
[72] [2005] Q.B. 643 at para.66.
[73] [2003] Fam. 16.

with the exercise of jurisdiction. However, in *R. v Immigration Officer at Prague Airport* ex p *European Roma Rights Centre*[74] Lord Bingham had the "very greatest doubt" that UK immigration officers at Prague airport "pre-clearing" Czech nationals who might wish to claim asylum in the UK were exercising jurisdiction over such individuals, even though the officers were formally treated as UK consular officials.

The European Court has also considered the territoriality of the Convention in the **3–21** important decision of *Bankovic v Belgium*[75] and held that, as a general rule, the notion of "jurisdiction" within the meaning of Art.1 must reflect the position under public international law. It is primarily territorial, but is presumed to be exercised throughout the State's territory. Territorial jurisdiction is not restricted to the national territory of the High Contracting Parties but extends to any area which, at the time of the alleged violation, is under the "overall control" of the contracting State concerned (*Loizidou v Turkey*[76]), including occupied territories (*Cyprus v Turkey*[77]) which lie outside Europe (*Issa v Turkey*[78]).

Article 1's sister provision Art.13, which guarantees the right to an effective **3–22** remedy before a national authority for any arguable violation of a Convention right, was omitted for essentially the same reason, namely that ss.7 to 9 were intended to lay down an appropriate remedial structure for giving effect to the Convention rights as defined by s.1(1).[79] This does not mean, however, that Arts 1 and 13 are irrelevant to the national courts' functions under the Human Rights Act. On the contrary, since the Human Rights Act is intended to give effect to Arts 1 and 13, national courts and tribunals are entitled to take these provisions into account when exercising the discretionary power to grant "just and appropriate" remedies under s.8 of the Act.[80] Moreover the Government made it clear on a number of occasions during the course of the Parliamentary debates that the obligation in s.2(1) of the Act (which requires national courts to take account of relevant Convention jurisprudence) was intended to include jurisprudence under

---

[74] [2005] 2 A.C. 1 at para.21: Lord Bingham thought the point had been assumed in *R. (B) v Secretary of State for the Foreign and Commonwealth Office* (above).

[75] (2001) 11 B.H.R.C. 435 at paras 59 to 67. See also *Gentilhomme and Others v France*, Applications 48205/99, 48207/99 and 48209/99 (14 May 2002) at para.20.

[76] March 23, 1995, Series A no.310. at paras 52 to 56.

[77] Application 25781/94, ECHR-2001 IV. See also, *Assanidze v Georgia* Application No.71503/01, April 8, 2004.

[78] Application No.31821/96 (November 16, 2004)—at para.74: Turkish military operations in northern Iraq potentially within Convention's jurisdiction.

[79] As the Lord Chancellor explained during debates, the Human Rights Act "gives effect to Art.13 by establishing a scheme under which Convention rights can be raised before our domestic courts": HL Debs, col.475 (November 18, 1997). See now *Montgomery v HM Advocate* [2003] 1 A.C. 641, PC; *Brown v Stott* [2003] 1 A.C. 681, PC; *R. (K) v Camden and Islington Health Authority* [2002] Q.B. 198, CA *per* Sedley L.J. at para.54. *Cf. Re S (Minors) (Care Order: Implementation of Care Plan)* [2002] 2 A.C. 291, HL *per* Lord Nicholls at paras 56, 59 to 60.

[80] It is a long established principle of interpretation that particular weight will be attached to Convention caselaw when the court is considering legislation which has been enacted in order to bring domestic law into line with the requirements of the Convention: *R. v Secretary of State for the Home Department ex parte Norney* (1995) 7 Admin.L.R. 861.

Art.13.[81] Article 13 has not been considered in any detail by the criminal courts. In *R. (D) v Central Criminal Court*,[82] a case engaging Art.2, the exceptions to s.29(3) of the Supreme Court Act 1981 (prohibiting judicial review on "matters relating to trial on indictment") identified in *Kebilene* were held to be sufficiently wide to permit judicial review of the decision to continue prosecution. Had it been otherwise, appeal following conviction or acquittal would not have provided an effective remedy in an Art.2 case. Nor would a declaration of incompatibility. Nevertheless, Art.13 does not create a general right to judicial review of matters relating to trial on indictment. Failure to award costs to successful defendants has raised Art.13 issues, which are discussed at 3–93 below.[83] In *Hobbs v UK*[84] the ECtHR concluded that a declaration of incompatibility was not an effective remedy within meaning of Art.13.

III. The relevance of Articles 16 to 18

3–23 Section 1(1) provides that the rights incorporated by the Act are to be read in conjunction with Arts 16 to 18 of the Convention. Article 16 relates to restrictions on the political activity of aliens. Article 17 provides that the rights contained in the Convention are not to be interpreted as implying for any state, group or person the right to engage in activity which is aimed at the destruction of the Convention rights of others, or their limitation to a greater extent than is provided for in the Convention.[85] The Commission has held, in reliance on Art.17, that extreme racist speech is outside the protection of Art.10 because of its potential to undermine public order and the rights of the targeted minority.[86] Thus a defence to the crime of inciting racial hatred, for example, based on Art.10 is unsustainable. Accordingly, the European Court held the application in

---

[81] During the Committee stage in the House of Commons, the Home Secretary acknowledged that "[T]he courts must take account of the large body of Convention jurisprudence when considering remedies . . . Obviously, in doing so, they are bound to take judicial notice of Art.13, without being specifically bound by it": HC Debs, col.981 (May 20, 1998). Similarly, the Lord Chancellor observed that "[T]he courts may have regard to Article 13. In particular, they may wish to do so when considering the very ample provisions of [section] 8(1).": HL Debs, col.477 (November 18, 1997). He went on to say: "One always has in mind *Pepper v Hart* when one is asked questions of that kind" (*ibid.*). See *Pepper v Hart* [1993] A.C. 593.

[82] *R. (D) v Central Criminal Court and another* [2004] 1 Cr.App.R. 41—Scott Baker L.J. called for Parliamentary consideration of an amendment to s.29(3) at para.35 of the judgment. See, most recently, *R. (Snelgrove) v Woolwich Crown Court* [2005] 1 W.L.R. 3223 on the ambit of s.29(3).

[83] cf. *R. v Canterbury Crown Court ex p Regentford* (*The Times* February 6, 2001) at paras 16 to 22) and *R. (Shields) v Liverpool Crown Court* [2001] U.K.H.R.R. 610, EWHC Admin. 90 DC at paras 20, 33 to 34, 53 to 58

[84] Application No.63684/00 (18.6.02). In *Dodds v UK* (App.59314/00 (8.4.03)) the ECtHR declined to re-visit or reverse *Hobbs* despite the UK's invitation. See also *Walker v UK* (Application No.37212/02, 16.3.04); *Pearson v UK* (Application No.8374/03, 27.4.04); *B&L v UK* (Application No.36936/02 29.6.04) and *PM v UK* (Application No.6638/02 19.7.05).

[85] See para.2–140 above. *Lawless v Ireland* (1961) 1 E.H.R.R. 1 at para.28.

[86] *Kühnen v Germany* 56 D.R. 205; *Glimmerveen and Haagenback v Netherlands* 18 D.R. 187 (1979); *Lehideux and Isorni v France* (1998) 30 E.H.R.R. 665 at paras 37–8 and 58. See also Cooper and Williams *Hate Speech, Holocaust Denial and International Human Rights Law* [1999] E.H.R.L.R. 593.

Norwood v UK[87] to be inadmissible. In *Norwood v DPP*[88] the applicant's conviction for the religiously-aggravated version of the offence of causing harassment, alarm or distress was upheld. He had displayed a poster showing the World Trade Centre in flames on "9/11" with the words "Islam out of Britain—Protect the British people". The Court held that Art.10 was to be read together with Art.17, whose purpose was "to prevent individuals or groups with totalitarian aims from exploiting in their own interests the principles enunciated in the Convention". The attack on all Muslims that the poster represented "linked the group as a whole with a grave act of terrorism" and was incompatible with the fundamental values of "tolerance social peace and non-discrimination" inherent in the Convention. In *Jersild v Denmark*[89] the journalist applicant was convicted of aiding and abetting the dissemination of racial insults by producing a documentary which included an interview with youths who expressed extreme racist views. The programme was broadcast without comment or disclaimer but consisted of good faith reporting and was not intended to promote racist attitudes but to expose them. The youths were convicted of making racist statements and the journalist of aiding and abetting them. The Court accepted unreservedly that the convictions of the youths were justified and that their speech was outside the protection of Art.10 but held that the conviction of the journalist was disproportionate to the protection of the rights of the targeted minorities. News reports based on interviews constituted one of the most important means by which the press was able to perform its "vital role as public watchdog". The punishment of a journalist for disseminating the statements of others in an interview would seriously hamper press freedom and "should not be envisaged unless there are particularly strong reasons for doing so".

Article 18 provides that the limitations permitted under the Convention to the rights guaranteed, may not be applied for any purpose other than the purpose for which they were prescribed.[90]

IV. Derogations

The Convention rights take effect in domestic law subject to any "designated derogation".[91] Article 15 of the Convention permits contracting states to derogate from their obligations under the Convention in times of war or "other public emergency threatening the life of the nation"; providing the derogation is "strictly required by the exigencies of the situation",[92] and is consistent with the state's other obligations under international law.[93] The United Kingdom's designated derogation to Art.5(3) was withdrawn by the Human Rights Act 1998

3–24

---

[87] (2005) 40 E.H.R.R. 11.

[88] [2003] Crim. L.R. 888. See also *DPP v Hammond* [2004] Crim. L.R. 851, DC. *cf. Percy v DPP* 166 J.P. 93 DC.

[89] 19 E.H.R.R. 1 at para.31. As to holocaust denial offences see *Lehideux and Isorni v France* 30 E.H.R.R. 665; *Witzsch v Germany* (unreported, 20.4.99) See also Recommendation No.20 of the Committee of Ministers to Member States on "Hate Speech" (adopted October 30, 1997) which reflects the ECHR case-law on Arts 10 and 17 of the Convention in Principle 4.

[90] See *Refah Partisi (The Welfare Party) v Turkey* (2003) 37 E.H.R.R. 1 at para.99 and 137.

[91] s.1(2).

[92] Art.15(1).

[93] Art.15(1). Note however that no derogation is permitted from Art.2 (save in respect of deaths resulting from lawful acts of war), Art.3, Art.4(1) or Art.7: Art.15(2).

(Amendment) Order 2001 which repealed parts of ss.14 and 16 and the whole of Pt I of Sch.3.[94] Under the Human Rights Act 1998, the Secretary of State may, by order, designate any future derogation (or proposed derogation[95]) from the Convention or its protocols.[96] Such an order must be approved by affirmative resolution of both Houses of Parliament within a period of 40 days, failing which it will cease to have effect.[97] Once approved a designation order remains in effect for a period of five years after it was made[98] unless, prior to its expiry, it is extended by order of the Secretary of State.[99] This power was exercised following 9/11 by making the Human Rights Act 1998 (Amendment No.2) Order 2001[100] under s.14. The Order amended Sch.3, setting out the terms of the derogation by the United Kingdom from Art.5(1), made in order to accommodate the controversial extended powers of detention (without trial) of foreign nationals in Pt IV of the Anti-Terrorism, Crime and Security Act 2001. As to the terms of the derogation itself, see the Human Rights Act 1998 (Designated Derogation) Order 2001.[101]

3–25 Under Pt IV, foreign (i.e. non-UK) nationals who could not be removed from the UK (because they would risk facing Art.3 treatment in the receiving country) and were believed to represent a national security risk and were suspected of links with terrorism were detained by order of the Home Secretary. Since no deportation was pending or foreseeable, detention under Pt IV would breach Art.5(1)(f)—hence the need for a derogation. An appeal from the Home Secretary's decision to detain lay to the Special Immigration Appeals Commission (SIAC), which sits without a jury. The standard of proof was "reasonable suspicion", which did not require any belief by the Minister that the allegation was true. Sensitive evidence was heard in a closed session, from which the detainee and his lawyers were excluded. A "special advocate" who represented the detainee's interests (but not the detainee) could make submissions on the closed evidence, but could not then communicate with the detainee. Specific allegations were not required; a general link to terrorism would suffice. Consequently, the detainee could not know much of the case against him. He was not interviewed about the allegations.

---

[94] S.I. 2001/1216. The derogation was entered in response to the judgment in *Brogan v United Kingdom* (1989) 11 E.H.R.R. 117 where the court held that detention for four days and six hours under the Prevention of Terrorism (Temporary Provisions) Act 1984 was incompatible with the requirement that a detained person should be brought promptly before a judge or judicial officer. The derogation preserved the power of the Secretary of State to extend the period of detention of persons suspected of terrorism in connection with Northern Ireland for a total of up to seven days. The derogation was subsequently held to be compatible with Art.15: *Brannigan and McBride v United Kingdom* (1994) 17 E.H.R.R. 539. The derogation was withdrawn since judicial control over the detention was introduced by Sch.8 to the Terrorism Act 2000 (in turn amended by s.306 of the Criminal Justice Act 2003).

[95] s.14(6).

[96] s.14(1)(b).

[97] s.16 (3) and (5). Note, however, that the lapsing of a designation order under s.16(3) does not affect anything done in reliance on the order during the interim period: s.16(4)(a). Nor does it prevent the Secretary of State from making a fresh designation order: s.16(4)(b).

[98] s.16(1)(b).

[99] s.16(2).

[100] S.I. 2001/4032.

[101] S.I. 2001/3644.

There was no equivalent detention procedure for those UK citizens whom the **3–26** Government accepted would be equally or more dangerous. Some detainees were incarcerated, in part, for their association with UK nationals who remained at liberty. Detention was used as an alternative to prosecution if, for example, the only evidence would be inadmissible in a criminal trial (because of the inadmissibility of intercept evidence); or if the evidence would require expert evaluation and was therefore incapable of meeting a criminal standard of proof (e.g. informant hearsay); or merely because a jury had previously failed to convict. In some cases, the Crown Prosecution Service had not been asked to consider whether a prosecution was possible

The derogation was quashed by an 8–1 majority of the House of Lords in *A and* **3–27** *others v Secretary of State for the Home Department.*[102] All of their Lordships except Lord Hoffmann considered that the SIAC (which had seen all the material available to the Government[103]) was entitled to reach the conclusion that there was a "public emergency" threatening the life of nation within the meaning of Art.15. However, seven of their Lordships held that the Pt IV measures were not "strictly required by the exigencies of the situation" as required by Art.15, primarily because the Government had not demonstrated that the steps (not involving detention) which were being taken in relation to UK nationals who represented a similar threat would not suffice to counter the threat from foreign nationals.[104] Since the Government had not derogated from Art.14, it remained in full force despite the derogation. Seven of their Lordships also held that Pt IV unjustifiably discriminated against the appellants in violation of Art.14 on the basis of their immigration status, which it was accepted, fell within "other status" under Art.14.[105] Lord Bingham also found a violation of the free-standing non-discrimination requirement in Art.26 of the ICCPR, which was part of the UK's international obligations under Art.15. The submissions that the Convention and international law sanctions the differential treatment, including detention, of aliens as compared with nationals in times of war or public emergency were rejected.[106] Accordingly, the Derogation Order was quashed, as it failed to meet the requirements of Art.15, and a declaration of incompatibility was made in respect of s.23 of the 2001 Act.

Lord Hoffmann, when rejecting the submission that there was a public emer- **3–28** gency, said: "Whether we would survive Hitler hung in the balance but there is no doubt that we shall survive Al-Qaeda". In his view, "[t]he real threat to the life of the nation, in the sense of a people living in accordance with its traditional laws and political values, comes not from terrorism but from laws such as these" and noted that "[s]omeone who has never committed any offence and has no intention of doing anything wrong maybe reasonably suspected of being a [terrorist] supporter on the basis of some heated remarks overheard in the pub". Lord Scott thought the scheme " . . . the stuff of nightmares, associated whether

---

[102] [2005] 2 A.C. 68.
[103] This included "closed" material not shown to the Appellants. The Attorney General was invited to show the "closed" material to the House but expressly declined to do so: para.27.
[104] paras 43–4, 85, 121–33, 155, 167, 188–9, 231 and 240.
[105] paras 45–68, 69–70, 78, 84, 105, 134–138, 157–9, 228, 232–8, 240.
[106] paras 55–70.

accurately or inaccurately with France before and during the Revolution, with Soviet Russia in the Stalinist era and now associated . . . with the United Kingdom". Lord Nicholls added that "detention without trial is anathema in any country which observes the rule of law". Lord Bingham emphasised the primacy of the courts as arbiters of fundamental human rights, a role which the Government had specifically tasked them to fulfil, and remarked that "[the Attorney General] is wrong to stigmatise judicial decision-making as in some way undemocratic".[107]

3–29   Whether SIAC complied with the civil and/or criminal requirements of Art.6 was not decided. The House of Lords subsequently unanimously ruled in *A and others v Secretary of State for the Home Department*[108] that evidence obtained by torture by non-UK agents was not admissible in SIAC proceedings, but was divided on the appropriate test to be applied in determining whether evidence was in fact obtained by torture. The submission that Pt IV detention was a "three-walled prison", since detainees were free to leave to any country that would have them, and therefore went no farther than was "strictly required", was rejected.[109]

3–30   In response to the decision on the derogation in *A and others v Secretary of State for the Home Department*, the Government did not seek to renew Pt IV of the 2001 Act but instead introduced the Prevention of Terrorism Act 2005, which applies to both foreign nationals and British citizens alike. It provides for two types of "control orders". "Derogating control orders" can require a person to remain under house arrest and would require a formal derogation from Art.5. At the time of writing, however, the Government's position was that there were no individuals (including those previously detained under Pt IV of the 2001 Act) for whom deprivation of liberty was strictly required, and therefore a formal Derogation Order was not made at the time the Bill passed through Parliament. It is questionable as a matter of Convention law whether creating a domestic legal framework which provides in advance for "derogating control orders" can itself be done without derogating from the Convention at the time of creating the framework. If so, this would require the Government to demonstrate the necessity for having such a framework at the level of threat which currently exists. The 2005 Act requires the Home Secretary to apply to a court[110] for a derogating control order, in contrast to the powers of detention without any prior judicial involvement in Pt IV of the 2001 Act. The Joint Committee on Human Rights was nevertheless concerned that the making of a derogating control order against an individual via the SIAC court model (involving special advocates and closed evidence) would breach the "lawful" requirements of Art.5.[111] It also questioned whether the imposition of such orders involved the determination of a criminal

---

[107] paras 96–7, 87, 155, 74 and 42 resp.
[108] [2006] 2 A.C. 221.
[109] paras 81, 123, 230.
[110] There is initially an *ex parte* hearing to determine if there is a *prima facie* case for imposition of a control order and if so an *inter partes* hearing (using special advocates in closed session).
[111] JCHR 10th report of 2004–5 on Prevention of Terrorism Bill (HL 68 HC 334) at [10].

charge and therefore that the SIAC model would violate the additional safeguards of Art.6.[112] The validity of any future derogation will also be open to challenge, whatever the prevailing conditions, particularly when evidence of intercepted communications remains inadmissible in criminal trials.

The Government has, however, sought to make a number of "non-derogating   **3–31**
control orders", which have no legislative limit on the restrictions they can impose, and a standard of proof which requires only "reasonable grounds to suspect". In *Secretary of State for the Home Department v MB*[113] the Home Secretary imposed a control order on a British citizen said to be an Islamic extremist involved in terrorist activities who intended to travel to Iraq to fight against British and coalition forces. No further information was provided to MB, although a "closed" statement was made available to the court. The terms of the control order required MB to reside at a specific address, surrender his passport and not leave the United Kingdom. Sullivan J. ordered that the control order remain in force, but issued a declaration of incompatibility under s.4(2) of the Human Rights Act on the basis that a hearing under s.3(10) of the 2005 Act was, contrary to Art.6 of the Convention, "conspicuously unfair", and provided only a "thin veneer of legality" to what was in reality "executive decision-making, untrammelled by any prospect of effective judicial supervision". The Court of Appeal set aside the declaration of incompatibility, finding that Sullivan J. was incorrect to conclude that s.3 only permitted an "historical" review of the Home Secretary's decision, without reference to new evidence that may have come to light since the initial decision. The Court of Appeal found that s.3 should be "read down" under s.3 of the Human Rights Act to so as to require a con-temporaneous review taking into account all evidence available to the court at the time of the hearing.

The second case to come before Sullivan J. under s.3(10), *Secretary of State for the Home Department v JJ and others*, concerned considerably more onerous control orders imposed on six individuals, including house curfews of 18 hours per day, geographical limitations on movements in the remaining six hours, electronic tagging, and severe restrictions in several other areas including visitors, pre-arranged meetings, use of communications equipment and bank accounts.[114] The matter was heard in the Administrative Court before the Court of Appeal's decision in *MB*. Sullivan J. quashed all six orders, finding that they imposed conditions which were the "antithesis of liberty" as protected under Art.5 of the Convention.[115] The Home Secretary had no power to make such orders, which could only be imposed following a designated derogation under s.14 of the Human Rights Act. The decision was upheld by the Court of Appeal.

---

[112] JCHR Preliminary report on the Prevention of Terrorism Bill (9th report of 2004–5): HL 61, HC 389. There are also Convention compatibility issues concerning the standard of proof ("balance of probabilities" for derogating control orders, "reasonable suspicion" for non-derogating control orders) for both types of control orders. For Ben Emmerson Q.C.'s published opinion on the Bill, see *http://www.statewatch.org/news/2005/feb/opinion-on-pta-bill.pdf*

[113] [2006] 3 W.L.R. 839.

[114] [2006] 3 W.L.R. 866.

[115] On the nature and extent of the Article 5 breach see para.5–02 below.

At the time of writing the decisions in *JJ* and *MB* are on appeal to the House of Lords.[116]

3-32   New emergency powers were also created under the Civil Contingencies Act 2004 in response to 9/11. Emergency regulations made under the Act, although potentially far-reaching, cannot amend the Human Rights Act.[117] Any new criminal offences created under the 2004 Act, for failing to comply with emergency regulations, are only triable using existing criminal procedures.[118]

V. Reservations

3-33   The Convention rights also take effect subject to any "designated reservation".[119] Article 57 of the Convention permits a state to enter a reservation at the time of signature or ratification of the Convention or a protocol, where a particular provision in its domestic law is considered to be incompatible with the obligations it is undertaking. Reservations must be specific, and must contain a brief statement of the law to which they relate.[120] They must be narrowly construed and temporary in nature.[121] They cannot be inconsistent with the object and purpose of the Convention, namely "an instrument for the protection of individual human beings [which] requires that its provisions be interpreted and applied so as to make its safeguards practical and effective".[122] The United Kingdom has entered a reservation to Art.2 of Protocol 1 (the right of parents to ensure that their children are educated in conformity with their own religious and

---

[116] At the time of going to press, there had recently been three further control orders decisions. In *Secretary of State for the Home Department v AF* [2007] EWHC 651 (Admin), Ouseley J. held that, while the case was "finely balanced", the restrictions imposed on the applicant by the control order (he was prevented from leaving his flat for more than 10 hours a day and could only visit a certain geographical area when out, had to wear an electronic tag, and required prior identification and approval for visitors to his flat) amounted to deprivation of liberty under Art.5, rendering the control order a nullity. Ouseley J. did hold, however, following *MB* in the Court of Appeal, that AF had had a fair hearing despite that fact that the case against him was, essentially, entirely undisclosed to him. The control orders at issue in *Secretary of State for the Home Department v E* [2007] EWHC 233 (Admin) and *Secretary of State for the Home Department v Abu Rideh* [2007] EWHC 804 were also quashed on the basis that they breached Art.5. Each of these three decisions also contains discussion of the Convention compliance of various aspects of the process by which control orders are made and reviewed.

[117] s.23(5)(b) Civil Contingencies Act 2004.

[118] ss.22(3) and 23(4).

[119] s.1(2).

[120] Art.57(1) and (2).

[121] On the permissible width and precision of reservations, see Art.64 of the ECHR. On the duration of reservations, see Ratification of Protocols and Withdrawal of Reservations and Derogations made in respect of the ECHR Recommendation 1671 (2004) Principle 7. "Such reservations are permitted to the extent that legislation in force at the time in the territory of the Contracting Party is not in conformity with a particular provision of the Convention. They should not therefore be of a permanent nature and should be confined to the period required to bring the legislation in question into conformity with the Convention".

[122] *Loizidou v Turkey* (1995) 20 E.H.R.R. 99 at para.72; *Marckx v Belgium* 2 E.H.R.R. 330, at para.31; *Airey v Ireland*, ante, at para.24; *Artico v Italy* 3 E.H.R.R. 1 at para.33; *Soering v UK* 11 E.H.R.R. 439, at para.87. Thus, the conditions imposed for the exercise of a Convention right must not impair its very existence or deprive it of its effectiveness (*Heaney and McGuinness v Ireland* (2001) 33 E.H.R.R. 12). See also Art.19(3) Vienna Convention on the Law of Treaties *cf.* HRC General Comment CCPR/C/21/Rev.1/Add. 6 (1995) 2 I.H.R.R. 10.

philosophical convictions). Referring to certain provisions of the Education Acts, the reservation states that this obligation is accepted "only in so far as it is compatible with the provision of efficient instruction and training, and the avoidance of unreasonable public expense".[123] The Human Rights Act gives domestic effect to this reservation[124] and invests the Secretary of State with power to designate any reservation which the United Kingdom may enter in the future.[125] Any designated reservation is subject to five yearly review by the appropriate Minister,[126] the result of which must be reported to Parliament.[127] There is, however, no requirement for periodic renewal or Parliamentary approval.[128]

VI. Protocols

The rights incorporated by the Act may be amended by order of the Secretary of **3-34** State to reflect the effect in relation to the United Kingdom of any protocol which has been ratified, or signed with a view to ratification.[129] This enables the Act to keep pace with any additional obligations which the United Kingdom may undertake in the future. Such an order may be made by statutory instrument,[130] but must be laid before, and approved by, both Houses of Parliament.[131] No such order may be made so as to come into force before the protocol to which it relates is in force in relation to the United Kingdom.[132] The protocols which confer additional substantive rights are:

(a) *Protocol 1.* This guarantees the protection of property,[133] the right to education,[134] and the right to free elections.[135] The United Kingdom has signed and ratified Protocol 1, and the rights which it enshrines are, subject to the reservation referred to above, incorporated into domestic law by s.1(1) of the Human Rights Act.[136]

(b) *Protocol 4.* This guarantees the prohibition on imprisonment for debt,[137] the right to freedom of movement,[138] the prohibition on expulsion of

---

[123] For the full text of the reservation see Human Rights Act 1998 Sch.3, Pt II.

[124] s.15(1)(a) and Sch.3, Pt II.

[125] s.15(1)(b). A state cannot enter a reservation after ratifying the Convention or protocol to which it relates. Accordingly, the power under s.15(1)(b) will arise in practice only in relation to any additional protocols which the United Kingdom may ratify, or if it should partially withdraw (or amend) the reservation to Art.2 of Protocol 1.

[126] s.17(1) and (2).

[127] s.17(3).

[128] *cf.* the position in relation to designated derogations.

[129] s.1(4) and (5).

[130] s.20(1).

[131] s.20(4).

[132] s.1(6).

[133] Art.1.

[134] Art.2.

[135] Art.3.

[136] See further Wadham, Mountfield and Edmundson *Blackstone's Guide to the Human Rights Act* (2003, 3rd edn) at paras 8.18.1 to 8.21.1.

[137] Art.1.

[138] Art.2.

nationals,[139] and the prohibition on the collective expulsion of aliens.[140] The United Kingdom signed Protocol 4 in 1963 but, unlike most Council of Europe members, has never ratified it. According to the White Paper *Rights Brought Home*, the Government had no intention of doing so on the grounds that "existing laws in relation to different categories of British nationals must be maintained".[141] In July 2004 the Department of Constitutional Affairs in its *Report on the UK Government's Inter-Departmental Review of the UK's Position under various International Human Rights Instruments* maintained that Protocol 4 should not be ratified.[142] In March 2005 the JCHR recommended that, at a minimum, consideration should be given to ratification with appropriate reservations to overcome the specific issues identified by the Government.[143]

3–35　　(c) *Protocol 6.* This provides for the abolition of the death penalty in peace-time.[144] The United Kingdom ratified Protocol 6 on January 27, 1999, following a successful backbench amendment to the Human Rights Act incorporating Arts 1 and 2 of Protocol 6 into s.1(1).[145] The Home Office Minister in the House of Lords, Lord Williams of Mostyn Q.C. explained during the debates that the amendment makes it "impossible for Parliament to reintroduce the death penalty in future, except for acts committed in time of war, or imminent threat of war, without denouncing the Convention itself".[146] Section 1(1)(c) of the Act has now been amended so as to incorporate Art.1 and 2 of Protocol 13 in place of Protocol 6 (see below).[147] The ECtHR considered the relationship between Protocol 6 and Arts 2 and 3 of the Convention in *Soering v UK*[148] and rejected an argument (by Amnesty International) that capital punishment (expressly preserved by Art.2) was *per se* inhuman and degrading, although the length of time and condition in which the applicant could expect to spend on death row prior to execution ("the death row phenomenon") did constitute a breach of Art.3. The Grand Chamber re-visited an allied issue in *Öcalan v Turkey*[149] and concluded that the Convention's living status and the current, almost universal, pan-European *de jure* abolition of the death penalty had resulted in an implied modification or abrogation of

---

[139] Art.3.
[140] Art.4.
[141] *Rights Brought Home*, Cmnd.3782, (1997), para.4.11.
[142] Appendix 6 at p.40.
[143] [31] JCHR 17th report of 2004–5 (HL 99/HC 264).
[144] The death penalty was abolished for murder by the Murder (Abolition of Death Penalty) Act 1965; for treason and piracy by the Crime and Disorder Act 1998, s.36. Any liability to the death penalty under the Army Act 1955, the Air Force Act 1955 and the Naval Discipline Act 1957 is abolished by s.21(5) of the Human Rights Act 1998, and replaced with a liability to imprisonment for life.
[145] HC Debs, cols 987–1013 (May 20, 1998). The amendment was moved by Kevin MacNamara M.P.
[146] HL Debs, col.2084 (October 29, 1998)
[147] S.I. 2004/1574 Art.2(1).
[148] (1989) 11 E.H.R.R. 439 at paras 101 to 4.
[149] Applic. No.46221/99 (12/5/05) at paras 163–5.

Art.2 (despite its clear and unambiguous words) such that "capital punishment in peacetime has come to be regarded as an unacceptable . . . form of punishment which is no longer permissible under Article 2."

(d) *Protocol 7*. This guarantees the right of an alien not to be expelled without due process of law,[150] the right of appeal against a conviction and sentence in criminal proceedings,[151] the right to compensation for a miscarriage of justice,[152] the protection against double jeopardy in criminal cases,[153] and the right to equality between spouses.[154] At the time of the White Paper *Rights Brought Home* the Government confirmed the United Kingdom's intention to sign, ratify and incorporate Protocol 7 once certain legislative changes, relating to the property rights of spouses, have been made.[155] The Government has now signed the Protocol. The Department for Constitutional Affairs' *Report on the UK Government's Inter-Departmental Review of the UK's Position under various International Human Rights Instruments*, July 2004, indicates that ratification will not be possible until an appropriate legislative vehicle is found by which to amend those property rights: see Appendix 4 to the Report.

(e) *Protocol 11*. This came into force on November 1, 1998, replacing the former part-time European Commission and Court of Human Rights with a single full-time court, reforming the enforcement procedures, and creating a right of access to the court after the exhaustion of effective domestic remedies.[156]

(f) *Protocol 12*. This came into force on April 1, 2005 and supplements Art.14 by guaranteeing a free-standing right to be protected against discrimination in the delivery of any right guaranteed under national law. The UK has not signed Protocol 12 and has given no indication that it is likely to do so in the near future. It currently considers that the text of Protocol 12 contains "unacceptable uncertainties", although the JCHR does not agree that such a cautious approach is warranted.[157]

(g) *Protocol 13*. This abolished the death penalty in all circumstances, closing the gap left by Protocol 6, which permits it in time of (imminent) war. The

---

[150] Art.1.

[151] Art.2.

[152] Art.3. See further *R. (Mullen) v Secretary of State for the Home Department* [2005] 1 A.C. 1 at paras 9, 39 to 55 and *R. (Murphy) v Secretary of State for the Home Department* [2005] EWHC 140 (Admin).

[153] Art.4.

[154] Art.5.

[155] *Rights Brought Home* Cmnd.3782, (1997), para.4.15. This commitment was re-iterated by the Government in an inter-departmental review of human rights instruments and welcomed by the JCHR in its 17th report of 2004–5 (HL 99/HC 264).

[156] This restructuring has, as a result, superseded the Second Protocol (Strasbourg, May 6, 1963; Cmnd.4551; Council of Europe, ETS 44) (now Arts 47–49 of the Convention); the Third Protocol (Strasbourg, May 6, 1963; Cmnd.4552; Council of Europe, ETS 45), the Fifth Protocol (Strasbourg, January 20, 1966; Cmnd.4963; Council of Europe, ETS 55), the Eighth Protocol (Vienna, March 19, 1985, Cmnd.9556; Council of Europe, ETS 118), the Ninth Protocol (Rome, November 6, 1990, Council of Europe, ETS 140) (now Art.34 of the Convention) and the Tenth Protocol (Strasbourg, March 25, 1992, Cmnd.2031; Council of Europe, ETS 146).

[157] See [31]–[33] JCHR 17th Report of 2004–5 (HL 99/HC 264).

Protocol is non-derogable and no reservations may be made in respect of it. Protocol 13 entered into force on July 1, 2003, having received the necessary 10 ratifications. At the time of writing, two member States had not signed this Protocol and nine have yet to ratify it. The rights which it enshrines are now incorporated directly into domestic law by virtue of an amendment to s.1(1)(c) of the Human Rights Act (which replaced Arts 1 and 2 of the Protocol 6 with Art.1 of Protocol 13).[158] The Grand Chamber in *Öcalan v Turkey* considered that the then large number of states (16) yet to sign or ratify Protocol 13 did not run counter to the argument that Art.2 had been impliedly amended so as to prohibit the death penalty in peacetime. It preferred not to decide the effect it had upon the argument that the death penalty was now contrary to Art.3 (which is non-derogable even in times of war).

(h) *Protocol 14.* This addresses the continued effectiveness of the European Court having regard to its steadily increasing workload.[159] The three main changes are: (i) single-judge final decisions on admissibility in clear-cut cases; (ii) a new, streamlined procedure for "manifestly well-founded" cases; and (iii) a new admissibility requirement for individual applications. Other measures include variation in judges' terms of office; greater flexibility in the Chamber's size and the appointment of ad hoc judges; joint decisions on admissibility and merits; a Commissioner for Human Rights able to intervene in all Grand Chamber decisions; a more flexible friendly settlement procedure and the possibility of the EU acceding to the Convention.[160] The Protocol was adopted on May 12, 2004, has been signed by all states and ratified by all but Russia. It will enter into force three clear months after this final ratification is received.

VII. Relevance of the Strasbourg jurisprudence

3–36   Section 2(1) provides that when determining a question which has arisen in connection with a Convention right, courts and tribunals must take into account the decisions of the Strasbourg institutions, whenever made or given,[161] so far as, in the opinion of the court or tribunal, they are relevant to the proceedings in which the question has arisen. This applies to judgments, decisions, declarations and advisory opinions of the European Court of Human Rights[162]; opinions of the former[163] Commission on Human Rights concerning the merits of a complaint,[164]

---

[158] S.I. 2004/1574 Art.2(1)—in force 22/6/04.

[159] e.g. nearly 40,000 applications were lodged in 2003—over 90 per cent of which were declared inadmissible.

[160] See further 1–171 *et seq.* below; Beernaert, *Protocol 14 and New Strasbourg Procedures. Towards Greater Efficiency? And at What Price?* [2004] E.H.R.L.R. 544; Greer, *Protocol 14 and the Future of the ECtHR* [2005] P.L. 83 and J.C.H.R. 1st report of 2004–5 on Protocol 14 to the ECHR (HL 8, HC 106).

[161] The inclusion of the words "whenever made or given" is intended to make it clear that the obligation applies to future decisions as well as past ones: HC Debs, col.405 (June 3, 1998).

[162] s.2(1)(a).

[163] The European Commission on Human Rights was abolished by Protocol 11.

[164] s.2(1)(b).

or its admissibility[165]; and rulings of the Committee of Ministers concerning the merits of a complaint or the supervision of a Court judgment.[166] Section 2(2) provides that evidence of any such decision is to be given in accordance with the relevant Rules of Court.

Under s.2(1) the courts are obliged to take the Convention caselaw into account, **3–37** but they are not bound to follow it. As the Lord Chancellor explained during the debates the domestic courts "may depart from existing Strasbourg decisions, and on occasion it might well be appropriate to do so, and it is possible they might give a successful lead to Strasbourg".[167] There are a number of factors which may affect the weight to be attached to a particular decision. A decision of a Chamber obviously carries less weight than a decision of the Grand Chamber; Commission decisions are less authoritative than decisions of the Court; admissibility decisions (of the Commission or the new Court) are less persuasive than binding judgments on the merits of a complaint; decisions relating to states with very different legal traditions may be of limited assistance[168]; the "living instrument" principle[169] means that older caselaw may no longer be a sure guide to the requirements of the Convention[170]; and decisions which are expressly based on the "margin of appreciation" doctrine are unlikely to give a reliable indication of the approach to be taken by a national court.[171] Moreover, in some circumstances it may be appropriate for the courts to recognise that there is also an area of judgment within which the judiciary will defer, on democratic grounds, to the considered opinion of the elected body or person whose act or decision is said to be incompatible with the Convention. It would be easier for the courts to recognise such a "discretionary area of judgment" where the Convention itself required a balance to be struck, or where questions of social or economic policy were involved; much less so where the Convention right in issue is stated in terms which are unqualified, is of high constitutional importance, or raises

---

[165] s.2(1)(c).

[166] s.2(1)(d). The references to the Articles of the Convention in s.2(1) are apt to confuse since s.2(1)(b) and (c) refer to the *former* Arts 26, 27(2) and 31 of the Convention (relating to the functions of the Commission prior to the abolition of the Commission under Protocol 11); whereas s.2(1)(d) refers to the function of the Committee of Ministers in supervising court judgments under Art.46 *as amended* by Protocol 11. However, s.21(3) of the Act provides that for the purposes of s.2(1)(d) the reference to Art.46 is to be taken to include a reference to former Arts 32 and 54. Former Art.32 was the provision under which the Committee of Ministers had jurisdiction to determine the merits of a complaint which was not referred to the court. This jurisdiction was abolished by Protocol 11. Former Art.54 conferred on the Committee of Ministers the responsibility for supervising the execution of court judgments, and is now to be found in Art.46.

[167] HL Debs, col.514 (November 18, 1997).

[168] Note, however, that during the Committee stage the Lord Chancellor made it clear that s.2 was intended to require courts to take account of Strasbourg decisions irrespective of the identity of the respondent state: HL Debs, col.513 (November 18, 1997).

[169] See para.2–18 above. *Tyrer v UK* [1978] Ser. A, No.26 at para.31; *Airey v Ireland* 2 E.H.R.R. 305 at para.26; *R. v H* [2004] 2 A.C. 134 at para.11. See, for example, the history of the evolving status of transsexual people detailed in *Chief Constable of the West Yorkshire Police v A (No.2)* [2005] 1 A.C. 51.

[170] A point made by the Lord Chancellor in debate: HL Debs, cols 1270–1271 (January 19, 1998).

[171] See, for example, the observations of Lord Hope in *R. v DPP ex parte Kebilene and ors* [1999] 3 W.L.R. 972 (HL). See also para.2–115 to 2–134 above.

questions which the court is especially well placed to determine.[172] In *R. v A (No.2)*[173] Lord Steyn observed that while the courts must give weight to the legislative policy adopted by Parliament, where the question arose whether, in a criminal statute, Parliament had adopted a legislative scheme which makes an excessive inroad into the right to a fair trial, the court would be qualified to make its own judgment, and must do so. Concerning absolute rights, such as Art.3, however, the House of Lords has recently re-emphasised that proportionality has no part to play and that Art.3 applies with equal force even when the ill-treatment occurs as a result of "legitimate government policy".[174]

3–38 It is clear that the judiciary must properly defer to the special expertise available to the executive in matters of national security. It is less clear that the fact that the executive is elected and can be removed is a relevant basis for deference. In *A v Secretary of State for the Home Department*[175] the House of Lords reviewed the deference owed by Parliament to the courts, and concluded that the courts were not precluded by any doctrine of deference from reviewing, on proportionality grounds, the Derogation Order made in order to enact Pt IV of the Anti-Terrorism Crime and Security Act 2001, even though national security issues were engaged. Lord Bingham held that the Human Rights Act gives the courts "a very specific, wholly democratic mandate" to delineate the boundaries of a rights-based democracy.[176] In particular, the courts are specifically required by Parliament to decide whether primary legislation is compatible with the Convention. The role of independent judges to interpret and apply the law "is universally recognised as a cardinal feature of the modern democratic state, a cornerstone of the rule of law itself".[177] "The court's role under the Human Rights Act is as the guardian of human rights. It cannot abdicate this responsibility".[178] Restraint inherent in the lack of democratic legitimacy of judges, developed by Lord Hoffmann in *Secretary of State for the Home Dept. v Rehman*[179] and *R. (ProLife Alliance) v BBC*,[180] or the existence of any jurisdictional barriers in certain classes of cases[181] both appear to be irreconcilable with the strong dicta of Lord Bingham in *A v Secretary of State for the Home Department* (with whom six of the majority agreed).[182] The position remains, however, that the courts may have to

---

[172] See *R. v DPP ex p Kebilene* [2000] 2 A.C. 326 *per* Lord Hope; *Brown v Stott* [2003] 1 A.C. 681, PC; *R. v Benjafield* [2003] 1 A.C. 1099; *McIntosh v Lord Advocate* [2003] 1 A.C. 1078, PC; and *International Transport Roth GmbH v Secretary of State for the Home Department* [2003] Q.B. 728, CA.

[173] [2002] 1 A.C. 45, HL at para.36. See also *R. v Lambert* [2002] 2 A.C. 545, HL.

[174] *R. v Secretary of State for the Home Dept. exp Adam, Limbulela & Tesema* [2006] 1 A.C. 396 at paras 55, 73, 90.

[175] [2005] 1 A.C. 68.

[176] Endorsing Prof. Jowell in *Judicial Deference: servility, civility or institutional capacity* [2003] P.L. 592 at 597.

[177] [2005] 2 A.C. 68. at paras 37–42, 81, 90, 107, 114, 131, 175 and 192. The case is considered further at para.3–27 below. See also *R. (ProLife Alliance) v BBC* [2004] 1 A.C. 185 at paras 75 to 76 and 144; *R. (Bloggs 61) v Secretary of State for the Home Department* [2003] 1 W.L.R. 2724.

[178] *per* Simon Brown L.J. in *International Transport Roth GmbH v Secretary of State for the Home Department* [2003] Q.B. 728 at para.78.

[179] [2003] 1 A.C. 153.

[180] [2004] 1 A.C. 185.

[181] See also Lord Hope's speech at para.108.

[182] See further Lord Steyn—*Deference: A Tangled Story* [2005] P.L. 346; *2000–5: Laying the Foundations of Human Rights Law in the UK*, B.I.I.C.L. 10/6/05.

make very difficult choices as to when they should defer to branches of government, having regard to the limits of their institutional capacity and the separation of powers principle.[183]

There is no doubt that domestic courts are free in appropriate cases to adopt a higher standard than the Strasbourg caselaw demands[184] but such provision should not be the product of interpretation of the Convention by national courts, since the meaning of the Convention should be uniform throughout the states party to it. The definitive explanation of the relevance of Strasbourg jurisprudence in the domestic courts was given by Lord Bingham in *R. (Ullah) v Special Adjudicator*: **3–39**

> "[a court] is required by section 2(1) of the Human Rights Act 1998 to take into account any relevant Strasbourg case law. While such case law is not strictly binding, it has been held that courts should, in the absence of some special circumstances, follow any clear and constant jurisprudence of the Strasbourg court: *R. (Alconbury Developments Ltd) v Secretary of State for the Environment, Transport and the Regions* [2003] 2 AC 295, para 26. This reflects the fact that the Convention is an international instrument, the correct interpretation of which can be authoritatively expounded only by the Strasbourg court. From this it follows that a national court subject to a duty such as that imposed by section 2 should not without strong reason dilute or weaken the effect of the Strasbourg case law. It is indeed unlawful under section 6 of the 1998 Act for a public authority, including a court, to act in a way which is incompatible with a Convention right. It is of course open to member states to provide for rights more generous than those guaranteed by the Convention, but such provision should not be the product of interpretation of the Convention by national courts, since the meaning of the Convention should be uniform throughout the states party to it. The duty of national courts is to keep pace with the Strasbourg jurisprudence as it evolves over time: no more, but certainly no less."[185]

---

[183] See Lester and Pannick, *Human Rights Law & Practice* 2nd edn at [3.19]n3. See also Professor Jowell, *Judicial Deference and Human Rights: A Question of Competence* in Craig, P. and Rawlings, R., eds, *Laws and Administration in Europe* (Oxford University Press, 2003); Richard Clayton Q.C. in *Judicial Deference and Democratic dialogue: the legitimacy of judicial intervention under the Human Rights Act 1998* [2004] P.L. 33.

[184] Sir Nicholas Bratza, the British judge on the Court has observed that:
"since the Convention provides a floor not a ceiling for rights throughout the Council of Europe, it is perfectly possible that the courts of this country will provide greater protection for human rights under the Act than is strictly required by case law emanating from Strasbourg . . . [I]t is thus possible that the courts of this country will disregard some of the more controversial case law of the Convention organs": Bratza, "Implications of the Human Rights Act 1998 for Commercial Practice" [2000] E.H.R.L.R. 1 at 4.
See also *Fitzpatrick v Sterling Housing Corporation* [2001] 1 A.C. 27 where the House of Lords, in defining the term "family" to include homosexual couples, departed from the more restrictive Convention caselaw on the point. Note, however, that in *Re Al-Fauwaz* [2000] All E.R. (D) 2052 Buxton L.J. observed that "it will only be very rarely that a national court feels able to rule on the meaning and reach of an article of the ECHR in terms different from those adopted, on the identical question, by one of the Convention organs".

[185] *R. (Ullah) v Special Adjudicator* [2004] 2 A.C. 323 at para.20 followed by Lord Hope in *N v Secretary of State for Home Department* [2005] 2 A.C. 296 at para.24. See also *R. (Alconbury) v Secretary of State for the Environment* [2003] 2 A.C. 295, HL at para.26 per Lord Slynn; *R. (Amin) v Secretary of State for the Home Department* [2004] 1 A.C. 653; *R. (Anderson) v Secretary of State for the Home Department* [2003] 1 A.C. 837, HL at para.18; *R. (Al Fawwaz) v Governor of Brixton Prison* [2001] 1 W.L.R. 1234, DC; *R. v Davis, Rowe and Johnson* [2001] 1 Cr.App.R. 8, CA; and *R. v Togher* [2001] 1 Cr.App.R. 33, CA.

3–40 The "no more" aspect of this approach was relied upon in *R. (Al-Jedda) v Secretary of State for Defence*[186] where the Court of Appeal held that internment in Iraq, which was required by Art.103 of the UN Charter, took precedence over the admitted violation of Art.5.

3–41 Although the House of Lords has not always adopted the law as stated by the European Court (e.g. relating to courts martial)[187] it is under a general duty to apply a clear decision by the Grand Chamber.[188] The situation may be somewhat different where the European Court has laid down a set of principles in relation to the general scope of Convention rights, but has left it to the national courts to develop their own procedures in order to implement those principles.[189] Conversely, the European Court has in turn responded to the jurisprudence of the House of Lords. In *Z and Others v United Kingdom*[190] the European Court, in the face of the decision of the House of Lords in *Barrett v Enfield London Borough Council*,[191] resiled from its earlier decision in *Osman v United Kingdom*[192] about the duty of care.

3–42 The United Kingdom remains bound by the supervisory jurisdiction of the European Court of Human Rights, and an unsuccessful litigant retains the right of individual petition under Art.34 of the Convention. A national court which departed from recent Convention jurisprudence, so as to adopt a lower standard of protection, would be acting contrary to the stated purpose of the Human Rights Act, which is to enable litigants to enforce their Convention rights without having to bring proceedings in Strasbourg.

VIII. Freedom of expression and freedom of religion

3–43 Section 12 of the Human Rights Act makes specific provision for cases involving freedom of expression. It does not, however, apply to a criminal court and is accordingly outside the scope of this work.[193] A criminal court is, nevertheless, a public authority under s.6 of the Act and is therefore obliged to act compatibly with Art.10, unless it is bound by the terms of primary legislation to do

---

[186] [2006] 3 W.L.R. 954. Permission to appeal has been sought.

[187] *R. v Spear* [2003] 1 A.C. 734, HL at para.12 (a national court need not follow a decision of the European court where it is clear that the decision was based on incomplete information); *R. v Lyons* [2002] UKHL 44 at para.46 (If the ECtHR has given a decision and the national court considers that it has misunderstood or been misinformed about English Law, the national court may wish to give a judgment inviting the ECtHR to reconsider).

[188] *R. (Alconbury) v Secretary of State for the Environment* [2003] 2 A.C. 295, HL at para.26 *per* Lord Slynn. As to the approach which the national courts should take to a decision which has been referred to (but not yet decided by) the Grand Chamber see *R. v H* [2004] 2 A.C. 134, HL at para.31.

[189] *R. v H* [2004] 2 A.C. 134, HL at para.33. See also the observations of Lord Bingham in *R. v Spear* [2003] 1 A.C. 734, HL.

[190] (2002) 34 E.H.R.R. 37.

[191] [2001] 2 A.C. 350—examples given by Lord Steyn in *2000–5: Laying the Foundations of Human Rights Law in the UK*, B.I.I.C.L. 10/6/05.

[192] (2000) 29 E.H.R.R. 245.

[193] See s.12(5). Section 12 itself does not therefore apply to decisions concerning reporting restrictions in criminal proceedings.

otherwise.[194] In *Re S (Identification: Restrictions on Publication)*[195] the House of Lords declined to grant an injunction restraining the publication by newspapers of the identity of a defendant in a murder trial. The injunction had been intended to protect the privacy of the defendant's son, who was not involved in the criminal proceedings. The House of Lords observed that "The glare of contemporaneous publicity ensures that trials are properly conducted. It is a valuable check on the criminal process." In *HM Attorney-General v Scotcher*[196] the House of Lords found s.8 of the Contempt of Court Act 1981 (which makes it a criminal offence to obtain, disclose or solicit any particulars of statements made, opinions expressed, arguments advanced or votes cast by members of a jury in the course of their deliberations in any legal proceedings) to be compatible with Art.10. Section 8(1) of the 1981 Act does not apply to a court when it considers a juror's complaints about misconduct during the jury's deliberations, since a court cannot be in contempt of itself. Section 13 provides that if a court's[197] determination of any question arising under the Act might affect the exercise by a religious[198] organisation[199] of the Convention right to freedom of thought, conscience and religion,[200] the court must have "particular regard" to the importance of that right.[201]

IX. Saving for existing rights

Section 11 provides that a person's reliance on a Convention right does not **3–44** restrict any other right or freedom conferred on him by or under any law having effect in any part of the United Kingdom.[202] Nor does it restrict his right to make any claim or bring any proceedings which he could make or bring apart from the Human Rights Act, ss.7 to 9.[203] Section 11 gives domestic effect to Art.53 of the Convention, which provides:

> "Nothing in this Convention shall be construed as limiting or derogating from any of the human rights and fundamental freedoms which may be ensured under the laws of any High Contracting Party or under any other agreement to which it is a Party."

During the Parliamentary debates on s.11 the Lord Chancellor explained that:

> "Convention rights are, as it were, a floor of rights; and if there are different or superior rights or freedoms conferred by or under any law having effect in the United Kingdom, this is a Bill which only gives and does not take away".[204]

---

[194] See the comments of the Home Secretary HC Debs, col.540 (July 2, 1998).

[195] [2005] 1 A.C. 593 at para.30.

[196] [2005] 1 W.L.R. 1867, applying *R. v Mirza* [2004] 1 A.C. 1118. See also *R. v Smith* [2005] 1 W.L.R. 704.

[197] The term "court" includes a tribunal: s.13(2).

[198] The Act provides no definition of religion, and there is some uncertainty in the Strasbourg caselaw about the boundaries of this term: see, for example, *Chappell v United Kingdom* (1987) 53 D.R. 241 (druidism); *Church of Scientology v Sweden* (1979) 16 D.R. 68.

[199] This extends to the organisation itself, or its members collectively: s.13(1).

[200] As to Art.9 see para.8–3 below.

[201] s.13(1).

[202] s.11(1).

[203] s.11(2). As to ss.7 to 9, see paras 3–74 *et seq.* below.

[204] HL Debs, col.510 (November 18, 1997). *cf.* e.g. Art.5(2) I.C.C.P.R. which contains a like provision in the Covenant.

The Human Rights Act cannot therefore be used to restrict rights which are directly enforceable in domestic law. Nor does it limit the extent to which litigants can invoke other international human rights instruments under the existing common law principles or via Art.53.[205]

E. APPLICATION TO PUBLIC AUTHORITIES

I. The duty to act compatibly

3–45   The guiding principle of the Human Rights Act is to be found in s.6(1). This provides that it is "unlawful for a public authority to act in a manner which is incompatible with a Convention right" unless required to do so by the terms of primary legislation which cannot be interpreted compatibly with the Convention.[206] An "act", for this purpose, includes a failure to act, but does not include a failure to legislate or make a remedial order.[207] Section 6(1) does not, however, apply to an act if, as the result of one or more provisions of primary legislation, the authority could not have acted differently[208]; or in the case of one or more provisions of, or made under, primary legislation which cannot be read or given effect in a way which is compatible with the Convention rights,[209] the authority

---

[205] In the absence of statutory incorporation, an international instrument does not form part of the law of England and Wales: *Chundawadra v Immigration Appeal Tribunal* [1988] Imm.A.R. 161; *Pan Amercian World Airways Inc. v Department of Trade* [1976] 1 Lloyd's Rep. 257. However, there is a presumption that Parliament does not intend to legislate in breach of the Crown's international obligations, and accordingly, it has long been established that an international treaty may be used to resolve an ambiguity in a statutory provision: *Waddington v Miah* [1974] 1 W.L.R. 683 (HL); *Garland v British Rail* [1983] A.C. 751 (HL); *Re M and H (Minors)* [1990] 1 A.C. 686 (HL) (*per* Lord Brandon at 721G); *R. v Secretary of State for the Home Department ex parte Brind* [1991] 1 A.C. 696. Particular weight will be attached to an international treaty obligation where the court is considering legislation which has been enacted in order to bring domestic law into line with the requirements thereof: *R. v Secretary of State for the Home Department ex parte Norney* (1995) 7 Admin.L.R. 861. An international human rights treaty which binds the United Kingdom may also be used as an aid to the development of the common law: see *Attorney-General v Guardian Newspapers Ltd (No.2)* [1990] 1 A.C. 109 (HL) (*per* Lord Goff at 283); *Derbyshire County Council v Times Newspapers* [1992] Q.B. 770 (CA) (*per* Butler-Sloss L.J. at 830); and *R. v Chief Metropolitan Stipendiary Magistrate ex parte Choudhury* [1991] 1 Q.B. 429 (DC) (*per* Watkins L.J. at 449). In *Rantzen v Mirror Group Newspapers (1986) Ltd* [1994] Q.B. 670 the Court of Appeal went further, and held that the European Convention on Human Rights, though unincorporated, could be deployed when a court is considering how to exercise a judicial discretion: see also *R. v Secretary of State for the Environment ex parte NALGO* (1992) 5 Admin.L.R. 785 (CA); *R. v Khan (Sultan)* [1997] A.C. 558 (HL) (*per* Lord Slynn at 165 and Lord Nicholls at 176). For a useful summary of the domestic courts' approach to the European Convention on Human Rights, prior to its incorporation, see Fatima, *Using International Law in Domestic Courts* (Hart Publishing, 2005); Beloff and Mountfield, "Unconventional Behaviour? Judicial Uses of the European Convention in England and Wales" [1996] E.H.R.L.R. 467. See further *R. v Lyons* [2003] 1 A.C. 976, HL.

[206] See s.6(2). As to the obligation to interpret primary legislation compatibly with Convention rights, see s.3(1) and para.3–58 *et seq.* below.

[207] s.6(6). S.6 thus preserves Parliamentary sovereignty and insulates the executive from challenge in relation to the introduction of legislation. As to remedial orders, see para.3–71 *et seq.* below.

[208] s.6(2)(a).

[209] As to the duty to interpret primary legislation compatibly with Convention rights, see s.3(1) and para.3–58 *et seq.* below.

was acting so as to give effect to or enforce those provisions.[210] This ensures that s.6 cannot be used as a means of mounting a collateral challenge to primary legislation which is irreconcilable with a Convention right.

II. Scope of the obligation imposed on public authorities

Where the body in question is plainly a public authority, such as the police, the   **3–46** Commissioners for Customs and Excise, or the Crown Prosecution Service, the duty in s.6(1) applics to all its activities, irrespective of whether the function in issue is public or private in nature. As the Lord Chancellor explained during the course of the Parliamentary debates[211]:

> "[Section 6(1)] refers to a 'public authority' without defining the term. In many cases it will be obvious to the courts that thcy will be dealing with a public authority. In respect of government departments, for example, or police officers, or prison officers, or immigration officers, or local authorities, there can be no doubt that the body in question is a public authority. Any clear case of that kind comes under [section 6(1)]; and it is then unlawful for the authority to act in a way which is incompatible with one or more of the Convention rights. There is no exemption for private acts such as is conferred by [section 6(5)] for [hybrid bodies]."

In *Aston Cantlow Parochial Church Council v Wallbank*,[212] for example, central   **3–47** to the House of Lords' determination that the appellant was not a "core/pure public authority" was the fact that it was not at all governmental and that it could not be a victim (within s.7) if it was.

A public authority will be liable even where the alleged violation arises from an   **3–48** act or omission of one of its employees which is beyond the scope of their authority. The Home Secretary made it clear in debate that the definition of public authority was intended to correspond with the notion of state responsibility under the Convention,[213] a notion which extends to the acts of subordinates, even where they have exceeded their mandate, or acted in defiance of express instructions.[214] Thus, the Commission has explained that "the obligations of a Contracting Party under the Convention can be violated by a person exercising an official function vested in him, even where his acts are outside or against instructions".[215]

---

[210] s.6(2)(b).

[211] HL Debs, col.811 (November 24, 1997).

[212] [2004] 1 A.C. 546 at paras 10, 59, 87 to 88, 129 and 166.

[213] "The principle of bringing rights home suggested that liability in domestic proceedings should lie with bodies in respect of whose actions the United Kingdom Government was answerable in Strasbourg . . . As a minimum, we must accept what Strasbourg has developed and is developing": HC Debs, cols 406–408 (June 17, 1998).

[214] *Ireland v United Kingdom* (1979–80) 2 E.H.R.R. 25 at para.159; *A v France* (1994) 17 E.H.R.R. 462; *Cyprus v Turkey* (1982) 4 E.H.R.R. 482; *Aydin v Turkey* (1998) 25 E.H.R.R. 251. *Cf. Makanjuola v Commissioner of Police for the Metropolis, The Times*, August 8, 1989. These decisions are discussed at para.1–79 above.

[215] *Wille v Lichtenstein* (1997) 24 E.H.R.R. CD 45.

III. Hybrid bodies

3–49 The term "public authority" in s.6(1) is deemed by s.6(3)(b) to include "any person certain of whose functions are of a public nature". This provision does not, however, apply where the act which is the subject of challenge is "private" rather than "public" in nature.[216] Thus, when hybrid bodies are under consideration "the focus should be on their functions and not on their nature as an authority".[217] During the Parliamentary debates the Lord Chancellor explained[218] that s.6(3)(b) was intended:

> " . . . to include bodies which are not manifestly public authorities, but some of whose functions only are functions of a public nature. It is relevant to cases where the courts are not sure whether they are looking at a public authority in the full-blooded . . . sense with regard to those bodies which fall into the grey area between public and private. The Bill reflects the decision to include as 'public authorities' bodies which have some public functions and some private functions."

3–50 Similarly, the Home Secretary explained[219] that the government:

> " . . . wanted a realistic and modern definition of the state so as to provide a correspondingly wide protection against the abuse of human rights. Accordingly, liability under the Bill would go beyond the narrow category of central and local government and the police—the organisations that represent a minimalist view of what constitutes the state."

This extended definition of "public authority" corresponds with the Strasbourg caselaw on state responsibility.[220] It is a fundamental principle of the Strasbourg

---

[216] s.6(5). De Smith, Woolf and Jowell suggest that a body is exercising a public function for the purposes of judicial review "when it seeks to achieve some collective benefit for the public, or a section of the public and is accepted by the public or that section of the public as having authority to do so": *Judicial Review of Administrative Action* (5th edn, 1995) para.3–024.

[217] HL Debs, col.797 (November 24, 1997), The Lord Chancellor. See also the Home Secretary at HC Debs col.433 (June 17, 1998), "As we are dealing with public functions and with an evolving situation, we believe that the test must relate to the substance and nature of the act, not to the form and legal personality." The government's aim was "to provide as much protection as possible to those who claim that their rights have been infringed": HL Debs, col.582 (November 3, 1997), the Lord Chancellor.

[218] HL Debs, col.811 (November 24, 1997).

[219] HC Debs, cols 406–408 (June 17, 1998).

[220] See the Lord Chancellor at HL Debs, cols 1231–1232 (November 3, 1997), where he observed that s.6(3)(b) "reflects the arrangements for taking cases to the Convention institutions in Strasbourg". Similarly, the Home Secretary explained during the debates that
"Under the Convention the government are answerable in Strasbourg for any acts or omissions of the state about which an individual has complaint under the Convention. The government has a direct responsibility for core bodies, such as central government and the police, but they also have responsibility for other public authorities, insofar as the actions of such authorities impinge on private individuals. The [Human Rights Act] had to have a definition that went at least as wide and took account of the fact that, over the past 20 years, an increasingly large number of private bodies, such companies or charities, have come to exercise public functions that were previously exercised by public authorities . . . it was not practicable to list all the bodies to which the [Human Rights Act's] provisions should apply. Nor would it have been wise to do so . . . [Section 6] therefore adopts a non-exhaustive definition of a public authority.": HC Debs, col.775 (February 16, 1998).

jurisprudence that a state cannot escape liability under the Convention by delegating its essentially public functions to private bodies. In *Costello-Roberts v United Kingdom*,[221] for example, the Court held that the United Kingdom would be liable under Art.3 for corporal punishment notwithstanding that it was inflicted in a private school. Examples of hybrid bodies falling within s.6(1) would thus include professional regulatory bodies such as the Law Society and the Bar Council, and a privatised company carrying out statutory functions[222] such as a private security company carrying out functions in relation to the management of a private prison or court security, (although not when providing security for commercial premises).[223] The Parochial Church Council in the *Aston Cantlow* case (above) was held not to be a hybrid public authority in relation to the private functions of enforcing of lay rectorial liability for chancel repairs, but could have been when carrying out public functions such as marriages or burials. Relevant factors in determining whether a function of a hybrid body was public included "the extent to which in carrying out the relevant function the body is publicly funded, or is exercising statutory powers, or is taking the place of central government, or local authorities, or is providing a public service".[224]

In *R. (Beer) v Hampshire Farmers' Markets Ltd*[225] the Court of Appeal held that **3–51** the House of Lords in *Aston Cantlow* had not over-ruled the (much criticised) decision in *Poplar Housing Association v Donoghue*[226] nor that in *R. (Heather) v Leonard Cheshire Foundation*[227] as to the proper test for determining whether a body was a "public authority". The Court of Appeal appeared to equate "functions of a public nature" under s.6(3)(b) of the Human Rights Act with the "exercise of a public function" test for amenability to judicial review under Civil Procedure Rules Pt 54.2. Nevertheless, the lack of clarity in the caselaw has led one academic commentator to argue that the latter is intended to be broader than the former.[228]

The Joint Committee on Human Rights is, at the time of writing, conducting a **3–52** short inquiry into the meaning of "public authority" under the 1998 Act. This follows on from the previous Committee's Report on the same topic in 2004, which concluded that the current state of the law is unsatisfactory, unfair and inconsistent with the intention of Parliament. The Report questioned whether the Act is providing effective protection for people whose rights are breached by private and voluntary sector bodies which provide "public" functions and services. The Committee noted that Parliament originally intended the term "public authority" to be interpreted widely, including private organisations which are

---

[221] (1995) 19 E.H.R.R. 112.
[222] *Rights Brought Home* Cmnd.3782, (1997), para.2.2. See also *DPP v Manners* [1978] A.C. 43 (HL).
[223] HL Debs, col.811 (November 24, 1997) the Lord Chancellor.
[224] *per* Lord Nicholls at para.11–12, considering *Hautanemi v Sweden* (1996) 22 E.H.R.R. CD 155.
[225] [2004] 1 W.L.R. 233 at para.25.
[226] [2002] Q.B. 48 at paras 65–66.
[227] [2002] 2 All E.R. 936.
[228] Oliver *Functions of a Public Nature under the Human Rights Act* [2004] P.L. 329 at 347.

active in the public sector. However, the courts have interpreted "public authority" relatively narrowly, relying on a largely "institutional" rather than "functional" approach to the question, thereby limiting the range of organisations which are expected to comply with the Human Rights Act. The Report urges the courts to take a more "flexible" and "generous" approach, and advises the government to intervene in cases where it can press for a broad interpretation.[229]

IV. Parliament is not bound by section 6(1)

3–53 The term "public authority" in s.6(1) does not include either House of Parliament (other than the House of Lords, sitting in its judicial capacity) or a person exercising functions in connection with proceedings in Parliament.[230] The Act thus prevents an individual from seeking to challenge incompatible primary legislation by alleging that Parliament has acted unlawfully in passing it. There is a complementary provision prohibiting potential challenges arising from a failure to legislate. Section 6(6) provides that a failure to introduce in, or lay before, Parliament a proposal for legislation, or to make any primary legislation or remedial order is excluded from the duty imposed by s.6(1).[231]

V. The position of the courts

3–54 The term "public authority" in s.6(1) includes a court or tribunal.[232] This ensures not only that the Convention rights afford an independent ground upon which to challenge the acts of external public authorities before an appropriate court or tribunal, but that the courts and tribunals themselves, as public authorities, are obliged to ensure that their own decisions are consistent with Convention rights (unless they are required to act otherwise by the terms of primary legislation, which cannot be interpreted compatibly[233]). In particular, in the Court of Appeal, a conviction following a trial in which the appellant's Art.6 rights have been violated is likely to be deemed "unsafe" within s.2(1) of the Criminal Appeal Act 1968: see *R. v Togher*[234]; *R. v Forbes*[235]; *R. v A. (No.2)*[236] and *Attorney-General's Reference (No.2 of 2001)*.[237] Some doubt has recently been cast on this proposition, however, following *R. v Lewis*[238] in which the appellant's conviction was upheld as safe even though Strasbourg had held it to have been obtained in breach of Art.6.[239] The unsatisfactory position now appears to be, as exemplified

---

[229] JCHR 7th report of 2003–4, (March 3, 2004, HL 39, HC 382).
[230] s.6(3) and (4). *Cf. R. v Parliamentary Commissioner for Standards ex parte Al Fayed* [1998] 1 W.L.R 669.
[231] As to the position where an applicant alleges a breach of a Convention right on the ground that an interference is unregulated by statute, see para.3–69 below.
[232] s.6(3)(a).
[233] As to the duty of compatible construction under s.3(1) see para.3–58 *et seq.* below.
[234] [2001] 1 Cr.App.R. 33 CA.
[235] [2001] 1 A.C. 473, HL.
[236] [2002] 1 A.C. 45, HL *per* Lord Steyn, at para.38.
[237] [2004] 2 A.C. 72, HL at paras 33 to 34. This issue is considered in detail in Ch.17 below.
[238] [2005] Crim. L.R. 796.
[239] *Edward and Lewis v UK* [2005] 40 E.H.R.R. 24.

by the Privy Council in *Randall*,[240] that the *extent* of the breach of Art.6 is relevant in determining safety—which is very difficult to reconcile with providing practical and effective safeguards against abuse of rights. However, the current uncertainty may be resolved, potentially at the expense of safeguarding rights, by the Government's intention *to amend the current appeal provisions to reflect its belief that* "the law should not allow people to go free where they were convicted and the Court are satisfied they committed the offence."[241] The Government is, at the time of writing, consulting on the legislative options for giving effect to this intention, including the possibility of reinstating a "proviso".[242] An examination of the many other implications of the inclusion of "court or tribunal" within s.6(1), including a detailed consideration of horizontality, is beyond the remit of this work.[243]

VI. Rules of common law

The inclusion of the courts within the definition of a "public authority" for the **3–55** purposes of s.6(1) has important implications for the common law. While the Act contains specific provisions insulating incompatible primary legislation from judicial override, there is no such saving for incompatible rules of common law.

Pre-existing common law rules which infringe Convention rights must therefore give way to the statutory duty imposed on the courts by s.6(1). *R. v Mushtaq*,[244] for example, concerned *inter alia* the common law rule about how a judge may direct a jury in cases where statements might have been obtained by oppression. The House of Lords held that a judge misdirected a jury when he said that, if they were sure that the defendant's confession was true, they might rely on it, even if it was, or might have been made as a result of oppression or other improper circumstances. Taking into account that the judge and the jury together constitute the tribunal but ultimately the jury is the primary decision maker on questions of fact, the House held that such a direction, however phrased, would always be inconsistent with the fair trial guarantee under Art.6. This displacement will also apply to private prosecutions as well as proceedings brought by a prosecuting authority. As the Lord Chancellor explained in debate[245]:

> "We ... believe that it is right as a matter of principle for the courts to have the duty of acting compatibly with the Convention not only in cases involving other public authorities but also in developing the common law in deciding cases between individuals. Why should they not? In preparing this Bill, we have taken the view that it is the other course, that of excluding Convention considerations altogether from cases between individuals which would have to be justified. The courts already bring the

---

[240] [2002] 1 W.L.R. 2237.
[241] *Quashing Convictions—Report of a review by the Home Secretary, Lord Chancellor and Attorney General, A Consultation Paper*, Office for Criminal Justice Reform, September 2006, at para.31.
[242] *Ibid.* at paras 31–39.
[243] See Clayton & Tomlinson, *The Law of Human Rights* (OUP, 2000 and annual update) at paras 5.38–5.99.
[244] [2005] 1 W.L.R. 1513.
[245] HL Debs, col.783 (November 24, 1997).

Convention to bear and I have no doubt that they will continue to do so in developing the common law."

3–56 This approach is consistent with the Convention jurisprudence on "positive obligations"[246] and state responsibility.[247] Under the former principle, a state can be held liable in Strasbourg when its substantive law (including its common law) fails to afford adequate protection against a violation of an individual's Convention rights by another private individual.[248] Under the latter principle, the state is answerable under the Convention for all its institutions, including the courts. Accordingly, a judicial decision which interferes with Convention rights will give rise to state liability, even where it was made in purely private litigation.[249] This principle was applied in a criminal context in *Venables and Thompson v News Group Newspapers and ors*[250] where the President of the Family Division held that Art.2 imposed a positive obligation on the court to grant an injunction against the private news media, in order to protect the identity of the two juveniles convicted of the murder of James Bulger, since there was compelling evidence that if their identities were revealed in the press, their lives would be put at serious risk. Although the defendants were not public authorities, the court was under an obligation to develop its equitable jurisdiction to grant injunctions in order to meet the requirements of the Convention. See also *Douglas v Hello!*[251] in which Brooke L.J. relied on Art.1 as the basis for horizontality. A comparable approach has been adopted by the UN Human Rights Committee in interpreting Art.2 of the ICCPR: a failure to ensure Covenant rights would give rise to violations by state parties of those rights, if they permitted or failed to take appropriate measures or to exercise due diligence to prevent, punish, investigate or redress the harm caused by such acts by private persons or entities.[252] However, the European Court in *Vo v France*[253] held that there was no requirement for a Contracting State to have in place a criminal offence for the negligent killing of a *foetus in utero* by a doctor, in order to comply with its positive obligations under Art.2. The possibility of a civil action for damages coupled with disciplinary measures against the negligent doctor would suffice.

---

[246] See para.2–53 above.

[247] See para.1–76 above.

[248] See *X and Y v Netherlands* (1988) 8 E.H.R.R. 235 (absence of a criminal offence prohibiting sexual abuse of mentally handicapped teenager found to violate Art.8); *A v United Kingdom* (1997) 27 E.H.R.R. 611 (common law offence of assault afforded insufficient protection to a child against a violation of Art.3 in view of the breadth of the defence of lawful correction); *Young, James and Webster v United Kingdom* (1982) 4 E.H.R.R. 38 (closed shop legislation in breach of Art.11); *Vo v France* (2005) 40 E.H.R.R. 259 (civil liability for negligent abortion sufficient to meet Art.2 positive obligations); *Bubbins v UK* (2005) 41 E.H.R.R. 458 (subjective belief by police officers acting in self-defence did not breach deceased's Art.2 rights); *Gul v Turkey* (2002) 34 E.H.R.R. 719; *McCann v UK* (1996) 21 E.H.R.R. 97; *Nachova v Bulgaria* (App.No.43577/98, 6/7/05) (Art.2 breached owing to lack of proportionality requirement in Bulgarian law which permitted lethal force to effect an arrest for minor offences).

[249] An obvious example is *Tolstoy v United Kingdom* (1995) 20 E.H.R.R. 442, where the United Kingdom was held responsible for an excessive award of damages in libel proceedings, which was held to violate Art.10.

[250] [2001] Fam. 430.

[251] [2001] Q.B. 967 at paras 82 to 83.

[252] HRC General Comment 31 *Nature of the General Legal Obligation on States Parties to the Covenant* UNDoc CCPR/C/21/Rev1/Add13 (2004) at para.8.

[253] (2005) 40 E.H.R.R. 259.

In certain circumstances, a defendant in criminal proceedings can enforce his   **3-57**
Art.6 rights "horizontally" by bringing an action against a private body which is
not a party to the criminal proceedings. For example, a Crown Court judge has
jurisdiction to grant a defendant an injunction against a third party preventing an
anticipated contempt of court, where, for example, the media is intending to
publish material which is prejudicial to the defendant.[254] In *Leary v BBC*[255] the
Master of the Rolls held that a private citizen with some special interest over and
above that enjoyed by all members of the public in the due administration of
justice (which included a defendant in a criminal trial) is entitled to seek an
injunction (from the High Court or the Crown Court) to prevent a contempt of
court, and in so doing does not need the consent of the Attorney-General. Other
civil cases decided under the Human Rights Act also confirm that, even though
the Act creates no new cause of action between purely private parties (i.e. the
Human Rights Act has no "direct horizontal effect"), such parties have enforceable Convention rights in international law which they can rely upon horizontally
if there is some pre-existing applicable cause of action ("indirect horizontal
effect"). Moreover, in adjudicating upon a purely private case, the court (as a
public authority) is required to act compatibly with both parties' Convention
rights[256]: see, e.g. *Ghaidan v Godin-Mendoza*[257]; *Campbell v MGN Ltd*[258]; *X v
Y.*[259] Furthermore the values and principles reflected in Convention rights may
shape the development of the common law and have a radiating effect on the
general law even if they cannot be relied upon with direct horizontal effect.[260]

F. APPLICATION TO LEGISLATION

I. The new approach to statutory interpretation

By s.3(1) primary and subordinate legislation[261] must[262] be read and given effect   **3-58**
in a way which is compatible with the Convention rights so far as it possible[263]
to do so. This obligation applies to past and future legislation.[264] As the White
Paper *Rights Brought Home* made clear,[265] s.3(1):

---

[254] *per* Aikens J. in *ex parte HTV Cyrmu (Wales) Ltd* (2002) E.M.L.R. 11.

[255] Unreported (Court of Appeal, Sep. 29, 1989).

[256] See Lord Hope in *Wilson v First County Trust Ltd (No.2)* at [2004] 1 A.C. 816 [94]–[95].

[257] [2004] 2 A.C. 557.

[258] [2004] 2 A.C. 457.

[259] [2004] U.K.H.R.R. 1172.

[260] Lord Steyn *2000–5: Laying the Foundations of Human Rights Law in the UK*, B.I.I.C.L. 10/6/05 p.11.

[261] The terms "primary legislation" and "subordinate legislation" are defined by s.21(1).

[262] The word "must" in s.3(1) makes it clear that the new approach to interpretation is mandatory. It follows that the court is under a duty to consider the obligation of compatible construction in every case, before considering the lawfulness of a public authority's action under s.6 (see para.3–45 above), or—where it has power to do so—the grant of a declaration of incompatibility under s.4 (see para.3–67 below).

[263] For discussion on the meaning of the term "possible" see Lord Lester of Herne Hill Q.C., "The Art of the Possible: Interpreting Statutes under the Human Rights Act" [1998] E.H.R.L.R. 665; Lord Irvine of Lairg, "The Development of Human Rights in Britain under an Incorporated Convention on Human Rights" [1998] Public Law 221; Lord Irvine of Lairg, "Activism and Restraint: Human Rights and the Interpretative Process" [1999] E.H.R.L.R. 350.

[264] s.3(2)(a).

[265] *Rights Brought Home*, Cmnd.3782, (1997) para.2.7.

" . . . goes far beyond the present rule which enables the courts to take the Convention into account in resolving any ambiguity in a legislative provision. The courts will be required to interpret legislation so as to uphold the Convention rights unless the legislation itself is so clearly incompatible with the Convention that it is impossible to do so."

3–59   The process of statutory interpretation is no longer dominated by a search for the intention of Parliament. Instead, the courts' first duty is to adopt any possible construction which is compatible with Convention rights.[266] Section 3(1) requires the courts to strive for compatibility,[267] if necessary by reading down over-broad legislation or reading necessary safeguards into an Act.[268] Section 3 was intended to supersede the pre-HRA principle that legislation had to be ambiguous before it was "possible" to interpret it compatibly with the Convention. Were it otherwise, the application of s.3 would be something of a "semantic lottery".[269] The courts are not mandated to "contort" words "to produce implausible or incredible meanings".[270] However they may be required to give a meaning to a statutory provision which it would not ordinarily bear,[271] to imply

---

[266] Writing extra-judicially Lord Steyn has explained that:
"Traditionally, the search has been for the one true meaning of a statute. Now the search will be for a possible meaning that would prevent the need for a declaration of incompatibility. The questions will be: (1) What meanings are the words capable of yielding? (2) And, critically, can the words be made to yield a sense consistent with the Convention rights? In practical effect, there will be a rebuttable presumption in favour of an interpretation consistent with Convention rights. Given the inherent ambiguity of language the presumption is likely to be a strong one." "Incorporation and Devolution: A Few Reflections on the Changing Scene" [1998] E.H.R.L.R. 153 at 155.
    As Lord Cooke of Thorndon explained during the second reading debate in the House of Lords, s.3(1) "will require a very different approach to interpretation from that to which the United Kingdom courts are accustomed. Traditionally, the search has been for the true meaning: now it will be for a possible meaning that would prevent the making of a declaration of incompatibility". HL Debs, col.1272 (November 3, 1997).
[267] During the Parliamentary debates the Government successfully resisted an amendment, which would have replaced the word "possible" with the word "reasonable", on the ground that this would unduly restrict the courts' powers of construction: HL Debs, cols 533–536 (November 18, 1997); HC Debs, cols 415 and 421 (June 3, 1998).
[268] cf. Attorney-General of Gambia v Momodou Jobe [1984] A.C. 689 at 700H PC; Flicklinger v Crown Colony of Hong Kong [1991] 1 N.Z.L.R. 439 at 440; Ministry of Transport v Noort [1992] 3 N.Z.L.R. 260.
[269] Ghaidan at [31] per Lord Nicholls. cf. e.g. R. v Navabi and Embaye [2005] EWCA Crim 2865, The Times, December 5 2005, where this approach was adopted in relation to an attempt to read s.2 of the Asylum & Immigration (Treatment of Claimants etc.) Act 2004 compatibly with the unincorporated Art.31 of the Refugee Convention 1951.
[270] See the comments of the Home Secretary during the Committee stage of the Bill in the House of Commons: HC Debs, col.422 (June 3, 1998). The Lord Chancellor has observed that "the Act, while significantly changing the nature of the interpretative process, does not confer on the courts a licence to construe legislation in a way which is so radical and strained that that it arrogates to the judges the power completely to rewrite existing law": Lord Irvine of Lairg, "Activism and Restraint: Human Rights and the Interpretative Process" [1999] E.H.R.L.R. 350 at 367.
[271] In R. v DPP ex parte Kebilene and ors [1999] 3 W.L.R. 972 Lord Cooke of Thorndon described s.3(1) as "a strong adjuration" which permits a court to depart from "the natural and ordinary meaning" of a statutory provision. Since it conveys "a rather more powerful message" than its counterpart in the New Zealand Bill of Rights Act 1990, it was "distinctly possible", within the meaning of s.3(1), to read the word "prove" in a criminal statute as imposing no more than an evidential burden (a construction which had been rejected in New Zealand: see R. v Phillips [1991] 3 N.Z.L.R. 175). Cf. Webb v EMO Air Cargo (UK) Ltd (No.2) [1995] 1 W.L.R. 1454 (HL).

words into a section[272] or to interpret general words as being subject to implied exceptions.[273] Only "in the last resort"[274] should a court conclude that a compatible construction is impossible.[275] The obligation in s.3(1) applies to all courts and tribunals.[276] Lower courts are thus no longer bound by a previous construction[277] which has been given to existing legislation by a higher court if, in the opinion of the inferior court, this construction would lead to a result which is incompatible with a Convention right. In assessing the policy objective of legislation, to determine if the proportionality requirement is satisfied, the courts are permitted to consider Ministerial statements, members' statements during Parliamentary debates and departmental Explanatory notes on a Bill as it progressed through Parliament. However, Parliamentary debates were not a matter for consideration in determining compatibility of legislation, nor were ministerial statements to be taken as indicative of Parliament's objective intention when enacting legislation.[278] Nevertheless, in *A and others v Secretary of State for the Home Department*[279] in deciding whether the derogating measures were "strictly required" within the meaning of Art.15 the House of Lords subjected the *choice* of immigration legislation as a response to the post 9/11 threat to intense scrutiny.

The leading case on s.3 is now *Ghaidan v Godin-Mendoza*.[280] In *Attorney*   **3–60**

---

[272] The Lord Chancellor has cited *Lister v Forth Dry Dock & Engineering Co. Ltd* [1990] 1 A.C. 546 (HL) as an example of the sort of implication which might be permitted by s.3(1): "The Development of Human Rights in Britain under an Incorporated Convention on Human Rights" [1998] Public Law 221. See also *Pickstone v Freemans plc* [1989] 1 A.C. 66 at 112D (HL). More radical approaches are sometimes permissible under Commonwealth Constitutions, see *Vasquez and O'Neil v R.* [1994] 1 W.L.R. 1304 at 1314D–G.

[273] In *R. v Secretary of State for the Home Department ex parte Simms and anor.* [2000] 2 A.C. 115 at 341–2 Lord Hoffmann equated the duty imposed by s.3(1) with the "principle of legality" under which a court will presume that primary or subordinate legislation expressed in general terms is to be read "subject to the basic rights of the individual". See also *R. v Secretary of State for the Home Department ex parte Pierson* [1998] A.C. 539 at 573G–575D, 587C–590A.

[274] See the observations of the Lord Chancellor during Committee stage in the House of Lords (HL Debs, col.535 (November 18, 1997)) and the Home Secretary during Committee stage in the House of Commons (HC Debs cols 415 and 421 (June 3, 1998)). The Home Secretary voiced the Government's belief that "in almost all cases the courts will be able to interpret legislation compatibly with the Convention" (HC Debs, col.780 (February 16, 1998).

[275] s.3(1) nevertheless requires a balance to be struck:
"If the courts were to adopt a very narrow view of this duty of consistent construction, their ability interpretatively to guarantee Convention rights would be severely curtailed. Instead of reading municipal law in a way which gave effect to individuals' rights, the courts would tend to discover irreconcilable conflicts between United Kingdom law and the Convention. In contrast, a judiciary which took an extremely radical view of its interpretative duty would be likely to stretch legislative language, beyond breaking point, if necessary, in order to effect judicial vindication of Convention rights . . . Both of these approaches would be wrong. The constitutional theory on which the Human Rights Act rests is one of balance." Lord Irvine of Lairg, "Activism and Restraint: Human Rights and the Interpretative Process" [1999] E.H.R.L.R. 350 at 367.

[276] Indeed, the duty in s.3(1) extends to the executive and any person or body with responsibility for interpreting or implementing legislation.

[277] i.e. a construction reached without the benefit of s.3(1).

[278] *Wilson v First County Trust (No.2)* [2004] 1 A.C. 816 at paras 61 to 7, 116 to 18, 140 to 145 and 173.

[279] [2005] 2 A.C. 68.

[280] [2004] 2 A.C. 557.

General's Reference (No.4 of 2002),[281] Lord Bingham explained the effect of *Ghaidan* as follows:

"The interpretative obligation of the courts under section 3 of the 1998 Act was the subject of illuminating discussion in *Ghaidan v Godin-Mendoza* [2004] 3 WLR 113. The majority opinions of Lord Nicholls, Lord Steyn and Lord Rodger in that case (with which Lady Hale agreed) do not lend themselves easily to a brief summary. But they leave no room for doubt on four important points. First, the interpretative obligation under section 3 is a very strong and far reaching one, and may require the court to depart from the legislative intention of Parliament. Secondly, a Convention-compliant interpretation under section 3 is the primary remedial measure and a declaration of incompatibility under section 4 an exceptional course. Thirdly, it is to be noted that during the passage of the Bill through Parliament the promoters of the Bill told both Houses that it was envisaged that the need for a declaration of incompatibility would rarely arise. Fourthly, there is a limit beyond which a Convention-compliant inter-pretation is not possible, such limit being illustrated by *R. (Anderson) v Secretary of State for the Home Department* [2002] UKHL 46, [2003] 1 AC 837 and *Bellinger v Bellinger* [2003] UKHL 21, [2003] 2 AC 467. In explaining why a Convention-compliant interpretation may not be possible, members of the committee used differing expressions: such an interpretation would be incompatible with the underlying thrust of the legislation, or would not go with the grain of it, or would call for legislative deliberation, or would change the substance of a provision completely, or would remove its pith and substance, or would violate a cardinal principle of the legislation (paras 33, 49, 110 to 113, 116). All of these expressions, as I respectfully think, yield valuable insights, but none of them should be allowed to supplant the simple test enacted in the Act: 'So far as it is possible to do so . . . '. While the House declined to try to formulate precise rules (para 50), it was thought that cases in which section 3 could not be used would in practice be fairly easy to identify."

Section 3 is therefore the principal remedial measure, and a declaration of incompatibility a measure of last resort. A linguistic approach which concentrates too much on the precise words used in the provision is inappropriate, and courts should concentrate on the substance and effect of the measure in question and adopt a purposive approach focussed on the importance of the fundamental right involved.[282] According to Lord Rodger, "however powerful the obligation in s.3(1) it does not allow the courts to change the substance of a provision completely, to change a provision from one where Parliament says that x is to happen into one saying x is not going to happen"[283] In Lord Nicholls' terms "the meaning imported by application of s.3 must be compatible with the underlying thrust of the legislation being construed".[284]

3–61   In *R. v A (No.2),*[285] Lord Steyn, with whom the majority of the House of Lords agreed, described the obligation imposed by s.3 in these terms:

"[T]he interpretative obligation under section of the 1998 Act is a strong one. It applies even if there is no ambiguity in the language in the sense of language being capable of

---

[281] [2005] 1 A.C. 264 at para.28.
[282] *Ghaidan v Godin-Mendoza* at paras 26 to 35, 37 to 52, 103 to 129.
[283] at para.110.
[284] at para.33.
[285] [2001] UKHL 25, [2002] 1 A.C. 45. See para.15–152 below.

two different meanings. It is an emphatic adjuration by the legislature ... The draftsman of the Act had before him the slightly weaker model in section 6 of the New Zealand Bill of Rights Act 1990 but preferred stronger language. Parliament specifically rejected the legislative model of requiring a reasonable interpretation. Section 3 places a duty on the court to strive to find a possible interpretation compatible with Convention rights. Under ordinary methods of interpretation a court may depart from the language of the statute to avoid absurd consequences: section 3 goes much further. Undoubtedly, a court must always look for a contextual and purposive interpretation: section 3 is more radical in its effect. It is a general principle of the interpretation of legal instruments that the text is the primary source of interpretation: other sources are subordinate to it. Section 3 qualifies this general principle because it requires a court to find an interpretation compatible with Convention rights if it is possible to do so ... In accordance with the will of Parliament as reflected in section 3 it will sometimes be necessary to adopt an interpretation which linguistically may appear strained. The techniques to be used will not only involve the reading down of express language in a statute but also the implication of provisions. A declaration of incompatibility is a measure of last resort. It must be avoided unless it is plainly impossible to do so".

Applying this approach, Lord Steyn held that s.3 required courts to "subordinate the niceties of the language" of the statutory restriction to broader considerations of relevance judged by logical and common sense criteria. This was achieved by implying into the section a judicial discretion to permit the admission of evidence which was necessary to secure a fair trial within the meaning of Art.6.[286] Lord Steyn's approach was expressly approved by Lord Bingham in *Attorney General's Reference (No.4 of 2002)*.[287]

An early illustration of the new approach to interpretation was the decision in *R. v Offen and ors*,[288] which Lord Woolf C.J. described as "a good example of how the 1998 Act can have a beneficial effect on the administration of justice, without defeating the policy which Parliament was seeking to implement". The case concerned s.2 of the Crime (Sentences) Act 1997 (subsequently s.109 of the Powers of the Criminal Courts (Sentencing) Act 2000, and since repealed by the Criminal Justice Act 2003) which provides for the imposition of an automatic life sentence following conviction for a second serious offence. The section obliged the court to impose such a sentence where the relevant qualifying offence is proved, regardless of whether the offender would otherwise have qualified for a discretionary life sentence. This was subject to a proviso that the court need not impose a life sentence where the circumstances are exceptional. Concerns had been voiced from an early stage that s.2 could lead to the imposition of a life sentence where the offender posed no serious risk to the public. In *Offen* the   **3–62**

---

[286] Lord Hope dissented on this issue, saying that he would find it "very difficult" to accept so substantial an implication by way of interpretation: "[T]he rule is only a rule of interpretation. It does not entitle the judges to act as legislators". For an equally far-reaching application of s.3 see *R. v Lambert* [2001] UKHL 37, [2002] 2 A.C. 545 where the House of Lords held that a provision requiring the accused to *prove* an issue of fact could be read as imposing a purely evidential burden of proof.

[287] [2005] 1 A.C. 264 at para.24.

[288] [2001] 1 W.L.R. 253.

appellants argued that to impose a life sentence on grounds of assumed dangerousness when it was clear that the defendant was not in fact dangerous would
result in arbitrary deprivation of liberty, and thus breach Art.5. Lord Woolf C.J.
agreed, and held that applying s.3 it was "possible" to read the expression
"exceptional circumstances" so as to prevent such a result:

> "The question of whether circumstances are appropriately to be regarded as exceptional
> must surely be influenced by the context in which the question is being asked. The
> policy and intention of Parliament was to protect the public against a person who had
> committed two serious offences. It therefore can be assumed the section was not
> intended to apply to someone in relation to whom it was established there would be no
> need for protection in the future. In other words, if the facts showed the statutory
> assumption was misplaced, then this, in the statutory context was not the normal
> situation and in consequence, for the purposes of the section, the position was
> exceptional."

3–63   Applying s.3 in *R. v Lambert*,[289] it was possible to read down "it shall be a
defence for the accused to prove [lack of guilty knowledge]" in s.28(2) of the
Misuse Drugs Act 1971 so as only to impose an evidential burden on the
accused.[290] A more recent example of the true potency of s.3 is the decision of
the House of Lords in *Attorney General's Reference (No.4 of 2002)*.[291] The
House of Lords held that s.11(2) of the Terrorism Act 2000, which placed the
legal burden on the accused to prove a defence that the terrorist organisation was
not proscribed or that s/he was inactive after (professed) membership, should be
read down so as only to impose an evidential burden. As Lord Bingham
explained, "[s]uch was not the intention of Parliament when enacting the 2000
Act, but it was the intention of Parliament when enacting section 3 of the 1998
Act."[292] In short, the words "so far as it is possible to do so" in s.3 may require
legislation to bear a meaning which departs from the unambiguous meaning
which the legislature intended.[293] Examples of the limit of the interpretative
power are *R. (Anderson) v Secretary of State for the Home Department*[294] and
Bellinger v Bellinger.[295] In *Anderson* it was impossible under s.3(1) for the courts
to devise a scheme to replace the Secretary of State's former power to decide on
the tariff to be served by mandatory life sentence prisoners. In *Bellinger*, redefin-
ing gender was held to be beyond the power of the courts under s.3(1). Both are
examples of the forbidden territory beyond the reach of s.3. Notably, in *Anderson*

---

[289] [2002] 2 A.C. 545.
[290] Strictly speaking this was *obiter* since the appeal failed on the non-retrospectivity of the HRA
(upheld in *R. v Kansal (No.2)* [2002] 2 A.C. 69). See also Lord Steyn in *Kebilene* [2000] 2 A.C. 326
at 370.
[291] [2005] 1 A.C. 264.
[292] at para.53. See also Lord Steyn at para.41 and Lord Rodger at paras 107, 123 to 4.
[293] *Ghaidan v Godin-Mendoza* at paras 29 to 31. See also *Re S. (Minors) (Care Order: Implementation of Care Plan)* [2002] 2 A.C. 291, HL (at [36–41] *per* Lord Nicholls); *R. (Anderson) v Secretary
of State for the Home Department* [2003] 1 A.C. 837, HL; *Poplar Housing and Regeneration
Community Association Ltd v Donoghue* [2002] Q.B. 48, CA (Civ. Div.); and *R. (Wooder) v Feggetter
and Mental Health Commission* [2003] Q.B. 219, CA (Civ. Div.)
[294] [2003] 1 A.C. 837.
[295] [2003] 2 A.C. 467.

Lord Steyn rowed back from his earlier apparent position in *R. v A (No.2)*, namely that there is a presumption that Convention rights override the provisions of other statutes unless there are *express* words to the contrary, and accepted that a s.3 interpretation "is not available where the suggested interpretation is contrary to express statutory words or *is by implication necessarily contradicted by the statute*".[296]

II. Legislation enacted after the Human Rights Act

A Minister of the Crown responsible for new legislation introduced in either **3–64** House of Parliament must, before second reading,[297] make a statement in writing to the effect that in his view the Bill is compatible with the Convention rights.[298] The JCHR has also succeeded in persuading the government to expand slightly the written information it supplies with a s.19 statement of compatibility.[299] If the Minister is unable to make such a statement,[300] he must inform Parliament that despite the potential incompatibility, the government nevertheless wishes to proceed with the Bill.[301] In *R. v A (No.2)*[302] Lord Hope emphasised that a s.19 statement of compatibility could not, in any way, bind the courts:

> "These statements may serve a useful purpose in Parliament. They may also be seen as part of the parliamentary history, indicating that it was not Parliament's intention to cut across a Convention right ... No doubt they are based on the best advice that is available. But they are no more than expressions of opinion by the Minister. They are not binding on the court, nor do they have any persuasive authority".

Following correspondence with the JCHR, revised guidance was issued advising **3–65** ministers to explain more fully which human rights were thought to be engaged by a Bill's provisions, and what considerations had led to the conclusion that a

---

[296] *Anderson* at [59].

[297] The statement should be included alongside the Explanatory and Financial Memorandum: *Rights Brought Home*, Cmnd.3782 (1997) para.3.3. The obligation to make a s.19 statement prior to second reading ensures that the implications of such a statement can be subject to effective Parliamentary scrutiny.

[298] s.19(1)(a). s.19 came into force on November 24, 1998: Human Rights Act 1998 (Commencement) Order 1998 S.I. 1998/2882. The government has undertaken to justify the inclusion of a statement of compatibility if the issue is raised in debate: See the answer of Lord Williams of Mostyn Q.C. HL Debs, col.186 (December 17, 1998).

[299] The Standing Orders of both Houses were amended in Nov. 2001 to require the memorandum attached to each Bill by the promoter to include "a statement of opinion ... as to the compatibility of the provisions of the Bill with the Convention rights ... ".

[300] This may be either because the Bill is plainly incompatible, or because its compatibility is uncertain.

[301] s.19(1)(b). The decision to make (or not to make) a statement of incompatibility is outside the control of the courts: s.6(3)(b) provides that "a person exercising functions in connection with proceedings in Parliament" is not a public authority for the purposes of the Act. See also *Mangawaro Enterprises Ltd v Attorney-General* [1994] 2 N.Z.L.R. 451 (equivalent provision in the New Zealand Bill of Rights Act 1990 held non-justiciable).

[302] [2002] 1 A.C. 45. See para.15–152 below.

s.19 statement could safely be made.[303] A Minister can only sign a certificate that he believes the Bill to be compatible if, after taking advice where necessary, "he is satisfied that it is more likely than not that the provisions will withstand legal challenge".[304] There have been only two situations to date where a certificate under s.19(1)(a) could not be given. The first related to the Local Government Bill, which repealed s.2A of the Local Government Act 1986 (more familiarly known as "section 28" of the Local Government Act 1988 which had introduced it). Section 2A provided that local authorities must not promote homosexuality. The Government Bill repealed this provision. The Bill was introduced into the House of Lords and a s.19(1)(a) statement was made in relation to it but the Opposition successfully amended the Bill to re-affirm the provisions of s.2A. Thus, when the Bill was introduced into the House of Commons, the Minister had to sign a certificate under s.19(1)(b) as real doubts existed as to the compatibility of s.2A with certain Convention rights. The second concerned the Communications Bill, which re-enacted the ban on political advertising. The Minister could not sign a statement under s.19(1)(a) owing to the Strasbourg decision in *Vgt Verein gegen Tierfabriken v Switzerland*.[305] Although the Government has contended that "the decision in the case is understandable on its facts, there is a strong possibility that . . . the courts would be persuaded not to follow it",[306] it nevertheless prevented the Minister from being satisfied that a court would be more likely than not to uphold the provision. Although the Minister believed that the Bill's provision would eventually be held to be compatible, he could not say it was at the time of enactment. A s.19 certificate was issued in relation to Pt 4 of the Anti-Terrorism Crime and Security Act 2001, since the Government believed that the derogation from Art.5 under Art.15 was valid, and therefore rendered Pt 4 Convention compatible. There is also considerable anecdotal evidence that s.19 statements have impacted on the consistency of advice given to ministers on the compliance of new policies and legislation with the HRA.[307]

III. Incompatible legislation

3–66   The courts have no power to strike down or disapply a provision in primary legislation which cannot be interpreted compatibly under s.3(1). Section 3(2)(b) provides that the duty of construction imposed by s.3(1) "does not affect the validity, continuing operation, or enforcement of any incompatible primary legislation".[308] The position of incompatible subordinate legislation is more

---

[303] JCHR 19th report (2004–5 HL 112, HC 552) at [75].

[304] Attorney General's lecture to Administrative Law Bar Association on October 2, 2003 "Human Rights Act—Three Years On".

[305] (2002) 34 E.H.R.R. 4 at paras 55 to 8.

[306] Attorney General's lecture to ALBA (above).

[307] e.g. Care Standards Act 2000, Gender Recognition Act 2004 and Mental Capacity Act 2005—examples from Starmer & Klug *Standing Back from the HRA: how effective is it five years on?* [2005] P.L. 716 at 719.

[308] Note, however, that the higher courts have power to grant a declaration of incompatibility: see para.3–67 below.

complex. If (disregarding the possibility of revocation) the parent statute prevents the removal of the incompatibility, then the courts must give effect to the incompatible subordinate legislation.[309] But where (as is often the case) the enabling provision is framed in general terms (and assuming it is impossible to read or give effect to the subordinate legislation in a manner which is compatible with Convention rights), the courts may then set a provision in subordinate legislation aside (either by striking it down, or by simply disapplying it).[310]

IV. Declarations of incompatibility

Where it is impossible[311] to interpret primary legislation compatibly with Convention rights, the higher courts,[312] may[313] grant a formal declaration of incompatibility under s.4(2). This power also applies to subordinate legislation in respect of which primary legislation prevents the removal of an incompatibility.[314] Section 4 is thus central to the constitutional balance which the Act strikes between Parliamentary sovereignty and the judicial protection of human rights. A declaration of incompatibility enables the courts to bring incompatible legislation to the attention of Parliament, and triggers the power to take remedial action in response.[315] It does not, however, affect the validity, continuing operation, or enforcement of the legislation.[316] Nor is it binding on the parties to the proceedings in which it was made.[317] It follows that a declaration of incompatibility in the Court of Appeal (Criminal Division) will not, of itself, afford a ground for quashing a criminal conviction, or reducing the sentence which would otherwise be appropriate. The effect of such a declaration in the course of a criminal appeal

3–67

---

[309] s.3(2)(c).

[310] As regards prior subordinate legislation, this result follows from the provisions of s.3(2)(c) read in conjunction with s.3(1). As regards future subordinate legislation, the Minister making the legislation will be acting unlawfully (within the meaning of s.6(1)), and thus *ultra vires*, if he enacts a provision which is incompatible with a Convention right, unless he is required to do so by the terms of primary legislation which cannot be interpreted in any other way. Note that in *R. v Lord Chancellor ex parte Witham* [1998] Q.B. 575 Laws L.J. adopted a similar approach to the common law right of access to court, holding invalid so much of the Supreme Court Fees (Amendment) Order 1996 as withdrew exemption from court fees for those on income support, and also withdrew the discretion to remit fees in cases of exceptional hardship.

[311] Within the meaning of s.3(1): see para.3–58 *et seq.* above.

[312] s.4(5) defines the courts with power to make a declaration of incompatibility. They are the House of Lords, the Privy Council, the Courts-Martial Appeal Court, the Court of Appeal, the High Court and, in Scotland, the High Court of Justiciary (sitting otherwise than as a trial court) and the Court of Session.

[313] The power is discretionary, but the courts will normally be expected to make such an order where legislation has been found to be incompatible, and it has not been possible to remove the incompatibility by construction. The Lord Chancellor suggested during the debates that the only circumstances in which a court might, in the exercise of its discretion, decline to make such a declaration would be where there is an alternative statutory appeal which the court considers ought to be utilised, or where there is another procedure which the court thinks an applicant should exhaust before a declaration is granted: See HL Debs, col.546 (November 18, 1997).

[314] s.4(3) and (4).

[315] See para.3–71 below.

[316] s.4(6)(a).

[317] s.4(6)(b).

is considered in Ch.17 below.[318] In *Hobbs v United Kingdom*[319] the European Court concluded that declaration of incompatibility was not an effective remedy within the meaning of Art.13.

3–68 In *Ghaidan v Godin-Mendoza*,[320] Lord Steyn analysed all the cases in which the courts had considered making a declaration of incompatibility.[321] In 10[322] cases the courts used their interpretative power under s.3, and in 15 cases the courts made declarations of incompatibility under s.4. In five cases the declarations of incompatibility were subsequently reversed on appeal[323]: in four of those cases it was held that no breach was established and in the fifth case[324] the exact basis for overturning the declaration of incompatibility was unclear. He concluded

> "Given that under the 1998 Act the use of the interpretative power under section 3 is the principal remedial measure, and that the making of a declaration of incompatibility is a measure of last resort, these statistics by themselves raise a question about the proper implementation of the 1998 Act. A study of the case law reinforces the need to pose the question whether the law has taken a wrong turning."

The House then went on to give the definitive interpretation (to date) of s.3. (See para.3–60 above.)

3–69 During the Parliamentary debates, an amendment was tabled which would have enabled courts to grant a declaration of incompatibility in cases where the applicant's complaint related to the *absence* of legislation governing an interference with a Convention right.[325] The Lord Chancellor explained that such a provision was unnecessary since the individual concerned would be able to

---

[318] Under para.2(aa) of the Criminal Appeal Rules 1968 (as amended) an appellant in criminal proceedings must include within his grounds of appeal written notice of any application for a declaration of incompatibility or of any issue which may lead the court to make such a declaration.

[319] Application No.63684/00 (18.6.02). In *Dodds v United Kingdom* (App.59314/00 (8.4.03)) the Court declined to re-visit or reverse *Hobbs* despite the UK's invitation. See also *Walker v United Kingdom* (Application No.37212/02, March 16, 2004); *Pearson v United Kingdom* (Application No.8374/03, April 27, 2004); *B&L v United Kingdom* (Application No.36936/03 June 39, 2004), *PM v United Kingdom* (Application No.6638/02 July 19, 2005) and *Upton v United Kingdom* (Application No.29800/04, April 11, 2006).

[320] [2004] 2 A.C. 557.

[321] At para.40 and Appendix to his opinion. See also Klug and O'Brien *The first two years of the Human Rights Act* [2002] P.L. 649. For a subsequent example of a declaration of incompatibility, see *Re MB* [2006] EWHC 1000 (Admin); [2006] H.R.L.R. 878, in which Sullivan J. held that the procedures for imposing a "non-derogating" control order under s.3 of the Prevention of Terrorism Act 2005 were incompatible with Art.6 of the EHCR. This decision was reversed on appeal: [2006] 3 W.L.R. 839, and at the time of writing, is on appeal to the House of Lords. See also *Westminster City Council v Morris* [2006] 1 W.L.R. 505, in which the Court of Appeal held that s.185(4) of the Housing Act 1996 was incompatible with Art.14 ECHR.

[322] There has since been a declaration in *Beaulane Properties Ltd v Terence Charles Palmer* [2005] H.R.L.R. 19.

[323] Which were *R. (Alconbury) v Secretary of State Environment* [2003] [2003] 2 A.C. 295; *Wilson v First County Trust (No.2)* [2004] 1 A.C. 816; *Matthews v MoD* [2003] 1 A.C. 1163; *R. (Uttley) v Secretary of State for the Home Department* [2004] 1 W.L.R. 2278. See also *R. (MH) v Secretary of State for Health* [2005] UKHL 60 *R. (Morris) v Westminster CC* [2005] 1 W.L.R. 865.

[324] *R. (Hooper) v Secretary of State for Work & Pensions* [2004] 1 W.L.R. 1681.

[325] HL Debs, cols 814–815 (November 24, 1997).

invoke his Convention rights in accordance with s.7 of the Act. The absence of legislation would mean that there was no legislative warrant for the interference, and "there is nothing to stop the courts providing a remedy" in such a case.[326]

V. Right of Crown to intervene

Where a court is considering whether to make a declaration of incompatibility, the Crown is entitled to notice in accordance with the Rules of Court.[327] Once notified, the relevant Minister,[328] or a person nominated by him, is entitled as of right to be joined as a party to the proceedings.[329] This right can be exercised by giving notice of an intention to be joined,[330] at any stage of the proceedings.[331] In criminal cases[332] a Minister who has been joined as a party may, with leave,[333] appeal to the House of Lords against any declaration of incompatibility made in the proceedings.[334] The interests of the Crown will not always be adequately represented by the prosecution in a criminal case, and in certain circumstances it will be appropriate for the responsible Minister to be separately represented: for example the intervention of the Lord Chancellor in *R. v Mirza*, when investigation of juror bias was under consideration.[335]

3–70

VI. Remedial orders

The government has indicated that a declaration of incompatibility will "almost certainly" prompt legislative change,[336] either by way of amending primary

3–71

---

[326] These comments relate to those situations in which an interference with a Convention right is required under the Strasbourg jurisprudence to be authorised by statute (see, for example, *Khan v United Kingdom*, (2001) 31 E.H.R.R. 45). In such a situation the courts would be able to provide a remedy because the complaint would be directed to the interference itself, rather than to the failure to legislate as such. Note, however, that a challenge directed to the legislature or the executive arising out of a failure to legislate is expressly excluded from the duty to act compatibly with Convention rights: s.6(6).

[327] s.5(1). As to the procedure to be followed for giving notice to the relevant Minister see the Criminal Appeal (Amendment) Rules 2000 (S.I. 2000/2056).

[328] In Scotland, the right to intervene applies to a member of the Scottish Executive (s.5(1)(b)). In Northern Ireland it applied to a Northern Ireland Minister (s.5(1)(c)), or a Northern Ireland department (s.5(1)(d)).

[329] s.5(2).

[330] s.5(2).

[331] s.5(3).

[332] There is no need for specific provision in civil proceedings since any person joined as a party to civil proceedings is entitled to exercise rights of appeal open to any other party.

[333] "Leave" means leave granted by the court making the declaration of incompatibility or by the House of Lords: s.5(5).

[334] s.5(4). The scope of any such appeal is confined to the grant of a declaration of incompatibility. Note: This provision does not apply to Scotland since there is no right of appeal to the House of Lords in relation to criminal proceedings in Scotland.

[335] [2004] 1 A.C. 1118. See also *R. v A (No.2)* [2002] 1 A.C. 45 (HL). The procedural issue is reported as *R. v A (Joinder of Appropriate Minister)* [2001] 1 W.L.R. 789.

[336] *Rights Brought Home* Cmnd.3782, (1997), para.2.9. See also the remarks of the Lord Chancellor during debate: HL Debs, col.1230 (November 3, 1997).

legislation, or under s.10 of the Act.[337] Section 10 confers a power on the relevant Minister of the Crown to amend incompatible primary legislation by remedial order. This power arises in three situations[338]:

    (i) Where a provision of primary legislation has been the subject of a declaration of incompatibility under s.4, and all parties to the proceedings have either exercised or abandoned any rights of appeal, or the time limit for appealing has expired.[339]

    (ii) Where it appears to a Minister of the Crown or Her Majesty in Council[340] that, having regard to a finding of the European Court of Human Rights made after October 2, 2000, in proceedings against the United Kingdom, a provision of legislation is incompatible with an existing obligation under the Convention.[341]

    (iii) In the case of incompatible subordinate legislation, where a Minister of the Crown considers that it is necessary to amend the parent legislation.[342]

3–72   In each case, if the Minister considers that there are "compelling reasons" for doing so,[343] he may by order make such amendments to the primary legislation as he considers necessary to remove the incompatibility.[344] A remedial order may contain "such incidental, supplemental, consequential or transitional provision" as the Minister "considers appropriate"[345]; may be made retrospective[346]; may make provision for the delegation of specific functions[347]; and may make different provision for different cases.[348] The relevant Minister must lay before Parliament a document containing a draft of the proposed order, an account of the incompatibility it is seeking to remove,[349] and an explanation for proceeding

---

[337] Note, however, that a failure to introduce legislation or to make a remedial order following a declaration of incompatibility cannot be challenged in the courts: see s.6(6).

[338] s.10 also applies where a provision of subordinate legislation has been quashed, or declared invalid, by reason of its incompatibility with Convention rights, and the relevant Minister intends to proceed under the power conferred to take remedial action in urgent cases under Sch.2 para.2(b).

[339] s.10(1)(a).

[340] If the legislation in question is an Order in Council, the power to make a remedial order is exercisable by Her Majesty in Council: s.10(5).

[341] s.10(1)(b).

[342] s.10(3).

[343] If there are no such compelling reasons, the Minister will be expected to proceed by way of amending primary legislation.

[344] s.10(2). See, e.g. Mental Health Act 1983 (Remedial) Order 2001 (S.I. 2001/3712)—made following the incompatibility identified in *R. (H) v Mental Health Review Tribunal* [2002] Q.B. 1 and Naval Discipline Act 1957 (Remedial) Order 2004.

[345] Sch.2, para.1(1)(a).

[346] Sch.2, para.1(1)(b). Note, however, that in order to avoid a violation of Art.7 of the Convention, no person is to be guilty of an offence solely as a result of the retrospective effect of a remedial order: Sch.2, para.1(4).

[347] Sch.2, para.1(1)(c).

[348] Sch.2, para.1(1)(d).

[349] As to the information required, see Sch.2, para.5.

under s.10, rather than by way of primary legislation.[350] He must then allow a period of 60 days to enable representations[351] to be made.[352] Following this consultation period, the draft must be formally laid before Parliament, together with a summary of any representations the Minister has received, and any amendments he has made in the light of those representations.[353] After a further interval of 60 days, the draft must be put to both Houses of Parliament for approval by affirmative resolution.[354] In urgent cases, the Minister may make a remedial order without the approval of Parliament.[355] In that event, the order must be laid before Parliament after it has been made,[356] together with the required information,[357] and must be approved within 120 days of the day on which it was made.[358] If, during the period of 60 days after the making of the order, representations have been made to the Minister, a summary of those representations must be laid before Parliament, together with the details of any changes the Minister considers appropriate in the light of the representations received.[359]

Section 4 has not proved to be the paper tiger predicted by some critics. In every **3–73** case where remedial actions had not been taken before the declaration of incompatibility was made, the government responded by repealing, amending or committing to repeal or amend, the relevant provision.[360] The most notable example was the House of Lords' declaration in December 2004 that Pt 4 of the Anti-terrorism, Crime and Security Act 2001 was incompatible with Arts 5 and 15. The government did not seek to renew the offending provision although when Pt 4 expired, but did replace it with a scheme which raises fresh compatibility issues.

---

[350] Sch.2, para.3(1). As to the information required, see Sch.2, para.5.

[351] "Representations" means representations about a remedial order (or proposed remedial order) made to the person making (or proposing to make) it and includes any relevant Parliamentary report or resolution: Sch.2, para.5.

[352] Sch.2, para.3(1)(b).

[353] Sch.2, paras 2(a) and 3(2).

[354] Sch.2, para.2(a).

[355] Sch.2, para.2(b).

[356] Sch.2, para.4(1).

[357] As to the information required, see Sch.2, para.5.

[358] Sch.2, para.4(4). If the order has not been so approved, it ceases to have effect. Para.4(4) makes it clear, however, that this does not affect the lawfulness of anything previously done under the order.

[359] Sch.2, para.4(2). If, in the light of representations, the Minister considers it appropriate to make changes to the order, then he must make a further order and lay it before Parliament in the ordinary way: Sch.2, para.4(3).

[360] In five cases the legislation has been amended after the declaration was made: *R. (H) v MHRT* [2002] Q.B. 1; *International Transport Roth GmbH v Secretary of State for the Home Department* [2003] Q.B. 728; *R. (D) v Secretary of State for the Home Department* [2003] 1 W.L.R. 1315; *Blood v Secretary of State for Health* (unreported); *Bellinger v Bellinger* [2003] 2 A.C. 467. In two cases the legislation was repealed after the declaration: *McR's application for judicial review* (2003) N.I.Q.B. 58 and *Anderson* (above). In one case the legislation was repealed before the declaration was made: *R. (Wilkinson) v Inland Revenue Commissioners* [2005] 1 W.L.R. 1718. In one case a commitment has been made to amend the legislation: [2003] A.C.D. 389 and in another case the incompatible legislation was not renewed (*A and others v Secretary of State for the Home Department*). List taken from Starmer and Klug (above).

G. CLAIMS AND REMEDIES

3–74 The procedural philosophy behind the Human Rights Act is that litigants should, wherever possible, use existing claims and remedies for enforcing Convention rights in the national courts. The White Paper *Rights Brought Home* explained that Convention arguments would normally arise in proceedings taken against individuals or already open to them, but that if none were available, it would be possible for a complainant to bring proceedings on Convention grounds alone.[361] This is reflected in ss.7 to 9 of the Act.

I. Free-standing claims

3–75 By s.7(1)(a) a person who claims that a public authority[362] has acted (or proposes to act) in a way which is made unlawful by s.6[363] may bring proceedings against that authority[364] in the appropriate court or tribunal.[365] This ensures that an individual is able to bring a claim alleging breach of a Convention right where there is no existing remedy available which is capable of adaptation. The expression "appropriate court or tribunal" is defined by the Civil Procedure (Amendment No.4) Rules 2000 (S.I. 2000/2092),[366] which make amendments to the CPR. CPR r.7.11 provides that a claim under s.7(1)(a) may be brought either in the County Court or in the High Court (subject to normal jurisdictional limits) unless it is a claim in respect of a judicial act, in which case it must be commenced in the High Court.

Proceedings under s.7(1)(a) must be brought within one year of the act complained of,[367] unless the court, in its discretion, considers that a longer period would be equitable, having regard to all the circumstances.[368] This is, however, subject to any rule imposing a stricter time limit in relation to the procedure in question.[369] Where, therefore, the proceedings are brought by way of judicial review, the time limit remains three months.

II. Reliance on Convention rights

3–76 By s.7(1)(b) a person who claims that a public authority[370] has acted (or proposes to act) in a way which is made unlawful by s.6[371] may rely on a Convention right in any legal proceedings. The term "legal proceedings" includes proceedings

---

[361] *Rights Brought Home*, Cmnd.3782, (1997), para.2.3.
[362] As to the meaning of "public authority", see s.6(3) and paras 3–45 *et seq.* above.
[363] See para.3–45 above.
[364] The term "proceedings against a public authority" in s.7(1)(a) includes a counter-claim or similar proceeding: s.7(2).
[365] s.7(1)(a).
[366] Made under s.7(2), (9) and (10).
[367] s.7(5)(a).
[368] s.7(1)(b).
[369] s.7(5).
[370] As to the meaning of "public authority", see s.6(3) and paras 3–45 *et seq.* above.
[371] See para.3–45 above.

brought by or at the instigation of a public authority,[372] and an appeal against the decision of a court or tribunal.[373] The Act adopts a deliberately broad and inclusive definition of "legal proceedings" so as to ensure that Convention arguments can be raised in all litigation, and at every level.[374]

III. The "victim" requirement

An individual may only bring proceedings under s.7(1)(a), or rely on his Conven-   3–77
tion rights in other proceedings under s.7(1)(b), if he is (or would be) a "victim" of the unlawful act[375] for the purposes of Art.34 of the Convention.[376] Under Art.34 the European Court of Human Rights has held that an applicant must have been directly affected by the measure in question.[377] However, this concept includes cases where the mere existence of a law is alleged to interfere with the exercise of a Convention right[378]; where there is a real threat of a future violation[379]; or where the victim is "indirect".[380] Special rules apply to cases involving secret surveillance, where it may be impossible for the individual to prove that the surveillance has occurred.[381] Where criminal proceedings have exceeded the reasonable time requirement, a reduction in sentence which has the express purpose of affording a remedy for the delay may deprive the defendant of his status as a "victim".[382]

If the Convention right is invoked in judicial review proceedings, the applicant   3–78
is to be taken to have "sufficient interest" only if he is, or would be, a "victim" of the unlawful act relied on.[383] In recent years the courts have adopted a more liberal approach to the "sufficient interest" test in judicial review proceedings, holding (for example) that responsible public interest organisations have standing to bring representative challenges where they are qualified to do so, and there is

---

[372] s.7(6)(a).

[373] s.7(6)(b). The reference to appeals ensures that Convention arguments can be raised for the first time on appeal against a decision of a court or tribunal where the applicant alleges the decision itself to be incompatible with a Convention right.

[374] This includes a collateral challenge to action taken by a public authority: *Boddington v British Transport Police* [1999] 2 A.C. 143. During debates the Home Office Minister Mike O'Brien M.P. confirmed that private prosecutions were included since the definition in s.7(6) was non-exhaustive: HC Debs, col.1057 (June 24, 1998). See further para.22.53ff Clayton & Tomlinson, *The Law of Human Rights* (OUP, 2000 and annual update).

[375] "Unlawful act" means an act made unlawful by s.6(1): s.6(6). As to s.6(1) see para.3–45 above.

[376] s.7(1), 7(3) and 7(7).

[377] See generally para.1–88 above. *Marckx v Belgium* (1979) 2 E.H.R.R. 330 at para.27; *Norris v Ireland* (1988) 13 E.H.R.R. 186 at paras 32–4; *Open Door Counselling and Dublin Well Woman v Ireland* (1992) 15 E.H.R.R. 244 at para.44; *Campbell and Cosans v UK* (1980) 3 E.H.R.R. 531 at para.116; *V, W, X, Y and Z v UK* (EcomHR admisibility decision 18/1/95 App. 22170/93)

[378] See para.1–89 above.

[379] See para.1–91 above.

[380] See para.1–94 above

[381] See para.1–93 above.

[382] *Eckle v Germany* 5 E.H.R.R. 1; *Bunkate v The Netherlands* 19 E.H.R.R. 477; *X v Germany* 25 D.R. 142; *Beck v Norway* (June 26, 2001).

[383] s.7(3). Similar provision is made in relation to petitions for judicial review in Scotland by s.7(4).

no obvious alternative challenger.[384] Although organisations which meet the "sufficient interest" test continue to have standing for the purposes of judicial review generally, they are not entitled to invoke the provisions of the Human Rights Act on behalf of the public (or a section of the public). Such organisations may nevertheless invoke the Act where it is their own rights as an organisation (or those of their members collectively) which are at stake.[385] And as the Lord Chancellor explained during the Parliamentary debates, they will have an important role to play in assisting and providing representation for individual victims, and in filing *amicus curiae* briefs.[386] Even before the Act was passed the House of Lords had permitted public interest organisations to file *amicus* briefs in a number of important criminal cases.[387] Moreover, since the Act preserves existing human rights,[388] such organisations may continue to invoke the Convention in accordance with the common law principles applicable before the Act came into force.[389]

3–79　The boundaries of Human Rights Act test litigation were reached in *Regina (Rusbridger and another) v Attorney General*.[390] In December 2000, *The Guardian* newspaper published a series of articles advocating republicanism and urging the abolition of the monarchy, but without inciting the use of unlawful force. The editor, aware that the prohibition against publication of articles advocating abolition of the monarchy in s.3 of the Treason Felony Act 1848 remained in force, albeit that no prosecutions had been brought since 1883, had written to the Attorney General seeking an assurance that he would either disapply s.3 as having fallen into desuetude, or on the ground that any prosecution would be contrary to Art.10. The Attorney General declined to give the assurance sought or to initiate any declaratory proceedings. Although no prosecutions ensued, the Guardian brought a judicial review of the Attorney General's decision, seeking declarations that he had acted unlawfully and on the compatibility of s.3 of the Treason Felony Act 1848. The House of Lords held that, although a court might as a matter of judgment hold that exceptional circumstances made it proper for a member of the public to bring proceedings against the Crown for a declaration that certain proposed conduct was lawful and to name the Attorney General as the formal defendant to the claim, since s.3(1) of the Human Rights Act 1998 placed it beyond doubt that s.3 of the Treason Felony Act 1848 could not be used

---

[384] See for example *R. v Secretary of State for Social Services ex parte CPAG* [1990] 2 Q.B. 540; *R. v Secretary of State for Employment ex parte EOC* [1995] A.C. 1; *R. v Her Majesty's Inspectorate of Pollution ex parte Greenpeace (No.2)* [1994] 4 All E.R. 329; *R. v Secretary of State for Foreign Affairs ex parte World Development Movement* [1995] 1 W.L.R. 386; *R. v Secretary of State for Social Security ex parte JCWI* [1997] 1 W.L.R. 275; *R. (Northern Cyprus Tourism Centre Ltd) and another v Transport for London* [2005] EWHC 1698 (Admin); [2005] U.K.H.R.R. 1231.

[385] See, for example, *Christians Against Racism and Fascism v United Kingdom* (1980) 21 D.R. 138; *Open Door Counselling and Dublin Well Woman v Ireland* (1993) 15 E.H.R.R. 244.

[386] HL Debs, col.810 (February 5, 1998). For example, see the interventions by Justice in *Brown v Stott* [2003] 1 A.C. 681, and *R. (Roberts) v Parole Board* [2005] 2 A.C. 738.

[387] *R. v Sultan Khan* [1997] A.C. 558 (Liberty); *R. v Secretary of State for the Home Department ex parte Venables and Thompson* [1998] A.C. 407 (Justice); *R. v Bow Street Stipendiary Magistrate ex parte Pinochet Ugarte* [1999] 2 W.L.R. 1015 (Amnesty and others).

[388] See s.11 and para.3–44 above.

[389] See para.3–21 above.

[390] [2004] 1 A.C. 357.

to mount a successful prosecution against a person publishing material advocating political change to a republic by peaceful and constitutional means, no purpose would be served by requiring the courts to accommodate unnecessary litigation seeking a formal declaration to that effect. Thus, even though *The Guardian's* application raised important constitutional issues, the claim for a declaration was refused.[391] Lords Hutton, Rodger and Walker opined that it was not the function of the courts to keep the statute book up to date—that was for Parliament and the executive.[392]

It was accepted that *The Guardian* did not have to demonstrate that it was a **3–80** "victim" under s.7. The House noted, however, the broad Strasbourg approach to the concept of victim. Thus, in *Norris v Ireland*[393] a gay man complained that the criminalisation of homosexual conduct in Ireland violated his Art.8 right to respect for his private life, although he accepted that the risk of being prosecuted was remote. The court accepted that he was a victim. The House observed that even an administrative policy of not prosecuting for the offence in question would not have made a difference. It was sufficient, therefore, that *The Guardian* had an interest and standing—the threshold requirement.[394]

IV. Remedies

In the context of criminal proceedings, s.7(1)(a) may be relevant where the **3–81** Magistrates Court or Crown Court has found that a public authority acted incompatibly with the defendant's Convention rights, and he then seeks damages for the breach. In this situation, the individual will be expected to pursue separate civil proceedings.[395] Usually, however the vehicle for invoking Convention rights in criminal proceedings is likely to be s.7(1)(b). This raises the question of the remedies which a criminal court is able to grant.

Section 8(1) provides that where a court finds that a public authority has acted (or **3–82** proposes to act) in a manner which is made unlawful by s.6, it may grant such relief or remedy, or make such order, *within its powers*, as it considers just and appropriate. The White Paper *Rights Brought Home* suggested that the remedy appropriate in any case would depend "on a proper balance being struck between the rights of the individual and the public interest".[396] In exercising this jurisdiction, the courts may have regard to the obligation under Art.13 of the Convention

---

[391] paras 8, 16, 18 to 20, 25, 28, 32–33, 38–40, 43–44, 51, 56, 59.
[392] paras 36, 58, 61. Seeking wide ranging declaratory relief in high-profile important cases was vigorously criticised in *R. (Burke) v GMC* [2006] Q.B. 273 where the Court of Appeal stressed that there were great dangers in the court grappling with abstract legal issues which were divorced from their factual context.
[393] (1988) 13 E.H.R.R. 186 at para.31 *cf. Klass v Germany* 2 E.H.R.R. 214 (applicant could claim to be a victim of secret surveillance without the necessity to prove conclusively that his telephone conversation had been intercepted); see also *Bowman v UK* 26 E.H.R.R. 1 (person may be a victim by virtue of a prosecution resulting in an acquittal); *Halford v UK* 24 E.H.R.R. 523; *Marckx v Belgium* 2 E.H.R.R. 330; *Karner v Austria* Application No.40016/98 (July 24, 2003).
[394] para.21 *per* Lord Steyn.
[395] See para.3–85 below.
[396] *Rights Brought Home*, Cmnd.3782 (1997), para.2.6.

to provide an effective remedy (notwithstanding that Art.13 is omitted from the list of incorporated rights). This is because the Act itself is intended to give effect to the United Kingdom's obligations under Art.13, and because the courts are required by s.2(1) to have regard to Convention jurisprudence under Art.13.[397] As the Lord Chancellor explained during the Parliamentary debates it is difficult to:

> "conceive of any state of affairs in which an English court, having held an act to be unlawful because of its infringement of a Convention right, would under [section] 8(1) be disabled from giving an effective remedy".[398]

In *B & L v United Kingdom*,[399] the court recalled that "a remedy which is not enforceable or binding or which is dependent on the discretion of the executive falls outside the concept of effectiveness as established in the Convention case-law". Lord Steyn suggested in *Ghaidan v Godin-Mendoza* that s.3 of the Human Rights Act was apt to provide a "remedy" (or avoid the need for one) in more cases than the courts had previously held.[400]

3–83 In criminal proceedings the courts have power under s.8 to quash an indictment, to stay the proceedings as an abuse of process, to allow a submission of no case to answer, to exclude evidence, or even to reflect the breach in the sentence which is imposed. The Court of Appeal (Criminal Division) has power to quash a conviction where the offence itself breaches a Convention right, or where there has been a breach of Art.6 in the course of the trial. Such a conviction is likely to be deemed "unsafe" within s.2(1) of the Criminal Appeal Act 1968: see *R. v Togher*[401]; *R. v Forbes*[402]; *R. v A. (No.2)*[403] and *Attorney-General's Reference (No.2 of 2001)*.[404] The latter case is particularly important in recognising the heirachy of remedies available where rights have been violated. Thus, the fact that the reasonable time requirement in Art.6 had been breached did not give rise to a corresponding right not to be tried—a pecuniary award, reduction in sentence or some lesser remedy might in some cases suffice as a just and proportionate remedy.

3–84 Strong recent pronouncements from the European Court about defendants' rights and remedies after an acquittal are difficult to reconcile with the domestic approach. In *Baars v Netherlands*[405] the court found a breach of Art.6(2) where a defendant had been refused a claim for his costs after proceedings had been

---

[397] See para.3–19 above. *cf. R. v Canterbury Crown Court ex p Regentford (The Times*, February 6, 2001) at paras 16 to 22 and *R. (Shields) v Liverpool Crown Court* [2001] U.K.H.R.R. 610 at paras 20, 33 to 34, 53 to 58.

[398] HL Debs, col.479 (November 18, 1997). See also the approach of the New Zealand Court of Appeal in *Simpson v Attorney-General* [1994] 3 N.Z.L.R. 667. As to what constitutes an effective remedy where the Art.6 right to trial within a reasonable time has been breached see *Attorney General's Reference (No.2 of 2001)* [2004] 2 A.C. 72.

[399] Application No.36536/02, (June 29, 2004).

[400] [2004] 2 A.C. 557 at para.40 and Appendix to his opinion.

[401] [2001] 1 Cr.App.R. 33 CA.

[402] [2001] 1 A.C. 473, HL.

[403] [2002] 1 A.C. 45, HL *per* Lord Steyn, at para.38.

[404] [2004] 2 A.C. 72, HL at paras 33 to 34. This issue is considered in detail in Ch.17 below.

[405] 39 E.H.R.R. 538.

stayed for excessive delay because he would in all likelihood have been convicted anyway. Similarly, in *Del Latte v Netherlands*[406] the refusal to pay compensation because the acquittal was "technical" (a lesser, un-indicted charge was made out) was held to violate the presumption of innocence in Art.6(2). The latter decision is in marked contrast to *R. (Mullen) v Secretary of State for the Home Department*[407] in which a defendant who had be unlawfully brought to the UK but had an otherwise fair trial was refused compensation. It made no difference that the trial judge would have been bound to stay the proceedings as an abuse had been aware of the manner in which the defendant had been brought into the jurisdiction.

V. Damages

Damages may only be awarded by a court which has power to award damages, **3–85** or to order the payment of compensation, in civil proceedings.[408] Damages may not therefore be awarded by a criminal court.[409]

An award of damages is only to be made where it necessary to afford "just **3–86** satisfaction" to the person in whose favour it is made.[410] In determining whether a monetary award is necessary, the court must have regard to all the circumstances including any other remedy or relief granted, or order made, in relation to the act in question (by that or any other court),[411] and the consequences of any decision (of that or any other court) in respect of that act.[412] If, therefore, a criminal court has excluded evidence or stayed criminal proceedings, or the Court of Appeal has quashed the applicant's conviction, this will be highly material in determining whether and to what extent an award of damages is necessary.[413]

In determining whether to make an award of damages against a public author- **3–87** ity,[414] and in fixing the amount of any such award, the court should take into

---

[406] 41 E.H.R.R. 176.

[407] [2005] 1 A.C. 1 at paras 9, 39 to 55 and *R. (Murphy) v Secretary of State for the Home Department* [2005] 1 W.L.R. 3516.

[408] s.8(2).

[409] During debates the Lord Chancellor explained that:
"it is not the Bill's aim that, for example, the Crown Court should be able to make an award of damages where it finds, during the course of a trial, that a violation of a person's Convention rights has occurred. We believe that it is appropriate for an individual who considers that his rights have been infringed in such a case to pursue any matter of damages through the civil courts where this type of issue is normally dealt with": HL Debs, col.855 (November 24, 1997).

[410] s.8(3).

[411] s.8(3)(a).

[412] s.8(3)(b).

[413] *cf. R. (Mullen) v Secretary of State for the Home Department* [2005] 1 A.C. 1 at paras 9 and 39 to 55.

[414] A public authority against which damages are awarded is to be treated for the purposes of the Civil Liability (Contribution) Act 1978 as liable in respect of damage suffered by the person to whom the award is made: s.8(5)(b). Accordingly, the normal principles of contribution apply to persons who are jointly and severally liable. Similar provision is made for Scotland by s.8(5)(a).

account the principles[415] applied by the European Court of Human Rights under Art.41 of the Convention.[416] The government's intention was that "people will be able to receive compensation from a domestic court equivalent to what they would have received in Strasbourg".[417] The decision of the Court of Appeal in *R. (KB) v Mental Health Review Tribunal*[418] sets out guidelines in relation to awards of Human Rights Act damages. The court followed the Strasbourg approach in holding that an award of damages may, in certain circumstances, be unnecessary where a finding of violation may itself constitute "just satisfaction". However, it went on to hold that Human Rights Act damages should be comparable with damages for tort claims—ultimately a more generous approach than Strasbourg.[419] In *Anufrijeva v Southwark London Borough Council*[420] Human Rights Act damages were not recoverable as of right for a Convention breach. It was held that courts dealing with claims for damages for maladministration should adopt a broad brush approach. Where no pecuniary loss was involved, the question whether the other remedies that had been granted to a successful complainant were sufficient to vindicate the right infringed, taking into account the complainant's own responsibility for what had occurred, should be decided without a close examination of the authorities or an extensive and prolonged examination of the facts. In many cases the seriousness of the maladministration and whether there was a need for damages should be capable of being ascertained by an examination of the correspondence and witness statements. In the absence of clear guidance from Strasbourg, the critical test under the Act was that the remedy had to be "just and appropriate" and "necessary" to afford "just satisfaction". The lack of Strasbourg guidance and the more restrictive approach generally taken by English courts compared with that adopted in Strasbourg have previously been the subject of some criticism.[421] However, the position was

---

[415] The paucity of reasoning in the court's rulings under Art.41 makes it difficult to identify a coherent set of principles capable of being applied by the national courts. Contrast, e.g. *Halford v UK* (1997) 24 E.H.R.R. 523 and *Kopp v Switzerland* (1998) 27 E.H.R.R. 91. See also *Kingsley v UK* (2002) 35 E.H.R.R. 177 at [40]. The Law Commission Report No.266 [3.12] *Damages Under the HRA* noted "It is rare to find a reasoned decision articulating principles on which a remedy is afforded. One former judge of the ECtHR privately states: 'We have no principles'. Another judge responds 'We have principles we just do not apply them'."

[416] s.8(4).

[417] *Rights Brought Home*, Cmnd.3782, (1997), para.2.6. See also HL Debs, col.1232 (November 3, 1997). In this rapidly changing area, see further: p.100–01 Wadham, Mountfield and Edmundson *Blackstone's Guide to the Human Rights Act* (2003, 3rd edn) at paras 6.2ff. and Clayton & Tomlinson, *The Law of Human Rights* (OUP, 2000 and annual update) at paras 21.10ff.

[418] [2003] 2 All E.R. 209—following which the Mental Health Act 1983 (Remedial) Order 2001 (S.I. 2001/3712) was made to rectify the incompatibility.

[419] Law Commission Report on *Damages under the Human Rights Act 1998* (Law Com. No.266) (Cm. 4853) (October 2000) suggests that the obvious analogy to a claim for damages under the 1998 Act is a claim against a public authority in tort (paras 4.14 and 4.15) but warns against the danger of drawing the analogy too strictly and says that "the exercise is difficult and the comparisons must be treated with care".

[420] [2004] Q.B. 1124 at [49]–[81]. See also *R. (Bernard) v Enfield LBC* [2003] H.R.L.R. 4; *R. (N) v Secretary of State for the Home Department* [2003] EWHC 193, 3 W.L.R. 185; *R. (Mambakasa) v Secretary of State for the Home Department* [2003] EWHC 319 (Admin); *Cullen v Chief Constable Royal Ulster Constabulary* [2003] 1 W.L.R. 1763 at [75]–[84]; *R. (H) v Secretary of State for the Home Dept.* [2004] 2 A.C. 253.

[421] See, e.g. Hartshorne, *The Human Rights Act 1998 and Damages for Non-Pecuniary Loss* [2004] E.H.R.L.R. 660.

clarified somewhat in *R. (Greenfield) v Secretary of State for the Home Department*[422] where the House of Lords held that in deciding whether and, if so, in what amount, to award damages under the Human Rights Act for a violation of the Convention, a domestic court had to take into account the principles applied by the European Court of Human Rights in awarding compensation under Art.41 of the Convention, including its ordinary practice of finding a violation of Art.6 to be, in itself, just satisfaction. The purpose of incorporating the Convention was to give victims the same remedies they could recover in the European Court without the delay and expense, rather than better remedies than they would recover in Strasbourg.

Section 4(6) of the Act enables the Government to continue argue in Strasbourg,   **3–88**
for example, that the legislative provision in question is not incompatible with Convention rights. It also means that no damages are available where a defendant has acted in accordance with a statute which has been declared to be incompatible.[423] In respect of the UK's derogation from Art.5, however, which the House of Lords found to be invalid in *A and others v Secretary of State for the Home Department*,[424] the unavailability of Human Rights Act damages for detainees (some of whom had been incarcerated for over three years) in breach of Art.5 raises the issue of whether this constitutes a breach of Art.5(5).[425] Whether a declaration of incompatibility amounts to an effective remedy within the meaning of Art.13 in such circumstances is also presently unresolved.

VI. Judicial acts

Where the complaint concerns a judicial act,[426] proceedings must be brought by   **3–89**
way of appeal[427] or judicial review,[428] or in such other forum as may be prescribed by rules.[429] The amendments to the CPR provide that a claim under s.7(1)(a) in respect of a judicial act must be commenced in the High Court.

The Act does not affect any rule of law which prevents a court from being subject   **3–90**
to judicial review.[430] Accordingly, the prohibition on judicial review of a matter arising out of trial on indictment, which is reflected in s.29(3) of the Supreme Court Act 1981,[431] continues to apply. Moreover, in the absence of bad faith or other exceptional circumstances, there is a strong presumption against judicial

---

[422] [2005] 1 W.L.R. 673 at [18]–[19].

[423] See *Re K* [2001] Fam. 377, CA at paras 45, 67 and 118–30.

[424] [2004] UKHL 56; [2005] 2 A.C. 68.

[425] cf. *R. (KB) Mental Health Tribunal* [2004] Q.B. 936 at paras 27–32.

[426] s.9(5) provides that term "judicial act" means a judicial act of a court and includes an act done on the instructions, or on behalf, of a judge; and the term "judge" includes a member of a tribunal, a justice of the peace and a clerk or other officer entitled to exercise the jurisdiction of a court.

[427] s.9(1)(a).

[428] s.9(1)(b).

[429] s.9(1)(c).

[430] s.9(2).

[431] As to the principles governing the application of s.29(3) see *In re Smalley* [1985] A.C. 622 (HL); *In re Sampson* [1987] 1 W.L.R. 194 (HL); *In re Ashton* [1994] 1 A.C. 9 (HL); *R. v Manchester Crown Court ex parte DPP* [1993] 1 W.L.R. 1524 (HL).

review of a decision to prosecute in criminal proceedings.[432] For an example of "exceptional circumstances" which were sufficient to displace the presumption, see *R. (D) v Central Criminal Court.*[433]

3–91   Damages may not be awarded in respect of a judicial act done in good faith[434] save to the extent required by Art.5(5) of the Convention.[435] Article 5(5) provides that any person whose arrest or detention was unlawful must have an enforceable right to compensation. Where a person has been imprisoned unlawfully by order of a court,[436] the United Kingdom is thus obliged under the Convention to afford a right to compensation, irrespective of fault.[437] In order to meet this obligation, whilst preserving the immunity of judges and magistrates from personal liability for judicial acts, any such award is to be made against the Crown.[438] Under CPR r.19.4A(3) a claim for damages in respect of a judicial act must be set out in the statement of case or appeal notice. An award of damages in respect of a judicial act may only be made after the "appropriate person", if not already a party, has been joined.[439] The Lord Chancellor, as the "appropriate person", will be notified of the claim when it is made, and has 21 days (or such other period as the court directs) in which to indicate whether he wishes to be joined at the outset, either to contest the substance of the claim, or to make representations on the quantum of damages.[440] Thereafter, he may be joined by the court at any time prior to the making of the award.[441] Where a claim is made under s.7 of the Act in respect of a judicial act which is alleged to have infringed the claimant's rights under Art.5 of the Convention, and that claim is based upon a finding by another court or tribunal that the claimant's Convention rights have been infringed, the court hearing the claim may proceed on the basis of the finding of the first court or

---

[432] *R. v DPP ex parte Kebilene and ors* [1999] 3 W.L.R. 972 (HL). See also *R. (Pepushi) v CPS* [2004] A.C.D. 47.

[433] *R. (D) v Central Criminal Court and another* [2004] 1 Cr.App.R. 41, [2003] EWHC 1212 (Admin)—Scott Baker L.J. called for Parliamentary consideration of an amendment to s.29(3) at para.35 of the judgment. See, most recently, *R. (Snelgrove) v Woolwich Crown Court* [2005] 1 W.L.R. 3223 on the ambit of s.29(3). *cf. R. v Canterbury Crown Court ex p Regentford* (*The Times*, February 6, 2001) at paras 16 to 22 and *R. (Shields) v Liverpool Crown Court* [2001] U.K.H.R.R. 610, at paras 20, 33 to 34, 53 to 58.

[434] Where a judicial act is done in bad faith, s.9(3) does not apply. As to the immunity of judges see *Sirros v Moore* [1975] 1 Q.B. 118. As to the liability of magistrates for acts in the performance of their judicial functions, see Justices of the Peace Act 1997 ss.51 and 52 (a magistrate may is only liable for acts done in excess of jurisdiction and in bad faith). *cf. R. (Mullen) v Secretary of State for the Home Department* [2005] 1 A.C. 1 at paras 9 and 39 to 55.

[435] s.9(3).

[436] As to the circumstances in which an error by a Magistrates Court will deprive the court of its jurisdiction to imprison see *Re McC* [1985] A.C. 528 (HL); *R. v Manchester City Magistrates Justices ex parte Davies* [1989] Q.B. 631.

[437] As to the application of Art.5(1) and (5) in these circumstances see *Benham v United Kingdom* (1996) 22 E.H.R.R. 293; *Poole v United Kingdom* (1998) Application No.28190/95; *Johnson v United Kingdom* (1998) Application No.28455/95; *Denson v United Kingdom* (1998) Application No.25286/94: *Perks and ors v United Kingdom*, (2000) 30 E.H.R.R. 33.

[438] s.9(4).

[439] s.9(4).

[440] CPR r.19.4A(3) and (4).

[441] CPR r.19.4A(4).

tribunal, but is not bound to do so. Instead, it may reach its own conclusion in the light of that finding and of the evidence heard in the earlier proceedings.[442]

H. MISCELLANEOUS PROVISIONS

I. Commencement

A number of the Act's procedural provisions came into force when it received the **3–92** Royal Assent on November 9, 1998.[443] Section 19, which makes provision for Ministerial statements of compatibility, came into force on November 24, 1998.[444] The remaining provisions came into force on October 2, 2000.[445]

II. Costs

The presumption that costs follow the event may not always be appropriate in **3–93** litigation under the Human Rights Act. The Privy Council has recognised that where the substance of a challenge involves important questions affecting fundamental rights, an award of costs against an unsuccessful applicant may be inappropriate since "*bona fide* resort to rights under the constitution ought not to be discouraged".[446] A similar approach has been taken by the Constitutional Court of South Africa. In *Motsepe v IRC*[447] Ackerman J. observed that:

" . . . one should be cautious in awarding costs against litigants who seek to enforce their constitutional rights against the state, particularly where the constitutionality of a statutory provision is attacked, lest such orders have an unduly inhibiting or "chilling" effect on other potential litigants in this category. This cautious approach cannot, however, be allowed to develop into an inflexible rule so that litigants are induced into believing that they are free to challenge the constitutionality of statutory provisions in this court, no matter how spurious the grounds for doing so may be."

The "cautious approach" is evidenced by the recent, increased willingness to **3–94** make costs orders in advance: e.g. *R. (Refugee Legal Centre) v Secretary of State for the Home Department*[448] where a full pre-emptive costs order in favour of the applicant charity was made and *R. (Campaign For Nuclear Disarmament) v Prime Minister and others*[449] in which a pre-emptive £25,000 maximum, unsuccessful costs limit was ordered. In *R. (Corner House Research) v Secretary of*

---

[442] CPR r.33.9(1) and (2).

[443] s.22(1): the provisions concerned were s.18 (appointment of judges to the European Court of Human Rights), s.20 (supplemental provisions and rule-making powers), s.21(5) (abolition of the death penalty in the armed forces) and s.22 (the commencement provisions).

[444] Human Rights Act 1998 (Commencement) Order 1998 S.I. 1998/2882.

[445] The Human Rights Act 1998 (Commencement No.2) Order 2000 (S.I. 2000/1851).

[446] *Ahnee and ors v DPP* (March 17, 1999) [1999] 2 A.C. 294.

[447] (1997) (6) B.C.L.R. 692 at 705 para.30.

[448] [2005] 1 W.L.R. 2219.

[449] [2002] EWHC 2777 (Admin), *The Times*, December 27, 2002.

State for Trade & Industry[450] the Court of Appeal gave guidance on the making of protective costs orders.

3–95   So far as successful defendants are concerned, the guidance in para.II.2.1 of the *Practice Direction (Costs: Criminal Proceedings)*[451] still permits a refusal to order costs to an acquitted defendant if:

> "there are positive reasons for not doing so. For example where the defendant's own conduct has brought suspicion on himself and has misled the prosecution into thinking that the case against him was stronger than it was".

Moreover, the Divisional Court held that the inability of to appeal or judicially review a refusal to order an acquitted defendant his costs is not a breach of Art.13: *R. v Canterbury Crown Court ex p Regentford.*[452] By contrast, in *Y v Norway*[453] a domestic civil court was criticised for refusing to order compensation to an acquitted man on the basis he had probably committed the offences in question.

III. The Act does not create criminal offences

3–96   Nothing in the Human Rights Act creates a criminal offence.[454] It does not necessarily follow that the Act is irrelevant to the scope of offences which already exist.[455] Moreover, where a claimant alleges that the very existence of a criminal offence interferes with his Convention rights, the High Court has jurisdiction, in an exceptional case, to make a declaration of incompatibility: *R. (Rusbridger) v Attorney General.*[456] See also *Re A. (Children) (Conjoined Twins: Surgical Separation)*[457] and *R. (Pepushi) v CPS.*[458] The Director of Public Prosecutions is under no obligation to indicate, prior to a person committing an offence, that such conduct will be immune from criminal proceedings purely on the basis that it is conduct potentially protected under the Convention: *R. (Pretty) v DPP*[459] (concerning the Suicide Act 1961, s.2(1)).

---

[450] [2005] 1 W.L.R. 2600: (largely approving guidelines set out by Dyson J. in *R. v Lord Chancellor, Ex parte Child Poverty Action Group* [(1999) 1 W.L.R. 347) i) A protective costs order could be made at any stage of the proceedings, on such conditions as the court thought fit, provided that the court was satisfied that (a) the issues raised were of general public importance; (b) the public interest required that those issues should be resolved; (c) the applicant had no private interest in the outcome of the case; (d) having regard to the financial resources of the applicant and the respondent and to the amount of costs that were likely to be involved it was fair and just to make the order; (e) if the order was not made the applicant would probably discontinue the proceedings and would be acting reasonably in so doing. (ii) If those acting for the applicant were doing so pro bono that would be likely to enhance the merits of the application for a protective costs order. (iii) It was for the court, in its discretion, to decide whether it was fair and just to make the order having regard to those considerations.

[451] [2004] 2 All E.R. 1070.

[452] [2001] H.R.L.R. 18 at paras 16 to 22.

[453] 41 E.H.R.R. 87.

[454] s.7(8).

[455] See, for example, *A v United Kingdom* (1999) 27 E.H.R.R. 611; *Bubbins v UK* (2005) 41 E.H.R.R. 458; *Gul v Turkey* (2002) 34 E.H.R.R. 719; *McCann v UK* (1996) 21 E.H.R.R. 97; *Nachova v Bulgaria* (2006) 42 E.H.R.R. 43.

[456] [2004] 1 A.C. 357, HL.

[457] [2001] Fam. 147, CA (Civ Div).

[458] [2004] A.C.D. 47.

[459] [2002] 1 A.C. 800, HL.

CHAPTER 4

THE DEFINITION OF A CRIMINAL CHARGE

A. INTRODUCTION

The most stringent of the Convention's due process guarantees are reserved for **4–01** those charged with a criminal offence. Whilst the right to a fair trial in Art.6(1) applies to civil as well as to criminal proceedings, its requirements are more extensive where the determination of a "criminal charge" is in issue.[1] In addition, there are a number of important due process rights which are expressly confined to criminal defendants: the presumption of innocence in Art.6(2); the "minimum rights" spelt out in Art.6(3); the requirement for legal certainty in the definition of an offence, the principle of restrictive interpretation, and the prohibition on retrospective offences and penalties in Art.7; the right of appeal in Art.2 of Protocol 4; and the prohibition on double jeopardy in Art.4 of that Protocol.[2] In order to determine whether an applicant can rely on any of these rights, it is necessary to have a clear understanding of what constitutes a criminal charge for the purposes of the Convention.[3]

Since the first edition of this book, a major characteristic of English law reform has been the tendency to adopt legislative techniques which seek to resolve

---

[1] Note, however, that in *Albert and LeCompte v Belgium* (1983) 5 E.H.R.R. 533 the Court held that where professional disciplinary proceedings have serious consequences for the individual, rights analagous to those set out in Arts 6(2) and 6(3) will be implied into Art.6(1): see para.4–43 below. The overall due process requirment of Art.6—whether civil or criminal—has been emphasised by the UK courts: see *McCann v Crown Court at Manchester* [2003] 1 A.C. 787, HL at para.29; *McIntosh v Lord Advocate* [2003] 1 A.C. 1078, PC at para.28; *R. v Benjafield and Rezvi* [2003] 1 A.C. 1099, HL at para.15; and *International Transport Roth GmbH v Secretary of State for the Home Department* [2003] Q.B. 728, at p.748. In *International Transport Roth*, Simon Brown L.J. emphasised (at p.748) that "the classification of proceedings between criminal and civil is secondary to the more directly relevant question of just what protections are required for a fair trial". See also *Gough v Chief Constable of Derbyshire Constabulary* [2002] Q.B. 1213, at paras 90–93.

[2] At the time that the Human Rights Bill was placed before Parliament, the Government signalled its intention to sign, ratify, and incorporate Protocol 7 as soon as practicable: *Rights Brought Home*, Cmnd.3782 (1997) paras 4.15–4.16. The Government has since signed the Protocol. The Department for Constitutional Affairs, *Report on the UK Government's Inter-Departmental Review of the UK's Position under various International Human Rights Instruments*, July 2004, indicates that ratification will not be possible until a legislative vehicle is found by which certain minor amendments can be made in family law (i.e. the terms of Art.5 protecting the right to equality between spouses): see Appendix 4 to the Report. To date this has not occurred.

[3] The "criminal charge" jurisprudence also has implications for Art.5(1): see para.4–56 below.

perceived procedural impediments in the criminal law by exporting its subject matter into civil proceedings. One such technique is to empower courts to grant injunctions prohibiting conduct deemed to be unacceptable, with breach of the injunction punishable by penalties. Football banning orders[4] and anti-social behaviour orders are key examples.[5] Another such technique, embodied in Pt 5 of the Proceeds of Crime Act 2002, is the power of the Asset Recovery Agency to bring civil proceedings for the recovery of unlawfully obtained property, irrespective of whether the holders of such property can be proved to have committed a criminal offence in obtaining it.[6] Finally, in the wake of the terrorist attacks on the United States on September 11, 2001, the Government has sought to use a number of legislative techniques including indefinite detention without trial, as contained in Pt IV of the Anti-Terrorism, Crime and Security Act 2001, and control orders as contained in the Prevention of Terrorism Act 2005.[7] All of these statutory schemes raise the question whether they count as the determination of a criminal charge within the meaning of Art.6; and consequently, whether the more stringent due process protections apply.

B. CRIMINAL PROCEEDINGS

I. General Principles

4–02   The Court has held that an autonomous definition of the term "criminal" is necessary in order to prevent contracting states from undermining the Convention's due process guarantees by reclassifying an offence as a disciplinary, administrative, regulatory, or civil penalty.[8] Adopting a realistic and substantive

---

[4] See para.4–47 below.

[5] See para.4–49 below.

[6] See para.4–19 below.

[7] See paras 4–54 below.

[8] For discussion, see Stavros, *The Guarantees for Accused Persons under Art.6 of the European Convention on Human Rights* (Martinus Nijhoff, 1993), pp.1–39. Harris D.J., O'Boyle M. and Warbrick C., *The Law of the European Convention on Human Rights* (Butterworths, 1995), pp.166–173. For the common law perspective on the definition of crime see Glanville Williams *The Definition of Crime in Current Legal Problems* (1995) at p.107; Hughes G., *The Concept of Crime, An American View* (1959) Crim.L.R. 239 *et seq.*; Seton Pollock, *The distinguishing Mark of Crime* (1929) 22 M.L.R. 4895; William Blackstone, *The Commentaries on the Laws of England*, Vol.IV, 4th edn (1876), pp.2–5. For the origins of the true crime/regulatory distinction in English law, see *Sherras v DeRutzen* [1895] 1 Q.B. 918. In *Proprietary Articles Trade Association v Attorney General for Canada* [1931] A.C. 310, 324 Lord Atkin observed:
"Criminal law connotes only the quality of such acts or omissions as are prohibited under appropriate penal provisions by authority of the state. The criminal quality of an act cannot be discerned by intuition; nor can it be discovered by reference to any standard but one: Is the act prohibited with penal consequences?"
In *Customs and Excise Comrs v City of London Magistrates' Courts* [2000] 1 W.L.R. 2020, 2025 Lord Bingham of Cornhill C.J. expressed himself in similar vein:
"It is in my judgment the general understanding that criminal proceedings involve a formal accusation made on behalf of the state or by a private prosecutor that a defendant has committed a breach of the criminal law, and the state or the private prosecutor has instituted proceedings which may culminate in the conviction and condemnation of the defendant."
However, in the Divisional Court judgment of *R. v Manchester Crown Court ex. parte McCann* [2001] 1 W.L.R. 358 at para.18, Lord Woolf C.J. noted that the distinction between criminal and civil proceedings may often, in practice, be difficult to determine:

approach, the Court will look behind the national classification, and inquire whether a proceeding which involves the determination of an accusation is "by its nature 'criminal' from the point of view of the Convention", or has exposed the person concerned to a sanction which "belongs in general to the 'criminal' sphere".[9] In the leading case of *Engel v Netherlands*[10] the Court explained its reasoning as follows:

> "The Convention without any doubt allows the States, in the performance of their function as the guardians of the public interest, to maintain or establish a disctinction between criminal law and disciplinary law, and to draw the dividing line, but only subject to certain conditions . . . If the Contracting States were able, at their discretion, to classify an offence as disciplinary instead of criminal, or to prosecute the author of a 'mixed' offence on the disciplinary rather than on the criminal plane, the operation of the fundamental clauses of Articles 6 and 7 would be subordinated to their sovereign will. A latitude extending thus far might lead to results incompatible with the purpose and object of the Convention. The Court thus has jurisdiction . . . to satisfy itself that the disciplinary does not improperly encroach upon the criminal".

The Court has since emphasised that there is nothing to prevent a state from decriminalising certain conduct, and prosecuting it instead as an administrative or regulatory offence, provided that in doing so it does not deprive the accused of the due process rights guaranteed by the Convention.[11]

II. The Engel Criteria

In *Engel* the Court established three criteria for determining whether proceedings **4–03** are "criminal" from the point of view of the Convention, namely: (a) the domestic classification; (b) the nature of the offence; and (c) the severity of the potential penalty which the person concerned risks incurring.[12] The Court's subsequent caselaw establishes that these criteria are to be assessed independently and that most importance is to be attached to the third.

The first criterion—domestic classification—"is of relative weight and serves **4–04** only as a starting point".[13] If domestic law classifies an offence as criminal, then this will be decisive,[14] even if the penalty imposed is relatively slight.[15] But if the

---

"There is no one overriding test within our domestic law for determining whether proceedings are civil or criminal. To some extent it is like describing an elephant; it is recognised when seen but it is difficult effectively to describe".

[9] *Lutz v Germany* (1988) 10 E.H.R.R. 182 at para.55; *Garyfallou AEBE v Greece* (1999) 28 E.H.R.R. 344 at para.33; *Lauko v Slovakia* (1998) 33 E.H.R.R. 40 at para.57.

[10] (1979–80) 1 E.H.R.R. 647 at para.81.

[11] *Ozturk v Turkey* (1984) 6 E.H.R.R. 409 at para.49.

[12] *Engel v Netherlands* (1979–80) 1 E.H.R.R. 647 at para.82; *Benham v United Kingdom* (1996) 22 E.H.R.R. 293 at para.56; *Garyfallou AEBE v Greece* (1999) 28 E.H.R.R. 344 at para.32; *Lauko v Slovakia* (1998) 33 E.H.R.R. 40 at para.56.

[13] *Benham v United Kingdom* (1996) 22 E.H.R.R. 293 at para.56; *Engel v Netherlands* (1979–80) 1 E.H.R.R. 647 at para.82; *Weber v Switzerland* (1990) 12 E.H.R.R. 508 at para.31; *Demicoli v Malta* (1992) 14 E.H.R.R. 47 at para.33; *Ozturk v Turkey* (1984) 6 E.H.R.R. 409 at para.52; *Campbell and Fell v United Kingdom* (1985) 7 E.H.R.R. 165 at para.71.

[14] *Engel v Netherlands* (1979–80) 1 E.H.R.R. 647 at para.82.

[15] As the Court put it in *Ozturk v Germany* (1984) 6 E.H.R.R. 409 at para.54: "The relative lack of seriousness of the penalty at stake cannot divest an offence of its inherently criminal character".

domestic law classifies the offence as civil, disciplinary, or administrative then the court will look behind the national classification and examine the substantive reality of the procedure in question.[16] In this respect, the indications given by national law have only "a formal and relative value".[17] As the Court said in *Engel*, "the autonomy of the concept of 'criminal' operates, as it were, one way only".[18]

4–05　　The second criterion—the nature of the offence—"carries more weight".[19] Here, the Court will examine whether the legal rule in question is addressed exclusively to a specific group, or is of a generally binding character[20]; whether the proceedings are instituted by a public body with statutory powers of enforcement[21]; whether there is a punitive or deterrent element to the process[22]; whether the imposition of any penalty is dependent upon a finding of culpability[23]; and how comparable procedures are classified in other Council of Europe member states.[24] The fact that an offence does not give rise to a criminal record may be relevant,[25] but is unlikely to be decisive, since it is usually a reflection of the domestic classification.[26] Statutory regimes can be classified as non-criminal even though

---

[16] See, for example, *Campbell and Fell v United Kingdom* (1985) 7 E.H.R.R. 165 where the Court defined prison disciplinary proceedings as "criminal" despite settled domestic authority to the effect that they were not a "criminal cause or matter" for the purposes of judicial review and appeal; and *Benham v United Kingdom* (1996) 22 E.H.R.R. 293 at para.56 where the same approach was taken in relation to proceedings for commitment to prison for non-payment of the community charge, despite the dicta of Henry J. in *R. v Highbury Corner Magistrates Court ex parte Watkins* [1992] R.A. 300 to the effect that such proceedings were "plainly legal proceedings other than criminal proceedings".

[17] *Ezeh and Connors v United Kingdom* (2004) 39 E.H.R.R. 1 at para.92.

[18] *Engel v Netherlands* (1979–80) 1 E.H.R.R. 647 at para.81.

[19] *Benham v United Kingdom* (1996) 22 E.H.R.R. 293 at para.56; *Ozturk v Germany* (1984) 6 E.H.R.R. 409 at para.52; *Campbell and Fell v United Kingdom* (1985) 7 E.H.R.R. 165 at para.71; *Ezeh and Connors v United Kingdom* (2004) 39 E.H.R.R. 1 at para.92.

[20] See, for example, *Bendenoun v France* (1994) 18 E.H.R.R. 54 at para.47; *Weber v Switzerland* (1990) 12 E.H.R.R. 508 at para.33; *Demicoli v Malta* (1992) 14 E.H.R.R. 47 at para.32; In *Benham v United Kingdom* (1996) 22 E.H.R.R. 293 at para.56 the Court attached importance to the fact that the obligation to pay the Community Charge, and the procedure for its enforcement, was of general application to all citizens. Similarly in *Campbell and Fell v United Kingdom* (1985) 7 E.H.R.R. 165 at para.71 the Court noted that the illegality of some acts which constituted offences against prison discipline "may not turn on the fact that they were committed in prison; certain conduct which constitutes an offence under the Rules may also amount to an offence under the criminal law".

[21] See *Benham v United Kingdom* (1996) 22 E.H.R.R. 293 at para.56.

[22] *Ozturk v Germany* (1984) 6 E.H.R.R. 409 at para.53; *Bendenoun v France* (1994) 18 E.H.R.R. 54 at para.47; *Benham v United Kingdom* (1996) 22 E.H.R.R. 293 at para.56.

[23] *Benham v United Kingdom* (1996) 22 E.H.R.R. 293 at para.56.

[24] *Ozturk v Germany* (1984) 6 E.H.R.R. 409 at para.53. See also *Maaouia v France* (2001) 33 E.H.R.R. 42, at para.39. *Cf. Ezeh and Connors v United Kingdom* (2004) 39 E.H.R.R. 1 at para.77, where the Government unsuccessfully sought to argue that the sanction of loss of early release for a breach of prison discipline was a common sanction of prison disciplinary regimes in many Council of Europe States.

[25] *Ravnsborg v Sweden* (1994) 18 E.H.R.R. 38.

[26] *Benham v United Kingdom* (1996) 22 E.H.R.R. 293; *Campbell and Fell v United Kingdom* (1985) 7 E.H.R.R. 165; *Lauko v Slovakia* (1998) 33 E.H.R.R. 40 at para.58. *Cf. Ravnsborg v Sweden* (1994) 18 E.H.R.R. 38; and *Pierre-Bloch v France* (1998) 26 E.H.R.R. 202 where the fact that a finding of guilt was not recorded as a criminal conviction was held to confirm the Court's view that the proceedings were not criminal in character.

they primarily deal with the subject matter of criminal law, provided that they are essentially preventative as opposed to penal in nature.[27]

The third criterion—the severity of the penalty—will often be decisive, partic-   **4-06**
ularly if the potential penalties include imprisonment. In *Engel* the Court held that a deprivation of liberty liable to be imposed as a punishment is, in general, a penalty that belongs to the "criminal" sphere, unless by its "nature, duration or manner of execution, [it] cannot be appreciably detrimental".[28] A criminal penalty may include any penalty contingent on a further act by the applicant.[29] Significant financial penalties may be sufficient, particularly if they are enforceable by imprisonment in default.[30] Even a minor financial penalty will suffice where it has a clearly deterrent and punitive purpose.[31] In each case, it is the potential penalty, rather than the actual penalty imposed which is decisive.[32]

The Court has emphasised in a number of cases that the second and third criteria   **4-07**
are alternative, and not necessarily cumulative.[33] For proceedings to be defined as "criminal" it suffices *either* that the offence in question is "criminal" in nature

---

[27] See for example *Maaouia v France* (2001) 33 E.H.R.R. 42, at para.39 (the exclusion of "aliens" for the puposes of immigration control); *Drozd and Janousek v France and Spain*, 14 E.H.R.R. 747, at para.10 (extradition); *Guzzardi v Italy* (1980) 3 E.H.R.R. 333 at para.108 (compulsory resident orders) and *M v Italy*, 70 D.R. 1991 (anti-mafia racketeering provisions). See also para.4–46 below.
Engel v Netherlands (1979–80) 1 E.H.R.R. 647 at para.82; See also *Benham v United Kingdom* (1996)
[28] E.H.R.R. 293 (Op. Comm) at para.67, where the Commission noted the Magistrates' power to imprison a person for up to 30 days for non-payment of the community charge, and said that "this alone would be sufficiently important to warrant classifying the 'offence' with which the applicant was charged as a criminal one under the Convention".
[29] See *Steel v United Kingdom* (1998) 28 E.H.R.R. 603 (Op. Comm) at para.66–68 (a bind over to keep the peace in the furture was held to constitute a criminal charge). See also *Hooper v United Kingdom*, *The Times*, November 19, 2005.
[30] *Bendenoun v France* (1994) 18 E.H.R.R. 54 at para.47. But this is not necessarily the case: *Ravnsborg v Sweden* (1994) 18 E.H.R.R. 38. Note also that in *Welch v United Kingdom* (1995) 20 E.H.R.R. 247 a confiscation order under the Drug Trafficking Offences Act 1985 was held to be a "criminal penalty" for the purposes of Art.7, partly because it was enforceable by imprisonment in default.
[31] *Schmautzer v Austria* (1995) 21 E.H.R.R. 511; *Pfarrmeier v Austria* (1996) 22 E.H.R.R. 175; *Umlauft v Austria* (1996) 22 E.H.R.R. 76; *Lauko v Slovakia* (1998) 33 E.H.R.R. 40.
[32] See *Engel v Netherlands* (1979–80) 1 E.H.R.R. 647 para.85 where the Court emphasised that "the final outcome of the appeal cannot diminish the importance of what was initially at stake"; and *Demicoli v Malta* (1992) 14 E.H.R.R. 47 at para.34 where the Court considered that it was the potential rather than the actual penalty which determined the importance of what was at stake for the accused.
[33] See, for example, *Lutz v Germany* (1987) 10 E.H.R.R. 182 at para.55; *Garyfallou AEBE v Greece* (1999) 28 E.H.R.R. 344 at para.33.

or that the penalty belongs to the "criminal sphere".[34] A cumulative approach may, however, be adopted where a separate analysis of the criteria does not make it possible to reach a clear conclusion as to the existence of a criminal charge.[35] In applying the above principles to English law in *R. (McCann) v Crown Court at Manchester*,[36] Lord Steyn emphasised the importance of looking at the substance rather than the form of the statutory scheme:

> "In a classic passage in *Proprietary Articles Trade Association v Attorney General for Canada* [1931] AC 310, 324 Lord Atkin observed: 'Criminal law connotes only the quality of such acts or omissions as are prohibited under appropriate penal provisions by authority of the state. The criminal quality of an act cannot be discerned by intuition; nor can it be discovered by reference to any standard but one: Is the act prohibited with penal consequences?' In *Customs and Excise Comrs v City of London Magistrates' Court* [2000] 1 WLR 2020, 2025 Lord Bingham of Cornhill CJ expressed himself in similar vein: 'It is in my judgment the general understanding that criminal proceedings involve a formal accusation made on behalf of the state or by a private prosecutor that a defendant has committed a breach of the criminal law, and the state or the private prosecutor has instituted proceedings which may culminate in the conviction and condemnation of the defendant.' "[37]

III. "Administrative" offences

4–08   A number of the member states of the Council of Europe have maintained a discrete category of "administrative" offences, which are subject to a separate enforcement regime, falling outside the ordinary criminal justice system. The leading case in this field is *Ozturk v Germany*[38] which involved the imposition of a fine for a minor road traffic offence. The offence in question had been decriminalised, and the power to impose a fine transferred to the administrative authorities. The first of the *Engel* criteria thus supported the government's argument that the criminal guarantees of Art.6 were inapplicable. However, the Court considered that the offence was criminal in nature.[39] Offences which give rise to deterrent penalties, typically including a fine or imprisonment, would usually come within the ambit of the criminal law. The Court noted that in the vast majority of contracting states, conduct of the kind alleged against the

---

[34] Thus, where an offence is plainly criminal in character, the relative lack of seriousness of the penalty actually imposed cannot deprive it of its inherently criminal character: *Ozturk v Germany* (1984) 6 E.H.R.R. 409 at para.54; *Lutz v Germany* (1987) 10 E.H.R.R. 182 at para.55; *Lauko v Slovakia* (1998) 33 E.H.R.R. 40 at para.57. Equally, the nature and severity of the penalty can be sufficient in itself to define an offence as criminal: *Engel v Netherlands* (1979–80) 1 E.H.R.R. 647 paras 82–85; *Benham v United Kingdom* (1996) 22 E.H.R.R. 293 (Op. Comm) at para.67; *Demicoli v Malta* (1992) 14 E.H.R.R. 47 at para.34.

[35] *Bendenoun v France* (1994) 18 E.H.R.R. 54 para.47; *Garyfallou AEBE v Greece* (1999) 28 E.H.R.R. 344 at para.34; *Lauko v Slovakia* (1998) 33 E.H.R.R. 40 at para.57. See also *Campbell and Fell v United Kingdom* (1985) 7 E.H.R.R. 165 at para.73.

[36] [2003] 1 A.C. 787, at para.20.

[37] See also *R. (Mundie) v Dover Magistrates Court* [2003] Q.B. 1238, CA, at para.36 *per* Laws L.J.: the application of the Engel criteria "should not distract the court from the question whether, given the three criteria, the proceedings in issue are in substance in the nature of a criminal charge. Are they an instance of the use of state power to condemn or punish individuals for wrong doing?"

[38] (1984) 6 E.H.R.R. 409.

[39] Para.53.

applicant would be treated as an ordinary criminal offence. Although the domestic legislation undoubtedly had the object of decriminalisation, its principal effect was to alter the procedural rules and the applicable penalties. The essence of the offence itself had "undergone no change in content". It was a rule of law directed towards all road users proscribing certain conduct and imposing a sanction for its breach. The penalty was intended to be punitive and deterrent in its effect. In the Court's view the general character of the rule, and the purpose of the penalty were sufficient to show that the offence was, in terms of Art.6 of the Convention, criminal in nature. The fact that it was of a minor character, and was unlikely to involve damage to the accused's reputation, was irrelevant, since there was "nothing to suggest that the criminal offence referred to in the Convention necessarily implies a certain degree of seriousness."[40] The "relative lack of seriousness of the penalty at stake" could not, in the Court's view "divest an offence of its inherently criminal character". The Court therefore found it unnecessary to apply the third of the *Engel* criteria.

The substantive right at issue in *Ozturk* was the guarantee of free interpretation **4–09** in Art.6(3)(e). In *Lutz v Germany*,[41] however, the Court reached a similar conclusion in relation to the presumption of innocence in Art.6(2). *Lutz* concerned a regulatory road traffic offence punishable by a fine and disqualification from driving for a period of up to three months. The proceedings against the applicant had been discontinued, but he had been refused his costs on the ground that the acquittal was technical in character. The Court held that since the proceedings were, in substance, criminal, he was entitled to invoke the protection of Art.6(2).[42]

The Court has taken a similar approach in relation to minor motoring offences **4–10** under Austrian and French administrative law.[43] In *Schmautzer v Austria*,[44] the applicant was stopped by police for failing to wear a seat-belt when driving. He received an order from the local police authority, obliging him to pay a fine. Under the relevant legislation there was a right of appeal, but no right to an adversarial trial. The Court held that although in Austrian law the procedure fell entirely within the administrative sphere, it should be treated as criminal for the purposes of the Convention. Austrian law referred ambiguously to "administrative *offences*", and the fine imposed on the applicant was accompanied by an order for his committal to prison in the event of his defaulting on payment.[45] In *Gradinger v Austria*[46] the Court applied the same autonomous approach to the definition of a criminal offence in Art.4 of Protocol 7 (the prohibition on double jeopardy). This was despite the fact that Austria had lodged a reservation when it ratified Protocol 7, with the specific object of preserving the administrative/

---

[40] Para.53.
[41] (1987) 10 E.H.R.R. 182.
[42] On the facts, however, the Court found no breach.
[43] *Schmautzer v Austria* (1995) 21 E.H.R.R. 511; *Pfarrmeier v Austria* (1996) 22 E.H.R.R. 175; *Umlauft v Austria* (1996) 22 E.H.R.R. 76.
[44] (1995) 21 E.H.R.R. 511.
[45] *ibid.*, at para.28.
[46] Judgment October 23, 1995; See also *Olivera v Switzerland* (1999) 28 E.H.R.R. 289 where the Court assumed the applicability of Art.4 of Protocol 7 in respect of a minor motoring offence prosecuted administratively.

criminal distinction.[47] A similar result was reached in *Malige v France*,[48] a case concerning the administrative imposition of penalty points on the applicant's driving licence for exceeding the speed limit. Since the sanction could result in the loss of the applicant's driving licence, it had a deterrent and punitive purpose sufficient to identify it as a criminal charge.

4–11   In *Lauko v Slovakia*,[49] the applicant was fined by a local admistrative office for a "minor offence" of causing a nuisance. He complained to the Slovakian Constitutional Court that there had been no judicial hearing of the allegation, but his complaint was dismissed on the ground that the offence was insufficiently serious to justify examination by a court. The Court held that the proceedings were criminal in nature because of the generally applicable character of the legal rule in issue, and because of the punitive purpose behind the fine imposed. Reiterating that the second and third of the *Engel* criteria were to be independently assessed, so that the relative lack of seriousness of the offence and its penalty could not deprive the charge of its essentially criminal character,[50] the court held that the applicant was entitled to the benefit of a fair procedure, including the right to appeal the penalty to a judicial tribunal.

IV. Tax and customs penalties

4–12   In *Bendenoun v France*[51] the applicant was prosecuted and fined by the French customs and tax authorities for various customs, exchange control and tax offences. He alleged that the non-disclosure of relevant evidence was in breach of Art.6(1). The Court observed that the contracting states must be free to empower their revenue authorities to impose penal surcharges in cases of bad faith, providing the taxpayer is able to bring any such decision before a court that affords the safeguards of Art.6. It rejected, however, the argument of the French government that such proceedings should be classified as falling outside the criminal sphere for the purposes of the Convention. In the Court's view there were four factors which pointed to the opposite conclusion. First, the offence belonged to a general tax code, applying to all citizens. Secondly, the surcharge was intended primarily as a punishment rather than as a measure of pecuniary compensation. Thirdly, the object of the power to impose a surcharge was both deterrent and punitive. And fourthly, the amount of the surcharge was substantial (a total of FF992,932) and it was enforceable by imprisonment in default. Whilst none of these factors would have been sufficient on its own to categorise the proceedings as criminal, their cumulative effect rendered the criminal guarantees of Art.6 applicable.

4–13   Similarly, in *JJ v Netherlands*[52] a fiscal penalty was imposed on the applicant for non-payment of income tax. During the course of the applicant's appeal to the

---

[47] The Court held that the terms of the Austrian reservation were insufficiently specific to meet the requirements of Art.57: See para.1–162 above.
[48] (1998) 28 E.H.R.R. 578.
[49] (1998) 33 E.H.R.R. 40.
[50] See para.54.
[51] (1994) 18 E.H.R.R. 54.
[52] (1999) 28 E.H.R.R. 168.

Supreme Court, the Advocate General submitted an advisory opinion which was made available to the court, but not to the applicant. The European Court held that the penalty constituted a criminal sanction, and accordingly that the applicant was entitled to a fully adversarial procedure which respected his rights under Art.6(1).[53] In view of the fact that he had not been afforded the opportunity to comment on the Advocate General's submissions, the proceedings had violated the applicant's right to a fair trial.[54] In *AP, MP, and TP v Switzerland*[55] the court held that measures taken against the heirs of the deceased in respect of the latter's evasion of tax amounted to a criminal charge. This was despite the fact that it was the guilt of the deceased, rather than the heirs, which had to be demonstrated.[56]

The leading case in this field is now *Garyfallou AEBE v Greece*,[57] in which the   **4–14**
Greek Deputy Minister of Commerce had used a statutory power to order the applicant to pay a large fine for breaching import regulations. The Court held that the sanctions available were sufficiently severe in themselves to justify classifying the proceedings as criminal, such that it was unnecessary to consider separately whether the offence was criminal in nature:

"[The company] risked a maximum fine equal to the value of the imported goods, that is, nearly three times the amount actually fined. In the event of non-payment, national law provided for the seizure of the applicant company's assets and, more importantly for the purposes of the Court's examination, the detention of its directors for up to one year."[58]

In *Georgio v United Kingdom*[59] the court held that penalty assessments in respect of VAT, and appeals therefrom, were criminal proceedings. This principle was applied in *King v Walden (Inspector of Taxes)*[60] where Jacobs J. held that the system of imposition of penalties for fraudulent or negligent delivery of incorrect income tax returns was likewise criminal for the purposes of Art.6. It was a system designed to punish defaulting taxpayers. The amount of the fine was potentially very substantial and on appeal the burden of proof lay on the Crown. Whilst the proceedings at issue had been protracted there was, on the facts, no breach of the right to trial within a reasonable time. However, it was highly desirable that such appeals should, in future, be distinguished from other determinations and appeals, and should be put on a "fast track". By contrast in *Goldsmith v Commissioners of Customs and Excise*[61] the Divisional Court held that proceedings for the condemnation of goods forfeited by Customs and Excise

---

[53] Para.37.
[54] Paras 41 to 43.
[55] (1998) 26 E.H.R.R. 541.
[56] Proceedings had to be issued against the heirs because under Swiss law the deceased's estate had no legal personality.
[57] (1999) 28 E.H.R.R. 344.
[58] (1999) 28 E.H.R.R. 344 at para.34.
[59] Application No.40042/98 [2001] S.T.C. 80. The case concerned the imposition of civil penalties for dishonest evasion of excise duties. See also *Han v Customs and Excise Commrs* [2001] 1 W.L.R. 2253, CA.
[60] *King v Walden* [2001] S.T.C. 822, Ch.D. (affirmed in *King v United Kingdom (No.2)* [2004] S.T.C. 911, ECtHR.). See also *Janosevic v Sweden* (2004) 38 E.H.R.R. 22.
[61] [2001] 1 W.L.R. 1673, D.C.

under s.139 of and Sch.3 to the Customs and Excise Management Act 1979 were not criminal proceedings for the purposes of the presumption of innocence in Art.6(2). The relevant provisions of the Excise Duties (Personal Reliefs) Order 1992 (as amended) provided that a certain quantity of specified goods should be presumed to have been imported for private purposes. If the amount actually imported exceeded that quantity, the Order created a presumption that the goods had been imported for commercial purposes, and placed the burden on the importer to prove otherwise. In the Court's view, the relevant considerations were that the legislation defined the proceedings as civil in nature; none of the usual consequences of a criminal conviction followed from condemnation and forfeiture proceedings; there was no conviction or finding of guilt; and the person concerned was not subject to any other penalty, apart from the forfeiture and loss of the goods.[62] However, even if the proceedings had been classified as criminal, the reverse burden of proof was proportionate, reasonable and justifiable.

V. Forfeiture orders and other penalties made against third parties

4–15 In *Allgemeine Gold- und Silberscheideanstalt v United Kingdom*[63] the applicant company was the owner of a quantity of Krugerrands which had been illegally imported into the United Kingdom without the company's knowledge. The dealers responsible for the importation were prosecuted by customs and convicted, and the coins were thereafter declared forfeit under the Customs Act 1952. The company brought an unsuccessful action against the Customs and Excise Commissioners for the return of the coins. Before the European Court it was argued that the proceedings were in violation of the presumption of innocence in Art.6(2). The Court rejected the submission:

> "The fact that measures consequential upon an act for which third parties were prosecuted affected in an adverse manner the property rights of AGOSI cannot of itself lead to the conclusion that, during the course of the procedures complained of, any 'criminal charge', for the purposes of Article 6 could be considered as having been brought against the applicant company."

4–16 The same reasoning was applied in *Air Canada v United Kingdom*[64] in which an aircraft was seized following the discovery that it was carrying a consignment of cannabis resin, and returned on payment of a £50,000 penalty. There was no requirement for a judicial finding of guilt or negligence on the part of the company. Although in one sense the procedure was intended to act as a deterrent, by encouraging airline companies to adopt more stringent security measures, it could not be characterised as the determination of a criminal charge. The forfeiture was a process *in rem*; it was consequent on the criminal activity of a third party rather than the applicant company; and there was no threat of criminal

---

[62] See also *R. (Mundie) v Dover Magistrates Court* [2003] Q.B. 1238, CA, where it was held that the seizure of a quantity of tobacco and the vehicle used for its transport, in accordance with ss.139 and 141 of the Customs and Excise Management Act 1979, did not consitute the determination of a criminal charge. Proceedings before the VAT and duties tribunal are not therefore required to comply with the full range of due process protections under Art.6(3): *Gora v Customs and Excise Commissioners* [2004] Q.B. 93.
[63] (1987) 9 E.H.R.R. 1 at 17–18.
[64] (1995) 20 E.H.R.R. 150.

proceedings against the company if it chose not to pay the penalty.[65] The principle that it is unnecessary to prove the criminal conduct of a person in possession of unlawfully obtained property was re-iterated by the Court in the admissibility decision of *Butler v United Kingdom*.[66] A confiscation order was made in the sum of almost £240,000 seized from the applicant pursuant to s.43(1) of the Drug Trafficking Act 1994, on the ground that customs officers believed the money was directly or indirectly the proceeds of drug trafficking and/or was intended for use in drug trafficking. The applicant had contended that a court, when considering whether to make a forfeiture order in the circumstances, "must effectively be asking itself whether the individual concerned was planning at some future stage to use the funds in question for drug-related activity". The Court declared the application inadmissible, stating:

"The court notes that criminal charges have never been brought against the applicant, nor against any other party. It is the applicant's contention that the forfeiture of his money in reality represented a severe criminal sanction, handed down in the absence of the procedural guarantees afforded to him under article 6 of the Convention, in particular his right to be presumed innocent. The court does not accept that view. In its opinion, the forfeiture order was a preventive measure and cannot be compared to a criminal sanction, since it was designed to take out of circulation money which was presumed to be bound up with the international trade in illicit drugs. It follows that the proceedings which led to the making of the order did not involve 'the determination . . . of a criminal charge' . . . "

In *International Transport Roth GmbH v Secretary of State for the Home Department*,[67] a penalty scheme created pursuant to s.32 of the Immigration and Asylum Act 1999 made carriers liable to a fixed penalty of £2,000 for every clandestine entrant found concealed in a vehicle. The owner, hirer and driver of a lorry containing illegant entrants, were liable unless they could establish: (i) that they were acting under duress; or (ii) that they had neither actual nor constructive knowledge of the clandestine entrant and that there was an effective system for preventing the carriage of clandestine entrants which was operated properly on the occasion in question. Once the Secretary of State had issued a penalty notice, a senior immigration officer could detain the vehicle if he considered there was a serious risk that the penalty would not be paid and no satisfactory alternative security had been given. In finding that the scheme constituted a criminal charge within the meaning of Art.6, the majority of the court emphasised that the underlying target of the scheme was dishonest and careless behaviour and the fixed penalty imposed was substantial.

VI. Criminal Confiscation Orders

In *McIntosh v Lord Advocate*[68] the High Court of Justiciary in Scotland held, by **4–17** a majority, that the presumption of innocence in Art.6(2) applied to confiscation

---

[65] *cf. Deweer v Belgium* ((1979–80) 2 E.H.R.R. 439) where the applicant was obliged to pay a sum of money under constraint of the provisional closure of his business in order to avoid criminal proceedings from being brought against him.

[66] Application No.41661/98, (unreported) June 27, 2002.

[67] [2003] Q.B. 728, CA.

[68] [2000] U.K.H.R.R. 751.

orders made under the Proceeds of Crime (Scotland) Act 1995 and the Drug Trafficking Offences Act 1994. In the opinion of the majority, a person against whom confiscation proceedings were brought was "charged with a criminal offence" for the purposes of Art.6. Drug trafficking was, on any view, criminal conduct, even if it was not the subject of a criminal charge in domestic law terms. Accordingly, the imposition of a sanction which is referable to such conduct amounted in substance to the determination of a criminal charge (albeit one which was not proved on the indictment). In *R. v Benjafield*[69] the same point was argued before the English Court of Appeal in connection with the provisions of the Drug Trafficking Act 1994 and the Criminal Justice Act 1988 (as amended by the Proceeds of Crime Act 1995). Following the approach in *McIntosh*, Lord Woolf C.J. accepted that Art.6(2) applied to the confiscation proceedings, notwithstanding that the person against whom the proceedings were brought had, by definition, been convicted of a qualifying criminal offence (or offences). He considered that:

> "The confiscation order is made in criminal proceedings. It is accepted by all the parties that it is penal. It must therefore be regarded for the purposes of Article 6(1) as at least part of the determination of a criminal charge since there is no other option for which Article 6(1) provides. The fact that a defendant who does not comply with a confiscation order, which may not be based on criminal conduct proved at the trial, may be ordered to serve a substantial consecutive sentence in default underlines that fact. A defendant threatened with consequences of this nature would be expected to be entitled to protection equivalent to that provided by Article 6(2) even if that paragraph did not exist, under Article 6(1)."

Shortly after the Court of Appeal's decision in *Benjafield* the Privy Council heard, and allowed, the prosecutor's appeal in *McIntosh*.[70] Lord Bingham rejected the argument that Art.6(2) applied to confiscation proceedings. Although the sentencing court was making an assumption that the defendant had engaged in other criminal conduct, that person was never formally charged or notified of a criminal charge relating to those offences, and "[t]he process involves no inquiry into the commission of drug trafficking offences". Unless the Strasbourg jurisprudence pointed to different result (which in his view, it did not), Lord Bingham was not prepared to "conclude that a person against whom application for a confiscation order is made is, by virtue of that application, a person charged with a criminal offence". The difficulty with this analysis is that a convicted defendant is undoubtedly a person charged with a criminal offence for the purpose of the other guarantees of Art.6, which are applicable both at the sentencing stage and during any appeal against conviction or sentence. The alternative route to the same conclusion would have been to hold that the presumption of innocence ceases to apply once a person has been proved guilty. This, indeed, seems to be the basis of Lord Hope's approach, when he said that the defence argument:

> " . . . overlooks the fact that the procedure on which the prosecutor is now engaged assumes that the accused has already been convicted of the offence with which he was

---

[69] [2003] 1 A.C. 1099, CA.
[70] [2003] 1 A.C. 1078, PC.

charged . . . Article 6(2) provides that everyone charged with a criminal offence shall be presumed innocent *until proved guilty according to law.* That stage is now passed. The court is concerned only with confiscation of the kind which the law prescribes where the conviction is for a drug trafficking offence. The respondent is not now being charged with another offence, nor is he at risk in these proceedings of being sentenced again for the offence of which he has been convicted."

This approach was subsequently followed by the European Court of Human Rights in *Phillips v United Kingdom.*[71] The majority of the Court held that the proceedings did not constitute a determination of a criminal charge:

4–18

"The purpose of this procedure was not the conviction or acquittal of the applicant for any other drugs-related offence. Although the Crown Court assumed that he had benefited from drug-trafficking in the past, this was not, for example, reflected in his criminal record, to which was added only his conviction for the November 1995 offence. In these circumstances, it cannot be said that the applicant was 'charged with a criminal offence'. Instead, the purpose of the procedure under the 1994 Act was to enable the national court to assess the amount at which the confiscation order should properly be fixed. The Court considers that this procedure was analogous to the determination by a court of the amount of a fine or the length of a period of imprisonment to impose upon a properly convicted offender . . . [W]hilst it is clear that article 6(2) governs criminal proceedings in their entirety, and not solely the examination of the merits of the charge . . . , the right to be presumed innocent under article 6(2) arises only in connection with the particular offence 'charged'. Once an accused has properly been proved guilty of that offence, article 6(2) can have no application in relation to allegations made about the accused's character and conduct as part of the sentencing process, unless such accusations are of such a nature and degree as to amount to the bringing of a new 'charge' within the autonomous Convention meaning . . . (see the *Engel v The Netherlands*, para 90)".[72]

This reasoning, and by extension the reasoning of the Privy Council in *McIntosh*, was disputed by the partly dissenting opinion of Judge Bratza and Judge Vajic:

"The view of the majority is based on the proposition that, while Article 6 (2) governs criminal proceedings in their entirety and not solely the examination of the merits of the charge, once an accused has been proved guilty of the offence charged Article 6 (2) can have no application in relation to allegations made about the accused's character and conduct as part of the sentencing process, unless the allegations are of such a nature and degree as to amount to the bringing of a new 'charge' within the autonomous meaning of Article 6. In our opinion, this is to take too narrow a view of the role of Article 6 (2) in the context of a trial of a criminal charge . . . . Here . . . [the] essential 'facts', namely whether property or assets in the applicant's possession were the proceeds of drug trafficking, are directly in issue. They are at the heart of the confiscation proceedings and are facts which the sentencing court is required to determine. Moreover, unlike the position in the *Engel* case, the underlying facts are determined and taken into account not merely for the purpose of assessing the applicant's personality in fixing the period of detention, but for the purpose of stripping him of substantial sums of money which the court determines, with the assistance of the statutory presumptions, have been derived from essentially criminal activities.[73]

---

[71] (2001) 11 B.H.R.C. 280.
[72] Para.34–35.
[73] Partly dissenting opinion by Judge Bratza joined by Judge Vajic.

Thereafter, the House of Lords considered the issue in the *R. v Benjafield and Rezvi*,[74] choosing to follow the Privy Council in *McIntosh* and the majority of the European Court in *Phillips*. In Lord Steyn's view "confiscation proceedings are part of the sentencing process following a conviction and do not involve a fresh criminal charge"[75] Lord Hope reaffirmed his position in *McIntosh*, that the procedure does not involve the the bringing of a fresh charge or charges against the defendant:

> "The process cannot begin until he has been convicted of the qualifying offences, and it is only those offences that may be taken into account in determining his sentence. The process which then follows is based upon the assumption that the criminal charges against the defendant in the indictment have been proved".[76]

VII. Civil Recovery Orders

4–19   Part 5 of the Proceeds of Crime Act 2002 introduced into English law for the first time a general power, outside of the customs and excise forfeiture procedures, to recover property obtained by criminal conduct in circumstances where the holder of the property cannot be shown to have committed a criminal offence.[77] In *R. (Director of the Assets Recovery Agency) v He and Chen*,[78] Collins J. held that the disposal of proceedings brought by the Asset Recovery Agency under Pt 5 of the 2002 Act did not constitute the determination of a criminal charge. Previous domestic decisions had established that statutory forfeiture proceedings are to be regarded as civil proceedings.[79] The court derived assistance from a number of European Court and Commision cases which dealt with the mafia. In *Arcuri v Italy*,[80] despite the fact that the Italian provisions were more draconian than Pt 5 by virtue of their reverse burden provisions, the Court held that the scheme did not engage the criminal protections of Art.6. Likewise in *M v Italy*,[81] the Commission came to the same conclusion. Collins J. concluded that both the domestic and European jurisprudence focuses upon the fact that the measures are primarily preventative; that the measures emphasise the unlawful nature of the property in question; and that they do not establish that the person in possession of the property is guilty of a criminal offence.

---

[74] [2003] 1 A.C. 1099, HL.

[75] para.13.

[76] para.30.

[77] As to the refusal of the English courts to recognise a right at common law to confiscate the proceeds of criminal conduct, see *Webb v Chief Constable of Merseyside Police* [2000] Q.B. 427 *per* May L.J., at pp.446–448, *per* Pill L.J., at p.449; *Costello v Chief Constable of Derbyshire Constabulary* [2001] 1 W.L.R. 1437; and *Attorney General v Blake* [2001] 1 A.C. 268, at p.289 *per* Lord Nicholls, and pp.292–293 *per* Lord Steyn.

[78] Unreported, December 7, 2004 [2004] EWHC 3021 (Admin).

[79] Para.51–52: i.e. *Goldsmith v Customs and Excise Commissioners* [2001] 1 W.L.R. 1673 and *R. (Mudie) v Dover Magistrates' Court* [2003] Q.B. 1238.

[80] Application No.52024/99, July 5, 2001.

[81] Application No.12386/86, April 15, 1991, (1991) 17 D.R. 59. See also *Guzzardi v Italy* (1980) 3 E.H.R.R. 333 and *Raimondo v Italy* (1994) 18 E.H.R.R. 237.

VIII. Competition law penalties

In *Societe Stenuit v France*[82] a fine of FF50,000 imposed by the French Minister　**4–20**
of Economy and Finance, following a finding by the Competition Commission,
was held to constitute a "criminal charge". It was the potential level of the
penalties at stake (five per cent of annual turnover for a firm, and FF5,000,000
for other contraventions) which identified them as deterrent in their effect.
However, in *Krone-Verlag GmbH and Mediaprint Anzeigen GmbH & Co. KG v
Austria*[83] the imposition of a fine for failing to obey an injunction, ordered in the
course of civil proceedings for unfair competition, was held not to involve a
criminal charge. The Commission emphasised that the fine and the injunction
were sanctions which belonged to civil procedural law.[84] Although the potential
penalties involved were not negligible, this was not in itself sufficient to lead to
the conclusion that the proceedings were criminal. As a result of the Enterprise
Act 2003, there are now a number of new criminal offences, in particular the
cartel offence contained in Pt 6 of the Act,[85] which will enjoy the full range of
criminal law protections under Art.6.

IX. Regulatory offences

It is difficult to generalise about the impact of the "criminal charge" jurispru-　**4–21**
dence on the regulatory process in the United Kingdom.[86] There are, however,
certain conclusions that can be drawn from the Strasbourg caselaw. The conduct
of an investigation by inspectors appointed under the Companies Act 1985 does
not, in itself, attract the protections of Art.6, since it cannot lead directly to an
adjudication, and is not inherently criminal in character.[87] The Court has held that
to rule otherwise "would in practice unduly hamper the effective regulation in

---

[82] (1992) 14 E.H.R.R. 509. The case was settled before the Court.

[83] (1997) 23 E.H.R.R. C.D. 152.

[84] The Commission drew an analogy with Art.5(1) which distinguishes between imprisonment
following conviction for a criminal offence (Art.5(1)(a)) and imprisonment "for non-compliance with
a lawful order of a court or in order to secure the fulfilment of any obligation prescribed by law"
(Art.5(1)(b)). Detention ordered by an "enforcement court" for non-compliance with an injunction
issued in unfair competition proceedings would, in the Commission's view, fall to be considered
under Art.5(1)(b) rather than Art.5(1)(a). Based on this somewhat circular reasoning, the Commission
therefore concluded that the fine involved the determination of a civil right or obligation rather than
a criminal charge.

[85] By s.190 of the Enterprise Act 2003, a person found guilty of the offence under s.188 of the Act
is liable to a term of imprisonment of up to five years and and/or an unlimited fine. The Act also
introduces an offence of providing false or misleading information to the the the OFT, which carries a
maximum sentence of two years imprisonment and/or an umlimited fine.

[86] See generally Paul Davies, *Self-Incrimination, Fair Trials, and the Pursuit of Corporate and
Financial Wrongdoing* in *The Impact of the Human Rights Bill on English Law* (Clarendon, 1998);
George Staple, *Financial Services and the Human Rights Act* in *The Human Rights Act and the
Criminal Justice and Regulatory Process* (Hart, 1999).

[87] *Fayed v United Kingdom* (1994) 18 E.H.R.R. 393, at para.61; *Saunders v United Kingdom*
(1997) 23 E.H.R.R. 313, para.67; *I.J.L., G.M.R. and A.K.P. v United Kingdom* (2001) 33 E.H.R.R. 11,
para.100.

the public interest of complex financial and commercial activities".[88] The same principle applies to an oral examination undertaken by a court under s.236 of the Insolvency Act 1986, or to the investigatory powers of the regulatory authorities.[89] The position is different, of course, if criminal proceedings are brought following such an investigation, and the fruits of the compulsorily obtained statements are admitted in evidence.[90]

4-22   Regulatory offences which can result only in disqualification are unlikely to be regarded as criminal. The legal rules in issue are not of general application, and the penalty of disqualification is not one which usually belongs to the criminal law. Thus, in *X v United Kingdom*,[91] where the Secretary of State had objected to the applicant's appointment as Chief Executive of an insurance company on the ground that he was not a "fit and proper person", as required by the Insurance Companies Act 1982, the Commission assumed that the proceedings were civil in nature. A similar conclusion was reached in *APB v United Kingdom*[92] in connection with the proceedings of IMRO (the insurance regulator). And in *Wilson v United Kingdom*[93] the Commission declared inadmissible an application arguing that the exercise of the power to disqualify a director under s.6 of the Company Director's Disqualification Act 1986 rendered proceedings criminal:

> "In the present case, the proceedings were classified as civil in domestic law, the disqualification of directors is a matter which is regulatory rather than criminal, and the penalty is neither a fine nor a prison sentence, but rather a prohibition on acting as a

---

[88] See *I.J.L., G.M.R. and A.K.P. v United Kingdom* (2001) 33 E.H.R.R. 11, para.100 where the Court confirmed explicitly that which it said had been impliedly held by the court in *Saunders* at para.67. The Court made a similar observation in *Allen v United Kingdom*, App.No.76574/01, December 10, 2001, when it held that the imposition of financial penalties for failing to answer a notice pursuant to s.20(1) of the Taxes Management Act 1970 did not engage the protections of Art.6. In so finding, the court relied upon the fact that "the obligation to make disclosure of income and capital for the purposes of the calculation and assessment of tax is . . . a common feature of the taxation systems of Contracting States and it would be difficult to envisage them functioning effectively without it". See also *R. v Allen* [2002] 1 A.C. 509, HL.

[89] See *Official Receiver v Stern* [2000] 1 W.L.R. 2230, CA (concerning statements obtained by the official receiver purusant to s.235 of the Insolvency Act 1986 being used in company director disqualification proceedings brought under s.6 of the Company Directors Disqualification Act 1986); *R. v Kearns* [2003] 1 Cr.App.R. 7, CA (concerning the the prosecution of a bankrupt person for an offence under s.354(3) of the Insolvency Act 1986 for failing to provide information to the official receiver); and *R. v Brady* [2005] 1 Cr.App.R. 5, CA (concerning the power under s.235 of the Insolvency Act 1986 to compel the office-holder of a company to provide statements at the time of the company's winding up). In *Brady*, statements were passed by the Official Receiver to the Inland Revenue, without notifying the maker of the statements, on the basis that they disclosed an income tax fraud. Ultimately, this led to a prosecution for conspiracy to cheat. On appeal, it was held that there was no principle under Art.6, or domestic law, which prohibits statements obtained under compulsory powers being passed from one law enforcement authority to another. Neither is there any obligation to provide the maker of the statement with notice that this has been done. See also *R. (Kent Pharmaceuticals Ltd) v Director of the Serious Fraud Office* [2005] 1 W.L.R. 1302, CA.

[90] *Saunders v United Kingdom* (1997) 23 E.H.R.R. 313, paras 68–76; *I.J.L., G.M.R. and A.K.P. v United Kingdom* (2001) 33 E.H.R.R. 11, paras 82–83 and 101. See also *R. v Allen* [2002] 1 A.C. 509, HL at para.35.

[91] (1998) 25 E.H.R.R. C.D. 88.

[92] Application No.30552/96 January 15, 1998.

[93] (1998) 26 E.H.R.R. C.D. 195.

company director without the leave of the court. None of these criteria indicates that the applicant was charged with a 'criminal offence'."[94]

Since the coming into force of the Human Rights Act, the domestic courts have **4–23** confirmed that disqualification or other disciplinary proceedings under regulatory law are not to be construed as determining a criminal charge. In *Official Receiver v Stern*,[95] the official receiver brought proceedings under s.6(1) of the Company Directors Disqualification Act 1986, seeking to disqualify two directors, and relied upon statements that were obtained from them pursuant to their obligation to provide statements under s.235 of the Insolvency Act 1986. Despite the fact that such proceedings "involve serious allegations and almost always carry a degree of stigma for anyone who is disqualified", the Court of Appeal concurred with the case law of the European Court and Commission that the directors were not subject to the determination of a criminal charge.[96] In *Porter v Magill*,[97] senior local government officers were made the subject of surcharges for losses incurred by wilful misconduct during their time in office, which were certified by the local authority's auditor in accordance with s.20 of the Local Government Finance Act 1982. These surcharges were made as a result of an audit hearing and a further opportunity thereafter to submit evidence on quantum. The officers subsequently appealed, raising various issues under Art.6, including a breach of the reasonable time requirement and a lack of independence and impartiality on the part of the auditor. The House of Lords held that the nature of the proceedings under s.20 of the 1982 Act was compensatory and regulatory, not punitive. In essence, the object of the auditing procedure was to compensate the body concerned, and the measure of the compensation was the amount of the loss suffered. According to Lord Hope:

"In the present case the amount certified was very large, but the nature of the proceedings does not alter depending on the amount certified. No fine is involved, nor does the section provide for a penalty by way of imprisonment. Section 20(4) provides for the respondents' disqualification from being members of a local authority. But this outcome is similar to that where a trustee is removed after being found to have been in serious breach of trust, or a person is disqualified from acting as a director of a company. In my opinion measures of the kind provided for by section 20, which apply to persons having a special status or responsibility and are compensatory and regulatory rather than penal in character, lie outside the criminal sphere for the purposes of article 6 of the Convention".[98]

---

[94] See also *D.C., H.S. and A.D. v United Kingdom* [2000] B.C.C. 710, at p.716.

[95] [2000] 1 W.L.R. 2230, CA, at p.2258.

[96] In finding that the proceedings did involve the determination of a civil right and obligation, the Court of Appeal refused to hold that evidence obtained under compulsory powers could never be admissible in civil proceedings, although it left open the possibility that in certain circumstances the admission of such evidence would cause a breach of Art.6. See also *R. (Fleurose) v Security and Futures Authority, The Times,* January 15, 2002, CA (disciplinary proceedings instituted by the Security and Futures Authority, where disqualification and an unlimited financial penalty were available sanctions, did not amount to a criminal charge).

[97] [2002] 2 A.C. 357, HL.

[98] Para.85.

X. Enforcement proceedings

4–24 The Commission has held that the imposition of a fine for refusing to obey an injunction issued in civil proceedings does not involve a criminal charge.[99] However, proceedings resulting in imprisonment for non-payment of criminal fines or disobedience to a court order to pay local government taxes are likely to be regarded as criminal proceedings. In *Benham v United Kingdom*,[100] the applicant had been committed to prison for failure to comply with a Magistrates Court order to pay the community charge (a "liability order"). Among the breaches of the Convention he alleged was a failure to provide legal aid for committal proceedings, as required by Art.6(3)(c). In order to bring his case within this provision he needed to establish that he had been "charged with a criminal offence." In English law it was plain that he had not: the proceedings for recovery of unpaid community charge were civil in nature.[101] However, the Court went on to consider the substance of the matter,[102] noting that the obligation to pay the community charge applied to all adults; that the enforcement proceedings were "brought by a public authority"; and that they had "punitive elements", since committal to prison was only possible after a finding of "wilful refusal to pay or culpable neglect". The sanction for disobedience was a "relatively severe" maximum penalty of three months' imprisonment (and an actual penalty of 30 days). The Court therefore concluded that the applicant had been charged with a criminal offence, and that the failure to provide a system of legal aid was in breach of Art.6(3)(c).[103]

XI. Contempt

4–25 The Court has not so far been called upon to determine the classification of contempt proceedings in the United Kingdom.[104] In *Weber v Switzerland*[105] the applicant journalist was fined in summary proceedings for having revealed during a press conference the existence of a confidential judicial investigation to which he was a party. He complained that the summary proceedings[106] had deprived him of the right to an adversarial hearing and, in particular, that he had

---

[99] *Krone-Verlag GmbH and Mediaprint Anzeigen GmbH & Co. KG v Austria* (1997) 23 E.H.R.R. C.D. 152.

[100] (1996) 22 E.H.R.R. 293.

[101] See *R. v Highbury Corner Magistrates Court ex parte Watkins* [1992] R.A. 300 *per* Henry J.

[102] At paras 55–56.

[103] See also *Perks v United Kingdom* (2000) 30 E.H.R.R. 33; *Beet v United Kingdom, The Times*, March 10, 2005, ECtHR.

[104] In *Harman v United Kingdom* (1984) 38 D.R. 53 the Commission declared admissible a complaint that the applicant's conviction for contempt, arising from the unauthorised disclosure of documents which had previously been read in open court, was in breach of Art.7. The case subsequently settled. Although the United Kingdom was not a party to *Kyprianou v Cyprus*, Application No.73797/01, December 15, 2005 (see para.4–29, below), its government was an intervenor in the case before the Grand Chamber, as were the Governments of Ireland and Malta. The basis upon which the United Kingdom Government intervened was that the judgment of the Court would have a direct bearing on all jurisdictions in the common law world.

[105] (1990) 12 E.H.R.R. 508.

[106] The proceedings were conducted in writing by the President of the Criminal Cassation Division of the Cantonal Court.

been afforded no opportunity to challenge the witnesses against him. The fact that the relevant provisions of domestic law used the word *"peine"* (punishment), was considered by the Court to be relevant, but not decisive. As to the nature of the offence, the Court drew a distinction between sanctions for the disclosure of confidential information imposed on judges, lawyers and "those closely associated with the functioning of the courts", on the one hand, and similar sanctions imposed on a party to litigation, on the other. In the former case, the sanction would be classified as a disciplinary measure taken against the person concerned on account of their membership of a particular profession.[107] But parties to litigation "only take part in the proceedings as people subject to the jurisdiction of the courts, and . . . therefore do not come within the disciplinary sphere of the judicial system". Since the relevant offence potentially affected the whole population it was to be regarded as criminal. The potential penalty (a substantial fine, enforceable by imprisonment in default) pointed in the same direction.[108]

The Court drew a similar distinction between criminal and disciplinary powers in **4–26** *Demicoli v Malta*,[109] a case concerning contempt of Parliament. The applicant was the editor of a political magazine which published an article criticising two Members of Parliament for their performance during a debate. The House of Representatives instituted proceedings against him for contempt (categorised as breach of privilege). At the conclusion of the proceedings, the applicant was found guilty and fined, and his appeal to the Constitutional Court was dismissed. Although the domestic classification was uncertain,[110] the Court considered that the offence was criminal in substance. The Court drew a distinction, similar to that drawn in *Weber*, between the powers of a legislature to regulate its own proceedings by disciplining Members for breach of privilege within the precincts of the House, on the one hand, and an extended jurisdiction to punish non-members for acts occurring elsewhere, on the other. Whilst the former might be categorised as disciplinary proceedings, the latter were properly regarded as criminal:

> "Mr Demicoli was not a Member of the House. In the Court's view, the proceedings taken against him in the present case for an act of this sort done outside the House are to be distinguished from other types of breach of privilege proceedings which may be said to be disciplinary in nature in that they relate to the internal regulation and orderly functioning of the House. [The relevant Ordinance] potentially affects the whole population since it applies whether the alleged offender is a Member of the House or not, and irrespective of where in Malta the publication of the defamatory libel takes place. For the offence thereby defined the Ordinance provides for the imposition of a penal sanction and not a civil claim for damages. From this point of view, therefore the particular breach of privilege is akin to a criminal offence."[111]

---

[107] As to wasted costs orders, see para.4–30 below.

[108] Switzerland had lodged a reservation to Art.6 designed to exclude any criminal charges "which, in accordance with the Cantonal legislation, are heard before an administrative authority". The court, however, found the reservation to be invalid since it did not append a statement of the laws concerned, as required by Art.57 (former Art.64).

[109] (1992) 14 E.H.R.R. 47.

[110] See para.32.

[111] See para.32.

4–27   This classification was confirmed by the severity of the potential penalty which could have been imposed on the applicant (imprisonment for up to 60 days and a fine of up to 500 Maltese liri). Since the proceedings were criminal for the purpose of the Convention the House of Representatives could not be regarded as an independent judicial tribunal because it was, in effect, judge in its own cause.[112]

4–28   In *Ravnsborg v Sweden*,[113] by contrast, the Court attached little significance to the fact that an applicant, who had been prosecuted for contempt of court, was a litigant rather than a professional participant in the judicial process. The applicant had been fined summarily for including in documents submitted to a court certain insulting statements about public officials. There were a number of factors suggesting that the jurisdiction to impose such fines belonged to the criminal law,[114] but there were also a number of factors pointing in the opposite direction.[115] The Court considered that the formal classification under domestic law was "open to different interpretations". In assessing the substantive nature of the offence, the Court attached importance to the fact that the charge applied only to statements made by a person participating in the proceedings. More importantly, it was for the court conducting the proceedings in which the statement was made to examine whether an offence had been committed;

> "In this respect the situation is different from those at issue in the cases of *Weber* and *Demicoli* . . . Rules enabling a court to sanction disorderly conduct in proceedings before it are a common feature of the legal systems of the Contracting States. Such rules and sanctions derive from the indispensable power of a court to ensure the proper and orderly functioning of its own proceedings. Measures ordered by courts under such rules are more akin to the exercise of disciplinary powers than to the imposition of a punishment for commission of a criminal offence. It is, of course, open to States to bring what are considered to be more serious examples of disorderly conduct within the sphere of the criminal law, but that has not been shown to be the case in the present instance as regards the fines imposed on the applicant."[116]

As to the severity of the sanction, the court held that neither the maximum penalty (Skr 1,000), nor the "theoretical possibility" of a term of imprisonment rendered the sanction a criminal one.[117] *Ravnsborg* was followed by the Court in *Putz v Austria*.[118] The applicant was a defendant in criminal proceedings who had been fined on three occasions for repeatedly making statements in open court

---

[112] The two Members allegedly defamed participated in the proceedings throughout.

[113] (1994) 18 E.H.R.R. 38.

[114] The code of judicial procedure referred to the fines as "*straff*" (punishment); the power to impose fines was to be found in a section of the code entitled "On the procedure in criminal cases"; academic opinion regarded the jurisdiction as criminal; and a fine could, in certain circumstances, be converted into a term of imprisonment.

[115] The court examined the allegation of its own motion, without the involvement of a prosecutor; the relevant provisions dealt only with offences against the good order of court proceedings, whilst improper behaviour of a more serious character was prosecuted as an ordinary criminal offence; and unlike an ordinary criminal fine in Swedish law, the amount was not calculated by reference to the defendant's means.

[116] Para.34.

[117] Para.35.

[118] Application No.18892/91, February 22, 1996.

accusing the presiding judge of improper conduct. The first fine was for 500 schillings; the second fine was for 700 schillings and the third fine was for 10,000 schillings. Two of the fines were converted into prison sentences, but the applicant did not have to serve them because he paid the fines. As in *Ravnsborg*, he complained that the hearing of the disciplinary offences was presided over by the judge who was the subject of his impugned comments. The complaint was similarly rejected on the grounds that Art.6 was inapplicable, because he had been the subject of disciplinary powers, rather than convicted of a criminal offence.[119] As to the imposition of the fines and prison sentences in default, the court reconised that there was a number of dissimilarities between the applicant's case and the *Ravnsborg* case, in which the amount of the fines could not exceed 1,000 Swedish kronor and the decision to convert them into custodial sentences required a prior hearing of the person concerned. However, these differences were insufficent to distinguish *Ravnsborg* for three reasons:

"Firstly, as in the *Ravnsborg* case, the fines are not entered in the criminal record; secondly, the court can only convert them into prison sentences if they are unpaid, and an appeal lies against such decisions, as it does against custodial sentences imposed straight away at the hearing where that course was essential for maintaining order; lastly, whereas in the *Ravnsborg* case the term of imprisonment into which a fine could be converted ranged from fourteen days to three months, in the instant case it cannot exceed ten days. However real they may be, the dissimilarities, which reflect the characteristics of the two national legal systems, therefore do not appear to be decisive. In both cases the penalties are designed to enable the courts to ensure the proper conduct of court proceedings. Having regard to all these factors the Court considers, like the Government, that what was at stake for the applicant was not sufficiently important to warrant classifying the offences as 'criminal' ".[120]

These decisions lay down the important principle that it is open to the Contracting States to establish summary procedures (such as the power of a judge to punish contempt of his own court) which do not fully meet the requirement under Art.6—and in particular the requirement for determination by an independent and impartial tribunal—provided they ensure that the penalties available to the tribunal do not cross the borderline which separates the disciplinary from the truly criminal.

The situation is different in the United Kingdom, because it is accepted that all **4–29** types of contempt proceedings, regardless of whether they concern misconduct in court, or a failure to comply with a court order, amount to a "criminal charge" within the autonomous meaning of that expression as it is used in Art.6.[121] Indeed, prior to the Human Rights Act coming into force, the case law on summary contempt proceedings was clear about the need to comply with the

---

[119] Para.33.
[120] Para.37.
[121] See *R. v MacLeod* [2001] Crim.L.R. 589, CA; *R. v Dodds* [2003] 1 Cr.App.R. 60, CA; and *Wilkinson v S* [2003] 1 W.L.R. 1254, CA. This includes contempt of court proceedings for breaches of injunctions of the civil courts: *Newman v Modern Bookbinders Ltd* [2000] 1 W.L.R. 2559, CA; *Mubarak v Mubarak* [2001] 1 F.L.R. 698; and *Raja v Van Hoogstraten* [2004] 4 All. E.R. 793, CA. See also *Mayer v H.M. Advocate* 2004 S.C.C.R. 734, dealing with the post-Human Rights Act summary jurisdiction in Scotland.

rules of natural justice, in particular the right to be tried by an impartial tribunal and to have prior notice of the nature of the accusation and an opportunity to counter it.[122] The summary jurisdiction to punish for contempt of court was reviewed by the Grand Chamber of the European Court of Human Rights in *Kyprianou v Cyprus*.[123] Both parties agreed that the proceedings constituted a determination of a criminal charge, and the Grand Chamber endorsed the finding of the Chamber that it did.[124] The governments of the United Kingdom, Ireland and Malta were given leave to intervene in the case on the basis that its ruling would bear directly on the conduct of contempt proceedings in their jurisdictions, and indeed throughout the common law world.[125] The principal importance of the Grand Chamber judgment in *Kyprianou* is that it gives clear guidance as to when it will be necessary for a tribunal to recuse itself from trying a contempt that has been committed in its presence.[126]

XII. Wasted costs orders[127]

4–30 In *B v United Kingdom*[128] the Commission considered that a wasted costs order made against a solicitor in criminal proceedings involved neither the determination of a criminal charge nor the determination of civil rights and obligations. The Commission considered that the proceedings consisted essentially of an investigation of the applicant solicitor's conduct of the defence case, in the exercise of judicial control over the proper administration of justice, with a view to preventing avoidable delay in criminal proceedings. Moreover, the maximum amount of the sanction was the equivalent of the costs thrown away. Accordingly, neither the nature of the proceedings, nor the severity of the potential penalty justified the classification of the proceedings as the determination of a criminal charge.

XIII. Tribunals of Inquiry

4–31 In *Goodman International and anor. v Ireland*[129] the applicants were a beef processsing company and its chief executive, whose activities were investigated by a Tribunal of Inquiry set up by Parliament to examine alleged illegalities in the industry. The Tribunal had powers to compel witnesses to give evidence, and

---

[122] *Balogh v Crown Court at St. Albans* [1975] Q.B. 73, at p.85 and p.90; *DPP v Channel Four Television Co. Ltd* [1993] 2 All. E.R. at pp.520–521; and *R. v Schot and Barclay* [1997] 2 Cr.App.R. 383, CA. See also *HM Advocate v Airs* 1975 S.L.T.

[123] Application No.73797/01, December 15, 2005.

[124] Paras 61–64.

[125] See the summary of the interventions at paras 43–59. As to the approach in other jurisdictions to the fair trial rights of those who are prosecuted for contempt of court, see *The State (DPP) v Walsh* [1981] I.R. 412 (Republic of Ireland); *R. v K. (B)* [1995] 4 S.C.R. 186 (Canada); *R. v Arradi* [2003] 1 S.C.R 280 (Canada); *Offutt v United States*, 348 US 11 (1954) (United States); *Mayberry v United States*, 400 US 455 (1971) (United States); *Vinay Chandra Mishra* [1995] 4 L.R.C. 1 (India); *Re Chinamasa* (2000) 9 B.H.R.C 519 (Zimbabwe); *State v Mamabolo* (2001) 10 B.H.R.C. 493 (South Africa); *State v Ntshwence* (2004) B.C.L.R. 392 (Tk) (South Africa).

[126] See a more detailed discussion of this case at 14–114 below.

[127] As to professional disciplinary proceedings, see para.4–43 below.

[128] (1984) 38 D.R. 213.

[129] (1993) 16 E.H.R.R. C.D. 26.

to make an award of costs against the applicants. In concluding that the proceedings could not involve the determination of a criminal charge, the Commission noted that the Tribunal's functions were limited to inquiring into the allegations, stating its conclusions and, if appropriate, making recommendations for the future. It had not applied the criminal standard of proof,[130] and its power to award costs could not be said to approach the standard required to identify the proceedings as criminal. Moreover, the tribunal had been at pains to emphasise that it would not interfere with the administration of criminal justice and that if there was a danger of this occurring, it would cease its investigation. It is well established under domestic law that an inquest conducted pursuant to s.8 of the Coroners Act 1988 does not constitute a determination of either a criminal charge or a civil right or obligation.[131] However, the conduct of such inquiries is subject to various due process guarantees, most notably a right of a witness under r.21(1) of the Coroners Rules 1984 not to answer a question that would tend to incriminate himself. More recently the courts have recognised the importance of clarity in the summing up to the jury, in terms of validating the reasonableness of their verdict.[132] The conduct of public inquiries in the United Kingdom have traditionally been subject to the so-called Salmon principles, which include, *inter alia*, the right of a witness to be informed of any potential allegation of wrong doing against them before attending the inquiry; a right to legal representation; a right to test evidence before the inquiry and a right to call additional evidence that might exonerate him.[133]

XIV. Offences against military discipline

In *Engel v Netherlands*[134] the court was concerned with a number of different **4–32** offences against military discipline. Certain of the offences were specific to the armed forces, whilst others "also lent themselves to criminal proceedings" under national law.[135] Applying the first and second of the criteria it had adopted, the court considered that "the choice of disciplinary action was justified".[136] When it came to analysing the third criterion, however, the court distinguished between the applicants, according to the level of penalty which the military tribunal had

---

[130] There is a certain circularity in the Commission's reasoning on this point.

[131] As a result of the judgment of the House of Lords in *R. (Middleton) v West Somerset Coroner* [2004] 2 A.C. 182, an inquest jury is able to return a verdict which describes by reference to the circumstances of the death the extent to which it might have been preventable.

[132] See for example, *R. (Anderson) v H.M. Coroner for Inner North Greater London* [2004] EWHC 2729 Admin at para.10; and *R. (Clayton) v H.M. Coroner for South Yorkshire (East District)* [2005] EWHC 1196 Admin at para.9. For a more general analysis of the importance of complying with the principles of natural justice in the context of public inquiries see *R. v Lord Saville of Newdigate ex parte A* [2000] 1 W.L.R. 1855 at para.38.

[133] See *R. v Chairman of the Inquiry into matters arising from the death of Stephen Lawrence ex. p. A'Court and Others*, unreported, June 18, 1998 (CO/2156/98 and 2173/98) (concerning the issue of what questions were permissible to ask those accused of killing Stephen Lawrence before an inquiry that was set up to examine the shortcoming of the police inquiry in the aftermath of the killing).

[134] (1979–80) 1 E.H.R.R. 647.

[135] Para.84.

[136] Para.84.

power to impose. The four penalties under consideration were "light arrest",[137] "aggravated arrest",[138] "strict arrest"[139] and "committal to a disciplinary unit".[140] In the Court's view neither "light arrest" not "aggravated arrest" constituted a deprivation of liberty and were insufficiently serious to render the proceedings "criminal" for the purposes of Art.6.[141]

4–33 Whilst "strict arrest" could in principle amount to a deprivation of liberty, the maximum period which could have been imposed on the facts was two days. In the context of military discipline, this was held to be "of too short a duration to belong to the 'criminal' law".[142] Three of the applicants, however, were liable to be committed to a disciplinary unit for periods of up to three and four months respectively. In the Court's view the charges against these applicants "did indeed come within the 'criminal' sphere since their aim was the imposition of serious punishments involving deprivation of liberty".[143] The fact that one of these three applicants was eventually sentenced only to 12 days aggravated arrest could not affect the classification of the proceedings against him, since the penalty actually imposed "cannot diminish the importance of what was initially at stake".[144]

4–34 The applicant in *Findlay v United Kingdom*[145] was a soldier who had developed post traumatic stress disorder as a result of his experiences during the Falklands war. After a bout of heavy drinking he held members of his own unit at gunpoint, and threatened to kill himself and others. The applicant pleaded guilty before a court-martial to three charges of common assault (a civilian offence), two charges of conduct to the prejudice of good order and discipline (a purely military offence), and two charges of threatening to kill (a civilian offence). Notwithstanding his medical condition the applicant was sentenced to two years' imprisonment, reduction in rank and dismissal from the army. In the Court's view, Art.6(1) was "clearly applicable to the court-martial proceedings, since

---

[137] See para.61: "Although confined during off duty hours to their dwellings or to military buildings or premises ... servicemen subjected to [light arrest] are not locked up and continue to perform their duties .... They remain, more or less, within the ordinary framework of their army life."

[138] See para.62: "Aggravated arrest differs from light arrest on one point alone: in off-duty hours soldiers serve the arrest in a specially designated place which they may not leave in order to visit the canteen, cinema or recreation rooms, but they are not kept under lock and key."

[139] See para.63: "Strict arrest ... differed from light arrest and aggravated arrest in that non-commissioned officers and ordinary servicemen served it by day and by night locked in a cell and were accordingly excluded from the performance of their normal duties."

[140] See para.64: "Committal to a disciplinary unit ... represented the most severe penalty under military disciplinary law in the Netherlands. Privates condemned to this penalty following disciplinary proceedings were not separated from those so sentenced by way of supplementary punishment under the criminal law, and during a month or more they were not entitled to leave the establishment. The committal lasted for a period of three to six months; this was considerably longer than the duration of the other penalties, including strict arrest which could be imposed for one to 14 days."

[141] Para.85.

[142] Para.85.

[143] Para.85.

[144] Para.85.

[145] (1997) 24 E.H.R.R. 221.

they involved the determination of Mr Findlay's sentence following his plea of guilty to criminal charges".[146]

XV. Offences against prison discipline

In a number of early cases the Commission held that prison disciplinary proceed- **4–35** ings were outside the scope of Art.6 altogether.[147] However, in *Campbell and Fell v United Kingdom*[148] the Court reversed the Commission's caselaw, holding that certain prison disciplinary offences were sufficiently serious to attract the criminal due process guarantees of Art.6. Campbell was charged with mutiny, incitement to mutiny, and doing gross personal violence to a prison officer. He was convicted by a Board of Visitors, and sentenced to 570 days loss of remission and 91 days loss of privileges. There was no doubt that the offences were regarded as disciplinary rather than criminal in national law.[149] The Court considered that some offences within prison were characteristic of a disciplinary system,[150] whilst others belonged simultaneously to the criminal and the disciplinary sphere. The Court emphasised the close connection between the offences which Campbell was convicted of, and the equivalent offences in the ordinary criminal law, as tending to show that the disciplinary charges at issue constituted criminal proceedings for the purpose of Art.6. In the Court's view;

" . . . these factors, whilst not of themselves sufficient to lead to the conclusion that the offences with which the applicant was charged have to be regarded as 'criminal' for Convention purposes, do give them a certain colouring which does not entirely coincide with that of a purely disciplinary matter."

Turning to the third criterion, the Court noted that the maximum penalty that **4–36** could have been imposed was the forfeiture of all remission of sentence available to the applicant at the time of the Board's decision (just under three years). Relying on the settled caselaw of the Commission,[151] the government argued that

---

[146] The government did not dispute the applicability of the "criminal" provisions of Art.6. See also *Thompson v United Kingdom* (2005) 40 E.H.R.R. 11; and *Grieves v United Kingdom* (2004) 39 E.H.R.R. 2. As to the anlysis of the court martial system in the light of the changes made to the law in the aftermath of the *Findlay* judgment, see *R. v Spear* [2003] 1 A.C. 734, HL.

[147] *X v United Kingdom* (1976) 2 Digest 241; *X v Switzerland* (1977) 11 D.R. 216; *X v United Kingdom* (1977) 2 Digest 243; *X v Germany* (1977) 2 Digest 243; Application No.7794/77 (1980) 2 Digest 247.

[148] (1985) 7 E.H.R.R. 165.

[149] Para.70.

[150] Such as the offence of making a false allegation against a prison officer, at issue in *Kiss v United Kingdom* (1976) 7 D.R. 55; or the offences of failure to wear prison uniform or to work, described in *McFeely v United Kingdom* (1980) 20 D.R. 44 at para.95 as "clearly disciplinary in nature".

[151] *X v United Kingdom* (1976) 2 Digest 241; *X v Switzerland* (1977) 11 D.R. 216; *X v United Kingdom* (1977) 2 Digest 243; *X v Germany* (1977) 2 Digest 243; Application No.7794/77 (1980) 2 Digest 247; *Eggs v Switzerland* (1978) 15 D.R. 35; *McFeeley v United Kingdom* (1980) 20 D.R. 44; *Hogben v Inited Kingdom* (1986) 46 D.R. 263; and *Borelli v Switzerland*, Application No.17571/90, September 2, 1993. The approach of the Commission in these early cases is illustrated by the decision in *Kiss v United Kingdom* (1976) 7 D.R. 55 at para.2. where it was held that:
"Loss of remission does not constitute deprivation of liberty. A prisoner, unlike a person doing military service, is deprived of his liberty for the whole of his sentence, and remission of that sentence for good behaviour is mere privilege, and loss of that remission does not alter the original basis for detention."

loss of remission did not constitute loss of liberty, as that term was used in *Engel*. The Court accepted that loss of remission was not, strictly speaking, to be categorised as a loss of liberty, but nevertheless held that it could amount to a criminal penalty where the consequences for the individual were sufficiently severe[152]:

> "The Court, for its part, does not find that the distinction between privilege and right is of great assistance to it for the present purposes; what is more important is that the practice of granting remission—whereby a prisoner will be set free on the estimated date for release given to him as the outset of his sentence, unless remission has been forfeited in disciplinary proceedings—creates in him a legitimate expectation that he will recover his liberty before the end of his term of imprisonment . . . By causing detention to continue for substantially longer than would otherwise have been the case, the sanction came close to, even if it did not technically constitute, deprivation of liberty, and the object and purpose of the Convention require that the imposition of a measure of such gravity should be accompanied by the guarantees of Article 6."

4–37   In *Ezeh and Connors*,[153] both of the applicants were awarded "additional days" of detention during governor adjudication proceedings.[154] *Ezeh* was accused of threatening to kill his probation officer if she failed to make various entries in his probation report. He eventually received a punishment of 42 additional days to his sentence. *Connors* was accused of assaulting a prison officer and received a punishment of seven additional days. The applicants argued that in the absence of an entitlement to legal representation at their adjudication hearings, they had not received a fair trial. The issue before the Grand Chamber was whether prison disciplinary proceedings resulting in a punishment involving up to a maximum of 42 additonal days of imprisonment amounted to the determination of a criminal charge. The Government argued that the sanction of loss of early release for a breach of prison discipline was a common sanction of prison disciplinary regimes in many Council of Europe States. Moreover, as recognised by the Court in *Campbell and Fell*, the unique need to enforce discipline effectively in prisons justified "broader parameters in a prison context for the disciplinary classification of proceedings".[155] Following *Campbell and Fell*, the Grand Chamber accepted that in applying the "*Engel* criteria" in determining where to place the dividing line between the "criminal" and the "disciplinary", the Court will do so in a manner that is consistent with the object and purpose of Art.6, while making "due allowance" for the prison context and for the "practical reasons and reasons of policy" in favour of establishing a special prison disciplinary regime. On that approach, however, the Grand Chamber was not satisified that the Government had shown compelling reasons why the loss by the governor of the power to

---

[152] Para.72.
[153] (2004) 39 E.H.R.R. 1.
[154] Note that the legal basis for detention following loss of remission has been changed by the Crime (Sentences) Act 1997 which replaced the system of discretionary remission with a statutory entitlement to release after serving one half or two thirds of the sentence (depending on the length of the overall term), and then the Criminal Justice Act 2003, which extended the entitlement to release at the half-way point to all prisoners serving 12 months or more. Instead of withdrawing remission, disciplinary sanctions now involve the imposition of "additional days".
[155] Para.83.

award additional days would undermine the prison disciplinary regime in England and Wales.[156] In particular, the Court found that it had not been convincingly explained why the availability of lesser sanctions (including forfeiture of privileges, exclusion from associated work and cellular confinement) would not have an impact comparable to awards of additional days in maintaining the effectiveness of the prison disciplinary system, including the authority of prison management.[157]

The Court then went on to apply the "*Engel* criteria". As to the domestic **4–38** classification of the offence as "disciplinary", the Court observed that "the indications so afforded by the national law have only a formal and relative value". Thus the fact, as pointed out by the Government, that a governor's findings would not form part of the applicants' criminal records was simply a natural consequence of the disciplinary classification of the offence.[158]

In considering the nature of the charge, the Court firstly rejected the Govern- **4–39** ment's argument that the the offences in question were directed towards a group possessing a special status, namely prisoners, as opposed to all citizens, which was sufficient to render the proceedings disciplinary only. In reality, the offences were characterised by the fact that they concerned conduct that was simultaneously an offence under the prison rules and under the criminal law.[159] Secondly, while it was not contested that the allegation against *Ezeh* corresponded to an offence in the criminal law, it was not sufficient for the Government to argue that the minor nature of the assault alleged against *Connors* might not necessarily have led to a prosecution outside of the prison context. While the extreme gravity of the offence might be indicative of its criminal nature, as indicated in *Campbell and Fell*, the converse, of itself, could not take it outside of the ambit of Art.6.[160] Thirdly, the Court rejected the Government's argument that the "punitive" element of the offence was secondary to the primary purpose of the "prevention" of disorder.

> "It does not find persuasive the government's argument distinguishing between the punishment and deterrent aims of the offences in question, these objectives not being mutually exclusive and being recognised as characteristic features of criminal penalties".[161]

---

[156] Para.88. The Scottish Prison Notice of June 8, 2001 had required governors to suspend awarding additional days prior to the Human Rights Act coming into force because of an anticipated challenge to the procedure as being incompatible with Art.6. Before the Grand Chamber, the Government argued that the award of additional days was made less often in Scotland and the Scottish Executive felt, therefore, less constrained by the abandonment of the system (see para.80).

[157] Para.88.

[158] Paras 90–91.

[159] Para.103.

[160] Para.104. The Court observed: "There is nothing in the Convention to suggest that the criminal nature of an offence, within the meaning of the second of the *Engel* criteria, necessarily requires a certain degree of seriousness".

[161] Para.106. See also para.102: as a matter of general principle, "criminal penalties have been customarily recognised as comprising the twin objectives of punishment and deterrence".

The Grand Chamber agreed with the conclusion of the judgment of the Chamber, that all these factors, even if they were not in themselves sufficient to lead to the conclusion that the offences with which the applicants were charged were to be regarded as "criminal" for Convention purposes, clearly gave them "a certain colouring which does not entirely coincide with that of a purely disciplinary matter".[162]

4–40 The decisive factor for the Court was, however, the third of the *Engel* criteria, namely the nature and severity of the penalty that was "liable to be imposed" on the applicants. In this respect the Court emphasised that although the actual penalty imposed is relevant to the determination, it cannot diminish the importance of what was initially at stake.[163] The Court then found that the reality of awards of additional days was that prisoners were detained in prison beyond the date on which they would otherwise have been released, as a consequence of separate disciplinary proceedings which were legally unconnected to the original conviction and sentence. Accordingly, the awards of additional days by the governor "constituted fresh deprivations of liberty imposed for punitive reasons after a finding of culpability".[164]

4–41 The decision in *Ezeh and Connors* was conceded by the Home Office to apply to English law when the House of Lords considered the appeal in *Greenfield v Secretary of State for the Home Department*.[165] It does not, however, follow that any disciplinary measure within the prison system involves the determination of a criminal charge. First, it is implict from the approach of the Grand Chamber in *Ezeh and Connors* that punishments for conduct which fall short of loss of liberty, such as cellular confinement or loss of privileges, would not be considered a criminal charge. Moreover, numerous offences under the Prison Rules simply do not carry an equivalent in the criminal law, but are specific to the maintenance of good order and discipline in a prison.[166] Finally, the principle in *Ezeh and Connors* does not apply to prison disciplinary proceedings against a life

---

[162] Para.107.

[163] Para.120.

[164] Para.124.

[165] [2005] 1 W.L.R. 673. The claimant was a prisoner who failed a mandatory drugs test and was charged with administering a controlled drug to himself, or failing to prevent the administration of a controlled drug to himself by another person, contrary to r.51(9) of the Prison Rules 1999. He was awarded 21 additional days' imprisonment. The Court of Appeal, prior to *Ezeh and Connors*, had concluded that the penalty imposed was a long way from the 570 days loss of remission in *Campbell and Fell*, and was effectively "a disciplinary sanction designed to ensure that prisoners comply with rules governing their conduct": see [2002] 1 W.L.R. 545 at para.53. See also *R. (Napier) v Secretary of State for the Home Department* [2004] 1 W.L.R. 3056, where the Secretary of State accepted than an adjudication of a prisoner who was charged with assaulting a prison officer and which led to a penalty of 35 additional days in custody was not compatible with Art.6. However, once the Respondent had remitted the imposition of the 35 additional days imprisonment, the governor's finding of guilt fell properly to be characterised as an administrative finding of fact without the stigma of a conviction. The claimant therefore failed, on his application for judicial review, to set the finding of guilt aside.

[166] *Galloway v United Kingdom* [1999] E.H.R.L.R. 119 (mandatory drug testing in prisons not criminal).

sentenced prisoner where, because of the nature of the life sentence, a punishment of "additional days" could not be imposed.[167]

There are other aspects of prison discipline, most notably the classification of a   **4–42**
prisoner as Category A, which do not constitute the determination of a criminal
charge.[168] Likewise, the House of Lords has held that more general determinations of the Parole Board do not amount to the determination of a criminal
charge, but nevertheless are likely to engage due process considerations of an
equivalent or near equivalent nature given the application of Art.5(4) to such
proceedings.[169]

XVI. Professional disciplinary proceedings

The Court's approach to professional disciplinary proceedings is less clear cut. In   **4–43**
Albert and LeCompte v Belgium,[170] the applicant doctors faced disciplinary
proceedings before the Belgian *Ordre des Médecins*. One was charged with
issuing false medical certificates (an offence which also had implications under
the criminal law), and the other with bringing the *Ordre* into disrepute (a purely
disciplinary matter). Dr Albert argued that the proceedings were criminal in
character. The Court considered it unnecessary to decide the point,[171] holding
that even if the proceedings were classified as civil for the purposes of Art.6, they
had sufficiently serious consequences to attract due process guarantees analagous
to those set out in Arts 6(2) and 6(3). In the Court's view the civil and criminal
aspects of Art.6 were not necessarily mutually exclusive,[172] and:

> " . . . the principles set out in paragraph 2 and in the provisions of paragraph 3 invoked
> by Dr. Albert . . . are applicable, *mutatis mutandis*, to disciplinary proceedings subject
> to paragraph 1 in the same way as in the case of a person charged with a criminal
> offence".[173]

Subsequent to *Albert and LeCompte*, the European Commission made a definitive ruling in *Wickramsinghe v United Kingdom*[174] that disciplinary proceedings
against a doctor for conduct amounting to an indecent assault under domestic
criminal law did not constitute a criminal charge for the purposes of Art.6. The
Commission was influenced by the fact that the most severe sentence that the
applicant risked was that which was in fact imposed by the General Medical

---

[167] *R. (Tangney) v Secretary of State for the Home Department, The Times*, August 30, 2005, CA
(Civ Div).
[168] *X v United Kingdom* (1979) 20 D.R. 202.
[169] *R. (West) v Parole Board; R. (Smith) v Parole Board (No.2)* [2005] 1 W.L.R. 350, HL; *R.
(Roberts) v Parole Board* [2005] 2 A.C. 738, HL, para.17. See also *Garcia Alva v Germany* (2001)
37 E.H.R.R. 335, at para.39.
[170] (1983) 5 E.H.R.R. 533.
[171] See para.30.
[172] See para.30.
[173] Para.39. See also para.30 where the court observed that the principles enshrined in Art.6(2) and
6(3)(a), (b) and (c) "are, for the present purposes, already contained in the notion of a fair trial as
embodied in paragraph 1". See also *Diennet v France* (1996) 21 E.H.R.R. 554 at para.28.
[174] Application No.31503/96 December 8, 1997.

Council: erasure of his name from the register. As a matter of general principle, the Commission observed:

> "professional disciplinary matters are essentially matters which concern the relationship between the individual and the professional association to which he or she belongs, and whose rules he or she has agreed to accept. They do not involve the State setting up a rule of general applicability by which it expresses disapproval of, and imposes sanctions for, particular behaviour, as is generally the case with 'criminal' charges".

However, the Commission in *Wickramsinghe* endorsed the approach of the Court in *Albert and LeCompte* in emphasising the need for procedural safeguards, given the importance of what was at stake. A similar approach has since been taken to the disciplinary proceedings of other professions regulated by law in the public interest, including lawyers[175] and architects.[176]

XVII. Disciplinary proceedings against civil servants

4–44   Whether disciplinary proceeding against civil servants involve the determination of a "criminal charge" depends on the classification of the act in domestic law, the nature of the offence and the potential punishment for the act in question.[177] Article 6(1) is not applicable to disciplinary proceedings following a criminal conviction when the disciplinary court limits itself to establishing that the commission of the criminal offence also constitutes a disciplinary offence and imposes a sanction provided for by disciplinary law.[178] Disciplinary proceedings brought against a police officer for failure to account for property received have been held not to amount to a "criminal charge", notwithstanding that the potential penalty was dismissal.[179]

XVIII. Election offences

4–45   In *Bowman v United Kingdom*,[180] where the applicant was prosecuted under the Representation of the People Act 1983 for incurring unauthorised election expenditure, there could be no dispute that the proceedings were criminal in nature, since they were so classified under domestic law.[181] However that is not necessarily the position, particularly where the penalty is imposed on a Parliamentarian. In *Pierre-Bloch v France*[182] the applicant was disqualified from

---

[175] *H v Belgium* (1988) 10 E.H.R.R. 339; *Ginikanwa v United Kingdom* (1988) 55 D.R. 251.

[176] *Guchez v Belgium* (1984) 40 D.R. 100.

[177] *Leiningen-Westerburg v Austria*, No.26601/95 88–A D.R. 85 citing *Ravnsborg v Sweden* (1994) 18 E.H.R.R. 38 (paras 30–35).

[178] *Kremzow v Austria*, No.16417/90 67 D.R. 307 at 309.

[179] *X v United Kingdom*, No.8496/79 21 D.R. 168. See also *Sygounis, Kotsis and others v Greece*, No.18598/91 78–A D.R. 71 (breach of police duty). Nor were such disciplinary proceedings found to be determinative of any "civil right or obligation".

[180] (1998) 26 E.H.R.R. 1.

[181] The applicant complained of a violation of Art.10. However, it is clear that the criminal guarantees of Art.6 were equally applicable to the proceedings, on the first of the *Engel* criteria.

[182] (1998) 26 E.H.R.R. 202.

standing in elections for the National Assembly, and fined for exceeding permitted election expenditure. Since the amount of the fine was equivalent to the excess expense incurred, the Court found that he was not subject to a "criminal charge":

"[T]he obligation to pay relates to the amount by which the Constitutional Council has found the ceiling to have been exceeded. This would appear to show that it is in the nature of a payment to the community of the sum of which the candidate in question improperly took advantage to seek the votes of his fellow citizens, and that it too forms part of the measures designed to ensure the proper conduct of parliamentary elections and in particular, equality of the candidates . . . [A]part from the fact that the amount payable is neither determined according to a fixed scale nor set in advance, several features differentiate this obligation to pay from criminal fines in the strict sense: no entry is made in the criminal record, the rules that consecutive sentences are not imposed in respect of multiple offences does not apply, and imprisonment is not available to sanction failure to pay . . . [T]he obligation to pay the Treasury a sum equal to the amount of the excess cannot be construed as a fine."

XIX. Measures adopted for the prevention of disorder or crime

In *Raimondo v Italy*[183] the Court held that the imposition of a special police supervision order in conjunction with criminal proceedings did not amount to a criminal sanction, since it was designed to prevent rather than to punish the commission of offences. While the criminal proceedings were still pending, the applicant was subject to 24-hour house arrest.[184] However, upon his acquittal in the criminal proceedings on January 30, 1986 on the grounds of insufficient evidence, the special police supervision order, which had previously been imposed, became effective. Thereafter, by the terms of the order the applicant was prohibited from leaving his home without informing the police; obliged to report to the police station on specified days; and obliged to return to his house by 9 p.m. and not to leave it before 7 a.m. unless he had valid reasons for doing so and had first informed the relevant authorities of his intention. Various goods belonging to him were seized and he was also required to lodge a security of 2,000,000 lire as a guarantee to ensure that he complied with the constraints attached to the supervision order.[185] He subsequently appealed against the order and on July 4, 1986, the Cantazaro Court of Appeal annulled the order referring to the "disconcertingly casual way in which the contested preventative measures concerning the person and property of Mr. Raimondo had been adopted thereby effectively decreeing his civil and economic death". The key issue that formed the basis for the subsequent complaint under the Convention was that the authorities then took over five months to communicate the decision of the court of appeal to the applicant and to return his goods and free him from the obligation

4–46

---

[183] (1994) 18 E.H.R.R. 237.

[184] For the potential to impose house confinement and curfews as bail conditions see *R. (CPS) v Chorley JJ.*, 166 J.P. 764, D.C. and *McDonald v Procurator Fiscal, Elgin, The Times*, April 17, 2003.

[185] Paras 10 and 12.

of the supervision order. On that basis, the court found that the continuation of the special police supervision order after the date of the appeal court judgment, and especially so in the period after it was filed with registry, amounted to a breach of Art.2 of Protocol 4.[186] In so finding, however, the court confirmed that the restriction on liberty encompassed by the supervision order was "not comparable to a criminal sanction because it was designed to prevent the commission of offences".[187] The Commission adopted a similar approach in *Ibbotson v United Kingdom*,[188] where the registration requirements of the Sex Offenders Act 1997 were found not to constitute a criminal penalty[189] since they were predominantly preventative rather than punitive in character. Similary, in *B. v Chief Constable of Avon and Somerset Constabulary*[190] Lord Bingham C.J. concluded that proceedings to obtain a sex offender order under s.2 of the Crime and Disorder Act 1998 were not criminal in character.[191]

4–47   In *Gough v Chief Constable of Derbyshire*,[192] the Court of Appeal held that proceedings under s.14B(4) of the Football Spectators Act 1989 did not constitute the determination of a criminal charge. Orders are made on a complaint to a magistrates' court by the chief officer of police. It must appear to him and he must prove to the court that the respondent has, within the last ten years, "at any time caused or contributed to any violence or disorder in the United Kingdom or elsewhere".[193] In rejecting the submission that the proceedings were criminal, the court held that they "neither require proof that an offence has been committed, nor involve the imposition of a penalty".[194] The court also adopted the reasoning of Lord Justice Laws in the Divisional Court that a football banning order did not constitute a penalty within the meaning of Art.7 of the Convention including, *inter alia*, that it was no part at all of the purpose of any such order to inflict punishment; and that the order was not made as part of a process of distributive criminal justice.[195]

---

[186] Paras 37 to 40. See also the Commission's decision at paras 95–108. The United Kingdom has signed but not ratified Art.2 of Protocol 4. The Court also held that, notwithstanding the applicant's assertion to the contrary, the measure in issue did not amount to a deprivation of liberty within the meaning of Art.5(1) of the Convention: "The mere restrictions on liberty of movement resulting from special supervision fall to be dealt with under Article 2 of Protocol No.4". *Cf. Guzzardi v Italy* (1980) 3 E.H.R.R. 333 at para.95, where the court found a violation of Art.5(1) in circumstances where the applicant was confined to 2.5 square kilometres on the Island of Asinara for 16 months.

[187] Para.43. See also the Commission's decision at para.112. A similar approach was taken by the court in *Guzzardi v Italy* (1980) 3 E.H.R.R. 333 at para.108.

[188] [1999] Crim.L.R. 153.

[189] The complaint was brought under Art.7 and concerned the retrospective nature of the registration requirement imposed by the 1997 Act. However, the criteria for determining whether a measure constitutes a criminal "penalty" for the purposes of Art.7 are directly analogous to the criteria established in *Engel* for the interpretation of the term "criminal charge" in Art.6(1): *Welch v United Kingdom* (1995) 20 E.H.R.R. 247.

[190] [2001] 1 W.L.R. 340.

[191] See also *Jones v Greater Manchester Police Authority* [2002] A.C.D. 4, DC concerning s.2 of the Crime and Disorder Act 1998 (repealed by the Sexual Offences Act 2003; now s.104 thereof).

[192] [2002] Q.B. 1213, CA.

[193] s.14B(2).

[194] Para.89.

[195] [2002] Q.B. 459 D.C. at paras 29 to 43.

XX. Breach of the peace

Proceedings in England and Wales whereby a defendant may be bound over to **4–48** keep the peace[196] or to be "of good behaviour"[197] involve the determination of a criminal charge for the purposes of Art.6. In *Steel and others v United Kingdom*[198] the Court explained that:

> "Breach of the peace is not classed as a criminal offence under English law. However, the Court observes that the duty to keep the peace is in the nature of a public duty; the police have powers to arrest any person who has breached the peace or whom they reasonably fear will breach the peace; and the magistrates may commit to prison any person who refuses to be bound over not to breach the peace where there is evidence beyond reasonable doubt that his or her conduct caused or was likely to cause a breach of the peace and that he or she would otherwise cause a breach of the peace in the future. Bearing in mind the nature of the proceedings and the penalty at stake, the Court considers that breach of the peace must be regarded as an 'offence' within the meaning of Article 5(1)(c)."

XXI. Anti-social Behaviour Orders

Section 1 of the Crime and Disorder Act 1998 enables a magistrates' court to **4–49** make an order prohibiting a defendant from certain forms of behaviour for a minimum of two years, as a result of proceedings that are classified as civil in domestic law. Section 1(10) then creates a strict liability offence of violating the prohibition in the order, without reasonable excuse, and provides a penalty of up to six months' imprisonment in summary proceedings, and up to five years on indictment. Moreover, s.1(11) prevents a court from granting a conditional discharge for this offence of breach. No doubt any proceedings under s.1(10) are criminal in nature, and legal representation would have to be provided before any sentence of imprisonment was imposed.[199] The more difficult question is whether the proceedings that result in the imposition of an anti-social behaviour order in the first place are themselves criminal proceedings.

On the one hand, there is an analogy with cases like *Krone-Verlag GmbH and* **4–50** *Mediaprint Anzeigen GmbH & Co. KG v Austria*,[200] involving civil injunctions. It might be thought that the order, though made by a criminal court, is no different in substance from a civil injunction. On the other hand there is an argument for treating the proceedings as a whole (including the "civil" stage at which the magistrates decide upon and frame the order) as criminal.[201] In terms of the criteria set out in *Benham* the proceedings are "brought by a public authority", they involve the application of a law applicable to society in general,

---

[196] *Steel and ors v United Kingdom* (1999) 28 E.H.R.R. 603 (paras 48–49 in context of Art.5).
[197] *Hashman and Harrap v United Kingdom* (1999) 30 E.H.R.R. 241.
[198] (1999) 28 E.H.R.R. 603 (para.48).
[199] s.21 Powers of Criminal Courts Act 1973, as applied (for example) in *Wilson* (1995) 16 Cr.App.R.(S) 997.
[200] (1997) 23 E.H.R.R. CD 152.
[201] The same conclusion is reached, on somewhat different reasoning, by White R.C.A., "Anti-social behaviour orders under section 1 of the Crime and Disorder Act 1998" (1999) 24 E.L. Rev. 55, at 59.

and the bridge between the making of the order and the undoubtedly severe maximum penalties does not require a separate finding of "wilful refusal" or "culpable neglect": Simple non-compliance is sufficient (unless the defendant proves "reasonable excuse"). The position can be contrasted with someone made subject to the sexual offenders register under s.2 of the Crime and Disorder Act 1998 (now s.104 of the Sexual Offences Act 2003). The sex offender has already had a fair trial to the criminal standard of proof on the conduct which gave rise to the jurisdiction to make the order. The sex offender order is a mechanism to control the further conduct of those already convicted of criminal offences. Thus the essential prerequisite for the order does not need to be proved in proccedings for making the order.[202] Moroever, a sex offender order is made against a very limited class of persons, those already convicted of sex offences, while the anti-social behaviour order is of general application.

4–51   The foundation for the strict liability offence is laid by the earlier proceedings in the magistrates' court, which have only the civil standard of proof and do not provide for full legal aid. In making an order the magistrates require proof of conduct that is criminal in nature, closely akin to offences under ss.4A and 5 of the Public Order Act 1986 and s.2 of the Protection of Harassment Act 1997. The Government's aim was to avoid granting to defendants the rights guaranteed by Art.6.[203] In *R. v Manchester Crown Court ex parte McCann and ors*[204] the Court of Appeal considered that this aim had been successfully carried into effect. The Master of the Rolls held that proceedings for obtaining anti-social behaviour orders were civil and not criminal and that they were accordingly outside the protection of Art.6(2) and (3). Lord Phillips accepted that the consequences of such an order may be severe but pointed out that many orders in civil proceedings had severe consequences. The court had to have regard not only to the consequences of the measure but to the purpose it was intended to serve. The purpose of an anti-social behaviour order was the restraint of those whose conduct founded a reasonable belief that a measure of restraint was necessary to protect members of the public. The position was thus directly analogous to that of a sex offender order imposed under s.2 of the Crime and Disorder Act 1998, which had been held to be civil in character for the purposes of Art.6.[205] Although the standard of proof to be applied was the civil standard, that was a flexible standard to be applied with greater or lesser strictness according to the seriousness of what had to be proved.

---

[202] See *R. (McCann) v Crown Court at Manchester; Clingham v Kensington and Chelsea Royal London Borough Council* [2003] 1 A.C. 787, at p.793D–E. Similar reasoning can be applied to the making of a confiscation order in the aftermath of a drug trafficking conviction. See *McIntosh v Lord Advocate* [2003] 1 A.C. 1078, PC; *R. v Benjafield and Rezvi* [2003] 1 A.C. 1099, HL; and *Phillips v United Kingdom* (2001) 11 B.H.R.C. 280. See now s.1C of the Crime and Disorder Act 1998, inserted by the Police Reform Act 2002, which allows allows a sentencing judge to impose a control order as part of the sentencing of certain types of comvicted offenders: *C. v Sunderland Youth Court* [2004] 1 Cr.App.R. (S.) 76; *R. v P. (Shane)* [2004] Cr.App.R. (S.) 63.

[203] The intention to avoid the normal procedural protections is apparent from the Labour Party's documents, *A Quiet Life* (1995) and *Protecting our Communities* (1996), which form the background for s.1 of the 1998 Act.

[204] [2001] 1 W.L.R. 1084. See also the judgment of Lord Woolf C.J. in the Divisional Court.

[205] *B. v Chief Constable of Avon and Somerset Constabulary* [2001] 1 W.L.R. 340.

On appeal to the House of Lords,[206] Lord Steyn described the social problem that **4-52** gave rise to the need for anti-social behaviour orders. There appeared to be a gap in the law. The criminal law offered insufficient protection to communities. Public confidence in the rule of law was undermined by a view in some communities that the law failed them.[207] He then turned to what he described as the "a model available for remedial legislation":

"Before 1998 Parliament had, on a number of occasions, already used the technique of prohibiting by statutory injunction conduct deemed to be unacceptable and making a breach of the injunction punishable by penalties. It may be that the Company Directors Disqualification Act 1986 was the precedent for subsequent use of the technique. The civil remedy of disqualification enabled the court to prohibit a person from acting as a director: s.1(1) of the 1985 Act: *R. v Secretary of State for Trade and Industry, Ex p. McCormick* [1998] BCC 379, 395C–F; *Official Receiver v Stern* [2000] 1 WLR 2230. Breach of the order made available criminal penalties: ss.13 and 14 of the 1986 Act. In 1994 Parliament created the power to prohibit trespassory assemblies which could result in serious disruption affecting communities, movements, and so forth: see s.70 of the Criminal Justice and Public Order Act 1994 which amended Part II of the Public Order Act 1986 by inserting s.14A. Section 14B which was introduced by the 1994 Act, created criminal offences in respect of breaches. In the field of family law, statute created the power to make residence orders, requiring a defendant to leave a dwelling house; or non molestation orders, requiring a defendant to abstain from threatening an associated person: ss.33(3) and (4) and s.42 of the Family Law Act 1996. The penalty for breach is punishment for contempt of court. The Housing Act 1996 created the power to grant injunctions against anti-social behaviour: s.152; s.153 (breach). This was, however, a power severely restricted in respect of locality. A broadly similar technique was adopted in the Protection from Harassment Act 1997: s.3; s.3(6) (breach). Post-dating the Crime and Disorder Act 1998, which is the subject matter of the present appeals, Parliament adopted a similar model in ss.14A and 14J (breach) of the Football Spectators Act 1989, inserted by s.1(1) of the Football (Disorder) Act 2000: *Gough v Chief Constable of the Derbyshire Constabulary* [2001] 3 WLR 1392. In all these cases the requirements for the granting of the statutory injunction depend on the criteria specified in the particular statute. The unifying element is, however, the use of the civil remedy of an injunction to prohibit conduct considered to be utterly unacceptable, with a remedy of criminal penalties in the event of disobedience."

Lord Steyn went on to note that proceedings under the first part of s.1 of the 1998 **4-53** Act were initiated by the civil process of complaint, and did not charge the defendant with any crime or involve the Crown Prosecution Service. Further, the making of such an order, the purpose of which was preventative not punitive, was not a conviction, did not appear on the defendant's criminal record and resulted in no penalty. He concluded that the proceedings could not classified as criminal for the purposes of Art.6 of the Convention.[208] Having reviewed the Convention caselaw applying the "*Engel* criteria", he concluded that there was no case in which the European Court had held proceedings to be criminal even though an adverse outcome for the defendant cannot result in any penalty:

---

[206] *R. (McCann) v Crown Court at Manchester; Clingham v Kensington and Chelsea Royal London Borough Council* [2003] 1 A.C. 787.
[207] Para.16.
[208] Para.22.

"It could be said, of course, that there is scope for the law to be developed in this direction. On the other hand, an extensive interpretation of what is a criminal charge under Article 6(1) would, by rendering the injunctive process ineffectual, prejudice the freedom of liberal democracies to maintain the rule of law by the use of civil injunctions".[209]

Although counsel for the Secretary of State reserved his position on the issue, Lord Steyn concluded that the proceedings did amount to a determination of a civil right or obligation for the purposes of Art.6.[210] Given the serious consequences attached to the making of an order, it was necessary for the magistrates court to be satisfied to a standard equivalent to the criminal standard of proof that the defendant has previously acted in an anti-social manner.[211] Subsequent case law has found that fundamental fairness additionally requires clarity as to the basis for, and the scope of, any order which the magistrates impose.[212] In *R. (Lonergan) v Crown Court at Lewes*, it was held that the imposition of a curfew as part of an order was not so stringent as to re-classify the procedure as the determination of a criminal charge. However, a court must consider carefully the need for and duration of a curfew when making an order. Moreover, just because an order under the 1998 Act must run for two years, it does not follow that each and every prohibition within a particular order has to endure for the life of the order.[213] Article 6 is not engaged by the decision of the magistates to make interim anti-social behaviour orders without notice, which are permitted by s.1D of the Crime and Disorder Act 1998 and r.5 of the Magistrates' Courts (Anti-social Behaviour Orders) Rules 2002. The Court of Appeal reached this conclusion in *R. (M.) v Secretary of State for Constituional Affairs*, because the order can only be made for a limited period, and can be reviewed or discharged on a return date, so that it cannot be characterised as constituting a final determination of a civil right or obligation.[214]

---

[209] Para.31.

[210] Para.29: "For my part, in the light of the particular use of the civil remedy of an injunction, as well as the defendant's right under Article 8 to respect for his private and family life, it is clear that a defendant has the benefit of the guarantee applicable to civil proceedings under Art.6.1. Moreover, under domestic English law they undoubtedly have a constitutional right to a fair hearing in respect of such proceedings". The European Court of Human Rights did not rule directly on this issue in either *Guzzardi v Italy* (1980) 3 E.H.R.R. 333 (see para.108); or *Raimondo v Italy* (1994) 18 E.H.R.R. 237 (at para.43).

[211] Para.37.

[212] *C. v Sunderland Youth Court* [2004] 1 Cr.App.R. (S.) 76, at paras 25 and 43, DC; *R. v P. (Shane)* [2004] Cr.App.R. (S.) 63, CA at para.19; *R. v Boness and Ors* [2005] EWCA Crim 2395 at para.20. In *Boness*, the Court of Appeal emphasised that each separate order prohibiting a person from doing a specified thing "must be necessary to protect persons from further anti-social acts *by* him" (para.29): "Any order should be tailor-made for the individual offender, not designed on a word processor for use in every case". As to the requirement that a prohibition under an ASBO not be unjustifiably wide, see *R. v McGrath* [2005] EWCA Crim 353.

[213] [2005] 1 W.L.R. 2570, Q.B.D. It was common ground in the case that the curfew was covered by Art.5 of the Convention: see para.6. *Cf. Guzzardi v Italy* (1980) 3 E.H.R.R. 333.

[214] [2004] 1 W.L.R. 2298, CA. Art.6 (and 8) also do not entitle the subject of a proposed control order to be consulted by the relevant authority, or heard, prior to the application by the authority to the magistrates court for the contol order to be imposed: see *R. (Carl Wareham) v Purbeck District Council* [2005] EWHC 358 Admin.

XXII Terrorism

The threat of terrorist attacks since September 11, 2001 has been met with the adoption of civil legislative schemes which attempt to circumvent the problems of obtaining admissible evidence for the purposes of a criminal trial. The crucial feature of these schemes is that they allow for the presentation of secret evidence in "closed" procedings in the absence of the suspect or his lawyers. The obvious unfairness of such a scheme is nominally remedied by the appointment of special advocates who represent the interests of the suspect as far as they are able to do so without disclosing the content of the evidence to him. Part IV of the Anti-Terrorist, Crime and Security Act 2001 introduced a scheme of detention based upon the Secretary of State's decision to certify that a foreign national subject to immigration control was a "suspected international terrorist". The scheme was eventually held by the House of Lords to be incompatible with the European Convention, because of its disproportionate and discriminatory nature.[215] In response to its defeat in the House of Lords the Government introduced a scheme of "derogating" and "non-derogating" control orders under the Prevention of Terrorism Act 2005. The distinguishing feature which differentiates a "derogating" from a "non-derogating" order is whether the obligations under the order cumulatively amount to a deprivation of liberty for the purposes of Art.5 of the Convention, in which case Parliament is required to derogate from the Convention.[216] Although control orders bear some comparison with anti-social behaviour orders, the principal difference is that the Secretary of State can impose an order if he has reasonable grounds to suspect that a person has been involved in terrorist related activity. The threshold for imposing an ASBO is significantly higher, because the applicant authority is required to show to a high civil standard of proof, which in reality is no different to the criminal standard, that the person has acted in an anti-social manner.[217]

The practical need and political justification for such measures has been intensely debated. The details of that debate are beyond the subject matter of this book. However, the preliminary question which arises in relation to counter-terrorist schemes is whether they in truth constitute the determination of a criminal charge. The House of Lords is yet to rule upon the issue, but thus far the lower courts have held that both the internment procedures under Pt IV of the 2001 Act and control orders under the 2005 Act are not criminal proceedings for the purposes of Art.6. The matter was first considered by the Court of Appeal in *A v Secretary of State for Home Department*.[218] The scheme had been introduced

4–54

---

[215] *A. v Secretary of State for the Home Department; X. v Same* [2005] 2 A.C. 68. The details of the extent to which the scheme constituted an unlawful derrogation from Art.5 of the Convention are dealt with in Ch.1.

[216] The issued was analysed *Secretary of State for the Home Department v JJ and Ors* [2006] 3 W.L.R. 866 upholding the detailed reasoning of Sullivan J. in the Administrative Court ([2006] EWHC 1623 (Admin)). See also Ch.1.

[217] In *Secretary of State for the Home Department v MB* [2006] 3 W.L.R. 839 the Court of Appeal held that despite the low evidential threshold required it was necessary for the court to determine at the time of the hearing whether there were objective grounds to justify the suspicion of terrorist related activity. In so finding, the court accepted that such a precondition was quite different from the test which applied under s.1(1)(a) of the Crime and Disorder Act 1998.

[218] *A. v Secretary of State for the Home Department; X. v Same* [2004] Q.B. 335, CA.

in Parliament on the basis of an undertaking that it would only be used if there was insufficient evidence to bring a criminal prosecution.[219] The effect of certification under the Act was, in reality, indefinite detention. The Court of Appeal held that the proceedings were "civil" for the purposes of Art.6, albeit without giving detailed reasons.[220]

4–55   The question of whether the imposition of a control order amounts to the imposition of a criminal charge has so far been considered in the context of an assumption that, by a process of strong analogy, the courts are bound by the judgment of the Court of Appeal in *A v Secretary of State for Home Department*. This was the position taken by Sullivan J. in *MB v Secretary of State for the Home Department*.[221] Had he considered himself free to decide the matter on his own, Sullivan J. indicated that he would have considerable sympathy for the position of the Joint Parliamentary Committee on Human Rights, which has concluded that the scheme does constitute a criminal procedure.[222] In particular, he was concerned about the extent of the control order restrictions, which in the examples referred to in the judgment were extremely severe. In those circumstances there were limits to the argument that the purpose of the obligations was to preventative rather than punitive:

> "The restrictions imposed by the ASBO in *McCann* upon activities that were prima facie lawful were relatively limited (a prohibition upon entering a particular area in Manchester). This must be contrasted with the obligations that have been imposed on most of other controlees, which have been described by the Independent Reviewer as falling 'not very far short of house arrest' (see paragraph 43 of his Report). I would pose the question, is there no limit to the severity of sanctions that may be imposed in civil proceedings without the safeguards afforded by Article 6.2 to 6.3 of the Convention if the purpose of the sanction is said to be prevention, not punishment? What if the state's ability to prosecute is due, at least in part, to a policy decision not to admit certain types of evidence, eg, intercept evidence, in criminal trials? I would reserve my position as to whether the ASBO regime is distinguishable from the control order regime in these, and other, respects which merit further consideration"[223]

On appeal, the Court of Apeal equally considered itself bound by the judgment in *A & Ors*. However, by way of a *per incuriam* observation the court indicated that proceedings under s.3 of the 2005 Act do not involve determination of a criminal charge. In reasoning thus, the court relied upon the requirement of a determination by a senior police officer, prior to the imposition of a control order, that it was not possible to bring criminal proceedings. Unlike the 2001 Act, s.8(2) of the 2005 Act creates a statutory duty to consider a prosecution. Under the

---

[219] See Hansard House of Lords (Lord Rooker), Motion of Approval, 27.11.01, Committee stage 29.11.01.

[220] [2004] Q.B. 335, para.57.

[221] The criminal charge issue was not determined by the House of Lords because the House found that the scheme was unlawful for other reasons. See [2005] 2 A.C. 68. In a separate judgment, concerning the use of evidence obtained from third parties as a result of torture by non-UK state agents, the House of Lords identified an exclusionary rule of evidence in the terms of Art.6, but again did not rule on whether the proceeedings were criminal or civil. See *A. and Ors (No.2) v Secretary of State for the Home Department* [2006] 2 A.C. 221.

[222] [2006] EWHC 1000 (Admin), paras 36–41.

[223] Para.41.

previous legislation that government had simply indicated that they would only use the civil powers where a prosecution was not possible. The Court of Appeal therefore held that,"It is implicit in the scheme that if there is evidence that justifies the bringing of a criminal charge, a suspect will be prosecuted rather than made the subject of a control order".[224]

XXIII. Issues arising under Article 5

There is a degree of confusion in the Convention caselaw as to the effect of the 4–56 "criminal charge" jurisprudence on the classification of detention under Art.5(1). So far as disciplinary offences are concerned, the Court has held that the "conviction" referred to in Art.5(1)(a) may be either a criminal or a disciplinary conviction.[225] The more difficult question is whether the fact that proceedings fall within Art.5(1)(b) (detention for non compliance with court orders or legal obligations) necessarily means that they are not "criminal" proceedings for the purposes of Art.6.[226] We have seen that in *Krone-Verlag GmbH and Mediaprint Anzeigen GmbH & Co. KG v Austria*[227] the Commission assumed that this was so.[228] However, this approach is hard to reconcile with the court's earlier decision in *Benham v United Kingdom*[229] where the applicant's detention was held to be justified under Art.5(1)(b),[230] despite the conclusion that it resulted from the determination of a criminal charge, for the purposes of Art.6. It follows from *Benham* that the categories of detention in Art.5(1) are not necessarily mutually exclusive, and that the Commission's reasoning in *Krone-Verlag* is open to doubt.

XXIV. Comparative law position

The classification of offences is not an area in which there is a clear international 4–57 or comparative consensus. It has been suggested that an autonomous approach to the definition of criminal proceedings is appropriate under Art.14 of the International Covenant on Civil and Political Rights.[231] On the other hand it appears that Art.8 of the American Convention on Human Rights is intended to apply only to offences of a certain level of gravity.[232]

---

[224] *Home Secretary v MB* [2006] 3 W.L.R. 839, para.53.

[225] *Engel v Netherlands* (1979–80) 1 E.H.R.R. 647 at para.68.

[226] Art.5(1)(a) permits lawful detention after "conviction by a competent court", whilst Art.5(1)(b) permits detention for disobedience to a lawful order of a court, or in order to secure the fulfilment of an obligation prescribed by law.

[227] (1997) 23 E.H.R.R. C.D. 152.

[228] See para.4–20 above.

[229] (1996) 22 E.H.R.R. 293.

[230] Para.39.

[231] Nowak, *UN Covenant on Civil and Political Rights* (Engel, 1993), p.243. Certain states have included regulatory offences and fiscal penalties in their reports on Art.14.

[232] Art.8 of the American Convention applies to "an accusation of a criminal nature". However, the *travaux préparatoires* indicate that the drafters intended to exclude minor offences, designated as *"faltas"* in the majority of Latin American systems: Burgenthal and Norris, *Human Rights, the Inter-American System* (Oceana, 1982), p.250.

4-58 Section 35 of the South African Constitution, which enshrines the right to a fair trial in criminal proceedings, has been held not to apply to statutory powers of compulsory questioning during a fraud inquiry,[233] or to professional disciplinary proceedings.[234] These decisions are broadly consistent with the approach taken in Strasbourg. A more restrictive approach is evident in Ireland[235] and New Zealand.[236]

4-59 Section 11 of the Canadian Charter applies only to persons charged with a criminal offence. In the leading case of *Wrigglesworth*[237] Wilson J. for a unanimous Supreme Court held that:

> "The rights guaranteed by section 11 of the Charter are available to persons prosecuted by the state for public offences involving punitive sanctions, *i.e.* criminal, quasi-criminal and regulatory offences, either federally or provincially enacted . . . It cannot seriously be contended that just because a minor traffic offence leads to a very slight consequence, perhaps only a small fine, that offence does not fall within section 11."

4-60 An offence would therefore attract the protection of s.11 either if it was "criminal" by its "very nature" or if it would lead to "true penal consequences". As to the former criterion, the Supreme Court distinguished between offences of "a public nature, intended to promote public order and welfare within a particular sphere of activity", which were criminal by their very nature, and "private, domestic or disciplinary matters which are regulatory, protective or corrective and which are primarily intended to maintain discipline, professional integrity and professional standards or to regulate conduct within a limited, private, sphere of activity". As to the relevance of the penalty imposed, a disciplinary offence would fall to be classified as "criminal" for the purposes of s.11 if it involved a punitive measure of sufficient severity, such as a fine or imprisonment.[238] In

---

[233] *Park Ross v The Director, Office for Serious Economic Offences* (1995) 2 B.C.L.R. 198 (applying s.25 of the Interim Constitution, the predecessor to s.35). The answers to such questions could not be used in any subsequent criminal proceedings: *cf. Saunders v United Kingdom* (1997) 23 E.H.R.R. 313.

[234] *Myburgh v Voorsitter van die Schoemanpark Ontspanningsklub Dissiplinere Verhoor* (1995) 9 B.C.L.R. 1145; *Cuppan v Cape Display Supply Chain Services* (1995) 5 B.C.L.R. 598 (both concerning s.25 of the Interim Constitution).

[235] *The State (Murray) v McRann* [1976] I.R. 133 (prison disciplinary proceedings); *Keady v Guarda Commissioner* [1992] 2 I.R. 197 (police disciplinary proceedings).

[236] See generally Butler "Regulatory Offences and the Bill of Rights" in Hushcroft and Rishworth (eds) *Rights and Freedoms: The New Zealand Bill of Rights Act 1990 and the Human Rights Act 1993* (Brookers, 1995).

[237] (1987) 60 C.R. (3d) 193 (S.C.C.).

[238] Applying these principles, the Canadian courts have held that s.11 rights would inapplicable to proceedings to determine fitness to obtain or maintain a licence, and to administrative proceedings to protect the public in accordance with the police of a statute (*R. v Wrigglesworth* (1987) 60 C.R. (3d) 193 (S.C.C.) at 210–211); police disciplinary proceedings which could lead to dismissal (*Trimm v Durham Regional Police Force* (1987) 37 C.C.C. (3d) 120 (S.C.C.); *Burnham v Ackroyd* (1987) 37 C.C.C. (3d) 118 (S.C.C.); *Trumbley v Metropolitan Police Force* (1987) 37 C.C.C. (3d) 120 (S.C.C.); to professional disciplinary proceedings of doctors (*Fang v College of Physicians and Surgeons of Alberta* [1986] 2 W.W.R. 380 (Alta CA) or lawyers (*Belhumeur v Discipline Committee of Quebec Bar Association*) (1983) 34 C.R. (3d) 279 (Que S.C.)). As to prison disciplinary proceedings, the Supreme Court has held that a charge resulting in five days solitary confinement and a restricted diet was insufficiently serious to qualify for s.11 protection: *Shubley* (1990) 74 C.R. (3d) 1 (S.C.C.).

terms which echo the Strasbourg jurisprudence, the Canadian Supreme Court has held that "[t]he characterisation of certain offences and statutory schemes as 'regulatory' or 'criminal', although a useful factor, is not the last word for the purposes of Charter analysis"[239]; and in *Wholesale Travel Group Ltd*[240] La Forest J., for the Ontario Court of Appeal, said that "what is ultimately important are not labels (though these are undoubtedly useful), but the values at stake in the particular context".

C. CHARGE

I. Autonomous Interpretation

The criminal guarantees of Art.6 apply only once the individual concerned has been "charged" with a criminal offence. In *Adolf v Austria*[241] the Court observed that:

> "The prominent place held in a democratic society by the right to a fair trial favours a 'substantive' rather than a 'formal' conception of the 'charge' referred to by Article 6; it impels the Court to look behind the appearances and examine the realities of the procedure in question in order to determine whether there has been a 'charge' within the meaning of Article 6."

4–61

Accordingly, the term "charge" has been given an autonomous Convention interpretation, and is defined as:

> "[T]he official notification given to an individual by the competent authority of an allegation that he has committed a criminal offence, a definition that also corresponds to the test whether the situation of the [suspect] has been substantially affected."[242]

4–62

Thus, there must be some formal notification of the accusation, but a "charge" can be constituted by any official act that carries such an implication.[243] This may be the date of formal charge by the police,[244] but in a case where the charge is delayed, or subsequent charges are added, it may be the date of the arrest,[245] "the date when the preliminary investigations were opened",[246] or the date on which the defendant becomes aware that he is being "seriously investigated" and that "immediate consideration" is being given to the possibility of a prosecution.[247] The Court and Commission have thus held Art.6 to be applicable from the date

4–63

---

[239] *Baron v Canada* (1993) 99 D.L.R. (4th) 350 at 370.

[240] (1989) 73 C.R. (3d) 320. *Wholesale Travel* has been applied in some English decisions analysing the proportionality of reverse burden of proof clauses: see *R. v Davies* [2003] I.C.R. 586.

[241] (1982) 4 E.H.R.R. 313 at para.30.

[242] *Eckle v FRG* (1983) 5 E.H.R.R. 1 at para.73; *Deweer v Belgium* (1979–80) 2 E.H.R.R. 439 at para.46.

[243] *Corigliano v Italy* (1983) 5 E.H.R.R. 334.

[244] *Ewing v United Kingdom* (1988) 10 E.H.R.R. 141.

[245] *Foti v Italy* (1983) 5 E.H.R.R. 313 at para.52.

[246] *Foti v Italy* (1983) 5 E.H.R.R. 313 at para.52.

[247] *X v United Kingdom* (1979) 14 D.R. 26; *X v United Kingdom* (1978) 17 D.R. 122.

on which an order was made for the closure of the applicant's business premises pending payment of a penalty as an alternative to prosecution,[248] the date on which the applicant was informed that his Parliamentary immunity had been lifted,[249] the date of an order for the production of evidence or the freezing of a bank account in the course of an investigation,[250] the date of a first interview by the Serious Fraud Office,[251] and the date of an initial search of the premises by the police.[252]

4–64   In certain circumstances a person may be "charged" within the meaning of Art.6 even before a decision to prosecute has been taken.[253] In *X v United Kingdom*[254] the applicant was convicted of burglary and handling in October 1973 and sentenced to four years imprisonment. At the time of his conviction, he was suspected of having procured arms and explosives for use in Northern Ireland, although there was insufficient evidence to prosecute him. Six months later, a witness came forward, and in October 1974 a decision was taken to prosecute the applicant on conspiracy charges. The indictment was issued in December of that year. The government argued that the applicant was not "charged" for the purposes of Art.6 until the indictment was preferred since, prior that time, his situation was unaffected (given that he was already serving a sentence of imprisonment). The Commission disagreed, holding that Art.6 was applicable from the moment the applicant was convicted on the first indictment:

> "In the Commission's opinion . . . the applicant's position was substantially affected as soon as the suspicion against him was seriously investigated and the prosecution case compiled. For it was from this moment onwards that uncertainty and anxiety as to his future began and he needed to consider and prepare his defence . . . [T]he commencement of the prospective conspiracy proceedings can be considered to be the end of the [first] Crown Court trial . . . immediate consideration having been given, and subsequent action taken, by the DPP as to the viability of further charges."

4–65   The question whether Art.6 is applicable during the early stages of an investigation appears to depend, at least in part, on the nature and powers of the authority conducting the investigation. In *Funke v France*[255] customs officers searched the applicant's home for evidence of his involvement in certain exchange control offences. When they were unable to find the documents they brought criminal proceedings against the applicant for the compulsory disclosure of bank statements relating to accounts which the applicant held with a number of foreign banks. The Court held Art.6 to be applicable, given the criminal character of the

---

[248] *Deweer v Belgium* (1979–80) 2 E.H.R.R. 439.
[249] *Frau v Italy* (1991) Series A No.195–E.
[250] *Funke v France* (1993) 16 E.H.R.R. 297.
[251] *Howarth v United Kingdom* (2005) 41 E.H.R.R. 2; *Massey v United Kingdom, The Times,* November 24, 2004, ECtHR. See also *King v United Kingdom (No.2)* [2004] S.T.C. 911, and *King v United Kingdom* (2005) 41 E.H.R.R. 2.
[252] *Neubeck v Germany*, 41 D.R. 13.
[253] A mere hearsay allegation to the police is not, however, sufficient to engage Art.6: *R. v HM Advocate*, 2000 J.C. 368 (High Court of Justiciary in Scotland).
[254] (1978) 14 D.R. 26.
[255] (1993) 16 E.H.R.R. 297.

investigation. However in *Saunders v United Kingdom*[256] Art.6 was held inapplicable to investigations conducted by DTI Inspectors appointed under the Companies Act 1985 since they were "essentially investigative in nature" and "did not adjudicate in form or in substance". The court noted that the purpose of the DTI investigation was to ascertain facts which might subsequently be used by *other* competent authorities—prosecuting, regulatory, disciplinary or even legislative.[257]

In *Attorney General's Reference (No.2 of 2001)*[258] it was held that time ran for the **4–66**
purposes of the reasonable time requirement from the earliest time when the defendant was officially alerted to the likelihood of criminal proceedings being taken against him, which would normally be when he was charged or served with a summons. However, it was wise not to lay down an inflexible rule in this area. Particular regard had to be given to the purposes of the reasonable time requirement: to ensure that criminal proceedings, once initiated, are prosecuted without undue delay; and to protect defendants from the trauma of awaiting trial for inordinate periods.[259] In so holding, Lord Bingham made the following observations about the Strasbourg case law:

> "The interviewing of a person for purposes of a regulatory inquiry in England and Wales will not meet the test laid down above: *Fayed v United Kingdom* (1994) 18 EHRR 393, 427–428, para 61; *IJL, GMR and AKP v United Kingdom* (2000) 33 EHRR 225, 258–259, para 131. Nor, ordinarily, will time begin to run until after a suspect has been interviewed under caution, since Code C made under section 66 of the Police and Criminal Evidence Act 1984 generally requires the charging process to be set in train once an interviewing officer considers that there is sufficient evidence to prosecute a detained person and that there is sufficient evidence for a prosecution to succeed. In *Howarth v United Kingdom* (2000) 31 EHRR 861 the European Court held that the period had begun with the first police interview of the defendant, but only 4 1/2 months separated that interview from the charge and attention was largely focused, at p 865, para 20, on the passage of time between sentence and final determination of a reference by the Attorney General under section 36 of the Criminal Justice Act 1988. Arrest will not ordinarily mark the beginning of the period. An official indication that a person will be reported with a view to prosecution may, depending on all the circumstances, do so."[260]

Providing the applicant has been "charged" in the extended sense described **4–67**
above, the guarantees of Art.6 will apply even if he is not finally brought to trial.

---

[256] (1997) 23 E.H.R.R. 313 at para.67.

[257] See also *R. v Hertfordshire County Council ex parte Green Environmental Industries Ltd and anor.* [2000] 2 W.L.R. 373 (HL) in which Lord Hoffmann held that the protection against self-incrimination in Art.6 was inapplicable to an investigation under the Environmental Protection Act 1990, since the investigation "did not form part, even a preliminary part, of any criminal proceedings" and did "not therefore touch the principle which prohibits interrogation of a person charged or accused".

[258] [2004] 2 A.C. 72.

[259] Para.27.

[260] Para.28. See also the opinion of Lord Hobhouse at para.128, which appeared to lay down a more specific division between an investigation and a prosecution, as characterised by Pts III and IV of the Police and Criminal Evidence Act 1984, which "draw a clear line between the investigating/arresting stage by the investigating police officers and the decision by a different independent police officer, the custody officer, whether a particular person should be charged and, if so, charging him: section 37 and Code C 16 (since amended)."

In *Allenet de Ribemont v France*,[261] the applicant was arrested for the murder of a French M.P. on December 29, 1976. On the same day, the French Interior Minister and two senior police officers gave a press conference in which they made comments suggesting that he was guilty of the offence for which he had been arrested. The applicant was charged on January 14, 1977, but released on bail two and a half months later. The proceedings were eventually discontinued without a trial in March 1980. The Court held that the applicant had been "charged" with a criminal offence for the purposes of Art.6 from the moment of his arrest, and that the remarks made during the press conference infringed the presumption of innocence in Art.6(2).

4–68   Where multiple offences are jointly tried, Art.6 will be applicable from the earliest date on which the defendant can be said to have been "charged". In *Ewing v United Kingdom*,[262] the applicant had been arrested in connection with dishonesty offences on December 5, 1979. He was charged with those offences on the same day, and subsequently released on bail. He was then re-arrested and charged with further related offences on March 13, 1980. He appeared in different Magistrates Courts on several occasions, and was subject to three separate committals, all arising out of the same sequence of events. In February 1991 the charges were amalgamated into a single indictment, and the applicant was thereafter tried and convicted. He complained of the length of the proceedings. The government argued that for the purposes of the reasonable time guarantee in Art.6 the proceedings began when the amalgamated indictment was signed. Perhaps unsurprisingly, the Commission rejected this view, and held that the proceedings had to be considered as a whole and that Art.6 was accordingly applicable with effect from December 5, 1979.

4–69   In *Callaghan and others v United Kingdom*[263] the Commission held that Art.6 applied to proceedings on appeal following a reference under s.17 of the Criminal Appeal Act 1968 (prior to its amendment by the Criminal Appeal Act 1995[264]). The case arose out of the first (unsuccessful) appeal by the six men convicted of the Birmingham pub bombings. Although the charge against the applicants had been finally determined, and their convictions had the quality of *res judicata*, the reference back had the effect of reopening the proceedings such that the applicants were, once again, "charged" with a criminal offence:

> "The Commission notes that in this case the criminal proceedings had long been completed and that the reference procedure was not a normal step. Nonetheless the proceedings on the Secretary of State's reference had all the features of an appeal against conviction, and could have resulted in the applicants being found not guilty or, as in fact happened, the convictions being upheld. They must therefore . . . be regarded as having the effect of determining, or redetermining, the charges against the applicants."

---

[261] (1995) 20 E.H.R.R. 557.
[262] (1988) 10 E.H.R.R. 141.
[263] (1989) 60 D.R. 296.
[264] ss.9 to 13 of the 1995 Act now govern the powers of reference back to the Court of Appeal or (in the case of a summary conviction) the Crown Court by the Criminal Cases Review Commission.

The Court has since held on numerous occasions that the autonomous meaning of a criminal charge includes the period taken by the determination of an appeal.[265]

Since the coming into force of the Human Rights Act the domestic courts have **4–70** recognised that Art.6 continues to apply to the appellate stage of the proceedings, such that a person can claim a breach of the reasonable time requirement for delays which take place at appeal stage.[266]

II. Comparative Law Position

The decisions of the Canadian and New Zealand courts afford less flexibility to **4–71** the notion of a criminal charge. In *Kalanj*[267] the Canadian Supreme Court held, by a majority of three to two[268] that a person is charged with a criminal offence for the purposes of s.11 of the Charter only when an information is sworn to a justice alleging an offence, or an indictment is laid.[269] The minority view, which was closer to the tests laid down in the Convention jurisprudence, was that the section should apply when the impact of the criminal justice system was felt by the accused through the service of a summons, notice of appearance or an arrest, with or without a warrant. Similarly the High Court of New Zealand has held that the term "charged" in the New Zealand Bill of Rights Act applies to "an intermediate step in the prosecutorial process", between arrest and appearance in court, "when the prosecuting authority formally advises an arrested person that he is to be prosecuted and gives him particulars of the charges he will face."[270]

---

[265] *Henworth v United Kingdom*, (2005) 40 E.H.R.R. 33.

[266] *Mills v HM Advocate* [2004] 1 A.C. 441, PC; *Attorney Generals Reference (No.2 of 2001)* [2004] 2 A.C. 72, applied in *R. v Ashton, Lyons and Webber, The Times*, December 10, 2002.

[267] (1989) 70 C.R. (3d) 260 (S.C.C.).

[268] This has since been confirmed as the position of the full court: *Morin* (1992) 12 C.R. (4th) 1 (S.C.R.).

[269] Note, however, that in *Heit* (1984) 11 C.C.C. (3d) 97 (Sask CA) the court suggested that the service of a traffic ticket which had not been sworn in court was sufficient to engage s.11.

[270] *Gibbons* [1997] 2 N.Z.L.R. 585, *per* Goddard J. at 595.

CHAPTER 5

RIGHTS RELATING TO ARREST AND DETENTION IN POLICE CUSTODY

A. INTRODUCTION

The core provision governing powers of arrest and detention is Art.5, which **5–01** protects the liberty and security of the person and occupies an important position in the Convention system.[1] The court has consistently emphasised that it is one of the fundamental principles of a democratic society that the state must strictly adhere to the rule of law when interfering with the right to personal liberty.[2] The underlying aim of Art.5 is "to ensure that no one should be dispossessed of [their] liberty in an arbitrary fashion".[3] In this chapter we examine the requirements of legality prescribed by Art.5(1), the power of arrest on reasonable suspicion, the power of arrest or detention for breach of a court order or to secure compliance with a legal obligation, the right to be informed of the reasons for an arrest, the information to be provided at the time of charge, the right to be produced promptly before a court after arrest, and the right to have the legality of a detention reviewed by a court in *habeas corpus* proceedings. Finally, we consider the Convention approach to allegations of ill-treatment in police custody under Art.3.

---

[1] *Brogan v United Kingdom* (1989) 11 E.H.R.R. 117, para.58; *De Wilde, Ooms and Versyp v Belgium* (1979–80) 1 E.H.R.R. 373, para.65.

[2] *Brogan v United Kingdom* (1989) 11 E.H.R.R. 117, para.58; *Engel v Netherlands* (1979–80) 1 E.H.R.R. 647, para.69.

[3] *Engel v Netherlands* (1979–80) 1 E.H.R.R. 647, para.58; *Winterwerp v Netherlands* (1979–80) 2 E.H.R.R. 387, para.37; *Guzzardi v Italy* (1981) 3 E.H.R.R. 333, para.92; *Bozano v France* (1987) 9 E.H.R.R. 297, para.54; *Van Droogenbroeck v Belgium* (1982) 4 E.H.R.R. 443, para.40; *Weeks v United Kingdom* (1988) 10 E.H.R.R. 293, para.49.

B. DEPRIVATION OF LIBERTY

I. The Strasbourg Caselaw

5–02 Article 5 contemplates individual liberty "in its classic sense, that is to say the physical liberty of the person".[4] It is concerned with the *deprivation* of liberty and not with mere *restrictions* on freedom of movement.[5] The distinction is not always easy to identify, since the difference is "merely one of degree or intensity, and not one of nature or substance".[6] In determining whether the level of restraint involved amounts to a detention, regard should be had to "a whole range of criteria such as the type, duration, effects and manner of implementation of the measure in question".[7] Thus, the Court has held that a person detained in a mental hospital under a compulsory detention order could rely on Art.5 even though he was kept in an open ward for part of the time and could leave the hospital unaccompanied on occasions.[8] On the other hand, a patient who, while remaining subject to a detention order, was provisionally released, was no longer deprived of her liberty.[9] In *X v Switzerland*[10] the Commission held that a disciplinary order confining a prisoner to his cell did not lead to an additional deprivation of liberty,[11] whereas in *Campbell and Fell v United Kingdom*[12] an order for the forfeiture of remission was held to have imposed an additional period of detention. In *Engel v Netherlands*[13] the Court held that "strict arrest" imposed on soldiers for disciplinary offences amounted to a deprivation of liberty despite the different standards which apply to military personnel. In *Pekov v Bulgaria*, the most recent in a number of 24 hour house arrest cases, the Court had to consider the submission by the Bulgarian Government that the fact that the Applicant was not being monitored, and could therefore have breached the house arrest order with impunity, meant that he was not "deprived of his liberty." The Court rejected this argument, finding that it was necessary to look at the "actual circumstance of the regime to which he or she was subject, as a matter of law and in fact . . . "[14]

---

[4] *Engel v Netherlands* (1979–80) 1 E.H.R.R. 647, para.58.

[5] *Engel v Netherlands* (1979–80) 1 E.H.R.R. 647, para.58; *Guzzardi v Italy* (1981) 3 E.H.R.R. 333, para.92; *Raimondo v Italy* (1994) 18 E.H.R.R. 237, para.39. Lesser restrictions on freedom of movement are governed by Art.2 of the Fourth Protocol, to which the United Kingdom is not a party.

[6] *Guzzardi v Italy* (1981) 3 E.H.R.R. 333, para.93; *Ashingdane v United Kingdom* (1985) 7 E.H.R.R. 528, para.41.

[7] *Guzzardi v Italy* (1981) 3 E.H.R.R. 333, para.92; *Ashingdane v United Kingdom* (1985) 7 E.H.R.R. 528, para.41; *Engel v Netherlands* (1976) 1 E.H.R.R. 647, paras 58–59.

[8] *Ashingdane v United Kingdom* (1985) 7 E.H.R.R. 528, para.42.

[9] *W v Sweden* 59 D.R. 158 (1988).

[10] Application 7754/77 (1977) 11 D.R. 216, para.2.

[11] cf. *R. v Deputy Governor of Parkhurst Prison ex parte Hague* [1992] 1 A.C. 58 where the House of Lords came to the same conclusion in relation to the tort of false imprisonment; however, in *Karagozlu v Commissioner of Police of the Metropolis* [2006] EWCA Civ 1691, the Court of Appeal held that the loss of residual liberty caused by a move to a prison of a higher security category was sufficient "damage" to found a claim in misfeasance.

[12] (1985) 7 E.H.R.R. 165, para.72.

[13] (1979–80) 1 E.H.R.R. 647.

[14] Application 50358/99, March 30, 2006, para.73.

The English courts have recently had cause to consider in some detail the decisions of the European Court on the ambit of "deprivation of liberty". The case of *Secretary of State for the Home Department v JJ and others*[15] concerned the imposition of a "non-derogating control order" on the Respondents under ss.2–3 of the Prevention of Terrorism Act 2005. The Respondents were suspected by the Government of involvement in terrorism. The terms of the control orders included an 18 hour curfew, geographical limitations on movement in the remaining six hours, the wearing of an electronic tag, severe restrictions on visitors and planned meetings, prohibitions on the use of communications equipment, with the exception of one landline, and a limit on banking facilities.[16] Sullivan J. concluded that there was a lacuna in the case law of the European court between 24 hour house arrest and a curfew of up to 12 hours per weekday and the entirety of the weekend, the former of which was a deprivation of liberty and the latter of which was a mere restriction.[17] However, he concluded that the restrictions imposed on the Respondents fell firmly within the category of deprivation of liberty. In reaching his decision he relied on the approach of the European Court in *Guzzardi* to take into account the effect of all the restrictions imposed on the Respondents, not simply those which confined them to their homes. Nonetheless, he took the view that even if the only obligation had been the 18 hour curfew, and its enforcement through tagging and reporting, there would still have been a deprivation of liberty.[18] Sullivan J. described the "concrete situation" of the Respondents as the "antithesis of liberty", and not a "borderline case": "The collective impact of the obligations . . . , could not sensibly be described as a mere restriction upon the respondents liberty of movement."[19] The Court of Appeal upheld the decision, and its reasoning, finding that the facts fell "clearly on the wrong side of the dividing line" between mere restrictions on liberty of movement and deprivation of liberty.[20] At the time of writing, the Home Secretary is appealing to the House of Lords.[21]

---

[15] [2006] EWHC 1623 (Admin); [2006] EWCA Civ 1141, [2006] 3 W.L.R. 866.

[16] For a full list of the obligations imposed on each of the Respondents, see Annex 1 to the judgment of Sullivan J.

[17] An assessment which was expressly upheld by the Court of Appeal: see para.21.

[18] Para.77.

[19] Paras 73–74. See also, the JCHR's 12th Report of 2005–06 and Lord Carlile of Berriew Q.C.'s First Report of the Independent Reviewer pursuant to s.14(3) of the Prevention of Terrorism Act 2005 (February 2, 2006), both cited by Sullivan J. at paras 3 and 80–81.

[20] Para.23.

[21] At the time of going to press, there had recently been three further control orders decisions. In *Secretary of State for the Home Department v AF* [2007] EWHC 651 (Admin), Ouseley J. held that, while the case was "finely balanced", the restrictions imposed on the applicant by the control order (he was prevented from leaving his flat for more than 10 hours a day and could only visit a certain geographical area when out, had to wear an electronic tag, and required prior identification and approval for visitors to his flat) amounted to deprivation of liberty under Art.5, rendering the control order a nullity. Ouseley J. did hold, however, following *MB* in the Court of Appeal, that AF had had a fair hearing despite that fact that the case against him was, essentially, entirely undisclosed to him. The control orders at issue in *Secretary of State for the Home Department v E* [2007] EWHC 233 (Admin) and *Secretary of State for the Home Department v Abu Rideh* [2007] EWHC 804 were also quashed on the basis that they breached Art.5. Each of these three decisions also contains discussion of the Convention compliance of various aspects of the process by which control orders are made and reviewed.

5-03 In this country, claims that a person was merely "helping the police with their inquiries" should be scrutinised with care. This anomalous category of quasi-detention is preserved by the Police and Criminal Evidence Act 1984,[22] but should it be regarded as amounting to a deprivation of liberty for the purposes of Art.5? There is no clear answer in the Convention caselaw, and the applicability of Art.5 in this context would appear to depend on the facts of the individual case. As a general proposition it can be said that Art.5 will not apply where the individual consents to the restriction, providing the consent is clearly established and unequivocal. But the fact that a person initially agreed to enter a custodial institution does not prevent him from relying on Art.5 if he subsequently wishes to leave.[23] In 1989, in the case of *Nielsen v Denmark*,[24] the Court held that where the detention of a child was in issue, consent of the parent or guardian might be sufficient, even if the detention was contrary to the child's wishes. The Court, however, noted that parental rights were not absolute and that it was incumbent on the State to provide safeguards against abuse.[25]

5-04 The duration of the detention is not necessarily decisive[26]: Art.5 has been held to apply to detention for the purposes of carrying out a compulsory blood test,[27] or for sobering up,[28] or during the course of a journey in a moving vehicle,[29] or an aircraft.[30] In *R. (Laporte) v Chief Constable of Gloucestershire Constabulary*[31] the Divisional Court found that the forcible return to London of protesters who were confined to their coach for a two and a half hour journey amounted to a deprivation of liberty under Art.5(1),[32] as did the High Court in considering the confinement for seven hours by police of several thousand protesters within cordons at Oxford Circus on May Day 2001.[33] In *R. (Gillan) v Commissioner of Police of the Metropolis*[34] the House of Lords took the view that a "short detainment" pursuant to the exercise of stop and search powers (in that case, under ss.44–45 of the Terrorism Act 2000) would not normally amount to a deprivation of liberty. Lord Bingham, with whom the rest of the House agreed, considered that

---

[22] The powers of the police in England and Wales to question a suspect without arrest are governed by the Police and Criminal Evidence Act 1984, s.29 *et seq.*
[23] *De Wilde, Ooms and Versyp v Belgium* (1979–80) 1 E.H.R.R. 373, para.65. See also *Amuur v France* (1996) 22 E.H.R.R. 533, para.48.
[24] (1989) 11 E.H.R.R. 175.
[25] The U.N. Convention on the Rights of the Child (1989) affords the child the right to be consulted over decisions affecting his or her future, and provides express protection against arbitrary deprivation of liberty.
[26] *X and Y v Sweden* (1976) 7 D.R. 123 (detention for one hour prior to deportation).
[27] Application 8278/78 *X v Austria* (1979) 18 D.R. 154.
[28] *Litwa v Poland* (2001) 33 E.H.R.R. 53; see also *DPP v Meaden* [2004] 1 W.L.R. 945 where Rose L.J. indicated that he was happy to accept that the detention by police of a man in a bathroom while his bedroom was being searched was a deprivation of liberty.
[29] *Bozano v France* (1987) 9 E.H.R.R. 297.
[30] *X and Y v Sweden* (1976) 7 D.R. 123.
[31] [2004] 2 All E.R. 874.
[32] The Art.5 issue was not resolved by the House of Lords.
[33] *Austin & Saxby v Commissioner of Police of the Metropolis* [2005] E.W.H.C. 480 at paras 501–512.
[34] [2006] 2 A.C. 307.

"the procedure will ordinarily be relatively brief. The person stopped will not be arrested, handcuffed, confined or removed to any different place. I do not think, in the absence of special circumstances, such a person should be regarded as being detained in the sense of confined or kept in custody, but more properly of being detained in the sense of kept from proceeding or kept waiting. There is no deprivation of liberty."[35]

In the past, the Commission has attached considerable (and perhaps undue) importance to the intention of the authorities. Thus, in *X v Germany*[36] the Commission held that a 10 year old girl who was questioned at a police station for two hours without being arrested, locked into a cell or formally detained was not deprived of her liberty for the purposes of Art.5. Together with another pupil, the applicant had been taken to the police station in the course of an investigation into thefts of stationery from other children, despite the fact that she was below the age of criminal responsibility. Somewhat unconvincingly the Commission observed that: " . . . in the present case the police action was not aimed at depriving the children of their liberty but simply to obtain information from them about how they obtained possession of the objects found on them and about thefts which had occurred previously at the school."

This formulation appears to turn entirely on the intentions of the police, a view **5–05** reinforced by the Commission's statement that it was "regrettable that the children may not have been able to understand the police action and may have felt that they were deprived of their liberty". This is surely an unsatisfactory (or at the very least an incomplete) test. It gives the appearance of depriving a person who is being interrogated by the police of the minimum rights guaranteed by Art.5, even where they are led to believe that they are being detained against their will.

II. Comparative Approaches

In Canada the Ontario Court of Appeal has held that whether or not a person who **5–06** has not been formally arrested is "detained" depends not solely on whether he or she believed that this was the case but more widely on a number of situational criteria.[37] These criteria were approved by the New Zealand High Court in *M*,[38] where it was held that the defendant had been detained when he had formed the belief, reasonably founded on police conduct, that he was not free to leave. The Chief Justice of New Zealand adopted the same approach in *P*:

"Arrest is defined as a communication or manifestation by the police of an intention to apprehend and to hold the person concerned in the exercise of authority to do so; or, as long as the conduct of the arrester, seen to be acting or purporting to act under legal authority, has made it plain that the subject had been deprived of the liberty to go where he pleased."[39]

---

[35] Para.25.
[36] Application 8819/79 (1981) 24 D.R. 158 at 161.
[37] *Moran* (1987) 36 C.C.C. (3d) 225.
[38] [1995] 1 N.Z.L.R. 242.
[39] *P* [1996] 3 N.Z.L.R. 132 at 136.

C. THE "LEGALITY" REQUIREMENTS OF ARTICLE 5(1)

5–07 Article 5(1) provides that everyone has the right to liberty and security of the person, and that no one is to be deprived of their liberty save in the circumstances prescribed in Art.5(1)(a) to (f). The list of exceptions set out in Art.5(1) thus provides an exhaustive[40] definition of the circumstances in which a person may be lawfully deprived of his liberty, and is to be given a narrow construction.[41] In addition to falling within sub-paras (a)–(f),[42] any detention must be: (i) "lawful" and (ii) carried out "in accordance with a procedure prescribed by law".[43] These terms refer to conformity with national law[44] and procedure and it is therefore "in the first place for the national authorities, notably the courts, to interpret and apply domestic law".[45]

5–08 Nevertheless, it remains the function of the European Court of Human Rights to determine whether Art.5 has been violated, and the Court therefore has the ultimate power to interpret and apply national law.[46] The scope of the Court's task in this connection "is subject to limits inherent in the logic of the European system of protection",[47] so that on the international level[48] a certain margin of appreciation will be afforded to the decisions of the domestic courts.[49] However, a detention which is unlawful under domestic law will be *a fortiori* in breach of Art.5.[50] On the other hand, a period of detention carried out pursuant to an order of a court which is subsequently found to have erred in law will not necessarily be retrospectively invalidated unless the court is found to have acted in excess of jurisdiction.[51]

---

[40] *Ireland v United Kingdom* (1979–80) 2 E.H.R.R. 25, para.194.

[41] *Guzzardi v Italy* (1981) 3 E.H.R.R. 333, paras 98 and 100; *Winterwerp v Netherlands* (1979–80) 2 E.H.R.R. 387, para.37; *Quinn v France* (1996) 21 E.H.R.R. 529, para.42.

[42] The grounds enumerated in sub-paras (a)–(f) are not mutually exclusive: *McVeigh, O'Neill and Evans v United Kingdom* (1981) 25 D.R. 15.

[43] *Winterwerp v Netherlands* (1979–80) 2 E.H.R.R. 387, para.39.

[44] The term also includes applicable international law; in *Ocalan v Turkey* (2005) 18 B.H.R.C. 293 at para.90) the court considered whether Turkey had acted inconsistently with Kenya's sovereignty and therefore contrary to international law in arresting the appellant in Kenya and concluded that it had not.

[45] *Bozano v France* (1987) 9 E.H.R.R. 297, para.58; *Winterwerp v Netherlands* (1979–80) 2 E.H.R.R. 387; *Wassink v Netherlands* (1990) Series A/185–A, para.24; *Benham v United Kingdom* (1996) 22 E.H.R.R. 293, para.41.

[46] *Gusinskiy v Russia* (2004) 16 B.H.R.C. 427, at para.66; *Bozano v France* (1987) 9 E.H.R.R. 297, para.58; *Benham v United Kingdom* (1996) 22 E.H.R.R. 293, para.41.

[47] *Bozano v France* (1987) 9 E.H.R.R. 297, para.58.

[48] As to the relevance of the "margin of appreciation" doctrine before the national courts see paras 2–123 to 2–134 above.

[49] *Weeks v United Kingdom* (1988) 10 E.H.R.R. 293, para.50; *Winterwerp v Netherlands* (1979–80) 2 E.H.R.R. 387, para.40.

[50] *Benham v United Kingdom* (1996) 22 E.H.R.R. 293; *cf. Poole v United Kingdom* (1998) Application No.28190/95; *Johnson v United Kingdom* (1998) Application No.28455/95; *Denson v United Kingdom* (1998) Application No.25286/94. See also *Steel and ors v United Kingdom* (1999) 28 E.H.R.R. 603, where the court, in determining the compatibility of the applicants' detention, distinguished between them by applying the relevant test under national law.

[51] *Lloyd & Others v United Kingdom, The Times,* March 10, 2005; *Perks v United Kingdom* (2000) 30 E.H.R.R. 33, para.62; *Benham v United Kingdom* (1996) 22 E.H.R.R. 293 at paras 39–44.

For a detention to comply with Art.5, it must conform to the general principles **5–09** contained in the Convention.[52] Thus the Court has held that;

> "[An] arrested or detained person is entitled to a review of the 'lawfulness' of his detention in the light not only of the requirements of domestic law, but also of the text of the Convention, the general principles embodied therein, and the aim of the restrictions permitted by Article 5(1)".[53]

A detention will be incompatible with the lawfulness requirement and the "very purpose" of Art.5 where there is no record detailing "such matters as the date, time and location of detention, the name of the detainee, the reasons for the detention and the name of the person effecting it": "the unacknowledged detention of an individual is a complete negation of the fundamentally important guarantees contained in Article 5 of the Convention and discloses a most grave violation of that provision.".[54]

The term "lawful" implies that the domestic law on which the detention is based **5–10** must itself be "accessible and precise".[55] In *Steel and others v United Kingdom*,[56] a case concerning arrest and detention for breach of the peace, the court held that given the importance of personal liberty, it is essential that national law governing detention be sufficiently precise to allow the citizen—if need be, with appropriate advice—to foresee, to a degree that is reasonable in the circumstances, the consequences which a given action of his may entail. In the Court's view the concept of breach of the peace had been clarified by judicial decision such that the applicable rules provided sufficient guidance, and were formulated with the degree of precision required by the Convention.[57]

Article 5 has been held to prohibit deprivation of liberty which is "arbitrary" in **5–11** its motivation or effect.[58] A detention will be arbitrary if it is not in keeping with

---

[52] *Winterwerp v Netherlands* (1979–80) 2 E.H.R.R. 387, para.37; *Herczegfalvy v Austria* (1993) 15 E.H.R.R. 437, para.63; *Bozano v France* (1987) 9 E.H.R.R. 297, para.54; *Weeks v United Kingdom* (1988) 10 E.H.R.R. 293, para.42. The "general principles" contained in the Convention include the "rule of law": *Engel v Netherlands* (1989) 11 E.H.R.R. 117, para.69; *Brogan v United Kingdom* (1989) 11 E.H.R.R. 117, para.58.

[53] *Jècius v Lithuania* (2002) 35 E.H.R.R. 400, para.56; *E v Norway* (1994) 17 E.H.R.R. 30, para.49.

[54] *Menesheva v Russia* Application 59261/00 (March 9, 2006), para.84. See also *Bazorkina v Russia* Application 69481/01 (July 27, 2006), para.146.

[55] *Gusinskiy v Russia* (2004) 16 B.II.R.C. 427, at para.62; *Dougoz v Greece* (2002) 34 E.H.R.R. 1480, para.55; Application 9174/80 *Zamir v United Kingdom* (1983) 40 D.R. 42; *Sunday Times (No.1) v United Kingdom* (1979–80) 2 E.H.R.R. 245, para.49; *Amuur v France* (1996) 22 E.H.R.R. 533, para.50.

[56] (1999) 28 E.H.R.R. 603.

[57] cf. *Hashman and Harrap v United Kingdom*, (2000) 30 E.H.R.R. 241, where the court reached the opposite conclusion in relation to an order to be bound over to be "of good behaviour".

[58] *Winterwerp v Netherlands* (1979–80) 2 E.H.R.R. 387, paras 37–39; *Van Droogenbroeck v Belgium* (1982) 4 E.H.R.R. 443, para.48; *Weeks v United Kingdom* (1988) 10 E.H.R.R. 293, para.49; *Bozano v France* (1987) 9 E.H.R.R. 297, para.54; *Ashingdane v United Kingdom* (1985) 7 E.H.R.R. 528, para.44. Cf. *Ong Ah Chuan v Public Prosecutor* [1981] A.C. 648, (PC).

the purpose of the restrictions permissible under Art.5(1) or with Art.5 generally.[59] An improperly motivated prosecution may violate Art.5(1)(c) read in conjunction with Art.18.[60] The absence of procedural safeguards leaving "effective and unqualified control" of a person's liberty in the hands of doctors will render detention arbitrary.[61] Detention which is ostensibly for the purpose of deportation but which is in reality a disguised illegal extradition is arbitrary.[62] Even if properly motivated, a detention may be arbitrary if it is disproportionate to the attainment of its purpose.[63] Thus, for example, imprisonment imposed on grounds of dangerousness by reference to characteristics which are susceptible to change with the passage of time will become arbitrary if those characteristics are no longer present.[64] Equally, the imposition of an automatic life sentence on an offender who is not considered a significant risk to the public may be arbitrary or disproportionate.[65] On the other hand, the fact that time spent in custody abroad is not taken into account in computing the length of a prison sentence does not render the additional period of detention arbitrary.[66] Nor does the fact that detention results from a "loss of time" order by the Court of Appeal Criminal Division under s.29(1) of the Criminal Appeal Act 1968.[67] In a striking example of the application of the principle of proportionality, the House of Lords held in *A v Home Secretary*[68] that the government's derogation from Art.5 in order to allow the indefinite detention of foreign nationals was disproportionate to the aim of the legislation, which was to address the security threat posed by Al-Qaeda, because it did not address the threat posed by United Kingdom nationals, it permitted foreign nationals suspected of being Al-Qaeda terrorists or their supporters to pursue their activities abroad and it permitted the detention of persons not suspected of posing a threat to the United Kingdom as Al Qaeda terrorists or supporters.

5–12 The requirements of the principle of legality in Art.5(1) were encapsulated by Lord Hope in *R. v Governor of HMP Brockhill ex parte Evans (No.2)*[69]:

---

[59] *Winterwerp v Netherlands* (1979–80) 2 E.H.R.R. 387, para.39; *Bouamar v Belgium* (1988) 11 E.H.R.R. 1, para.50; *Weeks v United Kingdom* (1987) 10 E.H.R.R. 293, para.42; *Ashingdane v United Kingdom* (1985) 7 E.H.R.R. 528, para.44; *Gusinskiy v Russia* (2004) 16 B.H.R.C. 427.

[60] *Gusinskiy v Russia* (2004) 16 B.H.R.C. 427 paras 70–78.

[61] *HL v United Kingdom* (2004) 17 B.H.R.C. 418 at paras 115 and 121.

[62] *Bozano v France* (1987) 9 E.H.R.R. 297.

[63] *Winterwerp v Netherlands* (1979–80) 2 E.H.R.R. 387 para.39; *Van Droogenbroeck v Belgium* (1982) 4 E.H.R.R. 443. *Bouamar v Belgium* (1989) 11 E.H.R.R. 1, para.53.

[64] *Van Droogenbroeck v Belgium* (1982) 4 E.H.R.R. 443; *Weeks v United Kingdom* (1988) 10 E.H.R.R. 293; *Thynne, Wilson and Gunnell v United Kingdom* (1991) 13 E.H.R.R. 666; *Abed Hussain v United Kingdom* (1996) 22 E.H.R.R. 1.

[65] *R. v Offen* [2001] 1 W.L.R. 253; *R. v Drew* [2003] 1 W.L.R. 1213.The mandatory life sentence for murder under the Murder (Abolition of Death Penalty) Act 1965 is not, however, arbitrary or disproportionate: *R. v Lichniak* [2003] 1 A.C. 903. See also *V and T v United Kingdom* (2000) 30 E.H.R.R. 121, paras 104–5.

[66] *C v United Kingdom* (1985) 43 D.R. 177.

[67] *Monnell and Morris v United Kingdom* (1988) 10 E.H.R.R. 205. Under the Criminal Appeals Act 1968, s.29(1) the Court of Appeal may, if it considers that an appeal is without merit, direct that time served between the imposition of the sentence and the disposal of the appeal should not count towards the accused person's sentence. As to the circumstances in which such an order may be made see *Practice Direction (Criminal Proceedings: Consolidation)* [2002] 1 W.L.R. 2870, para.II.16.1.

[68] [2005] 2 A.C. 68 at paras 43, 132–3, 189, and 231.

[69] [2001] 2 A.C. 19.

"The jurisprudence of the European Court of Human Rights indicates that there are various aspects to Article 5(1) which must be satisfied in order to show that the detention is lawful for the purposes of the article. The first question is whether the detention is lawful under domestic law. Any detention which is unlawful in domestic law will automatically be unlawful under Article 5(1)... The second question is whether, assuming that the detention is lawful under domestic law, it nevertheless complies with the general requirements of the Convention. These are based on the principle that any restriction on human rights must be prescribed by law... They include the requirements that the domestic law must be sufficiently accessible to the individual and that it must be sufficiently precise to enable the individual to foresee the consequences of the restriction... The third question is whether, again assuming that the detention is lawful under domestic law, it is nevertheless open to criticism on the ground that it is arbitrary because, for example, it was resorted to in bad faith or was not proportionate."

D. ARREST ON REASONABLE SUSPICION AND RELATED GROUNDS

I. General

Article 5(1)(c) authorises lawful arrest or detention for the purpose of bringing a   **5–13** person before the competent legal authority on reasonable suspicion of having committed a criminal offence, or when it is reasonably considered necessary to prevent him committing an offence or fleeing having done so. It has to be read in conjunction with Art.5(3), which provides additional protection for persons arrested in these circumstances.[70] When the period of detention commences before the entry into force of the Convention, the stage which the proceedings have reached should be taken into account. To that extent, reference may be made to the earlier period.[71]

II. Criminal Offences

Article 5(1)(c) is confined to criminal offences[72] within the extended Convention   **5–14** definition of that term.[73] The term "offence" means a criminal or disciplinary[74] offence which is "concrete and specified".[75] Article 5(1)(c) is not therefore capable of authorising a general power of preventative detention, since this would lead to "conclusions repugnant to the fundamental principles of the

---

[70] *Ciulla v Italy* (1989) 13 E.H.R.R. 346, para.38; *Lawless v Ireland (No.3)* (1979–80) 1 E.H.R.R. 15, para.14; *Smirnova v Russia* Application No.46133/99 and 48183/99, Judgment of July 24, 2003, para.56. On Art.5(3), see para.5–28.

[71] *Smirnova v Russia* Application No.46133/99 and 48183/99, Judgment of July 24, 2003, para.57.

[72] *Ciulla v Italy* (1991) 13 E.H.R.R. 346, para.38, where the court held that detention of the applicant in order to bring him before a competent legal authority in connection with a compulsory residence order did not fall within Art.5(1)(c).

[73] *Steel and ors v United Kingdom* (1999) 28 E.H.R.R. 603. As to the meaning of "criminal" proceedings for the purposes of Art.6, Ch.4 above.

[74] *De Jong, Baljet and Van Den Brink v Netherlands* (1986) 8 E.H.R.R. 20.

[75] *Guzzardi v Italy* (1981) 3 E.H.R.R. 333, para.102.

Convention".[76] In *Brogan v United Kingdom*[77] the applicants were detained for questioning in connection with alleged involvement in "acts of terrorism". The Court held that although an "act of terrorism" (which was defined as "the use of violence for political ends"[78]) was not a criminal offence in itself under domestic law, it was "well in keeping with the idea of an offence" for the purposes of Art.5(1)(c), particularly since the applicants had been questioned about specific offences immediately after their arrests. In *Steel and others v United Kingdom*[79] the Court held that breach of the peace fell to be regarded as an offence for the purposes of Art.5(1)(c).[80] The relevant test under domestic law was found to be sufficiently precise to meet the requirement of legal certainty implicit in Art.5.[81] The determination of the applicants' complaints therefore depended upon compliance with national law. The arrests of two of the applicants were found to comply with national law, but in the case of the remaining three applicants the court found a breach of Art.5(1)(c). In *Richards v Attorney-General of Jersey*[82] the Administrative Court held that the applicant's detention under a warrant issued under s.13 of the Indictable Offences Act 1848 for the purposes of her return for trial in Jersey satisfied Art.5(1)(c).

III. Competent Legal Authority

5–15 The requirement that detention must have been effected for the purpose of bringing a person before the competent legal authority is not confined to arrest on reasonable suspicion. It applies to all three grounds of detention in Art.5(1)(c).[83] Thus, in *Lawless v Ireland*[84] the court held that the internment of a suspected terrorist could not be justified under Art.5(1)(c) on the ground that it was necessary to prevent him committing an offence, since the detention was not effected for the purpose of initiating a criminal prosecution. The term "competent legal authority" has the same meaning as the term "judge or other officer authorised by law to exercise judicial power" in Art.5(3).[85] The competent legal authority in England and Wales is a Magistrates' Court.

IV. Reasonable Suspicion

5–16 In order for an arrest on reasonable suspicion to be justified under Art.5(1)(c) it is not necessary to establish either that an offence has been committed or that the

---

[76] *Lawless v Ireland (No.3)* (1979–80) 1 E.H.R.R. 15, para.14.
[77] (1989) 11 E.H.R.R. 117, para.51. *cf. Ireland v United Kingdom* (1979–80) 2 E.H.R.R. 25, para.196.
[78] See the Prevention of Terrorism (Temporary Provisions) Act 1984, s.14.
[79] (1999) 28 E.H.R.R. 603 (para.48).
[80] See para.4–48 above.
[81] Para.55 above. The approach in *Steel* was applied at the admissibility stage in *Lucas v United Kingdom*, Application No.39013/02, Decision of March 18, 2003; (2003) E.H.R.R. CD86.
[82] [2003] EWHC Admin 3365.
[83] *Lawless v Ireland (No.1)* (1979–80) 1 E.H.R.R. 15, para.14; *De Jong, Baljet and Van Den Brink v Netherlands* (1986) 8 E.H.R.R. 20, paras 43 and 44.
[84] (1979–80) 1 E.H.R.R. 15, paras 14 and 15.
[85] *Schiesser v Switzerland* (1979–80) 2 E.H.R.R. 417, para.29.

person detained has committed it.[86] Neither is it necessary that the person detained should ultimately have been charged or taken before a court. As the Court observed in *Murray v United Kingdom*,[87] the object of detention for questioning is to further a criminal investigation by confirming or discounting suspicions which provide the grounds for detention. However the requirement that the suspicion must be based on reasonable grounds "forms an essential part of the safeguard against arbitrary arrest and detention".[88] The fact that a suspicion is honestly held is insufficient.[89] The words "reasonable suspicion" mean the existence of facts or information which would satisfy an objective observer that the person concerned may have committed the offence.[90] This substantially accords with the test formulated by the Privy Council in *Shaaban Bin Hussien v Chong Fook Kam*[91]:

> "The circumstances of the case must be such that a reasonable man acting without passion or prejudice would fairly have suspected the person of having committed the offence . . . suspicion in its ordinary meaning is a state of conjecture or surmise where proof is lacking: 'I suspect but I cannot prove.' Suspicion arises at or near the starting point of an investigation of which the obtaining of *prima facie* proof is at the end."[92]

In *Austin & Saxby v Commisioner of Police of the Metropolis* the presence of persons, about whom there was reasonable suspicion, within a crowd of protesters was held by the Administrative Court to justify the detention of the entire crowd under Art.5(1)(c) until the individuals could be apprehended.[93]

What may be regarded as reasonable will depend on all the circumstances. In this   **5–17** regard, Art.5(1)(c) involves the same or a similar compromise between the reasonableness of a police officer's decision to arrest and the inidividual's right to liberty as that seen in s.24(6) of the Police and Criminal Evidence Act 1984.[94] Even in relation to offences with national security implications, however, the state must be in a position to provide evidence which is capable of satisfying a court that the arrested person was reasonably suspected of having committed the offence.[95] In *Fox, Campbell and Hartley v United Kingdom*[96] the Court had to consider a power of arrest under s.11 of the Northern Ireland (Emergency Provision) Act 1978, which provides that a constable may arrest "any person

---

[86] *X v Austria* (1989) 11 E.H.R.R. 112. *Gusinskiy v Russia* (2004) 16 B.H.R.C. 427 para.53.
[87] (1995) 19 E.H.R.R. 193, para.55. *Gusinskiy v Russia* (2004) 16 B.H.R.C. 427 at para.53.
[88] *Fox, Campbell and Hartley v United Kingdom* (1991) 13 E.H.R.R. 157, para.32. *Gusinskiy v Russia* (2004) 16 B.H.R.C. 427 at para.53.
[89] *Fox, Campbell and Hartley v United Kingdom* (1991) 13 E.H.R.R. 157, para.32. *Gusinskiy v Russia* (2004) 16 B.H.R.C. 427 at para.53.
[90] *Fox, Campbell and Hartley v United Kingdom* (1991) 13 E.H.R.R. 157, para.32. *Cf. Hussien v Kam* [1970] A.C. 942 at 946. *Gusinskiy v Russia* (2004) 16 B.H.R.C. 427 at para.53.
[91] [1970] A.C. 942.
[92] *Per* Lord Devlin at 948.
[93] [2005] E.W.H.C. 480, [2005] H.R.L.R. 20, para.513–6.
[94] *Fayed and others v Commissioner of Police of The Metropolis* [2004] EWCA Civ 1579, para.82.
[95] *Fox, Campbell and Hartley v United Kingdom* (1991) 13 E.H.R.R. 157, para.34. *Cf. Murray v United Kingdom* (1995) 19 E.H.R.R. 193, paras 56, 61–63.
[96] (1990) 13 E.H.R.R. 157, at para.32. See also *Murray v United Kingdom* (1995) 19 E.H.R.R. 193, at paras 56 and 61–2.

whom he suspects of being a terrorist". The power of arrest conferred by s.11 did not therefore include an objective test of "reasonableness" and could be satisfied by an honest belief.[97] The applicants argued that their detention in consequence of the exercise of this power of arrest violated Art.5(1)(c). The government declined to furnish the Court with all the evidence on which the suspicion was based, on the ground that the material and its sources were sensitive. The Court recognised that "terrorist crime falls into a special category", because the police often have to respond to an apparently urgent threat to life and limb, and stated that "Article 5(1)(c) of the Convention should not be applied in such a manner as to put disproportionate difficulties in the way" of state responses to terrorism.[98] But, despite this general affirmation, the Court went on to hold that "the exigencies of dealing with terrorist crime cannot justify stretching the notion of 'reasonableness' to the point where the essence of the safeguard in Article 5(1)(c) is impaired". Accordingly, the Court must be enabled to decide whether that safeguard had been secured in the particular case.[99] Since the necessary evidence was not adduced, the Court found a violation of Art.5(1)(c).[100]

E. ARREST OR DETENTION FOR BREACH OF A COURT ORDER

5-18   The first limb of Art.5(1)(b) provides for detention where the applicant has failed to comply with an injunction or other court order. The order must have been made by a court of competent jurisdiction,[101] it must be sufficiently precise to meet the Convention test of legal certainty,[102] and it must be capable of enforcement. Article 5(1)(b) has been held to permit detention for failure to pay a fine,[103] for refusal to undergo a blood test[104] or medical examination[105] ordered by a court; and for failure to observe a residence restriction.[106] In *Steel and others v United Kingdom*[107] the Court considered that the applicants' detention for refusing to be bound over to keep the peace fell within Art.5(1)(b) since it was imposed as a result of their refusal to comply with the court's order. As to the terms of the order, the Court observed that;

"... the orders were expressed in rather vague and general terms; the expression 'to be of good behaviour' was particularly imprecise and offered little guidance to the person bound over as to the type of conduct which would amount to a breach of the order. However, in each applicant's case the binding over order was imposed after a finding that she had committed a breach of the peace. Having considered all the circumstances,

---

[97] *McKee v Chief Constable for Northern Ireland* [1984] 1 W.L.R. 1358.
[98] (1991) 13 E.H.R.R. 157, at paras 32, 34.
[99] *ibid.*, paras 32 and 34.
[100] Note, however, that in *Murray v United Kingdom* (1995) 19 E.H.R.R. 193 the court went to considerable lengths to find that this requirement was met.
[101] A warning by the Chief of Police does not constitute an order of a Court for the purposes of Art.5(1)(b): *Guzzardi v Italy* (1981) 3 E.H.R.R. 333, para.101.
[102] *Steel and ors v United Kingdom* (1999) 28 E.H.R.R. 603 (paras 71 to 78).
[103] Application 6289/73 *Airey v Ireland* (1977) 8 D.R. 42.
[104] Application 8275/78 *X v Austria* (1979) 18 D.R. 154.
[105] Application 6659/74 *X v Federal Republic of Germany* (1975) 3 D.R. 92.
[106] Application 8916/80 *Freda v Italy* (1980) 21 D.R. 250.
[107] (1999) 28 E.H.R.R. 603 (paras 71 to 78).

the Court is satisfied that, given the context, it was sufficiently clear that the applicants were being requested to agree to refrain from causing further, similar, breaches of the peace during the ensuing 12 months."

The Court reached the opposite conclusion in *Hashman and Harrap v United*   5-19
Kingdom[108] in which a bind over order imposed on two hunt saboteurs, requiring them to be "of good behaviour" (not to act *"contra bonos mores"*) was held to be too vague to qualify as "law", and failed to provide any objective criteria against which their past and future actions could be judged.

F. DETENTION TO SECURE COMPLIANCE WITH A LEGAL OBLIGATION

The second limb of Art.5(1)(b) provides for a person's arrest or detention "in   5-20
order to secure the fulfilment of any obligation prescribed by law". In general, the obligation must be one which is "already incumbent on the person concerned".[109] However, in *McVeigh, O'Neill and Evans v United Kingdom*[110] the Commission held that in certain "limited circumstances of a pressing nature" a coercive power of detention may be permissible where it is necessary to secure fulfilment of a specific obligation at the time when it arises.[111] This principle may only be invoked where there is an immediate necessity for the fulfilment of the obligation, and where there is no reasonably practicable alternative means available for securing compliance.[112] In *R. (Laporte) v Chief Constable of Gloucestershire*,[113] preventing the occupants of a coach from disembarking by escorting their vehicle on a two and half hour journey, during which no stops were permitted, was not justified under Art.5(1)(c). The police had taken the course of action because they feared that the anti-war protestors on the coach would cause a breach of the peace. The Divisional Court held that there was no sufficiently imminent breach of the peace to merit even transitory detention, and even if there had been such immediacy, the period of detention went far beyond what could be described as transitory.[114] The Court of Appeal did not decide the Art.5 point in relation to the two and a half hour detention, but concluded that the initial actions of the police in preventing the protesters from proceeding to the protest site were not an interference with Art.5.[115] Once the case reached the House of Lords, the argument focussed on the rights to freedom of expresssion and assembly, Arts 10 and 11 of the Convention, rather than Art.5. It was accepted by the police that the police action had constituted an interference with the claimant's Art.10 and 11

---

[108] (2000) 30 E.H.R.R. 241. The case concerned a complaint under Art.10, but the applicable test for "lawfulness" is the same under Art.5.
[109] *Ciulla v Italy* (1991) 13 E.H.R.R. 346, para.36; *Guzzardi v Italy* (1981) 3 E.H.R.R. 333, para.101. Imprisonment for a failure to fulfil a contractual obligation is not a violation of Art.5(1) since it is separately protected under Art.1 of Protocol 4 to which the United Kingdom is not a party.
[110] (1983) 5 E.H.R.R. 71.
[111] (1983) 5 E.H.R.R. 71, paras 175 and 190–191.
[112] (1983) 5 E.H.R.R. 71, para.191.
[113] [2004] 2 All E.R. 874.
[114] [2004] 2 All E.R. 874, para.47.
[115] [2005] Q.B. 678, paras 51 and 56. No argument on Art.5 was pursued in the House of Lords: [2006] UKHL 55.

rights. The House of Lords concluded that the actions of the police in requiring the buses to be driven back to London was not "prescribed by law", and was also disproportionate, since it was premature and indiscriminate. The speeches of their Lordships are notable for their willingness to subject police decisions on public order issues to searching scrutiny, but leave the Art.5 issue unresolved. The decision does, however, establish that both the Divisional Court and the Court of Appeal were wrong to hold that there is a common law power to take steps to prevent a breach of the peace from *becoming* imminent: such a breach must actually *be* imminent before such steps can be taken. This is an important check on the power of the police to take "pre-emptive" action to stop protests at which a breach of the peace may take place at some unspecified future point.

Assuming that the criteria of necessity and lack of alternative means are satisfied, the importance and urgency of the obligation must nevertheless be balanced against the individual's right to liberty and the length of the detention. In *McVeigh* the Commission held that there was no breach of Art.5(1) where persons entering the United Kingdom were required to submit to "further examination" at the point of entry pursuant to the Prevention of Terrorism (Supplemental Temporary Provisions) Order 1976.[116] The applicants were detained for that purpose and released after 45 hours, having been questioned, searched, photographed and fingerprinted but not charged with any offence. In finding no violation the Commission attached importance to the fact that the obligation applied only on entering and leaving the United Kingdom and in order to verify the particular matters referred to in the legislation.[117] In *R. (Gillan) v Commissioner of Police for the Metropolis*,[118] the House of Lords considered the powers of stop and search authorised by the Assistant Commissioner of the Metropolitan Police in accordance with ss.44–45 of the Terrorism Act 2000. Searches carried out under such an authorisation do not require there to be reasonable suspicion. The ambit of the random stops is limited to searches for articles that could be used in connection with terrorist offences. The searches concerned two people, one student and one journalist, stopped on their way to an arms fair held in London in 2003, at which it was expected that there would be protesters. The House of Lords held that the normal exercise of these powers would not engage Art.5:

> "the procedure will ordinarily be relatively brief. The person stopped will not be arrested, handcuffed, confined or removed to any different place. I do not think, in the absence of special circumstances, such a person should be regarded as being detained in the sense of confined or kept in custody, but more properly of being detained in the sense of kept from proceeding or kept waiting. There is no deprivation of liberty."[119]

The same principle would presumably apply to other powers of temporary detention exercisable by the police without reasonable suspicion, such as the

---

[116] S.I. 1976/465.
[117] *Cf. Ireland v United Kingdom* (1979–80) 2 E.H.R.R. 25.
[118] [2006] 2 A.C. 307.
[119] At para.25, *per* Lord Bingham.

power to detain for the purpose of verifying ownership of a vehicle or the power to establish a roadblock. It might also be expected to apply to the burgeoning police "stop and search" powers under statutory provisions such as s.60 of the Criminal Justice and Public Order Act 1994,[120] s.8 of the Knives Act 1997, and ss.25–27 of the Crime and Disorder Act 1998. The detention of a person by use of reasonable force in a particular room of a house whilst the remainder of the property was searched in accordance with s.117 of the Police and Criminal Evidence Act 1984 was within the common law, and probably within Art.5(1)(b).[121]

G. The Right to be Given Reasons for Arrest

Article 5(2) requires that anyone arrested or detained should be "informed   **5–21** promptly, in a language which he understands, of the reasons for his arrest and of any charge against him". This principle is essentially the same as that contained in s.28 of the Police and Criminal Evidence Act 1984, which imposes a duty to give reasons for an arrest as soon as practicable, and makes this a condition precedent to a lawful detention.[122] The primary purpose of the obligation is to enable the detained person to apply to a court to challenge the lawfulness of the detention in accordance with Art.5(4).[123] Where a person has been arrested in connection with a criminal offence, Art.5(2) is also intended to enable him to deny the offence at the earliest opportunity.[124]

The detained person must be told "in simple, non-technical language that he can   **5–22** understand, the essential legal and factual grounds for his arrest".[125] The extent of the information required will depend on the circumstances.[126] Mere reference to the applicable statutory provision is generally insufficient.[127] Where the reason for the arrest is suspicion of involvement in a particular offence, the detainee must be informed of the facts which are the foundation of the decision to detain,

---

[120] Which caters for stop and search in reasonable anticipation of violence.

[121] *DPP v Meaden* [2003] EWHC Admin 3005, para.26.

[122] *Taylor v Chief Constable of Thames Valley Police* [2004] 1 W.L.R. 3155 at para.25. In making the lawfulness of an arrest dependent upon the provision of reasons, s.28 embodies the common law rule in *Christie v Leachinsky* [1947] A.C. 573.

[123] *Fox, Campbell and Hartley v United Kingdom* (1991) 13 E.H.R.R. 157, para.40. *Cf. Christie v Leachinsky* [1947] A.C. 573; the Police and Criminal Evidence Act 1984, s.28. On Art.5(4), see paras 5–33 to 5–35.

[124] *X v Germany* (1978) 16 D.R. 111 at 114.

[125] *Fox, Campbell and Hartley v United Kingdom* (1991) 13 E.H.R.R. 157, para.40. *Taylor v Chief Constable of Thames Valley Police* [2004] 1 W.L.R. 3155 at para.26. *Cf. Christie v Leachinsky* [1947] A.C. 573; the Police and Criminal Evidence Act 1984, s.28.

[126] *Fox, Campbell and Hartley v United Kingdom* (1991) 13 E.H.R.R. 157, para.40; *HB v Switzerland* (2003) 37 E.H.R.R. 52 at paras 47–9.

[127] *Ireland v United Kingdom* (1979–80) 2 E.H.R.R. 25, para.198; *Fox, Campbell and Hartley v United Kingdom* (1991) 13 E.H.R.R. 157, para.41; *Murray v United Kingdom* (1995) 19 E.H.R.R. 193, para.76.

and in particular he should be asked whether he admits or denies the allega-tion.[128] It will not always be necessary to inform a detained person of every charge which may later be brought, providing the information supplied is suffi-cient to justify the arrest.[129] Once a person has been charged, however, there is an additional entitlement under Art.6(3)(a) to be informed in detail of the nature and cause of the accusation against him.[130]

5–23   It is not always necessary for the relevant information to be given at the very moment of the arrest, provided it is given within a sufficient period following the arrest.[131] In a number of cases the Court and Commission have held that the obligation in Art.5(2) will be met if the information is provided during the course of questioning following an initial arrest.[132] In *Fox, Campbell and Hartley v United Kingdom*[133] the Court held that the offences in relation to which the applicants were being questioned by the police must have come to their attention through the questions being asked of them, even though they were not directly informed of the reasons for their arrest. The Court further held that the period of several hours during which the reasons for the arrest emerged from the police questioning "cannot be regarded as falling outside the constraints of time imposed by the notion of promptness in Article 5(2)".[134] In *Delcourt v Bel-gium*[135] an arrest warrant was issued in Dutch in respect of a French speaking detainee. The Commission found no violation because the subsequent question-ing, in which the reasons for the arrest became apparent, was conducted in French. Similarly, no violation was found where the detainee, a Turkish national, spoke Greek, and one of the interrogating officers spoke Turkish.[136]

H. INFORMATION TO BE PROVIDED AT THE MOMENT OF CHARGE

5–24   Article 6(3)(a) provides that an accused person should be informed promptly, in a language he understands and in detail, of the nature and cause of the accusation against him. What is the scope of this obligation? Article 6(3) applies when a person is "charged with a criminal offence". As we have seen,[137] the term "charge" has an autonomous meaning under the Convention. The court in *Eckle*

---

[128] *X v Germany* (1978) 16 D.R. 111, para.114.
[129] Application 4220/69 *X v United Kingdom* (1971) 14 Y.B. 250 at 278; *McVeigh, O'Neill and Evans v United Kingdom* (1983) 5 E.H.R.R. 71, para.210.
[130] See para.5–24.
[131] *Fox, Campbell and Hartley v United Kingdom* (1991) 13 E.H.R.R. 157, para.40. *Cf. Van der Leer v Netherlands* (1990) 12 E.H.R.R. 567 where a delay of 10 days was held to violate Art.5(2) in the context of detention of a mental patient.
[132] *Fox, Campbell and Hartley v United Kingdom* (1991) 13 E.H.R.R. 157, para.41; *Murray v United Kingdom* (1995) 19 E.H.R.R. 193, para.77.
[133] (1990) 13 E.H.R.R. 157.
[134] *ibid.*, at para.42. See also *Taylor v Chief Constable of Thames Valley Police* [2004] 1 W.L.R. 3155 at para.26.
[135] (1967) 10 Y.B. 238 at 270–272.
[136] *Egmez v Cyprus* (2002) 34 E.H.R.R. 29, para.85. See also *Conka v Belgium* (2002) 34 E.H.R.R 54, concerning the use of an interpreter at the time of arrest as satisfying Art.5(2).
[137] See para.4–61 above.

v Germany[138] held that a person may be "charged" within the meaning of Art.6:

" . . . on a date prior to the case coming before the trial court, such as the date of arrest, the date when the person concerned was officially notified that he would be prosecuted or the date when preliminary investigations were opened. 'Charge' for the purposes of Article 6(1), may be defined as 'the official notification given to an individual by the competent authority of an allegation that he has committed a criminal offence.' "[139]

This decision concerned the concept of delay in Art.6(1) rather than the informa-   **5–25** tion to be provided at the time of arrest (Art.5(3)) or "charge" (Art.6(3)(a)). The tests ought to be similar, but it is fair to say that the court in *Eckle* was not dealing with the kind of problem that may arise under Art.6(3)(a). Whilst it therefore provides authority for the suggestion that an arrest may amount to a "charge" for the purposes of determining whether or not Art.6 is applicable, the proposition that the two events are indistinguishable seems counter-intuitive in the present context, particularly in view of the fact that the Convention makes separate provision for the information to be provided at the moment of "arrest" and "charge". This conclusion draws some support from the ruling of the High Court of New Zealand, albeit in the slightly different context of the New Zealand Bill of Rights Act, that the term "charged" refers to "an intermediate step in the prosecutorial process", between arrest and appearance in court, "when the prosecuting authority formally advises an arrested person that he is to be prosecuted and gives him particulars of the charges he will face."[140]

The requirement that an accused person be informed "in a language he under-   **5–26** stands" was held to have been violated in *Brozicek v Italy*,[141] where the Italian authorities brushed aside the applicant's protest that he did not understand the documents sent to him in Italian. Turning to the level of detail to be given to the accused about the charges, the *Brozicek* decision interpreted Art.6(3)(a) some-what restrictively. The documents in that case: "sufficiently listed the offences of which he was accused, stated the place and date thereof, referred to the relevant Articles of the Criminal Code and mentioned the name of the victim."[142]

The information provided under English law by the issuing of a summons or the   **5–27** proffering of a charge will almost always be sufficient to meet the limited requirements of Art.6(3)(a). However, there may be circumstances in which greater detail is required. For example, in the Canadian case of *Lucas*[143] the information gave the date and place of the offence, but merely alleged the operating of an overweight vehicle contrary to a certain Act. In fact there were regulations made under that Act which set out eight different ways in which the offence might be committed, and the Supreme Court of Nova Scotia held that the accused had not been adequately "informed of the specific offence", as required

---

[138] (1983) 5 E.H.R.R. 1.
[139] *ibid.*, at para.73, quoting from *Deweer v Belgium* (1979–80) 2 E.H.R.R. 439, at para.46.
[140] *Gibbons* [1997] 2 N.Z.L.R. 585, *per* Goddard J. at 595.
[141] (1990) 12 E.H.R.R. 371.
[142] *ibid.*, at para.42. See also *X v Belgium* (1977) 9 D.R. 169.
[143] (1983) 6 C.C.C. (3d) 147.

by the Canadian Charter. He should have been informed which of the eight forms of the offence was to be relied upon by the prosecution.[144]

I. DETENTION IN POLICE CUSTODY

5–28   Article 5(3) provides that every person who has been arrested or detained in accordance with Art.5(1)(c) must be brought promptly before a judge or other judicial officer, and is entitled to trial within a reasonable time or to release pending trial. It applies only to criminal offences.[145] The twin aims of this provision are; (a) to limit the period of detention by the police before a detainee's first production in court; and (b) to establish a *prima facie* right to bail. The right to bail is considered in detail in Ch.13 below. This section is concerned with the permissible length of detention prior to an accused person's first appearance in court.

5–29   The requirements of Art.5(3) are to be construed in the light of the object and purpose of Art.5, which is "the protection of the individual against arbitrary interferences by the state with his right to liberty"[146] and in the context of the importance attached to Art.5 within the Convention legal order.[147] The term "judge or other officer authorised by law" has the same meaning as the term "competent legal authority" in Art.5(1)(c).[148]

5–30   In the case of a person arrested by the police this will be a magistrates' court. However, the detention of service personnel pending a court martial by order of the commanding officer does not meet the requirements of Art.5(3).[149] The tribunal must be independent of the investigating and prosecuting authorities,[150] and it must be impartial in the sense of being free from actual bias and from the appearance of bias.[151] It must also be empowered to review the merits of the

---

[144] A question might be raised about the wording of some indictments alleging complicity, in which, taking advantage of the Accessories and Abettors Act 1861, the prosecution charges a person with an offence without specifying whether he is alleged to be the principal or an accessory. It is well established in English law that the prosecution may then proceed on either basis (see the discussion in *Giannetto* [1997] 1 Cr.App.R. 1), but in at least one case the House of Lords has recognised that it is desirable for the prosecution to be as precise as possible (see *Maxwell v DPP for Northern Ireland* [1979] 1 W.L.R. 1350). The thrust of Art.6(3)(a) might suggest that precision should be the rule here.

[145] *De Wilde, Ooms and Versyp v Netherlands* (1979–80) 1 E.H.R.R. 373 para.71.

[146] *Brogan v United Kingdom* (1989) 11 E.H.R.R. 117, para.58.

[147] *Brogan v United Kingdom* (1989) 11 E.H.R.R. 117, para.58.

[148] *Lawless v Ireland (No.3)* (1979–80) 1 E.H.R.R. 15, paras 13–14; *Ireland v United Kingdom* (1979–80) 2 E.H.R.R. 25, para.199; *Schiesser v Switzerland* (1979–80) 2 E.H.R.R. 417, para.29. On Art.5(1)(c), see para.5–16.

[149] *Hood v United Kingdom* (2000) 29 E.H.R.R. 365; *Jordan v United Kingdom, The Times*, March 17, 2000; *Thompson v United Kingdom* ; (2005) 40 E.H.R.R. 11 at paras 33–4.

[150] *De Jong, Baljet and Van Den Brink v Netherlands* (1986) 8 E.H.R.R. 20, para.49; *Schiesser v Switzerland* (1979–80) 2 E.H.R.R. 417, paras 29 and 30.

[151] *Huber v Switzerland* (1990) Series A/188, para.43. *Cf.* the court's interpretation of the impartiality requirement in Art.6(1) (see paras 14–67 to 14–80 below). See also *HB v Switzerland*; (2003) 37 E.H.R.R. 52 at paras 55, 61–4; *Niedbala v Poland* ; (2001) 33 E.H.R.R. 48 at paras 53–7.

decision to detain,[152] and to make a legally binding decision ordering release.[153] In addition:

" . . . under Article 5(3) there is both a procedural and a substantive requirement. The procedural requirement places the 'officer' under the obligation of himself hearing the individual brought before him; the substantive requirement imposes on him the obligations of reviewing the circumstances militating for or against detention, of deciding, by reference to legal criteria, whether there are reasons to justify detention and of ordering release if there are no such reasons".[154]

The state is obliged to take the initiative for a detained person to be brought **5–31** before an appropriate tribunal. In *McGoff v Sweden*[155] the Commission held that Art.5(3) imposes an "unconditional obligation" on the State to bring the accused "automatically and promptly" before a court.[156] In *Egmez v Cyprus*, the Court held that Art.5(3) was fulfilled by the hearing taking place at a hospital where the applicant was being treated.[157]

In the context of Art.5(3) the Court has observed that "the degree of flexibility **5–32** attached to the notion of 'promptness' is limited".[158] While allowance will be made for the special features of each case, the Court has held that the significance attached to those features can never be taken to the point "of effectively negativing the state's obligation to ensure a prompt release or a prompt appearance before a judicial authority".[159] Although the Court and Commission have refrained from setting abstract time limits, it seems certain that the general regime established by the Police and Criminal Evidence Act 1984, ss.41–46 would be found to comply with Art.5(3). By contrast in *Brincat v Italy*[160] the Court held that detention for four days without being brought before a judicial officer was not "prompt" within the meaning of Art.5(3). Similarly, detention for four days and six hours under the Prevention of Terrorism (Temporary Provisions) Act 1976 was found to breach Art.5(3) in *Brogan v United Kingdom*.[161] Even accepting the considerable margin of appreciation allowed to states in the sphere of prevention of terrorism, the Court held that detention of this length

---

[152] *Sabeur Ben Ali v Malta* Application No.35892/97, Judgment of June 29, 2000; (2002) 34 E.H.R.R. 26 at para.30.

[153] *Ireland v United Kingdom* (1979–80) 2 E.H.R.R. 25, para.199.

[154] *Schiesser v Switzerland* (1979–80) 2 E.H.R.R. 417, para.31.

[155] (1982) 31 D.R. 72.

[156] This decision does not appear to have been cited in *Olotu v Home Office* [1997] 1 W.L.R. 328 where Lord Bingham C.J. held that detention following the expiry of custody time limits did not involve a breach of Art.5(3) because the relevant legislation placed the onus on the defendant to make an application for bail.

[157] (2002) 34 E.H.R.R. 29 at para.90.

[158] Note that the French text uses the word "aussitôt" which connotes a greater degree of immediacy: *Brogan v United Kingdom* (1989) 11 E.H.R.R. 117 paras 58–59. See also *Koster v Netherlands* (1992) 14 E.H.R.R. 396, para.24.

[159] *Brogan v United Kingdom* (1989) 11 E.H.R.R. 117, para.59; *Koster v Netherlands* (1992) 14 E.H.R.R. 396, para.24.

[160] (1993) 16 E.H.R.R. 591. See also *Salov v Ukraine* Application No.65518/01, Judgment of September 6, 2005 at para.59, and *Ocalan v Turkey,* judgment of March 12, 2003 ((2003) 15 B.H.R.C. 297) at para.110, upheld by the Grand Chamber in its decision of May 12, 2005 ((2005) 18 B.H.R.C. 293), where it was found that detention for seven days breached Art.5(3).

[161] (1989) 11 E.H.R.R. 117.

without being brought before a court ran counter to the principle of "judicial control of interferences by the executive with the individual's right to liberty."[162] *Brogan* was relied upon by the Administrative Court in *Austin & Saxby v Commissioner of Police of the Metropolis* as showing that seven hours satisfied the concept of "promptness" in Art.5(3).[163] Following the decision in *Brogan* the British government entered a derogation from Art.5(3), retaining the power of extended detention. A subsequent challenge to the derogation was defeated in *Brannigan and McBride v United Kingdom*,[164] where the court held the derogation to be compatible with the requirements of Art.15. This derogation was expressly incorporated into domestic law by s.14(1)(a) and Sch.3 to the Human Rights Act 1998, but was subsequently withdrawn by the Human Rights Act 1998 (Amendment) Order 2001, which repealed parts of ss.14 and 16 and the whole of Pt I of Sch.3.[165] A second derogation was made in accordance with the Anti-Terrorism, Crime and Security Act 2001, concerning powers of detention in relation to foreign nationals and Art.5(1)(f).[166] However, that derogation was quashed by an 8–1 majority of the House of Lords in *A and others v Secretary of State for the Home Department*.[167]

J. HABEAS CORPUS

5-33   Article 5(4) provides that everyone who is deprived of his liberty is entitled to take proceedings by which the lawfulness of his detention can be decided speedily by a court and his release ordered if his detention is not lawful.[168] This guarantees the right to *habeas corpus* in order to challenge the legality of executive detention. On any Art.5(4) review, the burden of proving the lawfulness of the detention rests with the state,[169] a principle which is fully observed in domestic *habeas corpus* proceedings. Thus, in *Brogan v United Kingdom*[170] the Court found that *habeas corpus* would have been an adequate procedure for challenging detention under Art.5(1)(c).

5-34   In the context of criminal proceedings, the right to challenge the legality of detention arises automatically on first appearance in court, when the accused has

---

[162] *ibid.*, at para.58.

[163] [2005] E.W.H.C. 480, [2005] H.R.L.R. 20, at para.516.

[164] (1994) 17 E.H.R.R. 539.

[165] S.I. 2001/1216. The derogation was withdrawn, since judicial control over the detention was introduced by Sch.8 to the Terrorism Act 2000 (in turn amended by s.306 of the Criminal Justice Act 2003).

[166] Human Rights Act 1998 (Designated Derogation) Order 2001 (S.I. 2001/3644).

[167] [2005] 2 A.C. 68, on which see further para.3–27.

[168] The term "lawfulness" in Art.5(4) has the same meaning as the term "lawful" in Art.5(1): *Brogan v United Kingdom* (1989) 1 E.H.R.R. 117, para.65.

[169] Application 9174/80 *Zamir v United Kingdom* (1983) 40 D.R. 42, para.58. The Court of Appeal made a declaration of incompatibility under s.4 of the Human Rights Act 1998 in *R. v Mental Health Review Tribunal, North and East London Region and anor* [2002] Q.B. 1, holding that ss.72 and 73 of the Mental Health Act 1983 were incompatible with Art.5 as they imposed the burden of proof on the patient to satisfy the tribunal that he was no longer suffering from a mental disorder warranting detention.

[170] (1989) 11 E.H.R.R. 117, para.65.

the right to apply for bail.[171] To that extent, the requirements of Art.5(4) intersect with the right to prompt production, and the right to bail in Art.5(3). As we have seen, the rights guaranteed by Art.5(3) are automatic, whereas Art.5(4) affords a right for the detained person to *initiate proceedings* to challenge the legality of a detention. In the context of arrest and detention in police custody, the principal relevance of Art.5(4) is that it guarantees the right of the accused to challenge the legality of his detention by the police prior to his first production in court. Although such applications are rare, the High Court will hear a *habeas corpus* application relating to a person in police custody as a matter of urgency where it is alleged that the police have no legal right to detain (or to continue the detention of) a suspect. A failure by the reviewing court to release a person where the lawful period of detention has expired, or where there is no order permitting continued detention, will breach Art.5(4).[172]

Under Art.5(4), the application for release must be determined "speedily".[173] In **5–35** *Sanchez-Reisse v Switzerland*[174] the court emphasised that the term "speedily" cannot be defined in the abstract. As with the "reasonable time" stipulations in Art.5(3) and Art.6(1) it must be determined in the light of the circumstances of the individual case. Relevant considerations include the diligence shown by the authorities, any delay caused by the detained person, and any other factors causing delay that do not engage the state's responsibility.[175] The speed with which a *habeas corpus* application is generally heard in the High Court undoubtedly meets the standards set by Art.5(4).[176]

K. Ill-Treatment in Custody

The admission in criminal proceedings of evidence obtained by ill-treatment in **5–36** breach of Art.3 will violate Art.6.[177] The House of Lords emphatically upheld this principle in *A and others v Secretary of State for the Home Department (No.2)*,[178] where it rejected the submission made on behalf of the Home Secretary that evidence which had or might have been obtained by torture inflicted by

---

[171] See Ch.13 below.

[172] *Ocalan v Turkey* (2005) 18 B.H.R.C. 293, at para.68.

[173] The requirement of "promptness" in Art.5(3) connotes a greater degree of urgency than the term "speedily" in Art.5(4): *E v Norway* (1994) 17 E.H.R.R. 30, para.64. For a discussion of "speedily" in the extradition context, see *R (Kashamu) v Governor of Brixton Prison* [2002] Q.B. 887.

[174] (1987) 9 E.H.R.R. 71, para.55.

[175] *Sanchez-Reisse v Switzerland* (1987) 9 E.H.R.R. 71, para.56.

[176] Periods of four days and 16 days have been held acceptable (*Egue v France* (1988) 57 D.R. 47 at 71; *Christenet v Switzerland* (1979) 17 D.R. 25 at 57), whereas delays of 31 days and 46 days have been held to violate Art.5(4) (*Sanchez-Reisse v Switzerland* (1987) 9 E.H.R.R. 71).

[177] *Jalloh v Germany* (2006) 20 B.H.R.C. 575, where the use in evidence of a plastic bag containing drugs obtained by the forcible administration of emetics was held to violate Art.6; *Austria v Italy* (1963) 6 Y.B. 740 at 748; *Montgomery v HM Advocate* [2003] 1 A.C. 641, 649 (PC); *R. (Ramda) v Secretary of State for the Home Department* [2002] EWHC 1278 at para.9; *P E v France* [2001] 10 I.H.R.R. 421 at para.6.3, a decision of the Committee against Torture, established by the UN Convention Against Torture.

[178] [2006] 2 A.C. 221.

foreign officials without the complicity of the British authorities ought to be admissible before the Special Immigration Appeals Commission. Lord Bingham concluded:

> "It trivialises the issue before the House to treat it as an argument about the law of evidence. The issue is one of constitutional principle, whether evidence obtained by torturing another human being may lawfully be admitted against a party to proceedings in a British court, irrespective of where, or by whom, or on whose authority the torture was inflicted. To that question I would give a very clear negative answer."

It is a settled principle of Art.3 jurisprudence that "where an individual is taken into police custody in good health, but is found to be injured at the time of release, it is incumbent on the state to provide a satisfactory and convincing explanation as to the cause of the injury".[179] In *Tomasi v France*[180] the applicant, a terrorist suspect, alleged that he had been slapped, kicked, punched, and ill-treated in other ways, over a two day period whilst he was being questioned in a police station. He adduced medical evidence establishing that he was injured at the time of his release. In the absence of any explanation from the government, the Court presumed the necessary causal connection, and found a violation of Art.3. This was despite the findings of the French courts that the officers concerned had no case to answer.[181] Similarly, in *Ribitsch v Austria*[182] the Court endorsed the Commission's statement that "it was for the Government to produce evidence establishing facts which cast doubt on the account of events given by the victim, particularly if this account was supported by medical certificates".[183] On the facts of that case, the Court considered that the government had "not satisfactorily established that the applicant's injuries were caused otherwise than . . . by the treatment he underwent while in police custody". The fact that the alleged perpetrator had been acquitted in criminal proceedings was not sufficient.[184]

---

[179] *Menesheva v Russia* [2006] ECHR 59261/00 at paras 49–50; *Tomasi v France* (1992) 15 E.H.R.R. 1; *Ribitsch v Austria* (1996) 21 E.H.R.R. 573 at para.38; *Aksoy v Turkey* (1996) 23 E.H.R.R. 553 at para.61; *Salman v Turkey* (2002) 34 E.H.R.R. 17 at para.113; *Yuksel v Turkey* (2005) 41 E.H.R.R. 19 at para.25 For an application of this principle in the context of a civil claim for damages arising from mistreatment by prison officers, see *Sheppard v Secretary of State for the Home Department* [2002] EWCA Civ 1921.

[180] (1993) 15 E.H.R.R. 1 at paras 104–116.

[181] *Tomasi* was distinguished in *Klaas v Germany* (1994) 18 E.H.R.R. 305 at paras 26–31 where the applicant's injuries were allegedly sustained *during the course of an arrest.* The applicant and the police officers involved gave conflicting accounts as to how the applicant's injuries had been sustained. The medical evidence was, in the Court's view, consistent with both accounts, and the court was not prepared to depart from the findings of the national courts in the absence of "cogent evidence". In the light of the Court's subsequent judgment in *Ribitsch v Austria* (1996) 21 E.H.R.R. 573, *Klaas* must now be regarded as confined to cases where injuries are sustained at the time of initial detention.

[182] (1996) 21 E.H.R.R. 573.

[183] Para.31.

[184] See *Ribitsch* at para.34, where the Court emphasised that an "acquittal in criminal proceedings by a court bound by the principle of the presumption of innocence does not absolve [the state] from its responsibility under the Convention". The judgment in *Ribitsch* draws a clear distinction between the standard of proof required for a criminal conviction and the standard adopted by the court under Art.3. This distinction is not easy to reconcile with the standard of proof beyond reasonable doubt referred to in *Ireland v United Kingdom* (1979–80) 2 E.H.R.R. 25 at para.161.

In *Selmouni v France*[185] the Court held that:

5–37

> "in respect of a person deprived of his liberty, recourse to physical force which has not been made strictly necessary by his own conduct diminishes human dignity and is in principle an infringement of the right set forth in Article 3".

Altering the boundaries of the treatment prohibited by Art.3, the Court held that the standards of treatment of those detained in custody had evolved, and that certain acts which would in the past have been classified as "inhuman and degrading treatment" should now be regarded as deserving the special stigma attached to the term "torture". In the Court's view, "the increasingly high standard being required in the area of the protection of human rights and fundamental liberties correspondingly and inevitably requires greater firmness in assessing breaches of the fundamental values of democratic societies." On the facts, the applicant had been subjected to serious assaults over a number of days in police custody. He had been struck several times, dragged along a corridor by his hair, made to run the gauntlet of a number of officers trying to trip him up, made to kneel, urinated upon and threatened with a blowtorch and a syringe. This was sufficient to amount to torture within the meaning of Art.3.[186]

L. ACCESS TO LEGAL ADVICE IN POLICE CUSTODY

Section 58 of the Police and Criminal Evidence Act 1984 provides that a detained person may have access to independent legal advice on request, unless delayed access is authorised in accordance with the section. A breach of s.58 may be a ground for exclusion of evidence under ss.76 or 78.[187] The relevant Convention standard is generally flexible enough to permit the restrictions established in s.58.[188] The right of access to a solicitor has been implied by the Commission and the court into Art.6(3), since it is "fundamental to the preparation of [an accused

5–38

---

[185] (2000) 29 E.H.R.R. 403 at para.99.

[186] See also, *Salman v Turkey* (2002) 34 E.H.R.R. 17 at paras 114–5; *Egmez v Cyprus* Application (2002) 34 E.H.R.R. 29, at paras 77–9.

[187] *R. v Samuel* [1988] Q.B. 615; *R. v Silcott and ors*, *The Times*, December 9, 1991; *R. v Alladice* (1988) 87 Cr.App.R. 380 and *R. v Absolam* (1989) 88 Cr.App.R. 332.

[188] In *Kennedy v Crown Prosecution Service* [2002] EWHC Admin 2297, [2004] R.T.R. 77, the appellant had been arrested on suspicion of driving whilst intoxicated. At the police station he said that he wanted to see a lawyer. Prior to the police contacting a solicitor on his behalf he was asked to provide a specimen of breath. He twice refused to do so, despite having been given a Notice warning him that the right to consult a solicitor did not permit him to delay the process. The court held that the procedural right to legal advice in Art.6 was not violated in these circumstances, as there was no requirement that legal advice be offered at any particular stage. The more precise rules in s.58 of the Police and Criminal Evidence Act 1984 were breached by the failure by the police to contact a solicitor immediately after the appellant had requested to consult a lawyer, but that breach was neither significant nor substantial, and did require the evidence to be excluded under s.78 of the 1984 Act. See also, *Campbell v DPP* [2002] EWHC Admin 1314, where the facts were similar, although in that case there was no question that the police had contacted a solicitor in advance of requesting the appellant to give breath specimens. The court concluded that the actions of the police were proportionate to the legitimate public interest served by requiring the appellant to give the specimens. There was no breach of Art.6 in these circumstances.

person's] defence".[189] However in *Bonzi v Switzerland*[190] the Commission observed that "in the absence of any explicit provision [in the Convention] it cannot be maintained that the right to confer with one's counsel and exchange confidential instructions or information with him is subject to no restriction whatsoever".[191] The Court has explicitly rejected the argument that the right to legal representation in Art.6(3)(c) only becomes relevant at the trial: although it forms part of the "fair trial" requirements, it "may also be relevant before a case is sent for trial if and in so far as the fairness of the trial is likely to be prejudiced by an initial failure to comply with them."[192] In *Imbroscia v Switzerland*, however, the Court held that the failure of the police and public prosecutor to notify the defence lawyers of the interrogations (with the result that the applicant was questioned in their absence) was remedied when the defence lawyer did attend the final interview, and made no objection to the record of the previous interviews.[193] In *Brennan v United Kingdom,* the applicant was denied access to legal advice for 24 hours. His lawyer did not arrive for a further 24 hours after the restriction had been lifted. During this second 24 hour period, the applicant made incriminating admissions. The European Court of Human Rights held that allowing these admissions in evidence did not breach Art.6 as they were made at a time when the State was no longer restricting access to legal advice.[194]

5–39   Against this general background, there are two potential areas of difficulty which deserve particular mention. The first concerns delay in access to a solicitor in the context of ss.34 to 37 of the Criminal Justice and Public Order Act 1994 (CJPOA), which permit juries to draw adverse inferences from a defendant's failure to answer questions in the police station, or failure to testify at trial. In *Murray v United Kingdom*[195] the Court held that where domestic legislation permits the drawing of adverse inferences from a decision not to answer questions in interview, the right of access to a solicitor in the police station is "of paramount importance"[196] such that a substantial delay on any ground will breach the right to a fair trial. In view of the adverse inference provisions of the Criminal Evidence (Northern Ireland) Order 1988, a delay in granting access to legal advice was held to amount to a breach of Art.6, even though it was carried out lawfully: "[E]ven a lawfully exercised power of restriction is capable of depriving an accused, in certain circumstances, of a fair procedure."[197] The Court held that:

---

[189] *Bonzi v Switzerland* (1978) 12 D.R. 185 at 190; *Ocalan v Turkey* judgment of March 12, 2003 ((2003) 15 B.H.R.C. 297), at paras 140–3, upheld by the Grand Chamber in its decision of May 12, 2005 ((2005) 18 B.H.R.C. 293). At paras 152–7 of the March 12, 2003 judgment the court held that restricting the duration and frequency of solicitor's visits during pre-trial detention impeded the applicant's ability to defend himself, and was therefore contrary to Art.6. The Grand Chamber saw no reason to depart from this finding.
[190] (1978) 12 D.R. 185.
[191] *ibid.,* at 190; *Brennan v United Kingdom* (2002) 34 E.H.R.R. 507 at para.45.
[192] *Imbroscia v Switzerland* (1994) 17 E.H.R.R. 441 at para.36; *Brennan v United Kingdom* Application No.39846/96, Judgment of October 26, 2001; (2002) 34 E.H.R.R. 18 at para.45.
[193] *ibid.; cf.* the vigorous dissenting judgment of Judge Pettiti.
[194] *Brennan v United Kingdom* (2002) 34 E.H.R.R. 507 at paras 46–8.
[195] (1996) 22 E.H.R.R. 29.
[196] *ibid.,* para.66; See also, *Averill v United Kingdom* (2001) 31 E.H.R.R. 36 at paras 44–52.
[197] *ibid.,* para.65.

"[T]he concept of fairness enshrined in Article 6 requires that the accused has the benefit of the assistance of a lawyer . . . at the initial stage of police interrogation. To deny access to a lawyer for the first 48 hours of police questioning, in a situation where the rights of the defence may well be irretrievably prejudiced, is—whatever the justification for such denial—incompatible with the rights of the accused under Article 6."[198]

That view has now been accepted by the government, as subsequent legislation demonstrates.[199] It was also used as a plank in the reasoning of the Court of Appeal decision in *Aspinall*,[200] where a schizophrenic defendant had been interviewed without the presence of an "appropriate adult" and after such a long delay in obtaining a duty solicitor that he agreed to be interviewed without legal advice. The Court of Appeal relied on *Murray* in concluding that the trial judge should have excluded the interview under his s.78 discretion.   **5–40**

Murray must be taken to have overruled earlier decisions on this point. In *G v United Kingdom*[201] the applicant had been refused access to a lawyer until he confessed, and the Commission left open the question whether Art.6(3)(c) guaranteed access to a lawyer at the pre-charge stage. This is surely inconsistent with, and displaced by, *Murray*. In *Di Stefano v United Kingdom*[202] the applicant's lawyer was present when he was charged and when his home and the lawyer's office were searched by police. He then spent over two days in custody, during which the police refused to allow him to see his lawyer. The lawyer made a bail application on his behalf, and there were many consultations during the lengthy period before his trial. The Commission noted that an accused person's right to communicate freely with a lawyer "cannot be said to be insusceptible of restriction," and that the general principle of fairness under Art.6 should be the guiding criterion. The comparatively short period during which the applicant was prevented from seeing his solicitor, after charge, was held not to violate either Art.6(3)(b) (preparation of defence) or Art.6(3)(c) (right to legal assistance).   **5–41**

The second area of difficulty concerns the facilities which are available for private telephone consultations in the police station. In *S v Switzerland*[203] the Court held that Art.6(3)(c) should be interpreted so as to guarantee confidentiality of communications between a detained person and his lawyer. Eavesdropping or interception by a third person (here, the government) was held to violate "one of the basic requirements of a fair trial in a democratic society".[204] There are   **5–42**

---

[198] *ibid.*, para.66.
[199] The right is recognised in s.58 of the Youth Justice and Criminal Evidence Act 1999 and s.109 of the Terrorism Act 2000.
[200] [1999] Crim. L.R. 741.
[201] (1984) 35 D.R. 75.
[202] (1989) 60 D.R. 182.
[203] (1992) 14 E.H.R.R. 670.
[204] *ibid.*, at para.48; See also, *Ocalan v Turkey* judgment March 12, 2003 ((2003) 15 B.H.R.C. 297), at paras 144–151 upheld by the decision of the Grand Chamber on May 12, 2005 ((2005) 18 B.H.R.C. 293).

other occasions on which the Court has emphasised the principle of the confidentiality of lawyer-client communications.[205] In *Brennan v United Kingdom* the Court made it clear that the right to confidentiality may be restricted, but that there must be compelling reasons for doing so. The purpose of the restriction in that case was to prevent the applicant from passing on information to suspects still at large. The Court held that this did not amount to a compelling reason on the facts, even though the restriction had only extended to the first meeting between the applicant and his solicitor, and not to later meetings.[206] The principle of lawyer-client confidentiality has the potential to raise significant practical problems since very few police stations in England and Wales are equipped with facilities to enable a detained person to consult a solicitor privately over the telephone. Telephone consultations are usually required to take place in the presence of the custody officer, who is then in a position to hear at least part of the conversation.

5–43   Finally, brief reference should be made to *Schonenberger and Durmaz v Switzerland*[207] where the Court emphasised the importance of enabling a person in police custody to consult a lawyer of his (or in this case his family's) choice. Whilst the second applicant was in police custody for drugs offences his wife instructed a lawyer (the first applicant) to represent her husband. The lawyer wrote a letter addressed to the suspect and sent it to the public prosecutor's office, asking that it be forwarded to his client. The letter contained forms of authority and also gave certain basic advice on the right to remain silent. Having read the letter the public prosecutor refused to pass it on, on the ground that it might impede the inquiry. In seeking to resist a finding that there had been a violation of the right to legal professional privilege in Art.6[208] the Swiss government argued that privilege did not attach since the lawyer had not been formally instructed by the suspect. The Court rejected this argument, noting that the lawyer had been instructed by the suspect's wife, and had subsequently made attempts to contact his client. In the Court's view, these contacts "amounted to preliminary steps intended to enable the second applicant to have the benefit of the assistance of a defence lawyer of his choice and, thereby, to exercise a right enshrined in another fundamental provision of the Convention, namely Article 6".

---

[205] *E.g. Niemietz v Germany* (1993) 16 E.H.R.R. 97, at para.37: "where a lawyer in involved, an encroachment on professional secrecy may have repercussions on the proper administration of justice and hence on the rights guaranteed by Article 6 of the Convention." See also *Kopp v Switzerland* [1998] E.H.R.L.R. 508.

[206] *Brennan v United Kingdom* (2002) 34 E.H.R.R. 507 at paras 59–63.

[207] (1989) 11 E.H.R.R. 202.

[208] See generally para.14–16 *et seq.* below.

CHAPTER 6

ENTRY, SEARCH AND SEIZURE

A. INTRODUCTION

I. The Common Law Principle

In *Entick v Carrington*[1] Lord Camden C.J. laid down the fundamental principle   **6–01**
that the executive cannot enter private premises without judicial or statutory
authority;

> "No man can set his foot upon my ground without my licence, but he is liable to an
> action, though the damage is nothing ... If he admits the fact, he is bound to show by
> way of justification, that some positive law has empowered or excused him. The
> justification is submitted to the judges, who are to look into the books and if such a
> justification can be maintained by the text of the statute law, or by the principles of the
> common law. If no such excuse can be found or produced, the silence of the books is
> an authority against the defendant ... Papers are the owner's goods and chattels ...
> and so far from enduring a seizure ... they will hardly bear an inspection; and though
> the eye cannot by the laws of England be guilty of trespass, yet where private papers
> are removed and carried away, the secret nature of those goods will be an aggravation
> of the trespass and demand more considerable damages in that respect. Where is the
> written law that gives any magistrate such a power? I can safely answer, there is none;
> and therefore it is too much for us without such authority to pronounce a practice legal,
> which would be subversive of all the comforts of society."

Accordingly, an entry and search carried out pursuant to an executive warrant   **6–02**
was held to be unlawful. The common law thus protects the principle, reflected
in Art.8 of the Convention, that any interference with the right to respect for
private life, home and correspondence, must be prescribed by law. This does not,
however, exhaust the requirements of Art.8 and there are numerous statutory, and
certain common law powers of entry which must be exercised in conformity with
the Human Rights Act.

---

[1] [1765] 19 State Trials 1029.

II. The Police and Criminal Evidence Act 1984

6–03   The Police and Criminal Evidence Act 1984 (PACE), Pt II, consolidated many but not all[2] of the statutory powers of entry, search and seizure in English law. It has been amended by the Serious Organised Crime and Police Act 2005 (SOCPA)[3] which has significantly broadened police powers in relation to search warrants.[4] Section 8 governs the power of a justice of the peace to issue a search warrant where there are reasonable grounds for believing that an indictable offence[5] or an immigration offence[6] has been committed, and that there is relevant evidence on the premises to be searched which is likely to be of substantial value to the investigation. A warrant may authorise the entry and search of one or more specified premises (in which case it is a "specific premises warrant")[7] or of any premises occupied or controlled by a person specified in the application (in which case it is an "all premises warrant").[8] An all premises warrant may be granted where there are reasonable grounds to believe that it is necessary to search premises connected to a specified person to locate the material sought and it is not reasonably practicable to specify in the application all the premises concerned which it might prove necessary to search.[9] A warrant may authorise entry to and search of premises on a single occasion or on multiple occasions,[10] and if multiple entries and searches are authorised, their number

---

[2] The police powers of entry not repealed by PACE include the warrant powers in the Obscene Publications Act 1959, s.3, the Theft Act 1968, s.26, and the Misuse of Drugs Act 1971, s.23. There are, in addition, numerous statutory powers of entry, search and seizure conferred on other public officials, including the Inland Revenue Commissioners, Customs and Excise officials and officers of central and local government: see generally Stone, *Entry, Search and Seizure* (3rd edn, 1997). Section 9(2) of PACE, Pt II provides that any Act under which a search of premises for the purposes of a criminal investigation could be authorised by the issue of a search warrant shall cease to have effect insofar as it relates to authorisation of searches for items subject to legal professional privilege, excluded material or special material.

[3] These amendments came into force on January 1, 2006; see Serious Organised Crime and Police Act 2005 (Commencement No.4 and Transitory Provision) Order 2005, SI 2005/3495.

[4] The Parliamentary Joint Committee on Human Rights have stated that the amendments gave rise to a significant risk of incompatibility with Art.8, describing them as giving "justices of the peace authority to issue a general warrant of a kind that has been anathema to the common law for centuries on account of the very wide discretion it confers on public officials, and the lack of effective prior judicial control over the decision to enter (if need be, by force) private premises including dwellings." (Joint Committee on Human Rights, Scrutiny: First Progress Report 2004–2005, HL Paper 26, HC 224, para.1.91)

[5] PACE, s.8(1)(a). The term "indictable offence" was substituted for "serious arrestable offence" by SOCPA, Sch.7, Pt 3, broadening the range of offences in relation to which arrest warrants may be granted. The change gives effect to the proposal in the Home Office Consultation Paper *Policing: Modernising Police Powers to Meet Community Needs* that the special powers—including the powers arising under s.8—arising in relation to serious arrestable offences be available in respect of all offences triable either way or on indictment when relevant, necessary and proportionate having regard to the rights of the individual and when their use will contribute to effectiveness and efficiency.

[6] PACE, s.8(6), as inserted by the Immigration and Asylum Act 1999. Relevant offences as defined in amended s.28D(4) of the Immigration Act 1971 include assisting unlawful immigration to a member state (s.25) and assisting an asylum-seeker to enter the United Kingdom (s.25A). An application for a warrant in relation to such offences would be made by an immigration officer (s.28D(4)(1)).

[7] PACE, s.8(1A)(a), as amended by SOCPA.

[8] PACE, s.8(1A)(b), as amended by SOCPA.

[9] PACE, s.8(1B), as amended by SOCPA.

[10] PACE, s.8(1C), as amended by SOCPA.

may be unlimited or limited to a maximum.[11] However, prior to granting a multiple entry warrant, a justice of the peace must be satisfied that multiple entries are necessary to achieve the purpose for which the warrant is being sought.[12] The power does not apply[13] to items subject to legal professional privilege,[14] excluded material (confidential personal records, medical samples, or journalistic material held in confidence),[15] or to "special procedure" material.[16] A search warrant is only to be granted under s.8 if it is impracticable to communicate with the person entitled to grant entry to the premises or access to the evidence, if entry would not be granted without a warrant, or if the purpose of the search would be frustrated or seriously impeded if police were unable to obtain immediate access.[17]

Section 9 and Sch.1 provide a "special procedure" for obtaining access to **6–04** excluded and special procedure material, either by means of a production order, or, in certain exceptional circumstances, by means of a warrant. An application is to be made to a circuit judge or a district judge for access to such material.[18] So far as production orders are concerned, Sch.1 provides two sets of "access conditions" which must be met as a precondition to the grant of such an order.[19] The first set of access conditions applies to special procedure material other than excluded material, and consists of three requirements. First, there must be reasonable grounds for believing[20] that an indictable offence[21] has been committed, that there is special procedure material on the premises specified or

---

[11] PACE, s.8(1D), as amended by SOCPA.

[12] PACE, s.8(1C), as amended by SOCPA.

[13] PACE, Pt II, s.8(1)(d). See also *R. v Guildhall Magistrates ex parte Primlaks Holdings* [1990] 1 Q.B. 261.

[14] As to the meaning of legal professional privilege see PACE, Pt II, s.10. See also para.6–14 below.

[15] As to the meaning of excluded material see s.11.

[16] Special procedure material is defined by PACE, Pt II, s.14 to be (a) journalistic material, other than material held in confidence, or (b) material held by a person a person who created or acquired it in the course of a trade, business, profession, occupation or office and which is held subject to an express or implied undertaking to hold it in confidence, or subject to a statutory restriction on its disclosure.

[17] PACE, Pt II, s.8(3); n.b. the Divisional Court held that there was no requirement arising under PACE or the ECHR for a justice of the peace to record his reasons for granting a warrant (*R. v Sheffield Magistrates Court, ex parte Cronin* [2002] EWHC 2568 Admin); an application to the ECtHR in the case was declared inadmissible on the facts of the case, the court having found that the Information contained all the relevant material on which the justices had based their decision. However, the ECtHR underscored the observation of the Divisional Court that in other cases additional information might be necessary to protect the interests of the person in relation to whom the warrant was issued (Application No.15848/03, Decision of January 6, 2004).

[18] Such an application may be heard in chambers: *R. v Central Criminal Court ex parte DPP, The Times*, April 1, 1998.

[19] The judge may not make an order unless he is personally satisfied that the access conditions are met: *R. v Lewes Crown Court ex parte Hill* 93 Cr.App.R. 60; *R. v Central Criminal Court, ex parte Bright, Alton, Rusbridger* [2001] 2 All E.R. 244 at 259. However, there is no requirement for the order to state on its face which access conditions were satisfied: *R. (on the application of Paul da Costa) v Thames Magistrates' Court and another* (2002) 152 N.L.J. 141.

[20] The requirement is for "grounds of belief"; grounds for suspicion are not sufficient (*R. v Central Criminal Court, ex parte Bright, Alton, Rusbridger* [2001] 2 All E.R. 244 at 260a).

[21] See footnote 1 above.

occupied or controlled by a person specified in the application,[22] and that the material consists of relevant evidence[23] which is likely to be of substantial value to the investigation.[24] Secondly, other methods of obtaining the material must have been tried without success or otherwise be bound to fail.[25] Thirdly, the judge must consider that the making of an order would be in the public interest, having regard to the benefit likely to accrue to the investigation if the material is obtained, and the circumstances in which it is held.[26] The second set of access conditions applies to special procedure *or* excluded material, and requires that the conditions for the grant of a warrant are otherwise met.[27] When either set of conditions is fulfilled, the judge may make an order requiring the person in possession of the material to produce it or give access to it,[28] which is enforceable through proceedings for contempt of court.[29] The power to make a production order is discretionary. In *R. v Central Criminal Court ex parte The Guardian, The Observer and Martin Bright*,[30] Judge L.J. held that in exercising this discretion, the judge should take account of fundamental rights, including the right to privacy, the right to freedom of expression and the protection against self-incrimination;

"This provision, as it seems to me, is the final safeguard against an oppressive order, and in an appropriate case, provides the judge with the opportunity to reflect on and take account of matters which are not expressly referred to in the set of relevant access conditions and, where they arise, to reflect on all the circumstances including, where appropriate, what can, without exaggeration, be described as fundamental principles . . . [I]n my judgment the judge must take account of an apparent disproportion between what might possibly be gained by the production of the material and the offence to which it is said to relate, and . . . in the case of journalistic material, to the potential stifling of public debate, and . . . to the risk of imposing an obligation requiring the individual to whom the order is directed to incriminate himself".[31]

---

[22] The applicant must set out a description of all the material sought: *R. v Central Criminal Court ex parte Adegbesan* 84 Cr.App.R. 219. There is a duty of full disclosure: *R. v Acton Crown Court ex parte Layton* [1993] Crim.L.R. 458.

[23] This means "anything that would be admissible in evidence at a trial for the offence": PACE, Pt II, s.8(4); The Divisional Court further qualified that the material sought must not be "merely general information which might be helpful to police inquiries, but evidence in the sense in which that term is applied in the Crown Court, relevant and admissible at trial." ((*R. v Central Criminal Court, ex parte Bright*, above)

[24] PACE, Sch.1 para.2(a); *cf. Re Moloney's Application for Judicial Review* [2000] N.I.J.B. 195, DC: a production order issued in respect of the journalist applicant's notebook in the context of the investigation into the murder of Belfast solicitor Pat Finucane was quashed on the ground that the police had not made out the case that the material contained within it was likely to be of "substantial value". *Cf.* also *R. v Central Criminal Court, ex parte Bristol Press and Press Picture Agency* [2001] 2 All E.R. 244; [2002] Crim.L.R. 64.

[25] PACE, Sch.1 para.2(b).

[26] PACE, Sch.1 para.2(c).

[27] PACE, Sch.1 para.3.

[28] PACE, Sch.1 para.4.

[29] PACE, Sch.1 para.15.

[30] [2001] 1 W.L.R. 662.

[31] See also *R. v Bristol Crown Court ex parte Bristol Press and Picture Agency Ltd* [1987] 85 Cr.App.R. 190.

This is an important principle,[32] suggesting as it does that the exercise of judicial **6–05** discretion prior to the authorisation of a power of entry, search and seizure, provides an opportunity for judicial consideration of the compatibility of such an entry with Convention rights.[33]

In certain circumstances a judge may, instead of making a production order, issue a warrant under s.9 and Sch.1 PACE.[34] Such a warrant is only to be issued where: (a) it is impracticable to communicate with the person entitled to give entry to the premises or access to the material[35]; (b) the service of a production order notice would seriously prejudice the investigation[36]; or (c) the search is necessary to prevent a person from disclosing information in breach of a statutory obligation.[37] In the case of an all premises warrant issued pursuant to s.9 and Sch.1, a judge must also be satisfied that there are reasonable grounds for believing that it is necessary to search non-specified premises in order to locate the material in question and it is not reasonably practicable to specifiy all the premises which might need to be searched.[38]

Sections 15 and 16 provide additional safeguards governing the grant and **6–06** execution of search warrants, whether issued under PACE or other legislation, and are to be read in conjunction with the detailed guidance set out in Code B (Code of Practice for the Searching of Premises by Police Officers and the Seizure of Property Found by Police Officers on Persons or Premises). The application must state the ground on which, and the legislation under which, it is made.[39] If authorisation is sought for entry and search on more than one occasion, it must also specify the grounds on which a multiple search warrant is being sought and must state the maximum number of entries desired or that an unlimited number of entries is required[40]; it must also specifiy, as far as practicable, the articles sought.[41] A specific premises warrant must also specify each set

---

[32] Judge L.J. was careful to emphasise that the decision applied only to PACE, Pt II, s.9 and Sch.1, but the principle would appear equally applicable to the power of a justice to grant or refuse a search warrant.

[33] *cf. Baron v Canada* [1993] 1 S.C.R. 416 where the Canadian Supreme Court held that the authorisation of a warrant must leave scope for judicial discretion if fundamental rights are to be respected. However, the Joint Committee on Human Rights has queried whether sufficient safeguards are in place to protect fundamental rights in relation to the grant of "all premises" and multiple search warrants introduced by SOCPA, stating: "safeguards external to the police are weak, because the justice of the peace is very unlikely to be able to assess properly the proportionality of a request to be allowed to enter and search unspecified premises on an unlimited number of future occasions over the following three months; and decisions of an inspector in relation to particular premises are unlikely to be subject to judicial or public scrutiny." (Joint Committee on Human Rights, Scrutiny: First Progress Report 2004–2005, HL Paper 26, HC 224, para.1.95).

[34] PACE, Sch.1 para.12.

[35] PACE, Sch.1 para.14(a) and (b).

[36] PACE, Sch.1 para.14(d).

[37] PACE, Sch.1 para.14(c).

[38] PACE, Sch.1, s.12A, as amended by SOCPA.

[39] PACE, ss.15(2)(a)(i) and (ii), as amended by SOCPA.

[40] (1) PACE, s.15(2)(a)(iii), as amended by SOCPA.

[41] PACE, Pt II, s.15(2)(c). See generally, *R. v Central Criminal Court ex parte AJD Holdings* [1992] Crim.L.R. 669; *R. v Reading Justices ex parte South West Meat Ltd* [1992] Crim.L.R. 672. See also *R. v Maidstone Crown Court ex parte Waitt* [1988] Crim.L.R. 384; *R. v Leeds Crown Court ex parte Switalski* [1991] C.O.D. 199.

of premises the entry to and search of which is authorised.[42] An all premises warrant must specify: (a) as many sets of premises which it is reasonably practicable to specify; (b) the person in occupation or control of those premises and of any other premises which might need to be entered and searched; (c) why it is necessary to search more premises than those specified; and (d) why it is not reasonably practicable to specifiy all the premises which it is desired to enter and search.[43] This information is to be included in the warrant, together with the name of the officer making the application.[44] A warrant which is too widely drawn, or which includes privileged material, is liable to be quashed.[45] The application is to be made *ex parte*, supported by an information in writing,[46] but the officer making it is to be available to give evidence on oath.[47] A warrant may authorise entry only on one occasion unless it specifies that it authorises multiple entries,[48] in which case it must also specify whether the number of entries authorised is unlimited or limited to a specified maximum.[49] A warrant authorises entry by any police constable or authorised civilian investigating officer,[50] together with any other person named or identified in the warrant.[51] However, in the case of warrants authorising multiple entries and searches, an officer of at least the rank of inspector must also authorise in writing any second or subsequent entry in order for it to be lawful.[52] Equally, in the case of an all premises warrant, no premises which are not specified in the warrant may be entered or searched unless specific written authorisation is given by an officer of at least the rank of inspector or above.[53] Any entry must take place within three months of the issue of the warrant,[54] and must be at a reasonable hour unless this would frustrate the purpose of the search.[55] Where the occupier or any other person is present the officer carrying out the search must identify himself and provide the person concerned with a copy of the warrant.[56] If no one is present a copy of the warrant is to be left in a prominent place on the premises.[57] The constable executing the warrant is required to endorse it with a record of the items found

---

[42] PACE, s.15(2A)(a), as amended by SOCPA.

[43] PACE, 15(2A), as amended by SOCPA.

[44] PACE, Pt II, s.15(6).

[45] *R. v Southampton Crown Court ex parte J and P* [1993] Crim.L.R. 962; however, see also *Bell v Chief Constable of Greater Manchester Police*, unreported, April 27, 2005 (Cooke J.); refusing permission to appeal [2005] EWCA Civ 902 (Potter P).

[46] PACE, Pt II, s.15(3).

[47] PACE, Pt II, s.15(4). As to the relevance of claims to public interest immunity in connection with the information provided, see *Taylor v Anderton, The Times*, October 16, 1986.

[48] PACE, Pt II, s.15(5), as amended by SOCPA.

[49] PACE, 15(5A), as amended by SOCPA.

[50] Police Reform Act 2002, Sch.4, Pt II.

[51] PACE, Pt II, s.16(2). Such a person has the same powers as the officer he or she is accompanying in respect of the execution of the warrant and the seizure of any materials to which the warrant relates (s.16(2A)); however, he or she may only exercise those powers in the company and under the supervision of an officer (section 16(2B)). Police Reform Act 2002, Sch.4, Pt II.

[52] PACE, s.16(3B), as amended by SOCPA.

[53] PACE, s.16(3A), as amended by SOCPA.

[54] PACE, Pt II, s.16(3), as amended by SOCPA, increasing the time limit from one month to three.

[55] PACE, Pt II, s.16(4).

[56] PACE, Pt II, s.16(5) and (6).

[57] PACE, Pt II, s.16(7).

and seized,[58] and must do so separately in respect of each set of premises entered and searched.[59] A warrant must be returned to the appropriate person[60] when it has been executed or, in the case of a non-executed specific premises warrant, an all premises warrant or a warrant authorising multiple entries, prior to its three-month expiry date.[61] The warrant must be retained by the appropriate person for a period of 12 months, during which time it is available for inspection by the occupier of the premises to which it relates.[62] One of the most important safeguards is that contained in s.16(8) which provides that: "[a] search under a warrant may only be a search to the extent required for the purpose for which the warrant was issued"—in effect a requirement that the warrant be executed in a manner proportionate to its objective. Code B provides that:

"Premises may be searched only to the extent necessary to achieve the object of the search, having regard to the size and nature of whatever is sought.[63] A search may not continue under:

- a warrant's authority once all the things specified in that warrant have been found
- any other power once the object of that search has been achieved.[64]

No search may continue once the officer in charge of the search is satisfied whatever is being sought is not on the premises[65] ... Searches must be conducted with due consideration for the property and privacy of the occupier of the premises searched and with no more disturbance than necessary ... "[66]

Further, a warrant to search premises does not authorise the search of persons on those premises,[67] unless that specific power is provided for in the warrant. Persons present on the premises may, however, be detained or restrained for the duration of the search where the warrant permits the search of persons as well as premises[68] or where such detention or restraint is necessary to ensure the "safe and effective exercise" of an express or necessary power to search the premises.[69]

Sections 17 and 18 of Pt II, PACE set out the powers of police officers to enter **6–07** private premises without a warrant to affect an arrest or to search for evidence.

---

[58] PACE, Pt II, s.16(9).
[59] PACE, s.16(9).
[60] PACE, s.16(10A). The appropriate person is (a) the designated officer for the local justice area in which the justice was acting (where the warrant was issued by a justice of the peace) or (b) the appropriate officer of the court (where the warrant was issued by a judge).
[61] PACE, s.16(10).
[62] PACE, Pt II, s.16(11) and (12).
[63] PACE, Code B, para.6.9.
[64] PACE, Code B, para.6.9A.
[65] PACE, Code B, para.6.9B.
[66] PACE, Code B, para.6.10B.
[67] *Hepburn v Chief Constable of Thames Valley* [2002] EWCA Civ 1841.
[68] *DPP v Meaden* [2004] 1 W.L.R. 904; [2004] Crim.L.R. 587.
[69] *Connor v Chief Constable of Merseyside Police* [2006] All E.R. (D) 293 (Nov.) where the restraint of the occupants of the premises searched was held to be necessary and proportionate for the execution of a search warrant granted under the Firearms Act 1968 on the grounds that it was reasonable to suspect that there were weapons on the premises and that those on the premises might themselves endanger lives or that their lives might be endangered.

Section 17 governs the power of entry for the purposes of executing an arrest warrant or a warrant of commitment[70]; for the purposes of arresting a person for an indictable offence,[71] offences pertaining to animal health[72] and certain specified non-indictable offences[73]; for the purpose of arresting a child or young person remanded or committed to local authority accommodation[74]; for the purpose of recapturing persons unlawfully at large[75]; or for the purpose of saving life or limb or preventing serious damage to property.[76] Where the object of the entry is to effect an arrest, the power may only be exercised if,[77] and to the extent that,[78] there are reasonable grounds for believing that the person sought is on the premises. The power of search conferred by s.17 is "only a power to search to the extent that is reasonably required for the purpose for which the power of entry is exercised".[79] Apart from the power of entry to deal with or prevent a breach of the peace,[80] all common law powers of entry without warrant are abolished.[81]

6–08   Section 18 provides a statutory power of entry and search following arrest for an indictable offence. The power may be exercised where there are reasonable grounds for suspecting that there is, on premises occupied or controlled by the

---

[70] PACE, Pt II, s.17(1)(a).

[71] PACE, Pt II, s.17(1)(b).

[72] PACE, s.17(1)(caa).

[73] PACE, Pt II, s.17(1)(c). These are offences under (i) s.1 of the Public Order Act 1936 relating to the prohibition of uniforms in connection with prohibited objects; (ii) any enactment contained in ss.6 or 8 of the Criminal Law Act 1977 relating to offences involving entering and remaining on property; (iii) s.4 of the Public Order Act 1986 pertaining to the creation of fear or provocation of violence; (iiia) ss.4 and 163 of the Road Traffic Act relating to driving under the influence of alcohol and drugs and failing to stop when required to do so by a constable in uniform; (iiib) s.27 of the Transport and Works Act 1992 relating to offences involving alcohol or drugs; (iv) s.76 of the Criminal Justice and Public Order Act 1994 pertaining to the failure to comply with an interim possession order; and (iv) selected sections of the Animal Welfare Act 2006 relating to the prevention of harm to animals. In relation to (ii) and (iv), the powers of entry and search are only exercisable by a constable in uniform (s.17(3)).

[74] PACE, s.17(1)(ca).

[75] PACE, Pt II, s.17(1) (cb) and (d).

[76] PACE, Pt II, s.17(1)(e);. This has been held not to authorise entry to premises to search for the address of the next of kin of an unconscious person who had been injured in a road traffic accident (R. v Veneroso [2002] Crim.L.R.306); in that case, the entry was found to amount to a breach of the right to privacy enshrined in Art.8 of the ECHR and, consequently, the evidence of drug offences found during the entry to the premises by the police was held to be inadmissible.

[77] PACE, Pt II, s.17(2)(a).

[78] PACE, Pt II, s.(2)(b) provides that, in relation to premises consisting of two or more separate dwellings, the powers of entry and search are limited to (i) any communal parts of the premises and (ii) any dwelling in which the constable has reasonable grounds to believe the person he is seeking may be.

[79] PACE, Pt II, s.(4).

[80] PACE, Pt II, s.17(6); further, entry to prevent a breach of the peace is only justified in "exceptional circumstances": the officer must be satisfied that there is an imminent threat of a breach of the peace of sufficient gravity to justify the entry (Friswell v Chief Constable of Essex Police [2004] EWHC Q.B. 2009).

[81] PACE, Pt II, s.17(5). S.II of PACE only applies to domestic offences. The police still retain a common law power to enter and search premises following a person's arrest for an extradition offence (R. v Metropolitan Police Commissioner, ex parte Rottman [2002] 2 A.C. 692). However, see also Hewitson v Chief Constable of Dorset Police [2003] EWHC 3296 (Admin) for the limitations placed on that common law power.

person under arrest, evidence (other than items subject to legal privilege) which relates to the offence for which he is under arrest or to another, connected or similar, arrestable offence.[82] A search under s.18 requires the written authorisation of an officer of the rank of inspector or above,[83] unless the accused's presence is required (in which case an inspector or above must be informed as soon as practicable).[84] The power of search may only be exercised "to the extent that is reasonably required for the purposes of discovering [the] evidence".[85] Any item which is evidence of an arrestable offence may be seized and retained.[86] Sections 19 to 21 make further provision for the seizure of evidence.

III. The Terrorism Provisions

The Terrorism Act 2000 (TA 2000) governs the powers of entry, search and   6–09
seizure in relation to suspected terrorism offences. A justice of the peace has the power to issue a search warrant in relation to specified premises if he is satisfied, having heard evidence on oath in relation to the matter, that there are reasonable grounds for suspecting that a person concerned in the commission, preparation or instigation of acts of terrorism is likely to be found on those premises.[87] Such a warrant authorises a police officer to enter and search the specified premises for the purpose of arresting the wanted person.[88] A justice of the peace also has the power to issue either a specific premises or an all premises search warrant[89] where he is satisfied that: (i) it is sought for the purpose of a terrorist investigation; (ii) there are reasonable grounds for believing that the material sought is likely to be of substantial assistance to such an investigation; (iii) that it does not include "excepted material"[90]; (iv) that the issue of a warrant is likely to be necessary in the circumstances of the case; and (v), in the case of an application for an all premises warrant, that it is not reasonably practicable to specify all the premises which the person specified in the application occupies or controls and which might need to be searched.[91] A warrant granted for the purposes of a terrorist investigation authorises any police officer to enter the premises, to search those premises and any person found there, and to seize and retain any

---

[82] PACE, Pt II, s.18(1).
[83] PACE, Pt II, s.18(4). S.18(7) provides that the authorising officer must record the grounds for the search and the nature of the evidence sought in writing. As to the effect of a breach of this provision see *Krohn v DPP* [1997] C.O.D. 345. S.18(8) provides that where the person concerned is in police custody this information is to be included in the custody record. A failure to comply does not however necessarily render the evidence so obtained inadmissible: *R. v Wright* [1994] Crim.L.R. 55.
[84] PACE, Pt II, s.18(5).
[85] PACE, Pt II, s.18(3).
[86] PACE, Pt II, s.18(2).
[87] TA 2000, s.42, read in conjunction with s.40(1)(b).
[88] TA 2000, s.42(2).
[89] TA 2000, Sch.5, Pt I, para.1(2A).
[90] TA 2000, Sch.5, Pt I, para.1(5)(b). "Excepted material" is defined by TA 2000, Sch.5, Pt I, para.4(a), (b) and (c) as excluded material, items subject to legal privilege and special procedure material, as *per* PACE, ss.11, 10 and 14 respectively.
[91] TA 2000, Sch.5, Pt I, para.1(5); *n.b.*, in cases involving non-residential premises, a warrant may be granted, even where the justice is not satisfied that the warrant is necessary in the circumstances of the case (as per para.1(5)(c), provided that the application is made by an officer of at least the rank of superintendent. However, where such a warrant is granted, it must be executed within 24 hours (TA 2000, Sch.5, Pt I, ss.2 and 2A).

relevant material found as a result of any such search.[92] Such a warrant does not apply to items subject to legal professional privilege,[93] nor does it confer the power to require a person to remove any clothing in public except for outer-garments.[94]

6–10 The TA 2000 also provides that a police officer of at least the rank of super-intendent can authorise, by way of a written authority signed by him, a search of specified premises that fall wholly or partly within a cordoned area.[95] An officer below that rank may also authorise such a search if he considers it necessary by reason of urgency.[96] As with a search conducted pursuant to a warrant, any authorisation so given permits a constable to enter and search the premises, to search any person found therein and to seize and retain any relevant material found,[97] but does not cover items subect to legal privilege, nor does it enable the officer to require a person to remove any clothing other than outergarments.[98] The authorisation must not be given unless the person giving it has reasonable grounds for believing that there is material on the premises which is likely to be of substantial value to a terrorist investigation which does not include excepted material.[99]

6–11 Paragraph 5 of Sch.1 provides a "special procedure" for obtaining access to both excluded and special procedure material by means of a production order or, in certain exceptional circumstances, by means of a warrant. It operates in a similar manner to the special procedure application process provided for under s.9 and Sch.1 of PACE. However, whereas a special procedure application under PACE is usually made *inter partes*, it is made *ex parte* under the Terrorism Act. An application for a production order must be made to a circuit judge or a district judge[100] who may grant the application if he is satisfied that: (i) the material[101] to which the application relates consists of or includes excluded or special procedure material[102]; (ii) it does not include items subject to legal privilege[103]; (iii) the order is sought for the purposes of a terrorist investigation and there are reasonable grounds for believing that the material is likely to be of substantial value any such investigation[104]; (iv) there are reasonable grounds for believing

---

[92] TA 2000, Sch.5, Pt I, para.1(2). As *per* TA 2000, Sch.5, Pt I, para.1(3), material is relevant if the constable has reasonable grounds for believing that it is likely to be of substantial value to a terrorist organisation and that it must be seized so as to prevent it from being concealed, lost, damaged, altered or destroyed.

[93] TA 2000, Sch.5, Pt I, para.1(4)(a).

[94] TA 2000, Sch.1, para.1(4)(b). The outer-garments specified are: headgear, footwear, outer-coats, jackets and gloves.

[95] TA 2000, Sch.5, Pt I, para.3(1).

[96] TA 2000, Sch.5, Pt I, para.3(2).

[97] TA 2000, Sch.5, Pt I, para.3(3).

[98] TA 2000, Sch.5, Pt I, para.3(5).

[99] TA 2000, Sch.5, Pt I, para.3(6).

[100] TA 2000, Sch.5, Pt I, para.5(1).

[101] The application must relate to "particular material or material of a particular description, which consists of or includes excluded material or special procedure material": TA 2000, Sch.5, Pt I, para.5(2).

[102] TA 2000, Sch.5, Pt I, para.6(1)(a).

[103] TA 2000, Sch.5, Pt I, para.6(1)(b).

[104] TA 2000, Sch.5, Pt I, para.6(2).

that it is in the public interest that the material should be produced or that access to it should be given, having regard to: (a) the benefit to any investigation that would accrue if the material is obtained; and (b) the circumstances under which the person in question holds any of the material in his possession, custody or control.[105] If the conditions are fulfilled, the judge may make an order requiring the specified person to produce the material or provide access to it, or, if he is not in possession of it, to supply details of its location to the best of his knowledge and belief.[106] Pursuant to para.11, a judge may issue a warrant instead of making a production order in certain specified circumstances.[107]

Exceptionally, para.15 of Sch.5 also permits a police officer of at least the rank **6–12** of superintendent to authorise a search which would otherwise require a search warrant where the case is one of great emergency, necessitating immediate action. Such authorisation must be made in writing and may apply to excluded or special procedure material.[108]

Paragraph 13 of Sch.1 provides that a judge may also make an order that a person **6–13** provide an explanation of any material seized or produced.[109] The order cannot require the breach of legal professional privilege, except that a lawyer can be required to provide the name and address of his clients.[110] Further, any statement made pursuant to such an order may not be used in evidence against that person, save in proceedings for the offence of deliberately or recklessly making an untrue statement pursuant to that order.[111]

B. THE CONVENTION APPROACH

I. General

The Convention differs from other constitutional instruments in failing to make **6–14** specific provision against unlawful entry, search and seizure. These issues are, however, addressed in the Court's caselaw under Art.8. In general, it can be said that any entry onto private premises will amount to an interference with the rights guaranteed by Art.8(1). This applies not only to a person's home, but also to business premises.[112] Such an interference must therefore meet the requirements of Art.8(2). Any entry or search must be "in accordance with the law" and proportionate to one of the legitimate aims there set out—typically the prevention of crime. This implies that the law must be accessible and foreseeable; it must afford adequate safeguards against abuse; there must be no other, less intrusive method, of obtaining the relevant evidence; and a power of search must be

---

[105] TA 2000, Sch.5, Pt I, para.6(3).
[106] TA 2000, Sch.5, Pt I, paras 5(3), 5(4) and 7.
[107] TA 2000, Sch.5, Pt I, para.11.
[108] TA 2000, Sch.5, Pt I, para.15.
[109] TA 2000, Sch.5, para.13.
[110] TA 2000, Sch.5, paras 13(2) and (3).
[111] TA 2000, Sch.5, paras 13(4) and 14.
[112] *Niemietz v Germany* (1993) 16 E.H.R.R. 97 at para.29.

exercised in practice in a manner which is proportionate. Prior judicial authorisation is not necessarily indispensible, but in the absence of such authorisation the court will closely scrutinise the safeguards in place in domestic law to prevent disproportionate interference with privacy rights,[113] paying particular attention to the manner in which the power has been exercised in practice.[114]

6–15   As we have seen, the framework established by the Police and Criminal Evidence Act 1984 broadly reflects the requirements of Art.8, at least so far as the warrant and production order procedures are concerned. The Act affords a statutory basis for entry into private premises; requires prior judicial authorisation where practicable; confines powers of entry to arrestable offences; requires that less intrusive methods should either have failed or be impracticable; affords added protection for confidential, journalistic and privileged material; and embodies the principle that searches may only be made to the extent reasonably required for the purpose. The powers of police officers and others to enter and search premises without a warrant are less secure in Convention terms.[115] But the important point in either case is that it is the *exercise* of those powers on a particular set of facts, and not merely the legislation itself, which must be examined for compatibility with the Convention. As the Strasbourg caselaw has shown, the powers conferred by PACE are capable of being exercised in a manner which amounts to a disproportionate interference with privacy rights.

II. Powers of Entry

6–16   Section 17(6) of PACE expressly preserves the common law power of entry to deal with or prevent a breach of the peace. The leading authority on the exercise of this power is *Thomas v Sawkins*.[116] In *McLeod v United Kingdom*[117] police officers had relied on this power in order to enter the applicant's home in her absence, so as to assist her former husband to remove property. The officers (wrongly) believed that the husband was entitled to remove the property in question under a court order made in the course of acrimonious matrimonial proceedings. The husband and his solicitor had asked the police to accompany them in order to prevent trouble occurring. The applicant complained that her right to respect for her private life and home under Art.8 had been violated. In the Court's view the officers' actions were "in accordance with the law", the power of entry to prevent a breach of the peace being defined with sufficient precision to meet the Convention standard of legal certainty.[118] As to the justification for the entry, the Court accepted that the prevention of disorder was a legitimate aim in this context, but held that the officers' actions were not "necessary in a democratic society". The Court concluded that the officers ought to have checked the court order themselves rather than taking the former husband's word for it.

---

[113] *Camenzind v Switzerland* (1999) 28 E.H.R.R. 458.
[114] *McLeod v United Kingdom* (1999) 27 E.H.R.R. 493.
[115] See the principle cited in *Camenzind v Switzerland* (1999) 28 E.H.R.R. 458 at para.45.
[116] [1935] K.B. 249.
[117] (1999) 27 E.H.R.R. 493.
[118] This finding corresponds with the Court's finding in *Steel v United Kingdom* (1999) 28 E.H.R.R. 603.

Had they done so, they would have realised that the applicant was not obliged to surrender the property at that time. Moreover, the officers ought to have realised that no breach of the peace was likely (only the applicant's elderly mother being in the house when the entry occurred).[119] In finding a violation of Art.8 on the facts, the Court emphasised that the power of entry to prevent a breach of the peace, must, in the same way as the power of arrest to prevent a breach of the peace, be regarded as an incursion into a citizen's private life and liberty which requires careful justification.

In *Keegan v United* Kingdom,[120] police officers, acting under the power of a **6–17** warrant, forcibly entered the applicants' home to search for cash stolen during the course of a number of robberies. The police were acting under a mistaken belief that the mother of one of the suspects in the investigation resided at the address. In fact, the applicants (parents and their three children) had moved into the premises some six months previously. The domestic court rejected the applicants' claim against the police for maliciously procuring a search warrant, unlawful entry and false imprisonment, finding that the police had not acted "maliciously" and that their entry into the premises had been made pursuant to a valid warrant. Importantly, the incident complained of had occurred in October 1999, prior to the coming into force of the Human Rights Act 1998. The domestic court highlighted that, had that Act been in force, its conclusions might have been different:

> "That an Englishman's home is said to be his castle reveals an important public interest, but there is another public interest in the detection of crime and the bringing to justice of those who commit it. These interests are in conflict in a case like this and on the law as it stood when these events occurred, which is before the coming into force of the Human Rights Act 1998, which may be said to have elevated the right to respect for one's home, a finding of malice on the part of the police is the proper balancing exercise."[121]

The applicants complained to Strasbourg that their rights under Art.8 had been violated. In accordance with the findings of the domestic court, the Court determined that the police had not effectively undertaken basic steps to verify the connection between the address and the offence under investigation. It therefore ruled that the resulting police action, which had caused the applicants considerable fear and alarm, could not be regarded as proportionate, stating: "Put in Convention terms, there might have been relevant reasons, but, as in the circumstances they were based on a misconception which could, and should, have been avoided with proper precautions, they cannot be regarded as sufficient."[122] Thus the interference was not justified under Art.8(2). Importantly, the Court did not cast doubt on the genuineness of the belief of the officers involved in obtaining or executing the warrant. Indeed, had the officers' belief been accurate and had the suspect's mother resided at the property, the entry would have been justified. However, it underscored that the absence of malice was not decisive under Art.8,

---

[119] *McLeod* judgment, para.57.
[120] [2006] All E.R. (D) 235 (Jul), App.No.28867/03.
[121] [2003] EWCA Civ 936.
[122] *ibid.*, para.33.

which was intended to protect against abuse of power, however motivated or caused.

III. Search and Seizure

6–18   The leading decision on search and seizure is *Funke v France*,[123] where customs officials had searched the applicant's house and had seized documents as part of an inquiry into exchange-control offences. The French government conceded that the applicant's Art.8 right had been interfered with. The Court held that the search pursued the legitimate aim of protecting "the economic well-being of the country", but emphasised that the exceptions in Art.8(2) should be interpreted narrowly and that, although judicial authorisation of search warrants was not a requirement of Art.8, "the relevant legislation and practice must afford adequate and effective safeguards against abuse." In the Court's view, the French customs law in force at that time failed to satisfy this standard. The powers of the customs officers were unduly wide since "they had exclusive competence to assess the expediency, number, length and scale of inspections". Moreover, "the restrictions and conditions provided for in law ... appear[ed] too lax and full of loopholes for the interferences with the applicant's right to have been strictly proportionate to the legitimate aim pursued."[124] With these strong words the Court found that the search was not "necessary in a democratic society" and constituted a violation of Art.8.

6–19   The Court pursued a similarly strong approach in *Niemietz v Germany*,[125] where the German police had searched a lawyer's offices, under a court warrant, in order to find evidence of the whereabouts of one of the lawyer's clients. The German government argued that the case did not engage Art.8 at all, on the ground that a person's professional activities do not fall within the notion of "private life." The Court dismissed this argument, holding that most people's business or professional lives are so intimately connected with their private lives that they should equally be protected from arbitrary interference.[126] The Court accepted that the interference was in accordance with German law and had the aim of preventing crime. But it nevertheless held that the search was disproportionate because the warrant was drawn in broad and unspecific terms (it referred to "documents" without any limitation) and because German law failed to provide any extra safeguards for searches of lawyers' offices where issues of professional confidentiality could be involved.[127] Moreover, the search had been carried out without the presence of an independent observer, and had been more extensive than was necessary for its stated purpose.

6–20   In *R. v Chesterfield Justices and anor., ex parte Bramley*[128] the Divisional Court applied the principles laid down in *Niemietz* in considering the scope of a police

---

[123] (1993) 16 E.H.R.R. 297.
[124] *ibid.*, paras 55–57.
[125] (1993) 16 E.H.R.R. 97.
[126] *ibid.*, paras 27–33.
[127] *ibid.*, para.37; see also *Kopp v Switzerland* [1998] E.H.R.L.R. 508. *Cf.* the "special procedure" under Sch.1 of PACE.
[128] [2000] 1 All E.R. 411.

officer's powers to seize and examine material which may be subject to legal professional privilege when executing a search warrant issued under s.8(1) of the Police and Criminal Evidence Act 1984. Under s.8(1) a magistrate may only issue a warrant if he has reasonable grounds for believing that the material on the premises does not consist of or include material subject to legal professional privilege. The court held that where the officer applying for a warrant makes no reference to privilege, the magistrate is required to ask whether the material sought included privileged material. If, having made inquiries on the point, the magistrate had reasonable grounds to believe that material sought included privileged material then the terms of the warrant must be redefined. Once the warrant had been issued, it was unnecessary for the police officer executing it to be independently satisfied that there were no reasonable grounds for believing that privileged material was included within the material sought. That qualification in s.8(1) is directed to the state of mind of the magistrate, not that of the officer executing the warrant. However, where the officer in fact has reasonable grounds for believing that material to be seized is covered by privilege, he has no power to seize it.[129] Moreover, the court held that an officer was not entitled to remove material for sifting outside the premises covered by the warrant. If he removed items which, on examination, turned out to be outside the scope of the warrant, then the 1984 Act afforded no defence to a claim in trespass. As Kennedy L.J. explained:

> "To put the matter in terms which would meet the requirements of the Convention, it seems to me that if in a democratic society it is necessary for the prevention of crime to invade privacy to a greater extent than is spelt out in the 1984 Act, then the limits of the invasion must be spelt out in the statute or in some regulations or code made thereunder, and there must be a convenient forum available for dealing with disputes. Meanwhile, in order to defend the right to privacy, I see no escape from the proposition that the words of the statute should be strictly applied."

Statutory authority for the practice of removal for sifting was subsequently given in the Criminal Justice and Police Act 2001.

The court has been especially cautious in considering searches conducted under executive warrant. In *Camezind v Switzerland*[130] the applicant was suspected of contravening telecommunications legislation by using an unauthorised cordless telephone. Under the relevant legislation the area director of the Post and Telecommunications Authority had power to issue a search warrant. The Court held that where a search took place without prior judicial authorisation, it was necessary to be "particularly vigilant" to ensure that the power was subject to very strict limits:

6–21

> "The Contracting States may consider it necessary to resort to measures such as searches of residential premises and seizures in order to obtain physical evidence of certain offences. The Court will assess whether the reasons adduced to justify such measures were relevant and sufficient and whether the aforementioned proportionality

---

[129] Although the court recognised in *Foxley v United Kingdom* (2001) 35 E.H.R.R. 637, at para.44, that in situations where the privilege is being abused or where there are other "exceptional circumstances", an interference with privileged communications might be justified.

[130] (1999) 28 E.H.R.R. 458.

principle has been adhered to. As regards the latter point, the Court must first ensure that the relevant legislation and practice afford individuals 'adequate and effective safeguards against abuse'; notwithstanding the margin of appreciation which the Court recognises the Contracting States have in this sphere, it must be particularly vigiliant where, as in the present case, the authorities are empowered under national law to order and effect searches without a judicial warrant. If individuals are to be protected from arbitrary interference by the authorities with the rights guaranteed under Article 8, a legal framework and very strict limits on such powers are called for. Secondly, the Court must consider the particular circumstances of each case in order to determine whether, in the concrete case, the interference in question was proportionate to the aim pursued."

6–22　　The safeguards in place in *Camezind* were similar to those imposed by ss.15 and 16 of PACE and Code B in respect of judicial warrants in England and Wales. The Court found these to be sufficient to meet the requirements of Art.8. In particular, the Court noted that a warrant could only be issued by officials of a certain level of seniority, and could only be executed by officials who had been specially trained for the purpose. Searches of dwellings had to take place at a reasonable time "except in important cases or where there is imminent danger". The person executing the search was required to produce evidence of identity, to inform the occupier of the purpose of the search, to permit the occupier to be present, to make a record of the search and to provide a copy of the record to the occupier. As to the facts, the applicant had been permitted to consult a lawyer and to read the file against him before the search began; the search had involved only one official and was confined to an examination of electrical equipment in the house. Having regard to the limited scope of the search, and the safeguards in place, the court found no violation of Art.8.

C. Comparative Approaches

6–23　　Decisions from other jurisdictions may assist in developing the principles on search and seizure under the Human Rights Act. Just as the European Court in *Funke* stated that the procedures for authorisation need not be judicial, so the Supreme Court of Canada has taken a similar view under the Charter. In *Hunter v Southam Inc*[131] the Supreme Court held that there must be a fair and independent procedure for prior authorisation of any search of premises. The authorisation need not be judicial, but it must be made by someone capable of acting judicially and independently, weighing the conflicting interests of law enforcement and individual liberty in an impartial way. This would rule out anyone connected with the investigatory or prosecutorial functions. In *Baron v Canada*[132] the Supreme Court made the further point that the process of authorisation must leave some discretion to the judge or other authorising person. A Canadian tax statute which provided that a judge "shall issue a warrant", if satisfied that there were reasonable grounds to believe that an offence under the statute had been committed, was therefore struck down as inconsistent with s.8 of the Charter.

---

[131] [1984] 2 S.C.R. 145.
[132] [1993] 1 S.C.R. 416.

Both these decisions make it clear that authorisation should only be given after 6–24 consideration of the rights of the person whose premises are to be searched, as well as the claims of the law enforcement agency. This point was elaborated in *Television New Zealand v Attorney-General*,[133] where the New Zealand Court of Appeal stated that, before issuing a search warrant in respect of the premises of a media organisation, courts must: (i) avoid, so far as possible, impairing the dissemination of news; (ii) only issue a warrant which might result in the "drying up" of confidential sources of information if this is "truly essential in the interests of justice"; and (iii) not grant a warrant unless the films to be seized are likely to have a direct and important place in any subsequent court case.[134] These three Commonwealth decisions demonstrate the need to give proper weight to the rights of the subject, including the right to freedom of expression and the right to privacy, when considering the grant of a search warrant.

---

[133] [1995] 2 N.Z.L.R. 641.
[134] *Per* Cooke P., at 648, on the last point following Lord Denning M.R. in *Senior v Holdsworth* [1976] Q.B. 23, at 34–35.

CHAPTER 7

COVERT INVESTIGATION

A. GENERAL PRINCIPLES

The decisions of the European Court establish a number of important principles **7–01** governing the use of covert investigative techniques, including secret surveillance. The exercise of such powers constitutes an "interference" with the right guaranteed by Art.8, and is tolerable in a democratic society only in so far as strictly necessary for safeguarding democratic institutions.[1] But in order to counter threats of espionage, terrorism or serious crime, secret surveillance can, in principle, be justified under Art.8(2).[2] Although states enjoy a certain latitude in deciding the conditions under which a system of surveillance can be operated, they do not enjoy an unlimited discretion to subject citizens to such forms of investigation. Since secret surveillance "can undermine or even destroy democracy on the ground of defending it", there must be adequate and effective safeguards against abuse.[3] It is not a requirement of Art.8 or Art.13 that supervision must be by a judge, but it should "normally be carried out by the judiciary, at least in the last resort, since judicial control affords the best guarantees of independence, impartiality and a proper procedure".[4] Supervisory bodies will be capable of providing an adequate and effective safeguard providing they enjoy sufficient independence to give an objective ruling.[5]

The requirement that covert investigation should be "in accordance with the **7–02** law" is not limited to an examination of whether a particular measure was permitted under domestic law. If it is conducted in breach of domestic law it will inevitably violate Art.8. In addition, however, the expression relates to the "quality" of the law governing the exercise of such powers. It must be "accessible and precise" and foreseeable as to its effects.[6] This does not entitle citizens to know in advance when the authorities are likely to observe or intercept their communications and thereby enable them to adapt their conduct. Nevertheless,

---

[1] *Klass v Germany* (1979–80) 2 E.H.R.R. 214; *Malone v United Kingdom* (1985) 7 E.H.R.R. 14; *Huvig v France* (1990) 12 E.H.R.R. 528.
[2] *Klass v Germany* (1979–80) 2 E.H.R.R. 214.
[3] *Klass v Germany* (1979–80) 2 E.H.R.R. 214.
[4] *Volokhy v Ukraine*, App.No.23543/02, Judgment November 2, 2006.
[5] *Klass v Germany* (1979–80) 2 E.H.R.R. 214.
[6] *Malone v United Kingdom* (1985) 7 E.H.R.R. 14.

the law must give an adequate indication of the circumstances in which, and the conditions under which, authorities are empowered to resort to "this secret and potentially dangerous interference with the right to respect for private life and correspondence".[7]

7–03   An unpublished non-statutory directive from a Department of State which is not legally binding is incapable of satisfying this requirement,[8] although it is not necessary that the framework of safeguards should be provided entirely by statute. If, however, the common law is relied upon then it must be sufficiently clear and unambiguous to enable a citizen to know the precise extent of his legal entitlements without the necessity for extrapolation.[9]

7–04   The rules must define with clarity the categories of citizens subject to orders authorising covert investigation techniques, the offences which might give rise to such orders and the permitted duration of any surveillance.[10] It should also indicate with precision the circumstances in which investigative authorities may store and use collected information, and when it should be destroyed.[11] Exhaustive definitions are not always necessary. It is sufficient for the law adequately to identify the types of activity which may fall within the scope of the power.[12] However, a constitutional provision which merely states that communications are to be private "unless the court decides otherwise" fails to indicate with sufficient certainty the extent of the authorities' discretion or the manner in which it is to be exercised.[13]

7–05   For the purposes of Art.8, it is unnecessary to establish that the contents of an intercepted conversation concerned matters of privacy.[14] However, additional safeguards apply where covert surveillance may intrude upon legal professional privilege. In *Kopp v Switzerland*[15] the Court emphasised the importance of protecting "a lawyer's work under instructions from a party to proceedings", and described it as "astonishing" that domestic law entrusted the authorisation of intrusive surveillance "in the sensitive area of the confidential relations between a lawyer and his clients" to an official "without supervision by an independent judge".

7–06   The Court has given an extended meaning to the term "victim" in this context. A relaxation of the "victim" requirement is necessary to ensure that the right of individual petition is effective. This is because it will usually be impossible for

---

[7] *Huvig v France* (1990) 12 E.H.R.R. 528; *Kruslin v France* (1990) 12 E.H.R.R. 547.
[8] *Hewitt and Harman v United Kingdom* (1992) 14 E.H.R.R. 657; *Khan v United Kingdom* (2001) 31 E.H.R.R. 1016.
[9] *Huvig v France* (1990) 12 E.H.R.R. 528.
[10] *Huvig v France* (1990) 12 E.H.R.R. 528; *Kruslin v France* (1990) 12 E.H.R.R. 547; *Valenzuela Contreras v Spain* (1999) 28 E.H.R.R. 483.
[11] *Amann v Switzerland* (2000) E.H.R.R. 843 para.50; *Rotaru v Romania* (2000) 8 B.H.R.C. 43; *Volokhy v Ukraine*, App.No.23543/02, Judgment 2 November 2006.
[12] In *Hewitt and Harman v United Kingdom* (1992) 14 E.H.R.R. 657 the Commission considered that it was unnecessary for legislation to define the term "interests of national security".
[13] *Valenzuela Contreras v Spain* (1999) 28 E.H.R.R. 483.
[14] *A v France* (1994) 17 E.H.R.R. 462.
[15] (1999) 27 E.H.R.R. 91 at para.74.

the individual to establish conclusively that he has been the subject of such measures. The Court has drawn a distinction here between complaints directed towards the existence of a regime which is alleged to fall short of the requirements of the Convention, and complaints concerning specific instances of unlawful activity by the state. In the former situation the Court has sometimes been prepared, in effect, to examine the impugned provisions of domestic law on their face. In the latter situation it has generally required the applicant to show a "reasonable likelihood" that he has been the subject of unlawful surveillance.

Thus, in *Klass v Germany*[16] the applicants' complaint concerned the absence of **7–07** legal safeguards governing intrusive surveillance in Germany. There was, however, no evidence to suggest that any of the applicants had been the subject of such surveillance (indeed, there was evidence to the contrary). The Court held that an applicant who seeks to challenge the compatibility of a regime authorising secret intelligence or surveillance techniques is not required to establish "any concrete measure specifically affecting him" since he will, by definition, be unaware of what has occurred. In order to ensure that the right of individual petition was effective in relation to such a complaint, any person who was potentially affected by secret surveillance could claim to be a "victim". This was held to include any user or potential user of the post or telecommunications systems:

"[A]n individual may, under certain conditions, claim to be the victim of a violation occasioned by the mere existence of secret measures or of legislation permitting secret measures, without having to allege that such measures were in fact applied to him. The relevant conditions are to be determined in each case according to the Convention right or rights alleged to have been infringed, the secret character of the measures objected to, and the connection between the applicant and those measures."

The Court adopted the same analysis in *Malone v United Kingdom*,[17] holding that **7–08** "the existence in England and Wales of laws and practices which permit and establish a system for effecting secret surveillance of communications amounted in itself to an 'interference' ".[18]

In *Halford v United Kingdom*,[19] by contrast, the Court applied a more restrictive **7–09** approach. There the applicant's complaint was not that the *regime* established by Interception of Communications Act 1985 was incompatible with Art.8,[20] but that her calls had been unlawfully intercepted, outside the Act's provisions. In this situation, the Court held, it was necessary for the applicant to establish a "reasonable likelihood" that the alleged interception had in fact occurred. Similarly, in *Hilton v United Kingdom*,[21] the Commission applied the "reasonable likelihood" test in determining whether a journalist could claim to be a victim of

---

[16] (1979–80) 2 E.H.R.R. 214.
[17] (1984) 7 E.H.R.R. 14.
[18] See para.63. See further *Iordachi v Moldova* App.No.25198/02, Admissibility decision of April 5, 2005.
[19] (1997) 24 E.H.R.R. 523 at paras 48 and 57.
[20] The 1985 Act had previously been found by the Commission to be compatible with the requirements of Art.8: *Christie v United Kingdom* (1994) 78A D.R. 119.
[21] (1986) 57 D.R. 108 at 118.

a violation of Art.8 arising out of the alleged retention of personal information on a security service file.

7–10   Where an invasion of privacy through secret surveillance infringes Art.8, it is immaterial that the complainant is not the primary victim of the invasion, providing that he has also been affected by it.[22] For the purposes of Art.8 therefore, it is irrelevant that the telephone or premises which are subject to surveillance did not belong to the victim.[23] In *Lambert v France*[24] the Court observed that any other conclusion; " . . . could lead to decisions whereby a large number of people are deprived of the protection of the law, namely all those who have conversations on a telephone line other than their own. That would in practice render the protective machinery largely devoid of substance." In this context, the regulation of surveillance should set out the necessary precautions as it affects those monitored "fortuitously" or as "necessary participants", even if they are not under suspicion themselves.[25]

7–11   Where surveillance has (or may have) occurred unlawfully, domestic law must provide an effective remedy before a national authority, whether or not the surveillance has resulted in a criminal prosecution.[26] Such an authority need not necessarily be judicial, and the nature of the remedy may be determined by the sensitivity of the information.[27]

7–12   The redress has to be as effective as it can be having regard to the restricted scope for recourse inherent in any system of secret surveillance.[28] However, it is not necessarily a requirement of a fair trial in Art.6 that evidence obtained in breach of Art.8 be excluded. The Court will examine the nature of the breach and the importance of the disputed evidence in the context of the proceedings as a whole. This issue is considered in further detail at para.7–62 below and in Ch.15.

B. EARLIER CHALLENGES TO THE UNITED KINGDOM'S COVERT SURVEILLANCE REGIME

7–13   Prior to the enactment of the Regulation of Investigatory Powers Act 2000 (RIPA),[29] the use of covert surveillance in the United Kingdom led to a number of adverse rulings in Strasbourg. The lack of an appropriate statutory regime was

---

[22] *Kruslin v France* (1990) 12 E.H.R.R. 547.

[23] *Khan v United Kingdom* (2001) 31 E.H.R.R. 1016.

[24] [1999] E.H.R.L.R. 123.

[25] See *Amann v Switzerland* (2000) E.H.R.R. 843 para.61.

[26] See generally Art.13 of the Convention. For a case in which a violation of Art.13 was found on this basis, see *Khan v United Kingdom* (2001) 31 E.H.R.R. 1016.

[27] *Klass v Germany* (1979–80) 2 E.H.R.R. 214 at para.67. This sits uneasily with the repeated statement that supervision should normally be by a judge "at least in the last resort", see para.7–01, above.

[28] *ibid.*, at para.69.

[29] Most parts of RIPA, with the notable exception of Pt III, came into force on October 2, 2000.

successfully challenged and the United Kingdom's response was piecemeal, reactive and inadequate. The Interception of Communications Act 1985, the Security Service Acts 1989 and 1996, the Intelligence Services Act 1994 and the Police Act 1997 were all introduced to redress or to forestall violations of Art.8, but left many issues unresolved.

RIPA has gone a long way towards meeting this country's obligations,[30] but it is **7–14** unfortunate that Parliament missed the opportunity to create a single unified regime providing for the consistent and coherent protection of privacy. Instead, RIPA sits alongside Pt III of the Police Act 1997 (which regulates powers connected with the interference with property) and the Intelligence Services Act 1994 (which governs authorisations for surveillance warrants for MI6 and GCHQ).[31] Accordingly, there remain different and overlapping procedures for authorisation, adding to the complexity of legal regulation in this area, rather than reducing it. This section outlines the evolution of the Court's case law in relation to the United Kingdom, and the legislative measures taken in response.

It begins with the position prior to the Interception of Communications Act 1985. **7–15** In *Malone v United Kingdom*[32] the Court held that the system under which telephone and mail interception was, at that time, conducted under a warrant issued by the Secretary of State, with no statutory framework, afforded insufficient legal protection to satisfy the requirements of Art.8. The Court held that:

> "[I]n its present state the law in England and Wales governing interception of communications for police purposes is somewhat obscure and open to differing interpretations . . . Detailed procedures concerning interception of communications on behalf of the police in England and Wales do exist. What is more, published statistics show the efficacy of those procedures in keeping the number of warrants granted relatively low, especially when compared with the rising number of indictable crimes committed and telephones installed. The public have been made aware of the applicable arrangements and principles through publication of the Birkett report and the White Paper and through statements by the responsible Ministers in Parliament. Nonetheless, on the evidence before the Court, it cannot be said with any reasonable certainty what elements of the powers to intercept are incorporated in legal rules and what elements remain within the discretion of the executive. In view of the attendant obscurity and uncertainty as to the state of the law in this essential respect, the Court cannot but reach a similar conclusion to that of the Commission [namely that Article 8 had been violated]. In the opinion of the Court, the law of England and Wales does not indicate with reasonable clarity the scope and manner of exercise of the relevant discretion conferred on the public authorities. To that extent the minimum degree of legal protection to which citizens are entitled under the rule of law in a democratic society is lacking."

The 1985 Act was a direct response to this ruling. It established a statutory **7–16** framework including a requirement for the prior issue of a warrant by the Secretary of State, and subsequent review by a Commissioner, acting as an

---

[30] This includes not merely its obligations to comply with the Convention, but, in this context, its obligations under Art.5 of the Telecommunications Data Protection Directive.
[31] See ss.5, 6 and 7 for the issuing of warrants under the Intelligence Services Act 1994.
[32] (1985) 7 E.H.R.R. 14.

independent tribunal. In passing the 1985 Act, Parliament endeavoured to limit the use to which the product of a telephone intercept would be put, and thus by extension, to protect rights of privacy. The Home Office White Paper[33] which preceded the 1985 Act, stated that; "The Bill will provide for controls over the use of intercepted material. By making such material generally inadmissible in legal proceedings it will ensure that interception can be used only as an aspect of investigation, not prosecution."[34]

7–17   However, secret surveillance of private property through the use of bugging devices remained entirely unregulated by statute until the Security Service Act 1989.[35] Such surveillance is of course as much an intrusion on privacy as a telephone interception. Indeed, it frequently involves a greater intrusion, since access is often gained to private property in order to "plant" a device. Prior to the 1989 Act, however, the Security Service had no statutory mandate for their activities in this respect. In *Hewitt and Harman v United Kingdom*[36] the Commission concluded that the absence of a legislative framework had led to a violation of the applicants' rights under Art.8. Based on an affidavit of a former MI5 agent, Cathy Massiter, the applicants alleged that personal information about them had been compiled by MI5 because of their positions as the General Secretary and Legal Officer of the National Council for Civil Liberties (now Liberty). The information derived in part from telephone and mail intercepts directed towards other people, and was retained because of their alleged left wing sympathies. Assuming the allegations to be correct, the Commission held that such activities required clear legal authority, which was absent:

> "The Commission notes that the activities of the Security Service are governed by a Directive of the Home Secretary to the Director-General of the Security Service dated 24 September 1952. Although the Directive is published, it is not claimed by the Government that it has the force of law or that its contents constitute legally enforceable rules concerning the operation of the Security Service. Nor does the Directive provide a framework which indicates with the requisite degree of certainty the scope and manner of the exercise of discretion by the authorities in the carrying out of secret surveillance activities. The Commission finds that in these circumstances the interference with the applicants' right to respect for private life was not 'in accordance with the law' ".

7–18   Following this decision, the 1989 Act was passed to place MI5 onto a statutory footing, and to provide a system of prior authorisation for intrusive surveillance. Under the Act an application for a warrant to enable the Security Services (MI5) to interfere with property or wireless telegraphy was to be made to the Secretary of State, and was subject to scrutiny by a Tribunal and Commissioner. This procedure was extended to encompass the Intelligence Services (MI6) and

---

[33] *The Interception of Communications in the United Kingdom* Cmnd.9438.
[34] Confirmed by the House of Lords in *R. v Preston* [1994] 2 A.C. 130 *per* Lord Mustill at 147. See, further, para.7–35, below.
[35] See now the Intelligence Services Act 1994, as amended by the Security Service Act 1996.
[36] (1992) 14 E.H.R.R. 657.

GCHQ by the Intelligence Services Act 1994.[37] In *Esbester v United Kingdom*[38] the Commission held that the new framework was sufficient to meet the requirements of Art.8:

> "In the absence of any evidence or indication that the system is not functioning as required by domestic law, the Commission finds that the framework of safeguards achieves a compromise between the requirements of defending a democratic society and the rights of the individual, which is compatible with the provisions of the Convention."

Subsequent challenges to the scope of the legislation were equally unsuccessful. **7–19** In *Hewitt and Harman v United Kingdom (No.2)*[39] the Commission dismissed as manifestly ill-founded a complaint that the term "national security" in the 1989 Act was unduly vague:

> "The principles [in Article 8(2)] do not necessarily require a comprehensive definition of the notion of 'the interests of national security' . . . the Commission considers that in the present case the law is formulated with sufficient precision to enable the applicants to anticipate the role of the Security Service."

And in *Christie v United Kingdom*[40] the Commission reached a similar conclu- **7–20** sion in relation to the term "economic well-being of the country" (in both the 1985 and the 1989 Acts):

> "It is compatible with the requirements of foreseeability that terms which are on their face general and unlimited are explained by administrative or executive statements and instructions, since it is the provision of sufficiently precise guidance to enable individuals to regulate their conduct, rather than the source of that guidance, which is of relevance."

By 1989, therefore, the United Kingdom had adopted acceptable legislation **7–21** governing interception of mail and telecommunications, and the conduct of intrusive surveillance by the Security Service. However, other forms of intrusive surveillance conducted by the *police* were not covered by either Act. Although bugging devices had been used routinely in major police investigations for many years, they had been subject only to non-statutory guidelines issued by the Home Office.[41] According to Home Office statistics in 1995 (the year the Interception of Communications Act was passed) there were approximately 2,100 authorisations by chief officers of intrusive surveillance operations in the United Kingdom undertaken by the police and customs.[42] This figure included 1,300 authorisations by police officers in England and Wales. Despite the prevalence of the practice, one former Home Secretary said during a Parliamentary debate in 1997

---

[37] S.5(3) of the 1994 Act originally prohibited the grant of a warrant in respect of criminal investigations which did not involve an element of national security where the action to be taken related to property in the British Isles. This prohibition was lifted so far as the Security Services were concerned by s.2 of the Security Services Act 1996.

[38] (1993) 18 E.H.R.R. CD 72.

[39] Application No.20317/92, September 1, 1993.

[40] (1994) 78–A D.R. 119 at 134.

[41] The Guidelines on the Use of Equipment in Police Surveillance Operations (December 19, 1984, Dep. NS 1579).

[42] HC Debs, col.512 (January 21, 1997).

that he had no knowledge of the scale of intrusive surveillance by the police during his term of office.[43]

7–22   The inadequacy of the Home Office guidelines as a system of supervising secret surveillance was brought into focus by the decision of the House of Lords in *R. v Khan*.[44] The defendant in that case was charged with importation of heroin. Acting on the authority of a chief constable, police officers placed a listening device in a house in which he was staying and recorded a series of highly incriminating conversations. At his trial the defendant argued that the tapes had been obtained in consequence of an act of criminal damage and/or trespass. In upholding the applicant's conviction, the Court of Appeal observed that;

> "There are, in the United Kingdom, no statutory provisions which govern the use by the police of secret listening devices on private property. This is to be contrasted with the position in relation to the interception of public telephone calls or postal communications . . . It is also to be contrasted with the controls on the use of surveillance devices by the security service, laid down in the Security Service Act 1989 . . . The Home Office guidelines, and other documents to which we have been referred, certainly prescribe criteria and procedures limiting such use. However, although not a legal rule, 'an Englishman's home is his castle' is a tenet jealously held and widely respected. It is, in our view, at least worthy of consideration as to whether the circumstances in which bugging a private home by the police can be justified should be the subject of statutory control. It may be thought that such control is, by analogy with the 1985 Act, just as desirable for bugging devices as for telephone tapping."

7–23   In the House of Lords, Lord Nolan similarly observed that;

> "The sole cause of this case coming to your Lordships' House is the lack of a statutory system regulating the use of surveillance devices by the police. The absence of such a system seems astonishing, the more so in view of the statutory framework which has governed the use of such devices by the Security Service since 1989, and the interception of communications by the police as well as by other agencies since 1985."

7–24   When the case was considered in Strasbourg, the absence of a statutory regime for the use of covert listening devices by the police was held to be conclusive of a violation of Art.8. In *Khan v United Kingdom*[45] the Court held that the Home Office guidelines were neither legally binding nor publicly accessible and the interference was therefore inadequately regulated by law.[46] Moreover, the Court held that there was no effective remedy for the violation, as required by Art.13 of the Convention. In the absence of a statutory scheme there was no procedure for determining complaints. The discretion to exclude evidence under s.78 of the Police and Criminal Evidence Act 1984 was held to be inadequate because, prior to the enactment of the Human Rights Act 1998, the national courts did not have jurisdiction under s.78 to determine the substance of the applicant's complaint, nor did they have power to grant appropriate relief for the violation. Significantly,

---

[43] Lord Callaghan HL Debs, col.401 (January 20, 1997).

[44] [1997] A.C. 558.

[45] (2001) 31 E.H.R.R. 1016.

[46] In accordance with *Khan v UK* the Court has found violations of that surveillance regime in *Allan v UK* (2003) 36 E.H.R.R. 12; *Hewiston v UK* (2003) 37 E.H.R.R. 31; *Chalkley v UK* (2003) 37 E.H.R.R. 30; *Perry v UK* (2004) 39 E.H.R.R. 3; *Lewis v UK* (2004) 39 E.H.R.R. 9 and *Wood v UK*, App.No.23414/02, Judgment of November 16, 2004.

the court also held that the system for investigating complaints against the police established in Pt IX of the 1984 Act failed to meet the standards of independence necessary to constitute sufficient protection against abuse of authority, and thus to provide an effective remedy within the meaning of Art.13.[47]

The journey of *Khan's* case through the courts was the immediate catalyst for Pt   **7–25** III of the Police Act 1997. As originally drafted, the Police Bill was plainly inadequate to meet the requirements of Art.8. In stark contrast to the previous legislation dealing with covert surveillance, the original proposals contained no requirement for prior independent authorisation. The decision was to reside with the authorising police officer alone. Following extensive political pressure in the House of Lords and in the media, amendments to the Bill were passed requiring certain types of surveillance to have the prior approval of an independent Commissioner, with the rank of a High Court judge or above. The scope of Pt III of the Act extends only to "entry on or interference with property or wireless telegraphy".[48] It does not therefore regulate other forms of covert surveillance which require no physical entry onto property, such as the use of long distance microphones. Initial authorisation may be given by an authorising officer, who must hold the rank of chief officer or above,[49] and may cover "the taking of such action, in respect of such property . . . as the authorising officer may specify".[50] This surprisingly broad formulation appears to impose no limits on the action which could be authorised. However, if the property to be entered is a dwelling, a hotel bedroom or an office then the authorisation will not take effect unless it has the prior approval of a Commissioner.[51] The same procedure applies if the surveillance is liable to reveal information subject to legal professional privilege, confidential personal information, or confidential journalistic material.[52] The Commissioner's prior approval is not, however, required if the authorising officer believes the case is urgent.[53]

Authorisation and approval is only to be given where the action to be taken is   **7–26** likely to be of substantial value in the prevention or detection of serious crime. Its purpose must be proportionate to what the action seeks to achieve, which includes considering whether it may be done by other means.[54] A crime is "serious" for this purpose if it would be likely to result in a sentence of three years imprisonment or more, or if it involves violence, results in substantial financial gain, or is "conduct by a large number of persons in pursuit of a common purpose".[55] This wording follows that of the Interception of Communications Act 1985 and the Intelligence Services Act 1994. However, as Lord

---

[47] See also *Govell v United Kingdom* [1999] E.H.R.L.R. 121, since affirmed by the Committee of Ministers (Resolution D.H. (98) 212. The framework for making complaints has since been changed by the Police Reform Act 2002 which replaced the Police Complaints Authority with a new Independent Police Complaints Commission.
[48] S.92.
[49] S.93.
[50] S.93(1).
[51] S.97(2)(a).
[52] S.97(2)(b).
[53] S.97(3).
[54] S.93(2).
[55] S.93(4).

Browne-Wilkinson pointed out during debates on the Bill,[56] the definition is wide enough to encompass many organised protest groups:

> "Suppose Mr A is one of a large number of protestors against making a new road; for example the Newbury bypass. The form of the protest, as in all these cases, is likely to involve the commission of a crime; for example criminal damage to property or obstruction of the police. Such crime will, to some eyes surprisingly, constitute a serious crime within the meaning of the Bill, because it is a large number of persons acting together".

7–27   It remains open to question whether the regime established by the 1997 Act complies with Art.8 in all respects. As to the legal framework, it is at least arguable that the absence of a general requirement for prior independent authorisation may, in certain cases, lead to a violation of the Convention. The Court's approach in *Lambert v France*[57] might suggest that confining the requirement for independent authorisation to the bugging of a person's home or office, or to specified categories of sensitive information, is inadequate. Moreover, the provisions permitting the use of a listening device in a lawyer's office without prior approval in cases of urgency are difficult to reconcile with the strong statements of principle in *Kopp v Switzerland*.[58] As to the ground for authorisation, it must be open to doubt whether that the Strasbourg Court would consider the use of intrusive surveillance powers against political protesters, in the circumstances envisaged by Lord Browne-Wilkinson, to be a proportionate response to the prevention of crime or disorder.

7–28   These issues aside, the 1997 Act left a number of significant holes in the statutory regime. In particular:

(1) A range of intrusive surveillance devices and other types of covert investigation techniques were already available to the police, which did not require either the interception of a telephone call or an entry onto property. Prior to RIPA, these techniques were not covered by legislation and lacked any system of authorisation or independent scrutiny. Their use was accordingly unlawful in Art.8 terms.

(2) Interceptions of calls on a private telecommunications network were not covered by the 1985 Act, notwithstanding that in *Halford v United Kingdom*[59] the court found a violation of Art.8 where the alleged interception occurred on a private network.

(3) In the case of portable telephones used in the home, the House of Lords had held that the interception of radio signals passing between the handset and the base unit were did not form part of a public telecommunications system.[60] The consequence of this ruling was that the

---

[56] HL Debs, cols 811–812 (November 11, 1996).
[57] [1999] E.H.R.L.R. 123.
[58] (1999) 27 E.H.R.R. 91 at para.74, see para.7–03 above.
[59] (1997) 24 E.H.R.R. 523.
[60] *R. v Effick* [1995] 1 A.C. 309. This principle does not apply to mobile telephones: HC Debs, cols 158–159 (March 11, 1997).

interception of calls ostensibly on a public network, but received on a portable handset, was also unregulated by statute.

C. THE REGULATION OF INVESTIGATORY POWERS ACT 2000

RIPA remedies many of the shortcomings in the previous regime outlined above,   7–29
and is reinforced by Codes of Practice which a court must take into account.[61] A detailed analysis of the provisions of RIPA is outside the scope of this work,[62] but its main provisions are summarised below.

I. Interceptions

Part I of RIPA replaces the Interception of Communications Act 1985[63] with a   7–30
statutory framework encompassing interception of communications on both public and private networks.[64] Pt I includes interception of postal communications[65] as well as telephone intercepts and email.[66] Pt I also establishes a regulatory structure for access to and handling of "communications data".[67]

---

[61] See S.I. 2002/1693 "Interception Code of Practice"; S.I. 2002/1933 "Covert Surveillance Code of Practice" and S.I. 2002/1932 "Covert Human Intelligence Sources Code of Practice" issued pursuant to s.71 of RIPA. For the potentially serious consequences of breach see *R. v Raymond Harmes and Gary Cranes* [2006] EWCA Crim. 928.

[62] For a critical assessment of the Act see the articles by Akdeniz, Taylor and Walker [2001] Crim. L.R. 73; Mirfield [2001] Crim. L.R. 91; Ormerod and McKay [2004] Crim. LR 15.

[63] Sch.5 of RIPA replaces ss.1–10, 11(3)–(5) and Sch.1 of the 1985 Act.

[64] A private telecommunications system is one which is attached, directly or indirectly to a public telecommunications system: s.2(1).

[65] The redirection of postal communications to a trustee in bankruptcy may is not an interception and therefore is in accordance with law, provided it is tightly constrained. In *Foxley v United Kingdom* (2000) 31 E.H.R.R. 25, a Receiver was appointed under s.80(2) of the Criminal Justice Act 1988 to enforce a confiscation order made following the applicant's conviction for offences of corruption arising out of his employment with the Ministry of Defence. The same individual was appointed as Trustee in Bankruptcy in parallel civil proceedings brought by the Ministry. An order for re-direction of the applicant's mail was made under s.371 of the Insolvency Act 1986 in favour of the Trustee in Bankruptcy. During the currency of the order letters passing between the applicant and his legal advisers were opened, and copies retained. The court observed that it could "see no justification for this procedure" and considered that "the action taken was not in keeping with the principles of confidentiality and professional privilege attaching to relations between a lawyer and his client". Accordingly, the opening and copying of these letters amounted to a disproportionate interference. In addition, certain packages had been opened after the order had expired, due to an administrative oversight. Here, the position was even more straightforward. The Trustee in Bankruptcy must have known the terms of the order she had applied for. Since that order had expired, there was no legal basis for the interference.

[66] See, for example, *R. v Ipswich Crown Court Ex parte NTL Group Ltd* [2002] 3 W.L.R. 1173.

[67] "Communications data" is defined to include the address or other information attached to a communication, any information (other than the contents of the communication) which records the use of postal or telecommunications systems, and any other information which is held the provider of post or telecommunications service about users of that service: s.21. It thus includes "cell site analysis" or what used to be known as "metering" information of the kind in issue in *Malone v United Kingdom* (1984) 7 E.H.R.R. 14. Under ss.22 and 23 a "designated person" may serve a notice requiring the production of such data on grounds which mirror the grounds on which the Secretary of State may grant an interception warrant. There are, however, no statutory restrictions on the disclosure in criminal proceedings or use in evidence of communications data.

7–31   Under s.1(1) it is an offence intentionally and without "lawful authority" to intercept any communication in the course of its transmission by a public postal service or public telecommunications system. It is similarly an offence to do so with regard to a private telecommunications system, unless it is done by or on behalf of a person who has the right to control or operate that system.[68] Even then, the interception would still give rise to civil liability.[69]

7–32   The "lawful authority" required for an interception may be provided by a warrant issued under Pt I of RIPA. Sections 5 to 11 set out the requirements relevant to the application and issuing of warrants under Pt 1. They are issued by the Secretary of State (other than in cases of emergency) and he must be satisfied that the warrant is necessary in the interests of national security; for the purpose of preventing or detecting serious crime (including giving effect to the provisions of any international mutual assistance agreement); or for the purposes of safeguarding the economic well-being of the United Kingdom. The latter reason only applies to obtaining information relating to acts or intentions of persons outside the British Islands. Mirroring the requirements of Art.8, a warrant should only be issued if to do so is proportionate to what it seeks to achieve, including taking into account whether that aim could be achieved by other means. Section 9 sets out the duration of Pt I warrants, including procedures for their extension.

7–33   Significantly, ss.3 and 4 of RIPA make it clear that some types of interceptions have lawful authority, but do not require a warrant. These include telephone communications to or from prisoners or patients in high security psychiatric institutions. There are two other categories worthy of note. The first applies where an interception is carried out with reasonable grounds for believing that both parties consent.[70] The second, more controversially, allows an interception to occur where one party consents, and the surveillance has been authorised under Pt II of RIPA. The importance of this provision is that it takes an interception that would need to meet the strict requirements of a warrant under Pt I, and places it under the much less stringent regime of Pt II.[71] Whether the fact that one party to the communication consents to the interception without the knowledge of the other, justifies placing this type of interception outside Pt I of RIPA is debateable.[72]

7–34   It is also important to note that the definition of a telecommunications "interception" only covers conduct which interferes or modifies a communication so as to make its contents available, while being transmitted, to a third party.[73] Therefore devices which allow for eavesdropping on conversations and which record the content of telephone conversations but do not interfere with a signal

---

[68] See s.1(2). For consideration of the meaning of "right to control or operate" see *R. v Stanford* [2006] 1 W.L.R. 1554.

[69] S.1(3).

[70] S.3(1).

[71] There has been some confusion as to whether recording by a participant in the call was a permitted interception, or whether it fell outside the definition of interception (see, for examples, *R. v Hammond, McIntosh and Gray* [2002] EWCA 1423, paras 6 and 7, considering the meaning of interception under the 1985 Act.).

[72] See Ormerod and McKay [2004] Crim. L.R. 15.

[73] See s.2(2).

in transmission, fall outside Pt I and potentially into Pt II.[74] This may even include a recording device in the ear of an officer making a telephone call, which records the conversation virtually at the instance it is received by the phone.[75]

Sections 15 and 16 of RIPA set out safeguards for the copying, storing and **7-35** destruction of intercept material. Intercept material must be destroyed when there are no longer grounds for retaining it for the "authorised purposes" set out at 15(4). Perhaps the most significant of these is at s.15(4(d), where retention is necessary "to ensure that a person conducting a criminal prosecution has the information he needs to determine what is required of him by his duty to secure the fairness of the prosecution". On one view, this should result in the retention of all intercept material that may be relevant to a criminal trial, until the end of the trial process. However, to do so would be contrary to the opinions of the House of Lords in *R. v Preston*.[76] In that case, their Lordships held that purposes for which the intercept was authorised under s.2(2) of the 1985 Act, "the prevention and detection of serious crime" did not include the prosecution of an offence.[77] Ensuring fairness at trial could not, therefore, be a reason for retention of the intercept material. Accordingly, intercept material would normally be destroyed at the point of charge.

The policy of early destruction emerging from *Preston* appears to be wholly **7-36** inconsistent with the competing policy considerations behind s.15(4)(d). Unfortunately, RIPA provides no specific, detailed guidance, even in the Codes of Practice, as to when intercept material should be destroyed in order to ensure that the authorised purpose in s.15(4)(d) can be fulfilled. What guidance there is, suggests that there is a real possibility that the *Preston* approach is still being followed. For example, the Interception of Communications Code of Practice[78] suggest that the in the normal course of events it would be "rare" for intercept material *not* to have been destroyed prior to the commencement of a criminal charge.[79]

If that is the case, the lack of clear guidance on this issue in Pt I of RIPA is a **7-37** serious oversight. Routine destruction of intercept material at the point of charge would mean that, in practice, a continuing assessment of the significance of the intercept material in ensuring the fairness of a prosecution would not be possible. This is particularly alarming since it may only be after charge, or during the trial itself, that the relevance and importance of intercept material to the fairness of a

---

[74] See, for example, *R. v Allsop* [2005] EWCA Crim 703; *R. v E* [2004] 1 W.L.R. 3279. At times there appears to have been definitional confusion in the judgments. For example, in *R. v Hardy and Hardy* [2003] 1 Cr.App.R. 30 the Court of Appeal indicated that recorded telephone conversations which did not interrupt the signal in transmission were not "interceptions" but went on to consider s.3(2) of RIPA, which would only be applicable if a recording was an "interception".

[75] See the first instance decision of *R. v McDonald*, Woolwich Crown Court, April 23, 2002, Astill J.

[76] [1994] 2 A.C. 130.

[77] The 1985 Act did not have any equivalent section to RIPA 15(4). Different considerations would apply for authorisations pursuant to the Intelligence Services Act 1994.

[78] S.I. 2002/1693, issued under s.71 of RIPA.

[79] See S.I. 2002/1693 para.7.2.

trial becomes clear. Furthermore, a miscarriage of justice caused by the prosecutor not having access to such material could not be identified because the material would not exist. For reasons set out in the following paragraph, this potential difficulty is exacerbated by a more fundamental problem.

Section 17 of RIPA and the prohibition of disclosure of intercept material

7-38 Section 17 of RIPA ensures that the United Kingdom interception regime remains unique in Europe and virtually alone in the world,[80] by preserving the principle contained in s.9 of the Interception of Communications Act 1985. It states that no evidence can be adduced, no question asked, assertion or disclosure made or other thing done in, for the purposes of, or in connection with any legal proceedings, which is likely to reveal the existence of or application for an interception warrant or the commission of an offence under s.1 by any public official.

7-39 The prohibition does not apply to all intercept material. For example, it does not prohibit the use in evidence, even by analogy of reasoning, of intercept material from a foreign jurisdiction[81] and it does not prohibit the use of intercept material obtained lawfully by way of ss.3 or 4.[82] However, in practice, it bans the disclosure and use of a whole category of potentially probative and important material in the context of a criminal prosecution. It is, unsurprisingly, a highly controversial provision.[83]

7-40 In an effort to reduce the obvious difficulties s.17 might present to a criminal trial, s.18 provides a range of measures to assist the prosecutor and court in their duties pursuant to Art.6. Section 18(7)(a) specifically provides that the prohibition on disclosure does not operate to prevent disclosure to a prosecutor for the purpose of enabling him "to determine what is required of him by his duty to secure the fairness of the prosecution". This must be read in conjunction with s.18(7)(b), (8) and (9) which together provide that a judge may order the prosecution to disclose the material to the court alone (presumably in the course of a public interest immunity hearing) but only where the "exceptional circumstances of the case make the disclosure essential in the interests of justice". Where the judge makes such an order he may, after having considered the material, direct the prosecutor to make any admission of fact which he considers essential in the interests of justice, but may not order the prosecutor to disclose the material itself, or facts relating to the circumstances in which it was obtained.[84] Quite how effective such a constrained admission could be in ensuring a fair trial, in practice, is questionable. A number of commentators have argued[85] that this procedure fails to secure equality of arms between the parties

---

[80] S.17(1). The only other legal system with a similar (but less draconian) provision is Hong Kong, which was a British colony until 1997.
[81] See *R. v Aujla* [1998] Cr.App.R 16; *R. v X, Y and Z, The Times* May 23, 2000.
[82] S.18(4).
[83] See Justice's report *Intercept Evidence: Lifting the Ban*, by Eric Metcalfe, October 2006, which provides a thorough analysis of the arguments in favour of abolition of the rule.
[84] S.18(10).
[85] [2001] Crim. L.R. 91.

and sits uneasily with the Court's judgment in *Rowe and Davis v United Kingdom*.[86] The problems that this rule creates in prosecutions following surveillance operations are discussed further in Ch.15.

II. Directed Surveillance, Intrusive Surveillance and the use of Covert Human Intelligence Sources

Part II of RIPA introduces regulatory procedures for many other types of investigative conduct, by technology or by human beings, that previously had no statutory basis. It is intended to regulate covert behaviour which does not involve a physical entry onto property and which is therefore outside the existing statutory authorisation powers in the Police Act 1997 and the Intelligence Services Act 1994 (the relevant provisions of which remain in force). There are three forms of "covert" conduct which are covered: "directed" surveillance, "intrusive" surveillance and the use of "covert human intelligence sources" (CHIS).   **7–41**

Surveillance is "covert" if, and only if, it is carried out in a manner calculated to ensure that persons who are subject to the surveillance are unaware that it is taking place.[87] Part II also defines a "covert purpose"[88] and the covert use of a relationship, or covert disclosure of information.[89]   **7–42**

Directed surveillance consists of covert (but not "intrusive") monitoring, observing or listening for the purposes of a specific investigation that is likely to reveal private information, including details of a person's private life.[90]   **7–43**

Intrusive surveillance is covert surveillance carried out in relation to anything taking place on residential premises[91] or in any private vehicle, whether carried out by a person or a device.[92] Where a device is used which is located outside the premises, it must be capable of providing information of the same quality and detail as might be expected from an internally placed device in order to qualify as intrusive.[93] It does not therefore include unaided visual observation from an external observation post. Electronic tracking devices are expressly excluded.   **7–44**

Covert human intelligence sources are persons who establish or maintain a personal or other relationship with another, for the "covert purpose" of using such a relationship to obtain information or to provide access to any information   **7–45**

---

[86] (2000) 30 E.H.R.R. 1.
[87] S.26(9)(a).
[88] S.26(9)(b).
[89] S.26(9)(c).
[90] S.26(2).
[91] The exclusion of business premises does not appear to cater for premises where there is a reasonable expectation of privacy, such as the business premises at issue in *Niemietz v Germany* (1992) 16 E.H.R.R. 97. See also *P.G. and J.H v United Kingdom* [2002] Crim. L.R. 308 and *Perry v United Kingdom* (2004) 39 E.H.R.R. 3, both of which held that there were reasonable expectations of privacy outside residential premises.
[92] S.26(3).
[93] S.26(5).

to another person.[94] The definition includes those who covertly disclose information obtained through the use of such a relationship.[95] The inclusion of this type of covert activity within an Art.8 compliant regime is welcomed. It has been encouraged by the Commission, but has been the subject of a number of conflicting decisions by the Court.[96]

7–46   Where a CHIS has been authorised, there must at all times be an office holder who is responsible for day to day dealings with the source and for their welfare and security (a designated handler); another office holder who has general oversight of the use made of the source (a designated controller); and a person who at all times is responsible for maintaining a record of the use made of the source.[97] As discussed above, where a source is used to make a telephone conversation which is recorded with the consent of the source, the resulting surveillance is to be treated as directed surveillance and is not subject to the controls of Pt I of the Act.

7–47   A variety of public authorities may authorise RIPA regulated surveillance under Pt II, depending on the type of surveillance in issue. In relation to "directed surveillance", this may involve a large group of relevant agencies listed in Pts I and II of Sch.1 to RIPA. In relation to CHIS, only those public authorities listed in Pt I of Sch.1 are included. In contrast, "intrusive surveillance" may only be authorised by an even more limited category of persons set out at s.32(6). Similarly, the authorisation procedure depends upon the type of surveillance being considered, and the appropriate authorisation officer within the relevant agency is determined by secondary legislation.

7–48   *Directed surveillance and the use of CHIS* may be authorised by an officer of the relevant agency holding the appropriate rank.[98] In the context of the police, this would be the rank equivalent to Superintendent or above, unless the case is urgent when it may be authorised by an officer of the rank of Inspector or above. The authorisation may be given only where it is necessary on one of the specified grounds and where the action to be authorised is proportionate to the end sought

---

[94] S.26(8).

[95] *Ibid.*

[96] See *Ludi v Switzerland* (1993) 15 E.H.R.R. 173; *Speckman v United Kingdom* Application No.27; *A v France* (1994) 17 E.H.R.R. 462; *Smith v United Kingdom* [1997] E.H.R.L.R. 277; *Allan v United Kingdom* (2003) 36 E.H.R.R. 12. For comparative cases in other jurisdictions, see *United States v White* 410 US 745 (1971); *Duarte* [1990] 1 S.C.R. 30; *Hebert* [1990] 2 S.C.R. 151; *Broyles* [1991] 3 S.C.R. 595; *Liew* [1999] 3 S.C.R. 227; *R. v Swaffield and Pavic* [1998] H.C.A. 1. The New Zealand Court of Appeal in *A* [1994] 1 N.Z.L.R. 429 accepted the reasoning in *Duarte* to the extent of holding that participant recording constitutes a "search and seizure", and then held that in deciding whether the intrusion was unreasonable a court should consider *inter alia* the seriousness of the crime under investigation. *Cf.* also *Barlow* (1995) 14 C.R.N.Z. 9.

[97] S.28(5).

[98] Regulation of Investigatory Powers (Prescription of Offices, Ranks and Positions) Order 2000, S.I. 2000/12417 (made under sub-ss.(1), (3)). Regulation of Investigatory Powers (Directed Surveillance and Covert Human Intelligence Sources) (Amendment) Order 2005, S.I. 2005/11084 (made under sub-ss.(1), (3), (5)(a), (b), (6)). Regulation of Investigatory Powers (Directed Surveillance and Covert Human Intelligence Sources) (Amendment) Order 2006, S.I. 2006/11874 (made under sub-ss.(1), (3), (5), (6)).

to be achieved.[99] The statutory grounds are national security, the prevention or detection of serious crime, the protection of the economic well-being of the United Kingdom, the interests of public safety, the protection of health, the assessment or collection of any tax or levy due to any government department, or for any other purpose which the Secretary of State may order.[100]

Intrusive surveillance is subject to a stricter authorisation procedure similar to   **7–49** that established under Pt III of the Police Act 1997. Authorisation may only be given on grounds of national security, the prevention or detection of serious crime or the economic well-being of the United Kingdom.[101] Authorisation is subject to the requirements of necessity and proportionality, including a mandatory consideration of whether the information could reasonably be obtained by other means.[102] The level of authorisation may be reduced in situations of urgency.

Once authorisation for intrusive surveillance has been given, a Surveillance   **7–50** Commissioner must be notified as soon as reasonably practicable. In general, the authorisation does not take effect until the Commissioner has granted prior approval. In urgent cases, the authorisation may take effect without prior approval, but the senior authorising officer must then notify the Commissioner as soon as reasonably practicable, setting out the reason for proceeding without prior approval. The Commissioner may quash any authorisation if he believes the statutory criteria have not been met or have since ceased to apply. A relevant senior officer has the right to appeal the decision of a Commissioner to the Chief Surveillance Commissioner.[103]

RIPA also contains provisions as to the information to be included within an   **7–51** application under Pt II, and provides that the authorisation must be given in writing unless the case is urgent. It sets out requirements for the duration of authorisations, extensions, and the keeping of records.

There is no equivalent of s.17 in relation to material obtained under Pt II. There   **7–52** is therefore no statutory restriction on the disclosure in criminal proceedings of information obtained under Pt II, nor on its use in evidence.

The Codes of Practice under both Pts I and II afford additional protection for   **7–53** material subject to legal professional privilege, confidential journalistic material and confidential personal information. They also require that those engaged in surveillance consider the potential "collateral intrusion" on those who are not the direct subjects of the investigation.

III. Investigation of electronic data protected by encryption

Part III provides new and potentially far-reaching powers for official access to   **7–54** electronic data protected by encryption, and includes an authorisation procedure

---

[99] S.28(2).
[100] S.28(3).
[101] S.32(3).
[102] S.32(2) and (4).
[103] S.35.

for requiring access to decrypted information, and the production of encryption keys. It sets the procedure for an authorisation of an order under 49 for the relevant production. It also creates offences of failing to comply with such a notice,[104] and of "tipping off" in relation to a notice.[105] At the time of writing, Pt III was still not in force.

IV. Scrutiny of Investigatory Powers

7–55　　Part IV establishes the machinery for scrutinising the investigatory powers conferred by RIPA. It created three commissioners—the Interception of Communications Commissioner[106] (to replace the Commissioner under s.8 of the Interception of Communications Act 1985), the Intelligence Services Commissioner (to replace the Commissioners under s.4 of the Security Service Act 1989 and s.8 of the Intelligence Services Act 1994) and an Investigatory Powers Commissioner for Northern Ireland. Each Commissioner must hold, or have held "high judicial office".[107] The Commissioners established by Pt III of the Police Act 1997 are given additional functions.

7–56　　Section 65 established a single Regulation of Investigatory Powers Tribunal replaced the tribunals under the Security Services Act, the Intelligence Services Act and the Police Act. The Tribunal has jurisdiction to determine[108];

(1)　any claim under s.7(1)(a) of the Human Rights Act 1998 in relation to an act or omission of the intelligence services or any public authority concerning the use of powers under the RIPA or any other entry on or interference with property or wireless telegraphy which is alleged to be incompatible with a Convention right;

(2)　any complaint concerning the use of powers under RIPA or any other entry on or interference with wireless telegraphy which is alleged to have been carried out by the intelligence services or by another public authority under a warrant, authorisation, authority or permission granted under the Act, or where the circumstances are alleged to be such that it would not have been appropriate for the conduct to take place without authorisation, or without proper consideration having been given to whether authorisation should have been sought;

(3)　any complaint alleging that the complainant has suffered detriment as the result of any prohibition under s.17 on his relying in, or for the purposes of, any civil proceedings on any matter; and

(4)　Proceedings against the intelligence services or their conduct, including proceedings relating to inclusion on the National Identity Register.

---

[104] S.53.
[105] S.54.
[106] S.57(1).
[107] S.57(5); 59(5), 61(8).
[108] S.65.

Subject to a one year time limit, the Tribunal must investigate whether the person   **7–57**
against whom the complaint is made has engaged in any such conduct; investigate the authority (if any) for the conduct; and determine the complaint by
reference to judicial review principles. In considering a complaint under the
Human Rights Act 1998 the Tribunal must apply the same principles as a court
would apply on an application for judicial review. The Tribunal may award
compensation or make any other order, including the quashing or cancellation of
a warrant or authorisation, and an order for the destruction of records of
information obtained as a result of the surveillance in issue. The Tribunal is
required to give notice to the complainant indicating either that a determination
has been made in his favour, in which case it must provide a summary of the
determination including any findings of fact, or that no determination has been
made in his favour. The Tribunal's procedure is set out in the Investigatory
Powers Tribunal Rules 2000.[109] In the first five years of its functioning the
Tribunal has found in favour of a complainant only once.[110]

D. CHALLENGES TO THE LAWFULNESS OF COVERT INVESTIGATIONS

Whether the framework set out by RIPA fully protects Art.8 rights is yet to be   **7–58**
tested in the Strasbourg Court. As a mechanism to assess and redress Art.8
complaints, RIPA and its Codes of Practice sit alongside the Human Rights Act
1998, independent of any criminal proceedings, in a way that did not previously
exist in English law.

Some features of RIPA remain problematic. The prohibition set out in s.17[111] and   **7–59**
the uncertainty about the timing of destruction of intercept material, discussed
above, are obvious concerns. Additionally, the level of authorisation required
under RIPA is open to criticism. Having chosen not to require judicial authority
for permitting such activity, notwithstanding the Strasbourg Court's comments
preferring that course, many surveillance and covert techniques under RIPA may
be authorised at a relatively low level. This potential flaw is compounded by the
fact that, at times, the standard of scrutiny and level of authorisation appears to
focus on the form of surveillance, rather than the quality of the infringement of
privacy (e.g. "participating informant" recording of phone conversations falls
outside Pt I).

Other than complaints about the surveillance regime itself, covert investigative   **7–60**
techniques are often challenged pursuant to Art.8 breaches in three ways. First,
allegations that flaws in an investigation caused breaches of Art.8 which have led
to unfairness contrary to Art.6. Secondly, there may be allegations of free-
standing breaches of Art.8, in the context of criminal investigations. Thirdly,
breaches of Art.8 may be claimed relating to retention and use of information
gathered during covert investigations. Each of these is considered below.

---

[109] S.I. 2000/2665.
[110] See Report of the Interception of Communications Commissioner for 2005–2006 para.39.
[111] A challenge to the prohibition was declared inadmissible in *Preston v United Kingdom*
App.No.24193/94, although that may be limited to its very specific facts.

The interplay between Article 8 and Article 6

7–61　Defendants in criminal cases may complain that unlawful or unfair practices during the course of an investigation breach their right to a fair trial under Art.6. Establishing a breach of Art.8 may be the first step in applying to exclude evidence or alleging an abuse of process.[112] While the admissibility of evidence is primarily a matter for regulation under national law,[113] and evidence obtained in breach of Art.8 does not, of itself render a trial unfair, it may do so.[114] The issues that arise in connection with Art.6, out of covert investigations and breaches of Art.8 are considered in further detail in Ch.15.

Freestanding Article 8 claims

7–62　A person may complain of a breach of Art.8 in the context of a criminal investigation, independent of any breach of Art.6. In *Perry v United Kingdom*,[115] the applicant was subject to secret filming while in police detention. The footage formed part of the evidence against him. Having declared his complaint under Art.6 inadmissible, the Court went on to consider Art.8. The Court noted that a person's private life may be concerned in measures effected outside a person's home or private premises, and that his reasonable expectation of privacy is a significant, but not necessarily a conclusive, factor. It also observed that the ploy adopted by the police went beyond the normal or expected use of a camera in a custody suite, and the footage in question had not been obtained voluntarily. In finding a breach of Art.8, the Court placed particular reliance on breaches by the police of the relevant codes of practice to the Police and Criminal Evidence Act 1984. This may have important implications for surveillance information gathered in breach of RIPA codes.

Complaints about the retention and use of investigatory material

7–63　The use of investigatory powers have consequences that go beyond considering infringements of privacy in the way it was gathered. Such information is often retained and may form part of a database of information.[116] Unfortunately in many areas of criminal investigation, there is insufficient clarity as to when investigative material must be destroyed and the purposes for which it can be used in the future.

7–64　There are circumstances where the initial gathering of information, even secretly, makes little infringement on Art.8(1), if any. In *Herbecq and Another v Belgium*[117] the Commission found that the monitoring of the actions of an individual

---

[112] See, for example, *P.G. and J.H. v United Kingdom*, App.No.44787/98 *Vetter v France* application No.59842/00, Judgment May 31, 2005.

[113] *Schenk v Switzerland* (1988) 13 E.H.R.R. 242 paras 45 and 46.

[114] See, for example, *PG and JH v United Kingdom*, App.No.44787/98, where breaches of Art.8 relating to covert surveillance did not lead to a breach of Art.6. However, in *Allan v United Kingdom*, the use of a police informant (the equivalent of a CHIS) to illicit incriminating comments after the applicant had relied on his right to silence, was a breach of Art.6.

[115] (2004) E.H.R.R. 3.

[116] This intersects with data protection issues which are beyond the scope of this chapter.

[117] Application Nos 32200/96 and 32201/96, Commission decision of January 14, 1998, D.R. 92–A, p.92).

in a public place by the use of photographic equipment that did not record the visual data did not, as such, give rise to an interference with Art.8. However, in *Leander v Sweden*,[118] it was held that the recording of data and the systematic or permanent nature of the record may do so.

The Court and Commission have consistently recognised the distinction between **7–65** the gathering of information and its retention for the purposes of Art.8. The retention of information gathered during a criminal investigation may be an interference, but in many circumstances would be easily justified.[119] In *Amann v Switzerland*[120] the fact of an intercepted telephone call from a woman from the Soviet Embassy (relating to purchasing a depilatory appliance) was retained by authorities in a secret card index for several years. The intercept had been in breach of Art.8. But, importantly, the lack of proper safeguards in the creation, storing and retention of the card, particularly the failure to indicate with sufficient clarity the scope and conditions of exercise of the authorities' discretionary power, was a further breach of Art.8.

Similarly in *Rotaru v Romania*[121] the applicant complained about the holding of **7–66** a secret register containing information about him, which was revealed during judicial proceedings in a different context. The Court held that the storing by a public authority of information relating to an individual's private life, the use of it, and the refusal to allow an opportunity for it to be refuted, amounted to an interference with the applicant's right under Art.8(1). In determining that such interference was not justified under Art.8(2), the Court focused on the absence of provisions setting out the manner in which information was obtained, and the lack of regulation of the state's power to gather, store and release such information.

The extent to which the retention of information requires careful assessment is **7–67** well illustrated by the Court's decision in *Segerstedt-Wiberg and Others v Sweden*.[122] The applicants objected to the storage of information in security police files. Having determined that the system of gathering and storing of information was in accordance with law, it strictly assessed each applicant's case and concluded that the continued storage of information was necessary in relation to the first applicant, but not for any of the remaining applicants.

The distinction between the gathering of information, and its retention and future **7–68** use arises frequently in relation to photographs, fingerprints and DNA material gathered during criminal investigations. In *Friedl v Austria*[123] the Commission considered whether the taking of photographs was an infringement of Art.8(1) and attached importance to whether the photographs amounted to an intrusion into the applicant's privacy; whether the photograph related to private or public

---

[118] See *Leander v Sweden* (1987) 9 E.H.R.R. 433. See *P.G. and J.H. v United Kingdom*, App. No.44787/98 para.57.
[119] See *McVeigh, O'Neill and Evans v United Kingdom* (1981) 5 E.H.R.R. 71.
[120] (2000) 30 E.H.R.R. 843.
[121] (2000) 8 B.H.R.C. 43.
[122] App.No.62332/00, Judgment September 20, 2005.
[123] (1995) 21 E.H.R.R. 83.

matters; and whether the material thus obtained was envisaged for a limited use or was likely to be made available to the general public. It concluded that there was no interference in the taking or retention. It placed particular weight on the fact that the photographs remained anonymous in that no names were noted down; the personal data recorded was not entered into a data processing system; and no action was taken to identify the persons photographed on that occasion by means of data processing.[124]

7-69   Different considerations would apply if such material was released to the public. In *Peck v United Kingdom*[125] the applicant had attempted to commit suicide in a public street late at night. The attempt itself was not recorded, but the immediate aftermath was, and was then released to media outlets. The Court emphasised the distinction between the gathering of information, which may not infringe Art.8(1), and its retention and use, which must be considered separately. The Court found that there was no justification for the disclosure of the recorded material to media outlets in the circumstances of that case.

7-70   An emerging concern is the extent to which many states, particularly the United Kingdom,[126] are retaining fingerprint, photograph and DNA information for storage and use on national databases. In *R. (Marper) v Chief Constable of South Yorkshire Police*[127] the House of Lords considered the lawfulness of provisions which allow the retention of such information gathered during the course of a criminal investigation, even if the suspected person was not charged or was acquitted after charge. While the Court of Appeal had been persuaded that the retention of such information had interfered with Art.8(1), it considered such interference justified.[128]

7-71   In the House of Lords, Lord Steyn considered both *McVeigh, O'Neill and Evans v United Kingdom* and *Kinnunen v Finland*, both of which had found no breach of Art.8 in the retention of photographs and fingerprints. He explicitly rejected the suggestion by the Court of Appeal that an interference with Art.8(1) could be assessed by taking into account the UK's cultural traditions of privacy. In Lord Steyn's opinion, such matters were relevant only to Art.8(2), and having considered the evidence of the procedure for storage and use of DNA samples, he concluded that:

---

[124] The recording and retention of information relating to the questioning of the applicant to establish his identity was an interference but was justified, in part because it had not been entered into a data processing system, but was in a general administrative file.

[125] (2003) 36 E.H.R.R. 41.

[126] See the Home Office Forensic Science and Pathology Unit publication "DNA Expansion Programme 2000–2005: Reporting Achievement" (para.6) which stated that the UK has, by far, the largest DNA database of any country and the largest proportion of its population's DNA held on a database. At the end of March 2005, it held 3,000,949 DNA profiles (taken from 2.71 million suspect offenders). 5.2 per cent of the UK population was on the Database, compared with 1.0 per cent in Austria, the second highest country, and 0.5 per cent in the USA.

[127] [2004] 1 W.L.R. 2196.

[128] [2002] 1 W.L.R. 3223. The reasoning for finding the interference justified was varied. Sedley L.J. contemplated the possibility that the merit of retaining information about a suspected person may need to be assessed on a case by case basis.

"looking at the matter in the round I incline to the view that in respect of retained fingerprints and [DNA] samples, Article 8(1) is not engaged. If I am wrong in this view, I would say any interference is very modest indeed."

He then found that any interference, if there was one, was justified. Importantly, **7–72** he placed emphasis on the details on the following points of evidence: (i) the fingerprints and DNA samples were kept only for the limited purpose of the detection, investigation, and prosecution of crime[129]; (ii) the fingerprints and DNA samples were not of any use without a comparator fingerprint or sample from the crime scene; (iii) the fingerprints and samples would not be made public; (iv) a person was not identifiable to the untutored eye simply from the profile on the database, and therefore any interference represented by the retention was minimal; (v) the resultant expansion of the database by the retention conferred enormous advantages in the fight against serious crime.

As for the concerns[130] that future scientific developments or internal reorganisa- **7–73** tion of databases might greatly expand the government's use of such information and the personal details it could disclose, Lord Steyn indicated that such issues, when they arose, may require future judicial decisions in order to ensure compliance with the Convention.

In a culture becoming more accepting of personal infringements of privacy which **7–74** might previously have been resisted, the balance may tip in favour of increasing the methods of surveillance and the quantity of personal data in the hands of government. It is therefore understandable that in *Marper* the need to provide law enforcement authorities with such powerful tools of detection prevailed over the arguments of principle about the presumption of innocence, or broad fears concerning the risk of future misuse of such information. It remains to be seen if the Strasbourg Court follows the reasoning of the House of Lords.

Marper demonstrates that the courts will make judgments on the basis of what *is* **7–75** being done with personal information, and not what *could* be done with it. In effect, the courts presume that the state agents who collect and store personal information will abide strictly by the limits of what is the admitted and permissible use of such information. The difficulty is that such an approach assumes that, in practice, state action will not overstep those boundaries. On one view, this is contrary to the very reasons why Art.8 protection is needed.

---

[129] For other decisions on the use or disclosure the DNA database for purposes other than its original collection, see *Lambeth London Borough Council (Applicant) v (1) S (2) C (3) V (4) J (by his children's guardian) (Respondents) & (1) Commissioner of Police for the Metropolis (2) Secretary of State for the Home Department (Intervenors)* [2006] EWHC 326 (Fam) and *Chief Constable of West Yorkshire and Others v Information Commissioner* (2005) Information Tribunal, October 12.
[130] Emphasised, in particular, in the intervention by Liberty in the Court of Appeal proceedings.

CHAPTER 8

THE SUBSTANTIVE CRIMINAL LAW

A. INTRODUCTION

As a general proposition it can be said that "the Convention leaves states free to   **8–01**
designate as criminal an act or omission not constituting the normal exercise of
one of the rights that it protects".[1] There are, however, a number of qualifications
to this principle. The first is that the state may not define as "criminal" any
conduct which constitutes an unjustified interference with the right to privacy, the
right to freedom of expression, the right to peaceful assembly and association, or
the right to peaceful enjoyment of possessions. This principle is the subject of the
present chapter. In addition, where an individual is prosecuted for a criminal[2]
offence, he is entitled to the protection of Arts 6 and 7 of the Convention. These
rights have implications for the elements of an offence as defined in domestic
law, which are discussed in Chs 9 and 10 below. The third main qualification is
that there are certain situations in which the state is under a *positive obligation*
to create an enforceable criminal offence, or to restrict available defences, so as
to protect the Convention rights of victims of crime.[3] The extent of this obligation is considered in Ch.18.

B. THE RIGHT TO PRIVATE LIFE

It can be argued that the Convention, and particularly Art.8, has been a significant   **8–02**
factor in bringing about the reform of the law of sexual offences. Shortly after the
enactment of the Human Rights Act a review of the law of sexual offences was
instituted. It reported in 2000, one of its main objectives being to bring the law
into line with the requirements of the Convention.[4] The Sexual Offences Act
2003 made sweeping changes to the law, removing some problems of compatibility but creating other possible problems.

---

[1] *Engel v Netherlands* (1979–80) 1 E.H.R.R. 647 at para.81.
[2] As to the meaning of a "criminal charge" for the purposes of the Convention, see Ch.4
above.
[3] As to positive obligations generally see para.2–53 above.
[4] *Setting the Boundaries: Reforming the Law on Sex Offences* (July 27, 2000).

I. General Principles

8–03   The European Court of Human Rights has frequently held that "sexual orientation and activity concern an intimate aspect of private life".[5] Accordingly,
"particularly serious reasons"[6] are required to justify a criminal prosecution
relating to consensual sexual activity in private. It is well established that not
only a criminal prosecution but even the threat of prosecution[7] may be sufficient
to constitute an interference with the rights guaranteed by Art.8. The central
question in each case will therefore be whether the prosecution, conviction and
sentence, taken individually or together, are proportionate to one of the legitimate
aims prescribed in Art.8(2).

8–04   It remains important to understand the court's approach and reasoning when
applying Art.8. One of the earliest criminal law challenges under this Article
concerned the offences of buggery[8] and gross indecency[9] in Northern Ireland. In
contrast to the laws elsewhere in the United Kingdom, the relevant legislation
allowed no exception for the acts of consenting adults in private. In *Dudgeon v
United Kingdom*[10] the Court held that the Northern Ireland legislation could not
be said to be "necessary in a democratic society" because there was no evidence
of a "pressing social need"[11] to use the criminal law in order to prohibit
consensual homosexual activity in private. The application of criminal sanctions
was disproportionate to any legitimate aim which was sought to be achieved. In
the Court's view, such justifications as there were for retaining the law in force
were outweighed by the detrimental effect it could have on the life of a person
of homosexual orientation. Although members of the public who regarded
homosexuality as immoral might be shocked, offended or disturbed by the
commission of homosexual acts in private, that could not, in itself, justify the
application of penal sanctions when both participants were consenting adults.[12]
The Court's judgment recognised that there are gradations of "private life" and
that sexual orientation, as one its most intimate aspects, should be given special
protection.[13]

8–05   In seeking to justify the legislation the government cited the strength of feeling
in Northern Ireland on the issue, arguing that there was a strongly held view that

---

[5] e.g. *Laskey v United Kingdom* (1997) 24 E.H.R.R. 39, para.36.
[6] *Dudgeon v United Kingdom* (1982) 4 E.H.R.R. 149.
[7] *Norris v Ireland* (1991) 13 E.H.R.R. 186.
[8] Under ss.61 and 62 of the Offences Against the Person Act 1861.
[9] Under s.11 of the Criminal Law Amendment Act 1885.
[10] (1982) 4 E.H.R.R. 149.
[11] The term "necessary" in Art.8(2) implies the existence of a pressing social need: see *Dudgeon*
at para.51: " '[N]ecessary,' in this context, does not have the flexibility of such expressions as
'useful', 'reasonable', or 'desirable', but implies the existence of a 'pressing social need' for the
interference in question." For the origin of the 'pressing social need' test see *Handyside v United
Kingdom* (1979–80) 1 E.H.R.R. 737 at para.48.
[12] At para.60.
[13] *cf.* the much more restrictive approach of the US Supreme Court in *Bowers v Hardwick* 478 US
186 (1986) and subsequent decisions, discussed extensively by Wintemute, *Sexual Orientation and
Human Rights*, (Clarendon) Ch.2.

the abolition of the offence "would be seriously damaging to the moral fabric" of society.[14] The Court was forthright in its rejection of this argument:

> "The Convention right affected by the impugned legislation protects an essentially private manifestation of the human personality. As compared with the era when the legislation was enacted, there is now a better understanding, and in consequence an increased tolerance, of homosexual behaviour to the extent that in the great majority of the member states of the Council of Europe it is no longer considered to be necessary or appropriate to treat homosexual practices of the kind now in question as in themselves a matter to which the sanctions of the criminal law should be applied; the Court cannot overlook the marked changes which have occurred in this regard in the domestic law of the member states."

As to the applicant's standing to challenge the legislation, the Court held that the   **8–06** "very existence of this legislation continuously and directly affects his private life: either he respects the law and refrains from prohibited sexual acts to which he is disposed ... or he commits such acts and thereby becomes liable to criminal prosecution".[15] *Dudgeon* was followed in *Norris v Ireland*.[16] In *Norris*, the Irish government directly challenged the applicant's status as a "victim",[17] arguing that he had never been prosecuted for the offence in question, and there had been no prosecutions in Ireland for many years, except where minors were involved, or where the acts occurred in public or without consent. The Court accepted that the risk of prosecution was "minimal" but pointed out that there was no stated policy on the part of the prosecuting authorities to refrain from enforcing the law. Whilst the offence remained on the statute book there was a possibility that it could be applied in the future if there was a change of policy. In the Court's view, the applicant ran the risk of being prosecuted, however slight that risk might be, and could therefore claim "victim" status under the Convention.[18]

II. Challenges to the former English Law

Two successful challenges to English law led to legislative changes. In *Suther-*   **8–07** *land v United Kingdom*[19] the applicant successfully relied upon Art.8, in conjunction with Art.14, in order to challenge the law on gross indecency, on the ground that the applicable age of consent was 18 whereas for heterosexual offences the age of consent was 16. While the age of consent itself falls, in principle, within a state's margin of appreciation,[20] the Commission held that different ages of consent for heterosexual and homosexual offences could no

---

[14] At para.46.
[15] At para.41.
[16] (1991) 13 E.H.R.R. 186.
[17] See para.1–84 above.
[18] A similar conclusion was reached in *Modinos v Cyprus* (1993) 16 E.H.R.R. 485 where the Court rejected an argument that the law in question was invalid (as being in conflict with the constitution) and thus inapplicable, noting that there was a statement to the contrary in the caselaw of the Supreme Court of Cyprus.
[19] (1997) 24 E.H.R.R. CD 22.
[20] *Dudgeon v United Kingdom* (1982) 4 E.H.R.R. 149, para.62.

longer be justified.[21] More generally, the Commission held that where there is a difference of treatment in the application of the criminal law on the grounds of a person's sexual orientation, the margin of appreciation is a "relatively narrow" one.[22] The law was changed by the Sexual Offences (Amendment) Act 2000, and the Sexual Offences Act 2003 abolished the offence of gross indecency altogether, the age of consent to sexual offences remaining at 16.

8–08　A second challenge was upheld by the court in *ADT v United Kingdom*.[23] The Sexual Offences Act 1967 exempted from criminalisation those homosexual offences committed by consenting adults in private, and defined "in private" as meaning where more than two persons were present. The applicant, convicted for consensual acts with a few friends, alleged a violation of Art.8 alone and in conjunction with Art.14, arguments that had been unsuccessful before the Commission some 20 years before.[24] The Court held that the applicant's activities with a few friends were "genuinely 'private', and the approach of the Court must be to adopt the same narrow margin of appreciation as it found applicable in other cases involving intimate aspects of private life." The Sexual Offences Act 2003 abolished the offence of gross indecency and, with it, the distinction between offences in public and in private, on the ground that it was not required in public policy terms and it was discriminatory in the sense that there was no equivalent offence for lesbian or heterosexual activities.[25]

III. The Compatibility of the Sexual Offences Act 2003

8–09　Questions of the compatibility of the 2003 Act with the Convention, and particularly Art.8, are beginning to come before the English courts. One focus of arguments is the cluster of offences designed to protect young children from sexual abuse. The Strasbourg case of *X and Y v Netherlands*[26] establishes that states have a positive obligation to create offences that protect vulnerable people (such as children) from invasions of their private life in the form of sexual molestation. The review of the law of sexual offences re-affirmed the purpose of

---

[21] A similar approach has been taken in Canada. In *Halem v Minister of Employment and Immigration* (1995) 27 C.R.R. (2d) 23 (Federal Court, Trial Division), a provision in the Criminal Code which fixed the age of consent for anal intercourse at 18 (whereas the age for other sexual activity was 14) was declared unconstitutional for being in breach of the equal protection clause of the Charter.

[22] Following the Commission's ruling the government indicated that it did not intend to contest the case before the court, and undertook to introduce legislation to equalise the age of consent. The prosecution of a man after the Commission's ruling in this case, but before the amendment to the law enacted by the Sexual Offences (Amendment) Act 2000 was found to be a violation of Art.14 taken together with Art.8: *B v UK* (2004) 39 E.H.R.R. 30.

[23] *The Times*, August 8, 2000; Judgment July 31, 2000.

[24] *X v United Kingdom* (1980) 19 D.R. 66, and also *Johnson v United Kingdom* (1986) 47 D.R. 72, discussed by Wintemute, *Sexual Orientation and Human Rights*, pp.102–103.

[25] Home Office, *Setting the Boundaries* (2000), para.6.6.3; see, however, *X v Y* (Employment: Sex Offender) [2004] EWCA Civ 662; [2004] I.C.R. 1634 where the Court of Appeal, with Brooke L.J. dissenting, held that sexual acts in a public toilet for which the appellant had received a caution for the offence of gross indecency did not engage the protection of Art.8.

[26] (1986) 8 E.H.R.R. 235, discussed fully at 18–56 below.

"child protection, both from predatory adults and from other children."[27] None-theless, Art.8 questions are raised by the configuration of offences in the 2003 Act,[28] which render criminal and subject to substantial maximum penalties a whole range of minor and exploratory sexual behaviour among children, as the case of G.[29] demonstrates. G, aged 15, was charged with rape of V, a child under 13. Section 5(1) of the 2003 Act states that "a person commits this offence if (a) he intentionally penetrates the vagina, anus or mouth of another person with his penis, and (b) the other person is under 13." G pleaded guilty on the basis that V had told him she was 15 too, and had been a willing participant. V subse-quently admitted that she had told G she was 15.

The challenge based on Art.8 was, in essence, that G should have been charged under s.9 (sexual activity with a child) combined with s.13, if at all; that charge and conviction under s.5 breached his right to respect for private life by labelling him publicly as a rapist, subjecting him to a maximum penalty of life imprison-ment and attracting sexual offender notification requirements. Compliance with Art.8 would require either: (a) no prosecution—the Government had given an assurance that consensual sexual activity between minors would not inevitably be prosecuted, but relied on prosecutorial discretion to achieve the correct balance, and this is not enough to ensure the protection of G's Art.8 rights; or (b) prosecution under ss.9 and 13, with the lower maximum penalty of five years and limited notification requirements.

The Court of Appeal accepted these submissions in part. It conceded that Art.8 was engaged, but said that the s.5 charge was proper in the first place (before V had admitted lying about her age), and that it was not the judge's duty to substitute a lesser charge:

"We accept the possibility that prosecution of a child under section 5 rather than section 13, or indeed prosecution at all, in relation to consensual sexual intercourse may, on the particular facts, produce consequences that amount to an interference with the child's Article 8.1 rights that are not justified under Article 8.2. Where, however, as here, no criticism can be made of an initial charge of breach of section 5, we do not consider that it follows that the judge must necessarily substitute an alternative charge of breach of section 13 if it transpires that the sexual activity was, or must be treated as, con-sensual."[30]

This judgment leaves open the argument that the prosecution breached s.6 of the Human Rights Act, since it should have sought the judge's approval to drop the charge of rape of a child under 13 when V largely conceded the facts underlying G's basis of plea. Moreover, it remains possible that a mere undertaking that the Crown Prosecution Service will use their discretion whether or not to charge a particular young person under the Sexual Offences Act is not a sufficient protection of the Art.8 rights of the young. Decisions such as *Norris v Ireland*

---

[27] Home Office, *Setting the Boundaries* (2000), para.3.5.6.
[28] *Cf.* the criticisms of Spencer J.R., "The Sexual Offences Act 2003—Child and Family Offences" [2004] Crim. L.R. 347.
[29] [2006] Crim. L.R. 930.
[30] At [46]. As discussed in 16-?? Below, the Court of Appeal went on to hold that the sentence of 12 months' detention in this case failed to allow for the fact that the offence interfered with G's Art.8 rights, and, bearing in mind that G had served five months already, it substituted a conditional discharge.

(8–06 above) and *Sutherland v United Kingdom* (8–07 above) suggest that this issue can be tested without a prosecution having been brought, and further challenges to the 2003 Act—particularly the over-broad and overlapping child sex offences—can be expected.

III. Sadomasochist "Assaults"

8–10   None of the cases so far considered involved any element of violence. The Review of sexual offences excluded sado-masochistic activities from its discussions, and the element of violence had been regarded as a major distinguishing feature when the Court came to decide on the Art.8 challenge in *Laskey and others v United Kingdom*,[31] the "Operation Spanner" case. The applicants had been charged with assaults arising out of consensual sadomasochistic activity involving the infliction of minor physical injuries to one another's genitals. They pleaded guilty after the trial judge ruled that they could not rely on the consent of their "victims" as a defence to the charge, and were sentenced to terms of imprisonment. The issue of consent was appealed to the House of Lords which ruled, by a three to two majority, that consent was no defence.[32] In Strasbourg the applicants argued that their convictions represented an unjustified intrusion into their right to respect for their private lives.

8–11   The Court unanimously concluded that the state was entitled to regulate, through the operation of the criminal law, activities which involved the infliction of physical harm, whether the injuries occurred in the context of sexual activity or otherwise. In the Court's view the English law on this point fell within the margin of appreciation left to member states in such matters, and none of the strong phrases used by the Court in *Dudgeon* and the subsequent decisions on consensual sexual offences are to be found in the judgment.[33] Instead, the Court held that the prosecution pursued the legitimate aim of the protection of health,[34] and possibly also of the protection of morals.[35] It was, in the first instance, for the domestic authorities, including the courts, to determine the level of physical harm which should be tolerated in situations where the victim consented. The Court noted that the injuries sustained were not insignificant, and that the factors at stake included public health considerations and the general deterrent effect of the criminal law. Accordingly, the Court rejected the applicants' arguments that their behaviour formed part of their private morality which it was not the state's business to regulate. Having regard to the fact that the Court of Appeal had reduced the sentences originally imposed by the trial judge, the prosecution and conviction was not disproportionate to the legitimate aim(s) of the protection of health and/or morals.

---

[31] (1997) 24 E.H.R.R. 39.

[32] *R. v Brown* [1994] 1 A.C. 212.

[33] *cf.* the critique by Moran L., "*Laskey v United Kingdom*: Learning the Limits of Privacy" (1998) 61 M.L.R. 77.

[34] See para.50.

[35] See para.51; for general discussion of the "public morals" exception to Arts 8–11, see Koering-Joulin R., "Public Morals", in Delmas-Marty M. (ed.), *The European Convention for the Protection of Human Rights: International Protection versus National Restrictions* (1992).

The emphasis which the court placed in *Laskey* on the severity of the injuries   **8–12**
inflicted led it to distinguish the English Court of Appeal decision in *Wilson*[36]
(albeit on tenuous grounds). In *Wilson* the Court of Appeal held that a defence of
consent was available to the defendant, who had branded his initials on to his
wife's buttocks. Consensual activity between husband and wife, in the privacy of
the matrimonial home, was held not to be a proper subject for criminal prosecution. The applicants in *Laskey* argued that if this were true for heterosexual
sadomasochism, it must be equally true for homosexuals. In an unconvincing
response, the Court held that there was no evidence of a difference in the
treatment of homosexuals, because it was the "extreme nature of the practices
involved" in *Laskey* that distinguished it, rather than the sexual orientation of the
participants. The facts of *Wilson* were "not at all comparable in seriousness" with
those in *Laskey*,[37] even though they amounted to assault occasionally actual
bodily harm.

In the case of *K.A. and A.D. v Belgium*[38] a magistrate and a doctor had been
convicted of offences of wounding, in respect of sado-masochistic practices
involving their wives. The Court unanimously followed *Laskey*, holding that,
although in principle the criminal law should not intervene in consensual sexual
practices, lack of respect for the rights of others was a reason why the state
should intervene. In this case, the "victims" had cried for mercy and told those
inflicting the pain to stop, and all parties were considerably intoxicated: such
circumstances showed that there had not been proper respect for choice and
autonomy. This was more important than the fact that the "victims" had not
made any official complaint. It remained essential that any sentence imposed for
the offence should not be disproportionate, and that condition was fulfilled here
(both applicants had been sentenced to short prison sentences, and had been
disqualified professionally for certain periods).

C. FREEDOM OF THOUGHT, CONSCIENCE AND RELIGION

I. General Principles

Article 9(1) accords unqualified protection to freedom of thought, conscience and   **8–13**
religion. It also protects the right to *manifest* one's religion or belief "in worship,
teaching, practice or observance". This latter right (of manifestation) may be
subject to limitations if the conditions in Art.9(2) are fulfilled. So far as organised
religions in the United Kingdom are concerned, the protection of Art.9 is
emphasised by s.13 of the Human Rights Act 1998.[39]

II. Religious exemptions

The Court and Commission have been generally unwilling to accept that individ-   **8–14**
uals can claim exemption from particular provisions of the criminal law on

---

[36] [1996] 2 Cr.App.R. 241.
[37] (1997) 24 E.H.R.R. 39 at para.47.
[38] App.No.42758/98, judgment of February 17, 2005.
[39] See para.3–20 above.

the grounds of their personal or religious beliefs. Thus, the Commission held that the protection of health criterion in Art.9(2) justified both the requirement of the criminal law that a sikh motorcyclist should wear a crash helmet,[40] and the prosecution of a farmer who had refused, on religious grounds, to participate in a compulsory vaccination scheme for farm animals.[41] In *Seven Individuals v Sweden*[42] the Commission held that a Swedish law which criminalised parental chastisement of children was compatible with Art.9, despite the parents' claim that their religious convictions required such measures. The protection of children from inhuman and degrading treatment under Art.3 was plainly a legitimate objective, within the meaning of Art.9(2), for restricting corporal punishment despite any suggested religious objections.

8–15   A similar reluctance to permit exceptions on religious grounds was evident in *Pendragon v United Kingdom*.[43] A prohibition order under the Public Order Act 1986 had been made to prevent all trespassory asssemblies within a radius of four miles of Stonehenge for the four days of the summer solstice. The applicant, a druid, claimed that his prosecution for breaching the prohibition notice (he was actually acquitted) violated his Convention rights. The Commission accepted that druidism was a religion for the purposes of Art.9 but, by a majority, declared the application inadmissible and held that the limitation on the rights in Arts 9 and 11 was necessary "for the prevention of disorder," taking account of the disturbances which had occurred in the Stonehenge area in previous years.

8–16   The Court of Appeal adopted a similar approach in *Taylor*,[44] where the defence to a charge of possessing cannabis with intent to supply was that smoking cannabis was part of the defendant's Rastafarian religion. It was further argued that s.139(5) of the Criminal Justice Act 1988 provides a religious defence to the carrying of a knife, and that the Misuse of Drugs Act 1971 was defective in failing to provide a similar defence for cannabis offences. The court held that Art.9 was engaged, but concluded that the offence was a justifiable interference with the defendant's Convention rights since it was "necessary in a democratic society" to criminalise drugs offences, and indeed international conventions require this.

III. Prosecution for Religious Activity

8–17   Prosecutions which directly involve religious activity have been more favourably received. In *Kokkinakis v Greece*[45] the Court held that the prosecution of a Jehovah's witness for "proselytism" was in breach of Art.9.[46] The law limited the applicant's right to "manifest his religion or belief . . . in practice," and the limitation was not proportionate to the protection of the rights and freedoms of

---

[40] *X v United Kingdom* (1978) 14 D.R. 234.
[41] *X v Netherland* 5 Y.B. 278.
[42] (1982) 29 D.R. 104 at 114.
[43] (1999) 27 E.H.R.R. CD 179; see also *Chappell v United Kingdom* (1987) 53 D.R. 241, where it was first accepted that Druidism qualifies as a religion for these purposes.
[44] [2002] Crim.L.R. 314.
[45] (1994) 17 E.H.R.R. 397.
[46] *ibid*., paras 49–50.

others. The Court distinguished "true evangelism" (which was the essential mission of the Christian religions) from "improper proselytism" (which was defined as an attempt to convert others by offering material or social benefits or taking advantage of the need, distress or incapacity of others).[47] The applicant, a Jehovah's Witness, had been persistent but had not acted improperly. He had done nothing more than attempt to persuade an adherent of another Christian religion of the virtues of his faith. In *D.P.P. v Hammond*[48] the Divisional Court expressed some hesitation in upholding the conviction of an evangelical Christian under s.5 of the Public Order Act 1986 for displaying a sign in a town centre which displayed the words "Stop Immorality" "Stop homosexuality" "Stop lesbianism", but found that the magistrates were entitled to conclude that the interference with the defendant's rights under Arts 9 and 10 was justified because the sign had been displayed on a Saturday afternoon provoking hostility, violence and disorder from members of the public.

IV. Ethical and Moral Values

Greater difficulty has been encountered when dealing with the manifestation of **8–18** non-religious moral convictions. Article 9(1) is not confined to recognised religions: it expressly mentions freedom of conscience and belief, and the Court has held that these freedoms are also; " . . . a precious asset for atheists, agnostics, sceptics and the unconcerned. The pluralism indissociable from a democratic society, which has been dearly won over the centuries, depends on it."[49]

In *Arrowsmith v United Kingdom*[50] the Commission accepted that pacifism fell **8–19** within the ambit of the right to freedom of thought and conscience. The applicant, who had distributed leaflets to soldiers urging them to go absent or refuse to serve in Northern Ireland, was prosecuted for incitement to disaffection. The Commission, however, held that the prosecution did not violate Art.9 since the applicant's actions did not amount to the "practice" of her pacifist beliefs.[51] The word "practice" in Art.9(1) did "not cover every act which is motivated or influenced by a religion or belief".[52] The Commission drew a slender and unconvincing distinction between the applicant's conduct on the one hand, and "public declarations proclaiming generally the idea of pacifism and urging the acceptance of a commitment to non-violence", on the other. The question of whether a conviction for refusing to undertake military service on the grounds of conscientious objection interferes with Art.9 has recently been considered in a number of cases. In *Thlimmenos v Greece*[53] the Court held that, where a Jehovah's witness had been convicted for refusing to wear a military uniform on account of his religious beliefs and was therefore barred (as a person convicted of a felony) from appointment as a chartered accountant, this amounted to a

---

47 *ibid.*, para.48.
48 [2004] Crim.L.R. 851.
49 In *Kokkinakis v Greece* (1994) 17 E.H.R.R. 397 at para.31.
50 (1978) 19 D.R. 5 at para.69.
51 *ibid.*, at para.75.
52 *ibid.*, at para.71.
53 (2001) 31 E.H.R.R. 15.

violation of Art.9 so as to engage Art.14, but expressly left open the question of whether the same action would have amounted to an interference with Art.9 considered alone. In the case of *Khan v Royal Air Force Summary Appeal Court*[54] the Court of Appeal, in considering the conviction of a Muslim who had objected to participation in the war against Iraq for the offence of being absent without leave, felt unable to depart from the House of Lords decision in *Sepet v Bulbur*[55] that the current state of Strasbourg jurisprudence was that a conviction for an offence committed on the grounds of conscientious objection to military service did not infringe Art.9(1), although it questioned whether this was correct in the light of the Commission's reasoning in *Thlimmenos*.[56]

D. Freedom of Expression

8–20 An offence penalising the medium of speech, publication or broadcasting amounts to an interference with the right to freedom of expression,[57] and such protection extends in principle to information or ideas that "offend, shock or disturb the State or any sector of the population,"[58] and indeed to matters that would be disturbing "to any person of ordinary sensibilities."[59] However, it is possible to justify an interference with freedom of expression if it can be "convincingly established"[60] that the interference is "necessary in a democratic society" under Art.10(2), which in this context has been said to assume a society characterised by "pluralism, tolerance and broad-mindedness."[61]

I. Obscenity Offences

8–21 The Convention caselaw establishes clearly that potentially obscene material is within the scope of Art.10, and that the compatibility of prosecution of such material is to be determined primarily by the likely audience. To that extent the Convention standard echoes the test in s.1 of the Obscene Publications Act 1959 Act that the material must be likely to deprave and corrupt "persons who are likely, having regard to all relevant circumstances, to read, see or hear the matter contained in [it]."

8–22 One of the earliest criminal cases under Art.10 was *Handyside v United Kingdom*.[62] The applicant was prosecuted under the Obscene Publications Acts 1959

---

[54] [2004] H.R.L.R. 40.
[55] [2003] 1 W.L.R. 856.
[56] Unreported, ,application 34369/97, decision of European Commission of Human Rights, December 4, 1998.
[57] See generally Barendt E., *Freedom of Speech* (1985).
[58] *Handyside v United Kingdom* (1979–80) 1 E.H.R.R. 737, para.40.
[59] *Per* Laws L.J. in *The ProLife Alliance v British Broadcasting Corporation* [2002] 2 All E.R. 756, at [39]. See generally Amos M., "Can we speak freely now? Freedom of Expression under the Human Rights Act", [2002] E.H.R.L.R. 750.
[60] *Otto Preminger Institut v Austria* (1995) 19 E.H.R.R. 34 at para.50; *Jersild v Denmark* (1995) 19 E.H.R.R. 1 at para.37.
[61] *Handyside v United Kingdom* (1979–80) 1 E.H.R.R. 737, para.49.
[62] (1979–80) 1 E.H.R.R. 276 at paras 59–67.

and 1964 for having obscene books in his possession for gain. He had acquired the distribution rights for a publication called *The Little Red Schoolbook*, an anti-authoritarian publication aimed at adolescents aged between 12 and 18, which contained a factually accurate—but explicit—section on sexual activity. The book was marketed so as to appear as if it were a schoolbook. The applicant was convicted by Lambeth magistrates' court and fined £100. The court also ordered the forfeiture and destruction of his remaining stock. The applicant's appeal to Inner London Quarter Sessions was dismissed. In Strasbourg he complained that his conviction was in breach of Art.10. The Court concluded that the prosecution amounted to an interference with the applicant's freedom of expression, contrary to Art.10(1). Turning to Art.10(2), the Court found that the interference was adequately "prescribed by law," and held that the legislation pursued the legitimate aim of the protection of morals. Noting that it was in the first place for the national authorities, including the courts, to determine the extent of the protection of morals required, the Court went on to establish the following important statement of principle:

> "Freedom of expression constitutes one of the essential foundations of a [democratic] society, one of the basic conditions necessary for its progress and for the development of every man. Subject to paragraph 2 of Article 10, it is applicable not only to information and ideas that are favourably received, or regarded as inoffensive, but also to those that offend, shock, or disturb the state or any sector of the population. Such are the demands of that pluralism, tolerance and broadmindedness without which there is no 'democratic society'."[63]

Nevertheless, the Court concluded that having regard to the potential audience **8–23** and the subject-matter of the book it was within the state's margin of appreciation to take criminal proceedings. It may be doubted whether the Court would take the same approach to such a publication today.

In *X and Y v Switzerland*[64] the Commission held that a prosecution for selling **8–24** obscene videos did not breach Art.10 because the case concerned a chain of video shops which were open to the general public. The Commission held that a "conviction for renting or selling the video films . . . would correspond to a pressing social need and would be proportionate to the legitimate aim pursued within the meaning of the Convention organs' case-law." In *Scherer v Switzerland*,[65] by contrast, the Court found that a conviction for publication of an obscene film did violate Art.10 because the films had only been shown at a cinema to which public access was restricted. The applicant ran a sex shop in Zurich for homosexuals, behind which was a small projection room used for showing video films of an explicit sexual nature. Applying the *Handyside* principle the Court held that the right to freedom of expression encompassed the publication of allegedly obscene material. The interference was prescribed by law (under Art.204 of the Swiss Criminal Code), and pursued the legitimate aim of protecting morals within the meaning of Art.10(2). The question was whether it was "necessary in a democratic society." The Court considered that it was of

---

[63] At para.49.
[64] 16564/90 April 8, 1991, (unreported).
[65] (1994) 18 E.H.R.R. 276 at paras 59–67.

particular relevance that the obscene material was not displayed to the general public. It was very unlikely that the projection room would be visited by persons who were unaware of the nature of the films shown, and there was control in the shop ensuring that minors could not gain access. In the opinion of the Court, the case did not concern the protection of the morals of Swiss society in general since no adult or child would be confronted with the films unintentionally or against his will. Where this is so, the Court held that there would have to be "particularly compelling reasons" justifying the interference. Since no such reasons had been shown, the Court held that the prosecution had amounted to a violation of Art.10.[66]

8–25   The application in *X Co. v United Kingdom*[67] related to the seizure of magazines under the Obscene Publications Act. The editor and publisher argued that the magazines were for export, so that the Art.10(2) justification of protecting the morals of United Kingdom citizens did not apply. To this the Commission replied that "the protection of morals" can extend to a state's interest in the diffusion of immoral publications from its territory. The applicant company also argued that the seizure of the magazines amounted to an unjustified deprivation of possessions and a violation of Art.1 of Protocol 1. The Commission found, however, that a measure that is "necessary" for one of the reasons stated in Art.10(2) satisfies the test of "public interest" for permitting deprivations of possessions in Art.1 of Protocol 1. The application was therefore declared inadmissible.

8–26   In *Hoare v United Kingdom*[68] the applicant was engaged in the publication and distribution of pornographic videotapes by post. The tapes depicted anal intercourse, bondage and the consumption of faeces. The applicant advertised in the *Sunday Sport* newspaper, and those responding to the advert would be sent a brochure describing the contents of the videos. The tapes would then be distributed on request. The applicant was charged with six counts of publishing obscene articles contrary to s.2(1) of the 1959 Act. He was convicted and sentenced to 30 months imprisonment. The applicant contended that the videos could not deprave or corrupt since only those who shared his interests would have purchased them from the brochure. He invited the Commission to have regard to the more liberal standards towards pornography applied in some Member States of the Council of Europe. In rejecting the application as manifestly ill-founded, the Commission again relied upon the protection of morals exception in Art.10(2). In the Commission's view, the sole question arising under the proportionality test was whether the sentence imposed was necessary. Although the Commission noted the precautions which the applicant had taken to prevent the tapes falling into the wrong hands, it nevertheless considered that there was no certainty that only the intended purchasers would have access to the material.

8–27   In considering analogous issues under the Charter, the Canadian courts have tended to focus on the inherent nature of the material, and the attitude of society generally to material in a certain category, rather than the likely audience for the

---

[66] *ibid.*, at paras 59–67.
[67] (1983) 32 D.R. 231.
[68] [1997] E.H.R.L.R. 678.

particular publication. In *Butler*[69] the Supreme Court was concerned with material depicting a variety of sexual and violent activities. The relevant section of the Canadian Criminal Code provided that "any publication a dominant characteristic of which is the undue exploitation of sex, or of sex and any one or more of . . . crime, horror, cruelty and violence, shall be deemed to be obscene." The question for the Supreme Court of Canada was whether this offence infringed the right to free expression in s.2(b) of the Charter. The court held that it did, but that the infringement was saved by s.1 of the Charter as being "a reasonable limit demonstrably justified in a free and democratic society". In the leading judgment, Sopinka J. held that, in a matter on which individual opinions differed considerably, judges should strive to ascertain the community view:

> "The courts must determine as best they can what the community would tolerate others being exposed to on the basis of the degree of harm that may flow from such exposure. Harm in this context means that it predisposes persons to act in an anti-social manner as, for example, the physical or mental mistreatment of women by men, or what is perhaps debatable, the reverse. Anti-social conduct for this purpose is conduct which society formally recognizes as incompatible with its proper functioning. The stronger the inference of a risk of harm the lesser the likelihood of tolerance. The inference may be drawn from the material itself or from the material and other evidence . . . In making this determination with respect to the three categories of pornography . . . the portrayal of sex coupled with violence will almost always constitute undue exploitation of sex. Explicit sex which is degrading or dehumanizing may be undue if the risk of harm is substantial. Finally, explicit sex that is not violent and neither degrading nor dehumanizing is generally tolerated in our society and will not qualify as undue exploitation unless it employs children in its production. If material is not obscene under this framework, it does not become so by reason of the person to whom it is or may be shown or exposed nor by reason of the place or manner in which it is shown."

II. Artistic Expression

Artistic expression has generally been afforded less stringent protection than political and journalistic speech.[70] In *Muller v Switzerland*[71] the applicant was a serious artist exhibiting at an exhibition to celebrate the 500th anniversary of Fribourg's entry into the Swiss Federation. He produced a series of large paintings, one of which included graphic depictions of sexual activity including homosexuality and bestiality. The paintings were displayed in a public exhibition with no warnings about their content. They were seen by a young girl visiting the exhibition with her father, who informed the public prosecutor. The applicant was convicted of publishing obscene items and fined. The paintings were confiscated, and not returned until almost eight years later.

8–28

In concluding that there had been no violation of Art.10, the Court placed considerable emphasis on the manner in which the paintings had been exhibited—in a gallery which sought to attract the public at large; which did not

8–29

---

[69] [1992] 1 S.C.R. 452.
[70] See generally Harris D.J., O'Boyle M. and Warbrick C., *The Law of the European Convention on Human Rights* (1995), pp.377–386; Paul Mahoney, "Universality versus Subsidiarity in Strasbourg Free Speech Cases" [1997] E.H.R.L.R. 364; and Lord Lester of Herne Hill, "Universality versus Subsidiarity: a Reply" [1998] E.H.R.L.R. 73.
[71] (1991) 13 E.H.R.R. 212.

warn visitors about the content of the exhibition; and which permitted admission without age restriction. The Court held that the conviction was justified for the protection of public morals and the rights of others. It was within the state's margin of appreciation to conclude that the conviction was a proportionate means of achieving that aim. Whilst conceptions of sexual morality had changed in recent years, the Swiss courts were not unreasonable in finding the paintings grossly offensive to persons of ordinary sensitivity and in imposing a fine.[72] However, the confiscation of an original work of art (as opposed to a reproduction) raised a rather different issue since the artist lost the opportunity of showing his work in places where the demands of the protection of morals were less strict. In the end the Court found that the confiscation did not violate Art.10 since the applicant could have applied for the return of the painting sooner than he did. Nevertheless, it is implicit in the decision that an order for the destruction of an original work of art or its permanent confiscation would require a particularly compelling justification.

III. Race Hate Speech and Holocaust Denial[73]

8-30   Section 18 of the Public Order Act 1986 creates the offence of incitement to racial hatred which is committed where a person uses abusive or insulting words, or displays abusive or insulting written material, which is likely to stir up racial hatred, providing the words have been spoken or the material displayed with that intention. Sections 19 to 22 apply the same principle to the publication or distribution of written material, to the public performance of plays, to the distribution, showing or playing of visual images or sounds, and to television broadcasts. Possession of such material with a view to its publication or broadcast is also an offence.[74] "Racial hatred" means hatred against a group of persons in Great Britain defined by reference to colour, race, nationality (including citizenship) or ethnic or national origins.[75]

8-31   The Racial and Religious Hatred Act 2006 inserts into the Public Order Act 1986 a new Pt IIIA, creating six religious hatred offences that correspond to those for racial hatred. These new offences clearly engage Art.10, but in many circumstances it will be held that the particular offence constitutes a proportionate interference with freedom of expression to an extent that is necessary in a democratic society. Leading Strasbourg decisions (dealing mostly with racial hatred) are discussed in the paragraphs that follow, but it is significant that a new s.29J, inserted by the Racial and Religious Hatred Act 2006, provides that:

"Nothing in this Part shall be read or given effect in a way which prohibits or restricts discussion, criticism or expressions of antipathy, dislike, ridicule, insult or abuse of particular religions or the beliefs or practices of their adherents, or of any other belief system or the beliefs or practices of their adherents, or proselytising or urging adherents

---

[72] On the relatively restrictive Swiss law, see Trechsel S., "Switzerland", in Delmas-Marty M. (ed.), *The European Convention for the Protection of Human Rights* (1992) at pp.254–256.
[73] See generally Cooper and Marshall Williams, "Hate Speech, Holocaust Denial and International Human Rights Law" [1999] E.H.R.L.R. 593.
[74] S.23.
[75] S.17.

of a different religion or belief system to cease practising their religion or belief system."

Despite this affirmation of Art.10, it will be necessary for prosecutors and for courts to assess the particular justifications, in a given situation, for applying one of the religious hatred offences.

Applying Art.17 of the Convention[76] the Commission has, in the past, held that **8–32** speech which is intended to incite race hatred is outside the protection of Art.10 altogether, because of its potential to undermine public order and the rights of the targeted minority.[77] In its later decisions, the Commission tended to reach the same conclusion via a slightly different route, accepting that such speech could, in principle, fall within Art.10(1), but referring to Art.17 as a factor relevant to the proportionality test in Art.10(2).[78] Thus, the Commission found no violation of Art.10 where the applicant was prosecuted for membership of a neo-fascist organisation,[79] or where prison authorities refused to deliver to a prisoner publications encouraging anti-semitism and racism.[80] In *Norwood v United Kingdom* the Court declared inadmissible an application made by a man who had been convicted under s.5 of the Public Order Act for displaying a poster in the window of his flat which contained a photograph of the Twin Towers in flame, the words "Islam out of Britain—Protect the British People" and a symbol of a crescent and star in a prohibition sign, on the grounds that the display was a vehement attack on a religious group and thus an act within the meaning of Art.17 which did not enjoy the protection of Art.10.[81]

Article 17 was also relied upon by the House of Lords when overruling the **8–33** Divisional Court in *D.P.P. v Collins*.[82] The defendant was convicted of sending a grossly offensive message through the public communications system, contrary to s.127 of the Communications Act 2003. He argued, *inter alia*, that the offence was an unjustified interference with his freedom of expression under Art.10. The House of Lords held that whether the message was "grossly offensive" is a question of fact for the Court, but that the offence was a proper restriction on the use of public communications networks to infringe the rights of others. Article 17 supported the conclusion that Art.10 could not be relied upon in this kind of case.

However, the scope of the criminal law prohibiting the publication of race hate **8–34** speech must not extend beyond that which is strictly necessary and proportionate. In *Jersild v Denmark*[83] the applicant was a journalist convicted of aiding and abetting the dissemination of racial insults. He had produced a short documentary

---

[76] See para.2–140 above.
[77] *Glimmerveen and Hagenback v Netherlands* (1979) 18 D.R. 187.
[78] *Kunen v Germany* (1982) 29 D.R. 194; *H, W, P and K v Austria* (1989) 62 D.R. 216; *Marais v France* (1996) 86A D.R. 184. But see the approach of the Court in *Lehideux and Isorni v France* (1998) 5 B.H.R.C. 540.
[79] *X v Italy* (1976) 5 D.R. 83.
[80] *Lowes v United Kingdom* (1988) 59 D.R. 244.
[81] (2004) 40 E.H.R.R. SE 111; cf. the domestic proceedings, *Norwood v DPP* [2003] Crim. L.R. 888.
[82] [2006] UKHL 40.
[83] (1995) 19 E.H.R.R. 1.

in which a television presenter interviewed three Danish youths about their avowedly racist views. The programme included extreme and offensive expressions of racism which were broadcast without any comment or disclaimer. The applicant had solicited the contributions and had edited the film so as to give prominence to the most extreme expressions of view. Nevertheless, it was common ground that the programme consisted of good faith reporting of current affairs and that the journalist did not intend to promote racist attitudes. The youths were convicted of making racist statements and the journalist of aiding and abetting them. The Court was quite clear that the convictions of the youths themselves were justified:

"There can be no doubt that the remarks in respect of which the [neo-nazis] were convicted were more than insulting to members of the targeted groups and did not enjoy the protection of Article 10."[84]

8–35 But the Court nevertheless held that the conviction of the journalist was not proportionate to the interest of protecting the rights of the minorities against whom the racism was directed.[85] News reports based on interviews constituted one of the most important means by which the press was able to perform its vital role of "public watchdog".[86] Although the Court declared the importance of combating racism in all its manifestations, it held that the punishment of a journalist for disseminating the statements of others in an interview would seriously hamper press freedom and "should not be envisaged unless there are particularly strong reasons for doing so."[87] As to the absence of an express disclaimer, the Court concluded that the form of the programme was essentially a matter of journalistic freedom.

8–36 In *Lehideux and Isorni v France*[88] the applicants were prosecuted for publishing a newspaper advertisement allegedly apologising for the war crimes of Marshall Petain. They represented two organisations that were campaigning for a review of the Petain trial, and the advertisement stated in terms that it was not seeking to excuse or minimise the atrocities of the Nazi regime. The Court observed that statements which sought to deny clearly established historical facts, such as the Holocaust, would be removed from the protection of Art.10 altogether, by the operation of Art.17. On the facts, however, the applicants' statements did not fall into this category, and the prosecution was therefore a breach of Art.10. These principles were applied by the Court in *Witzsch v Germany*[89] where the applicant had been convicted of an offence of disparaging the memory of the dead in connection with protests about the introduction of Holocaust denial legislation in Germany. Following *Lehideux and Isorni* the Court held that;

" . . . the public interest in the prevention of crime and disorder due to disparaging statements regarding the Holocaust, and the requirements of protecting the interests of

---

[84] *ibid.*, para.35.
[85] *ibid.*, para.37.
[86] *ibid.*, para.35; see generally on the role of the press, *Observer and Guardian Newspapers v United Kingdom* (1992) 14 E.H.R.R. 153.
[87] *Jersild*, para.35.
[88] (1998) 5 B.H.R.C. 540.
[89] Judgment April 20, 1999.

the victims of the Nazi regime, outweigh, in a democratic society the applicant's freedom to impart views denying the existence of the gas chambers and mass murder therein."

Similarly in *Garaudy v France*,[90] the Court found that the six months imprisonment of the applicant who had written a book entitled *The Founding Myths of Modern Israel* in which he disputed the existence of the crimes against humanity committed against the Jews by the Nazis did not violate the Convention. The court held that the denial or rewriting of this type of historical fact was one of the most severe forms of racial defamation and of incitement to hatred of Jews, that it undermined the values on which the fight against racism and anti-Semitism was based and constituted a serious threat to public order. The aims of the book therefore fell within the aims prohibited by Art.17 and the applicant could not rely on Art.10.

This emphasis on denial of established historical facts is echoed in the international and comparative caselaw. The United Nations Human Rights Committee has adopted a similar approach in relation to the right to freedom of expression in Art.19 of the International Covenant on Civil and Political Rights. In *Faurisson v France*[91] the applicant had been the subject of a private prosecution under French Gayssot Act 1990 (which creates a criminal offence of contesting the existence of the crimes against humanity tried at Nuremberg). In a magazine interview he had asserted a personal belief that there were no gas chambers for the extermination of Jews in the Nazi concentration camps. The Human Rights Committee held that the prosecution was a valid restriction on free expression, within the meaning of Art.19, because the statements were such as to raise or reinforce anti-semitic sentiment, and their suppression served the purpose of respecting the right of the Jewish community to live free from an atmosphere of fear.

8–37

Similarly, the German Constitutional Court has referred to the Basic Law to uphold the use of provisions in the Penal Code which criminalise Holocaust denial. In one case,[92] the police had banned a neo-Nazi meeting on the ground that, since a revisionist historian who denied the holocaust was due to speak, criminal offences were likely to be committed. The organisers of the meeting challenged the order as a restriction on the constitutional right of freedom of speech. The Constitutional Court held that, although the Basic Law protects expressions of opinion (even if they are untrue or irrational), it does not protect the utterance of "demonstrably untrue statements of fact". To hold that such speech is protected would violate the right of Jewish people to their personality and their human dignity, both of which are protected by the Basic Law.

8–38

The jurisprudence of the United States Supreme Court on these matters is extensive and detailed.[93] In *Beauharnais v Illinois*,[94] the Supreme Court held that

8–39

---

[90] Admissibility decision, 65831/01, July 7, 2003 (unreported).
[91] Communication No.550/1993, U.N. Doc. C.C.P.R./C/58/D/550/1993 (1996).
[92] (1994) 90 B.Verf.G.E. 241.
[93] Kommers D.P. and Finn J.E., *American Constitutional Law* (1998), p.463, and the treatise by Greenawalt K., *Speech, Crime and the Uses of Language* (1989).
[94] 343 US 250 (1952).

a statute criminalising group defamation did not infringe the First Amendment right of free speech. Later decisions seem to have placed greater emphasis on the First Amendment right, without actually overruling *Beauharnais*.[95] However, the matter is still attracting vigorous debate, and there is a formidable lobby in favour of interpreting the First Amendment so as to permit states to curb hate speech.[96]

8–40 The Canadian Supreme Court, for its part, has accepted that such restrictions are compatible with the free speech guarantee in the Charter. The point arose for consideration in *Keegstra*,[97] which concerned a schoolteacher who had communicated anti-semitic statements to his pupils. He was convicted of wilfully promoting hatred against an identifiable group, contrary to the Criminal Code, and argued that the offence contravened the Charter. The Supreme Court unanimously held, in the first place, that the offence is an infringement of the right to freedom of expression secured by s.2(b) of the Charter. That freedom should be upheld whatever the content of the expression: the only possible exception would be expressions communicated in a violent way. The court specifically declined to treat hate propaganda as analogous to violence, but nevertheless went on to hold, by a four to three majority, that the offence amounted to a "reasonable limit" on freedom of expression, and was therefore saved by s.1 of the Charter. The offence sent out a strong message of disapprobation to those who threatened the values of a multicultural society. This reasoning was strengthened by reference to s.27 of the Charter, which requires its provisions to be interpreted "in a manner consistent with the preservation and enhancement of the multi-cultural heritage of Canada".[98]

IV. Blasphemy

8–41 Blasphemy and blasphemous libel are indictable offences at common law.[99] Blasphemy is the publication of material which is "contemptuous, reviling, scurrilous or ludicrous" in relation to the objects of veneration of the Christian religion or of the Church of England.[100] It is not blasphemous to speak or publish

---

[95] Of the many Supreme Court decisions, see, e.g. *Cohen v California*, 403 US 15 (1971). Much discussed is the *Skokie* case, in which a local ordinance regulating assemblies in an area fraught with racial tension was struck down as unconstitutional: *Collin v Smith* (1978) F. 2d 1197.

[96] For a thoughtful comparative analysis, see Hare I., "Legislating against Hate—the Legal Response to Bias Crimes" (1997) 17 Oxford J.L.S. 415. See further Jacobs J.B. and Potter K., *Hate Crimes: Criminal Law and Identity Politics* (1998), discussed in relation to the new racially aggravated offences under the Crime and Disorder Act 1998 by Brennan F., "Racially Motivated Crime: the Response of the Criminal Justice System" [1999] Crim. L.R. 17; see also *Virginia v Black* (2003) 123 S Ct. 1536 where the US Supreme Court upheld a Virginia statute which criminalises cross-burning with intent to intimidate in the face of a challenge under the First Amendment, and the discussion of this decision in Hare I., "Inflammatory speech: cross-burning and the first amendment" [2003] P.L. 408.

[97] [1990] 3 S.C.R. 697.

[98] For a detailed analysis of the Canadian and European authorities, together with those under the I.C.P.P.R., see McGoldrick D. and O'Donnell T., "Hate-speech laws: consistency with national and international human rights law." (1998) 18 Legal Studies 453.

[99] See generally *Archbold* Ch.27.

[100] Stephen, *Digest of the Criminal Law* (9th edn) approved by Lord Scarman in *Whitehouse v Gay News* [1979] A.C. 617 at 665–666.

opinions hostile to the Church or to deny the existence of God, providing the expression of opinion is couched in "decent and temperate language."[101] Prosecutions for blasphemy are nowadays very rare in this country,[102] the most recent being in 1977.[103]

Although many European states have repealed blasphemy laws altogether, the **8–42** Commission has held that prohibition of blasphemy through the criminal law is not in violation of Art.10.[104] This view has been endorsed by the Court, which has shown a particular sensitivity to the religious concerns of certain sections of the community. In *Otto-Preminger-Institut v Austria*[105] the applicant institute announced the public showing of a satirical film which contained provocative and offensive portrayals of the objects of veneration of the Roman Catholic religion (the Eucharist was ridiculed, God the Father was portrayed as senile and impotent, the Virgin Mary was portrayed as a wanton woman with sexual interest in the devil, and Christ as mentally impaired). The film was based on a 19th century play which had been performed without censorship elsewhere. Before the first showing the public prosecutor instituted criminal proceedings against the manager and a judicial order was made for the seizure and forfeiture of the film. The Court accepted that the seizure was prescribed by law. Since Art.9 of the Convention protects the peaceful enjoyment of religious freedom it followed—in the Court's opinion—that the interference pursued the legitimate aim of protecting the rights of others. Although believers must tolerate and accept the denial of their beliefs by other people, and even the propagation of doctrines hostile to their faith, the manner in which such denial or opposition takes place could engage the responsibility of the state to take positive action. Respect for the religious beliefs of others could legitimately be thought to have been violated by "provocative portrayals of objects of religious veneration," which may be regarded as "malicious violation of the spirit of tolerance which must also be a feature of a democratic society."[106]

The Court went on to emphasise that those exercising freedom of expression also **8–43** undertake duties and responsibilities, amongst which was an obligation to avoid as far as possible expressions that are gratuitously offensive to others, and thus an infringement of their rights, and which do not contribute to any form of public debate. Since there was no discernible consensus throughout Europe on the significance of religion in society it was impossible to define comprehensively the interferences with anti-religious speech which might be permissible. In this instance, the fact that the applicant organisation had restricted admission by way of an age limit and an admission fee was not considered sufficient. The widely advertised nature of the film meant that its proposed screening must be considered sufficiently "public" to cause offence.[107] In the Court's opinion, the

---

[101] *ibid.*
[102] As the court noted in *Wingrove v United Kingdom* (1997) 24 E.H.R.R. 1 at para.57.
[103] *Whitehouse v Gay News Ltd* [1979] A.C. 617.
[104] *X Ltd and Y v United Kingdom* (1982) 28 D.R. 77.
[105] (1995) 19 E.H.R.R. 34; see the note by Pannick D., "Religious Feelings and the European Court" [1995] P.L. 7.
[106] (1995) 19 E.H.R.R. 34 at para.47.
[107] *ibid.*, at para.54.

Austrian authorities had acted to ensure religious peace and to prevent people feeling that their religion was being subjected to unwarranted attacks with the acquiescence of the state. The interference was accordingly proportionate to the legitimate aim which it pursued.

8–44   The Court's judgment in the *Otto Preminger Institut* case demonstrates the important relationship between Art.10 and Art.9 on these matters, holding that states have a "responsibility to ensure the peaceful enjoyment of the right guaranteed under Article 9 to the holders of those beliefs and doctrines" and also referring to "members of a religious majority or minority."[108] This approach may be thought to sit awkwardly with the limitation of the English law of blasphemy to the Christian faith, which is surely discriminatory since it fails to accord equal protection to minority faiths, and gives cause to doubt the earlier ruling of the Commission in *Choudhury v United Kingdom*[109] that this restriction on the English offence does not violate Art.9.[110]

8–45   Article 10 formed the basis of the challenge in *Wingrove v United Kingdom*,[111] where the British Board of Film Classification (BBFC) had denied a classification certificate to a short video film concerning St. Teresa of Avila, a 16th century nun who experienced powerful ecstatic visions of Christ. The work depicted a youthful nun having erotic fantasies involving sexual arousal with the crucified figure of Christ. The refusal to issue a classification certificate was based not upon the sexual imagery as such, but upon the view of the BBFC that the film infringed the criminal law of blasphemy. The Court held that there was no violation of Art.10 since the decision did not exceed the national authorities' margin of appreciation—a margin wider "within the sphere of morals or, especially, religion" than on matters such as political speech:

> "[B]lasphemy legislation is still in force in various European countries. It is true that the application of these laws has become increasingly rare and that several states have recently repealed them altogether ... Strong arguments have been advanced in favour of the abolition of blasphemy laws, for example that such laws may discriminate against different faiths or denominations ... or that legal mechanisms are inadequate to deal with matters of faith or individual belief ... However, the fact remains that there is as yet not sufficient common ground in the legal and social orders of the Member States of the Council of Europe to conclude that a system whereby a State can impose

---

[108] *ibid.*, at para.47. For further discussion of this relationship between Arts 9 and 10 see *Murphy v Ireland* (2004) 38 E.H.R.R. 13 which concerned legislation banning the broadcast of all religious advertising. The Court emphasised that the margin of appreciation was wider in restricting freedom of expression in relation to matters liable to offend intimate personal convictions within the sphere of morals or, especially, religion, than in restricting political speech, and held that Ireland was entitled to decide that "the exclusion of all religious groupings from broadcasting advertisements generates less discomfort than any filtering of the amount and content of such expression by such groupings."

[109] (1991) 12 H.R.L.J. 172. For the English proceedings, see *R. v Chief Metropolitan Stipendiary Magistrate ex parte Choudhury* [1991] 1 Q.B. 429.

[110] See further Idriss M. M., "Religion and the Anti-Terrorism, Crime and Security Act 2001", [2002] Crim.L.R. 890. For the Commission's approach following *Otto Preminger* see *Dubowska & Skup v Poland* (1997) 24 E.H.R.R. CD 75.

[111] (1997) 24 E.H.R.R. 1.

restrictions on the propagation of material on the basis that it is blasphemous is, in itself, unnecessary in a democratic society and thus incompatible with the Convention."[112]

This rather pusillanimous reasoning demonstrates the difficulties felt by the **8–46** Court on this subject. In principle it should be for the government to establish that there is a "pressing social need" to justify the censorship of a video film, according to the usual interpretation of Art.10(2), whereas the double negatives in the Court's reasoning betray unease and hesitation.[113] Although the Court placed considerable emphasis on the margin of appreciation allowed to states in these matters, it did at least point to "the breadth and open-endedness of the notion of blasphemy, and the risks of arbitrary or excessive interferences with freedom of expression under the guise of action taken against allegedly blasphemous material."[114] This leaves open the possibility of challenges under Art.10 against an over-restrictive or discriminatory use of blasphemy law in the future.

V. Defamatory Libel

Defamatory libel is a common law offence punishable with up to two years **8–47** imprisonment and/or a fine.[115] The offence may be committed through any publication of defamatory material in permanent form. The libel must be of a serious character,[116] and the offence is triable only on indictment. It is not necessary for the prosecution to prove either an intention to defame or knowledge that the information published is false.[117] However, it is necessary to prove that the defendant was aware of the allegedly libelous statement and not merely of the publication in which it appears.[118] Nevertheless if a defendant who was unaware of the presence of the libel was in such a position that he ought to have known of it, then the onus is on the defence to prove that he was not negligent.[119] A prosecution against the publisher, proprietor or editor of a newspaper requires leave,[120] and if the subject-matter involves a play then the consent of the Attorney-General is required.[121] Under the Human Rights Act, the caselaw under Art.10 should be the guiding principle in the grant or refusal of leave or consent, as well as in the scope of the offence itself and the potential defences available. In *Gleaves v Deakin*[122] Lord Diplock considered the offence to be altogether incompatible with Art.10:

> "[T]he truth of the defamatory statement is not in itself a defence to a charge of defamatory libel under our criminal law . . . No onus lies on the prosecution to show

---

[112] *ibid.*, para.57.

[113] See the forceful criticism of the decision by Gandhi S. and James J., "The English Law of Blasphemy and the European Convention on Human Rights" [1998] 4 E.H.R.L.R. 430.

[114] (1997) 24 E.H.R.R. 1 at para.58.

[115] Libel Act 1843, ss.4–5.

[116] *Gleaves v Deakin* [1980] A.C. 477 HL; *Desmond v Thorne* [1983] 1 W.L.R. 163 Q.B.D.

[117] If the defendant was not aware of the falsity of the information published, the maximum sentence is one year's imprisonment and/or a fine: Libel Act 1843, s.5.

[118] *Vitzelly v Mudie's Select Library Ltd* [1900] 2 Q.B. 170.

[119] *ibid.*

[120] Law of Libel Amendment Act 1888, s.8.

[121] Theatres Act 1968, s.8.

[122] [1980] A.C. 477 (HL).

that the defamatory matter was of a kind that it is necessary in a democratic society to suppress or penalise in order to protect the public interest. On the contrary, even though no public interest can be shown to be injuriously affected by imparting to others accurate information about seriously discreditable conduct of an individual, the publisher of the information must be convicted unless he himself can prove to the satisfaction of a jury that the publication of it was for the public benefit. That is to turn Article 10 of the Convention on its head."[123]

8–48   Prosecutions for criminal defamation are not uncommon in other Council of Europe member states. Such prosecutions will be compatible with Art.10 only insofar as they relate to untruthful and seriously damaging allegations of fact. In *Lingens and Leitgens v Austria*[124] the applicants were prosecuted for libel following the publication of an article which alleged that a politician had lied in a public speech. The Commission held that such a prosecution had the legitimate aim of protecting the reputations of others. A distinction had to be drawn "between the necessity of the legal regulations as such, and the necessity of their application in the particular case." In view of "the fundamental importance [of free expression] in the field of political discussion" the Commission considered it to be "of the utmost importance that these restrictive regulations should only be applied where it is really necessary in the particular case".[125] Politicians, in particular, must be prepared to accept even harsh criticisms of their public activities and statements. Such criticism could not be characterised as defamatory unless it threw considerable doubt on their character and integrity. However, since the article had presented as established fact the untruthful allegation that the politician had lied, a criminal prosecution was justified.

8–49   This conclusion is to be contrasted with the decision of the Court in a later case brought by the same applicant in respect of another prosecution for criminal defamation. In *Lingens v Austria*[126] the applicant wrote articles accusing the Austrian Chancellor of protecting former members of the Nazi S.S. for political reasons. He was convicted, fined and ordered to print the court's judgment in a subsequent issue of his magazine. The European Court of Human Rights emphasised the need to distinguish between assertions of fact and value judgments.[127] The offending passages in the articles were, in the Court's view, essentially expressions of opinion. It was therefore impossible to expect the applicant to prove their truth. In finding a violation of Art.10, the court emphasised that it was incumbent on the press to impart information and ideas on political issues, and accordingly that the limits of acceptable criticism are wider as regards politicians than for private individuals.

8–50   In *Oberschlick v Austria*[128] the applicant was the editor of a journal called *Forum*. He printed the text of a speech given by a politician which had glorified

---

[123] See *Worme v Commissioner of Police of Grenada* [2004] 2 A.C. 430 where the Privy Council distinguished the position under the English law of criminal libel and interpreted similar laws in the Criminal Code of Grenada as imposing a legal burden on the prosecution to prove both that the defamatory statement was untrue and that it was not in the public benefit that it be published.

[124] *Lingens and Leitgens v Austria* (1982) 4 E.H.R.R. 373 at 393.

[125] *ibid.*, at para.10c.

[126] (1986) 8 E.H.R.R. 407.

[127] *ibid.*, at para.40.

[128] [1997] E.H.R.L.R. 676.

all those who fought in the Second World War and argued that it was wrong to distinguish between "good" and "bad" soldiers. The speech was criticised in an article written by the applicant entitled "Idiot rather than Nazi." The article denounced the politician as a fool on the ground that he had suggested in the speech that those who did not fight in the war could not lay claim to democratic freedoms. The applicant was prosecuted for defamation and fined 200 Austrian schillings (with 10 days imprisonment in default). The domestic courts held that the word "idiot" was incapable of amounting to objective criticism. The Austrian Court of Appeal did not consider that Art.10 extended to the protection of defamatory speech aimed at politicians since this would lead to the general debasement of political debate. The European Court disagreed: the article had to be looked at in context, taking account of all the circumstances of the case and in particular of the extreme views expressed by the politician in his speech. Article 10 protected not only the substance of ideas but also the form in which they were conveyed. The limits of acceptable criticism were wider with regard to a politician acting in his public capacity than in relation to a private individual. The article, although polemical, was not a gratuitous attack on the politician because the author provided a rational basis for his criticism. Accordingly, the conviction and sentence had violated the applicant's rights under Art.10.

In *Thorgeir Thorgeirson v Iceland*[129] the applicant was prosecuted for two **8-51** articles he had published in a national newspaper alleging a pattern of brutality by unspecified members of the Rekjavíc police force. The Court held that the role of the press as a public watchdog was not confined to political discussion, but extended to other matters of public concern. The principal purpose of the articles was, in the Court's view, not to damage the reputation of the police, but to press for an independent investigation of allegations which had been made by others. In concluding that the defamation conviction violated Art.10 the Court emphasised that one of the instances of police brutality referred to was capable of proof. As to the broader picture, the articles had made it clear that the author was reporting allegations which had emanated from others and which had affected public opinion about the police. No police officers had been named, and the report emphasised that such brutality was the exception rather than the rule. In short, the articles had been prepared and presented responsibly and in good faith.

The role of the press as a public watchdog has been consistently emphasised by **8-52** the Court.[130] In *Cumpana and Mazare v Romania*[131] the Court held that the applicant journalists were on this basis entitled to inform the public about irregularities in the management of public funds by certain local elected representatives and public officials. The fact, however, that the applicants in addition directly accused specified individuals of mismanagement of public funds placed the applicants under an obligation to provide a sufficient factual basis for these

---

[129] (1992) 14 E.H.R.R. 842.
[130] See *Selistő v Finland*,(2006) 42 E.H.R.R. 144, finding a violation of Art.10 where a journalist had been convicted of defamation after exposing an allegedly alhocolic surgeon who operated on patients when drunk.
[131] Judgment of December 17, 2004; see also *Pedersen and Baadsgaard v Denmark*, judgment of December 17, 2004.

assertions particularly since these allegations were so serious as to amount to criminal offences. In this case the journalists had failed to take any steps before the national courts to substantiate their allegations. The Court concluded therefore that the state was entitled to conclude that the conviction of the applicants met a pressing social need. The seven-month prison sentence imposed on the applicants was, however, wholly unjustified, as was the order prohibiting the applicants from working as journalists for a year. In concluding that there had been a violation of Art.10, the Court observed that this was a classic case of defamation of an individual in the context of a debate on a matter of legitimate public interest; it stated that the imprisonment of a journalist for a press offence would only be justified in exceptional circumstances, where other fundamental rights had been seriously impaired, such as in cases involving hate speech or incitement to violence. The fact that the applicants did not serve their sentences because they had been pardoned by the President of Romania did not remove the chilling effect of the sanction.[132]

VI. Defamation of judges

8-53   In this country it is still a common law contempt of court to publish matter so defamatory of a judge or court as to be likely to interfere with the due administration of justice by seriously lowering the authority of the judge or the court.[133] The offence, known as "scandalising the court," is so infrequently used that it has been described as "virtually obsolescent."[134] Moreover, the restrictions which have been imposed on the scope of the offence are such that it almost certainly complies with the requirements of Art.10. The authorities establish that it is only in a clear case that this branch of the contempt jurisdiction may be exercised since any citizen must be free to criticise a decision of a court, even in an outspoken manner.[135]

8-54   Prosecutions for defamation of judicial officers do occur in a number of other Convention countries. In *Barford v Denmark*[136] the applicant journalist was prosecuted for defamation of two lay judges. He wrote an article suggesting that they "did their duty" in the course of litigation over which they were presiding by voting for the local authority by which both of them were employed. The article criticised the structural impartiality of having a case decided by a panel of

---

[132] In *Karhuvaara and Iltalehti v Finland* (judgment of November 16, 2004) where the applicants were prosecuted for reporting the criminal trial and conviction of the husband of a politician for assault, the Court noted that the public had a right to be informed about certain aspects of the private life of public figures. The Court held that, as the conviction of a politician's spouse could affect people's voting decisions, there was some degree of public interest involved in the reporting. The Court found that the applicants' conviction for the offence of infringement of the politician's privacy and in particular the fact that the politician's parliamentary status had been viewed as an aggravating factor in the offence violated Art.10; see also *Tammer v Estonia* (2003) 37 E.H.R.R. 43.

[133] *R. v Gray* [1990] 2 Q.B. 36; *R. v Editor of the New Statesman* (1928) 44 T.L.R. 301; see further *Arlidge, Eady and Smith on Contempt* (3rd edn, paras 5–204 to 5–274).

[134] Per Lord Diplock in *Secretary of State for Defence v Guardian Newspapers* [1985] A.C. 339 at 347.

[135] *Ambard v AG for Trinidad and Tobago* [1936] A.C. 322; *McCleod v St. Aubyn* [1989] A.C. 549; *R. v Metropolitan Police Commissioner ex parte Blackburn* [1968] 2 Q.B. 150.

[136] (1991) 13 E.H.R.R. 493.

judges including two employees of one of the litigants, and the personal integrity of the two individuals. The Court held that the prosecution was proportionate to the legitimate aim of protecting the reputations of others, and the authority and impartiality of the judiciary. The conviction had been based on the personal attacks which had been made on the judges, and not upon the structural unfairness of the tribunal (which would have been a legitimate subject of free public debate).[137] In *Skalka v Poland*[138] the applicant had been convicted of insulting a state authority and sentenced to eight months' imprisonment for sending letters in which, *inter alia*, he referred to the judges of the regional court as "irresponsible clowns," and to one unidentified judge as an "outstanding cretin." The Court held that to convict the applicant of an offence for his repeatedly derogatory remarks about the local judiciary was a justifiable interference with freedom of expression in a democratic society, but that Art.10 was violated because the sentence was far too severe. A similar approach was taken in *Lesnik v Slovakia*[139] with the opposite outcome: criticisms of the public prosecutor had included some veiled threats, and the Court concluded that the sentence—four months' imprisonment, suspended—was not disproportionate.

In considering whether prosecutions for defamation of prosecutors and state officials involved in the judicial process are violations of Art.10, the Court has balanced the need for the courts to enjoy public confidence against its finding that the limits of acceptable criticism may be wider in relation to civil servants exercising their powers than in relation to private individuals.[140] In *Nikula v Finland*[141] the Court found a violation of Art.10 in relation to the conviction of the applicant for criticising as unlawful two decisions taken by a public prosecutor in a trial in which the applicant was counsel for the defendants. Even though some of the terms of the applicant's criticism were inappropriate, it had been limited to the conduct of the prosecution as opposed to any personal qualities of the prosecutor. The Court noted that the distinction between the role of the prosecutor as the opponent of the accused and the role of the judge should provide increased protection for statements criticising the prosecutor as opposed to attacking the judge or the court as a whole,[142] and emphasised that it was only in exceptional cases that restriction of defence counsel's freedom of expression could be accepted as necessary in a democratic society.[143] Similarly, in finding a violation of Art.10 in *Raichinov v Bulgaria*[144] in convicting the applicant for alleging financial impropriety against another official, the Court emphasised the

---

[137] *cf. Schopfer v Switzerland* [1998] E.H.R.L.R. 646, where the Court held that there had been no breach of Art.10 when a lawyer was fined by his professional body for alleging that local judges knew of irregularities in their area and had been acting for years in flagrant disregard of human rights. See also *Hrico v Slovakia*, judgment of October 20, 2004, where the Court held that the limits of acceptable criticism are wider in respect of judges who enter political life and found a violation of Art.10 in relation to an award of damages against a journalist who had described as a "legal farce" the judgment given by a judge who was a prospective parliamentary candidate in a case which directly imvolved matters on which his political views were known.

[138] (2004) 38 E.H.R.R. 1.

[139] Judgment of March 11, 2003.

[140] For a discussion of these limits see *Thoma v Luxembourg* (2003) 36 E.H.R.R. 21, and the surprising decision of *Janowski v Poland* (2000) 29 E.H.R.R. 705.

[141] (2004) 38 E.H.R.R. 45.

[142] *ibid.*, at [25] and [50].

[143] See also *Steur v Netherlands* (2004) 39 E.H.R.R. 33.

[144] App.No.47579/99, judgment of April 20, 2006.

need for restraint in resorting to criminal proceedings in such cases rather than leaving individuals to bring civil actions.

VII. Speech Attacking the State

8–55 Turning to speech which is intended to undermine the state or its authorities, there are a number of statutory offences involving incitement to disaffection in the armed forces[145] or the police,[146] as well as the common law offence of seditious libel. The latter consists of the publication of words intended or tending to bring into hatred or contempt or to excite disaffection against the monarch, the government, Parliament or the administration of justice.[147] The offence requires proof of an intention to incite violence against constituted authority.[148] Lawful criticism which involves pointing out errors or defects in government with a view to encouraging change by lawful means is not seditious libel.[149]

8–56 Where such offences are involved the Strasbourg institutions require convincing evidence of a threat to national security or to the prevention of disorder. They will, however, take account of the context in which the speech has occurred. In *Engel v Netherlands*[150] the applicants were servicemen convicted of disciplinary offences following the publication and distribution of a journal which had been prohibited as being inconsistent with military discipline. The Court held that the term "disorder" in Art.10(2) encompassed not only public order, but the order required by membership of a specified group, such as the military. Since the publication had been in direct contravention of an order from a senior officer, the prosecution was based upon the legitimate requirement of preventing servicemen from undermining military discipline. More controversially, this principle has been extended to civilian defendants. In *Arrowsmith v United Kingdom*[151] the Commission rejected a complaint that a prosecution for incitement to disaffection amounted to a breach of Art.10. The applicant had distributed leaflets to soldiers advising them of ways to avoid serving in Northern Ireland. The Commission considered that the promotion of disaffection amongst soldiers could amount to a threat to national security, and accordingly that the restriction pursued a legitimate aim within Art.10(2). A prosecution was necessary because the applicant had expressed an intention to continue with the distribution.

8–57 On the other hand in *Grigoriades v Greece*[152] the Court found a breach of Art.10 where the applicant was convicted of an offence of insulting the army, and imprisoned. During his period of military service the applicant had written a letter critical of the army to his commanding officer. The Court held that the conviction was in breach of the right to freedom of expression. The letter, though it was expressed in harsh terms, addressed problems facing conscripts in general

---

[145] Under the Incitement to Disaffection Act 1934, s.1 *et seq.*
[146] See for example the Police Act 1997, s.43.
[147] Stephen's *Digest of Criminal Law* (9th edn), Art.114.
[148] *R. v Metropolitan Stipendiary Magistrate ex parte Choudhury* [1991] Q.B. 429 at 453.
[149] *R. v Burns* (1886) 16 Cox. 355.
[150] (1979–80) 1 E.H.R.R. 647.
[151] (1978) 19 D.&R. 5.
[152] (1999) 27 E.H.R.R. 464.

and did not insult any individual. It was sent only to the commanding officer and not to the press or other conscripts, so its potential to undermine army discipline was insignificant. In view of the penalty imposed, the conviction was neither "necessary in a democratic society" for the prevention of disorder in the army, nor proportionate to a legitimate aim.

Violations of Art.10 have been found in many of the cases arising out of the **8-58** Kurdish conflict in Turkey, where the government has used offences under the anti-terrorist legislation to prosecute people who have written articles critical of the government's approach.[153] However in *Surek v Turkey*[154] the Court found that Art.10 had not been violated. The applicant, the owner of a Turkish news journal, published two articles critical of the Turkish government's handling of the Kurdish situation. He was convicted under the anti-terrorism legislation of disseminating propaganda against the indivisibility of the state and provoking enmity and hatred among the people. The Court accepted that the right to freedom of expression was engaged, and held that the preservation of national security could only justify proportionate interference with the Art.10 right. However, the line is crossed when political polemics support unlawful violence, and the articles here could be taken as supporting the armed struggle and thereby encouraging further violence.

In *O'Driscoll v Home Secretary*[155] the applicant had been stopped by customs **8-59** officers when he returned from Belgium with 1,000 copies of a Turkish magazine, *Vatan*. He was arrested on suspicion of possessing property for use in terrorism, and although he was later released the copies of the magazine and some related property were confiscated. He sought judicial review of the confiscation, arguing that s.16 of the Terrorism Act 2000 was incompatible with his Art.10 rights, but was unsuccessful. Kennedy L.J. acknowledged the importance of freedom of expression, citing a passage from *Surek v Turkey*,[156] but held that s.16 is about possessing property with the intention that it be used for terrorist purposes, and not about freedom of expression. For a prosecution under s.16 to succeed, the prosecution would have to establish the necessary intention, and so it would be a question of whether the sale of the magazines was intended to provide funds for terrorism.

VIII. Disclosure of Official Secrets

The Court and Commission have accepted that where the disclosure of state **8-60** secrets is damaging to national security, and is not justified by an overriding public interest, the imposition of sanctions in respect of that disclosure is unlikely

---

[153] See *Zana v Turkey* (1997) 27 E.H.R.R. 667, the cases discussed at [1998] E.H.R.L.R. 645, see also *Sener v Turkey* (2003) 37 E.H.R.R. 34, *EK v Turkey* (2002) 35 E.H.R.R. 41, *Zarakolu v Turkey*, judgment of July 13, 2004 and *Okutan v Turkey*, judgment of July 29, 2004.

[154] [1999] E.H.R.L.R. 636. *Cf.* the series of cases decided on the same day and discussed at [1999] E.H.R.L.R. 637–639.

[155] [2002] EWHC Admin 2477.

[156] *ibid.*, at [17], citing para.57 of the *Surek* judgment.

to constitute a violation of Art.10.[157] In *Hadjianastassiou v Greece*[158] the applicant was an airforce officer in charge of a project to design and produce guided missiles, who complained that his conviction for "disclosing military information of minor importance" constituted a violation of Art.10. He had sold information from his work to a private company. He argued that the disclosure could not be regarded as damaging to national security since it was a routine technical study based entirely on his own documentation. The Court considered that the disclosure of a state's interest in a given weapons system and the corresponding technical knowledge could give an indication as to the state's progress in the manufacture of the weapon and that consequently it was capable of causing considerable damage to national security. Having regard to the "duties and responsibilities" incumbent on members of the armed forces and the obligation of confidentiality on the applicant, his conviction and suspended sentence did not constitute a violation of Art.10.

8–61   The Court's judgment in *Hadjianasstassiou* was cited by the House of Lords in *R. v Shayler*,[159] when it confirmed that the absence of a public interest defence to charges under ss.1(1) and 4(1) of the Official Secrets Act 1989 is compatible with Art.10. Those sections make it an offence for a member or former member of the security or intelligence services to disclose without lawful authority information which is in his possession by virtue of his position as such. There is no requirement for the Crown to prove that the information is damaging to the national interest,[160] and it is no defence for the accused to show that the disclosure was made in the public interest. Lord Hope approached the matter on the basis that the absence of a public interest defence in the 1989 Act appeared incompatible with Art.10, citing the opinions of textwriters to that effect.[161] When considering whether the Act's restrictions on freedom of expression met the test of proportionality, he concluded that "the scheme of the Act is vulnerable to criticism on the ground that it lacks the necessary degree of sensitivity" to the facts of each case, by ruling out entirely a public interest defence.[162] However, their Lordships pointed out the the defendant in this case had not attempted to take advantage of other procedures provided by the Act, such as a request for official authorisation. Even if one might be cynical about the probability that the security services would want to protect themselves by refusing all or most such requests, Lord Hope argued that decisions to refuse authorisation could be challenged by way of judicial review, and that this possibility met the requirement of proportionality in Art.10(2). Thus their Lordships concluded that the 1989 Act is compatible with Art.10, and that someone in Mr. Shayler's position, with his belief that certain citizens were being placed in danger by the activities

---

[157] *Vereniging Weekend Bluf! v Netherlands* (1995) 20 E.H.R.R. 189. The court has generally been prepared to recognise a wide margin of appreciation where measures taken to safeguard national security are at stake: *Leander v Sweden* (1987) 9 E.H.R.R. 433.

[158] (1992) 16 E.H.R.R. 219.

[159] [2002] UKHL 11.

[160] Where the disclosure is made by someone who is not a former member of the services, the offence is only made out if the disclosure is damaging. Accordingly, it is an offence for a member or former member of the services to disclose information notwithstanding that the disclosure of the same information would not be an offence if the disclosure was made by another person.

[161] At [42].

[162] At [70].

of MI5, should exercise his Art.10 right by applying for official authorisation to disclose and then challenging any refusal by way of judicial review.

"In favour of that choice there are a number of important factors. However well intentioned he or she may be, a member or former member of the security or inelligence services may not be equipped with sufficient information to understand the potential impact of any disclosure. It may cause far more damage than the person making the disclosure was ever in a position to anticipate. The criminal process risks compounding the potential for damage to the operations of these services, if the prosecution have to prove beyond reasonable doubt the damaging nature of the disclosures."[163]

IX. Free Speech and Public Order

In *Steel v United Kingdom*[164] five applicants claimed that their arrests for breach **8–62** of the peace violated their rights of freedom of expression. All of them were involved in protests, and in the cases of the first two applicants the protests took the form of physically obstructing the activities of others. The Court, citing *Chorherr v Austria*,[165] held that their conduct nonetheless constituted an expression of opinion within Art.10. In respect of two of the applicants, who had caused physical obstructions, the Court held that their arrest, conviction and subsequent imprisonment was a proportionate response in order to avert the danger of disorder and violence.[166] However, in relation to the other three applicants, who were merely distributing leaflets and holding a placard, the Court held that they were exercising their freedom of expression and (unanimously) that their arrest was a disproportionate response, which violated Art.10.

A similar issue arose in *Hashman and Harrup v United Kingdom*,[167] where the **8–63** applicants were hunt saboteurs who had blown a horn, and shouted at hounds during a fox-hunt. They were bound over to keep the peace by magistrates, and the Crown Court upheld the binding over on the ground that their conduct, although not involving either violence or the likelihood of a breach of the peace, was "*contra bonos mores*." The Court held that this amounted to a breach of Art.10. In the light of *Steel*, there was no doubt that the applicants' acts were forms of expression within Art.10(1). The more difficult question was whether the interference with their right was "prescribed by law", as required by Art.10(2). On this point the Court distinguished *Steel*. In *Steel* the Court had held that the concept of breach of the peace was sufficiently certain to fulfil the

---

[163] *Per* Lord Hope at [84].
[164] (1999) 28 E.H.R.R. 603; See also *McLeod v United Kingdom*, (1999) 27 E.H.R.R. 493 a decision of the court on the same day which also concerns the use of "breach of the peace" powers.
[165] (1994) 17 E.H.R.R. 358 cited at para.92 of *Steel*.
[166] The first applicant was held on arrest for 44 hours and then imprisoned for 28 days when she refused to be bound over to keep the peace. Four judges dissented from the finding that this was "not disproportionate" and held that her Art.10 right had been violated, two of them going so far as to describe the length of custody as "manifestly extreme."
[167] (2000) 30 E.H.R.R. 241.

"quality of law" test required by the Court.[168] Here, by contrast, the concept of behaviour *contra bonos mores* was not defined with sufficient clarity to enable citizens to regulate their conduct, and there was therefore a risk of arbitrary interference with the applicants' Art.10 rights. The Law Commission had reached the same conclusion in its inquiry into the subject,[169] but the government had not proposed any change in the law.

8–64 Less encouraging is the majority decision of the court in *Janowski v Poland*.[170] The applicant had been convicted of the offence of insulting civil servants. He was a journalist who witnessed two municipal guards directing stall holders to move their stalls to another place. Believing that they were acting unlawfully he intervened, eventually calling them "oafish" and "dumb". Overturning a finding of the Commission that Art.10 had been infringed, the Court observed that the applicants' remarks did not form part of an open discussion of matters of public concern, and that his conviction was based on the insults, rather than his criticisms of the officers' unlawful conduct. Whilst public servants should generally expect criticism of their actions, it could not be said that civil servants such as these municipal guards laid themselves open to the same degree of scrutiny as politicians. In the end the fact that the applicant had insulted the guards in front of a group of bystanders was held sufficient to justify his prosecution. In a strong dissenting opinion Sir Nicholas Bratza observed that there were good grounds for considering the guards' actions to be unlawful:

> "The applicant was, in these circumstances, amply justified in exercising his freedom of expression in remonstrating with [them]. The fact that, in the course of doing so, he used two insulting words which evidently reflected his sense of frustration with the attitude of the guards, could not in my view justify his prosecution ... [E]ven though the language used by the applicant may be considered exaggerated, it did not amount to a deliberate and gratuitous personal attack."

8–65 The relevance of Art.10 in a public order context was considered by the Divisional Court in *Redmond-Bate v Director of Public Prosecutions*.[171] The defendant and two others were Christian fundamentalists and were preaching from the steps of a cathedral. When some members of the crowd began to show hostility towards what they were saying, the police arrested the defendant for breach of the peace, and she was subsequently convicted of obstructing a police officer in the execution of his duty. The Divisional Court quashed the conviction, on an appeal by way of case stated, and placed considerable emphasis on the defendants' rights under Art.9, 10 and 11 of the Convention in doing so. Two points emerge from the decision. First, Sedley L.J. explicitly recognised that the right to freedom of expression extends to opinions that are controversial: "free speech includes not only the inoffensive but the irritating, the contentious, the heretical, the unwelcome and the provocative, provided it does not tend to provoke

---

[168] See para.10–17 below for discussion of certainty and the "quality of law" test.
[169] *Binding Over*, Law Com. No.222, (1994), paras 4.34 and 5.7.
[170] (2000) 29 E.H.R.R. 705.
[171] [1999] Crim. L.R. 998.

violence."[172] Secondly, the Divisional Court confirmed the principle in *Beatty v Gillbanks*[173] by holding that if the threat to the peace does not come from the defendants themselves but from hecklers, the police ought to arrest the hecklers and not the defendants. Both of them have a right to freedom of expression, of course, but the threat to public order comes from the heckler (unless the original speaker makes statements likely to provoke violence). This is a principle which the Strasbourg Court itself has articulated in the context of Art.11.[174]

In *Percy v Director of Public Prosecutions*[175] the defendant had been found   8-66
guilty of using insulting words or behaviour, contrary to s.5 of the Public Order Act 1986, when she wrote "Stop Star Wars" across a United States flag and, during a peaceful protest, waved the flag and then stood on it. The Divisional Court held that her conviction was incompatible with Art.10: in considering Art.10(2) the district judge had placed too much weight on the possibility of her making her protest in some other way, and too little emphasis on her right to freedom of expression. Protecting the feelings of American service personnel and their families was not sufficient justification for a criminal conviction. This decision does not mean that s.5 of the Public Order Act is in itself incompatible with Art.10, but it does suggest that there are situations in which a person may be able to rely on Art.10 by way of defence to a charge under that section, even where the elements of the offence are established.[176]

X. Election offences

In *Bowman v United Kingdom*[177] the defendant, a pro-Life campaigner, had   8-67
distributed leaflets during an election campaign setting out the candidates' voting record on abortion. She was prosecuted under s.75 of the Representation of the People Act 1983 for an offence of incurring unauthorised expenditure.[178] The Court held that the prosecution was a disproportionate interference with her right to freedom of expression. It accepted that the legislation pursued a legitimate aim, namely to control expenditure of individual candidates so as ensure, as far as possible, that they are on an equal financial footing. However, the Court found that the statutory restriction of expenditure to £5 in the weeks preceding an election was disproportionate to this aim. It was "particularly important in the period preceding an election that opinions and information of all kinds are permitted to circulate freely", and the applicant was therefore entitled to disseminate factually accurate information to the local electorate "during the crucial period when their minds were focussed on their choice of representative".

---

[172] [1999] Crim. L.R. 998 at 1000; *cf.* the similar statements in *Handyside v United Kingdom*, para.8–24 above, and generally Geddis A., "Free Speech Martyrs or Unreasonable Threats to Social Peace?" [2004] *Public Law* 853.

[173] (1882) 9 Q.B.D. 308.

[174] *Plattform "Artze fur das Leben" v Austria* (1991) 13 E.H.R.R. 204 at para.32.

[175] [2002] Crim.L.R. 835, on which see Rogers J., "Prosecutors, Courts and Conduct of the Accused which Engages a Qualified Human Right" (2005) 58 *Current Legal Problems* 101.

[176] See, however, *Hammond v DPP* [2004] Crim.L.R. 851, above, 8–17.

[177] (1998) 26 E.H.R.R. 1, noted at [1998] Public Law 592.

[178] See also *Holding* [2005] EWCA Crim 3185.

E. FREEDOM OF ASSEMBLY AND ASSOCIATION

I. General principles

8–68   The Convention protects the right to organise and to participate in peaceful public demonstrations[179] and marches.[180] The right extends to meetings which cause obstruction of public thoroughfares,[181] and to private meetings,[182] provided they are planned to be peaceful. The focus here is on the intention of the organisers. Thus, the Commission has held that:

> " . . . the right to freedom of peaceful assembly is secured to everyone who has the *intention* of organising a peaceful demonstration . . . [T]he possibility of violent counter-demonstrations, or the possibility of extremists with violent intentions . . . joining the demonstration cannot as such take away that right."[183]

8–69   A peaceful demonstration will be protected by Art.11(1) even if it is unlawful. Thus, for example, in *G v Federal Republic of Germany*[184] the Commission held that a non-violent unlawful sit-in which blocked the entrance to American barracks in Germany constituted "peaceful assembly", attracting the protection of Art.11.[185] The longer a demonstration goes on, however, the more likely it is that an interference will be justified under Art.11(2), particularly if it causes serious disruption to others. In *Friedl v Austria*[186] the applicant had organised a sit-in in a busy underpass in Vienna to publicise the plight of the homeless. The sit-in obstructed passers-by, and numerous complaints were made to the authorities. About 50 people were initially involved, and the demonstration continued for a week until the police dispersed it. The Commission concluded that the decision to disperse, after such a long period of time, fell squarely within the state's margin of appreciation.

8–70   Requirements to notify the authorities or to seek prior permission will not generally constitute an interference with the right to peaceful assembly.[187] The Court has, however, held that *ex post facto* criminal or disciplinary sanctions do amount to an interference. In *Ezelin v France*[188] a lawyer had carried a placard

---

[179] *Rassemblement Jurassien and Unite Jurassienne v Switzerland* (1979) 17 D.R. 93 at 119.

[180] *Christians against Racism and Fascism v United Kingdom* (1980) 21 D.R. 138 at 148.

[181] *Rassemblement Jurassien* (above) at 119.

[182] *ibid.*, although there is no elaboration of what constitutes a "private meeting" for this purpose.

[183] *Christians against Racism and Fascism v United Kingdom* (1980) 21 D.R. 138, emphasis added.

[184] (1989) 60 D.R. 256 at 263.

[185] In the event, the applicant's arrest and conviction were justified under Art.11(2) since the protest had caused "more obstruction than would normally arise from the exercise of the right to peaceful assembly".

[186] Application No.15225/89 (unreported) (Admissibility). A different aspect of the case was declared admissible under Art.8, and the court's judgment is at (1996) 21 E.H.R.R. 83.

[187] *Rassemblement Jurassien*, (1979) 17 D.R. 93 at 119. Obviously, if permission is refused then this will amount to an interference.

[188] (1992) 14 E.H.R.R. 362.

during a demonstration against the judicial system. His own conduct was peaceful, but when others began to hurl abuse and daub graffiti he failed to leave. The European Court held that his Art.11 rights had been violated despite the comparatively light the penalty subsequently imposed on him (a professional reprimand for "breach of discretion" as a lawyer).

The Court has held that there is some measure of positive obligation on the state **8–71** to protect those exercising their right of peaceful assembly from violent disturbance by counter-demonstrators. In *Plattform "Artze fur das Leben" v Austria*[189] the Court explained that "genuine, effective freedom of peaceful assembly cannot be reduced to a mere duty on the part of the State not to interfere", and that "Article 11 sometimes requires positive measures to be taken." If both demonstrations are peaceful, and thus entitled to protection, then the authorities must balance their rights. But if one demonstration is aimed at the disruption of the activities of another, then the authorities come under an obligation to protect those exercising the right of peaceful assembly. The threat of violence from an opposing demonstration does not of itself justify interference with a peaceful demonstration[190]:

> "A demonstration may annoy or give offence to persons opposed to the ideas or claims that it is seeking to promote. The participants must, however, be able to hold the demonstrations without having to fear that they will be subjected to physical violence by their opponents; such a fear would be liable to deter associations or other groups supporting common ideas or interests from openly expressing their opinions on highly controversial issues affecting the community. In a democracy, the right to counter-demonstrate cannot extend to inhibiting the right to demonstrate."

In the public order context, the principle of fair balance between competing **8–72** interests is easier to state than it is to apply.[191] In *Chorherr v Austria*,[192] the applicant held up banners at a military ceremony as a protest against the arms trade. Certain members of the crowd became agitated and threatened him with physical violence. The police asked him to desist and when he refused, he was arrested and subsequently fined. The Court found no violation, considering that the applicant's protest had been antagonistic. Given the occasion, there were no reasonable alternative means available to preserve public order, and the applicant's arrest was accordingly justified. However, in *Öllinger v Austria*[193] the Court found a violation of Art.11 when a counter-demonstration was unconditionally banned, not least because it was banned by reference to upholding the rights of ordinary visitors to a certain cemetery who were not involved in the demonstration at all. The Government had a positive obligation to preserve the applicant's right to peaceful assembly, by ensuring a sufficient police presence.

---

[189] (1991) 13 E.H.R.R. 204 at para.32.
[190] (1991) 13 E.H.R.R. 204 at para.32.
[191] See, however, *Redmond-Bate v DPP* [1999] Crim. L.R. 998, (considered at para.8–62 above) where the Divisional Court struck the balance firmly in favour of free expression.
[192] (1994) 17 E.H.R.R. 358.
[193] [2006] E.H.R.L.R. 583.

II. Offences under the Public Order Act 1986 and Criminal Justice and Public
Order Act 1994[194]

8–73   In England and Wales the carrying out of public demonstrations is regulated
primarily by Pt II of the Public Order Act 1986, as amended by the Criminal
Justice and Public Order Act 1994. Section 11 of the 1986 Act creates a duty of
advance notification to the police. Sections 12 and 14 create police powers to
impose conditions on processions and assemblies. Sections 13 and 14 (as
amended) create powers to prohibit processions and trespassory assemblies, and
to stop persons proceeding to trespassory assemblies. The Act creates a number
of summary offences of organising and participating in a prohibited demonstration.

8–74   Whilst the requirements for notice and the dependent offences appear on their
face to be compatible with Art.11 as interpreted, the issuance of a ban on
assemblies in a particular area raises more difficult issues. In *Christians against
Racism and Fascism v United Kingdom*[195] the Commission held that two separate
bans imposed under the Public Order Act 1936 on all marches in a particular area
were justified under Art.11(2). The bans were justified on the ground that there
was evidence of mounting tension in the area, and the police expected disorder
to occur. The Commission pointed to the limited duration of the ban and its
comparatively small geographical scope. Although it was drawn so as to encompass all processions in London, it had been aimed primarily at marches organised
by the National Front and was supported by evidence that such marches had
frequently degenerated into violence in the past.[196] In the light of the principles
subsequently stated by the court in *Plattform "Artze fur das Leben"*,[197] it is at
least open to question whether the case would be decided in the same way
today.

8–75   The application of Art.11 to the provisions of the Public Order Act 1986 arose
in *Rai, Allmond and "Negotiate Now" v United Kingdom*,[198] where the Secretary
of State had used a statutory power to make regulations requiring permission for
all demonstrations in Trafalgar Square, and had announced and adopted a policy
of refusing permission for all demonstrations relating to Northern Ireland that
were not "uncontroversial". The Commission held that this restriction could be
brought within Art.11(2), since its purpose was to prevent an outbreak of
violence. One interesting aspect in this application was that the Secretary of State

---

[194] See generally Fitzpatrick B. and Taylor N., "Trespassers might be Prosecuted: the European
Convention and Restrictions on the Right to Assemble" [1998] E.H.R.L.R. 292.
[195] (1980) 21 D.R. 138.
[196] The Commission in *Rassemblement Jurassien v Switzerland* (1979) 17 D.R. 93 had earlier
upheld a temporary local ban on demonstrations in a particular town in a Swiss canton, insisting that
such bans should be "proportionate" but also stating that the margin of appreciation in this field is
"fairly broad" when there is a foreseeable danger to public safety which requires prompt decisions.
[197] See para.8–71 above.
[198] (1995) 81 D.R. 146.

had reminded the applicants that permission was likely to be granted for a demonstration in Hyde Park.[199]

In *Pendragon v United Kingdom*[200] an order under s.14A of the Public Order Act **8–76** 1986 (as amended) had been made prohibiting all trespassory assemblies of 20 or more people within a four-mile radius of Stonehenge for a four-day period creating what was, in effect, an exclusion zone. The applicant was arrested and prosecuted for his part in breaching the order. He was acquitted, but alleged that his rights under Arts 9, 10 and 11 had been violated. The Commission declared the application inadmissible, noting that there had been disorder in previous years, which was capable of justifying the prohibition. Moreover, it remained possible for the applicant to exercise his right to freedom of religion by proceeding in a group of less than 20. These decisions clearly establish that it will be easier for the authorities to justify restrictions if there is a reasonably-founded fear of violence, but it is noticeable that both in *Pendragon,* and in *Rai, Allmond and "Negotiate Now"*, alternative means of exercising Convention rights were available.

The Criminal Justice and Public Order Act 1994 amended the 1986 Act, and **8–77** introduced further offences. The offence of aggravated trespass, contrary to s.68 of the 1994 Act, penalises persons who trespass on land and do acts intended, *inter alia*, to obstruct or disrupt an activity being lawfully conducted by others on that land. In the light of the Commission's decision in *G v Federal Republic of Germany*, discussed above,[201] it seems clear that a peaceful (albeit illegal) demonstration which is intended only to disrupt, and not to intimidate, constitutes an exercise of the Art.11(1) right to peaceful assembly.[202] This may give rise to difficult questions as to the applicability of Art.11 to private property.[203]

The 1994 Act also introduced various offences connected with trespassory **8–78** assemblies, (inserting ss.14A, B and C into the Public Order Act 1986).[204] In *DPP v Jones*[205] the defendant and others had been charged under s.14B(2) with holding a trespassory assembly in defiance of an order prohibiting such assemblies at Stonehenge. They were convicted in the magistrates' court but the Crown Court upheld their submission of no case to answer, on the ground that the demonstration had been peaceful and had not obstructed the highway. The prosecutor's appeal by way of case stated was allowed, the Divisional Court holding that the offence was committed even if the demonstration was peaceful and did not cause an obstruction. However, the House of Lords allowed the appeal and held that the defendants should not have been convicted of taking part

---

[199] The applicants sought to argue, albeit unsuccessfully, that if there was thought to be no danger to public safety from a meeting in Hyde Park it could not be said that a meeting in Trafalgar Square would be more liable to violence.

[200] [1999] E.H.R.L.R. 223; the Commission had earlier held in *Chappell v United Kingdom* (1988) 10 E.H.R.R. 510, that a ban on assemblies at Stonehenge was necessary for "the prevention of disorder or crime, or for the protection of the rights and freedoms of others."

[201] See para.8–69 above.

[202] See also *Ezelin v France* (1992) 14 E.H.R.R. 362.

[203] See para.8–75 below.

[204] As amended by ss.70 and 71 of the Criminal Justice and Public Order Act 1994.

[205] [1999] 2 A.C. 240.

in a trespassory assembly. The right to use a public highway was not restricted to passing and re-passing, but extended to a range of other activities such as taking photographs, handing out leaflets, collecting for charity, playing games on the pavement, or having a picnic, so long as the activity does not create a nuisance or an obstruction. This is an important decision in its own right, as a development of the common law, but it also chimes well with Arts 10 and 11 of the Convention. It moves towards the idea of the protection of the individual's rights as the court's starting point, whilst leaving room for the authorities to justify interference with the right on appropriate grounds.

8–79   The Public Order Act 1986 requires notice to be given to the police of a forthcoming demonstration, and s.13 of the Act allows a Chief Constable to apply for an order prohibiting all processions in a given area if ordinary police powers are thought insufficient to prevent the risk of serious disorder. In *R. (on the application of Laporte) v Chief Constable of Gloucestershire*[206] the police knew that there were to be demonstrations at the Fairford air base, but no application was made under s.13. Instead, on the day the police stopped coaches carrying demonstrators and ordered them back to London, providing a police escort that ensured their return to London without stopping. Although some of the passengers on the coach on which the appellant was travelling did belong to a group with a history of causing disruption, most did not and the appellant was merely a peaceful demonstrator. Lord Bingham held that:

> "There was no reason (other than her refusal to give her name, which however irritating to the police was entirely lawful) to view the claimant as other than a committed, peaceful demonstrator. It was wholly disproportionate to restrict her exercise of her rights under Articles 10 and 11 because she was in the company of others some of whom might, at some time in the future, breach the peace."[207]

Thus the House of Lords upheld the appeal, holding that the police had no right to turn the appellant away from Fairford because no breach of the peace by her was imminent, and also that the police had no right to restrict her liberty by forcing her to return to London.

III. A right to assemble on private property?

8–80   One question that is not yet fully resolved is whether the right of assembly conferred by Art.11 extends to meetings held on private premises. This may be important in any consideration of whether the offence of aggravated trespass (discussed above) is compatible with Art.11. The question was ventilated in *Anderson v United Kingdom*,[208] where the applicants had been excluded from a shopping centre by a letter from the owners alleging misconduct and disorderly behaviour. The lease granted to the owners of the shopping centre by the local authority required them to allow the public access to the centre during shopping

---

[206] [2006] UKHL 55.
[207] At [55].
[208] [1998] E.H.R.L.R. 218. For a comprehensive discussion of *Anderson* and the international and comparative law on the subject, see Kevin Gray and Susan Gray, "Civil Rights, Civil Wrongs and Quasi-Public Space" [1999] E.H.R.L.R. 46.

hours. The applicants alleged that their Art.11 rights had been violated. The Commission declared the application inadmissible, not on the ground that the premises were private, but on the ground that the right to peaceful assembly and freedom of association relates to gatherings of individuals "in order to attain various ends," and does not apply to people assembling for merely social purposes. The Commission appeared to consider that freedom of assembly in the Convention is confined to political purposes. This seems to be an unusually narrow reading of Art.11, and is more restrictive than the English law stated by the House of Lords in *DPP v Jones*.[209] It is one thing to accord special protection to the right to demonstrate on matters of public concern, but it is surely quite another thing to hold that there is no right at all to assemble for social purposes.[210]

Several common law jurisdictions have come to recognise that the law of trespass   **8–81** is subject a right of reasonable access to quasi-public spaces. Under this principle owners of large private areas which are generally accessible to the public may only exclude particular individuals on grounds which are objectively reasonable. In the United States, the principle was first established in the context of "company towns",[211] but has since developed to include shopping precincts and other quasi-public spaces.[212] A similar approach has been taken by the Supreme Court of Canada.[213]

The matter was considered by the Court in *Appleby v United Kingdom*[214] where the applicants had been prevented by the owners of a shopping mall in a town centre from setting up stands and collecting signatures in the entrances to the mall for a campaign against a local planning development. The Court considered the United States case-law but concluded that it did not reveal an emerging consensus on the right to free speech on privately owned land. The Court accepted that social and economic developments meant that there were changes in the way people came into contact with each other (and that shopping centres could assume the characteristics of the traditional town centre), but was not persuaded that this required the automatic creation of rights of entry to private property, or even, necessarily, to all publicly owned property (such as government offices and ministries, for instance). The Court did state, however, that where the bar on access to property had the effect of preventing any effective exercise of freedom of expression a positive obligation might arise to protect the enjoyment of the Convention rights by regulating property rights.[215] In this case the Court did not find that the applicants, who had managed to collect 3200

---

[209] See para.8–74 above.

[210] The application in *Anderson* was also brought under Art.14. The applicants were black and alleged that the exclusion was discriminatory, but the Commission found no evidence of this.

[211] *Marsh v Alabama* 326 US 501; 90 L. Ed. 265 (1946).

[212] *Amalgamated Food Employees Union Local 590 v Logan Valley Plaza* 391 US 308 at 319–320; 20 L. Ed. 2d. 603 at 612–613 (1968); *New Jersey Coalition Against War in the Middle East v JMB Realty Corporation* 650 A2d 757 (1994) at 777.

[213] See, for example, *The Queen in Right of Canada v Committee for the Commonwealth of Canada* (1991) 77 D.L.R. (4th) 385 at 393D-H.

[214] (2003) 37 E.H.R.R. 38.

[215] *ibid.* [47].

signatures notwithstanding their exclusion from the shopping centre, were effectively prevented from exercising their rights to freedom of expression or freedom of association.

IV. Freedom of Association

8–82 Article 11 safeguards not just the right of peaceful assembly but also the right to freedom of association with others. A decision to classify an organisation as a terrorist organisation (under Sch.2 to the Terrorism Act 2000, and s.3) renders its members liable to prosecution for various offences under that Act. In *R. (on application of the Kurdistan Workers' Party and others) v Home Secretary*[216] an action was brought for judicial review of the Home Secretary's decision to add various organisations to the list of proscribed organisations in Sch.2. The action failed for technical reasons not relevant here, but Richards J. accepted the relevance of Arts 10 and 11 in determining whether the proscription could be justified. In particular, the right to freedom of association under Article was engaged, which means that any interference with that right must be justified by being shown to be prescribed by law, pursuing a legitimate aim, and being proportionate to the aim pursued.

In *Refah Partisi (Welfare Party) v Turkey*[217] the Court found that the dissolution of the Refah Party on the basis that it advocated the adoption of sharia law was a proportionate interference with Art.11 because the aims espoused by the party were incompatible with the concept of a democratic society, because the Refah party did not exclude recourse to force in order to implement their plans and because there were real opportunities for the party to put its plans into practice which made the danger more immediate.[218] The reasoning employed by the Court in finding the interference with the applicant's rights justified under Art.11(2) could equally have supported an exclusion from reliance on that right under Art.17.[219] In *WP v Poland*,[220] in declaring inadmissible an application from Polish nationals who had been refused permission to set up an association called the National and Patriotic Association of Polish Victims of Bolshevism and Zionism, the Court concluded that the evidence in the case, which included the anti-semitic tenor of the submissions before the court, justified the need to bring Art.17 into play.

F. OTHER ISSUES

8–83 This Chapter has been concerned primarily with the rights guaranteed under Arts 8 to 11 of the Convention. In some cases a challenge based on one of those Articles has been combined with an Art.14 challenge; but it should be recalled that a challenge based on Art.14 alone cannot succeed, since that Article is only

---

[216] [2002] EWHC Admin 644.
[217] (2003) 37 E.H.R.R. 1.
[218] *ibid.* at [132].
[219] See *United Communist Party of Turkey v Turkey* (1998) 26 E.H.R.R. 121.
[220] (2005) 40 E.H.R.R. SE1.

engaged where the violation of another Convention right can also be demonstrated, and a challenge attempting to combine Art.6 with Art.14 has been unsuccessful.[221] However, issues may occasionally arise under other substantive guarantees. In *Family H v United Kingdom*,[222] for example, the applicants were convicted of failing to comply with an order requiring them to send their children to state school or provide evidence of their education at home. They had elected to educate their children at home because of learning difficulties. The family complained that the prosecution infringed their right to education under Art.2 of the First Protocol. The Commission rejected the complaint, holding that since the state is entitled to establish a system of compulsory state education, it did not breach Art.2 of the First Protocol by requiring parents to co-operate in an assessment of their children's educational standards.

---

[221] *Kirk and Russell* [2002] Crim.L.R. 756, alleging violations arising from the availability in s.6 of the Sexual Offences Act 1956 of a defence of reasonable mistake as to age for men under 24 but not for men over 24. See *Thlimmenos v Greece* (2001) 31 E.H.R.R. for successful reliance on Art.9 together with Art.14.
[222] (1984) 337 D.R. 105.

CHAPTER 9

THE BURDEN AND STANDARD OF PROOF

A. INTRODUCTION

The principles established in the Convention caselaw have to accommodate   **9–01**
criminal procedure systems as diverse as the former soviet legal systems of
Central and Eastern Europe, continental legal systems and common law systems,
judge-only trials and jury trials. It is inevitable that any constitutional standards
which are applicable to so many different legal traditions will sometimes be
insufficiently detailed to afford a comprehensive guide to the application of the
Convention in the United Kingdom criminal law. The burden and standard of
proof in criminal proceedings is one such area.

However, since the Human Rights Act came into force the English courts have
been developing their own pragmatic approach to the issues, as will appear
below.

B. REVERSE ONUS PROVISIONS

I. Introduction

The starting point in any analysis of reverse onus provisions in England and   **9–02**
Wales[1] is the well-known statement of Viscount Sankey L.C. in *Woolmington v
DPP*[2] that "throughout the web of the English criminal law one golden thread is
always to be seen, that is that it is the duty of the prosecution to prove the
prisoner's guilt." This principle is reflected in Art.6(2) of the Convention which
enshrines the presumption of innocence in criminal proceedings.[3] The only
common law exception to the *Woolmington* principle is the defence of insanity.[4]

---

[1] As to the position in Scotland, see *Slater v HM Advocate* 1928 J.C. 94 at 105.
[2] [1935] A.C. 462 at 481.
[3] Art.6(2) is an aspect of the defendant's right to a fair trial so that an infringement of the
presumption of innocence *a fortiori* renders a trial unfair within the meaning of Art.6. In *Deweer v
Belgium* (1979–80) 2 E.H.R.R. 439 at para.56 the European Court of Human Rights observed that the
rights contained in Art.6(2) and 6(3) " ... represent specific applications of the general principle
stated in paragraph 1 of the Article. The presumption of innocence embodied in paragraph 2 and the
various rights of which a non-exhaustive list appears in paragraph 3 ... are constituent elements,
amongst others, of the notion of a fair trial in criminal proceedings."
[4] See para.11–29 below.

There are, however, numerous statutory provisions which impose a burden of some kind on the accused in the course of a criminal trial. As Lord Hope observed in *R. v DPP ex parte Kebilene and others*[5]:

> "[I]t has always been open to Parliament by way of a statutory exception to transfer the onus of proof as to some matter arising in a criminal case from the prosecution to the accused ... [U]ntil now, under the doctrine of sovereignty, the only check on Parliament's freedom to legislate in this area has been political. All that will now change with the coming into force of the Human Rights Act 1998 ... [T]he change will affect the past as well as the future. Unlike the constitutions of many of the countries within the Commonwealth which protect pre-existing legislation from challenge under their human rights provisions, the 1998 Act will apply to all legislation, whatever its date, in the past as well as in the future."

9–03   The extent to which a statutory burden imposed on the accused encroaches on the presumption of innocence will depend on the legislative technique which has been adopted.[6] It is possible to identify three broad categories of reverse onus clause—persuasive (or ultimate) burdens, evidential burdens, and "special defences". A "persuasive" burden of proof requires the accused to prove, on a balance of probabilities, an ultimate fact necessary to the determination of guilt or innocence. Such a presumption may relate to an essential element (of greater or lesser importance) making up either the *actus reus* or the *mens rea* of the offence; and may be either mandatory[7] or discretionary[8] in its operation. Where a persuasive burden of proof is placed on the accused, it is possible for a conviction to be returned, even where the tribunal of fact entertains a reasonable doubt as to his guilt.[9] Such provisions require close scrutiny, in order to determine their compatibility with Art.6(2).

9–04   An "evidential" burden, by contrast, is not a burden of proof as such. It requires only that the accused must adduce sufficient evidence to raise an issue before it has to be determined by the tribunal of fact. Once the accused has adduced evidence sufficient to raise the issue, the burden of proving (or disproving) that issue rests on the prosecution. In the final assessment of guilt, the burden on the accused is thus no more than a burden to raise a reasonable doubt as to guilt. The

---

[5] [1999] 3 W.L.R. 972 (HL).

[6] See generally Glanville Williams, *The Proof of Guilt*, (3rd edn, Stevens, 1963), pp.183–186.

[7] Where a presumption operating against the accused is mandatory, the trier of fact has no discretion as to whether or not to apply the presumption, and it may therefore be possible to judge its compatibility with the presumption of innocence on the face of the statute, without reference to the facts of an individual case. In *R. v DPP ex parte Kebilene and ors* [1999] 3 W.L.R. 972 Lord Hope said "I can see no reason why, in a clear case, where the facts of the case are of no importance, a decision that a provision is incompatible [with Article 6(2)] should not be capable of being taken at a very early stage". Similarly, the US Supreme Court has held that where a mandatory reverse onus clause is in issue, the question of its constitutional compatibility is "logically divorced" from the facts of the case, so that the issue falls to be determined "facially" (i.e. on a consideration of the statute on its face): *County Court of Ulster County v Allen* 442 US 140 (1979).

[8] A discretionary presumption of guilt may breach the presumption of innocence, depending upon whether or not the tribunal of fact relies on the presumption in order to convict the accused. Accordingly, it will usually be necessary to consider the facts of a case before reaching a conclusion as to whether the presumption of innocence has been violated.

[9] This will occur where the accused adduces evidence which is sufficient to raise a reasonable doubt on the issue, but fails to discharge the burden of proof on the balance of probabilities.

imposition of an evidential burden on the accused is not incompatible with the presumption of innocence.[10]

A "special defence" arises where a statute prohibits the doing of an act save   9–05
where it is done with a licence or permission, or subject to an exemption or proviso. In *R. v Edwards*[11] Lawton L.J. said;

> "[O]ver the centuries the common law, as a result of experience and the need to ensure that justice is done both to the community and to defendants, has evolved an exception to the fundamental rule of our criminal law that the prosecution must prove every element of the offence charged. This exception, like so much else in the common law, was hammered out on the anvil of pleading. It is limited to offences arising under enactments which prohibit the doing of an act save in specified circumstances or with the licence or permission of specified authorities. Whenever the prosecution seeks to rely on this exception, the court must construe the enactment under which the charge is laid. If the true construction is that the enactment prohibits the doing of acts, subject to provisos, exemptions and the like, then the prosecution can rely upon the exception."[12]

Edwards was approved in *R. v Hunt*,[13] where the House of Lords held that it was   9–06
not a pre-requisite that the statute should specifically provide for the burden to rest on the defendant. Exceptions could be express or implied, and the relevant proviso did not need to appear in the section creating the offence. Where a linguistic construction did not clearly indicate on whom the burden should lie, the court could have regard to other considerations to determine the intention of Parliament, such as the mischief at which the offence was aimed, and practical considerations such as who is likely to be best able to discharge the burden. The distinguishing feature of a special defence is that the accused knows, at the time when he commits the act in question, that his conduct amounts to a criminal offence unless he can bring himself within the licence or permission requirements specified in the Act.[14] A special defence may breach the presumption of innocence,[15] but is less likely to do so than a persuasive burden on an important essential element of the offence.[16]

With these three broad categories in mind—persuasive burdens of proof, eviden-   9–07
tial burdens, and special defences—we turn to consider, first, the relevant Strasbourg caselaw; the approach of the English courts; then some constitutional decisions from other common law jurisdictions.

---

[10] See *R. v DPP ex parte Kebilene and ors* [1999] 3 W.L.R. 972 *per* Lord Hope (see below at para.9–23). The same conclusion has been reached in Canada and South Africa: see paras 9–57 and 9–61 below.

[11] [1975] Q.B. 27 (CA).

[12] A similar rule was introduced for summary proceedings by Magistrates' Courts Act 1980, s.101. This provides that wherever a statute creates a defence, exception, or proviso it must be proved by the defendant (on a balance of probabilities).

[13] [1987] A.C. 352.

[14] *Attorney-General for Hong Kong v Lee Kwong-kut and anor.* [1993] A.C. 951 (PC) *per* Lord Woolf at 962C–E; 964E–G.

[15] *R. v DPP ex parte Kebilene and ors* [1999] 3 W.L.R. 972, *per* Lord Hope, see para.9–23 below.

[16] See, for example, *R. v Schwartz* (1988) 55 D.L.R. (4th) 1 (S.C.C.).

II. The Strasbourg Caselaw

9–08   One of the earliest decisions was that in *X v United Kingdom*,[17] where the Commission upheld the rebuttable presumption that a man who was proved to be living with, or controlling a prostitute was knowingly living off immoral earnings. The Commission nevertheless observed that a presumption of law or fact " . . . could, if widely or unreasonably worded, have the same effect as a presumption of guilt. It is not, therefore, sufficient to examine only the form in which the presumption is drafted. It is necessary to examine the substance and effect."

9–09   In *Lingens and another v Austria*[18] the Commission was concerned with a "special defence"[19] under the Austrian penal code. The relevant section provided that it was an offence to publish defamatory material, unless the accused was able to prove the truth of the statement. The Commission considered that this offence did not violate Art.6(2) since all the essential elements of the offence of publishing a defamatory statement had to be proved by the prosecution. In the Commission's view the prosecution retained the overall burden of proving guilt, and "the mutual position of the parties to the criminal proceedings [was] exactly the same as in all other criminal proceedings."

9–10   The leading case on this issue is *Salabiaku v France*.[20] The applicant challenged a rule under the French Customs Code whereby an accused who was proved to have physically imported a consignment of prohibited drugs was presumed to have known that the drugs were in his possession, and therefore to be guilty of an offence of importation. The applicant had been acquitted of the criminal offence of knowingly importing drugs, but had been convicted of a strict liability "customs offence" of importing goods in breach of the Customs Code, which carried a much lighter maximum penalty (three months imprisonment). The Court made it clear that member states retain the power to create offences of strict liability:

> "As the Government and the Commission have pointed out, in principle the Contracting States remain free to apply the criminal law to an act where it is not carried out in the normal exercise of one of the rights protected under the Convention and, accordingly, to define the constituent elements of the resulting offence. In particular, and again in principle, the Contracting States may, under certain conditions, penalise a simple or objective fact as such, irrespective of whether it results from criminal intent or from negligence. Examples of such offences may be found in the laws of the contracting states."

This statement recognises that Art.6(2) is essentially a procedural guarantee. Indeed, Art.6 generally is designed to provide basic procedural protections for

---

[17] Application No.5124/71 (1975) 42 C.D. 135.
[18] (1982) 4 E.H.R.R. 373.
[19] See para.9–05 above.
[20] (1991) 13 E.H.R.R. 379.

those charged with criminal offences, and not to govern the substantive content of domestic criminal law.[21]

However, the judgment in *Salabiaku* also made it clear that states do not have   **9–11** complete freedom of action in this field. In a much-quoted passage, the Court held that:

> "Presumptions of fact or of law operate in every legal system. Clearly the Convention does not prohibit such presumptions in principle. It does, however, require the Contracting States to remain within certain limits in this respect as regards the criminal law . . . Article 6(2) does not therefore regard presumptions of fact or of law provided for in the criminal law with indifference. It requires States to confine them within reasonable limits which take into account the importance of what is at stake and maintain the rights of the defence."

The Court therefore held that the presumption of knowledge in this particular offence did not violate Art.6(2) since the prosecution bore the burden of proving the *actus reus* of the offence, and it was a defence for the accused to prove that he was unaware of the contents of the consignment. Moreover, the accused could avoid liability by proving *force majeure*, and the domestic courts had in fact found that he knew the drugs were in his possession (although not strictly required to do so). In the Court's view therefore the trial court had not been entirely deprived of "any genuine power of assessment."[22] However, the Court did not elaborate on the key phrases in the passage just quoted. The phrase "reasonable limits" has been left without elaboration, and it is unclear what the court meant by "the importance of what is at stake." This may be a reference to the objectives of the customs laws of which the offence formed part; but one would have thought that, in the context of determining what limits are reasonable, it ought also to refer to the maximum penalty faced by a convicted defendant. However, the maximum penalty for this offence was two years' imprisonment, and the Court appears to have concluded that deprivation of liberty for a significant period does not go beyond "reasonable limits" in relation to this customs offence.

Salabiaku was followed in *Pham Hoang v France*,[23] a case on very similar facts.   **9–12** The Court emphasised that it was not its function to consider whether the legislative presumptions in issue were compatible with Art.6(2). Its task was to examine the facts of the case in order to determine whether the legislation had been applied in a manner consistent with the presumption of innocence.[24] The court noted that the Paris Court of Appeal had made no express reference to the

---

[21] For a vigorous argument to the contrary, see Tadros V. and Tierney S., "The Presumption of Innocence and the Human Rights Act" (2004) 67 *Modern L.R.* 402; for a rebuttal, see Roberts P., "Strict Liability and the Presumption of Innocence: an Exposé of Functionalist Assumptions", in Simester A.P. (ed.), *Appraising Strict Liability (2005)*.

[22] A similar principle might apply to offences of strict liability in English law that have a "due diligence" exception, allowing a defendant to avoid liability by proving that reasonable precautions were taken. For examples and discussion, see Wasik M., "Shifting the Burden of Strict Liability" [1982] Crim.L.R. 567.

[23] (1993) 16 E.H.R.R. 53.

[24] At para.33.

presumptions in its judgment, but had taken account of "a cumulation of facts" and had; " . . . duly weighed the evidence before it, assessed it carefully and based its findings of guilt on it. It refrained from any automatic reliance on the presumptions . . . and did not apply them in a manner incompatible with Article 6(1) and (2) of the Convention."[25]

9–13 The Court's approach in *Salabiaku* and *Pham Hoang* demonstrates the difficulty of applying the Strasbourg jurisprudence directly in the national courts. The European Court of Human Rights has the luxury of a retrospective review of the domestic proceedings as a whole, and can examine *ex post facto* whether any presumption was in fact applied in a manner which failed to respect the rights of the defence. A national court, on the other hand, has to determine the issue on the case arising before it. In particular, it has to determine whether any particular burden of proof should be treated as evidential or persuasive in character. As the Commission's decision in *Hardy v Ireland*[26] shows, this question can be far from straightforward.

9–14 *Hardy* concerned a statutory explosives offence which provided that:

> "Any person who makes or knowingly has in his possession or under his control any explosive substance, under such circumstances as to give rise to a reasonable suspicion that he is not making it or does not have it in his possession or under his control for a lawful object, shall, unless he can show that he made it or had it in his possession or under his control for a lawful object, be . . . liable to penal servitude for a term not exceeding 14 years."

9–15 An identical provision in England and Wales (s.4 of the Explosive Substances Act 1883) had been held to impose a persuasive burden on the accused to prove a lawful object on the balance of probabilities.[27] In Ireland however the provision had been interpreted as imposing a merely evidential burden on the accused to raise a doubt as to whether he had the explosive in his possession for a lawful object.[28] In finding that the Irish provision was compatible with Art.6(2), the Commission attached particular importance to the principle that it was for the Crown to prove the guilt of the accused on each element of the offence to the requisite standard of proof, and that the burden on the accused was merely evidential:

> "The Commission further notes that, in the context of the constitutional challenge, the High Court and the Supreme Court emphasised that under Irish criminal law the persuasive burden of proof (that is, beyond all reasonable doubt) remains on the State and where an evidential burden of proof is transferred to the accused (as in section 4 of the 1883 Act) it is in a "saving or excusatory context" and the maximum obligation on

---

[25] At para.36.
[26] Application No.23456/94 (unreported).
[27] *R. v Berry (No.3)* [1985] A.C. 246; *R. v Fegan* [1972] N.I. 80; In *R. v DPP ex parte Kebilene and ors* [1999] 3 W.L.R. 972 (HL) Lord Hope identified the English provision as imposing a persuasive burden of proof, coupled with a mandatory presumption of guilt if it is not discharged, and falling outside the category of "special defences" identified in *Edwards*, see para.9–23 below.
[28] *Hardy v Ireland* (Irish Supreme Court, March 18, 1993).

the accused in such circumstances is merely to raise a doubt of substance in relation to the prosecution's case."

A number of other cases in the 1990s also went no further than the Commission. **9–16** In *H v United Kingdom*[29] the Commission held that the English rule that places on the accused the burden of establishing a defence of insanity was neither unreasonable nor arbitrary and does not infringe Art.6(2).[30] This approach was followed in *Robinson v United Kingdom*,[31] when the Commission dismissed as manifestly unfounded a complaint that the burden of proof is placed on the defendant to establish a partial defence of diminished responsibility on a charge of murder.

In *Bates v United Kingdom*,[32] the applicant was convicted of an offence under the **9–17** Dangerous Dogs Act 1991, which places on the defendant the burden of proving that a dog is not a member of the specified breed.[33] The Commission found no violation of Art.6(2). The applicant was found to have admitted that the dog was a member of the specified breed, and he had the opportunity to adduce evidence to disprove the presumption.

In *AG v Malta*[34] the Commission held that Art.6(2) was not violated by a **9–18** provision that placed on the defendant company director the burden of proving that the offence was committed without his knowledge and that he had exercised all due diligence. And in *Brown v United Kingdom*[35] it was held that there was no violation of Art.6(2) where the Sexual Offences (Amendment) Act 1976 placed the burden on a publisher to show that he was not at fault in relation to the publication that constituted the offence.

The principal Court judgment of the last decade on the presumption of innocence **9–19** is *Janosevic v Sweden*.[36] At issue here was a Swedish tax law that allowed the tax authorities to impose a surcharge on any taxpayer whom they judged to have under-stated his or her liability to tax. The law provided for the taxpayer to contest the surcharge by proving that the information supplied to the authorities was correct or that, if it was incorrect, this was excusable in the circumstances. The Court characterised the law as a presumption of fact that engaged Art.6(2). But it concluded that there was no violation of the presumption of innocence here, since the State's financial interests were at stake and this presumption was an effective and efficient method of enforcing the tax laws, and that the law on surcharges was confined within reasonable limits in the sense that it furnished taxpayers with possibilities of exculpation. In reaching this conclusion the Court

---

[29] App.No.15023/89.
[30] For critical analysis of this approach, see Jones T.H., "Insanity, Automatism and the Burden of Proof on the Accused" (1995) 111 L.Q.R. 475, and Ashworth A., "Four Threats to the Presumption of Innocence" (2006) 10 *Evidence & Proof* 241, at 263–266.
[31] App.No.20858/92.
[32] [1996] E.H.R.L.R. 312.
[33] The dog is presumed to be a member of the breed "unless the contrary is shown by the accused."
[34] App.No.1664/90.
[35] App.No.44233/98.
[36] (2004) 38 E.H.R.R. 473.

held that "the means employed have to be reasonably proportionate to the legitimate aim sought to be achieved",[37] and a significant difference between this case and *Salabiaku* is that the Swedish law did not provide for the use of imprisonment, even for non-payment of taxes.

III. The United Kingdom Case Law

9–20   As stated in 9–02 above, the famous decision in *Woolmington* declared the presumption of innocence to be a "golden thread" running through English criminal law, but also recognised that Parliament was free to create exceptions by imposing the burden on the defendant. In former years this was done with some frequency, sometimes as a kind of "half-way house" between imposing strict liability on the defendant and requiring the prosecution to prove full *mens rea*.[38] However, since the Human Rights Act came into force, the courts have been required to consider the compatibility of all reverse onus provisions with the presumption of innocence declared by Art.6(2). In responding to this challenge, the English courts have gone beyond the somewhat under-developed Strasbourg jurisprudence, while keeping faith with the proportionality test found in the *Salabiaku* and *Janosevic* judgments. Thus in *Attorney-General's Reference No.4 of 2002* Lord Bingham considered the Strasbourg cases and declared[39]:

> "Relevant to any judgment on reasonableness or proportionality will be the opportunity given to the defendant to rebut the presumption, maintenance of the rights of the defence, flexibility in application of the presumption, retention by the Court of a power to assess the evidence, the importance of what is at stake and the difficulty which a prosecutor may face in the absence of a presumption. Security concerns do not absolve member states from their duty to observe basic standards of fairness. The justifiability of any infringement of the presumption of innocence cannot be resolved by any rule of thumb, but on examination of all the facts and circumstances . . .
> There are now four decisions of the House of Lords, and a much larger number of cases in the Court of Appeal and Divisional Court, that have to be considered."

The Decision in Kebilene

9–21   The application of Art.6(2) to statutory reverse onus provisions in England and Wales arose for consideration by the House of Lords before the Human Rights Act came into force, in *R. v DPP ex parte Kebilene and others*. The applicants had applied for judicial review of the decision to prosecute them for offences under s.16A and 16B of the Prevention of Terrorism (Temporary Provisions) Act 1989. In giving and maintaining his consent to the prosecution, the DPP had obtained counsel's advice to the effect that the provisions were not incompatible with Art.6(2). The applicants challenged that conclusion, and the Divisional Court granted a declaration that the DPP had erred and that his decision was therefore unlawful. This ruling was overturned by the House of Lords on jurisdictional grounds. Lord Steyn, with whom the other members of the House

---

[37] *Ibid.*, at [101].
[38] See Lord Reid in *Sweet v Parsley* [1970] A.C. 132, at 150B–C, suggesting that more use might be made of this expedient.
[39] [2005] 1 A.C. 264, at [21].

of Lords agreed, held that in the absence of bad faith or other exceptional circumstances the Divisional Court should not entertain an application for judicial review of a decision to prosecute. The issue should be determined in the criminal trial and appeals process. Satellite litigation in criminal proceedings was to be discouraged.

In view of this conclusion, it was unnecessary for the House of Lords to rule on **9–22** the merits of the issue. Lord Hope nevertheless went on to consider the caselaw from Strasbourg and the common law jurisdictions where constitutional challenge is possible, and distilled a number of general principles which should govern such challenges in the United Kingdom. He noted the importance of identifying:

(i) whether merely an evidential burden rather than a persuasive/legal burden was transferred to the defendant;

(ii) whether the presumption was mandatory or discretionary (and, if discretionary, whether the effect was still to require the court to be satisfied beyond reasonable doubt of the relevant element of the offence, in which case there may be no infringement of the presumption of innocence at all); and

(iii) whether the presumed fact was an essential element of the offence or merely an "exemption" or "proviso".

Lord Hope held that the first stage in any inquiry as to whether a statutory reverse **9–23** onus provision is vulnerable to challenge under Art.6(2) is to identify the nature of the provision which is said to transfer a burden of proof. Some provisions would be more objectionable than others. A merely evidential burden, requiring the accused to do no more than raise a reasonable doubt on the issue to which it related, would not breach the presumption of innocence. Such provisions; " . . . take their place alongside the common law evidential presumptions which have built up in the light of experience. They are a necessary part of preserving the balance of fairness between the accused and the prosecutor in matters of evidence."However, a statute which imposed a persuasive burden, requiring the accused to prove, on a balance of probabilities, a fact which is essential to his guilt or innocence, required further examination. The court should determine whether the legislative technique which had been adopted was mandatory or discretionary, and whether it related to an essential element of the offence, or merely to an exemption or proviso. A mandatory presumption of guilt on an essential element of an offence would be inconsistent with the presumption of innocence. So far as "special defences"[40] were concerned, these "may or may not violate the presumption of innocence, depending on the circumstances".

It did not necessarily follow, however, that a provision which was incompatible **9–24** with the presumption of innocence would be found to violate Art.6(2). The Convention caselaw showed that although Art.6(2) is framed in absolute terms, it was not regarded in Strasbourg as imposing an absolute prohibition on reverse

---

[40] See para.9–05 above.

onus clauses. In each case, the question would be whether the presumption was confined within reasonable limits so as to be proportionate. The provisions which were the subject of challenge in *Kebilene* created a reverse onus on the two most important essential elements of the offence. Section 16A provides;

> "(1) A person is guilty of an offence if he has any article in his possession in circumstances giving rise to a reasonable suspicion that the article is in his possession for a purpose connected with the commission, preparation or instigation of acts of terrorism to which this section applies.
>
> (3) It is a defence for a person charged with an offence under this section to prove that at the time of the alleged offence the article in question was not in his possession for such a purpose as is mentioned in subsection (1) above.
>
> (4) Where a person is charged with an offence under this section and it is proved that at the time of the alleged offence (a) he and that article were both present in any premises; or (b) the article was in premises of which he was the occupier or which he habitually used otherwise than as a member of the public, the court may accept the fact proved as sufficient evidence of his possessing that article unless it is further proved that he did not at that time know of its presence in the premises in question, or if he did know, that he had no control over it."

Thus, s.16A(1) and (3) create a *mandatory* reverse onus on the issue of terrorist intent; and s.16A(4) creates a *discretionary* reverse onus on the issue of possession. Construed without the benefit of s.3(1) of the Human Rights Act 1998, both provisions would be taken to require proof by the accused on the balance of probabilities.In the Divisional Court Lord Bingham C.J. considered that this involved a "blatant and obvious" violation of Art.6(2), insofar as neither of the crucial ingedients of the offence (and notably the terrorist purpose) need be proved by the prosecution to the criminal standard. Laws L.J. concurred, concluding that the section "requires the defendant to disprove the offence's principal element." The Crown's plea was not, in truth, a plea for a fair balance. It was an argument that Art.6(2) should be disapplied; and that would be "an affront to the rule of law". In view of their ruling on the jurisdictional issue, it was not necessary for the House of Lords to decide the point. Lord Steyn, with whom Lord Slynn agreed, regarded the issue as "arguable" and "entirely open". Lord Cooke, however, was more forthright:

> "My Lords, I see great force in the Divisional Court's view that on the natural and ordinary interpretation there is repugnancy ... at best it is doubtful whether Article 6(2) can be watered down to an extent that would leave section 16A unscathed. The judgment of the Privy Council delivered by Lord Woolf in *Attorney-General of Hong Kong v Lee Kwong-kut* [1993] A.C. 951 strongly suggests that it cannot."

Lord Hobhouse thought the question was less clear than the Divisional Court believed it to be; "Surprising though it may seem to those trained in the common law and the English traditions of statutory construction, there is clearly room for some doubt as to the outcome, were the defendants to seek to challenge their convictions in Strasbourg."

9–25   Lord Hope elaborated on this more cautious approach. In reaching the conclusion that s.16A was not necessarily incompatible on its face, Lord Hope analysed it thus:

"What subsection (1) requires is *prima facie* proof, not mere suspicion. The prosecution must lead evidence which is sufficient to prove beyond reasonable doubt (a) that the accused had the article in his possession and (b) that it was in his possesion in circumstances giving rise to a reasonable suspicion that it was in his possession for a purpose connected with terrorism ... It should not be thought that proof to this standard will be a formality."

Much, therefore, depends on a correct analysis of the essence of the offence in s.16A. Professor Paul Roberts argues that Lord Hope's construction is to be preferred: the prosecution bears the burden of satisfying the court that there exist sufficient grounds for "reasonable suspicion", and the function of the defence in subs.(3) is to enable a defendant to be acquitted "even though reasonable grounds for suspecting that he has a terrorist purpose exist."[41] An alternative analysis would be that subs.(3) is not an affirmative defence but rather a simple negativing of the prosecution's case that grounds for "reasonable suspicion" exist. If that is correct, then once the prosecution has satisfied the court that those grounds exist, the question is whether the defendant must simply raise a doubt (the persuasive burden remaining on the prosecution) or must prove that there was no terrorist purpose (bearing a persuasive burden). It is submitted the latter is the natural meaning of s.16A, and that therefore Lord Cooke's view was right and that there was a conflict with Art.6(2).

The Decision in Lambert

In *R. v Lambert*[42] a majority of the House of Lords held that the statutory defence **9–26** contained in s.28(2) of the Misuse of Drugs Act 1971, which placed a legal burden on the accused to prove lack of knowledge that he possessed a controlled drug, undermined the presumption of innocence to an impermissible extent. Crucial to the reasoning of the majority was the fact that the offence in question carried a maximum penalty of life imprisonment.

Section 5(3) of the Misuse of Drugs Act 1971 provides that "subject to section **9–27** 28 of this Act, it is an offence for a person to have a controlled drug in his possession, whether lawfully or not, with intent to supply it to another." Section 28 provides various "defences" which the accused has to prove. In this case the defendant denied that he knew that what he had in his possession was a controlled drug. Section 28(3)(b) provides that the accused shall be acquitted:

"if he proves that he neither believed nor suspected nor had reason to suspect that the substance or product in question was a controlled drug."

The proper interpretation of ss.5 and 28 together lies at the heart of the *Lambert* decision. One straightforward approach would be that s.5 creates an offence of strict liability, and that s.28 introduces an affirmative defence, enabling the defendant to avoid conviction in limited circumstances.[43] That would mean that

---

[41] Roberts P., "The Presumption of Innocence Brought Home? *Kebilene* Deconstructed", (2002) 118 L.Q.R. 41, at 57.

[42] [2002] 2 A.C. 545.

[43] As argued by Roberts P., "Drug Dealing and the Presumption of Innocence: the Human Rights Act (almost) bites", (2002) 6 *Evidence and Proof* 17.

s.28 does not concern an "essential element" of the offence, and that its reverse onus is unobjectionable. However, Lord Steyn took a broader view, stating that:

> "The distinction between constituent elements of a crime and defensive issues will sometimes be unprincipled and arbitrary. After all, it is sometimes simply a matter of which drafting technique is adopted: a true constituent element can be removed from the definition of the crime and cast as a defensive issue whereas any definition of an offence can be reformulated so as to include all possible defences within it. It is necessary to concentrate not on technicalities and niceties of language but rather on matters of substance." [44]

Lord Steyn thus adopted the approach of Dickson C.J.C. in the Canadian case of *Whyte*, to the effect that:

> "If an accused is required to prove some fact on the balance of probabilities to avoid conviction, the provision violates the presumption of innocence because it permits a conviction in spite of a reasonable doubt in the minds of the trier of fact as to the guilt of the accused."

Sweeping aside all technical arguments as to the construction of ss.5 and 28, Lord Steyn therefore concluded that s.28 has a direct bearing on moral blameworthiness for the possession that lies at the centre of s.5, and indeed that the presumed culpability must be the true explanation for a maximum penalty as high as life imprisonment.

9–28   His Lordship then enquired whether this legislative interference with the presumption of innocence enshrined in Art.6(2) could be justified, i.e. "whether there was a pressing necessity to impose a legal rather than evidential burden on the accused." His review of the alleged evidential problems of proving knowledge led him to conclude that the imposition of a legal or persuasive burden on the defence in s.28 was "a disproportionate reaction to the perceived difficulties facing the prosecution in drugs cases." [45] The high maximum sentence probably played its part in this reasoning too. Although all of their Lordships accepted the importance of combatting the threat to social welfare posed by drugs, the majority found that the reverse onus provision constituted a degree of interference with the presumption of innocence that could not be justified.

9–29   Lord Hope reached a similar conclusion, arguing that "it is hard to see why a person who is accused of the offence of possessing a controlled drug and who wishes to use this defence should be deprived of the full benefit of the presumption of innocence." [46] He also shared Lord Steyn's view that it was appropriate to use the interpretative power in s.3 of the Human Rights Act rather than to make a declaration of incompatibility under s.4 of that Act. The key question is whether it is *possible*, within the meaning of s.3(1) to read the word "prove", where it relates to an onus on the accused, as imposing no more than an evidential burden.

---

[44] [2001] UKHL 37, at [35].
[45] *Ibid.*, at [41].
[46] *Ibid.*, at [89].

The basis for such a construction was explained, as long ago as 1988, by 9–30
Professor Glanville Williams, in an article entitled, "The Logic of Exceptions".
Many statutory reverse onus offences are cast in terms which provide that once
the prosecution "prove" fact A, fact B is to be presumed unless the defence
"prove" fact C. Despite the fact that such a provision uses the word "prove" to
apply both to the prosecution's burden, and to that of the defence, the courts
interpret the obligation differently according to where the burden lies. If it is the
prosecution which must "prove" a fact, then this requires proof beyond reasonable doubt. If it is the defence, then proof on the balance of probabilities is
required. Thus the courts give two different meanings to the same word, even
where it appears in the same subsection. Having swallowed this "camel", argues
Professor Williams, why should the courts "strain at the remaining gnat"? The
word "prove", when it applies to the defence, could be interpreted as requiring
the accused to adduce sufficient evidence to raise a reasonable doubt in the mind
of the court. Both Lord Steyn and Lord Hope explicitly adopted the Williams
reasoning, and Lord Slynn and Lord Clyde reached the same conclusion.

The Williams reasoning was found unpersuasive by judges in some subsequent 9–31
decisions. In *Daniel*[47] Simon Brown L.J. pointed out that the evidential burden
is not a burden of proof, but rather a burden of adducing sufficient evidence to
make an issue live,[48] and he quoted a passage from the Privy Council's decision
in *Jayasena v R.* (cited by Professor Birch)[49] to support the point. In *L v Director
of Public Prosecutions*[50] Pill L.J. stated that to describe the evidential burden as
a burden of "proof" deprived the word of any proper meaning.[51] Rose L.J. in
Sliney v London Borough of Havering[52] took the same point, and drew the same
inference from it.[53] The inference is that, *pace* the House of Lords in *Lambert*,
to construe "to prove" or "to show" as imposing only an evidential burden is not
an appropriate use of the power of interpretation provided by s.3 of the Human
Rights Act—because it does too much violence to the language—and that the
matter should have been dealt with by declarations of incompatibility under s.4
of that Act. However, in all those cases the courts went on to hold that they were
bound by *Lambert*.

A second point taken against *Lambert* in some subsequent decisions was that all 9–32
their Lordships' remarks on burden of proof are merely *obiter dicta*, since the
ratio of the decision is that the Human Rights Act does not have retrospective
effect. The courts have recognised this argument, but have continued to follow
the decision. Thus in *Attorney-General's Reference No.4 of 2002*[54] Latham L.J.
described the points made on burden of proof in *Lambert* as "strictly speaking
obiter" before going on to apply them,[55] and in *Sliney v London Borough of*

---

[47] [2002] EWCA Crim 959.
[48] At [26]; see above, 9–04.
[49] Commentary on *Lambert*, [2001] Crim.L.R. 807, at 809.
[50] [2002] 2 All E.R. 854.
[51] At [23].
[52] [2002] EWCA Crim 2558.
[53] At [40–42].
[54] [2003] EWCA Crim 762.
[55] At [10].

Havering, Rose L.J. held that the remarks in *Lambert* should be followed because they were "all considered views."[56]

The Decision in Johnstone

9–33   In *R. v Johnstone*[57] the House of Lords considered the reverse onus provision in the statutory defence to certain trade mark offences contained in s.92(5) of the Trade Marks Act 1994, and held that the balance struck was reasonable. Lord Nicholls stated (at para.50):

> "A sound starting point is to remember that if an accused is required to prove a fact on the balance of probability to avoid conviction, this permits a conviction in spite of the fact finding tribunal having a reasonable doubt as to the guilt of the accused . . . This consequence of a reverse burden of proof should colour one's approach when evaluating the reasons why it is said that in the absence of a persuasive burden on the accused, the public interest will be prejudiced to an extent which justifies placing a persuasive burden on the accused. The more serious the punishment which may flow from conviction, the more compelling must be the reasons. The extent and nature of the factual matters required to be proved by the accused and their importance relative to the matters required to be proved by the prosecution, have to be taken into account. So also does the extent to which the burden on the accused relates to facts which, if they exist, are readily provable by him as matters within his own knowledge or to which he has ready access."

9–34   Having laid down those general principles, Lord Nicholls went on (at para. 51):

> "In evaluating these factors the Court's role is one of review. Parliament, not the Court, is charged with the primary responsibility for deciding, as a matter of policy, what should be the constituent elements of a criminal offence. I echo the words of Lord Woolf in *Attorney-General of Hong Kong v Lee Kwong-Kut*[58]:
>
> > 'In order to maintain the balance between the individual and society as a whole, rigid and inflexible standards should not be imposed on the legislature's attempts to resolve the difficult and intransigent problems with which society is faced when seeking to deal with serious crime.'
>
> The Court will reach a difference conclusion from the legislature only when it is apparent the legislature has attached insufficient importance to the fundamental right of an individual to be presumed innocent until proved guilty."

9–35   In *Johnstone*, the factors which were held to justify the placing of a legal burden of proof on the accused included the dependence of the defence on facts within the defendant's own knowledge and the fact that those who trade in brand products are aware of the need to be on guard against counterfeit goods: "They are aware of the need to deal with reputable suppliers and keep records and of the risks they take if they do not." It was noted that if the prosecution had to prove that a trader acted dishonestly, fewer investigations would be undertaken and fewer prosecutions would take place. Thus, despite the principles stated by Lord

---

[56] [2002] EWCA Crim 2558, at [38].
[57] [2003] 1 W.L.R. 1736.
[58] [1993] A.C. 951, at 975.

Nicholls in 9–33 above, and despite the fact that this offence has a maximum penalty of 10 years' imprisonment, the House of Lords held that the reverse onus provision was "within reasonable limits."[59]

Further Appellate Decisions before Sheldrake

In *L v Director of Public Prosecutions*[60] the Divisional Court held that the   **9–36** statutory defence under s.139(4) of the Criminal Justice Act 1988, which cast upon the defendant the burden of proving good reason or lawful authority for the possession of a bladed article, did not infringe Art.6(2). The court (Pill L.J. and Poole J.) noted that there was a strong public interest in bladed articles not being carried in public without good reason and that the defendant was only required to prove something within his own knowledge.

In *Carass*[61] the Court of Appeal considered the statutory offence of concealing   **9–37** debts of a company in anticipation of winding up contrary to s.206(1)(a) of the Insolvency Act 1986, and the defence contained in s.206(4) for the defendant to prove that he had no intent to defraud. It was held that there was no justification for imposing a legal burden, rather than an evidential burden, on a defendant who relied on the statutory defence. However, the decision in *Carass* was overruled by a full Court of Appeal in *Attorney General's Reference (No.1 of 2004)*.[62]

Even before it was overruled, doubts had been cast on the decision in *Carass* by   **9–38** another division of the Court of Appeal in *Daniel*.[63] In that case, the accused was charged with concealing a debt contrary to s.354(i)(b) of the Insolvency Act 1986. This offence is subject to a statutory defence under s.352, which provides that a person is not guilty of an offence under s.354 "if he proves that, at the time of the conduct constituting the offence, he had no intent to defraud or to conceal the state of his affairs." Speaking for the Court of Appeal, Auld L.J. stated (at para.31):

> "Thus, where a bankrupt, knowing what is required of him, conceals a debt, how should the burden imposed on him of explaining his concealment be regarded? If he inadvertently 'concealed' the debt, he will not be guilty of an offence under section 354, regardless of the defence provided by section 352 because of lack of intent. Why should it be unreasonable to require a person, who has deliberately concealed a debt in circumstances where he knows he was obliged to disclose it, to prove that he did not intend to defraud or to conceal the state of his affairs. Such a burden does not seem to us, in the circumstance, we have mentioned, to contravene Article 6(2)."

This reasoning was approved by the full Court of Appeal in *Attorney General's Reference (No.1 of 2004)*.[64]

---

[59] The Court of Appeal had reached a similar conclusion in *S.* [2003] 1 Cr.App.R. 602.
[60] [2003] Q.B. 137.
[61] [2002] 1 W.L.R. 1714.
[62] [2004] 1 W.L.R. 2111. In *Sheldrake v D.P.P.* [2005] 1 A.C. 264 Lord Bingham agreed that *Carass* had been wrongly decided.
[63] [2003] 1 Cr.App.R. 6.
[64] Above, n.62.

9–39   In *Drummond*[65] the Court of Appeal held that the "hip flask" defence provided by s.15 of the Road Traffic Offenders Act 1988, whereby it is for the accused to prove that he consumed alcohol before providing a specimen and after the offence of driving while over the prescribed limit, was within reasonable limits. The evidence relied on by the accused was peculiarly within his own knowledge.

9–40   In *Attorney General's Reference (No.1 of 2004)*[66] the Court of Appeal sat as a full court of five judges (Lord Woolf C.J., Judge L.J., Gage, Elias and Stanley Burnton JJ.) to consider five cases. The court began by laying down 10 principles to guide judges in determining whether a reverse onus provision violated Art.6(2); but these principles were not endorsed by the House of Lords in *Sheldrake v D.P.P.*,[67] and one of them—the assumption that Parliament would not have made an exception to the presumption of innocence without good reason— was expressly rejected by Lord Bingham. It is therefore not advisable to refer to these principles, but it must equally be emphasised that the House of Lords in *Sheldrake* approved the particular decisions taken in the five cases that were the subject of the appeal. Thus both in the *Attorney General's Reference* itself and in *Edwards* the offence related to disposals of property by bankrupts in the period prior to their bankruptcy contrary to the provisions of the Insolvency Act 1986 ("the 1986 Act"). Under the 1986 Act, it is an offence if a bankrupt either: (i) does not inform the official receiver (or trustee) of disposals of property which would have comprised his estate but for the disposal; or (ii) disposes of his property by transfer or gift in the five years leading up to his bankruptcy. A limited reverse burden exception exists in that the offences shall not apply to a bankrupt who proves that at the time of the offences "he had no intent to defraud or to conceal the state of his affairs." The Court of Appeal concluded that it would be a normal inference from the failure to inform the official receiver of an unusual disposal that the bankrupt was intending to defeat the claims of creditors or to conceal the state of his affairs and that therefore is was no infringement of Art.6(2) to require a bankrupt to prove that this was not the case. However, the Court of Appeal went on to conclude that to require a bankrupt against whom it was proved only that he had made a gift or other disposal or created a charge within five years before his bankruptcy, to prove that he had no intent to defraud, is not justified and infringes Art.6(2).

9–41   The appeal of *Denton and Jackson* related to an alleged unlawful eviction contrary to the Protection from Eviction Act 1977. There is a limited reverse burden exception to unlawful eviction, namely that the defendant believed and had reasonable cause to believe that the occupier had ceased to reside in the premises from which he or she was evicted. The Court of Appeal concluded that the reverse burden struck a proper balance between the general interest of the community and the protection of the fundamental rights of the individual and that the infringement of Art.6(2) was wholly justified.

---

[65] [2002] 2 Cr.App.R. 352.
[66] [2004] 1 W.L.R. 2111.
[67] [2005] 1 A.C. 246, discussed in detail below.

The appeal of *Hendley* concerned an allegation of murder. It was alleged that the **9–42** accused had injected himself and his girlfriend with insulin. The appellant survived and his girlfriend did not. The appellant claimed that the injections were the result of a suicide pact. Pursuant to a limited reverse burden exception in s.4 of the Homicide Act 1957, an accused will be guilty of manslaughter where he can show that he was acting in pursuance of a suicide pact. The Court of Appeal concluded that the acts necessary to establish the defence would lie within the defendant's knowledge and, that the reverse legal burden provided protection for society from murder disguised as a suicide pact killing.

In *Crowley* the appellant was charged with witness intimidation pursuant to the **9–43** Criminal Justice and Public Order Act 1994. A reverse burden exception to such a charge exists where, once it is proved that a person does an act which intimidates another person, knowing that such person is a potential witness or juror, the defendant proves that he had no intention to pervert the course of justice. The Court of Appeal concluded that the legal burden of proof placed on the defendant was within reasonable limits.

The Sheldrake Decision

The House of Lords had a further opportunity to clarify the implications of **9–44** Art.6(2) of the Convention in the conjoined appeals in *Attorney General's Reference No.4 of 2002; Sheldrake v Director of Public Prosecutions*.[68] In the *Sheldrake* part of the decision, the House of Lords allowed the Director's appeal from a decision of the Divisional Court allowing the defendant's appeal against his conviction for being in charge of a motor vehicle in a public place after consuming so much alcohol that the proportion of it in his breath exceeded the prescribed limit, contrary to s.5(1) of the Road Traffic Act 1988. Section 5(2) of the 1988 Act contains a defence that there was no likelihood of the accused driving the vehicle whilst the proportion of alcohol in his breath, blood or urine remained likely to exceed the prescribed limit, the burden of proving which is placed on the accused. Lord Bingham stated (at para.41) that this section:

" . . . is directed to a legitimate object: the prevention of death, injury and damage caused by unfit drivers. Does the provision meet the tests of acceptability identified in the Strasbourg jurisprudence? In my view, it plainly does. I do not regard the burden placed on the defendant as beyond reasonable limits or in any way arbitrary . . . The defendant has a full opportunity to show that there was no likelihood of his driving, a matter so closely conditioned by his own knowledge and state of mind at the material time as to make it much more appropriate for him to prove on the balance of probabilities that he would not have been likely to drive than for the prosecutor to prove beyond reasonable doubt, that he would."

Lord Bingham added that the offence as originally enacted contained no such defence, and so the introduction of s.5(2) could be seen as a development favourable to defendants, which should not then be widened further by removing the reverse burden provided by Parliament.

---

[68] [2005] 1 A.C. 246.

9–45   In the conjoined appeal in *Attorney General's Reference (No.4 of 2002)* the House of Lords decided by a majority that the reverse burden in s.11(2) of the Terrorism Act 2000 impermissibly infringed the presumption of innocence. Section 11(1) of the 2000 Act provides that a person commits an offence if he belongs or professes to belong to a proscribed organisation. Section 11(2) provides that it is a defence for a person charged with an offence under s.11(1) to prove "(a) that the organisation was not proscribed on the last (or only) occasion on which he became a member or began to profess to be a member, and (b) that he has not taken part in the activities of the organisation at any time while it was proscribed." The essential reasoning, which led to the conclusion that s.11(2) was not a justifiable and proportionate response to the need to deter people from becoming members or taking part in the activities of terrorist organisation, may be summarised as follows:

(i)   A person who is innocent of any blameworthy or properly criminal conduct may fall within s.11(1) and might in effect be convicted on the basis of conduct which was not criminal at the date of commission.

(ii)   It might well be almost impossible for an accused to show that he had not taken part in the activities of the organisation at any time while it was proscribed, so as to satisfy s.11(2)(b).

(iii)   If the defendant failed to prove the matters specified in s.11(2), the court would have no choice but to convict him.

(iv)   The offence contrary to s.11(1) carried a maximum penalty of ten years' imprisonment.

9–46   From the decision in these two cases it is possible to state a general principle but not to indicate the weight or rank ordering of the various factors that courts ought to take into account when determining whether a reverse onus provision infringes the presumption of innocence in Art.6(2).[69] The general principle, as derived from the Convention jurisprudence and particularly from the *Salabiaku* and *Janosevic* decisions,[70] was set out by Lord Bingham in the following terms:

"The Convention does not outlaw presumptions of fact or law but requires that these should be kept within reasonable limits and should not be arbitrary. It is open to states to define the constituent elements of a criminal offence, excluding the requirement of *mens rea*. But the substance and effect of any presumption adverse to a defendant must be examined, and must be reasonable. Relevant to any judgment on reasonableness or proportionality will be the opportunity given to the defendant to rebut the presumption, maintenance of the rights of the defence, flexibility in the application of the presumption, retention by the court of a power to assess the evidence, the importance of what is at stake and the difficulty which a prosecutor may face in the absence of a presumption. Security concerns do not absolve member states from their duty to observe basic standards of fairness. The justifiability of any infringement of the presumption of innocence cannot be resolved by any rule of thumb, but on examination

---

[69] For detailed analysis of the House of Lords decision, see Dennis I., "Reverse Onuses and the Presumption of Innocence: In Search of Principle" [2005] Crim.L.R. 901, and Ashworth A., "Four Threats to the Presumption of Innocence" (2006) 10 *Evidence & Proof* 241.

[70] Above, 9–10 and 9–19.

of all the facts and circumstances of the particular provision as applied in the particular case."[71]

This statement gives pride of place to the assessment of reasonableness and proportionality, but then lists six relevant factors without assigning them any priority, weight or relative importance.

Moreover, the decision in this case demonstrates that other factors may also be relevant. The size of the maximum penalty was regarded as a significant factor in *Lambert*,[72] where the maximum of life imprisonment was held to tell against the reverse onus, and in the *Attorney-General's Reference No.4 of 2002*,[73] where the maximum of 10 years was held to tell against the reverse onus; but the same maximum of 10 years passed without comment when the reverse onus was upheld by the House of Lords in *Johnstone*.[74] Similarly there are several judgments that treat it as important, in upholding a reverse onus provision, that a particular matter can be said to lie "within the defendant's peculiar knowledge."[75] However, the "peculiar knowledge" doctrine has been exposed as illogical by other judges (intent and recklessness are within an accused's peculiar knowledge, but the law rightly does not require the defence to prove them).[76] Ease of proof by the defence may be relevant, as the sixth of Lord Bingham's factors recognizes, and in some cases (notably where the offence turns on whether or not the defendant has a licence) this is a good reason for placing an evidential burden on the defendant in relation to the licence or permit.[77]

9–47

The principal decision since *Sheldrake* is *Makuwa*,[78] where the charge was using a false instrument with the intention of inducing someone to accept it as genuine, contrary to s.3 of the Forgery and Counterfeiting Act 1981. The defence was that she was a refugee with good cause for illegal entry: s.31 of the Immigration and Asylum Act 1999. Two questions on the burden of proof arose. The first concerned the question whether the defendant is a refugee, i.e. a person who comes from a territory in which she has a well-founded fear of persecution. The court construed the 1999 Act by reference to its purpose and its structure, so as to hold that the defendant bears only an evidential burden:

9–48

> "as in the case of other more commonly raise defences, such as self-defence or alibi, provided that the defendant can adduce sufficient evidence in support of his claim to refugee status to raise the issue, the prosecution bears the burden of proving to the usual standard that he is not in fact a refugee."

Once this is established, however, s.31 provides a number of defences, such as that D had good cause for having no documents, that she presented herself to the

---

[71] [2005] 1 A.C. 246, at para.[21].
[72] Above, n.42.
[73] Above, n.68.
[74] Above, n.57.
[75] e.g. Lord Bingham in *Sheldrake v D.P.P.* [2005] 1 A.C. 246, at para.[41].
[76] For a full critique, see Dennis (op. cit.), 914–916.
[77] See *R. (on application of Grundy) v Halton Division* [2003] EWHC 272, and *D.P.P. v Barker* [2005] EWHC 2502.
[78] [2006] 2 Cr.App.R. 11; see also *Embaye* [2005] EWCA Crim 2865.

authorities without delay, and that she made her asylum claim as soon as reasonably practicable. The section starts: "it is a defence for a refugee to show that . . . " The Court of Appeal reviewed the House of Lords decisions above, and recognised that "the consequences of conviction . . . are severe" (maximum sentence of 10 years' imprisonment), but nonetheless held that:

> "the infringement of Article 6(2) is justifiable in this case since it represents a proportionate way of achieving the legitimate objective of maintaining proper immigration controls by restricting the use of false passports, which are one of the principal means by which they are liable to be overcome." [36]

The court was influenced by the fact that most of these matters of defence were "within the defendant's own knowledge" and that placing merely an evidential burden on the defence would render it "difficult, if not impossible, for the Crown to adduce positive evidence" in rebuttal. This decision may be taken to confirm two aspects of the current judicial approach—that a high maximum penalty is not determinative, and that ease of proof by the defence may lead a court to impose the legal burden (not just an evidential burden) on the defendant.

IV. Commonwealth and U.S. Jurisprudence

9–49 There is a considerable amount of constitutional jurisprudence from Commonwealth countries on the presumption of innocence and burdens of proof, and some of the leading decisions are discussed below. However, it is to be noted that in *Sheldrake* Lord Bingham made the following observations about this jurisprudence:

> "Some caution is . . . called for in considering different enactments decided under different constitutional arrangements. But, even more important, the United Kingdom courts must take their lead from Strasbourg. In the United Kingdom cases I have discussed our domestic courts have been trying, loyally and (as I think) successfully, to give full and fair effect to the Strasbourg jurisprudence."[79]

Important as this *caveat* is, it remains significant that some of the arguments relied upon in the English cases have been discussed and, sometimes, found wanting by judges in other countries that share the common law tradition.

V. Canada

9–50 In Canada the guarantee equivalent to Art.6 under the Canadian Charter of Rights and Freedoms is s.11(d), which provides: "Any person charged with an offence has the right . . . (d) to be presumed innocent until proven guilty according to law in a fair and public hearing by an independent and impartial tribunal." Section 1 provides that the Charter rights are subject to "such reasonable limits prescribed by law as can be demonstrably justified in a free and democratic society". This has led the Supreme Court to adopt a two stage test to the application of s.11(d), asking first whether a reverse onus clause infringes the

---

[79] [2005] 1 A.C. 246, at para.[33].

presumption of innocence protected by that provision, and if it does, going on to consider whether the interference is justified under s.1. The Canadian Supreme Court has emphasised the need to "keep sections 1 and 11(d) ... analytically distinct".[80] However, despite the fact that the process of reasoning is different from some of the other constitutional jurisdictions, the result is often the same.[81]

Applying these provisions, the Canadian Supreme Court has held that the **9–51** minimum requirement of s.11(d) is that the state must prove the guilt of the accused beyond a reasonable doubt. Thus, s.11(d) requires that the prosecution should bear the ultimate burden of proving each of the important essential elements of an offence. A provision requiring the accused to disprove an essential element on the balance of probabilities is incompatible with s.11(d) since it would be possible for a conviction to occur despite the existence of a reasonable doubt.[82] In such a situation, the state must advance a convincing justification under s.1 of the Charter if the provision in issue is to escape constitutional condemnation.

The facts of the leading case of *Oakes*[83] bear a passing resemblance to those of **9–52** *Salabiaku*.[84] Oakes was found in possession of eight grammes of cannabis in the form of hashish oil. He was charged with possession for the purpose of trafficking, and the prosecution relied on a statutory presumption in the Narcotic Control Act that a person found in possession of a narcotic is presumed to be trafficking unless he establishes to the contrary. The Supreme Court held unanimously that this provision violated Art.11(d) of the Charter, in that it required the accused to prove his innocence, albeit on a balance of probabilities, in relation to an important element of the offence. Dickson C.J., for the court, stated the guiding principle in these terms:

> "In general one must, I think, conclude that a provision which requires an accused to disprove on a balance of probabilities the existence of a presumed fact, which is an important element of the offence in question, violates the presumption of innocence ... If an accused bears the burden of disproving on a balance of probabilities an essential element of an offence, it would be possible for a conviction to occur despite the existence of a reasonable doubt. This would arise if the accused adduced sufficient evidence to raise a reasonable doubt as to his or her innocence but did not convince the jury on a balance of probabilities that the presumed fact was untrue."

The Supreme Court went on to consider whether, under s.1, the presumption was **9–53** "demonstrably justified in a democratic society". This required the court to examine whether the objectives of the Narcotic Control Act were sufficiently important to justify overriding a constitutionally protected right. In order to meet

---

[80] *R. v Oakes* 26 D.L.R. (4th) 200 at 223.

[81] *Attorney-General for Hong Kong v Lee Kwong-kut and anor.* [1993] A.C. 951 (PC), *per* Lord Woolf at 971H.

[82] *R. v Oakes* 26 D.L.R. (4th) 200; [1986] 1 S.C.R. 103. For applications of this principle see *R. v Driscoll* (1987) 60 C.R. (3d) 88 (Alta CA); *R. v Ireco Canada II Inc.* (1988) 65 C.R. (3d) 160 (Ont. CA); *R. v Shisler* (1990) 53 C.C.C. (3d) 531 (Ont. CA).

[83] 26 D.L.R. (4th) 200; [1986] 1 S.C.R. 103.

[84] See para.9–12 above.

this test, the court held that the measure in issue: (a) had to be carefully designed to achieve its objective and rationally connected to that objective; (b) had to impair the protected right to the minimum degree; and (c) had to be proportionate to the importance of the objective (so that the greater the incursions into a constitutionally protected right, the more persuasive the state's justification would have to be). The presumption of drug trafficking failed to satisfy this test, because there was insufficient rational connection between the possession of a small amount of drugs and engagement in trafficking.

9–54   In subsequent decisions the Canadian Supreme Court has held that a statutory provision which requires the accused to prove a matter which is *not* an essential element of the offence may also be *prima facie* inconsistent with s.11(d). In *R. v Whyte*[85] the court explained;

> "[T]he distinction between elements of the offence and other aspects of the charge is irrelevant to the s.11(d) inquiry. The real concern is not whether the accused must disprove an element or prove an excuse, but that an accused may be convicted while a reasonable doubt exists. When that possibility exists, there is a breach of the presumption of innocence. The exact characterisation of a factor as an essential element, a collateral factor, an excuse, or a defence should not affect the analysis of the presumption of innocence. It is the final effect of a provision on the verdict that is decisive. If an accused is required to prove some fact on the balance of probabilities to avoid conviction, the provision violates the presumption of innocence because it permits a conviction in spite of a reasonable doubt in the mind of the trier of fact as to the guilt of the accused."

9–55   However, a presumption will be easier to justify under s.1, if it relates not to an essential element of the offence, but to an exemption, proviso, excuse or the like. Thus, in *Whyte* the court upheld a presumption that a person found impaired in the driving seat of a vehicle had "care or control" so as to be guilty of an offence, unless he proved by way of defence that he did not intend to set the vehicle in motion. And in *Keegstra*[86] the court upheld a provision to the effect that a person who wilfully promotes hatred against an identifiable group is guilty of an offence unless the accused establishes by way of defence that the statements are true.

9–56   Statutory offences which require the accused to prove the existence of a certificate or licence have been held to be consistent with s.11(d). In *R. v Schwartz*[87] a provision requiring the accused to prove that he was the holder of a firearms certificate was held not to reverse the burden of proof. Under such a provision;

> "[The accused was] not required to prove or disprove any element of the offence or for that matter, anything related to the offence ... Although the accused must establish that he falls within the exemption, there is no danger that he could be convicted ... despite the existence of a reasonable doubt as to guilt, because the production of the certificate resolves all doubts in favour of the accused and in the absence of the certificate no defence is possible once possession has been shown. In such a case, where

---

[85] 64 C.R. (3d) 123 (S.C.C.) at 134–135 [1998] 2 S.C.R. 3.
[86] (1990) 1 C.R. (4th) 129 (S.C.C.) [1990] 3 S.C.R. 697.
[87] (1988) 55 D.L.R. (4th) 1 (S.C.C.).

the only relevant evidence is the certificate itself, it cannot be said that the accused could adduce evidence sufficient to raise doubt without at the same time establishing conclusively that the certificate had been issued. The theory behind any licencing system is that when an issue arises as to the possession of the licence, it is the accused who is in the best position to resolve the issue."

The Canadian Supreme Court has thus achieved a result in *Schwartz* which is equivalent to the "special defence" rule in *Edwards* and *Hunt*.[88]

On several occasions the Supreme Court has held that reverse onus offences **9–57** could be saved from constitutional invalidation by reading them as imposing a purely evidential burden. The case of *Downey*[89] has facts similar to those in *X v United Kingdom*.[90] The charge was living on the earnings of prostitution and the Canadian Criminal Code included a provision to the effect that evidence that a person "lives with or is habitually in the company of prostitutes" would be proof, "in the absence of evidence to the contrary", of living on the earnings of prostitution. By a majority of four to three the Canadian Supreme Court upheld the statutory presumption. Although it violated s.11(d) it could be saved by s.1 as a "reasonable limit" on the presumption of innocence, because it amounted merely to placing an evidential burden on the defendant in respect of an element that would be otherwise difficult to prove. That point was reinforced in *Laba*,[91] where a reverse onus provision was held not to satisfy the *Oakes* proportionality test because it imposed on defendants a burden of proving ownership on the balance of probabilities. The court held that the provision could take effect as imposing a mere evidential burden on the accused.

VI. South Africa

Since the present Constitution came into effect,[92] the Constitutional Court of **9–58** South Africa has developed a substantial body of case law on the compatibility of statutory reverse onus clauses with the constitutional presumption of innocence. The equivalent provision to Art.6(2) of the Convention is s.25(3)(c) of the Constitution which provides: "Every accused person shall have the right to a fair trial, which shall include the right . . . (c) to be presumed innocent . . . during plea proceedings or trial . . . ". Like the Canadian Charter, the South African Constitution contains a general savings clause (s.33(1)).[93] Applying these provisions, the South African Constitutional Court has followed the approach of the Canadian Supreme Court in holding that statutes which require the accused to

---

[88] See para.9–05 above.
[89] [1992] 2 S.C.R. 10.
[90] See para.9–08 above.
[91] [1994] 3 S.C.R. 965.
[92] On April 27, 1994.
[93] s.33(1) is in the following terms:"The rights entrenched in this Chapter may be limited by law of general application, provided that such limitation—(a) shall be permissible only to the extent that it is—(i) reasonable; and (ii) justifiable in an open and democratic society based on freedom and equality; and (b) shall not negate the essential content of the right in question and . . . shall . . . also be necessary."

disprove an important essential element of an offence on the balance of probabilities are in breach of the presumption of innocence, since they permit the conviction of an accused despite the existence of a reasonable doubt as to his guilt.

9–59   In *State v Mbatha*[94] the Constitutional Court was concerned with a statutory presumption which provided that the accused was deemed to be in possession of any firearm which was found at premises in which he was present, or of which he was the occupier, "until the contrary is proved". In the court's view, this presumption was in breach of s.25(3)(c) and was not saved by s.33(1). Giving the judgment of the court, Langa J. said[95]:

> "The effect of the provision is to relieve the prosecution of the burden of proof with regard to an essential element of the offence. It requires that the presumed fact must be disproved by the accused on a balance of probabilities ... [A] presumption of this nature is in breach of the presumption of innocence since it could result in the conviction of an accused person despite the existence of a reasonable doubt as to his or her guilt. No legal system can guarantee that no innocent person can ever be convicted. Indeed, the provision of corrective action by way of appeal and review procedures is an acknowledgement of the ever present possibility of judicial fallibility. Yet it is one thing for the law to acknowledge the possibility of wrongly but honestly convicting the innocent and then to provide appropriate measures to reduce the possibility of this happening as far as is practicable; it is another for the law itself to heighten the possibility of a miscarriage of justice by compelling the trial court to convict where it entertains real doubts as to culpability and then to prevent the reviewing court from altering the conviction even if it shares in the doubts."

9–60   As to the justification for the presumption, Langa J. observed:

> "The issue before us ... is not simply whether there is a pressing social need to combat crimes of violence—there clearly is—but also whether the instrument to be used in meeting this need is itself fashioned in accordance with specifications permitted by the Constitution ... The presumption of innocence is clearly of vital importance in the establishment and maintenance of an open and democratic society based on freedom and equality. If, in particular cases, what is effectively a presumption of guilt is to be substituted for the presumption of innocence, the justification for doing so must be established clearly and convincingly. It was argued that without the presumption it would be almost impossible for the prosecution to prove both the mental and physical elements of possession ... There will no doubt be cases in which it will be difficult to prove that a particular person against whom the presumption would have operated, was in fact in possession of the prohibited article. If that person was in fact guilty, the absence of the presumption might enable him or her to escape conviction. But this is inevitably a consequence of the presumption of innocence; this must be weighed against the danger that innocent people may be convicted if the presumption were to apply. In that process the rights of innocent persons must be given precedence."

9–61   Adopting the approach of the Canadian Supreme Court, Langa J. suggested that an evidential burden would meet many of the concerns which were said to justify the provision, without necessarily infringing the presumption of innocence:

---

[94] [1996] 2 L.R.C. 208.
[95] See 215G to 222D.

"I am not persuaded that the presumption, as it stands, satisfies the requirements of reasonableness and justifiability. I am fortified in this conclusion by the fact that it has also not been demonstrated that its objective, that is facilitating the conviction of offenders, could not reasonably have been achieved by other means, less damaging to constitutionally entrenched rights. Although the choice of appropriate measures necessary to address the need is that of the legislature, it has not been shown that an evidentiary burden, for example would not be as effective ... [B]y requiring the accused to provide evidence sufficient to raise a reasonable doubt, such a provision would be of assistance to the prosecution whilst at the same time being less invasive of section 25(3) rights."

In *State v Bhulwana*,[96] the Constitutional Court struck down a statutory offence **9–62** which provided that where it was proved that an accused had been found in possession of "dagga" exceeding 115g "it shall be presumed, until the contrary is proved, that the accused dealt in such dagga". O'Regan J., giving the judgment of the unanimous Court, held that[97]:

"The effect of the provision is that once the state has proved that the accused was found in possession of an amount of dagga in excess of 115g, the accused will, on a balance of probabilities, have to show that such possession did not constitute dealing as defined in the Act. Even if the accused raises a reasonable doubt as to whether he or she was dealing in the drug, but fails to show it on a balance of probabilities, he or she must nevertheless be convicted. The effect of imposing the legal burden on the accused may therefore result in a conviction for dealing despite the existence of a reasonable doubt as to his or her guilt."

Probably the most-cited South African decision is *State v Coetzee and Others*,[98] **9–63** where the Constitutional Court struck down two reverse onus clauses under the Criminal Procedure Act 1977. The first provided that if it was proved in a criminal proceeding that a false representation had been made by an accused, the accused was deemed, unless the contrary was proved, to have made the representation knowing it to be false. The second provided that a director or servant of a corporate body was guilty of an offence committed by that body unless it was proved that the person took no part in the commission of the offence and could not have prevented it. Both clauses were struck down on the ground that they were capable of permitting the conviction of an accused despite the existence of a reasonable doubt as to his guilt. In *Coetzee*[99] Langa J. observed:

"In a number of cases decided by this court, we have emphasised the importance of the rights entrenched in section 25(3)(c) of the Constitution, which include the right to be presumed innocent, in an open and democratic society based on freedom and equality ... Underlying the decisions in those cases is the recognition that a consequence of the value system introduced by the Constitution is that the freedom of the individual may not lightly be taken away. Presumptions which expose an accused person to the real risk of being convicted despite the existence of a reasonable doubt as to his or her guilt are not consistent with what is clearly a fundamental value in our criminal justice system."

---

[96] [1996] 1 L.R.C. 194.
[97] At 199H to 200A.
[98] [1997] 2 L.R.C. 593.
[99] At 604E–G.

9–64 In the same case Sachs J. was critical of the use made by some judges of what he termed "the ubiquity and ugliness argument" for approving a reverse onus provision because the offence is a serious one[100]:

> "Reference to the prevalence and seriousness of a crime therefore does not add anything new or special . . . The perniciousness of the offence is one of the givens, against which the presumption of innocence is pitted from the beginning, not a new element to be put into the scales as part of a justificatory balancing exercise."

VII. The United States Supreme Court

9–65 The United States Supreme Court has held that the due process clause in the US Constitution imposes limits on the power of Congress or that of a State legislature to "make the proof of one fact or group of facts evidence of the existence of the ultimate fact on which guilt is predicated". In *Tot v United States*[101] the test adopted by the Supreme Court for the constitutionality of such a provision was that there must be "a rational connection between the facts proved and the fact presumed". This basic standard has, however, developed over time into something resembling a proportionality test.

9–66 In *Leary v United States*[102] Harlan J., giving the opinion of the Supreme Court, held that "a criminal statutory presumption must be regarded as 'irrational' or 'arbitrary' and hence unconstitutional, unless it can at least be said with substantial assurance that the presumed fact is more likely than not to flow from the proved fact on which it is made to depend". Ten years later, in *County Court of Ulster County v Allen*[103] the Supreme Court distinguished between the approach appropriate to a discretionary (or permissive) presumption, on the one hand, and the approach appropriate to a mandatory presumption on the other. The "more likely than not" standard adopted in *Leary* was confined to cases where the presumption was "permissive". A permissive presumption was one which "allows, but does not require, the trier of fact to infer the elemental fact from proof by the prosecutor of the basic one, and which places no burden of any kind on the defendant". In that situation, "the basic fact may constitute *prima facie* evidence of the elemental fact", but the presumption "leaves the trier of fact free to credit or reject the inference". But a mandatory presumption was "a far more troublesome evidentiary device". Where a mandatory presumption was in issue, "the presumption must be rejected unless the evidence necessary to invoke the inference is sufficient for a rational jury to find the inferred fact beyond a reasonable doubt". In considering the constitutionality of a statutory criminal presumption there was thus a fundamental distinction:

> " . . . between a permissive presumption on which the prosecution is entitled to rely as one not necessarily sufficient part of its proof and a mandatory presumption which the jury must accept even if it is the sole evidence of an element of the offence . . . In the latter situation, since the prosecution bears the burden of establishing guilt, it may not

---

[100] 1997 (3) S.A. 527 at para.220.
[101] 319 US 463 (1943) at 467 *per* Roberts J.
[102] 395 US 6 23 (1969) L. Ed 2nd 57 at 36–37.
[103] 442 US 140 (1979).

rest its case entirely on a presumption unless the fact proved is sufficient to support the inference of guilt beyond reasonable doubt."

The court drew a further distinction between mandatory and discretionary provisions concerning the manner in which a constitutional challenge of this sort should be determined. The constitutionality of a mandatory provision could be determined without reference to the facts of an individual case:　9–67

"To the extent that the trier of fact is forced to abide by the presumption, and may not reject it based on an independent evaluation of the particular facts presented by the State, the analysis of presumption's constitutional validity is logically divorced from those facts and based on the presumption's accuracy in the run of cases".

However, where a discretionary or permissive presumption is in issue, the Supreme Court would require "the party challenging it to demonstrate its invalidity *as applied to him*". This would depend upon an examination of the record of the court of trial.

VIII. The Approach of The Privy Council

In *Attorney-General for Hong Kong v Lee Kwong-kut*[104] the Privy Council held　9–68
that a reverse onus provision in Hong Kong violated the presumption of innocence in Art.11(1) of the Bill of Rights Ordinance 1991 (which is in virtually identical terms to Art.6(2) of the Convention). Lord Woolf, delivering the opinion of the Board, said that the starting point for any court in determining whether a reverse onus provision respected the presumption of innocence was to identify the essential elements of the criminal liability which the offence imposed[105]: "In deciding what are the essential ingredients, the language of the relevant statutory provision will be important. However, what will be decisive will be the substance and reality of the language creating the offence rather than its form".[106]

Once the elements of the offence have been identified, the court should then go　9–69
on to apply the principle which lies at the heart of the decision, namely that it is impermissible for a statute to put the burden upon the defence to disprove an important essential element in the offence. Referring to *Salabiaku*, and the decisions of the Canadian Supreme Court, Lord Woolf pointed out that the

---

[104] [1993] A.C. 951.
[105] At 969H to 970A.
[106] For further references to the importance of considering the substance of the elements of the offence, rather than the form of the words used to create it, see 968E (" ... and if it is also remembered that it is the substance rather than the letter of the language of the statute which is important ... "); 972E (" ... by examining the substance of the statutory provision ... "); 973B (" ... their Lordships regard the answer as being relatively straightforward once the substance of the offences has been identified ... "); 973B–C (" ... the substantive effect of the statutory provision is to place the onus on the defence to establish that he can give an explanation as to his innocent possession of the property ... "); 973D (" ... the substance of the offence is contained in section 25(1) ... ").

presumption of innocence had been applied with an implicit degree of flexibility[107]:

> "This implicit flexibility allows a balance to be drawn between the interest of the person charged and the state. There are situations where it is clearly sensible and reasonable that deviations should be allowed from the strict application of the principle that the prosecution must prove the defendant's guilt beyond reasonable doubt. Take an obvious example in the case of an offence involving the performance of some act without a licence. Common sense dictates that the prosecution should not be required to shoulder the virtually impossible task of establishing that a defendant has not a licence when it is a matter of comparative simplicity for a defendant to establish that he has a licence . . . Some exceptions will be justifiable, others will not. Whether they are justifiable will in the end depend upon whether it remains primarily the responsibility of the prosecution to prove the guilt of the accused to the required standard and whether the exception is reasonably imposed, notwithstanding the importance of maintaining the principle which article 11(1) enshrines. The less significant the departure from the normal principle, the simpler it will be to justify an exception. If the prosecution retains responsibility for proving the essential ingredients of the offence, the less likely it is that an exception will be regarded as unacceptable . . . If the exception requires certain matters to be presumed until the contrary is shown, then it will be difficult to justify that presumption unless, as was pointed out by the United States Supreme Court in *Leary v United States* (1969) 23 L. Ed. 2d. 82, 'it can at least be said with substantial assurance that the presumed fact is more likely than not to flow from the proved fact on which it is made to depend' ".

9–70   On the first of the two appeals before the Board, the offence was that of possessing cash that is reasonably suspected of being stolen, and the Privy Council confirmed the ruling of the Hong Kong Court of Appeal that this was inconsistent with the presumption of innocence:

> "[T]he substantive effect of the statutory provision is to place the onus on the defence to establish that he can give an explanation as to his possession of the property. That is the most significant element of the offence. It reduces the burden on the prosecution to proving possession by the defendant and facts from which a reasonable suspicion can be inferred that the property has been stolen or obtained unlawfully, matters which are likely to be a formality in the majority of cases."[108]

On the second appeal, the offence required the prosecution to prove the defendant's involvement in dealing with another's drug trafficking proceeds, and the existence of reasonable grounds for believing that the other party was a drug trafficker, leaving the accused to prove one or more defences on a balance of probabilities. The Privy Council held that this provision was justifiable.

IX. Burdens of Proof post-Conviction

9–71   There is now a series of statutes containing powers relating to the confiscation of assets, running from the Drug Trafficking Offences Act 1986 through to the Proceeds of Crime Act 2002. Although some of the previous enactments remain

---

[107] At 969C to 970B.
[108] *ibid.*, at 973.

applicable, depending on the time of commission of the offence of conviction, the focus here will be on the Proceeds of Crime Act 2002. Section 6 of the Act provides that, where the Crown Court believes it appropriate to consider making a confiscation order, it must decide whether the offender has a "criminal life-style", and if so whether he has benefited from his "general criminal conduct"; or, if he does not have a criminal lifestyle, whether he has benefited from his particular criminal conduct.[109] The relevant proceedings occur after conviction, and the prosecution must satisfy the judge of these matters on a balance of probabilities. If the judge is so satisfied, certain statutory assumptions come into play in order to enable the court to calculate the amount of the confiscation order. The assumptions apply unless the offender can prove, on a balance of probabilities, that they should not.

These procedures raise at least two human rights questions—first, whether at this stage of proceedings the offender is a "charged with a criminal offence" so as to bring the case within Art.6(2) and 6(3); and secondly, how Art.6(2) would apply in such circumstances. In *McIntosh v Lord Advocate*[110] Lord Bingham stated: **9–72**

> "On this point I respectfully differ from the Court of Appeal.[111] The confiscation order procedure can only be initiated if the accused is convicted of a drug trafficking offence. The court is therefore dealing with a proven drug trafficker. It is then incumbent on the prosecutor to prove, as best he can, the property held by the accused and his expenditure over the chosen period up to six years, including any implicative gifts relied on . . . It is only if a significant discrepancy is shown between the property and expenditure of the accused on the one hand and his known sources of income on the other that the court will think it right to make the section 3(2) assumptions . . . If a significant discrepancy is shown, and in the first instance it is for the prosecutor to show it, I do not for my part think it unreasonable or oppressive to call on the accused to proffer an explanation."[112]

This passage runs together the two questions, but they were taken separately by the Strasbourg Court in *Phillips v United Kingdom*.[113] The majority held that Art.6(2) does not apply, partly because it does not apply at the sentencing stage and partly because confiscation proceedings do not involve charging the offender with another offence. The first reason is of doubtful strength, as the two dissenting judges argued, pointing to decisions of the court holding that Art.6 does apply to sentencing proceedings.[114] The second reason is not wholly convincing either, at least in relation to statutory procedures that reach back some six years and may involve allegations or assumptions that the offender has committed further offences (of which he has not been convicted). However, the majority went on to

---

[109] For a critical analysis of these provisions and their human rights implications, see Alldridge P., *Money Laundering Law* (2003), ch.7.

[110] [2001] 3 W.L.R. 107.

[111] *Sub nom. Benjafield* [2001] 2 Cr.App.R. 87.

[112] At [37].

[113] [2001] Crim.L.R. 817.

[114] Notably *Minelli v Switzerland* (1983) 5 E.H.R.R. 554, and *V and T v United Kingdom* (1999) 30 E.H.R.R. 121.

consider what the implications of applying Art.6(2) would be, and they concluded that on the facts of this case there was sufficient justification for admitting an exception to the presumption of innocence:

> "The Court notes that, had the applicant's account of his financial dealings been true, it would not have been difficult for him to rebut the statutory presumption: as the judge stated, the evidentiary steps which he could have taken to demonstrate the legitimate sources of his money were 'perfectly obvious and ordinary and simple' . . . Finally, when calculating the value of the realisable assets available to the applicant, it is significant that . . . the judge accepted the applicant's evidence. Whilst the Court considers that an issue relating to the fairness of the procedure might arise in circumstances where the amount of a confiscation order was based on the value of assumed hidden assets, this was far from being the case as regards the present applicant."[115]

Although the Court thus found that the application of the relevant provisions of the Drug Trafficking Act 1994 was "confined within reasonable limits, given the importance of what was at stake and that the rights of the defence were fully respected" (applying the *Salabiaku* decision),[116] the closing words of the quotation show that this was a decision on the facts of this case.[117]

9–73   In the House of Lords in *Revzi*,[118] Lord Steyn acknowledged the "powerful" dissenting opinion in *Phillips* to the effect that Art.6(2) should apply to confiscation proceedings, but commented that "if this view had prevailed it would in my respectful view have caused difficulties in English law and in other national legal systems", largely because other provisions such as Art.6(3)(a) would be hard to reconcile with the procedures of confiscation.[119] The House of Lords went on to hold that Art.6(2) did not apply, because confiscation proceedings do not involve a fresh criminal charge, but that even if the presumption of innocence did apply the statutory assumptions were a "proportionate response" to the problems of depriving offenders of their assets. The decision in *Revzi* concerned the confiscation provisions of the Criminal Justice Act 1988, and the House of Lords held in *Benjafield*[120] that the same applied, *mutatis mutandis*, to the confiscation provisions of the Drug Trafficking Act 1994.

X. Strict liability offences

9–74   It is important to distinguish strict liability offences (where criminal liability consists of the *actus reus* alone) from offences with a reverse onus of proof on *mens rea*.[121]

---

[115] Judgment of July 5, 2001, at [45–47].
[116] See 9–10 above.
[117] *Cf.* the comments of the Court of Appeal in *Barnham* [2006] 1 Cr.App.R. (S) 83, at [32]–[38].
[118] [2002] UKHL 1.
[119] At [12].
[120] [2002] UKHL 2.
[121] As to the importance of looking to the substance of the offence in determining its essential elements see para.9–68 above. See also the analysis of Lord Bingham C.J. and Laws L.J. in *R. v DPP ex parte Kebilene and ors* [1999] 3 W.L.R. 175.

On two occasions in recent years the House of Lords has pronounced that the presumption of mens rea, which applies to all statutory offences, is a "constitutional principle": *B v Director of Public Prosecutions*,[122] and *K*.[123] However, it is apparent that this approach, and the language of constitutionality, has no bearing on the relationship between the presumption of innocence and the imposition of strict criminal liability.

In *Barnfather v London Borough of Islington Education Authority*[124] the Divi-   **9–75**
sional Court heard a challenge to s.444(1) of the Education Act 1996 on school attendance, which states that "if a child of compulsory school age who is a registered pupil at a school fails to attend regularly at the school, his parent is guilty of an offence." This has been interpreted as a strict liability offence, but that was challenged primarily on human rights grounds. The argument for the appellants was that the decision in *Salabiaku v France*[125] also concerned a strict liability offence, and that the court held that Art.6.2 "requires States to confine [presumptions of fact in the criminal law] within reasonable limits which take into account the importance of what is at stake and maintain the rights of the defence."[126] In *Hansen v Denmark*[127] the court considered a strict liability offence which criminalized the employers of lorry drivers who falsified their tachograph records, and reached a decision that the application was inadmissible by deciding that the offence was "well within the limits which take into account what is at stake." However, Maurice Kay J. rejected the argument that courts are therefore required by Art.6.2 to make this assessment of every offence, holding that the Article is confined to procedural issues (i.e. burden of proof) and has no bearing on the absence or presence of a requirement of *mens rea*.

Both Maurice Kay J. and Elias J. went on to hold that strict liability was   **9–76**
justifiable for this offence. The former emphasised that it is only punishable with a fine, and that education authorities can be trusted not to prosecute if the parent is blameless. Elias J. relied on the contrast with the more serious offence under s.444(1A), which penalises a parent who *knows* that the child is not attending regularly and provides for a maximum of three months' imprisonment. Elias J. seemed more tempted by the argument that, if a State can avoid Art.6.2 by simply abolishing a defence rather than imposing a reverse onus in respect of it, this would drive a coach and horses through Art.6.2 and make the application of that Article random and capricious. But he too rejected this argument, concluding that Art.6 is about procedural protections and not substantive principles of liability.

A similar conclusion has been reached in other cases. For example, in *G(AR)*[128]   **9–77**
the Court of Appeal held that the Convention is not concerned with provisions of substantive criminal law, and is therefore not relevant to the imposition of strict

---

[122] [2000] 2 A.C. 428.
[123] [2002] 1 Cr.App.R. 121.
[124] [2003] EWHC Admin 418.
[125] (1988) 13 E.H.R.R. 379.
[126] At [28].
[127] App.No.28971/95.
[128] [2002] EWCA Crim 1992.

liability. In *R. v Halton Division Magistrates' Court*,[129] the Divisional Court held that the provision imposed strict liability, largely because it was not a truly criminal offence, and went on to hold that the Convention has no application to such issues of substantive law. Clarke L.J. quoted a passage from the *Salabiaku* decision in support:

"contracting States may, under certain conditions, penalise a simple or objective fact as such, irrespective of whether it results from criminal intent or from negligence. Examples of such offences may be found in the laws of the Contracting States."[130]

It was also this passage, and the practice of the Strasbourg Court, that led Lord Bingham to assert that it is open to states to define the constituent elements of criminal offences and to exclude mens rea.[131]

C. THE STANDARD OF PROOF

9–78   It has rightly been pointed out that the *standard* of proof required in criminal proceedings is largely unexplored in the Convention jurisprudence.[132] Nevertheless, it is implicit in the reasoning of the Strasbourg institutions that proof beyond reasonable doubt is necessary. The Court has emphasised on a number of occasions that "any doubt should benefit the accused".[133] In rejecting an application as inadmissible the Commission in one case observed that "the judge, in explaining that proof must be beyond reasonable doubt, also explained what was meant by a 'reasonable doubt' and told the jury that they must acquit if they had such a doubt".[134]

9–79   This assumption is also evident in other contexts. When considering whether state officials have deliberately tortured or inflicted inhuman and degrading treatment on a person in custody the Court has held that Art.3 requires proof beyond reasonable doubt, and has observed that "such proof may follow from the coexistence of sufficiently strong, clear and concordant inferences".[135] And in concluding that certain proceedings were not "criminal" within the autonomous interpretation given to the term "criminal charge" in Art.6,[136] the Commission has referred to the fact that a tribunal did not apply the criminal standard of proof beyond reasonable doubt.[137]

---

[129] [2003] EWHC Admin 272.

[130] *Ibid.* at [52], quoting from (1988) 13 E.H.R.R. 379, at [27].

[131] In *Sheldrake* [2005] 1 A.C. 246, at para.[21]; *cf.* the contrary argument of Tadros and Tierney, referred to in n.21 above.

[132] Sir Richard Buxton, "The Human Rights Act and the Substantive Criminal Law" [2000] Crim.L.R. 331.

[133] *Barbera, Messegue, and Jabardo v Spain* (1989) 11 E.H.R.R. 360 at para.77. See also *Austria v Italy* (1963) Y.B. VI 740 at 784, where the Commission observed that under Art.6(2) "the onus to prove guilt falls on the prosecution and any doubt is to the benefit of the accused."

[134] Application No.5768/72 (1975) 2 Digest 388.

[135] *Ireland v United Kingdom* (1979–80) 2 E.H.R.R. 25.

[136] See Ch.4 above.

[137] *Goodman v Ireland* (1993) 16 E.H.R.R. CD 26.

In practice this issue is only likely to arise in proceedings which are not classified **9–80** as criminal under domestic law, but which will fall to be so classified under Art.6. Where the proceedings concern a criminal offence recognised as such in domestic law, the criminal standard of proof beyond reasonable doubt will obviously apply. Any possible doubts on this issue are removed by s.11 of the Human Rights Act 1998 which provides that the Act does not restrict any right or freedom which is currently guaranteed under national law, including the common law.[138]

However, as shown in Ch.4 above, there are decisions in which the English **9–81** courts have held that proceedings are indeed civil, and not criminal under the autonomous meaning of that term in Art.6, and yet have also held that the standard of proof to be attained by the applicant or complainant is virtually indistinguishable from the criminal standard. Thus, for example, in *Gough v Chief Constable of Derbyshire*[139] the Court of Appeal had to consider the nature of football banning orders under s.14(B) of the Football Spectators Act 1989. Lord Phillips M.R. stated:

> "We find that the proceedings that led to the imposition of banning orders were civil in character. It does not follow from this that a mere balance of probabilities suffices to justify the making of an order. Banning orders under s.14(B) fall into the same category as antisocial behaviour orders and sex offenders' orders. While made in civil proceedings they impose serious restraints on freedoms that the citizen normally enjoys. While technically the civil standard of proof applies, that standard is flexible and must reflect the consequences that will follow if the case for a banning order is made out. This should lead the magistrates to apply an exacting standard of proof that will, in practice, be hard to distinguish from the criminal standard."[140]

This approach was confirmed by the House of Lords when dealing with antisocial behavior orders in *Clingham v Royal Borough of Kensington and Chelsea; R. v Crown Court at Manchester, ex parte McCann*,[141] where it was held that proceedings for the making of antisocial behaviour orders are civil not criminal, but that the criminal standard of proof is appropriate because of the possible consequences of breaching an order (i.e. up to five years' imprisonment).[142]

---

[138] See para.3–21 above.
[139] [2002] 2 All E.R. 985.
[140] At [89–90].
[141] [2002] UKHL 39.
[142] e.g. *per* Lord Steyn at [37] and *per* Lord Hope at [83].

CHAPTER 10

RETROSPECTIVITY AND THE PRINCIPLE OF LEGAL CERTAINTY

A. INTRODUCTION

The principle of legal certainty runs throughout the Convention,[1] and it manifests itself chiefly in two ways. First, it forms part of the "quality of law" test developed by the Strasbourg Court as a requirement when determining whether a detention is "lawful" for the purposes of Art.5,[2] and when assessing whether an interference with one of the qualified rights in Arts 8 to 11 is "prescribed by law" or "in accordance with the law".[3] Secondly, the principle of legal certainty is embodied in Art.7(1) (*no punishment without law*) which provides that: **10–01**

> "No one shall be held guilty of any criminal offence on account of any act or omission which did not constitute a criminal offence under national or international law at the time when it was committed ... "

The first limb of Art.7(1) thus prohibits the retroactive application of criminal offences so as to penalise conduct which was not criminal at the time when the relevant act or omission occurred. More generally, however, the Court has held that Art.7(1);   **10–02**

> " ... embodies ... the principle that only the law can define a crime and prescribe a penalty (*nullum crimen, nulla poena sine lege*) and the principle that the criminal law must not be extensively construed to an accused's detriment, for example by analogy; it follows from this that an offence must be clearly defined in law."[4]

The Court has emphasised the close relationship between the principle of legal certainty guaranteed by Art.7 and the "quality of law" requirement, applicable to   **10–03**

---

[1] See para.2–80 above.

[2] See paras 2–83 and 5–07 to 5–12 above.

[3] See para.2–86 above.

[4] *Kokkinakis v Greece* (1994) 17 E.H.R.R. 397 at para.52; reiterated in *K-HW v Germany* (2001) 36 E.H.R.R. 1081, at para.45, and in *Achour v France*, App.No.67335/01, judgment of Grand Chamber on March 29, 2006, at paras 41–43.

other provisions of the Convention, that an interference with an individual's fundamental rights must be governed by clear legal principles[5]:

> "When speaking of 'law' Article 7 alludes to the very same concept as that to which the Convention refers elsewhere when using the term, a concept which comprises written as well as unwritten law and implies qualitative requirements, notably those of accessibility and foreseeability."

10–04   Accordingly, for the purposes of the Convention;

> " . . . a norm cannot be regarded as 'law' unless it is formulated with sufficient precision to enable the citizen to regulate his conduct: he must be able—if need be with appropriate advice—to foresee, to a degree that is reasonable in the circumstances, the consequences which a given action may entail."[6]

10–05   The requirement of certainty flowing from Art.7 therefore encompasses two closely connected principles. The first is that the substantive criminal law should be sufficiently accessible and precise to enable an individual to know in advance whether his conduct is criminal; and the second is that developments of the criminal law by the courts (whether through the interpretation of statutory offences, or the development of common law offences) must be kept within the bounds of what is reasonably foreseeable.

B. CERTAINTY OF DEFINITION

I. At Common Law Generally

10–06   The principle that the criminal law must meet the requirements of reasonable certainty and accessibility has been said to be "deeply embedded" in English law.[7] Professor Glanville Williams explained the principle as an aspect of the Diceyan conception of the rule of law[8]:

> "'Englishmen are ruled by the law, and by the law alone', wrote Dicey. 'A man may with us be punished for breach of law, but he can be punished for nothing else'. In its Latin dress of *Nullum crimen sine lege, Nulla Poena sine lege*—that there must be no crime or punishment except in accordance with fixed, predetermined law—this has been regarded by most thinkers a self-evident principle of justice ever since the French

---

[5] *SW and CR v United Kingdom* (1996) 21 E.H.R.R. 363 at paras 32 (SW) and 34 (CR). In *Sunday Times (No.1) v United Kingdom* (1979–80) 2 E.H.R.R. 245 the applicants challenged contempt of court proceedings on the grounds of lack of legal certainty under Art.10, whilst in *Harman v United Kingdom* (1984) 38 D.R. 53 a similar challenge was mounted by reference to Art.7.

[6] *Silver v United Kingdom* (1983) 5 E.H.R.R. 347.

[7] See DeSmith, Woolf and Jowell, *Judicial Review of Administrative Action* (5th edn, 1995), para.13–026.

[8] *Criminal Law: The General Part* (2nd edn 1961) p.575. Similar sentiments were expressed by Laws L.J. in *Briffet and Bradshaw v Director of Public Prosecutions* [2001] EWHC 841 (Admin), a case about the clarity of definition of reporting restrictions imposed under s.39 of the Children and Young Persons Act 1933. Discussing the principle of legal certainty, Laws L.J. stated that "In the law of Europe this is a general principle; but however wide it runs, our domestic law has always applied it to the construction and effect of penal or criminal measures." [13].

Revolution. The citizen must be able to ascertain beforehand how he stands with regard to the criminal law; otherwise to punish him for breach of that law is purposeless cruelty."

This constitutional requirement, whether phrased in terms of the rule of law or the principle of legality, can be sub-divided into three related principles—the non-retrospectivity principle, the principle of maximum certainty, and the principle of strict construction of criminal statutes. Despite the strong statements above, none of these principles has been pursued with absolute consistency by the English criminal courts.[9] However, the principles now have a stronger foundation, and major decisions extending the criminal law and even creating new offences—notably *Shaw v Director of Public Prosecutions*[10] and *Knuller v Director of Public Prosecutions*[11]—would surely now be prohibited by the application of s.6 of the Human Rights Act and Art.7 of the Convention (see 10– below). **10–07**

II. The Treatment of Bye-Laws

The principle of legal certainty in criminal legislation has figured prominently in public law challenges to the validity of byelaws enforceable by criminal prosecution.[12] In *Staden v Tarjanyi*[13] Lord Lane C.J. explained that; **10–08**

" . . . to be valid, a byelaw, carrying as this one does penalties for infringement, must be certain and clear in the sense that anyone engaged upon [an] otherwise lawful pursuit . . . must know with reasonable certainty when he is breaking the law and when he is not breaking the law. That proposition scarcely needs demonstration or authority."

In this context, however, there is a presumption that an ambiguously worded byelaw "must, if possible, be given such a meaning as to make it reasonable and valid, rather than unreasonable and invalid".[14] The consequence, as Woolf J. pointed out in *R. v Secretary of State for Trade and Industry ex parte Ford*,[15] is

---

[9] See further Ashworth A., *Principles of Criminal Law* (5th edn, 2006), 68–83.
[10] [1962] A.C. 220.
[11] [1973] A.C. 435; see further the classic article by Smith A.T.H., "Judicial Lawmaking in the Criminal Law", (1984) 100 L.Q.R. 46.
[12] As long ago as 1898 it was established that " . . . a byelaw to be valid must, among other conditions, have two properties—it must be certain, that is, it must contain adequate information as to the duties of those who are to obey, and it must be reasonable": *Kruse v Johnson* [1898] 2 Q.B. 91 *per* Mathew J. at 108. The rationale for this principle was explained by Diplock L.J. in *Mixnam's Properties Ltd v Chertsey Urban District Council* [1964] 1 Q.B. 214 at 238 as deriving from Parliamentary intention: "[I]f the courts can declare subordinate legislation to be invalid for 'uncertainty' . . . this must be because Parliament is presumed not to have intended to authorise the subordinate legislation authority to make changes in the existing law which are uncertain."
[13] (1980) 78 L.G.R. 614 at 623.
[14] *Fawcett Properties Ltd v Buckingham County Council* [1961] A.C. 636 at 677. *Fawcett* was in fact concerned with the validity of a planning condition, but Lord Denning expressly equated the test with that to be applied to byelaws. The *Fawcett* test was expressly approved as applying to byelaw offences by the Court of Appeal in *Percy v Hall* [1997] Q.B. 924.
[15] (1984) 4 Tr. L. 150.

that "uncertainty of language rarely creates the necessary degree of invalidity to cause the courts to intervene".

10–09 It is important, however, to recall that the requirement for legal certainty takes colour from its context. Doubts as to the precise scope of a legal prohibition may be sufficient to afford a defence in criminal proceedings where the conduct in question falls within the penumbra of uncertainty surrounding a particular bye-law, without necessarily affording grounds for striking the byelaw down in its entirety. In *Bugg v DPP*[16] the Divisional Court found byelaws prohibiting entry onto military land to be insufficiently certain, and therefore "defective on their face", since they failed to refer to any plan or boundary setting out the precise limits of the area protected.

10–10 In *Percy v Hall*,[17] however, the Court of Appeal declined to follow *Bugg*, holding that "however narrow or precise the line on a map, there will always be, literally, a borderline of uncertainty". This would not be sufficient to invalidate the byelaws so as to render them void and unenforceable even against those who deliberately trespassed within the centre of the protected area. But that did not mean that uncertainty as to the boundary would be irrelevant to criminal liability. As Simon Brown L.J. appeared to accept,[18] if there were genuine uncertainty as to whether or not a byelaw applies at a particular point on or around the boundary, then the benefit of the doubt should be given to the individual, and he should not be convicted of a byelaw offence.

III. The Strasbourg Caselaw

10–11 As explained in 10–01 above, the European Court of Human Rights has developed the principle of certainty in two contexts—as part of the "quality of law" test, and as an aspect of the non-retrospectivity rule in Art.7. In doing so, however, it has recognised the need for some flexibility,[19] emphasising that the test of legal certainty must take account not only of the wording of the relevant provision, but also of the courts' interpretation of it, and of other readily available guidance as to its meaning and application. Moreover, in *Sunday Times v United Kingdom (No.1)*[20] the Court expressly recognised that absolute precision is unattainable, and observed that:

> " . . . whilst certainty is highly desirable, it may bring in its train excessive rigidity and the law must be able to keep pace with changing circumstances. Accordingly, many

---

[16] [1993] Q.B. 473.

[17] [1997] Q.B. 924.

[18] See counsel's submission at 936D, and Simon Brown L.J.'s response at 937H to 938B.

[19] Writing extra-judicially, Sir Richard Buxton has suggested that the Strasbourg caselaw "has disappointingly little to offer in practice" since "it is difficult to discern in the ECHR jurisprudence any general principle that the criminal law must be accessible and certain above a very modest level": Buxton R., "The Human Rights Act and the Substantive Criminal Law" [2000] Crim. L.R. 331. However, the question of the necessary degree of certainty is supremely difficult, since absolute certainty of definition is neither attainable nor desirable: Endicott T., "The Impossibility of the Rule of Law", (1999) 19 *Oxford J.L.S.* 1.

[20] (1979–80) 2 E.H.R.R. 245 at para.59.

laws are couched in terms which, to a greater or lesser extent, are vague and whose interpretation and application are questions of practice."

Similarly, in *Kokkinakis v Greece*[21] the Court held that the requirement for an offence to be clearly defined in law "is satisfied where the individual can know from the wording of the relevant provision *and, if need be, with the assistance of the courts' interpretation of it*, what acts and omissions will make him liable" (emphasis added).

Accordingly the Convention institutions have consistently looked to national **10–12** caselaw defining or interpreting an offence in order to determine whether the margin of uncertainty surrounding the essential elements of criminal liability is so wide that it is liable to deprive the affected individual of the information necessary to regulate his conduct. Thus, in *Handyside v United Kingdom*,[22] a case concerning the definition of obscenity in the Obscene Publications Acts 1959–1964, the Commission held that it was sufficient that the legislation provided a general description, which was then interpreted and applied by the courts. The Court has subsequently endorsed this view in relation to the concept of obscenity in Swiss law, stating that:

"the need to avoid excessive rigidity and to keep pace with changing circumstances means that many laws are invitably couched in terms which, to a greater or lesser extent, are vague ... criminal law provisions on obscenity fall within this category."[23]

The Court supported this view by referring to Swiss cases in which the concept had been applied and to some extent clarified. In the *Kokkinakis* case, a statutory offence of "proselytism" was held to have been clarified by a body of settled national caselaw on the meaning of the provision.[24] In reaching this conclusion the Court reiterated that "the wording of many statutes is not absolutely precise", and that "the interpretation and application of such enactments depend on practice." However, in *Wingrove v United Kingdom*[25] the Court held that there was no general uncertainty about the definition of the crime of blasphemy, and this has been applied to the concept of obscenity more recently, even though it is juries that make the key decisions here.[26]

---

[21] (1994) 17 E.H.R.R. 397 at para.52.
[22] (1974) 17 Y.B. 228. The court's judgment is reported at (1979–80) 1 E.H.R.R. 737.
[23] *Muller v Switzerland* (1991) 13 E.H.R.R. 212, at para.29.
[24] (1994) 17 E.H.R.R. 397 at paras 40–41 and 52. See also *Suggs and Dobbs v Sweden*, App. No.45934/99, where the court, in holding the application inadmissible, held that "the case-law, which had been published and was accessible, supplemented the letter of the legal provision and was such as to sufficiently enable the applicants to regulate their conduct." (p.4) The court also made it clear that being unfamiliar with the jurisdiction is not a defence: "The fact that the applicants had been in Sweden for only 12 hours when they were arrested cannot constitute an excuse for not complying with Swedish law." (p.4).
[25] (1997) 24 E.H.R.R. 1; see 8–45 above.
[26] See the English case of *Perrin* [2002] EWCA Crim 747, at [41–42], and *Chauvy and Others v France*, App.No.64915/01, decision of September 23, 2003: in convicting the applicants of defamation, the French courts had applied national caselaw dating back to 1881 and 1951, of which the publishers should have been aware, if necessary after taking legal advice.

10–13　　The relevance of external guidance was considered in *Ainsworth v United Kingdom*.[27] The applicant challenged his conviction under s.69 of the Army Act 1955 for engaging "conduct to the prejudice of good order and military discipline". As a lieutenant in the Royal Marines he had failed to prevent the consumption of alcohol by under-age recruits, one of whom had died from alcohol poisoning. He contended that the terms of s.69 were insufficiently specific to enable him to know in advance that he was committing a criminal offence, and argued that there had been a "blind eye" policy of allowing the consumption of alcohol by under-age recruits. In concluding that the standard set by Art.7 had been met, the Commission considered that s.69 had to be read in the light of "detailed and precise" standing orders which spelt out the duties of a supervising officer. Moreover, the adoption of a "blind eye" policy by more senior officers could not be said to amount to an "implicit abrogation" of the offence.

10–14　　On occasion, the court has been prepared to accept general wording, even in the absence of judicial interpretation or external guidance as to its meaning. In *Grigoriades v Greece*[28] the applicant challenged a Greek military offence of "insulting the armed forces", on the ground that it was not *lex certa* and was therefore in breach of Art.7. The Court held that, although "couched in broad terms", the offence met the required standard, since the ordinary meaning of the word "insult" (which was akin to the word "offend") was clear enough to encompass the applicant's conduct of writing a letter to a superior officer criticising the army.

10–15　　The Court has emphasised that a key issue is the individual's ability to foresee whether conduct will fall foul of the criminal law. Thus in *Chorherr v Austria*[29] the applicant had been arrested and fined for the offence of causing a breach of the peace "by conduct likely to cause annoyance", for mounting a demonstration during a military ceremony. In determining whether there had been a breach of Art.5 (right to liberty) or a justifiable interference with his Art.10 right (freedom of expression), the Court applied the quality of law test by thus describing the certainty requirement:

> "The Court reiterates that the level of precision required of the domestic legislation— which cannot in any case provide for every eventuality—depends to a considerable degree on the content of the instrument considered, the field it is designed to cover and the number and status of those to whom it is addressed."[30]

The Court concluded that, in the light of the wording of the offence, the applicant had been "in a position to foresee to a reasonable extent the risks inherent in his conduct" when he refused to comply with the police request to cease distributing leaflets.

---

[27] Application No.35095/97, unreported.
[28] (1999) 27 E.H.R.R. 464.
[29] (1993) 17 E.H.R.R. 358.
[30] At [26], with references to three previous court decisions.

A similar question arose in *Steel and others v United Kingdom*,[31] where the five   **10–16**
applicants had been arrested (in various situations) for breach of the peace. They
challenged the lawfulness of their arrests under Art.5, arguing that the concept of
breach of the peace was insufficiently certain. The Court recognised that "all law,
whether written or unwritten, must be sufficiently precise to allow the citizen—if
need be, with appropriate advice—to foresee, to a degree that is reasonable in the
circumstances, the consequences which a given action may entail."[32] The Court
concluded that recent decisions had clarified the concept of breach of the peace,
in terms of acting "in a manner the natural consequence of which would be to
provoke others to violence,"[33] and therefore that the grounds for arresting the
applicants satisfied the "quality of law" test.

The leading case in Strasbourg is now *Hashman and Harrup v United King-*   **10–17**
dom,[34] where the Court considered whether an order binding over the defendants
to be "of good behaviour" (that is, not to act *contra bonos mores*) was a lawful
interference with their right to freedom of expression under Art.10. The Court
concluded that the requirements of the bind-over failed to satisfy the certainty
requirement:

> "The Court next notes that conduct *contra bonos mores* is defined as behaviour which
> is 'wrong rather than right in the judgement of the majority of contemporary fellow
> citizens.'[35] It cannot agree with the Government that this definition has the same
> objective element as conduct 'likely to cause annoyance,' which was at issue in the case
> of *Chorherr*.[36] The Court considers that the question of whether conduct is 'likely to
> cause annoyance' is a question which goes to the very heart of the nature of the conduct
> proscribed: it is conduct whose likely conduct is the annoyance of others. Similarly, the
> definition of breach of the peace given in the case of *Percy v. Director of Public
> Prosecutions*[37]—that it includes conduct the natural consequences of which would be to
> provoke others to violence—also describes behaviour by reference to its effects.
> Conduct which is 'wrong rather than right in the judgement of the majority of
> contemporary citizens,' by contrast, is conduct which is not described at all, but merely
> expressed to be 'wrong' in the opinion of the majority of citizens."[38]

Thus, the Court's view was that the bind-over order was too vague to qualify as
"law", largely because it failed to indicate what description of conduct would fall
within it. On the facts of the case the result is perhaps not surprising, since the

---

[31] (1998) 28 E.H.R.R. 603.

[32] At [54] The relevance of legal advice in certain contexts was considered by the court in
Unterguggenberge v Austria, App.No.34941/97. The fact that the applicant in that case was acting in
his capacity as a member of the executive board of a company was influential in persuading the court
that he could have been expected to take legal advice on the complex domestic legislation under
which he had been prosecuted.

[33] At [55], referring to *Percy v Director of Public Prosecutions* [1995] 1 W.L.R. 1382 and other
decisions cited at [25–28].

[34] (1999) 30 E.H.R.R. 241.

[35] *Per* Glidewell L.J. in *Hughes v Holley* (1988) 86 Cr.App.R. 130 (footnote in original).

[36] See 10–15 above.

[37] [1995] 1 W.L.R. 1382 (footnote in original).

[38] (1999) 30 E.H.R.R. 241, at [38].

English Law Commission had reached the same conclusion some years earlier[39]; although it is important to point out that the Government had failed to act on the Law Commission's report. But the significance of this decision goes beyond the particular facts, since the Court spelt out in greater detail than before the kinds of criteria that should be applied in assessing the certainty of a rule or order.

The issue of foreseeability was further considered in *K.H. W. v Germany*.[40] The applicant was a GDR border guard who, after reunification, had been convicted of intentional homicide for shooting a man trying to cross the German border in 1972. The applicant was tried and convicted on the basis of the law of the GDR which had been applicable at the time of the offence. However, he complained that the trial court, when applying the defences available in 1972, interpreted them more restrictively than the courts of the GDR would have done. The Court took account of the fact that, even at the time of the killing, the GDR Criminal Code provided that obedience to orders was not a defence if the execution of the order manifestly violated the rules of public international law. It would have been foreseeable, by reference to international consensus at the time, that the killing violated such rules. There was therefore no violation of Art.7. The fact that the courts of the GDR may in practice have ignored those norms was held to be irrelevant. Similar issues arose in *Glassner v Germany*.[41] In that case the applicant was a former GDR prosecutor who had been involved in the prosecution of a political dissident, and had pressed for an extremely heavy sentence. After reunification, he was convicted of aiding and abetting a deliberate perversion of the course of justice and aiding and abetting a deprivation of liberty, under both the GDR and FRG penal codes applicable at the time. The Court, declaring the application inadmissible, stated that:

"It is legitimate for a State governed by the rule of law to bring criminal proceedings against persons who have committed crimes under a former regime; similarly, the courts of such a State, having taken the place of those which existed previously, cannot be criticised for applying and interpreting the legal provisions in force at the material time in the light of principles governing a State subject to the rule of law."[42]

These two decisions, although set against an unusual political background, are open to question on the basis that they require individuals to apply interpretations of international law which may be directly contradicted by the actual practice of the courts in their jurisdiction.

---

[39] Buxton R., "The Human Rights Act and the Substantive Criminal Law" [2000] Crim. L.R. 331.

[40] (2001) 36 E.H.R.R. 1081. See also *Streletz, Kessler and Krenz v Germany*, App.Nos 34044/96, 35532/97 and 44801/98.

[41] App.No.46362/99.

[42] At p.10. The Court also required of the applicant a degree of historical foresight, stating that "the parliament of the GDR democratically elected in 1990 had expressly requested the German legislature to ensure that criminal proseuctions would be brought in respect of the injustices committed by the SED. That makes it reasonable to suppose that, even if the reunification of Germany had not taken place, a democratic regime taking over from the SED regime in the GDR would have applied the GDR's legislation and prosecuted the applicant, as the German courts did after the reunification." (p.12).

IV. Comparative Approaches

A similar requirement of certainty may be found in most constitutional jurisdictions. Thus, criminal statutes can be (and have been) declared "void for vagueness" both in the United States and in Canada if they fail to provide an "intelligible standard" for the application of the prohibition. In *Connally v General Construction Co.*[43] the United States Supreme Court[44] held that a law is void on its face if it is so vague that persons "of common intelligence must necessarily guess at its meaning and differ as to its application". This principle has been explained on the basis that a law which fails to define clearly the conduct it proscribes "may trap the innocent by not providing fair warning" and may in practical effect impermissibly delegate "basic policy matters to policemen, judges and juries for resolution on an ad hoc and subjective basis, with the attendant dangers of arbitrary and discriminatory application".[45] Nevertheless, the constitutional presumption of validity will often save an otherwise vague law, by restricting its application in practice. In *Grayned v City of Rockford*[46] the Supreme Court was faced with an ordinance which provided that "no person on public or private grounds adjacent to any building in which a school [is] in session shall willfully make [any] noise or diversion which disturbs or tends to disturb the peace or good order of such school". The provision was held to be constitutionally valid, since state courts could be expected to apply it "to prohibit only actual or imminent interference" with the peace or good order of the school. Accordingly, it was clear what the ordinance prohibited.   **10–18**

A more searching standard seems to have been applied to criminal offences involving the right to free expression. In *Smith v Goguen*[47] the Supreme Court invalidated a statute which prohibited the public mutilation, defacement or contemptuous treatment of the American flag. Recognising that use of the flag for adornment or to attract attention had become commonplace, the court held that the legislation failed "to draw reasonably clear lines between the kinds of nonceremonial treatment that are criminal, and those that are not". Similarly, in *Stromberg v California*[48] the court declared unconstitutional a statutory provision which made it an offence to express "opposition to organised government" by displaying "any flag, badge, banner or device". Stressing the fundamental importance of the "opportunity of free political discussion", the court observed that; "A statute which upon its face, and as authoritatively construed, is so vague and indefinite as to permit the punishment of the fair use of this opportunity is repugnant to the guarantee of liberty contained in the Fourteenth Amendment".   **10–19**

---

[43] 269 US 385 (1926) at 391.

[44] See generally, Amsterdam, "The Void-for-Vaguenss Doctrine in the Supreme Court" 109 U. Pa. L. Rev. 67 (1960).

[45] *Grayned v City of Rockford* 408 US 104 (1972). These dicta were approved by Lord Phillips M.R. in *R. (ZL and VL) v Secretary of State for the Home Department* [2003] EWCA Civ 25, at [25].

[46] 408 US 104 (1972).

[47] 415 US 566 (1974).

[48] 283 US 359 (1931).

10–20 The Canadian Supreme Court has recognised a similar void for vagueness doctrine, grounded in the principles of fundamental justice guaranteed by s.7 of the Canadian Charter. In *Prostitution Reference*[49] the court rejected a challenge alleging that offences of keeping a "common bawdy house" and soliciting for the purposes of prostitution, were unconstitutionally vague. Lamer J. referred to the leading United States decisions and continued:

> "The principles expressed in these two citations are not new to our law. In fact they are based on the ancient Latin maxim *nullum crimen sine lege, nulla poena sine lege*—that there can be no crime or punishment unless it is in accordance with law that is certain, unambiguous and not retroactive. The rationale underlying this approach is clear. It is essential in a free and democratic society that citizens are able, as far as is possible, to foresee the consequences of their conduct in order that persons be given fair notice of what to avoid, and that the discretion of those entrusted with law enforcement is limited by clear and explicit legislative standards."

10–21 In words which find a strong echo in the Strasbourg jurisprudence, Lamer J.said that the void for vagueness doctrine did not "require that a law be absolutely certain: no law can meet this standard". The doctrine was not to be applied to the "bare words" of a statutory provision, but rather to "the provision as interpreted and applied in judicial decisions". The test in each case was "whether the impugned sections of the Criminal Code can be or have been given sensible meanings by the courts". Put another way, the court should ask whether the statute was "so pervasively vague" that it permits a "standardless sweep".

10–22 The Canadian decisions were reviewed in *R. v Nova Scotia Pharmaceutical Society*,[50] which concerned a statutory offence of conspiracy to lessen competition "unduly". Rejecting the challenge Gonthier J., for a unanimous Supreme Court, characterised the vagueness doctrine as being founded on the principles of fair notice to citizens and limitation of prosecution discretion, which were aspects of the rule of law. These principles had both a formal aspect (that citizens were presumed to know the law, such that ignorance of its requirements was no excuse) and a substantive aspect (that the citizen must in reality be able to ascertain whether particular conduct falls within the control of the law). A provision which was unintelligible gave insufficient guidance for legal debate (that is, for reaching a conclusion as to its meaning by reasoned analysis, applying legal criteria) and was therefore unconstitutionally vague. But the threshold for a finding of unintelligibility was a "relatively high" one. It could not be argued that a statute must provide sufficient guidance to predict the legal consequences of any given course of conduct in advance. All it could do was to enunciate the boundaries of risk with reasonable clarity.

10–23 The decisions in other constitutional jurisdictions are to broadly similar effect. In South Africa, a statutory offence of contempt in the face of the court has been held sufficiently clear and unambiguous,[51] as has a common law offence of

---

[49] (1990) 77 C.R. (3d) 1 (S.C.C.).
[50] (1992) 15 C.R. (4th) 1 (S.C.C.).
[51] *State v Lavhengwa* (1996) 2 S.A.C.R. 453. The court held that this issue had to be approached on the assumption that the statutory definition was directed at ordinary intelligent people who were capable of thinking for themselves.

fraud.[52] And in *Dharmarajen Sabapathee v The State*,[53] Lord Hope, on behalf of the Privy Council, held that a statutory provision in Mauritius which criminalised the "trafficking" of drugs was sufficiently precise to enable citizens to understand those transactions which fell within, and those which fell outside, the ordinary meaning of the expression. By way of contrast, in *Webster v Dominick*[54] the Scottish High Court of Justiciary considered the common law offence of "shameless indecency". The court held that the offence should no longer be used, since it

> "rests on an unsound theory, has an uncertain ambit of liability and lays open to prosecution some forms of private conduct the legality of which should be a question for the legislature."[55]

V. Legal Certainty under the Human Rights Act

It will be apparent from the discussion in the preceding paragraphs that the standard of certainty required by the "quality of law" test under the Convention, and under comparable constitutional principles, is relatively broad but not without limits. The significance of the Strasbourg decision in *Hashman and Harrup* remains to be seen, but on its face the Court has drawn the line at broad descriptions that do not define key elements of an offence by reference to their effects. More generally, the essential elements of the offence must be intelligible, and capable of interpretation in a manner which is reasonably clear. So far as offences created by primary and subordinate legislation are concerned, the wording of the relevant provision must be considered in conjunction with any interpretative caselaw. **10–24**

The common law principle of strict construction of criminal statutes (see 10–07 above) is now reinforced by the duty of compatible construction imposed by s.3 of the Human Rights Act (read in conjunction with Art.7). In the light of s.3, the circumstances in which it will be necessary to grant a declaration of incompatibility on grounds of vagueness will be few and far between. If the wording of primary or subordinate legislation is ambiguous, general, or objectionably vague, it will, almost by definition, be "possible", within the meaning of s.3, to adopt a narrow construction, limiting the scope of criminal liability so as to avoid the imposition of a penalty.[56] In the unlikely event that an offence created in primary legislation is truly unintelligible, or has no readily ascertainable meaning, it will **10–25**

---

[52] *State v Friedman* (1996) 1 S.A.C.R. 181.
[53] *Privy Council Appeal No.1 of 1999* (unreported).
[54] [2003] S.L.T. 975 (H.C.J.).
[55] [43], *per* Clerk L.J., citing *Paterson v Lees* [1999] S.C.C.R. 231, *per* Lord Justice General Rodger at 234D. See commentary by Blair S. at [2003] 20 *Scottish Human Rights Journal* 8.
[56] *cf. Fawcett Properties Ltd v Buckingham County Council* [1961] A.C. 636 at 662 where Lord Cohen said that the principle that "a man is not to be put in peril upon an uncertainty . . . involves that if a statutory provision is ambiguous, the court should adopt any reasonable interpretation which would avoid the penalty".

be unenforceable on ordinary common law principles,[57] and a declaration of incompatibility would seem both unnecessary and inappropriate.

10–26 The position of unintelligible byelaws is similar. Since the House of Lords decision in *Boddington v British Transport Police*[58] it has been clear that challenges to the validity of subordinate legislation may be mounted by way of defence in criminal proceedings, irrespective of the nature of the challenge. This principle is reflected in s.7(1)(b) of the Human Rights Act 1998. As we have seen, the English courts have elaborated a theory of vagueness which resembles the Canadian authorities, and which has (on occasion) resulted in the striking down of certain byelaw offences. Where a byelaw is intelligible but ambiguous, or where its precise boundaries are uncertain, the benefit of the doubt may be given to the accused without impugning the validity of the byelaw itself. The potential impact of the Human Rights Act on this line of authority was considered, *obiter*, by Brooke L.J. in *Westminster City Council v Blenheim Leisure (Restaurants) Ltd and others*.[59] The defendants had been charged with failing to "maintain good order" contrary to the City Council's Rules of Management for Places of Public Entertainment, by permitting prostitutes to offer sexual services for money. Brooke L.J. observed that the Council would "do well . . . to tighten up the language of [the relevant provision] if it wishes to be able to use it to prohibit activities like these on licensed premises after the Human Rights Act 1998 comes into force". He continued:

> "The extension of the very vague concept of the maintenance of good order to the control of the activities of prostitutes may have passed muster in the days when English common law offences did not receive critical scrutiny from national judicial guardians of a rights-based jurisprudence, but those days will soon be over. English judges will then be applying a Human Rights Convention which has the effect of prescribing that a criminal offence must be clearly defined in law. I do not accept [the] submission that it is impossible to define the kind of conduct [the Council] desire[s] to prohibit with greater precision, or that it is satisfactory to leave it to individual magistrates to decide, assisted only be some fairly arcane case law, whether or not activities of the type of which the Council complains in this case amount to a breach of good order so as to render the licensees liable to criminal penalties."

10–27 Turning from bye-laws to the substantive law, the years since the introduction of the Human Rights Act have seen several challenges based on the certainty requirement in the "quality of law" test. In *Tagg*[60] it was argued that an offence created by powers in the Civil Aviation Act 1982, "a person shall not enter any aircraft when drunk or be drunk in any aircraft", failed to meet the certainty requirements of the Convention. The Court of Appeal dismissed the appeal,

---

[57] See, for example, *Mixnam's Properties Ltd v Chertsey Urban District Council* [1964] 1 Q.B. 214 at 238 where Lord Diplock drew a distinction between the power of courts to declare subordinate legislation invalid for uncertainty and the power to treat legislation as being "*unenforceable*, as in the case of a clause in a statute to which it is impossible to ascribe a meaning" (emphasis added). See also *Fawcett Properties Ltd v Buckingham County Council* [1961] A.C. 636 at 662 where Lord Cohen recognised that a court could "strike a provision out of an Act on the ground of uncertainty" only where "it is impossible to resolve the ambiguity which it is said to contain".
[58] [1998] 2 All E.R. 203.
[59] (1999) 163 J.P. 401.
[60] [2001] EWCA Crim 1230.

finding that dictionary definitions of "drunk" (such as having consumed liquor "to an extent that affects steady self-control")[61] were sufficiently precise to meet Convention requirements. It may be noted that it is a feature of these definitions that they define the state of drunkenness by reference to its effects, which is consistent with the test in *Hashman and Harrup v United Kingdom* (above, 10–17), although that aspect of the decision was not mentioned in *Tagg*. In *R. v Muhamad*,[62] the foreseeability of consequences was again considered. In that case, the challenge was to the strict liability offence of materially contributing to the extent of insolvency by gambling (contrary to s.362(1)(a) of the Insolvency Act 1986). The appellant argued that one element of the actus reus—the presentation of a petition of bankruptcy within two years of the act of gambling—was outside the gambler's control and therefore unforeseeable. This violated the principle of legal certainty. The Court of Appeal rejected this argument:

"The answer to this submission is that it confuses factual uncertainty with legal uncertainty. Article 7 is concerned only with the latter. A person who is considering whether to gamble knows for certain that, if he gambles and loses, and if within two years a petition is presented based on insolvency to which the lost gamble has materially contributed, then he will have committed an offence . . . It is true that, when he places his bet, he does not know whether, if he loses, that will contribute to insolvency so as to trigger the section. But he does not even know that he will lose. . . . it is difficult to see why the fact that a bet may be lost does not render the offence uncertain, whereas the fact that a creditor's petition may result within two years does so. The short answer is that it is only legal uncertainty that offends against the principle enshrined in article 7."[63]

In *R. v Rimmington and Goldstein*[64] both appellants had been convicted of public nuisance, the first by sending over 500 postal packages with racist material, and the second by sending an envelope containing salt which leaked out and caused an anthrax scare. The House of Lords adopted the analysis of the certainty requirement in Art.7 put forward by Judge L.J. in *Misra* (below). The House narrowed the accepted common law definition of public nuisance by removing the reference to endangering "morals" (on the basis that this was not sufficiently certain to satisfy the requirements of Art.7) and by emphasising that the nuisance had to be caused to a "significant section of the public" rather than simply to a cumulation of individuals. The House quashed both convictions and recommended reform of the law; yet it also held that the rest of the definition of public nuisance was fully compatible with Art.7, despite its containing a vague phrase such as "endangering . . . the comfort of the public."

Concerns have long been expressed about the uncertainty of definition of the offence of manslaughter by gross negligence. The offence turns on the *degree* of the defendant's negligence, and it remains a question for the jury: **10–28**

---

[61] Quoted by Rose L.J. from the judgment of Goff L.J. in *Neale v RMJE* (1980) 80 Cr.App.R. 20.

[62] [2003] Q.B. 951.

[63] [29].

[64] [2005] UKHL 63.

"whether the extent to which the defendant's conduct departed from the proper standard of care incumbent on him, involving as it must have done a risk of death to the patient, was such that it should be judged criminal."[65]

This issue was addressed by the Court of Appeal in *R. v Misra*.[66] The appellant argued that the *Adomako* test, which requires the jury to be directed to find the defendant guilty if they are satisfied that his conduct was "criminal", was circular and therefore led to impermissible uncertainty.[67] After reviewing a range of authorities on legal certainty—Strasbourg, domestic and comparative—the court concluded that:

"it is not to be supposed that prior to the implementation of the Human Rights Act 1998, either this Court, or the House of Lords, would have been indifferent to or unaware of the need for criminal law in particular to be predictable and certain. Vague laws which purport to create criminal liability are undesirable, and in extreme cases, where it occurs, their very vagueness may make it impossible to identify the conduct which is prohibited by a criminal sanction. If the court is forced to guess at the ingredients of a purported crime any conviction for it would be unsafe. That said, however, the requirement is for sufficient rather than absolute certainty."[68]

Turning to the authorities on manslaughter by gross negligence, and in particular *Adomako*, the court concluded that the test was not in fact circular:

"On proper analysis, therefore, the jury is not deciding whether the particular defendant ought to be convicted on some unprincipled basis. The question for the jury is not whether the defendant's negligence was gross, and whether, *additionally*, it was a crime, but whether his behaviour was grossly negligent and *consequently* criminal. This is not a question of law, but one of fact, for decision in the individual case."[69]

This has been described as "the most perplexing aspect of the judgment . . . [which] does not meet the criticisms that the test is circular, nor that the test requires the jury to determine the scope of the criminal law."[70] In truth, it is a distinction without a difference. However, the court stated that "this represents one example, among many, of problems which juries are expected to address on a daily basis",[71] and concluded that:

"In our judgment the law is clear. The ingredients of the offence have been clearly defined, and the principles decided by the House of Lords in *Adomako*. They involve no uncertainty. The hypothetical citizen, seeking to know his position, would be advised that, assuming he owed a duty of care to the deceased which he had negligently broken, and that death resulted, he would be liable to conviction for manslaughter if, on the available evidence, the jury was satisfied that his negligence was gross. A doctor would

---

[65] *Per* Lord Mackay L.C. in *Adomako* [1995] 1 A.C. 171.

[66] [2005] 1 Cr.App.R. 21.

[67] The appellant relied on the Law Commission paper on Involuntary Manslaughter (Law Com. No.237), which had expressed doubts about the compatibility of the offence with the standards of certainty required by the Convention.

[68] [34], *per* Judge L.J.

[69] [62], emphasis in original text.

[70] By Professor D. Ormerod, commenting at [2005] Crim.L.R. 235–238.

[71] [63].

be told that grossly negligent treatment of a patient which exposed him or her to the risk of death, and caused it, would constitute manslaughter."[72]

This, too, is unconvincing. The court's review of the Strasbourg authorities omitted the leading decision in *Hashman and Harrup*. That decision, as we have seen, refines the test of legal certainty and allows vagueness to be cured either by describing behaviour by reference to its effects, or by embedding the vague requirement among other, more certain elements of an offence. The *Adomako* test which the Court of Appeal upheld in *Misra* does not describe the prohibited behaviour by reference to its effects, but rather to how serious the jury thinks the departure from relevant standards was. The Court of Appeal appeared to consider that the concept of breach of duty and "gross" negligence supplied a sufficiently certain context. However, the core uncertainty of the offence remains: it is not clear when a duty is imposed,[73] or what the extent of that duty is, or how great a breach of that duty is necessary before a conviction of manslaughter by gross negligence is appropriate.

There are grounds for concern about certainty in relation to various offences of **10–29** dishonesty. When the Law Commission was considering the case for introducing general offences of fraud and/or deception, it concluded as follows:

> "We consider the advantages of a general dishonesty offence, but take the provisional view that it is undesirable in principle that conduct should be rendered criminal solely because fact finders are willing to characterise it as 'dishonest.' It is also at least doubtful whether such an offence would be sufficiently certain to comply with the requirements of the European Convention on Human Rights."[74]

This is consistent with the test in *Hashman and Harrup*. However, in *Hashman and Harrup* it appears that part of the Government's argument was that the Court should be slow to condemn as insufficiently certain an order binding a person over to be of good behaviour, since that would have a chilling effect on all offences of dishonesty where, again, behaviour was described by reference to ordinary standards of decency rather than by reference to its effects. As is well known, the test of dishonesty was stated in *Ghosh*[75] to be "whether according to the ordinary standards of reasonable and honest people what was done was dishonest." The Court responded by drawing this distinction:

> "Nor can the Court agree that the Government's other examples of behaviour which is defined by reference to the standards expected of the majority of contemporary opinion are similar to conduct *contra bonos mores*, as in each case cited by the Government, the example given is but one element of a more comprehensive definition of the proscribed behaviour."[76]

---

[72] [64].

[73] Not least because the courts have taken to imposing a duty in situations where none would arise in the law of tort: see Ashworth A., *Principles of Criminal Law* (5th edn, 2006), 292–294.

[74] Law Commission Consultation Paper No.155, *Fraud and Deception* (1999), para.1.23; see the detailed examination of Convention jurisprudence at paras 5.33 to 5.51.

[75] [1982] Q.B. 1053.

[76] *Hashman and Harrup v United Kingdom* (2000) 30 E.H.R.R. 241, at [39]. For the Government's argument, which referred also to the offence of criminal libel, see [29].

This suggests that the test of certainty to be derived from *Hashman and Harrup* allows breadth or vagueness to be cured in one of two ways—first, by describing behaviour by reference to its effects, and secondly, by embedding the vague requirement among other, more certain elements of an offence. Quite how many other elements such an offence ought to have remains unclear, but the offence of theft has such elements as appropriation, property belonging to another, and an intention permanently to deprive the other of it—although the recent trend has been for the element of dishonesty to dominate and for the requirement of appropriation to become undemanding.[77]

10–30   It will be recalled that the justification for the certainty requirement in the "quality of law" test is to enable citizens to know the boundaries of permissible conduct. Two connected reasons were spelt out by the Strasbourg Court as long ago as 1979, in the *Sunday Times* case[78]:

> "First, the law must be adequately accessible: the citizen must be able to have an indication that is adequate in the circumstances of the legal rules applicable to a given case. Secondly, a norm cannot be regarded as a 'law' unless it is formulated with sufficient precision to enable the citizen to regulate his conduct: he must be able—if need be with appropriate advice—to foresee, to a degree that is reasonable in the circumstances, the consequences which a given action may entail."

The need for appropriate advice may be applicable where the law is complex, in the sense of requiring a number of statutory provisions to be read together.[79] But the *Sunday Times* formulation acknowledges, in its final reference to what is "reasonable in the circumstances", that an element of flexibility may have to remain. But its thrust supports the more focussed test developed in *Hashman and Harrup*.

It remains to be seen whether other offences will be vulnerable to attack on certainty grounds. It will emerge from 10–44 below that part, at least, of the challenge to the offence of perverting the course of justice relates to the essential uncertainty of its definition, although the argument has been conducted in the context of Art.7. The House of Lords decision in *Rimmington and Goldstein* (above, 10–27) opens up the possibility that other common law offences might also be challenged.

10–31   Before turning to the consideration of similar issues under Art.7, the relevance of another Convention provision must be mentioned. Article 6(3)(a) guarantees the right of a person charged with a criminal offence to be informed promptly "of the nature and cause of the accusation against him", and Art.6(3)(b) refers to adequate facilities for the preparation of a defence. In *Mercer*[80] a defendant who had been charged with robbery as part of a joint enterprise and convicted as a principal had his conviction quashed. At the re-trial he was charged again with robbery, but this time the prosecution put the case against him on the basis that he was the driver of the get-away car. The Court of Appeal dismissed the

---

[77] As a result of decisions such as *Gomez* [1993] A.C. 442 and *Hinks* [2001] 2 A.C. 241.
[78] *Sunday Times v United Kingdom (No.1)* (1979) 2 E.H.R.R. 245, at [49].
[79] Cf. *O'Driscoll v Home Secretary* [2002] EWHC Admin 2477, *per* Kennedy L.J. at [24–25].
[80] [2001] All E.R. (D) 187 (March).

argument that this amounted to a breach of Art.6(3)(a): the law of joint enterprise does not require the prosecution to specify in the indictment exactly what role a particular defendant is alleged to have undertaken. A similar point appears to have been dismissed in *Concannon*.[81] The Court of Appeal's view is therefore that the English law of complicity, which allows prosecutors to alter (even during the trial) the basis on which the case against a particular participant is put, satisfies the procedural requirement of certainty in Art.6(3)(a).[82]

It appears that the central concern under Art.6(3)(a) is to ensure that the time and   **10–32** place of the offence are set out as precisely as possible. This does not mean that such matters have to be specified in all cases—this is often difficult in child abuse cases, for example—but it does mean that if the prosecution has a detailed allegation and fails to put it, this may amount to a breach of the provision.[83]

C. JUDICIAL DEVELOPMENT OF THE ELEMENTS OF AN OFFENCE

I. Interpreting the Strasbourg Casclaw

In practical terms, it is unlikely that the courts will be faced with statutory   **10–33** offences which are expressly retrospective,[84] but difficult problems can arise when the elements of an offence are developed by judicial decision. In *X Ltd and Y v United Kingdom*[85] the Commission recognised that where an offence is created by the common law this "presents certain peculiarities for the very reason that it is, by definition, law developed by the courts". In determining whether such developments overstep the "margin of uncertainty"[86] the Commission suggested that Art.7:

" . . . implies that constituent elements of an offence such as e.g. the particular form of culpability required for its completion may not be essentially changed, at least not to the detriment of the accused, by the case law of the courts. On the other hand it is not objectionable that the existing elements of the offence are clarified and adapted to new circumstances which can reasonably be brought under the original concept of the offence".

In that case the House of Lords had held that the common law offence of   **10–34** blasphemous libel required only proof of an intention to publish, and not of an intention to blaspheme. In view of the absence of previous authority on the point,

---

[81] [2002] Crim.L.R. 213.

[82] *Cf.* also *Pattni, Dhunna, Soni and Poopalarajah* [2001] Crim.L.R. 570, where the trial judge, in rejecting a certainty challenge to the offence of cheating the Revenue, held that the offence of cheating "if properly particularised" met the necessary standard.

[83] *Mattocia v Italy* [2001] E.H.R.L.R. 89.

[84] In *Waddington v Miah* [1974] 1 W.L.R. 683 at 694 the House of Lords described as "hardly credible" the proposition that a Minister would propose or that Parliament would enact retrospective criminal legislation. Whilst this is undoubtedly true of legislation creating substantive offences, there are a number of examples of criminal statutes which impose retrospective penalties in breach of Art.7: see, for example, *Welch v United Kingdom* (1995) 20 E.H.R.R. 247.

[85] (1982) 28 D.R. 77 at para.9.

[86] *Zamir v United Kingdom* (1983) 40 D.R. 42 at para.91.

the Commission considered that the House of Lords ruling on the requisite *mens rea* for the offence was a clarification of the existing law, and not a change of the law to the applicant's detriment. In *Harman v United Kingdom*,[87] by contrast, the Commission declared admissible a complaint that the applicant had been convicted of contempt of court for showing documents to a journalist, even though the documents had been read out in open court, when (so it was submitted) it was not reasonably foreseeable that this would be regarded as a contempt. Under the Human Rights Act the courts may be called upon to determine whether certain common law offences have been extended in a way that breaches Art.7, or (more accurately) they may be constrained not to develop the law in that way.

10–35 The leading case on this issue is now *SW and CR v United Kingdom*,[88] in which the Court held that the removal of the marital rape exemption by the House of Lords in *R. v R.*[89] did not amount to a retrospective change in the elements of the offence. The Court emphasised that Art.7 does not prohibit the development of the criminal law through judicial decisions:

> "However clearly drafted a legal provision may be, in any system of law, including criminal law, there is an inevitable element of judicial interpretation. There will always be a need for elucidation of doubtful points and for adaptation to changing circumstances. Indeed, in the United Kingdom, as in the other Convention states, the progressive development of the criminal law through judicial law-making is a well entrenched and necessary part of legal tradition. Article 7 of the Convention cannot be read as outlawing the gradual clarification of the rules of criminal liability through judicial interpretation from case to case, providing the resultant development is consistent with the essence of the offence and could reasonably be foreseen."

10–36 Applying this dubiously elastic formulation, the Court unanimously found that the development of the law by the House of Lords "did no more than continue a perceptible line of case law development dismantling the immunity". There had been an evolution in the law creating a number of specific exceptions to the immunity, which "had reached a stage where judicial recognition of the absence of immunity had become a reasonably foreseeable development of the law."

10–37 The decision in *SW and CR* has been extensively criticised on the ground that the Court sacrificed an important constitutional principle in order to achieve a socially desirable result in the individual case.[90] It is certainly difficult to characterise such a significant development as a mere "clarification" of the law,

---

[87] (1984) 38 D.R. 53; the friendly settlement of this case, in which the Government undertook to change the law, is reported at (1986) 46 D.R. 57.

[88] (1996) 21 E.H.R.R. 363. See also *Schluga v Austria*, App.No.65665/01. The applicant had received a heavier sentence because of "particularly aggravating" circumstances. His application was declared inadmissible, the court holding that Art.7 could not be read as outlawing the gradual clarification of the rules of criminal liability through judicial interpretation from case to case, and in any event it would have been foreseeable—if necessary with legal advice—that the circumstances of the applicant's case might be treated as aggravating and therefore attract a heavier penalty.

[89] [1992] A.C. 599.

[90] See, for example, Craig Osborne, "Does the End Justify the Means? Retrospectivity, Article 7 and the Marital Rape Exemption" [1996] E.H.R.L.R. 406; the reasoning in *SW and CR* was followed by the court in *K-HW v Germany* (2001) 36 E.H.R.R. 1081 (above, 10–17) at paras 46 and 66, emphasising the supreme value of human life under the Convention.

given that an act which would previously have fallen outside the scope of the offence altogether was brought within it by the *ex post facto* removal of an established immunity which had until then defined the boundaries of criminal liability. It is far from clear that a hypothetical legal adviser would have understood the scope of the offence as the House of Lords subsequently declared it to be. Shortly before the issue arose in the courts, the Law Commission had expressed the view that the immunity was so well settled in English law that legislation would be required to remove it,[91] and a number of judges had considered themselves bound by the rule.[92] However, *SW* has subsequently been applied by the domestic courts to offences committed long before the decision in *R. v R.* In *R. v L (Graham)*[93] the Court of Appeal held that the appellant was properly convicted of raping his wife, even though the incident occurred before the decision in *R. v R.* In *R. v C*[94] the appellant, who had been convicted in 2002 of the rape of his wife in 1970, argued that Art.7 had been violated since the offence would not have been prosecuted in 1970, given the state of the common law at the time. He argued that *R. v R.* and *SW and CR* could be distinguished, on the basis that the offence in those cases took place in 1989, when attitudes were very different to those in 1970. The Court of Appeal held that the decision in *R. v R.*, as upheld by *SW and CR*, had not created a new offence but had merely removed a fiction of the common law. The debasing character of rape was so manifest that the decision in *R. v R.* could not be said to be at variance with the object and purpose of Art.7. In any event, the court held that, by 1970, a husband who sought legal advice on whether or not he could rape his wife would have been advised that:

> "notwithstanding the repetition of Hale's principle in the authorities, he might be liable for rape, probably liable for indecent assault, and certainly liable for the appropriate offence of violence. On this view therefore he would have been told that he could not rape his wife with complete impunity. To the extent that the European Court of Human Rights in *SW v United Kingdom* proceeded on the basis that he could, its analysis was not fully informed."[95]

This passage blurs the line between rape (the charge here) and other offences (conviction of which was indeed possible). As the law stood in 1970, it is highly unlikely that a husband seeking legal advice would have been told that a conviction for rape of his wife was foreseeable. For that reason, the decision in *C* is surely inconsistent with Art.7.

It is clear that the assessment of the issue by the courts in *SW and CR* and in *C*   **10–38**
was heavily influenced by the nature of the offence. As the court put it in *SW and CR*:

> "The essentially debasing character of rape is so manifest that the result of the decisions of the Court of Appeal and the House of Lords . . . cannot be said to be at variance with

---

[91] Law Commission Working Paper No.116, *Rape within Marriage* (1990), at para.2.08.
[92] See, for example, *R. v J.* [1991] 1 All E.R. 759.
[93] [2003] EWCA Crim 1512.
[94] [2004] 1 W.L.R. 2098.
[95] [19].

the object and purpose of Article 7 of the Convention . . . What is more, the abandonment of the unacceptable idea of a husband being immune against prosecution for rape of his wife was in conformity not only with a civilised concept of marriage but also, and above all, with fundamental objectives of the Convention, the very essence of which is respect for human dignity and human freedom."

10–39 It is understandable that the Court should have been reluctant to allow a human rights instrument to be invoked by a convicted rapist, so as to exclude criminal liability on the basis of an anachronistic conception of the rights of women *vis-á-vis* their husbands. But the nature of the offence should surely have been irrelevant when the Court came to lay down principles governing so important a right as the protection against retrospectivity in the development of the criminal law by judicial decision. The Court's appeal to the object and purpose of the Convention is especially unconvincing in this context since many criminal offences involve a violation of the Convention rights of the victim. If the "essentially debasing" nature of the offence were properly to be regarded as a consideration affecting the principles of retrospectivity, Art.7 would apply differentially to different categories of crime, and would be deprived of much of its purpose. It is difficult to believe that the court intended this result. The decision in *SW and CR* is perhaps best regarded as a salutory reminder that the European Court of Human Rights is as vulnerable as any other court to the accusation that hard cases make bad law.

10–40 The court followed *SW and CR* in its judgment in *KA and AD v Belgium*,[96] where two men had been convicted of wounding arising out of sado-masochistic practices. It was argued that, as there had never been a conviction under Belgian law of wounding in circumstances of sado-masochism, this amounted to retroactive law-making contrary to Art.7. The Court rejected this, on the basis that it was rare for a case to involve such a high degree of sado-masochistic harm as this one, and so the absence of authority for thus applying the criminal code was not crucial. The key question is whether it was foreseeable that the law would be applied in this way, and it surely was. Moreover there were two special factors— the fact that the "rules" of sado-masochism had been broken because of the high level of intoxication and the failure to respond to cries for mercy; and the fact that the applicants were both professionals, one of them a magistrate, who had ceased to frequent a sado-masochism club because they had not been allowed to carry out their own extreme practices. In these circumstances, the Court held, the application of the criminal law to their activities was reasonably foreseeable.

10–41 It may be argued that, even after *SW and CR*, Art.7 may nonetheless be interpreted as placing some outer limits on judicial creativity. In *Shaw v DPP*[97] the House of Lords notoriously created the offence of conspiracy to corrupt public morals, (whereas 10 years later in *Knuller v DPP*[98] the House foreswore the use of this power in future[99]). In *Tan*,[100] the Court of Appeal proclaimed that

---

[96] App.No.42758/98, judgment of February 17, 2005, discussed at 8–12 above.
[97] [1962] A.C. 220.
[98] [1973] A.C. 435.
[99] For discussion of the limits of judicial creativity, see Smith A.T.H., "Judicial Lawmaking in the Criminal Law" (1984) 100 L.Q.R. 46.
[100] [1983] Q.B. 1053.

"courts should not, or should at least be slow to create new offences". Where, as in that case, the prosecution is described as "novel", there may be a role for Art.7 to play. What is to happen if, for example, the Court of Appeal effectively narrows a defence so as to uphold the conviction of an accused? This was done in *Elbekkay*,[101] where the court held that it was no defence for a man to argue that his impersonation of the victim's boyfriend (as distinct from a husband) was insufficient to negative the woman's apparent consent. This decision was all the more remarkable because s.142 of the Criminal Justice and Public Order Act 1994 had recently re-defined rape but had repeated the reference to rape by impersonating a husband (without extending the reference to a partner or cohabitee), and because—as the court acknowledged—there was no previous decision or statute which required it to reach the conclusion it did. It might be argued that this development of the law by the courts was not reasonably foreseeable. Whereas in the case of marital rape there had at least been a series of lesser decisions suggesting that the courts might be moving in the direction of restricting a husband's immunity for rape of his wife, there was nothing in the law prior to *Elbekkay* to serve warning that a change might be imminent. The same observation may be made in relation to *Hasan*,[102] where the House of Lords narrowed the defence of duress (and thereby widened the scope of criminal liability). It is therefore suggested that there might be cases in which it can be argued that the expansion of an offence or the contraction of a defence would be contrary to Art.7, in the sense that the law has been developed "by analogy" in a way that is not foreseeable and which operates "to an accused's detriment".[103]

The Strasbourg Court has also considered cases where it is not the development   **10–42** of the common law but the interpretation of a statutory provision that is novel. In *Kyriakides v Cyprus*[104] the court held inadmissible an application based on the unprecedented interpretation given to a particular statutory provision by the Supreme Court of Cyprus. The Supreme Court had indeed departed from a previous decision in reaching the new interpretation, but that previous decision had taken place after the applicant had done the acts charged, and so the law did not operate retrospectively on his conduct. This decision leaves open the possibility that, if an appeal court reverses a previous construction of a statutory offence which had been handed down before the defendant did the act charged,

---

[101] [1995] Crim. L.R. 163, on which see Smith J.C. and Hogan B., *Criminal Law* (8th edn, 1996), p.469.

[102] [2005] UKHL 22.

[103] See the passage from *Kokkinakis v Greece* (1994) 17 E.H.R.R. 397, and similar statements (above, n.4) However, reasoning by analogy (in that case, finding a repeatedly broadcast statement analogous to a 'prior recording') was upheld by the Court in *Radio France v France*, App.No.53984/00, Judgment of March 30, 2004. In the broadcasting context, see also *Eurofinacom v France*, App.No.58753/00, where the application was held inadmissible under Art.7, on the basis that, although the Criminal Code did not expressly forbid the provider of a telecommunications network from assisting or benefiting from prostitution (a specific provision was added later), this was a foreseeable judicial interpretation of the Code. Interestingly, the Court did not gainsay the government's argument that a company involved as an internet provider ought to take particular care to obtain advice on the criminal law.

[104] App.No.53059/99, Admissibility Decision of December 11, 2001, [2002] E.H.R.L.R. 527.

the new ruling may be held to contravene Art.7 in its application to the defendant if it was not (with the assistance of legal advice) reasonably foreseeable.

II. Judicial Development after the Human Rights Act

10–43 A number of decisions since the Human Rights Act have considered the certainty requirements of Art.7, but many of them have done so in terms of whether the definition of the offence is sufficiently certain (considered in 10–24 to 10–32 above) rather than whether there are limits to the judicial development of the elements of offences. However, that matter has been judicially considered in relation to the common law crime of perverting the course of justice. In *Cotter, Clair and Wynn*[105] the appellants had been convicted of conspiracy to pervert the course of justice on the ground that they fabricated a story about a racist attack on the first appellant. Much of the argument concerned the ingredients of the offence, notably whether it was necessary to establish that the story was fabricated in order to bring about the arrest of a particular person. The Court of Appeal held that there was no such requirement, and that the offence was committed if the appellants had intended that their report of an attack should be taken seriously by the police and that an investigation shoulds be set in motion. The second challenge was to the definition of the offence, and its development by the courts. The court quoted from *SW and CR v United Kingdom* (above, 10–35), and concluded that the development of the offence since the offence was "clearly defined" by B. Pollock in *Vreones*[106] had been a "process of elucidation" which amounted to just the kind of "gradual clarification" held by the Strasbourg Court to be permissible.[107]

10–44 Professor Sir John Smith was strongly critical of the reasoning in *Cotter, Clair and Wynn*, arguing that the definition of the offence is far from settled, that there is a confusion over the requirements of the substantive offence as distinct from conspiracies or attempts to commit it, and that other elements of the crime remain uncertain.[108] In *Clark*[109] the Court of Appeal showed an awareness of the Art.7 issue, and declined to extend the offence to omissions rather than acts. The Court of Appeal had decided previously that the prosecution must show that there was an act or course of conduct by the defendant,[110] and the defence in this case was that Clark had done nothing to conceal evidence of the crime. He has merely failed to stop and to report the "accident". The court concluded that "there is little doubt that the offence has not so far been extended to cover facts such as those in this case," and added that:

> "if the ambit of this common law offence is to be enlarged it must be done step by step on a case by case basis and not with one large leap. The need for caution is underlined

---

[105] [2002] 2 Cr.App.R. 29.
[106] [1891] 1 Q.B. 360.
[107] [2002] 2 Cr.App.R. 29, at [36].
[108] Commentary at [2002] Crim.L.R. 826–828.
[109] [2003] EWCA Crim 991.
[110] *Headley* [1995] Crim.L.R. 738.

by Article 7 of the ECHR, which requires any criminal offence to be clearly defined by law."[111]

Whether or not the need for caution in developing offences has always been part of the common law, it is clear that the Human Rights Act has heightened awareness of it.

D. CRIMES UNDER INTERNATIONAL LAW

A conviction which results from the retrospective application of domestic law **10–45** will not breach Art.7(1) if the conduct of the accused was a crime under international law at the time that it occurred.[112] Certain offences, such as war crimes, piracy, torture and genocide are treated as crimes of universal jurisdiction under public international law. A state may prosecute individuals for such offences, wherever committed, solely on the basis that it has custody of the alleged offender. The United Kingdom has given effect to this principle in a number of statutes,[113] which can therefore be retrospectively applied[114] without violating Art.7. The court has also held that, in an appropriate case, international law principles can be relevant in determining whether the application of a statutory offence was sufficiently foreseeable.[115]

E. WAR CRIMES

Article 7(2) provides that the protection of Art.7(1);   **10–46**

" . . . shall not prejudice the trial and punishment of any person for any act or omission which, at the time when it was committed, was criminal according to the general principles of law recognised by civilised nations."

The exception created by Art.7(2) was intended to allow the application of national and international legislation enacted during and after the Second World War to punish war crimes, treason and collaboration with the enemy.[116] The practical effect of Art.7(2) is simply to make it clear that the international law exception in Art.7(1) is not confined to treaty-based or customary international law, but extends to conduct regarded as criminal under "the general principles of law recognised by civilised nations".

---

[111] [2003] EWCA Crim 991, at [13].

[112] Art.7(1) prohibits conviction or punishment for an act or omission which did not constitute a crime "under national *or international law*" at the time when it was committed.

[113] The War Crimes Act 1991, s.1 (offences of murder, manslaughter, or culpable homicide committed in German occupied territory during the Second World War to be triable in United Kingdom courts); the Criminal Justice Act 1988, s.134 (torture, wherever committed, to be triable in the United Kingdom); the Genocide Act 1969, s.1 (genocide, wherever committed, to be triable in the United Kingdom); the Geneva Conventions Act 1957, s.1 (grave breaches of the Geneva Conventions, wherever committed, to be triable in the United Kingdom).

[114] Providing the relevant rule of international law was in existence at the time of the offence.

[115] *K.-H. W. v Germany*, (2001) 36 E.H.R.R. 1081: see 10–17 above.

[116] *X v Belgium* (1957) 1 Y.B. 239.

CHAPTER 11

ISSUES OF CRIMINAL RESPONSIBILITY

A. THE AGE OF CRIMINAL RESPONSIBILITY

The age of criminal responsibility in England, Wales and Northern Ireland is 10 years.[1] Below this age, no child can be found guilty of a criminal offence. The age of 10 was endorsed by the Home Affairs Select Committee in October 1993[2] and again by Parliament in 1998.[3] It is, however, the lowest age of criminal responsibility in the European Union.[4] In Belgium and Luxembourg the age of criminal responsibility is 18. In Spain, Poland, Portugal and Andorra it is 16. In Denmark, Finland and Sweden, it is 15. In Germany, Austria, Italy, Liechtenstein and in many of the Central and Eastern states, it is 14. In France it is 13, and in Ireland, The Netherlands and Greece it is 12. There is not yet a clear European consensus on this issue, and some countries have set an even lower age than England and Wales. Scotland, for example, sets the age of criminal responsibility at eight, and in Switzerland it is currently set at seven although there is a proposal to raise it to 10. Nevertheless, the case for the UK being so out of line with prevailing practice in Europe is difficult to understand or defend,[5] especially when many European countries have recently increased the age of responsibility. In most Commonwealth countries the minimum age of criminal responsibility is either seven[6] or 10,[7] although all these countries have rebuttable presumptions like *doli incapax*. After recent changes, Canada has no such presumption, but criminal responsibility commences at 12.   **11–01**

Until 1998 a child in England and Wales was subject to the *doli incapax* rule, which presumed that between the ages of 10 and 14 he was not criminally responsible. That presumption could be rebutted by the prosecution proving beyond reasonable doubt that at the time of the offence the child knew that the   **11–02**

---

[1] S.50 of the Children and Young Persons Act 1933 as amended by s.16(1) of the Children and Young Persons Act 1963.

[2] *Juvenile Offenders*, Sixth Report of the Session (HMSO, 1992–3).

[3] See s.34 of the Crime and Disorder Act 1998 and para.11–02 below.

[4] Joint Committee Report on UN Convention on the Rights of the Child (10th report of 2002–3, HL 117, HC 81) at para.35 fn 64. Cyprus now has the age of responsibility commencing at 10 although below 12 there is a rebuttable presumption similar to *doli incapax*.

[5] J.C.H.R. 10th report at para.37.

[6] e.g. South Africa and India.

[7] e.g. Australia and New Zealand.

act in question was wrong as distinct from merely naughty or childish mischief.[8] However crude such a test may seem, it at least had the benefit of allowing for the phased introduction of criminal responsibility, so as to take account of the rapid development that occurs during the transition from childhood to early adolescence, and of the huge variation in emotional maturity between children in this group (even between children of the same chronological age). A child or young person in this developmentally diverse age group would only be held criminally responsible if he could be shown to have a real grasp of the difference between right and wrong. The *doli incapax* presumption was abolished with effect from September 20, 1998.[9] The UN Committee on the Rights of the Child considers that the abolition may violate the principles and provisions of the UN Convention on the Rights of the Child (the most widely ratified international convention in the world[10]). Following the removal of this safeguard, the Joint Committee on Human Rights recommended that the Government review the effects of the low age of criminal responsibility on children and crime and proposed that the minimum age be increased to 12.[11] This was firmly rejected by the Government.[12] The Department for Education and Skills asserted that the low age was justified as a way of intervening early in children's lives.[13]

11–03   Despite the absence of a settled international consensus on this issue, it is clear that there is an emerging international trend towards raising the age of criminal responsibility. Article 40(3)(a) of the United Nations Convention on the Rights of the Child requires states to establish a minimum age below which children shall be presumed not to have the capacity to infringe the criminal law.[14] Article 3 requires the best interest of the child to be a primary consideration in all actions take by courts of law, administrative authorities or legislative bodies. It is difficult to see how the ages of criminal responsibility in the UK can be justified as being in the child's best interests. The Government has indicated that it has no intention of incorporating the "aspirational" Convention into domestic law, despite the Joint Committee on Human Rights recommending this.[15] An attempt to introduce a provision into the Children Act 2004 requiring the Government to "rights-proof" legislation affecting children was rejected.[16] The United Nations Standard Minimum Rules for the Administration of Juvenile Justice (the Beijing Rules) recommend[17] that those countries which recognise an age for criminal responsibility of juveniles should not fix that age "at too low an

---

[8] See generally *C (a minor) v The Director of Public Prosecutions* [1996] A.C. 1.
[9] S.34 of the Crime and Disorder Act 1998.
[10] UNCRC/C/15/Add.188 (9 Oct. 2002) at paras 60(a), 62(b). The Convention was ratified by the United Kingdom in 1990 and entered into force in January 1992. It has been ratified by every country in the world except the United States of America and Somalia.
[11] J.C.H.R. 10th report of 2002–3 (above) at para.38, Recommendation 8.
[12] J.C.H.R. 18th report of 2003–3 (HL 187, HC 1279) at para.13–14.
[13] J.C.H.R. 10th report of 2002–3 (above) at Appendix 1.
[14] Although it does not state what that age should be.
[15] J.C.H.R. 10th report of 2002–3 (above) at p.14 fn 48; para.22. *cf.* Pt I of the Children Act 2004 (below).
[16] HL Deb June 21, 2004 c1 064.
[17] The court has accepted that Beijing Rules are not binding in international law. The Preamble invites states to adopt the standards laid down but does not oblige them to do so.

age level, bearing in mind the facts of emotional, mental and intellectual maturity".[18] The Commentary to this provision observes[19]:

"The minimum age of criminal responsibility differs widely, owing to history and culture. The modern approach would be to consider whether a child can live up to the moral and psychological components of criminal responsibility; that is whether a child, by virtue of her or his individual discernment and understanding, can be held responsible for essentially antisocial behaviour.[20] If the age of criminal responsibility is fixed too low or if there is no age limit at all, the notion of criminal responsibility becomes meaningless. In general, there is a close relationship between the notion of criminal responsibility for delinquent or criminal behaviour and other social rights and responsibilities (such as marital status, civil majority etc.) Efforts should therefore be made to agree on a reasonable lowest age limit that is applicable."

This equiparation between criminal responsibility and civil capacity points towards an age much higher than 10. It is thus not surprising that the United Nations Committee on the Rights of the Child[21] has recommended that "serious consideration be given to raising the age of criminal responsibility throughout the areas of the United Kingdom"[22]. In 2002 the Committee was "particularly concerned" at the low age of responsibility in the UK and recommended that the UK raise it "considerably".[23] The Committee has uniformly criticised countries with an age of responsibility of less than 12.[24] Lord Bingham in *R. (R) v Durham Constabulary*[25] noted the low age of criminal responsibility in England compared with other European countries. The House referred to both the Beijing Rules and the UN Convention on the Rights of the Child with approval. Baroness Hale noted that although the UN Convention was not binding in international law;

"it is reflected in the interpretation and application by the European Court of Human Rights of the rights guaranteed by the European Convention . . . to that extent at least, therefore, it must be taken into account in the interpretation and application of those rights in our national law."[26]

These issues came up for consideration in *T and V v United Kingdom*.[27] The applicants in that case were two juveniles charged with murder, who were 10 at the time of the offence, and 11 at the time of their trial. There was evidence that both of them were psychologically damaged, and that they were immature for their age. The *doli incapax* presumption was rebutted by evidence from their head teacher to the effect that the applicants, like any child over the age of about five, knew that it was seriously wrong to hit a younger child with a weapon. They

11–04

---

[18] r.4.1.

[19] Commentary to r.4.1.

[20] *cf.* The *doli incapax* presumption.

[21] The treaty body established to monitor the implementation of the United Nations Convention on the Rights of the Child.

[22] U.N. doc. CRC/C/15/add. 34, February 15, 1995, para.36. This recommendation was made prior to the abolition of the *doli incapax* presumption.

[23] UNCRC/C/15/Add.188 (9 Oct. 2002) at paras 59, 62(a).

[24] JUSTICE: *Children and Homicide—Appropriate procedures for juveniles in murder and manslaughter cases* (London, 1996) p.7.

[25] [2005] UKHL 21 at para.2.

[26] at para.26.

[27] (2000) 30 E.H.R.R. 121.

were each convicted of murder and sentenced to be detained at Her Majesty's Pleasure. In their application to Strasbourg they alleged that the cumulative effect of the low age of criminal responsibility in England and Wales and their trial in public, in an adult Crown Court, and under intense media scrutiny, reached the level of severity necessary to constitute a violation of Art.3. The Court rejected the argument, after careful consideration. In doing so, it noted that the trend towards raising the age of criminal responsibility had not yet hardened into a European consensus[28]:

> "The Court has considered first whether the attribution to the applicant of criminal responsibility in respect of acts committed when he was ten years old could, in itself, give rise to a violation of Article 3. In doing so, it has regard to the principle, well established in its caselaw that, since the Convention is a living instrument, it is legitimate when deciding whether a certain measure is acceptable under one of its provisions to take account of the standards prevailing amongst the member states of the Council of Europe . . . In this connection the Court observes that, at the present time, there is not yet a commonly accepted minimum age for the imposition of criminal responsibility in Europe. While most of the Contracting States have adopted an age limit which is higher than that in force in England and Wales, other States, such as Cyprus, Ireland, Liechtenstein and Switzerland, attribute criminal responsibility from a younger age . . . The Court does not consider that there is at this stage any clear common standard amongst the member states of the Council of Europe as to the minimum age of criminal responsibility. Even if England and Wales is among the few European jurisdictions to retain a low age of criminal responsibility, the age of ten cannot be said to be so young as to differ disproportionately from the age limit followed by other European States. The Court concludes that the attribution of criminal responsibility to the applicant does not in itself give rise to a breach of Article 3 of the Convention."

11–05   There are a number of points to make about this decision. The first and most obvious one is that the court laid emphasis on the existence or otherwise of an international consensus on the issue *at the present time*. The implication is that a convergence of European standards on this issue, which may well be on the horizon, could set a benchmark; and that the court might then find a violation of Art.3 if there were a disproportionate difference between the age adopted by a particular state and the standard prevailing in the Council of Europe. It is important in this context to recall that the decision in *T and V* related to a trial which took place prior to the abolition of the *doli incapax* presumption. To the extent that this rule mitigated the harshness of an indisputably low age of criminal responsibility, the present position is, if anything, less likely to comply with the emerging requirements of international human rights law.

11–06   The second point is that even in the absence of a European consensus, the low age of criminal responsibility in England and Wales undoubtedly contributed to the finding of a violation of Art.6 in *T and V.* The younger a state sets its age of criminal responsibility, the greater will be its obligation to ensure that real safeguards are put in place to promote the best interests of the child, to protect him from unnecessary harassment, publicity, and distress, and to provide the best

---

[28] At paras 72 to 74.

possible conditions for rehabilitation. As the Court explained[29]: "[I]t is essential that a child charged with an offence is dealt with in a manner which takes full account of his age, level of maturity and intellectual and emotional capacities, and that steps are taken to promote his ability to understand and participate in the proceedings."

Although the Crown Court had made a number of modifications to the procedure in *T and V*,[30] these were found insufficient in view of the applicants' age and emotional vulnerability, to meet the requirements of Art.6.

The third point relates to the anomalous consequences of the present age of criminal responsibility, as it applies to those charged with murder. The applicants in *T and V* argued before the Commission that the attribution of full criminal responsibility for murder to a child of 10 was incompatible with Art.14 in conjunction with Art.6. Their argument, in summary, was that a fixed age of 10 was arbitrary and disproportionate when the applicants' position was compared with that of a child just under 10, or an adult whose mental age was that of a 10 year old. Article 14 will, of course, only be violated where there is a difference in treatment between persons in a "relevantly similar" position which pursues no legitimate aim, or bears no reasonable relationship of proportionality to the aim which it pursues.[31] In *T and V* the underlying issue of proportionality fell to be considered in the context of the applicants' Art.6 complaint, and accordingly the Art.14 point was not pursued before the Court. It is nevertheless worth recalling the anomaly that a child of 10 whose mental age corresponds with his chronological age will be held fully responsible for murder in England and Wales, whereas a child who is a few months younger cannot be held criminally responsible at all, and an adult with a mental age of 10 would, almost certainly, be able to rely on the defence of diminished responsibility so as to reduce the offence to one of manslaughter.[32] This perhaps gives some indication of just how far out of line domestic law on this issue has become. The English courts have occasionally viewed Art.14 arguments concerning the differential treatment of similarly-aged offenders sympathetically: see e.g. Sedley L.J. in *R. (W) v Thetford Youth Court*.[33] **11–07**

In a strongly worded dissent on this point, five judges considered that the age of criminal responsibility was fixed so low as to violate Art.3: **11–08**

"As far as the age of criminal responsibility is concerned, we do not accept the conclusion of the Court that no clear tendency can be ascertained from the developments amongst European States and from international instruments. Only four Contracting States out of 41 are prepared to find criminal responsibility at an age as low as, or lower than, that applicable in England and Wales. We have no doubt that there is a

---

[29] Para.86.
[30] The applicants were seated next to social workers in a specially raised dock so that they could see the witnesses and the judge; their parents and lawyers were seated "within whispering distance"; the hearing times were shortened to reflect the school day; and they were permitted to spend time with their parents and social workers in a play area during adjournments.
[31] See para.2–135 above.
[32] s.2 of the Homicide Act 1957 specifically refers to abnormality of mind arising from *inter alia* "arrested or retarded development of mind".
[33] [2003] 1 Cr.App.R.(S) 323 at para.43.

general standard amongst the Member States of the Council of Europe under which there is a system of relative criminal responsibility beginning at the age of 13 or 14—with special court procedures for juveniles—and providing for full criminal responsibility at the age of 18 or above. Where children aged from 10 to about 13 or 14 have committed crimes, educational measures are imposed to try to integrate the young offender into society. Even if Rule 4 of the Beijing Rules does not specify a minimum age of criminal responsibility, the very warning that the age should not be fixed too low indicates that criminal responsibility and maturity are related concepts. It is clearly the view of the vast majority of the Contracting States that this kind of maturity is not present in children below the age of 13 or 14. In the present case we are struck by the paradox that, whereas the applicants were deemed to have sufficient discrimination to engage their criminal responsibility, a play area was made available for them to use during adjournments."

B. TRIAL OF YOUNG DEFENDANTS

11–09   In response to the *T and V* decision, Lord Bingham C.J. issued a Practice Direction on February 16, 2000, later re-issued as para.39 of the consolidated Practice Direction (Criminal Proceedings: Consolidation).[34] It requires Crown Courts to adapt their procedures to take "account of the age, maturity and development (intellectual and emotional) of the young defendant on trial and all other circumstances of the case". These include frequent breaks during trial, removal of wigs, an overall reduction in formality of proceedings, pre-trial court familiarisation visits, powers to prevent publicity, powers to reduce the number of persons in court during trial, requiring police co-operation to reduce any vilification, intimidation or abuse of young defendants, minimal visible police presence in court, permitting young defendants to sit with their families during trial and at the same level as all court participants and an ongoing explanation to the young defendant of what is happening in language s/he can understand.

11–10   In 1999, the 11-year old[35] S.C. was tried in an English Crown Court. The indictment alleged attempted robbery of an elderly woman together with an older boy. His defence was that he had acted under duress, having been threatened by the older boy. The youth court, having regard to S.C.'s previous convictions, which included robbery, burglary, theft and arson, thought a custodial sentence was a real possibility and had therefore committed him to the Crown Court for trial. During his Crown Court trial, S.C. was accompanied at all times by his supervising social worker, wigs and gowns were abandoned and the court took frequent breaks. His case had no publicity and generated no public anger. There was no evidence that the atmosphere in the courtroom was particularly tense or intimidating or that he was traumatised by the trial or that his psychological condition prevented him from understanding the nature of the wrongdoing of which he was accused or from instructing and consulting with his legal representatives. His social worker frequently conferred with him to try to explain the

---

[34] [2002] 1 W.L.R. 2870.
[35] He had just turned 11 at the time of the offence and was 11 at the date of trial.

processes. At trial it was not contended that he did not understand those explanations. Although the trial occurred prior to the 2000 Practice Direction, it complied with it. He was convicted, sentenced to 30 months' detention and subsequently refused leave to appeal against conviction and sentence by the Court of Appeal.

The European Court ruled in *SC v UK*[36] that the modifications to Crown Court **11–11** trial procedure were nevertheless insufficient to ensure compliance with Art.6(1). According to the Court, even where a young defendant understands his crime enough for him to be fit to plead, he may still be unable to participate enough in the trial to make it fair. SC had contended that he should not have been tried by a judge and jury, in a court open to the public and with free access to the press but in the privacy of a specialist Youth Court with proper sentencing powers. The European Court held that to participate effectively in a trial, a defendant needs to understand the broad thrust of what is going on, and SC did not—he had the mental age of a child aged between six and eight and was intellectually within the lowest two per cent of children in his age group. Having regard to the Convention's "living instrument" status and the lack of consensus concerning the lowest age of criminal responsibility, the Court reiterated its decision in *T and V*—that the attribution of criminal responsibility to, or the trial on criminal charges of, an eleven-year-old child does not in itself give rise to a breach of the Convention.[37] It stressed, however, that the right of a child defendant to effective participation in a criminal trial generally includes being dealt with in a manner which takes full account of the child's age, level of maturity and intellectual and emotional capacities, and that steps are taken to promote ability to understand and participate in the proceedings including conducting the hearing in such a way as to reduce, as far as possible, feelings of intimidation and inhibition. It accepted that Art.6(1) does not require that a child on trial for a criminal offence should understand or be capable of understanding every point of law or evidential detail. Given the sophistication of modern legal systems, many adults of normal intelligence are unable fully to comprehend all the intricacies and exchanges which take place in the courtroom hence the Art.6(3)(c) right to legal representation. However, *effective* participation in this context presupposes that the accused has a broad understanding of the nature of the trial process and of what is at stake for him or her, including the significance of any penalty which may be imposed. It also means that s/he, if necessary with the assistance of an interpreter, lawyer, social worker or friend, should be able to understand the general thrust of what is said in court. The defendant should be able to follow what is said by the prosecution witnesses and, if represented, to explain to his own lawyers his version of events, point out any statements with which he disagrees and make them aware of any facts which should be put forward in his defence.[38]

Central to the court's decision was the fact that, although the psychologist had **11–12** recommended, because of SC's very low intellectual level for his age, that the court process should be explained carefully in a manner commensurate with his

---

[36] (2005) 40 E.H.R.R. 10.
[37] para.27.
[38] paras 28 to 29.

learning difficulties, there remained evidence that that he did not (fully) comprehend the situation he was in:

> "Thus, the applicant seems to have had little comprehension of the role of the jury in
> the proceedings or of the importance of making a good impression on them[39]. Even
> more strikingly, he does not seem to have grasped the fact that he risked a custodial
> sentence and, even once sentence had been passed and he had been taken down to the
> holding cells, he appeared confused and expected to be able to go home with his foster
> father. In the light of this evidence, the Court cannot conclude that the applicant was
> capable of participating effectively in his trial . . . The Court considers that, when the
> decision is taken to deal with a child, such as the applicant, who risks not being able to
> participate effectively because of his young age and limited intellectual capacity, by
> way of criminal proceedings rather than some other form of disposal directed primarily
> at determining the child's best interests and those of the community, it is essential that
> he be tried in a specialist tribunal which is able to give full consideration to and make
> proper allowance for the handicaps under which he labours, and adapt its procedure
> accordingly."[40]

The Government also argued that SC had not exhausted his domestic remedies
since he had not contended during the domestic proceedings that he was unfit to
plead. The court, however, noted that the Government had unsuccessfully argued
the same point in *T and V*, and concluded that, although SC's level of understanding was not such as to render him unfit to plead (he understood guilt and
could instruct his lawyers), he was still incapable of participating effectively in
his trial to the extent required by Art.6(1).

11–13   Three months after the *SC v UK* decision, the Government announced its
intention to appeal to the Grand Chamber, officials stating that the Crown Court
is more experienced than the youth courts in sentencing for serious crimes, that
the jury trial is a central part of the justice system and should not be discarded
lightly, and to set up a dedicated specialist child court overcoming the drawbacks
of the present two tiers would add the complexity of an extra tier, and would be
expensive.[41]

11–14   In this respect, it is also worth noting that many European countries (including
those with lower minimum ages of responsibility than the UK) have specialized
youth courts, even for serious crimes, which are generally more sensitive to a
child's moral and intellectual maturity. Moreover, Art.40(3)(b) UN Convention
on the Rights of the Child[42] provides:

> "State Parties shall in particular seek to promote the establishment of law, procedures,
> authorities and institutions specifically applicable to children alleged as, accused of, or
> recognised as having infringed the penal law, and shall in particular, whenever appro-
> priate and desirable, measures for dealing with such children without resorting to
> judicial proceedings, providing that human rights and legal safeguards are fully
> respected."

---

[39] The court had accepted evidence that his short attention span antagonised the jury.
[40] paras 32 to 35.
[41] Reported in *The Crown Court: A fit place try a child? The Times*, Oct. 20, 2004.
[42] Cm 1976. Ratified by the United Kingdom in 1990 and entered into force in January 1992.
Ratified by every country in the world except the United States of America and Somalia.

Further, under s.44 of the Children and Young Persons Act 1933 the prosecution is obliged to consider the child's welfare in deciding whether it is in the public interest to prosecute. Prior to 1994, the child's age itself was a consideration in that decision. Sch.2, Pt I para.7(a)(ii) of the Children Act 1989 also places social services under a duty to provide resources to avoid the need for prosecution.

As Baroness Hale explained in *R. (R) v Durham Constabulary*,[43] the focus on prevention and diversion in the Beijing Rules and UN Convention on the Rights of the Child is:

"reinforced by the *United Nations Guidelines for the Prevention of Juvenile Delinquency (The Riyadh Guidelines)* 1990. The fundamental principles emphasize that 'Young persons should have an active role and partnership within society and should not be considered as mere objects of socialization or control' (I.3); delinquency prevention policies should 'avoid criminalizing and penalizing a child for behaviour that does not cause serious damage to the development of the child or harm to others' (I.5); and that official interventions should be 'pursued primarily in the overall interest of the young person and guided by fairness and equity' (I.5(c))."

Nevertheless, there is still no distinct criminal justice system for children in England and Wales. In Scotland, however, there exists a children's hearing system under the Social Work (Scotland) Act 1968 (and now contained in the Children (Scotland) Act 1995). This diverts children from the criminal justice system into a specialist child care system which also caters for children who have been ill-treated or neglected or present other causes for concern. The Scottish children's hearing system has been described as the "high water mark of the welfare-based approach to juvenile offending in the United Kingdom."[44] More recently, the Children Act 2004[45] created a Children's Commissioner, who when considering what constitutes "the interests of children", must have regard to the UN Convention. This the first incorporation into domestic law of any part of the UN Convention.

The effect of *SC v UK*, together with a number of recent domestic decisions **11–15** clarifying procedural rights of young defendants, ought to be that far fewer young defendants are tried in the Crown Court. In *R. (W) v Southampton Youth Court*[46] the Divisional Court stressed that it is the general policy of the legislature to try those under 18 in a youth court and that the exceptional power to detain very young defendant for grave offences under s.91 of the Powers of Criminal Courts (Sentencing) Act 2000 should not be used to dilute that principle. In *R. (on the application of P) v West London Youth Court*[47] a boy of 15 (mental age of 8) was charged in the youth court with robbery and attempted robbery. His counsel argued that the proceedings should be stayed because he could not participate effectively in the proceedings, but the District Judge ruled that he could have a fair trial if properly assisted by experienced and specialist representatives. The Divisional Court dismissed the application for judicial review. First, the court held that the burden of proving that it would be an abuse of

---

[43] [2005] UKHL 21 at para.28.
[44] *ibid.* at para.30.
[45] ss.1 to 9 came into force on November 15, 2004.
[46] [2003] 1 Cr.App.R.(S) 87.
[47] [2006] 1 All E.R. 477.

process to proceed with the trial lies on the defendant, on a balance of probabilities. That is the position in other abuse of process applications, and in unfitness to plead. The claimant contended that it should be sufficient to establish a "real possibility" that the defendant would be unable to participate effectively. The court's conclusion was that a prosecution should not be stayed at the outset unless the higher standard were met, and that it remained the judge's duty to stay the proceedings if, during the trial, it appeared that the defendant was unable effectively to participate. Secondly, the court agreed that the principles in *S.C. v United Kingdom* should be applied, but pointed out that that case concerned the Crown Court whereas this concerns the youth court. "Neither youth nor limited intellectual capacity necessary leads to a breach of Article 6." A number of steps should be taken during the trial:

> "These include (i) keeping the claimant's level of cognitive functioning in mind; (ii) using concise and simple language; (iii) having regular breaks; (iv) taking additional time to explain court proceedings; (v) being proactive in ensuring the claimant has access to support; (vi) explaining and ensuring the claimant understands the ingredients of the charge; (vii) explaining the possible outcomes and sentences; (viii) ensuring that cross-examination is carefully controlled so that questions are short and clear and frustration is minimised."[48]

The House of Lords refused leave to appeal, and so the Divisional Court's support for the approach in *S.C. v United Kingdom* remains authoritative.

11–16   However, the terms of the 2000 Practice Direction have not yet been altered, and other decisions suggest that the courts of England and Wales remain ambivalent in their approach to child defendants. In the case of *H.*,[49] a boy aged just 14 at the time of the Crown Court trial was tried and convicted on four counts of oral rape of a boy aged 5. The first ground of appeal was that the evidence of the alleged victim and two older boys was so inconsistent that the judge should have withdrawn the case from the jury, but this failed. The second ground concerned compliance with the *Practice Direction (Crown Court: Young Defendants)*, and the court observed that it was regrettable that no consideration was given at the plea and case management hearing to special steps to ensure that the defendant, then aged 13 and facing 4 counts of rape, could participate effectively in the trial. The court further held that it was not the responsibility of defence counsel alone to raise these matters. The court recognised that in this case there were several matters of concern. The court-room was large and forbidding in the old style, with a high dock, and people were coming in and out throughout the trial. H was assessed as being "at the lower level of maturity for his age." In his sentencing remarks the judge had commented on H's total indifference when the verdicts were announced. But the court concluded that these shortcomings were "not so grave" as to prevent a fair trial and effective participation, particularly because the judge ensured that there were frequent breaks in the proceedings. The case was decided without any discussion of *S.C. v United Kingdom* or the *West London* case above. Whereas the latter case concerned the youth court and was rightly distinguished by the Divisional Court on that ground, this case, like *S.C.*,

---

[48] *ibid.*, at [26].
[49] [2006] EWCA Crim 853.

relates directly to Crown Court trial. The defendant here was older but, as the court hinted, his lack of reaction to the verdicts may demonstrate low understanding. On the facts the case must be close to the borderline; in legal terms the failure to discuss the two previous decisions weakens it considerably.

The unavailability of "special measures" (e.g. evidence by video link) for **11–17** defendants,[50] while they were available under s.19 of the Youth Justice and Criminal Evidence Act 1999 for prosecution witnesses, was held by the House of Lords to be Art.6(3)(d) compatible in *R. (D) v Camberwell Green Youth Court.*[51] Baroness Hale, however, left open the possibility that refusing a young and particularly vulnerable defendant special measures might, in certain circumstances, violate Art.6. Recently the Office of Criminal Justice Reform has been appointing and paying for "intermediaries" for young defendants with communication needs. Most intermediaries are speech and language therapists, and all have received specialist training for the role. They will prepare an assessment report on a defendant's communications needs, and a court may permit an intermediary to be present assisting a defendant during a trial. This development may prove to be a significant step towards fairer trials for some young defendants.[52]

C. POSITIVE OBLIGATIONS TOWARDS JUVENILES

In *R. (R) v Durham Constabulary*[53] the House of Lords considered the Conven- **11–18** tion compatibility of the final warning and reprimand scheme contained in ss.65–66 of the Crime and Disorder Act 1998 (which replaced police cautions for young offenders). The issue was whether it was fair to subject a child to a formal diversion process with mandatory legal consequences without first obtaining his informed consent—the scheme contains no express requirement of parental or equivalent consent. Although Baroness Hale and Lord Steyn had "considerable misgivings" about the final conclusion and "grave doubts" as to whether the scheme was consistent with the child's rights under relevant international instruments, it unanimously held that the scheme did not involve the determination of a criminal charge against a young person within the meaning of Art.6. Had it done so, there would have been no valid waiver of fair trial rights.

The House of Lords decision *R. v G*[54] raised important issues concerning the **11–19** substantive obligations of the State in accommodating the special position of children within the criminal justice system. The appellants in *G* were two boys aged 11 and 12 who set fire to some newspapers in the backyard of a shop, threw

---

[50] S.17 of the Youth Justice and Criminal Evidence Act 1999.

[51] [2005] UKHL 4; [2005] Crim.L.R. 497.

[52] Further information can be obtained from the Better Trials Unit at the Office for Criminal Justice Reform.

[53] [2005] UKHL 21. See also the Joint Committee on Human Rights ("Scrutiny of Bills: Further Progress Report", Twelfth Report of Session 2002–03, HL Paper 119, HC 765, paras 2.26–2.37) which was concerned at the registration requirements imposed on young offenders reprimanded or warned for sex offences.

[54] [2003] UKHL 1, [2004] 1 A.C. 1034, HL(E).

them under a dustbin and left the yard without extinguishing the burning papers. The dustbin caught fire which spread to adjoining buildings, resulting in approximately £1 million worth of damage. The defendants were charged with arson under s.1 of the Criminal Damage Act 1971, being reckless as to whether property would be destroyed or damaged. At trial the defendants' case was that they expected the burning newspapers to extinguish themselves on the concrete floor of the yard. It was accepted that neither of the defendants appreciated that there was any risk of the fire spreading. The trial judge ruled that he was bound by the previous House of Lords authority in *R. v Caldwell*[55] to direct the jury that, in deciding whether the defendants had been reckless as to whether the property would be damaged or destroyed, the test to be applied was one of objective recklessness—i.e. when they created an obvious risk of damage/destruction, had they either not given any thought to the possibility of there being such a risk, or recognized that there was some risk involved but nevertheless gone on to do it? Whether there was an obvious risk was to be assessed by reference to the reasonable man and not by reference to a person endowed with the defendants' characteristics. Accordingly, the judge directed the jury that they could make no allowance for the defendants' youth, lack of maturity or any inability they might have to assess the situation. The Court of Appeal agreed that the direction was correct.

11–20   The House of Lords in *G* considered *Caldwell* wrongly decided. The compelling reasons for such a course, for Lord Bingham, were the requirement of subjective *mens rea* for conviction of a serious crime and that a failure to take account of individual characteristics in assessing mental state could led to results which might be "neither moral nor just".[56] Lord Steyn focused on the injustice of applying an objective (adult) state of mind to children[57]:

> "Ignoring the special position of children in the criminal justice system is not acceptable in a modern civil society. In 1990 the United Kingdom ratified the Convention on the Rights of the Child (Cm 1976) which entered into force in January 1992. Article 40(1) provides:
>
>> 'States parties recognise the right of every child alleged as, accused of, or recognised as having infringed the penal law to be treated in a manner consistent with the promotion of the child's sense of dignity and worth, which reinforces the child's respect for the human rights and fundamental freedoms of others and which takes into account the child's age and the desirability of promoting the child's reintegration and the child's assuming a constructive role in society.'
>
> This provision imposes both procedural and substantive obligations on state parties to protect the special position of children in the criminal justice system. For example, it would plainly be contrary to article 40(1) for a state to set the age of criminal responsibility of children at, say, five years. Similarly, it is contrary to article 40(1) to ignore in a crime punishable by life imprisonment, or detention during Her Majesty's pleasure, the age of a child in judging whether the mental element has been satisfied. It is true that the Convention became binding on the United Kingdom after *R v Caldwell* was decided. But the House cannot ignore the norm created by the Convention. This

---

[55] [1982] A.C. 341, HL(E).
[56] paras 32 to 33.
[57] paras 53 to 54.

factor on its own justified a reappraisal of *R v Caldwell*. If it is wrong to ignore the special characteristics of children in the context of recklessness under section 1 of the 1971 Act, an adult who suffers from a lack of mental capacity or a relevant personality disorder may be entitled to the same standard of justice. Recognising the special characteristics of children and mentally disabled people goes some way towards reducing the scope of section 1 of the 1971 Act for producing unjust results which are inherent in the objective mould into which the *Caldwell* analysis forced recklessness."

The argument that *Caldwell* objective recklessness was, in itself, a breach of Art.6 of the Convention was not pursued.[58]

The same issue of ignoring the special characteristics of children (and also of   **11–21** mentally disabled people) arises in connection with anti-social behaviour orders under s.1 of the Crime and Disorder Act 1998. Although the Government originally stated that ASBOs were not intended for children, around a half such orders are made on children, and the consequences of breach can be severe. Among the particular issues raised by ASBOs made on children is the terms of the prohibition(s) contained in the order: in *R. (on application of W) v Director of Public Prosecutions*,[59] one of the conditions of the order made on the youth was to refrain from "committing any criminal offence", and in striking down this broad prohibition Brooke L.J. commented that "at this age he might well not know what was a criminal offence and what was not."

Section 11 of the Children Act 2004 requires certain bodies to discharge their   **11–22** functions having regard to the need to safeguard and promote the welfare of children. Police authorities, local probation boards, youth offending teams and prison or secure training centre governors (and the directors of privately run prison or secure training centres) are included in this new duty. A consideration of the many human rights issues concerning the treatment of children within the criminal justice system is outside the scope of this work.[60]

D. INSANITY

In Convention terms, the detention of persons found not guilty by reason of   **11–23** insanity falls to be considered under Art.5. The key provision is Art.5(1)(e), which permits "the lawful detention of . . . persons of unsound mind." The guiding principles were first laid down in *Winterwerp v Netherlands*,[61] where the court had to consider a number of basic questions about the application of Art.5(1)(e). Three of the points made by the court have potential implications for the insanity defence in English criminal law.

---

[58] para.40.
[59] [2005] EWHC Admin 1333.
[60] For a helpful summary, see the Children's Rights Alliance for England *Annual Report* (Nov. 2004).
[61] (1979–80) 2 E.H.R.R. 387. See also *Luberti v Italy* (1984) 6 E.H.R.R. 440.

11–24   First, whilst the court declined to lay down a definition of unsoundness of mind and recognised that the meaning of the term is changing as psychiatry evolves,[62] it laid emphasis on the importance of a close correspondence between expert medical opinion and the definition of mental disorder used in the domestic law.[63] In this country a close correspondence does not exist on certain issues. Thus the courts have tried to draw a distinction between insanity and automatism by developing the notion that "diseases of the mind" which spring from "internal" causes should be classified as insanity whereas those that spring from "external" factors should be classified as automatism. Not only is this distinction unknown to, and probably rejected by, current medical opinion; it has also led to special verdicts of insanity in cases of epilepsy,[64] diabetes leading to hyperglycaemia,[65] and sleep-walking,[66] none of which would be regarded as forms of mental disorder by current psychiatric opinion.[67] There is therefore a strong argument for reforming the insanity verdict so as to avoid this wide divergence between medical opinion and the existing law, developed as it has been from the *M'Naghten* Rules of 1843.[68] The inadequacy of the *M'Naghten* Rules as the basis for a finding of insanity was recognised by the Royal Commission on Capital Punishment in 1953, by the Butler Committee on Mentally Abnormal Offenders in 1975, and in the Law Commission's draft Criminal Code in 1989. As Professor Mackay has observed,[69] "the manner in which the judiciary have interpreted 'disease of the mind' is largely governed by policy considerations, and has little or nothing to do with the practice of psychiatry".[70] In the absence of legislative reform, courts should at least refrain from depriving of his liberty a defendant who is acquitted on grounds of insanity in a case falling outside current psychiatric definitions. Committal to hospital in such cases could well violate the defendant's Art.5 rights.[71] In *Attorney General v Prior*,[72] the Royal Court of

---

[62] At para.37.

[63] At paras 37 to 39.

[64] *Sullivan* [1984] 1 A.C. 156.

[65] *Hennessy* [1989] 1 W.L.R. 287.

[66] *Burgess* [1991] 2 Q.B. 92.

[67] In this context it is worth noting that the Supreme Court of Canada has categorised sleepwalking as a form of non-insane automatism, on the basis that it is not a neurological, psychiatric or other illness. Although the court did not support the internal/external distinction, it pointed out that sleepwalking does not fall clearly on either side of the line: *Parks* (1993) 15 C.R. (4th) 289.

[68] See Sutherland P.J. and Gearty C.A., "Insanity and the European Court of Human Rights" [1992] Crim. L.R. 418, for an elaboration of this and other relevant arguments.

[69] Professor R.D. Mackay, *Mental Condition Defences in the Criminal Law* (Oxford, 1995).

[70] Professor H.L.A. Hart explained the evolution of this conflict between law and psychiatry in *Punishment and Responsibility, Essays in the Philosophy of Law*: "This dispute raged throughout the nineteenth century and was certainly marked by some curious features. In James Fitzjames Simon's great *History of the Criminal Law* the dispute is vividly presented as one between doctors and lawyers. The doctors are pictured as accusing the lawyers of claiming to decide a medical or scientific issue about responsibility by out of date criteria when they limited legal inquiry to the question of knowledge. The lawyers replied that doctors, in seeking to give evidence about other matters, were attempting illicitly to thrust upon juries their views on what should excuse a man when charged with a crime; illicitly because responsibility is a question not of science but of law."

[71] Since the Criminal Procedure (Insanity and Unfitness to Plead) Act 1991, the disposal decision has been at the discretion of the court in all cases in which the penalty is not mandatory: see further para.11–12 below.

[72] Unreported, February 2001. See Mackay and Gearty, *On being Insane in Jersey—the case of Attorney General v Jason Prior* [2001] Crim.L.R. 560.

Jersey declined to adopt the *M'Naghten* rules as the basis for the defence of insanity[73] holding that they were arguably inconsistent with Art.5:

"It is true that the Convention jurisprudence is looking at the matter from the perspective of the lawfulness of detaining a person of unsound mind rather than from the perspective of exculpation from criminal liability by reason of insanity. But these are simply different ends of the same spectrum. If a person is excused from responsibility for a criminal act by his insanity, he is liable to be detained during Her Majesty's Pleasure.[74] That detention will be unlawful unless it complies with the requirements of the Convention."

On appeal, the Jersey Court of Appeal declined to address the Convention **11–25** compatibility of the *M'Naghten Rules* but doubted the correctness of the Bailiff's ruling below. Giving no reasons, it thought the argument was not "correctly based" and was troubled by the Royal Court of Guernsey's opposite conclusion on the point (it having considered the Royal Court of Jersey decision).[75] The Jersey Court of Appeal thought that a different insanity defence between the islands was "highly undesirable". On the mainland, the Scottish Law Commission has proposed reform of the definition of insanity in Scots law, which it takes to be Convention compatible.[76] It is not known whether similar changes in English law will be recommended if the Law Commission reconsiders the defence as part of its codification project.[77]

A second point made by the court in *Winterwerp* is that decisions on unsoundness **11–26** of mind "call for objective medical expertise" and that a defendant deprived of liberty under Art.5(1)(e) should be "reliably shown to be 'of unsound mind'". The Criminal Procedure (Insanity and Unfitness of Plead) Act 1991 has improved matters somewhat, in that s.1(1) prohibits a court from returning an insanity verdict "except on the written or oral evidence of two or more registered medical practitioners at least one of whom is duly approved." This brings English law closer to compliance with the requirements of Art.5, although the wording states only that the court should receive such evidence, not that it should follow it. It would be a bold course of reasoning to go further and argue that s.3(1) of the Human Rights Act 1998, read in conjunction with s.1 of the 1991 Act, opens the way for the courts to bring the substantive definition of the defence of insanity closer to current psychiatric opinion.[78] Currently, in homicide cases, for example, psychiatrists consider that there is a "profound mismatch" between the thinking of the law and psychiatry.[79] There are also practical difficulties in performing a sufficiently detailed medical assessment of defendants in custody on murder

---

[73] Within the meaning of the Criminal Justice (Insane Persons) Jersey Law 1964.

[74] There is no equivalent in Jersey of the sentencing discretion afforded in England and Wales by the Criminal Procedure (Insanity and Unfitness to Plead) Act 1991.

[75] *Law Officers of the Crown v Derek Lee Harvey* (unreported, Royal Court of Guernsey, Aug. 3, 2001).

[76] Scot Law Com No.195, 2004.

[77] See Mackay, "On being Insane in Jersey Part Two—the appeal in Jason Prior v Attorney General" [2002] Crim.L.R. 728 at 734 and Editorial in [2004] Crim. L.R. 681.

[78] This bold course is examined by Baker E., "Human Rights, *M'Naghten* and the 1991 Act" [1994] Crim. L.R. 84.

[79] Royal College of Psychiatry response to *Law Commission Final Report on Partial Defences to Murder* (2004, Law Com. 290) at para.5.44 of the Report.

charges, for example, if they have not been observed and treated over an extended period in a mental hospital.[80]

11-27   A third point concerns cases in which committal to hospital follows automatically from a special verdict. Although the 1991 Act conferred on the courts a discretion in the disposal of most special verdict cases,[81] committal to hospital indefinitely remains mandatory where "the offence to which the special verdict [relates] is an offence the sentence for which is fixed by law."[82] The court in *Winterwerp* held that, before a person is deprived of liberty, "the mental disorder must be of a kind or degree warranting compulsory confinement".[83] Mandatory committal to hospital leaves no opportunity for such a finding. Moreover, in cases where the special verdict is based on the "internal factors" doctrine (e.g. epilepsy, hyperglycaemia, sleep-walking), it is highly unlikely that compulsory confinement would be necessary. This yields two possible conclusions. First, if the 1991 Act cannot be read compatibly with Art.5(1)(e) in cases where the sentence for the offence is fixed by law,[84] there may be grounds for the issue of a declaration of incompatibility under s.4 of the Human Rights Act 1998.[85] Secondly, even in cases where the court has a discretion as to disposal under the 1991 Act, it ought to be satisfied that the defendant's disorder is "of a kind or degree warranting compulsory confinement" before it makes such an order, if Art.5 is to be complied with.

11-28   The House of Lords held in *R. v H.*[86] that Unfitness to Plead proceedings under ss.4 and 4A of the Criminal Procedure (Insanity) Act 1964 (as inserted by s.2 of the 1991 Act) do not involve the determination of a criminal charge within the meaning of Art.6 of the ECHR as they cannot result in a conviction or in any order that could be seen as a significant penalty.[87] Provided that the procedure is properly conducted, with scrupulous regard for the interests of the defendant, it is compatible with his other rights under Art.6. In such cases, the defence may not raise any issues relating to intent (including provocation). Any subsequent compulsory detention (in cases where the sentence is fixed by law) does not engage Art.6 and may comply with Arts 5(1)(e) and 5(4) having regard to the

---

[80] See *Law Commission Final Report on Partial Defences to Murder* (2004) at para.5.30.

[81] For discussion, see White S., "The Criminal Procedure (Insanity and Unfitness to Plead) Act 1991" [1992] Crim. L.R. 4.

[82] There was an argument that the "automatic life sentence" created by s.2 of the Crime (Sentences) Act 1997 created a "sentence fixed by law"; but that provision has now been repealed, and the dangerousness sentences created by the Criminal Justice Act 2003 are accompanied by provisions stating that they are not sentences fixed by law—see, for imprisonment for public protection, s.225(5) of the Act.

[83] In *Winterwerp* the court expressed its full agreement with the view that "no one may be confined as a 'person of unsound mind' in the absence of medical evidence establishing that his mental state is such as to justify his compulsory hospitalisation", (1979–80) 2 E.H.R.R. 387, para.39, quoting from para.76 of the Commission's report.

[84] It may well be possible for the House of Lords to overrule previous decisions such as *Sullivan* [1984] 1 A.C. 156 and to alter the common law so as to align the definition of insanity with current psychiatric opinion.

[85] See para.3–35 above.

[86] [2003] 2 Cr.App.R. 25, HL.

[87] For critical comment on this last point, see [2003] Crim.L.R. 818.

Mental Health Review Tribunal's powers although questions "of some difficulty" arise if the person is not assessed to be sufficiently mentally ill to warrant detention or in-patient treatment but is nevertheless unable to instruct lawyers: *R. (Grant) v DPP.*[88]

One final point about the insanity defence concerns the burden of proof. The **11-29** general issues raised by Art.6(2) in the context of "reverse onus" provisions are considered in Ch.9, but it is convenient at this point to mention the burden of proof where insanity is raised. In the leading case of *Woolmington v DPP,*[89] insanity was identified as the only common law exception to the principle that the prosecution should prove guilt beyond reasonable doubt. In general, where a common law defence is in issue, the defendant bears no more than an evidential burden to raise the defence, and then the prosecution must disprove the defence beyond reasonable doubt. The imposition of a purely evidential burden does not infringe the presumption of innocence in Art.6(2) of the Convention.[90] But if insanity is the defence, the accused must go further than discharging an evidential burden, and must prove on a balance of probabilities that he or she comes within the *M'Naghten* Rules: *R. v Smith (Oliver).*[91]

It may be thought that this would infringe the presumption of innocence, but **11-30** when the argument was put to the Commission in 1990, it declared the application inadmissible.[92] The current position may or may not be justifiable under Art.6(2), but the Commission's reasoning on the point was apparently a long way wide of the mark. It held that "requiring the defence to *present evidence* concerning the accused's mental health at the time of the offence" was compatible with the presumption of innocence. But this, of course, neglects the difference between the presentation of evidence, which may be equated with an evidential burden, and the ultimate burden proving insanity to the court on the balance of probabilities. The Commission went on to remark that "in English law the burden of proof remains with the prosecution to prove beyond reasonable doubt that the accused did the act or made the omission charged". This may be true as a general principle, but it does not alter the fact that the defendant bears the burden of proving insanity. In an attempt to square this circle, the Commission characterised the existing rule as relating to the presumption of sanity, rather than the presumption of innocence. Once again, this a highly questionable distinction given that a person found insane, in the *M'Naghten* sense is, as a matter of English law, not guilty of any offence. The best justification for the Commission's conclusion lies in its observation that the burden imposed on the accused in insanity cases is neither arbitrary nor unreasonable. This is a point which has been taken up in some of the Canadian decisions.[93]

---

[88] [2002] 1 Cr.App.R. 528, DC and CA.
[89] [1935] A.C. 462.
[90] *R. v DPP ex parte Kebilene and ors* [1999] 3 W.L.R. 972 (HL) *per* Lord Hope.
[91] 6 Cr.App.R. 19, CCA.
[92] *H v UK* Application No.15923/89 noted at (1990) 87 Law Society Gazette 31.
[93] For a wide-ranging examination of this topic, see Jones T.H., "Insanity, Automatism and the Burden of Proof on the Accused" (1995) 111 L.Q.R. 475.

11–31 In Canada the reverse onus in insanity cases was challenged under the Charter in the leading case of *Chaulk*.[94] A majority of the Supreme Court found that the reverse onus provision was incompatible with the presumption of innocence declared by the Charter, but was saved by s.1 of the Charter as being a "reasonable limit" on the presumption of innocence which was "demonstrably justifiable" because the burden of the prosecution would otherwise be virtually impossible. The *Oakes* test of proportionality[95] was held to be fulfilled, and so the reverse onus survives. Whilst there were other issues in the case,[96] it must be said that the majority's reasoning on this point fails to grapple with the practical or theoretical basis for distinguishing insanity from the other defences on the issue of burden of proof. There would appear to be no insurmountable obstacle to a rule which places a merely evidential burden on the accused. This would require the introduction by the defence of medical evidence sufficient, if left uncontradicted, to raise a reasonable doubt as to the sanity of the accused. It would then be for the prosecution to call evidence to disprove this. In *R. v DPP ex parte Kebilene* Lord Hope pointed out that the courts had declined to impose a persuasive onus in cases of non-insane automatism, despite the conceptual proximity of the two defences. Lord Hope cited the words of Lord Devlin in *Hill v Baxter*[97]:

> "As automatism is akin to insanity in law there would be a great practical advantage if the burden of proof was the same in both cases. But so far insanity is the only matter of defence in which, under the common law, the burden of proof has been held to be completely shifted."

11–32 One might equally ask the question the other way around—why should the law impose a persuasive burden in cases of insanity, when this has not been found necessary in cases of automatism?[98] In the United States it seems that about half of the states place only an evidential burden on the defendant in insanity cases, whereas the other half go further and impose a legal burden of proof.[99] The United States Supreme Court has, however, held that it is not contrary to the Constitution to place the legal or persuasive burden on the accused.[100]

11–33 The Scottish Law Commission has recently changed its position, and argued that a legal burden on the accused to prove the "mental disorder defence" (which will replace the Scottish equivalent of the insanity defence) is justified by the practical difficulties of disproof if the burden were on the Crown and the need to deal with the problem of false claims of mental disorder.[101] It relied, primarily, on the problematic Canadian decision in *Chaulk* but also reasoned that, irrespective of the type of burden imposed, medical evidence would generally have to be

---

[94] [1990] 3 S.C.R. 1303.
[95] See para.9–20 above.
[96] Notably the exploration of the view that the insanity defence is not a mere negation of *mens rea* or *actus reus* but relates to a basic precondition of all criminal responsibility, expounded in the judgment of McLachlin J.
[97] [1958] 1 Q.B. 277 at 285.
[98] *Bratty v Attorney General for Northern Ireland* [1963] A.C. 386.
[99] Kadish S.H. and Schulhofer S.J., *Criminal Law and its Processes* (6th edn, 1995), p.936.
[100] *Patterson v New York* 432 US 197 (1977).
[101] Scot Law Com No.195, 2004.

produced to demonstrate insanity thus eroding the practical difference between evidential and legal burdens.[102]

In contrast, the South Africa Law Commission came to a different conclusion on **11–34** the compatibility of insanity in South African law with defendants' constitutional entitlement to the presumption of innocence.[103] "[T]he task of disproving insanity in South African law is not so arduous" as it was in Canada (*Chaulk*) because a defendant thought to be mentally ill must be referred for examination to a panel of psychiatric practitioners who prepare a report which includes a finding of whether, at the relevant time, the accused's capacity to distinguish right from wrong was affected by mental illness. Thus, it could not be argued that it was "virtually impossible" for the State to disprove insanity.[104]

It has been suggested that since the English Courts have already upheld the legal **11–35** burden on the accused to prove diminished responsibility, it is unlikely they would take a different view in relation to insanity.[105] The difficulty in placing a legal burden on the accused is not as acute where the defence takes the form that the defendant did not know that his act was wrong (within the second limb of the *M'Naghten Rules*). Here s/he is setting up the existence of facts which are wholly outside the prosecution's case and it is not obviously unjustified to place the onus on the defendant.[106]

E. DIMINISHED RESPONSIBILITY

Section 2 of the Homicide Act 1957 introduced the defence of diminished **11–36** responsibility, so as to reduce homicide from murder to manslaughter where the accused was suffering from such abnormality of mind (whether arising from a condition of arrested or retarded development of mind or any inherent causes or induced by disease or injury) as substantially impaired his mental responsibility. Section 2(2) provides that "it shall be for the defence to prove that the person charged is by virtue of this section not liable to be convicted of murder". The compatibility of this onus of proof was considered in *R. v Lambert and Ali*.[107] The court held that since proof of diminished responsibility was pre-eminently a matter for defence evidence, and since proof of the contrary was extremely difficult for the prosecution, s.2 of the 1957 Act was compatible with Art.6(2). A

---

[102] For critical discussion of the Scottish Law Commission's reasoning, see Ashworth A., "Four Threats to the Presumption of Innocence", (2006) 10 *Evidence & Proof* 241 at 263–266.

[103] South African Law Commission Report Project 101—*The Application of the Bill of Rights to Criminal Procedure* (discussed in Criminal Law, the Law of Evidence and Sentencing: May 2001).

[104] *cf.* Lord Woolf C.J. in *R. v Lambert and Ali* [2002] Q.B. 1112; [2001] Cr.App.Rep. 14 at paras 18 to 19 (See para.11–18 below).

[105] *R. v Lambert and Ali* [2001] 2 W.L.R. 211 at para.18. See para.11–18 below. A view expressed in [2004] Crim.L.R. 68.

[106] *R. v Carr-Briant* [1943] K.B. 607, 29 Cr.App.R. 76; *Sodeman v R.* [1936] 2 All E.R. 1138. See further *Smith & Hogan, Criminal Law* (10th edn, Butterworths) at p.227.

[107] [2002] Q.B. 1112, [2001] Cr.App.Rep. 14 at paras 18–19 (CA).

key factor in Lord Woolf C.J.'s reasoning was the fact that a defendant cannot be required to submit to an examination by a doctor.[108]

11–37 The Commission also reached the same conclusion in *Robinson v UK*,[109] being unable to distinguish its previous decision on insanity in *H v UK*[110]: "both cases presume the accused's ability to understand what he was doing at the time of the crime unless he can show there was some serious mental impairment of a permanent or transient kind." A five-judge Court of Appeal followed *R. v Lambert and Ali* in *Attorney-General's Reference (No.1 of 2004)*, holding that the partial homicide defence of killing in pursuance of a suicide pact included a justified reverse burden.[111]

11–38 Nevertheless, following the recent, detailed re-examination of the Convention compatibility of reverse burdens by the House of Lords in *Attorney General's Reference (No.4 of 2002)*,[112] the position is not absolutely settled. Lord Bingham expressed himself as "inclined to agree", in the absence of argument on the point, that the Court of Appeal's conclusion on the reverse burden in the partial defence of killing in pursuance of a suicide pact would not have been affected by the Lords' decision.

11–39 There remains the potential anomaly that where the partial defence to murder is provocation, the defendant bears an evidential burden and the prosecution must disprove the defence, whereas if the partial defence to murder is diminished responsibility the burden of proof lies on the defendant. In its report on partial defences to murder, the Law Commission did not recommend any change to the burden of proof in diminished responsibility cases.[113] It also rejected a suggestion that the burden could be placed on the prosecution if their psychiatrist were afforded access to the defendant.[114] A small majority the Commission's consultees was in favour of the defence only bearing an evidential burden. The judiciary was evenly split, but the legal professions were in favour of retaining the current arrangement.[115] In its final report on Murder, Manslaughter and Infanticide, the Law Commission confirms its recommendation that the burden of proving diminished responsibility should be on the defendant; indeed, it makes a similar proposal in relation to the burden of proving duress as a defence,[116] although the position would be unchanged for the partial defence of provocation (only an evidential burden on the accused).

---

[108] at para.18.
[109] Application 20858/92 (unreported, May 5, 1993).
[110] Application 15023/89 (unreported, April 4, 1990)—see n.43 above.
[111] at paras 130 to 132.
[112] [2004] UKHL 43. See further, Ch.9 on Reverse Onus Provisions.
[113] *Law Commission Final Report on Partial Defences to Murder* (2004, Law Com. 290) paras 5.91 to 5.92.
[114] A suggestion from JUSTICE at para.5.90 of the Report.
[115] para.5.88+ of the Report.
[116] Law Com. No.304, *Murder, Manslaughter and Infanticide* (2006), Ch.8.

CHAPTER 12

DOUBLE JEOPARDY

A. INTRODUCTION

In its report on *Double Jeopardy and Prosecution Appeals*[1] the Law Commission **12–01** recommended that the Court of Appeal should have power to set aside an acquittal for murder and order a retrial where there is compelling new evidence of guilt and the Court is satisfied that it would be in the interests of justice to do so. The Law Commission concluded that the introduction of such a procedure would be compatible with the provisions of the Convention and, in particular, with Art.4 of Protocol 7. Art.4 provides:

"1. No one shall be liable to be tried or punished again in criminal proceedings under the jurisdiction of the same state for an offence for which he has already been finally acquitted or convicted in accordance with the law and penal procedure of that state.

2. The provisions of the preceding paragraph shall not prevent the reopening of the case in accordance with the law and penal procedure of the state concerned, if there is evidence of new or newly discovered facts, or if there has been a fundamental defect in the previous proceedings, which could affect the outcome of the case.

3. No derogation from this article shall be made under Art.15 of the Convention."

Protocol 7 was adopted in order to bring the Convention into line with the **12–02** broader range of rights protected under the International Covenant on Civil and Political Rights[2] (I.C.C.P.R.). In its White Paper, *Rights Brought Home*,[3] the Government expressed its intention to sign, ratify and incorporate Protocol 7 once certain provisions of national law, relating to property rights of spouses and outside the scope of the present work, had been amended. The Government has now signed the Protocol. The Department for Constitutional Affairs, *Report on the UK Government's Inter-Departmental Review of the UK's Position under various International Human Rights Instruments*, July 2004, indicates that ratification will not be possible until an appropriate legislative vehicle is found by

---

[1] *Double Jeopardy and Prosecution Appeals*, Law Commission No.267, January 24, 2001.
[2] See *Rights Brought Home*, Cmnd. 3782, paras 4.9 and 4.14.
[3] Cmnd.3782, (1997), para.4.15.

which to amend those property rights.[4] In order to understand the impact of Art.4 of Protocol 7 on domestic law, it is necessary to consider the practice of other states, the current approach in England and Wales, the approach taken under the I.C.C.P.R., and the caselaw under the Convention.

B. THE APPROACH IN OTHER JURISDICTIONS

12–03 All European states recognise the principle that once ordinary appellate remedies have been exhausted, or the relevant time limit for appealing has expired, a conviction or acquittal is to be regarded as irrevocable, and acquires the quality of *res judicata*.[5] However, many states permit a final decision to be reopened if fresh evidence becomes available which demonstrates that the original verdict was wrong or if there has been a fundamental defect in the original proceedings. Provisions which permit the reopening of a final conviction or acquittal generally require the involvement of an appellate court. Where the original verdict is set aside in accordance with such a procedure the appellate court may, in some states, order a retrial. The power of an appellate court to reopen criminal proceedings, and to order a retrial, is thus to be distinguished from the concept of double jeopardy as it is understood in common law systems. In many European jurisdictions, the prohibition on double jeopardy operates to prevent prosecuting authorities from commencing a fresh prosecution on their own initiative. It does not necessarily prevent an appellate court from overturning a final conviction or acquittal and ordering a retrial.

12–04 There is considerable variation in the practices adopted on this issue in the criminal procedure systems which make up the Council of Europe. In Italy, for example, once ordinary appellate remedies have been exhausted, a judgment becomes final and an acquitted or convicted person may not be tried again for the same offence, even if relevant new facts or evidence have become available.[6] In Finland, on the other hand, any criminal proceedings can be reopened if an acquittal has been obtained through fraud; and an acquittal in respect of an aggravated offence can be reopened if, within a year, fresh evidence becomes available which could have led to a conviction or a penalty which is substantially more severe than that which was actually imposed.[7]

12–05 Provisions permitting a final conviction or acquittal to be reopened are to be found in the criminal procedure systems of a number of Western European states.[8] In some states the rules apply in the same way whether it is the prosecution which is seeking to overturn a final acquittal, or the defence which is seeking to overturn a final conviction. In other states the right to apply to an

---

[4] See Appendix 4 to the Report.
[5] See Explanatory Report to Protocol 7 of the Convention, CE Doc H (83) 3, para.22.
[6] See generally Van Den Wyngaert, *Criminal Procedure Systems in the European Community* (Butterworths, 1993), p.258.
[7] See Finland's Reservation to the I.C.C.P.R., para.6, cited in Nowak, *CCPR Commentary* (Engel, 1993), p.753.
[8] See generally Nowak, pp.272–273.

appellate court to reopen a criminal verdict which has the force of *res judicata* is available only to the defence.

Article 50 of the Charter of Fundamental Rights of the European Union includes a right not to be tried twice in criminal proceedings for the same offence. This is qualified by Art.52.1 which permits limitations on Charter Rights subject to proportionality principles. Article 52.3 provides that, in so far as the Charter provides rights corresponding to Convention rights, Charter rights shall be the same as Convention rights. This does not prevent EU law providing greater protection than the Convention (each is only a "floor of rights") but it would be unlikely if the Charter prohibited any new evidence exceptions to double jeopardy. The Charter is part of EU law but is not yet directly enforceable by the EU courts or national courts. It will become directly enforceable only when the Constitutional Treaty is ratified by all 25 member states.[9]

The European developments, in particular the move towards a Framework Decision, harmonising and recognising the high status of the law of double jeopardy in European jurisdictions contrast with the English law changes in the opposite direction under Pt 10 of the Criminal Justice Act 2003. It remains unclear whether the Framework decision may operate to prevent an English retrial following a non-UK acquittal and whether there will also be associated extradition difficulties in such circumstances.

The absence of a European consensus on these procedural issues has inhibited the adoption of a uniform double jeopardy principle in international human rights law. However, a clear distinction is drawn in most states between the power of an appellate court to reopen proceedings and to order a retrial; and the prohibition on a second prosecution for the same offence, initiated by the prosecuting authorities without the involvement of an appellate court. **12–06**

The position in other jurisdictions is somewhat mixed. In eight other countries (including New Zealand and Scotland) no retrial following acquittal is possible in any circumstances. In Canada, an acquittal is final and can only be appealed by the Crown on a matter of law. If successful, the case can be sent back for retrial. The Crown's right to appeal on a question of law alone survived the double jeopardy provision in s.11(h) of Canadian Charter of Rights.[10] However, the Canadian Supreme Court has also held that others provisions in Quebec, which permitted a wider scope for Crown appeal, are unconstitutional.[11] Fresh evidence is not a ground for Crown Appeal. Australia has a procedure equivalent to an Attorney General's Reference on a point of law in English law,[12] whereby the prosecution can appeal for clarification of the law but the appellate decision cannot affect the finality of the acquittal. In *R. v Carroll*,[13] the High Court of

---

[9] Nevertheless, the Charter has already become an important reference document, and the ECJ has referred to it on several occasions in order to identify the fundamental rights which must be respected by the Community.

[10] *R. v Morgentaler, Smoling and Scott* [1988] 1 S.C.R. 30.

[11] *Corporation Professionnele des Medecins du Quebec v Thibault* [1988] S.C.R. 1033.

[12] Under s.36 of the Criminal Justice Act 1972.

[13] (2002) 194 A.L.R. 1.

Australia held that, where the defendant had given evidence at his trial for murder and his conviction had been quashed on appeal, his subsequent prosecution for perjury at his murder trial (the false evidence alleged being his denial of the killing) should have been stayed as an abuse because the prosecution inevitably sought to controvert the earlier acquittal regardless of the cogency and weight of any new evidence that the prosecution had. In South Africa, the Law Commission proposed restrictions on the prosecution's right of appeal against an acquittal on fact and it is *anticipated that they will be enacted*.[14]

In the United States the double jeopardy rule is so fundamental that it is afforded the highest legal status in the Fifth Amendment to the US Constitution: "nor shall any person be subject for the same offence to be twice put in jeopardy of life or limb".[15] In the international sphere, Art.10 of the International Criminal Tribunal for the Former Yugoslavia and Art.9 of the Special Court for Sierra Leone, for example, allow for the trial of a person by the international court for acts for which s/he has already been tried by a national court if these acts were characterised by the national court as ordinary crimes but go on to state that "No person shall be tried before a national court for acts for which he or she has already been tried by the [international] court".[16]

The wide international variation in definition, qualification and restriction of the double jeopardy or *ne bis in idem*[17] rule both in domestic laws and in many international conventions makes it currently impossible to describe it as a generally accepted principle of fairness, criminal justice or customary international law.[18] Moreover, protections in international human rights instruments do not generally extend to convictions (or equivalent) of foreign courts. Where two States have concurrent jurisdiction over an individual, international law does not prevent either State from re-prosecuting after an acquittal or conviction has been obtained in the other, unless treaty obligations can be applied to enforce *ne bis idem* with horizontal effect.[19]

C. ENGLAND AND WALES

12–07 The position in England and Wales is a hybrid. The defence may seek to reopen criminal proceedings which have resulted in a final verdict of guilty, even where

---

[14] South African Law Commission: *The Right of the Director of Public Prosecutions to Appeal on a Question of Facts* (Project 73—*Simplification of Criminal Procedure*) December 2000.

[15] See Brennan J. in *Ashe v Swenson* 397 US 435 at 451: "a guarantee that the State with all its resources and power [shall] not be allowed to make repeated attempts to convict an individual for an alleged offence, thereby subjecting him to embarrassment, expense and ordeal and compelling him to live in a continuing state of anxiety and insecurity".

[16] See para.12–16 below for the position in the International Criminal Court.

[17] "Not twice at the same thing".

[18] Van den Wyngaert C., and Ongena T., "*Ne bis in idem* Principle, Including the Issue of Amnesty" in Caessese A., Gaeta P. and Jones J.W.R.D., *The Rome Statute of the International Court: A Commentary* (OUP, 2002) at 705.

[19] See Ian Dennis *Prosecution Appeals and Retrial for Serious Offences* [2004] Crim. L.R. 619, 637 and Van den Wyngaert C, and Stessens G, *The International non bis in idem Principle: Resolving Some of the Unanswered Questions* (1999) 48 I.C.L.Q. 779.

all ordinary remedies have been exhausted and the verdict has acquired the force of *res judicata*. This power is exercised through the jurisdiction of the Court of Appeal to entertain an appeal out of time, and through the powers of the Criminal Cases Review Commission to refer a case back to the Court of Appeal. On such an appeal, the Court of Appeal may quash the conviction on the basis of fresh evidence, or a fundamental defect (such as material non-disclosure), subject always to the requirement that the new consideration is such as to render the conviction unsafe. In either case the Court of Appeal has, since 1988, had the power to order a retrial without infringing the prohibition on double jeopardy.

The rule against double jeopardy only operates to prevent re-prosecution on (substantially) the same facts as gave rise to an earlier acquittal. The House of Lords held in *R. v Z*[20] that the rule does not prevent evidence being adduced at a subsequent trial for a different offence which tends to show that the accused was in fact guilty of the offence for which he had been earlier acquitted.

Sections 54 to 56 of the Criminal Procedure and Investigations Act 1996 **12–08** introduced a new procedure whereby the prosecution may apply to reopen an acquittal which has acquired the force of *res judicata*, if there is convincing evidence that the acquittal was tainted by intimidation of a witness or juror. Again, the consequence of such an order is that the accused may be retried without infringing the prohibition on double jeopardy. The procedure applies where a person has been acquitted of an offence and either the defendant or another person has been convicted of an administration of justice offence involving the intimidation of a juror or witness in the proceedings which led to the acquittal.[21] In those circumstances, if it appears to the court before which the latter was convicted that "there is a real possibility that, but for the interference or intimidation, the acquitted person would not have been acquitted" the court shall certify that it so appears.[22] The power is not, however, to be exercised if, because of the lapse of time, or for any other reason, it would be contrary to the interests of justice to take proceedings against the acquitted person for the offence of which he has been acquitted.[23] Where such a certification is issued, the prosecution may apply to the High Court for an order quashing the acquittal.[24] The High Court is required to quash the acquittal if, but only if, four conditions are satisfied:

(a) It appears to the High Court that it is *likely* that, but for the interference or intimidation, the acquitted person would not have been acquitted[25];

(b) It does not appear to the High Court that, because of the lapse of time or for any other reason, it would be contrary to the interests of justice to take

---

[20] [2000] 2 A.C. 483, 2 Cr.App.R. 281—followed in New Zealand in *R. v Degman* [2001] 1 N.Z.L.R. 280 (CA) at 291, but not in Canada. *Cf. United States v Dowling* (1990) 493 US 342 at 347–50. See *R. v Terry* [2004] EWCA Crim 3252 for the precise ambit of *R. v Z*.
[21] S.54(1).
[22] S.54(2).
[23] Ss.54(2)(b) and 54(5).
[24] S.54(3).
[25] S.55(1).

proceedings against the acquitted person for the offence of which he has been acquitted[26];

(c) The acquitted person has been given a reasonable opportunity to make written representations to the court[27]; and

(d) It appears to the court that the conviction for the administration of justice offence will stand.[28]

The effect of an order quashing a conviction is that "proceedings may be taken against the acquitted person *for the offence of which he was acquitted*".[29] The Act does not permit the prosecution to bring proceedings for another offence based upon the same facts, even if that offence is less serious than the offence of which the accused was originally convicted.

Part 9 of the Criminal Justice Act 2003[30] introduces new rights of prosecution appeal against adverse rulings. The existing interlocutory rights of appeal to the Court of Appeal (for prosecution and defence) from rulings in preparatory hearings in serious fraud cases and cases of exceptional complexity are preserved.[31] Section 58 of the 2003 Act creates a general right of appeal (exercisable in all trials on indictment) against a terminating ruling by the trial judge—that is, a ruling which would otherwise result in the defendant's acquittal (e.g. a ruling of no case to answer). The prosecution can also appeal subsidiary non-terminating rulings if they are appealing a ruling of no case to answer. There are powers to expedite the appeal, and the trial continues pending the determination of appeal. The Court of Appeal can order a fresh trial or resumption of the trial. Section 62 also creates a prosecution right of appeal in respect of qualifying evidentiary rulings. These are rulings to exclude evidence which result in a substantial weakening of the prosecution case in a trial for a qualifying offence. The list of qualifying offences include various serious offences against the person, sexual and drug offences, robbery, criminal damage, war crimes and terrorism.[32] The list is narrower than that applicable to Pt 10. It is doubtful that an error of law by the trial judge in respect of an evidentiary or terminating ruling would constitute a "fundamental defect" in the proceedings (*cf.* tainted acquittals under ss.54 to 56 of the 1996 Act[33]). However, the defendant is not in fact acquitted by the terminating ruling until the prosecution appeal has failed,[34] so that the trial judge's ruling lacks finality. The Pt 9 prosecution rights of appeal are

---

[26] S.55(2).

[27] S.55(3).

[28] S.55(4). The court should not quash the conviction if, at the time the application is made, the time limit for appeal against conviction for the administration of justice offence has not expired, or an appeal is pending: s.55(6).

[29] S.54(4).

[30] Ss.57–61 were brought into force from April 4, 2005 (with transitional provisions) by S.I. 2005/150.

[31] By s.9 of the Criminal Justice Act 1987 and s.35 Criminal Procedure and Investigations Act 1996 respectively.

[32] Pt I of Sch.4.

[33] See further 12–08 above.

[34] S.58(11).

therefore unlikely to breach the double jeopardy protections of the Convention or the I.C.C.P.R.[35]

I. Part 10 of the Criminal Justice Act 2003

Part 10 of the Criminal Justice Act 2003[36] provides for the possibility of retrial **12–09** following acquittal by a jury or on appeal against conviction, verdict or finding for qualifying serious criminal offences where there is "new and compelling" evidence against the acquitted person and a retrial is "in the interests of justice". The power to quash an acquittal and order a retrial is not based on any defect or irregularity in the original trial. Although not explicit, the concept of an "unsafe acquittal" appears to underpin Pt 10. This far-reaching and controversial change to English law applies to 30 qualifying offences (including rape, murder, manslaughter, trafficking in Class A controlled drugs, terrorist offences, crimes against humanity, specified war crimes and genocide[37]) all punishable with life imprisonment.[38] The list is far wider than the Law Commission recommended.[39]

Unlike the 1996 Act, Pt 10 is of fully retrospective effect: it applies whether the acquittal was before or after the passing of the Act.[40] This will not necessarily contravene Art.7 of the Convention, which does not prohibit retrospective changes in the rules of criminal procedure so as to remove a bar or obstacle to a prosecution. Article 7 requires that the conduct in question constituted a crime at the time when the offence was committed: it is immaterial that the procedural rules in existence at the time of an acquittal or conviction prevented it from being reopened.[41] However, there will be no violation if the applicable law at the time of the retrial is the same as at the time of the original acquittal and the sentence imposed is no more severe than that which might originally have been imposed. The Law Commission did not consider Art.7 an obstacle to Pt 10's retrospectivity and the Joint Committee on Human Rights formed a similar view.[42] Nevertheless, the Law Commission had justified its recommendation for legislative retrospectivity by reference to new scientific techniques unavailable at the time (e.g. DNA), whereas Pt 10 does not limit "new evidence" to this category (see below). A long period of "double jeopardy" between the acquittal and the retrial ought to make it make a retrial less likely to be "in the interests of justice": as recognised in s.79(2). Although the retrospective effect of Pt 10 might not

---

[35] See 12–31 and 12–25 below (respec.).

[36] Bought into force from April 4, 2005 by S.I. 2005/150.

[37] Offences of hijacking, robbery with a firearm and s.18 wounding with intent were removed from the list included in the original Bill.

[38] Pt 1 of Sch.5.

[39] Law Com. No.267 (24.1.01) which, in general, was much weaker in its support of the rule against double jeopardy than its earlier *Double Jeopardy* Consultation Paper Law Com. No.156 (except that the latter proposed that the legislation apply to all offences). For a full discussion of the Report see paras 12–30 *et seq.* of the previous edition of this book.

[40] s.75(6).

[41] *cf. R. v Offen* [2001] 1 W.L.R. 253 at paras 84 to 90. See generally para.2–85 and Ch.10 above.

[42] Para.4.52 Law Com. No.267 and J.C.H.R. 2nd Report of 2002–03 on the Criminal Justice Bill at para.44. See in general para.2–85 and Ch.10 above.

infringe Art.7, a retrial might violate Art.6 or constitute an abuse of process in certain circumstances on grounds linked to the retrospectivity.

The legislative history of Pt 10 began with a recommendation in the Macpherson report into Stephen Lawrence's death that re-prosecution be considered where fresh and viable evidence is presented.[43] Nevertheless, it now seems there is no possibility that Pt 10 will ever be invoked against those suspected of his murder.[44] The subsequent Law Commission Consultation Papers and final Report and a Home Affairs Select Committee Report[45] all recommended reform of the double jeopardy rule. The proposals attracted substantial public interest at all stages. The responses from consultees revealed a deep division of opinion on the issue. A majority of individual judges who responded supported the new exception, but the Council of H.M. Circuit Judges was against it. A majority of individual practitioners who responded supported the change, but it was opposed by the Criminal Bar Association, the London Criminal Courts Solicitors Association and the Criminal Law Committee of the Law Society. The police and prosecuting authorities were in favour of change, most of the academic community against it. The public were equally divided. In the end, the Law Commission appears to have opted for a middle path—a pragmatic compromise between the two opposing views. Lord Justice Auld's review of the criminal courts[46] endorsed the Law Commission's proposals, which were adopted in White Papers[47] and duly became Pt 10.

12–10   There are a number of preconditions before an acquittal can be quashed and a re-trial ordered under Pt 10. The prosecutor must apply to the Court of Appeal[48] for an order quashing an acquittal and ordering a re-trial. The DPP's written consent is required, and may only be given if he is satisfied that there is "new and compelling" evidence against the acquitted person on the qualifying offence, that a retrial is in the public interest, and that any retrial would not be inconsistent with the United Kingdom's obligations under Arts 31 and 34 of the Treaty on European Union relating to the *ne bis in idem* principle.[49] The DPP also has powers to limit or prevent further investigation into the qualifying offence.[50] The Court of Appeal may only quash the acquittal and order a retrial if it is satisfied that there is "new and compelling" evidence against the acquitted person on the qualifying offence and that a retrial is "in the public interest".[51] Only one

---

[43] Recommendation 38 of *The Stephen Lawrence Inquiry—Report* Cm 4262–1 (1999).

[44] See, e.g. *The Observer*, June 5, 2002. There has been a great deal of publicity surrounding the three prime suspects, the original investigation was flawed and there was a private prosecution which resulted in acquittals because of the absence of any reliable (identification) evidence.

[45] *Double Jeopardy Rule* 3rd Report of 1999–2000 by the Home Affairs Committee of the House of Commons.

[46] *Review of the Criminal Courts of England & Wales: Report* (TSO London, 2001) pp.627 to 634.

[47] *Criminal Justice: The Way Ahead* (2001) Cm 5074; *Justice for All* (2002) Cm 5563.

[48] *cf.* Under the CPIA 1996, the application is to the High Court.

[49] S.76(3)–(4).

[50] S.85.

[51] S.77–9.

application to the court on any acquittal is possible: there can be no triple jeopardy.[52]

Part 10 also includes detailed provisions concerning authorisation of investigations after acquittal, reporting restrictions in retrials, arrest, custody and bail of acquitted persons being re-investigated.

Part 10 is thus a far-reaching exception to the ancient plea in bar of *autrefois*   **12–11**
acquit going beyond the exception first created in the 1996 Act, and never yet applied, relating to tainted acquittals. Part 10 does not attempt to codify the law of double jeopardy or any of the exceptions identified in *Connelly v DPP* or *R. v Beedie (Thomas Sim)*.[53] The primary justification for the *autrefois acquit* rule is one of finality, upon which critics of the legislation relied heavily. Finality is a safeguard against oppression[54] and unfair delay, and promotes probity and diligence in the investigation of crime. The Government remained unpersuaded and opted for a much wider list of qualifying offences than was originally proposed. It placed greater weight on the accuracy of outcome of proceedings[55] than finality and, consistent with its self-professed desire to "re-tilt" the criminal justice system away from defendants,[56] appears to be seeking a greater symmetry between convictions and acquittals.[57] Clearly these are issues of principle and go to the heart of criminal procedural law.[58] To date only one application, *R. v D*,[59] has been heard by the Court of Appeal under Pt 10. The Respondent's acquittal for murder was quashed and a re-trial was ordered. D was tried twice in 1991 for a murder committed in 1989. On both occasions, the jury failed to agree and the Respondent was formally acquitted. In 1999 he confessed to the murder, and was charged with two counts of perjury relating to his evidence at his earlier trials. He pleaded guilty and was sentenced to six years' imprisonment. Following the

---

[52] S.76(5). Unless the final acquittal was in a retrial under Pt 10 and was "tainted" under the CPIA 1996: see Law Com No.267 at paras 4.97, 5.31 and 5.33(2).

[53] [1964] A.C. 1254, [1998] Q.B. 356 (respec.) and Law Commission Report Pt 2. *R. v Beedie* was applied most recently in *R. v Phipps* [2005] EWCA Crim 33, where a prosecution for dangerous driving was stayed as an abuse of process because it arose out of the same facts as had led to a conviction for driving with excess alcohol.

[54] "Towards the 13th century the [double jeopardy] rule attained particular significance in England. As the state began to institute action against an individual at its own discretion, certain restraints were placed on the prosecutor's power to institute criminal proceedings. The rule then began to realise its most important function: protection of the accused against arbitrary exercise of state power . . . the idea is that the accused ought to be protected against harassment by the state . . . The rule's broader purpose . . . is to prevent abuse by the state of the criminal process": Jordan, *Appeal by the prosecution and the right of the accused to be protected against double jeopardy: A Comparative Perspective* (1999) C.I.L.S.A. 1.

[55] Accuracy is not the only value at stake, hence the principle that "a conviction may be unsafe even where there is no doubt about guilt but the trial process has been vitiated by serious unfairness or significant misdirection" *R. v Davis, Rowe and Johnson* [2001] 1 Cr.App.R. 115. See generally paras 17–25 *et seq.* below.

[56] See, e.g. the White Paper *One Step Ahead: A 21st Century Strategy to Defeat Organised Crime* (2004) Cm 6167 at para.6.3.

[57] *cf.* the rights of prosecution appeal against adverse rulings in Pt 9 of the Criminal Justice Act 2003.

[58] Roberts, *Double Jeopardy Law Reform: A Criminal Justice Commentary* (2002) 65 M.L.R. 393.

[59] [2006] EWCA 1354, [2007] 1 All E.R. 593.

coming into force of Pt 10, the DPP sought to quash D's acquittal for murder on the basis that his confession was "new and compelling" evidence. D accepted that this was "new" evidence and made no submission, or concession, as to whether it was "compelling". D's case was predicated on the interests of justice pre-condition, which he argued was not fulfilled.[60]

Acquittals

12–12 An acquittal for the purposes of Pt 10 is defined by s.75, and includes an acquittal by a jury or on appeal against conviction, but excludes a finding that the accused was unfit to plead but did the act in question or a verdict of not guilty by reason of insanity. What remains unclear, however, is where the accused is acquitted of an offence but convicted of a lesser alternative offence, whether there could be an application to quash the acquittal and permit a retrial where there is new evidence that the accused was guilty of the more serious offence. Thus although Pt 10 would appear to permit a retrial for murder, for example, where the accused was previously only found guilty of manslaughter, only the "rule" in *R. v Elrington*[61] and the uncertain "interests of justice" test would seems to militate against it: *cf. R. v Hoogstraten.*[62] In such circumstances, an application to stay of proceedings on the ground of abuse of process (which is possible in wider circumstances than the narrow *autrefois acquit* rule itself permits: see, e.g. *Connelly*) is also likely. It is a little unclear whether on a Pt 10 retrial for murder following an acquittal of murder, the jury would be entitled to return a manslaughter verdict: the quashing of an acquittal under the Act does not explicitly quash all acquittals of lesser alternative verdicts and so conviction of the lesser offence might still be prohibited by *autrefois acquit.*[63]

The evidence pre-conditions

Central to the new double jeopardy exception in Pt 10 is a requirement of "new and compelling evidence", of which the DPP must be satisfied[64] before he can give consent for an application to quash an acquittal, and of which the Court of Appeal must be satisfied[65] before it can make any such order and order a re-trial. The current Code for Crown Prosecutors refers to these cases as "exceptional".[66]

12–13 Evidence is "new" if "it was not adduced in the proceedings in which the person was acquitted (nor, if those were appeal proceedings, in earlier proceedings to which the appeal related)".[67] The "new" evidence need not have existed or come to light only after the acquittal—it may have been within the prosecution's knowledge or possession before trial but not adduced. Although the Attorney

---

[60] On which see below at para.12.15.
[61] (1861) 121 E.R. 170.
[62] [2003] EWCA 3642.
[63] See ss.75(1), (2), (7) and 76(1).
[64] Ss.76(4)(a) and 78.
[65] Ss.77(1)(a) and 78.
[66] Para.12.3 of the Code for Crown Prosecutors (5th edn)—November 16, 2004.
[67] Ss.78(2).

General gave an undertaking (agreed with the DPP) that an application for retrial would not be made where the "new evidence" was not originally deployed merely for tactical reasons,[68] as Lord Bingham has noted in another context, "it is not however acceptable that interpretation and application of a statutory provision bearing on the liberty of the subject should be governed by implication, concession and undertaking".[69] Under the Bill as originally drafted, evidence was "new" if "it was not available or known to an officer or prosecutor at or before the time of the acquittal". Section 78(2) as enacted, however, contains a much broader definition of "new". However, s.79(2)(c) requires the Court of Appeal, when deciding whether to quash an acquittal and order a re-trial, to consider whether the new evidence would have been adduced in the earlier proceedings but for the failure by the prosecution to act with due diligence or expedition. The due diligence requirement relates both to the discovery of the evidence (is it likely that the evidence would have been discovered by diligent/expeditious investigators?) and its use (had it been discovered, would it have been used by a diligent prosecutor?). The categories of new evidence are not limited: unsolicited confessions, relevant witnesses who come forward after trial, new scientific evidence (using new techniques or existing techniques on new samples which were not previously available) are all possibilities.

Evidence is "compelling" if it is "reliable, substantial and, in the context of the **12–14** outstanding issues, it appears highly probative of the case against the accused person".[70] Outstanding issues are defined as those in dispute in the proceedings in which the person was acquitted (or, in appeal proceedings, any other issues remaining in dispute from earlier proceedings to which the appeal related).[71]

The evidence pre-conditions do not, therefore, expressly require the Court of Appeal to predict the likelihood of the new evidence affecting the outcome of the original trial or the likelihood of conviction on a re-trial. The court need not hypothesise about effects of evidence on juries—its own evaluation of the strength of the evidence suffices. It is noteworthy that Pt 10 rejects both the test of "new and viable" evidence, suggested in the Macpherson Report, and the test of "evidence of new or newly discovered facts . . . which could affect the outcome of the case", contained in ECHR Art.4(2) of Protocol 7.

Interests of justice pre-condition

Under s.79 the Court of Appeal must also be satisfied that it is in the "interests **12–15** of justice" to quash an acquittal and order a retrial. In so doing, it must have regard to, in particular: (a) whether existing circumstances make a fair trial unlikely: (b) the length of time since the qualifying offence was allegedly committed: (c) the likelihood that the new evidence would have been adduced in the earlier proceedings but for the failure by the prosecution to act with due diligence or expedition; and (d) whether, since those proceedings (or, if later,

---

[68] Hansard HL col.710 (Nov 4, 2003): Taylor *et al.*, *Blackstone's Guide to the Criminal Justice Act 2003* (OUP, 2004) at p.113.
[69] *A and others v Home Secretary* [2005] 2 A.C. 68.
[70] S.79(3).
[71] S.78(4).

since the commencement of Pt 10), the prosecution has failed to act with due diligence or expedition. The inherent difficulties in s.79(a) in assessing in advance whether prejudicial publicity prevents a fair trial are apparent when contrasting cases such as *R. v Taylor*[72] with *R. v Stone*.[73] It is difficult exactly to reconcile s.79(b) with the decision in *Attorney-General's Reference (No.2 of 2001)*[74] that a trial should only be stayed following a breach of the reasonable time guarantee within Art.6 if a fair trial is impossible; other remedies can often adequately compensate for delay. Would a retrial be less likely to be fair because of lapse of time than a first trial? Under s.79(c) the Court is obliged to consider the competence of the original investigation and prosecution and whether the new evidence could competently have been obtained earlier. It is notable that a negligent failure to obtain and adduce the new evidence is not a pre-condition to quashing an acquittal, only a factor to be taken into account. There is obviously a heightened tension between the State seeking to re-try a person acquitted following a negligent prosecution or investigation and the desire of the victim, or their family, to see justice done, particularly in such cases. In *R. v D*, the Respondent argued that his re-trial was not in the interests of justice for three reasons: (1) D's confessions were made in the reliance on the belief, induced by his legal advisors and the police, that he could not be prosecuted for murder; (2) a fair trial was unlikely given the prejudicial publicity since acquittal, including programmes broadcast on national television, and the unavoidable reference at any retrial to the previous trials; (3) the 17-year delay between the offence and retrial, the seven-year delay between confession and trial and the nine-month delay between the coming into force of the Act and the application for a re-trial. The Court of Appeal rejected all three arguments, concluding in particular that D was not induced to make his confessions by being told that he could not be re-tried for murder.

Note that if the Court is satisfied that it is in the interests of justice to quash an acquittal and order a retrial, there is no residual discretion not to do so. The "quasi-discretion" in s.79 obliges the Court to make an order once the pre-conditions have been satisfied.

Foreign acquittals

12–16 Part 10 also applies to acquittals in non-UK courts, if the offence would amount to a qualifying offence in the UK.[75] The Human Rights Committee has held that equivalent provisions do not breach Art.14(7) of the I.C.C.P.R.[76] This is to be contrasted with the *ne bis in idem* principle as set out in Art.20 of the Rome Statute of the International Criminal Court, which prohibits a State from re-trying someone for the same crimes for which they have already been tried by the

---

[72] (1994) 98 Cr.App.R. 361.

[73] [2001] Crim. L.R. 465: see Taylor *et al.*, *Blackstone's Guide to the Criminal Justice Act 2003* (OUP, 2004) at p.114.

[74] [2004] 2 W.L.R. 1.

[75] S.75(4). *Cf.* the concept of "double criminality" in extradition law. Note that the Scottish "not proven" verdict is not an acquittal for the purposes of s.75(1) and cannot be quashed to enable a retrial.

[76] *AP v Italy* (204/86) at para.7.3, followed in *ARJ v Australia* (692/96) at para.6.4: Art.14(7) "only prevents double jeopardy with regard to an offence adjudicated in a given state"

International Criminal Court, and also prohibits the court from trying someone who has already been tried by the State for the same conduct. Article 20(3) permits a second trial on the same facts only where the first trial "was designed to shield a suspect from prosecution elsewhere, or was not independent, impartial, or consistent with an intent to bring the perpetrator to justice".[77] Section 75(4) of the 2003 Act is much more open-ended, and it is unclear precisely which factors the DPP or Court of Appeal would have to consider when deciding whether to order a retrial. It is possible that there might be circumstances in which it would be easier to reopen a foreign acquittal than one obtained in an English court. The s.75 grounds for reopening foreign acquittals are wider than the Law Commission recommended, and lack international comity. If, for example, a foreign court did not take into account material held in England which was not (for whatever reason) passed on to the foreign investigators, s.75 is so ambiguous and sparse that it is unclear whether this would be at all relevant. More fundamentally, it is difficult to understand how s.75 will operate in respect of acquittals from Schengen states, when Art.54 of the Schengen Convention contains no reservation equivalent to that created by Pt 10 or Art.4(2) of Protocol 7 of the European Convention.[78] In practice, there are likely to be a small number of cases where the English courts would have jurisdiction to retry someone in England following an acquittal abroad, given that relatively few offences committed abroad are within English jurisdiction. There may also be extradition issues where there has been an acquittal abroad.

The position in relation to Scottish acquittals is anomalous.[79] Scottish law does not permit a retrial in Scotland following an acquittal in Scotland in any circumstances. In recognition of the high status of double jeopardy in Scottish law and the lack of any border control between England and Scotland, Pt 10 does not permit a retrial for the same offence in England following an acquittal in Scotland, when, in equivalent circumstances, a foreign (non-UK) acquittal would not operate as an absolute bar to retrial.[80] Even the Scottish "not proven" verdict is an absolute bar to any retrial in England under Pt 10.   **12–17**

Procedurally, a prosecutor in seeking a retrial following a foreign acquittal for the same conduct applies for an order determining whether the foreign acquittal is an *autrefois acquit* or a *ne bis in idem* bar to re-trial in the UK and, if so, to have the bar removed.[81] Parallel conditions concerning the DPP's consent apply. The DPP must consider s.76(4)(c) (which refers to Arts 31 and 34 of the Treaty of European Union) when granting consent to re-prosecute. This is wide enough to   **12–18**

---

[77] See Law Commission Report (above) at para.6.14.
[78] Art.54: "A person who has been finally judged by a Contracting Party may not be prosecuted by another Contracting Party for the same offences provided that, where he is sentenced, the sentence has been served or is currently being served or can no longer be carried out under the sentencing laws of the Contracting Party". See also Arts 55 to 58.
[79] The English law status of murders in Scotland complicates the position further: *Hirst* [1995] C.L.J. 488: Taylor *et al.*, *Blackstone's Guide to the Criminal Justice Act 2003* (OUP, 2004) at p.103.
[80] S.75(4).
[81] Ss.77(4), 78, 79 and 77(3).

include EU agreements between States on double jeopardy and attempts to reflect the mutual recognition of decisions and judgments in criminal matters. Were it otherwise, the UK would have been politically handicapped in negotiations with foreign states on co-operation in law enforcement matters, particularly since *ne bis in idem* is revered in many jurisdictions as a significant safeguard against excessive action by one state to reach out and punish nationals of another.

12–19   As detailed below, *ne bis in idem* is to be the subject of legislative measures across the European Union as part of the attempted harmonisation of criminal law. Central to many international instruments are the twin components of mutual trust and confidence in the legal systems to which the instruments relate, which necessarily includes minimum procedural safeguards and invariably *ne bis in idem*.[82] EU states, however, are not alone in applying this principle, but there is no mandatory requirement for the Court of Appeal to consider *ne bis in idem* treaty obligations (equivalent to Arts 31 and 34 of the Treaty of the European Union) when considering an application under Pt 10 in relation to an acquittal in a non-EU state.

European *ne bis in idem* developments

12–20   Articles 31 and 34 of the Treaty of the European Union refer to the EU powers to extend criminal and judicial cooperation, in particular, by the creation of an Area of Freedom, Security and Justice (AFSJ) as set out in the Amsterdam Treaty (to be amended by the Constitution on Europe). The EU's objective is to create a judicial zone within the Union by harmonisation and approximation of law and the mutual recognition of criminal judgments via the primary mechanism of Framework Decisions. A fundamental feature of the creation of the AFSJ is the establishment of basic protections for the defendant.[83] *Ne bis in idem* is a key provision in this regard, being allied to the concept of a Europe without internal frontiers and based on mutual trust. Accordingly, there is currently a proposal for a Framework Decision on *ne bis in idem*.[84] If implemented, all EU countries will have to bring their laws into line with this approximating decision. This is the reason for the proposals within the Criminal Justice Act 2003 allowing for this to happen, although it is not entirely clear whether Pt 10 could conform with it.

---

[82] *Current Law Statutes Guide to the Criminal Justice Act 2003* (Sweet & Maxwell, 2004) at pp.44–88.

[83] *cf. Programme of Measures to Implement the Principle of Mutual Recognition of Decisions in Criminal Matters*, O.J. (2001) C 12/10. Under the chapter heading *Taking Account of Final Criminal Judgements Already Delivered by the Courts in Another Member State*, Art.1.1. states "*Ne bis in idem* Aim: To strengthen legal certainty in the Union by ensuring that a final conviction handed down by a criminal court in one Member State is not challenged in another Member State. The fact that such a decision has been handed down in one Member State must preclude a further prosecution in another Member State for the acts that have already been judged. This aim has been partially realised in Articles 54 to 57 of the Convention implementing the Schengen Agreement."

[84] Initiated by Greece: Initiative of the Hellenic Republic with a view to adopting a Council Framework Decision concerning the application of the *ne bis in idem* principle *Official Journal* C–100, 26/04/2003 P. 0024–0027.

However, the negotiations on the Framework Decision have been suspended **12-21** pending a ruling by the European Court of Justice on the *Miraglia* case,[85] which concerns the definition of "final decision". A mutual assistance request was made by Italy to the Netherlands in a drugs case. The Netherlands had previously closed the case in view of the Italian proceedings, and refused the request as, under its law, the closure of the case rendered it a "final decision". The case will consider Art.54 of the Schengen Convention[86] which governs *ne bis in idem* in respect of the area of Europe governed by the Schengen Convention. It has so far been difficult to achieve consensus on the definition of "final decision" but the *Miraglia* decision may provide the necessary breakthrough. In addition, on December 23, 2005 the Commission issued a Green Paper on Conflicts of Jurisdiction and the Principle of *ne bis in idem* in Criminal Proceedings. The Green Paper canvassed views on the scope of the *ne bis in idem* principle, and the meaning of "final decision", in relation to which the Commission put forward the following definition: "a decision, which prohibits a new criminal prosecution according to the national law of the Member State where it has been taken, unless this national prohibition runs contrary to the objectives of the TEU."[87] The consultation process was completed on March 31, 2006 and the intention at the time of writing is to present a proposal for a new Framework Decision. In its response to the Green Paper, the United Kingdom Government made clear its concern to ensure that the exceptions in Pt 10 of the Criminal Justice Act 2003 are accommodated within any new European framework.[88]

When the European Court of Justice previously considered the meaning of "final **12-22** decision"in the joint cases of *Gozutok and Brugge*,[89] it ruled:

"Article 54 of the CISA [*ne bis in idem*], the objective of which is to ensure that no one is prosecuted on the same facts in several Member States on account of his having exercised his right to freedom of movement, cannot play a useful role in bringing about the full attainment of that objective unless it also applies to decisions definitively discontinuing prosecutions in a Member State, even where such decisions are adopted without the involvement of a court and do not take the form of a judicial decision."

The Court also pointed to the incongruity that would arise if Art.54 CISA were **12-23** confined to judicial decisions: in reality only serious offences would be covered and there would be no scope for allowing simplified methods of administering justice for less serious crimes. These cases have raised concerns as to whether forum shopping will emerge for the trial of criminal matters, particularly where

---

[85] Case C–469/03 (Mar 15, 2005, 5th chamber). The E.C.J. will also consider Schengen commencement issues in the *van Esbroeck* case (C–442/04—reference for preliminary ruling): prosecution in Belgium for drugs offence of which defendant was already convicted by and served sentence in Norway, prior to the latter's implementation of Schengen acquis. The reference also concerns whether an import offence in one country is the "same offence" (under Art.54) as an export offence in another.

[86] Art.54: "A person who has been finally judged by a Contracting Party may not be prosecuted by another Contracting Party for the same offences provided that, where he is sentenced, the sentence has been served or is currently being served or can no longer be carried out under the sentencing laws of the Contracting Party." See also Arts 55 to 58.

[87] COM (2005) 696.

[88] Available at *http://europa.eu*.

[89] Cases C–187/01 and C–385/01 [2003] E.C.R. I–1345 (February 11, 2003).

more lenient treatment or various forms of sanctions are available. Will a "Brussels Convention" become necessary to determine the choice of law in such cases?

12–24 It is seems clear from the *Gozutoic and Brugge* decision, above, that *ne bis in idem*, when applied within a context of mutual recognition in criminal proceedings in the EU, should be given a broad interpretation allowing for the differences in what is perceived to be a "final decision" in the various Member States. Indeed, the Court has also stated that the *ne bis in idem* principle constitutes a general principle of Community law which is applicable regardless of any legislative provision.[90]

D. ARTICLE 14 OF THE INTERNATIONAL COVENANT ON CIVIL AND POLITICAL RIGHTS

12–25 The drafting of the I.C.C.P.R. was carried out by the United Nations Human Rights Commission in parallel with the drafting of the Convention by the Council of Europe in the immediate aftermath of the Second World War. The two organisations worked closely together on the texts, and the Council of Europe relied in part on the drafts prepared by the Human Rights Commission.[91] The I.C.C.P.R. was not, however, finally adopted by the General Assembly of the United Nations until 1966, and did not enter into force until 1976. It was ratified by the UK in 1976 and is part of its international law obligations, but it has not been incorporated nor is there any individual right of petition to the Human Rights Committee under the Optional Protocol. There are 67 signatories and 160 State Parties to the Covenant. The rights contained in the I.C.C.P.R. are broadly similar in their content to those contained in the Convention, although there are a number of significant differences.

12–26 Article 14(7) of the I.C.C.P.R. provides that:

> "No one shall be liable to be tried or punished again for an offence for which he has already been finally convicted or acquitted in accordance with the law and penal procedure of each country."

Article 14 applies both to the reopening of a conviction and to the reopening of an acquittal. Read literally, it therefore prohibits even the power of an appellate court to quash a criminal conviction and to order a retrial if fresh evidence or a procedural defect is discovered after the ordinary appeals process has been concluded.

12–27 In the drafting process which led to the adoption of the I.C.C.P.R. the Committee of Experts of the Council of Europe noted that in many European states it was permissible to reopen criminal proceedings which had acquired the force of *res judicata*, where there had been serious procedural flaws or fresh evidence had

---

[90] *X v European Central Bank.* Case T–333/99 (October 18, 2001).

[91] The interrelation between the I.C.C.P.R. and the Convention is explained in Cohen-Jonathon, *La Convention Europeenne des Droits de L'Homme* (Paris, 1989), at p.15ff.

become available.[92] They considered such procedures to be arguably inconsistent with Art.14(7) and recommended that states which permitted the reopening of criminal proceedings should submit a formal reservation. Reservations were submitted by Austria,[93] Denmark,[94] Finland,[95] Iceland,[96] the Netherlands,[97] Norway[98] and Sweden.[99]

In its General Comment on Art.14(7)[100] however, the United Nations Human   **12–28**
Rights Committee, the treaty body charged with implementing the I.C.C.P.R., expressed the view that the reopening of criminal proceedings "justified by exceptional circumstances", did not infringe the principle of double jeopardy (*ne bis in idem*), even in respect of those states which had not lodged a reservation. The Committee drew a distinction between the "resumption" of criminal proceedings, which it considered to be permitted by Art.14(7), and "retrial" which was expressly forbidden:

> "In considering state reports, differing views have often been expressed as to the scope of paragraph 7 of Article 14. Some states parties have even felt the need to make reservations in relation to procedures for the resumption of criminal cases. It seems to the Committee that most states parties make a clear distinction between a resumption of a trial justified by exceptional circumstances and a retrial prohibited pursuant to the principle of *ne bis in idem* as contained in paragraph 7. This understanding of the meaning of *ne bis in idem* may encourage states parties to reconsider their reservations to Article 14, paragraph 7."

The distinction between "resumption" and "retrial" is not one which has pre-   **12–29**
viously been expressly recognised in the law of England and Wales.[101] However, as we have explained above, it is a distinction which is, in substance, reflected in the power of the Court of Appeal to order a retrial following an appeal brought out of time or on a reference by the Criminal Cases review Commission, and in the statutory provisions permitting the reopening of an acquittal tainted by

---

[92] CE Doc H (70) 7, 40f. para.149.
[93] Nowak pp.750–751, para.4(c).
[94] Nowak p.753, para.2(b).
[95] Nowak pp.753–754, para.6.
[96] Nowak pp.757–758, para.4.
[97] Nowak p.765.
[98] Nowak p.765.
[99] Nowak p.766.
[100] Gen C 13/21. Para.19, reproduced in Nowak pp.857–861. There have been over 200 Human Rights Committee cases on Art.14 I.C.C.P.R. Most are complaints from prisoners on death row about the fairness of their trials.
[101] The distinction between resumption and retrial has been expressly rejected by the Inter-American Commission of Human Rights (IAC). Article 8(4) of the American Convention on Human Rights (A.C.H.R.) provides: "An accused person acquitted by a non-appealable judgment shall not be subjected to a new trial for the same cause". In the *Garcia Case* (Case No.10.006 (Peru) 1994 Annual Report 71 at 102) the Commission observed that on a literal reading Art. 8(4) referred only to a "new trial" and did not therefore expressly prohibit the "reopening" of criminal proceedings. The Commission held however that the protection afforded by Art. 8(4) "implicitly includes those cases in which reopening a case has the effect of reviewing questions of fact and law which have come to have the authority of *res judicata*". The approach of the IAC may be explained by the fact that Art. 8(4) of the A.C.H.R. applies only in relation to acquittals, and not in relation to convictions.

intimidation.[102] The Crown Prosecution Service can also resume or "re-start" *discontinued* proceedings without infringing the rule against double jeopardy, because in discontinued prosecutions there has been no final determination of guilt or innocence. The current guidance gives examples of "rare cases where a new look at the original decision [to discontinue] shows that it was clearly wrong",[103] "cases which are stopped so that more evidence which is likely to be available in the fairly near future can be collected and prepared" and "cases which are stopped because of a lack of evidence but where more significant evidence is discovered later".[104]

12–30 The dividing line between what is permitted by Art.14(7) and what is forbidden thus rests primarily upon the involvement of an appellate court. Article 14(7) permits a state's prosecuting authorities to apply to "reopen" an acquittal, in exceptional circumstances, after it has the quality of *res judicata*; but it prevents the prosecuting authorities from bringing fresh criminal proceedings on their own initiative. This distinction has taken firm root in European human rights law, and is now reflected in Art.4(2) of Protocol 7 to the European Convention.

E. ARTICLE 4 OF PROTOCOL 7

I. General

12–31 When the Convention was drafted in 1950, the original signatory states made no express reference to the prohibition on double jeopardy. In its early caselaw the Commission left open the question whether the principle could be implied into the right to a fair trial in Art.6.[105] However, in 1983, in *S v Federal Republic of Germany*,[106] the Commission held that "the Convention guarantees neither expressly nor by implication the principle of *ne bis in idem*". Shortly after this decision, on November 22, 1984, Protocol 7 to the Convention was opened for signature. It entered into force, in respect of those states which had ratified it, on November 1, 1988. The UK has not ratified it, is not bound by it in international or national law, but has said that it intends to ratify it.[107]

12–32 Article 4(1) embodies the principle of double jeopardy as it applies to the unilateral action of a prosecuting authority, or private prosecutor. The Explanatory Report to Protocol 7[108] makes it clear that the words "under the jurisdiction of the same state" are intended to limit the operation of Art.4 to the national

---

[102] *viz.* The Criminal Procedure and Investigations Act 1996, ss.54 to 56 and Pt 10 of the Criminal Justice Act 2003.
[103] Para.12.2 (a) of the Code for Crown Prosecutors (5th edn)—November 16, 2004. *Cf. DPP v Taylor* [2004] EWHC Admin 1554.
[104] Paras 12.2 (b) to (c) of the Code for Crown Prosecutors (5th edn)—November 16, 2004.
[105] See, for example, *X v Austria* (1970) 35 C.D. 151.
[106] (1983) 39 D.R. 43.
[107] *Rights Brought Home* Cmnd.3782, (1997), para.4.15. It is due to be signed after laws concerning spousal inequality have been amended.
[108] CE Doc H (83) 3.

level.[109] Article 4(1) does not therefore prohibit successive prosecutions for the same offence in different countries,[110] and thus appears to be narrower than the domestic rules on double jeopardy, which have been assumed to encompass a conviction before a foreign court.[111]

As to the degree of finality required before Art.4(1) can be invoked, the Explana-   **12–33** tory Report states that "the principle established in this provision applies only after the person has been finally acquitted or convicted in accordance with the law and penal procedure of the state concerned".[112] A decision is to be regarded as final;

> "if, according to the traditional expression, it has acquired the force of *res judicata*. This is the case when it is irrevocable, that is to say when no further ordinary remedies are available or when the parties have exhausted such remedies or have permitted the time limit to expire without availing themselves of them".[113]

Article 4(2) permits a case to be "reopened", in accordance with the provisions   **12–34** of domestic law, "if there is evidence of new or newly discovered facts", or if there has been "a fundamental defect in the previous proceedings". In either case the new consideration must be such as could have an affect on the outcome of the case. It thus preserves the power of an appellate court to overturn an acquittal or conviction outside the ordinary appeals process, and to order a retrial. So far as the prosecution are concerned, this exceptional power may only be exercised on the two grounds specified in Art.4(2). However, the Explanatory Report makes clear that Art.4 imposes no limitation on the grounds upon which an appellate court may reopen criminal proceedings to the benefit of the defence.[114]

The exceptions permitted by Art.4(2) have their origins in the practice of those   **12–35** European states which submitted reservations to Art.14(7) of the I.C.C.P.R.,[115] and in the approach taken by the United Nations Human Rights Committee in its General Comment on Art.14.[116] In relation to acquittals, the fundamental defect exception is now reflected in ss.54 to 56 of the Criminal Procedure and Investigations Act 1996 (CPIA), which provide a means of reopening an acquittal which is tainted by intimidation.

There is very little guidance in the Court's caselaw concerning the scope of the   **12–36** fresh evidence exception in Art.4(2). There are, however, two limitations in the

---

[109] Explanatory Report at para.27.

[110] The United Nations Human Rights Committee has adopted the same construction in relation to Art.14(7) of the I.C.C.P.R. *AP v Italy* (Application No.204. 1986, para.7.3).

[111] *R. v Roche* (1775) 1 Leach 134; *R. v Aughet* 13 Cr.App.R. 101; *R. v Lavercombe* [1988] Crim. L.R. 435; *R. v Thomas* [1985] Q.B. 604. *Cf. R. v Beedie* [1998] Q.B. 356, where the Court of Appeal held that the plea of *autrefois acquit* was confined to a prosecution for the same offence in law.

[112] Explanatory Report at para.29.

[113] Explanatory Memorandum at para.22, adopting the commentary on Art.1(a) of the European Convention on the International Validity of Criminal Judgments (1970).

[114] Para.31 states: "Furthermore, this article does not prevent a reopening of the proceedings in favour of the convicted person and any other changing of the judgment to the benefit of the convicted person".

[115] See para.12–27 above.

[116] See para.12–28 above.

wording of Art.4(2) itself. The evidence must be such as "could affect the outcome of the case" and it must be evidence of "a new or newly discovered fact". The first requirement is analogous to the condition in s.55(1) of the CPIA in relation to tainted acquittals: the evidence must be such that it is *likely* that if it has been presented to the trial court, the accused would not have been acquitted. This obviously involves a requirement that the evidence must be credible and relevant. But it also involves a requirement that the evidence must be sufficiently probative of guilt to have a significant and substantial effect on the outcome of the case.

12–37   Turning to the requirement for evidence of "new or newly discovered facts", this requirement is not intended to confine the operation of Art.4(2) to wholly new factual elements in the case. The Explanatory Memorandum makes it clear that the term "new or newly discovered facts" includes "new means of proof relating to previously existing facts".[117] However, in using the words "new or newly discovered", Art.4(2) obviously contemplates evidence which was not available to the prosecuting authorities at the time of the trial. This caters for the position where a new witness comes forward, or new scientific techniques produce incriminating evidence which was not previously available. A further possible consequence relates to changes in the rules governing the admissibility of evidence. If the law were amended so as to render admissible evidence which the prosecution had previously been unable to adduce, such evidence might be thought to constitute a "new means of proof relating to previously existing facts", in the words of the Explanatory Report. This would of course involve a retrospective application of the criminal law, but the Commission has in the past held that the retrospective application of an important precedent in the law of evidence was not in violation of Art.7.[118] Article 4(2) does not appear to extend to new evidence which was, or could have been, available at trial but was not adduced by the prosecution for some other reason, as is permitted under s.78(2) Criminal Justice Act 2003.[119] Contrary to the Law Commission's Report, under s.78(5), the admissibility of the new evidence at the original trial is irrelevant. Thus, for example, intercept evidence, which is inadmissible in a criminal trial (by the Regulation of Investigatory Powers Act 2000) but the admissibility of which is currently under review,[120] might be deployable to retry an acquitted person under Pt 10, subject only to the "interests of justice" test.

II. The Strasbourg Caselaw

12–38   The first case in which the European Court of Human Rights considered Art.4 of Protocol 7 was *Gradinger v Austria*.[121] The applicant was convicted of a criminal

---

[117] Explanatory Report at paras 30–31.

[118] *X v United Kingdom* (1976) 3 D.R. 95.

[119] See paras 12–08 *et seq.* above.

[120] See e.g. White Paper: *One Step Ahead, a 21st Century Strategy to Defeat Organised Crime* (March 2004; Cmnd. Paper 6167). The Joint Committee on Human Rights concluded that "the case for relaxing the absolute ban on the use of intercept evidence is overwhelming. It is in our view a disproportionate and unsophisticated response to the legitimate aim of protecting intelligence sources and methods." 56 J.C.H.R. 18th Report of 2003–4 HL Paper 158, HC 713.

[121] Judgment October 23, 1995, unreported.

offence of causing death by negligent driving, but acquitted of the aggravated form of the offence. The offence of which he was acquitted required proof that the amount of alcohol in his blood exceeded the prescribed limit at the time of the offence. It was not in dispute that the applicant had consumed alcohol on the day of the offence, but the Court accepted medical evidence which placed his blood/alcohol level at the time of the collision beneath the prescribed limit. The local administrative authorities subsequently acquired a medical report which contradicted the evidence adduced by the applicant at his trial. On the basis of the new report the authorities imposed an administrative penalty (a fine) on the applicant for driving with excess alcohol.

The Court concluded that Art.4(1) was applicable in these circumstances.   **12–39**
Although the second set of proceedings were classified as "administrative" for the purposes of national law, they fell to be categorised as criminal proceedings for the purpose of the Convention.[122] In determining whether Art.4(1) had been violated, the Court adopted a substantive rather than a formalistic approach to the double jeopardy principle. Although the elements of the two offences were different, and they pursued different aims, the blood/alcohol level required for the two offences was the same. Since both charges were "based on the same conduct" the Court concluded that there had been a violation of Art.4.

There is no discussion in the judgment of the effect of Art.4(2), and it seems clear   **12–40**
that the Court did not consider it to be relevant. The imposition of the administrative penalty did not involve a "reopening" of the earlier proceedings because: (a) there was no requirement for the authorities to seek a ruling from an appellate court overturning the acquittal; and (b) the subsequent proceedings involved a different charge. It appears that if, instead of imposing an administrative penalty for the less serious offence, the authorities had been able to apply to a court to reopen the applicant's acquittal for the aggravated criminal offence, this would have complied with the requirements of Art.4(2). This apparently anomalous result reflects the limits inherent in Art.4 itself.

The Court of Appeal distinguished *Gradinger v Austria* in *R. v Kerry Young*.[123]   **12–41**
It held that where a defendant had previously been convicted of wounding with intent and acquitted of attempted murder, a subsequent prosecution for murder following the death of the victim from her injuries was not in breach of Art.4 since the "new fact" of the death of the victim had emerged since the first trial.

In *Oliveira v Switzerland*[124] the European Court recognised that successive   **12–42**
prosecutions will not violate Art.4 if they relate to two separate offences arising out of the same course of criminal conduct. The applicant was involved in a road traffic accident in which another motorist was seriously injured. As the result of an administrative error, her case was dealt with by the police magistrate, whose

---

[122] Applying the criteria laid down by the court in *Engel v Netherlands (No.1)* (1979–80) 1 E.H.R.R. 647 and *Ozturk v Germany* (1984) 6 E.H.R.R. 409.
[123] 24/10/05 (unreported) Case No.0405955 D2—extempore judgment.
[124] Judgment July 30, 1998, unreported.

jurisdiction was limited to minor offences. The magistrate convicted the applicant of a minor offence of failing to control her vehicle, and imposed a fine of CHF 200. He had no jurisdiction to consider the more serious offence of negligently inflicting physical injury, and he failed to refer the case to the district attorney, as he was required to do under the relevant provisions of Swiss law. The district attorney's office subsequently issued a penal order fining the applicant CHF 2,000 for the more serious offence of negligently injuring the other motorist. The applicant appealed against the order to the Zurich District Court and subsequently to the Zurich Court of Appeal. The conviction was upheld, but the fine was reduced, and the applicant was given credit for the fine imposed by the magistrate.

12–43   The applicant complained that she had been prosecuted twice in respect of the same offence. The Court rejected this complaint, holding that this was "a typical example of a single act constituting various offences". As the Court explained:

> "The characteristic feature of this notion is that a single criminal act is split up into two separate offences, in this case the failure to control the vehicle and the negligent causing of physical injury. In such cases, the greater penalty will usually absorb the lesser one. There is nothing in that situation which infringes Article 4 of Protocol No. 7 since that provision prohibits people being tried twice for the same offence, whereas in cases concerning a single act constituting various offences, one criminal act constitutes two separate offences."

12–44   The Court observed that it would have been more consistent with the principles governing the proper administration of justice for sentence in respect of both offences to have been passed by the same court in a single set of proceedings. Nevertheless, the fact that this had not occurred was irrelevant to the issues arising under Art.4 since;

> " . . . that provision does not preclude separate offences, even if they are all part of a single criminal act, being tried by different courts, especially where, as in the present case, the penalties were not cumulative, the lesser being absorbed by the greater."

12–45   The decision in *Olivera* confirms the previous practice of the Commission, which has consistently distinguished between successive prosecutions for the same offence, and prosecutions for multiple offences arising out the same facts. In *Palaoro v Austria*,[125] for example, the Commission rejected as manifestly ill-founded a complaint brought under Art.4 by an applicant who had been convicted of two offences of exceeding the prescribed speed limit in the course of a single journey, since the two offences had been committed on separate sections of road. Similarly, in *Iskandarani v Sweden*,[126] the Commission rejected a complaint under Art.4 where the applicant had previously been convicted of abducting his daughter, and was subsequently prosecuted for withholding the child from its legal custodian after the abduction had occurred. These were separate offences arising out the same course of criminal conduct. Article 4 of Protocol 7 did not prohibit separate proceedings for such offences. In *Gotken v*

---

[125] Application No.16718/90, unreported.
[126] Application No.23222/94, unreported.

France[127] the Court considered whether a penalty imposed for a drugs offence and one for a customs matter in respect of the same incident amounted to a breach of Art.4 but concluded that they were two separate offences arising out of the same conduct, and accordingly found no violation. In *Nikitin v Russia*[128] the Court concluded that a "supervisory review" did not amount to a second trial in breach of Art.4. Relevant factors in the assessment included whether there had been a final decision before the supervisory hearing, whether the issue was being tried again, whether the defendant was liable to be tried again by a decision of this body, and whether there was a duplication of proceedings. However, following *Franz Fischer v Austria*,[129] the Court may have broadened its approach slightly from the *Olivera* judgment by distinguishing a case of drink driving which incurred both administrative as well as criminal penalties:

"The Court observes that the wording of Article 4 of Protocol No. 7 does not refer to "the same offence" but rather to trial and punishment "again" for an offence for which the applicant has already been finally acquitted or convicted. Thus, while it is true that the mere fact that a single act constitutes more than one offence is not contrary to this Article, the Court must not limit itself to finding that an applicant was, on the basis of one act, tried or punished for nominally different offences. The Court, like the Austrian Constitutional Court, notes that there are cases where one act, at first sight, appears to constitute more than one offence, whereas a closer examination shows that only one offence should be prosecuted because it encompasses all the wrongs contained in the others . . . An obvious example would be an act which constitutes two offences, one of which contains precisely the same elements as the other plus an additional one. There may be other cases where the offences only slightly overlap. Thus, where different offences based on one act are prosecuted consecutively, one after the final decision of the other, the Court has to examine whether or not such offences have the same essential elements."

F. PART 10 CRIMINAL JUSTICE ACT 2003—COMPLIANCE WITH ECHR PROTOCOL 7, ARTICLE 4 AND I.C.C.P.R. ARTICLE 14(7)

The new evidence pre-conditions in Pt 10 of the Criminal Justice Act 2003   **12–46** (detailed in paras 12–09 *et seq.* above) are to be contrasted with Art.4(2) of Protocol 7 to the ECHR.[130] Part 10 includes evidence which need not have

---

[127] (2002) Application 33402/96.

[128] (2004) Application 50178/99. See also, *Bratyakin v Russia* (2006) Application 72776/01, where the application was declared inadmissible because the supervisory review constituted a reopening of the case owing to a fundamental defect in the previous proceedings, within the scope of Art.4(2) of Protocol 7.

[129] (2001) Application 37950/97 at para.25—followed in *WF v Austria* (2004) 38 E.H.R.R. 39 and *Sailer v Austria* (2002) Application 38237/97. See also, *Nilsson v Sweden* (2005) Application 73661/01, where the Applicant claimed that the administrative removal of his driving licence following his conviction and sentence for driving while drunk amounted to a second set of criminal proceedings and punishment, contrary to Art.4 of Protocol 7. The application was ruled inadmissible on the basis that, "While the different sanctions were imposed by two different authorities in different proceedings, there was nevertheless a sufficiently close connection between them, in substance and in time, to consider the withdrawal to be part of the sanctions under Swedish law for the offences of aggravated drunken driving and unlawful driving."

[130] See para.12–31 above.

existed or come to light only after the acquittal—the evidence may have been within the prosecution's knowledge or possession before trial but simply not adduced. The Art.4(2) definition of "evidence of new or newly discovered facts" does not appear to include evidence which existed pre-trial but was not adduced. Even if the "interests of justice" requirement in s.79 is read sufficiently narrowly, reliance only on judicial discretion to prevent a retrial in cases where the evidence was (or could have been) available to the prosecution at trial but was not adduced or discovered because of prosecutorial negligence, is unlikely to ensure compliance with Art.4 of Protocol 7 (which at the time of writing has still not been ratified).[131] The additional Pt 10 requirements that the new evidence be "compelling" and the non-inclusion of a retrial following a "fundamental defect" or equivalent mean that *in those respects* English law gives greater protection to the defendant than Art.4 of Protocol 7 of the Convention.

12–47   Article 4 of Protocol 7 appears to give the State somewhat greater leeway than I.C.C.P.R. Art.14(7) in permitting retrial where the "new" evidence was available to the prosecution at trial.[132] As noted above, although the UN Human Rights Committee has permitted reopening or resumption of a criminal trial in "exceptional circumstances", it would not sanction straightforward retrial.[133] Thus, it seems likely that the possibility of retrial based on evidence which was (or could have been) available at the original trial renders s.78 incompatible with I.C.C.P.R. Art.14(7), even assuming that ECHR Art.4(2) of Protocol 7 is "read into" I.C.C.P.R. Art.14(7). The Joint Committee on Human Rights concluded that clause 72 in the Criminal Justice Bill, which became s.78 of the 2003 Act, appeared "likely to be incompatible" with the UK's international law obligations under I.C.C.P.R. Art.14(7).[134] It rejected the argument that judicial discretion under s.79 (which expressly requires the Court of Appeal to take into account prosecutorial negligence, but not Art.4 of Protocol 7 nor Art.14(7) I.C.C.P.R.) would be sufficient to remedy the incompatibility.[135]

---

[131] The Government has defended the s.78 definition and reliance on judicial discretion to "weed out cases where the original investigation or prosecution had simply been conducted in a sloppy way". The Minister contended that it had proved difficult to find a test which covered evidence which had existed before only where it could not have been found, or its significance could not have been understood at the time, even with reasonable diligence on the part of officers and prosecutors. See Joint Committee on Human Rights, 11th report of 2002 (HL 118, HC 724) on the Criminal Justice Bill at para.32.

[132] The Convention should, so far as possible, be interpreted in harmony with other rules of public international law of which it forms part (*Al Adsani v UK* (2002) 34 E.H.R.R. 11).

[133] See para.12–28 above.

[134] J.C.H.R. 11th Report of 2002–3 at paras 27 to 38.

[135] See further Lord Bingham in *A and others v Home Secretary* [2004] UKHL 56, [2005] 2 A.C. 68, at para.33.

CHAPTER 13

BAIL

A. INTRODUCTION

The right to apply for bail pending trial is governed by Arts 5(3) and 5(4) of the **13–01** Convention, and by the presumption of innocence in Art.6(2). The compatibility of the Bail Act 1976 with the Convention caselaw under these provisions was considered in detail by the Law Commission in a consultation paper published in November 1999.[1] The consultation paper recommended the amendment or repeal of a number of statutory provisions, the publication of detailed guidance on the application of others and the provision of training for judges and magistrates on making and recording of bail decisions in a way which is compliant with Arts 5 and 6. The enactment of the New Zealand Bill of Rights Act led to similar calls for a tightening of remand procedures so as to give greater weight to the presumption of innocence,[2] and there were a number of successful challenges to bail legislation under the Canadian Charter.[3] Following consultation the Law Commission adopted an altogether more cautious approach in its final report, *Bail and the Human Rights Act 1998*.[4] In this Chapter we consider the Convention caselaw, and the decisions reached by the domestic courts under the 1998 Act, against the background of the criticisms made in the Law Commission's original consultation paper and its final recommendations.[5]

B. GENERAL PRINCIPLES

Article 5(3) provides that every person who has been arrested or detained in **13–02** accordance with Art.5(1)(c) must be brought promptly before a judge or other judicial officer and is entitled to trial within a reasonable time or to release pending trial. In some cases this duty may extend to taking steps to bring about

---

[1] Consultation Paper No.157, *Bail and the Human Rights Act 1998*.
[2] See the discussion of the judgment in *Gillbanks v Police* [1994] 3 N.Z.L.R. 61 by the New Zealand Court of Appeal in *Tonihi* [1995] 1 N.Z.L.R. 154.
[3] Padfield, "The Right to Bail: a Canadian Perspective" [1993] Crim. L.R. 510.
[4] Law Commission No.269, June 21, 2001.
[5] See notes 1 and 4 above.

conditions to allow for a detainee's release before the right to be brought before a court crystallises.[6] In *McGoff v Sweden*[7] the Commission held that Art.5(3) imposes an "unconditional obligation" on the state to bring the accused "automatically and promptly" before a court.[8] The term "judge or other officer authorised by law" has the same meaning as the term "competent legal authority" in Art.5(1)(c).[9] The tribunal must be independent of the investigating and prosecuting authorities,[10] and it must be impartial in the sense of being free from actual bias and from the appearance of bias.[11] In addition:

" . . . under Article 5(3) there is both a procedural and a substantive requirement. The procedural requirement places the 'officer' under the obligation of himself hearing the individual brought before him; the substantive requirement imposes on him the obligations of reviewing the circumstances militating for or against detention, of deciding, by reference to legal criteria, whether there are reasons to justify detention and of ordering release if there are no such reasons".[12]

13–03 Whilst a criminal court, acting in accordance with the Bail Act 1976, will generally meet these structural requirements, a number of domestic exceptions to the right to bail raise issues under Art.5.[13] And the United Kingdom has been held to be in breach of these procedural requirements in Strasbourg—the detention of service personnel pending a court martial by order of the commanding officer was held to violate the independence and impartiality standard implicit in Art.5(3).[14]

In a number of cases the European Court has suggested that the court reviewing bail must also be empowered to make a legally binding decision ordering release.[15] The matter was however reconsidered in the recent case of *McKay v UK*,[16] which concerned s.67(2) Terrorism Act 2000,[17] a Northern Ireland provision which removes the right of magistrates to grant bail in a number of

---

[6] See *Vasileva v Denmark* 40 E.H.R.R. 681, where the Court found that it had been no breach of Art.5 to detain the applicant for failing to give her paritculars, but the state had been in breach of Art.5(3) during a six hour period when the police allowed her to sleep without making their own enquiries to determine her identity.

[7] (1982) 31 D.R. 72. This decision does not appear to have been cited in *Olotu v Home Office* [1997] 1 W.L.R. 328 where Lord Bingham C.J. held that detention following the expiry of custody time limits did not involve a breach of Art.5(3) because the relevant legislation placed the onus on the defendant to make an application for bail.

[8] The court suggested that this should be within four days—*Brogan v UK* (1988) 8 E.H.R.R. S.23 Terrorism Act 2006, which allows for a 28-day period, is clearly open to challenge under Art.5.See also *TW v Malta, Aquilina v Malta* 29 E.H.R.R. 185.

[9] *Lawless v Ireland (No.3)* (1979–80) 1 E.H.R.R. 15, paras 13–14; *Ireland v United Kingdom* (1979–80) 2 E.H.R.R. 25, para.199; *Schiesser v Switzerland* (1979–80) 2 E.H.R.R. 417, para.29. On Art.5(1)(c), see para.5–13 above.

[10] *De Jong, Baljet and Van Den Brink v Netherlands* (1986) 8 E.H.R.R. 20, para.49; *Schiesser v Switzerland* (1979–80) 2 E.H.R.R. 417, paras 29 and 30.

[11] *Huber v Switzerland* (1990) Series A/188, para.43. *Cf.* the Court's interpretation of the impartiality requirement in Art.6(1) (see paras 14–67 *et seq.* below).

[12] *Schiesser v Switzerland* (1979–80) 2 E.H.R.R. 417, para.31.

[13] See para.xxx below.

[14] *Hood v United Kingdom,*(1999) 29 E.H.R.R. 365; *Jordan v United Kingdom, The Times,* March 17, 2000.

[15] *Ireland v United Kingdom* (1979–80) 2 E.H.R.R. 25, para.199. See also *TW v Malta, Aquilina v Malta* 29 E.H.R.R. 185

[16] (2006) 44 E.H.R.R. 827.

[17] And its predecessor provision, s.3(2) Northern Ireland (Emergency Provisions) Act 1996.

scheduled offences. Bail applications must instead be made to the High Court. The applicant was a young offender who was arrested for a robbery which was plainly unconnected with terrorism, in circumstances where the officer in the case had indicated that he would have no objection to bail if there were a power to grant it. The applicant remained in custody until the High Court could hear the application, three days after his arrest, and 36 hours after the magistrates' court hearing.

The Court reviewed the authorities, with the majority concluding that it was **13–04** unnecessary for the initial review of detention to include any consideration that the defendant be released for any other reason than the detention was unlawful on Art.5(1)(c) grounds. The Court observed that the *Scheisser* decision had made no specific reference to bail, and that it was authority only for the proposition that the judicial officer must have power to review the lawfulness of the arrest and detention under domestic law under Art.5(1). The majority observed

"... in order to ensure that the right guaranteed is practical and effective, not theoretical and illusory, it is not only good practice, but highly desirable in order to minimise delay, that the judicial officer who conducts the first automatic review of lawfulness and the existence of a ground for detention, also has the competence to consider release on bail. It is not however a requirement of the Convention and there is no reaons in principle why the issues cannot be dealt with by two judicial officers, within the requisite time-frame. In any event, as a matter of interpretation, it cannot be required that the examination of bail take place with any more speed than is demanded of the first automatic review, which the Court has identified as being a maximum of four days."[18]

Six members of the Court disagreed with this surprising interpretation of **13–05** Art.5(3).[19] Judges Rozakis, Tulkens, Botoucharova, Myjer and Ziemele thought that the judicial officer should have "full jurisdiction"—the competence to order release if appropriate. They were of the view that the decision of the majority was not in conformity with the "very purpose" of Art.5(3), to protect against unlawful or unnecessary detention throught prompt judicial control.

The second limb of Art.5(3) expressly entitles an accused person "to trial within **13–06** a reasonable time or to release pending trial". The use of the word "or" does not indicate that prompt trial is an alternative to release on bail.[20] As the Court explained in *Wemhoff v Germany*[21]:

"[S]uch an interpretation would not conform to the intention of the High Contracting Parties. It is inconceiveable that they should have intended to permit their judicial authorities, at the price of release of the accused, to protract proceedings beyond a reasonable time."

---

[18] para.47, citing *Brogan v UK*, above.
[19] Although five of these members agreed with the outcome of the case, on the ground that the release within 36 hours was sufficiently prompt for the purposes of Art.5(3). Judge Jebens disagreed on this point.
[20] *Neumeister v Austria (No.1)* (1979–80) 1 E.H.R.R. 91, para.4; *Wemhoff v Germany* (1979–80) 1 E.H.R.R. 55, paras 4–5.
[21] *Wemhoff v Germany* (1979–80) 1 E.H.R.R. 55.

13–07 Accordingly, the Court has held that the proper construction of Art.5(3) is that a person charged with an offence must always be released pending trial unless the state can show that there are "relevant and sufficient" reasons to justify his continued detention.[22] The Court requires the state to show "special diligence" in its conduct of proceedings, in order to justify detain a person pending trial.[23] The Court will be prepared to look at the eventual sentence received, with a view to determining whether the time spent on remand was reasonable.[24] Moreover, the state must show that detention in penal custody is required, and that it has considered other methods of ensuring appearance at trial.[25] Where an accused person is suffering from mental disorder, a therapeutic *measure* (such as supervision in the community or committal to a mental hospital) is more likely to comply with Art.5.[26]

13–08 Article 5(3) applies throughout the period from the arrest of an accused to his conviction or acquittal by the trial court, but not to detention pending appeal.[27] The procedural requirements imposed by Art.5(4) where a court is considering bail in criminal proceedings are discussed in detail below. In brief, the defence must be afforded adequate access to the evidence in the possession of the prosecution, and the procedure must ensure equality of arms and be "truly adversarial".[28] The court is obliged to pay due regard to the presumption of innocence and must record the arguments for and against release in a reasoned ruling.[29]

C. GROUNDS FOR REFUSAL OF BAIL

I. The Strasbourg Principles

13–09 Article 5(1) lists six separate grounds for a state to detain an individual. These grounds are exhaustive and have been restrictly applied[30]: the Court has insisted on many occasions that not only the right to liberty but also the presumption of innocence is at stake here. Thus it is for the state to establish that one of these grounds applies—any burden on the detained person to show why he should be

---

[22] *Wemhoff v Germany* (1979–80) 1 E.H.R.R. 55, para.12; *Yagci and Sargin v Turkey* (1995) 20 E.H.R.R. 505, para.52.

[23] *Stogmuller v Austria* (1969) 1 E.H.R.R. 155; *Ilowielki v Poland* 37 E.H.R.R. 546, *Bartuss v Czech Republic* 34 E.H.R.R. 948; *Punzelt v Czech Republic* (2001) 33 E.H.R.R. 1159.

[24] See for example *Latasiiewicz v Poland* (2005) ECtHR June 23, where the court found a breach of Art.5(3) where the applicant had been on remand for 18 months before receiving a sentence of two and a half years.

[25] *Ilowielki v Poland* 37 E.H.R.R. 546.

[26] *Clooth v Belgium* (1992) 14 E.H.R.R. 717 at para.40.

[27] *Wemhoff v Germany* (1979–80) 1 E.H.R.R. 55, paras 7–9; *B v Austria* (1991) 13 E.H.R.R. 20, paras 36–40.

[28] *Lamy v Belgium* (1989) 11 E.H.R.R. 529, para.29.

[29] *Letellier v France* (1992) 14 E.H.R.R. 83, para.35; *Yagci and Sargin v Turkey* (1995) 20 E.H.R.R. 505, para.52. For a recent re-statement of the principle, see *Weinsztal v Poland* (2006) May 30, ECtHR.

[30] *Jablonski v Poland* 36 E.H.R.R. 455.

released will be in breach of Art.5(4).[31] In *Ilijkov v Bulgaria*, the Court said at para.85.

> "Shifting the burden of proof to the detained person in such matters is tantamount to overturning the rule of article 5 of the Convention, a provision which makes detention an exceptional departure from the right to librtty and one that is only permissible in exhaustively enumerated and strictly defined cases."

Amongst those exhaustive cases where detention is permissible, Art.5(1)(c) provides for the detention of a criminal suspect on "reasonable suspicion of having committed an offence or when it is reasonably considered necessary to prevent his committing an offence or fleeing after having done so." The Court has been willing to engage in the issue of whether there was sufficient suspicion to justify detention,[32] stressing that the facts grounding suspicion under Art.5(1)(c) do not need to be at the same level as that required to base a charge, but should amount to "facts or information which would satisfy an objective observer that the accused may have committed an offence."[33]

The European Court of Human Rights has recognised four principal grounds   **13–10**
upon which a national court may legitimately rely in refusing bail under Art.5(3), once reasonable suspicion of having committed an offence has been made out. Whilst these reasons broadly coincide with certain of the grounds specified under the Bail Act 1976, they do not overlap entirely, and the Human Rights Act has had a significant impact upon the way the domestic courts approach decisions about bail.[34] The Court has consistently stressed the need for concrete evidence in bail decisions, and the need to avoid abstract or generalised reasoning. As we shall see, the Law Commission's audit of bail law for compatibility with the Convention identified a number of areas of mismatch.

Risk that the accused will fail to appear for trial

The Court has held that a defendant may be remanded in custody pending trial,   **13–11**
consistently with Art.5(3), where there is well-founded fear that if released on bail he would fail to surrender. Refusal of bail on this ground requires "a whole set of circumstances . . . which give reason to suppose that the consequences and hazards of flight will seem to him to be a lesser evil than continued imprisonment".[35] Relevant considerations are those "relating to the character of the person involved, his morals, his home, his occupation, his assets, his family ties, and all kinds of links with the country in which he is being prosecuted".[36] The severity of the potential sentence, though important, is not an independent ground

---

[31] *Ilijokov v Bulgaria* [2001] 7 Archbold News 1, ECtHR July 26, 2000; *Niklovka v Bugaria* (1999) 31 E.H.R.R. 64, *Hutchinson-Reid v UK* [2003] 1 M.H.L.R. at 237.

[32] *Fox, Campbell and Hartley v UK* (199) 13 E.H.R.R. 157, *Guzzardi v Italy* (1980) 3 E.H.R.R. 333, *Berktay v Turkey* (2001) at paras 199–201.

[33] *Ergadoz v Turkey* 32 E.H.R.R. 473.

[34] Although there is no evidence that these changes have improved a defendant's chances of being granted bail. The proportion of people being committed in custody for Crown Court trial rose from 28 per cent in 1999 to 30 per cent in 2004.

[35] *Stögmüller v Austria* (1979–80) 1 E.H.R.R. 155, para.15.

[36] *Stögmüller v Austria* (1979–80) 1 E.H.R.R. 155, para.15.

and cannot itself justify the refusal of bail.[37] The fact that it is possible for the accused to escape from the jurisdiction does not necessarily warrant the conclusion that he would abscond if released.[38] If the risk of absconding is the only justification for the detention, release of the accused pending trial should be ordered if it is possible to impose adequate and enforceable bail conditions. In *Wemhoff v Germany*[39] the Court held that:

> "[T]he concluding words of Art.5(3) of the Convention show that, when the only remaining reason for continued detention is the fear that the accused will abscond and thereby subsequently avoid appearing for his trial, his release pending trial must be ordered if it is possible to obtain from him guarantees that will ensure such appearance."

In *Jablonski v Poland*[40] the Court held that this will amount to a positive duty upon the State to show that it has given condideration to all measures which might provide an alternative to custody, and to explain why these would not suffice to guarantee appearance at court.

13–12 More controversially, the Court has held that the risk of a defendant absconding diminishes as the trial approaches, a view which some English judges may find difficult to accept. In *Neumeister v Austria*[41] the Court explained its reasoning as follows:

> "The danger of flight necessarily decreases as the time spent in detention passes by, for the probability that the length of detention on remand will be deducted from the period of imprisonment which the person concerned may expect, if convicted, is likely to make the prospect seem less awesome to him and reduce his temptation to flee".

Interference with the course of justice

13–13 Bail may be refused under Art.5(3) where there is a well-founded risk that the accused, if released, would take action to prejudice the administration of justice.[42] The risk may involve interference with witnesses, warning other suspects, or the destruction of relevant evidence.[43] However, the Court has held that a generalised risk is insufficient. The risk must be identifiable and there must be evidence in support.[44] Further, the court must bear in mind that this risk will often

---

[37] *Neumeister v Austria (No.1)* (1979–80) 1 E.H.R.R. 91, para.10; *Letellier v France* (1992) 14 E.H.R.R. 83, para.43. For a Privy Council authority affirming these principles see *Hurnam v State of Mauritius* [2006] 1 W.L.R. 857.
[38] *Neumeister v Austria (No.1)* (1979–80) 1 E.H.R.R. 91, para.10; *Letellier v France* (1992) 14 E.H.R.R. 83, para.43.
[39] *Wemhoff v Germany* (1979–80) 1 E.H.R.R. 55.
[40] (2003) 36 E.H.R.R. 455 at para 84.
[41] *Neumeister v Austria (No.1)* (1979–80) 1 E.H.R.R. 91, For a recent re-statement of this principle, see *Jablonski v Poland*, above, n.40.
[42] *Wemhoff v Germany* (1979–80) 1 E.H.R.R. 55, para.14.
[43] *Letellier v France* (1992) 14 E.H.R.R. 83, *Wemhoff v Germany* (1979–80) 1 E.H.R.R. 55
[44] *Clooth v Belgium* (1992) 14 E.H.R.R. 717, para.44; *Tomasi v France* (1993) 15 E.H.R.R. 1, paras 84 and 91. This does not necessarily have to be evidence which would be admissable at trial: *R. v Havering Magistrates Court, ex parte DPP* [2001] 1 W.L.R. 805.

diminish with time, once the investigation has concluded.[45] In *Letellier v France*, for example, the Court accepted that "a genuine risk of pressure being brought on the witnesses may have existed initially", but took the view that this risk had "diminished and indeed disappeared with the passing of time."[46] In particular, if the accused has previously been on bail and there is no evidence that he or she interfered with the course of justice during that period, this will be a strong factor militating against a custodial remand on this ground.[47]

Prevention of further offences

The public interest in the prevention of crime may justify detention on remand   **13–14**
where there are good reasons to believe that the accused, if released, would be likely to commit further offences.[48] However, the danger must be "a plausible one" and the appropriateness of a remand in custody on this ground must be considered "in the light of the circumstances of the case and, in particular, the past history and the personality of the person concerned".[49] A risk of further offences cannot be automatically assumed from the fact that the accused has a criminal record. The court should consider whether any previous convictions are "comparable, either in nature or in the degree of seriousness to the charges preferred against [the accused]".[50] The Court has also emphasised that a risk of minor offences is insufficient.[51] Where the mental condition of a person charged with murder is cited as a ground for refusal of bail, steps should be taken to provide him with the necessary psychiatric care whilst on remand.[52]

The preservation of public order[53]

Where the nature of the crime alleged and the likely public reaction to it are such   **13–15**
that the release of the accused may give rise to public disorder, then temporary detention on remand may be justified.[54] In *Letellier v France*,[55] the Court emphasised that this ground was confined to exceptional offences which "by reason of their particular gravity and public reaction to them . . . may give rise to

---

[45] *Clooth v Belgium*(1992) 14 E.H.R.R. 717, para.43; *W v Switzerland* (1994) 17 E.H.R.R. 60, para 35, *Letellier v France* (1992) 14 E.H.R.R. 83 para.39.

[46] (1992) 14 E.H.R.R. 83.

[47] *Ringeisen v Austria (No.1)* (1979–80) 1 E.H.R.R. 455 at para.106; after the accused had been on bail for five months, the Austrian court used this reason in support of a custodial remand, without referring to any particular evidence in support. The European Court commented that this "does not stand up to examination."

[48] *Matznetter v Austria* (1979–80) 1 E.H.R.R. 198, para.9; *Toth v Austria* (1992) 14 E.H.R.R. 551, para.70; *Clooth v Belgium* (1992) 14 E.H.R.R. 717, para.40.

[49] *Muller v France* 1997–II, para.44.

[50] *Clooth v Belgium* (1992) 14 E.H.R.R. 717, para.40.

[51] *Matznetter v Austria* (1979–80) 1 E.H.R.R. 198 at para.9 On the facts, the Court referred to "the very prolonged continuation of reprehensible activities and the huge extent of the loss sustained by the victims"

[52] *Clooth v Belgium* (1992) 14 E.H.R.R. 717, para.40.

[53] It should be noted that a provision in the Canadian Criminal Code which allowed courts to refuse bail on the ground that it was "necessary in the public interest" was struck down as unduly vague and contrary to the Canadian Charter: *Morales* [1992] 3 S.C.R. 711. For an accessible discussion, see Padfield N., "The Right to Bail: a Canadian Perspective" [1993] Crim. L.R. 510.

[54] *Letellier v France* (1992) 14 E.H.R.R. 83, para.51

[55] (1992) 14 E.H.R.R. 83. See also *Dumont-Malverg v France* (2005) May 31, ECtHR.

a social disturbance". The Court has held that a premeditated act of terrorism by an organisation which has caused death or serious injury may qualify as such a risk.[56] In *AI v France*[57] the Court observed that there may be cases in which; " . . . the safety of a person under investigation requires his continued detention, for a time at least. However, this can only be so in exceptional circumstances having to do with the nature of the offences concerned, the conditions in which they were committed and the context in which they took place." Detention on this ground may only continue for as long as the threat to public order remains.[58]

II. Application to the Bail Act 1976

13–16 Section 4 of the Bail Act 1976 provides that a person brought before a magistrates' court or a Crown Court charged with a criminal offence has a right to be released on bail, unless one of the grounds for refusing bail set out in Pt 1 of Sch.1 applies. There are eight such grounds listed in the schedule. The first three grounds, which are most commonly invoked, are contained in para.2. This provides that a defendant need not be granted bail if the court is satisfied that there are substantial grounds for believing that if released on bail he would; (a) fail to surrender to custody; (b) commit an offence whilst on bail, or; (c) interfere with witnesses or otherwise obstruct the course of justice. It is not necessary for the court to conclude that one of these consequences will occur, or even that it is more likely than not. The court merely has to be satisfied that there are *substantial grounds for believing* that one of them would occur.[59] In considering any objection under para.2 the court is required to "have regard" to; (a) the nature and seriousness of the offence and the probable sentence; (b) the character, antecedents, associations and community ties of the defendant; (c) the defendant's history of compliance with any bail conditions previously imposed on him; and (d) the strength of the evidence.

13–17 Statutory provisions have created a number of exceptions to the right to bail. Section 25(1) of the Criminal Justice and Public Order Act 1994, as amended, imposes a statutory restriction on the grant of bail in respect of certain serious offences, where the defendant has a relevant previous conviction,[60] and the Criminal Justice Act 2003 further amended the Bail Act in a number of significant respects. Some of these provisions raise issues of compatibility with the Convention, and will be discussed below in more detail. Under the current law a defendant "may not be granted bail unless the court is satisfied that there is no significant risk of his committing an offence while on bail" where he is charged with any offence when already on bail for another offence,[61] or if he has absonded, "unless the court is satisfied that there is no significant risk that, if

---

[56] *Clooth v Belgium* (1992) 14 E.H.R.R. 717, para.40.
[57] 1998-IV Judgment September 23, 1998, para.108.
[58] *Letellier v France* (1992) 14 E.H.R.R. 83, para.51; *Tomasi v France* (1993) 15 E.H.R.R. 1, para.91.
[59] *R. v Nottingham Justices ex parte Davies* [1981] Q.B. 38.
[60] See para.13–20 below.
[61] Bail Act 1976, Sch.1, Pt I, para.2A as amended by s.13 Criminal Justice Act 2003.

released on bail . . . he would fail to surrender to custody."[62] Further exceptions apply where it is necessary for a defendant be kept in custody for his own protection, or if he is a child or young person, for his own welfare[63]; if he is already serving a sentence of imprisonment[64]; if there is insufficient time to obtain the information necessary to make a bail decision[65]; or if he has been arrested for a Bail Act offence and the court is not satisfied that there is no significant risk that he will abscond.[66] New restrictions apply to the grant of bail to adult offenders who have tested positive for specified Class A drugs, who are before the court for Class A drug-related offences or offences which the court believes are drug-related, and who refused to participate in treatment for drug-dependency.[67]

Paragraph 2(b): Risk of further offences

The criteria for a refusal of bail under paras 2(a) and (c) appear to correspond   **13-18** closely with the Strasbourg caselaw. Providing there is convincing evidence in support of the alleged risk, and the decision is adequately reasoned,[68] it is unlikely that a refusal of bail on either of these grounds will violate Art.5(3). However, the refusal of bail on the ground that there is a risk that the accused would commit further offences (para.2(b)) requires more detailed consideration, particularly when an accused was already on bail for another offence. As we have seen, the court has laid particular emphasis on the seriousness of the anticipated crimes and the need for real grounds establishing the likelihood of their commission,[69] and has stressed the need to consider each case on its individual merits. This contrasts with para.2(b), which contains no requirement that the potential offence(s) must be serious. It is notable in this connection that an amended Irish Constitution provides for pre-trial detention where reasonably necessary "to prevent the commission of a *serious* offence by that person".[70]

In considering the compatibility of para.2(b) with the Strasbourg caselaw, the   **13-19** Law Commission suggested that a defendant's previous convictions would be relevant only where they were comparable to the offence which it is feared that the defendant might commit. It recommended that guidance be issued to judges and magistrates emphasising that bail should only be refused on this ground, where the offence feared might properly be characterised as "serious", and was likely to attract a custodial sentence; where it could be shown that there is a *real risk* of the defendant committing the offence; and where detention was the appropriate measure in the light of that risk, and all the circumstances of the case. In its final report the Law Commission suggested specific guidance to this effect. The amendments to the Bail Act by the Criminal Justice Act 2003 did not address this point.

---

[62] Bail Act 1976, Sch.1, Pt 1, para.6 as amended by s.15 Criminal Justice Act 2003.
[63] Bail Act 1976, Sch.1, Pt 1, para.3.
[64] Bail Act 1976, Sch.1, Pt 1, para.4.
[65] Bail Act 1976, Sch.1, Pt 1, para.5.
[66] Bail Act 1976, Sch.1, Pt 1, para.6 as amended by s.15 Criminal Justice Act 2003.
[67] Bail Act 1976, Sch.1, Pt 1, para.6A, as amended by s.19 Criminal Justice Act 2003.
[68] see para.13-58 below.
[69] *Matznetter v Austria* (1979-80) 1 E.H.R.R. 198 (para.44).
[70] For analysis and discussion, see Uni Raifeartaigh, "Reconciling Bail Law with the Presumption of Innocence." (1997) 17 Oxford J.L.S. 1.

Section 25(1) of the Criminal Justice and Public Order Act 1994

13–20 In *Caballero v United Kingdom*[71] the European Commission of Human Rights concluded that s.25(1) of the Criminal Justice and Public Order Act 1994 was in breach of Art.5(3). As then drafted, the section imposed an absolute prohibition on the grant of bail on a charge of murder, attempted murder, manslaughter, rape or attempted rape where the accused had a prior conviction for such an offence. It deprived the court of any jurisdiction to consider the individual circumstances of the case or of the accused. As the Commission pointed out, it imposed an obligation to refuse bail even in the theoretical case of a person who was totally paralysed. In the Commission's view:

> "[T]he exclusion from the risk assessment of a consideration of all the particular circumstances and facts of each accused's case (other than the two facts contained in section 25) exposes, of itself, accused persons to an arbitrary deprivation of liberty."

13–21 The Government accepted the Commission's conclusion, and conceded the alleged violation before the Court. *Caballero* was followed by a decision of the European Court in *SBC v United Kingdom*,[72] which found the UK in violation for exactly the same reasons. As a consequence, s.25 was amended (by s.56 of the Crime and Disorder Act 1998), so as to restore an element of judicial discretion. It now provides that: "A person who in any proceedings has been charged with or convicted of an offence to which this section applies . . . shall be granted bail in those proceedings only if the court . . . considering the grant of bail is satisfied that there are *exceptional circumstances* which justify it." The offences appear to be selected on grounds of seriousness, as a step towards public protection, and it is established that the seriousness of the offence charged is not itself sufficient to justify a substantial period of detention on remand.[73]

13–22 Despite the amendment, s.25 continued to generate controversy under the Human Rights Act. On its face the amended provision appeared to create a presumption (or a reverse onus), and there is no statutory definition of the term "exceptional circumstances".[74] At one extreme, therefore, the provision might be read as depriving the court of any real discretion to grant bail in all but the most unusual cases. At the other extreme it might be read as entitling a court to grant bail where, having taken account of the matters referred to in the section, the court would otherwise consider the grant of bail to be appropriate. The Law Commission provisionally concluded that without amendment or judicial guidance, s.25 was liable to misunderstood as having dispensed with the need to take all relevant circumstances into account. In the Commission's view, in order to comply with Art.5(3), s.25 would have to be read in such a way as to give appropriate weight to the statutory criteria whilst retaining a true judicial discretion—in effect, a middle path. Applying this approach, the court could legitimately attach special weight to the factors identified in the section, and might even treat them as decisive in the balance it had to perform. But it should not treat them as

---

[71] (2000) 30 E.H.R.R. 643.
[72] (2001) 34 E.H.R.R. 619
[73] *Nakhmanovich v Russia*, App.No.55669/00, judgment of March 2, 2006.
[74] See *Offen* [2001] 1 W.L.R. 253, for some guidance on the phrase "exceptional circumstances" in the case of "automatic" life sentences.

conclusive for the grant of bail since that would, in substance, involve returning s.25 to its original form.

In *Ilijkov v Bulgaria*[75] the Court found a violation of Art.5(4) where the national **13–23** courts applied a strong presumption in domestic law against the grant of bail, without addressing specific submissions put to them. It is noteworthy that the presumption could only be rebutted if the detainee established exceptional circumstances. In addition, in *Reid v UK*[76] the Court made clear that any imposition of a burden of proof on the detained person to show why he should be released is incompatible with Art.5(4) of the Convention. The Court in that case expressly rejected an argument by the UK government that notwithstanding clear statements to the applicant that the onus was on him to show why he should not be detained, "issues of the burden of proof were largely irrelevant for the Sheriff in reaching his findings . . . "

The House of Lords has now provided guidance for the interpretation of s.25, in **13–24** the decision of *R. (O) v Crown Court at Harrow and Governor HMP Wormwood Scrubs*.[77] In that case the applicant, who was charged with rape and had a previous conviction for that offence, had been refused bail notwithstanding a refusal by the trial judge to extend custody time limits after delay by the prosecution in complying with its disclosure obligation. The House of Lords upheld the decision of the Administrative Court,[78] which had endorsed the judge's decision to refuse bail.

All parties to the appeal agreed that it would be inconsistent with Art.5(3) to read **13–25** s.25 as imposing a persuasive or ultimate burden of proof on a defendant to make out exceptional circumstances. That would be incompatible with the principle established in the European Court's jurisprudence that the State must bear the burden of justifying any pre-trial remand in custody. Two alternative ways of reconciling the language of the section with the Convention jurisprudence had been suggested in the judgments of the Administrative Court.

Kennedy L.J. had concluded that the term "exceptional circumstances" should **13–26** be regarded as establishing a norm or presumption that an accused who was charged with murder, rape or manslaughter and who had a previous conviction for such an offence, was to be generally to be regarded as representing an unacceptably high risk to the public if released on bail. This norm or presumption did not prevent the judge from reviewing all relevant circumstances and granting bail if, on the facts, the accused did not pose such a risk. On this analysis, the section did not impose a burden on the accused to justify his release. The burden of justifying a remand in custody remained on the prosecution, and s.25 was part of the means by which the prosecution discharged that burden. Lord Brown, giving the leading speech in the House of Lords, expressed a "mild preference"

---

[75] (2002) July 26, unreported.
[76] [2004] M.H.L.R. 226, at para.73. See also *Rokhlina v Russia*, App.No.54071/00, judgment of April 7, 2005.
[77] [2006] 3 W.L.R. 195.
[78] [2003] 1 W.L.R. 2756.

for the approach adopted by Hooper J. in the Divisional Court. According to this approach, s.25 was capable of being Art.5 compliant only if it was interpreted as imposing an evidential burden on the defendant. This could be achieved by reading the section down under s.3 Human Rights Act 1998.[79] Once the accused had discharged the burden of raising an issue as to the existence of exceptional circumstances, the burden would then shift to the prosecution to prove that such circumstances did not exist on the facts. Lord Carswell expressed a stronger preference for the Hooper approach, concluding that this was the most appropriate way to secure compatibility with the Convention.

Defendant already on bail

13–27 Paragraph 2A[80] of Sch.1, Pt 1, provides that a defendant need not be granted bail if he is charged with an offence, and he was already on bail for another offence on the date of the commission of the offence for which he is before the court. The Criminal Justice Act 2003 amended para.2A to apply to all imprisonable offences[81]—as originally worded, it did not cover cases where the new offence could only be tried summarily, which it is submitted was more in keeping with the emphasis in Strasbourg caselaw that anticipated further crimes should be serious.[82]

13–28 The new wording requires a court to "give weight" to the fact that a defendant was on bail at the time of the further arrest, when assessing whether there is a substantial risk of further offences being committed were the defendant released on bail. The court may re-bail a defendant only if it is "satisfied that there is no significant risk of committing an offence on bail," and bail does not follow automatically even if the court is so satisfied.[83]

13–29 Even in its narrower incarnation, the Law Commission raised a note of caution, rightly pointing out that this scenario did not fall within the *grounds* recognised in the Strasbourg caselaw as "relevant and sufficient". Whilst being on bail at the date of a further arrest *may* give reason to believe that there is a likelihood that he will commit further offences if released, this is by no means a necessary inference in every case. As the Law Commission observed:

> "In the first place, the court cannot simply assume, for the purpose of the bail decision, that the defendant did commit the offence charged: it must bear in mind the presumption of innocence under Article 6(2). Secondly, where there are substantial grounds for believing that the defendant would commit an offence if given bail, the right to bail is excluded by paragraph 2(b) anyway. If the fact that the defendant was on bail at the time of the alleged offence did justify the belief that he or she would commit an offence if given bail again, paragraph 2A would add nothing to paragraph 2(b). It is redundant unless that fact does *not* justify that belief. But in that case it is hard to see what legitimate purpose paragraph 2A serves."

---

[79] para.99 of Administrative Court judgment.
[80] As amended by s.15 Criminal Justice Act 2003.
[81] And in cases where the new offence is not imprisonable, but the offence for which the offender was originally bailed was imprisonable.
[82] *Maznetter v Austria* (1979–80) 1 E.H.R.R. 198 (para.44).
[83] S.14 Criminal Justice Act 2003.

Accordingly, the Law Commission provisionally recommended that this exception be repealed, and included instead amongst the list of factors which a court should take into account in deciding whether there is a risk that the accused will commit further offences. In passing the new version of para.2A, Parliament took a step in the other direction.

The Joint Committee on Human Rights expressed considerable reservation about **13–30** s.15, observing that:

> "the court would be prevented from granting bail in at least some cases even though it were not satisfied that there is a sufficient public interest in detaining the defendant pending trial. Instead, the court would have to detain him or her unless satisfied that there is no significant risk that he or she would abscond. In some cases . . . the court would be prevented from granting bail where detaining the defendant in custody would be self-evidently disporportionate to any purpose, and in other cases it might be clear that the public interest in detaining the defendant is outweighed by other considerations . . . "[84]

Although less strongly worded than s.25 of the Criminal Justice and Public Order **13–31** Act, this provision can be seen as creating an effective presumption against bail. In most cases where there has been a further arrest, it may be an almost impossible hurdle for a defendant to satisfy even the most robust court that there is no significant risk of further offences. Unlike the old law, where the prosecution had to show a substantial risk that the accused would re-offend, it is difficult to read the provision as conveying anything other than a burden on the accused to show that he will not re-offend, and this carries with it a risk of arbitrary decisions being made with insufficient consideration of the individual circumstances of a defendant.

Defendant absconding whilst on bail

Section 15 creates a similar exception to the right to bail in cases where an adult **13–32** defendant has failed without a reasonable excuse to surrender[85] in the same proceedings, providing that a court "may not" grant bail in these circumstances. Similar reservations apply about its compatibility with Art.5. It is interesting to note that the Solicitor-General, in debate about this particular provision, described it as "creating a presumption against bail. It requires the court to refuse bail to an adult defendant who fails without reasonable cause to answer bail in the same proceedings unless the court is satisifed that there is no significant risk that he would again fail to surrender if released on bail."[86]

Again, this raises issues under the Convention, and any curb on a court's **13–33** discretion to grant bail may fall foul of Art.5. The "presumption against bail" would appear to offend the principles laid down by the European Court in *Hutchinson-Reid*, and if the provisions are interpreted so as to make the fact that

---

[84] 2002–3 Session, Eleventh Report, para.68.
[85] or, even if he may have a reasonable excuse, to surrender as soon as it was reasonably practicable to do so—Bail Act 1976, Sch.1, Pt 1, para.6(3) as amended by s.15 Criminal Justice Act 2003.
[86] HC Consideration of Amendments, May 19, 2003, col.719.

the defendant absconded only a relevant factor to be taken into account when deciding whether to grant bail, the new provision adds nothing at all to existing law.

13–34   The provision was considered by Collins J. in the Administrative Court in *R. (on the application of Wiggins) v Harrow Crown Court*.[87] In that case a defendant who had answered his bail on other occasions during the same proceedings forgot his trial date and turned up one and a half hours late. The judge remanded the defendant in custody, not referring to para.6(3), but clearly having it in mind when she expressed a fear that if the defendant felt like not turning up on the day he would not do so. The Practice Direction *Bail: Failure to Surrender and Trials in Absence*[88] was not followed, and the judge did not embark upon proceedings to enquire into the Bail Act offence before revoking the bail.

13–35   An attempt by the applicant to argue that the provisions did not apply unless there had been a conviction for failing to surrender to his bail was unsurprisingly unsuccessful. Of greater significance are the court's views on the applicant's argument that, notwithstanding the directory language of the statute, there was no practical difference between the exceptions to the right to bail in s.4 (the court "need not" grant bail) and the further exceptions in para.6 (the court "may not" grant bail). Collins J. observed:

> " 'Need not' manifestly conveys a discretion. 'May not' is prohibitive and makes it plain that what was intended was that if a failure to surrender was established then the court should not grant bail unless the court was satisfied that there was no risk of a further failure to surrender to custody –as I say, putting, as it were, the burden the other way round . . . . Having said that, one still must bear in mind the overall principle that bail should only be refused if there is a good reason to refuse it, and the approach that must remain is that it is in all the circumstances proportionate to refuse bail. That is the test that has to be adopted by the Crown Court judge."

13–36   On the facts of this case, Collins J. held that decision could not withstand the *Wednesbury* test, in the absence of any evidence to justify the judge's fear that the defendant would abscond. Notwithstanding the finding in favour of the applicant, the language of the judgment may be thought to sit a little uncomfortably with Strasbourg case law, and could benefit from further clarification. The apparent "presumption against bail", and the suggestion that there is a burden on the applicant to establish a right to release, would appear to run counter to the principles laid down by the European Court, as authoritatively interpreted by the House of Lords in *R. (O) v Crown Court at Harrow and Governor HMP Wormwood Scrubs*.[89] In *Hutchinson-Reid v UK*[90] the European Court made clear that any imposition of a burden of proof on the detained person to show why he should be released is incompatible with Art.5(4) of the Convention. And in *Niklovka v Bulgaria*[91] a strong statutory presumption against the grant of bail was declared incompatible with Art.5.

---

[87] [2005] EWHC 882 (Admin), unreported.
[88] [2004] 1 W.L.R. 539.
[89] [2006] 3 W.L.R. 195.
[90] [2004] 1 M.H.L.R. 236.
[91] Judgment March 25, 1999. See also *Ilijokov v Bulgaria* [2001] *Archbold News 1* ECHR.

The defendant's own protection

Under para.3 of Sch.1, Pt 1, bail need not be granted if the court is satisfied that   **13–37**
the defendant should be kept in custody for his own protection. As the Law
Commission has observed, this ground "might be invoked where the defendant
is at risk of self-harm, or of harm from criminal associates, or where public
feeling is running high because of the nature of the alleged offence".[92] In the
light of the Convention caselaw, the Law Commission concluded that guidance
should be issued to judges and magistrates making it clear this exception could
only be compatible with the Convention if there are exceptional circumstances
relating to the nature of the offence or the conditions or context in which it is
alleged to have been committed. In its final report the Law Commission suggested specific guidance on this issue. As to a decision to remand an accused
person in custody to protect him against a risk of self-harm, the Law Commission
considered that this would be compatible with Art.5 provided the court was
satisfied that the risk was real and that a proper medical examination would take
place promptly.

The Criminal Justice Act 2003 amended para.3 in a way which appears to meet   **13–38**
the Law Commission's concerns,[93] and appears to be in line with a recent
decisions of the European Court.[94] The court may now impose bail conditions
upon an offender for his own protection or welfare, and this power extends to
defendants under the age of 18.[95] Whilst this may divert young and vulnerable
defendants from spending time on remand, it should be noted that the power to
impose conditions is very widely drafted, with no definition of what amounts to
a measure for a defendant's own protection, or a young person's welfare. The
provisions may have the effect of interfering with defendants' liberty, by encouraging courts to attach extensive conditions which may in turn be easily
breached.

Defendant arrested for a Bail Act offence

Paragraph 5 of Sch.1, Pt II, as amended by Criminal Justice Act 2003[96] provides   **13–39**
that bail need not be granted if the defendant has previously been granted bail in
the same proceedings, and has been arrested under s.7 of the Act (which relates
to failure to surrender, absconding or breaching a bail condition), if the court is
satisfied that there are substantial grounds for believing that the defendant, "if
released on bail . . . would fail to surrender to custody, commit an offence or bail
or interfere with witnesses or obstruct the course of justice". The former wording
of para.6 of Sch.1, Pt I, which simply provided that bail need not be granted after
a defendant has been arrested under s.7 of the Bail Act, has been repealed. This
is a welcome change, although it may be of limited significance in the light of
other new exceptions brought in by the Criminal Justice Act 2003.[97] It formalises
the approach suggested by the cases of *R. v Havering Magistrates Court ex parte*

---

[92] Consultation Paper No.157, *Bail and the Human Rights Act 1998*.
[93] S.13 Criminal Justice Act 2003.
[94] See for example *Nawicka v Poland* [2003] 1 F.L.R. 417.
[95] Ss.3 and 3A Bail Act 1976.
[96] S.13(4).
[97] See above at para.13–27.

DPP,[98] and *R (on the application of Vickers) v West London Magistrates' Court*,[99] which provided guidance to the courts about how to interpret the old provisions in a way which did not faul foul of Art.5. The provision as worded assumed that merely because the accused has breached his bail conditions in the past, he was likely to do so again in the future, and applied to arrests under section for anticipatory breach of bail conditions. The Law Commission recommended repeal of the provisions, concluding that a refusal of bail under para.6 was likely to infringe Art.5. The provisions as amended change the emphasis in cases where there has been an arrest under s.7 in line with the *Havering Justices* and *Vickers* decisions, reducing the arrest to a factor to be taken into account when the court is deciding if there is a risk of failure to surrender, further offences or obstruction of the course of justice.

Class A drug users

13–40   Section 19 Criminal Justice Act 2003 amends Sch.1 of Bail Act 1976[100] to impose a new restriction on the grant of bail to an adult offender who has tested positive for specified Class A drugs and are either: (i) before the court in relation to possession, or possession with intent to supply Class A drugs; or (ii) the court satisfied that there are substantial grounds for believing that Class A drug use "caused or contributed to the offence or (even if it did not) that the offence was motivated wholly or partly by the drug use"[101]; and (iii) that the defendant has refused to agree to participate in assessment or follow-up in relation to drug dependency. Bail "may not be granted unless the court is satisfied that there is no significant risk of his committing an offence while on bail".

13–41   It would be difficult to argue against the proposition that Class A drug addiction increases the risk of a defendant re-offending on bail, either by procuring the drugs themselves, or by committing further offences to fund the addiction—a defendant who continues to take Class A drugs, and refuses to co-operate with available treatment would be likely to provide a court with real grounds for believing that further offences would be committed in all but the most exceptional cases. Accordingly, it is unlikely that this provision will offend Art.5 in most cases, so long as the courts do not interpret it as a strict presumption against the grant of bail, and there remains a discretion to grant bail in those cases where no good grounds exist for believing that that further serious offences will be committed. If the provision is correctly applied, this is yet another example of a new provision which appears to add little to existing law—even without it, a court which was aware of a positive drug sample, in a drug-related case, with a defendant who was not co-operating with drug agencies, would in any event been likely to refuse bail on the ground that the there was a substantial risk of further offences.

---

[98] [2001] 1 W.L.R. 805.
[99] 167 J.P. 473.
[100] By inserting para.6A into Pt 1.
[101] Bail Act, Sch.1, Pt 1, para.6B(1).

D. CONDITIONS OF BAIL

Article 5(3) expressly provides that "release may be conditioned by guarantees **13–42**
to appear for trial". The court in *Wemhoff* implied that, wherever conditional bail
would be a satisfactory solution, it is to be preferred to a custodial remand—a
point particularly relevant where the risk of absconding is the primary reason for
continued detention.[102] Permissible conditions of bail under Art.5(3) include a
requirement to surrender travel documents and driving documents,[103] the imposition of a residence requirement,[104] and the provision of a sum of money as a
surety or security.[105] Where a financial condition is imposed the figure must be
assessed by reference not to the financial loss occasioned by the alleged
offence[106] but by reference to the means of the accused, if it is a security, or of
the person standing surety, and of the relationship between the two.[107] If the
accused refuses to furnish the necessary information to enable an assessment to
be made of his assets, it is permissible to establish a bail figure based on
hypothetical assets.[108] Where a person is charged with a minor public order
offence, the practice of imposing a bail condition prohibiting the defendant from
attending a demonstration or a picket may raise issues under Arts 10 or 11.[109]

Convention law permits the imposition of bail conditions when necessary to **13–43**
secure attendance at trial, and where custody may be the only other alternative.
The European Court has also looked at very restrictive bail conditions, holding
that the difference between deprivation of and restriction upon liberty is "merely
one of degree or intensity, and not one of nature or substance."[110] There will
come a point where the restrictions on liberty are sufficient to constitute detention
under Art.5.

Domestically, we have seen more and more conditions being added to bail as a **13–44**
means of avoiding remand custody. Aside from general conditions of bail such as
residence, signing at the police station, surrender of passport, the Bail Act 1976,
as amended,[111] now allows for many conditions: for example, tagging of children
and young persons, a requirement that a defendant undergoes a psychiatric
examination, or that s/he is assessed for whether s/he is dependent on drugs.
Some practices are not set out in statute: the domestic courts have also sanctioned
a "doorstep" condition (where the defendant is obliged to present himself at the

---

[102] (1979–80) 1 E.H.R.R. 55 at para.15.
[103] *Stögmüller v Austria (No.1)* (1979–80) 1 E.H.R.R. 155, para.15; Application No.10670/83
Schmid v Austria (1985) 44 D.R. 195.
[104] Application No.1067/83 *Schmid v Austia* (1985) 44 D.R. 195.
[105] *Wemhoff v Germany* (1979–80) 1 E.H.R.R. 55.
[106] *Can v Austria* (1984) E.H.R.R 121.
[107] *Neumeister v Austria* (1979–80) 1 E.H.R.R. 91, para.14, *Schertenlieb v Switzerland* (1980) 23
D.R. 137 at 196.
[108] *Bonnechaux v Switzerland* (1979) 18 D.R. 100 at 144.
[109] By analogy with *Steel v United Kingdom* (1999) 28 E.H.R.R. 603.
[110] *Guzzardi v Italy* (1981) 3 E.H.R.R. 333. see also *Pekov v Bulgaria* (2006) March 30,
ECtHR.
[111] S.3.

door of his home to show that he is observing a curfew).[112] The Criminal Justice Act provides for the imposition of yet more conditions, including conditions added for the protection of a defendant or, if the defendant is a child, his or her welfare.[113] Whilst this would appear to be in keeping with the Strasbourg caselaw,[114] care should be taken to avoid too many conditions being attached to the bail of a young person, which may in turn be easily breached. The power to impose conditions is very widely drafted, and contains no definition of what amounts to a measure for a defendant's own protection or a young person's welfare.

13–45 It should be noted that under s.16 of the Criminal Justice Act 2003 there is now a right of appeal to the crown court against the imposition of certain bail conditions by magistrates, perhaps in recognition that bail conditions are likely to multiply. Whilst the imposition of individual conditions may not fall foul of Art.5, the courts should be wary of imposing too many conditions, and placing undue restrictions on liberty or placing a person under effective house arrest.[115] Yet in the Scottish case of *McDonald v Procurator Fiscal, Elgin*,[116] a condition to remain at home at all times except between 10am and midday was upheld by the courts. The High Court of Justiciary specifically found that it did not amount to a "deprivation of liberty" so as to engage Art.5. However, the reasoning in the "control orders" decision of the Court of Appeal in *Secretary of State for the Home Department v JJ*[117] suggests that such restrictions would probably be held to amount to a deprivation of liberty. The Court of Appeal held that a curfew of 18 hours per day, restricting the applicant to a single room, with controls on visitors to the room and controls on any arranged meetings outside the room, amounted to a deprivation of liberty within the meaning of Art.5.[118]

E. PROCEDURAL REQUIREMENTS

I. General

13–46 Article 5(4) of the Convention provides that everyone who is deprived of his liberty is entitled to take proceedings by which the lawfulness of his detention can be decided speedily by a court and his release ordered if his detention is not

---

[112] *R (on the application of the CPS) v Chorley Justices* (2002) EWHC 2162 Admin, 166 J.P. 764. See also *McDonald v Procurator Fiscal, Elgin, The Times* April 17, 2003, where a condition to remain at home at all times except between 10am and midday was upheld by the courts.
[113] S.3(6) Bail Act 1976 as amended by S.13 Criminal Justice Act 2003.
[114] See for example *Nawicka v Poland* [2003] 1 F.L.R. 417.
[115] It is for this reason that the Terrrorism Act 2005 recognises that particularly onerous "control orders" have to be in derogation of a persons Art.5 rights—see *MB* [2006] 3 W.L.R. 839.
[116] *The Times* April 17, 2003.
[117] [2006] EWCA Civ 1141.
[118] Applying *Guzzardi v Italy* (1980) 3 E.H.R.R. 333.

lawful.[119] This guarantees the right to *habeas corpus* in order to challenge the legality of executive detention. It also applies to other proceedings in which a court is called upon to determine whether a person should be detained, including a bail application in criminal proceedings. In this context therefore, Art.5(4) overlaps with the requirements of Art.5(3). The former entitles the individual to apply to a court for his release and imposes certain procedural requirements, including the right to make repeated applications, whilst the latter governs the circumstances in which a court may extend pre-trial detention. The procedural requirements for a bail application in England and Wales are accordingly to be derived from a consideration of Arts 5(3) and 5(4) together. Art.6 does not apply directly, although the court has been prepared to imply analogous procedural protection under Art.5(3) and (4). The extent of the analogy was considered in *R. v Havering Magistrates Court ex parte DPP*[120] where Latham L.J. observed:

> "[T]he Court has been prepared to borrow some of the general concepts of fairness in judicial proceedings from Article 6. But that does not mean that the process required for conformity with Article 5 must also be in conformity with Article 6. That would conflate the Convention's control over two separate sets of proceedings, which have different objects."

Art.5(4) does not guarantee a right to appeal from a refusal of bail. However, where domestic law provides such a procedure, then the appeal hearing should itself be Art.5(4) compliant.[121]

II. A fully adversarial hearing

The minimum requirements for a "court" are the same under Art.5(4) and Art.5(1)(a),[122] namely independence of the executive and the parties, impartiality,[123] and a power to determine the lawfulness of the detention for the purposes of Art.5(1)(c). On any Art.5(4) review, the burden of proving the lawfulness of the detention rests with the state.[124] If the state provides a right of appeal against a refusal to order release, the appeal body must itself comply with the requirements of Art.5(4).[125] The European Court of Human Rights has held that Art.5(4) requires procedural guarantees appropriate to the kind of deprivation of liberty in   **13–47**

---

[119] The term "lawfulness" in Art.5(4) has the same meaning as the term "lawful" in Art.5(1); *Brogan v United Kingdom* (1989) 11 E.H.R.R. 117, para.65.

[120] [2001] 1 W.L.R. 805.

[121] *Grauzinis v Lithuania* (2004) 35 E.H.R.R. 144.

[122] See Ch.xx above.

[123] In *K v Austria* (1993) Series A/255-B the commission ruled that the requirement for impartiality was not satisfied where a judge who imposed a fine later ruled upon a person's detention for failure to pay the fine.

[124] *Zamir v United Kngdom* (1983) 40 D.R. 42 para.58.

[125] See *Toth v Austria* (1992) 14 E.H.R.R. 551, para.84, where the court held that although Art.5(4) does not require states to establish a second level of jurisdiction for applications for release from detention, where a system of appeal is established it "must in principle accord to the detainees the same guarantees on appeal as at first instance"; *Navarra v France* (1994) 17 E.H.R.R. 594, para.28.

question.[126] The "equality of arms" principle which has been implied by the Court into Art.6, also applies to Art.5(4) review[127]: the procedure adopted must "ensure equal treatment" and be "truly adversarial".[128] The detained person must be told the reasons for his detention[129] and be given disclosure of all relevant evidence in the possession of the authorities.[130] He must also have adequate time to prepare an application for release.[131] In *Lamy v Belgium*[132] the Court held that the requirements of Art.5(4) had not been fulfilled when:

" . . . the investigating judge and crown counsel had had an opportunity to make their submissions in full knowledge of the contents of a substantial file, while the defence could only argue its case on the vaguest of charges made on an arrest warrant."[133]

13–48　　In *Nikolova v Bulgaria*,[134] the Court held that "equality of arms is not ensured if counsel is denied access to those documents in the investigation file which are essential in order effectively to challenge the lawfulness of his client's detention." This right exists irrespective of whether it can be shown that the material is relevant to the preparation of the defendant's defence.[135] Procedural standards of this kind pose problems for the English adversarial system, where little information may be available to the defence before service of the Crown's primary case, and where it is unlikely that the defence will have had sight of the contents of the file on which the prosecutor's representations are based. The Law Commission rightly pointed out that there was no legal requirement in English law for disclosure in bail hearings,[136] but the absence of a legal obligation of disclosure for the purposes of bail hearings was to some extent remedied by *R.*

---

[126] *Wassink v Netherlands* (1990) Series A/185–A, para.30. See also *Winterwerp v Netherlands* (1979–80) 2 E.H.R.R. 387, para.60 (the procedural guarantees required by Art.5(4) are "not always" the same as those required by Art.6(1) for criminal or civil litigation). *Cf. Lamy v Belgium* (1979–80) 11 E.H.R.R. 529, para.29 (the appraisal of the need for a remand in custody in a criminal case and the subsequent assessment of guilt are "too closely linked" to permit a wholly different approach to the duty of prosecution disclosure); *De Wilde Ooms and Versyp v Belgium* (1979–80) 1 E.H.R.R. 373, paras 78–79 (procedural guarantees appropriate to a criminal prosecution required in proceedings leading to the detention of vagrants).

[127] See, *e.g. Toth v Austria* (1992) 14 E.H.R.R. 551, para.84 (prosecutor present at an appeal on the question of detention while the applicant was not: violation of Art.5(4)). There are suggestions in some of the early cases that the "equality of arms" guarantee does not apply in Art.5(4) proceedings: *Neumeister v Austria (No.1)* (1979–80) 1 E.H.R.R. 91 at 132, paras 22–25; approved in *Matznetter v Austria* (1979–80) 1 E.H.R.R. 198 at 228, para.13. These decisions have not, however, been followed: see *Toth v Austria* (1992) 14 E.H.R.R. 551, para.84; *Lamy v Belgium* (1989) 11 E.H.R.R. 529, para.29; *Sanchez-Reisse v Switzerland* (1987) 9 E.H.R.R. 71, paras 52–52.

[128] *Toth v Austria* (1992) 14 E.H.R.R. 551, para.84; *Lamy v Belgium* (1989) 11 E.H.R.R. 529, para.29, *EMK v Bulgaria* (2005) January 18, E.C.H.R.

[129] *X v United Kingdom* (1982) 4 E.H.R.R. 188, para.66.

[130] *Lamy v Belgium* (1989) 11 E.H.R.R. 529, para.29; *Weeks v United Kingdom* (1988) 10 E.H.R.R. 293, para.66. *Cf. Wassink v Netherlands* (1990) Series A/185–A, para.28.

[131] *Farmakopoulos v Belgium* (1993) 16 E.H.R.R. 187.

[132] (1989) 11 E.H.R.R. 529.

[133] *ibid.*, para.27.

[134] 31 E.H.R.R. 64, E.C.H.R.

[135] *Garcia Alva v Germany* (2003) 37 E.H.R.R. 335, where the Euorpean Court found a violation where material had not been shown to the defence for fear for prejudicing the investigation. The authority is in marked contrast to the Scottish case of *Procurator Fiscal, Glasgow v Burn and McQuilken* 2000 J.C. 043.

[136] Consultation Paper No.157, *Bail and the Human Rights Act 1998*, para.11.19.

v DPP ex parte Lee[137] where the Divisional Court held that for a bail application to be effective in a complex case there must be some residual duty of disclosure.[138]

The Attorney General's Guidelines on Disclosure 2005 provide[139] that:　　　**13-49**

> "Investigators must always be alive to the potential need to reveal and prosecutors to the potential need to disclose material, in the interests of justice and fairness in the particular circumstances of any case, after the commencement of proceedings but before their duty arises under the Act. For instance, disclosure ought to be made of significant information that might affect a bail decision or that might enable the defence to contest the committal proceedings."

The Guidelines are subject to the *caveat* that disclosure "will depend on what the accused chooses to reveal about the defence" and a statement that disclosure should not exceed anything which is obtainable under the CPIA. This probably raises no issues under the Convention—the scope of the disclosure obligation imposed by Art.5(4) is plainly less extensive than the obligation of disclosure imposed by Art.6 in relation to the trial.[140] However, the test adopted in *Nikolova* suggests that the defence must, as a minimum, have access to the documents necessary to enable an effective bail application to be made. Prosecutors will need to be vigilant to ensure compliance in individual cases, particularly where the case against the defendant is of some complexity and there may be considerable delay before the applicant may be able to challenge whether there is a *prima facie* case against him.

III. Legal representation

Article 5(4) requires the provision of legal assistance, whenever this is necessary　　**13-50**
to enable the detained person to make an effective application for release.[141] In *Woukam Moudefo v France*[142] the Commission considered that legal assistance should be available prior to the hearing as well as during it. The onus is on the

---

[137] [1999] 2 All E.R. 237.

[138] See also *Procurator Fiscal, Glasgow v Burn and McQuilken* 2000 J.C. 403, where the High Court of Justiciary held that whilst a prosecutor should be in a position to explain the basis for any fears that the accused may interfere with witnesses, he was not required to disclose sensitive operational information. *Cf. Garcia Alva v Germany*, Judgment February 13, 2001, where the European Court of Human Rights found a violation of Art.5(4) arising from a failure of the prosecutor to disclose relevant evidence on grounds of its sensitivity.

[139] Paras 55 and 56.

[140] In *Rowe and Davies v United Kingdom* (2000) 30 E.H.R.R. 1 (Op. Comm.) at para.71, the Commission observed that the disclosure requirements imposed by Art.6 are "more extensive" than those imposed by Art.5(4). As to the obligation of disclosure under Art.6 see generally paras 14–87 *et seq.* below.

[141] *Winterwerp v Netherlands* (1979–80) 2 E.H.R.R. 387, para.60; *Bouamar v Belgium* (1988) 11 E.H.R.R. 1, para.60; *Megyeri v Germany* (1993) 15 E.H.R.R. 584, paras 23–25; *Woukam Moudefo v France* (1988) 13 E.H.R.R. 549.

[142] (1988) 13 E.H.R.R. 549.

state to take the initiative to provide legal representation[143] and to provide legal aid where representation is necessary and the detained person has insufficient means to pay for it.[144] Art.5(4) generally requires that a detained person or his legal representative be permitted to participate in an oral hearing,[145] and the European Court has found states in violation of the Convention where bail has been considered in the absence of both.[146]

IV. Presence of the accused

13–51 The European Court has said that the judge determining bail "must himself or herself hear the detained person before taking the appropriate decision,"[147] but this appears to mean the hearing of representations from the defendant or his or her lawyer, rather than hearing oral evidence. Old authorities suggesting that the accused has a right to be present whether or not he is represented by a lawyer do not appear to represent the current state of the law.[148]

13–52 The Convention probably does not require the presence of a defendant at a hearing under Art.5(4), so long as he or she is represented and there is no risk of injustice from this.[149] If the proceedings are to be adversarial, then the defendant must know the nature of the prosecution objections to his or her release, and be given the opportunity to comment on it.[150] The representations made should be oral rather than in writing,[151] and the applicant and a representative from the defence should be physically present to hear any representations made by the prosecution.[152] If there is any dispute as to the matters relied upon, or any new materials raised in court, then the accused should be given a right to attend the hearing: in *Gruzinis v Lithuania*[153] the Court said there is a right to be present and to give instructions if any new grounds are relied upon at a bail hearing[154] In keeping with this, the Law Commission's final report suggested that participation through a legal representative will generally be sufficient, although a court should

---

[143] *Megyeri v Germany* (1993) 15 E.H.R.R. 584, para.27; *Winterwerp v Netherlands* (1979–80) 2 E.H.R.R. 387, para.66.

[144] Application 9174/80 *Zamir v United Kingdom* (1983) 40 D.R. 42 at 60.

[145] *Keus v Netherlands* (1991) 13 E.H.R.R. 700, para.27; *Farmakopoulos v Belgium* (1992) 16 E.H.R.R. 187, (para.46); *Winterwerp v Netherlands* (1979–80) 2 E.H.R.R. 387, para.60; *Bouamar v Belgium* (1989) 11 E.H.R.R. 1, para.60; *cf. Sanchez-Reisse v Switzerland* (1987) 9 E.H.R.R. 71, para.51 (written proceedings held sufficient in a case under Art.5(1)(f)).

[146] *EMK v Bulgaria* (2005) January 18, Applicantion No.00043231/98.

[147] *TW v Malta* (1999) 29 E.H.R.R. 185.

[148] *Winterwerp v Netherlands* (1979–80) 2 E.H.R.R. 387.

[149] *Sanchez-Reisse v Switzerland* (1986) 9 E.H.R.R. 71. *Cf.* the domestic authority of *R (Gardner) v Parole Board* [2005] EWHC 2985.

[150] See *Toth v Austria* (1991) 14 E.H.R.R. 551 at para.84.

[151] *Kotsaridis v Greece* (2004) ECHR September 14, *Todorov v Bulgaria* (2005) October 20, ECtHR. Both judgments are only available in French.

[152] *Wloch v Poland* (2000) October 19, ECtHR.

[153] (2002) 35 E.H.R.R. 144.

[154] In the *Havering Justices* case, above para.13–46, the Administrative Court placed some reliance on the fact that a defendant could give evidence if he wished to do so.

not finally dispose of a bail application in the absence of the defendant "where the defendant's presence is essential to fair proceedings".[155]

Under English law, a defendant has no express right to be present at a bail **13–53** application. Section 122 of the Magistrates' Courts Act 1980 entitles magistrates to proceed in the absence of a defendant, provided he is legally represented.[156] In practice, however, magistrates generally treat an accused person as entitled to be present, unless he or his legal representative invite the court to proceed in his absence. The Law Commission suggested that magistrates "would expect the procedure to be challenged by judicial review if they gave their decision in the defendant's absence against his or her wishes".[157]

For some time it has been standard procedure for Crown Court bail applications **13–54** take place in chambers, where the defendant is not produced.[158] The procedure was clearly open to challenge under the ground that it offended the principles of open justice and the right of the defendant to participate effectively under Art.6,[159] particularly as courts are now able to conduct hearings with the defendant being present via a live television link.[160] In *R. (Malik) v Central Criminal Court and Crown Prosecution Service*,[161] the Administrative Court reviewed a judge's refusal to hear a bail application in open court in the presence of the defendant. Although it was persuaded by the applicant's arguments that bail applications should generally be held in open court, the court held that a defendant should have a "burden of persuading the Crown Court that he should be given leave to be present."

It is unclear how this judgment may be interpreted in practice, and the extent to **13–55** which it will secure Convention rights in every case. There are often good reasons why the defendant may need to be present, in person or via a video link. Although there are rules mandating the prosecution to give written notice of its objections to bail and to serve a copy of this on the defence[162] these are rarely followed, and it is common for defence lawyers to be met with new material at court, when it is impossible to take instructions from the defendant or counter the allegation. Put at its lowest, the Convention obliges the Crown to put the defence on detailed notice of their objections to bail, and grounds in support of these, in advance of the hearing, to allow for the defence to meet the objections and avoid unnecessary adjournments and further remands in custody. This may be difficult to achieve in a system where bail applications are often listed for hearing at the crown court within 48 hours of notification.

---

[155] Guidance to Bail Decision-Takers, para.27.
[156] r.19.13, Criminal Procedure Rules 2005.
[157] Consultation Paper No.157, *Bail and the Human Rights Act 1998*, para.11.14, n.18.
[158] r.19.18 Criminal Procedure Rules 2005. The defendant may seek leave to be present. On appeal to the Crown Court following decisions by magistrates the defndant has no right to be present unless he is represnting himself: r.19.17.
[159] See for example *Scarth v UK* [1999] EHRLR 332, where the hearing of arbitration hearings in private on the basis of administrative convenience was said to be in breach of Art.5. But see *Campbell and Fell v UK* (1984) 7 E.H.R.R. 164, where there were considerations of security.
[160] S.57 Crime and Disorder Act 1998.
[161] [2006] 4 All E.R. 1141.
[162] Criminal Procedure r.19.18(3).

V. A hearing in public?

13–56   In its early decisions the Court held that there was no requirement under Art.5(4) that bail proceedings must take place in public. In *Neumeister v Austria*[163] the Court observed that "publicity in such matters is not . . . in the interest of accused persons as it is generally understood". However, this was before the Court had developed its current emphasis on a fully adversarial procedure. In later decisions, the Court has implied that Art.5(4) hearings should ordinarily take place in public.[164]

Crown Court bail applications were heard almost exclusively in private, until the recent decision in *R.(Malik) v Central Criminal Court.*[165] The Law Commission's final report pointed out that this procedure probably offended Art.5(4), and recommended that if the defendant requested that a bail hearing take place in public, then it should be held in public unless there are good reasons for not doing so.[166]

13–57   A domestic challenge was long in coming. Quashing a refusal for a public hearing of a bail application where a defendant was charged with terrorist offences, the Administrative Court in *Malik* observed that in the light of the principle of open justice there could be no presumption in favour of bail applications being held in private. The correct approach would be for the court to consider whether it was necessary to depart from the ordinary rule of open justice in an individual case. The court went on to observe that there was nothing objectionable to the Crown Court listing bail applications as private hearings so long as any application to have it heard in public should be acceded to unless there was good reason for excluding the public. It is likely that this listing practice will change if enough defendants and interested parties insist on a public hearing.

VI. The duty to give a reasoned ruling

13–58   The Convention caselaw under Art.5(3) and (4) imposes an obligation on a court considering bail to give reasons for its decision. In *Letellier v France*,[167] the Court explained that, in considering an application for bail, domestic courts:

> " . . . must examine all the facts arguing for and against the existence of a genuine requirement of public interest justifying, with due regard to the principle of the presumption of innocence, a departure from the rule of respect for individual liberty and set them out in their decisions on the applications for release. It is essentially on the basis of the reasons given in these decisions and of the true facts mentioned by the

---

[163] (1979–80) 1 E.H.R.R. 91 at 132, para.23. *Cf. De Wilde Ooms and Versyp v Belgium* (1979–80) 1 E.H.R.R. 373 at 409, para.79, where the Court suggested that a requirement for a public hearing and public pronouncement of judgment were "judicial features" required by Art.5(4).

[164] *Assenov v Bulgaria* [1999] E.H.R.L.R. 225 where the court held that the fact that a hearing was held in a closed court was one of several factors contributing to a breach of Art.5(4). See also *Nikolova v Bulgaria*, March 25, 1999, unreported.

[165] [2006] 4 All E.R. 1141.

[166] Guidance to Bail Decision-Takers, para.28.

[167] (1992) 14 E.H.R.R. 83 at para.35.

applicant in his application for release and his appeals that the Court is called upon to decide whether or not there has been a violation of Article 5(3) of the Convention."

The Court has stated on a number of occasions that the reasoning of the domestic courts will be regarded as inadequate if it is "abstract" or "stereotyped".[168] In *Van der Tang v Spain*[169] the Court found no breach of Art.5(3) where the applicant's detention in custody was justified on the facts, and he was aware of the reasons on which it was based. Nevertheless, the Court emphasised the need for adequate reasoning. In response to the applicant's contention that "the decisions refusing to grant conditional release contained very poor reasoning", the Court stated that "it would certainly have been desirable for the Spanish courts to have given more detailed reasoning as to the grounds of the applicant's detention."[170] In *Jablonski v Poland*[171] the Court suggested that the Polish courts should have gone so far as to give reasons why bail with conditions would not have secured the accused's presence at trial.

Since the coming into force of the Human Rights Act, English courts have   **13–59** adopted the practice of giving reasoned judgments on bail.[172] This is a sea-change from the pre-HRA position, noted by the Law Commission as follows[173]:

> "In practice . . . we understand that bail decisions are commonly recorded on forms which require only the ticking of boxes to indicate both the grounds on which bail is denied and the statutory reasons for that conclusion . . . Our view of the Strasbourg case law is that reasons recorded simply by repeating the statutory wording on a standard form are likely to be considered 'abstract' or 'stereotyped' . . . [T]he Strasbourg Court assumes that the quality of the reasons given indicates the quality of the decision-making process recorded. As a result, any refusal of bail which is recorded in standard form is in danger of being held to violate Article 5."

Moreover, the Law Commission could see no good reason in principle why bail decisions should not be subject to the administrative law principle that when a duty to give reasons arises, those reasons must be "clear and adequate and deal with the substantial issues in the case".[174] Such principles are incontrovertible now that a right of judicial review lies in respect of a refusal of bail in the Crown Court,[175] following the abolition of the right to apply to a High Court judge for bail under s.17(3) Criminal Justice Act 2003.

---

[168] *Clooth v Belgium* (1992) 14 E.H.R.R. 717, para.44; *Yagci and Sargin v Turkey* (1995) 20 E.H.R.R. 505, para.52; *AI v France* 1998–IV Judgment September 23, 1998, para.108.

[169] (1996) 22 E.H.R.R. 363.

[170] *ibid.*, para.60.

[171] (2003) 36 E.H.R.R. 455 at para.84.

[172] See for example *R.(Shergill) v Harrow Crown Court* [2005] EWHC, for a confirmation of this practice.

[173] Consultation Paper No.157, *Bail and the Human Rights Act 1998*, paras 4.20 to 4.21.

[174] *R. v Immigration Appeal Tribunal ex parte Jebunisha Kharvaleb Patel* [1996] Imm.A.R. 161 at 167.

[175] *R (N) v Isleworth Crown Court and HM Customs and Excise*, March 2, 2005.

VII. Practical obstacles

13–60   It is worth recalling that the remedy required by Art.5(4) must be available in practice as well as in theory. In *RMD v Switzerland*,[176] a prisoner on remand was moved from one prison to another and across a number of Swiss cantons. Although there was a procedure in each canton through which he could challenge the lawfulness of his detention, the procedure had to be re-started each time the prisoner was transferred from one canton to another. The Court held that although appropriate procedures were theoretically available, the procedural obstacles involved in using them were so great that the remedy was not effective in practice, and there had accordingly been a violation of Art.5(4).

VIII. Periodic reconsideration of remand in custody

13–61   In *Bezicheri v Italy*,[177] the Court held that a person who is detained before trial should have the opportunity to test the lawfulness of continued detention at reasonable intervals. The Italian government had argued that in cases of pre-trial detention the intervals need not be so frequent as, for example, where a mentally disordered person is detained. The Court rejected this approach in clear terms: "The nature of detention on remand calls for short intervals; there is an assumption in the Convention that detention on remand is to be of strictly limited duration . . . because its *raison d'etre* is essentially related to the requirements of an investigation which is to be conducted with expedition."[178] In that case the accused had re-applied within a month, and the Court regarded that as a reasonable interval, taking account of the need for the judge to examine the evidence and the fact that the accused was deprived of his liberty.[179] Other decisions lay emphasis on the possibility that the strength of reasons for refusing bail may diminish over time, and also on the insufficiency of courts relying on stereotyped formulae for continued remands in custody.[180]

13–62   It is open to question whether English law fully meets this requirement. In *R. v Nottingham Justices ex parte Davies*[181] the Divisional Court held that a person may only make a renewed application for bail if there has been a "material change of circumstances". The Criminal Justice Act 1988 inserted a new Pt IIA into Sch.1 to the Bail Act. Paragraph 2 provides that this requirement does not apply to the second application for bail:

> "At the first hearing after that at which the court decided not to grant the defendant bail he may support an application for bail with any argument as to fact or law that he desires (whether or not he has advanced that argument previously)."

---

[176] (1999) 28 E.H.R.R. 225.
[177] (1990) 12 E.H.R.R. 210.
[178] *ibid.*, at para.21.
[179] The judge did not rule on the renewed bail application for over five months, and the court held that to be a violation of Art.5(3).
[180] See *Clooth v Belgium* (1992) 14 E.H.R.R. 717 and *Mansur v Turkey* (1995) 20 E.H.R.R. 535 at para.55, for example. *Cf.* the domestic courts' approach in *W v Switzerland* (1994) 17 E.H.R.R. 60, which was detailed and well-documented.
[181] [1981] Q.B. 38.

However, para.3 goes on to provide that at any *subsequent* hearing, "the court **13–63** need not hear arguments as to fact or law which it has heard previously". In *R. v Barking Justices ex parte Shankshaft*,[182] the Divisional Court held that where a new argument for bail was advanced by the defendant, the court should consider that new argument in addition to any arguments which had previously been advanced. Applying this principle to para.3, it would appear that where the accused is able to advance a new argument, he is entitled to rely on arguments previously considered as well. The fact remains, however, that there is no entitlement under English law to periodic reconsideration of bail on the ground of the passage of time. If the defendant is unable to advance any fresh arguments of fact or law after the second hearing, the court is not obliged to entertain the application. This appears to be inconsistent with Art.5(4).

In light of the Strasbourg caselaw, the Law Commission considered that an **13–64** accused should be able to re-apply for bail at 28-day intervals, without having to advance any fresh arguments[183]:

> "Article 5(4) requires that the defendant should be able to mount a legal challenge to the grounds for detention, and, after the lapse of a reasonable time, should be able to do so again—even, it would seem, if there has been no change of circumstances other than the lapse of time. Yet the [Bail] Act expressly says that, after the second hearing, the court need not hear arguments which it has already heard . . . [I]f there is no new argument, the court has a discretion not to hear any arguments at all. And if it does refuse to hear argument, we think it most unlikely that the hearing could be regarded as giving the defendant sufficient opportunity for challenge to satisfy Article 5(4) . . . Our provisional view is that where, after a remand in custody of 28 days, the defendant makes a further application for bail, and the court refuses to hear arguments that were put forward at the previous hearing, the Strasbourg Court might well find an infringement of the defendant's rights under Article 5(4). It follows that in these circumstances a magistrates' court should be willing to hear such arguments again."

In order to achieve this result without the need for legislative amendment, the Law Commission proposed that "courts should be given guidance to the effect that a lapse of 28 days since the last fully argued bail application should itself be treated as an argument which the court has not previously heard". The Law Commission's final report makes specific proposals for such guidance, noting in particular the possibility that time served on remand may have reduced the risk of the defendant absconding.[184]

F. CUSTODY TIME LIMITS

Where the court orders that a person should remain in custody pending trial there **13–65** will be a breach of Art.5(3) if the proceedings are not conducted with appropriate

---

[182] (1983) 147 J.P. 399.
[183] Consultation Paper No.157, *Bail and the Human Rights Act 1998*, paras 12.17 *et seq.*
[184] Guidance to Bail Decision-Takers, para.27. As to the Strasbourg approach to this question, see para.13–08 above.

expedition[185]: the fact that an accused has been refused bail requires special diligence in the conduct of the proceedings[186] and entitles him to have his case treated as a priority by the prosecution and the court.[187] There is however no absolute limit to the permissible period of pre-trial detention; the reasonableness of the length of the proceedings depends on the facts of the case.[188] The requirement for expedition has to be balanced against the duty of the court to ascertain the facts and to allow both parties to present their case,[189] and continued detention can only be justified if there are specific indications of a genuine requirement of public interests which outweighs the rule of respect for individual liberty.[190]

13–66 The standard which the court has imposed is not a particularly exacting one, although it may be difficult for a state to justify a remand period which is longer than the eventual sentence for an offence.[191] In *W v Switzerland*[192] the Court (by a narrow majority) found no violation of Art.5(3) where an accused person had been detained for four years before his trial. The case was a particularly complex fraud, which required lengthy preparation and the court held that there were valid reasons for refusing bail.

13–67 Against this background, it seems certain that the regime established by the Prosecution of Offences Act 1985, and the Prosecution of Offences (Custody Time Limits) Regulations 1987[193] would be found to satisfy Art.5(3). The court's power to extend the time limit when satisfied that there is "good and sufficient cause for doing so" and that "the prosecution has acted with all due expedition" is also likely to comply with the Convention, especially if the court's discretion is exercised according to the guidance laid down by Lord Bingham C.J. in *R. v Manchester Crown Court ex parte McDonald*,[194] where the Divisional Court considered the Convention authorities. In *Wildman v DPP*[195] the High Court held that the principles established in *R. v Havering Magistrates Court ex parte DPP*[196] applied equally to applications to extend custody time limits. Thus, neither the strict rules of evidence, nor the requirement for formal disclosure[197]

---

[185] The standard of diligence required is the same as under Art.6(1): *Abdoella v Netherlands* (1995) 20 E.H.R.R. 585, para.24.

[186] *Clooth v Belgium* (1992) 14 E.H.R.R. 717, para.36; *Tomasi v France* (1993) 15 E.H.R.R. 1, para.84; *Herczegfalvy v Austria* (1993) 15 E.H.R.R. 437, para.71.

[187] *Wemhoff v Germany* (1979–80) 1 E.H.R.R. 55, para.17.

[188] *W v Switzerland* (1994) 17 E.H.R.R. 60 (four years: no breach of Art.5(3)); *Toth v Austria* (1992) 14 E.H.R.R. 551 (two years and one month: violation of Art.5(3)); *Tomasi v France* (1993) 15 E.H.R.R. 1 (five years and seven months: violation of Art.5(3)), *Kotsaridis v Greece* (2004) September 23, E.C.H.R. (five years and five months: violation of Art.5(3) and 6(1), *Wesolowski v Poland* (2004) Application No.0029687/96 (three years, two months: violation).)

[189] *Wemhoff v Germany* (1979–80) 1 E.H.R.R. 55, para.17.

[190] *Illowecki v Poland* 37 E.H.R.R. 546.

[191] *Goral v Poland* (2003) Application No.00038654/97.

[192] (1994) 17 E.H.R.R. 60.

[193] S.I. 1987/299.

[194] [1999] 1 W.L.R. 841.

[195] *The Times*, February 8, 2001.

[196] [2001] 1 W.L.R. 805, see para.13–39 above.

[197] Note, however, that para.56 of the Attorney General's Guidelines on *Disclosure of Information in Criminal Proceedings* (2005) provides that "disclosure ought to be made of significant information that might affect a bail decision": see para.13–49 above.

applied. The court did, however, recognise that insofar as it may be necessary for a defendant to test any aspect of the application, the procedural means must be made available to enable him to do so. The House of Lords held in *R. v Leeds Crown Court ex parte Wardle*,[198] by a 3–2 majority, that Reg.4(4) of the Prosecution of Offences (Custody Time Limits) Regulations,[199] which state that each offence attracts its own custody time limit, is compatible with Art.5.

One might have assumed that if a defendant were to be detained in breach of the **13–68** custody time limits, this would amount to a violation of Art.5(3), and thus to give rise to a right to compensation under Art.5(5). This issue arose for consideration in *Olotu v Home Office*,[200] where the claimant had been detained beyond the expiry of the custody time limits. As the result of an oversight, her case had not been brought before the Crown Court. Lord Bingham C.J., for the Court of Appeal, held that the detention did not amount to a violation of Art.5(3) since expiry of the custody time limits did not entitle a defendant to be released, but merely to apply to the Crown Court for bail. Although the court would have been under an obligation to grant bail, the failure of the claimant's solicitor to apply for bail meant that the detention, though unlawful, did not give rise to a violation of Art.5(3). Nor, therefore, did it give rise to a right to compensation under Art.5(5). There are a number of difficulties with the reasoning in this decision. Lord Bingham accepted in terms that the claimant's detention was unlawful as a matter of domestic law. If that analysis is correct,[201] then it is difficult to see how the detention could have met the requirements of legality in Art.5(1) or (3). Moreover, the Court of Appeal does not appear to have been referred to *McGoff v Sweden*[202] where the Commission held that Art.5(3) imposed an "unconditional" obligation on the state to bring the accused automatically before a court.

The issue arose again in *R. (O) v Crown Court at Harrow and Governor HMP* **13–69** *Wormwood Scrubs*,[203] where a Crown Court judge had refused bail after refusing to extend a custody time limit, because the defendant was subject to s.25 of Criminal Justice and Public Order Act 1994.[204] It was argued in the House of Lords that, because a refusal to extend a custody time limit involves a judge finding that the prosecution has lacked "due diligence", the court cannot go on to refuse bail without violating Art.5(3). Under Art.5(3), the state must show "special diligence" in progressing cases where a defendant is in custody.[205] The appellant argued that the test for "due diligence" and "special diligence" are the same, and similarly that the significance attached in the Strasbourg case law to "relevant" and "sufficient" grounds was akin to the expression "good and

---

[198] [2001] 2 W.L.R. 865.
[199] S.I. 1987/299.
[200] [1997] 1 W.L.R. 328.
[201] It was of course open to the Court of Appeal to hold that the detention was lawful on the ground that until a bail application was made, the defendant was in lawful custody by order of the Crown Court. This is not, however, how the decision is expressed.
[202] (1982) 31 D.R. 72.
[203] [2006] 3 W.L.R. 195.
[204] For further discussion about this section and the decision in *O*, see para.13–24 above.
[205] *Stogmuller v Austria* (1969) 1 E.H.R.R. 155; *Punzelt v Czech Republic* (2001) 33 E.H.R.R. 49.

sufficient cause" in s.22(3) (a) Prosecution of Offenders Act 1985. The House of Lords rejected this attractive argument, finding no automatic equation between a lack of due diligence for the purposes of custody time limits and the reasonable time requirement in Art.5(3). Referring to the approach adopted in *Grisez v Belgium*,[206] where the European Court found no breach of Art.5(3) notwithstanding culpable delays on the part of the state, Lord Brown said that the Strasbourg approach was to look at a case as a whole, deciding at a later point in the proceedings where the reasonable time guarantee had been breached.

13–70 Again, the reasoning is problematic. Applying the Convention directly, domestic courts of first instance do not have the luxury of being able to look from the endpoint of the proceedings. Instead, the domestic courts are obliged at an earlier point to make decisions in accordance with the Convention. The crucial question at the earlier stage is not whether after the event the Strasbourg Court would find a violation of Art.5(3) later down the line, but whether it is permissible to deny bail to a defendant whose custody time limit has not been renewed. The fact that domestic law sets an exacting standard in the custody time limits, and that these have been breached should weigh heavily at this point, as should the presumption of liberty.

---

[206] (2003) 36 E.H.R.R. 854.

ASPECTS OF CRIMINAL PROCEDURE

A. Legal Representation and Related Matters

I. Introduction

Article 6(3)(c) guarantees the right of a defendant in criminal proceedings "to **14–01** defend himself in person, or through legal assistance of his own choosing or, if he has not sufficient means to pay for legal assistance, to be given it free when the interests of justice so require". The purpose of this provision is to secure "equality of arms" so as "to place the accused in a position to put his case in such a way that he is not at a disadvantage *vis-à-vis* the prosecution."[1] We have already seen[2] that denial of access to a solicitor during police detention may violate Art.6(3)(c) in conjunction with Art.6(1), particularly if adverse inferences are subsequently drawn from a defendant's failure to answer questions in an interview.[3] In this section, we examine the right to legal representation more generally, including the imposition of mandatory representation requirements, issues surrounding the appointment and dismissal of counsel, the standard of representation and the adequacy of the time allowed for preparation of the defence case, legal professional privilege and the right to legal aid in criminal proceedings.

II. Mandatory Representation

Subject to the requirement to provide legal aid in appropriate cases[4] it is, in the **14–02** first place, for the national authorities to determine whether the accused should

---

[1] *X v FRG* (1984) 8 E.H.R.R. 225; *Bonisch v Austria* (1987) 9 E.H.R.R. 191.
[2] See para.5–38 above.
[3] *Murray v United Kingdom* (1996) 22 E.H.R.R. 29.
[4] See paras 14–27 *et seq.* below.

have the right to defend himself in person, or through a lawyer. In *X v Austria*[5] the Commission observed that:

> "While [Article 6(3)(c)] guarantees to an accused person that proceedings against him will not take place without an adequate representation of the case for the defence, [it] does not give an accused person the right to decide for himself in what manner his defence should be assured ... [T]he decision as to which of the two alternatives should be chosen, namely the applicant's right to defend himself in person or to be represented by a lawyer of his own choosing, or in certain circumstances one appointed by the court, rests with the competent authorities concerned."

14–03 Thus, the Court has recognised that there may be circumstances in which domestic law might justifiably insist on legal representation.[6] In *Croissant v Germany*[7] the applicant was charged in connection with his activities as the lawyer of various members of the Red Army Faction. The relevant German legislation required that he be legally represented at all stages of the proceedings. He was initially represented by two court-appointed lawyers of his own choosing. Because of the complexity of the case the court then appointed a third lawyer to whom the applicant objected on political grounds. In finding no violation of Art.6 the Court considered that a requirement for legal representation could not breach Art.6(3)(c): "The requirement that a defendant be assisted by counsel at all stages of the Regional Court's proceedings—which finds parallels in the legislation of other contracting states—cannot, in the Court's opinion, be deemed incompatible with the Convention."

14–04 Similarly in *Imbroscia v Switzerland*[8] the Court held that a requirement of legal representation is in the first instance a question for the national authorities, the court considering the matter in the light of the overall fairness of the trial. The Commission has expressed a similar view in relation to appeal proceedings.[9] Moreover, it is to be noted that mandatory professional defence in the case of serious offences was considered permissible by most members of the United Nations Human Rights Committee.[10]

14–05 It is against this background that domestic courts will have to evaluate statutory provisions requiring a defendant to be legally represented for the purposes of cross-examining a child victim of assault, cruelty or sexual abuse or an adult rape victim. Section 34A of the Criminal Justice Act 1988 prohibits a defendant in person from cross-examining any child witness who is alleged to be a victim of or witness to a sexual or violent offence.[11] Similar restrictions were introduced in relation to adult rape victims by the Youth Justice and Criminal Evidence Act 1999. Providing the accused has been given a proper opportunity to cross-

---

[5] Application No.1242/61.
[6] In Italy, for example, it seems that only legal representatives are able to attend appeal proceedings in the Court of Cassation: *Tripodi v Italy* (1994) 18 E.H.R.R. 295 at para.30. As to the practice of the European Court of Human Rights on this issue, see para.1–30 above.
[7] (1993) 16 E.H.R.R. 135.
[8] (1994) 17 E.H.R.R. 441.
[9] *Philis v Greece* (1990) 66 D.R. 260.
[10] U.N. Docs. CCPR/C/SR. 132 (May 16, 1994). Report on Jordan.
[11] Within the meaning of s.32(2) of that Act.

examine through counsel,[12] we consider that it is unlikely that such a provision would be found to breach Art.6. Although some commentators have assumed that the prohibition might infringe defendants' rights under the Convention, this neglects the point that such rules are intended to strike a proper balance between the rights of the accused and those of the victim.[13] Indeed, it is arguable that obliging a victim to be cross-examined by the person alleged to have abused them has the potential to violate the Art.3 rights of the victim.[14]

III. Choice of Representation

In general, an accused's choice of lawyer should be respected,[15] and an appoint- **14–06**
ment made against the wishes of the accused will be "incompatible with the notion of a fair trial . . . if it lacks relevant and sufficient justification".[16] Factors to be taken into account include the basis of the accused's objection to the appointment and the existence or absence of prejudice. Article 6(3)(c) does not however guarantee the accused the right to choose a court-appointed lawyer, nor to be consulted with regard to the choice of an official defence counsel.[17] This principle has been held to apply to legally aided defendants in the United Kingdom.[18] A lawyer may be excluded by the court for good reason.[19] Thus, in *X v United Kingdom*[20] the Commission found no violation of Art.6(3)(c) where the Professional Conduct Committee of the Bar Council had ruled that it would be improper for defence counsel to represent his father in a criminal trial. A defendant does not have an absolute right to be represented by lay relatives either.[21]

The fact that an accused has failed to attend the hearing does not entitle the court **14–07**
to proceed in the absence of his lawyer.[22] Indeed, if neither the defendant nor the legal representative is duly informed of the hearing, it is a violation of Art.6 for the court to proceed.[23] Similarly, there may be a violation if the lawyer is not

---

[12] The Youth Justice and Criminal Evidence Act 1999 makes provision for the appointment of a "special counsel", where this is necessary in the interests of justice, to conduct cross-examination of a complainant where the accused is unrepresented. As the role of "special counsel" in criminal proceedings generally, see para.14–154 below.

[13] See *Doorson v Netherlands* (1997) 23 E.H.R.R. 330.

[14] Such a complaint was made in *M v United Kingdom* (Unreported) see para.18–57 below.

[15] *Goddi v Italy* (1984) 6 E.H.R.R. 457.

[16] *Croissant v Germany* (1993) 16 E.H.R.R. 135 (para.27).

[17] *X v Germany* (1976) 6 D.R. 114.

[18] *X v United Kingdom* (1983) 5 E.H.R.R. 273; *Balliu v Albania*, App.No.74727/01, judgment of 16 June 2005.

[19] *X v United Kingdom* Application No.6298/73, (1975) 2 Digest 831 (disrespect to the court); *Ensslin, Baader and Raspe v Federal Republic of Germany* (1978) 14 D.R. 64 (breach of professional ethics); *cf. Bothwell* [2006] N.I.C.A. 35, (chosen lawyers did not have rights of audience, no violation of Art.6 in excluding them).

[20] (1978) 15 D.R. 242 (paras 243–244).

[21] *Mayzit v Russia* (2006) 43 E.H.R.R. 38, *Popov v Russia*, App.No.26853/04, judgment of July 13, 2006.

[22] *Lala v Netherlands* (1994) 18 E.H.R.R. 586.

[23] *Metelitsa v Russia*, App.No.33132/02, judgment of June 22, 2006 (not notified of appeal hearing—prosecution represented, defence not); *Kehayov v Bulgaria*, App.No.41035/98, judgment of January 8, 2005 (lawyer barred from pre-trial remand hearing).

allowed to see the case file, since this is likely to reduce the effectiveness of the legal representation.[24]

14–08   The accused's right to representation by a lawyer can be undermined by a breakdown in the relationship between counsel and his client or by professional embarrassment. How far does the court have to go in permitting the instruction of alternative counsel in such circumstances? The problem of professional embarrassment arose in *X v United Kingdom*.[25] In the course of evidence given on a *voir dire* the defendant departed from his instructions and admitted that certain incriminating statements which he was alleged to have made were true. Despite this, he wished defence counsel to continue to represent him on the basis that the statements were untrue. Defence counsel withdrew. The judge took the view that given the extent of the admissions which the defendant had made on the *voir dire*, any fresh counsel appointed would be unavoidably embarrassed. Accordingly, he declined to permit the appointment of new counsel and required the defendant to continue unrepresented, albeit with the assistance of his solicitors. The Commission considered that "the trial judge offered the applicant every assistance and advice in the presentation of his case,"[26] and took account of the fact that the applicant's solicitors continued to act for him and were available to advise and assist him during the trial; the fact that the defendant in person was permitted the opportunity to cross-examine witnesses and call evidence; the fact that the judge had offered the defendant the opportunity to make an unsworn statement from the dock; the fact that the judge gave clear directions on the burden and standard of proof; and the fact that the judge had directed an acquittal on three of the counts. The Commission observed that:

> "[A]n accused person cannot require counsel to disregard basic principles of his professional duty in the presentation of his defence. If such an insistence results in the accused having to conduct his own defence, any consequent 'inequality of arms' can only be attributable to his own behaviour ... [S]uch was the nature, scope and specificity of the incriminating statements made by the applicant, [that] it was not unreasonable for the trial judge to have formed the opinion that fresh counsel could not continue to act on his behalf in a manner consistent with his professional duty not to mislead the court."[27]

14–09   In *Kamasinski v Austria*[28] the applicant expressed to the judge on several occasions his dissatisfaction with his counsel, and eventually, as a result of a dispute in court, counsel asked the judge to discharge him from his function. The request was refused, and the applicant was convicted. The Court held that even though the trial could have been conducted differently, and even if counsel had sometimes acted in a way that the applicant thought contrary to his best interests, there had been no violation of Art.6(3)(c). There was no manifest failure to

---

[24] *Ocalan v Turkey*, App.No.46221/99, judgment of Grand Chamber on May 12, 2005; *Kehayov v Bulgaria* (previous note: lawyer not allowed access to case file); *cf. Klimentyev v Russia*, App. No.46503/99, judgment of November 16, 2006 (lawyer had access to case file: no violation).
[25] (1980) 21 D.R. 126.
[26] *ibid.*, at para.16.
[27] *ibid.*, at paras 6–8.
[28] (1991) 13 E.H.R.R. 36.

provide effective legal representation in this case.[29] In *Frerot v France*[30] the applicant had dismissed his lawyer towards the end of a trial. The first replacement lawyer declined to act, so a second lawyer was assigned to him. That lawyer then applied for an adjournment but the French court, taking account of the procedural difficulties this would cause, refused the request. The Commission held that this did not amount to a violation of Art.6(3)(c), because the applicant had been advised and represented by the same counsel for all but the last day of the trial, and the late change did not render the trial unfair.

IV. The Right to Effective Representation

In order to meet the requirements of Art.6(3)(c), representation provided by the state must be effective. The state will not generally be responsible for shortcomings in the way a legal aid lawyer performs his duties,[31] but the relevant authorities may be required to intervene where the failure to provide effective representation is manifest and has been brought to their attention.[32] Thus in *Artico v Italy*[33] the accused had been sentenced to custody for various fraud offences in his absence and without his knowledge. Wishing to appeal, he applied for legal aid and was assigned counsel. The lawyer declined to act, pleading ill-health and the onerous nature of the brief. The accused's various efforts to have a new lawyer appointed met with no success for some months, and by the time he succeeded his appeal had already been dismissed. The Court gave short shrift to the Italian government's argument that it had complied with Art.6 by appointing the first lawyer, holding that "the Convention is intended to guarantee not rights that are theoretical or illusory but rights that are practical and effective." In the Court's view, the authorities should have either compelled the lawyer to act or appointed a new one. Nor was it necessary for the applicant to establish that the result of the proceedings would have been different if he had been effectively defended. Whilst the existence or absence of prejudice was relevant to extent of the remedy required by way of just satisfaction, it was not a pre-requisite for a finding that Art.6(3)(c) had been violated. The Court found a violation on a similar basis in *Daud v Portugal*[34]:

14–10

> "The first appointed lawyer had not taken any steps before reporting sick and the second did not have the necessary time to study the file, visit the client and prepare the defence. The time between the notification of the replacement of the lawyer and the hearing was too short for a serious, complex case in which there had been no judicial investigation and which led to a heavy sentence."[35]

In those circumstances the state, or the court itself, ought to have ensured that the trial was adjourned until counsel had had adequate time for preparation.

---

[29] *cf. Pakelli v Germany* (1984) 6 E.H.R.R. 1.
[30] (1996) 85–B D.R. 103.
[31] *Artico v Italy* (1981) 3 E.H.R.R. 1, para.36.
[32] *Artico v Italy* (1981) 3 E.H.R.R. 1; *Kamasinki v Austria* (1991) 13 E.H.R.R. 36, para.65.
[33] (1981) 3 E.H.R.R. 1.
[34] [1998] E.H.R.L.R. 634.
[35] *ibid.*, at 635.

14–11   Where counsel has been instructed so late as to leave insufficient time to master the brief, the accused's right under Art.6(3)(b) to adequate time and facilities for the preparation of his defence may be violated. However, the Court is unlikely to find a violation on this ground unless an application has been made for an adjournment to enable the case to be prepared.[36] The adequacy of the time allowed will obviously depend upon the complexity of the case.[37] The defence lawyer must be appointed in sufficient time to enable the case to be properly prepared.[38] Where there is a change of legal representation, the newly-appointed lawyers must be permitted additional time to prepare.[39] Although it was formerly the practice of the Commission to examine a case to determine if the late appointment of the defence lawyer had actually prejudiced the accused,[40] the current emphasis in the court's case-law is upon the necessity for criminal proceedings to have the appearance of fairness, and upon "the increased sensitivity of the public to the fair administration of justice."[41] The provision of legal assistance does not, however, require unlimited access by a defendant to a lawyer. It may be acceptable for the lawyer to limit the number of consultations so as to ensure that the legal aid budget is not exceeded.[42]

14–12   The approach of the Commission to the question of state responsibility was not always consistent. In *F v United Kingdom*[43] defence counsel had to withdraw the day before the trial, and the defendant met new counsel only on the morning of the trial. Although the trial was for attempted murder, and the new counsel declined to apply for an adjournment to ensure fuller preparation of the case, the Commission dismissed the application on the basis that the conduct of counsel could not be attributed to the state.[44] In *Daud v Portugal*,[45] however, new counsel was appointed only three days before the hearing of a complex drugs case, at the conclusion of which the applicant was sentenced to nine years' imprisonment. The Court found a breach of Art.6(3)(c). While respecting the independence of the Bar, the court held that it was the state's duty to ensure that everyone received "the effective benefit of his right". On the facts of this case it should have been obvious to the authorities that the legal representation offered was inadequate.

14–13   The English authorities have traditionally assumed that shortcomings in legal representation must cross the threshold of "flagrant incompetence" before they are capable of amounting to a ground of appeal against conviction.[46] That

---

[36] *Murphy v United Kingdom* (1972) 43 C.D. 1; 2 Digest 794.

[37] See generally *Albert and Le Compte v Belgium* (1983) 5 E.H.R.R. 533 at para.41.

[38] *X and Y v Austria* (1978) 15 D.R. 160; *Perez Mahia v Spain* (1987) 9 E.H.R.R. 145.

[39] *Goddi v Italy* (1984) 6 E.H.R.R. 457.

[40] *X v United Kingdom* (1970) 13 Y.B. 690; *Murphy v United Kingdom* (1972) 43 C.D. 1.

[41] See, in another context, *Borgers v Belgium* (1993) 15 E.H.R.R. 92 at para.24.

[42] *M v United Kingdom* (1984) 36 D.R. 155; see also the Canadian decision in *Munroe* (1990) 59 C.C.C. (3d) 446.

[43] (1992) 15 E.H.R.R. CD 32.

[44] See also the court in *Kamasinski v Austria* (1991) 13 E.H.R.R. 36 at para.65: "It follows from the independence of the legal profession of the State that the conduct of the defence is essentially a matter between the defendant and his counsel, whether counsel be appointed under a legal aid scheme or be privately financed."

[45] [1998] E.H.R.L.R. 634.

[46] *R. v Ensor* 89 Cr.App.R. 139 (CA) considering *R. v Irwin* 85 Cr.App.R. 294 (CA) and *R. v Gautam* [1988] Crim.L.R. 109 (CA).

approach appeared to be softening somewhat in *R. v Clinton*[47] where the Court of Appeal observed that "it is probably less helpful to approach the problem via the somewhat semantic exercise of trying to assess the qualitative value of counsel's alleged ineptitude, but rather to seek to assess its effect on the trial and the verdict". However in *R. v Donnelly*[48] the court retreated to its former position, holding that the practice of criticising trial counsel on appeal without alleging flagrant incompetence should not be followed. This rather arid debate seems to have been put to rest by the Human Rights Act. In *R. v Nangle*[49] the Court of Appeal observed that in view of the requirements of the Convention, flagrant incompetence may no longer be regarded as the appropriate measure of when the court will quash a conviction for the alleged error of legal representatives: "What Article 6 requires in this context is that the hearing of the charges against the accused should be fair. If the conduct of the legal advisers has been such that this objective is not met, then this Court may be compelled to intervene." In the Scots case of *James v H.M. Advocate*,[50] the defendant came to be represented by the same firm as one of two co-defendants, both of whom had incriminated him. It was found that his individual defence was not properly put, and his conviction was quashed since his right to fair trial had been violated.

In the New Zealand case of *Shaw*,[51] defence counsel informed the Crown of his **14–14** unavailability on the trial date, but it was not until five days before the trial that the Crown sent a reply objecting to any alteration of the trial date. The judge refused an adjournment at the start of the trial, and the accused was left to conduct his own defence. He was found guilty and sentenced to six months' imprisonment. The Court of Appeal found that the defendant's right to legal representation had been violated, not least because counsel's understanding of the law and ability to cross-examine might have influenced the outcome of the trial.[52]

There is considerable North American jurisprudence on the provision of "effec- **14–15** tive assistance" by counsel. In the United States the test is whether counsel's performance fell below a reasonable standard, bearing in mind the Bar's standards of conduct.[53] A similar approach has been adopted in the Canadian cases,[54] where a two-stage test is now applied. The court should enquire: (a) whether counsel's conduct showed a lack of competence; and (b) whether it is probable that, but for that lack of competence, the result of the proceedings would have been different.[55]

---

[47] 97 Cr.App.R. 320; See also *R. v Fergus* 98 Cr.App.R. 313.

[48] [1998] Crim.L.R. 131.

[49] [2001] Crim. L.R. 506.

[50] 2006 S.C.C.R. 170.

[51] [1992] N.Z.L.R. 652.

[52] Under the Strasbourg jurisprudence the requirement to show prejudice is considered as relevant only to the extent of the remedy required: See *Artico v Italy* (1981) 3 E.H.R.R. 1 at para.35.

[53] *Strickland v Washington* 466 US 668 (1984).

[54] E.g. two cases from Ontario, *Silvini* (1991) 68 C.C.C. (3d) 251 and *Collier* (1992) 77 C.C.C. (3d) 570, and the Nova Scotia decision in *Schofield* (1996) 148 N.S.R. (2d) 175.

[55] See *McAuley* (1996) 150 N.S.R. (2d) 1 (counsel relied on submission of no case; no incompetence proved); *B (LC)* (1996) 46 C.R. (4th) 368 (counsel refused to visit defendant in prison; even if incompetent, not established that result would probably have been different.)

V. Legal Professional Privilege

14–16   The inviolability of legal professional privilege in English law was re-affirmed by the House of Lords in *R. v Derby Magistrates' Court ex parte B*,[56] where Lord Taylor described it as "a fundamental human right protected by the European Convention". B was arrested for murder, and admitted in interview with the police that he was solely responsible. Shortly before his trial he retracted his confession and alleged that the murder had been committed by his step-father (A). B was acquitted, and the police thereupon arrested A and charged him with the murder. At committal proceedings against A, his counsel sought an order for the disclosure of statements made by B to his solicitor. B declined to waive privilege. The magistrate made the order, considering that B no longer had an interest in maintaining his privilege (since he could not be prosecuted for the murder a second time), and holding that the public interest in the acquittal of the innocent outweighed the public interest in protecting solicitor and client communications. The House of Lords overturned the magistrate's order, Lord Taylor explaining that it breached the "long established rule that a document protected by privilege continues to be protected so long as the privilege is not waived by the client: once privileged, always privileged":

> "[T]he privilege is the same whether the documents are sought for the purpose of civil or criminal proceedings, and whether by the prosecution or the defence, and ... the refusal of the client to waive his privilege, for whatever reason, or for no reason, cannot be questioned or investigated by the court ... [T]he privilege is that of the client, which he alone can waive, and ... the court will not permit, let alone order, the attorney to reveal the confidential communications which have passed between him and his former client. His mouth is shut forever."

14–17   Having reviewed the English authorities, he continued;

> "The principle which runs through all these cases ... is that a man must be able to consult his lawyer in confidence, since otherwise he might hold back half the truth. The client must be sure that what he tells his lawyer in confidence will never be revealed without his consent. Legal professional privilege is thus much more than an ordinary rule of evidence, limited in its application to the facts of a particular case. It is a fundamental condition on which the administration of justice as a whole rests ... Nobody doubts that legal professional privilege could be modified, or even abrogated, by statute, subject always to the objection that legal professional privilege is a fundamental human right protected by the European Convention for the Protection of Human Rights and Fundamental Freedoms."

14–18   For its part, the European Court of Human Rights has recognised that a high degree of protection is to be afforded to the confidentiality of communications passing between a lawyer and his client. Breach of professional privilege can involve a violation of the right to privacy in Art.8, as well as having implications for the right to a fair trial in Art.6(1) and, in particular, for the right to effective legal representation in Art.6(3)(b). In *Schonenberger and Durmaz v Switzerland*[57] the second applicant had been arrested for drugs offences. Whilst he was

---

[56] [1996] A.C. 487.
[57] (1989) 11 E.H.R.R. 202.

in police custody his wife instructed a lawyer, the first applicant, to represent her husband. Mr Schonenberger wrote a letter addressed to Mr Durmaz and sent it to the public prosecutor's office, asking that it be forwarded to his client. The letter contained forms of authority and also advised Mr Durmaz that he was not obliged to answer questions, that his answers could be used in evidence, and that it would be to his advantange to maintain his silence. The public prosecutor read the letter and decided to withhold it from Mr Durmaz on the ground that it might jeopardise the proper conduct of the investigation. The Court was in no doubt that this constituted a violation of Art.8:

> "[T]he Government relies in the first place on the contents of the letter in issue: according to the Government, it gave Mr Durmaz advice relating to pending criminal proceedings which was of such a nature as the jeopardise their proper conduct. The Court is not convinced by this argument. Mr Schonenberger sought to inform the second applicant of his right 'to refuse to make any statement', advising him that to exercise it would be to his 'advantage'. In that way, he was recommending that Mr Durmaz adopt a certain tactic, lawful in itself since, under the Swiss Federal Court's case law—whose equivalent may be found in other contracting states—it is open to an accused person to remain silent. Mr Schonenberger could also properly regard it as his duty, pending a meeting with Mr Durmaz, to advise him of his right and of the possible consequences of exercising it. In the Court's view, advice given in these terms was not capable of creating a danger of connivance between the sender of the letter and its recipient and did not pose a threat to the normal conduct of the prosecution."

Neither did the Court accept the argument that the communication did not attract privilege since Mr Schonenberger had not been formally instructed by Mr Durmaz. He had received instructions from Mrs Durmaz and had made attempts to contact his client. In the Court's view, these contacts "amounted to preliminary steps intended to enable the second applicant to have the benefit of the assistance of a defence lawyer of his choice and, thereby, to exercise a right enshrined in another fundamental provision of the Convention, namely Article 6". **14–19**

The passing reference to Art.6 in *Schonenberger and Durmaz* was taken up in *S v Switzerland*,[58] where the Court implied into Art.6(3)(c) the right of an accused person to consult with his lawyer in private, without the risk of infringements of privilege by the state. Although Art.6 makes no explicit reference to legal professional privilege, the Court noted that this right was guaranteed under the national law of a number of contracting states, and expressly enshrined in Art.8(2)(d) of the American Convention on Human Rights. The Court also attached importance to the fact that within the Council of Europe, an equivalent protection was recognised by Art.93 of the Standard Minimum Rules for the Treatment of Prisoners.[59] This provides that "interviews between [a] prisoner and his legal adviser may be within the sight, but not within the hearing, either direct or indirect, of a police or institution official". On the strength of these comparative and international standards, the Court concluded that: **14–20**

---

[58] (1992) 14 E.H.R.R. 670, para.48.
[59] Annexed to Resolution (73) 5 of the Committee of Ministers.

"[A]n accused's right to communicate with his advocate out of the hearing of a third person is one of the basic requirements of a fair trial in a democratic society and follows from Article 6(3)(c) of the Convention. If a lawyer were unable to confer with his client and receive confidential instructions from him without such surveillance, his assistance would lose much of its usefulness, whereas the Convention is intended to guarantee rights that are practical and effective."

14–21   As a result, the monitoring of the applicant's correspondence with his lawyer, and the supervision of visits to him in custody, constituted a breach of Art.6(3)(c). The possibility that defence lawyers might co-ordinate their strategies could not justify such supervision since there was nothing unusual or unethical about such an approach. Neither was it necessary for the applicant to prove that he had been in any way prejudiced in the preparation of his case since "[a] violation of the Convention does not necessarily imply the existence of injury".

14–22   The leading decision is now *Brennan v United Kingdom*,[60] where the principal complaint was that, when the applicant was eventually allowed to consult his lawyer, this was only permitted in the presence of a police officer. The Court stated the basic principle of confidentiality, reasoning that "if a lawyer were unable to confer with his client and receive confidential instructions from him without surveillance, his assistance would lose much of its usefulness, whereas the Convention is intended to guarantee rights that are practical and effective." However:

> "the Court's case law indicates that the right of access to a solicitor may be subject to restrictions for good cause and the question in each case is whether the restriction, in the light of the entirety of the proceedings, has deprived the accused of a fair hearing. While it is not necessary for the applicant to prove, assuming such were possible, that the restriction had a prejudicial effect on the course of the trial, the applicant must be able to claim to have been directly affected by the restriction in the exercise of the rights of the defence."[61]

In this case a police officer was present only at one interview, but this was the first interview between lawyer and client. Noting that the decision in *John Murray v United Kingdom*[62] recognised the significance of an early decision not to answer police questions, the Court found a violation of Art.6(3)(c) in conjunction with Art.6(1):

> "The Court cannot but conclude that the presence of the police officer would have inevitably prevented the applicant from speaking frankly to his solicitor and given him reason to hesitate before broaching questions of potential significance to the case against him. Both the applicant and his solicitor had been warned that no names should be mentioned and that the interview would be stopped if anything was said which was perceived as hindering the investigation . . . It is indisputable that he was in need at that time of legal advice, and that his responses in subsequent interviews, which were to be carried out in the absence of his solicitor, would continue to be of potential relevance to his trial and could irretrievably prejudice his defence."[63]

---

[60] (2002) 34 E.H.R.R. 507.
[61] *Ibid.*, para.58.
[62] (1996) 22 E.H.R.R. 29, discussed in 15–102 below.
[63] (2002) 34 E.H.R.R. 507, at para.62.

In *Ocalan v Turkey*[64] the Grand Chamber reiterated the principles in *Brennan* and found a violation where the applicant had only been allowed to consult his lawyers in the presence of military personnel, and then for restricted periods of time.

The approach of the English courts has been more equivocal. In the *La Rose* case[65] the complaint was that the applicant had to speak to his solicitor from a telephone on the custody desk in the police station, within the earshot of police officers. The Divisional Court dismissed the application on the ground that no prejudice had been shown, and that there was no evidence that a police officer had overheard L's conversation with his lawyer. However, this was the applicant's first contact with his lawyer, and the case was decided before *Brennan*. It should now be approached differently. At the other end of the scale is *Grant*,[66] the Court of Appeal quashed a conviction where communications between solicitors and their clients in the exercise yard of a police station were recorded by the police. Such recordings had been made in relation to suspects in three major cases. In the other two cases the proceedings were stayed for abuse of process, and the Court of Appeal held that the same remedy should have been applied here. The decision in *Brennan* was cited, but the judgment was founded on the common law and the proposition that deliberate interference with a detained suspect's right to the confidence of privileged communications with his solicitor seriously undermines the rule of law. Irrespective of the gravity of the crimes alleged, and prosecution would be an abuse of process even though it could not be known what prejudice the defendant suffered as a result of the recordings.   **14–23**

The close relationship between Art.6 and Art.8 was emphasised in *Niemietz v Germany*[67] which concerned the execution of a search warrant at the offices of a lawyer in order to ascertain the whereabouts of a third party who was under investigation for a criminal offence. The Commission and the Court both held that the concept of "privacy" extended to a lawyer's dealings with his clients. After noting the principle of professional secrecy guaranteed under the German Federal Regulations for Lawyers, the Commission observed: **14–24**

"These features of privacy are particularly strong as regards the lawyer's activities in his own law office. There he exercises domestic authority and general access by the public is excluded. Such privacy is a necessary basis for the lawyer-client relationship ... The interference complained of affected the applicant in his position as a lawyer *i.e.* as an independent organ in the administration of justice and as independent counsel of his clients, with whom he must entertain a relationship of confidentiality, ensuring the secrecy of information received from his clients and documents relating thereto. Such are also the demands of the right to a fair trial and the effective use of defence rights as envisaged by Article 6(1) and (3) of the Convention in cases of representation by counsel."

---

[64] App.No.4622/99, judgment of May 12, 2005, paras 131–137.
[65] *R. (on the application of La Rose) v Commissioner of Police for the Metropolis* [2002] Crim.L.R. 215.
[66] [2005] Crim.L.R. 955.
[67] [1999] Q.B. 966 at 977 to 978.

In finding a violation of Art.8, the Court explained that:

"[T]he search impinged on professional secrecy to an extent that appears disproportionate in the circumstances; it has, in this connection, to be recalled that, where a lawyer is involved, an encroachment on professional secrecy may have repurcussions on the proper administration of justice and hence on the rights guaranteed by Article 6 of the Convention."

14–25   The privilege is free-standing, and it is not necessary to show that particular lawyer-client communications were directly concerned with pending proceedings.[68] Moreover in *Foxley v United Kingdom*[69] the Court treated Art.8 and Art.6 as effectively interchangeable where a violation of legal professional privilege was alleged. In that case, a Receiver and Trustee in Bankruptcy, appointed in the context of proceedings for the enforcement of a confiscation order under the Criminal Justice Act 1988, had obtained an order from the county court under the Insolvency Act 1986,[70] authorising the re-direction of the applicant's mail. The letters opened and copied included correspondence with the applicant's legal advisers. The Court found a violation of Art.8, observing that it could find "no justification" for the actions of the Receiver, which were contrary to "the principles of confidentiality and professional privilege attaching to relations between a lawyer and his client". It noted that the government had not sought to argue that "the privileged channel of communication was being abused". Nor were there "any other exceptional circumstances" justifying the intrusion. Having found a violation of Art.8, the Court held that it was unnecessary to examine the same complaint under Art.6 of the Convention.

14–26   Legal professional privilege does not extend to communications made to a solicitor by his client for the purpose of being guided or helped in the commission of crime,[71] or to communications which are themselves in furtherance of a criminal enterprise.[72] This principle applies whether or not the solicitor is aware of his client's unlawful purpose.[73] It is implicit in the *Schonenberger and Durmaz*, *Campbell* and *Foxley* cases that abuse of a privileged relationship is capable of affording a ground for restricting the protection afforded to legal professional privilege. Nevertheless, the Court has emphasised the need to ensure that the exception is narrowly and carefully defined, and that procedures are in place to ensure that any interference is kept within this limited category. Thus, in *Kopp v Switzerland*[74] the Court held that even where it is alleged that the lawyer himself is involved in criminal activity, special safeguards are required to ensure

---

[68] *Campbell v United Kingdom* (1993) 15 E.H.R.R. 137, paras 46–48.

[69] [1999] 1 W.L.R. 2130 at 2144, para.25, and 2148, para.39.

[70] At 2140, para.5.

[71] *Pretto v Italy* (1984) 6 E.H.R.R. 182, para.21.

[72] *Axen v Germany* (1984) 6 E.H.R.R. 195, para.25; *Pretto v Italy* (1984) 6 E.H.R.R. 182, para.21.

[73] In *T and V v United Kingdom* (2000) 30 E.H.R.R. 121 the presence of the media during a trial of two juveniles, and an order made by the judge lifting reporting restrictions to permit the publication of their identities and their photographs was held to have contributed to a violation of Art.6(1). The court referred to the possibility that procedures such as publicity, which are generally considered to safeguard the rights of adults on trial, could have the opposite effect on young defendants, and may need to be abrogated in order to ensure their understanding and participation.

[74] (1995) 20 E.H.R.R. 557.

that a proper distinction is drawn between "matters specifically connected with a lawyer's work under instructions from a party to proceedings and those relating to activity other than that of counsel". The applicant was a lawyer under investigation in connection with the disclosure of official secrets. The Court considered that the absence of independent judicial authorisation for the interception of the applicant's telephone calls was "astonishing", especially "in this sensitive area of the confidential relations between a lawyer and his clients, which directly concern the rights of the defence".

VI. Legal aid in criminal cases

The second limb of Art.6(3)(c) imposes a requirement to provide legal aid in **14–27** criminal cases. The wording of the English text appears to suggest that the right to free legal representation is an alternative to the right of an accused person to represent himself. This is not however how it has been interpreted by the Court. In *Pakelli v Germany*[75] the Court held that Art.6(3)(c) guarantees three related but independent rights to a person charged with a criminal offence: first, the right to defend himself in person; secondly, the right to defend himself through legal assistance of his own choosing; and thirdly, on certain conditions being met, the right to free legal assistance and representation:

> "Having regard to the object and purpose of this Article, which is designed to secure effective protection of the rights of the defence ... a person charged with a criminal offence who does not wish to defend himself in person must be able to have recourse to legal assistance of his own choosing; if he does not have sufficient means to pay for such assistance, he is entitled under the Convention to be given it free when the interests of justice so require."

The "interests of justice" criterion will take account of the complexity of the **14–28** proceedings, the capacity of the individual to represent himself, and the severity of the potential sentence.[76] Legal aid is not necessarily required where the factual and legal issues in the case are straightforward, and there is no requirement for expert cross-examination.[77] On the other hand, the Court has rejected the argument that a violation of Art.6(3)(c) will only arise where the absence of legal assistance can be shown to have actually prejudiced the accused.[78]

Where the accused faces imprisonment, this will usually be sufficient in itself to **14–29** require the grant of legal aid.[79] However, the requirements of the Convention go further than this. In *Pham Hoang v France*[80] the Court found a violation of Art.6 where the French courts had denied legal aid to the applicant, despite the fact that "the proceedings were clearly fraught with consequences" for him, because he had been convicted of importing drugs and was ordered to pay a substantial fine. This decision suggests the restriction of legal aid to cases where custody is a real possibility may not be honouring the "interests of justice" criterion in

---

[75] *ibid.*, at paras 35–41.
[76] *X v Austria* (1963) 11 C.D. 31 at 43.
[77] *X v Norway* (1970) 35 C.D. 37 at 48.
[78] Application No.9433/81 (unreported), (1981) 2 Dig. 738.
[79] *ibid.*, at 738.
[80] *Ensslin, Baader and Raspe v Germany* (1978) 14 D.R. 64.

Art.6(3)(c).[81] Thus, where a Scottish magistrate peremptorily refused legal aid on the ground that it was not in the interests of justice to grant it in cases of breach of the peace and resisting arrest, the case proceeded to a friendly settlement.[82]

14–30   In practice, the European Court of Human Rights adopts a strict approach to the requirement to provide free legal assistance in criminal cases, which is illustrated by a series of cases against the United Kingdom. In *Granger v United Kingdom*,[83] a Scottish case, the court held that a refusal of legal aid for the applicant's appeal against a conviction for perjury violated Art.6(3)(c) taken together with Art.6(1). Legal aid had been refused on the ground that the appeal was without substance and had no reasonable prospect of success. The court however held that the interests of justice criterion had to be assessed in the light of all the circumstances of the case. The applicant was serving a five year prison sentence so that there was no doubt about the importance of what was at stake for him. The Court of Appeal had been addressed at length by the Solicitor General who appeared for the Crown. One of the issues which arose was of considerable complexity, but the applicant was not in a position to understand the prepared statement he read out, or the opposing arguments. Nor could he reply to those arguments or answer questions from the bench.

14–31   At first sight the court's decision in *Granger* may appear to turn on the complexity of the issues which arose in the appeal. However, in *Boner v United Kingdom*[84] and *Maxwell v United Kingdom*[85] the court unanimously found a violation of Art.6(3)(c) despite concluding that the legal issues were straightforward. Under Scots law there was, at the time, no requirement for leave to appeal. But the decision as to whether legal aid should be granted lay with the Scottish Legal Aid Board which had to decide whether an applicant for legal aid had substantial grounds for appealing and whether it was in the interests of justice that he should be granted legal aid. The Board could therefore refuse legal aid on the ground that the appeal was unmeritorious. The European Court of Human Rights held that the interests of justice required free legal assistance. This was despite the fact that the legal issues in the case were not complex, no point of substance had arisen in the appeal, and prosecution counsel had not addressed the Court of Appeal. The court held that in the absence of legal representation the applicants had been unable to address the court on the issues raised in the appeal and thus had been deprived of the opportunity to defend themselves effectively.

14–32   It is now quite clear that the requirement for effective legal representation will be mandatory not only in the higher courts but in all courts or tribunals where loss of liberty may be at stake. In *Benham v United Kingdom*,[86] the Court was called upon to determine whether the "interests of justice" criterion in Art.6(3)(c) was satisfied in Magistrates' Court proceedings leading to imprisonment for non-

---

[81] *Cf.* Young R. and Wilcox A., "The Merits of Legal Aid Revised" [2007] Crim. L.R.
[82] *McDermite v United Kingdom* (1987) 52 D.R. 244.
[83] (1990) 12 E.H.R.R. 469, at paras 42–48.
[84] (1995) 19 E.H.R.R. 246.
[85] (1995) 19 E.H.R.R. 97.
[86] (1996) 22 E.H.R.R. 293, at paras 61–64.

payment of the community charge. Under the applicable regulations there was no right to full legal aid, but a debtor was entitled to Green Form advice and assistance and, in the discretion of the Magistrates' Court, to representation under the ABWOR[87] scheme. The Government submitted that this level of provision was adequate in the circumstances. In the Government's submission, the proceedings were intended to be straightforward and amounted, in effect, to a means inquiry at which full legal representation was unnecessary. The Court disagreed:

> "[W]here deprivation of liberty is at stake, the interests of justice in principle call for legal representation. In this case B faced a maximum term of three months imprisonment . . . Furthermore, the law which the magistrates had to apply was not straightforward. The test for culpable negligence in particular was difficult to understand and operate, as was evidenced by the fact that, in the judgment of the Divisional Court, the magistrates' finding could not be supported on the evidence before them."

The Court went on to hold that the existing provision was inadequate since under Art.6(3)(c) the applicant was entitled to representation at the hearing *as of right*:   **14–33**

> "The Court has regard to the fact that there were two types of legal aid provision available to B. Under the Green Form scheme he was entitled to up to two hours advice and assistance from a solicitor prior to the hearing, but the scheme did not cover legal representation in court. Under the ABWOR scheme the magistrates could, at their discretion, have appointed a solicitor to represent him, if one had happened to be in court. However, B was not entitled as of right to be represented . . . In view of the severity of the penalty risked by B, and the complexity of the applicable law, the Court considers that the interests of justice demanded that, in order to receive a fair hearing, B ought to have benefitted from free legal representation during the proceedings before the magistrates."

Despite the Court's reference to the complexity of the domestic proceedings, it   **14–34**
is clear that the decisive criterion in *Benham* was the seriousness of what was at stake for the applicant in terms of the potential penalty that the court could impose.[88] On the same principle the Strasbourg Court has held that Art.6 requires legal representation before a person is bound over to keep the peace, since imprisonment is the penalty for default.[89] The approach of the United Nations Human Rights Committee under Art.14 of the I.C.C.P.R. appears to be broadly the same. In *OF v Norway*[90] the Committee held that a defendant who had been convicted of two minor motoring offences which could only lead to a small fine had not shown that the interests of justice in the particular case required the assignment of a defence lawyer at the state's expense.[91] The Strasbourg Court

---

[87] Advice by way of representation.
[88] The court has subsequently ordered the payment of compensation to several others who were denied legal representation in such proceedings prior to 1997: see *Beet v United Kingdom* (2005) 41 E.H.R.R. 23, and *Lloyd v United Kingdom*, App.No.29798/96, judgment of March 1, 2005.
[89] *Hooper v United Kingdom* (2005) 41 E.H.R.R. 1.
[90] Application No.158/1983.
[91] *Cf. Robinson v Jamaica*, App. No.223/1987.

has likewise held that Art.6.(3)(c) does not require the grant of legal assistance in minor cases.[92]

14–35   In *Procurator Fiscal, Fort William v McLean and anor*[93] the High Court of Justiciary held that a fixed fee for certain summary prosecutions was not incompatible with Art.6. The relevant regulation[94] provided for a flat fee of £550 for all work done in summary proceedings up to and including a diet at which a plea of guilty was made and accepted, or a plea in mitigation was made, and the first 30 minutes of any summary trial. The lawyer would receive the same fee regardless of the work done or of how essential or costly any outlays may have been. The defence argued that such a rigid system of payment, with no safeguard to allow for the actual requirements of a given case, imported a substantial risk that even an honourable solicitor acting in good faith might allow professional standards to fall below an acceptable minimum. The court accepted that the system produced what could properly be called a conflict of interest since it was in the interests of the defence lawyer to keep outlays and work done to a minimum. However, on the facts, there was no actual prejudice to the defendants since there was no suggestion that their lawyers had omitted to do anything which was necessary for the presentation of their defence. The court was not persuaded by the more general argument that all defendants were necessarily prejudiced by the regulations since they were at risk of receiving inadequate representation. The suggestion that a lawyer would betray his client's interests was unacceptably speculative. Whether the matter was approached in terms of "conflict of interest" or in terms of "equality of arms" there was no basis for holding that what might be the case in particular circumstances was inevitably the case in all circumstances.

B. CAUTIONING AND DISCONTINUANCE

14–36   Neither the presumption of innocence in Art.6(2), nor the right of access to court implicit in Art.6(1), entitles an accused to insist that any criminal charge which has been brought be carried through to its conclusion in order to enable him to establish his innocence. In *X, Y and Z v Austria*[95] the Commission held that Art.6(2) does not:

> " . . . prevent the Public Prosecutor's Office from deciding not to prosecute or to withdraw the indictment and the judge from terminating the proceedings without a ruling. In other words Article 6(2) does not confer on the accused an absolute right that the charge brought against him should be determined by a court."[96]

---

[92] *Gutfreund v France* (2006) 42 E.H.R.R. 48.
[93] *The Times*, August 11, 2000.
[94] Criminal Legal Aid (Fixed Payments) (Scotland) Regulations (S.I. 1999/491).
[95] (1980) 19 D.R. 213 at 217–8.
[96] *ibid.*, at 217.

The Commission noted that if the decision had involved any suggestion that the applicant was guilty this would be different. Recent re-affirmed by the Court,[97] these principles were applied when declaring inadmissible the complaint in *Withey v United Kingdom*,[98] where the applicant had been charged with offences of indecency with children. When the case came to court the prosecution offered no evidence (the principal witness having declined to testify), and the judge ordered that the case should "lie on the file" and might be revived if there was any repetition of the alleged acts. The applicant complained that he was denied the opportunity of establishing his innocence, but the Court held that Art.6 does not guarantee a right to be tried.

Notwithstanding this general principle the Court has held that any compromise of **14–37** criminal proceedings (such as the administration of a caution or the acceptance of a plea of guilty to a lesser offence) must be truly voluntary and free from constraint. In the leading decision of *Deweer v Belgium*[99] the applicant was a butcher who was alleged to have been selling over-priced pork. The public prosecutor issued an order requiring the provisional closure of the applicant's business pending the conclusion of the criminal prosecution, or until the applicant paid a penalty of B. Fr. 10,000 by way of "settlement". The applicant opted to pay the penalty under protest. In Strasbourg, he complained that the procedure had denied him the right to a fair trial. The Court began by observing that "the 'right to a court', which is a constituent element of the right to a fair trial, is no more absolute in criminal than in civil matters". It was subject to implied limitations. Without wishing to elaborate a general theory of such limitations, the Court pointed to a decision not to prosecute, and an order for discontinuance of proceedings as being obvious examples. The Court held that by agreeing to pay the penalty the applicant had waived his right to a trial. That did not, however, exhaust the requirements of Art.6. The right to a fair trial was of such importance that any compromise reached between the state and the accused had to be free from constraint. In the present case the amount of the fine was minimal when compared to the consequences of contesting the proceedings. Had the applicant elected to proceed to trial, his business would have remained closed throughout the period, and he would have been exposed to the risk of a far more substantial penalty in the event of a conviction. In the Court's view, there was a "flagrant disporportion" between the two alternatives facing the applicant. This created a pressure so compelling that it was hardly surprising that he had yielded. As a result the procedure was held to be "tainted by constraint" and to have amounted to a breach of Art.6. These principles may prove relevant to the development of conditional cautions under the Criminal Justice Act 2003.[100]

C. SEVERANCE

The principles of English law governing severance of defendants who are **14–38** properly joined in the same indictment are reasonably settled. The fact that

---

[97] *Soini v Finland*, App.No.36404/97, judgment of January 17, 2006, para.67.
[98] App.No.59493/00, decision of August 26, 2003.
[99] (1979–80) 2 E.H.R.R. 439.
[100] Criminal Justice Act 2003, ss.22–27; for further discussion of *Deweer*, see 16–77 below.

evidence which is admissible against one defendant may be inadmissible against another is a relevant consideration, but is not in itself generally sufficient to require the court to order separate trials since the risk of unfairness can be countered by clear directions to the jury.[101] Similarly, the fact that the defence of one accused inevitably involves an attack on a co-accused, whilst material to the exercise of the discretion, is not decisive.[102]

14–39 The Strasbourg institutions have generally held that admissibility of evidence is primarily a matter for domestic law.[103] Nevertheless, the admission of certain types of evidence is capable of rendering the trial as a whole unfair.[104] Where evidence inadmissible against one defendant is admitted against another in a joint trial, the Commission appears to accept that a refusal to order severance *may* exceptionally raise an issue under Art.6 if the evidence which has been elicited puts the fairness of the trial in jeopardy. In one unreported decision[105] the applicant complained that evidence elicited during cross-examination of a co-defendant was prejudicial to his defence. He had not however applied for severance before or during the trial. In rejecting the complaint, the Commission observed that:

> " . . . in a trial, like the present, where four co-defendants are tried together, it is inevitable that some evidence elicited from or in relation to one of the defendants may be considered prejudicial to another defendant by his counsel. In the present case, however, the applicant does not appear to have applied to be tried separately from his co-defendants, and the Commission does not find that the evidence given by this co-defendant was such as to jeopardise the fairness of the applicant's trial."[106]

14–40 A challenge to the constitutionality of severance provisions under the South African Constitution failed in *State v Shuma*.[107] The court held that the existing provisions in the Criminal Procedure Act, which enabled severance at any point during the proceedings where this was in the interests of justice, struck a fair balance between the interests of the accused and those of the state. Erasmus J. observed that "courts should not readily declare well-established procedure offensive to the constitution". The issue had to be judged "in the real context of criminal trials in general and the facts of the particular case".

D. DELAY

14–41 Article 6(1) guarantees a right to a hearing within a reasonable time in both civil and criminal cases. Its purpose is to protect all parties from excessive procedural

---

[101] See, e.g. *R. v Lake* (1976) 64 Cr.App.R. 172 at 175 (C.A.).
[102] *R. v Grondkowski and Malinowski* [1946] K.B. 369; *R. v Miller* (1952) 36 Cr.App.R. 169.
[103] See generally Ch.15 below.
[104] See, e.g., *Austria v Italy* (1963) 6 Y.B. 740 at 784, and more recently *Teixeira de Castro v Portugal* (1999) 28 E.H.R.R. 101.
[105] Application No.10159/82, 2 Dig. Supp. 6.1.1.4.4.5, at 6.
[106] *ibid.*, at 7.
[107] [1994] 4 S.A. 583 E.

delays.[108] In guaranteeing a trial within a reasonable time Art.6(1) underlines "the importance of rendering justice without delays which might jeopardise its effectiveness and credibility".[109] In criminal cases it serves the additional function of protecting individuals from "remaining too long in a state of uncertainty about their fate".[110] It is thus a guarantee of expedition in the conduct of the proceedings themselves. In determining what constitutes a "reasonable time" for the purposes of Art.6, regard must be had to the circumstances of each case including, in particular, the complexity of the factual or legal[111] issues raised by the case; the conduct of the applicant and of the competent administrative and judicial authorities; and what is "at stake" for the applicant.[112] Article 6(1) operates in conjunction with other Convention guarantees against undue delay, such as Art.5(3) requiring an arrestee to be "brought promptly before a judge" and Art.5(4) declaring that a detained person is "entitled to take proceedings by which the lawfulness of his detention shall be decided speedily by a court".

States are obliged to organise their legal systems so as to allow the courts to **14-42** comply with the requirements of these Articles.[113] Thus, breaches of the Convention have been found in cases where excessive delays resulted from a long-term backlog of work in the court system coupled with the failure of the state to take remedial measures.[114] A lack of resources is unlikely to amount to a sufficient justification for delay in a trial,[115] particularly where the detention or continued detention of the defendant is at stake.[116]

I. When does Time begin to Run?

For the purposes of both Art.5 and Art.6, it was established by the Strasbourg **14-43** Court in *Deweer v Belgium*[117] that time begins to run from point of charge and runs until its final determination, including the exhaustion of all ordinary avenues of appeal. However, as confirmed in the subsequent judgment in *Eckle v Germany*,[118] the term "charge" has an autonomous meaning in this context which approximates to whether the suspect has been "officially notified" of the allegation or "the situation of the [suspect] has been substantially affected" by the official actions in respect of the case. The *Deweer-Eckle* approach was applied by

---

[108] *Stogmuller v Austria* (1979–80) 1 E.H.R.R. 155.

[109] *H. v France* (1990) 12 E.H.R.R. 74.

[110] *Stogmuller*, at para.5.

[111] If a particular case will have important repercussions on the national case-law in a particular area, this may be a relevant consideration: *Katte Klitsche de la Grange v Italy* (1994) 19 E.H.R.R. 368, para.62.

[112] *Zimmermann and Steiner v Switzerland* (1984) 6 E.H.R.R. 17, para.24.

[113] *Muti v Italy* (1994), A. 281–C, para.15; *Sussman v Germany* (1998) 25 E.H.R.R. 64, paras 55–56; *Reid v United Kingdom* (2003) 37 E.H.R.R. 211, at para.77.

[114] *Zimmermann and Steiner v Switzerland* (1984) 6 E.H.R.R. 17, paras 27–32; *Guincho v Portugal* (1985) 7 E.H.R.R. 223, paras 40–41.

[115] *Hentrich v France* (1994) 18 E.H.R.R. 440, para.61.

[116] *Mansur v Turkey* (1995) 20 E.H.R.R. 535, para.68; *Zana v Turkey* (1999) 27 E.H.R.R. 667, para.84.

[117] (1980) 2 E.H.R.R. 30.

[118] (1982) 5 E.H.R.R. 1; see also *Serves v France* (1999) 28 E.H.R.R. 265, and *Fryckman v Finland*, App.No.36288/98, judgment of October 10, 2006.

the court in *Heaney and McGuinness v Ireland*,[119] holding that the applicants had been "charged" for this purpose when served with a notice requiring them to account for their movements, prior to being formally charged with an offence. It was also applied in *Barry v Ireland*,[120] so as to hold that the applicant had been "charged" on the date when his home was searched under a warrant, because at that stage he became "substantially affected" by the official action against him.

14–44 Much depends on the characterisation of the procedures to which a person has been subjected. Thus in *Howarth v United Kingdom*[121] the charge was conspiracy to defraud, and the Court held that time began to run from the date when the applicant was first interviewed by the Serious Fraud Squad (March 1993), and not from the time when he was charged (July 1993). The former fell within the *Deweer* meaning of "charge". However, in *IJL, GMR and AKP v United Kingdom*[122] the applicants, who had been prosecuted for alleged involvement in a share support scheme during the Guinness takeover bid for Distillers, contended that time should be taken to run from the date upon which they had been called in for interview by Inspectors from the Department of Trade and Industry (DTI). The Court disagreed. Since the DTI investigation did not involve the determination of a criminal charge, time was held to run from the commencement of the criminal proceedings proper. In respect of the first two applicants, this meant the date of charge. In respect of the third it was the date of his arrest in the United States on an extradition warrant.

14–45 It is not clear that the British courts have fully accepted this approach. In *Attorney-General's Reference (No.2 of 2001)*[123] Lord Bingham, with whom all their Lordships concurred on this point, held that time usually begins to run from the point at which a person is charged or summoned. However, he added, referring to *Howarth v United Kingdom* (above), that this will not always be the case. Without engaging with that decision or the other Strasbourg jurisprudence, Lord Bingham commented that "arrest will not ordinarily mark the beginning of that period. An official indication that a person will be reported with a view to prosecution may, depending on the circumstances, do so."[124] The difficulties with the House of Lords' position are: (a) that Lord Bingham appeared to depart from the Strasbourg approach without giving reasons for doing so—he is entitled to do this, but when s.2 of the Human Rights Act states that a British court "must take into account" the Strasbourg jurisprudence one would expect a discussion of the relevant decisions and good reasons to be offered for taking a different approach; and (b) that the decision leaves it unclear under what circumstances an English court will hold that time begins to run before the point of charge. For prosecutors and other criminal practitioners this is hardly satisfactory: should they be guided by the Strasbourg decisions (such as *Deweer*, *Howarth* and

---

[119] (2000) 33 E.H.R.R. 264.
[120] App.No.18273/04, judgment of December 15, 2005.
[121] (2001) 31 E.H.R.R. 861.
[122] (2001) 33 E.H.R.R. 225.
[123] [2003] UKHL 68.
[124] *Ibid.*, at para.28.

Heaney and McGuinness), or was Lord Bingham signalling an approach that is more flexible (from the prosecutor's point of view)?

The Divisional Court followed the *Deweer-Eckle* approach when deciding the **14-46** point at which the applicant had been "charged" in *Department of Work and Pensions v Costello*.[125] At an official interview the applicant had been given a form recording that "you may be prosecuted for the offence shown below": Keene L.J. held that this was an "official indication" that placed the person "under the stress of waiting to hear whether he or she is in fact going to be prosecuted", and so classified it as a "charge" for the purposes of time beginning to run.

II. When does time cease to run?

The Strasbourg jurisprudence indicates that the "reasonable time" guarantee **14-47** applies from the time of arrest through to the final stage of appeals. Thus in *Howarth v United Kingdom*[126] a two-year delay in dealing with an appeal was held to breach Art.6(1); in *Mellors v United Kingdom*[127] a three-year delay between trial and appeal in Scotland was held unreasonable; and in *Reid v United Kingdom*[128] the Court held that:

> "The delays which appear in this case cannot be justified either by the complexity of the case or the exigencies of internal procedure. While one year per instance may be a rule of thumb in Art.6(1) cases, Art.5(4) concerning issues of liberty requires particular expedition."[129]

The Reid case concerned review of the justification for continued detention of a mental patient under Art.5(4), but the decision demonstrates that the contrast is not so much between the "reasonable time" guarantees in that Article and Art.6(1), as between whether the appellant was in custody or not—custody cases call for greater expedition, whichever Article is applicable.

Is the guarantee in Art.6(1) applicable to the enforcement of sentences and **14-48** ancillary orders made on sentence? In *R. (on the application of Lloyd) v Bow Street Magistrates' Court*[130] the Divisional Court held that it does apply. Dyson L.J. found no difficulty in applying Art.6(1) to the enforcement of a confiscation order made on conviction for conspiracy to handle stolen goods: "such proceedings are part and parcel of the confiscation proceedings, which in turn are part and parcel of the original criminal proceedings". This has now been confirmed by *Crowther v United Kingdom*,[131] where the Court applied Art.6(1) to delays in enforcing a confiscation order made on conviction.

---

[125] [2006] EWHC 1156 Admin.
[126] (2001) 31 E.H.R.R. 861.
[127] App.57836/00, judgment of July 17, 2003.
[128] (2003) 37 E.H.R.R. 211.
[129] *Ibid.*, para.78.
[130] [2004] Crim.L.R. 136.
[131] App.53741/00, judgment of February 1, 2005.

14–49   If an accused is not finally brought to trial, Art.6 ceases to apply as at the date of discontinuance.[132] Where charges have been left to "lie on the file", Art.6 ceases to apply if the prosecution undertake not to proceed with them[133] or if it is the settled practice of the prosecuting authorities not to do so.[134] Thus in *L v United Kingdom*[135] the applicant argued that, when a court ordered that five charges should "lie in the file" following a plea of guilty to a specimen charge of indecent assault, this deprived him of the right to trial within reasonable time on those counts. The Commission held that "the established practice in English law of not proceeding with other charges so long as the first conviction remains undisturbed, coupled with the judicial control over any further proceedings, means that in fact the accused is no longer faced with any criminal charges which require determination."[136] Where a case is referred back to the Court of Appeal by the Criminal Cases Review Commission time is taken to run from the date of the referral.[137] In order to ascertain whether the proceedings as a whole were determined within a reasonable time, the Court will aggregate the length of the first proceedings with the time taken to determine the appeal following the reference back, but will disregard the period in between.[138]

III. What amounts to a breach?

14–50   In order to establish a breach of Art.6(1) on the ground of excessive delay, it is unnecessary to show that the accused has suffered prejudice in the preparation or presentation of his defence. The right to trial within a reasonable time is a free-standing right safeguarded by Art.6(1), as recognised by the House of Lords in *Porter v Magill*.[139] The factors to be taken into account are well established:

> "The reasonableness of the length of proceedings is to be assessed in the light of the particular circumstances of the case, regard being had to the criteria laid down in the Court's case law, in particular the complexity of the case, the applicant's conduct and the conduct of the competent authorities."[140]

A failure on the part of the defendant to co-operate with the judicial authorities is not necessarily to be held against him since Art.6 does not require active co-operation[141]: indeed, the Strasbourg Court has re-asserted that a defendant is not to be blamed for taking advantage of whatever procedural possibilities are provided by the domestic legal system for defence against a criminal charge.[142]

---

[132] *Orchin v United Kingdom* (1984) 6 E.H.R.R. 391 (entering of a *nolle prosequi*).

[133] *X v United Kingdom* (1979) 17 D.R. 122.

[134] *X v United Kingdom* (1983) 5 E.H.R.R. 508.

[135] (1990) 65 D.R. 325. This case was argued under Art.5(3) (trial within a reasonable time of arrest), but the issue is the same.

[136] *Ibid.*, para.2.

[137] *IJL, GMR and AKP v United Kingdom* (2001) 33 E.H.R.R. 225.

[138] *Ibid.*, paras 130–131.

[139] [2002] 2 A.C. 357.

[140] *Pelissier and Sassi v France* (2000) 30 E.H.R.R. 715, para.67.

[141] *Zana v Turkey* (1999) 27 E.H.R.R. 667, para.79.

[142] See *Kajas v Finland*, App.No.64436/01, judgment of March 7, 2006, para.25; *Holomiov v Moldova*, App.No.30649/05, judgment of November 7, 2006, para.143.

A more rigorous standard applies when the defendant is in custody.[143] Thus in **14–51** *Albo v Italy*[144] the court emphasised the duty of "special diligence" where the defendant is in custody, and even though the evidence against him was strong, the Court found a violation of the special duty and therefore of Art.5(3) when some 16 months elapsed while a preliminary issue was resolved. Where the case is complex, that may justify some delay: complexity may arise from the number of charges, from the difficulty of the legal issues involved, from the need to obtain evidence from abroad,[145] from the volume of evidence,[146] or from excusable delays in the obtaining of expert evidence.[147] Thus in *IJL, GMR and AKP v United Kingdom*[148] the Court held that four and a half years to determine complex fraud charges (which included the determination of a reference back to the Court of Appeal) was not unreasonable:

> "The Court observes that the criminal proceedings were of undoubted complexity. The applicants were each charged with multiple offences arising out of an alleged unlawful and highly complicated share support operation. The applicants' trial lasted 75 days during which the jury heard ten days of speeches by counsel and a five day summing up by the trial judge. The trial itself was prefaced by a lengthy trial on the *voir dire* in the course of which the applicants sought to have transcripts of their interviews with the Inspectors ruled inadmissible. As a further example of the case's complexity, it is to be observed that the Court of Appeal's second judgment delivered on 27 December 1995 ran to 113 pages, following a ten day hearing."[149]

As a general proposition it is accepted that prosecutions for economic crime are more complex and may take longer,[150] although this is a question of fact in each case. In comparison, the Court found in *Mellors v United Kingdom*[151] that a delay of three years and two weeks in dealing with an appeal was unreasonable because the case was not unduly complex, and although the defence contributed in a small way to the delays, the major problem was one of listing the appeal. Similarly in *Ahmed v Birmingham Magistrates' Court and the CPS*[152] a Divisional Court (consisting only of Hooper J.) held that a delay of some three years in enforcing a simple summons for dangerous driving and bringing the case to court breached Art.6(1). This was too long "for the trial of a very simple, uncomplicated case of dangerous driving". The causes lay in the court's failure to notice that it was sending letters to the wrong address, and in certain periods of unexplained inactivity, and there was no evidence that the defendant was trying to avoid or escape trial.

---

[143] *Abdoella v Netherlands* (1992) 20 E.H.R.R. 585, para.24; *Reid v United Kingdom* (2003) 37 E.H.R.R. 21, para.78.

[144] (2006) 43 E.H.R.R. 27.

[145] *Neumeister v Austria (No.1)* (1979) 1 E.H.R.R. 91.

[146] *Wemhoff v Germany* (1968) 1 E.H.R.R. 55.

[147] *Ibid.*

[148] (2001) 33 E.H.R.R. 225; see also the earlier Commission decision in *X v United Kingdom* (1979) 17 D.R. 122, at para.73.

[149] (2001) 33 E.H.R.R. 225, at para.134.

[150] *Lehtinen v Finland (No.2)*, App.No.41585/98, judgment of June 8, 2006.

[151] App.57836/00, judgment of July 17, 2003.

[152] [2003] EWHC Admin 72.

14–52   The state is not responsible for delays attributable to the defendant or his lawyers[153] and periods spent unlawfully at large are to be disregarded in determining the overall length of the proceedings.[154] The state is, however, responsible for delays attributable to the court or the prosecution. Unexplained delays in the progress of court proceedings are the responsibility of the state, and it is well established that states should organize their judicial systems so as to avoid undue delay.[155] In *Orchin v United Kingdom*[156] three years of delay (out of a total period of five years and three months during which the charges were outstanding) were attributed by the government to an administrative oversight. The Northern Ireland DPP had decided not to proceed with the charges, but failed to notify the applicant or to enter a *nolle prosequi* for another three years. The Commission held that it was "the sole responsibility of the prosecuting authorities to take steps to terminate proceedings reasonably promptly after they had decide not to proceed". Violations of the reasonable time guarantee have been found in relation to a delay to enable an appeal court to deal with four appeals together,[157] and excessive time taken for the hearing of appeals.[158]

14–53   Two decisions demonstrate the application of these principles to the enforcement of ancillary orders on sentence, and also show the reasons for applying Art.6(1). Thus in *R. (on the application of Lloyd) v Bow Street Magistrates' Court* it took some five years for the Crown Prosecution Service to ensure that proceedings were brought against the applicant to enforce the confiscation order in respect of the unpaid portion. Among other delays were two years during which the receiver appointed by the court did nothing, and a further year's delay before the final summons could be heard at Bow Street. Dyson L.J. stated:

> "Convicted criminals who are the subject of confiscation orders do not attract sympathy, and are not entitled to favoured treatment. But there is nothing surprising about the requirement that, if the prosecuting authorities/magistrates court seek to enforce a confiscation order, they should do so within a reasonable time. It is potentially very unfair on a defendant that he should be liable to be committed to prison for non-payment of sums due under a confiscation order many years after the time for payment has expired, and long after he has been released from custody and resumed work and family life."[159]

Likewise in *Crowther v United Kingdom*[160] the court found that there was "a period of four years, three months of almost total inactivity . . . until Customs took any effective steps to enforce the [confiscation] order, by requesting a warrant for the applicant to be questioned about his financial circumstances." The Government's case was that the applicant was liable to pay this sum

---

[153] *Cf. Konig v Federal Republic of Germany (no.1)* (1980) 2 E.H.R.R. 170.

[154] *Girolani v Italy* (1991) A. 196–E.

[155] E.g. *Simonavicius v Lithuania*, App.No.37415/02, judgment of June 27, 2006; *Altun v Turkey*, App.No.66354/01, judgment of October 19, 2006, and *Apicella v Italy*, App.No.64890/01, judgment of the Grand Chamber, March 29, 2006, para.72.

[156] (1984) 6 E.H.R.R. 391.

[157] *Hentrich v France* (1994) 18 E.H.R.R. 440, para.61.

[158] *Howarth v United Kingdom* (2001) 31 E.H.R.R. 861, *Mellors v United Kingdom*, App.57836/00, judgment of July 17, 2003.

[159] [2004] Crim.L.R. 136, [2003] EWHC Admin. 2294, para.25.

[160] App.53741/00, judgment of February 1, 2005.

throughout, but the court responded that this does not absolve the authorities from taking timely steps towards enforcement. Finding a breach of Art.6(1), the court found that the period of inactivity was "inexcusable and, given that somebody's liberty was involved [imprisonment in default, 18 months], unconscionable."

IV. Remedies for Breach of the "Reasonable Time" Guarantee

It will be apparent from the preceding paragraphs that the right to trial within a **14–54** reasonable time in Art.6(1) is a fundamentally different concept from the common law jurisdiction to stay a prosecution as an abuse of process on grounds of delay, as that jurisdiction was earlier understood in England and Wales. The absence of a requirement to show prejudice in order to establish a breach of Art.6(1) is in direct conflict with the pre-Human Rights Act principle that a court should stay an indictment on grounds of delay only in exceptional circumstances, and only where the accused has been so prejudiced in the conduct of his defence that a fair trial is no longer possible.[161] In the absence of prejudice (in the narrow sense), domestic case law had, prior to the Human Rights Act, treated the hardship flowing from procedural delay as a factor in mitigation of sentence.[162] Thus, since decisions on abuse of process were concerned with the risk of prejudice to the defence, the jurisdiction focussed upon the period between the commission of the offence and the start of the trial. However, Art.6(1) is concerned with a much wider time-frame, from the moment that the defendant was first affected by the proceedings, to the final determination of any appeal.

British courts soon had to contend with the argument that proceedings must be **14–55** stayed, or convictions quashed, wherever the "reasonable time" guarantee in Art.6(1) had been breached. The judicial response has not been utterly clear, an uncertainty foreshadowed by two Privy Council decisions at the turn of the century. Thus in *Darmalingum v The State*[163] the Privy Council held that the right to trial within a reasonable time in the constitution of Mauritius (modelled on Art.6) is a free-standing right, distinct from the right to a fair trial. Breach of the right does not depend on proof of prejudice, and occurs whenever there is an "inordinate and oppressive" delay. As to remedy, their Lordships held that it would ordinarily be right to quash the conviction. This was despite a submission from the prosecutor that the case should have been remitted to the Supreme Court with a direction to impose a non-custodial sentence in recognition of the breach:

"The normal remedy for a failure of this particular guarantee, *viz.* the reasonable time guarantee, would be to quash the conviction. That is, of course, the remedy for a breach of the other two requirements of section 10(1) ... Their Lordships do not wish to be overly prescriptive on this point. They do not suggest that there may not be circumstances in which it might arguably be appropriate to affirm the conviction but substitute a non-custodial sentence, e.g. in a case where there had been a plea of guilty or where

---

[161] The leading authority then was *Attorney-General's Reference No.1 of 1990* [1992] Q.B. 630.
[162] *R. v Derby Crown Court, ex parte Brooks* (1984) 80 Cr.App.R. 164, at 169.
[163] [2000] 2 Cr.App.R. 445.

the inexcusable delay affected the convictions on some counts but not on others. But their Lordships are quite satisfied that the only disposal which will properly vindicate the constitutional rights of the appellant in the present case would be the quashing of the conviction."

14–56 Soon afterwards, however, a differently constituted Board of the Privy Council delivered judgment in *Flowers v The Queen*,[164] rejecting the principle that there was a presumption that unconstitutional delay should result in the quashing of a conviction. Lord Hutton held that in assessing the impact of delay it was necessary to have regard to: (a) the length of the delay; (b) the reason for the delay; (c) whether or not the accused had asserted the right to a speedy trial in the course of the proceedings; and (d) the extent of any prejudice. In assessing prejudice, the court should take account not only of evidential prejudice, but also of: (i) the need to prevent oppressive pre-trial detention; (ii) the need to minimise the anxiety and concern of the accused; and (iii) the need to limit the possibility that the presentation of the defence would be evidentially impaired. The right to trial within a reasonable time had to be balanced against the public interest in the conviction of the guilty. Although the delay had been "lengthy and regrettable" it did not afford grounds for quashing the conviction where the accused had been convicted on strong evidence of a serious murder in the course of a robbery. Lord Hutton distinguished *Darmalingum* on the ground that the appellant in that case did not pose a serious threat to society. This appears to suggest that the remedy should depend on the gravity of the crime, reasoning that finds no reflection either in the Strasbourg principles or in the leading Commonwealth decisions.

14–57 The difficulty of reconciling the two Privy Council decisions has been recognised by Lord Bingham,[165] and also by Lord Carswell.[166] But when the British courts came to deal with the issue, there was also a division of opinion. The Privy Council decided *H.M. Advocate v R.*[167] on the wording of the Scotland Act 1998. It was held that for a trial to take place following a breach of Art.6(1) would require the court to do an act incompatible with a Convention right. Since courts have no power to act in that way, the only remedy for breach should be a stay of the proceedings. An indication of the possibly wide ramifications of such a decision in England is that in the leading case the House of Lords sat with nine members. In *Attorney-General's Reference (No.2 of 2001)*[168] the House held by a majority of 7–2 that it will rarely be appropriate to stay the proceedings if they have not yet begun, because there is a strong public interest in having charges tried. A court should therefore consider lesser remedies such as compensation or mitigation of sentence. Lord Bingham held:

"The appropriate remedy will depend on the nature of the breach and all the circumstances, including particularly the stage of the proceedings at which the breach is established. If the breach is established before the hearing, the appropriate remedy may be a public acknowledgement of the breach, action to expedite the hearing to the greatest extent practicable and perhaps, if the defendant is in custody, his release on

---

[164] [2000] 1 W.L.R. 2396.
[165] In *Dyer v Watson* [2004] 1 A.C. 379, at para.29.
[166] In *Boolell v State* [2006] U.K.P.C. 46, at para.21.
[167] [2002] U.K.P.C. D3.
[168] [2003] UKHL 68.

bail. It will not be appropriate to stay or dismiss the proceedings unless (a) there can no longer be a fair hearing or (b) it would otherwise be unfair to try the defendant. The public interest in the final determination of criminal charges requires that such a charge should not be stayed or dismissed if any lesser remedy will be just and proportionate in all the circumstances. The prosecutor and the court do not act incompatibly with the defendant's Convention right in continuing to prosecute or entertain proceedings after a breach is established in a case where neither of conditions (a) or (b) is met, since the breach consists in the delay which has accrued and not in the prospective hearing." [169]

Is this a faithful application of the Convention? It is true that the Strasbourg Court has said that breach of the right does not necessarily render the whole proceedings a nullity, [170] but of course that court has never had to consider the proper approach to a case in which the delay means that the trial has not yet taken place—applications to Strasbourg tend to come towards the end of domestic proceedings. In a strongly worded dissenting speech, Lord Hope went so far as to say that the majority's decision "empties the reasonable time guarantee almost entirely of content". [171] In his view, there are many cases where mitigation of sentence or compensation would not be sufficient recognition of the Art.6(1) right. Lord Bingham's condition (b) would presumably be satisfied by such things as bad faith, unlawfulness or executive manipulation of the kind seen in *R. v Horseferry Road Magistrates' Court, ex parte Bennett*. [172] His Lordship did accept that there may be "very exceptional" cases, lying outside categories (a) and (b) above, where a stay of proceedings might be appropriate, [173] so the door is not absolutely shut to "abuse of process" arguments.

Lord Bingham held that the same general approach should apply where the **14–58** matter is raised on appeal:

"If the breach of the reasonable time requirement is established retrospectively, after there has been a hearing, the appropriate remedy may be a public acknowledgement of the breach, a reduction in the penalty imposed on a convicted defendant or the payment of compensation to an acquitted defendant. Unless (a) the hearing was unfair or (b) it was unfair to try the defendant at all, it will not be appropriate to quash any conviction. Again, in any case where neither of conditions (a) or (b) applies, the prosecutor and the court do not act incompatibly with the defendant's Convention right in prosecuting or entertaining the proceedings but only in failing to procure a hearing within a reasonable time." [174]

This approach was followed by the Privy Council when dealing with a petition **14–59** from Mauritius in *Boolell v State* [175]: Lord Carswell stated that unreasonable delay might be found in the absence of prejudice to the defendant, but where a breach is found the case should not be stayed or a conviction quashed on account of delay alone unless: (a) the hearing was unfair; or (b) it was unfair to try the

---

[169] *Ibid.*, at para.24.
[170] *Bunkate v Netherlands* (1993) 19 E.H.R.R. 477.
[171] [2003] UKHL 68, at para.46.
[172] [1994] 1 A.C. 41.
[173] [2003] UKHL 68, para.25.
[174] *Ibid.*
[175] [2006] U.K.P.C. 46, para.32.

defendant at all. In this case unreasonable delay was found, but the Privy Council held that reduction of sentence was the most appropriate remedy.

14–60 It is therefore evident that the normal approach to remedies for delays during the appeal process is to grant compensation (if the conviction is quashed on appeal) or a reduction in sentence. However, it is clear from *Yetkinsekerci v United Kingdom*[176] that, if the Court of Appeal makes such a reduction, it should state clearly the extent to which the reduction is intended as compensation for the breach. In that case there was an unexplained delay in the Criminal Appeal Office which meant that it took just under three years for his appeal to be heard. The court acknowledged the failure to hear the appeal within a reasonable time, and also mentioned that greater allowance should have been made for the fact that the offence was only an attempt, and reduced the sentence from 14 to 12 years. The Government argued that the applicant was therefore no longer a "victim" and therefore had no standing to make the application, but the Strasbourg Court disagreed:

> "It cannot be said, even approximately, what proportion of the two years' reduction in sentence was related to the fact that the applicant's offence was limited to an attempt, and what proportion was due to the time spent waiting for the appeal to come on. As it is not able with any precision to ascertain to what extent the applicant's sentence was reduced [sc. in response to the delay], the Court cannot accept the Government's contention that the sentence was reduced sufficiently to render the applicant 'no longer a victim.'"[177]

Although this part of the judgment is directed chiefly at a procedural issue, it suggests that a court (trial or appellate) that reduces a sentence in order to compensate for delay ought to declare the magnitude of that reduction.

14–61 The application of these principles to the enforcement of orders made at the sentencing stage is not clear. In *R. (on the application of Lloyd) v Bow Street Magistrates' Court*,[178] where the enforcement of part of a confiscation order was delayed for some five years, the Divisional Court placed emphasis on the fact that the prison sentence had been served and the confiscation order was still capable of being enforced by other means. Thus:

> "Against that background, we reach the conclusion that the only proper remedy for the breaches of Article 6.1 in this case is to order that the proceedings to commit the claimant to prison for default in paying be stayed . . . The only proportionate response to the breaches of Article 6.1 which have occurred is to say that this weapon in the armoury (viz imprisonment in default) is no longer available."[179]

The *Lloyd* case was decided before the House of Lords decision in *Attorney-General's Reference No.2 of 2001*, and its style of reasoning is somewhat different, but it is not inconsistent with what Lord Bingham stated in that case.

---

[176] (2005) 43 E.H.R.R. 67.
[177] *Ibid.*, at para.14.
[178] [2004] Crim.L.R. 136, [2003] EWHC Admin 2259 above, 14–53.
[179] *Ibid.*, para.34.

Some states have introduced schemes for redress for those who suffer unreason- **14-62**
able delays. In Italy there is a compensation system for this purpose, but the
Grand Chamber held in *Apicella v Italy* that it is open to the court to "verify
whether the way in which the domestic law is interpreted and applied produces
consequences that are consistent with the principles of the Convention as interpreted in the light of the Court's case law."[180] The Grand Chamber found that in
the present case the compensation was not prompt enough and was insufficient
in amount. This judgment confirms that the British decisions on delay may be
subject to Strasbourg review in an appropriate case.

So-called "systemic delay" has been recognised as a ground for constitutional **14-63**
challenge under the Canadian Charter and the New Zealand Bill of Rights Act.
In *R. v B* the New Zealand Court of Appeal criticised a delay of 23 months for
largely institutional reasons (a backlog of cases to be heard) but stopped short of
quashing the appellant's conviction. The leading Canadian decision is *Morin*,[181]
where the Supreme Court set out a number of factors that have a bearing on
whether a delay should be regarded as "unreasonable". The court should have
regard to the length of the delay; any waiver of time periods by the defence; the
reasons for the delay (including the inherent time requirements of the case, the
actions of the accused, the actions of the Crown, and the limits on institutional
resources); and the existence or absence of any resulting prejudice to the
accused."[182] In relation to the requirement to show prejudice, it is to be noted that
this concept has a wider ambit under most constitutional instruments than under
the doctrine of abuse of process at common law. Thus in the leading United
States case of *Barker v Wingo*[183] Justice Powell recognised a broad conception of
prejudice flowing from procedural delays. The object of the sixth Amendment
right to a "speedy trial" was "(i) to prevent oppressive pre-trial incarceration; (ii)
to minimize anxiety and concern of the accused; and (iii) to limit the possibility
that the defence will be impaired." Similarly, in *Doggett v United States*[184] the
Supreme Court observed that:

> "Between diligent prosecution and bad faith delay, official negligence in bringing an
> accused to trial occupies the middle ground. While not compelling relief in every case
> where bad faith delay would make relief virtually axiomatic, neither is negligence
> automatically tolerable simply because the accused cannot demonstrate exactly how it
> has prejudiced him."

This approach has been widely adopted in common law countries.[185] Thus the
Canadian and the New Zealand courts have taken the view that the psychological

---

[180] App.No.64890/01, judgment of March 28, 2006, para.80; *cf.* para.75 on systems in other
member states.
[181] (1992) 12 C.R. (4th) 1, followed by the New Zealand Court of Appeal in *Martin v District
Court at Tauranga* [1995] 2 N.Z.L.R. 419.
[182] (1992) 12 C.R. (4th) 1 at 12–13, *per* Sopinka J.
[183] 407 US 514 (1972) at 532.
[184] (1992) 120 L. Ed. 2d. 520.
[185] E.g. by the Supreme Court of Zimbabwe in *Re Miambo* [1993] 2 L.R.C. 28.

effects of delay on a defendant may constitute a strong argument that the delay is unreasonable, even if a fair trial could still be held.[186]

E. PUBLICITY, FAIR TRIALS AND CONTEMPT

I. General

14–64   Adverse publicity concerning a criminal prosecution carries an inevitable risk of prejudice to the fair trial of the accused, particularly if the case is to be tried by a jury. English courts have responded to this risk by holding that prejudicial publicity may lead to the stay of a criminal prosecution on grounds of abuse of process where no fair trial is possible,[187] and may in certain instances lead to the quashing of a criminal conviction.[188] The publication of prejudicial matter may also render the publisher liable to prosecution under the Contempt of Court Act 1981.[189] If proceedings are *active* (in the sense that there has been an arrest, summons or the issue of an arrest warrant), it will be an offence to publish material which creates a substantial risk that the course of public justice will be seriously impeded or prejudiced.[190] In *Attorney General v BBC*,[191] the BBC was held to be in contempt for broadcasting an inaccurate report of a trial that had just started. The Divisional Court held that there was a substantial risk of prejudice, despite the judge's ruling that it was unnecessary to discharge the jury (since the interests of the accused could be secured by a strong direction to ignore the broadcast). Under s.4(2) of the Contempt of Court Act 1981 a trial judge may order the postponement of contemporary reporting of court proceedings where this is necessary to avoid a substantial risk of prejudice to the administration of justice in those proceedings, or in any other proceeding pending or imminent. The power to make orders under s.4(2) does not extend to reporting which goes beyond the content of court proceedings, such as opinion pieces. Those reports are covered by the strict liability rule under s.1 of the 1981 Act.[192] Additional reporting restrictions are automatically imposed in respect of committal proceedings,[193] applications to dismiss a charge and preparatory hearings ordered in

---

[186] *cf. Askov.* [1990] 2 S.C.R. 1199, and *Martin v District Court at Tauranga* [1995] 2 N.Z.L.R. 419. For an analysis of the English, Canadian and other authorities up to 1993, see Choo A., *Abuse of Process and Judicial Stays of Criminal Proceedings* (1993).

[187] *R. v Reade* October 15, 1993, Central Criminal Court (Garland J.) (prosecution for perjury arising out of the conviction of six men for the Birmingham pub bombings); *R. v Magee and ors* January 24, 1997, Belmarsh Crown Court, (Kay J.) (escape from HMP Whitemoor).

[188] *R. v McCann and ors* (1991) 92 Cr.App.R. 239; *R. v Taylor and Taylor* (1994) 98 Cr.App.R. 361; *R. v Wood* [1996] 1 Cr.App.R. 207. For discussion of these and other cases, see Corker D. and Levi M., "Pre-Trial Publicity and its Treatment in English Courts" [1996] Crim.L.R. 622.

[189] The 1981 Act was, of course, passed following the decision of the European Court in *Sunday Times v United Kingdom (No.1)* (1979–80) 2 E.H.R.R. 245 that the common law of contempt violated Art.10 on freedom of expression.

[190] S.2(2) of the Contempt of Court Act 1981. For fuller discussion, see *Arlidge, Eady and Smith on Contempt* (3rd edn, 2005), Ch.4.

[191] [1992] C.O.D. 264.

[192] *R. v B* [2006] EWCA Crim 2692 and *Scarbruck and Galbraith v HM Advocate*, High Ct of Justiciary, unreported, September 7, 2000.

[193] See s.8(4) of the Magistrates Courts Act 1980.

serious or complex fraud cases under the Criminal Justice Act 1987,[194] and in respect of preparatory hearings and pre-trial rulings under the Criminal Procedure and Investigations Act 1996.[195]

More generally, it is a settled principle of English criminal procedure that all   **14-65** evidence and argument must take place in public, with access being afforded to the press, unless a departure from the principle of open justice is strictly necessary. In *Attorney General v Leveller Magazine*[196] Lord Diplock explained that:

> "As a general rule the English system of administering justice does require that it be done in public: *Scott v Scott* [1913] AC 417. If the way that courts behave cannot be hidden from the public ear and eye this provides a safeguard against judicial arbitrariness or idiosyncrasy and maintains the public confidence in the administration of justice. The application of this principle of open justice has two aspects: as respects proceedings in the court itself, it requires that they should be held in open court to which the press and public are admitted and that, in criminal cases at any rate, all evidence communicated to the court is communicated publicly. As respects the publication to a wider public of fair and accurate reports of proceedings that have taken place in court the principle requires that nothing should be done to discourage this."

The importance of this principle was reaffirmed in *R. v Legal Aid Board ex parte*   **14-66** *Kaim Todner (a firm)*.[197] Lord Woolf M.R. explained that the courts should be especially vigilant when considering departures from the principle of open justice:

> "The need to be vigilant arises from the natural tendency for the general principle to be eroded and for exceptions to grow by accretion as the exceptions are applied by analogy to existing cases. This is the reason it is so important not to forget why proceedings are required to be subjected to the full glare of a public hearing. It is necessary because the public nature of the proceedings deters inappropriate behaviour on the part of the court. It also maintains the public's confidence in the administration of justice. It enables the public to know that justice is being administered impartially. It can result in evidence becoming available which would not become available if the proceedings were conducted behind closed doors or with one or more of the parties' or the witnesses' identity concealed. It makes uninformed and inaccurate comment about the proceedings less likely ... Any interference with the public nature of court proceedings is therefore to be avoided unless justice requires it. However Parliament has recognised there are situations where interference is necessary ... In deciding whether to accede to an application for protection from disclosure of the proceedings it is appropriate to take into account the extent of the interference with the general rule which is involved. If the

---

[194] See s.11(12) of the Criminal Justice Act 1987.

[195] See ss.37, 41 and 42 of the Criminal Procedure and Investigations Act 1996. Where automatic reporting restrictions apply, there is no requirement for the judge to balance the risk of prejudice to the trial against the rights of the media to report the proceedings or the right of the public to receive such information. For a critique of these provisions by reference to the Convention, see Cram, "Automatic Reporting Restrictions in Criminal Proceedings and Art.10 of the ECHR" [1998] E.H.R.L.R. 742.

[196] [1979] A.C. 440.

[197] [1999] Q.B. 966, at 977–8.

interference is for a limited period that is less objectionable than a restriction on disclosure which is permanent. If the restriction relates only to the identity of a witness or a party this is less objectionable than a restriction which involves proceedings being conducted in whole or in part behind closed doors."

14–67 In *Ex parte Guardian*[198] the Court of Appeal accepted that the first of the principles in *Kain Todner* should be more broadly expressed, and that:

"Open justice promotes the rule of law. Citizens of all ranks in a democracy must be subject to transparent legal restraint, especially those holding judicial or executive offices. Publicity, whether in the courts, the press, or both, is a powerful deterrent to abuse of power and improper behaviour."

Consistent with the Convention approach, the court emphasised that whatever order is made should be proportionate to the risk which the court considers to be attendant upon disclosure and should be balanced against the rights of the press and the public.[199]

14–68 From the perspective of the Convention, these issues involve a delicate interplay between the right to a fair trial in Art.6 (and especially the presumption of innocence in Art.6(2)), and the right to freedom of expression in Art.10. Article 6(1) generally requires that the hearing of criminal charges should take place in public. The purpose of this guarantee is to protect litigants "against the administration of justice in secret with no public scrutiny" and to maintain public confidence.[200] The Court has held that access for the press is of particular importance in this context, and that media reporting of criminal proceedings plays an important part in the public administration of justice.[201] Nevertheless, the right to a public hearing is subject to the express qualifications set out in the second sentence of Art.6(1). The press may be excluded from all or part of a trial in the interests of morals, public order or national security, where the interests of juveniles[202] or the protection of the private lives of the parties so require, or to the extent strictly necessary in the opinion of the court in special circumstances where publicity would prejudice the interests of justice. Article 10(2) contains a similar, though less specific, qualification, referring to the maintenance of "the authority and impartiality of the judiciary" as a legitimate aim for restricting freedom of expression. The two issues are closely inter-related, but it is necessary to identify the separate considerations that the court has taken into account under Art.6 and Art.10 respectively. Ultimately, if there is a balance to be struck, it would appear to come down in favour of preserving the right to a fair trial. This is because the restictions on open justice in Art.6(1) and the focus upon preserv-

---

[198] [1999] 1 W.L.R. 2130, at 2144.
[199] At 2140.
[200] *Pretto v Italy* (1984) 6 E.H.R.R. 182.
[201] *Ibid.*, para.21.
[202] *Cf. T and V v United Kingdom* (2000) 30 E.H.R.R. 121, where the Court referred to international conventions requiring privacy for juvenile defendants (paras 76–79 and 87).

ing the independence of the judiciary in Art.10(2) share the same purpose of maintaining fairness.[203]

II. Pre-Trial Publicity and the Presumption of Innocence

In *Allenet de Ribemont v France*,[204] the French Interior Minister and a number of **14–69** senior police officers held a press conference shortly after the applicant's arrest, in which they named him as one of the instigators of the murder of a French MP. Their statements were widely reported in France. The applicant was later charged but subsequently released without trial. The court held that the making of the statements, which carried with it the clear implication that the applicant was guilty of the charge, violated the presumption of innocence in Art.6(2). In its judgment the court laid down the following principles on pre-trial statements of this nature:

> "The presumption of innocence enshrined in paragraph 2 of Article 6 is one of the elements of a fair criminal trial that is required by paragraph 1 ... The Court considers that the presumption of innocence may be infringed not only by a judge or court but also by other public authorities ... Freedom of expression, guaranteed by Article 10 of the Convention, includes the freedom to receive and impart information. Article 6(2) cannot therefore prevent the authorities from informing the public about criminal investigations in progress, but it requires that they do so with all discretion and circumspection necessary if the presumption of innocence is to be respected.
>
> The Government maintained that [the Minister's] remarks came under the head of information about criminal proceedings in progress and were not such as to infringe the presumption of innocence, since they did not bind the courts ... The Court notes that in the instant case some of the highest ranking officers in the French police referred to Mr Allenet de Ribemont, without any qualification or reservation, as one of the instigators of a murder, and thus an accomplice in that murder. This was clearly a declaration of the applicant's guilt which, firstly, encouraged the public to believe him guilty and, secondly, prejudged the assessment of the facts by the competent judicial authority. There has therefore been a breach of Article 6(2)".[205]

It has long been established that even without official statements of this kind, a **14–70** "virulent press campaign against the accused" is capable of violating the right to a fair trial, particularly where the trial is to take place with a jury.[206] Nevertheless, the Commission will take account of the fact that some press comment on a trial involving a matter of public interest is inevitable.[207] As the Commission has observed[208]:

---

[203] See, for example, *Axen v Germany* (1984) 6 E.H.R.R. 195, para.25: "By rendering the administration of justice visible, publicity contributes to the achievement of the aims of Article 6, namely a fair trial ... ". A similar view was expressed by the Commission in the Art.10 case *Hodgson, Woolf Productions and the N.U.J. v United Kingdom*, (1987) 10 E.H.R.R. 505.

[204] (1995) 20 E.H.R.R. 557.

[205] *Ibid.*, paras 35–41.

[206] *X v Austria* (1963) 11 C.D. 31 at 43.

[207] *X v Norway* (1970) 35 C.D. 37 at 48.

[208] App. No.9433/81, (1981) 2 Dig. 738.

"[T]he mass media and even the authorities responsible for crime policy cannot be expected to refrain from all statements, such as the mere existence of criminal proceedings or the fact that a suspicion exists. What is excluded however is a formal declaration that somebody is guilty."[209]

In one case the Commission went slightly further, holding that it would be unreasonable to require either the press or the authorities to refrain from referring to the dangerous character of an accused person when they are in possession of uncontested facts.[210]

14–71 A number of inadmissibility decisions illustrate the differing approaches of the Commission, according to the nature of the tribunal. In one unreported case[211] newspaper and television reports referred to the fact that the applicant had previously been tried for the same offence, and that the jury had been unable to agree. One of the reports incorrectly stated that the applicant had pleaded guilty at the first trial. At the end of the retrial the judge summoned the newspaper proprietors for contempt of court, and acknowledged that the reports might have prejudiced the trial. The judge had not given the jury specific warnings which would have drawn their attention to the contents of the reports but gave them a general warning to ignore any press statements they might have seen. The Commission considered that there was no appearance of a violation. In particular, it considered that the report of the fact that the jury at the first trial had been unable to agree was more likely to prejudice the prosecution than the defence. In *X v Austria*[212] the Commission observed that:

"in certain cases, and in particular in cases where laymen participate as jurors in the proceedings, [the right to a fair trial] may be seriously impaired by a virulent press campaign against the accused, which so influences public opinion, and thereby the jurors, that the hearing can no longer be considered to be a 'fair hearing' within the meaning of Article 6 of the Convention."

A similar argument was raised in relation to the trial of Rosemary West, but the application foundered on procedural grounds.[213]

14–72 The Commission has often emphasised that where the hearing is to take place before judges the risk of prejudice is substantially reduced, and the latitude afforded to the press will be correspondingly greater. Where press reports of statements by the Public Prosecutor alleged that the applicant had committed offences other than those listed on the indictment, and the case was tried at first instance and on appeal by judges, the Commission considered that the judges were unlikely to be affected by the publicity[214]:

"In the present case the Court of Appeal comprised no jurors who were likely to be influenced by such a campaign; neither the charge nor the conviction of the judges was

---

[209] *Ibid.*, at 738.
[210] *Ensslin, Baader and Ruspe v Germany* (1978) 14 D.R. 64.
[211] App. No.5768/72, (1975) 2 Dig. 684.
[212] App. No.1476/62, (1963) 11 C.D. 31 at 43.
[213] *West v United Kingdom* [1998] E.H.R.L.R. 204.
[214] App. No.7748/76, (1977) Dig. 688.

founded upon the statements of an influenceable witness. Nothing, moreover, suggests that the judges hearing the case at first instance and on appeal, before whom the existence of the facts was scarcely challenged, might have been really influenced by a press campaign of this kind. The mere fact that they sentenced the applicant to the maximum term (6 months) does not permit the Commission to conclude that the Public Prosecutor's statements of which he complains led the judges to believe that the applicant had accorded more substantial advantages to Mr X than those recorded in the indictment."[215]

The same principle has been applied to the English Court of Appeal. In rejecting   **14–73** one complaint,[216] the Commission took account of the fact that the Court of Appeal sits without a jury, and had extensively examined the merits of the case and found the conviction to be safe. In the Commission's opinion, any risk of bias in the jury had been rectified by the hearing before the Court of Appeal,[217] which had paid specific regard to the publicity as a factor affecting the safety of the conviction. The Court of Appeal had concluded that "there was no real risk that the jury was influenced by the publicity," and that "the case for the Crown was so overwhelming that no jury could conceivably have returned any different verdicts." The Commission saw no reason to take a different view. Where the case has not achieved national coverage, the risk of unfairness caused by adverse publicity is sometimes dealt with by means of an order for change of venue. In *Austria v Italy*[218] the Commission held that an application for a change of venue, on the grounds of legitimate suspicion of bias, could constitute a remedy which was effective and sufficient.

Recommendations issued by the Committee of Ministers of the Council of   **14–74** Europe to member states "on the provision of information through the media in relation to criminal proceedings"[219] have sought to deal with "the possibly conflicting interests protected by articles 6, 8 and 10 of the Convention". The Committee recommends, *inter alia*,

> Principle 2—Respect for the principle of the presumption of innocence is an integral part of the right to a fair trial. Accordingly, opinions and information relating to on-going criminal proceedings should only be communicated or disseminated through the media where this does not prejudice the presumption of innocence of the suspect or the accused;
>
> Principle 10—In the context of criminal proceedings, particularly those involving juries or lay judges, judicial authorities and police services should abstain from publicly providing information which bears a risk of substantial prejudice to the fairness of the proceedings;

---

[215] *Ibid.*, at 688.
[216] (1969) 30 C.D. 70 at 74–75.
[217] *Cf.* para.17–08 below.
[218] (1961) 4 Y.B. 116; see also *Jespere v Belgium* (1980) 22 D.R. 100 at 126–127.
[219] Council of Europe Rec (2003) 13E, July 10, 2003.

Principle 11—Where the accused can show that that the provision of information is highly likely to result, or has resulted, in a breach of his or her right to a fair trial, he or she should have an effective legal remedy.

14–75   The Convention caselaw on adverse publicity and jury bias[220] was extensively reviewed by Lord Hope for the Privy Council in *Montgomery and Coulter v HM Advocate and anor.*[221] Under Scots law the test for staying a criminal prosecution on grounds of prejudicial media coverage, laid down in *Stuurman v HM Advocate*,[222] was whether the continuation of the prosecution would be oppressive in the sense that the risk of prejudice was so grave that no direction by the trial judge could reasonably be expected to remove it. In judging that issue, the court was to take account of all the circumstances of the case, including the length of time since publication, the focusing effect of listening to evidence over a prolonged period, and the likely directions of the trial judge. Applied in that way, the test was "well-suited for use in the context of a complaint which is made under Article 6(1) of the Convention". In Lord Hope's view the *Stuurman* test fitted in well with the Strasbourg caselaw on jury bias[223] which took account of the adequacy of safeguards against a lack of impartiality. Article 6 did not require the issue of objective impartiality to be resolved with mathematical accuracy. Rather, it called for "sufficient" guarantees and safeguards, and for the exclusion of any "legitimate doubt" of bias. However, there was one respect in which the approach under Scots law required modification. The concept of "oppression" had been held to involve a balancing exercise between the interests of the defendant in having a fair trial, and the public interest in ensuring that serious crime is prosecuted.[224] Lord Hope held that there was no scope for the concept of balance when the matter was approached from the standpoint of Art.6:

> "The right of an accused to a fair trial by an independent and impartial tribunal is unqualified. It is not to be subordinated to the public interest in the detection and suppression of crime. In this respect it might be said that the Convention right is superior to the common law right ... [T]he only question to be addressed in terms of Article 6(1) of the Convention is the right of the accused to a fair trial. An assessment of the weight to be given to the public interest does not enter the exercise. Provided this point of principle is recognised, I see no reason why the *Stuurman* test should not continue to be used in this context. The logical justification for doing so is that it directs attention to the effectiveness of the principal measures ... which the tribunal itself can provide. The likely effect of any warnings or directions given to the jury by the trial judge, in the light of the other circumstances of the trial, will in most cases be the critical issue."[225]

---

[220] See para.14–81 below.
[221] [2003] 1 A.C. 641.
[222] 1980 J.C. 111 at 122.
[223] See para.14–93 above.
[224] *X v Sweeney* 1982 J.C. 70.
[225] [2003] 1 A.C. 641, PC at p.673D.

The views expressed by the Privy Council in *Montgomery* must be read together   **14–76**
with an established line of English authority which recognises that criminal
proceedings can be stayed in circumstances where a defendant can no longer
recive a fair trial as a result of adverse publicity.[226] The remedy is only applied
in exceptional circumstances,[227] and in particular, only when other remedies such
as a change of trial venue, or the discharge of a juror would not suffice.[228] In
addition, there have been cases where convictions were quashed because of a
failure to discharge jurors in the face of prejudicial publicity during the course of
the trial.[229] In *R. v Reade* (the trial of officers involved in the investigation of the
Birmingham 6), Garland J. emphasised that adjournments and change of trial
venue would often be a sufficient response to the problem of adverse publicity.
However, in some cases media reporting would be "so irresponsible and prejudicial as to make the unfairness irreparable and the administration of justice
impossible". In those circumstances he found there was "quite literally nowhere
to go". This was the case because it was "more important to retain the integrity
of the system of justice than to ensure the punishment of even the vilest
offender".[230] A similar sentiment was expressed in the dissenting opinion of Mr.
Justice Frankfurter in *Stroble v California*[231]:

"Such passion as the newspapers stirred in this case can be explained (apart from mere
commercial exploitation of revolting crime) only as want of confidence in the orderly
course of justice. To allow such use of the press by the prosecution as the California
court here left undisciplined, implies either that the ascertainment of guilt cannot be
left to the established processes of law or impatience with those calmer aspects of the
judicial process which may not satisfy the natural, primitive, popular revulsion
against horrible crime but do vindicate the sober second thoughts of a community. If
guilt here is clear, the dignity of the law would be best enhanced by establishing that
guilt wholly through the processes of law unaided by the infusion of extraneous
passion. The moral health of the community is strengthened by according even the most
miserable and pathetic criminal those rights which the Constitution has designed for
all".

---

[226] *R. v Reade* October 15, 1993, Central Criminal Court (Garland J.) (prosecution for perjury
arising out of the conviction of six men for the Birmingham pub bombings); *R. v Magee and ors*
January 24, 1997, Belmarsh Crown Court, (Kay J.) (escape from HMP Whitemoor). For an example
of a jury being discharged as a result of what was published during the course of a trial see *Attorney
General v MGN*, [2002] EWHC 907 Admin; *R. v Woodgate and others*, Crown Court at Hull, April
9, 2001 (Poole J.) (public order trial of the footballers, Lee Bowyer and Jonathan Woodgate).

[227] *R. v West* [1996] 2 Cr.App.R. 374, 386.

[228] *R. v Stone* [2001] EWCA 297 Crim (alternative venue); *R. v Meziane and Benmerzouga* [2004]
EWCA Crim 1768 (discharge of individual jurors who had sight of particular publications). There
will also be circumstances where evidence is exluded on the basis that its prejudicial effect (inflated
by adverse inadmissible media) outweighs its probative value. This has occurred in a number of
terrorist trials since September 11, 2001 in relation to evidence of tangential association with Abu
Hamza and the Finsbury Park Mosque.

[229] *R. v McCann and ors* (1991) 92 Cr.App.R. 239; *R. v Taylor and Taylor* (1994) 98 Cr.App.R.
361; *R. v Wood* [1996] 1 Cr.App.R. 207.

[230] *R. v Reade*, unreported, October 15, 1993. The judgment is endorsed by the Court of Appeal in
R. v Stone [2001] EWCA 297 Crim, para.44 and the Supreme Court of Zimbabwe in *Banana v
Attorney General* [1999] 1 L.R.C. 120, at 127.

[231] (1952) 343 US 181.

Set against such views is a strong presumption that juries will adhere to their oath and try cases only on the evidence before them.[232] As Lord Taylor C.J. observed in the *West* case, "to hold otherwise would means that if allegations of murder are sufficiently horrendous so as inevitably to shock the nation, the accused cannot be tried".[233] This proposition has been put under strain by the events of September 11, 2001 and thereafter, which have had a traumatic effect on the type of negative publicity which surrounds terrorist trials in this and other countries. In *R. v Wood* (an IRA case), the Court of Appeal recognised the dangers of a person not receiving a fair trial because of what it described as "the special stigma of terrorism".[234] Unlike other trials the jury are the potential victims of the crime. In *Meziane and Benmerzouga*,[235] a number of jurors wrote notes to the judge which were read out in open court indicating that they felt unable to try a case of two men alleged to be associated with Al Qaeda. The Court of Appeal accepted that the development of Islamic terrorism was unprecedented, and it followed that the coverage attached to it was "unprecedented and intense". Nevertheless, the courts have responded to this problem by emphasising the critical role which juries play in maintaining the right to a fair trial.[236] Perhaps most notably, in *R. v Hamza*,[237] the court upheld a conviction of a Muslim cleric who had been the subject of a virulent tabloid campaign for many years, aimed at persuading the authorities either to imprison him or remove him from the country. The court accepted that there was a degree of tension between the presumption that a jury could follow their oath and other aspects of criminal procedure such as contempt of court orders and the requirement to direct juries on alternative verdicts, which suggested otherwise.[238] In effect, these aspects of criminal procedure were designed to engage with the reality that "the risk that members of a jury may be affected by prejudice is one that cannot wholly be eliminated". Even so, the court held that

> "the fact . . . that adverse publicity may have risked prejudicing a fair trial is no reason for not proceeding with the trial if the judge concludes that, with his assistance, it will be possible to have a fair trial. In considering this question it is right for the judge to have regard to his own experience and that of his fellow judges as to the manner in which juries normally perform their duties."

III. Freedom of Expression

14–77   Section 12 of the Human Rights Act 1998 makes special provision for the rights of the media, restricting the making of *ex parte orders* and requiring the courts

---

[232] *R. v Kray* (1969) 53 Cr.App.R. 412 at pp.414–415, *R. v West* [1996] 2 Cr.App.R. 374, 385–386, *R. v Coughlin and Young* (1976) 63 Cr.App.R. 33 at 37, *Montgomery v H.M. Advocate* [2003] 1 A.C. 641, PC at p.674, *R. v Meziane and Benmerzouga* [2004] EWCA Crim 1768, para.47; *R. v B* [2006] EWCA Crim 2692, para.32; and *R. v Hamza* [2006] EWCA Crim 2918, paras 89–92.

[233] [1996] 2 Cr.App.R. 374, 386.

[234] [1996] 1 Cr.App.R. 207.

[235] [2004] EWCA Crim 1768, para.55.

[236] *R. v B* [2006] EWCA Crim 2692, para.32. The Vice President descibes the role of the jury in this capacity as its "birthright".

[237] [2006] EWCA Crim 2918.

[238] Para.92. The relevant case on alternative verdicts is *R. v Coutts* [2006] 1 W.L.R. 2154.

to pay particular regard to the importance of the Convention right to freedom of expression.[239] For reasons which are not entirely clear, criminal proceedings are excluded from the scope of the duty imposed by s.12.[240] A criminal court is, nevertheless, a public authority under s.6 of the Act and is therefore obliged to act compatibly with Art.10, unless it is bound by the terms of primary legislation to do otherwise.

Any restriction on the reporting of a criminal investigation, charge or prosecution   **14–78**
will involve an interference with the right to freedom of expression in Art.10(1) of the Convention.[241] However, such restrictions will be justifiable under Art.10(2) where they are necessary and proportionate to ensure the fair trial of an accused. In *Sunday Times v United Kingdom*[242] the Court observed that;

> "[I]nsofar as the law of contempt may serve to protect the rights of litigants, this purpose is already included in the phrase 'maintaining the authority and impartiality of the judiciary': the rights so protected are the rights of individuals in their capacity as litigants, that is as persons involved in the machinery of justice, and the authority of that machinery will not be maintained unless protection is afforded to all those involved in or having recourse to it."

The Court emphasised, however, that any given restriction must be strictly necessary on the particular facts of the case before the court:

> "[W]hilst the mass media must not overstep the bounds imposed in the interests of the proper administration of justice, it is incumbent on them to impart information and ideas concerning matters that come before the courts just as in other areas of public interest. Not only do the media have the task of imparting such information and ideas: the public also has a right to receive them ... The Court is faced not with a choice between two conflicting principles, but with a principle of freedom of expression that is subject to a number of exceptions which must be narrowly interpreted ... It is not sufficient that the interference involved belongs to that class of exceptions listed in Article 10(2) which has been invoked. Neither is it sufficient that the interference was imposed because its subject-matter fell within a particular category or was caught by a legal rule formulated in general or absolute terms. The Court has to be satisfied that the interference was necessary having regard to the facts and circumstances prevailing in the specific case before it."[243]

Hodgson, Woolf Productions and the NUJ v United Kingdom[244] concerned a   **14–79**
proposal to broadcast daily reconstructions of the trial of Clive Ponting for Official Secrets Act offences arising from the disclosure of information about the

---

[239] See para.3–20 above.
[240] See s.12(5).
[241] *Hodgson, Woolf Productions and the NUJ v United Kingdom* (1988) 10 E.H.R.R. 503.
[242] (1980) 2 E.H.R.R. 245.
[243] See also *R. v Home Secretary ex parte Simms* [1999] 3 W.L.R. 328 at 336, where Lord Steyn emphasised that any interference with freedom of expression must be "measured in specifics".
[244] (1988) 10 E.H.R.R. 503.

sinking of the *General Belgrano* during the Falklands war. Channel Four proposed to broadcast a programme entitled *Court Report* each day during the trial, which would take the form of studio readings from a transcript that had been carefully checked for accuracy and fairness. The trial judge made an order under s.4(2) of the Contempt of Court Act 1981, prohibiting the broadcast until the conclusion of the trial. Whilst he had no doubt that the broadcasters would make a sincere attempt present a balanced picture of the day's events, he held that if five hours of court proceedings were condensed into a 25 minute reading, it was inevitable that the programme would focus on certain parts of the evidence at the expense of other parts. As a result of the ruling, Channel Four altered the format of the programme, using newsreaders instead of actors, and presenting the broadcast as an extended news report.

14–80   The journalists and the production company complained that their rights under Art.10 had been violated. Notwithstanding the fact that Channel Four had been able to broadcast substantially the same information in a news format, the Commission was satisfied that there had been an interference with the applicants' right to freedom of expression:

> "The Commission considers that the effect of the court order was to transform the television programme as initially devised by the applicants. It was no longer permissible for them to use actors to play the role of the participants in the trial and the transcript of the court proceedings had to be read by a newsreader. In the Commission's view, such an interference with the manner of conveying information to the public, as opposed to the content of the information, constitutes an interference with freedom of expression ... In reaching this view the Commission has attached particular importance to the role played by production and presentation techniques in the making of television programmes."

14–81   However, the restriction was held to be justified by the need to ensure the fairness of the *Ponting* trial. The Commission attached particular weight to the role of the trial judge in assessing the risk of prejudice:

> "[T]he need to ensure a fair trial and to protect members of the jury from exposure to prejudicial influences corresponds to a 'pressing social need'. Such an interpretation is reflected in the importance attached in a democratic society to the right to a fair trial. Furthermore, where a trial judge is confronted, in the opening of a highly publicised and controversial trial, with a potentially prejudicial media report, great weight must be attached to his on-the-spot assessment of the dangers of prejudicing the jury and thereby harming the fairness of the trial ... It is true that there may have been other less objectionable courses open to the trial judge, short of prior restraint, such as instructing the jury not to watch the programme or watching it himself before taking the decision. However the Commission considers that where there is a real risk of prejudice the appropriate response, in the circumstances, is one which must lie, in principle, with the person responsible for ensuring the fairness of the trial, namely, the trial judge."

14–82   In *Atkinson, Crook and The Independent v United Kingdom*[245] the applicants were journalists and a national newspaper who complained that their Art.10 rights had been violated by a court's decision to exclude public and press from

---

[245] (1990) 67 D.R. 244.

sentencing proceedings. The Commission declared the application inadmissible, holding that since Art.6(1) provides explicitly for the possibility of holding proceedings *in camera* it followed that Art.10 must, in appropriate circumstances, give way. The leading decision of the Court is *Worm v Austria*,[246] in which the applicant was a journalist who had written an article asserting that Hannes Androsch, the former Austrian Vice Chancellor and Minister of Finance, was guilty of tax evasion. The article was published whilst the criminal proceedings were still in progress and the applicant was charged and convicted of an offence of "exercising a prohibited influence on criminal proceedings", a decision upheld by the Vienna Court of Appeal. The Court re-iterated that it was the task of journalists to impart such information, and that the public also had a right to receive it:

> "There is general recognition of the fact that the courts cannot operate in a vacuum. Whilst the courts are the forum for the determination of a person's guilt or innocence on a criminal charge, this does not mean that there can be no prior or contemporaneous discussion of the subject-matter of criminal trials elsewhere, be it in specialised journals, in the general press or amongst the public at large. Provided that it does not overstep the bounds imposed in the interests of the proper administration of justice, reporting, including comment, on court proceedings contributes to their publicity and is thus perfectly consonant with [the] requirement under Article 6(1) of the Convention that hearings be public."

This was all the more so when a public figure, and especially a former politician, **14–83** is involved since in that context "the limits of acceptable comment are wider."[247] The Court however emphasised that the limits of permissible comment did not extend to statements that were likely to prejudice a fair trial, even where public figures were involved. The objectionable feature of the article in question was that the assertion of Mr Androsch's guilt was made in such absolute terms that it conveyed the impression that the court could not do otherwise than convict him, and indeed it appeared to be intended to influence the outcome of the case.[248] The national courts had a margin of appreciation in determining whether it was necessary to restrict the publication of such an article for the purpose of "maintaining the authority and impartiality of the judiciary". The breadth of that margin was circumscribed by the fact that there was a substantial measure of common ground on the issue in the member states of the Council of Europe. However, the Austrian courts were entitled to guard against the risk that the public would become "accustomed to the regular spectacle of pseudo-trials in the news media [which] might in the long run have nefarious consequences for the acceptance of the courts as the proper forum for the determination of a person's guilt or innocence". Insofar as the applicant was quoting the words of the prosecutor in opening the case against the accused, he should have indicated that the words were a quotation, rather than appearing to adopt them as a statement of his own. Accordingly the Court was satisfied that the reasons given by the Austrian courts were sufficient, and that the journalist's right to freedom of expression was not—in the manner in which it was exercised—so great as to

---

[246] (1998) 25 E.H.R.R. 454.
[247] *Stögmüller v Austria* (1979–80) 1 E.H.R.R. 155.
[248] *H v France* (1990) 12 E.H.R.R. 74.

outweigh the adverse consequences for the authority of the Austrian judicial system.[249]

14-84 In *Montgomery v HM Advocate*, Lord Hope expressed the view that as a matter of Convention law, it was to be doubted that the right to a fair trial fell to be balanced against other Convention rights:

> "Reference was also made to *Baragiola v Switzerland* (1993) 75 DR 76. In that case the Commission observed, at p 120, that, while particular importance should be attached to the freedom of the press because of the public's right to information, a fair balance must nevertheless be struck between that freedom and the right to a fair trial guaranteed by article 6 of the Convention and that a restrictive interpretation of article 6.1 would not correspond to the aim and purpose of that provision. As I understand these observations, however, they were intended to emphasise the point that primacy must be given to the right to a fair trial. Article 6, unlike articles 8 to 11 of the Convention, is not subject to any words of limitation. It does not require, nor indeed does it permit, a balance to be struck between the rights which it sets out and other considerations such as the public interest. In so far as the *Baragiola* case may be taken as suggesting that in the application of article 6.1 a balance must be struck between the right of the individual to a fair trial and the freedom of the press or the public's right to information, I would be inclined not to follow it on the ground that this suggestion is inconsistent with the wording of the Convention. The suggestion is not, so far as I am aware, supported by any other authority."[250]

This passage in the speech of Lord Hope in *Montgomery* conflicts with the subsequent decision of the Court of Appeal in *Ex Parte Telegraph Group*.[251] In that case it was suggested in the context of a decision as to whether to impose an order under s.4(2) of the Contempt of Court Act that it would still be necessary to balance the right to a fair trial against other rights:

> "Suppose that the judge concludes that there is indeed no other way of eliminating the perceived risk of prejudice; it still does not follow *necessarily* that an order has to be made. The judge may still have to ask whether the degree of risk contemplated should be regarded as tolerable in the sense of being 'the lesser of two evils'. It is at this stage that value judgments may have to be made as to the priority between 'competing public interests'".[252]

14-85 There appears to be no settled international consensus as to the relative weight to be attached to the competing factors at stake when it is alleged that media coverage may prejudice a fair trial. One influential decision is that of the Supreme Court of Canada in *Re Dagenais and Canadian Broadcasting Corporation*.[253] The accused, members of a Catholic order who were being tried for various offences of sexual and physical abuse against boys at a training school, sought to prevent the CBC from screening a programme that gave a fictional

---

[249] *Stögmüller v Austria* (1979–80) 1 E.H.R.R. 155, para.5.
[250] [2003] 1 A.C. 641, PC at p.673D.
[251] [2001] 1 W.L.R. 1983, CA, para.22 (*per* Longmore L.J.).
[252] The conflict between the view of Lord Hope in *Montgomery* and the Court of Appeal in *Ex Parte Telegraph* was identified in *R. v B* [2006] EWCA Crim 2692, without deciding the issue.
[253] If a particular case will have important repercussions on the national case-law in a particular area, this may be a relevant consideration: *Katte Klitsche de la Grange v Italy* (1994) 19 E.H.R.R. 368, para.62.

account of physical and sexual abuse at a Catholic institution. A publication ban was made by the courts, but the Supreme Court held that this failed to provide sufficient protection for the right of freedom of expression. The existing law on publication bans was held to go too far in protecting the right of fair trial over the right to freedom of expression, when the Charter accorded equal status to the two rights. Such a ban would only be in accordance with the Charter if there was a substantial risk to the fairness of the trial, which could not be avoided by other means (such as an adjournment, a change of venue, or strong judicial direction to jury), and if the deleterious effects of a ban were clearly outweighed by its benefits for the administration of justice.

That approach was considered but not followed by the New Zealand Court of **14–86** Appeal in *Gisborne Herald v Solicitor General*.[254] In that case a local newspaper had published details of a man recently arrested for wounding a police officer, stating that he was on bail on other charges and setting out his previous convictions. The New Zealand courts held that the newspaper was guilty of contempt, particularly because in a small community it was unlikely that people would forget what had been written. The Court of Appeal adopted the view that, where freedom of expression and the right to a fair trial come into conflict, it would be appropriate to curtail temporarily the former right in order to secure the latter. The alternative methods of ensuring a fair trial mentioned in the Canadian case of *Dagenais* were not considered to be adequate to guard against prejudice at the trial.

IV. Protection of the Identity of Offenders

In *Venables and Thompson v News Group Newspapers and ors*,[255] the President **14–87** of the Family Division held that the High Court had jurisdiction to grant a lifelong injunction against the world where there was compelling evidence that this was strictly necessary to protect the new identities to be given to the two juveniles convicted of the murder of James Bulger. The claimants were due to be released and there was clear evidence before the court that attempts would be made to identify them in the community, leading to potentially fatal reprisal attacks. Whilst emphasising that the facts of the case were wholly exceptional, Butler-Sloss L.J. held that there was a positive obligation[256] on the courts, under Art.2 of the Convention, to take steps to prevent the dissemination of information which could expose their lives to unnecessary risk. A similar order was made in relation to the child of Mary Bell, by reference to her Convention rights under Art.8.[257]

---

[254] *Zimmermann and Steiner v Switzerland* (1984) 6 E.H.R.R. 17, para.24.
[255] [2001] 1 All E.R. 908.
[256] Above, para.2–53.
[257] *X. (formerly known as Mary Bell) v S*, *The Daily Telegraph*, May 29, 2003, Q.B.D.

F. THE RIGHT TO AN INDEPENDENT AND IMPARTIAL TRIBUNAL

I. General Principles

14–88   Article 6(1) guarantees the right to trial by an independent and impartial tribunal. The concepts of independence and impartiality are closely linked, and it will often be appropriate to consider them together.[258] A tribunal must be independent of the executive, of the parties, and of the legislature.[259] In determining whether this requirement is met, regard must be had to the manner of appointment of a tribunal's members, their term of office, the existence of guarantees against outside pressures, and the question whether the body presents an appearance of independence.[260] It is doubtful whether the requirements of independence and impartiality can be waived, in view of their importance for confidence in the judicial system.[261] Thus, in *Bulut v Austria*[262] the Court considered itself bound to examine the impartiality of a tribunal, irrespective of an alleged waiver by the applicant.[263]

14–89   It has been held that the right to a fair trial before an independent and impartial tribunal is a right to a fair trial at first instance.[264] The right therefore carries with it a correlative right not to be subjected to a hearing by a tribunal which does not possess those characteristics.[265] Failure to accord the right is therefore "irremediable".[266] The reason for this was expressed by Lord Steyn in *Brown v Stott* when he observed that "it is a basic premise of the Convention system that only an entirely neutral, impartial, and independent judiciary can carry out the primary task of securing and enforcing Convention rights".[267] Citing that dictum in *Millar v Dickson*, Lord Bingham said of the right, "It is a safeguard which should not, least of all in the criminal field, be weakened or diluted, whatever the

---

[258] *Hentrich v France* (1994) 18 E.H.R.R. 440, para.61.

[259] *Campbell and Fell v United Kingdom* (1985) 7 E.H.R.R. 165, para.78; *Crociani and ors v Italy* No.8603/79 22 D.R. 147 (independence of Parliament) and *Demicoli v Malta* (1992) 14 E.H.R.R. 47 (Comm. Rep. para.40); *McGonnell v United Kingdom* (2000) 30 E.H.R.R. 289.

[260] *Langborger v Sweden* (1990) 12 E.H.R.R. 416 para.32; *Campbell and Fell v United Kingdom* (1985) 7 E.H.R.R. 165, para.78; *Findlay v United Kingdom* (1997) 24 E.H.R.R. 22; *Incal v Turkey* (2000) 29 E.H.R.R. 449; *Piersack v Belgium* (1983) 5 E.H.R.R. 169, para.27; *Delcourt v Belgium* (1979–80) 1 E.H.R.R. 355, para.31; *Bryan v United Kingdom* (1996) 21 E.H.R.R. 342, para.37. As to the requirement for an appearance of independence and impartiality, see para.14–95 below.

[261] *Oberschlick v Austria* (1995) 19 E.H.R.R. 389, para.51 (waiver "in so far as it is permissible" must be established in unequivocal manner).

[262] (1996) 24 E.H.R.R. 84, para.30.

[263] The Government's argument in this regard was also rejected in *McGonnell v United Kingdom* (2000) 30 E.H.R.R. 289. *Cf.* the approach of the Court of Appeal to the question of waiver in *Locobail (UK) Ltd v Bayfield Properties Ltd and anor* [2000] Q.B. 451 (para.14–80 below).

[264] *Findlay v United Kingdom* (1997) 24 E.H.R.R. 22 (at paras 78–79), *Incal v Turkey* (2000) 29 E.H.R.R. 449 (at para.72); *De Cubber v Belgium* (1984) 7 E.H.R.R. 23 (at paras 32 and 34); *R. (Hammond) v Secretary of State for the Home Department* [2005] 3 W.L.R. 1229 (*per* Lord Bingham at paras 12–15 and *per* Lord Brown at para.42).

[265] *Dyer v Watson* [2004] 1 A.C. 379, PC (*per* Lord Millett at para.

[266] *R. (Hammond) v Secretary of State for the Home Department* [2005] 3 W.L.R. 1229 at para.47.

[267] [2003] 1 A.C. 681, PC.

administrative consequences."[268] Thus, even if a tribunal which lacks the requisite independence has conducted the trial in a manifestly fair manner, this is irrelevant to the overriding requirement to quash the conviction.[269] If the test for bias, dealt with below, is satisfied, there is no question of a balancing exercise between the right to a fair trial and the public interest in prosecuting serious crimes. The express words of Art.6 are unqualified and are not to be subordinated to public policy.[270]

Appointment by the executive or the legislature is permissible under Art.6,   **14–90** provided the appointees are free from influence or pressure when carrying out their adjudicatory role.[271] In order to establish a lack of independence in the manner of appointment, it is necessary to show that the practice of appointment as a whole was unsatisfactory, or alternatively, that the establishment of the particular court, or the appointment of the particular judge (or jury member) gave rise to a risk of undue influence over the outcome of the case.[272] A relatively short term of office has been held acceptable for unpaid judicial appointments.[273] However, a renewable four year appointment for a judge who is a member of a national security court was considered "questionable".[274] Any direct involvement in the passage of legislation or executive rules is likely to be sufficient to cast doubt on the judicial impartiality of a person subsequently called upon to determine a dispute as to the existence of reasons for permitting a variation from the legislation or the rules.[275] In *Starrs and Chalmers v Procurator Fiscal*,[276] the High Court of Justiciary in Scotland held the post of temporary sheriff to be incompatible with Art.6 since the appointment was for a fixed period of 12 months, and its renewal was within the unfettered discretion of the executive. The court considered that security of tenure was the cornerstone of judicial independence, and that such independence could be threatened not only by interference, but also by a judge being influenced, consciously or unconciously, by his hopes and fears about possible treatment by the executive in the future. The same conclusion was not reached by the Privy Council in *Kearney v H.M. Advocate*.[277] A temporary judge had been appointed by the Lord President on the advice of the Scottish Executive, of which the Lord Advocate, the head of the prosecution service, was a member. Unlike the appointment of the temporary

---

[268] [2002] 1 W.L.R. 1615, para.26.

[269] *Millar v Dickson* [2002] 1 W.L.R. 1615, PC (*per* Lord Hope at paras 63 and 65).

[270] *Montgomery v H. M. Advocate* [2003] 1 A.C. 641, *per* Lord Hope at 673D. This proposition was accepted by the Court of Appeal (Criminal Division) in *R. v Meziane and Benmerzouga* [2004] EWCA Crim 1768 and the Court of Appeal (Civil Division) in *AWG Group Ltd v Morrison* [2006] 1 W.L.R. 1163.

[271] *Campbell and Fell v United Kingdom* (1985) 7 E.H.R.R. 165, para.79; *Crociani v Italy* No.8603/79 22 D.R. 147.

[272] *Zand v Austria* (1978) 15 D.R. 70 at 81 (para.78).

[273] *Campbell and Fell v United Kingdom* (1984) 7 E.H.R.R. 165, para.80 (e.g. a term of three years for prison visitors).

[274] *Incal v Turkey* (2000) 29 E.H.R.R. 449.

[275] *McGonnell v United Kingdom* (2000) 30 E.H.R.R. 289 and *Davidson v Scottish Ministers* ([2004] UKHL 34), *The Times*, February 22, 2004. See 14–102.

[276] *The Times*, December 17, 1999, (2000) 8 B.H.R.C. 1, [2000] H.R.L.R. 191; 2000 S.L.T. 42. The decision was subsequently endorsed by the Privy Council in *Millar v Dickson* [2002] 1 W.L.R. 1615.

[277] (2006) 20 B.H.R.C. 157, PC.

sheriff in *Starrs*, security of tenure was not an issue. The employment and deployment of the judge was primarily administered by the Lord President and not the Lord Advocate. Lord Bingham endorsed the observation in *Starrs* that as a matter of principle there was nothing inherently objectionable in the appointment of judges by the Executive, which was the practice in much of the world: it made practical sense that judges should be appointed by the body which was thereafter responsible for paying them, accommodating them and servicing their professional requirements.[278] In Canada there have been several challenges under the equivalent section of the Charter against part-time judges and justices of the peace, but the leading decision of the Supreme Court upholds the existing system of appointment and training and discounts fears (particularly in relation to part-time judges) about conflicts of interest arising from their other professional duties.[279]

14–91 In *Campbell and Fell v United Kingdom*,[280] a case concerning disciplinary adjudications under the former prison visitors regime, the Court held that members of a tribunal must, as a very minimum, be protected against removal *during* their term of office:

> "[T]he irremovability of judges by the executive during their term of office must in general be considered as a corollary of their independence and thus included in the guarantees of Article 6(1). However, the absence of a formal recognition of this irremovability in the law does not in itself imply lack of independence provided that it is recognised in fact and that the other necessary guarantees are present."

In *Campbell*, the Court held that the Board of Visitors was sufficiently independent and impartial. However, in *Whitfield v United Kingdom*,[281] the independence of the the tribunal under a new system was successfully challenged on the basis that persons answerable to the Home Office (whether as prison officer, governor or controller in the applicants' prisons) drafted and laid the charges against the applicants, investigated and prosecuted those charges and determined the applicants' guilt or innocence together with their sentences.[282]

14–92 Independence requires that each judge and tribunal member be free from outside pressure, whether from the executive, legislature, parties to the case or other members of the court or tribunal. Thus where a tribunal's members "include a person who is in a subordinate position, in terms of his duties and the organisation of his service, *vis à vis* one of the parties, litigants may entertain a legitimate doubt about that person's independence."[283] In *Findlay v United Kingdom*[284] the

---

[278] Para.5.

[279] See *Quebec (AG) v Lippe* (1991) 64 C.C.C. (3d) 513, and other authorities discussed by Stuart D., *Charter Justice in Canadian Criminal Law* (2nd edn, 1996), pp.349–354.

[280] (1985) 7 E.H.R.R. 165, para.80.

[281] (2005) 41 E.H.R.R. 44, para.45.

[282] See to the same effect, *R. (Al Hassan) v Secretary of State for the Home Department; R. (Carroll) v Same* [2005] 1 W.L.R. 688, HL. The deputy governor who witnessed the attempt to conduct an intimate search of a prisoner, sat as the adjudicator in subsequent disciplinary proceedings where the issue was whether the decision to carry out the search had been lawful.

[283] *Sramek v Austria* (1985) 7 E.H.R.R. 351.

[284] *Findlay v United Kingdom* (1997) 24 E.H.R.R. 221, paras 73–77.

Court found that there were objectively justified doubts as to the independence and impartiality of a court martial, where a "convening officer" was responsible for arranging the court martial, and for appointing the members of the court, the prosecuting and defending officers (who were all subordinate in rank, and fell within his chain of command). He also had the function of "confirming" the conviction and sentence imposed by the court.

The requirement for an impartial tribunal embodies the protection against actual   **14–93** and presumed bias. The Court has adopted a dual test, examining first the evidence of actual bias, and then making an objective assessment of the circumstances alleged to give rise to a risk of bias.[285] In *Hauschildt v Denmark*[286] the Court expressed the test in these terms:

> "The existence of impartiality for the purpose of Article 6(1) must be determined according to a subjective test, that is on the basis of the personal conviction of a particular judge in a given case, and also according to an objective test, that is ascertaining whether the judge offered guarantees sufficient to exclude any legitimate doubt in this respect."[287]

The onus of establishing actual bias on the subjective test is a heavy one.[288]   **14–94** There is a presumption that the court has acted impartially, which must be displaced by evidence to the contrary.[289] In applying the objective test, the question is whether a legitimate doubt as to the impartiality of the tribual can be "objectively justified".[290] The Court will inquire whether the tribunal offered guarantees sufficient to exclude such a doubt,[291] or whether there are "ascertainable facts" that may raise doubts as to a tribunal's impartiality.[292] In making an assessment of a tribunal's impartiality, "even appearances may be important".[293] Where there is legitimate doubt as to a judge's impartiality, he must withdraw from the case.[294]

An appearance of independence and impartiality is important because "what is at   **14–95** stake is the confidence which the courts in a democratic society must inspire in

---

[285] *Piersack v Belgium* (1983) 5 E.H.R.R. 169, para.30 applied in *Ferrantelli and Santangelo v Italy* (1997) 23 E.H.R.R. 288, para.56; *Bulut v Austria* (1997) 24 E.H.R.R. 84, para.31; *Thomann v Switzerland* (1997) 24 E.H.R.R. 553, para.30.

[286] (1990) 12 E.H.R.R. 266.

[287] *ibid.*, at para.46.

[288] The test adopted by the court is that the members of a tribunal must be "subjectively free of personal prejudice or bias": *Findlay v United Kingdom* (1997) 24 E.H.R.R. 221, para.73.

[289] *Hauschildt v Denmark* (1989) 12 E.H.R.R. 266, para.47; *Piersack v Belgium* (1983) 5 E.H.R.R. 169, para.30(a); *Thomann v Switzerland* (1997) 24 E.H.R.R. 553, para.31.

[290] *Hauschildt v Denmark* (1990) 12 E.H.R.R. 266, para.48; *Ferrantelli and Santangelo v Italy* (1997) 23 E.H.R.R. 288, para.58; *Incal v Turkey* (2000) 29 E.H.R.R. 449 (para.71); *Castillo Agar v Spain* (2000) 30 E.H.R.R. 827, para.46.

[291] *Piersack v Belgium* (1983) 5 E.H.R.R. 169, para.30; *Incal v Turkey* (2000) 29 E.H.R.R. 449, para.65.

[292] See for example, *Hauschildt v Denmark* (1990) 12 E.H.R.R. 266, para.48.

[293] *Piersack v Belgium* (1983) 5 E.H.R.R. 169, para.30; *Sramek v Austria* (1985) 7 E.H.R.R. 35, para.42; *Findlay v United Kingdom* (1997) 24 E.H.R.R. 221, para.76.

[294] *Hauschildt v Denmark* (1990) 12 E.H.R.R. 266, paras 46, 48; *Castillo Algar v Spain* Judgment September 28, 1998, para.45. As to the test to be applied in English law, see *Locobail (UK) Ltd v Bayfield Properties Ltd and anor.* [2000] Q.B. 451 (CA) (guidance on judicial impartiality).

the public".[295] The applicable test has been described in the following ways: whether the public is "reasonably entitled" to entertain doubts as to the independence or impartiality of the tribunal[296]; whether there are "legitimate grounds for fearing" that the tribunal is not independent or impartial[297]; whether "there are ascertainable facts that may raise doubts" as to independence or impartiality[298]; or whether such doubts can be "objectively justified".[299]

14–96   The fact that a trial judge or appeal judge has made pre-trial decisions in a case, including those concerning detention on remand, cannot in itself be held to justify fears as to the judge's impartiality, since:

> "[Q]uestions which the judge has to answer when taking such pre-trial decisions are not the same as those which are decisive for his final judgment. When taking a decision on detention on remand and other pre-trial decisions of this kind the judge summarily assesses the available data in order to ascertain whether *prima facie* the police have grounds for their suspicion; when giving judgment at the conclusion of the trial he must assess whether the evidence that has been produced and debated in court suffices for finding the accused guilty. Suspicion and formal finding of guilt are not to be treated as being the same."[300]

14–97   Where, however, the issues determined at the pre-trial stage are closely related to those which arise at a final determination, the court's impartiality is capable of appearing open to doubt.[301] While it is not contrary to Art.6(1) for the same judge to take part in different proceedings against several persons accused of the same offence,[302] the position is otherwise where the judge has previously expressed views suggesting that he has formed an opinion as to the accused's guilt.[303]

14–98   There is no general rule resulting from the obligation to be impartial that a superior court which sets aside a decision of an inferior tribunal is bound to send the case back to a differently constituted bench.[304] The same principle applies where the first trial was held *in absentia* since:

> "[J]udges who retry in the defendant's presence a case that they have first had to try *in absentia* on the basis of the evidence that they had available to them at the time are in no way bound by their first decision. They undertake a fresh consideration of the whole

---

[295] *Incal v Turkey* (2000) 29 E.H.R.R. 449, para.71; *Fey v Austria* (1993) 16 E.H.R.R. 387, para.30 (confidence of accused also essential in context of criminal trial).

[296] *Campbell and Fell v United Kingdom* (1985) 7 E.H.R.R. 165, para.81.

[297] *Langborger v Sweden* (1990) 12 E.H.R.R. 416, para.35; *Procola v Luxembourg* (1996) 22 E.H.R.R. 193, para.45; *McGonnell v United Kingdom* (2000) 30 E.H.R.R. 289.

[298] *Castillo Algar v Spain* (2000) 30 E.H.R.R. 827.

[299] *Hauschildt v Denmark* (1990) 12 E.H.R.R. 266, para.48.

[300] *Hauschildt v Denmark* (1990) 12 E.H.R.R. 266, para.50. See also *Bulut v Austria* (1997) 24 E.H.R.R. 84, paras 33–34 (role of judge in pre-trial proceedings restricted to questioning of two witnesses, but no assessment as to applicant's involvement in offence—no objective justification for lack of impartiality); *Sainte-Marie v France* (1993) 16 E.H.R.R. 116, paras 32–34; *Fey v Austria* (1993) 16 E.H.R.R. 387, paras 31–33; *Padovani v Italy* Judgment February 26, 1993, para.28; *Nortier v Netherlands* (1994) 17 E.H.R.R. 273, paras 33–35.

[301] *Hauschildt v Denmark* (1990) 12 E.H.R.R. 266, paras 51–52.

[302] *Ferrantelli and Santangelo v Italy* (1997) 23 E.H.R.R. 288 (Comm. Rep.) para.57.

[303] *Ferrantelli and Santangelo v Italy* (1997) 23 E.H.R.R. 288, paras 59–60.

[304] *Thomann v Switzerland* (1997) 24 E.H.R.R. 553, paras 33–36; *Ringeisen v Austria (No.1)* (1979–80) 1 E.H.R.R. 455, para.97; *Diennet v France* (1996) 21 E.H.R.R. 554, paras 37–38.

case; all the issues raised by the case remain open and this time are examined in adversarial proceedings with the benefit of the more comprehensive information that may be obtained from the appearance of the defendant in person ... [I]f a court had to alter its composition each time that it accepted an application for a retrial from a person who had been convicted in his absence, such person would be placed at an advantage in relation to defendants who appeared at the opening of their trial, because this would enable the former to obtain a second hearing of their case by different judges at the same level of jurisdiction."[305]

Where a trial judge was previously the head of the section of the public   **14–99**
prosecutor's department which had investigated the applicant's case and commenced proceedings against him, the Court, not surprisingly, held that the "impartiality of the 'tribunal' which had to determine the merits ... was capable of appearing open to doubt".[306] It was not necessary for the applicant to establish that the judge had been directly involved in the case:

"In order that the courts inspire the confidence which is indispensable, account must also be taken of questions of internal organisation. If an individual, after holding in the public prosecutor's department an office whose nature is such that he may have to deal with a given matter in the course of his duties, subsequently sits in the same case as a judge, the public are entitled to fear that he does not offer sufficient guarantees of impartiality."[307]

However, the Court considered that: **14–100**

"[I]t would be going too far ... to maintain that former judicial officers in the public prosecutor's department were unable to sit on the bench in every case that had been examined initially by that department, even though they had never had to deal with the case themselves. So radical a solution, based on an inflexible and formalistic conception of the unity and indivisibility of the public prosecutor's department would erect a virtually impenetrable barrier between that department and the bench. It would lead to an upheaval in the judicial system of several Contracting States where transfers from one of those offices to the other are a frequent occurrence. Above all, the mere fact that a judge was once a member of the public prosecutor's department is not a reason for fearing that he lacks impartiality".[308]

In determining an application to stay proceedings or to exclude evidence, it may   **14–101**
be incompatible with Art.6 for a judge to be shown material which is wholly adverse to the interests of a defendant during an *ex parte* public interest immunity application, without the defendant's legal representatives (or in exceptional cases, a special advocate) having an opportunity to comment upon the material.[309]

---

[305] *Thomann v Switzerland* (1997) 24 E.H.R.R. 553 at 556–557 (paras 35–36).

[306] *Piersack v Belgium* (1983) 5 E.H.R.R. 169 at 181, para.31.

[307] *Piersack v Belgium* (1983) 5 E.H.R.R. 169 at 180 (para.30(d)).

[308] *Piersack v Belgium* (1983) 5 E.H.R.R. 169 at 179 (para.30(d)).

[309] *Edwards and Lewis v United Kingdom* (2005) 40 E.H.R.R. 24; and *R. v H and C* [2004] 2 A.C. 132, HL. See para.14–122a–122d. The principle identified in *Edwards and Lewis* was not applied in *R. v May* [2005] 3 All. E.R. 523, CA (judge in confiscation proceedings expressly indicating that he had ignored any material revealed to him in the PII hearings during the trial), or in the case of *R. v Lewis* [2005] EWCA Crim 859 (when the Grand Chamber case was reconsidered by the Court of Appeal).

14–102 Where a judge has a financial or personal interest in the case, a party is objectively justified in fearing lack of impartiality.[310] Any direct involvement in the passage of legislation or the enactment of executive rules is likely to be sufficient to cast doubt on the judicial impartiality of a person subsequently called upon to determine a dispute as to the existence of reasons for permitting a variation from the legislation or rules at issue. In *McGonnell v United Kingdom*[311] the Bailiff of Guernsey, when sitting in his judicial capacity, was held not to be "independent" since he had performed a presiding role in the local legislature when it adopted the measure in dispute. As a result of the original decision in *McGonnell*, various questions arose as to how the Lord Chancellor and the Law Lords would exercise their dual roles as judges and parliamentarians. The Lord Chancellor at the time, Lord Irvine, gave a written answer to a parliamentary question on February 23, 2000,[312] in which he declined to step down as head of the judiciary and distinguished his role from that of the Bailiff of Guernsey, but added:

> "The Lord Chancellor would never sit in any case concerning legislation in the passage of which he had been directly involved nor in any case where the interests of the executive were directly engaged."

This response was supplemented by a collective reply by the Lords of Appeal in Ordinary on June 22, 2000[313]:

> "As full members of the House of Lords the Lords of Appeal in Ordinary have a right to participate in the business of the House. However, mindful of their judicial role they consider themselves bound by two general principles when deciding whether to participate in a particular matter, or to vote; .... secondly the Lords of Appeal in Ordinary bear in mind that they might render themselves ineligible to sit judicially if they were to express an opinion on a matter which might later be relevant to an appeal to the House."

McGonnell was subsequently followed by the House of Lords in *Davidson v Scottish Ministers*.[314] The issue in the case turned upon the extent to which ministerial immunity in the Crown Proceedings Act 1947 had been altered by the Scotland Act 1998. One of the judges, Lord Hardie, when holding the office of Lord Advocate in Her Majesty's Government and in the context of promoting the Scotland Bill in the House of Lords, advised the House on the effect of s.21 of the Crown Proceedings Act on the remedies which might be available to the courts in Scotland against the Scottish Ministers. Various statements which he made were in conflict with the prisoner's claim in the subsequent case.

14–103 Both before and after the Human Rights Act came into force, the test of judicial bias in domestic law was considered by the House of Lords and by the Court of

---

[310] See *Demicoli v Malta* (1992) 14 E.H.R.R. 47 (paras 36–42) (members of the House of Representatives who were the subject of alleged offence of breach of parliamentary privilege were among those who sat in Judgment); *Langborger v Sweden* (1990) 12 E.H.R.R. 416, para.35 (lay members of tribunal adjudicating on deletion of clause in tenancy agreement were nominated by organisations having an interest in the clause's continued existence).

[311] (2000) 30 E.H.R.R. 289.

[312] HL Hansard, Vol.610, February 23, 2000, W.A. 33.

[313] HL Hansard, Vol.614, June 22, 2000, col.419.

[314] ([2004] UKHL 34) *The Times*, July 16, 2004.

Appeal. In *R. v Bow Street Metropolitan Stipendiary Magistrate ex parte Pinochet Ugarte (No.2)*,[315] the House of Lords held that Lord Hoffmann's connection with Amnesty International, which had intervened in the appeal, violated the principle that a person may not be a judge in his own cause. That principle goes wider than financial interests, and encompasses the promotion of a cause in which the judge is involved with one of the parties. Following the *Pinochet* ruling there was a sharp increase in the number of applications for recusal, and in *Locobail (UK) Ltd v Bayfield Properties Ltd and another* the Court of Appeal gave guidance, in a series of linked appeals, on the approach to be adopted where it is alleged that a judge has a personal interest in the outcome of the proceedings.[316] Referring to Art.6, the Court of Appeal held that the right to a fair hearing by an impartial tribunal was fundamental. This pointed to a rule of automatic disqualification when a judge had a direct pecuniary or proprietary interest in the subject-matter of a proceeding, however small,[317] and where the matter at issue was concerned with the promotion of a cause and the judge is involved with one of the parties seeking to promote that cause.[318] In other cases, there was no rule of automatic disqualification. The question was whether a reasonable, objective and informed person would, on the correct facts, reasonably apprehend that the judge will not bring an impartial mind to bear on the adjudication of the case, that is a mind open to persuasion by the evidence and the submissions of counsel.[319] The religion, ethnic or national origin, gender, age, class, means or sexual orientation of a tribunal member could not conceivably form the basis of a sound objection. Nor could an objection generally be based on matters of social, educational, service or employment background or history, nor that of the tribunal member's family. Other factors which would generally be irrelevant were previous political associations, previous judicial decisions, extra-judicial comment, previous instructions to act for or against any party, as solicitor or advocate engaged in the case, or membership of the same Inn of Court, circuit, local Law Society or chambers. By contrast a real danger of bias might arise from personal friendship or animosity between the tribunal member and any other person involved in the case, or a close acquaintance (especially where credibility is in issue).[320] It would generally be appropriate for a tribunal member to recuse himself if, in a previous case, he had rejected the evidence of a witness in such

---

[315] [2000] 1 A.C. 119; see also the High Court of Australia in *Webb v R.* (1994) 181 C.L.R. 41, where the test was whether the judge's interests or affiliations would give rise to a suspicion, in a fair-minded and informed member of the public, that the judge might be biased.

[316] [2000] 1 All E.R. 65 (C.A.). As to police disciplinary proceedings, see *Regina (Bennion) v Chief Constable of Merseyside Police*, *The Times*, June 12, 2001 (no breach of Art.6 where the Chief Constable adjudicated on disciplinary proceedings under Reg.13(1) of the Police (Disciplinary) Regulations 1985, despite the fact that the officer being disciplined had brought a sex discrimination claim against the relevant force in which the chief constable was cited as defendant. The disciplinary function of a chief constable was to be distinguished from that of a judge.

[317] See *Dimes v The Proprietors of the Grand Junction Canal* (1852) 3 HL Cas 759.

[318] *R. v Bow Street Metropolitan Stipendiary Magistrate ex parte Pinochet Ugarte (No.2)* [2000] 1 A.C. 119.

[319] *R. v Gough* [1993] A.C. 646; *President of the Republic of South Africa & ors v South African Rugby Football Union & ors* 1999 (7) B.C.L.R. (C.C.) 725.

[320] See the authorities dealing with the possibility that jurors decided their verdicts on the basis of their attitudes to the barristers in the case, rather than the evidence: *R. (Dawson) v H.M. Coroner for East Riding and Kingston upon Hull* [2001] EWHC Admin 352; *Hardiman v United Kingdom* [1996] E.H.R.L.R. 425.

outspoken terms as to throw doubt on his ability to approach that witness's evidence in subsequent proceedings with an open mind; if he had expressed views on any question at issue in the case in such strong and unbalanced terms as to throw doubt on his ability to try the case with an objective mind; or if, for any reason, there were real grounds to doubt his ability to ignore extraneous considerations, prejudices and predilections, and bring an objective mind to bear on the issues.[321] In any case of doubt, that doubt was to be resolved in favour of recusal. If an appropriate disclosure has been made to the parties, and no objection is taken, the party affected will be taken to have waived his right to complain (other than in cases requiring automatic disqualification).[322]

II. Jury Bias

14–104   The requirement of independence and impartiality applies equally to juries.[323] Article 6(1) imposes an obligation on every court to check whether, as constituted, it is an "impartial tribunal" within the meaning of that provision when there is an allegation of bias that does not immediately appear manifestly devoid of merit.[324] The common law test for bias was originally established by the House of Lords in *R. v Gough.*[325] Prior to *Gough* there was inconsistent domestic authority as to whether the test was one of actual bias (which was the test applied to jurors) or appearance of bias (which was the test applied to magistrates). The House of Lords ruled that the same test should apply to both. The court should inquire into the circumstances, and then ask itself whether there was "a real danger" of bias on the part of the relevant member of the tribunal in the sense that he might unfairly regard with favour or disfavour the case of one of the parties. Stating the test in terms of "real danger" rather than "real likelihood" was intended to ensure that the court is thinking in terms of possibility rather than probability. In the case of *In Re: Medicaments and Related Classes of Goods (No.2),*[326] the Court of Appeal held that the test for bias under the common law required some modification in order to comply with the Art.6 jurisprudence:

> " . . . The difference is that, when the Strasbourg court considers whether the material circumstances give rise to a reasonable apprehension of bias, it makes it plain that it is applying an objective test to the circumstances, not passing judgment on the likelihood that the particular tribunal under review was in fact biased . . . "

---

[321] See *R. v Inner West London Coroner ex parte Dallaglio and Lockwood Croft* [1994] 4 All. E.R. 139 (where a coroner described a bereaved relative of someone who had died on the Marchioness as "unhinged"); and *Hoestra v H.M. Advocate, The Times,* April 14, 2000, High Ct. of Justiciary (where a judge in a criminal appeal concerning Human Rights Act arguments published an article in a newpaper which used language which clearly indicated a deep-seated and long-standing hostility to the Convention). See also *Prosecutor v Sesay* (2004) 16 B.H.R.C. 245, a decision of the Special Court for Sierra Leone (Appeals Chamber) concerning the recusal of a judge on the basis that he had written a book in which he accused the organisation to which the appellants belonged of having perpetrated crimes against humanity.

[322] This approach to waiver does not appear to sit comfortably with the approach of the European Court of Human Rights: see para.14–67 above.

[323] *Pullar v United Kingdom* (1996) 22 E.H.R.R. 391, para.30.

[324] *Remli v France* (1996) 22 E.H.R.R. 253, paras 46–48.

[325] [1993] A.C. 646.

[326] [2001] 1 W.L.R. 700, CA (Civ. Div), para.83.

In Re: Medicaments was subsequently approved by the House of Lords in *Porter v Magill*[327] The common law *Gough* "real danger" test was found by Lord Hope:

" . . . no longer to serve a useful purpose here, and . . . [is] not used in the jurisprudence of the Strasbourg Court . . . The applicable test from henceforward was to be as follows: . . . whether a fair-minded and informed observer, having considered the facts, would conclude that there was a real possibility that the tribunal was biased . . . ".

The standard adopted in Strasbourg appears to have strengthened over the years, **14–105** consistent with the court's emphasis on the increasing sensitivity of the public to an appearance of fairness. In *X v Norway*[328] the Commission declared inadmissible a complaint that a jury member was the godchild of an interested party. Similarly, in *X v Austria*[329] a complaint that the jury foreman was employed by the organisation which owned the shop where a robbery had taken place was also rejected by the Commission. But in *Holm v Sweden*[330] the Court found a violation of Art.6(1) where a number of jury members were also members of a political party that owned a publishing company which was one of the defendants in the case. In *Pullar v United Kingdom*,[331] a Scottish case, the defendant discovered after his conviction that one of the jurors who had tried him was an employee of the principal prosecution witness, and was acquainted with another of the prosecution witnesses. Surprisingly, the Court held, by five votes to four, that there was no evidence of prejudice to the defence, and no violation of Art.6(1). The fact that the juror would have been discharged if the trial court had been aware of the connection was not sufficient to provide "objective justification" for the applicant's fear of bias. The Court appeared to require a higher standard of proof to oblige the domestic courts to disturb a conviction on this ground than would be required for the discharge of a juror during the trial:

"[I]t is by no means decisive that (as the High Court of Justiciary observed) the sheriff would probably have dismissed F. from the jury had he known about the connection between the latter and M. It is natural that a presiding judge should strive to ensure that the composition of the jury is beyond any reproach whatsoever, at a time when this is still possible, before or during the trial. However, once the trial is over and a verdict had been given, it became material whether F's continued presence on the jury constituted a defect grave enough to justify setting aside that verdict."[332]

After examining the circumstances, the Court held that the risk of bias was not **14–106** objectively justified. The court placed reliance upon the fact that the juror was a junior employee of the firm owned by the witness, that he had not worked on the project which formed the background to the accusations, and that he had been served with a redundancy notice three days before the trial began.

Where the risk of bias has been brought to the court's attention before or during **14–107** the trial, the key question will usually be whether the judge took adequate steps

---

[327] [2002] 2 A.C. 357, para.103.
[328] (1970) 35 C.D. 37 at 49.
[329] (1978) 13 D.R. 38.
[330] (1994) 18 E.H.R.R. 79.
[331] (1996) 22 E.H.R.R. 391.
[332] *ibid.*, at para.36.

to investigate the source of the potential bias, and to remedy the defect. In *Remli v France*[333] one of the jurors in the Rhone Assize Court was overheard expressing racist attitudes towards the defendant, but the trial judge failed to conduct any examination of the allegation or take steps to remedy the situation. The Court held that this failure was sufficient in itself to give rise to a violation of Art.6:

> "Article 6(1) of the Convention imposes an obligation on every national court to check whether, as constituted, it is an 'impartial tribunal' within the meaning of that provision where, as in the instant case, this is disputed on a ground that does not immediately appear to be manifestly devoid of merit. In the instant case [the court] did not make any such check, thereby depriving [the applicant] of the possibility of remedying—if it proved necessary—a situation contrary to the requirements of the Convention. This finding (regard being had to the confidence which the courts must inspire in those subject to their jurisdiction) suffices for the Court to hold that there has been a breach of Article 6(1)."[334]

14–108   *Remli* is to be contrasted with *Gregory v United Kingdom*,[335] where the Court found no violation of Art.6. During the trial of a defendant who was black, the judge received a note from one jury member indicating that at least one other member of the jury was "showing racial prejudice." The Court held that it was sufficient that the judge had investigated the matter, had consulted both counsel, and had then given the jury a clear direction to decide the case on the evidence, free from any prejudice. The fact that the judge had not considered it necessary to discharge the jury did not give rise to a violation of Art.6, because he had recognised the problem and had dealt with it in a satisfactory way. It was the French court's refusal to examine the matter at all that led to the finding of a violation in *Remli*. The court had failed to offer guarantees sufficient to exclude any legitimate doubt about the juror's impartiality.

14–109   In *Miah v United Kingdom*[336] a statement emanating from a member of the jury, produced one year after the trial, alleged that some members had decided on the defendant's guilt at an early stage, and did so on the basis of racist assumptions. The Court of Appeal concluded that the statement "lacked substance". The Commission similarly held that there was "no convincing evidence of actual or subjective bias on the part of one or more jurors." In the Commission's view, the Court of Appeal's enquiries into the origins and content of the statement were adequate. However, in *Sander v United Kingdom*[337] the Court found a violation of Art.6 where, during the trial of two Asian defendants, one member of the jury sent a note to the judge alleging that at least two other members of the jury were making racist jokes and remarks. On examination, there was evidence confirming that such remarks had been made, although the juror concerned dismissed them as a joke. The Court considered that this was sufficient to give rise to a legitimate doubt as to the impartiality of the jury. Such a doubt could not be dispelled by a direction from the judge to try the case on the evidence, or to put prejudice

---

[333] (1996) 22 E.H.R.R. 253.
[334] *ibid.*, at para.48.
[335] (1998) 25 E.H.R.R. 577.
[336] (1998) 26 E.H.R.R. CD 199.
[337] (2001) 31 E.H.R.R. 44.

aside, however strongly the direction was worded. Accordingly, there had been a violation of Art.6.

These authorities were considered by the Court of Appeal in *R. v Lewis*.[338] Three **14–110** days after the appellant's conviction by unanimous verdict, the Crown Court received a letter from one of the jurors stating that the jury had not in fact been unanimous. The Court of Appeal declined to order that inquiries be made of the jury. Keene L.J. held that the principles established in *R. v Millward*[339] remained valid, notwithstanding the coming into force of the Human Rights Act 1998. In *R. v Mirza*; *R. v Connor and Rollock*,[340] the House of Lords held that the common law rule on the inadmissibility of evidence relating to jury deliberations was compatible with Art.6, notwithstanding that it would prevent a court from considering material that would indicate that a defendant was denied an impartial hearing.[341] In the *Mirza* case, a letter was written by a juror after the verdict, which complained of racist remarks during the course of the jury's deliberations. In the *Connor and Rollock* case, a juror had written directly to the court after the verdict and indicated that the jury failed to treat each of the cases seperately despite a direction to do so and only reached a final verdict because some of their number wanted to go home. In choosing to uphold the secrecy rule the majority of their Lordship's' House relied on its two-fold historic justification: first, to promote candour in discussion and second, to promote finality once a verdict has been given.[342] They also took account of the extent to which the Strasbourg courts had endorsed the rule, in particular in *Gregory v United Kingdom*, where the Court acknowledged that that the rule "is a crucial and legitimate feature of English trial law which serves to reinforce the jury's role as the ultimate arbiter of fact and to guarantee open and frank deliberations among jurors on the evidence which they have heard."[343] The rule turns completely upon timing, because it only relates to jury deliberations after their retirement and before the delivery of the verdict.[344] It does not constrain a juror from contacting a judge prior to the verdict and registering a complaint.[345] Neither does it remove from a judge the requirement to appropriately investigate and/or remedy an allegation of impartiality if it is drawn to his attention at any time before the verdict.[346]

---

[338] *The Times*, April 26, 2001.

[339] [1999] 1 Cr.App.R. 61.

[340] [2004] 1 A.C. 1118, HL.

[341] Subject to certain differences in its scope, a similar exclusionary rule has prevailed in Commonwealth countries: Canada: *R. v Pan* [2001] 2 S.C.R. 344; Australia: *R. v Andrew Brown* (1907) 7 N.S.W.S.R. 290; *R. v Medici* (Court of Criminal Appeal, Victoria, June 5, 1995); New Zealand: *R. v Papadopoulos* [1979] 1 N.Z.L.R. 621.

[342] [2004] 1 A.C. 1118, paras 47, 61, 99 and 142.

[343] (1998) 25 E.H.R.R. 577, para.44.

[344] The common law has always tolerated inquiries by the Court of Appeal in relation to irregular occurrences after retirement, but which are extraneous to the actual deliberations on the verdict: see *R. v Young (Stephen)* [1995] Q.B. 324 (juror used a ouija board to contact the deceased victim in the case during an overnight stay in a hotel).

[345] *The Practice Directions (Guidance to Jurors)* [2004] 1 W.L.R. 665 was issued in response to the *Mirza* judgment. It requires judges to invite juries to bring any matters of concern to the attention of the court prior to any verdict, with an appropriately worded indication that it may not be possible to do so afterwards.

[346] See *Remli v France* (1996) 22 E.H.R.R. 253, *Gregory v United Kingdom* (1998) 25 E.H.R.R. 577, *Sander v United Kingdom* (2001) 31 E.H.R.R. 44.

Where necessary, jurors must be discharged and/or directions given in comprehensive and emphatic terms with sufficient particularity and emphasis.[347] Such an investigation by the court, of its own process, will not constitute a contempt within the meaning of s.8 of the Contempt of Court Act, even if the result of the judge's investigations are disclosed to counsel.[348] However, to the extent that s.8 of the 1981 Act prohibits the publication of matters relating to the jury room to the wider public, it constitutes a legitimate interference with Art.10. This is the case even if a juror discloses the information with the bona fide aim of preventing a miscarriage of justice.[349]

14–111   Focus upon the composition of juries has arisen more acutely as a result of s.321 of the Criminal Justice Act 2003, which has removed certain categories of persons from those previously ineligible for jury service (the judiciary and others concerned with the administration of justice). In *R. v Abdroikov*[350] the Court of Appeal held that members of the prosecution service or other persons involved in the administration of justice should not, because that was their occupation, be automatically regarded as being disqualified from a jury. However, the question of whether a particular eligible person should be prevented from sitting on a particular jury at a particular place, is a question to be investigated on a case by case basis.If an issue arises as to whether, despite the precautions that are taken, a member of the jury has knowledge which makes him or her unsuitable to sit on that jury, the usual test as indicated by Lord Hope in the *Porter* case has to be applied in all the circumstances to determine whether the requirements of fairness have been met or not.[351]

III. Summary Proceedings for Contempt of Court

14–112   Prior to the Human Rights Act coming into force, the case law on summary contempt proceedings was clear about the need to comply with the rules of natural justice, in particular the right to be tried by an impartial tribunal and to have prior notice of the nature of the accusation and an opportunity to counter

---

[347] *R. v Smith (Patrick); R. v Mercieca* [2005] 1 W.L.R. 704. The judgment of Lord Carswell summarises all of the principles in relation to jury inquiries at para.16.

[348] [2004] 1 A.C. 1118, para.93 and 139, which disapproved of the previous observations by Lord Taylor C.J. in *R. v Young (Stephen)* [1995] Q.B. 324, 330F–H.

[349] *Attorney-General v Scotcher* [2005] 2 Cr.App.R. 35, HL. On the facts of the case, the sole purpose of a letter written to a the mother of a convicted defendant after a verdict was to prevent a perceived violation of Article 6. The House of Lords relied upon the terms of the *Practice Directions (Guidance to Jurors)* [2004] 1 W.L.R. 665 and the further guidance given in *Smith* and *Mercieca* in order to justify the prohibition on any disclosure after the veridict.

[350] [2006] 1 Cr.App.R. 1.

[351] Paras 25–37. It has been held that the principle of random jury selection will not offend the right to an independent and impartial tribunal if it leads to an ethnic minority defendant being tried by an all white jury: *R. v Smith (Lance Percival)* [2003] 1 W.L.R. 2229 upholding *R. v Ford (Royston)* [1989] Q.B. 868, CA. *Cf.* the situation considered by the Privy Council in *Rojas v Berllaque (Attorney General for Gibraltar intervening)* [2004] 1 W.L.R. 201, where only male citizens of Gibraltar were liable to sit on juries, and women could merely volunteer to sit.

it.[352] Thus, in *R. v Schot and Barclay*,[353] the Court of Appeal overturned a conviction for contempt of court imposed by a judge upon two jurors who had indicated prior to the jury being discharged that they were not prepared to return a verdict according to their oaths. It did so, because the judge had expressed a view that a serious contempt had been committed prior to ordering them to return in 12 days to "show cause" as to why they should not be fined. It was held that the judge's premature expression of the appellants' guilt was in breach of the presumption of innocence and created a risk of apparent bias. In those circumstances the judge was obliged to recuse himself. The Court of Appeal also held that the procedure was, in any event, fundamentally flawed by the fact that "the contempt was never clearly defined in the manner which, as it seems to us, is essential for a proper inquiry . . . in the context of the criminal or quasi-criminal nature of contempt of court".

The principal case decided under the Human Rights Act is *Wilkinson v S.*[354] The **14-113** case involved an assault by one party to a custody dispute (the father) on the other party (the mother) as the judge was delivering her judgment. Lady Justice Hale reviewed English legal procedure in the light of the fact that it was accepted that the criminal safeguards of Art.6 were engaged. She concluded that the correct test as to whether the judge should recuse herself from trying the contempt of her own court was the test of apparent bias approved by the House of Lords in *Porter v Magill*. On the facts of *Wilkinson* there was held to be no real possibility of bias. The judge herself was not the target of the contempt. Although the judge had witnessed the assault, she took care to ascertain that there was no dispute on the facts, and that the defendant admitted his guilt, before deciding that it was appropriate to hear the case herself. Applying the same principles a different decision was reached on the facts of *Mayer v H.M. Advocate*.[355] The case concerned a barrister who was alleged to have provided false information to a trial judge about his professional commitments in another case. The trial judge questioned the barrister about the matter and, being dissatisfied with the explanations, he fixed a date for a contempt hearing. The alleged contempt consisted of deliberately misleading the court. The judge subsequently found the barrister guilty of contempt and fined him. The court found that the position of the judge as a result of the first hearing is that he had already formed the view that that the barrister's demeanour "was not suggestive of someone doing his best to be frank" and that if the barrister had been a witness he "would not have believed his explanations" and concluded that he may have been "deliberately misleading the court by providing false information".

The summary jurisdiction to punish for contempt of court was reviewed by the **14-114** Grand Chamber of the European Court of Human Rights in *Kyprianou v*

---

[352] *Balogh v Crown Court at St. Albans* [1975] Q.B. 73, at p.85 and p.90; *DPP v Channel Four Television Co. Ltd* [1993] 2 All. E.R. 517, at pp.520–521; and *R. v Schot and Barclay* [1997] 2 Cr.App.R. 383, CA.

[353] [1997] 2 Cr.App.R. 383.

[354] [2003] 1 W.L.R. 1254, CA.

[355] 2004 S.C.C.R. 734, dealing with the post-Human Rights Act summary jurisdiction in Scotland.

Cyprus.[356] The applicant was conducting a trial before a tribunal of three judges in Limassol and accused the male and female judge of interfering with his cross-examination by passing *ravasakia* between each other. In Greek Cypriot that word is capable of two meanings, either notes or love letters. The tribunal immediately indicated that what had been said was a contempt of court. The applicant was told that he should either withdraw what he had said or immediately be sentenced. When the applicant subsequently asked for details of the alleged offence, the court passed judgment describing the applicant as having, amongst other things, created a climate of terror and intimidation within the court. The applicant was sentenced to five days imprisonment. The Grand Chamber found that the confusion of roles between complainant, witness, prosecutor and judge could obviously prompt objectively justified fears as to the conformity of the proceedings with the principle that no one should be a judge in his own cause and, consequently, as to the impartiality of the bench. On that basis the applicant's fears of bias were objectively justified.[357] As regards the subjective test of bias, the statement of the tribunal indicated a sense of indignation and shock which ran counter to the detached approach expected of judicial pronouncements. The judges had also imposed an immediate sentence of five days imprisonment, which indicated a disproportionate response to the events, and had expressed the opinion, before any trial of the issue, that they considered the applicant to be guilty of contempt.[358] On that basis the applicant's misgivings about the impartiality of the Bench were also found to be justifed under the subjective test.[359]

G. DISCLOSURE AND PUBLIC INTEREST IMMUNITY

I. Introduction

14–115 Prior to 1996, the duty of disclosure in England and Wales was governed solely by common law.[360] It was a broad duty which was capable of applying to any material "that has, or might have, some bearing on the offences charged."[361] In determining whether an item of evidence was *prima facie* discloseable the central criterion was "materiality". This was inclusively defined in *R. v Keane*[362] as:

---

[356] (2007) 44 E.H.R.R. 28.

[357] Paras 127–128.

[358] Paras 130–133. The Grand Chamber also found that the length of the sentence constituted a breach of Art.1 (paras 170–183).

[359] See also *Chmelíř v the Czech Republic* (2007) 44 E.H.R.R. 20 where the applicant was deemed not to have had a fair and impartial appeal tribunal where the applicant made a number of allegations against an appeal court judge which were found to be false and merely delaying tactics, who was subsequently held in contempt and fined as a result of those allegations, and then brought a libel action against the judge in question. In the circumstances it was deemed to be a breach of Art.6 that the judge failed to recuse himself.

[360] *R. v Banks* [1916] 2 K.B. 621, *Dallison v Caffrey* [1965] 1 Q.B. 348, *R. v Ward* [1993] 1 W.L.R. 619; *R. v Livingstone* [1993] Crim.L.R. 597; *R. v Saunders*, September 29, unreported, C.C.C. (Henry J.); *R. v Keane* [1994] 1 W.L.R. 746, *R. v Brown (Winston)* [1998] A.C. 367, HL; *R. v Mills and Poole* [1998] A.C. 382, HL.

[361] *R. v Saunders, ibid.*

[362] [1994] 1 W.L.R. 746.

"that which can be seen on a sensible appraisal by the prosecution (1) to be relevant or possibly relevant to an issue in the case; (2) to raise or possibly raise a new issue whose existence is not apparent from the evidence which the prosecution proposes to use; (3) to hold out a real (as opposed to fanciful) prospect of providing a lead on evidence which goes to (1) or (2)."

The Criminal Procedure and Investigations Act 1996 (CPIA) created a statutory **14–116** framework which has significantly restricted the prosecution duty of disclosure. Under the Act, primary disclosure (of material which, in the view of the police disclosure officer, might undermine the case for the prosecution) was automatic; but secondary disclosure (of material which might assist the accused's defence) was originally dependent upon the disclosure of a defence case statement by the accused.[363] In the first edition of this book it was doubted whether this regime fully met the requirements of Art.6. As a result of an amendment enacted by s.32 of the Criminal Justice Act 2003, the test for primary disclosure was developed to include material which might reasonably be considered capable of assisting the case for the accused.[364] This removed the risk that the disclosure officer might withold material that would assist a potential defence which had not been formally disclosed in a defence case statement. In additon, case law in the domestic courts and in Strasbourg has subsequently identified a range of principles in an attempt to ensure that the CPIA is applied in a Convention compatible fashion. In the sections which follow, we examine the general principles governing the duty of disclosure under Art.6, the issues arising under the CPIA, and the position in the magistrates court. After brief reference to the approach adopted in Canada, we consider the specific problem posed by *ex parte* public interest immunity hearings.

II. The Strasbourg Caselaw

The most extensive consideration of the impact of the equality of arms principle **14–117** on the pre-trial disclosure of evidence is to be found in the decision of the Commission in *Jespers v Belgium*,[365] a decision which is now over 25 years old. The applicant was a Belgian judge who had been prosecuted and convicted for the attempted murder of his wife and other serious offences. He complained before the Commission that a "special folder" containing relevant evidence had been withheld from the defence. Although the Commission found no grounds for concluding that the folder contained material that would have assisted in the preparation of the defence, it nevertheless took the opportunity to consider and explain the scope of the disclosure obligation imposed by Art.6(1) and (3)(b).

---

[363] s.3. For brief analysis, see Sprack J., "The Duty of Disclosure" [1997] Crim.L.R. 308; for fuller discussion, see Leng R. and Taylor R., *The Criminal Procedure and Investigations Act 1996*. The amendments to the CPIA brought about by the CJA 2003 are analysed in Mike Redmayne, "Criminal Justice Act 2003 (1): Disclosure and its Discontents" [2004] Crim.L.R. 441.

[364] The amendment was introduced as a result of a recommendation made in Auld L.J.'s "Review of the Criminal Courts of England and Wales" (October 2001), Ch.10, para.171. See also para.162: "The differently formulated tests for disclosure, suggesting a subjective and narrow approach at the primary stage, are logically indefensible, confusing and the cause of much unnecessary pre-trial dispute and delay".

[365] (1981) 27 D.R. 61.

The Commission noted the disparity in resources between prosecution and defence, and elaborated the implications of the principle of "equality of arms" in these terms:

"As regards the interpretation of the term 'facilities' [in Article 6(3)(b)], the Commission notes firstly that in any criminal proceedings brought by a state authority, the prosecution has at its disposal, to back the accusation, facilities deriving from its powers of investigation supported by judicial and police machinery with considerable technical resources and means of coercion. It is in order to establish equality, as far as possible, between the prosecution and defence that national legislation in most countries entrusts the preliminary investigation to a member of the judiciary or, if it entrusts the investigation to the public prosecutor's department, instructs the latter to gather evidence in favour of the accused as well as evidence against him. It is also, and above all, to establish that same equality that the 'rights of the defence' of which Article 6 paragraph (3) of the Convention gives a non-exhaustive list, have been instituted. The Commission has already had occasion to point out that the so called 'equality of arms' principle could be based not only on Article 6 paragraph (1) but also on Article 6 paragraph (3), especially sub-paragraph (b) ... In particular, the Commission takes the view that the 'facilities' which everyone charged with a criminal offence should enjoy include the opportunity to acquaint himself, for the purpose of preparing his defence, with the results of investigations carried out throughout the proceedings. Furthermore, the Commission has already recognised that although a right of access to the prosecution file is not expressly guaranteed by the Convention, such a right can be inferred from Article 6 paragraph 3(b) ... It matters little moreover, by whom and when the investigations are ordered or under whose authority they are carried out ... Any investigation [the prosecution] causes to be carried out in connection with criminal proceedings and the findings thereof consequently form part of the 'facilities' within the meaning of Article 6 paragraph 3(b) of the Convention ... In short, Article 6 paragraph 3(b) recognises the right of the accused to have at his disposal, for the purposes of exonerating himself or of obtaining a reduction in his sentence, all relevant elements that have been or could be collected by the competent authorities. The Commission considers that, if the element in question is a document, access to that document is a necessary facility ('facilité necessaire') if ... it concerns acts of which the defendant is accused, the credibility of testimony etc."[366]

14–118   In *Edwards v United Kingdom*,[367] the applicant had been convicted of robbery, the evidence against him consisting primarily of admissions he was alleged to have made to the police. The applicant's case was that the admissions had been fabricated. Following an independent police inquiry, the case was referred back to the Court of Appeal by the Secretary of State under s.17(1)(a) of the Criminal Appeal Act 1968. The principal ground of appeal was that the conviction was rendered unsafe by non-disclosure of relevant evidence during the trial. Two areas of non-disclosure were relied upon. The first related to fingerprint evidence. During the course of the trial one of the officers to whom the applicant was alleged to have confessed gave evidence that no fingerprints had been found at the scene of the robbery. The police inquiry uncovered two fingerprints which had been found during the original investigation but had not been disclosed to the defence. The finger marks were attributable to a neighbour who was a frequent

---

[366] *Jespers v Belgium* (1981) 27 D.R. 61 at 87–88.
[367] (1993) 15 E.H.R.R. 417, on which see Field S. and Young J., "Disclosure, Appeals and Procedural Traditions" [1994] Crim.L.R. 264.

visitor to the house where the robbery took place. The applicant argued on appeal that the existence of the fingerprint evidence showed that the officer concerned had lied on this aspect of the case, which in turn cast doubt upon his credibility in relation to the disputed admissions. He did not however apply to the court to exercise its powers to hear a fresh cross-examination of the officer on the basis of the new evidence. In addition, the elderly victim of the robbery had made witness statements in which she said that she had had a brief glimpse of the robber's face and thought that she would be able to identify him if she saw him again. She did not give evidence at the trial but her statements were read to the jury by consent. A police inquiry later discovered that during the investigation the victim had been shown an album of photographs which included the applicant, and had failed to pick him out. This information had not been disclosed to the defence. The Court of Appeal dismissed the appeal, concluding that the new evidence did not cast doubt on the safety of the conviction.

In proceedings before the European Court of Human Rights, the failure of the **14–119** prosecution to disclose the material evidence at trial was held to have given rise to a defect in the proceedings. However the Court attached considerable importance to the fact that the undisclosed evidence had been discovered by the time of the appeal hearing and the Court of Appeal had therefore been able to assess its impact on the safety of the conviction:

> "The Court considers that it is a requirement of fairness under Article 6, indeed one which is recognised under English law, that the prosecution authorities disclose to the defence all material evidence for or against the accused and that the failure to do so in the present case gave rise to a defect in the trial proceedings. However, when this was discovered, the Secretary of State, following an independent police investigation, referred the case to the Court of Appeal, which examined the transcript of the trial including the applicant's alleged confession, and considered in detail the impact of the new evidence on the conviction. In the proceedings before the Court of Appeal the applicant was represented by senior and junior counsel who had every opportunity to seek to persuade the Court that the conviction should not stand in view of the evidence of non-disclosure. Admittedly, the police officers who had given evidence at the trial were not heard by the Court of Appeal. It was, nonetheless, open to counsel for the applicant to make an application to the Court—which they chose not to do—that the police officers be called as witnesses ... Having regard to the above, the Court concludes that the defects of the original trial were remedied by the subsequent procedure before the Court of Appeal. Moreover, there is no indication that the proceedings before the Court of Appeal were in any respect unfair."

In *Rowe and Davis v United Kingdom*,[368] which is considered in detail below, the **14–120** evidence which was the subject of the application had been withheld at trial *and on appeal*. The court distinguished *Edwards* on the ground that there had been no opportunity for adversarial argument before the Court of Appeal. In *IJL, GMR and AKP v United Kingdom*[369] the applicants relied on *Rowe and Davis* where the prosecution had wrongly withheld evidence at trial and on their first appeal to the Court of Appeal. However, by the time the case was considered in Strasbourg, the applicants' convictions had been referred back to the Court of

---

[368] (2000) 30 E.H.R.R. 1.
[369] (2001) 33 E.H.R.R. 11.

Appeal by the Home Secretary (prior to the establishment of the Criminal Cases Review Commission). On the second appeal, the Court of Appeal considered the fresh evidence, and held that whilst it should have been disclosed at trial, the procedural irregularity had caused no prejudice to the accused since the jury's verdict would inevitably have been the same if disclosure had been given. In finding no violation of Art.6, the Court reverted to the analysis adopted in *Edwards*:

> "[A]ll of the materials at issue were disclosed to the applicants before the start of the Court of Appeal proceedings. The applicants had a full opportunity to persuade the Court of Appeal that their convictions were unsafe on account of the prosecution's failure to disclose materials which may have assisted their defence. The Court of Appeal extensively reviewed the materials at issue and considered the possible prejudice which their non-disclosure may have had on the fairness of the trial ... In the Court's opinion, the particular defect identified by the Court of Appeal was remedied by the subsequent and extensive review of the issue conducted by the Court of Appeal in the reference proceedings ... The Court observes that the applicants' case is to be distinguished from the circumstances underlying the case of *Rowe and Davis v the United Kingdom* in which the Court found that the prosecution's failure to lay evidence before the trial judge to permit him to rule on the question of disclosure deprived the latter applicants of a fair trial. It notes in this connection that, and in contrast to the position in the *Rowe and Davis* case, the present applicants had received all the materials which had not been disclosed to them by the stage of the second set of appeal proceedings and the Court of Appeal was able to consider the impact of the new material on the safety of the conviction in the light of detailed argument from their defence lawyers."

14–121   A similar conclusion was reached by the Court in *Dowsett v United Kingdom*,[370] where discrete items of relevant evidence which were not available during the first instance proceedings were made available and were subject to full adversarial argument at the appellate stage:

> "As regards the material disclosed by the prosecution prior to the appeal, the so-called 'Actions' and the fraud inquiry materials, the Court observes that the applicant was able to make use of it to support his arguments before the Court of Appeal and that the Court of Appeal was assisted by defence counsel in its assessment of the nature and significance of this material in reaching its conclusion as to whether or not the applicant's conviction should stand. This procedure was, in the Court's view, sufficient to satisfy the requirements of fairness as regards the late disclosed material".

14–122   *Bendenoun v France*[371] was an unusual case since three different sets of proceedings had been brought against the applicant on account of his cross-border art dealings. The French customs authorities had used their powers to fine him, and he had been prosecuted in the criminal courts and imprisoned for tax evasion. The application to Strasbourg concerned administrative proceedings brought by the French tax authorities. The Court rejected the applicant's claim that the tax authorities had acted in breach of Art.6 by failing to disclose certain documents which should have been disclosed. This conclusion turned on two issues of fact. First, the undisclosed documents were not relied upon by the tax authorities in

---

[370] (2004) 38 E.H.R.R.41, para.46.
[371] (1994) 18 E.H.R.R. 54.

relation to the administrative proceedings, and the applicant had given no specific reasons for wishing to see them. And secondly, the applicant and his lawyers were aware of the content of most of the documents because they had been given access to the complete file in the proceedings before the criminal courts. The second point may well have coloured the Court's approach to the first, and so the implications of this case are uncertain.

In *Hardiman v United Kingdom*[372] a rather different issue arose. The applicant   **14–123** was jointly charged with murder. He and his co-accused sought to blame one another for the killing. The co-accused gave evidence implicating the applicant. After the applicant's conviction, his lawyers discovered the existence of prison psychiatric report on the co-accused which could have cast serious doubt on his credibility as a witness. The report was in the possession of the judge, the prosecution and the co-accused's defence team but had not been disclosed to the applicant or his lawyers. The Commission found no violation of Art.6 because of the special circumstances in which the report had come into existence. The co-accused was not cautioned before the interview with the psychiatrist, and did not have his solicitor present. Given the settled practice of not referring to such reports unless a medical issue arose in the trial, and given that the purpose of this practice was to protect the rights of defendants (by obtaining information about them as to their mental capacity), the refusal to disclose the material to a co-defendant was held not to be either unfair or arbitrary. The Commission's decision was heavily influenced by the need to guarantee the protection of one accused person's legal professional privilege, and the confidential relationship between the accused and the psychiatrist preparing the report.

In *Preston v United Kingdom*[373] the applicants complained that telephone inter-   **14–124** cept material obtained pursuant to a warrant issued under the Interception of Communications Act 1985 had not been disclosed to the defence. The Commission dismissed the application as manifestly ill-founded on the ground that the material could not, in any event, be introduced into evidence due to the statutory prohibition on the use of such material under the 1985 Act. Moreover, the applicants had failed to show how the material could have assisted or harmed the defence case.[374] The Court confirmed this approach in *Jasper v United Kingdom*[375]:

> "[T]he applicant has alleged that his trial had been unfair because the product of a telephone intercept had been withheld from the defence without being placed before the trial judge. However, the Court notes that it is not established any such material existed at the time of the trial. Moreover, since under section 9 of the 1985 Act both the

---

[372] [1996] E.H.R.L.R. 425.

[373] [1997] E.H.R.L.R. 695.

[374] This observation shows again that the ultimate concern of the Strasbourg organs when reviewing conformity with Art.6 is whether in fact the criminal process as a whole was fair in this case. For a similar holding, see the unusual case of *F v United Kingdom* (1986) 47 D.R. 230, where the applicant had complained that the seizure, retention and examination of his defence documents by the police deprived him of a fair trial and prevented adequate preparation of his defence. In declaring the application manifestly ill-founded, the Commission attached particular importance to the fact that no information from the documents was used against the applicant during his trial.

[375] (2000) 30 E.H.R.R. 441.

prosecution and the defence were prohibited from adducing any evidence which might tend to suggest that calls had been intercepted by the state authorities, the principle of equality of arms was respected. It would, further, have been open to the applicant himself to testify, or to call evidence from other sources, as to the fact and contents of the instructions he allegedly received by telephone the day before his arrest."

III. The Criminal Procedure and Investigations Act 1996

14–125 It is notable that there have been only a few successful applications in Strasbourg relating to the non-disclosure of evidence by the prosecution.[376] Moreover, it is clear that certain propositions have been stated without the kind of detailed exploration of arguments that is to be found in some of the English decisions on disclosure. It is important to appreciate the context in which those statements have been made. The notion of a case file as an open document has no parrallel in English criminal procedure. To some extent this arises from the difference between adversarial and inquisitorial systems of criminal justice. Thus, the Commission in *Jespers* observed that, in order to achieve equality of arms, "most countries" entrust the preliminary investigation to "a member of the judiciary or, if it entrusts the preliminary investigation to a member of the Public Prosecutor's Department, instructs the latter to gather evidence in favour of the accused as well as against him."[377] English criminal procedure fits neither of these descriptions.[378] Prior to the CPIA coming into force, the important principle that the police should seek evidence for a defendant as well as evidence against him finds only a weak reflection in English practice,[379] and the idea of the police as trustees of the information they uncover had not yet established itself as fundamental.[380]

14–126 With these caveats, the courts invariably had to consider whether United Kingdom practices under the CPIA were compatible with Art.6. Three areas of potential incompatibility arise. First, under the Act, if the prosecutor considers that the material will neither undermine the prosecution case, nor advance the defence, then it need not be disclosed. This does not appear to conform to the "common pool" principle, referred to in *Edwards* and the other Strasbourg cases, under which the prosecution should disclose all of the evidence in its possession, or to which it could gain access, including evidence which is neutral or harmful to the defence. The Commission appears, for example, to have assumed that the duty of disclosure extends to material which may undermine the credibility of a

---

[376] The court did find a violation of Art.6 due to non-disclosure in *Foucher v France* (1997) 25 E.H.R.R. 36 and in *Rowe and Davis v United Kindgdom* (2000) 30 E.H.R.R. 1. These decisions are considered in detail below.

[377] (1981) 27 D.R. 61 at 87.

[378] *R. v H and C* [2004] 2 A.C. 134, *per* Lord Bingham, at para.13.

[379] The Royal Commission on Criminal Justice argued that it is "important that the police should see it as their duty when conducting investigations to gather and consider all the relevant evidence, including any which may exonerate the suspect" (*Report*, Cmnd.2263 (1993), p.10). Some changes in investigation techniques have been noted in more recent times, but it is not clear how widespread they are. *Cf.* the Royal Commission's recommendations on disclosure, *ibid.*, pp.95–97. See also the observations of the Court of Appeal in *R. v Fergus* 98 Cr.App.R. 313.

[380] *cf.* O'Connor P., "Prosecution Disclosure: principle, practice and justice" [1992] Crim.L.R. 464.

defence witness.[381] This is a category of disclosure which the House of Lords, in *R. v Brown (Winston)* expressly declined to recognise at common law,[382] holding that the principle of fairness that lies at the heart of the duty of disclosure; " . . . has to be seen in the context of the public interest in the detection and punishment of crime. A defendant is entitled to a fair trial, but fairness does not require that his witnesses should be immune from challenge as to their credibility."[383] Subject to this qualification, the House of Lords and the Court of Appeal made it clear that there ought to be no conflict between the right to disclosure at common law and the same right under Art.6.[384] In the subsequent case of *R. v H. and C.*,[385] Lord Bingham held that, whether in its amended or unamended form, s.3 of the CPIA does not require disclosure of material which is either neutral in its effect or which is adverse to the defendant, whether because it strengthens the prosecution or weakens the defence. This, he considered, was not in conflict with any principle of fairness, "since a defendant cannot complain that the defence (and the judge and the jury) are not alerted to the existence of material which, if revealed, would lessen his chance of acquittal.[386]

The concern that the 1996 Act adopts a test of relevance which is narrower than the test under Art.6 also arises in relation to the principle, now well-settled in the Art.6 case law, that the prosecution must disclose not only material which is relevant to guilt or innocence, but any material which may assist an accused in obtaining a reduction in sentence.[387] This is an aspect of the disclosure obligation which has not, thus far, been thoroughly explored in English law. Moreover, the Convention duty of disclosure encompasses any material to which the prosecution or the police could gain access,[388] a principle which points to a broad duty of third party disclosure.[389] The problem is partly dealt with in the Codes of Practice at para.3.4, which requires an investigator "to pursue all reasonable lines of inquiry, whether these point towards or away from the supsect". The code further states that "what is reasonable in each case will depend on the particular circumstances". Generally this provision has been read restrictively.[390] The one area where it tends to give rise to a potential application for a stay is where the prosecution negligently fails to secure relevant evidence, which is then

14–127

---

[381] *Jespers v Belgium* (1981) 27 D.R. 61.

[382] *R. v Brown* [1998] A.C. 367.

[383] *ibid., per* Lord Hope at 456. This principle is unaffected by the Attorney General's Guidelines on Disclosure of Information in Criminal Proceedings (2000). See para.14–134 below.

[384] *R. v Brown* [1998] A.C. 367, 381. See Steyn L.J. to the same effect in the Court of Appeal (*R. v Winston Brown* [1995] 1 Cr.App.R. 191 at 198E–F).

[385] [2004] 2 A.C. 132.

[386] Para.17.

[387] *Jespers v Belgium* (1981) 27 D.R. 61.

[388] See *Jespers v Belgium* (1981) 27 D.R. 61.

[389] Note, however, that in *Z v Finland* (1998) 25 E.H.R.R. 371 the Court recognised that the disclosure of confidential medical information relating to a witness in criminal proceedings is protected by Art.8. For a very narrow reading of the word "prosecutor" in s.2(3) of the CPIA, see *DPP. v Wood; DPP. v Mc Gillicuddy* 170 J.P. 177, DC. In a prosecution by the CPS for an offence of driving with excess alcohol, the police and the third-party company which held a contract to provide the police with breath testing devices were held to be third parties.

[390] *DPP v Metten*, unreported, CO/2005/98, January 22, 1998 CD.

destroyed, resulting in demonstrable prejudice to the defence.[391] One issue which has become increasingly controversial is the lengths to which the police and the prosecution are required to go in circumstances where they rely on evidence obtained from foreign law enforcement agencies and it is not possible to say definitively whether a consideration of potentially exculpatory material has been adequately carried out.[392]

14–128   The second area of potential incompatibility between the CPIA and Art.6 arises from the fact that the 1996 Act vests a very wide discretion in the prosecuting authorities to determine relevance. At the stage of primary disclosure it is the police who take the decision whether or not an item of evidence "might undermine the case for the prosecution against the accused." It may be argued that the absence of adequate safeguards against abuse falls short of the requirements of Art.6.[393] The fairness of the current regime depends on the judgment, diligence and honesty of the disclosure officer and the impartiality of the CPS reviewing lawyer. In the context of adversarial litigation, the potential for a serious conflict of interest is obvious. The Convention caselaw suggests that where potentially relevant evidence may be withheld from the defence, there should a measure of scrutiny which is independent of the executive.[394] The involvement of independent prosecution counsel might be said to afford such a safeguard. However this is doubtful for a number of reasons. Surveys conducted during 1999 by the Law Society and the Criminal Bar Association suggest that prosecution counsel does not always view all of the unused material personally, particularly in less serious cases.[395] The DPP has publicly recognised that prosecutors have not always complied with their obligations.[396] Since that time steps were taken both by the Crown Prosecution Service and the courts to improve the manner in which the primary disclosure scheme was operated. In particular, it was made clear that

---

[391] *R. (Ebrahim) v Feltham Magistrates' Court; Mouat v DPP* [2001] 2 Cr.App.R. 23, DC; *DPP v S* [2002] EWHC 2982 (Admin), *R. v Boyd* [2004] R.T.R. 2, CA. See also *Sofri v Italy* [2004] Crim.L.R. 846, EctHR, where it was held that the destruction of evidence, for which the State authorities were responsible, did not of itself give rise to a violation of Art.6; it was necessary to establish that the loss of evidence put the defendant at a disadvantage compared with the prosecution.

[392] See *R. v Allibhai* [2004] EWCA Crim 681; *State v Michael McKevitt* [2005] I.E.C.A. 139 (December 9, 2005).

[393] See the argument of Sharpe S., "Art.6 and the Disclosure of Evidence in Criminal Trials" [1999] Crim.L.R. 273 at 280–281, relying on *Miailhe v France (No.2)* (1997) 23 E.H.R.R. 491 at paras 43–44.

[394] *Rowe and Davis v United Kingdom* (2000) 30 E.H.R.R. 1; *Jasper v United Kingdom* (2000) 30 E.H.R.R. 441 Application No.27052/95; *Fitt v United Kingdom* (2000) 30 E.H.R.R. 1 Application No.29777/96. See further para.14–129 below.

[395] The surveys were published in a series of papers presented to the British Academy of Forensic Sciences on December 1, 1999 (see Med. Sci. Law (2000) Vol.40. No.2).

[396] At his first meeting with 42 newly appointed Chief Crown Prosecutors in May 1999 the DPP David Calvert-Smith Q.C. said there was proveable evidence that prosecutors were still not complying with the obligations imposed on them by the 1996 Act, and that as a result there was a risk of wrongful convictions. He subsequently commissioned a review by the CPS Inspectorate. See Inspectorate's *Report on the Thematic Review of the Disclosure of Unused Material* (CPSI, London 2000). See also other reports criticising the workings of the CPIA: Plotnikoff J. and Woolson, R. "A fair trial in the balance"? Evaluation of the Disclosure Laws, RDS Occasional Paper No.76 (Home Office, London, 2001); and Review of Criminal Investigations and prosecutions Conducted by HM Customs and Excise by Hon. Mr Justice Butterfield, Ch.12.

prosecuting lawyers must be satisfied that "scrupulous accuracy" has been applied to disclosure questions.[397] In *H and C*,[398] the House of Lords further emphasised that the duty of prosecution counsel, in this area, is not to obtain a conviction at all costs but to act as a minister of justice.[399]

Thirdly, the duty of disclosure under Art.6 of the Convention is not dependent   **14–129**
upon disclosure of the defence case. The duty to serve a defence case statement may, in itself, be thought to sit uncomfortably with the Convention caselaw on freedom from self-incrimination.[400] Certainly, it is open to question whether such an obligation can be a precondition to the grant of other fair trial guarantees, such as the duty of disclosure. To some extent, this depends on the statutory construction of what degree of disclosure is required under the a defence case statement. In this context, the remarks of the Solicitor-General in the Parliamentary debate on what is now s.5(6) of the CPIA are apposite. He said: "There is no suggestion that in giving the reason [why it takes issue with the prosecution], detail of the evidence to support that reason should be given". In particular, he stated (no doubt bearing *Pepper v Hart* in mind) that "the fear that this might require the defence to set out its oral cross-examination is not well founded. That is not intended at all".[401] Section 5 is a provision relating to criminal law that limits, without removing, the privilege against self-incrimination. In that respect it must not be read over-extensively and certainly not beyond the concepts of "generalities" and "issues" that are contained in its wording and supported by the statement of its sponsoring minister.[402] Bearing in mind that "it is a general principle that where a power is given for a particular purpose it is not permissible to use that power for a collateral purpose",[403] there is no basis in law upon which a defence statement should be construed as anything remotely approaching the disclosure of the defence case. Once these matters are recognised, it becomes less corrosive of fair trial principles to require a defendant, in relation to material which is *prima facie* irrelevant, to give, if only briefly, specific reasons as to why material should be disclosed.[404] This is particularly the case given that the Strasbourg case law recognises that some limitation upon the right to silence will

---

[397] *R. v Jackson* [2000] Crim.L.R. 377, CA.
[398] [2004] 2 A.C. 132, para.13.
[399] *Randall v The Queen* [2002] 1 W.L.R. 2237, para.10. See also *Boucher v The Queen* [1955] S.C.R. 16, 23–24: "Counsel have a duty to see that all available legal proof of the facts is presented: it must be done firmly and pressed to its legitimate strength but it must be done firmly".
[400] See Ch.15 below.
[401] Hansard, House of Commons Committee, May 16, 1996, cols 66–69. The Auld Report made the similar observation in relation to s.5(6): "It does not require him to set out his defence other than by reference to what he disputes . . . the sooner he tells the court and the prosecutor the better, so that both sides know the battleground and its extent (para 153)"
[402] *R. (Sullivan) v Maidstone Crown Court* [2002] 2 Cr.App.R. 31, DC (concerning the practice of a presiding judge to order that defendant sign the statements personally). For other examples of the courts indicating the need for a strict limitation upon statutes and regulations that require the disclosure of potentially incriminating details see *General Mediterranean Holdings SA v Patel* [2000] 1 W.L.R. 272 at 291 (in relation to wasted costs orders under the Civil Procedure rules) and *R. (Morgan Grenfell) v Special Commissioner for Tax* [2003] 1 A.C. 563 *per* Lord Hobhouse at paras 45–48 (dealing with the continuing role of legal professional privilege in relation to the duty of disclosure by the tax paying client). See also *Bowman v Fels* [2005] 2 Cr.App.R. 19, CA (restricted reading of s.328 of the Proceeds of Crime Act 2002.
[403] *R. (Morgan Grenfell) v Special Commissioner for Tax* op cit *per* Lord Hobhouse at para.48.
[404] *Bendenoun v France* (1994) 18 E.H.R.R. 54.

be permissible, by way of evidential inferences being drawn from a failure to provide a response to matters which clearly call for an answer.[405] The critical concern under Art.6 is that such provisions must be kept within reasonable limits.[406] Various practitioner groups, including the Bar Council and the Criminal Bar Association, have formed the view that defence statements are an acceptable limitation upon the right to silence as a mechanism for rationalising disclosure and generally focussing all sides on the issues for trial.[407] It is for this reason that Lord Justice Auld describes as "an arid debate" the question of whether the statements are seen as a precondition for further disclosure or a logical means of identifying issues.[408] The Court of Appeal has criticised a defence statement that consisted in a general denial of the counts on the indictment accompanied by the assertion that the defendant took issue with any witness purporting to give evidence contrary to his.[409] Clearly, however, there is a significant difference between a mere denial statement or a far reaching allegation without particularity, and a document which indicates what aspects of the prosecution evidence are in issue and why, albeit in general terms.

14–130　　In its admissibility decision in *Glover v United Kingdom*[410] the European Court held that the requirement for a defendant to establish by way of service of a defence case statement that material, which appeared to a prosecutor to be irrelevant, was disclosable did not violate established principles. The case concerned a drugs prosecution where the crown relied on a small extract of many hundreds of hours of covert recordings, and where the defendant had sought access to transcripts of the unused recordings. Both the first instance tribunal and the Court of Appeal dismissed the applicant's arguments that an unfair trial had resulted from the application of the test for primary and secondary disclosure provided for under the CPIA. The Court distinguished the case from its previous jurisprudence, because in cases such as *Rowe and Davis* and *Jasper* it was accepted that the withheld evidence—which formed no part of the prosecution case against the accused—could be relevant to the defence case. The question was then whether the non-disclosure to the defence of the unused evidence was compatible with Art.6 of the Convention. In the present case, the issued turned not on the non-disclosure of relevant (but unused) material, but on the non-disclosure of unused material which—according to the prosecution—was not at all relevant to the defence. In those circumstances, the Court analysed the CPIA regime to consider whether it was inherently incompatible with the rights of the defence. It made no conclusive observation to that effect, but did find the application manifestly ill-founded. This was because the applicant had not made

---

[405] *Murray v United Kingdom* (1996) 22 E.H.R.R. 29, para.47.

[406] *Condron v United Kingdom* (2001) 31 E.H.R.R. 1.

[407] "Review of the Criminal Courts (AULD): The Bar Council Response", Ch.10, para.40.

[408] Auld L.J.'s "Review of the Criminal Courts of England and Wales" (October 2001), Ch. 10, para.156.

[409] *R. v Bryant* [2005] EWCA Crim. 2079. S.6E(2) of the CPIA (as inserted by s.36 of the CJA 2003) a judge is empowered to give the defence a warning that the defence statement has failed to comply with the statute and there is a possibility of comment being made or inference drawn under s.11(5) of the Act. The judge is also entitled to direct that a copy of the statement or any part of it is placed before the jury. See Mike Redmayne, "Criminal Justice Act 2003 (1): Disclosure and its Discontents" [2004] Crim.L.R. 441.

[410] (2005) 40 E.H.R.R. SE18.

any submissions which could cast doubt on the validity either of the prosecution's conclusion that the unused material in question was not relevant, or of the domestic courts' acceptance of that conclusion. *Glover* does not necessarily amount to a full scale endorsement of the CPIA in every circumstance. However, it does provide some authority for the argument that unfettered access to the "common pool" of prosecution material is no longer considered a basic entitlement under Art.6.[411] In *H and C*,[412] the House of Lords emphasised that the Art.6 jurisprudence was specifically not designed to create a "straight jacketing" approach:

> "The overriding requirement is that the guiding principles should be respected and observed, in the infinitely diverse situations with which trial judges have to deal, in all of which the touchstone is to ascertain what justice requires in the circumstances of the particular case".

The Criminal Justice Act 2003 added a new duty of defence disclosure in relation   **14–131** to supplying the names of any intended lay witness and any expert witness who was instructed.[413] The provisions have not yet been brought into force. They go very far beyond the requirement of the defence to identify core issues in a defence case statement on pain of inference. They are not simply limited to alibi witnessess or expert witness reports which the defence intend to rely upon, both of which have historically been recognised as an exceptional categories requiring pre-trial defence disclosure. The expert witness provision is designed to asecertain indirectly whether the defence have obtained adverse expert opinions which they do not wish to use at trial. On the basis that there is no property in a witness, the prosecution are then in a position to approach them, although acute problems arise in so far as the witnesses are bound by litigation privilege.[414] These provisions disturb a principle of legal advice privilege, in requiring provisional decisions between a lawyer and his client with regard to witnesses to be disclosed prior to the start of a trial. If ever brought into force, it is likely that they could be successfully challeged under common law principles[415] and Art.6.[416]

As to cases in which the evidence in question has subsequently been disclosed,   **14–132** the position is relatively straightforward. The non-disclosure of evidence which is significantly helpful to the defence would, if a conviction resulted, involve a

---

[411] *Cf. Jespers v Belgium* (1981) 27 D.R. 61.

[412] [2004] 2 A.C. 132, para.33.

[413] S.6C C.P.I.A., inserted by s.34 of the C.J.A. 2003, deals with the requirement to provide notification to call defence witnesses. S.6D, inserted by s.35 of the C.J.A. 2003, deals with the rquirement to provide notification of the names of experts instructed by the accused.

[414] *R. v Reid* [2001] 8 Archbold News 3; *R. v Davies* [2002] EWCA Crim 85 and *S County Council v B* [2000] 3 W.L.R. 51.

[415] *R. (Morgan Grenfell) v Special Commissioner for Tax* [2003] 1 A.C. 563, *Three Rivers District Council v Governor and Company of the Bank of England (No.6)* [2005] 1 A.C. 610; and *Bowman v Fels* [2005] 2 Cr.App.R. 19, CA.

[416] *S. v Switzerland*, (1991) 14 E.H.R.R. 670, *Ocalan v Turkey*, (2005) 41 E.H.R.R. 45. A similar recognition of the lawyer-client relationship has been made under Art.8: *Campbell v UK* (1992) 15 E.H.R.R. 137; and *Foxley v U.K.*, (2001) 31 E.H.R.R. 25. For the recognition of the same principles under EC law see *A M & S Europe Ltd v Commission of the European Communities* (Case 155/79) [1983] Q.B. 878).

breach of Art.6. But it would now also justify the quashing of a conviction under the current interpretation of s.2 of the Criminal Appeal Act. In the context of disclosure the Court of Appeal has held that once the court is satisfied that disclosure should have been made at first instance then, "It must be for the prosecution to show that the conviction is nonetheless safe: that is, the disclosure of the evidence would not reasonably have affected the verdict".[417]

14-133   The CPIA only applies from the moment in which the prosecution formally serves its case, whether by way of committal pursuant to the Magistrates' Courts Act 1981, or service of papers under the Crime and Disorder Act 1998 or the Criminal Justice Act 1988. Before that time both the common law and Art.6 recognise the duty of the prosecution to consider advanced disclosure of material which would, for instance, assist in a bail application, the preparation of a dismissal application, or resisting further applications for the adjournment of service.[418] The CPIA does not apply to post-trial disclosure, but the obligation upon the Crown to make dislosure of relevant material continues on the basis of the common law duty of the the prosecution to act fairly and assist the administation of justice.[419] This position is strengthened by the long line of Convention case law which has held that Art.6 applies from the moment of charge to the final determination of the proceedings, including any appeal.[420]

IV. The Attorney General's Guidelines (2000)

14-134   Certain of the shortcomings of the 1996 Act were addressed in the Attorney General's *Guidelines on the Disclosure of Information in Criminal Proceedings*.[421] The foreword to the Guidelines notes that in the three years since the Act came into force "concerns have been expressed about the operation of the provisions by judges, prosecutors and defence practitioners". The Guidelines were intended to improve the operation of the Act and acknowledged in terms that the guidance given in some areas "goes beyond the requirements of the legislation where experience suggests that such guidance is desirable". The introduction refers directly to Art.6, observing that a fair trial is "the proper object and expectation of all participants in the trial process", that fair disclosure to the accused is "an inseparable part" of a fair trial, and that disclosure which fails to ensure timely preparation and presentation of the defence case "risks preventing a fair trial taking place".

---

[417] *R. v Allan (Richard Roy)* [2004] EWCA Crim 2236, para.141.
[418] *R. v DPP ex p Lee* [1999] 2 Cr.App.R. 304, D.C. See also *DPP v Ara* [2002] 1 W.L.R. 815 (the police were under a duty to disclose to the defendant's solicitor material which assist him in advising his client whether or not to accept a caution). The European Court has held that the "equality of arms" principle inherent in Art.6, also includes bail hearings: *Woukam Moudefo v France* 13 E.H.R.R. 549; *Wloch v Poland* (2002) 34 E.H.R.R. 9. See also *R. (DPP) v Havering Justices* [2001] 2 Cr.App.R. 2, and *Wildman v DPP* [2001] EWHC Admin 14.
[419] *R. v Makin* (2004) 148 S.J. 821, CA.
[420] *Delcourt v Belgium*, (1979–1980) 1 E.H.R.R. 355, para.25, *Adolf v Austria* (1982) 4 E.H.R.R. 313, *Edwards v United Kingdom* (1993)15 E.H.R.R. 417.
[421] November 29, 2000.

In order to improve the existing arrangements, and bring them closer into line   **14–135**
with the requirements of Art.6, the Guidelines established a series of principles,
among the most important of which are the following:

(a) An individual must not be appointed as disclosure officer, or continue in
    that role, if that is likely to result in a conflict of interest.[422]

(b) Where investigators have seized a large volume of material, but have
    decided not to examine it because it seems unlikely to be relevant, the
    existence of the material should be made known to the defence, and
    permission given for its inspection.[423]

(c) Prosecutors should review disclosure schedules for completeness and
    accuracy, and should take steps to make good any deficiencies.[424] If they
    conclude that a fair trial cannot take place because of a failure to disclose
    information which cannot or will not be remedied, the prosecution should
    be discontinued.[425]

(d) Prosecutors should not adduce evidence of a defence case statement, other
    than in the circumstances permitted by s.11 of the Act or to rebut alibi
    evidence.[426]

(e) The practice of "counsel to counsel" disclosure, where it occurs, should
    cease.[427]

(f) Where a Government department or other Crown body appears to be in
    possession of material which may be relevant to an issue in the case,
    reasonable steps should be taken to identify and consider the material.[428]
    Where it appears that a non-governmental third party is in possession of
    material which might be discloseable if it were in the possession of the
    prosecution, the prosecutor must take appropriate steps to seek access to
    the material.[429] If access is denied then the prosecutor should apply for a
    witness summons[430] if it considered that it is reasonable to seek produc-
    tion of the material.

(g) The duty of primary disclosure should be treated as extending not only to
    material which directly contradicts a prosecution witness's version of
    events, but also to material which could be useful in cross-examination, or
    which could lead to the exclusion of evidence, the grant of a stay of the
    proceedings or a finding that a public authority has acted incompatibly

---

[422] Para.7. The example given, however, appears unduly narrow—"if the disclosure officer is the
victim of the alleged crime which is the subject of criminal proceedings".
[423] Para.9.
[424] Paras 14 to 17, and 23 to 24.
[425] Para.21.
[426] Para.18.
[427] Para.26.
[428] Para.29.
[429] Para.30. The Guidelines emphasise that it will be especially important to seek access to third
party material if it is likely to undermine the prosecution case or assist the defence.
[430] Assuming the conditions of s.2 of the Criminal Procedure (Attendance of Witnesses) Act 1965
or s.97 of the Magistrates Courts Act 1980 are met.

with the rights of the accused under the Human Rights Act 1998.[431] Any material which relates to the defendant's mental or physical health, his intellectual capacity or any alleged ill-treatment whilst in custody should be treated as relevant to the reliability of a purported confession.[432]

(h) The duty of secondary disclosure should be treated as applying to certain categories of "linked" material which "relates to" a defence being put forward, whether or not it directly supports such a defence. The categories include[433] scientific findings which relate to the accused; records of all previous descriptions or identification procedures carried out, including any photographs taken of the accused at the time of his arrest; information concerning rewards received or requested by or promised to a prosecution witness; plans or video recordings of the scene of a crime; names of witnesses with relevant information who have not been interviewed; and records of any information provided by other individuals.

(i) The prosecution should serve on the defence all evidence upon which the Crown intends to rely in summary proceedings.[434]

(j) The prosecution should consider disclosing any material which is relevant to sentence, such as information which might mitigate the seriousness of the offence or assist the accused to lay blame in whole or in part on a co-accused or another person.[435]

A protocol for the control and management of unused material in the Crown Court issued in 2006 notes that although the Guidelines do not have the force of law "they should be given due weight".[436] Perhaps the most important aspect of the Guidelines is that the prosecution are required to disclose material that would assist in the exclusion of evidence, a stay of proceedings or a argument under the Human Rights Act.[437] The requirement to make disclosure in these areas is recognised under the common law.[438] Many of the most significant prosecutorial failures to make disclosure concern the covering up of executive misconduct, and more often than not, aggravate any potential abuse of process in doing so.[439]

---

[431] Para.36.
[432] Para.38.
[433] Para.40.
[434] Para.43.
[435] Para.44.
[436] Disclosure: A Protocol for the control and management of unused material in the Crown Court, para.10. Other aspects of this Protocol are in tension with the spirit of the Attorney General's Guidelines, because it insists on a more rigorous and technical application of the law, which the guidelines were in part designed to relax. For a criticism of the fact that protocols, such as this one, are now being issued without clear reference to the power and authority upon which they are based, see the Preface to the 2007 edition of Archbold Criminal Pleading, Evidence and Practice.
[437] Para.38.
[438] *R. v Smith (Brian)* [1995] Crim.L.R. 658; *R. v Mullen* [2000] Q.B. 520; *R. v Togher* [2001] 1 Cr.App. 457.
[439] *R. v Patel and Villiers*, [2001] EWCA Crim 2505; *R. v Early* [2003] 1 Cr.App.R. 19; and *R. v Choudhury and Ors* [2005] EWCA Crim 1788.

V. The Magistrates' Courts

The European Court of Human Rights has held that the right of access to the   **14–136**
prosecution file applies even to minor offences. Thus in *Foucher v France*[440] the
applicant and his father had been charged with insulting behaviour towards
persons entrusted with public service duties. The case was to be tried in the local
police court, and they were to represent themselves. The public prosecutor refused
them access to their files on the ground that a copy could not be supplied to a
private individual, except through a lawyer. The Court held that this constituted a
violation of Arts 6(1) and 6(3)(b). Although the decision turned chiefly on the
point that defendants should not be denied access to documents simply because
they are representing themselves, it also demonstrates that the general principles
discussed above apply even at the lowest level of criminal courts.

This approach may be compared to the position in the magistrates' court in   **14–137**
England and Wales. Where a defendant is charged with a summary only offence,
the Magistrates' Court (Advance Information) Rules 1985 do not require the
prosecution to disclose even the evidence upon which it intends to rely. In some
areas the CPS were prepared to give voluntary disclosure, but in others they were
not. In *R. v Stratford Justices ex parte Imbert*,[441] the Divisional Court (*per*
Buxton L.J. and Collins J.) held that advance disclosure in the magistrates' court
was not a requirement of the right to a fair trial, and expressed the view *obiter*,
that their decision would be unaffected by the implementation of the Human
Rights Act. The practical importance of this point was substantially diminished
by the Attorney General's *Guidelines on Disclosure of Information in Criminal
Proceedings (2000)*,[442] which provide that;

> "The prosecutor should, in addition to complying with the obligations under the CPIA,
> provide to the defence all evidence upon which the Crown proposes to rely in a
> summary trial. Such provision should allow the accused or their legal advisers sufficient
> time properly to consider the evidence before it is called. Exceptionally, statements may
> be withheld for the protection of witnesses or to avoid interference with the course of
> justice."

This change of practice was absolutely essential to ensure that the CPIA was   **14–138**
workable in the magistrates' court. Under the Act the defendant in the magistrates' court has the right to "primary" disclosure of evidence which might
undermine the prosecution case.[443] But—in view of the absence of any right to
advanced information—he did not have the right to see the statements of the
witnesses whom the prosecution proposed to call. The right to secondary
disclosure—that is, of material which may advance the defence case—is dependent upon the service by the defendant of a case statement setting out the matters
upon which he takes issue with the prosecution witnesses, and the reasons he
takes issue with them.[444] In the magistrates' court the service of such a statement

---

[440] (1998) 25 E.H.R.R. 234.
[441] [1999] 2 Cr.App.R. 276.
[442] November 29, 2000, at para.42. See paras 14–105 to 14–106 above.
[443] Ss.1(1)(a) and 3(1)(a).
[444] S.5(6).

is voluntary, but the Crown's duty of secondary disclsoure is nevertheless contingent upon such a statement having been served.[445] It was obviously impossible for the defendant to take advantage of this opportunity—and thereby to avail himself of a fundamental protection—if he had not seen the prosecution evidence in the first place. The *Imbert* decision has never been overturned. However, the position recognised in Stone's Justices Manual is that there is nothing to prevent a magistates' court ordering disclosure where fairness dictates that such a step be taken.[446]

VI. Canada

14–139   In the leading Canadian case of *Stinchcombe*[447] Sopinka J., speaking for a unanimous Supreme Court, stated that: "[T]he fruits of the investigation which are in the possession of counsel for the Crown are not the property of the Crown for use in securing a conviction but the property of the public to be used to ensure that justice is done." He went on to hold that the overriding concern of the courts is to ensure that the accused can "make full answer and defence", which he described as "one of the pillars of criminal justice on which we heavily depend to ensure that the innocent are not convicted."[448]

14–140   Sopinka J. also delivered the judgment in the unanimous Supreme Court decision in *Chaplin*.[449] He reiterated that the Crown's obligation is only to disclose relevant evidence, although one test of relevance is whether the material is "of some use to the defence." Where the existence of relevant information was established, "the Crown must justify non-disclosure by demonstrating either that the information sought is beyond its control, or that it is clearly irrelevant or privileged." Where, on the other hand, the Crown denies the existence of the material sought, "the defence must establish a basis which could enable the presiding judge to conclude that there is in existence further [identifiable] material which is potentially . . . useful to the accused in making full answer and defence." Once the defence overcome this threshold, designed to exclude "fishing expeditions and conjecture," the Crown once again bears the burden of justifying non-disclosure.

14–141   The leading Canadian case on third party disclosure is *O'Connor*.[450] The question in that case was whether the defence should be granted an order to compel the complainants, prior to a trial for sexual offences some 25 years previously, to authorize their therapists and other counsellors to pass their reports to the Crown, and the Crown then to disclose them to the defence. The application was originally granted by a judge, but Crown counsel thought it unduly wide and delayed compliance. The trial judge then stayed the prosecution for abuse of process. On appeal the Supreme Court held by a five to three majority that the

---

[445] Ss.6 and 7.
[446] Butterworths Stone's Justices Manual, Vol.1, 2006, 1–3581.
[447] [1991] 3 S.C.R. 326.
[448] *ibid.*, at 336.
[449] [1995] 1 S.C.R. 727.
[450] (1996) 103 C.C.C. (3d) 1; see also the decision in *A (LL) v B (A)* [1995] 4 S.C.R. 536, handed down on the same day.

stay should not have been granted because the defendant's right to make full answer and defence had not been impaired on the facts. The court went on to determine the appropriate procedure for dealing with applications for third party disclosure. The first stage places a threshold burden on the defence to satisfy the judge that the evidence will be relevant to the defendant's case.[451] The second stage requires the judge to examine the records to decide whether, and to what extent, they should be disclosed to the defence. Both L'Heureux-Dube J. and Lamer C.J.C., agreed, in their separate judgments, that in balancing the competing rights at stake the following factors should be considered:

"(1) The extent to which the record is necessary for the accused to make full answer and defence; (2) the probative value of the record in question; (3) the nature and extent of the reasonable expectation of privacy vested in that record; (4) whether production of the record would be premised upon any discriminatory belief or bias; . . . and (5) the potential prejudice to the complainant's dignity, privacy or security of person that would be occasioned by production of the record in question."[452]

Although little is said about the weight to be assigned to these factors and how they should be balanced, the process is securely tied to the range of rights declared in the Charter. Similar reasoning, arising from Convention rights, might now be appropriate in this country. In *Z v Finland*,[453] for example, the Court held that the lawful seizure of a third party's medical records and an order that her medical advisers give evidence in criminal proceedings did not violate Art.8, but that the threatened disclosure to the public of her identity and medical condition did constitute a violation.   **14–142**

VII. Public Interest Immunity

The Court in *Edwards*[454] specifically left open the question whether the rules of public interest immunity, as applied to criminal proceedings in England and Wales, conform to the requirements of Art.6. As Judge Pettiti explained in his dissenting opinion[455]:   **14–143**

"[T]he principle of public interest immunity . . . in English law allows the prosecution, in the public interest, not to disclose or communicate to the defence all the evidence in its possession and to reserve certain evidence . . . The Court made no express statement of its views on this point and its silence might be understood as approval of this principle, which is not the case. The Court had regard primarily to the failure by the defence to rely on this ground of appeal. To be sure, it is understandable that the plea of 'defence secrets' should be invoked at the stage of duly authorised telephone taps.

---

[451] The standard of the threshold, and the notion of relevance, are similar to those established in *Stinchcombe*.

[452] (1996) 103 C.C.C. (3d) 1 at para.156 (L'Heureux-Dube J.) and at para.31 (Lamer C.J.C.); at para.32 Lamer C.J.C. declined to associate himself with other factors that L'Heureux-Dube J. regarded as relevant, such as the wider social interest in encouraging people to report sexual offences against them.

[453] (1998) 25 E.H.R.R. 371. The court recognised at para.97, that the confidentiality of medical data might be trumped, in appropriate cases, by the importance of investigating and prosecuting crime.

[454] (1993) 15 E.H.R.R. 417.

[455] (1993) 15 E.H.R.R. 417 at 433.

But once there are criminal proceedings and an indictment, the whole of the evidence, favourable or unfavourable to the defendant, must be communicated to the defence in order to be the subject of adversarial argument in accordance with Article 6 of the Convention ... Under the European Convention an old doctrine, such as that of 'public interest' must be revised in accordance with Article 6."[456]

14–144   The issue arose for consideration in *Rowe and Davis v United Kingdom*.[457] The applicants had been convicted of a murder and a series of robberies committed in 1988. An important part of the evidence against them was given by three men, one of whom (as it subsequently turned out) was a police informer who had claimed and been paid a reward. The evidence relating to the role of the informer was withheld by the Crown, without reference to the judge, in accordance with guidelines on prosecution disclosure issued by the Attorney General in 1981.[458] On their appeal against conviction, the Court of Appeal established a procedure for judicial supervision of the decision to withhold evidence on grounds of public interest immunity. In *R. v Davis, Johnson and Rowe*[459] the court held that it was not necessary in every case for the prosecution to give notice to the defence when it wished to claim public interest immunity, and outlined three different procedures to be adopted. The first procedure, which had generally to be followed, was for the prosecution to give notice to the defence that they were applying for a ruling by the court and indicate to the defence at least the category of the material which they held. The defence would then have the opportunity to make representations to the court. Secondly, however, where the disclosure of the category of the material in question would in effect reveal that which the prosecution contended should not be revealed, the prosecution should still notify the defence that an application to the court was to be made, but the category of material need not be disclosed and the application should be made *ex parte*. The third procedure would apply in an exceptional case where to reveal even the fact that an *ex parte* application was to be made would in effect be to reveal the nature of the evidence in question. In such a case, the prosecution should apply to the court *ex parte* without notice to the defence. Having laid down these procedural guidelines, the Court of Appeal then proceeded to view the material in issue in the case, and endorsed the decision of the Crown to withhold it.

14–145   The applicants argued in Strasbourg that the procedure adopted was in breach of Art.6. Whilst accepting that it may be legitimate, in certain circumstances, to withhold relevant evidence on grounds of national security or the protection of vulnerable witnesses, they submitted that the *ex parte* procedure lacked the

---

[456] *ibid.*, at 433–435.

[457] (2000) 30 E.H.R.R. 1.

[458] (1982) 74 Cr.App.R. 302. As to the Guidelines issued in 2000 see para.14–134 above. In its Opinion on the merits in *Rowe and Davis* ((2000) 30 E.H.R.R. 1 at 18 *et seq.*) the Commission held that the Attorney-General's guidelines (as they stood at that time) "include at least three [categories of sensitive material] where the interests of the State in maintaining confidentiality for the purposes of encouraging information to be given to the police would *prima facie* rarely if ever outweigh the interests of the accused in having access to information of possible help to the defence." The three categories mentioned were (e) information supplied by banks, etc; (f) evidence relating to serious allegations against, or convictions of, other persons; and (g) matters of private delicacy that might cause domestic strife.

[459] [1993] 1 W.L.R. 613.

necessary safeguards to ensure that the rights of the accused were adequately protected. In the present case the evidence had been withheld at trial without judicial supervision. This amounted, in itself to a breach of Art.6. The resulting defect was not cured by the *ex parte* hearing before the Court of Appeal, which offered no procedural safeguards and which did not result in the disclosure of the evidence sought. The applicants argued that in order to counterbalance the exclusion of the accused from the procedure it was necessary to introduce an adversarial element, such as the appointment of an independent "special counsel" who could advance argument on behalf of the defence as to the relevance of the undisclosed evidence, test the strength of the claim to public interest immunity, and act as an independent safeguard against the risk of judicial error or bias. They pointed to four situations in which such a "special counsel" procedure had been introduced in English law as a means of safeguarding sensitive information whilst affording a party to litigation a measure of procedural justice.[460] Under these procedures an independent lawyer is appointed, subject to security vetting, to *represent the interests* of the accused. The "special counsel" is not, however, instructed by, nor directly accountable to the accused, and is under a duty to maintain the confidentiality of the proceedings.

The Court held that while Art.6 generally requires the prosecution to disclose to the defence all material evidence for or against an accused, considerations of national security or the protection of vulnerable witnesses may, in certain circumstances, justify an exception to this rule: **14–146**

> "It is a fundamental aspect of the right to a fair trial that criminal proceedings, including the elements of such proceedings which relate to procedure, should be adversarial and that there should be equality of arms between the prosecution and the defence. The right to an adversarial trial means, in a criminal case, that both the prosecution and defence must be given the opportunity to have knowledge of and comment on the observations filed and the evidence adduced by the other party. In addition, Article 6(1) requires, as indeed does English law, that the prosecution authorities should disclose to the defence all material evidence in their possession for or against the accused. However, as the applicants recognised, the entitlement to disclosure of relevant evidence is not an absolute right. In any criminal proceedings there may be competing interests, such as national security or the need to protect witnesses at risk of reprisals or keep secret police methods of investigation of crime, which must be weighed against the rights of the accused. In some cases it may be necessary to withhold certain evidence from the defence so as to preserve the fundamental rights of another individual or to safeguard an important public interest."

---

[460] Following *Chahal v United Kingdom* (1997) 23 E.H.R.R. 413, and *Tinnelly v United Kingdom* (1999) 27 E.H.R.R. 249 a "special counsel" procedure had been introduced into immigration appeals and employment discrimination cases involving national security issues by the Special Immigration Appeals Commission Act 1997 and the Northern Ireland Act 1998. A similar provision was again made by s.5 of the Terrorism Act 2000 in relation to proscription proceedings before the Proscribed Organisations Appeal Commission; s.70 of the Anti-Terrorism, Crime and Security Act 2001 in realtion to proceedings before the the Pathogens Access Appeal Commission; and by the Northern Ireland (Sentences) Act 1998, Sch.2, para.7(2) and the Life Sentences (Northern Ireland) Order 2001 in realtion to post-Good Friday release prisoner release proceedings. Special Counsel are also appointed under the schedule of the Prevention of Terrorism Act 2005 in relation to control order proceedings in the High Court.

14–147 However, the Court went on to apply the important principle that any departure from a system of open adversarial justice had to be "strictly necessary". The consequent handicap imposed on the defence required the adoption of compensating procedural safeguards;

> "[O]nly such measures restricting the rights of the defence which are strictly necessary are permissible under Article 6(1). Moreover, in order to ensure that the accused receives a fair trial, any difficulties caused to the defence by a limitation on its rights must be adequately counterbalanced by the procedures followed by the judicial authorities."

14–148 On the facts, the court unanimously found a violation of Art.6. Since the prosecution had withheld relevant evidence on public interest immunity grounds, without first submitting it to the trial judge, the requirements of a fair procedure were not met. In contrast to the position in *Edwards*,[461] the resulting defect could not be cured by submitting the material to the Court of Appeal in the course of an appeal against conviction (unless, of course, the Court of Appeal ordered disclosure of the material):

> "During the applicants' trial at first instance the prosecution decided, without notifying the judge, to withhold certain relevant evidence on grounds of public interest. Such a procedure, whereby the prosecution itself attempts to assess the importance of concealed information to the defence and weigh this against the public interest in keeping the information secret, cannot comply with the above-mentioned requirements of Article 6(1) ... It is true that at the commencement of the applicants' appeal prosecution counsel notified the defence that certain information had been withheld, without however revealing the nature of this material, and that on two separate occasions the Court of Appeal reviewed the undisclosed evidence and, in *ex parte* hearings with the benefit of submissions from the Crown but in the absence of the defence, decided in favour of non-disclosure. However, the Court does not consider that this procedure before the appeal court was sufficient to remedy the unfairness caused at the trial by the absence of any scrutiny of the withheld information by the trial judge. Unlike the latter, who saw the witnesses give their testimony and was fully versed in all the evidence and issues in the case, the judges in the Court of Appeal were dependent for their understanding of the possible relevance of the undisclosed material on transcripts of the Crown Court hearings and on the account of the issues given to them by prosecuting counsel. In addition, the first instance judge would have been in a position to monitor the need for disclosure throughout the trial, assessing the importance of the undisclosed evidence at a stage when new issues were emerging, when it might have been possible through cross-examination seriously to undermine the credibility of key witnesses and when the defence case was still open to take a number of different directions or emphases. In contrast, the Court of Appeal was obliged to carry out its appraisal *ex post facto* and may even, to a certain extent, have unconsciously been influenced by the jury's verdict of guilty into underestimating the significance of the undisclosed evidence."

14–149 In *Atlan v United Kingdom*[462] the court rejected an attempt to distinguish *Rowe and Davis*. The government argued that the applicants in that case were in a different position since they were unable to show that the evidence which had

---

[461] See para.14–118 above.
[462] (2001) 34 E.H.R.R. 33.

been the subject of an *ex parte* hearing before the Court of Appeal was relevant to the defence they had advanced at trial. The government also pointed out that the Court of Appeal had postponed its ruling on the application for disclosure until it had heard argument on the merits of the appeal, and that before dismissing the appeal it had made a number of factual assumptions in the applicants' favour. The Court, however, considered that there was a "strong suspicion" that the evidence was relevant, and noted that the applicants had asked for access to any undisclosed material at the time of their trial. The principle in *Rowe and Davis* meant that it was for the trial judge rather than the Court of Appeal to rule on the issue of public interest immunity. Moreover, the court considered that if the evidence had been put before the judge he may have summed the case up differently to the jury.

In *PG and JH v United Kingdom*,[463] the prosecution had sought to withhold on public interest grounds certain information relating to the installation of a listening device. A police officer declined to answer questions put to him in cross-examination by defence counsel because his answers might reveal sensitive material. The judge then, with the consent of the defence, put questions to the officer in the absence of the defendants and their lawyers, and concluded that the benefit of the answers to the defence was slight, if any, while the damage to the public interest if the answers were made public would be great. The judge refused to exclude the evidence derived from the device. It was unanimously held, partly on the same grounds as in *Jasper* and *Fitt* that the withholding of the officer's report and the procedure adopted to examine him had not violated Art.6. The Court held, at para.71: **14–150**

> "The court also notes that the material which was not disclosed in the present case formed no part of the prosecution case whatever, and was never put to the jury. The fact that the need for disclosure was at all times under assessment by the trial judge provided a further, important safeguard in that it was his duty to monitor throughout the trial the fairness or otherwise of the evidence being withheld. It has not been suggested that the judge was not independent and impartial within the meaning of article 6(1). He was fully versed in all the evidence and issues in the case and in a position to monitor the relevance to the defence of the withheld information both before and during the trial."

However, in two judgments handed down on the same day as *Rowe and Davis* (*Fitt v United Kingdom*[464] and *Jasper v United Kingdom*[465]) the Court held, by the narrowest of majorities (nine votes to eight), that there was no violation of Art.6 where the material in question had been submitted to the trial judge at an *ex parte* hearing of which the defence had been given notice. In each case, evidence had been withheld following a "type two" hearing under the guidelines issued by the Court of Appeal in *R. v Davis, Johnson and Rowe*.[466] In *Jasper* the majority explained its conclusion as follows: **14–151**

---

[463] [2002] Crim.L.R. 308. See also *Mansell v United Kingdom* (2003) 36 E.H.R.R. CD 221.
[464] (2000) 30 E.H.R.R. 1.
[465] (2000) 30 E.H.R.R. 441.
[466] [1993] 1 W.L.R. 613.

"The Court is satisfied that the defence were kept informed and permitted to make submissions and participate in the above decision-making process as far as was possible without revealing to them the material which the prosecution sought to keep secret on public interest grounds. Whilst it is true that in a number of different contexts the United Kingdom has introduced, or is introducing, a 'special counsel', the Court does not consider that such a procedure was necessary in the present case. The Court notes, in particular, that the material which was not disclosed in the present case formed no part of the prosecution case whatever, and was never put to the jury. This position must be contrasted with the circumstances addressed by the [legislation making provision for 'special counsel'], where impugned decisions were based on material in the hands of the executive, material which was not seen by the supervising courts at all.

The fact that the need for disclosure was at all times under assessment by the trial judge provided a further, important safeguard in that it was his duty to monitor throughout the trial the fairness or otherwise of the evidence being withheld. It has not been suggested that the judge was not independent and impartial within the meaning of Article 6(1). He was fully versed in all the evidence and issues in the case and in a position to monitor the relevance to the defence of the withheld information both before and during the trial. Moreover it can be assumed—not least because the Court of Appeal confirmed that the transcript of the *ex parte* hearing showed that he had been 'very careful to ensure and to explore whether the material was relevant, or likely to be relevant to the defence which had been indicated to him'—that the judge applied the principles which had recently been clarified by the Court of Appeal, for example that in weighing the public interest in concealment against the interest of the accused in disclosure, great weight should be attached to the interests of justice, and that the judge should continue to assess the need for disclosure throughout the progress of the trial. The jurisprudence of the English Court of Appeal shows that the assessment which the trial judge must make fulfils the conditions which, according to the Court's caselaw, are essential for ensuring a fair trial in instances of non-disclosure of prosecution material. The domestic trial court in the present case thus applied standards which are in conformity with the relevant principles of a fair trial embodied in Article 6(1). Furthermore, during the appeal proceedings the Court of Appeal also considered whether or not the evidence should have been disclosed, providing an additional level of protection for the applicant's rights."

14–152   The minority, by contrast, considered that in the absence of "special counsel" the *ex parte* procedure had to be considered fundamentally unfair:

"We note that, although the defence in this case were notified that an *ex parte* application was to be made by the prosecution for material to be withheld on grounds of public interest immunity, they were not informed of the category of material which the prosecution sought to withhold, they were not—by definition—involved in the *ex parte* proceedings, and they were not informed of the reasons for the judge's subsequent decision that the material should not be disclosed. This procedure cannot, in our view, be said to respect the principles of adversarial proceedings and equality of arms, given that the prosecuting authorities were provided with access to the judge and were able to participate in the decision-making process in the absence of any representative of the defence. We do not accept that the opportunity given to the defence to outline their case before the trial judge took his decision on disclosure can affect the position, as the defence were unaware of the nature of the matters they needed to address. It was purely a matter of chance whether they made any relevant points.

The fact that the judge monitored the need for disclosure throughout the trial cannot remedy the unfairness created by the defence's absence from the *ex parte* proceedings. In our view, the requirements ... that any difficulties caused to the defence by a limitation on defence rights must be sufficiently counterbalanced by the procedures followed by the judicial authorities, are not met by the mere fact that it was a judge who decided that the evidence be withheld ... Our concern is that, in order to be able to fulfil his judicial functions as the judge in a fair trial, the judge should be informed by the opinions of both parties, not solely the prosecution. The proceedings before the Court of Appeal were, in our view, inadequate to remedy these defects, since, as at first instance, there was no possibility of making informed submissions to the court on behalf of the accused ...

We accept that there may be circumstances in which material need not be disclosed to the defence, but we find that the way in which the United Kingdom courts dealt with the sensitive material in the present case was not satisfactory. It is not for this Court to prescribe specific procedures for domestic courts to follow, but we note that, in the light of two Convention cases, a 'special counsel' system has been introduced in the United Kingdom where it is necessary to withhold evidence from one of the parties to litigation, and that other examples are likely to be introduced. These examples do not exactly match the circumstances of the present case, but we have no doubt that the practical problems raised by the Government can be solved ... [These procedures] show that legitimate concerns about confidentiality can be accommodated at the same time as according the individual a substantial measure of procedural justice."

When the Human Rights Act first came into force, the Court of Apeal held that the procedure for *ex parte* public interest immunity applications was unaffected by the case law summarised above.[467] The court came to the same conclusion in *Botmeh*,[468] even when the Crown sought to conduct public interest immunity applications before the Court of Appeal in realtion to material that had not be shown to the trial judge. In those circumstances, it was still open to the Court of Appeal to determine that the proceedings were compliant with Art.6 where it satisfied itself that the undisclosed material could have no possible impact on the fairness of the proceedings.[469] The conflict of this decision with *Rowe and Davis* and *Atlan*, in so far as a court determined an issue without adversarial argument at all, is the subject of an outstanding application to the European Court of Human Rights. In the course of the hearing in *Botmeh* the court considered whether counsel could give a personal undertaking not to disclose the content of sensitive material to his client. Having consulted his professional body and taken his clients' instructions, he declined to give such an undertaking:

14-153

"He gave six reasons: a substantial risk of undermining public confidence and the clients' confidence in the profession; the inability of counsel to perform his duty of advising his clients as to their best interests; proper instructions from a client not in a position to appreciate the significance of the material would be precluded; counsel might receive material adverse to his clients about which he could not obtain proper instructions; counsel would have serious practical difficulties in conducting the case without accidentally disclosing confidential material; and, if the material could not be disclosed to counsel's instructing solicitors, the matter could be compounded because of the solicitor's unrivalled knowledge of the case and professional duty of disclosure to the lay clients. This approach has subsequently been endorsed in AG's Guidance on the Disclosure of Information in Criminal Proceedings (2000). In the light of these considerations, this court proceeded to examine the matter ex parte"[470]

---

[467] *R. v Davis, Rowe and Johnson (No.2)*, *The Times*, April 24, 2000.
[468] [2002] 1 W.L.R. 531, CA.
[469] Para.20 See also *R. v Craven* [2001] 2 Cr.App.R. 12.
[470] [2002] 1 W.L.R. 531, para.26.

In the aftermath of *Botmeh*, the Court of Appeal invited the appointment of a special advocate when hearing an appeal against a decision of the Special Immigration Appeals Commission.[471] Subsequently the House of Lords recognised that this procedure might be appropriate if it were necessary to examine very sensitive material on an application for judicial review by a member or former member of a security service.[472] During his review of Criminal Courts, Lord Justice Auld recommended that consideration be given to appointing special advocates in *ex parte* proceedings before the Crown Court.[473] In its response to Lord Justice Auld, the Bar Council endorsed his proposal.[474]

14–154   This was the domestic law context in which the European Court of Human Rights considered the case of *Edwards and Lewis v United Kingdom*.[475] In both cases the applicants alleged that the proceedings against them should be stayed because undercover police officers and/or informants had acted as agents provocateurs. The key evidence in relation to the status of the police informants was produced in *ex parte* hearings, but remained undisclosed to the defence. The difference between these cases and the previous authorities which had found *ex parte* hearings to be acceptable was that the judge who conducted the hearings was also the tribunal of fact for the purposes of the application to stay. The Chamber considered it to be particularly significant that, in Mr Edwards' case, the British Government disclosed for the first time during the ECHR proceedings that the original trial judge had been shown material which suggested that the applicant was previously involved in drug trafficking.[476] In the circumstances, the Court was not satisified that "the procedure employed to determine the issues of disclosure of evidence and entrapment complied with the requirements to provide adversarial proceedings and equality of arms and incorporated adequate safeguards to protect the interests of the accused."[477] The decision was upheld by the Grand Chamber,[478] by which time the House of Lords had considered the first instance Chamber decision, in *H and C*.[479]

14–155   *Edwards and Lewis* provides authority for the proposition that it may be incompatible for a trial judge seized with the task of deciding whether to stay proceedings or exclude evidence to see material which is potentially relevant to the issue but is not the subject of adversarial argument. That principle applies where the material sought to be withheld is potentially relevant to an application to stay a prosecution as an abuse of process or to exclude evidence under s.78 of the

---

[471] *Secretary of State for the Home Department v Rehman* [2003] 1 A.C. 153, paras 31–32.

[472] *R. v Shayler* [2003] 1 A.C. 247, para.34. See also *R. (on the application of the Kurdistan Workers Party and Others) v SSHD* [2002] EWHC 644 (Admin) *per* Richards J. at para.76 and *R. v Customs and Excise Commissioners ex p Popley* [1999] STC 1016.

[473] Auld L.J.'s "Review of the Criminal Courts of England and Wales" (October 2001), Ch.10, paras 476–478.

[474] "Review of the Criminal Courts (AULD): The Bar Council Response", Ch.10, paras 91–95.

[475] (2005) 40 E.H.R.R. 24 (Grand Chamber). The decision of the Fourth Section of the Chamber is App.Nos 39647/98;40461/98, July 22, 2003, but its relevant sections are copied in the report of the Grand Chamber judgment ((2005) 40 E.H.R.R. 24).

[476] App.Nos 39647/98;40461/98, July 22, 2003, para.58.

[477] Para.59.

[478] (2005) 40 E.H.R.R. 24.

[479] [2004] 2 A.C. 134. See para.14–122c.

Police and Criminal Evidence Act 1984 on grounds of entrapment.[480] But the principle is broader, and applies equally where the material is potentially relevant to such applications made on grounds of serious executive illegality or misconduct amounting to an affront to the public conscience.[481] There was a pre-existing authority from the Criminal Division of the Court of Appeal (*R. v Smith (Joe)*)[482] that had held such an outcome to be acceptable in the context of a decision as to the admissibility of DNA evidence which it was submitted was unlawfully obtained. The trial judge relied on material shown to him on an *ex parte* basis to conclude that the police were in possession of sufficient information in order to justify the taking of a DNA sample.[483] In keeping with its general approach, the European Court in *Edwards and Lewis* had not dictated that it was necessary to introduce the safeguard of a special advocate in order to protect against any potential unfairness to a defendant. At the same time, the court recognised the role of special advocates as a potential solution, and noted that Lord Justice Auld had supported their introduction in his report.

In *H and C*, a trial judge sought to appoint independent counsel as a result of an   **14–156**
application by the defendants that he should do so in the context of deciding an entrapment argument. The Court of Appeal overruled the decision, and the House of Lords subsequently conducted a wide ranging review of the issue. The judgment of Lord Bingham represents the considered opinion of the whole committee. It starts by recognising a "cardinal and overriding requirement" that the trial process, viewed as a whole, must be fair. Any issue relating to the potential disclosure of sensitive material to a defendant must be governed by that principle.[484] Fairness, however, is an evolving concept, such that practices acceptable 100 years ago, or even 20 years ago, are not acceptable now.[485] Bitter experience had shown that miscarriages of justice had occurred because of failure to make disclosure of relevant material. The common law had recognized a duty to make disclosure of relevant material whether it was asked for or not.[486] The test for relevance under the CPIA, whether in its original or amended form, did not require the disclosure of material which was "either neutral in its effect or adverse to the interests of the accused".[487] Circumstances may arise in which material held by the prosecution and tending to undermine the prosecution or assist the defence cannot be disclosed to the defence, fully or even at all, without the risk of serious prejudice to an important public interest:

"In such circumstances some derogation from the golden rule of full disclosure may be justified but such derogation must always be the minimum derogation necessary to

---

[480] *R. v Looseley* [2001] 1 W.L.R. 2060, HL.
[481] *R. v Latif* [1996] 1 W.L.R. 104, HL. The Court of Appeal appointed a special advocate to represent the interests of the defence in *R. v Choudhury and Ors* [2005] EWCA Crim 1788.
[482] [2001] 1 W.L.R. 1031, CA.
[483] *Cf. Lamothe v Comr of Police of the Metropolis* (unreported) October 25, 1999.
[484] [2004] 2 A.C. 134, para.10.
[485] Para.11.
[486] Paras 14–16. See *R. v Ward (Judith)* 1993] 1 W.L.R. 619, 674; and *R. v Keane* [1994] 1 W.L.R. 746, 752.
[487] Para.17. See some support for this approach in the admissibility decision of *Glover v United Kingdom* (2005) 40 E.H.R.R. SE18.

protect the public interest in question and must never imperil the overall fairness of the trial."[488]

This problem was catered for in the ex parte procedure introduced by *Davis, Johnson and Rowe*. The years since that judgment had seen the development of novel procedures involving the use of special advocates outside the criminal sphere.[489] The fact that there was little express sanction for the use of such a procedure in English law was not of itself a bar to their appointment. The House then embarked upon a qualified endorsement of the use of special counsel, but only in exceptional circumstances:

"Such an appointment does however raise ethical problems, since a lawyer who cannot take full instructions from his client, nor report to his client, who is not responsible to his client and whose relationship with the client lacks the quality of confidence inherent in any ordinary lawyer-client relationship, is acting in a way hitherto unknown to the legal profession. While not insuperable, these problems should not be ignored, since neither the defendant nor the public will be fully aware of what is being done. The appointment is also likely to cause practical problems: of delay, while the special counsel familiarises himself with the detail of what is likely to be a complex case; of expense, since the introduction of an additional, high-quality advocate must add significantly to the cost of the case; and of continuing review, since it will not be easy for a special counsel to assist the court in its continuing duty to review disclosure, unless the special counsel is present throughout or is instructed from time to time when need arises. Defendants facing serious charges frequently have little inclination to co-operate in a process likely to culminate in their conviction, and any new procedure can offer opportunities capable of exploitation to obstruct and delay. None of these problems should deter the court from appointing special counsel where the interests of justice are shown to require it. But the need must be shown. Such an appointment will always be exceptional, never automatic; a course of last and never first resort. It should not be ordered unless and until the trial judge is satisfied that no other course will adequately meet the overriding requirement of fairness to the defendant. In the Republic of Ireland, whose legal system is, in many respects, not unlike that of England and Wales, a principled but pragmatic approach has been adopted to questions of disclosure and it does not appear that provision has been made for the appointment of special counsel: see *Director of Public Prosecutions v Special Criminal Court* [1999] 1 IR 60."[490]

14–157   The House of Lords then reviewed the Convention jurisprudence summarised above. The judgment rejects the proposition that a special advocate will always be necessary in circumstances where a judge sits as a tribunal of fact on an application to stay and/or exclude evidence. To accept such a proposition would be to "place the trial judge in a straightjacket".[491] The consistent approach of the Strasbourg jurisprudence was to declare principles and apply those principles on a case-by-case basis. Overall there was no dissonance between the principles of domestic law and those recognised by the Convention case law.[492] The court then emphasised that the circumstances when *ex parte* procedures ought to take place,

---

[488] Para.18.
[489] Para.22. See para.14–122.
[490] Para.22.
[491] Para.33.
[492] Para.35.

still less when a judge would need to recuse himself, could be limited if certain principles were faithfully followed. Chief amongst them was that the material which does not weaken the prosecution case or strengthen the defence case gives rise to no duty of disclosure. Claims for disclosure must be carefully analysed by reference to the actual issues in the case. The trial process "is not well served" if the defence are permitted "to make general and unspecified allegations and then seek far-reaching disclosure in the hope that material may turn up to make them good". Only in truly borderline cases should the prosecution seek an *ex parte* ruling. When any issue of derogation from the golden rule of full disclosure comes before it, their Lordships ruled that the court must address a series of questions[493]:

(1) What is the material which the prosecution seek to withhold? This must be considered by the court in detail.

(2) Is the material such as may weaken the prosecution case or strengthen that of the defence? If No, disclosure should not be ordered. If Yes, full disclosure should (subject to (3), (4) and (5) below) be ordered.

(3) Is there a real risk of serious prejudice to an important public interest (and, if so, what) if full disclosure of the material is ordered? If No, full disclosure should be ordered.

(4) If the answer to (2) and (3) is Yes, can the defendant's interest be protected without disclosure or disclosure be ordered to an extent or in a way which will give adequate protection to the public interest in question and also afford adequate protection to the interests of the defence? This question requires the court to consider, with specific reference to the material which the prosecution seek to withhold and the facts of the case and the defence as disclosed, whether the prosecution should formally admit what the defence seek to establish or whether disclosure short of full disclosure may be ordered. This may be done in appropriate cases by the preparation of summaries or extracts of evidence, or the provision of documents in an edited or anonymised form, provided the documents supplied are in each instance approved by the judge. In appropriate cases the appointment of special counsel may be a necessary step to ensure that the contentions of the prosecution are tested and the interests of the defendant protected. In cases of exceptional difficulty the court may require the appointment of special counsel to ensure a correct answer to questions (2) and (3) as well as (4).[494]

(5) Do the measures proposed in answer to (4) represent the minimum derogation necessary to protect the public interest in question? If No, the court should order such greater disclosure as will represent the minimum derogation from the golden rule of full disclosure.

---

[493] Para.36.
[494] A special advocate was appointed to represent the interests of the defence in *R. v Bourgass and Ors*, Central Criminal Court, April 2005. The Court of Appeal used a special advocate in *R. v Greaves and Ors* [2004] EWCA Crim 822; and *R. v Choudhury and Ors* [2005] EWCA Crim 1788.

(6) If limited disclosure is ordered pursuant to (4) or (5), may the effect be to render the trial process, viewed as a whole, unfair to the defendant? If Yes, then fuller disclosure should be ordered even if this leads or may lead the prosecution to discontinue the proceedings so as to avoid having to make disclosure.

(7) If the answer to (6) when first given is No, does that remain the correct answer as the trial unfolds, evidence is adduced and the defence advanced? It is important that the answer to (6) should not be treated as a final, once-and-for-all, answer but as a provisional answer which the court must keep under review.

In dealing with these questions the judge should involve the defence to the maximum extent possible, without disclosing that which the general interest requires to be protected, but taking full account of the specific defence which is relied on. It followed that there will be very few cases indeed in which some measure of disclosure to the defence will not be possible, even if this is confined to the fact that an ex parte application is to be made. If even that information is withheld and if the material to be withheld is of significant help to the defendant, there would inevitably be a very serious question whether the prosecution should proceed, since special counsel, even if appointed, cannot then receive any instructions from the defence at all.[495] On this basis, their Lordships agreed with the Court of Appeal that the trial judge had prematurely appointed a special advocate on the facts of the extant appeals, because he had not considered the material in order to decide whether it warranted such an appointment. At the same time, it was not clear on the face of the disclosed material whether an *ex parte* application by the Crown was actually warranted in any event.[496] Their Lordships dealt with two further matters. First, the procedure adopted in the case of *Joe Smith*[497] where the legality of the taking of a DNA sample was decided entirely on an *ex parte* basis without involving the defence in any way was not to be followed in the future. No efforts had been made to ascertain the core questions to ask of the officer or to devise a a procedure capable of exposing the matter to as much inter parties scrutiny as possible. Finally, the principles articulated in relation to Crown Court proceedings would apply equally to magistrates court proceedings. The court's duty of continuing review would militate against the tribunal recusing itself, although there might be circumstances where this would need to occur. Wherever possible, the court should transfer matters to the Crown Court.[498]

---

[495] Para.37.

[496] Para.38. It is to be noted that when the case of *R. v Lewis* [2005] EWCA Crim 859 was heard by the Court of Appeal in the aftermath of the Grand Chamber judgment, no violation of Art.6 was found because the disclosed material indicated that there was no reasonable possibility of a finding that the defendant had been the subject of an agent provocateur. In that respect, the fact that the judge had considered material which was damaging to the defence on an ex parte basis did not undermine the safety of his finding that there had been no entrapment.

[497] [2001] 1 W.L.R. 1031, CA. Paras 41–42. See *P.G. and J.H. v United Kingdom* [2002] Crim.L.R. 208 ECtHR.

[498] Paras 43–44. See *R. v Stipendiary Magistrate for Norfolk, Ex p Taylor* (1997) 161 J.P. 773, and *R. (DPP) v Acton Youth Court* [2001] 1 W.L.R. 1828.

The consequence of *H and C* is that it brings new clarity to the *ex parte*   **14–158**
procedure, which has suffered continuous problems since its inception. By
emphasising the limited situations in which an *ex parte* application is permissible, it is hoped that applications will take place less often.[499] When they do
occur, there is a tension between competing principles of justice. On the one hand
there are dicta which suggest that disclosure requests must be scrutinised with
care in order to deal robustly with attempts to embarrass the prosecution.[500] On
the other hand, there is a long line of authority which indicates that an expansive
interpretation must be placed upon the type of material which would assist a
defendant in the context of a criminal trial before a jury.[501] That is because, in the
words of Lord Simon in *DPP v Shannon*[502]:

> "The law in action is not concerned with absolute truth, but with proof before a fallible
> human tribunal to a requisite standard of probability in accordance with formal rules of
> evidence."

Outside the immediate realm of the criminal courts, the use of special advocates   **14–159**
and closed proceedings is increasingly becoming a conventional process for
justifying interfence with human rights in circumstances where the evidence
upon which the interference is based cannot be disclosed because of reasons of
national security. Statutory procedures were developed under Pt IV of the Anti-
Terrorism, Crime and Security Act 2001 in order to detain terrorists suspects who
according to the government could not be prosecuted because it would be
contrary to the public interest to disclose the evidence upon which their alleged
criminalty was based. Although that system was subsequently repealed by
Parliament as a result of the declaration of incompatibility with Art.5 and 14
made by the House of Lords,[503] the same regime of closed proceedings has been
adopted in relation to control order proceedings under the Prevention of Terrorism Act 2005.[504] As time goes on evidence is emerging that prosecutions that

---

[499] *R. v Preston* [1994] 2 A.C. 130: *Ex Parte* hearings are "objectionable in principle and in
practice" and should not take place unless "absolutely necessary": (*per* Lord Mustill at p.153). For
earlier authority about the prohibition upon seeing the judge ex parte for any matter other than a
ruling on PII material, see *R. v Smith (David James)* [1998] 2 Cr.App.R. 1, CA.

[500] *R. v Turner (Paul)* [1995] 1 W.L.R. 264, 267.

[501] See the various tests identifying the test for discloseability in the case law: *Marks v Beyfus*
[1890] 25 Q.B.D.494 ("if the disputed material *may* prove the defendant's innocence or avoid a
miscarriage of justice, then the balance comes down resoundingly in favour of disclosing it"; *R. v
Hallett* [1986] Crim.L.R. 462 *per* Lord Lane (documents should be disclosed "in order to prevent the
possibility that a man may . . . be deprived the opportunity of casting doubt on the case against him")
and *R. v Agar* 90 Cr.App.R. 318, 324 (the defendant should be allowed to put forward a tenable case
in its best light). Sir Richard Scott V.C.'s *Report of the Inquiry into the Export of defence equipment
and Dual-Use Goods in Iraq and related Prosecutions,* concluded that if the material had the potential
to assist the defence case then it should always be disclosed. In effect Scott V.C. asserts that the notion
of a "balancing exercise" is imprecise because a document which might be of assistance to the
defence cannot remain undisclosed in favour of some notional higher public interest: see paras 6.12
to 6.14 and 6.18 (viii). The approach of the House of Lords in *H and C* does not disssent from this
view, but it recognises the possibility that the admissions can be made by the Crown, without having
to disclose all of the material to which sensitivity attaches.

[502] (1974) 59 Cr.App.R. 250, 268.

[503] *A and Ors (No.1) v Secretary of State for the Home Department* [2005] 2 A.C. 68. See Ch.4
above.

[504] *Secretary of State for the Home Department* [2006] 3 W.L.R. 839, CA.

were said to be foreclosed by public interest immunity considerations are either taking place[505] or the CPS were never properly consulted as to whether they could take place.[506] In *Roberts v Parole Board*[507] the House of Lords recognised that it was not inherently wrong in principle that a special advocate might be appointed by the Parole Board to determine a key issue in a parole hearing in the absence of the prisoner. Nothing in *H and C* has indicated that criminal trials can rely on closed evidence to determine guilt or innocence of an offence. In many ways, the judgment may be important in the future for preventing a development which was not advocated by any of the parties in the case and which has not yet entered the mainstream of law reform debate. Fortunately, for the time being, no one could sensibly advocate that the *ex parte* procedure could be used in criminal proceedings for anything other than discrete and exceptional questions of disclosure.

H. The Protection of Vulnerable Witnesses

I. Introduction

14–160   The protection of the identity of a police informant who does not give evidence is one of the principal grounds for claiming public interest immunity. As we have seen,[508] the Court has held that the withholding of evidence which might expose such a witness to a risk of reprisals is not necessarily incompatible with Art.6. However, prosecuting authorities may also wish to protect the identity of witnesses who *are* called to give evidence. A variety of methods may be employed to achieve this, and the court's powers have been extended and re-structured by Pt II of the Youth Justice and Criminal Evidence Act 1999. A witness may be permitted to give evidence anonymously (using a letter in place of his/her name); screens may be used to prevent the witness being seen by the defendant or the public; a witness may be allowed to give evidence by live link; permission may be given to use video-recorded examination or cross-examination; or the court may be asked to sit *in camera*. The 1999 Act does not deal specifically with witness anonymity, but it provides new procedures for the approval of the other four methods of witness protection.

II. Anonymity

14–161   In its early decisions the European Court of Human Rights adopted a stringent approach to anonymity and kindred measures, relying exclusively on the rights of the accused under Art.6. Thus in *Kostovski v Netherlands*[509] the court drew attention to the different standards applicable in the investigation phase and the trial phase:

---

[505] *R. v Hamza* [2006] EWCA Crim 2918.
[506] *E. v Secretary of State for the Home Department* [2007] EWHC 233 (Admin) 36kk [2005] 2 A.C. 738.
[507] [2005] UKHL 45.
[508] See para.14–117 above.
[509] (1990) 12 E.H.R.R. 434.

"The Government stressed the fact that case law and practice in the Netherlands in the matter of anonymous evidence stemmed from an increase in the intimidation of witnesses and were based on a balancing of the interests of society, the accused and the witnesses ... [T]he Court does not underestimate the importance of the struggle against organised crime. Yet the Government's line of argument, whilst not without force, is not decisive ... [T]he right to a fair administration of justice holds so prominent a place in a democratic society that it cannot be sacrificed to expediency. The Convention does not preclude reliance, at the investigation stage, on sources such as anonymous informants. However, the subsequent use of anonymous statements to found a criminal conviction ... is a different matter. It involved limitations on the rights of the defence which were irreconcilable with the guarantees contained in Article 6."[510]

The Court further observed that if the defence are deprived of information **14–162** necessary to challenge a witness's credibility, then this may amount to an insurmountable obstacle to a fair trial:

"If the defence is unaware of the identity of the person it seeks to question, it may be deprived of the very particulars enabling it to demonstrate that he or she is prejudiced, hostile or unreliable. Testimony or other declarations inculpating an accused may well be designedly untruthful, or simply erroneous and the defence will scarcely be able to bring this to light if it lacks the information permitting it to test the author's reliability or cast doubt on his credibility. The dangers inherent in such a situation are obvious."[511]

Likewise, in *Windisch v Austria* the Court held that[512]:

"[T]he defence was confronted with an almost insurmountable handicap: it was deprived of the necessary information permitting it to test the witnesses' reliability or cast doubt on their credibility."

However, a change of approach was signalled in *Doorson v Netherlands*.[513] The **14–163** Court began by noting that in certain circumstances, the disclosure of a witness's identity could put his right to physical security, or even his life, at risk. Against this background the Court considered it necessary to balance the interests of the witness against the interests of the accused:

"It is true that Article 6 does not explicitly require the interests of witnesses in general, and those of victims called upon to testify in particular, to be taken into consideration. However, their life, liberty or security of person may be at stake, as may interests coming generally within the ambit of Article 8 of the Convention ... Contracting States should organise their criminal proceedings in such a way that those interests are not unjustifiably imperilled. Against this background, principles of fair trial also require that in appropriate cases the interests of the defence are balanced against those of witnesses or victims called upon to testify."[514]

In the *Doorson* case itself there was no evidence that any of the witnesses had **14–164** been threatened by the defendant. On the other hand there was evidence that drug

---

[510] *ibid.*, at para.44.
[511] *ibid.*, at para.42.
[512] (1991) 13 E.H.R.R. 281 at para.28.
[513] (1996) 22 E.H.R.R. 330.
[514] *ibid.*, at para.70.

dealers in general often resorted to threats of or actual violence against persons who testified against them. Moreover, one of the witnesses in the case had suffered violence at the hands of a different drug dealer against whom he had given evidence in the past. The Court held that these factors were sufficient to justify maintaining anonymity, provided that there was an adequate system of safeguards in place to ensure that the rights of the defence were respected:

> "The maintenance of the anonymity of the witnesses ... presented the defence with difficulties which criminal proceedings should not normally involve. Nevertheless, no violation of Article 6(1) taken together with Article 6(3)(b) of the Convention will be found if it is established that the handicaps under which the defence laboured were sufficiently counterbalanced by the procedures followed by the judicial authorities."

14–165 The safeguards approved by the Court in *Doorson* were that the anonymous witnesses had been questioned in the presence of counsel by an investigating magistrate; the magistrate was aware of their identity; the magistrate noted in the official report the circumstances on the basis of which the court was able to draw conclusions as to the reliability of the evidence; counsel was able to ask the witnesses whatever questions he considered to be in the interests of the defence except those which might lead to the disclosure of their identity, and all questions had been answered. The Court emphasised that;

> "[E]ven when 'counterbalancing' procedures are found to compensate sufficiently the handicaps under which the defence labours, a conviction should not be based either solely or to a decisive extent on anonymous statements ... Furthermore, evidence obtained from witnesses under conditions in which the rights of the defence cannot be secured to the extent normally required by the Convention should be treated with extreme care."

On the facts the Court held that the trial had not been unfair when two prosecution witnesses remained anonymous and were questioned by the judge in the presence of both counsel (but not the accused).

14–166 In *Van Mechelen v Netherlands*,[515] by contrast, the Court found a violation of Art.6 when 11 police officers gave evidence for the prosecution, remained anonymous, and were questioned by the judge whilst prosecution and defence counsel were kept in another room, with only a sound link to the judge's chambers. The Court began by distinguishing *Doorson* on the ground that the position of police officers is different from that of ordinary members of the public (since it is part of their duty to give evidence in court). Only exceptionally, when there was clear evidence of direct threats, would it be proper to grant anonymity in respect of professional witnesses of this kind. In the *Van Mechelen* case the defendants and their counsel were not only unaware of the identity of the witnesses, "but were also prevented from observing their demeanour under direct questioning, and thus from testing their reliability". In finding a violation of Art.6, the Court restated the principle established in *Doorson* that any measure restricting the rights of the defence must be "strictly necessary". The Court in *Van Mechelen* interpreted this to mean that "[i]f a less restrictive measure can

---

[515] (1998) 25 E.H.R.R. 647.

suffice, then that measure should be adopted". On the facts, the Court considered that the government had failed to offer a satisfactory explanation as to why it was necessary to resort to such extreme limitations on the rights of the defence, or why less far-reaching measures had not been not considered.

The existing practice in England and Wales does not appear to conform fully with **14–167** the criteria established by the court in *Doorson* and *Van Mechelen*. In particular, the Strasbourg case-law appears to prohibit reliance on anonymous witnesses whose evidence is likely to be "decisive" to the outcome of the case. The equivalent domestic law rules point in the opposite direction: anonymity is only to be permitted where the evidence is sufficiently important to make it unfair to oblige the Crown to proceed without it.[516] Applications for witness anonymity have long been made in blackmail cases, and have now become common in terrorist cases involving security service witnesses, in prosecutions involving child witnesses, and in cases involving serious or organised crime. The House of Lords has held that in rare and exceptional circumstances a judge may permit a witness to conceal his identity entirely from the accused.[517] In *R. v Taylor (Gary)*[518] the Court of Appeal held that whether such circumstances exist was for the discretion of the trial judge. The following factors were held to be relevant to the exercise of the discretion:

(a) There must be real grounds for fear of the consequences if the identity of the witness were revealed. It might not be necessary for the witness himself to be fearful, or to be fearful for himself alone.

(b) The evidence must be sufficiently important to make it unfair for the Crown to proceed without it. A distinction can be drawn between cases where a witness's credit is in issue and cases where it is the witness's accuracy which is at stake.

(c) The Crown must satisfy the court that the creditworthiness of the witness has been fully investigated and disclosed.

(d) The court must be satisfied that there will be no undue prejudice to the accused.

(e) The court should balance the need for the protection of the witness, including the extent of that protection, against the unfairness or appearance of unfairness to the accused.

A Home Office committee considered the *Taylor* principles, without reference to the Convention, and pronounced them satisfactory.[519]

---

[516] *Taylor (Gary)* [1995] Crim.L.R. 253.

[517] For the general rule, see *Scott v Scott* [1913] A.C. 417, and *Attorney-General v Leveller Magazine* [1979] A.C. 440.

[518] [1995] Crim.L.R. 253; *The Times*, August 17, 1994. As to the need for that anonymity applications are scrutinised with care, see *R. v Legal Aid Board ex parte Kaim Todner (a firm)* [1999] Q.B. 966. See also paras 14–51a to 14–51c above.

[519] Report of the Interdepartmental Working Group on the treatment of Vulnerable or Intimidated Witnesses in the Criminal Justice System, *Speaking Up for Justice* (Home Office, 1998), para.8.32.

14–168   More recently, in *R. v Davis*, the Court of Appeal sought, after examining the relevant Convention jurisprudence, to provide detailed guidance on the issue of witness anonymity:

> " . . . In our judgment the discretion to permit evidence to be given by witnesses whose identity may not be known to the defendant is now beyond question. The potential disadvantages to the defendant require the court to examine the application for witness anonymity with scrupulous care, to ensure that it is necessary and that the witness is indeed in genuine and justified fear of serious consequences if his true identity became known to the defendant or the defendant's associates. It is in any event elementary that the court should be alert to potential or actual disadvantages faced by the defendant in consequence of any anonymity ruling, and ensure that necessary and appropriate precautions are taken to ensure that the trial itself will be fair. Provided that appropriate safeguards are applied, and the judge is satisfied that a fair trial can take place, it may proceed. If not, he should not permit anonymity. If he does so, and there is a conviction, it is not to be regarded as unsafe simply because the evidence of anonymous witnesses may have been decisive."[520]
>
> "Among the safeguards, first, is the decision of the trial judge whether to exercise his discretion to allow some or all the witnesses against the defendant to give their evidence anonymously. If the only evidence against the defendant consists of wholly unsupported anonymous witnesses, whose evidence is demonstrably suspect, the judge may decide . . . that the Crown should not adduce it. Again, if the decisive evidence comes from an unidentified witness who cannot be cross-examined (for example, anonymous witnesses whose evidence was admitted in documentary form only, and who will not be called to give oral testimony), the judge may decide that the evidence should not be admitted. As we emphasise, these are issues for judicial decision in case-specific situations, after allowing for the disclosure process, any public interest immunity decisions, and the ability to cross-examine together with the deployment of material helpful to the defendant in the course of cross-examination, or even when cross-examination may not be possible. For example, the judge may be satisfied that a wholly independent, understandably terrified witness, a stranger to the defendant, and with no possible motive to implicate him, may have made a note of a crucial car number plate at the scene of the crime. If satisfied that this witness is indeed independent, but unfit to give live evidence, the judge may admit his or her evidence, anonymously, and in statement form."[521]
>
> "At the end of the prosecution case, the judge may decide that it would be unsafe for the evidence of the anonymous witnesses to be considered further by the jury, or indeed, that the case as a whole should be withdrawn from their consideration. We are not seeking to formulate a scheme, merely to identify appropriate safeguards currently in place to ensure the fairness of the trial. Thereafter, if the case is fit to go to the jury, when the evidence is concluded, and to enable the jury properly to approach its task, the judge must give appropriate directions in his summing up, sufficient to identify the particular disadvantages under which the defence may have been labouring. . . . The judge would probably suggest that the jury should consider whether there is any independent, supporting evidence, tending to confirm the credibility of the anonymous witnesses, and the incriminating evidence they have given. We are not reinstating outdated principles relating to corroboration, nor implying that such independent evidence is a prerequisite to conviction. We are simply reflecting the obvious consideration that independent evidence consistent with the defendant's guilt would be likely to

---

[520] [2006] EWCA Crim 1155, [2006] 1 W.L.R. 3130, [59].
[521] *ibid.*, [60].

increase confidence in the truthfulness and accuracy of incriminating anonymous witnesses."[522]

The importance of this decision lies not just in the guidance given by the Court of Appeal but also in the clear references to Convention jurisprudence.

Some mention should be made in this context of the approach of the International **14–169** Criminal Tribunal for the former Yugoslavia (ICTY). The ICTY has sought to apply the Convention case law in the difficult context of trying war criminals. There are two significant points for present purposes. First, the ICTY has not chosen to adopt the Strasbourg approach which holds that convictions should not be based solely or to a decisive extent on the evidence of anonymous witnesses. Instead, it has followed the same course as the United Kingdom courts, holding that one of the criteria *in favour* of allowing anonymity is that the evidence must be of importance in proving the prosecution case. Secondly, the ICTY has not expressly adopted the principle in *Doorson* that evidence from an anonymous witness should be treated with "extreme care."

In the *Blaskic (Protective Measures)* decision[523] the Trial Chamber issued guide- **14–170** lines allowing witness anonymity under the following conditions:

"First and foremost, there must be real fear for the safety of the witness or her or his family. Secondly, the testimony of the particular witness must be important to the Prosecutor's case. Thirdly, the Trial Chamber must be satisfied that there is no *prima facie* evidence that the witness is untrustworthy. Fourthly, the ineffectiveness or non-existence of a witness protection programme is another point that . . . has considerable bearing on any decision to grant anonymity . . . Finally, any measures taken should be strictly necessary. If a less restrictive measure can secure the desired protection, that measure should be applied."

In the *Tadic First Instance (Witness Protection)* decision the Trial Chamber made **14–171** three further points[524]:

"Firstly, the Judges must be able to observe the demeanour of the witness, in order to assess the reliability of the testimony . . . Secondly, the Judges must be aware of the identity of the witness in order to test the reliability of the witness . . . Thirdly, the defence must be allowed ample opportunity to question the witness on issues unrelated to his or her identity or current whereabouts, such as how the witness was able to obtain the incriminating information, but still excluding information that would make the new name traceable. Finally, the identity of the witness must be released when there are no longer reasons to fear for the security of the witness."

The Chamber accepted that the general rule must be that, in the words of the **14–172** European Court in *Kostovski*, "in principle, all the evidence must be adduced in the presence of the accused at a public hearing with a view to adversarial argument." Having stated this general rule however, the Chamber went on to hold that:

---

[522] *ibid.*, [61].
[523] U.N. Docs. IT–95–14–T (November 5, 1996).
[524] U.N. Docs. IT–94–1–T (August 10, 1995) at para.71.

"The interest in the ability of the defendant to establish facts must be weighed against the interest in the anonymity of the witness. The balancing of these interests is inherent in the notion of a fair trial. A fair trial means not only fair treatment to the defendant but also to the prosecution and to the witnesses ... The European Court of Human Rights, when determining whether non-disclosure of the identity of a witness constitutes a violation of the principle of fair trial looks at all the circumstances of the case (see *Kostovski* paras 43, 45). The Court identifies any infringement of the rights of the accused and considers whether the infringement was necessary and appropriate in the circumstances of the case."[525]

14–173   Some of the language used by the Trial Chamber in these two cases will be familiar to British judges and lawyers. But it should be stressed that the ICTY's guidelines are not—and are not intended to be—a reflection of the Strasbourg case law applicable to criminal procedure at the national level. The correct test under Art.6 remains that established in the *Doorson/Van Mechelen* line of cases, and considerable caution should be exercised in drawing any analogies with the procedural rules of the ICTY. Writing extra-judicially, the former President of the ICTY, Professor Antonio Cassese, has emphasised that the guidelines were the product of the wholly exceptional conditions under which the Tribunal is obliged to carry out its duties[526]:

"The Trial chamber [in *Tadic First Instance (Witness Protection)*] noted that only in exceptional circumstances may the Trial Chamber restrict the accused's right of cross-examination. In support of its findings that 'exceptional circumstances *par excellence*' exist in former Yugoslavia in view of the conflict which was then ongoing, the Trial Chamber cited Article 15 of the European Convention which allows for derogation in 'time of war or other public emergency threatening the life of the nation' ... In the words of the Trial Chamber 'The fact that some derogation is allowed in cases of national emergency shows that the rights of the accused guaranteed under the principle of the right to a fair trial are not wholly without qualification ...'

The Majority Opinion of the Trial Chamber was, of necessity, selective in its reliance on the *Kostovski* case. Indeed, it must be borne in mind that the finding of the majority in *Tadic First Instance (Witness Protection)* was that fair trial guarantees were not violated with anonymous witnesses, whereas the finding of the European Court in *Kostovski* was that such guarantees were violated. The majority of the trial chamber saw its task as providing guidelines to ensure fair trial based *inter alia* on the guidance provided by the case-law of the European Court of Human Rights, but only as subject to 'the unique object and purpose of the International Tribunal, particularly recognising its mandate to protect victims and witnesses'."

14–174   Section 2 of the Human Rights Act expressly requires domestic courts to have regard to the decisions of the European Court and Commission of Human Rights. Insofar as the standards adopted by ICTY offer weaker protection for the accused than those adopted by the European Court of Human Rights, it is submitted that the latter should prevail. However, as we have seen, the drift of the European Court's jurisprudence has been away from strict insistence on Art.6 rights and towards greater recognition of the rights of witnesses and victims.

---

[525] *ibid.*, at paras 55–56.
[526] Cassese, "The International Criminal Tribunal for the Former Yugoslavia and Human Rights" [1997] E.H.R.L.R. 329.

III. Screens

In *R. v X and others*[527] the Court of Appeal approved the erection of a screen in   **14–175**
a courtroom to prevent young children from seeing, or being seen by, the
defendants. The test in each case is whether the interests of justice require the use
of screens in the sense that it would seriously inhibit the calling of relevant
evidence if the appearance of the witness was to become known to the accused
and/or the public. In practice it has become routine for security service officers
giving evidence in terrorist trials to do so from behind screens.[528] The same is
true of trials involving serious sexual offences, especially where the offence
involves a child complainant. In *R. v Cooper and Schaub*[529] the Court of Appeal
held that the use of screens should generally be confined to cases involving child
witnesses, and that in the case of an adult witness such a course should be
adopted only in the most exceptional cases, because it could be prejudicial even
if the judge gave an appropriate direction. The matter was held to be one for the
discretion of the trial judge, however, and the use of a screen in this particular
rape trial was held not to have been unreasonable. In *Foster*,[530] a differently
constituted Court of Appeal took a distinctly more flexible approach than that in
Cooper and Schaub. The point of the trial judge's discretion is to ensure that
justice is done, and where the judge decides that this requires the use of a screen,
a proper judicial warning should remove the risk of prejudice. In *R. (DPP) v West
London Youth Court* it was noted that "neither security services nor . . . undercover police officers have any passport to [the use of screens]. The issue has to
be considered on a case by case basis."[531]

Section 23 of the Youth Justice and Criminal Evidence Act 1999 now provides   **14–176**
for the screening of a witness from the accused, in cases where the witness falls
into one of the special categories established by ss.16 and 17 of the Act. Failure
to adhere fully to the requirements of s.23 will not necessarily render a trial
unfair. Thus in *Attorney-General for the Sovereign Base Areas of Akrotiri and
Dhekelia v Steinhoff* the Privy Council held that, in the circumstances of the case,
the requirements of a fair trial had not been compromised by the breach of s.23
arising from the fact that

> "the arrangement of the courtroom and screen were such that the witness could not be
> seen by both counsel at once. Accordingly, it was decided that counsel should change
> places, so that each could see the witness while questioning her. Both could, of course,
> hear her throughout . . . ".[532]

By a similar token, a late application for the use of a screen is not necessarily
inappropriate:

---

[527] (1990) 91 Cr.App.R. 36.
[528] See, e.g., *O'hAdhmaill* (C.C.C., 1994, Rougier J.); *Friars and Jack* (C.C.C., 1995, Ebsworth J.);
McHugh et al. (C.C.C., 1997, Smedley J.).
[529] [1994] Crim.L.R. 531; *The Times*, December 3, 1993.
[530] [1995] Crim.L.R. 333.
[531] [2005] EWHC 2834 (Admin), [24].
[532] [2005] U.K.P.C. 30, [2].

"It often arises that applications for special measures are made in the courts within the rules well before a trial, but there are some instances where a witness, at the moment of giving evidence comes to court, experiences fear and apprehension and asks for the protection of screens and it is then the duty of the Crown to make an application to the judge. If the judge is satisfied on the evidence he grants it. The manner in which the screens are erected and dealt with can then only be pursued as the circumstances present themselves in that particular courtroom at that particular time."[533]

The Court of Appeal has also noted: "Provided the jury [are] correctly instructed as to the implications of the use of screens, . . . it cannot possibly be the case . . . that the fact that a witness gives evidence without screens requires all the rest to do so as well."[534]

14–177   In the European context the issue came up for consideration by the Commission in *X v United Kingdom*.[535] The applicant was convicted of a murder of two soldiers in Northern Ireland during a Republican funeral. Parts of the incident had been captured on film and the Crown wished to conceal the identity of the journalists, cameramen and photographers who had witnessed the incident and taken the film. The case was tried by judge alone. The witnesses were shielded so that the accused, the press and the public were unable to see them, but they could be seen by the judge and by counsel. In rejecting the applicant's complaint, the Commission stressed that far from being decisive in the conviction, the evidence of the screened witnesses was neutral as to his guilt:

"The Commission recalls the case-law of the European Court of Human Rights that in principle all evidence must be adduced in the presence of the accused at a public hearing with a view to adversarial argument, but this does not mean that a statement from a witness must always be made in court and in public if it is to be admitted in evidence. The defendant must be given an adequate and proper opportunity to challenge and question the witnesses against him. In the present case the witnesses whose identity was not disclosed to the public or the accused were present in court and could be seen by the judge and by the representatives of both prosecution and defence. The evidence itself concerned not the question of identification of the applicant (which evidence was given by police officers whose identity was not withheld), but merely the making of certain filmed and photographic evidence. It was accepted by the defence that the evidence did not implicate the applicant.

Accordingly, given that the applicant was able, through his representatives who could see the witnesses, to put all questions he wished to the witnesses in question, and that far from being the only item of evidence on which the trial court based its decision to convict, the evidence in question did not implicate the applicant at all, the Commission finds no indication that the decision to screen witnesses from the applicant interfered with his rights under either Article 6(1) or Article 6(3)(d) of the Convention.

Moreover, to the extent that the public was not able to see the screened witnesses, the Commission notes that the interference with the right to publicity was kept to a minimum by the fact that the public was not excluded from the proceedings, but could hear all the questions put to and answers given by those witnesses. The Commission finds that the screening was 'in the interests of . . . public order or national security'

---

[533] *R. v Adeloye* [2005] EWCA Crim 2969, [21].
[534] *R. v Brown* [2004] EWCA Crim 1620, [12].
[535] (1992) 15 E.H.R.R. CD 113.

and 'to the extent strictly necessary in the opinion of the court in special circumstances where publicity would prejudice the interests of justice'."[536]

The Commission also held that a trial judge should be made aware of the names **14-178** and addresses of the witnesses whose identities had been withheld. *X v United Kingdom* does not of course establish that screening of witnesses in a terrorist case is always compatible with Art.6. The fact that the case was tried without a jury substantially reduced any risk of prejudice. Moreover, the Commission attached considerable weight to the fact that the evidence in issue was of a purely formal character. Where the screened witnesses are decisive to the case against an accused, different considerations—of the kind set out in *Van Mechelen v Netherlands*[537]—should be borne in mind.

IV. Hearings in camera

The general principle of English criminal procedure is that all evidence must be **14-179** given in public unless a departure from the general rule is strictly necessary.[538] However, s.25 of the Youth Justice and Criminal Evidence Act 1999 now provides that a court may make a "special measures direction", where a witness falls into one of the categories in ss.16 and 17 of the Act, requiring "the exclusion from the court, during the giving of the witness's evidence, of persons of any description specified in the direction." Section 25 only applies where the offence is a sexual one, or where there are reasonable grounds for believing that the witness has been or will be subject to intimidation. The 1999 Act also introduces further possibilities, such as the giving of evidence by live link or the use of video-recorded testimony, which may be used in appropriate cases so as to protect the rights of witnesses.

This is an area in which the Convention establishes no more than a minimum **14-180** standard. The right to a public hearing "protects litigants against the administration of justice in private with no public scrutiny,"[539] and is intended to maintain public confidence in the administration of justice.[540] However, the terms of Art.6(1) are considerably broader and more permissive than the relevant principles of domestic law, providing that the press and public may be excluded "in the interests of morals, public order or national security in a democratic society, where the interests of juveniles or the protection of the private life of the parties so require, or to the extent strictly necessary in the opinion of the court in special circumstances where publicity would prejudice the interests of justice." Applying these restrictions, the Commission has upheld the exclusion of the public from the trial of an accused for sexual offences against children.[541]

---

[536] *ibid.*
[537] (1998) 25 E.H.R.R. 647.
[538] See para.14–65 above.
[539] *Pretto v Italy* (1984) 6 E.H.R.R. 182 at para.21.
[540] *Diennet v France* (1996) 21 E.H.R.R. 554 at para.31.
[541] *X v Austria* (1965) Application No.1913/63; 2 Dig. 438.

I. THE RIGHT TO A HEARING IN THE PRESENCE OF THE ACCUSED

14–181   It is the almost invariable practice in the Crown Court and magistrates' courts for the accused to be present throughout the proceedings. In *R. v Lee Kun* Lord Reading C.J. explained that[542]:

> "There must be very exceptional circumstances to justify proceeding with the trial in the absence of the accused. The reason why the accused should be present at the trial is that he may hear the case against him and have the opportunity ... of answering it. The presence of the accused means not merely that he must be physically in attendance, but also that he must be capable of understanding the proceedings."

14–182   More recently, both the Court of Appeal and the House of Lords have given detailed consideration to the issue. In *R. v Hayward, Jones and Purvis* the Court of Appeal emphasised that an accused person had a fundamental right to be present and represented, but could waive that right by absenting himself. The court then set out the principles to be applied when a trial court is considering whether to proceed in the absence of the defendant:

> "(1) A defendant has, in general, a right to be present at his trial and a right to be legally represented.
>
> (2) Those rights can be waived, separately or together, wholly or in part, by the defendant himself. They may be wholly waived if, knowing, or having the means of knowledge as to, when and where his trial is to take place, he deliberately and voluntarily absents himself and/or withdraws instructions from those representing him. They may be waived in part if, being present and represented at the outset, the defendant, during the course of the trial, behaves in such a way as to obstruct the proper course of the proceedings and/or withdraws his instructions from those representing him.
>
> (3) The trial judge has a discretion as to whether a trial should take place or continue in the absence of a defendant and/or his legal representatives.
>
> (4) That discretion must be exercised with great care and it is only in rare and exceptional cases that it should be exercised in favour of a trial taking place or continuing, particularly if the defendant is unrepresented.
>
> (5) In exercising that discretion, fairness to the defence is of prime importance but fairness to the prosecution must also be taken into account. The judge must have regard to all the circumstances of the case including, in particular: (i) the nature and circumstances of the defendant's behaviour in absenting himself from the trial or disrupting it, as the case may be and, in particular, whether his behaviour was deliberate, voluntary and such as plainly waived his right to appear; (ii) whether an adjournment might result in the defendant being caught or attending voluntarily and/or not disrupting the proceedings; (iii) the likely length of such an adjournment; (iv) whether the defendant, though absent, is, or wishes to be, legally represented at the trial or has, by his conduct, waived his right to representation; (v) whether an absent defendant's legal representatives are able to receive instructions from him during the trial and the extent to which they are

---

[542] [1916] K.B. 337 at 341.

able to present his defence; (vi) the extent of the disadvantage to the defendant in not being able to give his account of events, having regard to the nature of the evidence against him; (vii) the risk of the jury reaching an improper conclusion about the absence of the defendant; (viii) the seriousness of the offence, which affects defendant, victim and public; (ix) the general public interest and the particular interest of victims and witnesses that a trial should take place within a reasonable time of the events to which it relates; (x) the effect of delay on the memories of witnesses; (xi) where there is more than one defendant and not all have absconded, the undesirability of separate trials, and the prospects of a fair trial for the defendants who are present.

(6) If the judge decides that a trial should take place or continue in the absence of an unrepresented defendant, he must ensure that the trial is as fair as the circumstances permit. He must, in particular, take reasonable steps, both during the giving of evidence and in the summing up, to expose weaknesses in the prosecution case and to make such points on behalf of the defendant as the evidence permits. In summing up he must warn the jury that absence is not an admission of guilt and adds nothing to the prosecution case."[543]

Jones appealed to the House of Lords, with the following question certified for the Lords' consideration: "Can the Crown Court conduct a trial in the absence, from its commencement, of the defendant?" The question was answered in the affirmative, Lord Bingham of Cornhill noting:

"The Court of Appeal's checklist of matters relevant to exercise of the discretion (see paragraph 22(5)) is not of course intended to be comprehensive or exhaustive but provides an invaluable guide. I would add two observations only.[544]

First, I do not think that 'the seriousness of the offence, which affects defendant, victim and public', listed in paragraph 22(5)(viii) as a matter relevant to the exercise of discretion, is a matter which should be considered. The judge's overriding concern will be to ensure that the trial, if conducted in the absence of the defendant, will be as fair as circumstances permit and lead to a just outcome. These objects are equally important, whether the offence charged be serious or relatively minor.[545]

Secondly, it is generally desirable that a defendant be represented even if he has voluntarily absconded. The task of representing at trial a defendant who is not present, and who may well be out of touch, is of course rendered much more difficult and unsatisfactory . . . But the presence throughout the trial of legal representatives, in receipt of instructions from the client at some earlier stage, and with no object other than to protect the interests of that client, does provide a valuable safeguard against the possibility of error and oversight."[546]

An attempt to bring the case before the European Court of Human Rights proved unsuccessful.[547]

---

[543] [2001] EWCA Crim 168, [2001] Q.B. 862, [22].
[544] [2002] UKHL 5, [2003] 1 A.C. 1, [13].
[545] *ibid.*, [14].
[546] *ibid.*, [15]. See generally Ferguson P.W., "Trial in Absence and Waiver of Human Rights" [2002] Crim.L.R. 554.
[547] *Jones v United Kingdom (Admissibility)* (2003) 37 E.H.R.R. CD269.

14–183   The approach described in the preceding paragraph has been adopted in several subsequent cases.[548] In *Campbell v R.*[549] the Privy Council applied *Jones* in the context of the absence of the defendant from the hearing of the Attorney-General's appeal against the defendant's sentence on the ground that it was unduly lenient.

14–184   The *Practice Direction (Bail: Failure to Surrender)* contains the following observations on trials in the absence of the defendant:

> "A defendant has a right, in general, to be present and to be represented at his trial. However, a defendant may choose not to exercise those rights by voluntarily absenting himself and failing to instruct his lawyers adequately so that they can represent him and, in the case of proceedings before the magistrates' court, there is an express statutory power to hear trials in the defendant's absence: section 11 of the Magistrates' Courts Act 1980. In such circumstances, the court has discretion whether the trial should take place in his/her absence.[550]
> The court must exercise its discretion to proceed in the absence of the defendant with the utmost care and caution. The overriding concern must be to ensure that such a trial is as fair as circumstances permit and leads to a just outcome.[551]
> Due regard should be had to the judgment of Lord Bingham of Cornhill in *R. v Jones (Anthony)* [2003] 1 A.C. 1 in which Lord Bingham identified circumstances to be taken into account before proceeding, which include: the conduct of the defendant, the disadvantage to the defendant, public interest, the effect of any delay and whether the attendance of the defendant could be secured at a later hearing. Other relevant considerations are the seriousness of the offence and likely outcome if the defendant is found guilty. If the defendant is only likely to be fined for a summary offence this can be relevant since the costs that a defendant might otherwise be ordered to pay as a result of an adjournment could be disproportionate. In the case of summary proceedings the fact that there can be an appeal that is a complete rehearing is also relevant, as is the power to reopen the case under section 142 of the Magistrates' Courts Act 1980."[552]

The treatment of the seriousness of the offence as a relevant consideration would appear to contradict the views of Lord Bingham quoted above.

14–185   The power to continue a trial in the absence of the accused must of course be exercised in conformity with the Human Rights Act. The European Court of Human Rights has held that the right of an accused person to be present at the hearing of a criminal charge is fundamental to the fairness of the proceedings.[553] An individual may waive his right to be present by failing to attend, having been given effective notice.[554] Trial *in absentia* may also be permitted where the state has acted diligently, but unsuccessfully, to give an accused effective notice of the

---

[548] See *R. v Singh* [2003] EWCA Crim 3712; *R. v Liburd* [2005] EWCA Crim 951; *R. v Thompson* [2005] EWCA Crim 2032; *R. (Webb,Johnson) v DPP* [2005] EWHC 3123 (Admin); *R. v O'Hare* [2006] EWCA Crim 471; *R. v Williams* [2006] EWCA Crim 1457; *R. v Smith* [2006] EWCA Crim 2307.
[549] [2006] U.K.P.C. 56.
[550] [2004] 1 W.L.R. 589, [I.13.17].
[551] *ibid.*, [I.13.18].
[552] *ibid.*, [I.13.19].
[553] *Ekbatani v Sweden* (1988) 13 E.H.R.R. 504 (para.25).
[554] *C v Italy* (1988) 56 D.R. 40 at 59–60.

hearing.[555] Where a court proceeds in the accused's absence, the hearing must be "attended by minimum safeguards commensurate to its importance".[556] In particular, the absent individual must be afforded effective legal representation.[557]

In *Colozza v Italy*[558] the Court held that a defendant who absconds with the **14–186** intention of evading justice has not waived his right to be present at the hearing, since the right to a fair trial is absolute and applies to an accused person who has absconded as much as it does to any other defendant who has not expressly waived the right to be present. Accordingly, the accused must be able to obtain "a fresh determination of the merits of the charge" when he later learns of the proceedings which took place in his absence.[559] This suggests that the fact that a trial has proceeded *in absentia* should, in itself, be a ground for quashing a conviction and ordering a retrial.[560]

Exceptionally, a court may proceed where the accused is absent through illness, **14–187** provided the accused's interests are fully protected.[561] Thus where defendants went on hunger strike, the Commission held that there was no absolute right to be present in all circumstances. The point of Art.6(3)(c) was to ensure that the defence had the opportunity to present its arguments adequately, and this right had been secured because they were able to receive practically unlimited visits from their lawyers.[562]

The right to be present implies not merely physical presence, but the ability to **14–188** hear and follow the proceedings,[563] to understand the evidence and argument, to instruct lawyers, and to give evidence.[564] The state is under an obligation to give

---

[555] *Colozza v Italy* (1985) 7 E.H.R.R. 516 (paras 28–29); *Rubinat v Italy* (1985) 7 E.H.R.R. 512. This was not established in *FCB v Italy* (1992) 14 E.H.R.R. 909.

[556] *Poitrimol v France* (1994) 18 E.H.R.R. 130 (para.31).

[557] *Lala v Netherlands* (1994) 18 F.H.R.R. 586; *Pelladoah v Netherlands* (1994) 19 E.H.R.R. 81; *Van Geyseghem v Belgium* Judgment January 21, 1999; *Karatas v France* (2002) 35 E.H.R.R. 37 (p.1253).

[558] (1985) 7 E.H.R.R. 516 at para.28. The issue was actually left open by the court because the applicant in *Colozza* had not absconded but had simply left his last known address. The applicant in *Rubinat v Italy*, a case that was originally joined with *Colozza*, had absconded deliberately, and had taken no part in proceedings. The Commission's finding of a violation in *Rubinat* was unanimous, because the Italian courts had refused to re-open the proceedings: (1985) 7 E.H.R.R. 512 at para.13.

[559] *Colozza v Italy* (1985) 7 E.H.R.R. 516 (paras 28–29); *Rubinat v Italy* (1985) 7 E.H.R.R. 512.

[560] It should be noted that the Ontario Court of Appeal has taken a similar view to that of the English courts, holding in *Czuczman* (1986) 49 C.R. (3d) 385 that a defendant who absconds during the trial may be deemed to have waived the right to be present during the trial, a right stemming from s.7 of the Charter. This decision has been strongly criticised (see Stuart D., *Charter Justice in Canadian Criminal Law* (2nd edn, 1996), p.168) on the ground that it gives insufficient weight to the Charter right—a critique in line with the Strasbourg jurisprudence.

[561] *Ensslin, Baader and Raspe v Federal Republic of Germany* (1978) 14 D.R. 64 at 115–116 (hunger strike (para.22)).

[562] *Ensslin, Baader and Raspe v Germany* (1978) 14 D.R. 64.

[563] *Stanford v United Kingdom* (1994) Series A No.282-A (No violation where a defendant who was hard of hearing had failed to raise objection at the appropriate time).

[564] *T and V. v United Kingdom* (2000) 30 E.H.R.R. 121.

the accused adequate notice of a hearing and, if he is in custody, to take steps to secure his attendance.[565]

14–189   In *R. v Preston*[566] the trial judge conducted a number of hearings *in camera* concerning the products of telephone interceptions under the Interception of Communications Act 1985. The hearings took place in the presence of counsel but in the absence of the accused and their solicitors. The judge directed that counsel must not inform the accused of what had occurred. The House of Lords heavily criticised the procedure which the judge had adopted but dismissed the appeal. The appellants brought a complaint to the Commission, alleging *inter alia* that their exclusion from parts of the trial constituted a violation of Art.6. In rejecting the complaint the Commission noted that the applicants had been excluded for 30 hours during a trial lasting three and a half months, and that they were legally represented during their absence (although their counsel were ordered not to divulge to them what was said).[567] The Commission was not satisfied that the exclusion of the applicants was strictly necessary but found no violation of Art.6, relying in particular on the fact that the hearings *in camera* concerned matters of law, and the jury were not present.

14–190   The right of an absent appellant to be legally represented on appeal is considered in detail in Ch.17. In brief, however, the Court has held that:

> "The right of everyone charged with a criminal offence to be effectively defended by a lawyer is one of the basic features of a fair trial. An accused does not lose that right merely on account of not attending a court hearing. Even if the legislature had to be able to discourage unjustified absences, it may not penalise them by creating exceptions to the right to legal assistance."[568]

By refusing counsel leave to make submissions on the applicant's behalf, the Court of Cassation had violated her right under Arts 6(1) and 6(3)(c). Similarly, in *Omar v France*[569] the Court held that a rule which required an appellant in criminal proceedings to surrender to custody, in accordance with an order made by a lower court, before he could be heard on appeal against the decision, was incompatible with the right of access to court. In the light of this decision, the Court of Appeal has held that it is no longer appropriate to treat as ineffective an application for leave to appeal made on behalf of a defendant who has absconded.[570]

J. TRIAL OF JUVENILES IN THE CROWN COURT

14–191   This topic was discussed fully in Ch.11 above, at 11–09 to 11–17.

---

[565] *Goddi v Italy* (1984) 6 E.H.R.R. 457.
[566] [1994] 2 A.C. 130.
[567] *Preston and ors v United Kingdom* [1997] E.H.R.L.R. 695 at 698.
[568] *Van Geyseghem v Belgium* Judgment January 21, 1999.
[569] (2000) 29 E.H.R.R. 210.
[570] *R. v Charles, R. v Tucker, The Times*, February 20, 2001.

CHAPTER 15

CRIMINAL EVIDENCE

A. THE EVALUATION OF EVIDENCE

In general, the *assessment* of evidence is a matter for the domestic courts, and the **15–01** European Court of Human Rights will not substitute its own view of the facts for an assessment that has been fairly reached by an impartial and independent tribunal. This is an important application of the court's "fourth instance" doctrine,[1] under which recourse to Strasbourg is characterised as a *review* of domestic practice for compliance with the Convention, rather than an *appeal* against the national courts' decisions. Thus, the European Court of Human Rights will only interfere with a conclusion of fact where there is an indication that the domestic courts have drawn unfair or arbitrary conclusions from the evidence before them.[2] As the Commission observed in *Stewart v United Kingdom*[3]:

> "[T]he national judge, unlike the Commission, has had the benefit of listening to the witnesses at first hand and assessing the credibility and probative value of their testimony after careful consideration. Accordingly, in the absence of any new evidence having been brought before the Commission and of any indications that the trial judge incorrectly evaluated the evidence before him, the Commission must base its examination of the Convention issues before it on the facts as established by the national courts."

---

[1] See para.2–114 above.
[2] *Schenk v Switzerland* (1991) 13 E.H.R.R. 242; *Edwards v United Kingdom* (1993) 15 E.H.R.R. 417 at para.34; *Van Mechelen v Netherlands* (1998) 25 E.H.R.R. 647 at para.50.
[3] (1984) 39 D.R. 162 at 168.

15–02   In *IJL, GMR and AKP v United Kingdom*[4] the applicants complained that there had been improper collusion between Inspectors of the Department of Trade and Industry and police officers investigating their involvement in an alleged share support scheme, a complaint which had previously been rejected by the Court of Appeal. The Court held that "when faced with a dispute over facts it must turn in the first place to the facts as found by the domestic authorities". After referring to the Court of Appeal's conclusion on the issue, the judgment continued:

> "The Court, for its part must give due weight to this finding, reached as it was after lengthy adversarial argument and in the light of all the materials assembled by the applicants' lawyers in support of their case. On the basis of its own careful examination of these materials the Court does not consider that the Court of Appeal's assessment of the evidence or establishment of the facts can be impeached on the ground that they were manifestly unreasonable or in any other way arbitrary."

15–03   However, in an exceptional case the Court will be prepared to assess the weight of the evidence before a national court in determining whether a trial was fair. In *Barbera, Messegue and Jabardo v Spain*[5] the applicants were convicted of serious terrorist offences allegedly committed on behalf of a Catalan separatist organisation. The defendants alleged that their confessions had been obtained through torture. However they were not permitted to give evidence orally to this effect; their evidence was taken by letters rogatory. The allegation of torture was rejected by the domestic courts. In finding a violation of Art.6, the Court noted that the defendants had allegedly confessed after a long period of incommunicado detention, and expressed "reservations" about the confession evidence and the manner in which it had been considered.[6] The Court concluded that "very important pieces of evidence were not adequately adduced and discussed at the trial in the applicants' presence and under the watchful eye of the public."[7]

15–04   Over the years there have been numerous attempts, usually by unrepresented applicants, to persuade the Commission to examine the evidence which had led to a conviction. These attempts have almost all been unsuccessful. In one case[8] the applicant had been convicted of murder by a 10 to two majority verdict on visual identification by a single eyewitness. The applicant complained that his conviction on identification alone was unfair, and that an important alibi witness had not been called in his defence. The Commission appeared to take the view that visual identification evidence does call for special caution, but nevertheless rejected the application as manifestly ill-founded on the ground that the judge had adequately directed the jury on the issue:

> "The case before the court was by no means simple as is shown by the fact that the jury reached its verdict of guilty by a majority decision of 10 to 2. The crucial issue in the evidence was the identification of the applicant by one witness at the material time and place, but the judge in his summing up took trouble to explain to the jury the problems which arose thereby and the difficulties of their decision on this evidence. Furthermore, one of the relevant witnesses whom the applicant says should have been called to prove

---

[4] (2000) 33 E.H.R.R. 255.
[5] (1989) 11 E.H.R.R. 360.
[6] *ibid.*, at para.87.
[7] *ibid.*, at para.89.
[8] Application No.6208/73 (1975, unpublished), 2 Dig. 389.

an alibi had made a statement which was in itself inconclusive as to the critical periods of time and was not even mentioned by the applicant in his own testimony before the court of first instance."

B. RULES OF ADMISSIBILITY

The Convention does not lay down a comprehensive set of rules for the admissi-   **15–05**
bility of evidence, which is primarily a matter for regulation through national law. The Court's function is to determine whether the proceedings in question, taken as a whole, were fair, and whether the rights of the defence under Art.6 were adequately respected.[9] Thus, in a major entrapment case, the Court stated that it was "essential" to "examine the *procedure* whereby the plea of entrapment was determined, to ensure that the rights of the defence were adequately protected."[10] Applying this approach, the Court and the Commission have considered the application of Art.6 in the context of evidence which has been obtained unlawfully or in breach of Convention rights,[11] evidence obtained by ill-treatment in custody,[12] or by powers of compulsory questioning,[13] the drawing of adverse inferences from a defendant's silence under police questioning where there are insufficient safeguards against unfairness,[14] the admission of evidence obtained by entrapment,[15] the evidence of accomplices who have been offered immunity from prosecution, or undercover agents placed in a prison to eavesdrop on conversations involving the accused,[16] the admission of a co-defendant's plea of guilty pursuant to s.74 of the Police and Criminal Evidence Act 1984, the admission of anonymous witnesses,[17] or important hearsay evidence without an opportunity to cross-examine,[18] and the refusal to call a witness central to the defence case.[19] These issues are considered in detail in the sections which follow.

C. UNLAWFULLY OBTAINED EVIDENCE

I. The Strasbourg Caselaw

Article 6 and Art.13, taken together, have been held to imply that there must be   **15–06**
an effective procedure during a criminal trial by which to challenge the admissibility of evidence which has been obtained unlawfully or in breach of the

---

[9] *Miailhe v France (No.2)* (1997) 23 E.H.R.R. 491, para.43.
[10] *Edwards and Lewis v United Kingdom* [2003] Crim.L.R. 891, Chamber judgment of July 22, 2003, para.51. Affirmed by the Grand Chamber, (2005) 40 E.H.R.R. 24.
[11] See para.15–06 below.
[12] See para.15–32 below.
[13] See para.15–79 below.
[14] See para.15–101 *et seq.* below.
[15] See para.15–33 below.
[16] *X v Federal Republic of Germany* Application No.12127/86 (1989) 11 E.H.R.R. 84.
[17] See para.15–139 below.
[18] *Unterpertinger v Austria* (1991) 13 E.H.R.R. 175: see Art.6(3)(d) at paras 15–123 *et seq.* below. As to hearsay evidence relied upon by the defence, see para.15–144 below.
[19] See para.15–150 below.

Convention.[20] Where a breach of domestic law is relied upon, the existence of the *voir dire* procedure has been held to be sufficient to comply with this procedural obligation,[21] and the same will generally be true of an application to exclude evidence under ss.76 and 78 of the Police and Criminal Evidence Act 1984. However, where it is alleged that the evidence was obtained in breach of a Convention right, these procedures will only afford an effective remedy if that breach is capable in practice of affording a ground for the exclusion of the evidence.[22]

15–07 The admission of evidence obtained in breach of Art.3 will inevitably violate Art.6.[23] In *Austria v Italy*[24] the Commission held that where "the accused, during the preliminary investigation, has been subjected to any maltreatment with the aim of extracting a confession from him", Art.6(2) will be violated "if the Court subsequently accepted as evidence any admissions extorted in this manner." The principle has now been confirmed by the Grand Chamber in *Jalloh v Germany*,[25] holding that the measures taken against the applicant (four police officers holding him down and forcibly administering emetics so as to make him regurgitate a packet of drugs he had swallowed) amounting to inhuman and degrading conduct under Art.3 to such a degree as to render a fair trial impossible under Art.6. However, there was a difference of emphasis in the judgments. The judgment of the majority held that the use of evidence obtained by torture would always render the trial unfair, but left open the broader question:

> " 'It cannot be excluded that on the facts of a particular case the use of evidence obtained by intentional acts of ill-treatment not amounting to torture will render the trial against the victim unfair irrespective of the seriousness of the offence allegedly committed, the weight attached to the evidence and the opportunities which the victim had to challenge its admission and use at his trial.'
>
> 'In the present case, the general question whether the use of evidence obtained by an act qualified as inhuman and degrading treatment automatically renders a trial unfair can be left open.' "[26]

The majority held that relevant factors, in holding that the trial was unfair in this case because of the violation of Art.3, included the fact that this was the decisive

---

[20] *Schenk v Switzerland* (1991) 13 E.H.R.R. 242, para.47; *Khan v United Kingdom* (2000) 31 E.H.R.R. 45.

[21] *G v United Kingdom* (1983) 35 D.R. 75, where the applicant's case was that the police had refused to allow him to see his solicitor until he signed a confession. The Commission held that the trial was not unfair, since he had been able to ventilate his concerns at the *voir dire* and the judge had considered them before making an adverse ruling.

[22] In *R. v Sultan Khan* [1997] A.C. 558, the House of Lords held that the opportunity to rely on the Convention in an application under s.78 complied with the duty to provide an effective domestic remedy under Art.13 of the Convention. The European Court of Human Rights disagreed, holding that since there was no legally enforceable right to privacy in English law prior to the enactment of the Human Rights Act 1998, s.78 was incapable of meeting the requirements of Art.13: see paras 15–12 and 15–26 below.

[23] As to the relationship between this principle and the duty to exclude evidence obtained by oppression under s.76 of the Police and Criminal Evidence Act 1984, see para.15–32 below.

[24] (1961) 4 Y.B. 116 at 784; 2 Digest 722. See also *Barbera, Messegue and Jabardo v Spain* (1989) 11 E.H.R.R. 360. *Cf. Ferrantelli and Santangelo v Italy* (1997) 23 E.H.R.R. 288, paras 49–50.

[25] App.No.54810/00, judgment of July 11, 2006.

[26] *Ibid*, paras 106–107.

evidence against the applicant, and that the crime charged was merely street dealing in drugs. In his concurring opinion, Judge Bratza argues that fidelity to the Convention as a whole would require the Court to go further than this:

"The use of evidence obtained by treatment violating the fundamental valuies enshrined in Article 3 appears to me to offend against the whole concept of a fair trial, even if the admission of such evidence is not—as it was in the present case—decisive in securing a conviction. As in the case of the use of coerced confessions, it is the offensiveness to civilised values of fairness and the detrimental effect on the integrity of the judicial process, as much as the unreliabillity of any evidence which may be obtained, which lies at the heart of the objection to its use.

It is true that the treatment to which the appellant was subjected has been found to be inhuman and degrading rather than torture . . . However, not only is the borderline between the various forms of ill-treatment neither immutable nor capable of precise definition, as the Court has previously recognised, but the fairness of the judicial process is in my view irreparably damaged in any case where evidence is admitted which has been obtained by the authorities of the State concerned in violation of the prohibition in Article 3."[27]

We have seen that the majority was not prepared to go so far as to hold that every breach of Art.3 should render evidence inadmissible at a trial, because it would inevitably lead to an unfair trial under Art.6, but Judge Bratza's view may be thought more persuasive.[28]

As we shall see, the court has held that the admission of evidence obtained by **15–08** entrapment may violate Art.6,[29] and the same is true of evidence obtained by powers of compulsory questioning, enforceable by criminal proceedings in default.[30] However, it does not necessarily follow that the admission of evidence obtained in breach of other Convention rights, such as Art.8, will render the trial unfair. Whether or not it does so will depend on the circumstances of the case.[31]

In *Scheichelbauer v Austria*[32] the Commission appeared to establish the basis for an exclusionary rule, when it observed that in a legal system based on respect for the individual, a suspect can legitimately demand that the law should give him suitable protection against interference with other substantive rights in the evidence-collection process. On the facts of that case, however, the Commission found no violation, emphasising that the recording of a telephone intercept was shown to be an accurate record of the conversation, and concluding that the trial as a whole was not unfair.

In *Schenk v Switzerland*,[33] the Court adopted an altogether stricter line on the **15–09** issue. The Swiss government had conceded that intercept evidence used against

---

[27] *Ibid.*, Concurring Opinion of Judge Bratza.
[28] *Cf.* the suggestion of Lord Bingham, below, para.15–24.
[29] See para.15–37 below.
[30] See para.15–74 below.
[31] *Schenk v Switzerland* (1991) 13 E.H.R.R. 242, paras 46–48; *X v Federal Republic of Germany* (1989) 11 E.H.R.R. 84; *Khan v United Kingdom* (2000) 31 E.H.R.R. 45.
[32] (1970) 14 Y.B. 902.
[33] (1991) 13 E.H.R.R. 242.

the applicant in a trial for attempted incitement to murder had been obtained without the requisite authority, and therefore both unlawfully in domestic law and in contravention of Art.8 of the Convention. The Court found no violation of Art.6:

> "While Article 6 of the Convention guarantees the right to a fair trial, it does not lay down any rules on the admissibility of evidence as such, which is therefore primarily a matter for regulation under national law. The Court cannot therefore exclude as a matter of principle and in the abstract that unlawfully obtained evidence of the present kind may be admissible. It has only to ascertain whether Mr Schenk's trial as a whole was fair. Like the Commission it notes first of all that the rights of the defence were not disregarded. The applicant was not unaware that the recording complained of was unlawful because it had not been ordered by a competent judge. He had the opportunity—which he took—of challenging its authenticity and opposing its use . . . The fact that his attempts were unsuccessful makes no difference . . . The Court also attaches weight to the fact that the recording of the telephone conversation was not the only evidence on which the conviction was based . . . . [The Rolle Criminal Court] carefully stated in several passages of its judgment that it relied on evidence other than the recording but which corroborated the reasons based on the recording for concluding that Mr Schenk was guilty . . . It emerges clearly from [the judgment] that the criminal court took account of a combination of evidential elements before reaching its opinion."[34]

15–10 The court's judgment in *Schenk* appeared to place considerable emphasis on the existence of other evidence implicating the accused.[35] However, in *Khan v United Kingdom*[36] the Court held that the admission of evidence obtained by means of a listening device in breach of Art.8 did not render the proceedings unfair, despite the fact that the prosecution case rested entirely on the disputed tape recording. The Court held that where unlawfully obtained evidence was relied upon to secure a conviction, the compatibility of the proceedings with Art.6 would depend upon an examination of the nature of the unlawful activity alleged and, if it involved a violation of another Convention right, the nature of the violation found. The Court noted that the use of a listening device was not unlawful under domestic law since there was, at the time, no legally enforceable right to privacy in English law. The police had acted compatibly with Home Office guidelines on intrusive surveillance and the breach of Art.8 related solely to the absence of a statutory basis for the surveillance. Moreover, the incriminating statements had been made voluntarily and without inducements. Whilst the Court would attach weight to the existence of other evidence implicating the accused, the relevance of independent evidence depended on the circumstances. Where the contested evidence was compelling, and there was no challenge to its reliability, the need for supporting evidence would be correspondingly weaker. The applicant had had the opportunity to challenge both the authenticity and the

---

[34] See also *Smith v United Kingdom* [1997] E.H.R.L.R. 277 where the Commission declared inadmissible a complaint based on the use in evidence of a conversation between the applicant and a disguised security service officer, on the ground that it did not go to the heart of the matter and as such was to be regarded as a ruse in the public interest.

[35] This is in line with the court's decisions on the admission of hearsay evidence without an opportunity for cross-examination (see para.15–121 *et seq.* below) and with the court's approach to entrapment evidence (see para.15–33 below).

[36] (2001) 31 E.H.R.R. 1016.

admissibility of the tape recording. After it was ruled admissible he pleaded guilty. At each stage of the domestic proceedings the courts had assessed the impact of the admission of the evidence on the fairness of the proceedings and if they had concluded that its admission would have led to substantive unfairness, they would have had a discretion to exclude it. In those circumstances, the proceedings as a whole were fair.

In a strongly worded dissenting judgment, Judge Loucaides expressed the argu-   **15-11**
ment in favour of an exclusionary rule thus:

> "This is the first case which comes before the Court where the only evidence against an accused in a criminal case which also led to his conviction, was evidence obtained in a manner contrary to Article 8 of the Convention . . . I cannot accept that a trial can be 'fair', as required by Article 6, if a person's guilt for any offence is established through evidence obtained in breach of the human rights guaranteed by the Convention . . . I do not think one can speak of a 'fair' trial if it is conducted in breach of the law . . . If violating Article 8 can be accepted as 'fair' then I cannot see how the police can be effectively deterred from repeating their impermissible conduct . . . Breaking the law, in order to enforce it, is a contradiction in terms and an absurd proposition."

Despite its principal finding that the proceedings did not involve a violation of   **15-12**
Art.6, the majority of the Court in *Khan* held that Art.13 of the Convention required an effective remedy before a national authority for the alleged violation of Art.8. In the Court's view, the discretion to exclude evidence under s.78 of the Police and Criminal Evidence Act 1984 was inadequate to meet this requirement because, prior to the enactment of the Human Rights Act 1998 there was no legally enforceable right to privacy in English law. The national courts therefore lacked the necessary jurisdiction to rule on the substance of the applicant's Art.8 complaint, or to grant appropriate relief if the complaint was well-founded. There had accordingly been a violation of Art.13. The implications of this finding for English law were considered by the House of Lords in *R. v P.*[37] On one view, the violation of Art.13 in *Khan* could be taken to support the proposition that a breach of Art.8 should now be remediable through the exclusion of evidence, since the Human Rights Act has introduced a legally enforceable right to privacy in English law. This reading of the judgment was however rejected by Lord Hobhouse, in the leading speech in *P*. In his view, the European Court's decision in *Khan* that there had been a violation of Art.13 confirmed the existing position in English law that the power to exclude evidence under s.78 was concerned with the fairness of the trial and not with providing a remedy for a breach of Art.8. If the evidence could be admitted in a manner consistent with Art.6, then there was no basis for its exclusion in order to afford a remedy for a breach of Art.8. The criterion to be applied was the criterion of fairness and the Human Rights Act did not require s.78 to be read as affording any broader remedial jurisdiction:

> "[T]he ECHR decision that any remedy for a breach of Article 8 lies outside the scope of the criminal trial and that Article 13 does not require a remedy for a breach of Article to be given within that trial shows that their Lordships [in *R. v. Sultan Khan* [1997] A.C. 558] were right to say that a breach of Article 8 did not require the exclusion of

---

[37] [2002] 1 A.C. 146, (HL).

evidence. Such an exclusion, if any, would have to come about because of the application of Article 6 and section 78."

15–13   The Court revisited the relationship between Art.6 and a breach of Art.8 in *PG and JH v United Kingdom*.[38] The Court found that the surveillance methods had violated Art.8 and, indeed, that the case had "strong similarities to that of *Khan*." The Court went on to state that this case was stronger than *Khan* because there was other evidence tending to confirm the applicants' involvement, a point that serves to emphasise that *Khan* constitutes a departure from the Court's general principle that a conviction should not be based solely or mainly on evidence obtained through a breach of another Convention right. The reason for finding no violation of Art.6 here was the same as in the *Schenk* and *Khan* cases, namely that the applicants "had ample opportunity to challenge both the authenticity and the use of the recordings."[39] As in *Khan*, the majority's judgment was followed by a sharp dissent, this time from Judge Tulkens. She pointed out that the Court has declared many times that "the Convention must be interpreted as a coherent whole", and she argued that "it is the Court's very duty, where the taking of evidence is concerned, to ensure that the commitments entered into under the Convention are honoured by Contracting States." Associating herself with the dissenting opinion of Judge Loucaides in *Khan*, she concluded by asking:

> "Will there come a point at which the majority's reasoning will be applied where the evidence has been obtained in breach of other provisions of the Convention, such as Article 3 for example? Where and how should the line be drawn? According to which hierarchy in the guaranteed rights?"

The majority has yet to confront the points made by the two judges who dissented in these cases.[40]

15–14   The admission of evidence obtained by methods contrary to Art.8 was held to amount to a breach of Art.6 in *Allan v United Kingdom*,[41] but the important difference was that the unlawful recording was not simply of a spontaneous conversation but of a conversation manipulated by a police informer (H) who had been put in a cell with the applicant and told to "push him for what you can." The Court found that the statements:

> "were induced by the persistent questioning of H, who, at the instance of the police, channelled their conversations into discussions of the murder in circumstances which can be regarded as the functional equivalent of interrogation, without any of the safeguards which would attach to a formal police interview . . . In those circumstances, the information gained by the use of H in this way may be regarded as having been obtained in defiance of the will of the applicant and its use at trial impinged on the applicant's right to silence and privilege against self-incrimination."[42]

---

[38] [2002] Crim.L.R. 308, judgment of September 25, 2001.
[39] *Ibid*, para.79.
[40] The admissibility decision in *Chalkley v United Kingdom* [2003] Crim.L.R. 51 applied the majority view again.
[41] (2002) 36 E.H.R.R. 143.
[42] *Ibid*, para.52.

In effect, therefore, the case was treated as involving a direct violation of an Art.6 right.

II. Comparative Approaches

The courts in New Zealand developed a *prima facie* exclusionary rule where   **15–15** evidence had been obtained in breach of the Bill of Rights Act.[43] In *Simpson v Attorney-General (Baigent's Case)*[44] Hardie Boys J. said:

> "The New Zealand Bill of Rights Act, unless it is to be no more than an empty statement, is a commitment by the Crown that those who in the three branches of government exercise its functions, powers and duties will observe the rights that the Bill affirms. It is, I consider, implicit in that commitment, indeed essential to its worth, that the Courts are not only to observe the Bill in the discharge of their own duties, but are able to grant appropriate and effective remedies where rights have been infringed . . . In the limited range of cases that have thus far come before it, this Court has been consistent in the view that the terms of the Covenant and the terms of the Bill of Rights Act itself require a rights-centred response to infringements. That is not to exclude other objectives: to ensure compliance in the future, and to secure the wider public interest. But the primary focus has been on providing an appropriate remedy to a person whose rights have been infringed . . . Thus, the Courts have responded to breaches of [the Bill of Rights Act] by adopting a rule of *prima facie* exclusion of evidence obtained in consequence of the breach. This has certainly had the effect of securing general recognition by law enforcement authorities of the rights affirmed by those sections. And while there are doubtless those who believe that this has favoured criminals to the detriment of the public interest, it may also have advanced that interest in other ways by emphasising the importance of what is often taken for granted, and by demonstrating that the Courts will not be party to breaches, but will insist on preserving the integrity of the administration of justice."[45]

Similarly, in *Te Kira*[46] Sir Robin Cooke P. observed that: **15–16**

> "In affirming certain rights and freedoms the New Zealand Bill of Rights Act does not merely repeat the old law. In so far as the rights and freedoms concerned coincide with the old law, the legislature has given them an added emphasis. It would be inconsistent with the concept of a Bill of Rights to relegate them to be matters to be given some weight in the exercise of judicial discretion."

Subsequently, however, the New Zealand courts began to dilute this approach,   **15–17** and ulitmately in *Shaheed*[47] a seven-member Court of Appeal replaced the *prima facie* exclusionary rule with a broad balancing approach to admissibility. A majority of the court aligned itself with the position taken by the Privy Council in *Allie Mohammed v State*,[48] declaring that:

---

[43] *Simpson v Attorney-General* [1994] 3 N.Z.L.R. 667; *R. v H* [1994] 2 N.Z.L.R. 143; *R. v Goodwin* [1993] 2 N.Z.L.R. 153 at 191–194.

[44] [1994] 3 N.Z.L.R. 667.

[45] At 702–703.

[46] [1993] 3 N.Z.L.R. 257 at 262.

[47] [2002] 2 N.Z.L.R. 377, on which see J. Ip, "The End of the Prima Facie Exclusionary Rule" (2002) 9 *Auckland University Law Review* 1016; Mahoney R., "Abolition of New Zealand's Prima Facie Exclusionary Rule", [2003] Crim.L.R. 607. See also *R. v Pou* [2002] 3 N.Z.L.R. 637.

[48] [1999] 2 A.C. 111; below, para.15–28.

"the proper approach is to conduct a balancing exercise in which the fact that there has been a breach of the accused's guaranteed right is a very important but not necessarily determinative factor. The breach of a right would be given considerable weight (the Privy Council in *Mohammed* called it 'a cogent factor militating in favour of exclusion'). But it might, in the end, be held to be outweighed by the accumulation of other factors."[49]

Evidence obtained through a breach of the Bill of Rights Act may be admitted nonetheless if, for example, there was insufficient causal link between the breach and the obtaining of the evidence,[50] where the defendant was aware of the right but waived it,[51] where it is inevitable that the evidence would have been discovered apart from the violation of the right,[52] or where the breach was trivial or technical.[53]

15–18 In Canada, the exclusion of evidence obtained in breach of the Canadian Charter of Rights and Freedoms 1982 is expressly provided for.[54] Section 24(1) provides that a person whose rights or freedoms have been infringed may apply to a court for a remedy. Section 24(2) provides:

"Where, in proceedings under subsection (1) a court concludes that evidence was obtained in a manner that infringed or denied any rights or freedoms guaranteed by this Charter, the evidence shall be excluded if it is established that, having regard to all the circumstances, the admission of it in the proceedings would bring the administration of justice into disrepute."

15–19 This creates an exclusionary rule, rather than a discretion, but the operation of the rule depends on a finding that admission of the evidence would "bring the administration of justice into disrepute." This rather open-ended formulation has been refined in subsequent decisions. In *Stillman*[55] the Supreme Court held that, for these purposes, evidence could be classified either as "conscriptive" (where the accused has been compelled to incriminate himself orally or by the giving of bodily samples) or as "non-conscriptive" (where the evidence was obtained without the participation of the accused). The admission of conscriptive evidence obtained in breach of the Charter would generally be taken to render the trial

---

[49] [2002] 2 N.Z.L.R. 377, at para.144.

[50] *Grant* (1992) 8 C.R.N.Z. 483.

[51] *Wojcik* (1994) 11 C.R.N.Z. 463.

[52] *Butcher* [1992] 2 N.Z.L.R. 257; *cf. H* [1994] 2 N.Z.L.R. 143, where Richardson J. (at 150) argued against this exception on the ground that it "would encourage warrantless searches and seizures" and might therefore undermine the very purpose of the Bill of Rights.

[53] E.g. *Goodwin* [1993] 2 N.Z.L.R. 153, *per* Cooke P. at 171.

[54] For brief discussion, see Mirfield P., *Silence, Confessions and Improperly Obtained Evidence* (1997), pp.365–370; for fuller treatment, see Stuart D.R., *Charter Rights in Canadian Criminal Law* (2nd edn, 1996), Ch.24.

[55] (1996) 113 C.C.C. (3d) 321; this decision was applied in, for example, *Law* [2002] 1 S.C.R. 227, *Fliss* [2002] 1 S.C.R. 535 and *Buhay* [2003] 1 S.C.R. 631. See generally Cory P., "General Principles of *Charter* Exclusion (Exclusion of Conscriptive and Non-Conscriptive Evidence)" (1998) 47 *UNB Law Journal* 229; Delaney W. D., "Exclusion of Evidence under the *Charter: Stillman v The Queen*" (1997) 76 *Canadian Bar Review* 521; Stuart D., "*Buhay*: No Automatic Inclusionary Rule under Section 24(2) When Evidence is Non-Conscripted and Essential to Crown's Case" (2003) 10 *Criminal Reports (6th)* 233; D. Stuart, "*Stillman*: Limiting Search Incident to Arrest, Consent Searches and Refining the Section 24(2) Test" (1997) 5 *Criminal Reports (5th)* 99.

unfair, unless the evidence could have been discovered by other means. So far as "non-conscriptive" evidence is concerned, at least three factors have been identified as relevant in deciding whether admission would bring the administration of justice into disrepute. First, the court should ask whether the breach of the Charter was serious (which depends on "the deliberate or non-deliberate nature of the violation by the authorities, circumstances of urgency and necessity, and other aggravating or mitigating factors"[56]). Secondly, the court should ask whether other investigatory techniques, compatible with the Charter, could have been used. Thirdly, the nature of the breach will be relevant. If the violation of the defendant's right was relatively minor compared with the seriousness of the offence, then its admission would be less likely to bring the administration of justice into disrepute.[57] The relevance of good or bad faith on the part of law enforcement officers has been narrowly circumscribed in Canada. Thus, in *Elshaw*[58] Iacobucci J. held that:

> "[T]he bad faith of the police may strengthen the case for exclusion because . . . it may tend to show a 'blatant disregard for the Charter.' However, the good faith of the police will not strengthen the case for admission to cure an unfair trial. The fact that the police thought they were acting reasonably is cold comfort to an accused if their actions result in a violation of his or her right to fair criminal process."

The United States jurisprudence on unlawfully obtained evidence has, in the past, **15–20** tended towards an absolute exclusionary rule—the so-called "fruit of the poisoned tree" doctrine—although a measure of flexibility has been introduced in recent years.[59] The Fourth Amendment to the United States Constitution establishes the right not to be subjected to an unlawful search or seizure. In the landmark decision of *Mapp v Ohio*[60] the Supreme Court declared that evidence obtained in breach of this provision should be excluded automatically from the trial. Subsequent decisions have supported this rule for its deterrent effect on the police, but have nevertheless recognised a "good faith" exception where, for example, a search warrant is invalid because of some error by the issuing authority—an error which *ex hypothesi* is unlikely to be relevant to the rationale of deterring police misconduct.[61] The other principal United States rule flows from the Fifth Amendment privilege against self-incrimination. The right to counsel, recognized in *Miranda v Arizona*,[62] is supported by a rule of exclusion

---

[56] *Elshaw* [1991] 3 S.C.R. 24, *per* Iacobucci J. at 39–40.

[57] *Collins* [1987] 1 S.C.R. 265.

[58] [1991] 3 S.C.R. 24 at 43. This was a case where the accused had been questioned by an officer in the police van immediately after arrest, at which stage he made admissions. On arrival at the police station he was charged and told of his right to a lawyer, and no subsequent admissions were made. The Supreme Court held that the violation of his Charter right to a lawyer before being questioned was such as to adversely affect the fairness of the trial and bring the administration of justice into disrepute.

[59] For an accessible and thoughtful discussion, see Mirfield P., *Silence, Confessions and Improperly Obtained Evidence* (1997), pp.319–339.

[60] 367 US 643 (1961); in *Pennsylvania Board of Probation and Parole v Scott* 524 US 357 (1998) the Supreme Court confirmed that the exclusionary rule is not a constitutional principle, but rather "a judicially created means of deterring illegal searches and seizures."

[61] See the discussion of *United States v Leon* 468 US 897 (1984) and other cases cited by Mirfield, *op. cit.*, pp.322–324.

[62] 384 US 436 (1966); the Supreme Court in *Dickerson v United States* 120 S.Ct. 2326 (2000) declined to overturn *Miranda* and indeed held that it is a constitutional decision.

of evidence obtained in breach. Subsequent Supreme Court decisions have tempered the absolute nature of the exclusionary rule, creating a more finely calibrated approach. In *New York v Quarles*,[63] for example, the Supreme Court held that exclusion of evidence should not follow inexorably when the police asked questions in breach of *Miranda* in a situation in which public safety was at issue.

15–21　　The Supreme Court of Ireland has taken the view that, where evidence has been obtained by intentional breach of a constitutional right, there is a much stronger presumption that the evidence should be excluded than where there has merely been some other unlawful act during the investigation. Thus in *The People (AG) v O'Brien*[64] the Supreme Court held that evidence obtained in "deliberate and conscious" breach of a constitutional right was inadmissible except in "extraordinary excusing circumstances".[65] Among the decisions which followed this approach is *The People (DPP) v Kenny*,[66] where some of the prosecution evidence had been obtained through an unlawful search which violated the defendant's right, under Art.40 of the Constitution, to the inviolability of his dwelling. Finlay C.J. held that evidence obtained through breach of a personal constitutional right "must be excluded" unless the breach was "accidental" or there were other exceptional circumstances affording an excuse. The court held that it was immaterial that the police officer was unaware that the warrant was defective.[67] However, in *People v Balfe*[68] the Court of Criminal Appeal took a less stringent approach, and held that where the police seized evidence in innocent reliance on a defective search warrant, the evidence need not be excluded. The prevailing rationale for exclusion in Ireland is that the courts have a duty "to defend and vindicate" constitutional rights. The Irish courts have thus rejected the deterrent rationale adopted in the United States.

15–22　　The rules and exceptions developed by the courts in these jurisdictions raise questions about the rationale for excluding evidence for breach of a fundamental right. One prominent rationale is often said to be the deterrence of law enforcement officers: if they know that the evidence is likely to be excluded, they will acquire greater respect for the rights of the individuals with whom they deal. This is in one sense a rights-centred rationale, in that it regards respect for rights as the goal and selects deterrence as the means to achieving it. Another prominent rationale is the protective principle, that individuals should not be disadvantaged if one of their declared rights is infringed in the investigation process. This

---

[63] 467 US 649 (1984), discussed by Mirfield, *op. cit.*, pp.335–336.

[64] [1965] I.R. 142.

[65] An approach based on *People v O'Brien* has also been followed in South Africa. Thus, in *S v Motloutsi* [1996] 1 S.A.C.R. 78, the court held that a strict approach to exclusion would be appropriate where there had been a deliberate breach of a constitutional right. In such cases the evidence should only be admitted if "extraordinary excusing circumstances" existed, such as the imminent destruction of vital evidence or the need to rescue a victim in peril, or when the evidence was obtained by "a search incidental to and contemporaneous with a lawful arrest although made without a valid search warrant."

[66] [1990] I.R.L.M. 569.

[67] *Larkin v O'Dea* [1995] 2 I.R.L.M. 1.

[68] [1998] 4 I.R. 50. See further Fennell C., *The Law of Evidence in Ireland* (2nd edn, 2003), Ch.4.

approach aims to vindicate the declared importance of individual rights in constitutions or human rights documents. A further rationale is that it would undermine the integrity of the criminal justice system if a court were to act on evidence obtained unlawfully or through violation of a constitutional right.[69] To proclaim certain rights and then to act on evidence obtained through breaches of those rights is said to be a contradiction in terms and to undermine the rule of law.

Each of the three remedial rationales has its weaknesses,[70] and the courts in New **15–23** Zealand, Canada and the United States have all begun to move in the direction of greater recognition of "the public interest" and "public safety" in recent years. However, it is important to note that in all those jurisdictions the movement amounts to the development of exceptions to what remains an accepted starting point, which is that in principle a violation of a constitutional right ought to be followed by exclusion of the resulting evidence. Where such exceptions are permitted, reliance on "the public interest", or "the interests of the wider community", generally requires careful analysis, including a discussion of whether the protection of individual rights is not itself in the interests of the community and its members.

III. Exclusion of Evidence under the Human Rights Act 1998

In its important decision in *A and Others v Secretary of State for the Home* **15–24** *Department*,[71] the House of Lords held that there was a common law rule rendering any evidence obtained by torture automatically inadmissible. The House had been pressed by the Secretary of State to accept that the evidence should be admissible at trials, and that to reject it would be an affront to certain foreign governments. Lord Bingham responded thus:

> "The English common law has regarded torture and its fruits with abhorrence for over 500 years, and that abhorrence is now shared by over 140 countries which have acceded to the Torture Convention. I am startled, even a little dismayed, at the suggestion (and the acceptance by the Court of Appeal majority) that this deeply-rooted tradition and an international obligation solemnly and explicitly undertaken can be overridden by a statute and a procedural rule which make no mention of torture at all . . . It trivialises the issue before the House to treat it as an argument about the law of evidence. The issue is one of constitutional principle, whether evidence obtained by torturing another human being may lawfully be admitted against a party to proceedings in a British court,

---

[69] This approach has been reflected in a number of English decisions on abuse of process: See *R. v Horseferry Road Magistrates ex parte Bennett* [1994] 1 A.C. 42; *R. v Mullen* [2000] Q.B. 520. cf. *Latif and Shahzad* [1996] 1 W.L.R. 104. As to the appropriateness of abuse of process as a remedy in these circumstances see Choo A., *Abuse of Process and Judicial Stays of Criminal Proceedings* (1993), and Choo A., "Halting Criminal Prosecutions: the Abuse of Process Doctrine Revisited" [1995] Crim.L.R. 864.

[70] For argument, see Mirfield, *op. cit.*, Ch.2, and Ashworth A., "Exploring the Integrity Principle in Evidence and Procedure", in Mirfield P. and Smith R. (eds), *Essays for Colin Tapper* (2003).

[71] [2005] UKHL 71, [2006] 2 A.C. 221. See generally Grief N., "The Exclusion of Foreign Torture Evidence: A Qualified Victory for the Rule of Law" [2006] E.H.R.L.R. 201; N. Rasiah, "*A. v Secretary of State for the Home Department (No.2)*: Occupying the Moral High Ground?" (2006) 69 M.L.R. 995.

irrespective of where, or by whom, or on whose authority the torture was inflicted. To that question I would give a very clear negative answer."[72]

However, Lord Bingham qualified this principle by suggesting that it might be necessary to draw a distinction between evidence obtained by torture, reliance on which would always render a trial unfair contrary to Art.6, and inhuman or degrading treatment, which ranked as a less serious invasion of rights and might not always have that effect.[73] It was noted earlier that, in its subsequent decision in *Jalloh v Germany*, the majority judgment of the Grand Chamber hinted at a similar distinction.[74] As for evidence obtained by other means, special principles apply to evidence obtained through the interception of communications, as will be explained in the next section. Generally, however, English law has not regarded the fact that evidence was obtained illegally as a ground for exclusion in itself.[75] The focus has always been on the effect of the evidence on the fairness of the trial. How, then, should the English courts approach the exercise of their exclusionary discretions, under s.78 of the Police and Criminal Evidence Act 1984, and at common law, under the new constitutional framework established by the Human Rights Act? Section 8 of the Act provides that where a public authority has acted in a manner which is incompatible with a complainant's Convention rights, a court may grant any remedy, within its powers, which it considers "just and appropriate". In the context of a criminal trial, this obviously includes an order for the exclusion of evidence (as well as, in extreme circumstances, an order for the stay of criminal proceedings as an abuse of process).

15–25   In exercising the remedial jurisdiction under s.8 of the Human Rights Act, the Strasbourg approach cannot be transplanted directly into English law. The Court and Commission have always adhered strictly to the "fourth instance" doctrine,[76] when dealing with Art.6 applications, and have been reluctant to disturb the findings of domestic courts so long as the hearing itself was procedurally fair. Consistent with the Court's general approach to the evaluation of evidence,[77] the emphasis is on ensuring that questions concerning the admissibility of unlawfully obtained evidence are addressed effectively *at the national level*. Thus, the Court has required an effective procedure within the trial for examining allegations of illegality, and for excluding evidence obtained unlawfully or in breach of Convention rights.[78] In *Khan v United Kingdom*,[79] as we have seen, the Court found a violation of Art.13 on the ground that—prior to the Human Rights Act—there was no legally enforceable right to privacy in English law. Accordingly a breach of Art.8 was not, in itself, a sufficient basis for the exclusion of evidence under s.78, and there was therefore no effective remedy in national law. Although Art.13 is not amongst the rights specifically incorporated by s.1 of the Human Rights Act, the courts are expected to take the Convention caselaw under Art.13

---

[72] [2006] 2 A.C. 221, at [51], referred to in *Ahmad and Aswat v Government of the United States of America* [2006] EWHC Admin 2927.
[73] *Ibid*, at [53].
[74] Above, para.15–07.
[75] *R. v Sang* [1980] A.C. 402 (HL); *R. v Sultan Khan* [1997] A.C. 558 (HL).
[76] See para.2–114 above.
[77] See paras 15–06 to 15–12 above.
[78] See para.15–08 and para.15–09 above.
[79] [2000] Crim.L.R. 684. See para.15–12 above.

into account when exercising their remedial powers under s.8 of the 1998 Act.[80] For s.8 remedial powers to be exercised in conformity with the Convention, an English court must, as a minimum, have jurisdiction to rule on the alleged violation and to exclude evidence if the violation is well-founded. However, as the House of Lords emphasised in *R. v P*,[81] the dominant consideration in the exercise of this jurisdiction remains the fairness of the proceedings, and their compatibility with Art.6. A breach of Art.8 is not regarded as sufficient, in itself, to require the exclusion of evidence. Depending on the nature of the breach it may nonetheless be an important factor in the court's determination of whether the admission of the evidence would be fair for the purposes of s.78.

English courts have to fulfil their duty under s.6 to act in a way which is **15-26** compatible with Convention rights (unless they are obliged to do otherwise by the terms of incompatible primary legislation which cannot be construed compatibly under s.3). This means that they have to apply the Convention directly to the case before them, and to afford "just and appropriate" remedies where a violation is found on the facts, rather than following the residual or supervisory approach adopted by the Strasbourg institutions. Under s.3, they also have to interpret *and give effect* to s.78 of the Police and Criminal Evidence Act in a manner which is compatible with the Convention rights "so far as it is possible to do so". The open-textured wording of s.78 is plainly capable of being construed in a manner which is compatible with Art.6 jurisprudence. Even before the Act came into force, Lord Nicholls had observed, in *R. v Sultan Khan*,[82] that s.78 and Art.6 are both in effect directed towards the same question:

> "[T]he discretionary powers of the trial judge to exclude evidence march hand in hand with Article 6(1) of the European Convention on Human Rights. Both are concerned to ensure that those facing criminal charges receive a fair hearing. Accordingly, when considering the common law and statutory discretionary powers under English law, the jurisprudence on Article 6 can have a valuable role to play."

In determining whether exclusion of evidence is the "just and appropriate" **15-27** remedy for a breach of Convention rights, there is thus an important distinction to be drawn between two categories of complaint. The first category concerns evidence, the admission of which would breach Art.6. This would apply, for example, to the admission of evidence obtained by ill-treatment in custody[83] or improper entrapment,[84] to the admission of statements or evidence obtained by compulsory questioning powers,[85] and to the admission of certain forms of hearsay evidence.[86] Here, the trial court retains a theoretical power under s.78 to admit the evidence, but it is a power which can, in practice, only be exercised one way. As Lord Nicholls put it in *R. v Sultan Khan*, Art.6 and s.78 "march hand in hand". If the admission of certain evidence would result in a breach of the right to a fair trial, as interpreted in Strasbourg, then the judge, as a public authority,

---

[80] See para.3–81 above.
[81] [2002] 1 A.C. 146, (HL). See further para.15–12 above.
[82] [1997] A.C. 558 at 583.
[83] See para.15–07 (above and para.15–28 below).
[84] See para.15–33 below.
[85] See *Allan v United Kingdom* (above, para.15–14).
[86] See para.15–121 below.

will be acting unlawfully within the meaning of s.6 of the Human Rights Act if he exercises his power under s.78 in favour of admitting the evidence.[87] To quote Sir John Laws, s.78 "will look less like a general discretion (which anyway it is not), and more like a means of vindicating concrete requirements of fairness".[88]

15–28 The second category concerns evidence which has been obtained in breach of a Convention right other than Art.6, such as the right to privacy in Art.8. Here, the position is more subtle, and the trial court has a genuine discretion to examine all the circumstances before ruling under s.78. In accordance with the Court's decision in *Khan v United Kingdom*, the judge will wish to take account of the nature of the unlawful activity alleged, the gravity of the breach of Convention rights, any element of inducement or compulsion, the existence of other evidence implicating the accused, the probative weight of the disputed evidence and its reliability.[89] Breach of a Convention right is inherently more serious than breach of a rule of domestic law, for the simple reason that the right in issue has been accorded the status of a basic or fundamental right, deserving of special protection by the courts. This is the point emphasised in the dissenting judgments of Judges Loucaides and Tulkens in *Khan* and in *PG and JH*, discussed above.[90] At present, such a breach does not necessarily require the exclusion of evidence obtained in consequence, but the constitutional nature of the right should weigh heavily in the "balancing process". This approach appears consistent with the decision of the House of Lords in *R. v P*,[91] where the appellants had argued that evidence obtained by telephone interception according to the law of another jurisdiction should be excluded under s.78 because its admission would involve a breach of Art.6. The House of Lords found no violation of Art.8 in the way the evidence had been obtained or used, and held that under both Art.6 and s.78 of PACE a defendant was entitled, not to the exclusion of the evidence, but to the opportunity to challenge its use in evidence, and to a judicial assessment of the effect of its admission upon the fairness of the proceedings. This may be compared to the somewhat stronger approach of Lord Steyn, for the Privy Council, in *Allie Mohammed v The State*.[92] Here the appellant had unsuccessfully challenged the admissibility of a statement made to the police on the ground that he had been denied his constitutional right to consult with a solicitor in the police station. Relying on the now abandoned New Zealand approach of *prima facie* exclusion of evidence obtained in breach of constitutional rights, the appellant argued that his conviction should be quashed. Lord Steyn held that where there had been a breach of the constitutional right to a fair trial it would always be right

---

[87] As Kennedy L.J. accepted in *Attorney-General's Reference No.3 of 2000* [2001] 2 Cr.App.R. 472, [2001] Crim.L.R. 645 (May 17, 2001) (CA), where the admission of evidence would violate Art.6 the court is bound to afford a remedy.

[88] *The Human Rights Act and the Criminal Justice and Regulatory Process* (Hart Publishing, 1999), p.xiv.

[89] See para.15–10 above.

[90] See paras 15–11 to 15–13.

[91] [2002] 1 A.C. 146; see further para.15–12 above.

[92] [1999] 2 A.C. 111 at 123–124.

for a conviction to be quashed.[93] Where other rights were violated, the court should recognise the added value attached to breach of a constitutional right but was not bound to apply a presumption in favour of exclusion:

"On balance, their Lordships have arrived at a view that does not entirely accord with the view which has prevailed in New Zealand . . . [T]he discretion of a trial judge is neither *prima facie* exclusionary, nor *prima facie* inclusionary. It is, however, not a completely open-textured discretion . . . On the one hand the judge has to weigh the interest of the community in securing relevant evidence on the commission of serious crime so that justice can be done. On the other hand, the judge has to weigh the interest of the individual who has been exposed to an illegal invasion of his rights . . . It is a matter of fundamental importance that a right has been considered important enough . . . to be enshrined in [the] Constitution. The stamp of constitutionality on a citizen's right is not meaningless: it is clear testimony that added value is attached to the protection of the right . . . On the other hand, it is important to bear in mind the nature of a particular constitutional guarantee and the nature of a particular breach. For example, a breach of a defendant's constitutional right to a fair trial must inevitably result in the conviction being quashed. By contrast, the constitutional provision requiring a suspect to be informed of his right to consult a lawyer, although of great importance, is a somewhat lesser right and potential breaches can vary greatly in gravity. In such a case, not every breach will result in a confession being excluded. But their Lordships make clear that the fact that there has been a breach of a constitutional right is a cogent factor militating in favour of the exclusion of the confession. In this way the constitutional character of the infringed right is respected and accorded a high value. Nevertheless, the judge must perform a balancing exercise in the context of all the circumstances of the case."

Subsequent English decisions appear not to regard a breach of the Convention as a cogent factor militating in favour of exclusion. In *Mason et al*[94] the four defendants were arrested for various robberies and burglaries when the police felt that they needed more evidence against them, and so the Chief Constable authorised the covert recording of their conversations in the cells. The Court of Appeal held that there was a breach of Art.8, since the recording was not "in accordance with the law" in the absence of a legal framework for authorisation at that time. The court held nonetheless that the police acted in good faith, even though it was doubtful that they had complied with the procedures that were in place,[95] and it followed the Strasbourg decision in *PG and JH v United Kingdom* in deciding that the judge was right not to exclude the evidence under s.78 of the Police and Criminal Evidence Act 1984. The Court of Appeal insisted that it recognised the breach of Art.8 and was providing a remedy, as required by Art.13:

15–29

"the remedy does not have to be the exclusion of evidence. The remedy can be the finding, which we have now made, that there has been a breach of Article 8 or it can be an award of compensation. The European Court of Human Rights recognises that to

---

[93] The implications of this decision for the jurisdiction of the Court of Appeal (Criminal Division) are discussed in para.17–28 below. It is important, however, to note that the scope of the right to a fair to a fair trial under the Constitution of Trinidad and Tobago which was at issue in *Allie Mohammed* is considerably narrower than Art.6 as interpreted in Strasbourg.

[94] [2002] 2 Cr.App.R. 628.

[95] *Ibid*, at [61–62].

insist on the exclusion of evidence could in itself result in a greater injustice to the public than the infringement of Article 8 creates for the defendant."[96]

It is not clear that this rationalisation of the Strasbourg position is correct, but the result is certainly consistent with *Khan* and with *PG and JH*.

15–30   In *Lawrence et al*[97] evidence had been obtained against several men (subsequently charged with conspiracy to cheat) by the covert use of "probes" in order to eavesdrop on their conversations. The trial judge held that there was an interference with the men's Art.8 rights but that this was not unlawful and was "necessary in a democratic society" for the prevention of crime. Agreeing with this ruling, the Court of Appeal suggested that a breach of Art.8 in the gathering of evidence could in certain circumstances amount to a justification for staying the proceedings, rather than affecting the admissibility of the evidence. The court did not specify the types of case in which this more far-reaching remedy might be used, but one example is provided by *Grant*.[98] Listening devices placed in the exercise yard at a particular police station resulted in the recording of conversations between Grant and his legal advisers. The Court of Appeal held that the deliberate interference with a suspect's right to the confidence of privileged communications with his solicitor seriously undermined the rule of law, and justified a stay of proceedings for abuse of process even without proof of prejudice to the defendant. This may be regarded as a much stronger case than either *Mason* or *Lawrence*, because the right to confidential access to legal advice is regarded as a central principle under Art.6.[99] The case therefore concerns not simply a breach of Art.8 but also a breach of an Art.6 right, and decisions such as *Allan v United Kingdom*[100] suggest strongly that the judge's ruling was correct.

15–31   In the controversial case of *Attorney-General's Reference No.3 of 1999*,[101] the House of Lords found no breach of Art.8 and therefore did not have to confront these issues. In this case a DNA sample had been retained, despite the defendant's acquittal, contrary to s.64 of PACE. Although the use of that sample would have been contrary to Art.8, because it was not in accordance with the law, Lord Steyn held that it was not in breach of Art.8 to use a subsequent DNA sample (which had been matched with the wrongly retained sample, in order to identify the defendant as the perpetrator) as evidence against the defendant. Although it amounted to an interference with the defendant's right to privacy under Art.8(1), the later sample had been obtained in accordance with the law (because it did not breach s.64) and its admission was necessary in a democratic society for the investigation and prosecution of serious crime. The interference with the Art.8(1) right was therefore justified according to Art.8(2).

---

[96] *Ibid*, at [75].
[97] [2002] Crim.L.R. 584.
[98] [2005] Crim.L.R. 955. See also the trial ruling in *Sutherland*, (Nottingham Crown Court), reported in *The Times*, January 30, 2002; on this and related issues, see Ormerod D., "ECHR and the Exclusion of Evidence: Trial Remedies for Art.8 Breaches?" [2003] Crim.L.R. 61.
[99] See e.g. *Brennan v United Kingdom* (2002) 34 E.H.R.R. 18, discussed in para.14–22 above.
[100] Above, para.15–14.
[101] [2001] 2 W.L.R. 56.

Turning finally to evidence obtained by ill-treatment, we have seen that the   **15–32**
admission of such evidence is *a fortiori* in breach of Art.6.[102] It seems to have
been accepted by the House of Lords that the regulation of confession evidence
by s.76 of the Police and Criminal Evidence Act 1984, subs.(2) of which creates
a statutory test of voluntariness as a condition precedent to the admissibility of
a confession, satisfies the requirements of Art.6.[103] One element in that condition
precedent is that a confession which is represented to have been obtained by
oppression is not to be admitted into evidence unless the prosecution proves that
it was not so obtained. Section 76(8) defines oppression so as to include "torture,
inhuman or degrading treatment, or the use or threat of violence (whether or not
amounting to torture)".[104] This lays the foundation for a close correspondence
between English law and the Convention. It should be noted, however, that the
decision of the House of Lords in *R. v Mushtaq*[105] imposes an important
obligation on trial judges. In this case the following question was certified for
consideration by the House of Lords:

> "Whether, in view of Article 6 of the Convention for the Protection of Human Rights
> and Fundamental Freedoms, a Judge, who has ruled pursuant to Section 76(2) of the
> Police and Criminal Evidence Act 1984 that evidence of an alleged confession has not
> been obtained by oppression, nor has it been obtained in consequence of anything said
> or done which is likely to render unreliable any confession, is required to direct the jury,
> if they conclude that the alleged confession may have been so obtained, they must
> disregard it."

This question was answered in the affirmative. In the words of Lord Rodger of
Earlsferry:

> "the logic of section 76(2) of PACE really requires that the jury should be directed that,
> if they consider that the confession was, or may have been, obtained by oppression or
> in consequence of anything said or done which was likely to render it unreliable, they
> should disregard it".[106]

IV. Intercept Evidence

Special considerations apply to evidence obtained through the interception of
communications. Following criticism by Strasbourg of the lack, at the time, of
proper legal regulation in the United Kingdom of such interceptions,[107] the
Interception of Communications Act 1985 was introduced. The relevant provisions of that Act have since been replaced by ss.17 and 18 of the Regulation of
Investigatory Powers Act 2000 (RIPA) (considered in detail in Ch.7).

---

[102] See para.15–07 above.
[103] *Hasan* [2005] UKHL 22.
[104] See, for example, *Fulling* [1987] Q.B. 426, *Paris, Abdullahi and Miller* (1993) 97 Cr.App.R.
99.
[105] [2005] UKHL 25, [2005] 1 W.L.R. 1513.
[106] *ibid.*, [47].
[107] *Malone v United Kingdom* (1985) 7 E.H.R.R. 14.

"The obvious purpose of [the] prohibition [in section 17(1)]", the House of Lords has acknowledged, "was to preserve the secrecy of what had, to be effective, to be a covert operation."[108] To put it at greater length:

" . . . the purpose of section [17] can be seen as the protection, not of the fruits of the intercepts, but of information as to the manner in which they were authorised and carried out. . . . the defendant was not to have the opportunity to muddy the waters at a trial by cross-examination designed to elicit the Secretary of State's sources of knowledge or the surveillance authorities' confidential methods of work. Evidently the proscription of questioning on the existence of warrants was seen as an economical means of achieving this result."[109]

Although the legislation does not expressly provide for the inadmissibility of intercept evidence, it has been held to do so impliedly. As Lord Hope of Craighead explained:

" . . . evidence of material obtained by the interception by the persons mentioned in section [17(3)] of the [2000] Act of communications of the kind described in section 1(1) of that Act . . . will always be inadmissible. It is not possible to say that section [17(1)] of the Act provides for this in express language. But, in the context of the Act as a whole, the prohibitions which it contains lead inexorably to that result. So I would hold that it has that effect by necessary implication."[110]

The exclusionary rule only applies, however, to intercepts made in the United Kingdom: "Where . . . the intercept was made in a foreign country by the authorities of that country and the [2000] Act accordingly has no application", the exclusionary rule likewise does not apply.[111] The evidence would simply be capable of being excluded in the exercise of discretion in accordance with the usual principles.

The inadmissibility of intercept evidence is controversial and there have been frequent calls for the reversal of this rule.[112] The statutory prohibition on disclosure of the existence of a telephone intercept or the use of evidence from it, even during the course of a criminal trial, has been considered by the House of Lords and the European Court of Human Rights. In *R. v Preston*, the House of Lords did not find the rule inconsistent with a fair trial, and the Commission declared the ensuing application to Strasbourg inadmissible.

Those decisions must be examined carefully to appreciate their full implications. First, they rested strongly on the facts of that case. The prosecution informed the

---

[108] *Attorney-General's Reference (No.5 of 2002)* [2004] UKHL 40, [2005] 1 A.C. 167, [6] *per* Lord Bingham of Cornhill.
[109] *R. v Preston* [1994] 2 A.C. 130, 167 *per* Lord Mustill. See also *Attorney-General's Reference (No.5 of 2002)* [2004] UKHL 40, [2005] 1 A.C. 167, [7].
[110] *Morgans v DPP* [2001] 1 A.C. 315, 338.
[111] *R. v P* [2002] 1 A.C. 146, 165 *per* Lord Hobhouse of Woodborough.
[112] For a comprehensive account of the issues see generally JUSTICE, *Intercept Evidence: Lifting the Ban—A JUSTICE Report* (2006); *http://www.justice.org.uk/images/pdfs/JUSTICE%20Intercept%20Evidence%20report.pdf*. In November 2006 a private member's bill to amend RIPA was introduced in the House of Lords: see the Interception of Communications (Admissibility of Evidence) Bill.

judge and defence counsel that police officers who had considered the content of the intercept evidence knew it would not assist the defence. Under current provisions, it would not have been permissible for such an explicit disclosure to be made to the defence.[113] Secondly, by the time of trial, the intercept material had been destroyed, and therefore no appellate court was in a position to make its own assessment of the value of that material. Although the House of Lords approved that course (with some hesitation), RIPA would now almost certainly prevent such destruction.[114] Therefore, while the conclusions in *Preston* are not surprising on the facts of that case, many cases would need to be considered on a different basis.

In dealing with the prohibition itself, Lord Mustill found that it was compatible with the right to a fair trial, but in doing so acknowledged that it involved a compromise that imposed an unusually heavy burden on the prosecutor:

" . . . counsel for the defendants have forcefully and rightly emphasised some disturbing problems [with the prosecution position] which may, I believe, fairly be seen as having two aspects. Firstly, to what extent may favourable materials (i.e. those which point to the possibility that the defendant is innocent) be disclosed to those who have it in their power to see that injustice is avoided? Second, if the prosecutor's argument is sound, by whom does the statute contemplate that this power will be exercised? The dilemma will already be plain. At the one extreme the only intellectual ground ever advanced for saying that the materials should not be disclosed at all, namely the Attorney General's argument on admissibility [i.e. inadmissible material need not be preserved or disclosed] does not hold water. At the other, the notion that the intercepted material should be disclosed in the same way as other unused material, subject to the same restrictions (mediated by prosecuting counsel) as in the case of any other 'sensitive' material is inconsistent with the hypothesis on which we currently proceed [that intercept material cannot be disclosed], and must be discarded. There must accordingly, so the argument runs, be some intermediate solution whereby someone in the chain consisting of telephone engineer—transcriber—notetaker—officer in the intelligence unit-senior police officer in the case—Crown Prosecution Service official, decides the material is favourable to the defendant, and causes (by some mechanism not explained) a prosecution which would otherwise have been brought to be aborted. . . .[115]"

Lord Mustill went on to accept the compromise proposed by the Crown:

"In the end, however, I consider that the very real apprehension voiced by counsel for the defendants cannot prevail over the plain intent and wording of the Act. The need for surveillance and the need to keep it secret is undeniable. So also is the need to protect to the feasible maximum the privacy of those whose conversations are overheard without their consent. Hence sections 2 and 6 [of the Interception of Communications Act 1985]. These policies are in flat contradiction to current opinions on the 'transparency' of the trial process. Something has to give way, and the history, structure and terms of the statute leave me in little doubt that this must be the duty to give complete

---

[113] See RIPA s.17(1). Before the House of Lords the Crown also indicated that the indication passed down from the relevant officer should not, in fact, have occurred (at 168G). Lord Mustill considered that disclosure of the existence of an intercept may need to be disclosed (at 172F), which would now be prohibited by RIPA.

[114] RIPA s.15(4)(d).

[115] 167F–168B.

disclosure of the unused materials. The result is a vulnerable compromise, but it may be the best that can be achieved . . . "

Accordingly, even if an intercept contains material that may undermine the prosecution or assist the defence, the prosecutor cannot disclose it. He cannot even make a public interest immunity application. Given the importance of proper disclosure to the fairness of a trial, the prosecutor would be forced to halt the prosecution. The only other alternative may be to ask the trial judge to sanction an admission that may reduce the unfairness caused by the non-disclosure.[116] But given that such an admission must not, even indirectly, reveal the existence of a telephone intercept,[117] in most circumstances it will be very difficult for a meaningful admission to be made.[118]

This extreme approach is, in accordance with *Preston*, the only way that the intercept prohibition can be consistent with fair trial. But the handicap on the prosecutor and the resultant risk to the proper administration of justice is obvious. If, within thousands of hours of prejudicial telephone intercept material, in what would otherwise be an overwhelming case against a defendant, there is one short conversation that might assist the defence, the prosecution must be halted.

There is no way of assessing how rigorously prosecutors have observed this rule, since no part of that assessment can be disclosed to a defendant. Police officers first have to preserve and then identify potentially significant telephone intercept material. Prosecutors then have to consider the implication of any material, in the knowledge that even intercept material that is only marginally helpful to the defence, or is open to two interpretations, may still require the prosecution to be halted.

Furthermore, it is not just explicitly exculpatory intercept material that may require a prosecution to be halted. In the context of disclosure, it is often emphasised that "neutral" material is not material which either assists the defence or undermines a prosecution. Accordingly, a prosecutor's failure to disclose neutral material would not prevent a fair trial. However, the effect of intercept evidence needs to be assessed holistically. If, during thousands of hours of telephone intercepts, two alleged conspirators only discussed trivial matters and never discussed the alleged conspiracy, this is not necessarily "neutral". It may assist the defendants in establishing their innocence, by inferring that their interaction over the relevant period was not connected with a conspiracy as alleged. In such circumstances the statutory prohibition that prevents the prose-cutor from disclosing the existence of that material, or even being able to

---

[116] RIPA s.18.

[117] RIPA s.18(10).

[118] Annex I to the Crown Prosecution Service Disclosure Manual sets out the circumstances of how such an admission might be made. It does not grapple with the practical difficulty of making a s.18 admission consistent with s.18(10). Rather it states that it would be "rare" to require any form of s.18 admission and "very rare" not to be able to make that admission without offending s.18(10). Whether this is correct, in practice, is not clear.

summarise its contents for the defence, may prevent a fair trial. The prosecution could not continue.

This rule, placing the UK in an almost unique position in the world,[119] is the subject of much debate and at the time of writing is under renewed scrutiny and criticism.[120] Whether the reasoning behind the prohibition on intercept evidence being used in English cases can survive much longer is questionable. Not least, if a prosecutor is faithful to the principles in *Preston* then from time to time important and serious prosecutions have to be abandoned. That alone would appear to be a threat to the proper administration of justice, quite apart from any impact on the fair trial rights of a defendant.

D. ENTRAPMENT

I. The Strasbourg Caselaw Under Article 6

In *Ludi v Switzerland*[121] an undercover agent had posed as a potential purchaser **15–33** of 2 kg of cocaine and the applicant offered to sell the drugs to him. His conviction depended heavily upon tape recorded telephone conversations which had occurred during the course of the negotiations. The applicant's complaint that the investigation violated his right to privacy was rejected on the ground that he had knowingly run the risk of encountering an undercover police officer, and could not therefore invoke the protection of Art.8.[122] The Court went on to find a violation of Art.6 on the ground that there had been no opportunity to cross-examine the undercover officer in the criminal proceedings. There was, however, no suggestion in the judgment that the admission of the evidence would have violated Art.6 if the officer had been called to give oral evidence at the trial.

The approach to Art.8 adopted by the court in *Ludi* placed great emphasis on **15–34** whether the defendant was already engaged in criminal activity before he was approached. This issue was considered by the Commission in the context of Art.6 in *Radermacher and Pferrer v Germany*.[123] The applicants had been convicted of dealing in counterfeit currency. There was no dispute that a police informer (W) and an undercover agent had played "an important and active part" during the long series of events which finally resulted in the delivery of the counterfeit notes, but there was a conflict of evidence as to the precise nature of that role.

---

[119] The only other jurisdiction with a similar (but less severe) rule is Hong Kong, which was a UK colony until 1997.

[120] For recent detailed and conflicting observations on the value of preserving the prohibition on intercept evidence, see Attorney Generals comments of September 21, 2006 in favour of abolition of the rule, subject to qualifications; *Report of the Interception of Communications Commissioner* 2005–2006, para.45, (published February 19, 2007)—strongly in favour of preserving the rule; and Justice's report *Intercept Evidence: Lifting the Ban* (above, n.112), which provides a thorough analysis of the arguments in favour of abolition of the rule.

[121] (1993) 15 E.H.R.R. 173.

[122] See also *Speckman v United Kingdom* Application No.27007/95 (unreported).

[123] Application No.12811/87 (unreported).

The Commission was unwilling to elaborate any general principles governing the use of undercover officers or informants, but nevertheless described the question of whether the offences had been instigated by W as "crucial" to its decision. Since there was conflicting evidence on the point, the Commission found no violation of Art.6:

"The Commission notes that, according to the Government's . . . account of events, the police informer W has not taken the initiative to arrange a delivery of counterfeit money, but only reacted to an offer by G who visited him on 12 December 1982. Furthermore, W had not incited the second applicant to commit the offence but the second applicant had already been prepared to participate in the delivery of counterfeit money and had, together with G and on their own initiative, come to see W in order to follow up G's earlier offer . . . In the absence of any evidence to the contrary . . . the Commission accepts this version of the origin of the offences as corresponding to the truth. It follows that W cannot be regarded as the real initiator of the offences. Consequently, it is not necessary to examine further the question whether there was a violation of Article 6(1) on the ground that the offences had been brought about by the activities of an undercover agent."

15–35   In *Teixeira de Castro v Portugal*[124] the issue could not be so easily avoided. Two undercover police officers approached a man (S) who was suspected of small scale drug trafficking and asked him to supply them with several kilogrammes of cannabis. When he was unable to find a supplier, they said that they were interested in buying heroin. S mentioned the applicant's name as a possible supplier of heroin. S took the officers to the applicant's home and the officers told the applicant that they wished to buy 20 grams of heroin and produced a roll of banknotes. The applicant agreed and went, without the officers, to the home of another man (O). O obtained three wraps of heroin amounting to a total of 20 grams and handed them to the applicant, who took the drugs to another location where he was intending to meet the officers. On producing the heroin he was arrested, and subsequently charged.

15–36   The Commission concluded, by 30 votes to one, that the proceedings as a whole violated Art.6. In reaching this conclusion it referred to the approach adopted in the United States:

"[T]he Commission considers that, even if it is not its task to give an opinion on the lawfulness of police provocation, it does nonetheless have a duty to ascertain whether the proceedings, considered as a whole, were fair. To this end, the Commission must consider whether the role played by the police officers was so decisive in the commission of the offence with which the applicant was charged that it affected the fairness of the proceedings in question . . . [I]t is clear . . . that an issue as to the fairness of the proceedings may arise in this type of situation. This might be the case where a criminal offence is committed and the accused convicted purely as a result of the conduct of the officers in question. The Commission notes, moreover, that the same approach is adopted by the courts of a number of member states of the Council of Europe, such as Germany, and by the Supreme Court of the United States, which held, in *Sherman v. United States* (1958) 356 U.S. 369 that evidence obtained by inciting someone to commit an offence which they would not otherwise have committed is inadmissible."

---

[124] (1999) 28 E.H.R.R. 101.

The Commission attached importance to the fact that the officers were conduct- **15–37**
ing the operation without judicial supervision; that there was nothing in the
evidence to "pinpoint any conduct of the applicant, prior to his arrest, which
would suggest that he would have committed the offence in question even if the
police officers had not provoked him"; and that the verdict of guilty was based
"mainly" on the evidence of the officers concerned. The Commission continued:

> "All the foregoing circumstances lead the Commission to consider that the police
> officers' actions were essentially, if not exclusively, the cause of the offence being
> committed and the applicant being sentenced to a fairly heavy penalty. They thus
> incited the applicant to commit a criminal offence which he might not have committed
> if he had not been provoked. In the Commission's opinion, this situation irremediably
> affected the fairness of the proceedings."

The Court agreed, by eight votes to one. It held explicitly that the seriousness of **15–38**
the offence could never justify a conviction obtained as a result of police
incitement:

> "The use of undercover agents must be restricted and safeguards put in place even in
> cases concerning the fight against drug-trafficking. While the rise in organised crime
> undoubtedly requires that appropriate measures be taken, the right to a fair administra-
> tion of justice nevertheless holds such a prominent place that it cannot be sacrificed for
> the sake of expedience. The general requirements of fairness embodied in Article 6
> apply to proceedings concerning all types of criminal offence, from the most straight-
> forward to the most complex. The public interest cannot justify the use of evidence
> obtained as a result of police incitement."

The Court distinguished the facts of *Teixeira* from those of *Ludi*, noting that in **15–39**
the latter case there was already a criminal investigation underway into the
applicant's activities, the officer had been subject to judicial supervision, and his
role had been limited to acting as an undercover officer, as distinct from an *agent
provocateur*:

> "In the instant case it is necessary to determine whether or not the two police officers'
> activity went beyond that of undercover agents. The Court notes that the Government
> have not contended that the officers' intervention took place as part of an anti-drug
> trafficking operation ordered and supervised by a judge. It does not appear either that
> the competent authorities had good reason to suspect that Mr Teixeira de Castro was a
> drug trafficker; on the contrary, he had no criminal record and no preliminary investiga-
> tion concerning him had been opened. Indeed, he was not known to the police officers,
> who only came into contact with him through intermediaries . . . Furthermore, the drugs
> were not at the applicant's home; he obtained them from a third party who had in turn
> obtained them from another person. Nor does the [domestic court judgment] indicate
> that, at the time of his arrest, the applicant had more drugs in his possession than the
> quantity the police officers had requested thereby going beyond what he had been
> incited to do by the police. There is no evidence to support the government's argument
> that the applicant was predisposed to commit offences. The necessary inference from
> these circumstances is that the two police officers did not confine themselves to
> investigating Mr Teixeira de Castro's criminal activity in an essentially passive manner,
> but exercised an influence such as to incite the commission of the offence."

The Court thus attached prime importance to two linked factors: (i) the absence **15–40**
of evidence to suggest that the applicant was already engaged in drug trafficking,

or was otherwise predisposed to commit the offence and (ii) the undoubted fact that the officers had instigated the commission of this particular offence:

"[T]he Court concludes that the two police officers' actions went beyond those of undercover agents because they instigated the offence and there is nothing to suggest that without their intervention it would have been committed. That intervention and its use in the impugned criminal proceedings meant that, right from the outset, the applicant was definitively deprived of a fair trial."[125]

15–41 Since the applicant had been convicted "mainly" on the basis of the statements of the two police officers, there had been a violation of Art.6. The force of the Court's condemnation is underlined by its approach to the award of just satisfaction. It is rare for the Court to award compensation in respect of a violation of Art.6 since the necessary causation is difficult to establish.[126] In *Teixeira*, however, the court held that the applicant's detention had resulted directly from the use of evidence that was incompatible with Art.6. In those circumstances he was entitled to recover loss of earnings for the period of his sentence, and an additional sum in non-pecuniary loss to reflect the damage he had suffered and the difficulties he had faced in finding employment after his release.

15–42 *Teixeira* was distinguished by the Commission in *Shahzad v United Kingdom*[127] (the Strasbourg proceedings in *R. v Latif and Shahzad*[128]) and more recently by the court in *Shannon v United Kingdom (Admissibility)*[129] and *Eurofinacom v France (Admissibility)*.[130] The Commission held in *Shahzad* that although the particular importation in respect of which the applicants had been convicted would not have occurred without the assistance of undercover officers, the offence had been instigated by S himself, without any prompting. Moreover, S was proved to have had a history of involvement in heroin trafficking:

"[T]he Commission notes that, as the House of Lords observed, undercover agents gave the applicant the opportunity to attempt to commit the crime of importing heroin into the United Kingdom and that the particular importation would not have taken place when and how it did without the assistance of undercover agents. However, the Commission also notes that, as accepted by the national courts, the undercover agents did not take the initiative to contact the applicant with a view to importing heroin into the United Kingdom, but only reacted to an offer by the applicant. In this respect, the applicant's case is distinguishable from *Teixeira de Castro v. Portugal*, where the Commission found a violation of Article 6(1) of the Convention because of the role played by "agents provocateurs" in bringing about that applicant's conviction. As opposed to *Teixeira de Castro v. Portugal*, in the present case, it has not been established that the undercover agents were the real initiators of the offences. The Commission also notes that, as opposed to the applicant in *Teixeira de Castro v. Portugal*, the applicant in the present case had a long-term involvement in the heroin trade and was ready and willing to commit crime even without the involvement of the

---

[125] *ibid.*, at paras 38–39.
[126] See paras 1–140 to 1–146 above.
[127] Application No.34225/96. See also *KL v United Kingdom* Application No.32715/96, both reported at [1998] E.H.R.L.R. 210.
[128] [1996] 1 W.L.R. 104. See n.69 above.
[129] Application No. 67537/01, April 6, 2004, [2005] Crim.L.R. 133.
[130] Application No.58753/00, September 7, 2004, [2005] Crim.L.R. 133.

undercover agents. Moreover, the testimony of the undercover agents did not form the exclusive basis of the applicant's conviction, which was also supported by other evidence such as tape and video recordings."

There is no doubt that the judgment in *Teixeira de Castro* is now established in the Strasbourg jurisprudence. Thus in *Edwards and Lewis v United Kingdom*,[131] where the application concerned the use of public interest immunity to prevent disclosure of evidence vital to an entrapment submission, the Court began by recalling that:

15–43

"although the admissibility of evidence is primarily a matter for regulation by national law, the requirements of a fair criminal trial under Article 6 entail that the public interest in the fight against crime cannot justify the use of evidence obtained as a result of incitement."[132]

This statement was supported by a reference to the *Teixeira* decision, which was then summarised.

II. In English Law

Two decisions of the House of Lords establish that, if it is proved that the defendant was entrapped into the conduct which is the subject of the charge, it may be appropriate to stay the prosecution or, if not, to exclude the evidence under s.78 of the Police and Criminal Evidence Act 1984. In *R. v Latif and Shahzad*[133] the appellants had been involved in a scheme for the importation of heroin into the United Kingdom. S had approached a man (H) in Pakistan who, unknown to him, was an informer for the United States Drugs Enforcement Agency. S offered to supply drugs for importation into the United Kingdom, and subsequently delivered 20 kilogrammes of heroin to H. The drugs were physically imported by a British Customs officer, and some time later S arrived in this country. He was arrested, together with L, as he took possession of a dummy consignment. In their defence L and S argued that they had been lured into the crime by undercover officers acting as agents provocateurs. The House of Lords rejected both the argument that the proceedings should have been stayed as an abuse of process, and an alternative argument that the evidence should have been excluded under s.78. In respect of the abuse of process argument Lord Steyn said:

15–44

"Weighing countervailing considerations of policy and justice, it is for the judge in the exercise of his discretion to decide whether there has been an abuse of process which amounts to an affront to the public conscience and requires the criminal proceedings to be stayed . . . The speeches in *R. v Horseferry Road ex parte Bennett* conclusively establish that proceedings may be stayed . . . not only where a fair trial is impossible, but also where it would be contrary to the public interest in the integrity of the criminal justice system that a trial should take place . . . [The] judge must weigh in the balance the public interest in ensuring that persons charged with grave crimes should be tried

---

[131] [2003] Crim.L.R. 891, judgment of July 22, 2003. Affirmed by the Grand Chamber, (2005) 40 E.H.R.R.
[132] Judgment, para.49.
[133] [1996] 1 W.L.R. 104.

and the competing public interest in not conveying the impression that the court will adopt the approach that the end justifies any means."

15–45 S had taken the initiative at the crucial meeting with H when the importation was agreed. He was in no way vulnerable, and had been an organiser in the heroin trade in the past. He had indicated from the start that he was ready and willing to arrange the importation. While it was true that this particular importation would not have occurred in the way, and at the time it did without the involvement of the undercover officers, the actions of the officer were not so unworthy or shameful as to make it an affront to the public conscience to allow the prosecution to proceed. As noted above, the appellants' subsequent application to Strasbourg was held by the Commission to be manifestly ill-founded.[134] However, there is a marked difference between Lord Steyn's broad reference in the House of Lords to "balancing" the public interest against the defendant's right to a fair trial, and the much less compromising declaration of the Strasbourg Court in *Teixeira de Castro* that the fight against organised crime cannot justify the sacrifice of the right to a fair trial.[135]

15–46 These points were taken further in the second and more important House of Lords decision, *Looseley; Attorney-General's Reference No.3 of 2000*.[136] In these cases, the House held that in *Looseley* the trial judge had rightly refused to stay the prosecution, because there were reasonable grounds to suspect the defendant (or at least those who frequented the particular public house) of involvement in the supply of class A drugs and the undercover officer had done no more than give him an opportunity to commit the offence; whereas in the *Attorney General's Reference No.3 of 2000* the trial judge had been right to stay the prosecution (and the Court of Appeal wrong to allow the appeal)[137] because the police officers had no reasonable grounds to suspect the defendant of involvement in the supply of class A drugs, and moreover had first supplied him with cheap cigarettes and thus prepared the ground for their request for class A drugs to appear as a "favour for a favour."[138]

15–47 Their Lordships' speeches contain explicit declarations of the importance of ensuring that it is fair to try the particular defendant. Thus Lord Nicholls stated:

> "It is simply not acceptable that the state through its agents should lure its citizens into committing acts forbidden by the law and then seek to prosecute them for doing so. That would be entrapment. That would be a misuse of state power, and an abuse of the process of the courts. The unattractive consequences, frightening and sinister in extreme

---

[134] *Shahzad v United Kingdom* Application No.34225/96. See also *KL v United Kingdom* Application No.32715/96, both reported at [1998] E.H.R.L.R. 210.

[135] Above, para.15–38.

[136] [2001] UKHL 53; for discussion, see Ashworth A., "Re-Drawing the Boundaries of Entrapment", [2002] Crim.L.R. 161.

[137] [2001] 2 Cr.App.R. 472, [2001] Crim.L.R. 645. For a searching analysis of the issues in entrapment, written largely before the House of Lords decision, see Ormerod D. and Roberts A., "The trouble with *Teixeira*: developing a Principled Approach to Entrapment", (2002) 6 E. & P. 38.

[138] As noted by Lord Hutton, [2001] UKHL 53, para.116.

cases, which state conduct of this kind could have are obvious. The role of the courts is to stand between the state and its citizens and make sure this does not happen."[139]

The House of Lords went on to hold that the proper remedy for entrapment is usually a stay of the proceedings, consistently with the decision in *Teixeira de Castro v Portugal* that entrapment deprives a person "from the outset" of a fair trial. If the argument for a stay of the prosecution fails, it will still be open to the defence to argue for the exclusion of the evidence.

Before discussing the concept of entrapment developed by the House, it is **15–48** necessary to recall the words of Lord Bingham in *Nottingham City Council v Amin*,[140] with which their Lordships agreed. In that case two plain clothes police officers hailed the defendant driver, and asked him to take them to a particular destination, which he did. No element of persuasion was necessary. He was prosecuted under the Town Police Clauses Act for an offence of plying for hire without a licence. Having heard submissions on *Teixeira de Castro* the stipendiary magistrate acquitted him. On a prosecution appeal by way of case stated, the decision was overturned. The Divisional Court allowed the appeal. Lord Bingham C.J. summarised the position thus:

"On the one hand it has been recognised as deeply offensive to ordinary notions of fairness if a defendant were to be convicted and punished for committing a crime which he only committed because he had been incited, instigated, persuaded, pressurised or wheedled into committing it by a law enforcement officer. On the other hand, it has been recognised that law enforcement agencies have a general duty to the public to enforce the law and it has been regarded as unobjectionable if a law enforcement officer gives a defendant an opportunity to break the law, of which the defendant freely takes advantage, in circumstances where it appears that the defendant would have behaved in the same way if the opportunity had been offered by anyone else."

The House of Lords in *Looseley* adopted this broad distinction, and developed **15–49** the doctrine further. Whether the acts of the undercover officer or informant are characterised as "active" or "passive" is no longer relevant.[141] More important are two tests: first, whether what was done amounted to nothing more than providing the defendant with an "unexceptional opportunity" to commit the offence or, as Lord Nicholls put it, "whether the police conduct preceding the commission of the offence was no more than might be expected from others in the circumstances."[142] And secondly, where a person has been targeted by the police, whether there were reasonable grounds for suspecting either the defendant or persons frequenting a particular place of being involved in offences of the kind committed.[143] This marks a difference from the *Teixeira* judgment, which refers to evidence that the defendant was pre-disposed to the type of offence. The House of Lords opposed the pre-disposition test because it would tend to penalise those with previous convictions against whom there may be no current grounds

---

[139] *Ibid*, para.1.
[140] [2000] 1 Cr.App.R. 426.
[141] See Lord Hoffmann at [65] and Lord Hutton at [110]; this displaces the former "guideline" judgment in *Smurthwaite and Gill* (1994) 98 Cr.App.R. 437.
[142] [2001] UKHL 53, at [23].
[143] *Ibid, per* Lord Hoffmann at [55].

for suspicion. Lord Hoffmann also emphasised the need to ensure that an operation was duly authorised and compliant with the relevant codes of practice,[144] a point that echoes the requirements of authorisation articulated in *Teixeira de Castro*.[145]

15–50   English law has been clarified by the *Looseley* decision and brought more closely into alignment with the *Teixiera* judgment, which remains the most significant Strasbourg pronouncement on entrapment. However, the two decisions leave a number of uncertainties about the definition of entrapment—such as the types of crime for which undercover methods are permissible; the limits to which the police may properly go in drugs cases; the lawfulness of "reverse sting" operations; and whether an operation becomes lawful if initially unsubstantiated beliefs are confirmed by subsequent facts. *Looseley* was applied in *R. v Moon* where the Court of Appeal held that:

> "whether the matter is looked through the lens of the proper safeguards of authorisation, or through the lens of the appellant's absence of predisposition or antecedents, or through the lens of the actual nature of the police activities in relation to this appellant, the conclusion to which we are driven is that this appellant was lured into crime or was entrapped, and that it was a case of causing crime rather than merely providing an opportunity for it, and ultimately that it would be unfair for the State to prosecute her for this offending. In these circumstances, the application to stay for abuse should, we think, have been accepted."[146]

15–51   Still controversial is the decision in *Williams v DPP*[147] in which police officers set up a "virtue-testing operation" by leaving a van load of cigarette cartons unsecured and unattended in a public street. Two members of the public who came across the van, and began to unload the cartons, were arrested. It was held that the police had done nothing to force, persuade, encourage or coerce them into doing what they had done. They had been free to decide whether or not to succumb and were victims not of a trick, but of their own dishonesty. This was despite the fact that there was no evidence of prior involvement in offences. The officers had gone out of their way to create the conditions in which the accused were able to commit a purely opportunistic offence which they would not otherwise have committed. Lord Hoffmann's view in *Looseley* was that this was "an authorised investigation into actual crime, and the fact that the defendants may not previously have been suspected or even thought of offending was their bad luck."[148] However, his Lordship also held that if a police officer left a wallet on a park bench in order to see who picked it up and whether they stole it, this would amount to entrapment. The distinction between these two types of case may need to be revisited.

---

[144] *Ibid*, at [66].
[145] It may be noted that Lord Bingham had said in *Nottingham City Council v Amin* (above) that such factors were not relevant in English law, but since the Regulation of Investigatory Powers Act 2000 they are.
[146] [2004] EWCA Crim 2872, [51].
[147] [1993] 3 All E.R. 365.
[148] [2001] UKHL 53, at [65].

III. Comparative Approaches

The strong stand taken in Strasbourg against entrapment finds echoes in other   **15–52**
jurisdictions outside Europe. In the United States it is the question of predisposi-
tion that is crucial. If there is evidence that the defendant was predisposed
towards the type of offence alleged, active incitement by undercover officers
does not ground a defence of entrapment, whereas in the absence of predisposi-
tion it does.[149] It is to be noted that the American approach is to provide a full
defence to crime, which assigns the crucial decision to the jury rather than to the
judge. In Canada, the courts have held that police incitement may be acceptable
where there is objective evidence of reasonable suspicion that the defendant was
involved in some connected criminal activity.[150] However, the Canadian courts
remain willing to stay the prosecution where entrapment is found, as it was in the
"reverse sting" case of *Shirose and Campbell v R.*[151] In Australia the High Court
has held that entrapment is a ground for excluding evidence.[152]

E. ADMISSIONS OBTAINED BY SUBTERFUGE

The issues considered in the previous section concerned conduct by undercover   **15–53**
officers which is alleged to have had a causal connection with the commission of
the offence. A related but discrete question is the use of undercover officers to
obtain admissions to past offences. Thus the case of *R. v Christou,*[153] which is
often cited in the entrapment context, was not really a case of entrapment at all,
since the subterfuge used (the setting up of a shop purporting to deal in stolen
goods) was intended primarily as a means of gathering intelligence concerning
offences of theft and handling which had already occurred.

When this issue arose for consideration in Strasbourg some 18 years ago the   **15–54**
Commission held that it is not a breach of Art.6 to admit the evidence of an
undercover agent placed in a prison to eavesdrop on conversations involving the
accused, so long as the evidence was not unlawfully obtained, and there was no
element of coercion or covert interrogation involved. In *X v Federal Republic of
Germany*[154] two German citizens had been arrested in Italy for drugs offences.
An undercover Italian police officer was placed in their cell, posing as a remand
prisoner. Not knowing that their "cellmate" could speak German the two men
had a conversation in which the applicant admitted to murder. He subsequently
repeated his confession to the Italian and German police, and to an Italian
investigating magistrate. He was then extradited to Germany. Before the German

---

[149] The leading case is *Jacobson v United States* 503 US 540 (1992). For discussion of the
American and Canadian decisions, see Choo A., *Abuse of Process and Judicial Stays of Criminal
Proceedings* (1993), Ch.6, and Mirfield P., *Silence, Confessions and Improperly Obtained Evidence*
(1997), pp.199–209.
[150] *Mack* (1988) 44 C.C.C. (3d) 513.
[151] (1999) 133 C.C.C. (3d) 257; *Cf. now Canada's Bill C–24 of 2001, which authorised various
methods for combatting organised crime.*
[152] E.g. *Ridgeway v R.* (1995) 184 C.L.R. 19, and *Nicholas v R.* (1998) 193 C.L.R. 173.
[153] [1992] 4 All E.R. 559.
[154] Application No.12127/86 (1989) 11 E.H.R.R. 84.

court of trial he retracted his formal confessions, and challenged the admissibility of the cell confession on the ground that the evidence was unlawfully obtained. The Commission rejected his complaint, observing that:

> "The applicant had an interest in not talking to his accomplice about the crime in the presence of a third person. If he nevertheless freely did so it is his own responsibility that this turned against him. He has not alleged that the undercover agent in any way caused him to talk about the killing of the businessman. In these circumstances it cannot be found that the applicant's freedom of will was affected by the action of the Italian police so as to make the use of the evidence obtained from the Italian undercover agent deprive the applicant of his right to a fair trial as guaranteed by Article 6 of the Convention."

15–55 The last point marks the difference from *Allan v United Kingdom*,[155] where the Court held that the police informant had been placed in the cell with a view to eliciting details of the offence from the applicant, and did so in a way that violated his privilege against self-incrimination. However, the Commission's finding in *X v Federal Republic of Germany* might have to be reconsidered followed the Court's ruling in *PG and JH v United Kingdom*[156] that the recording of a suspect's voice in a police cell did amount to a breach of Art.8(1), on the ground that:

> "Private life considerations may arise once any systematic or permanent record comes into existence of such material from the public domain. It is for this reason that files gathered by the security services on a particular individual fall within Article 8 even where the information has not been gathered by any intrusive or covert method."[157]

This does not mean that a violation of Art.8 will necessarily be found in such cases, merely that the interference must be justified in the terms of Art.8(2). Thus, so long as the interference was lawful (which, in this country, now means compliant with the Regulation of Investigatory Powers Act 2000[158]), a court has to decide whether the interference was "necessary in a democratic society" for the prevention of crime.

15–56 In *Smith v United Kingdom*,[159] MI5 officers secretly taped a telephone conversation between the defendant and an undercover security service officer. The Commission distinguished this situation from one in which the evidence has been obtained unlawfully. The conversation had been conducted with the consent of one party; it was brief; and it did not go to the heart of the matter. The Commission therefore held that it had to be regarded as a ruse in the public interest, and declared the application inadmissible.

15–57 The leading decisions of the Supreme Court of Canada distinguish between conduct which is passive (where an undercover officer simply records what is

---

[155] (2002) 36 E.H.R.R. 143, above, para.15–14.
[156] [2002] Crim.L.R. 308, above, para.15–13
[157] Judgment, para.57.
[158] Police surveillance operations that took place prior to the Act have been found not to be "in accordance with the law" and hence to violate Art.8: see e.g. *Lewis v United Kingdom* (2003) 39 E.H.R.R. 9 (p.213); *Wood v United Kingdom*, Application No.23414/02, November 16, 2004.
[159] [1997] E.H.R.L.R. 277.

said without posing questions to the suspect),[160] and conduct which amounts to an active attempt to elicit comments or admissions about the case.[161] These decisions were followed in the New Zealand case of *Barlow*,[162] where the Court of Appeal admitted tape recordings of conversations between the defendant and a friend of his. The friend had initially been telephoned by the defendant, but then contacted the police and thereafter followed police instructions, so as to avoid deliberately eliciting comments about the alleged offence.

F. ACCOMPLICES AND PARTICIPANT INFORMERS

For several years the use of participant informers was governed by the 1969   **15–58**
Home Office guidelines and the 1984 guidelines of the Association of Chief Police Officers.[163] The latter made it clear that no police officer or informant should counsel, procure or incite the commission of crime. The guidelines emphasised that where police allowed an informant to participate in an offence, the informer's role was to be passive and minor, and his participation had to be absolutely necessary to enable police to frustrate and arrest the principal offenders. No undertaking was to be given which would necessitate misleading a court in subsequent criminal proceedings; the role of the participant informer was to be disclosed to the prosecution and to the defence; and payments were to be supervised by a senior officer. There was compelling evidence, however, that these guidelines were not always followed.[164] ACPO issued revised and more detailed "Codes of Practice" which came into force in January 2000, when the Home Office circular was withdrawn. The use of "covert human intelligence sources" is now subject to a statutory framework under the Regulation of Investigatory Powers Act 2000.[165]

The English courts have long recognised that accomplice evidence is inherently   **15–59**
vulnerable. Where the accomplice has "an obvious and powerful inducement" to implicate an accused person in order to advance his own position, the Court of Appeal has previously held that it may be necessary for the trial judge to exercise his discretion to exclude the evidence.[166] In *R. v Pipe*[167] the prosecution had called an accomplice who had been charged for his part in the offence alleged against the accused, but against whom the proceedings had not been concluded. The Court of Appeal held that this procedure was "wholly irregular", saying:

> "It may well be . . . that in strict law [the accomplice] was a competent witness, but for years now it has been the recognised practice that an accomplice who has been charged,

---

[160] *Hebert* (1990) 57 C.C.C. (3d) 1, evidence admitted.

[161] *Broyles* [1991] 3 S.C.R. 595, evidence excluded. In *Broyles*, the person eliciting the information was a friend of the suspect, acting at the instigation of the police, but the principles are the same as for an undercover officer.

[162] (1995) 14 C.R.N.Z. 9.

[163] Home Office Circular 97/1969, "Informants who Take Part in Crime".

[164] For evidence and discussion, see JUSTICE, *Under Surveillance: Covert Policing and Human Rights Standards* (1998), pp.38–51.

[165] See paras 7–29 *et seq.* above.

[166] *R. v Pipe* (1966) 51 Cr.App.R. 17; *R. v Turner (BJ)* (1975) 61 Cr.App.R. 67.

[167] (1966) 51 Cr.App.R. 17.

either jointly in the indictment with his co-accused or in the indictment though not under a joint charge shall not be called by the prosecution, except in limited circumstances. Those circumstances are set out correctly in *Archbold*, in paragraph 1297 of the current edition, where it is said that where it is proposed to call an accomplice at the trial, it is the practice (a) to omit him from the indictment or (b) take his plea of Guilty on arraignment, or before calling him either (c) to offer no evidence and permit his acquittal or (d) to enter a *nolle prosequi* . . .

This Court is quite satisfied that if this case had to go on, and the prosecution were still minded to call [the accomplice], they must have let it be known that in no event would proceedings be continued against him. In the judgment of this court it is one thing to call for the prosecution an accomplice, a witness whose evidence is suspect, and about whom the jury must be warned in the recognised way. It is quite another to call a man who is not only an accomplice, but is an accomplice against whom proceedings have been brought which have not been concluded. There is in his case an added reason for making his evidence suspect."[168]

15–60 By contrast, in *R. v Turner (BJ)*[169] the Crown relied upon a supergrass against whom there was no realistic prospect of further prosecution. The Court of Appeal observed that where there was a very powerful inducement operating on the mind of the accomplice, the judge could secure a fair trial by exercising his discretion to exclude the evidence. On the facts however the Court of Appeal held that the admission of the evidence did not result in an unfair trial. The accomplice was no longer at risk of being prosecuted for his part in the offences, regardless of whether he chose to give evidence or not, and regardless of the nature of the evidence which he gave. The court pointed out that: "These facts distinguished this case from *Pipe*, and would have justified the judge in refusing to exercise his discretion to exclude [the accomplice's] evidence."[170]

15–61 The court further held that the rule in *Pipe* was:

" . . . confined to a case in which an accomplice who has been charged, but not tried, is required to give evidence of his own offence in order to secure the conviction of another accused. *Pipe*, on its facts, was clearly a right decision. The same result could have been achieved by adjudging that the trial judge should have exercised his discretion to exclude [the accomplice's] evidence on the ground that there was an obvious and powerful inducement for him to ingratiate himself with the prosecution and the court and that the existence of this inducement made it desirable in the interests of justice to exclude it . . . If the inducement is very powerful, the judge may decide to exercise his discretion."[171]

15–62 When one of the defendants in *Turner* subsequently applied to the European Commission of Human Rights, alleging *inter alia* a violation of Art.6(1) arising from the admission of the accomplice's evidence, the Commission in *X v United Kingdom*[172] established the principle that the introduction of the evidence of an accomplice who has been offered immunity may "put in question" the fairness

---

[168] *ibid.*, at 21.
[169] (1975) 61 Cr.App.R. 67.
[170] *ibid.*, at 79.
[171] *ibid.*, at 78.
[172] (1976) 7 D.R. 115.

of a trial under Art.6.[173] Whether or not it did so was to be determined by a consideration of the circumstances of the domestic proceedings as a whole. The Commission held that there was no violation of Art.6 on the facts of the case since the defence and the jury had been made fully aware of the circumstances in which the evidence was obtained; the evidence had been treated with appropriate caution and subjected to accomplice warnings; and the Court of Appeal had fully evaluated the whole of the evidence in considering an appeal against conviction. The Commission observed that:

> "[T]he manner in which the evidence . . . was obtained was openly discussed with counsel for the defence and before the jury. Furthermore, the Court of Appeal examined carefully whether due account was taken of these circumstances in the assessment of the evidence and whether there was corroboration. The Commission concludes, therefore, that an examination of the trial as a whole does not disclose any appearance of a violation of Article 6(1) of the Convention."[174]

The Commission also emphasised that the immunity which had been granted did **15–63** not amount to an inducement to give testimony favourable to the Crown since the accomplice could not in any event be prosecuted:

> "As regards the complaint that the trial was not fair because S. in giving evidence was influenced by the inducements contained in the letter of . . . April 1973, from the Director of Public Prosecutions to S's solicitors, the Commission observes that:
>
> (a) At the time he gave evidence, there was no possibility of S. being prosecuted because;
>
> > (i) he had been acquitted of certain charges at the Central Criminal Court before the proceedings against the applicant were commenced at the magistrates' court,
> > (ii) if other charges were later brought against S, his statements could not have been given in evidence against him because they had been obtained from him as a result of inducements."[175]

Once again, the chief concerns of the Commission lay with the safeguards in **15–64** place and the fairness of the trial as a whole.[176] However, it is noteworthy that one element to which the Commission appeared to attach importance was that the trial judge had warned about the dangers of accomplice evidence and that the Court of Appeal had made sure that there was corroboration. Since 1994 the trial judge's *duty* to give a warning about the dangers of acting on an accomplice's evidence without corroboration has been abrogated, in favour of a *discretion* to

---

[173] "The Commission observes in this connection that the use at the trial of evidence obtained from an accomplice by granting him an immunity from prosecution may put in question the fairness of the hearing granted to an accused person, and thus raise an issue under Art.6(1) of the Convention." *Ibid.*, at 118.

[174] *ibid.*, at 118.

[175] *ibid.*, at 118.

[176] On this, see also *MH v United Kingdom* [1997] E.H.R.L.R. 279, where a co-defendant's guilty plea was admitted into evidence on a conspiracy charge. The judge had warned the jury but had declined to exclude the guilty plea by using the s.78 discretion. The Commission did not find the trial as a whole unfair, and declared the application inadmissible.

warn (where appropriate) of the dangers of acting on unsupported evidence.[177] It is likely that most judges would give some kind of warning in cases where an accomplice has given evidence for the Crown,[178] but the absence of an adequate warning has the potential to violate the defendant's right to a fair trial under Art.6.

15–65   A similar point arose in *Charlene Webb v United Kingdom*,[179] where the applicant had been charged with drugs offences in Bermuda.[180] Two prosecution witnesses (who were servicemen) had pleaded guilty before a court martial and had been sentenced for their part in the offence. They received lenient treatment in return for agreeing to co-operate with the military authorities by providing information on civilians involved. The defendant was arrested and charged on the basis of the information which the accomplices had provided. The two accomplices then entered into a further agreement with the civilian authorities that they would not be prosecuted in the civilian courts provided that: (a) they agreed to give evidence for the prosecution of the applicant; (b) neither of them committed perjury in the course of giving evidence; and (c) the testimony they gave was consistent with the statements that they had previously made to the Bermuda police implicating the applicant. Despite the obvious risks associated with condition (c), and its potential inconsistency with (b), the Commission declared the application inadmissible:

> "The Commission notes that [the accomplices] had been charged, convicted and sentenced by the US court martial prior to giving evidence. Further [they] were granted immunity from prosecution in the civil jurisdiction. With regard to the condition imposed on [them] that they give evidence in accordance with their statements to the Bermuda police, the Commission notes that there was also an express obligation on [them] not to commit perjury. The judge further gave a clear direction on assessing the credibility of witnesses and the dangers of convicting on uncorroborated evidence, and the Court of Appeal confirmed this. The Commission considers that in these circumstances the exercise of the judge's discretion to admit the evidence of [the accomplices] cannot be said to have rendered the trial unfair within the meaning of Article 6(1)."

15–66   Whilst this decision shows a certain reluctance to intervene in accomplice cases, it is notable that the Commission again referred to the warnings which had been given to the jury as an important safeguard for the accused. Similarly, in *Baragiola v Switzerland*[181] the Commission emphasised the importance of careful scrutiny of accomplice evidence, but held that there was no objection in principle to allowing the prosecution to rely on the evidence of co-defendants who had already received reduced sentences for their co-operation:

> "[T]he sentences imposed on the co-defendants who had given evidence for the prosecution were considerably reduced and alleviated in other ways under the Italian legislation . . . As they ran the risk of losing the advantages they had been given if they

---

[177] S.32 of the Criminal Justice and Public Order Act 1994 For analysis, see Dennis I., *The Law of Evidence* (3rd edn 2006), Ch.15, and Choo A., *Evidence* (2006), 299–307.

[178] See *Makanjuola* [1995] 1 W.L.R. 1348.

[179] (1997) 24 E.H.R.R. CD 73.

[180] The United Kingdom has made a declaration under Art.63 of the Convention extending the application of the Convention to certain overseas territories, including Bermuda.

[181] (1993) 75 D.R. 76.

went back on their previous statements or retracted their confessions, their statements were open to question. It was therefore necessary for the Swiss courts to adopt a critical approach in assessing the statements of the [accomplices]."

The Commission held that so long as that testimony was open to challenge and   **15–67**
was not the only evidence, the trial was likely to be fair. However, in a case where there was evidence that police officers had spoken to the accomplice during his evidence, and another accomplice witness (who was in prison) had been allowed to read newspaper reports of the evidence given at trial before he was called, the Commission considered that the fairness of the trial was called into question.[182]

G. THE PRIVILEGE AGAINST SELF-INCRIMINATION

I. The Strasbourg Caselaw

In *Funke v France*[183] the Court held that the right to a fair trial in a criminal case   **15–68**
includes "the right of anyone charged with a criminal offence . . . to remain silent and not to contribute to incriminating himself".[184] Customs officers made a search of the applicant's house and, finding evidence that he had foreign bank accounts, they issued orders requiring him to produce certain details of those accounts. Failure to produce the documents was an offence, for which he was prosecuted, convicted and fined. It was submitted on his behalf that his conviction infringed his right to a fair trial under Art.6(1). He claimed that there was a right not to give evidence against oneself in the legal orders of the Contracting States, under the European Convention on Human Rights, and under the International Covenant on Civil and Political Rights (I.C.C.P.R.). The French authorities had brought criminal proceedings calculated to compel M. Funke to co-operate in a future prosecution to be mounted against him.

The French Government submitted that the customs and exchange control regime   **15–69**
operated in France saved taxpayers from having their affairs systematically investigated, but imposed duties in return, such as the duty to keep papers concerning their income and property, and the duty to make them available to the authorities on request. The customs, the argument continued, had not required M. Funke to confess to an offence or to provide evidence of one himself. They had merely asked him to give particulars of bank statements and cheque-books discovered during a search of his house.

The Commission held that the applicant's right to a fair trial under Art.6 had not   **15–70**
been breached. It could not "choose to ignore the special character of inquiries of an economic and financial nature", which are necessary "to protect the

---

[182] *X v United Kingdom* (1978, unpublished) 2 Dig. 393.
[183] (1993) 16 E.H.R.R. 297.
[184] Compare the statement of the common law privilege against self-incrimination by Browne-Wilkinson V.C. in *Tate Access Floors v Boswell* [1991] Ch. 512 at p.529: "a man is not bound to provide evidence against himself by being forced to answer questions or produce documents."

country's vital economic interests." In this context "coercion to supply information or produce documents is not as such exceptional," and indeed it can be regarded as "a *quid pro quo* for the trust reposed by the State in every citizen, which enables it to forego the adoption of more restrictive measures of control and supervision."[185]

15–71   The Court, on the other hand, took the view that the customs officers, being unable or unwilling to obtain the desired evidence by alternative means, had attempted to compel the applicant himself to provide evidence of the offences he had allegedly committed. In "discovering" a right to silence in Art.6, the Court said this:

> "The special features of [French] customs law . . . cannot justify such an infringement of the right of anyone charged with a criminal offence, within the autonomous meaning of this expression in Article 6, to remain silent and not to contribute to incriminating himself. There has accordingly been a breach of Article 6(1). The foregoing conclusion makes it unnecessary for the Court to ascertain whether M. Funke's conviction also contravened the presumption of innocence in Article 6(2)."[186]

15–72   With this statement, the Court established the accused's right to remain silent as a requirement of a fair trial under Art.6. Moreover, it established that the right is one that cannot easily be brushed aside by "public interest" considerations, since the court departed clearly from the Commission's view that any interests of the applicant must be subordinated to the importance of protecting a country's economic interests.

15–73   The operative passage of the *Funke* decision has been described as "brief and Delphic."[187] It left several questions unanswered. It was not clear whether the right "to remain silent and not to contribute to incriminating himself" was intended to apply only in court, or also at the investigation stage. The facts of the case were distributed across the two possibilities, since the applicant was fined for the non-production of documents, but those proceedings (although criminal) were ancillary to the prosecution that the customs authorities were intending to institute. However, since the original prosecution had never been brought (the first applicant having died), the case tends to suggest that the court regarded the right as applicable at the investigatory stage. As Sir Nicolas Bratza has pointed out, "the Court appears to have considered that the mere fact that a sanction is imposed for a refusal to produce potentially self-incriminating evidence constitutes a violation of the right to a fair hearing."[188] Further, the Court appears to have treated the right as applying not only to answers to questions but also to the compulsory production of documents or other real evidence.

---

[185] *ibid.*, at pp.313–314.
[186] *ibid.*, at paras 44–45.
[187] By Sir Nicolas Bratza, "The Implications of the Human Rights Act 1998 for Commercial Practice" [2000] E.H.R.L.R. 1 at 10.
[188] *ibid.*, at 11.

A different approach to these issues is evident in the subsequent decision in   **15-74**
Saunders v United Kingdom.[189] In this case the Court considered that the
admission in evidence at the applicant's trial of transcripts of interviews with
Inspectors of the Department of Trade and Industry, appointed to carry out an
investigation under ss.432–436 of the Companies Act 1985, violated Art.6(1)
since at the time of the interrogation the applicant was under a duty to answer the
inspectors' questions, which was enforceable by proceedings for contempt. The
British Government argued that the principle in *Funke* was not strictly relevant
because in that case the applicant was punished for refusal to incriminate himself,
whereas Ernest Saunders had co-operated with the Inspectors without incurring
any penalty. The response of the Commission was that anyone "who incriminates
himself under threat of punishment . . . and provides evidence for use against
himself at trial may be as seriously prejudiced, perhaps more so, as the applicant
who incurs the punishment for refusing to incriminate himself."

The Commission did observe that "the right to silence is not expressly guaran-   **15-75**
teed by Art.6 of the Convention, and accept[ed] that the right may not be
unqualified." Nevertheless, the Commission went on:

> "[T]he privilege against self-incrimination is an important element in safeguarding an
> accused from oppression and coercion during criminal proceedings. The very basis of
> a fair trial presupposes that the accused is afforded the opportunity of defending himself
> against the charges brought against him. The position of the defence is undermined if
> the accused is under compulsion, or has been compelled to incriminate himself. . . .
> Whether a particular applicant has been subject to compulsion to incriminate himself
> and whether the use made of the incriminating material has rendered criminal proceed-
> ings unfair will depend on an assessment of each case as a whole."[190]

The Government argued that "the right to silence or the privilege against self-   **15-76**
incrimination is not absolute, and that any departure from it [was] justified . . .
having regard . . . to the special status of persons conducting affairs of public
companies, who enjoy a fiduciary position towards the public." Here again, the
Commission decisively rejected the argument: "The right to silence, to the extent
that it may be contained in the guarantees of Article 6 must apply as equally to
alleged company fraudsters as to those accused of other types of fraud, rape,
murder or terrorist offences."[191]

The Court agreed with the conclusion of the Commission, holding that the right   **15-77**
to silence and the right not to incriminate oneself are generally recognised
international standards which lie "at the heart of a notion of a fair procedure"
under Art.6. The Court continued:

> "The right not to incriminate oneself, in particular, presupposes that the prosecution in
> a criminal case seek to prove their case against the accused without resort to evidence
> obtained through methods of coercion or oppression in defiance of the will of the

---

[189] (1997) 23 E.H.R.R. 313.
[190] *ibid.*, Commission, para.70.
[191] *ibid.*, para.71; *cf.* the similar rejection, by the court in *Teixeira de Castro v Portugal* (above,
para.15–37), of the proposition that an exception to the Art.6 right should be made for drug-
trafficking investigations.

accused. In this sense the right is closely linked to the presumption of innocence contained in Article 6(2) of the Convention."[192]

15–78   Before the Court the Government submitted that the admission of the interviews could not violate the right to self-incrimination because nothing said by the applicant was overtly harmful to his interests. He had merely given exculpatory answers which, if true, supported his defence. The Court held that the prohibition on the admission of evidence obtained by compulsory questioning did not depend on a confession of guilt:

> "[T]he right not to incriminate oneself cannot reasonably be confined to statements of admission of wrongdoing or to remarks which are directly incriminating. Testimony obtained under compulsion which appears on its face to be of a non-incriminating nature—such as exculpatory remarks or mere information on questions of fact—may later be deployed in criminal proceedings in support of the prosecution case, for example to contradict or cast doubt upon other statements of the accused or evidence given by him during the trial, or otherwise to undermine his credibility. Where the credibility of an accused must be addressed by a jury the use of such testimony may be especially harmful. It follows that what is of the essence in this context is the use to which evidence obtained under compulsion is [put] in the course of the criminal trial."[193]

On the facts, the Court concluded that the prosecution had used the transcripts during the trial in a manner which sought to incriminate the applicant. Accordingly their use was held to have rendered the trial unfair and in breach of Art.6.[194] *Saunders* remains the key Strasbourg judgment on the privilege against self-incrimination and, as will be apparent in the next section, its ambit has been much discussed in subsequent English decisions. Five questions arising from *Saunders* may be discussed at this stage.

15–79   *(i) Does the Privilege against Self-Incrimination apply universally?* It appears from *Saunders* that the privilege relates only to the admission of the evidence in criminal proceedings. It does not, in itself, prohibit the use of compulsory questioning powers in the course of a *purely administrative* investigation. The court emphasised that the role of the DTI investigation was essentially regulatory, and was thus distinct from that of the investigation or prosecution of crime. The role of the Inspectors was " . . . to ascertain and record facts which might subsequently be used as the basis for action by other competent authorities—prosecuting, regulatory, disciplinary or even legislative."[195] In *Abas v Netherlands*[196] the applicant had given information to the tax authorities when required to do so. Subsequently his family home was searched, and evidence thereby obtained was used in a prosecution for fraud and tax evasion. He was convicted and sentenced to imprisonment. The Commission declared the application inadmissible, on the basis that the obligation to answer the tax

---

[192] *ibid.*, court, para.68.
[193] *ibid.*, para.71.
[194] See also *Kansal v United Kingdom* (2004) 39 E.H.R.R. 31 (p.645).
[195] Para.67.
[196] [1997] E.H.R.L.R. 418.

inspector's questions did not infringe the right to silence (and the answers were not used in the criminal prosecution). The Commission also mentioned that compulsory powers are regarded as necessary in most countries to allow tax inspectors to carry out their functions. The Court considered the very point in *IJL, GMR and AKP v United Kingdom*,[197] an application by other defendants in the first Guinness trial. The applicants argued that the proceedings before the DTI inspectors should be treated as part of the prosecution process because of collusion between the inspectors and the prosecuting authorities, and that therefore they should have been accorded the rights of persons "charged with a criminal offence" during the DTI hearings. The Court rejected this argument, and with it the view that "a legal requirement for an individual to give information demanded by an *administrative body* necessarily infringes Article 6 of the Convention."[198] The use of the evidence at the subsequent trial infringed Art.6, but the compulsory questioning by inspectors did not.

Where the investigation is criminal rather than administrative, however, **15–80** the privilege against self-incrimination applies even at the early stages. Thus in *Heaney and McGuinness v Ireland*[199] the two applicants had been arrested on suspicion of terrorist acts and had been questioned by the police, under compulsory powers, as to their whereabouts at the time. They refused to answer: they were then prosecuted for and convicted of withholding information, and were sentenced to the maximum term of six months imprisonment. The Court held that the privilege against self-incrimination implied into Art.6 had been breached. In its judgment the Court referred to and indeed relied upon the early decision in *Funke v France*,[200] stating that "both cases concerned the threat and imposition of a criminal sanction on the applicants in question because they failed to supply information to authorities investigating the alleged commission of criminal offences."[201] In *Shannon v United Kingdom* the Court held "that the requirement for the applicant to attend an interview with financial investigators [appointed under the Proceeds of Crime (Northern Ireland) Order 1996] and to be compelled to answer questions in connection with events in respect of which he had already been charged with offences was not compatible with his right not to incriminate himself. There has therefore been a violation of Art.6(1) of the Convention."[202] However, a qualification appears to have been placed on the *Heaney and McGuinness* principle (without citing *Heaney and McGuinness*) in *King v United Kingdom*,[203] where the Court held (in an admissibility decision) that a

---

[197] (2001) 33 E.H.R.R. 225.
[198] *ibid.*, para.100.
[199] (2001) 33 E.H.R.R. 264.
[200] Above, at 15–71.
[201] 33 E.H.R.R. 264, at para.49.
[202] (2006) 42 E.H.R.R. 31 (p.660), [41].
[203] April 8, 2003.

compulsory requirement to provide information did not violate the privilege, since he was then prosecuted for failing to respond to that requirement and not for "an offence due to acts or omissions in which he had been involved prior to that moment." This decision may be regarded as further destabilising the law on the point.

15–81   *(ii) Does the Privilege apply in all circumstances of Compulsion to provide Evidence?* After stating that the right not to incriminate oneself is closely linked to the presumption of innocence, forming part of fair procedure and contributing to the avoidance of miscarriages of justice, the Court went on to draw a distinction between the provision of "real" evidence and the provision of oral or testimonial evidence:

> "The right not to incriminate oneself is primarily concerned, however, with respecting the will of an accused person to remain silent. As commonly understood in the legal systems of the Contracting Parties to the Convention and elsewhere, it does not extend to the use in criminal proceedings of material which may be obtained from the accused through the use of compulsory powers but which has an existence independent of the will of the suspect such as, *inter alia*, documents acquired pursuant to a warrant, breath, blood and urine samples, and bodily tissues for the purpose of DNA testing."[204]

This distinction seems to amount to little more than a pragmatic attempt to rein back the possible implications of the privilege against self-incrimination. It is true that the laws of many Contracting States contain provisions for the compulsory taking of blood samples and other samples, in motoring cases and for other crimes. In terms of practical law enforcement, it is difficult to resist the pressure to allow some such procedures.[205] This may also account for earlier decisions of the Commission which point in the same direction. In a 1962 case the Commission held that a legal obligation to undergo a medical examination in the course of a criminal investigation is not, in itself, incompatible with Art.6(2).[206] And in *X v Netherlands*[207] the Commission adopted the same approach in relation to a statutory requirement to provide an evidential breath specimen, in the context of an investigation into an offence of driving with excess alcohol. Accordingly, a complaint that the applicant's prosecution for failure to provide a specimen was in breach of Art.6(2) was declared manifestly ill-founded.[208]

---

[204] (1997) 23 E.H.R.R. 313 at para.69. In *J.B. v Switzerland* [2001] Crim.L.R. 748, the Court (para.68) added that the compulsory fitting of a tachograph to a lorry would not engage the privilege; in *PG and JH v United Kingdom* [2002] Crim.L.R. 308 the Court held (para.80) that voice samples obtained for comparison (not for their content) did not engage the privilege.

[205] For discussion of the American authorities, see Easton S., "Bodily Samples and the Privilege against Self-Incrimination" [1991] Crim.L.R. 18, and Dennis I., "Instrumental Protection, Human Right or Functional Necessity? Reassessing the Privilege against Self-Incrimination" (1995) 54 Camb. L.J. 342 at 373–375.

[206] *X v Germany* (1962) 5 Y.B. 193 at 199.

[207] (1978) 16 D.R. 184.

[208] *cf. HM Advocate v Brown* [2001] 2 W.L.R. 817.

However, neither in *Saunders* nor in any other decision have the Stras- **15–82** bourg organs offered a rationale for the distinction between the application of the privilege to testimonial evidence and its non-application to real evidence.[209] In *Jalloh v Germany*,[210] where evidence had been obtained by forcibly administering emetics to the applicant, the Grand Chamber distinguished the case from the above paragraph from *Saunders* on three grounds—first, that the obtaining of the evidence was plainly "in defiance of the applicant's will"; secondly, the degree of force was great, involving four police officers; and thirdly, the procedure was such as to violate Art.3.[211] However, the Grand Chamber went on to suggest that the weight of the public interest in securing a conviction for this offence was a factor to be taken into account.[212] This ruling adds to the collection of uncertainties surrounding the privilege against self-incrimination in European human rights law. Thus, insofar as the Art.8 right to respect for private life is concerned, one might have thought that compulsory submission to blood, breath or other bodily tests represents a greater interference than forced speech.[213] Moreover, the application of the distinction to documentary evidence has not been explained convincingly. As we have seen,[214] the Court found a violation in *Funke* in respect of the failure to provide documents which, one would have thought, had an existence independent of the will of the accused. The ruling in *Funke* was approved by the Court in *Heaney and McGuinness v Ireland*,[215] although without reference to the *Saunders* distinction. In *JB v Switzerland*[216] the Court found a breach of Art.6 where the applicant was fined for failing to hand over financial records to the tax authorities: the Court distinguished such documents from the blood or urine samples referred to in *Saunders*, noting that the latter "had an existence independent of the person concerned and [were] not, therefore, obtained by means of coercion and in defiance of the will of that person".[217] Several points call for further elaboration by the Court. On the one hand, documents have an existence independent of the person concerned; on the other hand, a requirement to produce documents operates on the will of the subject, but so does a requirement to submit to certain bodily tests. Alternatively, does the true distinction lie between compulsion to produce pre-existing documents and compulsion to give written details put together specifically in

---

[209] See the doubts expressed by Lord Bingham in *Brown v Scott* [2001] 2 W.L.R. 817, discussed at para.15–94 below.

[210] App.No.54810/00, judgment of July 11, 2006; above, 15–07.

[211] *Ibid*, paras 116–117.

[212] *Ibid*, para.119; *cf.* the Concurring Opinion of Judge Bratza, disagreeing on this point.

[213] See Ashworth, *Human Rights, Serious Crime and Criminal Procedure* (2002), pp.18–23, for further discussion and references.

[214] See para.15–68 above.

[215] Above, n.199 and text.

[216] [2001] Crim.L.R. 748. Judgment May 3, 2001 at para.68.

[217] *cf. Attorney-General's Reference No.7 of 2000* [2001] EWCA Crim 888, [2001] 2 Cr.App.R. 19 (p.286), where the Court of Appeal held that documents delivered to the Official Receiver under compulsion fell within the *Saunders* exception for "real evidence" and, unlike statements made by the accused under compulsion, were outside the privilege against self-incrimination. See also the discussion of a production order under PACE in the judgment of Judge L.J. in *R. v Central Criminal Court ex parte The Guardian, The Observer and Bright* [2001] 1 W.L.R. 662.

response to the requirement? On the last point, *Saunders* seems to favour reserving the privilege to the latter form of compulsion, but the decisions in *Funke* and in *J.B. v Switzerland* appear to adopt the contrary view, although without analysis.[218]

15–83　　*(iii) Where the Privilege does apply, is it Absolute or Not?* The privilege against self-incrimination is an implied right that forms part of the right to a fair hearing embodied in Art.6. The scope of the right is likely to be developed through decisions of the Court, and in *Saunders* the Court did not "find it necessary . . . to decide whether the right not to incriminate oneself is absolute or whether infringements of it may be justified in particular circumstances."[219] This should not be taken to suggest that the privilege can simply be "outweighed" by considerations of the public interest, as the Court immediately made clear:

> "It does not accept the Government's argument that the complexity of corporate fraud and the vital public interest in the investigation of such fraud and the punishment of those responsible could justify such a marked departure as that which occurred in the present case from one of the basic principles of fair procedure."[220]

Indeed, it was the Court's view that both the fairness requirements of Art.6 generally and the privilege itself "apply to criminal proceedings in respect of all types of criminal offences without distinction from the most simple to the most complex." This point is strongly underscored by the decision in *Heaney and McGuinness v Ireland*,[221] where the Irish government had argued that the compulsion to answer questions was a proportionate response to the threat to public security arising from terrorism. The Court disagreed, and evidently took the view that "proportionality" of this kind was not the issue:

> "The Court . . . finds that the security and public order concerns of the Government cannot justify a provision which extinguishes the very essence of the applicants' right to silence and their right not to incriminate themselves guaranteed by Article 6(1) of the Convention."[222]

Thus, the essence of the privilege must be preserved, and in both *Saunders* and *Heaney and McGuinness* the Court was careful to state that the particular departures from the privilege could not be justified.[223] This brings one back to the point left open in *Saunders*: if the privilege against self-incrimination is not absolute, in what circumstances might an exception be made? To this there is no answer at present, save that the decisions

---

[218] The Court of Appeal in *Attorney-General's Reference No.7 of 2000* [2001] EWCA Crim 888, [2001] 2 Cr.App.R. 19 (p.286) preferred the *Saunders* position: see further Ward T. and Gardner P., "The Privilege against Self-Incrimination: in Search of Legal Certainty", [2003] E.H.R.L.R. 388.

[219] (1997) 23 E.H.R.R. 313, at para.74.

[220] *Ibid.*

[221] (2001) 33 E.H.R.R. 264, above, para.15–80.

[222] *Ibid*, para.58.

[223] The "very essence" test in *Heaney and McGuinness* was reiterated by the court in *Allan v United Kingdom* (2002) 36 E.H.R.R. 143, again without any suggestion that the privilege could be "balanced" against the public interest or the seriousness of the crime.

in *Saunders* and *Heaney and McGuinness* do establish that simply balancing the privilege against considerations of the public interest (and even public security) is not a legitimate route. The Court has stated that the privilege "does not act as a prohibition on the use of compulsory powers to require taxpayers to provide information about their financial affairs,"[224] but it is not clear whether this is regarded as an exception.

(iv) Are there other Authorities inconsistent with these? Two decisions might   **15–84**
be discussed briefly. The Commission's ruling in *Tora Tolmos v Spain*[225]
appears inconsistent with the above version of the privilege. The applicant's car was photographed breaking the speed limit, and the police sent him a notice requiring him to state who was driving his car at that particular time and place. He contended that his conviction for the offence of failing to comply with this notice breached his privilege against self-incrimination. The Commission declared the application inadmissible, holding that a law of this kind is not necessarily incompatible with Art.6:

> " . . . the person concerned is not inevitably obliged to admit his or her own
> guilt or to incriminate a relative. Depending on the circumstances, they may be
> able to show that they had nothing to do with the offence committed by the
> driver, for instance by establishing that the vehicle was being used by someone
> whose identity is unknown to them or whom they had not authorised to use
> it."

In reaching this conclusion the Commission did not discuss *Funke*, which ought to have had a bearing on the reasoning adopted[226]; and in any event the *Tora Tolmos* ruling must now be read in the light of the reference in *Heaney and McGuinness* to ensuring that the "very essence" of the privilege against self-incrimination is protected. Some may argue, however, that this may be an infringement that can be justified as necessary for practical law enforcement, perhaps on the ground that the benefits to society are so much greater than the relatively small obligation placed on citizens. The Court has not yet accepted such a line of argument.

Secondly, in *Serves v France*[227] the Court found no violation of Art.6   **15–85**
where the applicant was fined after refusing to take the oath as a witness. The Court, disagreeing with the Commission's ruling, drew a distinction between the solemn act of taking the oath—a necessary foundation for judicial proceedings—and any subsequent obligation to answer questions or to incriminate oneself:

> "Whilst a witness's obligation to take the oath and the penalties imposed for
> failure to do so involve a degree of coercion, the latter is designed to ensure that
> any statements made to the judge are truthful, not to force witnesses to give
> evidence. In other words, the fines imposed on Mr Serves did not constitute a

---

[224] *King v United Kingdom*, April 8, 2003, para.2. See also *Allen v United Kingdom* (2002) 35 E.H.R.R. CD 289.
[225] (1995) 81 D.R. 82.
[226] As suggested in the article by Sir Nicolas Bratza (above, n.187), at 11–12.
[227] (1999) 28 E.H.R.R. 265.

measure such as to compel him to incriminate himself as they were imposed before such a risk ever arose."[228]

In this case the applicant had been called as a witness in the investigation of two other men involved in an alleged murder, and his argument was that the decision to call him as a witness was a subterfuge to avoid according to him his privilege against self-incrimination under French law. The Court held that the applicant was to be treated as a "person charged", for the purposes of Art.6, because a case file was still open against him; but the decision to find no violation of Art.6 implies that he should have taken the oath but may then have chosen not to answer questions that might incriminate him. On that analysis, the decision is not inconsistent with the privilege.

15–86   (v) *How has the Saunders judgment been applied and interpreted?* It is apparent from the foregoing paragraphs that the Strasbourg Court has yet to reach a clear position on the ambit of the privilege against self-incrimination. Several areas of uncertainty—whether the privilege applies only to the use of evidence in criminal proceedings, or also to compulsory obtaining of evidence than may be so used; the extent to which the privilege applies to documents; what circumstances might found an exception to the privilege; and so forth—have been identified. Where legal doctrine is being developed judicially, uncertainties are not unusual. The difficulty here is that the Court appears to cite different authorities on different occasions, and has avoided opportunities to review the subject and to take some steps towards greater clarity. When it did cite most of the authorities in a single judgment, that of the Grand Chamber in *Jalloh v Germany*,[229] it did little to resolve the uncertainties. Similarly, the Court's decision that the application in *Allen v United Kingdom*[230] was inadmissible is also more of a judgment on the facts. In this case the applicant had responded to a coercive demand by giving false information to the tax authorities, and on that basis it was easy for the Court to distinguish the previous decisions and to hold that the privilege against self-incrimination does not confer a right to tell lies. The Court did nothing to resolve a further strand of uncertainty—how much compulsion is permissible in order to ensure that obligations to pay taxes are not avoided?—since it appeared to hold that a fine of up to £300 might not be regarded as "coercion" for the purposes of invoking the privilege, contrasting that with the possible prison sentence in *Saunders* but failing to reconcile it with the holding in *J.B. v Switzerland*[231] to the effect that a potential fine of some £700 would amount to "coercion". The same point is left unresolved in *King v United Kingdom*,[232] where the Court held that one reason why the privilege was not violated was that "the applicant faced the risk of, at most, a financial penalty for refusal to

---

[228] *ibid.*, para.47.
[229] Above, notes 214 and 216.
[230] (2002) 35 E.H.R.R. CD 289, [2003] Crim.L.R. 280.
[231] [2001] Crim.L.R. 748, above, para.15–82.
[232] April 8, 2003, para.2.

declare his assets, in contrast to the position faced by the applicants in *Saunders* and *J.B. v Switzerland*," an extraordinary interpretation of the latter decision.

II. Self-Incrimination and the Human Rights Act

The practical effects of the *Saunders* decision have been significantly reduced by s.59 and Sch.3 to the Youth Justice and Criminal Evidence Act 1999 which amend many of the statutory provisions creating exceptions to the privilege against self-incrimination,[233] and introduce restrictions on the use of answers obtained under compulsion. Thus, for example, s.434 of the Companies Act 1985 is amended as follows: **15–87**

> "In criminal proceedings in which that persons is charged with an offence to which this subsection applies—
>
> (a) no evidence relating to the statement may be adduced, and
> (b) no question relating to it may be asked,
>
> by or on behalf of the prosecution, unless evidence relating to it is adduced, or a question relating to it is asked, in the proceedings by or on behalf of that person."

It is apparent that the amendment leaves untouched the compulsion to answer an Inspector's questions, but provides that answers may not be referred to by the prosecution in criminal proceedings.

One of the statutory provisions which was not amended by the 1999 Act is s.71(2) of the Environmental Protection Act 1990. The House of Lords had the opportunity in *R. v Hertfordshire County Council ex parte Green Environmental Industries Ltd*[234] to consider the relationship between that provision and the Strasbourg authorities. When clinical waste was found on an unlicensed site used by the applicants, the Council served on them a notice under s.71(2)(b), which empowers a waste regulation authority "by notice in writing served on him, [to] require any person to furnish such information specified in the notice as the authority reasonably considers it needs . . . ". Failure to comply with the notice is an offence triable either way. The applicants asked for an undertaking that the information would not be used in a subsequent prosecution, but the Council declined to give one. The applicants then challenged the validity of the notice. Lord Hoffmann, in the leading speech in the House of Lords, held that the notice was not in breach of Art.6 of the Convention, because the case raised the question of the duty to provide information, whereas the Strasbourg authorities were concerned with the use to which answers were put in criminal proceedings. If a prosecution had been brought, an English judge would have the opportunity to exclude the evidence under s.78 of the Police and Criminal Evidence Act 1984; but that would not affect the validity of the statutory notice itself. Lord Hoffmann based his conclusion on *Saunders v United Kingdom*[235]: **15–88**

---

[233] On which see Jackson J.D., "The Right of Silence: Judicial Responses to Parliamentary Encroachment", (1994) 57 M.L.R. 270.
[234] [2000] 2 W.L.R. 373.
[235] Above, para.15–74.

"The European jurisprudence under Article 6(1) is firmly anchored to the fairness of the trial and is not concerned with extrajudicial inquiries. Such impact as Article 6(1) may have is upon the use of such evidence at a criminal trial. Although it is true that the council, unlike the DTI inspectors, had power to prosecute in criminal proceedings, I do not think that the request for information under section 71(2) could be described as an adjudication . . . "[236]

15–89   When he came to consider *Funke v France*,[237] Lord Hoffmann found "obscurities" in the Court's reasoning. He pointed out that Funke had not been obliged to incriminate himself in the proceedings for failure to produce the documents, since he could be convicted of that offence simply for the non-production; and no further prosecution had been brought. Although this approach may be thought to draw some support from *IJL, GMR and AKP v United Kingdom*,[238] where the Court held that "whether or not information obtained under compulsory powers by such a body violates the right to a fair hearing must be seen from the standpoint of the use made of that information at the trial," it has now been strongly disavowed by the court's subsequent decision in *Heaney and McGuinness v Ireland*.[239] Where a person stands to be convicted for failing to produce a document or to answer questions, that amounts to compulsion sufficient to violate the privilege against self-incrimination in relation to the more serious offence, be it tax evasion, terrorism or an environmental offence.

15–90   Lord Hoffmann supported his conclusion by reference to the decision of the European Court of Justice in *Orkem v Commission of the European Communities*.[240] By a Regulation the Commission was empowered to obtain information in relation to price-fixing activities, in order to enforce competition laws. The court drew a distinction between questions "intended only to secure factual information . . . and the requirement of disclosure of documents", which were permissible, and questions designed to secure admissions that the company had been involved in price fixing, which were invalid as infringing the "need to safeguard the rights of the defence which the court had held to be a fundamental principle of the Community legal order."[241] Lord Hoffmann noted that in *Green* all the Council's requests were for factual information. None invited any admission of wrongdoing.

15–91   The unanimous decision of the House of Lords in *Green* is therefore based on the finding that, because a request under s.71(2) of the 1990 Act "does not itself form a part, even a preliminary part, of any criminal proceedings," it does not "touch the principle which prohibits interrogation of a person charged or accused." Much therefore depends on the characterisation of the particular procedure. One could regard the decision in *Ex parte Green* as turning on the *administrative* nature of the investigation which was underway[242] (although the council did have the power to prosecute). It might then be contrasted with the Court's subsequent

---

[236] [2000] 2 W.L.R. 373 at 381–382.
[237] Above, para.15–79.
[238] (2001) 33 E.H.R.R. 225.
[239] (2001) 33 E.H.R.R. 264, above, para.15–80.
[240] [1989] E.C.R. 3283.
[241] *ibid.*, at 3351, para.52.
[242] See para.15–79 above.

decision in *Heaney and McGuinness v Ireland*,[243] which holds that if a person is prosecuted for an offence arising out of a failure to answer questions in a *criminal* investigation there will be a breach of Art.6. The connection with possible prosecution is much stronger if one considers a production order for special procedure material under the Police and Criminal Evidence Act 1984. Such an order may only be granted if there are reasonable grounds for believing that the material will be of substantial value to the investigation of a serious arrestable offence. In *R. v Central Criminal Court ex parte The Guardian, The Observer and Bright*,[244] Judge L.J. held that a production order of this kind may breach the privilege against self-incrimination insofar as it obliges a journalist to hand over items of evidence to the police which may be incriminating.

The connection between requiring a person to furnish information and the use of   **15–92** that information in subsequent proceedings came into sharp focus in relation to s.172(2) of the Road Traffic Act 1988. We have already seen that in *Tora Tolmos v Spain*[245] the European Commission of Human Rights held that such a requirement is not necessarily inconsistent with the privilege against self-incrimination because it is possible to fulfil it without incriminating oneself. This issue has now been discussed by both the High Court of Justiciary and the Privy Council in *Brown v Procurator Fiscal, Dunfermline*,[246] where the appellant was arrested for theft from a supermarket and then observed to smell of alcohol. She was asked who had been driving her car about an hour earlier and, on answering that it was her, was then breathalysed and arrested for driving with excess alcohol. At her trial she challenged this use of the power in s.172 of the Road Traffic Act 1988 on the ground that it infringed her rights under Art.6. In a lengthy and detailed judgment delivered by the Lord Justice General, the High Court of Justiciary upheld her challenge.

Whereas in *Saunders* the statements made by the applicant to the DTI inspectors   **15–93** were taken to have been made in an *administrative* investigation before a criminal investigation was in train, in this case the power under s.172 had been used by the police as part of their criminal investigation. In response to the argument that s.172 forms a necessary part of a regulatory scheme, the Lord Justice General followed the Supreme Court of Canada in *White*[247] in holding that the privilege against self-incrimination applies where compelled self-incriminatory statements are admitted in evidence, whether part of a "regulatory" scheme or otherwise:

> "I am satisfied that the applicant was subject to compulsion to make an incriminating reply under threat of being found guilty of an offence and punished with a fine. The Crown propose to use evidence of the answer given by the appellant as a significant part of the prosecution case against her at her trial. For the reasons which I have given, the use that the Crown propose to make of the appellant's answer would offend her right

---

[243] (2001) 33 E.H.R.R. 264.
[244] [2001] 1 W.L.R. 662.
[245] Above, para.15–78 (???).
[246] High Court of Justiciary, February 4, 2000; [2001] 2 W.L.R. 817.
[247] [1999] 2 S.C.R. 417, *per* Iacobucci J. at 450. Cf. *R. v SAB* [2003] 2 S.C.R. 678.

not to incriminate herself, which is a constituent element of the basic principles of fair procedure inherent in Article 6(1)."

15–94 The Privy Council unanimously allowed the prosecutor's appeal in *Brown v Stott*.[248] In the leading speech Lord Bingham surveyed the Convention jurisprudence in a general fashion, and then articulated three reasons why neither s.172 itself, nor the use at a subsequent trial of evidence obtained by invoking s.172, is contrary to Art.6:

> "(1) Section 172 provides for the putting of a single, simple question . . . the section does not sanction prolonged questioning about the facts alleged to give rise to criminal offences such as was understandably held to be objectionable in *Saunders*, and the penalty for declining to answer under the section is moderate and non-custodial. There is in the present case no suggestion of improper coercion or oppression . . . "

This first reason appears to draw the line between permissible and improper coercion by reference to two considerations, the length of questioning and the size of the penalty for not answering. The "single, simple question" argument cannot stand with the subsequent Strasbourg decision in *Heaney and McGuinness v Ireland*,[249] where there was also a single question to be asked. The possible penalty was greater than Lord Bingham allowed, since he failed to mention disqualification from driving, and there are other decisions to the effect that a fine may amount to sufficient compulsion to engage Art.6.[250]

> "(2) While the High Court was entitled to distinguish between the giving of an answer under section 172 and the provision of physical samples, and had the authority of the European Court in *Saunders* for doing so, this distinction should not in my opinion be pushed too far. It is true that the respondent's answer, whether given orally or in writing, would create new evidence which did not exist until she spoke or wrote. In contrast, it may be acknowledged that the percentage of alcohol in her breath was a fact . . . "

In this passage Lord Bingham points to an obvious weakness in the *Saunders* judgment: why should compulsion to submit one's body to tests be regarded as less significant or intrusive than the compulsion to speak? The only reason advanced in *Saunders* was that all legal systems find the former to be necessary, which is a pragmatic reason rather than a principled justification. As argued in 15–82 above, the Strasbourg authorities on this point need to be re-worked if they are to be convincing.

> "(3) All who own or drive motor cars know that by doing so they subject themselves to a regulatory regime . . . , imposed because the possession and use of cars (like, for example, shotguns, the possession of which is very closely regulated) are recognised to have the potential to cause grave injury . . . If . . . one asks whether section 172 represents a disproportionate legislative response to the problem of maintaining road safety, whether the balance between the interests of the community at large and the interests of the individual is struck in a manner unduly prejudicial to the individual, whether (in short) the leading of this evidence would infringe a basic human right of the respondent, I would feel bound to give negative answers."

---

[248] [2001] 2 W.L.R. 817.
[249] Above, para.15–80.
[250] See *J.B. v Switzerland* [2001] Crim.L.R. 748.

All their Lordships recognised the force of the *Saunders* decision but felt able to distinguish it on the facts. As Lord Bingham put it, "the High Court interpreted the decision in *Saunders* as laying down a more absolute standard than I think the European Court intended." Lord Steyn made exactly the same point. However, this approach fails to take account of the clear statements in *Saunders*, since repeated in *Heaney and McGuinness*, to the effect that the seriousness of the offence or complexity of the case has no bearing on the application of the privilege against self-incrimination. It must also now be read in the light of the Court's insistence in *Heaney and McGuinness* that the "essence" of the privilege must be protected.[251]

The decision of the Privy Council in *Brown v Stott* stands as a significant   **15–95**
landmark in British human rights law. It was the first decision at the highest level on the Human Rights Act. The judgments are suffused with the assumption that an Art.6 right (or, at least, this implied right) can simply be "traded off" against considerations of public interest and then discarded. The use of the "proportion-ality" concept in this context was particularly unfortunate. Not only is it plain from *Saunders* and other decisions that infringements of the privilege against self-incrimination cannot be justified on a bare test of proportionality, but the Privy Council's actual reasoning relied to some extent on a quotation from the Strasbourg Court's dictum in *Sporrong and Lonnroth v Sweden*[252] that relates to a right that has an explicit "public interest" exception (Art.1 of Protocol 1). It is well established that interference with one of the rights declared in Arts 8–11 may be justified by reference to what is "necessary in a democratic society", but the justification has to conform with the conditions set out in the Article. Article 6 declares a stronger right that contains no express justifications for interference, and it was therefore quite inappropriate for the Privy Council to invoke a simple "balancing" test—which is less demanding than the conditions for justifying an interference with Arts 8–11. The characterisation of the privilege against self-incrimination as an implied right does not weaken this point. All these criticisms are strengthened by the Court's subsequent decision in *Heaney and McGuinness v Ireland*, to which frequent reference has been made in the foregoing para-graphs, both for its general approach to the issue of proportionality and its conclusion on the particular point.

There are also two internal British criticisms of the Privy Council's judgment.   **15–96**
First, there appears to be no reference to the House of Lords decision in *R. v Hertfordshire County Council ex parte Green Environmental Industries*,[253] where similar issues were discussed in the Convention context. It is not clear what remains of the distinction drawn in that case between "extra-judicial inquiries" on the one hand and the admission of evidence at trial on the other, and what impact the subsequent decision in *Heaney and McGuinness* has on the relevance of that distinction to the facts of *Ex parte Green*. Secondly, it could also be argued that many of the provisions for compulsory powers that were amended by s.59 and Sch.3 of the Youth Justice and Criminal Evidence Act 1999 need not

---

[251] Above, para.15–80.
[252] (1982) 5 E.H.R.R. 35.
[253] Above, para.15–88.

have been amended if the restrictive interpretation of *Saunders* adopted in *Brown* had been thought plausible, which it was clearly not.

15–97   How might the Strasbourg Court be expected to respond to an application on the facts of *Brown v Stott*? This would be very much a case of first impression. If the Court followed its own dictum in *Saunders*, then the same standards of fair procedure should apply to all types of case, whether serious or minor, whether complex or simple. On the other hand, the Court might be persuaded to reflect the general consensus among member states (if such it is) that compulsory questioning powers in relation to the owners of motor vehicles are justifiable as necessary in the interests of public safety and practicality. If some such argument could be mounted,[254] then it might become the first recognised exception to the privilege against self-incrimination—or, perhaps, the second exception, if cases of bodily samples etc. are properly to be characterised as an exception to the privilege rather than as simply lying outside its ambit.

15–98   Three subsequent decisions should be mentioned. First, in *Allen*[255] the House of Lords dismissed the argument based on self-incrimination and upheld the appellant's conviction for cheating the revenue. Compulsory powers had been used to require him to furnish details, and the House held that the powers were permissible, citing Lord Bingham's sweeping reference to the acceptability of "limited qualification of these rights . . . if reasonably directed by national authorities towards a clear and proper public objective," a point criticised above as inconsistent with the Strasbourg jurisprudence.[256] As we have seen,[257] the Strasbourg Court also found no violation of Art.6, but did so by focussing on the fact that the applicant had responded not with silence but with false information.

15–99   Secondly, in *Attorney-General's Reference No.7 of 2000*[258] the Court of Appeal held that a requirement in the Insolvency Act which imposed on a bankrupt a duty to deliver up certain documents (on pain of imprisonment for failure) did not

---

[254] For a sophisticated argument on this and related issues, see Sedley S., "Wringing Out the Fault: Self-Incrimination in the 21st Century", (2001) 52 N.I.L.Q. 107. Following the decision in *Brown v Stott*, the Divisional Court in *D.P.P. v Wilson* [2001] EWHC 198 (Admin), (2001) 165 J.P. 715 referred to the limited nature of the information required of the vehicle owner, compared with the general interest of the community. This still does not confront the nature and extent of the coercion implicit in the Road Traffic Act provisions. *Wilson* has, however, been followed in *Charlebois v DPP*, where it was held that "the use of sections 172(2)(a) and (b) for alleged offences of speeding and going through a red light is a proportionate legislative response to the problem of maintaining road safety. Offences of speeding and going through a red light not only lead to the endorsement of a licence and the award of penalty points, but may, in certain circumstances, lead to a driver being disqualified from driving": [2003] EWHC 54 (Admin), [12]. The argument that these were not serious offences but merely offences of a regulatory nature was accordingly rejected: *ibid.* [13]. Similarly, it has been stated in *Mawdesley v Chief Constable of Cheshire*: "Speeding may present the gravest danger to the public. It cannot sensibly be argued that it is disproportionate to admit an incriminating answer to a section 172 request in a speeding case, but not in a drink/driving case": [2003] EWHC 1586 (Admin), [2004] 1 W.L.R. 1035, [41].
[255] [2001] UKHL 45.
[256] *Ibid*, para.30. Lord Bingham's approach was criticised at 15–94 above.
[257] Above, para.15–86.
[258] [2001] 2 Cr.App.R. 286.

violate the privilege, even if the documents so delivered were used in a subsequent prosecution, because the privilege does not apply to pre-existing documents. The court purported to follow *Saunders* as distinct from *Funke* on this point, but the subsequent decision in *J.B. v Switzerland*[259] holds that the privilege can apply to the coerced delivery of existing documents. This is one of the points of uncertainty (see 15–82 above) that requires clarification by the Strasbourg Court.

Thirdly, in *Kearns*[260] the defendant had been convicted of, being a bankrupt,   **15–100** failing to account for the loss of certain property as required by s.354 of the Insolvency Act 1986. The court upheld the conviction and dismissed the argument that the defendant's privilege against self-incrimination had been violated. After an extensive review of the decisions both in Strasbourg and in this country, the court adopted the distinction emphasised by Lord Hoffmann in *R. v Hertfordshire County Council ex parte Green Environmental Industries*, between criminal proceedings and administrative or extra-judicial enquiries. Thus Aikens J. held:

> "(5) A law will not be likely to infringe the right to silence or not to incriminate oneself if it demands the production of information for an administrative purpose or in the course of an extra-judicial enquiry. However, if the information so produced is or could be used in subsequent judicial proceedings, whether criminal or civil, then the use of the information in those proceedings could breach those rights and so make that trial unfair.
> (6) Whether that is the case will depend on all the circumstances of the case, but in particular (a) whether the information demanded is factual or an admission of guilt, and (b) whether the demand for the information and its subsequent use in proceedings is proportionate to the particular social or economic problem that the relevant law is intended to address."[261]

Consistent as these propositions are with the British authorities, they remain difficult to reconcile with some of the Strasbourg decisions. Thus Aikens J. mentions, without comment, the Strasbourg Court's conclusion in *Heaney and McGuinness v Ireland* that the requirement to answer questions could not be accepted as a proportionate response to the terrorist threat[262]—not noticing that it sits awkwardly with *Brown v Stott*. Aikens J. makes much of the point that the purpose of the questioning in *Heaney and McGuinness* was to provide evidence for a subsequent prosecution, and states that the same purpose explains the decision in *J.B. v Switzerland*. It remains for the Strasbourg Court to articulate its true position on these issues. Its failure to give a single authoritative judgment has encouraged the British courts to pursue their own, apparently different path.

---

[259] [2001] Crim.L.R. 748, above, para.15–82.
[260] [2002] EWCA Crim 748, [2002] Crim.L.R. 650.
[261] *Ibid*, para.53.
[262] In fact, as appears from para.15–83 above, the Court did not accept that "proportionality" was the issue: that is a concept that the British courts have imported into discussions of the privilege against self-incrimination.

H. ADVERSE INFERENCES FROM SILENCE

I. The Strasbourg Caselaw

15–101 The precise relationship between the privilege against self-incrimination and the right of silence depends on the scope of each, and there are no agreed definitions. The above discussion of self-incrimination assumes, as the Strasbourg Court implies, that the privilege relates to cases where there is a significant penalty for failure to answer questions—such as a conviction or finding of contempt of court, together with a substantial fine or heavier penalty. The so-called right of silence refers to the limitations on drawing adverse inferences from a defendant's failure to answer questions, usually questions from the police or other agency at the investigation stage, but also at trial.

15–102 The first of the important decisions is *Murray v United Kingdom*,[263] where the Court found that the Criminal Evidence (Northern Ireland) Order 1988,[264] as applied to the facts of that case, did not constitute a violation of Art.6(1). The applicant had remained silent under police questioning and in court, and failed to account for his presence at the scene of the alleged crime. The Court emphasised that the independent evidence of guilt was strong, and that the Northern Ireland legislation incorporated a number of safeguards: in particular, the adverse inferences had been drawn by a judge sitting without a jury, and his decision was recorded in a reasoned judgment which was susceptible to scrutiny on appeal.[265]

15–103 The Court went on to hold that whether the drawing of adverse inferences is compatible with Art.6 will depend on the degree of compulsion inherent in the situation and the nature of any inferences which are drawn:

> "On the one hand, it is self-evident that it is incompatible with the immunities under consideration to base a conviction solely or mainly on the accused's silence or on a refusal to answer questions or to give evidence himself. On the other hand, the Court deems it equally obvious that these immunities cannot and should not prevent that the accused's silence, in situations which clearly call for an explanation from him, be taken into account in assessing the persuasiveness of the evidence adduced by the prosecution."[266]

15–104 The Court in *Murray* nevertheless found a breach of Art.6 arising out of the denial of access to a solicitor in the course of police detention. Since the relevant legislation permitted adverse inferences to be drawn from a failure to answer questions, access to legal advice was of "paramount importance" to ensure that the position of the detained person was not "irretrievably prejudiced". In the light of this finding, s.24 of the Youth Justice and Criminal Evidence Act 1999 was enacted so as to provide that an adverse inference cannot be drawn under s.34 of the Criminal Justice and Public Order Act 1994 in respect of a person who

---

[263] (1996) 22 E.H.R.R. 29.
[264] S.I. 1988/1987.
[265] *cf. Dermot Quinn v United Kingdom* [1997] E.H.R.L.R. 167.
[266] *ibid.*, para.47.

is at an authorised place of detention and who has not been allowed an opportunity to consult a solicitor prior to interview.

The possible problems of applying the *Murray* approach in the context of trial by jury were first identified in the opinion of Nicolas Bratza Q.C., then the British member of the Commission: **15–105**

> "In reaching the view that there has been no violation of the Convention, I attach considerable importance to the fact that adverse inferences under the 1988 Order are drawn by a judge sitting without a jury. Not only is a judge, by his training and legal experience, likely to be better equipped than a lay juryman to draw only such inferences as are justified from a defendant's silence but, as pointed out by the Commission, a judge in Northern Ireland gives a reasoned judgment as to the grounds on which he decides to draw inferences, and the weight he gives to such inferences in any particular case . . . The same safeguards against unfairness do not appear to me to exist in the case of a jury trial. When it is a jury which must decide, without giving reasons, what adverse inferences, if any, to draw against an accused from his silence, and what weight to attach to such inferences in arriving at a verdict, the risk of unfairness seems to me to be substantially increased, however carefully formulated a judge's direction to the jury might be."[267]

In a number of subsequent decisions the Court has had the opportunity to consider the limits imposed by Art.6 on the drawing of adverse inferences. In *Condron and Condron v United Kingdom*,[268] adverse inferences had been drawn in a jury trial. The applicants, who were heroin addicts, were certified fit to be interviewed. Their solicitor did not believe that they were fit, and advised them not to answer the questions put by the police. On appeal against conviction, the Court of Appeal accepted that the judge's direction to the jury was inadequate, but nevertheless held that the convictions were safe in the light of the other evidence in the case. The European Court of Human Rights held that the direction given to the jury had failed to strike the balance required by Art.6. In particular, the jury should have been directed, as a matter of fairness, that if there might be an innocent explanation for the applicants' silence at interview, no adverse inference should be drawn. The unfairness which resulted from such a misdirection could not be cured on appeal. Whilst it was possible, in some cases, for a defect at trial to be remedied at the appellate level, that was not the position in the instant case, since the Court of Appeal had no means of knowing whether the applicants' silence had played a significant role in the jury's decision to convict them.   **15–106**

The decision in *Condron* is founded on *Murray*, but goes beyond it in a number of respects. The Court in *Murray* laid great emphasis on access to legal advice, and found a breach of Art.6 on this point. The court in *Condron* held that the same principle requires courts to have due regard to the content of any legal advice that is given: **15–107**

> "The very fact that an accused is advised by his lawyer to maintain his silence must also be given appropriate weight by the domestic court. There may be good reason why such advice may be given. The applicants in the instant case state that they held their silence

---

[267] (1996) 22 E.H.R.R. 29, Commission at para.37.
[268] (2000) 31 E.H.R.R. 1.

on the strength of their solicitor's advice that they were unfit to answer questions."[269]

15–108 The Court accepted that it was not contrary to Art.6 to leave the drawing of adverse inferences from the accused's silence to a jury, but held that the directions of the trial judge must be scrutinised carefully. In this case the trial judge failed to "reflect the balance which the Court in its *John Murray* judgment sought to strike between the right to silence and the circumstances in which an adverse inference may be drawn from silence." The trial judge drew the jury's attention to the applicants' explanation that they remained silent in reliance on legal advice, but:

> "he did so in terms which left the jury at liberty to draw an adverse inference notwithstanding that it may have been satisfied as to the plausibility of the explanation ... In the Court's opinion, as a matter of fairness, the jury should have been directed that if it had been satisfied that the applicants' silence at the police interview could not sensibly be attributed to their having no answer or none that would stand up to cross-examination they should not draw an adverse inference. Unlike the Court of Appeal, the Court considers that a direction to that effect was more than merely 'desirable'."[270]

15–109 In *Averill v United Kingdom*[271] the applicant had been detained near the scene of a double murder. He was initially denied access to his solicitor whilst being questioned. He did not reply to questions about his movements at the time of the murder, or offer an explanation for the finding of fibres on his hair and clothing which matched fibres on clothing discarded by the gunmen. The Court found a violation of Art.6(3)(c) in the denial of access to a lawyer, but held that the drawing of inferences from the applicant's failure to answer questions was not in breach of Art.6. The trial in Northern Ireland had been by judge alone, and he had given a reasoned judgment on the drawing of inferences. In particular, he had cited the strength of the forensic evidence linking the applicant with the murders, and the failure to respond to other police questioning.

15–110 Four main points emerge from the judgment in *Averill*. First, the court recognised that the caution administered to persons about to be questioned, under the Northern Ireland order and under the Criminal Justice and Public Order Act, to the effect that adverse inferences may be drawn from failure to mention facts, "discloses a level of indirect compulsion."[272] Secondly, the Court was clear in its recognition that the drawing of adverse inferences from a failure to answer police questions must be limited. The Court accepted that provisions such as those in Northern Ireland and in the Criminal Justice and Public Order Act 1994 are intended:

> "to prevent the hampering of police investigations by accused who take advantage of their right to silence by waiting until trial to spring exculpatory explanations, in circumstances in which the accused has no reasonable excuse for withholding an

---

[269] *ibid.*
[270] *ibid.*, paras 61–62.
[271] (2000) 31 E.H.R.R. 36 (p.839)
[272] *Ibid*, para.46.

explanation. Notwithstanding these justifications, the Court considers that the extent to which adverse inferences can be drawn from an accused's failure to respond to police questioning must necessarily be limited. While it may no doubt be expected in most cases that innocent persons would be willing to co-operate with the police in explaining that they were not involved in any suspected crime, there may be reasons why in a specific case an innocent person would not be prepared to do so."[273]

Thirdly, the Court suggested that there is a range from acceptable to unacceptable **15–111** reasons for silence. Silence following a lawyer's advice will usually be acceptable, but in this case the applicant's explanation was that he had a policy of not co-operating with the police:

"the applicant did not contend at his trial that he remained silent on the strength of legal advice. His only explanation was that he did not co-operate with the Royal Ulster Constabulary for reasons of policy . . . It must also be noted that the applicant was fully apprised of the implications of remaining silent and was therefore aware of the risks which a policy based defence could entail for him at his trial."[274]

This passage implies that the Court did not regard such a policy as a respectable reason for failing to answer police questions, despite the fact that the same explanation might equally have been expressed as an insistence on putting the prosecution to proof.

Fourthly, the *Averill* judgment develops the observation in *Murray* that there may **15–112** be circumstances which "call for an explanation". In this case it was "the presence of incriminating fibres in the applicant's hair and clothing" which was held to call for an explanation, and the Court considered that it was fair to draw adverse inferences in the absence of any explanation from the applicant when the matter was put to him. The Court points out that the finding of the fibres was put to the applicant after he had consulted his lawyer; it does not state whether, if the lawyer had advised him not to respond, the Court would have regarded the lawyer's advice as a more powerful factor than the presence of circumstances calling for an explanation. The tone of the judgment suggests not.

In *Telfner v Austria*[275] the Court reiterated that the drawing of adverse inferences **15–113** cannot be permissible unless and until the prosecution has established "a convincing prima facie case against" the defendant. Otherwise the effect is to shift the burden of proof to the defendant and to violate Art.6(2). The Court also repeated the point that, although the right of silence is not absolute and allows for the drawing of inferences in circumstances calling for an explanation, adverse inferences should only be drawn where "the only common-sense inference to be drawn from the accused's silence is that he had no answer to the case against him," and a conviction should not be based solely or mainly on such an inference.

The Court also found a violation of the right of silence in *Beckles v United* **15–114** *Kingdom*.[276] The applicant had answered "no comment" throughout the police

---

[273] *ibid.*, para.47.
[274] *ibid.*, para.49.
[275] (2002) 34 E.H.R.R. 207.
[276] (2002) 36 E.H.R.R. 162.

interview on the advice of his solicitor. However, before the solicitor's arrival he had told the police that the victim jumped and was not pushed, which was the line of defence at the trial. When asked at trial whether he would divulge the terms of his lawyer's advice he had agreed to do so, but he was never asked. The Court unanimously found a breach of Art.6, because in his direction the trial judge had not given proper weight to the applicant's explanation for his silence at interview, and had invited the jury to consider whether the explanation for silence was "a good one" rather than emphasising that it must be consistent only with guilt. Among the Court's general observations was the following re-statement of the *Murray-Condron* position:

> "It would be incompatible with the right to silence to base a conviction solely or mainly on the accused's silence or on a refusal to answer questions or to give evidence himself. Nevertheless, it is obvious that the right cannot and should not prevent that the accused's silence, in situations which clearly call for an explanation from him, be taken into account in assessing the persuasiveness of the evidence adduced by the prosecution."[277]

It follows from the Strasbourg decisions that, although the right of silence is not "absolute", the drawing of adverse inferences is permissible only in carefully defined circumstances where the failure to answer questions is consistent only with guilt.

II. Adverse Inferences and the Human Rights Act

15–115   Section 36 of the Criminal Justice and Public Order Act 1994 allows the drawing of an adverse inference from a person's failure to explain marks on his clothing or objects in his possession when arrested close to the scene of the alleged offence. Section 37 allows adverse inferences from a person's failure to explain his presence at or near the scene. In the light of the *Averill* judgment it is likely that a case falling within either of these sections will be regarded under the Human Rights Act as "calling for an explanation", and therefore as justifying an adverse inference in the absence of a plausible explanation. However, it should be noted that ss.36 and 37 do not contain an explicit requirement to consider the circumstances obtaining at the time of the failure to provide an explanation, or to consider the reasonableness of the defendant's refusal to offer an explanation at that time. There is a strong argument, based on the Strasbourg judgments in *Condron* and *Beckles*, that juries should be directed to consider these issues in deciding whether the defendants' silence could fairly be attributed to their guilt rather than to some other reason.

15–116   Section 34 permits the drawing of an adverse inference where the accused fails to mention when questioned a fact which he later relies on in his defence and which he could reasonably have been expected to mention when questioned by the police. It is fair to recall that there is a range of cases in which s.34 does not

---

[277] *Ibid*, para.58.

apply,[278] but where its terms do apply, as the Court of Appeal recognised in *Birchall*,[279] its application in a jury trial could lead to violations of Art.6 unless the judge's directions are carefully framed. The Court in *Beckles v United Kingdom* made this absolutely clear: because it is "impossible to ascertain the weight, if any, given by the jury to the applicant's silence," it is "crucial that the jury [is] properly directed."[280] The Judicial Studies Board's Specimen Direction now attempts to express the Strasbourg principles in a form that can be drawn upon by judges when directing juries, and includes (for example) the points that the prosecution's case must be so strong that it clearly calls for an answer from the defendant, that the jury must be satisfied that the only sensible explanation for the failure to mention certain facts is that he had no satisfactory answer to the questions, and that even if the jury does draw inferences it must not convict "wholly or mainly on the strength" of those inferences.

More problematic is the treatment of silence on a legal adviser's advice. In *Betts*   **15–117**
and Hall,[281] the Court of Appeal stated that it was the genuineness of the defendant's decision not to answer questions, rather than its reasonableness, that was crucial. The same court began to distance itself from this approach in *Howell*,[282] suggesting that there is a public interest in suspects disclosing their explanations at an early stage and that reliance on legal advice should not be allowed to thwart this objective. Similarly in the later cases of *Knight*,[283] *Hoare*[284] and *Beckles*[285] the court stated that *Betts and Hall* should not be read as allowing a defendant who decides to follow a lawyer's advice thereby to immunise himself from later adverse inference, whatever the quality of the advice. The Specimen Direction was revised in December 2004 to take account of this latest development in the law. The relevant part of the Direction now provides:

> "If, for example, you considered that he had or may have had an answer to give, but genuinely and reasonably relied on the legal advice to remain silent, you should not draw any conclusion against him. But if, for example, you were sure that the defendant remained silent not because of the legal advice but because he had no answer or no satisfactory answer to give, and merely latched onto the legal advice as a convenient shield behind which to hide, you would be entitled to draw a conclusion against him, subject to the direction already given."[286]

However, the latest decisions (and the consequent revision to the Specimen Direction in December 2004) fail to give adequate weight to the importance

---

[278] See Birch D.J., "Suffering in Silence: a Cost-Benefit Analysis of s.34 of the Criminal Justice and Public Order Act 1994" [1999] Crim.L.R. 769 at 782–783, and Dennis I., "Silence in the Police Station: the Marginalisation of Section 34", [2002] Crim.L.R. 25.

[279] [1999] Crim.L.R. 311.

[280] (2002) 36 E.H.R.R. 162, para.65.

[281] [2001] EWCA Crim 224; [2001] 2 Cr.App.R. 16 (p.257).

[282] [2003] EWCA Crim 1, [2005] 1 Cr.App.R. 1 (p.1). See generally Choo A.L.T. and Jennings A.F., "Silence on Legal Advice Revisited: *R. v Howell*" (2003) 7 *E & P* 185.

[283] [2003] EWCA Crim 1977, [2004] 1 W.L.R. 340. See generally Choo A.L.T., "Prepared Statements, Legal Advice and the Right to Silence: *R. v Knight*" (2004) 8 *E & P* 62.

[284] [2004] EWCA Crim 784.

[285] [2004] EWCA Crim 2766.

[286] Judicial Studies Board, *Specimen Directions*, December 2004.

under the Convention of access to legal advice, and they place defendants in the invidious position in having to evaluate their own lawyer's advice in order to decide whether it is safe to rely upon it.[287] Both the *Condron* and *Averill* judgments emphasise the importance of legal advice under the Convention, and it might be thought that the latest strand of Court of Appeal decisions go too far in inviting juries to drawn adverse inferences in cases of genuine reliance on a lawyer's advice.

15–118   Another piece of recent legislation to make a statutory inroad on the "right of silence" is the Criminal Justice (Terrorism and Conspiracy) Act 1998, passed when Parliament was recalled for a single day in September 1998 following the bombing at Omagh.[288] Section 1 of the Act amends the provision in s.2 of the Prevention of Terrorism (Temporary Provisions) Act 1989 for an offence of belonging to a proscribed organisation. Among its provisions is s.1(6), which allows courts to draw inferences from an accused's failure "to mention a fact which is material to the offence and which he could reasonably be expected to mention", but which also states that no committal for trial, submission of no case or conviction should be based solely on the inferences.[289] At the time the Government stated that it had been advised that this was ECHR-proof, and satisfied the points made by the European Court in the *Murray* decision.[290] It is true that the 1998 Act states that inferences may only be drawn if the defendant was permitted to consult a solicitor before the questioning from which adverse inferences are drawn. But, on the other hand, the 1998 Act also allows the admission in evidence of a senior police officer's opinion that the accused belongs to a proscribed organisation; and the various points just made in relation to the proper assessment of failures to answer questions remain to be taken into account. In particular, it should be made clear that no conviction or other finding should be based solely *or mainly* on adverse inferences from silence. The relevant provisions are now to be found in section 109 of the Terrorism Act 2000.

15–119   Finally, the effect of the Privy Council's decision in *Brown v Stott*[291] must be considered. The decision that the compulsory power of enquiry under s.172 of the Road Traffic Act 1988 is compatible with Art.6, if correct,[292] raises the further question of whether adverse inferences may be drawn from a failure to reply. If the circumstances giving rise to the s.172 enquiry, and the failure to reply, are regarded as a situation "calling for an explanation", then it would seem

---

[287] The court in *Knight* appears to have recognised that for "distinctly weak or vulnerable" suspects this may not be fair. But this may be thought to give insufficient recognition to the inherent tensions involved in being questioned by the police, with or without a legal adviser, and to impose too great a burden on the suspect at this time.

[288] For full analysis, see Campbell C., "Two Steps Backwards: the Criminal Justice (Terrorism and Conspiracy) Act 1998" [1999] Crim.L.R. 941.

[289] This is a parallel provision to s.38(3) of the Criminal Justice and Public Order Act 1994. It does not however appear to prevent a conviction being based "mainly" on such an inference: see para.15–101.

[290] (1996) 22 E.H.R.R. 29, discussed above, para.15–104.

[291] Above, paras 15–94 *et seq.*; but *cf. Heaney and McGuinness* para.15–80.

[292] *Cf.* the criticisms at **15–95** above.

to follow that adverse inferences will be permissible, so long as the prosecution case does not rest "wholly or mainly" on the inferences.

III. Comparative Approaches

Finally, reference should be made in this context to the approach of the United Nations Human Rights Committee in interpreting the parallel provisions of the International Covenant on Civil and Political Rights. Article 14 of the I.C.C.P.R. guarantees the right to a fair trial. Article 14(3)(g) expressly provides that in the determination of any criminal charge the accused has "the right not to be compelled to testify against himself or to confess guilt."[293] In July 1995 the Human Rights Committee considered the United Kingdom's fourth periodic report under the I.C.C.P.R. and addressed directly the question whether the relevant provisions of the 1988 Order and the 1994 Act conformed to the requirements of Art.14. The Committee concluded that the adverse inference rules "violate various provisions in Article 14 of the Covenant [fair trial], despite a range of safeguards built into the legislation and the rules enacted thereunder." In accord with the I.C.C.P.R. approach are the laws of the United States and Canada. In the former, the landmark Supreme Court decision in *Griffin v California*[294] established that the Fifth Amendment to the United States Constitution forbids both comments by the prosecution on the accused's silence and instructions by the court that such silence may be evidence of guilt. Similarly, it is well established under s.4(6) of the Canada Evidence Act that a trial judge may not comment on the accused's silence, and similarly the prosecution may not rely on evidence of the accused's silence either under police questioning or in court.[295] In this respect the Charter changed nothing.

15–120

I. HEARSAY, CONFRONTATION AND WITNESS STATEMENTS

I. The general Strasbourg approach

Article 6(3)(d) provides that everyone charged with a criminal offence has the right: "to examine or have examined witnesses against him and to obtain the attendance and examination of witnesses in his behalf under the same conditions as witnesses against him." The term "witness" has an autonomous meaning under the Convention, which includes a person whose statements are produced as evidence before a court, even though the maker is not called to give oral evidence.[296] The opportunity to cross-examine need not be available at the trial itself, provided the witness was available for cross-examination at an earlier

15–121

---

[293] To that extent the I.C.C.P.R. mirrors exactly the protection implied into Art.6 of the ECHR in *Funke* and *Saunders*.

[294] 380 US 609 (1965).

[295] See, *e.g. Chambers* [1990] 2 S.C.R. 1293.

[296] *Kostovski v Netherlands* (1990) 12 E.H.R.R. 434; *cf. Bonisch v Austria* (1987) 9 E.H.R.R. 191, where the Court declined to make a ruling on whether a court-appointed expert fell within the definition of a witness in Art.6(3)(d).

stage, such as a full committal.[297] In this sense Art.6(3)(d) has much in common with the "right of confrontation" under the Constitution of the United States,[298] and the European Court has occasionally referred to "the lack of any confrontation" as the reason for finding a trial unfair.[299]

15–122   The starting point of the Strasbourg interpretation of Article 6(3)(d) is that "all the evidence must in principle be produced in the presence of the accused at a public hearing with a view to adversarial argument."[300] In certain situations the admission of depositions or other witness statements for the prosecution, without the presence of the maker, may be inconsistent with the right to confrontation. However, the Court has not applied the rule inflexibly. In keeping with the general approach to Art.6, the Court will examine the reasons advanced for the non-attendance of the witness; any compensating safeguards; the opportunity, if any, which the defence has had to confront the witness at an earlier stage of the proceedings; the possibility of introducing the evidence in a manner less intrusive to the rights of the accused; whether the defence requested the attendance of the witness; and the importance of the prohibited hearsay evidence in the context of the proceedings as a whole.[301]

15–123   Four decisions illustrate the circumstances in which the court may find a violation. In *Unterpertinger v Austria*[302] the prosecution's case was based largely on the formal statements of two witnesses who, as relatives of the defendant, were non-compellable and exercised their privilege not to give oral evidence. Their statements were read out at the trial, and the Court held that "in itself the reading out of statements in this way cannot be regarded as being inconsistent with Article 6". However, the Court added that "the use made of them as evidence must nevertheless comply with the rights of the defence, which it is the object of Article 6 to protect."[303] The applicants' inability to cross-examine the witnesses, and the court's refusal to hear evidence attacking the credibility of the witnesses, meant that the defence rights were "appreciably restricted",[304] in breach of

---

[297] *Kostovski v Netherlands* (1990) 12 E.H.R.R. 434 at para.41.

[298] The Sixth Amendment right "to be confronted with the witnesses against him": on the parallels between this and the ECHR jurisprudence, see Friedman R., "Thoughts from across the water on Hearsay and Confrontation" [1998] Crim.L.R. 697. The most recent decision of the US Supreme Court on the right of confrontation is *Crawford v Washington* 124 S. Ct. 1354 (2004). See generally Choo A., "Crawford v Washington: A View from Across the Atlantic", *http://www.bepress.com/ice/vol2/iss1/art4/*; HL Ho, "Confrontation and Hearsay: A Critique of *Crawford*" (2004) 8 *E & P* 147; Summers S. J., "The Right to Confrontation after *Crawford v Washington*: A 'Continental European' Perspective", *http://www.bepress.com/ice/vol2/iss1/art3/*

[299] E.g., *Saidi v France* (1994) 17 E.H.R.R. 251 at para.44.

[300] *Barbera, Messegue and Jabardo v Spain* (1989) 11 E.H.R.R. 360 at para.78, a passage repeated in many later judgments, e.g., *Ludi v Switzerland* (1993) 15 E.H.R.R. 173 at para.47, and *Van Mechelen v Netherlands* (1998) 25 E.H.R.R. 647 at para.51.

[301] See *Unterpertinger v Austria* (1991) 13 E.H.R.R. 175; *Kostovski v Netherlands* (1990) 12 E.H.R.R. 434; *Windisch v Austria* (1991) 13 E.H.R.R. 281; *Lüdi v Switzerland* (1993) 15 E.H.R.R. 173; *Barberà, Messegué and Jabardo v Spain* (1989) 11 E.H.R.R. 360; *Bricmont v Belgium* (1990) 12 E.H.R.R. 217; *Delta v France* (1993) 16 E.H.R.R. 574; *Saidi v France* (1994) 17 E.H.R.R. 251; *Asch v Austria* (1993) 15 E.H.R.R. 597; *Artner v Austria* (1992) Series A No./242–A; *Isgro v Italy* (1990) Series A No./194.

[302] (1991) 13 E.H.R.R. 175.

[303] *ibid.*, para.31.

[304] *ibid.*, at para.33.

Art.6(1) in conjunction with Art.6(3)(d). Although there was other evidence in the case, the court had clearly treated the witnesses' written statements as "proof of the truth" of their accusations, basing the conviction on their (untested) statements.[305]

A breach of Art.6 was also found in *Kostovski v Netherlands*,[306] where the conviction was based "to a decisive extent" on the statements of two anonymous witnesses who gave evidence but whom neither the defendant, nor defence counsel, nor the trial court was able to observe.[307] The right to confrontation, held the Court: **15–124**

> "does not mean, however, that in order to be used as evidence statements of witnesses should always be made at a public hearing in court: to use as evidence such statements obtained at the pre-trial stage is not in itself inconsistent with paragraphs (3)(d) and (1) of Article 6, provided the rights of the defence have been respected. As a rule, these rights require that an accused should be given an adequate and proper opportunity to challenge and question a witness against him, either at the time the witness was making his statement or at some later stage in the proceedings."[308]

In this case the defence had been able to submit questions, which an examining magistrate had then put to one of the two witnesses (the other was only questioned by police), but the Court held that "it cannot be said that the handicaps under which the defence laboured were counterbalanced by the procedures followed by the judicial authorities."[309] The Court's comments on the difficulties facing a defendant against whom witnesses testify anonymously demonstrate its belief in the value of cross-examination:

> "If the defence is unaware of the identity of the person it seeks to question, it may be deprived of the very particulars enabling it to demonstrate that he or she is prejudiced, hostile or unreliable. Testimony or other declarations inculpating an accused may well be designedly untruthful or simply erroneous and the defence will scarcely be able to bring this to light if it lacks the information permitting it to test the author's reliability or to cast doubt on his credibility. The dangers inherent in such a situation are obvious."[310]

The *Kostovski* judgment was followed in *Windisch v Austria*,[311] where there had been no opportunity for the defence to question the two anonymous witnesses and, since the trial court had relied "to a large extent" on their written statements, the Court held that the restrictions on defence rights deprived the applicant of a fair trial.[312]   **15–125**

> "The collaboration of the public is undoubtedly of great importance to the police in their struggle against crime. In this connection the Court notes that the Convention does

---

[305] *ibid.*, at para.33.
[306] (1991) 12 E.H.R.R. 434.
[307] *ibid.*, at para.44.
[308] *ibid.*, at para.41, citing the *Unterpertinger* judgment.
[309] *ibid.*, at para.43.
[310] *ibid.*, at para.42.
[311] (1991) 13 E.H.R.R. 281.
[312] *ibid.*, at para.31.

not preclude reliance, at the investigative stage, on sources such as anonymous informants. However, the subsequent use of their statements by the trial court to found a conviction is another matter. The right to a fair administration of justice holds so prominent a place in a democratic society that it cannot be sacrificed."[313]

The same conclusion was reached in *Ludi v Switzerland*,[314] where the written statement of an undercover agent had "played a part" in the conviction, and where the anonymity of the undercover agent could and should have been preserved without denying the applicant his rights of defence.[315]

15–126 On the other side lies *Asch v Austria*,[316] a case of alleged domestic violence in which the accused's partner had called the police, described the assault to the police officer, gone to hospital and been medically examined, but later withdrew her complaint and exercised her right (under Austrian law) not to testify. The prosecution continued with the case, and at the trial the police officer testified to what the woman had said to him at the time (on the basis of the statement he had recorded), and also told the court about the bruises he had seen and described her frightened state. The Court found no violation of Art.6 on the facts, since the defendant had not taken the opportunity to cross-examine the police officer, the defendant himself gave conflicting accounts, and there was corroborative medical evidence:

> "It would clearly have been preferable if it had been possible to hear her [the victim] in person, but the right on which she relied in order to avoid giving evidence should not be allowed to block the prosecution . . . The fact that it was impossible to question [the victim] at the hearing did not therefore, in the circumstances of the case, violate the rights of the defence."[317]

In *SN v Sweden*, the Court, speaking in the context of a child complainant of sexual abuse, M, held:

> "Nor can it be said that the applicant was denied his rights under Art. 6(3)(d) on the ground that he was unable to examine or have examined the evidence given by M during the trial and appeal proceedings. Having regard to the special features of criminal proceedings concerning sexual offences, this provision cannot be interpreted as requiring in all cases that questions be put directly by the accused or his or her defence counsel, through cross-examination or by other means. The Court notes that the videotape of the first police interview was shown during the trial and appeal hearings and that the record of the second interview was read out before the District Court and the audiotape of that interview was played back before the Court of Appeal. In the circumstances of the case, these measures must be considered sufficient to have enabled the applicant to challenge M's statements and his credibility in the course of the criminal proceedings. Indeed, that challenge resulted in the Court of Appeal reducing

---

[313] *ibid.*, at para.30.
[314] (1993) 15 E.H.R.R. 173.
[315] See to similar effect: *Barbera, Messegue and Jabardo v Spain* (1989) 11 E.H.R.R. 360; *Bricmont v Belgium* (1990) 12 E.H.R.R. 217; *Delta v France* (1993) 16 E.H.R.R. 574; *Saidi v France* (1994) 17 E.H.R.R. 251; *PS v Germany* (2001) 36 E.H.R.R. 61 (p.1139); *Lucà v Italy* (2001) 36 E.H.R.R. 46 (p.807).
[316] (1993) 15 E.H.R.R. 597.
[317] (1993) 15 E.H.R.R. 597 at para.31.

the applicant's sentence because it considered that part of the charges against him had not been proved."[318]

What appears from these and other decisions[319] is a complex mixture of at least   **15–127** three major factors. First, the Court's chief concern is the fairness of the trial as a whole: the defendant's right to "confront" or cross-examine every prosecution witness is important, but not absolute. Or, to express the point differently, reliance on pre-trial witness statements is not contrary to the Convention, so long as the rights of the defence are respected.[320] Secondly, the Court's judgment on overall fairness is much affected by the significance of the written or reported statements for the prosecution case: a trial has typically been regarded as unfair if the conviction rested "solely or mainly" on the disputed statement. *SN v Sweden* stands as an exception to this; in that case, a violation was not found by the Court notwithstanding that "the statements made by M were virtually the sole evidence on which the courts' findings of guilt were based".[321] At the other end of the spectrum, however, there are some decisions in which the test is expressed in terms that appear very favourable to the defence. Thus in *Ludi v Switzerland*[322] the Court thought it sufficient to render the trial unfair that the written evidence had "played a part" in the conviction.

However, the version of the test adopted in *Ludi* may be explained by a third   **15–128** factor: that the Court has regard to the practical possibility of according greater recognition to defence rights than was done at the trial. In other words, there are some cases where the impracticability of producing the witness at the trial might lead the court to adopt a more flexible approach to Art.6(3)(d) (as, for example, in *Artner v Austria*,[323] where the witness had gone missing and was untraceable; or in *Asch v Austria*,[324] where the witness exercised her right not to testify). But the national court should always look for alternative safeguards. As the Court put it in *Van Mechelen v Netherlands*, "any measures restricting the rights of the defence should be strictly necessary. If a less restrictive measure can suffice then that measure should be applied."[325]

II. Applying the Strasbourg jurisprudence to the Criminal Justice Act 1988

The provisions of the Criminal Justice Act 1988 dealing with hearsay evidence   **15–129** were on April 4, 2005 replaced by the relevant provisions of the Criminal Justice Act 2003, discussed below at paras 15–146—15–149. The provisions of the 1988

---

[318] (2004) 39 E.H.R.R. 13 (p.304) (judgment of 2002), [52]. See generally Ellison L., "The Right of Challenge in Sexual Offence Cases: *SN v Sweden*" (2003) 7 *E & P* 62. See also *Magnusson v Sweden (Admissibility)*, Application no. 53972/00, December 16, 2003; *Laukkanen v Finland*, Application No.50230/99, February 3, 2004.
[319] E.g., *Isgro v Italy* (1990) A–194, *Artner v Austria* (1992) A–242–A, and the many decisions discussed at paras 15–122 to 15–125 above. For earlier discussion, see Osborne C., "Hearsay and the European Court of Human Rights" [1993] Crim.L.R. 255.
[320] See particularly *Windisch v Austria* (1990) 13 E.H.R.R. 281 at para.26.
[321] (2004) 39 E.H.R.R. 13 (p.304) (judgment of 2002), [46].
[322] (1993) 15 E.H.R.R. 173.
[323] (1992) A–342.
[324] (1993) 15 E.H.R.R. 597.
[325] (1998) 25 E.H.R.R. 647 at para.59.

Act will still be relevant, however, in any appeals in respect of trials which had commenced prior to April 4, 2005. Section 23 of the 1988 Act provides four sets of circumstances in which a witness statement (first-hand hearsay) may be admitted in the absence of its maker, and s.26 provides that a court should give leave for the admission of such evidence only if this would be in the interests of justice.[326] The four sets of circumstances are:

"(2)(a) that the person who made the statement is dead or by reason of his bodily or mental condition unfit to attend as a witness;

(b) that (i) the person who made the statement is outside the United Kingdom and (ii) it is not reasonably practicable to secure his attendance; or

(c) that all reasonable steps have been taken to find the person who made the statement, but he cannot be found;

(3) (a) that the statement was made to a police officer or some other person charged with the duty of investigating offences or charging offenders; and (b) that the person who made it does not give oral evidence through fear or because he is kept out of the way."

The relevance of Strasbourg decisions to the interpretation of these provisions under the Human Rights Act is considered in the paragraphs which follow.

15–130   The first set of circumstances is where "the person who made the statement is dead or by reason of his bodily or mental condition unable to attend as a witness": s.23(2)(a). In *Bricmont v Belgium*[327] the Court found a breach of Art.6 on the ground that there had been no opportunity for confrontation of the principal witness against the applicant,[328] who had not given oral evidence in court owing to ill-health. The Court attached importance to the possibility that arrangements could have been made to enable the witness to be examined at his home, which "would have made it possible to clarify certain facts and to lead the [witness] to give further particulars of—or even withdraw—one or more of his charges."[329] Since it appeared that the courts had relied to some extent on the witness's statements, Art.6 had been breached. By way of contrast, the Court held in *Ferrantelli and Santangelo v Italy*[330] that the evidence of a witness who had died could be admitted, despite the impossibility of confrontation. The Court concluded that the statements were "corroborated by a series of other items of evidence" and so found no violation of Art.6(3)(d).

15–131   Two subsequent decisions of the Commission considered the issue. In *MK v Austria*[331] the trial court had admitted the statements of two witnesses, one the young victim of the alleged sexual abuse, and the other his younger sister. Both were in psychiatric care and the trial court held that requiring them to testify

---

[326] See generally *Archbold*, (2005), paras 9–126 to 9–142.

[327] (1990) 12 E.H.R.R. 217.

[328] The witness in question was the Prince of Belgium. The Court considered that special procedures for taking evidence from "high-ranking persons of State" were not, in themselves, incompatible with Art.6, provided the rights of the defence were adequately respected.

[329] (1990) 12 E.H.R.R. 217 at para.81.

[330] (1997) 23 E.H.R.R. 288 at para.52; *cf. Bricmont v Belgium* (last note), where the Court found a breach where the trial court had "frequently referred" to the statements of the absent witness, and had "relied on" them (paras 83–84), even though there was other evidence.

[331] (1997) 24 E.H.R.R. CD 59.

could lead to irreparable psychological harm. The course adopted was to appoint as a court expert a psychiatrist who interviewed the victim and then gave evidence and was cross-examined by the defence. The Commission reiterated that the Convention in principle protects the rights of victims and witnesses, as well as those of the accused. In concluding that there had been no violation of Art.6, the Commission attached importance to the ability of the defence to cross-examine the expert, and to the existence of independent evidence of guilt.

The other decision is *Trivedi v United Kingdom.*[332] The applicant was a general   **15–132**
practitioner who was charged with false accounting in respect of claims which he had made for night visits to a patient C. The prosecution relied on the evidence of C that the applicant had often provided him with several prescriptions on a single visit, and had not attended on each of the occasions for which he had made claims. C was elderly and suffered from a number of illnesses. Before the trial began the prosecution served a medical report indicating that his condition had deteriorated and that he would never be able to attend to give oral evidence. Despite defence objections, the trial judge admitted two statements made by C pursuant to ss.23 and 26 of the 1988 Act. The applicant was convicted and his appeal was dismissed.

In his application to the Commission the applicant complained that the admission   **15–133**
of C's witness statements violated Art.6(1) and 6(3)(d). The Commission recalled that the use of statements obtained at a pre-trial stage would not violate Art.6, provided the rights of the defence had been properly respected. Those rights meant that the defendant had to have an adequate opportunity to challenge and question the witness, either at the time when the statement was made or at a later stage of the proceedings. In the present case the Commission laid particular emphasis on the fact that the trial judge had conducted a detailed inquiry into C's condition, including his memory, at the material time. It noted that the statements were "not the only" evidence in the case to show that the applicant had claimed for visits which had not occurred. Evidence relevant to C's reliability had been admitted and the defence had had the opportunity to comment on this to the jury. Finally, the judge had specifically warned the jury in his summing up that less weight should be attached to C's evidence. For these reasons the Commission, by a majority, declared the application inadmissible.

It is particularly important not to over-emphasise the effect of this ruling. It does   **15–134**
not establish that ss.23–26 are "Convention-proof". It merely demonstrates that there may be situations in which evidence may be admitted under this part of s.23 without rendering the trial as a whole unfair, and it spells out some of the conditions under which that will be so. If a key witness is claimed to be too ill to attend court, consideration should be given to arranging the confrontation at his residence, in order to respect defence rights.[333] If a key witness has died

---

[332] (1997) 89 A.D.R. 136.
[333] See *Bricmont v Belgium* (1990) 12 E.H.R.R. 217 at para.81.

before the trial, it may be satisfactory to admit his statement in evidence so long as the rights of the defence are as well respected as they were in *Trivedi*.[334]

15–135   The second set of circumstances, in s.23(2)(b), is that the maker of the statement is outside the United Kingdom and it is not reasonably practicable to secure his attendance. There is a Commission ruling to the effect that, if the witness can be located, defence rights may be respected by having evidence taken by a judicial officer of the other country:

> "The Commission recalls that Art. 6(3)(d) of the Convention does not grant the accused an unlimited right to secure the appearance of witnesses in court. Its purpose is rather to ensure equality between the defence and the prosecution as regards the summoning and examining of witnesses ... It does not exclude the possibility that witnesses residing abroad whose presence at the trial cannot be enforced by the trial court are examined on commission by a court at their place of residence."[335]

15–136   Provisions for mutual assistance and mutual recognition among member states of the European Union may render this more practicable in future, and the Crime (International Co-operation) Act 2003 makes provision for the obtaining of evidence abroad. In *Radak*[336] a key witness refused to leave the United States in order to give evidence at a fraud trial in this country. The Court of Appeal explored various possibilities, such as making use of a mutual assistance treaty with the United States to set up an examination of the witness before an appointed judge, which might possibly be on a live link. Since the prosecuting authorities in England had taken no steps to avail themselves of this possibility, but had applied to have the witness's written statement admitted under s.23, the court held that the trial judge had wrongly exercised his discretion under s.26 of the 1988 Act to admit the statement. The court held that the Convention jurisprudence "coincides with the proper application of the [English] statute".

15–137   The third set of circumstances is where "all reasonable steps have been taken to find the person who made the statement, but ... he cannot be found": s.23(2)(c). Two decisions of the Court are relevant here. In *Delta v France*[337] the prosecution relied on the statements of the victim and another witness: they were summoned to attend but failed to do so, and the judge did not take any steps to have them brought before the court. On appeal the defence asked for the two witnesses to be produced, but the request was refused. The Court held that Art.6(3)(d) had been violated: the defence had never had an adequate opportunity to examine the witnesses or to test their reliability, and it was the only evidence against the applicant.[338] To be contrasted with this is *Doorson v Netherlands*,[339]

---

[334] See the Scottish decision in *McKenna v HM Advocate*, 2000 J.C. 291, where the High Court of Justiciary based its judgment on *Trivedi*, and noted that Scots law's requirement of corroboration means that a conviction would rarely, in any event, be based "solely or mainly" on a statement admitted under ss.23–26. See also *Kennedy v United Kingdom* (1999) 27 E.H.R.R. CD 266.

[335] *X v Germany* (1988) 10 E.H.R.R. 503: the ruling is somewhat vague on the rights of the parties to attend and to put questions directly in the foreign proceedings.

[336] [1999] 1 Cr.App.R. 187.

[337] (1993) 16 E.H.R.R. 574.

[338] *ibid.*, at para.37.

[339] (1996) 22 E.H.R.R. 330.

where efforts to have a particular witness brought before the court were made on three separate occasions, and when he was brought to court by force he absconded. The Court held that "in these circumstances it was open to [the Dutch court] to have regard to the statement obtained by the police, since it could consider that statement to be corroborated by other evidence before it."[340]

The fourth set of circumstances is where the maker "does not give oral evidence   **15–138**
through fear or because he is kept out of the way," and the statement was made previously to a police officer or other investigator: s.23(3). At least four Strasbourg cases have a bearing on this. In *Windisch v Austria*[341] the two witnesses declined to give evidence for fear of reprisals and remained anonymous, which meant that the defence could not even attack their credibility (since it did not know who they were). The Court held that this was too great a restriction on the applicant's right to a fair trial.[342] In *Saidi v France*[343] fear of reprisals was the justification advanced for not requiring the witnesses to give oral evidence (identifying the accused) in a case of drug trafficking and involuntary homicide. Finding a violation, the Court observed that the written witness statements:

"constituted the sole basis for the applicant's conviction . . . Yet neither at the stage of the investigation nor during the trial was the applicant able to examine or have examined the witnesses concerned. The lack of any confrontation deprived him in certain respects of a fair trial. The Court is fully aware of the undeniable difficulties of the fight against drug-trafficking—in particular with regard to obtaining and producing evidence—and of the ravages caused to society by the drug problem, but such considerations cannot justify restricting to this extent the rights of the defence . . . "[344]

This may be regarded as a strong decision, in view of the emphasis placed by the French government on the importance of protecting the safety of witnesses. But it was the absence of any corroborating evidence that weighed heavily with the Court.

In *Doorson v Netherlands*[345] the Court accepted that the witnesses had previously   **15–139**
been threatened by drug dealers and declared that the interests of witnesses (for example, under Art.8) should be taken into account by trial courts.[346] The witnesses had been allowed to remain anonymous, and had been questioned by an investigating judge (in the absence of defence lawyers), their statements then being admitted at trial. The Court held that in this case there were certain "counter-balancing" procedures (the earlier judicial questioning, the opportunity for the defence to cast doubt on the reliability of the witnesses, which they did) "to compensate sufficiently for the handicaps under which the defence labours",[347] and that there was sufficient other evidence against the defendant, to justify the conclusion that there had been no violation. In *Van Mechelen v*

---

[340] *ibid.*, para.88, referring to *Artner v Austria* (1992), Series A–242–A at para.22.
[341] (1990) 13 E.H.R.R. 281.
[342] See para.15–125 above.
[343] (1994) 17 E.H.R.R. 251.
[344] *ibid.*, at para.44; to similar effect, *Windisch v Austria* (1991) 13 E.H.R.R. 281 at para.30.
[345] (1996) 22 E.H.R.R. 330.
[346] The key passage (*ibid.*, para.70) is considered at paras 14–163 *et seq.* above.
[347] *ibid.*, para.76.

Netherlands,[348] the critical factors pointing towards a violation of Art.6(3)(d) were that the witnesses were police officers who should be expected to give evidence, that there had been no investigation of the risk of reprisals against the officers, that the measures taken at trial did not adequately respect defence rights, and that the convictions were based "to a decisive extent" on the identification evidence of the officers.

15–140 The distinction between *Doorson* and *Saidi* seems to turn largely on the strength of the other evidence in the case. This may have important but novel implications for English law. Under s.26 of the 1988 Act the judge has to determine whether it would be in the interests of justice to admit the s.23 statement as evidence. The Human Rights Act requires courts to take account of the decisions of the court, summarised above. To do this faithfully will require that the judge consider the range of factors identified in the Strasbourg decisions. In two cases where the Court of Appeal discussed the relevance of the Convention to ss.23–26, albeit prior to the coming into force of the Human Rights Act, it drew attention to the provisions in Sch.2 to the Criminal Justice Act 1988 which provide a procedure for the credibility of an absent witness to be attacked, and to the principles in s.25 relating to the authenticity of the statement and the extent to which it supplies evidence not otherwise readily available.

15–141 Thus in *Gokal*[349] the prosecution at a fraud trial wished to introduce statements made by the defendant's brother-in-law, who was overseas and unwilling to return to this country. The statements implicated the defendant in material ways. The Court of Appeal upheld the trial judge's ruling that the statement should be admitted under ss.23–26. Ward L.J. gave brief consideration to some of the Strasbourg decisions discussed above: he stated that *Unterpertinger*[350] was distinguishable because the Austrian court had there refused to allow the defendant to attack the credibility of the absent witnesses, whereas English law would allow that; and he stated that *Kostovski*[351] was "a far cry from the facts before us" since it concerned an anonymous witness.

15–142 As we have seen, the Strasbourg decisions suggest that a conviction should not rest solely or mainly on evidence adduced under provisions such as those in the 1988 Act, even if the judge is as meticulous as the trial judges in *Gokal* and in *Trivedi*. In the latter case the European Commission was able to find that there had been other confirmatory evidence.[352] In *Gokal* the Court of Appeal made no such enquiry and no such finding. Indeed, it might be said that the wording of s.25(2)(b) points in the opposite direction: it requires the court to have regard to the extent to which "the statement appears to supply evidence which would otherwise not be readily available". Whether the facts of *Gokal* were such that the prosecution case rested mainly on the statement is difficult to say: it appears that some of the contents of the witness statement did coincide with notes written by the witness and obtained from a different source. But other decisions may now

---

[348] (1998) 25 E.H.R.R. 647.
[349] [1997] 2 Cr.App.R. 266.
[350] Above, para.15–123.
[351] Above, para.15–124.
[352] To the same effect, see *Kennedy v United Kingdom* (1999) 27 E.H.R.R. CD 266.

be more doubtful—for example *Dragic*,[353] where the prosecution for burglary rested on the identification of the defendant (by recognition) in a statement from a witness who was now too ill to attend court, and there was no scientific or other supporting evidence.

In *Thomas*[354] the trial judge, in a case of conspiracy to supply heroin in which the   **15–143** defence claimed that the prosecution witnesses were the true heroin dealers, decided to admit the statement of one witness who refused to attend court because of fear. The Court of Appeal upheld his decision, on the basis that he had taken account of all the relevant considerations. The court added, citing *Trivedi*, that ss.23–26 were not in themselves contrary to the Convention. The court appears not to have considered whether the statement was the sole or main basis for the conviction, but Professor Birch commented that this requirement would "reduce statements admitted under the [1988] Act to the level of an inferior form of evidence which at best could be corroborative of direct testimony."[355] This is a classification to which English lawyers may have to become accustomed: it applies also, as we have seen, to the admissibility of improperly obtained evidence, to the drawing of adverse inferences from silence, and to reliance on accomplice evidence.[356] Evidence can certainly tip the balance in favour of conviction, and may indeed contribute significantly to that outcome; but there is consistent Strasbourg authority that it should not be the sole or even the main evidence supporting conviction. It does not have to be supported by *direct* testimony, since there are cases where the other evidence has been circumstantial,[357] but English courts may have to modify their approach to ss.23 and 26 to take account of this approach.

The presumption against hearsay embodied in Art.6(3)(d) is worded so as to   **15–144** apply only to witnesses who give evidence against the accused. There is no equivalent rule against the introduction of hearsay evidence by the defence. Where the admission of such evidence is permitted under national law there is nothing in Art.6 to prevent this. On the other hand, there is no obligation in Art.6 for a court to admit hearsay evidence which purports to exonerate the accused.[358]

In *Bricmont v Belgium*[359] the Court observed that whilst the assessment of   **15–145** evidence was generally a matter for the domestic courts, there could be exceptional circumstances in which a failure to call witnesses helpful to the defence would amount to a violation of Art.6.[360] In *Vidal v Belgium*[361] the Court found

---

[353] [1996] 2 Cr.App.R. 232.
[354] [1998] Crim.L.R. 887.
[355] In her commentary on *Thomas et al.* [1998] Crim.L.R. 887, 889; she adds that the effect of this would be "particularly unfortunate if the Act could not be invoked in circumstances where the only possible prosecution witness has been frightened out of giving evidence."
[356] Above, paras 15–1015–103 and 15–67.
[357] E.g., the domestic violence case of *Asch v Austria* (1993) 15 E.H.R.R. 597, above, para. 15–126.
[358] *Blastland v United Kingdom* (1988) 10 E.H.R.R. 528; 52 D.R. 273.
[359] (1990) 12 E.H.R.R. 217.
[360] On the facts, however, the failure to call certain defence witnesses was not found to violate Art.6.
[361] (1992) Series A No.235–B.

such a violation where the national courts had refused without reason to call the key witness upon whom the defence case rested. In the court's view, the "complete silence" of the national court's judgment on this central issue was not consistent with the concept of a fair trial.

III. Applying the Strasbourg jurisprudence to the Criminal Justice Act 2003

15–146 The previous law of criminal hearsay in England and Wales was superseded on April 4, 2005 by the relevant provisions of the Criminal Justice Act 2003. Section 116 of the 2003 Act is closely modelled on s.23 of the 1988 Act. A significant difference is that, while s.23 applies only to statements made by a witness in a document, s.116 applies not only to such statements but also to statements made orally. There are five conditions under which a statement may be admissible in evidence under s.116. These are set out in s.116(2):

> "The conditions are—
>
> (a) that the relevant person is dead;
> (b) that the relevant person is unfit to be a witness because of his bodily or mental condition;
> (c) that the relevant person is outside the United Kingdom and it is not reasonably practicable to secure his attendance;
> (d) that the relevant person cannot be found although such steps as it is reasonably practicable to take to find him have been taken;
> (e) that through fear the relevant person does not give (or does not continue to give) oral evidence in the proceedings, either at all or in connection with the subject matter of the statement, and the court gives leave for the statement to be given in evidence."

The unavailability of the maker of the out-of-court statement for one of the five reasons specified in s.116(2) must not have been brought about by the party seeking to give the statement in evidence in order to prevent him or her from giving oral evidence. For the purposes of s.116(2)(e), "fear" "is to be widely construed and (for example) includes fear of the death or injury of another person or of financial loss". Moreover, leave may be given under s.116(2)(e) "only if the court considers that the statement ought to be admitted in the interests of justice, having regard; (a) to the statement's contents; (b) to any risk that its admission or exclusion will result in unfairness to any party to the proceedings (and in particular to how difficult it will be to challenge the statement if the relevant person does not give oral evidence); (c) in appropriate cases, to the fact that a direction under section 19 of the Youth Justice and Criminal Evidence Act 1999 (c 23) (special measures for the giving of evidence by fearful witnesses etc) could be made in relation to the relevant person; and (d) to any other relevant circumstances".

15–147 Another provision of the Criminal Justice Act 2003 that may raise questions of compliance with Art.6 is s.114(1)(d). This provides that hearsay evidence will be admissible if "the court is satisfied that it is in the interests of justice for it to be admissible".[362] In deciding whether a statement should be admitted in evidence on this basis:

"the court must have regard to the following factors (and to any others it considers relevant)—

  (a) how much probative value the statement has (assuming it to be true) in relation to a matter in issue in the proceedings, or how valuable it is for the understanding of other evidence in the case;
  (b) what other evidence has been, or can be, given on the matter or evidence mentioned in paragraph (a);
  (c) how important the matter or evidence mentioned in paragraph (a) is in the context of the case as a whole;
  (d) the circumstances in which the statement was made;
  (e) how reliable the maker of the statement appears to be;
  (f) how reliable the evidence of the making of the statement appears to be;
  (g) whether oral evidence of the matter stated can be given and, if not, why it cannot;
  (h) the amount of difficulty involved in challenging the statement;
  (i) the extent to which that difficulty would be likely to prejudice the party facing it".[363]

There is a specific power to exclude hearsay evidence under s.126(1)(b) of the   **15–148** Criminal Justice Act 2003 if "the court is satisfied that the case for excluding the statement, taking account of the danger that to admit it would result in undue waste of time, substantially outweighs the case for admitting it, taking account of the value of the evidence". Additionally, s.125(1) provides:

"If on a defendant's trial before a judge and jury for an offence the court is satisfied at any time after the close of the case for the prosecution that—

  (a) the case against the defendant is based wholly or partly on a statement not made in oral evidence in the proceedings, and
  (b) the evidence provided by the statement is so unconvincing that, considering its importance to the case against the defendant, his conviction of the offence would be unsafe,

the court must either direct the jury to acquit the defendant of the offence or, if it considers that there ought to be a retrial, discharge the jury."

It may be expected that the approach adopted by the domestic courts in assessing   **15–149** the Art.6—compliance of the hearsay provisions of the Criminal Justice Act 1988, discussed in the preceding section, will be repeated in relation to the hearsay provisions of the Criminal Justice Act 2003. Thus it may be expected that the provisions of the 2003 Act will not, in themselves, be considered to violate Art.6; what will be required is that they can be seen, in the context of the case as a whole, to have been appropriately used. In *Sellick*, decided in March 2005, when the commencement of the new law was imminent, the Court of Appeal summed up the relevant principles emerging from the European Court jurisprudence as follows:

---

[362] S.114(1)(d).
[363] S.114(2). See generally Durston G., "Hearsay Evidence and the New Inclusionary Discretion" (2004) 168 *Justice of the Peace* 788.

"(i)   The admissibility of evidence is primarily for the national law;

(ii)   Evidence must normally be produced at a public hearing and as a general rule Article 6(1) and (3)(d) require a defendant to be given a proper and adequate opportunity to challenge and question witnesses;

(iii) It is not necessarily incompatible with Article 6(1) and (3)(d) for depositions to be read and that can be so even if there has been no opportunity to question the witness at any stage of the proceedings. Article 6(3)(d) is simply an illustration of matters to be taken into account in considering whether a fair trial has been held. The reasons for the court holding it necessary that statements should be read and the procedures to counterbalance any handicap to the defence will all be relevant to the issue, whether, where statements have been read, the trial was fair.

(iv) The quality of the evidence and its inherent reliability, plus the degree of caution exercised in relation to reliance on it, will also be relevant to the question whether the trial was fair.

[(v)] ... it ... cannot be right for there to be some absolute rule that, where compelling evidence is the sole or decisive evidence, an admission in evidence of a statement must then automatically lead to a defendant's Article 6 rights being infringed."[364]

The court in *Sellick* also made specific observations on the possible use by the prosecution of the statements of persons allegedly kept away by fear:

"Our view is that certainly care must be taken to see that sections 23 and 26, and indeed the new provisions in the Criminal Justice Act 2003, are not abused. Where intimidation of witnesses is alleged the court must examine with care the circumstances. Are the witnesses truly being kept away by fear? Has that fear been generated by the defendant, or by persons acting with the defendant's authority? Have reasonable steps been taken to trace the witnesses and bring them into court? Can anything be done to enable the witnesses to be brought to court to give evidence and be there protected? It is obvious that the more 'decisive' the evidence in the statements, the greater the care will be needed to be sure why it is that a witness cannot come and give evidence. The court should be astute to examine the quality and reliability of the evidence in the statement and astute and sure that the defendant has every opportunity to apply the provisions of Schedule 2. It will, as section 26 states, be looking at the interests of justice, which includes justice to the defendant and justice to the victims. The judge will give warnings to the jury stressing the disadvantage that the defendant is in, not being able to examine a witness."[365]

In *R. v Xhabri*[366] the Court of Appeal specifically addressed the hearsay provisions of the 2003 Act, reiterating that "Article 6(3)(d) does not give a defendant an absolute right to examine every witness whose testimony is adduced against him. The touchstone is whether fairness of the trial requires this."[367] The argument that, given its potential to permit hearsay evidence where the maker of the statement was unavailable for cross-examination, s.114 was incompatible with Art.6, was rejected:

"The discretion granted by section 114 is not restricted to the admission of a hearsay statement the maker of which is not available for cross-examination. To the extent that

---

[364] [2005] EWCA Crim 651, [50], [53].

[365] *ibid.*, [57].

[366] [2005] EWCA Crim 3135, [2006] 1 All E.R. 776. See generally Malik B., "The Hearsay Rule under the Criminal Justice Act 2003: *R. v Xhabri (Agrol)*" (2006) 10 *E & P* 316.

[367] [2005] EWCA Crim 3135, [2006] 1 All E.R. 776, [44].

Article 6 would be infringed by admitting such evidence, the court has a power to exclude the evidence under section 126 and a duty so to do by virtue of the Human Rights Act. There can thus be no question of section 114 being incompatible with the Convention."[368]

Furthermore, the court considered that the hearsay provisions of the 2003 Act did not violate the "equality of arms" principle inherent in Art.6(3)(d) of the Convention: "The hearsay provisions of the 2003 Act apply equally to prosecution and defence, so there is no inherent inequality of arms arising out of those provisions."[369]

J. Admission of a Co-Defendant's Plea of Guilty

Sections 74 and 75 of the Police and Criminal Evidence Act (PACE)[370] provide **15–150** a mechanism for admitting evidence of a criminal conviction of any person other than the accused, in order to prove the commission by that person of the offence, where this "is relevant to any issue in those proceedings". The commission by another person of an offence may be relevant to an issue in the proceedings because it is an essential element of the offence with which the accused is charged[371]; or it may be relevant in order to show the purpose of a joint enterprise to which the Crown allege that the accused was a party[372]; or to show that the accused was seen at the relevant time in company with a person who has admitted being involved in the commission of the offence charged.[373] This provision is subject to the discretionary power of exclusion in s.78. In *R. v Curry*[374] the Court of Appeal endorsed the views expressed in *R. v Robertson and Golder*[375] to the effect that s.74 should be sparingly used, especially in relation to joint offences such as conspiracy and affray. Where the evidence sought to be put before the jury under s.74 expressly or by necessary inference involved the guilt of the person on trial[376] the evidence should be excluded under s.78.

The application of s.74 arose for consideration by the Commission in *MH v* **15–151** *United Kingdom.*[377] The applicant was charged with conspiracy to cheat the Inland Revenue in relation to the tax affairs of a company of which he was director and the second largest shareholder. The total sum involved was £85 million. His co-defendant (who was named as a co-conspirator) pleaded guilty to a substantive offence arising out of the same transaction. The judge permitted the co-defendant's plea to be proved in evidence under s.74 of PACE, and declined to exercise his discretion under s.78 to exclude it. The applicant complained that

---

[368] *ibid.*, [42].
[369] *ibid.*, [43].
[370] See generally *Archbold* (2005) para.9–82 *et seq.*
[371] E.g., proof of theft on a charge of handling; or proof of the guilt of another on a charge of assisting an offender.
[372] *Robertson and Golder* [1987] Q.B. 920.
[373] *Grey (Kenneth)* (1988) 88 Cr.App.R. 375 (C.A.); *Kempster* (1989) 90 Cr.App.R. 14 (C.A.).
[374] [1988] Crim.L.R. 527.
[375] [1987] Q.B. 920.
[376] As where the person concerned has pleaded guilty to conspiring *with the defendant.*
[377] [1997] E.H.R.L.R. 279.

the admission of the plea denied him the opportunity to cross-examine the co-defendant and in effect reversed the burden of proof by requiring him to prove that he did not know of the fraud which the co-accused had admitted. The Commission concluded that the admission of the plea did not render the trial unfair. The judge had made it clear to the jury that the co-defendant's plea did not prove the existence of a conspiracy, and there were no grounds to criticise the judge's refusal to exercise his discretion to exclude the evidence under s.78. The defence could have called the co-defendant and could have examined him, albeit that cross-examination would only have been possible if the witness had been declared hostile. Whilst the admission of the co-defendant's plea strengthened the case against the applicant, it did not alter the burden of proof. The Commission's response here is consistent with the Strasbourg institutions' general unwillingness to review decisions on the admissibility of evidence so long as the procedures adopted seem fair as a whole.

K. CROSS-EXAMINATION OF RAPE COMPLAINANTS ON SEXUAL HISTORY

15–152 In 1975 the Heilbron Committee reviewed the law on rape and recommended restrictions on the cross-examination of complainants, on the basis that a woman's sexual experience with chosen partners does not indicate either untruthfulness or a general willingness to consent to intercourse.[378] The reform was accomplished by s.2 of the Sexual Offences (Amendment) Act 1976, but a subsequent Home Office report concluded that there was "overwhelming evidence that the present practice in the courts is unsatisfactory and that the existing law is not achieving its purpose."[379] The evidence was that judges were giving leave to cross-examine too frequently, and that strictly irrelevant evidence was being admitted, to the considerable distress of complainants. This view was strongly contested by some judges,[380] but the Government pressed ahead with legislation.

15–153 Section 41(1) of the Youth Justice and Criminal Evidence Act 1999 provides that in proceedings for a sexual offence no evidence may be adduced or question asked by or on behalf of the accused about any sexual behaviour of the complainant without leave of the judge. The restriction thus applies to previous sexual activity of the complainant, whether it is alleged to have occurred with a third party or with the accused himself. Subsections (2) and (3) together provide that the judge may not give leave where the evidence or question is said to relate to the issue of consent, unless either; (i) the sexual behaviour to which the evidence relates is alleged to have occurred "at or about the same time" as the event which is the subject of the charge (s.41(3)(b)); or (ii) the alleged past sexual behaviour of the complainant is so similar to the behaviour of the complainant at the time

---

[378] Home Office, *Report of the Advisory Group on the Law of Rape* (1975).

[379] Home Office, *Speaking Up for Justice* (1998), para.9.64.

[380] See, e.g., Judge L.J., interviewed in *The Guardian*, July 21, 1998, p.7, and Lord Bingham C.J. in the second reading debate in the House of Lords, who stated that "no one has rights coterminous with those of the defendant because it is he alone who is at risk of being punished by the state." For further discussion, see Kibble N., "The Sexual History Provisions" [2000] Crim.L.R. at 289–292.

of the alleged offence that the similarity cannot be explained by coincidence. The rationale behind the provision is that each act of sexual intercourse requires a separate consent, and accordingly the fact that the complainant has, in the past, given her consent to sex with the accused is logically irrelevant to the issue of whether she consented on the occasion in question. There is of course a *non-sequitur* in this reasoning. As enacted, the section had two anomalous consequences. First, where the issue is not consent but the accused's erroneous belief that the complainant was consenting, the section does not apply and the evidence can be admitted. In these circumstances the judge has to direct the jury that the past sexual history is relevant to the accused's state of mind (*i.e.* his belief in consent) but not to the state of mind of the complainant (*i.e.* whether she was in fact consenting).[381] More importantly, the section prevented evidence being adduced of a long term sexual relationship between the complainant and the accused unless there was some feature of their sexual activity which was so strikingly similar in its pattern that it could not be explained by coincidence (in effect, a similar fact principle).

The compatibility of this provision with Article 6 was considered by the House of Lords in *R. v A*.[382] The appellant had been denied leave to adduce evidence of previous sexual relations between himself and the complainant, which had taken place over a number of weeks before the alleged offence. Lord Steyn reviewed the Canadian jurisprudence on rape shield provisions.[383] He concluded that: **15–154**

"[T]he 1999 Act deals sensibly and fairly with questioning and evidence about the complainant's sexual experience with other men. Such matters are almost always irrelevant to the issue whether the complainant consented to sexual intercourse on the occasion alleged in the indictment, or to her credibility. To that extent the scope of the reform of the law by the 1999 Act was justified. On the other hand, the blanket exclusion of prior sexual history between the complainant and the accused in section 41(1), subject to narrow categories of exception in the remainder of section 41, poses an acute problem of proportionality. As a matter of common sense, a prior sexual relationship between the complainant and the accused may, depending on the circumstances, be relevant to the issue of consent. It is a species of prospectant evidence which may throw light on the complainant's state of mind. It cannot, of course, prove that she consented on the occasion in question. Relevance and sufficiency of proof are different things. The fact that the accused a week before an alleged murder threatened to kill the

---

[381] It is notable that the new substantive law on sexual offences, contained in the Sexual Offences Act 2003, renders the defendant liable to conviction only if his belief in consent was reasonable rather than simply honest. The extent to which sexual history evidence may be regarded as relevant in establishing a reasonable belief in consent may be expected to be rather more limited than the extent to which it is relevant in establishing a merely honest belief. See generally McEwan J., "Proving Consent in Sexual Cases: Legislative Change and Cultural Evolution" (2005) 9 *E & P* 1.

[382] [2001] 2 W.L.R. 1546. See generally Birch D., "Rethinking Sexual History Evidence: Proposals for Fairer Trials" [2002] Crim.L.R. 531; Birch D., "Untangling Sexual History Evidence: A Rejoinder to Professor Temkin" [2003] Crim.L.R. 370; McEwan J., "The Rape Shield Askew? *R. v A*" (2001) 5 E & P 257; Mirfield P., "Human Wrongs?" (2002) 118 L.Q.R. 20; Redmayne M., "Myths, Relationships and Coincidences: The New Problems of Sexual History" (2003) 7 E & P 75; Spencer J. R., "'Rape Shields' and the Right to a Fair Trial" [2001] Camb. L.J. 452; Temkin J., "Sexual History Evidence—Beware the Backlash" [2003] Crim.L.R. 217; J. Temkin, *Rape and the Legal Process* (2nd edn 2002) Ch.4.

[383] Especially *R. v Seaboyer* (1991) 83 D.L.R. (4th) 193 and *R. v Darrach* (2000) 191 D.L.R. (4th) 539.

deceased does not prove an intent to kill on the day in question. But it is logically relevant to that issue. After all, to be relevant the evidence need merely have some tendency in logic and common sense to advance the proposition in issue. It is true that each decision to engage in sexual activity is always made afresh. On the other hand, the mind does not usually blot out all memories. What one has engaged on in the past may influence what choice one makes on a future occasion. Accordingly, a prior relationship between a complainant and an accused may sometimes be relevant to what decision was made on a particular occasion."

15–155   A majority[384] of the House of Lords agreed that Parliament had adopted a legislative scheme which made an "excessive inroad" into the right to a fair trial. Read according to ordinary cannons of construction, it amounted to a blanket exclusion of potentially relevant evidence, subject only to narrow exceptions. This denied to the accused in a significant range of cases the right to put forward a full and complete defence. Whilst the statute had pursued desirable goals the method adopted amounted to "legislative overkill" when applied to a sexual relationship between the complainant and the accused. Applying the test of proportionality adopted in *De Freitas v Permanent Secretary of Ministry of Agriculture, Fisheries, Lands and Housing*[385] Lord Steyn held that the reach of the section went beyond what was necessary to achieve its legitimate purpose and was therefore incompatible with Art.6.

15–156   Lord Steyn then went on to consider whether it was possible, within the meaning of s.3 of the Human Rights Act 1998,[386] to resolve the incompatibility by construction. He considered first whether the words "at or about the same time" in s.41(3)(b) could be stretched to include past sexual activity which was probative of the issue of consent but had taken place several weeks before the alleged offence. He held that these words could extend to an act which had taken place earlier the same evening, but that even with the benefit of s.3 they could not encompass events occurring days, weeks or months beforehand. Lord Steyn went on, however, to consider the exception in s.41(3)(c) for sexual behaviour which was so similar to the alleged behaviour of the complainant at the time of the offence that it could not be explained by coincidence. On ordinary canons of construction the subsection pointed to a narrow exception resembling the old common law (i.e. pre-Criminal Justice Act 2003) test for the admissibility of similar fact evidence—either the *Boardman*[387] test or, at the very least, the test of high probative force subsequently laid down by the House of Lords in *DPP v P*.[388] Even adopting the latter approach, the threshold test would be too high. It was therefore necessary to turn to the Human Rights Act. In His Lordship's view it was possible, applying s.3, to achieve a compatible construction. Section 3 required the court to "subordinate the niceties of the language of section 41(3)(c), and in particular the touchstone of coincidence, to broader considerations of relevance judged by logical and common sense criteria of time and circum-stances". It was reasonable to assume that the legislature, if alerted to the

---

[384] Lord Hope dissented, holding that the restriction was within the "discretionary area of judg-ment" which the courts should accord to the legislature. See further paras 2–132—2–133 above.
[385] [1999] 1 A.C. 69. See para.2–110 above.
[386] See para.3–58 above.
[387] [1975] A.C. 421.
[388] [1991] 2 A.C. 447.

problem, would not have wished to deny the accused the right to put forward a full and complete defence. It was therefore possible to read the section as subject to an implied provision that evidence or questioning which is required to ensure a fair trial under Art.6 should not be treated as inadmissible. The result would be that sometimes logically relevant sexual experiences between a complainant and accused would be admitted, although a judge would still be justified in excluding evidence of an isolated incident distant in time and circumstances. By introducing a judicial discretion, the section could be saved from a declaration of incompatibility.[389] It would have achieved a major part of its objective but its excessive reach would be attenuated in accordance with the will of Parliament as expressed in the Human Rights Act.

This decision seems consistent with the balance required by the Convention   **15–157** caselaw. In *Baegen v Netherlands*,[390] the applicant had not been allowed to question the complainant directly in a rape trial, although he had been offered the opportunity to put written questions (which he declined). The Commission recognised that proceedings for sexual offences "are often conceived of as an ordeal by the victim", and stated:

> "In the assessment of the question whether or not in such proceedings an accused received a fair trial, account must be taken of the right to respect for the victim's private life. Therefore, the Commission accepts that in criminal proceedings concerning sexual abuse certain measures may be taken for the purpose of protecting the victim, provided that such measures can be reconciled with an adequate and effective exercise of the rights of the defence."

L. SPECIAL MEASURES DIRECTIONS AND THE YOUTH JUSTICE AND CRIMINAL EVIDENCE ACT 1999

The Youth Justice and Criminal Evidence Act 1999 permits, or requires, courts   **15–158** to make special measures directions to assist vulnerable or intimated witnesses. Section 21 of the Act creates a presumption that all child witnesses give their evidence in chief by means of a video recording of an interview of the witness and that the rest of their evidence is given by live link. Special provision is made, however, in relation to child witness "in need of special protection". A child witness is in need of special protection if the offence to which the proceedings relate is a sexual offence under a number of specified statutes, kidnapping, false imprisonment or child abduction, cruelty to a child, or any offence "which involves an assault on, or injury or a threat of injury to, any person".[391] In the case of a child who is *not* in need of special protection, the presumption mentioned above is rebuttable "to the extent that the court is satisfied that compliance with it would not be likely to maximise the quality of the witness's

---

[389] See para.3–67 above.
[390] (1995) A.327–B.
[391] S.35(3).

evidence so far as practicable".[392] In cases where the child is in need of special protection, however, the presumption is irrebutable.[393] In *R. (D) v Camberwell Green Youth Court*[394] the House of Lords held that this irrebuttability did not constitute a violation of the general fair trial guarantee of Art.6 or of Art.6(3)(d). Baroness Hale of Richmond stated:

> "All the evidence is produced at the trial in the presence of the accused, some of it in pre-recorded form and some of it by contemporaneous television transmission. The accused can see and hear it all. The accused has every opportunity to challenge and question the witnesses against him at the trial itself. The only thing missing is a face to face confrontation, but . . . the Convention does not guarantee a right to face to face confrontation."[395]

It is notable that the provisions on special measures in the Youth Justice and Criminal Evidence Act 1999 do not apply to defendants. In *R.(S) v Waltham Forest Youth Court*[396] it was confirmed that a special measures direction could not be given in respect of a 13-year-old defendant even if she was intending to give evidence against her co-defendants. This state of affairs was not thought to constitute a violation of the defendant's right to a fair trial under Art.6.[397]

M. Evidence of the Accused's Previous Convictions

15–159　　There are of course a number of circumstances in which the previous convictions of an accused may be introduced into evidence in a criminal trial in England and Wales. The law on this topic is now encapsulated in the provisions of the Criminal Justice Act 2003. This is not an area of criminal procedure in which there is any consensus between Member States of the Council of Europe. For example, a section of the Austrian Code of Criminal Procedure which provides for the accused's criminal record to be read out at the hearing has been quoted by the court without comment.[398] It is therefore most unlikely that the admission of a defendant's previous convictions would be found in Strasbourg to violate the right to a fair hearing under Art.6. In *X v Denmark*[399] the jury were informed of the previous convictions of the defendant during a trial on two charges of rape. The Commission held that:

> "When interpreting such fundamental concepts as 'fair hearing' within the meaning of Article 6(1) and 'presumption of innocence' within the meaning of Article 6(2), the Commission finds it necessary to take into consideration the practice in different countries which are members of the Council of Europe . . . [Since it is] clear that in a

---

[392] S.21(4)(c).
[393] S.21(5).
[394] [2005] UKHL 4, [2005] 1 W.L.R. 393.
[395] *Ibid.* [49].
[396] [2004] EWHC 715 (Admin), [2004] 2 Cr.App.R. 21 (p.335).
[397] In *R. (D) v Camberwell Green Youth Court* [2005] UKHL 4, [2005] 1 W.L.R. 393, [63], Baroness Hale of Richmond reserved her position on whether the *Waltham Forest* case was correctly decided. These issues were discussed further in Ch.11, above.
[398] See *Asch v Austria* (1993) 15 E.H.R.R. 597 at para.21.
[399] (1965) 18 C.D. 44 at 45; 2 Dig 739.

number of these countries information as to previous convictions is regularly given during the trial, before a court has reached a decision as to the guilt of the accused . . . the Commission is not prepared to consider such a procedure as violating any provision of Article 6 of the Convention, not even in cases where a jury is to decide on the guilt of an accused."

This suggests that the provisions of the Criminal Justice Act 2003, which allow for the wider admissibility of evidence of previous misconduct than was previously the case, are unlikely to encounter Convention problems.[400]

N. PSYCHIATRIC EVIDENCE RELATING TO A CO-DEFENDANT

In *Hardiman v United Kingdom*[401] the Commission rejected a complaint arising out of the non-disclosure of a psychiatric report relating to a co-accused who was running a "cut-throat" defence on a murder charge. From the report of the decision it does not appear that the Commission specifically addressed the "equality of arms" problem raised by this case. In *R. v Smith (SI)*[402] the Court of Appeal held that the prosecution could cross-examine an accused person on the contents of a psychiatric report where his account in evidence differed from his account to the psychiatrists. The court also approved the trial judge's decision to allow the prosecution to call the psychiatrists to give evidence in rebuttal. It is difficult to see how the considerations of confidentiality and the absence of a caution, mentioned by the Commission in its decision, could be sufficient to render such reports immune from disclosure to a co-accused when they could be used by the prosecution. In this respect the *Hardiman* decision does not sit comfortably with the declaration of the court in *Edwards v United Kingdom* that "it is a requirement of fairness under Article 6 . . . that the prosecution authorities disclose to the defence all material evidence for or against the accused."[403]

15–160

O. POLYGRAPH EVIDENCE

Article 6 does not entitle the accused to insist on the introduction of polygraph evidence, where this is not permitted under domestic law. *Archbold* states as settled law the principle that "evidence produced by the administration of a mechanically or chemically or hypnotically induced test on a witness so as to show the veracity or otherwise of that witness is not admissible in English law."[404] However, the authority cited in support of that proposition, *Fennell v*

15–161

---

[400] *cf.* Law Commission Consultation Paper No.141, *Evidence in Criminal Proceedings: Previous Misconduct of a Defendant* (1996).

[401] [1996] E.H.R.L.R. 425. See para.14–123 above.

[402] (1979) 69 Cr.App.R. 378.

[403] (1993) 15 E.H.R.R. 417 at para.36, discussed in detail (with *Hardiman*) in paras 14–118 *et seq.*; for a further application of the principle of "equality of arms" to experts' reports, see *Mantovanelli v France* (1997) 24 E.H.R.R. 370 at paras 33–36.

[404] *Archbold* (2005), para.8–158.

Jerome Property Maintenance Ltd,[405] is concerned only with "truth drug" evidence.

15–162   In *Application No.9696/82*[406] the applicant was convicted of murder on the basis of circumstantial evidence. The trial judge refused his request to be examined by polygraph and the applicant alleged that this violated his right to a fair trial. The Commission rejected the application as manifestly ill-founded:

> "In the opinion of the Commission the rejection of the applicant's request to be interrogated with the use of a lie detector does not make the proceedings unfair . . . [I]t is, according to the present state of knowledge, not possible to obtain fully reliable results by the use of a lie detector. Under those circumstances the Commission considers it justified that no general right for the use of a lie detector is granted to suspected persons or to convicted persons. The authorisation of some persons to use a lie detector would inevitably influence the position of other persons who would refuse to be subjected to a lie detector. Their refusal might be interpreted as a sign of guilt."

P. Expert Evidence

15–163   The use of "independent" or court-appointed experts in criminal proceedings can have significant implications for the equality of arms guarantee in Art.6 if the expert expresses a firm opinion adverse to one of the parties. In *Bonisch v Austria*[407] a court-appointed expert, who had drafted the report relied upon to institute criminal proceedings against the applicant, was afforded preferential status over an expert witness appointed by the defence. He was permitted to attend throughout the hearing, to put questions to the accused and the witnesses, and to make comments on their replies (facilities which were denied to the defence expert). In view of the fact that his evidence was adverse to the accused, the Court considered that he should have been treated as a prosecution witness. Accordingly, the failure to maintain equality of treatment violated Art.6. However, in *Brandstetter v Austria*[408] the Court held that the mere fact that the court-appointed expert was employed by the same institute as the expert whose report had led to the commencement of the prosecution was insufficient to give rise to legitimate doubts as to his impartiality.

Q. Retrospective Changes in the Law of Evidence

15–164   In *X v United Kingdom*[409] the Commission held that it is not a breach of Art.7 of the Convention for the Court of Appeal to uphold a conviction by reference to a precedent in the law of evidence decided after the applicant's conviction. Article

---

[405] *The Times*, November 26, 1986.
[406] (1983, unpublished) 2 Dig. Supp. 6.1.1.4.4.5 at 6.
[407] (1987) 9 E.H.R.R. 191.
[408] (1993) 15 E.H.R.R. 378.
[409] (1976) 3 D.R. 95.

7 prohibits the retroactive application of criminal offences so as to penalise conduct which was not criminal at the time when the relevant act or omission occurred. It does not apply to the law of evidence.

CHAPTER 16

SENTENCING AND RELATED ISSUES

In this chapter we examine the relevance of the Human Rights Act 1998 to the **16–01** sentencing process. Under s.6 of the Act judges and magistrates are obliged to exercise their sentencing discretion in conformity with Convention rights. There is a considerable Strasbourg jurisprudence on the application of the Convention to sentencing issues, and the British jurisprudence is now developing quickly. The chapter begins by exploring several grounds for challenging the severity of sentences, taking account of the changes to the English sentencing system introduced by the Criminal Justice Act 2003. It then discusses the application of the Convention to aspects of sentencing procedure, and concludes by considering the principle of non-retrospectivity in sentencing, and the impact of Art.8 on the rights of an accused with family ties in the United Kingdom who is facing a recommendation for deportation.

Running through the chapter is the distinction, developed by the Strasbourg **16–02** Court, between preventive sentences and punitive sentences. Article 7 uses the word "penalty", and that has been given an autonomous meaning by the Court when deciding whether the principle of non-retrospectivity applies to a particular order or measure. Other decisions, as we shall see, apply different rules to punitive and to preventive sentences—and, indeed, to the punitive and preventive components of a single sentence that can be regarded as partly preventive and partly punitive. These distinctions will be developed as the chapter progresses.

A. CHALLENGES TO THE SEVERITY OF SENTENCES

No article of the Convention provides a specific right to question the severity of **16–03** a sentence imposed following conviction for a criminal offence.[1] However, there are two possible ways in which a disproportionately severe sentence can be

---

[1] *X v United Kingdom* (1974) 1 D.R. 54 at 55 (application in respect of four-year sentence for arson). It should be noted, however, that Art.49(3) of the Charter of Fundamental Rights of the European Union (2001) provides that "The severity of penalties must not be disproportionate to the criminal offence."

challenged under the Convention. First, the Commission and Court have indicated that the overall length of a custodial sentence could, in principle and in appropriate circumstances, amount to inhuman punishment contrary to Art.3 of the Convention. Although the Court would undoubtedly hesitate before making such a finding,[2] it has on occasions raised doubts about the length of sentences imposed. Secondly, whenever the government attempts to rely on the second paragraph of Arts 8 to 11 to justify an interference with the declared right, a disproportionately severe sentence would make that justification difficult to sustain.[3]

16–04 Questions of proportionality of sentence do not only arise in cases where imprisonment is imposed. They may also arise in cases where a non-custodial sentence or a penalty such as forfeiture is involved.[4] They may even be an issue where there is a legislative provision for the administrative imposition of penalty points on a driver's licence following an on-the-spot fine. Convention jurisprudence has long required that a person who is liable to such a penalty must have the right to challenge that penalty in a court.[5] In *Malige v France*[6] the Court held that the applicant, who received an on-the-spot fine with four penalty points for grossly exceeding the speed limit, did have the opportunity to challenge this in a court. The Court was also satisfied that the sanction was sufficiently proportionate: "the legislation itself makes provision to a certain extent for the number of points deducted to vary in accordance with the seriousness of the offence committed by the accused."[7]

16–05 However, for the question of proportionality to arise there must be a "penalty," as distinct from a preventive measure. This distinction is examined fully below,[8] but it is worth signalling at this point that a notification requirement under the Sexual Offences Act 2003[9] and a requirement to attend a driver re-training course[10] would be classified as preventive measures whereas a confiscation order has been held to be a "penalty."[11]

I. Disproportionately Severe Sentences as "Inhuman" Punishment under the Convention

16–06 Observations on the possibility of challenging the length of a punitive sentence are to be found in *Weeks v United Kingdom*.[12] The applicant (then aged 17) had

---

[2] See, e.g. *Treholt v Norway* (1991) 71 D.R. 168 at 191: "the prospects of serving a 20-year sentence [imposed for espionage] may well cause severe problems for the applicant and his family without necessarily coming within Art.3 of the Convention."

[3] See paras 16–12 to 16–20 below.

[4] See paras 16–19 and 16–20 below, and also the decision of the New Zealand Court of Appeal in *Lyall v Solicitor-General* [1997] 2 N.Z.L.R. 641.

[5] *Ozturk v Germany* (1984) 6 E.H.R.R. 409.

[6] (1999) 28 E.H.R.R. 578.

[7] *ibid.*, at para.49.

[8] Paras ? 16–63 to 16–68.

[9] See the consideration of the previous legislation, the Sex Offenders Act 1997, in *Ibbotson v United Kingdom* (1999) 27 E.H.R.R. CD 332.

[10] *Blokker v Netherlands* [2001] E.H.R.L.R. 328.

[11] *Welch v United Kingdom* (1995) 20 E.H.R.R. 247.

[12] (1988) 10 E.H.R.R. 293.

been sentenced to life imprisonment for an offence of armed robbery, by threatening the owner of a pet shop with an unloaded starting pistol and stealing 35 pence. The trial judge, in passing sentence, indicated that he had imposed a discretionary life sentence because of the applicant's dangerousness, and not because of the gravity of his offence. The sentence was intended to protect the public and it was to be a matter for the Secretary of State to determine when it was safe to release the applicant. The European Court accepted that subject to appropriate safeguards[13] indeterminate detention of this nature could be justified by the need to protect society. However, the Court held that if a term of life imprisonment had been imposed for this offence on purely punitive grounds "one could have serious doubts as to its compatibility with Article 3 of the Convention which prohibits *inter alia* inhuman punishment."[14] This is a significant statement, even though the Court has not yet acted upon it. In *Abed Hussain v United Kingdom*[15] the Court expressed a similar opinion in relation to a sentence of detention during Her Majesty's Pleasure[16] imposed on a juvenile convicted of murder.[17] There is some evidence that the English courts may be willing to treat gross disproportionality as contrary to Art.3: in his judgment on the automatic sentence of life imprisonment in *Offen (No.2)*,[18] Lord Woolf C.J. stated that a "wholly disproportionate" punishment might contravene Art.3, as well as being a "arbitrary and disproportionate" and thus in breach of Art.5. The example given was a sentence of life imprisonment imposed on a person convicted of manslaughter resulting from a simple unjustified push which gave rise to a fatal head injury, the sentence for which would normally be no more than one or possibly two years' imprisonment. However, the House of Lords has held that the imposition of a mandatory life sentence upon a person convicted of murder who is not considered to present a danger to the public does not contravene Art.3 or Art.5.[19]

The general principle is that, in order to constitute a violation of Art.3, the **16–07** punishment complained of "must attain a minimum level of severity."[20] Thus, for example, the Court had no difficulty in concluding that judicial corporal punishment on the Isle of Man was in breach of Art.3.[21] Whether a custodial sentence imposed on an adult would be found to be "inhuman or degrading punishment"[22] will depend on the "sex, age and state of health" of the defendant.[23] In determining the standard to be applied, some assistance can be gained from decisions of the Court and Commission in the extradition context. The

---

[13] In particular the court held that such a sentence gives rise to a right of periodic access to a court under Art.5(4) to review the justification for continued detention: *ibid.*, at paras 58–59.
[14] *ibid.*, at para.47.
[15] (1996) 22 E.H.R.R. 1.
[16] Under s.53(1) of the Children and Young Persons Act 1933.
[17] (1996) 22 E.H.R.R. 1, at para.53.
[18] [2001] 1 W.L.R. 253, approved by the House of Lords in *Drew* [2003] UKHL 25.
[19] *R. v Lichniak and Pyrah* [2003] 1 A.C. 903, discussed in para.16–46 below.
[20] See, e.g. *Ireland v United Kingdom* (1979–80) 2 E.H.R.R. 25 at para.162.
[21] *Tyrer v United Kingdom* (1979–80) 2 E.H.R.R. 1.
[22] *X v Germany* (1976) 6 D.R. 127, and *Treholt v Norway*, above, n.6.
[23] *Ireland v United Kingdom* (1979–80) 2 E.H.R.R. 25 at para.162; see also *Campbell and Cosans v United Kingdom* (1982) 4 E.H.R.R. 293 at para.28, and *A v United Kingdom* (1999) 27 E.H.R.R. 611 at para.20.

Court has held that a proposed extradition can give rise to inhuman treatment under Art.3 where there is a "real risk" that the sentence which is liable to be imposed in the requesting state will be "disproportionate to the gravity of the crime committed."[24] The fact that a person extradited or deported may face prosecution for a criminal offence which carries a severe sentence, or one that is more severe than would apply in other European states, is not sufficient.[25] In *Altun v FRG*[26] the Commission held that a violation of Art.3 could arise from the risk that criminal proceedings abroad would lead to an "unjustified or disproportionate sentence,"[27] whereas the Commission subsequently held that "only in exceptional circumstances could the length of a sentence be relevant under Article 3."[28]

16–08   There are two particular types of case in which English courts may need to draw upon the Convention. Inasmuch as severity and disproportionality, in the context of Art.3, turn on the "sex, age and state of health" of the offender, this raises questions about certain sentences imposed on young offenders and on mentally disordered offenders. The leading cases discussed above, *Weeks* and *Hussain*, both involved young offenders. In certain circumstances—broadly speaking, for crimes carrying a maximum sentence of 14 years or more for an adult—a court may impose on an offender aged between 10 and 18 a sentence under s.91 of the Powers of Criminal Courts (Sentencing) Act 2000. That sentence may be longer than the normal maximum for offenders under 18, which stands at two years' detention. In his guideline judgment on the subject, *Mills*,[29] Lord Bingham C.J. emphasised that custodial sentences for young offenders should be no longer than is necessary. But there are other authorities suggesting that it is proper to impose deterrent sentences on young offenders under the s.91 powers,[30] and this raises the possibility of a sentence whose length is based on deterrence and is disproportionate in relation to the offence itself. Such a sentence might be open to challenge under Art.3.

16–09   In *T and V v United Kingdom*[31] the applicants argued that the sentence of detention during Her Majesty's Pleasure (HMP), imposed on a child as young as 11, amounted to a breach of Art.3. However, the Court held that there was no violation. The punitive element inherent in the "tariff" did not, of itself, give rise to a breach of Art.3. The court recognised:

"that Article 37 of the U.N. Convention [on the Rights of the Child] . . . provides that the detention of a child 'shall be used only as a measure of last resort and for the shortest appropriate period of time,' and that r.17.1(b) of the Beijing Rules recommends

---

[24] *Soering v United Kingdom* (1989) 11 E.H.R.R. 439 at para.104.
[25] *C v FRG* (1986) 46 D.R. 179.
[26] (1983) 36 D.R. 209.
[27] *ibid.*, at 233.
[28] *C v Germany* (1986) 46 D.R. 179.
[29] [1998] 2 Cr.App.R.(S) 128.
[30] See, for example, *Ford* (1976) 62 Cr.App.R. 303; *cf. Cunningham* (1993) 14 Cr.App.R.(S) 444, which prohibits exemplary sentences but upholds deterrent sentencing based on, for example, the "prevalence of the offence."
[31] (2000) 30 E.H.R.R. 121.

that 'restrictions on the personal liberty of the juvenile shall . . . be limited to the possible minimum'."[32]

In this case the applicants had already been detained for six years from the age of 11, but the court did not consider: "that in all the circumstances of the case including the applicant's age and his conditions of detention, a period of punitive detention of this length can be said to amount to inhuman or degrading treatment."[33]

Turning to mentally disordered offenders, the law provides a range of special **16–10** disposals under the Mental Health Act 1983 and other statutes. Despite s.82 of the Powers of Criminal Courts (Sentencing) Act 2000,[34] courts find themselves sending mentally disordered offenders to prison (or, in the case of young offenders, detention) for various reasons—for example, because there is no hospital willing to offer a bed to an offender, or because an offender diagnosed as suffering from mental impairment or psychopathic disorder is regarded as "untreatable".[35] For some mentally disordered offenders, prison is likely to be such an adverse and damaging environment, even if the offender is held in the prison hospital, that it may amount to "inhuman treatment" under Art.3.[36]

In *Aerts v Belgium*[37] the applicant, a mentally disturbed arrestee, had been **16–11** detained for nine months in the crowded psychiatric wing of a prison before transfer to a mental hospital. The European Committee for the Prevention of Torture and Inhuman or Degrading Conduct (CPT) had reported on this particular prison in 1994, concluding that "keeping mental patients for long periods in the conditions [which apply in the Lantin psychiatric annexe] carries an undeniable risk of causing their mental state to deteriorate." At the Commission's hearing on the merits, a majority held that the applicant's treatment had been in breach of Art.3:

---

[32] *ibid.*, at para.97.

[33] Taken from the judgment in *T and V v United Kingdom, ibid.*, para.99.

[34] In broad terms, the section requires courts to obtain reports before sentencing persons who appear mentally disordered, and to consider the likely effect on the offender's condition of imposing a custodial sentence.

[35] For evidence of the numbers and needs of mentally disordered persons in prison, see Gunn J., Maden A. and Swinton M., "Treatment Needs of Prisoners with Psychiatric Disorders" (1991) 303 *British Medical Journal* 338. For discussion of the Mental Health Act provisions and relevant case-law, see Ashworth A., *Sentencing and Criminal Justice* (4th edn, 2005), pp.370–379.

[36] An application based on the effects of prison overcrowding and inadequate facilities failed in *Delazarus v United Kingdom* (Application No.17525/90, discussed by Harris, O'Boyle and Warbrick, *The Law of the European Convention on Human Rights* (1995), pp.70–71), but in *Peers v Greece* [2001] E.H.R.L.R. 719 the court found a violation of Art.3 where the cell was cramped, there was an unscreened and malfunctioning toilet, and ventilation was inadequate for the hot conditions. In *Zhu v United Kingdom* [2001] E.H.R.L.R. 231 an application was held inadmissible on the ground that the applicant had not established beyond reasonable doubt that the conditions of detention attained the "minimum level of severity" needed for a violation of Art.3. *Cf. Keenan v United Kingdom* (2001) 33 E.H.R.R. 38, where the Court found a violation of Art.3 through failure adequately to supervise a prisoner who was a known suicide risk; and *Price v United Kingdom* (2002) 34 E.H.R.R. 53; [2001] Crim.L.R. 916, where the Court found a violation of Art.3 where a severely disabled person was committed to prison without ensuring that there were facilities appropriate to the nature and degree of her disabilities.

[37] (2000) 29 E.H.R.R. 50.

"By failing to take, within a reasonable time, the steps necessitated by the applicant's particular state of mental suffering caused by his extreme anxiety, the State caused him, by omission, to be treated in a manner which cannot be justified on any ground— certainly not on the ground of financial exigencies—and which, in the circumstances of the case, was 'inhuman' or, at the very least, 'degrading'."[38]

16–12 A majority of the Court, however, held that "the living conditions on the psychiatric wing at Lantin do not seem to have had such serious effects on [the applicant's] mental health as would bring them within the scope of Article 3." The conclusion suggests that the standard of proof had not been reached:

"Even if it is accepted that the applicant's state of anxiety, described by the psychiatric report of 10 March 1993, was caused by the conditions of detention in Lantin, and even allowing for the difficulty Mr Aerts may have had in describing how these had affected him, it has not been conclusively established that the applicant suffered treatment that could be classified as inhuman or degrading."[39]

The terms of this conclusion suggest a narrow basis for the decision, and the issue of the length of detention is much intertwined with the conditions of detention. This part of the *Aerts* decision was reached by a majority of seven to two, and the dissenting opinion argues strongly, with reference to the CPT report on conditions at Lantin prison, that the suffering caused to the applicant "by keeping him in the above-described conditions for such a long time exceeds . . . the minimum level of severity required for inhuman treatment under Article 3 of the Convention."

16–13 Along similar lines to the judgment of the majority in *Aerts v Belgium* is the decision of the House of Lords in *Drew*.[40] The appellant had pleaded guilty to two offences of causing grievous bodily harm with intent. There was a psychiatric report on him that recommended a hospital order, but the case fell within the automatic life sentence provisions in s.109 of the Powers of Criminal Courts(Sentencing) Act 2000.[41] He was therefore sentenced to life imprisonment and, because of his mental condition, was transferred from prison to mental hospital some eight days after sentence. He argued that the imposition of the automatic life sentence on a person with his mental condition amounted to "inhuman and degrading punishment" contrary to Art.3. In dismissing the appeal, Lord Bingham made three main points. First, while it may be wrong in principle to punish those who are unfit to be tried or who, although fit, are not responsible for their conduct because of insanity, it was not the case that a mentally disordered offender was necessarily absolved of all responsibility for his offence.[42] And the court had regarded the appellant as criminally culpable. Secondly, Lord Bingham

---

[38] *ibid.*, Commission report, para.82.

[39] *ibid.*, court, para.66. See also *Kudla v Poland* [2001] E.H.R.L.R. 352, to similar effect.

[40] [2003] 1 W.L.R. 1213; [2004] 1 Cr.App.R.(S) 8 at 65.

[41] The provisions on automatic life sentences were repealed by the Criminal Justice Act 2003 and replaced by wider provisions for sentences of life imprisonment and sentences of imprisonment for public protection, discussed in paragraphs 16–50 to 16–51 below.

[42] Where the offender does lack criminal responsibility then his detention can only be justified under Art.5(1)(e), not 5(1)(a). He must be detained in a place and under conditions that are appropriate given that he is detained on grounds of mental disorder, not for punitive purposes. A prison is not appropriate: *Aerts v Belgium* (2000) 29 E.H.R.R. 50 at para.46.

conceded that there would be a conflict with Art.3 if the automatic life sentence were to have the effect of denying medical treatment to a prisoner. However, he went on:

"that is not a necessary result of these provisions, since section 47 of the [Mental Health Act 1983] gives the Home Secretary power to transfer a defendant sentenced to imprisonment to a hospital where he will receive any medical treatment he needs, and the Home Secretary is obliged to act compatibly with the Convention. Thus, as the Recorder observed in this case, the effect of the sentence may be very much the same whether he is sentenced to imprisonment or made subject to a hospital order."[43]

This is an important consideration, but it is not compelling. It may be argued that in many cases the judge is entitled to assume that the Secretary of State will use the power to transfer the offender to a mental hospital if that is the proper course; but is that assumption a sufficient assurance that the judge is acting compatibly with the Convention rights of the offender? Certainly there may be some cases where the judge must recognise the strong probability that the Secretary of State will not be able to ensure the offender's transfer or otherwise to ensure that the offender's Convention rights are respected, and in that kind of situation the Strasbourg Court has suggested a different approach.[44] And thirdly, Lord Bingham accepted that the confinement of the appellant in prison for eight days without the proper medication "caused him ill effects" but, like the majority in *Aerts*, concluded that "these were not in our opinion of sufficient severity to engage the operation of Article 3."[45] The reasoning in *Drew* was applied by the Court of Appeal in *Staines*,[46] where the sentence was custody for life with a hospital and limitation direction under s.45A of the Mental Health Act 1983.

II. Constitutional Disproportionality in other Jurisdictions

In many other jurisdictions, disproportionality of sentence may of itself raise   **16–14**
constitutional issues. In 1992 the Council of Europe approved, through its Council of Ministers, a recommendation on sentencing that includes the principle that, whatever fundamental rationales for sentencing are adopted, there should be no disproportionality between the sentence and the seriousness of the crime.[47] The Charter of Fundamental Rights of the European Union, approved in 2000, declares in Art.49(3) that "the severity of penalties must not be disproportionate to the criminal offence." Some European jurisdictions already recognise such a right at a constitutional level: for example, the fundamental right to human

---

[43] *Ibid*, para.[18]. Art.5 is also relevant here. The right not to be deprived arbitrarily under Art.5(1) gives rise to the principle that a person must be detained in a place and under conditions appropriate to the ground of detention. However, this principle is itself subject to the need to strike a reasonable balance bewteen the competing interests involved , so allowing some, albeit strictly limited, recognition of the friction between available and needed capacity in hospitals. That recognition permits of some delay in transferring a patient from prison to hospital: *Brand v Netherlands* 17 B.H.R.C. 398 at paras 62–5.
[44] See *Price v United Kingdom* (2002) 34 E.H.R.R. 53; [2001] Crim.L.R. 917, discussed in n.36 above.
[45] [2003] 1 W.L.R. 1213, ; [2004] 1 Cr.App.R.(S) 8 at 65, para.19.
[46] [2006] 2 Cr.App.R.(S) 376.
[47] Principle A4, Recommendation R (92) 17, *Consistency in Sentencing* (Strasbourg, 1992).

dignity under the German Constitution has been interpreted as prohibiting disproportionate punishments.[48]

16–15   In many jurisdictions the question has arisen in the context of a constitutional right not to be subjected to "cruel and unusual punishment." Section 12 of the Canadian Charter of Rights is in these terms and has been interpreted by the Supreme Court of Canada as prohibiting disproportionate sentences. Thus in *Smith*[49] the court held that a mandatory minimum sentence of seven years' imprisonment for drug importatation contravened s.12, since it was disproportionate to some forms of the offence for which it would have to be imposed. In *Lyons*[50] the court held that an indeterminate sentence of preventive detention imposed under a "dangerous offender" provision was capable of conformity with s.12, on the ground that it was not grossly disproportionate because the particular offence was serious and the provisions for review and release would ensure that in actual cases the detention was not disproportionately long. However, release decisions are based on assessments of risk, which are (a) notoriously fallible and (b) not necessarily related to the seriousness of the offence, which is the key issue in respect of disproportionality.[51] In *M (CA)*[52] the Supreme Court again confirmed that grossly disproportionality would amount to "cruel and unusual punishment", but went on to affirm that the totality principle in sentencing law should operate so as to prevent disproportionate sentences for multiple offences.[53]

16–16   Section 12 of the Constitution of South Africa declares the right "not to be deprived of freedom . . . without just cause", and in the leading decision of *S v Dodo*[54] the Constitutional Court held that a prohibition on gross disproportionality of sentence was inherent in this right. As Ackerman J. expressed it:

> "To attempt to justify any period of penal incarceration, let alone imprisonment for life as in the present case, without inquiring into the proportionality between the offence and the period of imprisonment, is to ignore, if not to deny, that which lies at the very heart of human dignity. Human beings are not commodities to which a price can be attached; they are creatures with inherent and infinite worth; they ought to be treated as ends in themselves, never merely as a means to an end. Where the length of a sentence, which has been imposed because of its general deterrent effect on others, bears no relation to the gravity of the offence . . . the offender is being used essentially as a means to another end and the offender's dignity is assailed. So too where the reformative effect of the punishment is predominant and the offender is sentenced to lengthy imprisonment, principally because he cannot be reformed in a shorter period, but the

---

[48] BverfGE 1, 346, on which see van Zyl Smit D., *Taking Life Imprisonment Seriously in National and International Law* (2002), Ch.4. For a general review and analysis, see van Zyl Smit D. and Ashworth A., "Disproportionate Sentences as Human Rights Violations" (2004) 67 MLR 541.
[49] [1987] 1 S.C.R. 1045.
[50] [1987] 2 S.C.R. 309.
[51] For further discussion see Manson A., *The Law of Sentencing* (Toronto, 2001), p.300ff.
[52] [1996] 1 S.C.R. 500, upholding a total sentence of 25 years for a series of sex offences which did not carry life imprisonment.
[53] In English law the totality principle is re-stated in s.166(3) of the Criminal Justice Act 2003.
[54] 2001 (3) S.A. 382 (CC).

length of imprisonment bears no relationship to what the committed offence merits."[55]

This passage indicates that where a longer sentence is imposed for deterrent purposes this may violate the prohibition on (gross) disproportionality. The prohibition may also be violated where an indefinite or very long sentence is imposed for a non-serious offence in order to incapacitate an offender believed to be dangerous: as stated in *S v Bull*,[56] the index offence "must clearly be of such a nature as to justify a present determination of continued dangerousness in the future which . . . requires a pattern of persistent or repetitively aggressive or violent behaviour."

The Supreme Court of the United States has also interpreted the right not to be **16–17** subjected to "cruel and unusual punishment" as prohibiting grossly disproportionate punishments, but its application of the principle has varied considerably. For example, in *Rummel v Estelle*[57] the Supreme Court held by a majority that the imposition of life imprisonment for a third minor and non-violent theft did not infringe the proportionality test, whereas in *Solem v Helm*[58] the Supreme Court held by a majority that life imprisonment for a seventh minor non-violent offence was so disproportionate as to constitute "cruel and unusual punishment." More recently in *Ewing v California*[59] the Supreme Court held by a majority that a sentence of life imprisonment with a 25 year non-parole period for the third felony (theft of three golf clubs) under a "three strikes and you're out" law was not so disproportionate as to infringe the constitutional right. The majority was able to reach this conclusion by arguing that the California legislature's policy of incapacitation had to be taken into account when considering disproportionality, an approach that misunderstands the proportionality principle and emasculates its connection with the seriousness of the offence. Likewise in *Lockyer v Andrade*[60] the Supreme Court held by a majority that a sentence of twice life imprisonment with a minimum non-parole period of 50 years for two incident of theft involving a total of 11 blank video tapes was not grossly disproportionate. As the dissenting judgment commented, "If Andrade's sentence is not grossly disproportionate, the principle has no meaning."[61] It is submitted that the reasoning of the Constitutional Court of South Africa (16–16 above) is much more persuasive.

III. Disproportionately Severe Sentences and Articles 8 to 11

Where it is alleged that criminal proceedings have involved a violation of Arts 8 **16–18** to 11, the severity of the sentence imposed will be highly material in determining whether the interference was "necessary in a democratic society" within the meaning of the second paragraph of each article, and to the proportionality of the

---

[55] *Ibid*, at para.[38].

[56] 2001 (2) SACR 681.

[57] (1980) 445 US 263; for analysis and discussion, see van Zyl Smit D., *Taking Life Imprisonment Seriously in National and International Law* (2002), Ch.2.

[58] (1983) 463 US 277.

[59] (2003) 12 S.Ct. 1179.

[60] (2003) 123 S.Ct. 1166.

[61] Justice Souter at p.1179, Stevens, Ginsburg and Breyer J.J. concurring.

measure.[62] There is also authority from Commonwealth courts to support the view that an interference with a particular right may be held disproportionate if the severity of the sentence is not justified by the purpose it is intended to serve.[63]

16–19 Under the Convention the principle was stated in the early case of *Handyside v United Kingdom*[64] emphasising the importance attached to the ability of citizens to exercise their freedom of expression under Art.10, and hence the Court's need to enquire "whether the 'restrictions' or 'penalties' were necessary for the 'protection of morals'." This principle was reiterated by the Commission in *Arrowsmith v United Kingdom*,[65] where one of the questions was whether the applicant's conviction for incitement to disaffection violated her right to freedom of expression. In determining whether the interference with her right was "necessary in a democratic society", the Commission stated that it:

> "must finally consider the severity of the sentence. [The Commission] is of the opinion that the sentence which the applicant finally received and served (seven months' imprisonment), although admittedly severe, was not in the circumstances so clearly out of proportion to the legitimate aims pursued that this severity in itself could render unjustifiable such an interference which the Commission otherwise had held justified."[66]

This is an important statement of the need to distinguish between a sentence that is severe and one that is significantly out of proportion to the seriousness of the offence.

16–20 The question came up for decision in connection with Art.8 in *Laskey and others v United Kingdom*.[67] The applicants had been convicted of assaults arising out of consensual sadomasochistic activity involving the infliction of minor physical injuries to one another's genitals. The acts consisted of maltreatment of the genitalia (with, for example, hot wax, sandpaper, fish hooks and needles) and ritualistic beatings with either bare hands or a variety of implements, including stinging nettles, spiked belts and a cat-o'nine tails. There were instances of branding and infliction of injuries which resulted in the flow of blood and which left scarring. Laskey was sentenced to four years imprisonment for keeping a disorderly house (together with concurrent sentences for aiding and abetting assault occasioning actual bodily harm). Jaggard was sentenced to three years imprisonment for assaults occasioning actual bodily harm and unlawful wounding. Brown was sentenced to two years and nine months imprisonment for assault occasioning actual bodily harm. The defendants appealed to the Court of Appeal against conviction and sentence. Their appeals against conviction were dismissed but the Court of Appeal reduced their sentences to 18 months in the case of

---

[62] For a fuller discussion see Ch.8 above.
[63] E.g. *R. v Edwards Books and Art Ltd* [1986] 2 S.C.R. 713 (Supreme Court of Canada).
[64] (1979–80) 1 E.H.R.R. 737 at para.49.
[65] (1978) 19 D.R. 5, discussed in para.8–21 above.
[66] *ibid.*, at para.99.
[67] (1997) 24 E.H.R.R. 39.

Laskey, six months in the case of Jaggard and three months in the case of Brown.

The Strasbourg Court considered that the prosecution itself did not amount to a   **16–21**
violation of Art.8 since the domestic authorities were entitled to conclude that a
prosecution was necessary in a democratic society for the protection of health
and/or morals (within Art.8(2)).[68] The Court then went on to consider whether
the sentences imposed were disproportionate to that objective. The Court's
reasoning on this point appears to suggest that the original sentences imposed by
the trial judge may well have been held to be a disproportionate measure. But
having regard to the reductions ordered by the Court of Appeal, the sentences did
not violate Art.8:

> "[The Court] notes that in recognition of the fact that the applicants did not appreciate
> their actions to be criminal, reduced sentences were imposed on appeal. *In these
> circumstances*, bearing in mind the degree of organisation involved in the offences, the
> measures taken against the applicants cannot be regarded as disproportionate."[69]

This is important recognition that, even where it is held that there is sufficient
justification for interfering with one of the rights in Arts 8–11, through prosecution and conviction, it is still necessary to ensure that any sentence imposed takes
account of the fact that a fundamental right is being thereby restricted.

A similar conclusion was reached in *K.A. and A.D. v Belgium*,[70] where the Court   **16–22**
held that a Belgian law penalising extreme sado-masochism was "necessary in a
democratic society". The Court recognised that the applicants' Art.8 rights were
engaged, however, and held that the sanctions imposed in this case were not
disproportionate in that context (short prison terms, and periods of professional
disqualification).

A similar principle appears to have been applied by the Court of Appeal in *G.*,[71]   **16–23**
where a boy of 15 was convicted of rape of a child under 13, contrary to s.5 of
the Sexual Offences Act 2003, in circumstances where the other participant had
stated that she was 15 and appeared to consent. The court recognised that s.5 was
not intended for such cases: "we accept the possibility that prosecution of a child
under section 5 . . . in relation to consensual intercourse may, on the facts,
produce consequences that amount to an interference with the child's Article 8.1
rights that are not justified under Article 8.2." The court held that this should
have been taken into account by passing a light sentence. The sentence of 12
months' detention was quashed and, bearing in mind that G. had served five
months already, a conditional discharge was substituted.

The general proportionality requirement in cases engaging Arts 8–11 is sup-   **16–24**
ported by other Strasbourg decisions. In *Hoare v United Kingdom*[72] the applicant

---

[68] See para.8–13 above.
[69] (1997) 24 E.H.R.R. 39 at para.49 (emphasis added).
[70] App.No.42758/98, February 17, 2005.
[71] [2006] EWCA Crim 821.
[72] [1997] E.H.R.L.R. 678.

was engaged in the publication and distribution of pornographic videotapes by post. The applicant was convicted of six counts of publishing obscene articles contrary to s.2(1) of the Obscene Publications Act 1959 and sentenced to 30 months imprisonment. In the Commission's view, the sole question arising under the proportionality test was whether the sentence imposed was necessary in a democratic society. Although the Commission noted that the tapes had only been sent to people who had obtained a catalogue and placed a specific order, it nevertheless considered that there was no certainty that only the intended purchasers would have access to the material. The Commission accordingly concluded that the sentence was proportionate to the aim of protecting morals, and dismissed the application as manifestly ill-founded.

16–25   In *Worm v Austria*,[73] the Court held that it could be said to be "necessary in a democratic society" to punish a journalist for writing critical comments about a person currently being tried for serious offences. The Court went on to consider whether the sentence was "disproportionate to the legitimate aim pursued" and held that it was not: it was a substantial fine, for which the publishing company was jointly and severally liable. Similarly in *Steel v United Kingdom*[74] the Court held that it was not a disproportionate interference with the first applicant's Art.10 rights to bind her over to keep the peace and to fine her £70. She was then imprisoned for 28 days when she declined to be bound over. A majority of the court held that this was not a disproportionate period of detention, taking account both of "the public interest in deterring such conduct" (i.e. disruptive protests against fox-hunting, held to create a risk of disorder and violence) and of the "importance in a democratic society of maintaining the rule of law and the authority of the judiciary." Four judges recorded strong dissents from this conclusion, holding that Art.10 had been violated in the case of the first applicant because the deprivation of liberty had been disproportionately long, or indeed "manifestly extreme", for "a person who, albeit in an extreme manner, jumped up and down in front of a member of the shoot to prevent him from killing a feathered friend."[75]

16–26   A clear illustration of the principles may be found in *Skalka v Poland*,[76] where the applicant had written a letter insulting the local judiciary and referring to one unidentified judge as an "outstanding cretin." He was convicted of insulting the state authorities and sentenced to eight months' imprisonment. The Court held that Art.10 was engaged, that it may be justifiable to interfere with the right to freedom of expression in order to safeguard the authority of the judiciary, but that Art.10 was violated here because of the severity of the penalty:

> "It is the Court's assessment that the sentence of eight months' imprisonment was disproportionately severe. Even if it is in principle for the national courts to fix the sentence, in view of the circumstances of the case, there are common standards which this Court has to ensure with the principle of proportionality. These standards are the

---

[73] (1998) 25 E.H.R.R. 454 at para.57.
[74] (1999) 28 E.H.R.R. 603 at paras 106–109.
[75] *ibid.*, at pp.650–651.
[76] (2004) 38 E.H.R.R. 1; discussed at para.8–51. *Cf. Lesnik v Slovakia*, judgment of March 11, 2003, where the court upheld a sentence of 4 months in somewhat similar circumstances.

gravity of the guilt, the seriousness of the offence, and the repetition of the alleged offences.

In the Court's view, the severity of the punishment applied in this case exceeded the seriousness of the offence. It was not an open and overall attack on the authority of the judiciary, but an internal exchange of letters of which nobody of the public took notice."[77]

The decisions thus far discussed demonstrate the relevance of custodial sentences   **16–27** to decisions about compliance with, or violation of, Arts 8 to 11. But the issue is one of proportionality generally, and there has been scrutiny of other types of penalty imposed on an offender, such as forfeiture orders.[78] Thus in *X Co. v United Kingdom*[79] the Commission declared inadmissible a complaint relating to seizure and forfeiture of magazines under the Obscene Publications Act. The applicant alleged that the forfeiture order breached Art.10 and Art.1 of the First Protocol to the Convention (the right to peaceful enjoyment of property). The Commission considered that the "protection of morals" exception in Art.10(2) was not confined to the moral standards of likely readers, but extended to the state's general interest in preventing the diffusion of immoral publications within its territory. Forfeiture was therefore in the public interest and "necessary" within the meaning of Art.10(2).

Orders for the forfeiture of allegedly obscene original works of art, on the other   **16–28** hand, require a particularly compelling justification. In *Muller v Switzerland*[80] the applicant exhibited a series of large paintings in a public gallery, one of which included graphic depictions of sexual activity including homosexuality and bestiality. He was convicted of publishing obscene items and fined. The paintings were confiscated, but returned almost eight years later. The Court held that the conviction itself was justified for the protection of public morals and the rights of others. However, the confiscation order was different since the artist lost the opportunity of showing his work in a less sensitive location. On the facts, the court found that the confiscation did not violate Art.10 since the applicant could have applied for the return of the painting sooner than he did.

III. Disproportionality and Protocol 1

Disproportionality arguments have also been rested on Art.1 of Protocol 1, which   **16–29** declares a right not to be deprived of one's property "except in the public interest and subject to the conditions provided for by law." In *May*[81] one of the arguments was that the orders for confiscation of D's property were disproportionate:

---

[77] *Ibid.*, paras 41–42.
[78] The question was also raised by the Commission in connection with the duty to register under the Sex Offenders Act 1997. In *Adamson v United Kingdom* (1999) 28 E.H.R.R. CD 209, discussed in s.H below, the Commission satisfied itself that the duty to register, which required information in breach of Art.8, was "proportionate to the aims pursued" so as to be necessary in a democratic society for preventive purposes. The confiscation provisions contained in the Criminal Justice Act 1988 have been held by the Court of Appeal to comply with Art.8: *R. v Goodenough* [2004] EWCA Crim 2260; [2005] Crim. L.R 71.
[79] (1983) 32 D.R. 231.
[80] (1991) 13 E.H.R.R. 212.
[81] [2005] 3 All E.R. 523.

in demanding the full loss from each co-conspirator, they went beyond what was necessary to satisfy the public interest. The court's reply recognises the legitimacy of this approach:

> "We see force in that point as a general proposition, and in some circumstances it may lead the court to adopt an apportionment approach. For example, there may be cases where the defendants have substantial assets, with the result that making orders for the full benefit in each case would lead to the Revenue recovering far more than the conspiracy or joint enterprise had obtained. In such a case the court may be prepared to apportion the benefit. But that situation does not apply here."[82]

In other confiscation cases, arguments based on disproportionality and Protocol 1 have fared less well.[83]

IV. Disproportionate Penalties and European Community Law

16-30 Finally, brief reference should be made to the possibility that a disproportionate sentence may be held contrary to European Community Law. In *Sofia Skanavi and Konstantin Chryssanthakopoluos*[84] the two defendants were prosecuted in Germany for driving without a valid German driving licence, an offence punishable with up to one year's imprisonment. The European Court of Justice held that, because they had valid Greek driving licences, their offences were merely administrative in nature. The prosecution breached the right to freedom of movement, especially as "Member States may not impose a penalty so disproportionate to the gravity of the infringement that this becomes an obstacle to the free movement of persons, [which] would be especially so if the penalty consisted of imprisonment."[85] Thus, where an offence and its penalty tend to restrict a right protected by European Community Law, the question of proportionality of sentence becomes an important consideration. It remains to be seen what regard the European Court of Justice will have to the Charter of Fundamental Rights of the European Union, Art.49(3) of which proclaims that "the severity of penalties should not be disproportionate to the criminal offence."

B. PREVENTIVE SENTENCES

16-31 All the sentences considered in A, above (with the exception of the discretionary sentence of life imprisonment in *Weeks*) were punitive rather than preventive sentences, for Convention purposes; the grounds for challenging punitive sentences are relatively narrow. With those sentences which are either wholly or partly preventive in purpose, i.e. based solely or partly on some characteristic of the offender which is thought to render him dangerous, and not solely on the need

---

[82] At para.[41].
[83] *Cf. Sharma* [2006] EWCA Crim 16 and *Carter* [2006] EWCA Crim 416.
[84] [1996] E.C.R. I–929, discussed by Baker E., "Taking European Criminal Law Seriously" [1998] Crim. L.R. 361 at pp.371–373.
[85] [1996] E.C.R. I–929 at para.36.

to impose punishment for the offence, the main concern of the Strasbourg organs has been to ensure compliance with the Art.5(4) requirements on periodic judicial review and related safeguards. Hospital orders are an example of preventive sentences, and the position of restricted patients was analysed in *X v United Kingdom*.[86] Where the sentence is an indeterminate sentence with a mixed punitive-preventive purpose, the punitive element must comply with the requirements for punitive sentences and the preventive element must comply with the requirements for preventive sentences. Discretionary sentences of life imprisonment, an example of an indeterminate partly preventive sentences, are discussed in para.I below. By contrast, determinate sentences which are partly punitive and partly preventive have been held, despite their preventive component, to be governed by the rules applicable to purely punitive terms.[87]

Under Art.5(4) of the Convention, everyone deprived of liberty by detention 16–32 "shall be entitled to take proceedings by which the lawfulness of his detention shall be decided speedily by a court." It is not sufficient that the detention was ordered by a court following conviction, if the duration of continued detention turns on characteristics of the offender that may change over time (e.g. dangerousness and/or immaturity), so that it can be said that "the very nature of the deprivation of liberty . . . appears to require a review of lawfulness at reasonable intervals."[88] At least six forms of sentence under English law fall to be considered here, and they are discussed in turn.

I. Discretionary Sentences of Life Imprisonment

One area where the Convention has been held to impose important safeguards is 16–33 preventive detention on grounds of dangerousness (as for example in the post-tariff phase of a discretionary life sentence or sentence of detention at Her Majesty's Pleasure). Under Art.5(4) such sentences have been held to carry a right to periodic review by a judicial tribunal and to release if the offender is no longer dangerous.[89] This is because the justification for imposing such a sentence relates not so much to the gravity of the crime itself, as to characteristics of the offender which are "susceptible of change with the passage of time."[90] Thus, the continued detention of a discretionary life sentence prisoner beyond the expiry of the judicially imposed tariff period requires regular independent review by a judicial body.[91]

---

[86] (1982) 4 E.H.R.R. 188.

[87] See *R. (Giles) v Parole Board* [2004] 1 A.C. 1 discussed at para.16–40.

[88] *Winterwerp v Netherlands* (1979–80) 2 E.H.R.R. 387 at para.55.

[89] *Van Droogenbroeck v Belgium* (1982) 4 E.H.R.R. 443 paras 48–49.

[90] *Thynne, Wilson and Gunnell v United Kingdom* (1991) 13 E.H.R.R. 666 at para.70; the Supreme Court of Canada has also recognised the validity, under s.12 of the Charter (prohibition on "cruel and unusual punishment"), of indeterminate sentences for dangerous serious offenders who satisfy certain criteria: *Lyons* [1987] 2 S.C.R. 309.

[91] *Weeks v United Kingdom* (1988) 10 E.H.R.R. 293 at para.58; *Thynne, Wilson and Gunnell v United Kingdom* (1991) 13 E.H.R.R. 666 at para.76.

16–34 In *Thynne, Wilson and Gunnell v United Kingdom*[92] the Court observed that:

> "[T]he discretionary life sentence has clearly developed in English law as a measure to deal with mentally unstable and dangerous offenders; numerous judicial statements have recognised the protective purpose of this form of life sentence.[93] Although the dividing line may be difficult to draw in particular cases, it seems clear that the principles underlying such sentences, unlike mandatory life sentences, have developed in the sense that they are composed of a punitive element and subsequently of a security element designed to confer on the Secretary of State the responsibility for determining when the public interest permits the prisoner's release . . . [T]he factors of mental instability and dangerousness are susceptible to change over the passage of time and new issues of lawfulness may thus arise in the course of detention. It follows that at this phase in the execution of their sentences the applicants are entitled under Art.5(4) to take proceedings to have the lawfulness of their continued detention decided by a court at reasonable intervals."[94]

16–35 As a result of the decision in *Thynne* s.34 of the Criminal Justice Act 1991 introduced a procedure for Art.5(4) review of the post-tariff phase of a discretionary life sentence.[95] It also formalised the sentencing procedure so that a judge imposing a discretionary life sentence must now specify in open court the "relevant part" or tariff which is to be served to meet the requirements of retribution and deterrence.[96] The *Practice Direction (Criminal Proceedings: Consolidation)*[97] makes it clear that it is only in very exceptional circumstances that a judge would be justified in not specifying a relevant part or tariff. Such circumstances would arise only where the judge considers that the offence is so serious that detention for life is justified by the gravity of the offence alone, irrespective of the risk to the public. In such a case the judge should state this in open court when passing sentence.[98] The specified period is a "sentence" for the purposes of the Criminal Appeal Act 1968 and so may be subject to appeal.[99]

16–36 Once the tariff period has expired the applicant's case is referred automatically to the Parole Board which must hold an oral hearings before a "Discretionary Lifer Panel" (DLP), at which the applicant is legally represented and has a right to give evidence and to cross-examine. The Act provides for two year intervals between DLP hearings.[100] However in *AT v United Kingdom*[101] the Commission held that periodic review under Art.5(4) should—on the facts of the case—have been more frequent than the two years specified in the Act. This conclusion, which was subsequently endorsed by the Committee of Ministers, was based partly on evidence that the applicant was no longer mentally ill, and partly on a

---

[92] *ibid.*

[93] The court here referred to *R. v Hodgson* (1967) 52 Cr.App.R. 113 (CA); *R. v Wilkinson* (1983) 5 Cr.App.R.(S) 105 (CA); *R. v Secretary of State ex parte Bradley* [1991] 1 W.L.R. 134 (DC).

[94] (1991) 13 E.H.R.R. 666 at paras 73, 76.

[95] The procedure is now governed by s.82A of the Powers of Criminal Courts (Sentencing) Act 2000.

[96] S.34(1) and (2); For the position under s.82A of the Powers of Criminal Courts (Sentencing) Act 2000, as amended by the Criminal Justice Act 2003, see *Archbold* (2005) paras 5.310 to 5.312.

[97] para.IV.47 [2002] 1 W.L.R. 2870.

[98] See *Practice Direction,* para.IV.47.3.

[99] *R. v Dalton* [1995] 2 Cr.App.R. 340 (CA).

[100] S.34(5)(b).

[101] [1996] E.H.R.L.R. 92.

recommendation from the previous DLP for an earlier review. Similarly, in *Oldham v United Kingdom*[102] a recalled life sentence prisoner attended courses to address his problems in the first eight months after recall, but was then informed that it would be a further 16 months before the need for his continued detention could be reviewed. The Court held that, given that the applicant's condition was subject to change over time, the period of two years between reviews was not sufficiently "speedy" to comply with Art.5(4). However, that decision was confined to its own facts in *R. v Parole Board ex parte MacNeil*,[103] where Peter Gibson L.J. held that an interval of two years between reviews by the Parole Board did not constitute a breach of Art.5(4) on the facts of the case.

II. Detention during Her Majesty's Pleasure

In *Abed Hussain v United Kingdom*[104] the European Court of Human Rights held **16–37** that juveniles convicted of murder and detained during Her Majesty's Pleasure under s.53(1) of the Children and Young Persons Act 1933 are entitled to the same regular periodic review by the Parole Board as discretionary life sentence prisoners. Although their sentence is partly punitive, the imposition of an indeterminate sentence on a young person "can only be justified by considerations based on the need to protect the public." There must therefore be provision for regular review after the expiry of the tariff or minimum term, in order to "take into account any developments in the young offender's personality and attitude as he or she grows older."[105] Parliament gave effect to this decision in s.28 of the Crime (Sentences) Act 1997, which extended to juveniles sentenced to HMP detention the same rights in the post-tariff phase of detention as those which apply to a discretionary life sentence prisoner (i.e. a right to periodic review by way of an oral hearing before an HMP panel of the Parole Board.)

Two aspects of the HMP procedure were challenged successfully by the appli- **16–38** cants in *T and V v United Kingdom*.[106] The Court held unanimously that the fixing of the tariff by the Home Secretary, a member of the Executive, violates the applicants' right under Art.6(1) to a "fair and public hearing . . . by an independent and impartial tribunal." The Court held that the fixing of the tariff period "amounts to a sentencing exercise,"[107] and that the Home Secretary "was clearly not independent of the executive."[108] The applicants also challenged the sentence under Art.5(4), alleging that there was no provision for periodic judicial review of the lawfulness of continued detention. Once again, the Court unanimously found a violation:

> "Given that the sentence of detention during Her Majesty's Pleasure is indeterminate and that the tariff was initially set by the Home Secretary rather than the sentencing judge, it cannot be said that the supervision require by Article 5(4) was incorporated in

---

[102] [2000] Crim. L.R. 1011.
[103] *The Times*, April 18, 2001.
[104] (1996) 22 E.H.R.R. 1.
[105] *ibid.*, at paras 53–54.
[106] (2000) 30 E.H.R.R. 121.
[107] *T and V v United Kingdom, ibid.*, para.111.
[108] *ibid.*, para.114.

the trial court's sentence.[109] . . . Moreover, the Home Secretary's decision setting the tariff was quashed by the House of Lords on 12 June 1997 and no new tariff has since been substituted. This failure to set a new tariff means that the applicant's entitlement to access to a tribunal for periodic review of the continuing lawfulness of his detention remains inchoate. It follows that the applicant has been deprived, since his conviction in November 1993, of the opportunity to have the lawfulness of his detention reviewed by a judicial body in accordance with Article 5(4)."[110]

16–39   As a result of the judgment the Home Secretary relinquished his power, and the tariff is now set by the trial judge in the same way as for adults subject to discretionary life sentences.[111] A transitional policy ensured that the minimum period for existing detainees was set according to the Lord Chief Justice's recommendation. The Lord Chief Justice also issued a Practice Direction setting out the various factors which judges should take into account when setting tariff periods for murder by offenders of all ages.[112]

16–40   However, the Home Secretary retains a duty to keep under continuing review the minimum term of every child detained during Her Majesty's Pleasure. The House of Lords so held in *R. (Smith) v Secretary of State for the Home Department*,[113] where it was emphasised that, even though the Home Secretary cannot lengthen the minimum term, the prerogative of mercy can be used to shorten it, and should be used by directing early release if clear evidence of exceptional and unforeseen progress was reasonably judged to justify it. This is part of the special duty towards children and young persons deprived of their liberty under HMP, and it continues after they come of age.

III. Mandatory Life Sentences for Murder

16–41   The mandatory sentence of life imprisonment for murder was first analysed as ordering lifelong punitive detention in the Myra Hindley case,[114] and this approach was followed in *Thynne, Wilson and Gunnell v United Kingdom*.[115] In *Wynne v United Kingdom*[116] the Court considered but rejected the argument that the distinction between mandatory and discretionary life sentences had narrowed to the extent that the rights accorded to those subject to discretionary life sentences in *Thynne* should be extended to those convicted of murder and sentenced to a mandatory life sentence. The Court held to the view that the

---

[109] The court here referred to *De Wilde, Ooms and Versyp v Belgium* (1979–80) 1 E.H.R.R. 373, para.76, and to *Wynne v United Kingdom* (1995) 19 E.H.R.R. 353, para.36.

[110] *T and V v United Kingdom*, paras 120–122.

[111] As noted at para.16–09 above the Strasbourg Court held that it was not contrary to Art.3 to impose a punishment on a young offender convicted of murder. The sentencing court must conduct the same exercise under s.82A of the Powers of Criminal Courts (Sentencing) Act 2000 as it does in relation to discretionary life sentence prisoners by specifying a relevant part which is necessary to meet the requirements of retribution and deterrence.

[112] *Practice Statement (Life Sentences for Murder)* [2000] 2 Cr.App.R. 457; cf. also *Practice Statement as to Life Sentences* [2002] 1 W.L.R. 2870.

[113] [2006] 1 A.C. 159.

[114] *X v United Kingdom* (1975) 3 D.R. 10.

[115] (1991) 13 E.H.R.R. 666.

[116] (1995) 19 E.H.R.R. 333.

mandatory life sentence was unique because it was imposed as a punishment for the offence and irrespective of considerations of the dangerousness of the offender. The essential rationale of the mandatory life sentence remained that the crime of murder was so serious that the offender must be considered to have forfeited his liberty to the state for life.[117]

The *Wynne* approach was abandoned by the court in 2002: in *Stafford v United Kingdom*[118] the Grand Chamber decided unanimously that it should recognise the "emerging European consensus" and hold that decisions on the minimum term and on the release of mandatory life sentence prisoners should be taken by a judicial body. The Court justified its departure from its previous decision by arguing that "a failure by the Court to maintain a dynamic and evolutive approach would risk rendering it a bar to reform or improvement."[119] The precise issue in *Stafford* was the exercise of the power of release. The Court held that mandatory life sentences, like their discretionary counterparts, have two portions—a minimum term based on punitive considerations, and then a preventive portion based on public protection and assessments of risk. This reversed *Wynne,* and had the immediate consequence that release from the preventive part of the sentence must be subject to periodic review by a judicial body under Art.5(4). The Home Secretary is not a judicial body, and so his exclusive power of release violated the Convention. **16–42**

As for the minimum term itself, the Court reached the clear conclusion that "the Secretary of State's role in fixing the tariff is a sentencing exercise."[120] It did not have to decide whether the Home Secretary is an "independent and impartial tribunal" within Art.6, although it did state that the Home Secretary's role "has become increasingly difficult to reconcile with the notion of separation of powers between the executive and the judiciary."[121] The final step was taken by the House of Lords in its decision in *R. v Secretary of State for the Home Department, ex parte Anderson.*[122] The Home Secretary argued that the House should not follow *Stafford* because the Strasbourg Court had given inadequate reasons for departing from its previous decision in *Wynne,* but the House of Lords held that it would not decline to follow a decision of the Court sitting as a Grand Chamber "without good reason." In this case it saw no good reason, and entirely accepted the seven steps in the argument of counsel for the appellant: **16–43**

(1) Under Art.6(1) of the Convention a criminal defendant has a right to fair trial by an independent and impartial tribunal.

---

[117] For a similar conclusion, see the decision of the Supreme Court of Canada in *Arkell* [1990] 2 S.C.R. 695.

[118] (2002) 35 E.H.R.R. 1121.

[119] *ibid.,* at [68]

[120] *ibid.,* at [87]

[121] *ibid.,* at [78]; see also *Benjamin and Wilson v United Kingdom* (2002) 36 E.H.R.R. 1, an application concerning Art.5(4) and release procedures for "technical" lifers who had been transferred to mental hospital, where the government had sought to argue that the Home Secretary always exercised his power of release in accordance with the recommendation of the mental health review tribunal, and the court replied that "this is not a matter of form but impinges on the fundamental principle of the separation of powers and detracts from a necessary guarantee against the possibility of abuse" (at [36]).

[122] [2003] 1 A.C 837.

(2) The imposition of sentence is part of the trial.

(3) Therefore sentence should be imposed by an independent and impartial tribunal.

(4) The fixing of a tariff of a convicted murderer is legally indistinguishable from the imposition of a sentence.

(5) Therefore the tariff should be fixed by an independent and impartial tribunal.

(6) The Home Secretary is not an independent and impartial tribunal.

(7) Therefore the Home Secretary should not fix the tariff of a convicted murderer.

16–44   The House of Lords also gave some consideration to the lawfulness of "whole life" minimum terms. The Strasbourg Court in *Stafford* stated that "a whole life tariff may, in exceptional cases, be imposed where justified by the gravity of the particular offence,"[123] and Lord Steyn in *Anderson* confirmed that this is still the position taken by the House:

> "there is nothing logically inconsistent with the concept of a tariff by saying that there are cases where the crimes are so wicked that even if the prisoner is detained until he or she dies it will not exhaust the requirements of retribution or deterrence."[124]

This, with respect, is an argument that would need to be constructed with care. It may be noted that when in 1977 the German Constitutional Court considered the constitutionality of the mandatory life sentence for murder under German law,[125] and held that life imprisonment does not infringe the fundamental right to human dignity guaranteed by Art.1 of the German Constitution,[126] there was support for the conclusion that "life means life" would be inhuman. However, in its 1983 decision it accepted that this would not be incompatible with the constitutional right.[127] But the court took seriously the argument that the psychological effects of life imprisonment could be crushing and recognised a duty on the State to provide a prison regime aimed at resocialization, in order to respect human dignity.

16–45   The changed approach to mandatory life sentences, evident in the *Stafford* decision, must also apply to the sentence of custody for life that is the required sentence for an offender aged 18–20 convicted of murder. The Commission in Strasbourg had previously held, in *Bromfield v United Kingdom*[128] and in *Ryan v United Kingdom*,[129] that this sentence was more akin to the adult life sentence

---

[123] (2002) 35 E.H.R.R. 1121, at [79]

[124] [2003] 1 A.C 837at [47], quoting from his own speech in *R. v Secretary of State for the Home Department, ex parte Hindley* [2001] 1 A.C. 410, at p.417.

[125] For discussion, see van Zyl Smit D., "Is Life Imprisonment Constitutional? The German Experience" [1992] *Public Law* 263.

[126] *B.Verf.G.E.* 45 187 of June 21, 1977.

[127] *B.Verf.G.E.* 64 261 of June 28, 1983.

[128] (1998) 26 E.H.R.R. CD 138.

[129] (1999) 27 E.H.R.R. CD 204.

than to the HMP sentence imposed on younger offenders. This assimilation now has different consequences following the *Stafford* and *Anderson* decisions.

A challenge to the mandatory life sentence for murder was mounted in *R. v* **16–46** *Lichniak and Pyrah*[130] on the basis of Arts 3 and 5. Both the appellants were of previous good character and were convicted of murders in circumstances which led each trial judge to state that the appellants did not present a danger to the public. The House of Lords heard the case at the same time as *Anderson*, and the argument for the appellants was that the mandatory life sentence contravenes the Convention because even if there is no danger to the public the sentence requires detention beyond the point warranted on punitive grounds and subjects the offender to lifelong supervision on licence and the risk of recall. The House of Lords unanimously rejected the argument that the mandatory life sentence is disproportionate and arbitrary, adopting the view of the Strasbourg Court in *V v United Kingdom* that the possibility of continued detention after the expiry of the minimum term is appropriate where a serious crime has been committed,[131] and regarding it as sufficient that the question whether the offender poses a continuing danger to the public should be determined by the Parole Board on the expiry of the minimum term rather than by the judge at the time of trial.[132]

Section 269 of the Criminal Justice Act 2003 and Sch.21 are designed to **16–47** constrain the breadth of the court's sentencing discretion in murder cases. The provisions specify categories of murder according to their seriousness and set three different starting points, of a whole life minimum term (e.g. murders of children, or of two or more people, involving abduction or sexual or sadistic motivation), 30 years (e.g. murders of police or prison officers, murders involving firearms or aggravated by factors relating to race, religion or sexual orientation), or 15 years (the remainder). The court can increase or reduce the period according to whether identified aggravating or mitigating factors are present. In the leading case of *Sullivan*,[133] Lord Woolf C.J. emphasised that the principal task is "to determine the period the court considers appropriate. Thus notwithstanding the statutory guidance, the decision remains one for the judge," who retains "the discretion to determine any term of any length as being appropriate because of the particular aggravating and mitigating circumstances that exist in that case."[134]

Schedule 22 of the Act contains transitional provisions for mandatory lifers **16–48** whose offences were committed before the Act came into force. In *Sullivan*[135] the Court of Appeal considered the operation of the legislation in relation to a number of offenders who were convicted after the legislation came into force but whose offences were committed before. The court considered that in general the Secretary of State's practice in December 2002 was reflected in the 2000 and

---

[130] [2003] 1 A.C 903; see also n. above.
[131] (1999) 30 E.H.R.R. 121, at para.98, quoted by Lord Hutton at [2003] 1 A.C. 903 at [27].
[132] See Lord Bingham in [2003] 1 A.C. 903, at [16].
[133] [2005] 1 Cr.App.R.(S) 308.
[134] *Ibid*, at [11]—[16]. The effect of reduction for a guilty plea in murder cases was considered in *Last* [2005] 2 Cr.App.R.(S) 381.
[135] [2005] 1 Cr.App.R.(S) 308, above, n.133.

2002 Practice Directions and that these should be applied. The exceptions were the first two most serious categories of murder contained in Sch.21 where the Secretary of State did on occasion fix higher tariffs. The court also considered that except in these two most serious categories of case, there would be little difference between an application of the Practice Statements and the statutory guidelines, but accepted that the lower figure should be selected if there were a difference.[136]

16–49   In those transitional cases where the offender was both convicted and sentenced before the 2003 Act came into force, Sch.22 creates a special procedure for the minimum term to be determined by a High Court judge. Paragraph 11 of Sch.22 provides that the minimum term must be fixed by the High Court judge without an oral hearing. In *R. (Hammond) v Secretary of State for the Home Department*[137] the House of Lords held that a literal reading of para.11 would be incompatible with the Convention because it would prohibit an oral hearing even when this is required to comply with the lifer's rights under Art.6(1). In the light of this ruling, the Secretary of State accepted that an implied condition should be read into para.11 to the effect that a judge has the discretion to order an oral hearing where such a hearing is required to comply with the mandatory lifer's rights under Art.6(1).

IV. Indeterminate Sentences for Dangerous Offenders

16–50   In *Offen et al*[138] the Court of Appeal assessed the Convention compatibility of the (now abolished) automatic sentence of life imprisonment for the second serious sexual or violent offence. The court held that the automatic life sentence was a partly or wholly preventive sentence, and that therefore the task of the courts should be to ensure that such a sentence is only passed where there is evidence of the need for prevention. Lord Woolf, C.J., therefore held that such a sentence will not contravene Convention rights if courts apply the statutory provision, and particularly the "exceptional circumstances" proviso, so that "it did not result in offenders being sentenced to life imprisonment when they did not constitute a significant risk to the public." Thus: "If the offences were of a different kind, or if there was a long period which elapsed between the offences during which the offender had not committed other offences, that might be a very relevant indicator as to the degree of risk to the public that he constituted." Lord Woolf held that, by relating "exceptional circumstances" directly to a judicial assessment of the need for public protection from the defendant, courts would prevent an offender from being subjected to arbitrary detention in breach of Art.5.

16–51   The Criminal Justice Act 2003 abolished the automatic life sentence in favour of new "dangerousness" measures introduced by ss.224–229 of that Act. These provisions introduce two forms of indeterminate sentence for "dangerous" offenders—life imprisonment or, if that sentence is unavailable for the offence, imprisonment for public protection (IPP) for those convicted of a "serious

---

[136] *Ibid* [35].
[137] [2005] UKHL 69.
[138] [2001] 1 W.L.R. 253.

specified offence" who are assessed as dangerous. A court is bound to impose a life sentence or an IPP sentence in such cases whenever it is satisfied that there is a significant risk to members of the public of serious harm occasioned by the commission by him of further specified offences. Section 229 provides that where the offender is over 18 and has a previous conviction for a specified violent or sexual offence, there is a rebuttable presumption of dangerousness and the burden shifts to him to show that he is not dangerous; where the offender is under 18 or has no such previous conviction, the court's discretion is not contrained by any such presumption. The dangerousness provisions were the subject of guidance from the Court of Appeal in *Lang*[139]: although the legislation was drafted with the requirements of the judgment in *R. v Offen*[140] in mind, it remains to be seen whether the rebuttable presumption of dangerousness—based as it may be on the commission of a single previous specified offence (some of which are not high on the scale of seriousness) which may be neither recent nor relevant—is regarded as constraining a court's decision to the extent of incompatibility with either Art.3 or Art.5. Moreover, the judgments in *Weeks v United Kingdom*[141] and in *Offen*[142] suggest that there might be a disproportionality argument in relation to the difference between a given specified offence and an IPP sentence. For young offenders, even though the presumption does not apply, the argument may be no less strong.[143]

V. Hospital Orders with Restrictions without Limit of Time

Under ss.37 and 41 of the Mental Health Act 1983 a court may, on receiving the **16–52** necessary psychiatric evidence, impose a hospital order with a restriction order without limit of time. This is a purely preventive order, to be made only after certain procedural requirements have been fulfilled and where it is held necessary in order to "protect the public from serious harm from" the offender.[144] Its predecessor was considered by the Strasbourg Court in *X v United Kingdom*[145] and found to be in breach of Art.5(4), in that release was in the hands of the Home Secretary and there was no means of testing the lawfulness of detention before a court.[146] The law was changed in the 1983 Act, and a Mental Health Review Tribunal (chaired by a judge) is now regarded as a court for this purpose and has the power to direct release without requesting the leave of the Home Secretary.[147] Section 45A of the Mental Health Act 1983 (introduced by s.46 of

---

[139] [2006] 2 Cr.App.R.(S) 13.

[140] [2001] 1 W.L.R. 253.

[141] Above, at 16–50.

[142] Above, at 16–50.

[143] See the remarks in *Lang* [2006] 2 Cr.App.R.(S) 13, at [17], on young offenders.

[144] *cf. Erkalo v Netherlands* (1999) 28 E.H.R.R. 509, where the court found a violation in respect of the Netherlands procedure, where the government had failed to make a timely application for the continuation of the applicant's detention, even though he was eligible for early release.

[145] (1982) 4 E.H.R.R. 188.

[146] See also *Gordon v United Kingdom* (1986) 47 D.R. 36 (Commission) and 46 (Committee of Ministers).

[147] The tribunal has a duty to discharge a patient in certain circumstances: *cf.* the recent decision in *Johnson v United Kingdom* (1999) 27 E.H.R.R. 296, finding a violation where the conditional discharge of an unrestricted patient had been ordered subject to finding a place at a hostel where he could reside, but where no hostel place was forthcoming and he remained in detention for a further three years.

the Crime (Sentences) Act 1997) provides for a hybrid form of order, the hospital and limitation direction, which, in the case of an offender suffering from psychopathic disorder,[148] may be added to a prison sentence (including a discretionary or automatic life sentence) in certain circumstances.[149] In *R. v Mental Health Review Tribunal, North and East London Region and anor.*[150] the Court of Appeal issued a declaration of incompatibility, holding that ss.72 and 73 of the Mental Health Act 1983 were incompatible with Art.5 since they reversed the burden of proof by requiring the patient to satisfy the tribunal that he was no longer suffering from a mental disorder warranting detention. Sections 72 and 73 have since been amended to require discharge of the patient unless the tribunal is satisfied of the conditions justifying continued detention.[151]

VI. Extended Sentences

Section 85 of the Powers of Criminal Courts (Sentencing) Act 2000 introduced the extended sentence aimed at ensuring greater public protection from offenders convicted of certain violent or sexual offences who pose a risk of future offending. Sections 227 and 228 of the Criminal Justice Act 2003 introduced a slightly modified form of extended sentence, as part of the dangerousness provisions in that Act. In addition to the appropriate custodial term, the court must—if the offender satisfies the criteria of dangerousness in s.229—impose an extension period of a length sufficient to protect members of the public from the significant risk of serious harm from him, up to five years in the case of a violent offence and eight years in the case of a sexual offence, subject to the statutory maximum for the offence in question. The sentence operates so that the offender is released on licence in the usual way, but the licence remains in force and the offender remains subject to recall beyond the end of the custodial component until the expiry of the extension period. In *R. (Sim) v Parole Board*[152] the Court of Appeal held that, though determinate, the sentencing court does not order the offender's detention throughout the period of the sentence. Detention is only ordered by the court during the custodial period. Once the extension period is entered the offender must be released on licence. Any decision by the Secretary of State to revoke the licence does not result in a period of detention that has already been ordered by the passing of the sentence, and therefore recall to prison engages Art.5(4) and its requirement of assessment by an impartial tribunal. This is a major difference from the position in relation to the former long-than-normal sentences for public protection.[153]

---

[148] Under s.45A(10) of the Mental Health Act 1983 the Secretary of State is empowered to extend the categories of mental disorder in respect of which a hospital and limitation direction may be made, but has so far chosen not to do so. For judicial consideration of s.45A, see *Staines* [2006] 2 Cr.App.R.(S) 376.

[149] For further discussion, see Eastman N. and Peay J., "Sentencing Psychopaths: is the 'Hospital and Limitation Direction' an Ill-Considered Hybrid?" [1998] Crim. L.R. 93.

[150] [2001] 3 W.L.R. 512.

[151] See the Mental Health Act 1983 (Remedial) Order 2001, S.I. 2001/3712.

[152] [2004] Q.B 1288.

[153] On which see the Commission decision in *Mansell v United Kingdom* [1997] E.H.R.L.R. 666, criticised in paras 16–39 and 16–40 of the first edition of this work. The House of Lords in *R. (Giles) v Parole Board and Home Secretary* [2003] UKHL 43 gave the authoritative decision on this (now superseded) provision.

C. CUSTODIAL SENTENCES: CREDIT FOR TIME SERVED

The question of making allowance for time already served in custody has arisen, **16–53** in respect of the Convention, in two different situations—custody abroad, and custody pending appeal. First, there are persons who have already served a period in prison abroad. Section 47 of the Criminal Justice Act 1991 allows a court which is dealing with an offender who has been extradited to the United Kingdom to order that the whole or part of the time spent in foreign custody should count as a "relevant period" in computing the length of his sentence under s.67 of the Criminal Justice Act 1967.[154] Alternatively, a court can take account of the time served abroad by reducing the length of the sentence imposed rather than exercising the power under s.47. Whichever procedure is followed, the matter is within the discretion of the trial judge, and the authorities establish that an offender who has deliberately prolonged his time in custody abroad should not be given credit for the full period.[155]

In *C v United Kingdom*[156] the time spent by the applicant in custody abroad **16–54** awaiting extradition was not taken into account by the trial judge in computing the length of his prison sentence. The Commission held that this did not render the additional period of detention "arbitrary" for the purposes of Art.5. On the other hand, where detention prior to extradition from another signatory state was found by the court to have exceeded the reasonable time guarantee in Art.5(3), the fact that the Crown Court judge who sentenced the applicant *had* taken the period into account in fixing the length of his sentence was held to be a ground for refusing to award compensation under Art.50.[157]

The question of time in custody in this country awaiting appeal was raised in **16–55** *Monnell and Morris v United Kingdom*,[158] where the applicants complained that the decision of the Court of Appeal, that time spent awaiting appeal should not count towards sentence because they had both persisted in unmeritorious appeals, breached Art.5(1)(a). The Court recognised that the Court of Appeal had exercised its statutory power for deterrent reasons, and that this had no connection with the offences committed, but held that nonetheless the statutory power was "an inherent part of the criminal appeal process following conviction" and that it "pursues a legitimate aim" within Art.5(1)(a).[159] Also relevant was the fact that in many continental systems a sentence of imprisonment does not start to run until the appeal process has been terminated. The Court in *Monnell and Morris* did not directly consider the inhibiting effect which this power may have on the exercise of a right of appeal in borderline cases. In the light of the court's subsequent decision in *Omar v France*,[160] it is open to serious doubt whether the

---

[154] See, e.g. *Ireland v United Kingdom* (1979–80) 2 E.H.R.R. 25 at para.162.

[155] *R. v Scalise and Rachel* (1985) 7 Cr.App.R.(S) 395; *R. v Stone* (1988) 10 Cr.App.R.(S) 332; *R. v Peffer* (1991) 13 Cr.App.R.(S) 150.

[156] (1985) 43 D.R. 177.

[157] *Scott v Spain* (1997) 24 E.H.R.R. 391.

[158] (1988) 10 E.H.R.R. 205, criticised in paras 17–21 to 17–22 below.

[159] *ibid.*, at para.46.

[160] (2000) 29 E.H.R.R. 210. In *Papon v France* (2004) 39 E.H.R.R. 10 the Strasbourg Court found a violation even where the requirement to surrender to custody was imposed in respect of a very serious offence.

loss of time provisions[161] would be regarded as compatible with the right of access to an appellate court if the issue were to be reconsidered today. In *Omar* the Court held that a rule which required an appellant to surrender to custody before he could be heard on appeal against his conviction was incompatible with Art.6 since it imposed a disproportionate restriction on the exercise of his right of appeal.[162] The same principle should surely apply where the court considering the appeal has power to impose what is, in effect, an additional prison sentence as a deterrent against appeals which turn out, on examination, to be unmeritorious.

D. EQUAL TREATMENT IN SENTENCING

16–56   Article 14 of the Convention provides that Convention rights are to be secured "without discrimination on any ground such as sex, race, colour, language, religion, political or other opinion, national or social origin . . . property, birth or other status." Article 14 must be pleaded in conjunction with another Convention right, but it is not necessary to establish that the substantive right concerned has been violated.[163] In order to rely on Art.14, the applicant need only establish that his claim falls "within the ambit" of the right concerned.[164] Once this hurdle is overcome, the applicant must then show that there has been a difference in treatment *in the delivery* of the right as between himself and another person in a relevantly similar position. If such a difference in treatment is established then there will be a violation of Art.14 if *either* (a) the difference does not pursue a legitimate aim (in the sense that there is no "objective and reasonable justification" for it) *or* (b) there is no reasonable relationship of proportionality between the means employed and the end sought to be achieved. Thus in the *Belgian Linguistics* case the Court observed: "[A] difference in treatment in the exercise of a right laid down in the Convention must not only pursue a legitimate aim: Article 14 is likewise violated when it is clearly established that there is no reasonable relationship of proportionality between the means employed and the end sought to be realised."[165] The difference in treatment need not be on grounds analogous to race or sex. The use of the words "on any such grounds as", and the inclusion of "any other status" in the non-exhaustive list of prohibited grounds within Art.14 permits comparisons to be made on the basis of any

---

[161] Under the Criminal Appeal Act 1968, s.29(1) the Court of Appeal may, if it considers that an appeal is without merit, direct that time served between the imposition of the sentence and the disposal of the appeal should not count towards the accused person's sentence. As to the circumstances in which such an order may be made see *Practice Direction (Crime: Sentences: Loss of Time)* [1980] 1 W.L.R. 270.

[162] For the effect of this decision on the practice of the Court of Appeal (Criminal Division) see *R. v Charles, R. v Tucker, The Times*, February 20, 2001 (the Registrar should no longer treat an application for leave to appeal on behalf of a defendant who has absconded as ineffective).

[163] *Belgian Linguistics Case (No.1)* (1979–80) 1 E.H.R.R. 241, and *(No.2)* (1979–80) 1 E.H.R.R. 252.

[164] *Abdulaziz, Cabales and Balkandali v United Kingdom* (1985) 7 E.H.R.R. 471 at para.71; *Inze v Austria* (1988) 10 E.H.R.R. 394 at para.36; *Van der Mussele v Belgium* (1984) 6 E.H.R.R. 163 at para.43.

[165] (1979–80) 1 E.H.R.R. 252 at para.10.

abiding characteristic.[166] Four examples may be briefly discussed—AIDS, race, sex, and age.

The potential application of Art.14 in the sentencing context is illustrated by *RM*   **16–57**
v United Kingdom.[167] In that case the applicant, who was suffering from HIV/ AIDS had been sentenced to imprisonment for drugs offences. He sought to rely on his illness as a mitigating factor. The sentencing judge held that he was bound by the Court of Appeal decision in *R. v Stark*[168] to ignore HIV/AIDS as a mitigating circumstance. In *Stark* the Court of Appeal had held that HIV/AIDS was a matter not for mitigation, but for the Secretary of State in exercising the power of compassionate release. *M* appealed against sentence but the Court of Appeal, again applying *Stark*, confirmed that the illness was immaterial to sentence.[169]

In his application to the Commission, *M* alleged a violation of Art.14 of the   **16–58**
Convention in conjunction with Art.5. The sentencing decision clearly fell "within the ambit" of Art.5(1)(a) which permits deprivation of liberty "after conviction by a competent court". The applicant pointed to a range of sentencing precedents which established that other debilitating fatal illnesses were regularly treated as mitigating circumstances by the domestic courts. Accordingly he submitted that there had been an unjustified difference in treatment between the sentencing of a defendant with HIV/AIDS and the sentencing of defendants with other comparable illnesses. In its response the Government argued that this difference in treatment had an objective and reasonable justification. HIV/AIDS —so the argument went—was less predictable in its outcome than the other terminal illnesses which the applicant had relied upon as comparators. The Commission accepted that Art.14 was capable of applying in conjunction with Art.5 so as to prohibit discrimination in sentencing. Nevertheless, on the facts the Commission found that the difference in treatment was justified for the reasons advanced by the Government. The Court of Appeal has subsequently reaffirmed the principle that a medical condition which may at some future date affect either life expectancy or the prison authorities' ability to treat the prisoner satisfactorily is not a reason to alter the sentence, and should be left for the Home Office and Parole Board to deal with appropriately.[170]

In *Grice v United Kingdom*[171] the Commission declared inadmissible an applica-   **16–59**
tion based on alleged violations of Arts 3 and 14. The applicant's case was that his continued imprisonment amounted to "inhuman punishment", but the Commission found no evidence that the detention of an AIDS sufferer has any long term effect on his health or life expectancy. The applicant also alleged that the Home Office discriminated against him, as an AIDS sufferer, in failing to grant

---

[166] *Kjeldsen, Busk, Madsen and Pederson v Denmark* (1976) 1 E.H.R.R. 711, para.56 and *R. (S and Marper) v Chief Constable of the South Yorkshire Police* [2004] 1 W.L.R. 2196.
[167] (1994) 77A D.R. 98.
[168] (1992) 13 Cr.App.R.(S) 548.
[169] *Moore* (1993) 15 Cr.App.R.(S) 97.
[170] *Bernard* [1997] 1 Cr.App.R.(S) 135; *cf. Green* (1992) 13 Cr.App.R.(S) 613 for an exceptional case.
[171] (1994) 77 D.R. 90.

compassionate early release when it did so more readily for prisoners suffering from cancer or senile dementia. The Commission held that if release procedures did discriminate there would indeed be a case under Arts 5 and 14, but it found no evidence of discrimination on the facts.

16–60   The Commission had earlier recognised that "where a settled sentencing policy appears to affect individuals in a discriminatory fashion . . . this may raise issues under Article 5 read in conjunction with Article 14".[172] In general, however, the more insidious forms of discrimination, such as race and sex discrimination, do not manifest themselves in settled sentencing policy. Under the Human Rights Act, an individual needs to be able to demonstrate that he or she is a "victim" of a violation of the Convention.[173] In the context of sentencing discrimination, this is likely to raise almost insurmountable difficulties. Research into race and sentencing has found that offenders from an Afro-Caribbean background were, after taking account of the seriousness of their offences and their criminal records, some five per cent more likely to be sent to prison, with an even higher probability at one court and a lower probability at another.[174] These findings consist of strong statistical inferences, but they do not demonstrate discrimination in any particular case. This would of course be extremely difficult to prove, unless injudicious remarks were made at the sentencing stage.

16–61   Although the general statistical evidence suggests elements of leniency rather than greater severity in the sentencing of women,[175] there have been several findings that suggest undue severity against certain types of woman offender who, it is alleged, receive longer sentences because of their "inappropriate" lifestyle.[176] Here too, however, discrimination is likely to be difficult to prove in an individual case, although it may be easier to demonstrate that a particular sentence has a disproportionate impact where the female defendant has children. It should be recalled that the question whether a sentence is so disproportionately severe as to be an "inhuman punishment" contrary to Art.3 depends to some extent on the "sex, age and state of health" of the offender.[177] The imposition of a custodial sentence on the mother of a young child (which enforces separation between the two) might be thought to raise proportionality issues in certain cases[178]; as might the imposition of a custodial sentence on a pregnant woman, which may mean that she gives birth whilst serving a prison sentence.[179]

16–62   Age-based arguments are most likely to arise where the offender is very young. However, we have already noted that this was one of the unsuccessful grounds

---

[172] *Neilson v United Kingdom* (1986) 49 D.R. 170.
[173] See para.3–43 above.
[174] Hood R., *Race and Sentencing* (1992), p.78; see also Hood R., "Race and Sentencing—a Reply" [1995] Crim. L.R. 272.
[175] Hedderman C. and Gelsthorpe L. (eds.), *Understanding the Sentencing of Women* (Home Office, 1997).
[176] See, for example, Morris A., "Sex and Sentencing" [1988] Crim. L.R. 163 at 166–167.
[177] *Ireland v United Kingdom* (1979–80) 2 E.H.R.R. 25 at para.162.
[178] In *Togher v United Kingdom* [1998] E.H.R.L.R. 636 the Commission declared admissible a complaint, under Art.3, by a young mother remanded in custody and separated from her new-born child, whom she had been breast-feeding. For broader evidence, see the report by Caddle D. and Crisp D., *Mothers in Prison*, Home Office Research Findings No.38 (1997).
[179] See, e.g. *Scott* (1990) 12 Cr.App.R.(S) 23.

of challenge in *T and V v United Kingdom*.[180] The Court recited the provision in Art.37 of the United Nations Convention on the Rights of the Child, to the effect that detention of a child "shall be used only as a measure of last resort and for the shortest appropriate time", and also r.17(1)(b) of the Beijing Rules, recommending that "restrictions on the personal liberty of the juvenile . . . shall be limited to the possible minimum." Nevertheless, the Court concluded that, taking account of all the circumstances including the fact that the two applicants were aged only 11 when sentenced, punitive detention for six years could not be said to amount to inhuman or degrading treatment.[181]

E. CONSENT TO COMMUNITY PENALTIES

Article 4(2) of the Convention declares that "no one shall be required to perform forced or compulsory labour", and Art.4(3) lists various forms of work to which Art.4(1) does not apply. Compulsory labour ordered by a court following conviction of an offence is not listed. When the community service order was introduced into English law in 1972, it was thought necessary to insert a requirement that the offender should consent to the order, so as to comply with Art.4(2) of the Convention. In 1995 the Government took the view that this had been an "over-cautious" interpretation,[182] and s.38 of the Crime (Sentences) Act 1997 removed the consent requirement. Does an unpaid work requirement forming part of a community sentence (as introduced by the Criminal Justice Act 2003) breach the Convention in this respect? In *Van der Mussele v Belgium*,[183] the Court held that compulsory labour would only violate Art.4(2) if it was both against the person's will and "unjust or oppressive". **16–63**

It is well known that the giving of consent to a community penalty was in many cases a sham, since the probable alternative sentence would be immediate custody. To that extent the 1997 amendment merely gave statutory effect to the existing reality. Article 4(3) expressly cites work carried out in prison or on conditional release as examples which fall outside the notion of compulsory labour. The Court in *Van der Mussele* emphasised that the categories set out in Art.4(3) are not to be regarded as an exhaustive list of exceptions, to be restrictively construed. Rather, they are illustrative of the limits to the concept of compulsory labour as it is understood in Art.4(1). This opens the way to analogical analysis, especially since the sentence of community punishment is less intrusive of individual rights than work required to be performed as part of a prison sentence. The omission of unpaid work orders from Art.4(3) is best explained by the fact that they were not generally available as a sentence within Europe when the Convention was drafted. Applying the "living instrument" principle,[184] the Court would doubtless be influenced by their current availability **16–64**

---

[180] (2000) 30 E.H.R.R. 121.
[181] *T and V v United Kingdom, ibid.*, paras 97–99.
[182] Home Office, *Strengthening Punishment in the Community*, Cmnd. 2780, (1995), para.4.20, citing the *Van der Mussele* decision (next note).
[183] (1984) 6 E.H.R.R. 163.
[184] See para.2–18 above.

in many European states, and would find it possible to regard compulsory orders as not violating Art.4.

F. PROCEEDINGS AGAINST FINE DEFAULTERS

16–65   When a fine defaulter is brought back to a magistrates' court for enforcement proceedings, it is normal for the justices' clerk or a court clerk to put questions to the offender. There is no prosecutor present, and so the clerk acts as inquisitor. When the justices consider what action to take, it is the clerk who advises them on the law. In *Corby JJ ex parte Mort*[185] the impartiality of the clerk's role in such proceedings was challenged, but the Divisional Court held that on the facts the clerk had not assumed a partisan role. The court stated that fine enforcement proceedings are neither civil nor criminal, and that they could see no alternative to the clerk putting questions. However, the involvement of the clerk as an inquisitor, and then as adviser to the justices on the law, is potentially incompatible with Art.6. The proceedings are surely "criminal", in Convention terms.[186] A Practice Direction attempts to explain and to limit the clerk's role in enforcement proceedings, and to emphasise the overriding duty of impartiality.[187]

G. SENTENCING PROCEDURE

16–66   In *X v United Kingdom*[188] the Commission emphasised that Art.6 continues to apply at the sentencing stage.[189] Thus, the entitlements to *inter alia* legal representation and legal aid, a public hearing, equality of arms, adequate time and facilities, and free interpretation would all continue at a sentencing hearing:

> "The Commission considers that complaints concerning proceedings on sentence, even after a plea of guilty, could raise issues under Article 6 of the Convention; so that for example a defendant should have the opportunity of being represented where the prosecution gives evidence in relation to sentence. In the opinion of the Commission, the determination of a criminal charge, within the meaning of Article 6(1) of the Convention, includes not only the determination of the guilt or innocence of the accused, but also in principle the determination of his sentence; and the expression 'everyone charged with a criminal offence' in Article 6(3) includes persons who, although already convicted, have not been sentenced. The Commission observes that questions of sentence may be closely related to questions of guilt or innocence, and that in the Criminal Procedure of many States Parties to the Convention, they cannot be separated at this stage of the proceedings."

16–67   The application of Art.6 to the sentencing stage has been accepted by the Commission and the Court, and was not regarded as a matter for dispute in the

---

[185] (1998) 162 J.P. 310.

[186] See *Benham v United Kingdom* (1996) 22 E.H.R.R. 293; and see generally para.4–20 above.

[187] *Practice Direction (Justices' Clerk to the Court)* [2001] 1 Cr.App.R. 147, para.11.

[188] (1972) 2 Digest 766.

[189] This observation can not of course apply to the presumption of innocence in Art.6(2). See para.16–68 below.

decision of the court in *T and V v United Kingdom*.[190] Thus in *Cuscani v United Kingdom*[191] the Court had no doubt that the right to an interpreter in Art.6(3)(e) applies fully at the sentencing stage, and the Court held that the applicant's right had been violated even though the defence lawyer had suggested that the applicant's brother might suffice if no professional interpreter were available. The applicant had pleaded guilty and was subsequently sentenced to four years' imprisonment. In this context, the Court stated that the trial judge as "the ultimate guardian of the fairness of the proceedings" should have insisted on the presence of an interpreter. In general, however, the Court's chief concern is to assure the minimum procedural guarantees provided by Art.6 and its attendant jurisprudence. Thus, for example, Art.6 does not prevent a judge from taking account at the sentencing stage matters that would not be admissible at the trial, such as the offender's previous convictions.[192] As noted in 16–41 above, Art.6 applies equally to the transitional procedure established in the High Court under Sch.22 of the Criminal Justice Act 2003 for fixing the minimum terms of existing mandatory life sentence prisoners. This is a sentencing exercise.

I. Confiscation of the Proceeds of Crime

Questions about the burden of proof at the sentencing stage have arisen in stark **16–68** form in relation to the confiscation legislation. Provisions in the Drug Trafficking Act 1994, the Proceeds of Crime (Scotland) Act 1995 and now the Proceeds of Crime Act 2002 state that, after a person has been convicted of a drug trafficking offence, the court may make certain assumptions, "except insofar as any of them may be shown to be incorrect"in the particular offender's case. The presumption is that any property transferred to him in the six years before indictment represented the proceeds of drug trafficking, and is therefore liable to be confiscated. In *McIntosh v HM Advocate*[193] the High Court of Justiciary held that the assumptions required by the legislation violate Art.6(2). The prosecution bears no burden of proof at any stage, and the statutory assumptions are "in a quite literal sense baseless," Lord Prosser held. The statute could have made them contingent on the raising of a reasonable suspicion by the prosecution, but it did not—the assumptions are automatic. However, the Privy Council allowed the prosecutor's appeal.[194] Lord Bingham held that Art.6(2) does not apply to confiscation proceedings because the person against whom the application for an order is made is not "by virtue of that application a person charged with a criminal offence." This approach is problematic, because there is no doubt that a convicted defendant is a person charged with a criminal offence for the purpose of the other guarantees in Art.6, which are applicable both at the sentencing stage and during any appeal against conviction and sentence. A preferable approach would have been to hold that Art.6 is engaged, but that the specific guarantee in Art.6(2) cannot apply at this stage because, as Lord Hope pointed out, it states only that a person charged shall be presumed innocent "until proved guilty

---

[190] (2000) 30 E.H.R.R. 121.
[191] (2003) 36 E.H.R.R. 2.
[192] *Albert and le Compte v Belgium* (1983) 5 E.H.R.R. 533.
[193] Judgment of October 13, 2000.
[194] *McIntosh v Lord Advocate* [2003] 1 A.C. 1078; [2001] 2 Cr.App.R. 27.

according to law." This leaves the difficulty that, when there has been an application for a confiscation order, there are underlying allegations that the offender has been concerned in other drug trafficking. Lord Hope responded by arguing that confiscation proceedings are more in the nature of a civil process which does not require the court to assume criminal wrongdoing. This assumes that the confiscation proceedings are part of the sentencing process flowing from the offence of conviction, whereas in reality they involve allegations of other offences which yielded the proceeds at which the confiscation order is aimed. However, their Lordships went on to hold that, even if Art.6(2) were relevant, the drug trafficking legislation was "approved by a democratically elected Parliament and should not be at all readily rejected."

16–69   The issue was considered by the Strasbourg Court in *Phillips v United Kingdom*.[195] The Court held that confiscation proceedings do amount to sentencing procedures, but that Art.6(2) is not applicable to the presumptions embodied in the Drug Trafficking Act unless they are such as to amount to the bringing of a further "criminal charge" against the applicant, which (the Court held) they are not. On this point there was a spirited dissent by two judges (including Sir Nicolas Bratza, the British judge), who pointed out that there is established authority to the contrary. In *Minelli v Switzerland*,[196] a case involving an award of costs, the Court stated that "Article 6(2) governs criminal proceedings in their entirety." The majority's judgment on this point seems unpersuasive. However, both the majority and the minority in *Phillips* went on to hold that, even if Art.6(2) were applicable, the presumptions in the legislation were compatible with the rather elastic principles on burden of proof enunciated in *Salabiaku v France*.[197] In particular, there was no compulsion on the judge to make the statutory presumptions; the defendant did have the opportunity to rebut them; and in this case the judge only applied the confiscation order to property in respect of which the applicant's ownership was proved (rather than merely suspected).

16–70   Two further cases have come before the House of Lords. In *Revzi*[198] an important fact was that the appellant had been charged with 14 offences of theft from his employer, and that, when the prosecution accepted his plea of guilty to two counts, the prosecution originally insisted on a trial of the other 12 counts. However, the prosecution then served a notice under the confiscation legislation and decided not to proceed with the other 12 counts, which were ordered to lie on the file. The defence argued that the judge should not make the statutory assumptions in respect of any of the matters covered in the 12 counts lying on the file, since they remained in dispute. However, the judge decided to reject the defence argument and, having applied the statutory presumptions and having heard defence evidence in rebuttal, made a confiscation order that went well beyond the sums involved in the two offences to which there had been a guilty plea. The House of Lords held unanimously that this procedure was compatible with the Convention. Lord Steyn reviewed the difference of opinion between the

---

[195] [2001] Crim.L.R. 817.
[196] (1983) 5 E.H.R.R. 554.
[197] (1988) 13 E.H.R.R. 379, discussed at para.9–10 above.
[198] [2003] 1 A.C. 1099, [2002] 2 Cr.App.R.(S) 3000, a decision on the confiscation provisions in ss.71 and 72 of the Criminal Justice Act 1988.

majority and the minority in *Phillips v United Kingdom*, and commented only that "if Article 6(2) is held to be directly applicable, it will tend to undermine the effectiveness of confiscation procedures generally"—not a principled proposition, but a pragmatic one.[199] However, Lord Steyn went on to hold that the confiscation laws were a proportionate response to an internationally recognised problem, and adopted the Court of Appeal's view that judges have a duty to ensure that the application of the confiscation laws does not result in injustice. The decision in *Revzi* should be read in conjunction with that in *Benjafield*,[200] handed down on the same day and following the same course of reasoning.

There remains a difficulty which arises from the facts of *Revzi*. Counsel for the appellant argued that it was an abuse of process for the judge to make a confiscation order based on evidence from undetermined counts. Lord Steyn simply replied that "the premise of this argument is wrong: the judge rightly relied on the evidence before him in relation to confiscation and not on any undetermined counts." His Lordship added that "the application by the Crown to apply primary legislation (subject to control by the court and subject to a full right of appeal on the part of a convicted defendant) could not amount to an abuse of the process of the court."[201] This appears difficult to reconcile with Lord Bingham's enunciation in *Canavan and Kidd*[202] of the fundamental principle that "a defendant should [not] be sentenced for offences neither admitted nor proved by verdict." This principle was stated in the context of prosecutions based on specimen counts, and that was the position both in *Canavan* and in *Revzi*. No doubt the reply, implicit in *Revzi*, is that the defendant is being sentenced only for the offence(s) of conviction, and that the confiscation order may be based on other "facts" without determining that those other facts involve the commission of offences. However, it must be evident that there is a disjunction here between procedure and substance. It may be true, as a matter of procedure, that the confiscation order is not a sentence for the other unprosecuted offences. But in substance that is what it appears to be: a confiscation order is certainly a sentence,[203] and it is a sentence that runs beyond the fact of the offence(s) of conviction. If at this stage it is re-asserted that this is the procedure ordained by a democratically elected legislature, then this begs and does not answer the question of compatibility. The Strasbourg Court would surely scrutinise the substance of the process, as it has often done when determining whether a case involves a "criminal charge."[204] For example, the Court has affirmed the principle that a person should be sentenced in relation to the indictment presented, and to which the defence was prepared, and not on wider allegations that have not

16–71

---

[199] And probably incorrect, in the sense that the whole court in *Phillips* held that, even if Art.6(2) did apply, the legislation would be held proportionate and within the broad approach permitted by *Salabiaku v France* (although it is true that Lord Steyn had adopted a more discerning view of Art.6(2) in *Lambert*, above, para.9–27).

[200] [2003] 1 A.C. 1099, [2002] 2 Cr.App.R.(S) 313, dealing with slightly different confiscation provisions in the Drug Trafficking Act 1994.

[201] [2003] 1 A.C. 1099, p.1154, at [20].

[202] [1998] 1 Cr.App.R.(S) 243, at p.247.

[203] Reliance can be placed on the quotation from *Welch v United Kingdom* in para.16–81 below, both for this proposition and (indirectly) for the next proposition too.

[204] See Ch.4 above.

been charged and proved in the proper way.[205] Important as it is that the European and international initiatives against organised crime, money laundering and so forth should be supported, it does not follow that they have to be pursued by methods that infringe the Convention rights of those involved.

16–72   A second issue that has arisen under Art.6 is as to the application of its reasonable time requirement. Cases have been decided which concern delays in enforcement proceedings[206] and in commencing an application for a certificate increasing the offender's realisable assets.[207] In *R. (Lloyd) v Bow Street Magistrates' Court* the claimant was made subject to a confiscation order in 1996 and had paid part of it when enforcement proceedings began in 1997. Due to a series of delays the matter remained unresolved by 2002, at which point the claimant sought a stay. The Divisional Court upheld his complaint that there had been a violation of the reasonable time requirement under Art.6(1) and by way of remedy prohibited the use of committal to prison in default. The Strasbourg Court decision of *Crowther v United Kingdom* is to similar effect. In the case of *In Re Saggar*[208] the appellant had in 1995 been made subject to a confiscation order of £1,370 following his conviction for drug trafficking offences, this being the amount which the court assessed to be his realisable assets. Some seven years later after he had paid the sum in full, the Commissioners applied under s.16 of the Drug Trafficking Offences Act 1994 for a certificate increasing the amount of realisable assets to be recovered. It was accepted that the reasonable time requirements of Art.6(1) apply to any alleged delay by HM Commissioners of Customs and Excise in seeking to re-open a confiscation order so as to increase the amount which might be realised under it. The issue in the case was whether the period of time for the purposes of Art.6(1) is the whole period of the criminal proceedings or the time since the institution of the s.16 application. The Court of Appeal held that it was the whole period of the criminal proceedings, despite the terms of the legislation according to which the criminal proceedings had terminated with the making of the confiscation order and the application for a certificate under s.16 amounted to fresh proceedings which carried no limitation period.[209]

16–73   Issues under Art.8 have also arisen in confiscation proceedings. Section 71 of the Criminal Justice Act 1988 (as amended by the Proceeds of Crime Act 1995) removed any discretion in the sentencing court whether to impose a confiscation order or as to the amount of any order, where it was concerned that the full amount of the order might adversely affect the rights of others by, for example, forcing the sale of the matrimonial home. In *R. v Ahmed and Qureshi*[210] the Court of Appeal held that under the provisions relating to the imposition of the confiscation order the sentencing court is only concerned with the arithmetical exercise of computing what is, in effect, a statutory debt. This is a process which

---

[205] See *Ecer and Zeyrek v Turkey* (2002) 35 E.H.R.R. 672, at [35].
[206] *R. (Lloyd) v Bow Street Magistrates' Court* [2004] 1 Cr.App.R. 11 and *Crowther v United Kingdom, The Times*, February 11, 2005.
[207] *In Re Saggar* [2005] EWCA Civ 174.
[208] [2005] EWCA Civ 174.
[209] *Ibid* at paras 37–41.
[210] [2005] 1 W.L.R. 122, [2005] 1 All E.R. 128.

does not involve any judgment of how that debt might ultimately be paid. Accordingly, no question arises at this stage under Art.8. However, that is not true at the enforcement stage. Relying on the decision of the House of Lords in *In Re Norris*[211] the Court of Appeal held that at this stage of the procedure the rights of third parties can be considered and resolved. Where an issue arose as to the sale of the matrimonial home then Art.8 rights would clearly be involved and a determation required whether it would be proportionate to to make an order selling the home.[212]

II. Guilty Pleas and Defendants' Rights

The procedure whereby a defendant may plead guilty and be sentenced without **16–74** a trial or examination of the evidence has been held compatible with the right to a fair trial under Art.6, although until recently no such procedure was available in most European countries. In *X v United Kingdom*[213] the Commission noted that:

> "[U]nder English criminal procedure, if a person pleads guilty there is no trial in the usual sense; if the judge is satisfied that the accused understands the effect of his plea, his confession is recorded, and the subsequent proceedings are concerned only with the question of sentence. The Commission having examined this practice in the context of English criminal procedure, and also in other systems among those State Parties to the Convention where a similar practice is found, is satisfied that the procedure as such is not inconsistent with the requirements of Article 6(1) and (2) of the Convention. In arriving at this conclusion the Commission has had regard to the rules under which the practice operates and in particular to the safeguards which are provided to avoid the possibility of abuse."

The safeguards to which the Commission was adverting presumably include the **16–75** rules governing fitness to plead, equivocal pleas, and the availability of legal representation. In *R.O. v United Kingdom*[214] the Commission recognised that it was fair to have rules disallowing change of an unequivocal and voluntary plea, and this was applied by the Divisional Court in *Revitt, Borg and Barnes v D.P.P.*,[215] holding that the defendants were rightly prevented from changing their unequivocal pleas but that the discretion might have been exercised otherwise if there had been doubt about the basis for their conviction. Another safeguard is the potential for a *Newton*[216] hearing—in which the burden of proof is on the prosecution—whenever a factual issue relevant to sentence is in dispute. Thus in *De Salvador Torres v Spain*[217] the Court held that a defendant must be given due warning, to comply with Art.6(3)(a), of any circumstance to be alleged by the prosecution as constituting a factor aggravating sentence.[218] In this case the

---

[211] [2001] 1 W.L.R. 1388.

[212] *ibid.*, at [12].

[213] (1972) 40 C.D. 64 at 67; 2 Dig. 744.

[214] App.No.23094/93, Commission decision of May 11, 1994.

[215] [2006] EWHC Admin 2266.

[216] (1982) 77 Cr.App.R. 13.

[217] (1997) 23 E.H.R.R. 601.

[218] *cf.* the decision of the Supreme Court of Canada in *Lyons* [1987] 2 S.C.R. 309, to the effect that the Crown's failure to give the defendant notice that they intended to invite the sentencer to impose an extended sentence on grounds of public protection did not infringe s.7 of the Charter.

aggravating factor was that the defendant was a public official in a position of trust, which gave the court access to a higher sentence, and the Court found that he must have been well aware that that was regarded as an aggravating factor. Proper application of the extensive case-law following the *Newton* decision[219] should ensure that an offender is given the opportunity to contest any significant aggravating factor alleged by the prosecution.[220]

16–76   In the third case entitled *X v United Kingdom*[221] the trial judge had observed in passing sentence that a guilty plea would have constituted a mitigating circumstance. The applicants argued in Strasbourg that this amounted to the imposition of a heavier sentence on the grounds that they had contested the charge and accordingly that the sentence was in breach of Art.6. In rejecting the application as manifestly ill-founded the Commission observed:

> "It is clear from the statements by the trial judge that he did not increase the applicants' sentence on the ground that they had affirmed their innocence throughout the trial, but rather refrained from reducing what he deemed to be the proper sentence, having regard to the gravity of the offences concerned."

This is consistent with the theory behind the guilty plea discount in English law.[222]

16–77   However, the compatibility of a discount for pleading guilty may depend on the extent of the inducement involved. In *Deweer v Belgium*[223] the court found a violation of Art.6 where the applicant had been offered the choice between paying a relatively modest fine by way of "compromise" or facing lengthy criminal proceedings. If he had chosen to contest the charge his butcher's shop would have remained closed by administrative order, thus depriving him of income. The Court held that a procedure under which an accused can waive the right to a hearing on payment of a penalty is not necessarily inconsistent with Art.6, but that such a settlement must be free from "constraint." In the present case there was such disproportionality between the fine and the consequences of contesting the proceedings that the settlement was tainted by constraint and therefore in breach of Art. 6. The current guidelines on reduction of sentence for pleading guilty indicate a maximum reduction of one-third and recognise that there may be borderline cases in which the effect of pleading guilty might make the difference between a custodial sentence and a community sentence.[224] The practice of advance indication of sentence also has the capacity to exert pressure on the accused.[225] The question, in all these situations, is whether the decision to plead guilty that results is sufficiently free from "constraint."

---

[219] See *Archbold*, Ch.5.
[220] It seems likely that the approach to sentencing persons convicted on specimen counts was contrary to Art.6 before the decision in *Canavan and Kidd*, above, n.202.
[221] (1975) 3 D.R. 10 at 16.
[222] See, for example, *Harper* [1968] 1 Q.B. 108.
[223] (1979–80) 2 E.H.R.R. 439.
[224] Sentencing Guidelines Council, *Reduction of Sentence for a Guilty Plea* (2004).
[225] *Goodyear* [2006] 1 Cr.App.R.(S) 23.

III. Disclosure and Sentencing

In relation to mitigation of sentence, it will be recalled that the prosecution's duty **16–78** of disclosure under Art.6 and the doctrine of "equality of arms" extends to the disclosure of "any material in their possession . . . which may assist the accused in exonerating himself *or in obtaining a reduction in sentence*."[226] The Attorney-General's *Guidelines on the Disclosure of Information in Criminal Proceedings*[227] now recognise that the prosecution should consider disclosing any material which is relevant to sentence, such as information which might mitigate the seriousness of the offence or assist the accused to lay blame in whole or in part on a co-accused or another person.[228]

H. THE PROHIBITION ON RETROSPECTIVE PENALTIES

The second limb of Art.7(1) prohibits a court from imposing a heavier penalty **16–79** than the one which was applicable at the time the offence was committed. It should be recalled that Art.7 is one of the few Convention rights from which no derogation is possible (Art.15). Article 7 only prohibits an increase in the penalty for the offence, and so it is first necessary to determine what amounts to a "penalty", and then to determine when it is heavier than the one "applicable at the time of the offence".

I. The Meaning of "Penalty"

The term "penalty" has an autonomous meaning, defined by reference to criteria **16–80** analogous to those which apply to the term "criminal charge" in Art.6.[229] The domestic classification is no more than a starting point, and the Court has held that[230]:

> "To render the protection offered by Art.7 effective, the Court must be free to go behind appearances and assess for itself whether a particular measure amounts in substance to a 'penalty' within the meaning of this provision . . . [T]he starting point in any assessment of a penalty is whether the measure in question is imposed following conviction for a 'criminal offence'. Other factors that may be taken into account as relevant in this connection are the nature and purpose of the measure in question; its characterisation under national law; the procedures involved in the making and implementation of the measure and its severity."

In *Welch v United Kingdom*[231] a confiscation order was made under the Drug **16–81** Trafficking Offences Act 1986 in respect of an offence committed before the Act entered into force. Section 38(4) of the Act expressly gave retroactive effect to

---

[226] *Jespers v Belgium* (1981) 27 D.R. 61, discussed in para.14–89 above.
[227] November 29, 2000.
[228] Para.44. No Rules have yet been made under Pt 22 of the Criminal Procedure Rules 2005 S.I. 2005/384, in respect of disclosure by the prosecution.
[229] *Welch v United Kingdom* (1995) 20 E.H.R.R. 247 at paras 27–35.
[230] *ibid.*, at paras 27–28.
[231] (1995) 20 E.H.R.R. 247.

the powers of confiscation, provided the defendant had been *charged* after the Act came into force. The Government argued that the confiscation order was not a penalty but rather a preventive measure "designed to bleed the drug trafficking economy of its lifeblood." The Court held unanimously that the confiscation order was an additional penalty, and therefore in violation of Art.7(1). It noted that the measure had punitive as well as preventive and reparative aims; that the order was calculated by reference to "proceeds" rather than profits, and therefore had a reach beyond the mere restoration of the *status quo ante*; that the amount of the order could take account of the offender's culpability; and that the order was enforceable by a term of imprisonment in default. Subsequent decisions on confiscation orders start from the proposition that it constitutes a penalty, and have, as described in paras 16–67 to 16–70 above, gone on to hold that a confiscation order is a penalty for the offence of conviction and that, although it extends to the proceeds of "crime" over a period of six years, it does not involve any further "criminal charge" within the meaning of Art.6.[232]

16–82   It emerges from *Welch* that, even if a major part of the purpose of a measure is preventive, it may be held to have a punitive effect and therefore to fall within the autonomous meaning of "penalty". An attempt was made to invoke this reasoning in *Ibbotson v United Kingdom*[233] in respect of the provisions for the registration of sex offenders introduced by the Sex Offenders Act 1997. The principal issue was whether the requirement to register is a "penalty" within the autonomous meaning of the term under the Convention. The Commission ruled that, whereas in *Welch* it was held that confiscation of assets was partly punitive in nature, here the restrictions on sex offenders were purely preventive, "in the sense that the knowledge that a person has been registered with the police may dissuade him from committing further offences." It was also relevant that the registration requirement was far less "severe" than a confiscation order,[234] and that there was no provision for imprisonment in default[235]: any proceedings for breach of the 1997 Act would have to be brought independently. This reasoning[236] must apply equally to notification requirements under Pt 2 of the Sexual Offences Act 2003.

16–83   The English courts have also held that a football banning order, made under s. 14B of the Football Spectators Act 1989 as amended, is a preventive order rather than a penalty. In *Gough v Chief Constable of Derbyshire*[237] the Court of Appeal conducted an extensive review of the compatibility of such orders with the principle of freedom of movement in the European Union, but on the question

---

[232] In Strasbourg the decision in *Phillips v United Kingdom* [2001] Crim.L.R. 817; in this country, *McIntosh v Lord Advocate* [2001] 2 Cr.App.R. 27 and *Revzi* [2002] UKHL 1; above, para.16–

[233] (1999) 27 E.H.R.R. CD 332. See also *B v Chief Constable of Avon and Somerset Constabulary* [2001] 1 W.L.R. 340 (considered at para.4–35 above).

[234] The Commission rejected the applicant's argument that the hostility of the public towards persons on the Sex Offenders Register should be considered as part of the severity of the penalty.

[235] This is a feature of the confiscation regime.

[236] Also applied in *Adamson v United Kingdom* (1999) 28 E.H.R.R. CD 209. The severity of the notification requirements was challenged on Art.8 grounds, unsuccessfully, in *Forbes v Secretary of State for the Home Department* [2006] EWCA Civ 962.

[237] [2002] 2 All E.R. 985.

whether such orders are "penalties" within Art.7 the court agreed with the reasoning of Laws L.J. in the Divisional Court, where he said:

"The order is not made as part of the process of distributive criminal justice. Under section 14B there is no requirement of a criminal conviction, so that the starting point in *Welch v United Kingdom* is not met. In section 14A, the existence of a relevant conviction is in my judgment no more than a gateway criterion for the making of the order, equivalent to the provision in section 14B(4)(a) when no conviction is involved."[238]

When the House of Lords came to consider whether an anti-social behaviour   **16–84** order under s.1 of the Crime and Disorder Act 1998 constitutes a penalty, in *Clingham v Royal Borough of Kenginston and Chelsea; R. v Crown Court at Manchester, ex parte McCann*,[239] it too concluded that the proceedings do not involve a criminal charge and that the order is essentially preventive and not punitive. As Lord Hope stated:

"An anti-social behaviour order may well restrict the freedom of the defendant to do what he wants and to go where he pleases. But these restrictions are imposed for preventive reasons, not as punishment. The test that has to be applied under section 1(6) is confined to what is necessary for the purpose of protecting persons from further anti-social acts by the defendant. The court is not being required, nor indeed is it permitted, to consider what an appropriate sanction would be for his past conduct."[240]

The substance of this decision has been discussed in an earlier chapter.[241] Given the reasoning and conclusion of the House of Lords, it seems that the same classification will be applied to an anti-social behaviour order when it is imposed after conviction of an offence.[242] The argument to the contrary based on the criteria used by the Commission in *Ibbotson* (above, 16–82)—that the terms of some anti-social behaviour orders are more severe than the mere obligation to notify the police under the Sex Offenders Act and that, although proceedings for breach of the order must be brought independently, they involve a strict liability offence with a high maximum penalty of five years' imprisonment—has not yet met with any success.

The question whether an order disqualifying an adult from working with chil-   **16–85** dren, under s.28 of the Criminal Justice and Court Services Act 2000, constitutes a penalty was considered by the Court of Appeal in *Field and Young*.[243] The court analysed the issues in some detail, but the point it found most persuasive was that the order should be made (if the qualifying conditions are fulfilled) either on conviction or on a finding of unfitness to plead or not guilty by reason of insanity. As Kay L.J. reasoned:

---

[238] [2001] 3 W.L.R. 1392, para.[42]

[239] [2003] 1 A.C. 787.

[240] At 76.

[241] See Ch.4.

[242] This possibility was introduced by the Police Reform Act 2002, and orders made on conviction now form the majority of ASBOs being made: see Ashworth A., *Sentencing and Criminal Justice* (4th edn 2005), 203–206.

[243] [2003] 1 W.L.R. 882.

"It seems to us of considerable importance that a conviction is not a necessary condition for the making of such an order. When one considers the nature and purpose of such an order it points overwhelmingly to this being for preventative rather than punitive effect. Precisely the same order is made whether a person is convicted or not and the making of an order has no regard to the extent or seriousness of the offending but rather to whether a repetition of the conduct is likely."[244]

It is open to question whether this goes too far. Whilst it is true that s.28 requires a court to make an order unless it is satisfied that it is unlikely that the individual will commit any further offence against a child—which makes clear the chiefly preventive purpose—this requirement only arises in cases of conviction where a custodial sentence of 12 months or more has been imposed. This suggests that the order is related to the seriousness of the past offence. Of course no such condition is relevant where there is a finding of not guilty by reason of insanity, because a punitive sentence may not be imposed in those cases. But the possibility of an insanity verdict in a small number of cases, and the availability of the disqualification order in those cases, can hardly be said to negative the punitive element in the order itself. The enactment of a provision that confiscation orders may be made on persons found not guilty by reason of insanity would surely not have altered the court's decision in *Welch*, since that would be to place form before substance. However, the legislature has now gone further in the provisions applicable to certain new orders: the Sexual Offences Act 2003 has introduced three orders (sexual offences prevention orders, foreign travel orders, and risk of sexual harm orders) that may be made by a court without a conviction, so long as it it satisfied of certain past events and future dangers.[245]

16–86   In *Field and Young* Kay L.J. also discussed disqualification from driving, which does not restrict liberty or make a financial demand but which, he concluded, "is clearly penal in nature [because] it is imposed by reference to the conduct that led to the conviction and without necessarily any relationship to the danger a person may represent when driving a motorcar."[246] The latter point may be disputed by some; and the implication of the remainder of the judgment in *Field and Young* is that disqualification from driving could become classified as preventive simply by inserting a provision empowering or requiring a court to impose disqualification in cases where a driver is found unfit to plead or not guilty by reason of insanity. There is certainly authority that disqualification may be preventive if the power is exercised by another authority. In *Blokker v Netherlands*[247] a driver was convicted of drunk driving and disqualified from driving for six months. Dutch law permitted the Minister of Transport to require a driver to attend an Education Measure on Traffic and Alcohol, in effect a three-day course on the effects of alcohol on driving, for which the driver had to pay, and the applicant was subjected to such an order. He argued that it was a penalty, largely because of the

---

[244] At [58].

[245] S.33 of the Criminal Justice and Police Act 2001 introduced a power to include within the sentence of a drug trafficker a travel restriction order. The provision has no retrospective reach, no doubt in recognition of strong possibility that the order would qualify as a penalty for the purpose of Art.7(1). As to the principles to be applied in making such an order see *Mee* [2004] 2 Cr.App.R.(S) 434.

[246] At [35].

[247] [2001] E.H.R.L.R. 328.

Minister's power to revoke a driving licence if the driver failed to complete the course satisfactorily. The Court declared the application inadmissible, on the basis that this was clearly a preventive measure and its administrative operation could be compared with the procedure for granting a driving licence in the first place.

However, in *Malige v France*[248] the question arose in relation to French law's **16–87** system of penalty points, which is regarded as separate from the criminal law and as a "secondary penalty" of a purely administrative nature. The Court held that, since the docking of points was an automatic consequence of conviction, it had a sufficiently punitive and deterrent character to qualify as a penalty. Unlike disqualification itself, it could not be regarded as chiefly preventive in purpose.

II. Retrospectivity—the meaning of "applicable at the time the offence was committed"

The decision whether to classify a measure as a penalty or merely as a preventive **16–88** order is of great significance, since under Art.7 penalties may not operate retrospectively whereas there is no such prohibition relating to preventive orders. Thus, once the Court of Appeal in *Field and Young* had decided that an order of disqualification from working with children is not a penalty, it proceeded quickly to hold that orders could properly be imposed on those convicted in respect of offences committed before the Act came into force.[249] But where a measure is classified as a penalty, the protection afforded by Art.7 becomes central:

> "The guarantee enshrined in Article 7, which is an essential element of the rule of law, occupies a prominent place in the Convention system of protection, as is underlined by the fact that no derogation from it is permissible under Article 15 in time of war or other public emergency. It should be construed and applied, as follows from its object and purpose, in such a way as to provide effective safeguards against arbitrary prosecution, conviction and punishment."[250]

This principle was applied in *Ecer and Zeyrek v Turkey*,[251] where the applicants had been convicted on an indictment charging them with acts assisting terrorism "in 1988 and 1989." They were given a higher sentence than was applicable in those years: a statute of 1991 had increased the maximum penalty by one-half, and the court had made use of the higher maximum stating that the applicants had confessed to involvement in assisting terrorism in 1992–93. The Court unanimously found a breach of Art.7, because they had never been charged with or convicted of offences later than 1989, and so it was wrong to apply the higher maximum retrospectively. This decision confirms the significance of what is in

---

[248] (1999) 28 E.H.R.R. 578.
[249] [2003] 1 W.L.R. 882, at [59].
[250] *Ecer and Zeyrek v Turkey* (2002) 35 E.H.R.R. 672, at [29], repeated in *Veeber v Estonia* (2004) 39 E.H.R.R. 6, at [29].
[251] *Ecer and Zeyrek v Turkey* (2002) 35 E.H.R.R. 672.

the indictment, and raises questions about specimen charges in the English setting.[252]

16–89   The principles above apply no less where the charge relates to a continuing offence that began before the change of law and continued afterwards, as the court held in *Puhk v Estonia*.[253] Thus in *Greenwood and Greenwood*[254] the Court of Appeal held that, where the conspiracy with which the appellants were charged was expressed to run from 1990 to 1999, the judge was bound to sentence within the maximum of five years, and not the maximum of seven years (to which it had been raised in 1994).

16–90   Just as it is vital to identify whether a measure amounts to a penalty or is merely preventative, so too the application of Art.7 depends upon whether the increase in the sentence which is identified amounts to an increase in "the sentence applicable at the time the offence was committed". There is no difficulty in a case such as *Ecer and Zeyrek* where there has been an increase in the statutory maximum. But in *R. (Uttley) v Secretary of State for the Home Department*[255] the question arose whether Art.7(1) had a more extensive reach, to cover circumstances where the offender is required to serve longer can he could have expected to serve at the time the offence was committed. In *Uttley* this arose in the following way. The appellant was sentenced to 12 years for offences of rape. The statutory maximum at the time the offences were committed in the 1970s and the date of conviction in 1992 was the same, namely life imprisonment. But the administration of the sentence was fundamentally different. Under the regime applicable at the time the offence was committed, the appellant would have been released as soon as he had served two thirds of the sentence imposed by the court, at which time that sentence would have expired. His 12 year sentence was, in substance, an eight year term since the coercive impact of the sentence ended completely at that point. But, under the regime governed by the Criminal Justice Act 1991 which was in force when he was convicted and sentenced, while he would still be released at the two thirds point of his sentence, the release would be on licence. He could therefore be recalled to prison to serve his sentence under s.39 of the Criminal Justice Act 1991. And in the event that he committed a further offence before the sentence expired, he could be returned to prison to serve the remainder of the term outstanding at the date of commission of the further offence, under s.116 of the Powers of Criminal Courts (Sentencing) Act 2000. Under the 1991 Act regime, the impact of the sentence continues throughout the 12 year term and the prisoner may be required to serve the whole of that term. The House of Lords held that Art.7 is not engaged in this situation. It does no more than prohibit the imposition of a penalty that is greater than the statutory maximum applicable at the time the offence was committed.

---

[252] See the discussion in para.16–70 above. *Cf. Pardue* [2004] 1 Cr.App.R.(S) 105 and *Attorney-General's Reference (No.82 of 2002)* [2003] 2 Cr.App.R.(S) 673, where the Court of Appeal appears to have approved a procedure that falls below proper standards, with *Tovey and Smith* [2005] 2 Cr.App.R.(S) 606.

[253] App.No.55103/00, judgment of May 10, 2004.

[254] [2005] EWCA Crim 2686, applying *Hobbs* [2002] 2 Cr.App.R.(S) 92.

[255] [2004] 1 W.L.R. 2278.

In giving this narrow meaning to "applicable at the time" their Lordships relied   **16–91**
upon the case of *Coëme v Belgium*[256] where at para.145 it was said that:

> "The Court must therefore verify that at the time when an accused person performed the
> act which led to his being prosecuted and convicted there was in force a legal provision
> which made that act punishable, and that the punishment imposed did not exceed the
> limits fixed by that provision . . . "[257]

Further support for this restrictive construction was found by the House of Lords   **16–92**
in *Flynn v HM Advocate*.[258] That was a case concerning the transitional provisions introduced to judicialise the mandatory life sentence. In Scotland, prior to
judicialisation, no term was ever fixed to mark the punitive part of the sentence.
Instead the Secretary of State simply referred the case to the Parole Board to
consider whether to recommend release. Even with such a recommendation
release could be refused by the Secretary of State on the ground that he
considered the lifer had been insufficiently punished. Under the new regime, a
punitive part was to be retrospectively fixed in line with the judicial recommendation. The appellants complained because under the old regime their cases
had already been referred to the Parole Board for consideration of release. Yet the
punitive periods fixed under the new regime had not yet expired with the result
that they could not, under the new regime, apply for parole for some time. The
appellants argued that the introduction of the new regime aggravated the penalty
because under the new system they were likely to spend substantially longer
periods in custody. Their Lordships upheld the appellants' challenge on divergent
grounds, but all expressed a view about Art.7. Lords Carswell and Rodger
construed Art.7 in accordance with their later speeches in *Uttley* and considered
that Art.7 was not engaged because under the new regime the appellants were
required to serve a longer period than would have been likely under the old
regime, but not than would have been competent. Three other Law Lords were
very sympathetic to the Art.7 argument. Baroness Hale was among them and she
also sat in *Uttley* where she agreed that Art.7 was not engaged. In her speech, she
sought to distinguish *Flynn* on the ground that the regime for the administration
of the sentence did in fact alter the nature of the sentence itself. In her view, the
mandatory life sentence, under the old regime, was in truth an indeterminate
sentence. Baroness Hale noted that in England the transitional provisions contained in the Criminal Justice Act 2003,[259] by which the minimum terms of
existing mandatory lifers in England and Wales fall to be judicialised, do prevent
a greater term being fixed than the one previously notified by the Secretary of
State. There is no doubt that the regime was introduced on the assumption

---

[256] Reports of Judgments and Decisions 2000-VII, p.75.

[257] Their Lordships could equally have relied upon *Taylor v United Kingdom* Admissibility
decision of December 3, 2002, reported at [2003] E.H.R.L.R. 238 at p.9. Here the Court recalled that
"that it has had occasion to stress in the context of its judgments under Art.7 that only the law can
define a crime and prescribe a penalty (*nullum crimen, nulla poena sine lege*), from which it follows
that an offence must be clearly defined in law. This condition is satisfied where the individual can
know from the wording of the relevant provision, if need be with the assistance of the domestic
courts' interpretation of it, what acts and omissions will make him liable and, it would add for the
purposes of the instant case, what penalties can be imposed."

[258] [2004] H.R.L.R. 17 at 447; [2004] U.K.P.C. D1; 2004 S.C.C.R. 281, PC.

[259] The transitional provisions are contained in Sch.22.

that Art.7 was engaged.[260] However, in light of the narrow construction given to this guarantee, it would appear that this was unnecessary. Just as life is the maximum penalty authorised by the legal provision governing the sentence of rape, so too is life the maximum minimum term authorised by s.1 of the Murder (Abolition of Death Penalty) Act 1965 in respect of the punitive component of the indeterminate sentence: *R. v SSHD ex parte Hindley.*[261] Any change in the regime governing the administration of the mandatory life sentence, which results in an individual prisoner serving longer than he could previously have expected, is indistinguishable from the situation of Mr Uttley; it does not engage Art.7.

16–93 This narrow construction of Art.7 produces some very strange results. Article 7 will protect an offender from being subjected to a sentence which was unavailable at the time the offence was committed however minor the penalty might be. Thus, there will be a violation if in addition to a term of imprisonment the new sentencing powers enable a court to impose a small confiscation order, or a single day's community order.[262] On the other hand, if the parole arrangements applicable to Mr Uttley's sentence had been altered to his detriment the day before he was due for release, Art.7 would not be engaged.[263]

16–94 The House of Lords construction of Art.7 is consistent with the approach taken by the Court of Appeal when it found no incompatibility where a sentencer imposed a sentence higher than that which would have been imposed if the offender had been convicted soon after the commission of the offence, because the tariff had increased in the intervening years.[264] It is further supported by the Court's decision in *Taylor v United Kingdom.*[265] In this case a boy was charged with robbery just a month after his 14th birthday. Because of lengthy delays, arising from a change in the charge, adjournments at the prosecution's request, failure of co-defendants and (on one occasion) the defendant to attend court, the applicant was eventually convicted and sentenced after his 15th birthday. He was sentenced to 18 months' detention in a young offender institution, whereas if he had been convicted and sentenced before his 15th birthday it would not have been possible to impose a custodial sentence. The Court held that an application based on Art.7 was inadmissible, on the ground that it had been known to the defendant (or at least to his legal advisers) that the sentencing powers of the

---

[260] It is notable that much legislation which alters the impact of a sentence is drafted upon the assumption that it would be contrary to Art.7 to apply it to offenders whose offences were committed before that date, e.g. s.85(1)(a) of the 2000 Sentencing Act. These appear to have been unnecessary precautions. By contrast secitions 225 and 226 of the Criminal Justice Act 2003 which introduce new indeterminate sentences for dangerous offenders properly have no retrospective reach. These provisions increase the statutory maximum for some sentences from 10 years to an indeterminate term, which could be as long as life.

[261] [2001] A.C. 410.

[262] E.g. *Welch v United Kingdom* [1995] 20 E.H.R.R 247.

[263] See S. Atrill, *"Nulla Poene Sine Lege* in Comparative Perspective", [2005] *Public Law* 127. Of course an issue might well arise under Arts 3 and 6.

[264] *Alden v Wright* [2001] 2 Cr.App.R.(S) 359; c.f the view of Hoffman L.J. in *Ex parte McCartney, The Times*, May 25, 1994, judgment May 19, 1994 that the imposition of a tarff on discretionary life prisoner whose offences were committed in the 1970s violated Art.7 because it took into account an increase in the tariff for terrorist offences in the 1980s.

[265] Admissibility decision of December 3, 2002, reported at [2003] E.H.R.L.R. 238 at p.9.

courts would change significantly on his 15th birthday. The relevant statute "defined the sentencing powers of the domestic courts with respect to young offenders convicted of such offences as well as the age of the offender for the determination of the sentence."[266] There was never any guarantee that the proceedings would be completed before his 15th birthday, nor was there evidence of delays brought about in order to produce that result. The Court went on to consider whether there had been unreasonable delay and held that there had not.

In this admissibility decision the court relied on a line of English cases starting   **16–95**
with *Danga*,[267] which (it stated) articulate "the age at date of conviction rule, as opposed to the date of sentence." However, in *Danga* and several later decisions the Court of Appeal has qualified that principle in a material way, stating that the sentence that would have been imposed if the case had been dealt with promptly is a "powerful factor to be taken into account" when determining sentence at a later date.[268] This point was pressed strongly in *Ghafoor*,[269] where it was argued on behalf of the appellant that Art.7 should be interpreted so that the "penalty applicable at the time the offence was committed" are treated as referring to the penalty "applicable to the offence and the offender." The argument was that:

> "The philosophy of restricted sentencing powers for juveniles reflects society's accep-
> tance that young offenders are less responsible for their actions and therefore less
> culpable. The culpability of a young offender should not be affected by the date of trial
> or conviction."[270]

The court held that "the relevant age for determining a defendant's age ... is the date of conviction", which appears to be congruent with the Strasbourg decision in *Taylor*. However, the court softened the impact of that ruling considerably, by accepting the above argument about the philosophy behind the different sentencing powers for young offenders. The sentence that would have been passed at the date of the offence is not only a "powerful factor" but "there have to be good reasons for departing from the starting point", and a perusal of the Court of Appeal decisions reveals no departure from that point. "Justice requires there to be good reason to pass a sentence higher than would have been passed at the date of the offence."[271] The Court of Appeal reached its conclusion by means of English sentencing principles rather than by interpreting Art.7 in the way proposed by counsel for the appellant. The conclusion is, however, hard to reconcile with the outcome in *Taylor v United Kingdom*, a case in which the Court of Appeal had already dismissed the appeal against the sentence of detention, even though no custodial sentence would have been available if he had been sentenced for assault occasioning actual bodily harm at the age of 14.

---

[266] (2005) 41 E.H.R.R. 751.

[267] (1992) 13 Cr.App.R.(S) 408.

[268] *Cuddington* (1995) 16 Cr.App.R.(S) 246. The point has particular resonance in cases of hisorical child abuse, and in sentencing mature adults for sex offences committed in their teens the Court of Appeal has held that the probable sentence if they had been sentenced as youths must be a strong factor: *Bowers* [1999] 2 Cr.App.R.(S) 97, *Fowler* [2002] 2 Cr.App.R.(S) 463.

[269] [2003] 1 Cr.App.R.(S) 428.

[270] At [17].

[271] At [32].

16–96   In *Achour v France*[272] the offender received a 12 year term on grounds of recidivism following his conviction for drug offences. The relevant statute allowed the sentencing court to treat the offender as a recidivist if the offence was committed within ten years of the expiry of another sentence for a similar offence. When sentencing under the recidivism provisions the court could impose a sentence of up to double the statutory maximum for the offence, and the applicant was sentenced to 12 years, above the 10 year statutory maximum. However, when he had been sentenced for the first offence, the law relating to recidivism only allowed an earlier offence to count for a period of five years following the expiry of the sentence, and so he claimed that the increase in penalty was retrospective and contrary to Art.7. The Grand Chamber found no violation of Art.7: there is no right to have a conviction disregarded after a number of years, and it was established French law that, when new recidivism provisions are introduced, it is sufficient for the second offence to be committed after the entry into force of the new law. The effect of the law was therefore foreseeable, with appropriate legal advice. The question here was one of successive statutes, not retroactive legislation.

16–97   This appears to be consistent with the Court of Appeal's decision in *R. v Offen*[273] that Art.7(1) was not engaged in the (now repealed) automatic life sentence provisions contained in s.2 of the Crime (Sentences) Act 1997.[274] The Court of Appeal held that the first offence did not fall to be considered at all because the sentence was imposed for the second offence and thus no issue of retrospectivity arose. Indeed, under those provisions (unlike French law in *Achour*) the maximum penalty for the offence remained unchanged.

16–98   The Drug Trafficking Offences Act 1986 (DTOA), challenged successfully under Art.7 in *Welch v United Kingdom*, was unusual in this country since its provisions for confiscation of assets were explicitly retrospective. However, Dr Thomas has argued that nonetheless the provisions challenged in *Welch* could have been held to comply with Art.7.[275] The purpose of the prohibition on retrospective increases in sentence is to ensure that people are not punished more heavily than they contemplated when they committed the crime. Dr Thomas argues that under the pre-1986 law the offender in *Welch* could easily have been ordered to pay a sum similar to the £60,000 he was ordered to pay under the confiscation order: he could have been fined that amount, for example, and the enforcement procedure for unpaid fines would be similar to those for confiscation orders. There are, however, some counter-arguments: it is questionable whether an Art.7 challenge to the law relied on by the sentencing court (confiscation) can be answered by reference to a law that the court did not rely upon (fine).

16–99   Retrospective confiscation provisions identical to s.38(4) of the DTOA have been included in subsequent confiscation legislation.[276] A challenge to the equivalent

---

[272] (2005) 41 E.H.R.R. 751.
[273] [2001] 1 W.L.R. 253.
[274] The same provisions were later re-enacted in s.109 of the 2000 Sentencing Act.
[275] [1996] Crim. L.R. 276–278.
[276] See, e.g. s.102 of the Criminal Justice Act 1988.

provisions in the Criminal Justice Act 1988 foundered on procedural grounds.[277] A challenge to s.38 of the DTOA was unsuccessful before the Commission in *Taylor v United Kingdom*,[278] where confiscation orders had been made in respect of drug trafficking in 1974–79 (for which he had been convicted previously without a confiscation order being made) and further drug trafficking in 1990–93. The Commission declared the application inadmissible, on the ground that Taylor must have known when committing the 1990–93 offences that he would be liable under the DTOA for confiscation of proceeds from the 1974–79 offences, and on the ground that he had admitted "benefiting" from drug trafficking during 1974–79. Whether challenges to the Proceeds of Crime Act 2002 will be successful, notably in relation to the making of confiscation orders on the basis that an offender has a "criminal lifestyle" (ss.6 and 75), remains to be seen.

In *RC v United Kingdom*[279] the applicant had been convicted on a charge of   **16–100** conspiracy to import cannabis. The conspiracy period as laid in the indictment began long before the coming into force of the DTOA, but ended shortly afterwards. There had been a number of substantive importations in furtherance of the conspiracy. The majority of these had occurred before the relevant date but one had occurred thereafter. The evidence showed conclusively that the applicant had withdrawn from the conspiracy before it came to an end, and the prosecution accepted that he had not participated in the importation which occurred after the DTOA had come into force. Relying on the rationale behind Art.7 the applicant argued that he should have been exposed only to the range of penalties which were available at the time of his last participation in the conspiracy. It should not, in other words, have been open to the state to impose a heavier penalty by reference to the criminal acts of others committed after he had withdrawn from the conspiracy. The Commission, by a majority, ruled the complaint inadmissible, on the unconvincing basis that the relevant dates should be determined by reference to the conspiracy period laid in the indictment:

> "[N]otwithstanding the specific acts in which the applicant participated, the offence in respect of which the applicant was charged and convicted was a conspiracy which existed between the dates of 1 January 1983 and 29 February 1988. The relevant provisions of the 1986 Act came into force during the subsistence of this conspiracy. The Commission finds therefore that since the conspiracy was in existence at and after the date on which the legislation came into force, it cannot be said that a heavier penalty was imposed on the applicant than the one which was applicable at the time."[280]

The principle in *Welch*, as developed in *Taylor*, may require courts to apply the   **16–101** stronger provisions of the Human Rights Act. When *Taylor*[281] had been before the Court of Appeal, in view of the fact that s.38(4) is unambiguous, it held that under the then rules governing the relevance of the Convention it had no power to apply *Welch*. Accordingly the Court of Appeal could not overturn a retrospective confiscation order, even if it had been imposed in clear breach of

---

[277] *Foxley v United Kingdom* 8 B.H.R.C. 571.
[278] [1998] E.H.R.L.R. 90.
[279] Unreported, April 6, 1994 (Application No.22668/93).
[280] *Cf.* the decisions relating to ongoing conspiracies in *Puhk v Estonia* and *Greenwood and Greenwood*, discussed in para.16–89 above.
[281] [1996] 2 Cr.App.R. 64.

Art.7.[282] However, the interpretation section of the Human Rights Act, s.3(1), requires courts to read and give effect to primary legislation in a way which is compatible with the Convention "so far as it is possible to do so." Given the strength of the interpretive obligation,[283] courts must now read and give effect to provisions of this kind by implying into the legislation a safeguard that it is not to be enforced if this would violate Art.7. Alternatively, the higher courts will be obliged to grant a declaration of incompatibility.

16–102   Article 7 is likely to have a continuing relevance largely because of the the increasing number of prosecutions in respect of offences committed many years previously, particularly sex offences. Where a person is prosecuted for an offence allegedly committed several years before, it will be important for both the prosecution and the defence to acquaint themselves with relevant maximum sentences then and now. It would be contrary to Art.7 for a person convicted of an offence committed many years previously to be liable now to a higher penalty than would have been lawful at the time of the offence. However, where the maximum sentence remains the same but wider sentencing powers have been introduced (such as imprisonment for public protection and extended sentences under ss.224–229 of the Criminal Justice Act 2003), it appears that no issue under Art.7 will arise. Even though the significance of an earlier conviction of a "specified offence" is now gar greater than it was when the conviction occurred—since under s.229 it raises a presumption of dangerousness, and becomes a gateway to a more severe sentence—the clear import of the decisions in *Offen* and in *Achour v France*[284] is that this does not violate Art.7 so long as sentence is passed for an offence committed after the new statutory regime came into force. The maximum penalty for the offence is unchanged by the IPP provisions but can be exceeded by the "extension period" (i.e. extended licence period) that constitutes part of an extended sentence.

I. Recommendation for Deportation

16–103   Section 3(6) of the Immigration Act 1971 provides that a non-British citizen who is convicted of an offence punishable with imprisonment is liable to deportation if he is recommended for deportation by the sentencing court.[285] Sections 6 and 7 of the Act provide supplementary procedural guarantees. Where a defendant has family ties in the United Kingdom, a recommendation for deportation may involve a violation of the right to family life in Art.8 of the Convention.

16–104   For many years the leading case was *Nazari*[286] where the Court of Appeal gave guidance on the exercise of the power to recommend deportation. For present purposes the relevant passage reads:

---

[282] In determining whether there has been a breach of the Convention, a court will now be obliged to take account of the distinctions drawn by the Commission in *Taylor* (above, n.85).

[283] *Ghaidan v Godin-Mendoza* [2004] 2 A.C. 557.

[284] See paras 16–96 to 16–97 above.

[285] See generally *Archbold* Ch.5.

[286] [1980] 1 W.L.R. 1366.

"The next matter [which courts should keep in mind] is the effect that an order recommending deportation will have upon others who are not before the court and who are innocent persons. This Court and all other courts would have no wish to break up families or impose hardship on innocent people."[287]

However, the Court of Appeal has now decided that a court does not have to **16–105** consider the defendant's Art.8 rights before making an order for deportation. In *Carmona*[288] Stanley Burnton J. held:

"It is only if there is any unjustified *interference* with the rights conferred by Article 8 that it is infringed. If the recommendation [for deportation] is not followed by the Home Secretary, and he decides before the expiry of the custodial sentence not to make a deportation order, on expiry of his custodial sentence his private and family life will resume and he will be free to live in his home. The Article 8 rights may be affected by the decision of the Home Secretary to deport the offender, but not by what is only a recommendation. Thus in, for example, *Samaroo and Sezek v Home Secretary* [2001] EWCA Civ 1139 the claimant had been convicted of a drug offence and sentenced to imprisonment; a recommendation for deportation had been made. The claimant's challenge on the grounds of an alleged infringement of his Article 8 rights was to the Home Secretary's order, not to the recommendation for deportation."

The last point seems inconclusive, because the question is whether the order could have been challenged at trial. An alternative view to that taken by the Court of Appeal would emphasise that the making of a deportation order by a court is an important step that has, in itself, an effect on a person's private and family life—even if it is not determinative—and that a court would be violating s.6 of the Human Rights Act 1998 if it made such an order in circumstances that were not consistent with the defendant's Art.8 rights. The House of Lords refused leave to appeal in *Carmona*, but it remains possible that legislation on the subject will be forthcoming.

The impact of Art.8 has been considered in various Strasbourg decisions: to **16–106** amount to a justifiable interference within Art.8(2), the interference must be justified by a "pressing social need" and, in particular, it must be proportionate to the legitimate aim pursued. In *Beldjoudi v France*[289] the applicant, an Algerian national, was a professional criminal who had been convicted of numerous criminal offences and had served a total of 10 years in prison (approximately half of his adult life). The French Government proposed his deportation to Algeria. In holding that the proposed deportation would violate Art.8, the Court emphasised that the applicant had lived in France all his life and had married a French woman. He had been educated in France and all of his close relatives had lived there for many years. He had had no contact with Algeria and did not speak Arabic. The Court held that in those circumstances the applicant's criminal record had to be balanced against the interference with his family life. The deportation would imperil his marriage and damage his relationship with his immediate family. As such, it could not be regarded as proportionate to the threat which he posed to public order in France.

---

[287] *ibid.*, at 95.
[288] [2006] EWCA Crim 508.
[289] (1992) 14 E.H.R.R. 801.

16–107   By contrast, in *Boughanemi v France*[290] the applicant was a Tunisian national convicted of living on the earnings of prostitution. He was sentenced to three years imprisonment and ordered to be deported. He had previous convictions for burglary, serious assault, and driving offences. The applicant, who was 36, had lived in France since the age of eight. His parents and 10 siblings lived in France, and he had a child by a relationship with a French woman (although he did not live with the mother). The Court accepted that the applicant's relationship with his child constituted family life despite the absence of cohabitation. Exceptional circumstances were required to break the parent/child tie so as to take the relationship outside the protection of Art.8. Nevertheless, the court held that the proposed deportation was proportionate to the aim of the prevention of disorder or crime. The Court attached particular significance to the seriousness of the applicant's offence, and to his criminal record. It also noted that he had retained some ties with Tunisia which went beyond the mere fact of his nationality. There was no evidence to suggest that he was unable to speak Arabic. Nevertheless, *Boughanemi* must be regarded as a borderline case, if only because the Commission had concluded by the clearest of majorities that the deportation did violate Art.8.

16–108   In *Bouchelkia v France*[291] the Court found no violation of Art.8 where an Algerian national who had lived in France since the age of two was deported following his conviction for rape. The fact that he was married to a French woman with whom he had a child was held insufficient to outweigh the seriousness of his offence. The applicant had maintained real links with Algeria, where a number of close family members still lived, and was able to speak Arabic.

16–109   A further important question about the application of Art.8 is whether a recommendation for deportation may be made solely on the basis of past offences, or whether it is necessary to show that the applicant is likely to re-offend. This arose in the case of *Samaroo and Samek*, cited in the passage from *Carmona* quoted in **16–105** above. It was accepted by the Secretary of State that the appellant, who had been convicted of serious drug trafficking offences, posed no risk of further re-offending. It was further accepted that he had very substantial and long standing ties to this country—he was married with a child and it was unlikely that they would follow him to Guyana—and no meaningful family ties in Guyana where he had not lived since 1983. The Secretary of State stated that he had given great weight to the compassionate factors weighing against deportation but these were outweighed by the importance he attached to the deterrent effect of deportation when combined with the crucial part the appellant played in the trafficking organisation. It is implicit in the Court of Appeal's judgment that the legitimate aim of preventing crime can be served where the offender himself poses no future risk and the purpose is one of general crime prevention by the use of measures intended to deter others. However, it must be said that the court took a very restrictive view of its role under the Human Rights Act in assessing the proportionality of a measure which interferes with Art.8 rights. The court reviewed the Strasbourg jurisprudence including *Boughanemi* and identified the relevant

---

[290] (1996) 22 E.H.R.R. 228.
[291] [1997] E.H.R.L.R. 433.

question as whether the decision struck a fair balance between the rights of the appellant and the interests of the wider community. It rejected the appellant's argument that this was the wrong approach because it was based upon the notion that as an international tribunal the Strasbourg Court should afford states a margin of appreciation. The Court of Appeal held that in assessing whether the Secretary of State had struck a fair balance it must recognise and allow him a discretionary area of judgment, which, in a case such as this, should be wide. This was because it is the Secretary of State and not the courts who has the expertise in judging how effective a deterrent is a policy of deportation. While the Court of Appeal stated that its assessment of whether the Secretary of State had struck a fair balance required it to review his decision with more intensity that under a traditional *Wednesbury* approach, the inevitable result of allowing such a wide area of discretion was an assessment of proportionality that was not discernibly different.[292] This decision, taken together with that in *Carmona*, suggests that it has become more difficult to challenge deportation orders since the Human Rights Act.

However, there has also been a change in the relevant EU law. Article 48 of the **16–110** EC Treaty remains, but Council Directive 64/221, as interpreted by the European Court of Justice in its well-known decision in *R. v Bouchereau*,[293] has been replaced since April 30th, 2006, by Directive 2004/38/EC. This applies to "measures concerning entry into their territory, issue or renewal of residence permits, or expulsion from their territory, taken by Member States on grounds of public policy, public security or public health." The new Directive confers enhanced residence rights on EU citizens within EU countries, and therefore restricts the use of deportation and any other forms of expulsion between EU Member States. Referring to the new Directive, the Court of Appeal in *Carmona* held that it "will have a significant effect on the exercise by the courts of the power to make a recommendation for deportation, since it would not be right to make a recommendation for deportation in circumstances where the Directive precludes actual deportation."[294] We noted in 16–105 above that the court was unwilling to apply similar reasoning to the application of Art.8 of the Convention.

---

[292] The Court of Appeal accepted that in many cases the starting point is not to assess whether a fair balance has been struck between the competing interests, but to ascertain whether a less restrictive measure was available. However, the court understandably found that this first question was not relevant here. This is because the sole issue that arose was whether the Secretary of State should exercise his power to deport. There were no other measures available.

[293] [1978] Q.B. 732; [1978] 2 W.L.R. 251.

[294] [2006] EWCA Crim 508, at [3].

CHAPTER 17

APPEALS

A. GENERAL PRINCIPLES

I. Application of Article 6 to Appeals

Article 6 of the Convention does not guarantee a right of appeal as a component **17–01** of the right to a fair hearing. But where domestic law provides for an appeal against conviction or sentence, whether on grounds of fact or law, then the appeal proceedings will be treated as an extension of the trial process, and accordingly will be subject to the requirements of Art.6. Thus in *Delcourt v Belgium* the Court held:

> "A criminal conviction is not really 'determined' as long as the verdict of acquittal or conviction has not become final. Criminal proceedings form an entity and must, in the ordinary way, terminate in an enforceable decision ... The Convention does not, it is true, compel the Contracting States to set up courts of appeal or of cassation. Nevertheless, a State which does institute such courts is required to ensure that persons amenable to the law shall enjoy before these courts the fundamental rights guaranteed in Article 6."[1]

Several subsequent decisions of the Court affirm the principle that, in applying **17–02** Art.6, "account must be taken of the entirety of the proceedings in the domestic legal order and the role of the appellate courts therein."[2] Article 6 applies not only to the determination of a substantive appeal, but also to proceedings for leave to appeal: the Court confirmed in *Monnell and Morris v United Kingdom*[3] that "applications for leave to appeal ... constituted part of the determination of the criminal charges."

It is safe to assume that Art.6 would also be held to apply on an appeal which has **17–03** been referred to the Court of Appeal by the Criminal Cases Review Commission,

---

[1] (1979–80) 1 E.H.R.R. 335 at para.25.
[2] *Helmers v Sweden* (1993) 15 E.H.R.R. 285 at para.31; to similar effect, see, e.g. *Edwards v United Kingdom* (1993) 15 E.H.R.R. 417, para.34.
[3] (1988) 10 E.H.R.R. 205 at para.54.

despite the fact that the criminal charge has been finally "determined", and the conviction and sentence have acquired the quality of *res judicata*. In *Callaghan and others v United Kingdom*[4] the Commission held that Art.6 was applicable to a Home Secretary's reference to the Court of Appeal under s.17 of the Criminal Appeal Act 1968 (prior to its amendment). The Commission recognised that the procedure was not part of the ordinary appeals process and took place long after the criminal proceedings had finally been determined. Nevertheless:

> "the proceedings on the Secretary of State's reference had all the features of an appeal against conviction, and could have resulted in the applicants being found not guilty or . . . their convictions being upheld. They must therefore, in the Commission's view, be regarded as having the effect of determining, or re-determining, the charges against the applicants."

The Commission's approach was confirmed by the court in *IJL, GMR and AKP v United Kingdom*[5] where, in assessing a complaint that proceedings had extended beyond a reasonable time for the purposes of Art.6(1), the Court aggregated the time taken to hear and dispose of the original prosecution and appeal with the time taken to dispose of a further appeal following a reference by the Home Secretary.[6]

17–04 In the White Paper *Rights Brought Home*, published in October 1997, the Government indicated its intention to sign, ratify and incorporate Protocol 7 to the Convention once it had rectified some inconsistencies in the law relating to property rights of spouses which would also be affected.[7] At the time of writing, more than nine years on, the Government has signed but still not ratified the Protocol, but has again reiterated its intention to do so.[8] Article 2 of Protocol 7 provides:

> "2(1) Everyone convicted of a criminal offence by a tribunal shall have the right to have his conviction or sentence reviewed by a higher tribunal. The exercise of this right, including the grounds on which it may be exercised, shall be governed by law.
>
> (2) This right may be subject to exceptions in regard to offences of a minor character, as prescribed by law, or in cases in which the person concerned was tried in the first instance by the highest tribunal or was convicted following an appeal against acquittal."

17–05 The terms of Protocol 7 give rise to two practical points. First, the term "criminal offence" has the same extended definition here as the term "criminal charge" in

---

[4] (1989) 60 D.R. 296. *Callaghan* must be taken to have overruled the much earlier decision in *X v Austria* (1962) 9 E.H.R.R. CD 17.

[5] [2001] Crim.L.R. 133.

[6] See para.14–44 above.

[7] Cm 3782, at para.4.15.

[8] Department for Constitutional Affairs, Report on the UK Government's Inter-Departmental Review of the UK's Position under various International Human Rights Instruments, July 2004, Appendix 4.

Art.6.[9] It follows that the right of appeal in Art.2 of Protocol 7 may apply to proceedings which are not currently defined as "criminal" in domestic law. Secondly, the additional guarantees of Protocol 7 cannot be read as intended in any way to limit the applicability or the requirements of Art.6 in appellate proceedings. This is expressly confirmed in the Explanatory Report to Protocol 7, cited with approval by the court in *Ekbatani v Sweden*.[10]

II. Retrospective Application of the Human Rights Act

Prior to the House of Lords decision in *Lambert*[11] the Court of Appeal had held   **17–06** on a number of occasions that the Act would operate retrospectively on appeal, requiring the Court to approach the safety of a conviction as if the Act had been in force at the time of the trial.[12] The mounting judicial concern which arose from those decisions was put to rest in *Lambert*, where a majority of the House of Lords held that the Act did not permit an appellant to mount a retrospective challenge on appeal to the decision of a trial court which was lawful at the time when it was made. The speeches of the majority reflect different processes of reasoning on the point. Lord Hope, in particular, held that where the challenge was directed not to an act of the trial court, but to an act of the prosecuting authority, the Act would operate retrospectively on appeal. He thus distinguished *Lambert*, which was a challenge to the way in which the judge had directed the jury on a reverse onus clause, from *Kebilene*,[13] which was a challenge to the decision of the DPP to consent to a prosecution for an offence which contained such a clause. The issue was considered again by the House of Lords in *Kansal (No.2)*,[14] where a majority of their Lordships held that the decision on retrospectivity in *Lambert* was wrong, but nonetheless should be followed out of deference to judicial precedent.[15]

Some commentators have suggested that this absolutist stance can occasionally contribute to surprising results. In *Lyons and others*,[16] the appellants contended that their convictions were unsafe as their answers in interview had been given under threat of criminal penalty. The European Court had ruled that the use of such evidence infringed their right to a fair trial.[17] Notwithstanding the fact that Parliament had acknowledged the finding of a breach of Art.6 by the Court and redrafted the offending statute, the effect of the decisions of the majority in *Lambert* and *Kansal* was to bar any submission that a serious breach of Art.6 could be invoked retrospectively.

---

[9] *Gradinger v Austria*, October 23, 1995, (unreported).
[10] (1991) 13 E.H.R.R. 504 at para.26.
[11] [2002] 2 A.C. 545.
[12] *R. v Lambert and Ali* [2001] 2 W.L.R. 211; *R. v Benjafield and ors.* [2003] 1 A.C. 1099; *R. v Kansal* [2001] 3 W.L.R. 1562.
[13] [2000] 2 A.C. 326 at 362.
[14] [2002] 2 A.C. 69.
[15] See also *R. v Benjafield* [2003] 1 A.C. 1099.
[16] [2003] 1 A.C. 976.
[17] *Kansal v United Kingdom* (2004) 39 E.H.R.R. 645.
5 Youth Justice and Criminal Evidence Act 1999 s.59, Sch.3.

B. THE REQUIREMENTS OF ARTICLE 6

I. The General Position

17–07 The requirements of fairness will not necessarily be the same on appeal as they would be at first instance. In *Monnell and Morris v United Kingdom*[18] the Court pointed out that the manner of application of Art.6 to appellate proceedings depends upon the special features of the proceedings involved, seen in their domestic law context, and taking account of the role and functions of the appeal court. In order to determine whether the requirements of Art.6 were met, the Court held that it was necessary to consider matters such as;

— the significance of appellate procedure in the context of the criminal proceedings as a whole;

— the scope of the powers of the Court of Appeal; and

— the manner in which the appellant's interests were presented and protected in practice.

It follows that the guarantees of Art.6 require adaptation in the context of appeal proceedings, particularly where the appeal concerns only a point of law.

17–08 On the other hand, in *Ekbatani v Sweden*[19] the Court held that where an appellate court is called upon to examine the facts of the case, and to make an assessment of the probative weight of evidence adduced by the prosecution, the requirements of fairness are more akin to those of a criminal trial. In view of the test under the Criminal Appeal Act, s.2, as amended—which requires the court to allow an appeal only if it considers that the conviction is "unsafe"—there is an argument that all criminal appeals involve some consideration of the evidence.[20]

II. The right to free legal representation and a public hearing in the presence of the accused

17–09 As a general rule Art.6(1) and Art.6(3)(c), taken together, require a public hearing at which the accused person is entitled to be present, and to be legally represented, with legal aid if necessary. The Court has insisted in several cases that it is "of crucial importance for the fairness of the criminal justice system that the accused be adequately defended, both at first instance and on appeal".[21] The application of these general principles to appeal proceedings in the United Kingdom has been considered by the Court in four cases.

---

[18] (1988) 10 E.H.R.R. 205.
[19] (1991) 13 E.H.R.R. 504.
[20] See, for example *R. v Craven, The Times*, February 2, 2001, where the court found irregularities at trial but upheld the conviction in the light of fresh DNA evidence.
[21] *Lala v Netherlands* (1994) 18 E.H.R.R. 586 at para.33; *Pelladoah v Netherlands* (1995) 19 E.H.R.R. 81 at para.40.

In *Monnell and Morris v United Kingdom*[22] the Court examined the procedure   **17–10**
whereby the Court of Appeal may determine an application for leave to appeal
against conviction "on the papers", without the accused being present or represented by counsel, and without hearing oral argument on the merits of the appeal.
The Court found that this procedure was compatible with Art.6, noting that on an
application for leave, the Court of Appeal did not re-hear the facts of the case,
and no witnesses were called, even where the grounds involved mixed questions
of law and fact. The sole issue before the Court of Appeal was whether the
applicant had demonstrated arguable grounds which would justify a hearing on
the merits. In the Court's view, the limited nature of this issue did not, in itself,
call for oral argument at a public hearing in the presence of the applicants. The
Court attached importance to the fact that the prosecution were unrepresented;
that the applicants had received legally aided advice on appeal from counsel; and
that the applicants had had the opportunity of submitting written grounds of their
own with argument in support. The Court went on:

> "Under paragraph 3(c) of Article 6, they were guaranteed the right to be given legal
> assistance free only so far as the interests of justice so required. The interests of justice
> cannot, however, be taken to require an automatic grant of legal aid whenever a
> convicted person, with no objective likelihood of success, wishes to appeal after having
> received a fair trial at first instance in accordance with Article 6. Each applicant, it is
> to be noted, benefited from free legal assistance both at his trial and in being advised
> as to whether he had any arguable grounds of appeal. In the Court's view, the issue to
> be decided in relation to section 29(1) of the Criminal Appeal Act 1968 did not call, as
> a matter of fairness, for oral submissions on behalf of the applicants in addition to the
> written submissions and material already before the Court of Appeal."[23]

This decision has been criticised, and some of the Court's subsequent judgments
appear to have taken a stricter line.

In *Granger v United Kingdom*,[24] a Scottish case, the Court held that a refusal of   **17–11**
legal aid for the applicant's appeal against a conviction for perjury violated Art.6.
Under Scots law there was, at that time, no requirement for leave to appeal. But
the decision as to whether legal aid should be granted lay with the Legal Aid
Committee of the Scottish Law Society, which had to decide whether an applicant for legal aid had substantial grounds for appealing, and whether it was in the
interests of justice that s/he be granted legal aid. The Committee could therefore
refuse legal aid on the ground that the appeal was unmeritorious. Following an
unfavourable advice from counsel, legal aid was refused. The applicant appeared
at the hearing in person and read out a statement prepared by his solicitor. The
Court noted that Art.6(3)(c) only guarantees a right to legal aid where the
interests of justice require this. However, the interests of justice criterion must be
assessed in the light of all the circumstances of the case. The applicant was
serving a five year prison sentence, so that there was no doubt about the
importance of what was at stake for him. The Court of Appeal had been
addressed at length by the Solicitor General who appeared for the Crown. One of

---

[22] (1988) 10 E.H.R.R. 205.
[23] *ibid.*, at para.67.
[24] (1990) 12 E.H.R.R. 469 at paras 42–48.

the issues which arose was of considerable complexity, but the applicant was not in a position to understand the prepared statement he read out. He could neither understand nor reply to the arguments against him, nor could he answer questions from the bench. It was therefore held that the proceedings had breached Art.6, irrespective of the merits of the applicant's case.

17–12 In *Maxwell v United Kingdom*[25] and *Boner v United Kingdom*,[26] two further Scottish cases, the Court unanimously found a violation of Art.6 despite concluding that the legal issues in the appeal were straightforward. Here again, legal aid had been refused on the ground that the appeal was without merit. In the light of *Granger*, the Government had introduced a new provision in Scotland which enabled the Court of Appeal to grant legal aid if, on examination, it considered that there was a point of substance in the appeal. This was held to be insufficient to meet the requirements of Art.6. The Court accepted that the legal issues were not complex, that no point of substance had arisen in the appeal, and that prosecution counsel had not been called upon to address the Court of Appeal. The Court nevertheless held that in the absence of legal representation the applicants had been unable to address the court on the issues raised in the appeal and thus had been deprived of the opportunity to defend themselves effectively.[27]

17–13 One interpretation of these cases is that the right to be present and represented by counsel applies only once leave to appeal has been granted. However, the Court has offered a different rationale. In *Ekbatani v Sweden*[28] the Court suggested that the decisive consideration in *Monnell and Morris* was not that the proceedings in that case had involved applications for leave (as distinct from a full appeal) but that the appeals were concerned with questions of law alone and not with questions of fact. In *Ekbatani*, the applicant's appeal against conviction was determined on written submissions made by the prosecutor and the defence. The court noted that the "equality of arms" principle in Art.6 had been maintained, but emphasised that this was "only one feature of the wider concept of a fair trial in criminal proceedings". The Swedish appellate court in *Ekbatani* had had the function of considering both fact and law, and "had to make a full assessment of the applicant's guilt or innocence". Accordingly, in the absence of a public and adversarial procedure, there had been a violation of Art.6.

17–14 The Court held that in order to justify a departure from the requirement of a public hearing in the presence of the accused there had to be some "special feature" of the appeal proceedings. It explained that the "underlying reason" for the finding of no violation in *Monnell and Morris* "was that the court concerned did not have the task of establishing the facts of the case, but only of interpreting

---

[25] (1995) 19 E.H.R.R. 97.
[26] (1995) 19 E.H.R.R. 246.
[27] In reaching a similar conclusion, the courts have not always found it necessary to invoke Art.6. In *Fa'Afete Taito v the Queen* [2002] UKPC 15 the Privy Council held the appellate arrangements then in force in New Zealand, which effectively barred the appellants from being heard on appeal once their applications for legal aid had been dismissed on paper, were "contrary to fundamental conceptions of fairness and justice" (*per* Lord Steyn).
[28] (1991) 13 E.H.R.R. 504 at paras 25–33.

the legal rules involved."[29] It is fair to say that the Court's judgment in *Monnell and Morris* does not appear to attach the same degree of importance to this aspect of the case as the Court subsequently suggested it had in *Ekbatani*, and therefore that the latter decision may demonstrate a change of approach. However, in *Belziuk v Poland*[30] the Court held that the personal attendance of the accused does not necessarily take on the same significance for an appeal hearing, and Art.6 does not always entail the right to a public hearing or the right to be present in person, even when the appellate court has full jurisdiction to review the case on questions of both fact and law.[31] Moreover, in the case of *Cookson v United Kingdom*,[32] the Court dismissed an argument that the refusal of legal aid for a renewed application for leave to appeal was incompatible with Art.6.

The *Cookson* approach has been affirmed by the domestic courts, most recently in *R. v Oates*,[33] where it was submitted again that a refusal of legal aid to cover a renewed application for leave to appeal against conviction was incompatible with Art.6. Having considered the Convention authorities, the Court of Appeal applied *Monnell and Morris*, holding that the principle that an appellant should be legally represented on an appeal did not extend to an application for leave. The Court of Appeal noted that the appellant had received legal aid to cover representation at trial, the provision of advice by counsel following conviction, and the drafting of grounds of appeal. In addition, the grounds in that case involved questions of law which could fairly be considered by the full court on the basis of written submissions alone.

What are the implications of these decisions for the application of the Human Rights Act? Five conclusions may be suggested: **17–15**

— A consideration of an application for leave on the papers by the single judge is unlikely to raise a serious issue under Art.6 since the application can be renewed to the full court.

— The dismissal of an application for leave by the full court in the non-counsel list *may* raise an issue under Art.6 in an exceptional case if the case is a complex one, or if it involves a detailed consideration of the evidence. However, it would be necessary for the applicant to persuade the court to depart from *Monnell and Morris*, or to distinguish it by pointing to a real unfairness on the facts of the case.

— Where an oral hearing for leave is held, there *may* be an argument for the presence of the accused (despite the presumption in s.22(2) of the 1968 Act) and for the grant of legal aid if the accused would otherwise be unrepresented. As regards legal aid, however, it should be noted that

---

[29] *ibid.*, para.31.
[30] (2000) 30 E.H.R.R. 614.
[31] See also *Kucera v Austria* (2002) (Application No.40072/98) where the Court referred to its "constant case-law" that a court of second instance should order that an accused be brought before it "if his personal presence appears necessary in the interest of justice" (Kremzow judgment, op. cit., para.68; *Cooke v Austria*, op. cit., para.43; *Pobornikoff v Austria*, No.28501/95, para.32, 3.10.2000).
[32] Decision on admissibility, May 4, 2001, Application No.56842/00.
[33] [2002] EWCA Crim 1071.

Art.6(3)(c) guarantees a right to legal representation and not a right to free legal aid as such. If counsel in fact appears on a *pro bono* basis on an application for leave, the requirements of Art.6(3)(c) will have been met in that case. Article 6 does not assist counsel who has appeared *pro bono* to argue that the court is obliged to grant retrospective legal aid for the hearing.

— On a full hearing of an appeal the appellant is generally entitled to be present and to be represented on legal aid (subject to means) in cases of any seriousness.

— Where an appeal involves the consideration of fresh evidence called by either side, compliance with Art.6 will generally require the provision of safeguards akin to those required in a criminal trial.

III. Reasons in appeal proceedings

17–16   It is a general principle of Art.6(1) that a court (including an appellate court) must give reasons for its decision. All courts must "indicate with sufficient clarity the grounds on which they based their decision."[34] The purpose of this requirement is partly to enable the unsuccessful litigant to exercise any (further) right of appeal, and partly to maintain public confidence in the administration of justice.

17–17   The practice of the Court of Appeal in this respect is fully in compliance with Art.6. Reasons are given not only for the dismissal of a substantive appeal, but also for a refusal of leave. However, in those cases where the Court of Appeal has certified a point of public importance but has refused leave to appeal to the House of Lords, the position is different. It is not the usual practice of the Appellate Committee of the House of Lords to give reasons when refusing an application for leave to appeal. Similarly, it is common practice for courts of cassation in some European jurisdictions to give the briefest of reasons for refusing leave to appeal. In some instances, the Commission has regarded as acceptable reasoning which does little more than refer to the applicable provision under which the appeal was refused.[35] As the Commission has put it:

> "where a supreme court refuses to accept a case on the basis that the legal grounds for such a case are not made out, very limited reasoning may satisfy the requirements of Article 6 of the Convention (see, for example, *Muller-Eberstein v Germany*[36] concerning the Federal Constitutional Court of Germany, which rejects decisions in summary proceedings by reference to the statutory provisions governing the Federal Constitutional Court)."[37]

17–18   Although the House of Lords' current practice has not been significantly affected by the Human Rights Act, it may, exceptionally, be arguable that reasons are

---

[34] *Hadjianatassiou v Greece* (1993) 16 E.H.R.R. 219 at para.33.
[35] Application 9223/80 October 15, 1981 (unpublished); Application No.9982/82 May 18, 1984 (unpublished).
[36] Application No.29752/96, November 27, 1996 (unpublished).
[37] *Webb v United Kingdom* (1997) 24 E.H.R.R. CD 73 at 74.

required for a refusal of leave on the facts of a particular case. Thus the Court has held that the extent of the duty to give reasons varies according to the nature of the decision in issue and the applicable substantive law and procedure, and that "the question whether a court has failed to fulfil the obligation to state reasons ... can only be determined in the light of the circumstances of the case."[38]

In *Webb v United Kingdom*[39] the applicant complained that Privy Council had **17–19** failed to give reasons for refusing an application for special leave to appeal against her conviction in Bermuda on drug trafficking charges. The Commission declared the application inadmissible. It noted that appeal to the Privy Council was limited to points of "great and general importance" or a "grave injustice", and held that in these circumstances very limited reasoning may satisfy the requirements of Art.6 since "it must be apparent to litigants who have been refused leave that they have failed to satisfy the Privy Council that their case involves [such a point]". Where, on the other hand, an appeal is allowed, the appellant is ordinarily entitled to a detailed explanation of why the conviction has been quashed. However, in *R. v Guney*[40] the Court of Appeal held that: "as was recognised by this court in *Doubtfire* [2001] Crim.L.R. 813, there can be cases where the balance of conflicting interests comes down in favour of revealing very little of the reasoning which has persuaded this court to allow an appeal ... "

IV. Loss of Time and other Procedural Sanctions on Appeal

Under s.29(1) of the Criminal Appeal Act 1968 the Court of Appeal may, if it **17–20** considers that an appeal is without merit, direct that time served between the imposition of the sentence and the disposal of the appeal should not count towards sentence. The circumstances in which such an order may be made are set out in a *Practice Direction*.[41]

The most surprising aspect of the Court's decision in *Monnell and Morris v* **17–21** *United Kingdom*[42] was its conclusion that a loss of time order made in that case, following an application for leave to appeal which had been dismissed in the non-counsel list, was compatible both with Art.5 and with Art.6. The Court recognised that the order effectively imposed an additional period of imprisonment on the applicants, and that it was ordered for reasons unconnected with the facts of the offence or with the character or antecedents of the applicants. Nevertheless, the Court held that the order for loss of time was lawful under Art.5(1)(a), as being detention after conviction by a competent court. Although it was not treated under domestic law as part of the sentence, it did form a component part of the period of detention which resulted from the applicants' conviction. The Court therefore found a sufficient connection between the conviction and the loss of time to prevent the detention from being characterised as "arbitrary". The

---

[38] *Ruiz Torija v Spain* (1995) 19 E.H.R.R. 553 at para.29.
[39] (1997) 24 E.H.R.R. CD 73.
[40] [2003] EWCA Crim 1502.
[41] *Practice Direction (Criminal Proceedings: Consolidation)* [2002] 1 W.L.R. 2870, para. II.16.1.
[42] (1988) 10 E.H.R.R. 205.

Court reasoned that the power to make the order, which had the express policy of deterring unmeritorious appeals, was part of the domestic machinery for ensuring that criminal proceedings were concluded within a reasonable time, as required by Art.6(1).

17–22 Moreover, the fact that the Court of Appeal had power to (and did) make such an order was held to be insufficient to tip the balance in favour of a requirement for legal representation for the application for leave. The applicants had been given the benefit of free legal advice after conviction about the prospect of an appeal, and that advice has been negative. The applicants were able to present written grounds of appeal to the court, which they did. No question of inequality of arms arose, because the Crown was not represented on the appeal either. The Court concluded that "the interests of justice and fairness" were met by the applicants' ability to make written submissions, and that, despite the significant period of extra detention ordered by the court, no oral hearing was necessary to comply with Arts 5 and 6.[43] The renewed application for leave in *Monnell and Morris* was made contrary to the advice of counsel. The fact that grounds have been settled (or even argued) by counsel is not, of itself, an absolute bar to a loss of time order, although the Court of Appeal would doubtless hesitate long and hard before making an order in such circumstances. It is certainly difficult to see how such an order could be compatible with the right to counsel or with the duty to attach "appropriate weight" to legal advice.[44] More generally, however, it is open to doubt whether this aspect of the decision in *Monnell and Morris* is consistent with the court's subsequent decision in *Omar v France*.[45]

17–23 Where domestic law goes further, and provides for an appeal to be disallowed in response to unacceptable conduct by the would-be appellant, the Court has held that this may contravene Art.6. Thus in *Poitrimol v France*[46] the French appellate courts had refused to allow the applicant's appeals because he had absconded to another country: his trial had been conducted *in absentia*, but the Cour de Cassation refused to allow his appeal to be heard in that way or to allow him to be legally represented at such hearings. The Court held that this denial was disproportionate, having regard to the importance of the rights of the defence. In *Omar v France*[47] the Cour de Cassation had declared the applicants' appeal on points of law inadmissible, on the ground that they had failed to comply with warrants for their arrest, in accordance with the order made by the trial court. The Court held that to compel a person to subject himself to deprivation of liberty before an appeal on a point of law can be heard is incompatible with Art.6:

> "This impairs the very essence of the right of appeal, by imposing a disproportionate burden on the appellant, thus upsetting the fair balance that must be struck between the legitimate concern to ensure that judicial decisions are enforced, on the one hand, and the right of access to the Court of Cassation and the exercise of the rights of the defence on the other."[48]

---

[43] *ibid.*, paras 62–68.
[44] *Condron and Condron v United Kingdom* (2001) 31 E.H.R.R. 1.
[45] See para.16–55 above and para.17–23 below.
[46] (1994) 18 E.H.R.R. 130.
[47] (2000) 29 E.H.R.R. 210.
[48] *ibid.*, para.40.

In *R. v Charles, R. v Tucker*[49] the Court of Appeal held that the Registrar of Criminal Appeals should no longer treat an application for leave to appeal on behalf of a defendant who has absconded as ineffective, considering the practice to be potentially incompatible with Art.6(1) in the light of the judgment in *Omar*. In *Vacher v France*[50] the Court emphasised that it was the duty of the state to ensure that an appellant was notified of time limits and other procedural restrictions, in order to ensure his effective participation in an appeal.[51]

V. Appeals and the Reasonable Time Guarantee

Since the Art.6 guarantee of fair trial applies to the proceedings as a whole, from **17–24** arrest through to the final determination of any appeal, it follows that appeals should be heard within a reasonable time. There is authority for the proposition that this requirement applies less strictly to a constitutional court or other final court of appeal. The constitutional role of such a court justifies a more flexible approach, since it is reasonable for a final appellate court to give priority to considerations other than "the mere chronological order in which cases are entered on the list, such as the nature of a case and its importance in political and social terms."[52] Whilst this principle would undoubtedly apply to the House of Lords, the Court of Appeal is expected to operate within tighter time constraints, as appears from *Howarth v United Kingdom*.[53] Following his conviction after a lengthy fraud trial, the applicant lodged his notice of appeal against conviction in March 1995. In April 1995 the Attorney General made a reference to the Court of Appeal for review of his sentence, a community service order. Perfected grounds of appeal were lodged in September 1995, but the Court of Appeal did not hear his appeal until March 1997, dealing with the Attorney General's reference the following day. In view of the unexplained delay of 19 months, in which there was no judicial activity, the Strasbourg Court held that the applicant's right to a hearing "within a reasonable time" had been breached, and thus that there had been a violation of Art.6(1). The time taken to deal with the Attorney General's reference (which ordered him to serve a sentence of 20 months imprisonment) was the subject of unreasonable delay; that depended on the disposal of the applicant's appeal against conviction; and that was complicated by the complexity of the fraud trial and the appeals of co-defendants. However, the Court found "no convincing reasons" for the delays. Furthermore, in the case of *Weir*[54] the House of Lords refused an application by the prosecution for leave to appeal out of time on the grounds that the accused is entitled to know whether a decision favourable to him is to be challenged or not within a reasonable time.[55]

---

[49] *The Times*, February 20, 2001.

[50] (1996) 24 E.H.R.R. 482.

[51] See also *Khalfaoui v France* (2001) 31 E.H.R.R. 42, applied in *Papon v France* Application 54210/00, (July 25, 2002) where it was held that the requirement on the applicant to surrender to custody before his appeal was disproportionate.

[52] *Sussmann v Germany* (1998) 25 E.H.R.R. 64 at paras 55–60.

[53] [2001] Crim.L.R. 229; see also *Bunkate v Netherlands* (1995) 19 E.H.R.R. 477.

[54] [2001] 1 W.L.R. 421.

[55] For the most recent domestic consideration of the reasonable time requirement in Art.6(1), not limited to delay post conviction, see *Attorney-General's Reference (No.2 of 2001)* [2004] 2 A.C. 72 and *R. v S* 170 JP 434; [2006] All E.R. (D) 73 (CA).

VI. Substituted Verdicts

By s.3 of the Criminal Appeal Act 1968, the Court of Appeal may, instead of allowing or dismissing an appeal, substitute a verdict of guilty of another offence provided it is an offence of which the jury could, on the indictment, have found the accused guilty. We have already seen that the availability of lesser alternative verdicts at trial has been held compatible with the right in Art.6(3)(a) to be informed promptly and in detail of the nature and cause of the accusation.[56] There is no obvious reason why the same principle should not apply on appeal, although it will obviously be important to ensure that the appellant has had an adequate opportunity to meet the allegation. In *Pélissier v France*,[57] for example, the Court found a violation of Art.6 where a conviction for aiding and abetting an offence had been substituted on the applicant's appeal against his conviction as a principal. On the facts, the Court held that the applicant had not been given an effective opportunity to deal with what was, in effect, a new allegation. The risk of a similar violation occurring in this jurisdiction is substantially mitigated by the Court of Appeal's practice. Under s.3 the court may only substitute a verdict where the ingredients of the lesser offence are, in law, subsumed within those of the offence of which the appellant was convicted: it is not sufficient that the evidence adduced at trial could have supported a conviction for a different offence in law.[58] Moreover, the section provides that the court must, before exercising its powers, first conclude that from their verdict the jury must have been satisfied of the facts upon which the substitute verdict depends. The court will not generally exercise its powers if the jury received an inadequate direction on the alternative charge, or if the conduct of the defence could have been materially affected if the appellant had been charged with the alternative.[59]

C. UNFAIR TRIALS AND UNSAFE CONVICTIONS

17–25　Is a conviction which has been obtained in breach of a Convention right, and especially Art.6, for that reason alone to be regarded as "unsafe", within the meaning of s.2 of the Criminal Appeal Act 1968 as amended? The term "unsafe" must, like any other statutory provision, be read in a way which conforms with Convention rights, so far as it is possible to do so.[60] The question is thus whether and in what circumstances the fact that a trial was "unfair" for the purposes of Art.6 means that the resulting conviction must be regarded as "unsafe" within the meaning of s.2 of the 1968 Act, when that provision is read with the benefit of s.2 of the Human Rights Act 1998.

I. Reinterpreting the Criminal Appeal Act

17–26　In many European jurisdictions, there are two ways in which a defendant can challenge his conviction: appeal (which goes to the *correctness* of the verdict)

---

[56] Para.14–162 above.
[57] (2000) 30 E.H.R.R. 715.
[58] *R. v Cooke* [1997] Crim.L.R. 436 (CA).
[59] *R. v Caslin* 45 Cr.App.R. 47 (CA); *R. v Graham and ors.* [1997] 1 Cr.App.R. 302 (CA).
[60] Human Rights Act 1998, s.3.

and cassation (which goes to the *legality* of the proceedings which resulted in the conviction). Under the pre-1995 formulation of s.2, it could be said that the Court of Appeal was exercising both jurisdictions simultaneously. A conviction could be quashed for misdirection or for error of law, but subject to the application of the proviso. Then the Criminal Appeal Act 1995 replaced the old phrase "unsafe or unsatisfactory" with the single word "unsafe."

The Court of Appeal initially inclined to the view that the 1995 Act had, in effect, **17–27** abolished the court's jurisdiction to quash a conviction simply on the ground that it was procedurally defective or otherwise tainted with unfairness, and that the sole question for the court was whether the conviction was "safe".[61] However, in subsequent decisions the court began to move away from this stance,[62] and the judgment of Lord Woolf C.J. in *Togher, Doran and Parsons*[63] effectively overrules the narrower view and restores the pre-1995 position.

Although many believed that the narrower view of the term "unsafe" was wrong **17–28** as an interpretation of the 1995 Act,[64] the coming into force of the Human Rights Act 1998 and the Strasbourg decision in *Condron and Condron v United Kingdom*[65] made it necessary for the Court of Appeal to review its approach urgently after October 2, 2000. One of the arguments for the Government in *Condron* was that the applicants had received a fair trial because, whatever errors might have been made by the trial judge, the Court of Appeal had been able to review matters and to ensure overall fairness. The response of the Strasbourg Court was this:

> "The Court must also have regard to the fact that the Court of Appeal was concerned with the safety of the applicants' conviction, not whether they had in the circumstances received a fair trial. In the Court's opinion, the question whether or not the rights of the defence guaranteed to an accused under Article 6 of the Convention were secured in any given case cannot be assimilated to a finding that his conviction was safe in the absence of any enquiry into the issue of fairness."[66]

This decision therefore recognised that, at that time, it was possible for the English Court of Appeal to uphold a conviction as safe even if it was satisfied that the trial had been unfair. The Court did not consider that this amounted to an adequate remedy for a serious misdirection concerning the adverse inferences which could be drawn from the appellants' silence at interview. The Court of Appeal had acknowledged the misdirection, but had dismissed the appeal on the ground that there was other compelling evidence of guilt. In the Court's view, this was no answer to the complaint of a breach of Art.6. In the absence of a reasoned judgment from the jury the Court of Appeal had no means of knowing

---

[61] *R. v Chalkley and Jefferies* [1998] 2 Cr.App.R. 79 (CA).

[62] See, for example, *Mullen* [2000] Q.B. 520, and the opinion of Lord Steyn in *Allie Mohamed v The State* [1999] 2 A.C. 111 that "it is important to bear in mind the nature of the particular constitutional breach. For example, a breach of the defendant's constitutional right to a fair trial must inevitably result in a conviction being quashed."

[63] [2001] Crim.L.R. 124.

[64] See, e.g. Sir John Smith, "The Criminal Appeal Act 1995" [1995] Crim.L.R. 920, and his note on *Chalkley and Jeffries* at [1999] Crim.L.R. 215.

[65] [2000] Crim.L.R. 677.

[66] *ibid.*, at para.65.

how significant a role the applicants' silence had played in the jury's decision to convict them, and was therefore driven to speculate about the jury's process of reasoning.

Similar reservations about the role of the Court of Appeal were voiced in *Rowe and Davis v United Kingdom*,[67] where the Court suggested that there was a risk of the Court of Appeal being unconsciously influenced by a jury's guilty verdict into underestimating the significance of fresh evidence. That case, it will be recalled, turned on the non-disclosure of relevant evidence on public interest immunity grounds. In *Edwards v United Kingdom*[68] the Court had previously held that where relevant evidence was wrongly withheld at trial, its disclosure prior to an appeal, and the subsequent consideration by the Court of Appeal of its impact on the safety of the conviction, was capable of curing the defect which had arisen at first instance. The government argued that the same principle should apply where there had been an *ex parte* public interest immunity hearing before the Court of Appeal. The Court disagreed;

"[T]he Court does not consider that this procedure before the appeal court was sufficient to remedy the unfairness caused at the trial by the absence of any scrutiny of the withheld information by the trial judge. Unlike the latter, who saw the witnesses give their testimony and was fully versed in all the evidence and issues in the case, the judges in the Court of Appeal were dependent for their understanding of the possible relevance of the undisclosed material on transcripts of the Crown Court hearings and on the account of the issues given to them by prosecuting counsel. In addition, the first instance judge would have been in a position to monitor the need for disclosure throughout the trial, assessing the importance of the undisclosed evidence at a stage when new issues were emerging, when it might have been possible through cross-examination seriously to undermine the credibility of key witnesses and when the defence case was still open to take a number of different directions or emphases. In contrast, the Court of Appeal was obliged to carry out its appraisal *ex post facto* and may even, to a certain extent, have unconsciously been influenced by the jury's verdict of guilty into underestimating the significance of the undisclosed evidence."

17–29 The question came before the Court of Appeal in *Davis, Johnson and Rowe*.[69] The Court of Appeal accepted that the Strasbourg Court's determination was obviously relevant, and that it would be difficult to go behind that ruling "without doing serious injury to the intent and purpose" of the Human Rights Act, but pointed out that English courts are bound only to take account of, and not strictly to follow, judgments from Strasbourg:

"We are required to review the safety of convictions resulting from a trial which the ECHR has adjudged to have been unfair. It may be the first case of its kind; it certainly will not be the last. How should we proceed? . . . We see no difficulty in giving effect to the 'right to a fair trial' when discharging our duty to consider the safety of a conviction . . . The Court is concerned with the safety of a conviction. A conviction can never be safe is there is doubt about guilt. However, the converse is not true. A conviction may be unsafe even where there is no doubt about guilt but the trial process has been 'vitiated by serious unfairness or significant legal misdirection' . . . Usually,

---

[67] (2000) 30 E.H.R.R. 1. See para.14–120 above.
[68] (1992) 15 E.H.R.R. 417. See para.14–118 *et seq*. above.
[69] (2001) 1 Cr.App.R. 115.

it will be sufficient for the court to apply the test in *Stirland*[70] which, as adapted ...
might read: 'Assuming the wrong decision on law or the irregularity had not concurred
and the trial had been free from legal error, would the only reasonable and proper
verdict have been one of guilty?' That being so, there is no tension between section
2(1)(a) of the Criminal Appeal Act 1968 as amended and section 3(1) of the Human
Rights Act 1998."

The court went on to note that a decision of the European Court of Human Rights
does not involve any express finding on the nature and quality of a breach of
Art.6 or its impact on the safety of a conviction. In view of this limitation on the
European Court's function, it would remain necessary for the Court of Appeal
itself to assess the impact which a particular breach of Article 6 might have on
the safety of a conviction:

"We are satisfied that the two questions [of fairness and safety] must be kept separate
and apart. The ECHR is charged with inquiring into whether there has been a breach of
a Convention right. This court is concerned with the safety of a conviction. That the first
question may intrude upon the second is obvious. To what extent it does so will depend
on the circumstances of the particular case. We reject therefore the contention that a
finding of a breach of Article 6(1) by the ECHR leads inexorably to the quashing of a
conviction. Nor do we think it helpful to deal in presumptions. The effect of any
unfairness upon the safety of a conviction will vary according to its nature and degree.
At one end of the spectrum [counsel] cites the example of an appropriate sentence
following a plea of guilty passed by a judge who for some undisclosed reason did not
constitute an impartial tribunal. At the other extreme there may be a case where a
defendant is denied the opportunity to give evidence on his own behalf."

A leading decision is that of the Court of Appeal in *Togher, Doran and Parsons*,[71]   **17–30**
where Lord Woolf C.J. delivered the judgment. Having reviewed the varied case
law since *Chalkley and Jeffries*, Lord Woolf concluded that, even if there was
previously a difference of approach:

"Now that the European Convention is part of our domestic law, it would be most
unfortunate if the approach identified by the European Court of Human Rights and the
approach of this Court continued to differ unless this is inevitable because of provisions
contained in this country's legislation or the state of our case law. As a matter of first
principles, we do not consider that either the use of the word 'unsafe' in the legislation
or the previous cases compel an approach which does not correspond with that of the
ECHR. The requirement of fairness in the criminal process has always been a common
law tenet of the greatest importance ... Fairness in both jurisdictions is not an abstract
concept. Fairness is not concerned with technicalities. If a defendant has not had a fair
trial and as a result of that injustice has occurred, it would be extremely unsatisfactory
if the powers of this Court were not wide enough to rectify that injustice. If, contrary
to our expectations, that has not previously been the position, then it seems to us that
this is a defect in our procedures which is now capable of rectification under section 3
of the Human Rights Act 1998 ... The 1998 Act emphasises the desirability of taking
a broader rather than a narrower approach as to what constitutes an unsafe conviction.
In *R. v Davis, Rowe and Johnson* this Court acknowledged that there could still be a
distinction between its approach and the approach of the European Court of Human

---

[70] [1944] A.C. 315.
[71] [2001] Crim.L.R. 124.

Rights. However, in the later case of *R. v Francom*[72] this Court indicated ... that we would expect, in the situation there being considered, that the approach of this Court, applying the test of lack of safety would produce the same result as the approach of the ECHR applying the test of lack of fairness. We would suggest that, even if there was previously a difference of approach, that since the 1998 Act came into force, the circumstances in which there will be room for a different result before this Court and before the ECHR because of unfairness based on the respective tests we employ will be rare indeed. Applying the broader approach identified by Rose L.J.,[73] we consider that if a defendant has been denied a fair trial it will almost be inevitable that the conviction will be regarded as unsafe. Certainly, if it would be right to stop a prosecution on the basis that it was an abuse of process, this court would be most unlikely to conclude that if there was a conviction despite this fact, the conviction should not be set aside."

The Court of Appeal has since held that the protection offered by the Art.6 right is indistinguishable from that offered by the common law right to a fair trial in the great majority of cases.[74]

17–31   The effect of applying the interpretative obligation in s.3 of the Human Rights Act is thus to widen the meaning given to the term "unsafe" so as to include unfairness. Circumstances that ought to have led to a stay of the prosecution for abuse of process would clearly afford a strong example of when a conviction should be quashed as unsafe. But the judgment in *Togher* left the possibility of a small gap between the Strasbourg test and the Court of Appeal's test.

17–32   An early indication from the House of Lords pointed to a strong line being taken by the appellate courts. In *Forbes*,[75] the House of Lords appeared to suggest that *any* significant breach of Art.6 ought to be sufficient to render a conviction unsafe:

"Reference was made in argument to the right to a fair trial guaranteed by Article 6 of the ECHR. That is an absolute right. But as the Privy Council pointed out in *Brown*,[76] the subsidiary rights comprised within that Article are not absolute, and it is always necessary to consider all the facts and the whole history of the proceedings in a particular case to judge whether a defendant's right to a fair trial has been infringed or not. If on such consideration it is concluded that a defendant's right to a fair trial has been infringed, a conviction will be held to be unsafe within the meaning of section 2 of the Criminal Appeal Act 1968."

This approach was confirmed in *R. v A*[77] where Lord Steyn observed that it was;

" ... well-established that the guarantee of a fair trial under Article 6 is absolute: a conviction obtained in breach of it cannot stand. The only balancing permitted is in respect of what the concept of a fair trial entails: here account may be taken of the familiar triangulation of interests of the accused, the victim and society".

---

[72] [2000] Crim.L.R. 1018.
[73] In *Mullen* [2000] Q.B. 520.
[74] *R. v Abdroikov* [2005] 1 W.L.R. 3538, at para.37.
[75] [2001] 1 A.C. 473. See also *Brown v Stott* [2003] 1 A.C. 681.
[76] [2002] 1 A.C. 45.
[77] [2002] 1 A.C. 45.

Applying these principles in *Millar v Dickson*[78] the Privy Council held that, by continuing to prosecute the defendants before a body which had been held not to consitute an independent and impartial tribunal, the Lord Advocate had infringed their rights under Art.6(1); and although the defendants could not show that they had suffered any substantial injustice, the right to a fair trial before an independent tribunal was absolute and could not be compromised unless validly waived.[79] The decision of the High Court *inter alia* not to dismiss Millar's appeal against conviction was reversed, and all four cases were remitted to the High Court.

Thus, the view which now seems to have taken root is that the relative importance of a particular defect in the trial may be taken into account when the Court of Appeal is considering whether the proceedings, taken as a whole, were unfair. But once that threshold is crossed, the conviction is necessarily unsafe.

In more recent cases the appeal courts have been described as "beating a retreat"[80] from this "absolutist" stance. That may be to put it too high. Judges have tended to be careful to draw a distinction between *an* unfairness at trial, which " . . . is not always fatal to a conviction[81]" (even where the court has found a breach of the defendant's right to a fair trial[82]) and unfairness which requires the Court of Appeal to "rectify injustice".[83]

In *Pendleton*,[84] albeit a case concerned with the presentation of fresh evidence **17–33** before the Court of Appeal, the House of Lords considered the scope of s.2 of the Criminal Appeal Act 1968, and the function of the Court of Appeal in applying the test. The decision of the House of Lords in *Stafford v Director of Public Prosecutions*[85] was relied on by the Crown; Lord Bingham accepted the submissions of the Crown, which he summarised as follows:

> "Section 2 of the 1968 Act imposes on the Court of Appeal, in cases which involve fresh evidence as in cases which do not, a duty of judgment. If the court thinks the conviction is unsafe they must allow, otherwise they must dismiss, the appeal. It is their judgment which matters: "if they think . . . ". They may find it usefel when forming that judgment to consider what impact the evidence, if called before the jury, might have had, but that is not a necessary step nor is it the only or final question the court must ask."[86]

Lord Bingham later identified the correct approach to the question of safety in a fresh evidence case:

> "I am not persuaded that the House laid down any incorrect principle in *Stafford*, so long as the Court of Appeal bears very clearly in mind that that the question for its consideration is whether the conviction is safe and not whether the accused is guilty. But the test advocated by counsel in *Stafford* and by [the Appellant's counsel] in this

---

[78] [2002] 1 W.L.R. 1615.
[79] *ibid.*, at 1624.
[80] *Mind the Gaps: Safety, Fairness and Moral Legitimacy* [2004] Crim.L.R. 266, at 275.
[81] *R. v Lambert* [2001] 3 W.L.R. 206, para.43 *per* Lord Steyn.
[82] *R. v Lewis* [2005] Lawtel 7/4/2005 (unreported elsewhere).
[83] *R. v Hanratty (Deceased)* [2002] 2 Cr.App.R. 30.
[84] [2001] UKHL 66.
[85] [1974] A.C. 878.
[86] Para.14.

appeal does have dual virtue to which the speeches I have quoted perhaps give somewhat inadequate recognition. First, it reminds the Court of Appeal that it is not and should never become the primary decision-maker. Secondly, it reminds the Court of Appeal that it has an imperfact and incomplete understanding of the full processes which led the jury to convict. The Court of Appeal can make its assessment of the fresh evidence it has heard, but save in a clear case it is at a disadvantage in seeking to relate that evidence to the rest of the evidence which the jury heard. For those reasons it will usually be wise for the Court of Appeal, in a case of any difficulty, to test their own provisional view by asking whether the evidence, if given at trial might reasonably have affected the decision of the trial jury to convict. If it might, the conviction is unsafe."[87]

Lord Hobhouse stated:

" . . . the sole criterion which the Court of Appeal is entitled to apply is that of what it thinks is the safety of the conviction. It has to make the assessment. That is made clear by the use of the words 'if they think'. The change in the language of the statute has reinforced the reasoning in *Stafford* and shows that appeals are not to be allowed unless the Court of Appeal has itself made the requisite assessment and has itself concluded that the conviction is unsafe."[88]

and continued:

"Unless and until the Court of Appeal has been persuaded that the verdict of the jury is unsafe, the verdict must stand. Nothing less will suffice to displace it. A mere risk that it is unsafe does not suffice: the appellant has to discharge a burden of persuasion and persuade the Court of Appeal that the conviction *is* unsafe."[89]

17–34 In *Beckles*,[90] a case where the Criminal Cases Review Commission had referred a conviction to the Court of Appeal following a finding of a violation of Art.6 by the European Court in relation to judge's direction to the jury regarding his failure to answer questions in interview, Lord Woolf. C.J. indicated that the approch of the Court of Appeal was as follows:

"The HRA was not in force at the time of the Appellant's trial and the Act is not retrospective. However, the fact that the Act is not retrospective does not mean that decisions of the ECtHR should be ignored or regarded as irrelevant. The general effect of Article 6 is to guarantee a fair trial. This has long been a requirement of our domestic law. There is a problem, however, in that section 2 of the Criminal Appeal Act 1968 (as amended), when setting out the test for determining whether an appeal should be allowed, does not expressly refer to the fairness of the trial. Instead the test is whether the Court 'think that the conviction is unsafe'. While there is this distinction in language, its importance should not be overemphasized.
    39. The distinction in language was considered in a manner which both parties accept in *R. v Hanratty (Deceased)* [2002] 2 Cr.App.R. 30. In the judgment in that case, reference is made to the speech of Lord Bingham of Cornhill in *R. v Pendleton* [2002] 1 Cr.App.R. 34. The Court then said; 'the most important lesson to be learnt from this part of Lord Bingham's speech is that Parliament's overriding intention . . . in the 1968

---

[87] Para.19.
[88] para.35.
[89] para.36.
[90] [2005] 1 W.L.R. 2829.

Act, is that it should be this Court's central role to ensure that justice has been done and to rectify injustice'. Considering the effect of the passage of time, this Court went on to say [at paragraph 98 and 100]:

'The non-technical approach is especially important in references by the Commission such as this since standards may have changed because of the passage of time. For understandable reasons, it is now accepted in judging the question of fairness of a trial, and fairness is what rules of procedure are designed to achieve, we apply current standards irrespective of when the trial took place. But this does not mean that because contemporary rules have not been complied with a trial which took place in the past must be judged on the false assumption it was tried yesterday. Such an approach could achieve injustice because the non-compliance with rules does not necessarily mean that a defendant has been treated unfairly. In order to achieve justice, non-compliance with rules which were not current at the time of the trial may need to be treated differently from rules which were in force at the time of trial. If certain of the current requirements of, for example, a summing up are not complied with at a trial which takes place today this can almost automatically result in a conviction being set aside but this approach should not be adopted in relation to trials which took place before the rule was established. The fact that what has happened did not comply with a rule which was in force at the time of trial makes the non-compliance more serious than it would be if there was no rule in force. Proper standards will not be maintained unless this Court can be expected, when appropriate, to enforce the rules by taking a serious view of a breach of the rules at the time they are in force. It is not appropriate to apply this approach to a forty year-old case.

The question of whether a trial is sufficiently seriously flawed, so as to make a conviction unsafe because it does not comply with what would be regarded today as the minimum standards, must be approached in the round, taking into account all the relevant circumstances . . . ' "

In *Randall* [2002] U.K.P.C. 19, the Privy Council commented that: **17–35**

"There will come a point when the departure from good practice is so gross, or so persistent, or so prejudicial, or so irremediable that an appellate court will have no choice but to condemn a trial as unfair and quash a conviction as unsafe, however strong the grounds for believing the defendant to be guilty."

Guidance on when the threshold has been passed is inevitably rather lacking; it seems that each case will turn on its own facts.[91] It seems that the European Court is prepared to endorse such an approach. In *C.G. v United Kingdom*[92] the European Court found that there was no breach of Art.6 where the Court of Appeal had dismissed an appeal even where it had found "some substance" in the appellant's criticism of the nature and frequency of the trial judge's interventions. In particular, it observed that in four other Court of Appeal cases the conviction of the defendant was quashed as "unsafe" on the basis of the

---

[91] In *R. v Lewis*, for example, the Court of Appeal rejected the appellant's appeal, despite the fact that the ECtHR had held (in *Edwards and Lewis v United Kingdom* (2005) 40 E.H.R.R. 24) that the PII hearings during the appellant's trial had breached his Art.6 rights. The Court of Appeal noted that the ruling on the abuse argument, of which the appellant complained, was based in part on evidence disclosed by the prosecution, and there was nothing to suggest the decision was tainted by anything learnt at the PII hearing. The court considered that there was overwhelming evidence that on arrest, the appellant was in possession of a large quantity of counterfeit notes, which established the offences, and noted that he had unambiguously pleaded guilty to the offences.

[92] (2002) 34 E.H.R.R. 31.

excessive interventions of the judge, notwithstanding the acknowledged strength of the evidence against the defendants.

17–36   There is a limited range of cases in which the European Court has held that a fundamental defect which has occurred at trial has been *cured* by the proceedings on appeal. This may occur, as in *Edwards v United Kingdom*,[93] where evidence undisclosed at trial has been admitted on appeal, and subjected to adversarial argument.[94] This principle was pressed into service in *Craven*[95] where a conviction was upheld despite a number of irregularities at trial. Referring directly to *Edwards* the Court held that it was entitled to have regard not only to the evidence which had been wrongly withheld at trial, but also to fresh DNA evidence which pointed strongly to the appellant's guilt. The duty of the Court was to evaluate all the evidence available to it in deciding whether a conviction was safe. In that way, the Court held that the rights of the defence under Art.6 were properly secured.[96]

17–37   If the Court of Appeal were to find that there has been a breach of a defendant's Convention rights, but does not consider it necessary or appropriate to quash a conviction, is it able to afford any other remedy? Section 8 of the Human Rights Act enables a court to grant any remedy which is *within its existing powers* and which it considers just and appropriate. One possibility might be for the Court of Appeal to grant a remedy in damages whilst leaving the conviction intact. This would depend upon treating the Court of Appeal as a single court which sits in two divisions, and which therefore already has jurisdiction to award compensation. Apart from any technical objections, there is an obvious risk that this would be seen by the public and the appellant as an unsatisfactory and inadequate remedy.

17–38   It seems likely that the courts will follow the approach of the South African Constitutional Court, which has held that a breach of constitutional rights which has caused no prejudice to the accused can be marked by a real, as opposed to nominal, reduction in the sentence imposed.[97] The Privy Council in *Mills v HM Advocate*[98] considered the case of an appellant whose sentence of eight and a half years imprisonment was reduced by nine months following a finding of unreasonable delay (and consequent breach of Art.6(1)) in hearing his appeal. Having

---

[93] (1992) 15 E.H.R.R. 417.

[94] See paras 14–18 *et seq.* above. Whilst the European Court has been prepared to adopt this approach in relation to undisclosed evidence, this appears to be the exception rather than the rule. Thus, in *Findlay v United Kingdom* (1997) 24 E.H.R.R. 221, a case involving a lack of structural independence and impartiality, the court held that since the applicant was charged with a serious offence he was "entitled to a first instance tribunal which fully met the requirements of Article 6". See also *Condron and Condron v United Kingdom* (2001) 31 E.H.R.R. 1, above para.17–28 (Court of Appeal unable to remedy misdirection on adverse inference from silence); and *Rowe and Davis v United Kingdom* (2000) 30 E.H.R.R. 1, above para.17–29 (Court of Appeal unable to remedy unfairness arising from non-disclosure through an *ex parte* public interest immunity hearing).

[95] *The Times*, February 2, 2001.

[96] See also *Dallos v Hungary* (2003) 37 E.H.R.R. 524, and *Sipavicius v Lithuania* (2002) L.T.L. 21/2/2002.

[97] *Wild and anor v Hoffert and ors* (1998) 6 B.C.L.R. 656; (1998) 2 S.A.C.R. 1 (CC).

[98] [2004] 1 A.C. 441.

reviewed the jurisprudence of the European Court, Lord Hope held that such an approach provided an "appropriate and sufficient remedy".[99] Lord Steyn expressly recanted his earlier dictum[100] that the "normal remedy" in such cases should be the quashing of the conviction.[101] This is an approach also taken in cases where the police have overstepped the mark in encouraging the commission of the offence, but their conduct is held to fall short of the level required to exclude evidence on grounds of entrapment. Mitigation of sentence may be substantial.[102]

The position as set out above is, however, currently the subject of a fundamental **17–39** review by the Government. In September 2006, the Office for Criminal Justice Reform published its Consultation Paper, *Quashing Convictions—Report of a Review by the Home Secretary, Lord Chancellor and Attorney General.* The Government has taken the following view:

> "The dominant and settled legal interpretation of the statutory test in the Criminal Appeal Act 1968 (as amended) appears to mean that the Court of Appeal may quash a conviction if they are dissatisfied with some aspect of procedure at the original trial, even if the person pleaded guilty or the Court are in no doubt that he committed the offence for which he was convicted. The Government believes that the law should not allow people to go free where they were convicted and the Court are satisfied they committed the offence."[103]

While the Report is presented as a "Consultation Paper", the Foreword by the Home Secretary makes it very clear that it is only the method of effecting the changes on which responses are invited: "whilst the Government is open to suggestions about *how* we achieve the aims, we are not consulting on the aims themselves or therefore on *whether* the law should be changed. It is our firm view that the present system risks outcomes which are unacceptable to the law-abiding majority." (emphasis in the original).

The options on which the Government invites comment are: **17–40**

A. re-instate a proviso similar to that which was part of the original statutory test . . . so as to provide that the appeal should not be allowed, even if there is a procedural irregularity, if the court consider no miscarriage of justice actually occurred;

B. replace the proviso with another formulation, designed to achieve the same end, and perhaps addressing more directly the court's view (where they have reached one) of the guilt of the appellant;

C. recast the test and the task of the Court of Appeal so as to require a substantial re-examination of the evidence (akin to the task of the jury).[104]

---

[99] *ibid.*, p.1616.
[100] See *Darmalingum* [2000] 1 W.L.R. 2303 at 2310.
[101] *ibid.*, p.1605.
[102] E.g. *Beaumont* (1987) 9 Cr.App.R.(S) 342; *Tonnessen* [1998] 2 Cr.App.R.(S) 328.
[103] Para.31.
[104] Para.33.

The Government favours either option B or C, as it takes the view in relation to option A "that the concept of 'miscarriage of justice' itself requires considerable interpretation and that this legal process may overlay and obscure the essential matter of the guilt of the appellant."[105] The compatibility with Art.6 of any of these three options, or indeed the motives that underpin them, is highly questionable in light of the case law set out above and will no doubt be the subject of challenge should the Government succeed in implementing its proposal.

II. The Duty to Reopen Proceedings

17–41   In January 2000 the Committee of Ministers adopted Recommendation No. R (2000) 2 on the re-examination or reopening of certain cases at domestic level following judgments of the European Court of Human Rights. Paragraph II of the Recommendation;

> "Encourages the Contracting Parties, in particular, to examine their national legal systems with a view to ensuring that there exist adequate possibilities of re-examination of the case, including reopening of proceedings, in instances where the Court has found a violation of the Convention, especially where:
>
> (i) the injured party continues to suffer very serious negative consequences because of the outcome of the domestic decision at issue, which are not adequately remedied by the just satisfaction and cannot be rectified except by re-examination or re-opening, and
>
> (ii) the judgment of the Court leads to the conclusion that (a) the impugned domestic decision is on the merits contrary to the Convention, or (b) the violation found is based on procedural errors or shortcomings of such gravity that a serious doubt is cast on the outcome of the domestic proceedings complained of."

The European Parliamentary Assembly in a July 2000 report by the Committee on Legal Affairs and Human Rights Rapporteur on the execution of judgments also recommended that those states without legislation in place to permit reopening in individual cases should seek to remedy this as a matter of priority.[106] In February 2006 the J.C.H.R. recommended "that the Government should investigate the possibility of reform of the law to allow for the re-opening of proceedings in appropriate cases following judgments of the ECtHR, in order to allow for effective implementation of judgments in all cases."[107]

17–42   The question is whether English law makes provision for such reopening at present. It seems that, to an extent, this can be achieved through the Criminal Cases Review Commission considering a case and deciding to refer it to the Court of Appeal. The Recommendation by the Committee of Ministers falls short of imposing an absolute obligation to make such a reference, although one might expect that in all but the most exceptional case the Criminal Cases Review Commission should be expected to refer back to the Court of Appeal a case in

---

[105] Para.34.
[106] Committee on Legal Affairs and Human Rights, *Report on the Execution of Judgments of the European Court of Human Rights*, Doc 8808, paras 12.i.d and 76.
[107] 13th Report of 2004–05, para.23.

which a violation has been found in Strasbourg. However, this will not be possible in those cases where the violation arises from the substantive rather than procedural law. For example, in *ADT v United Kingdom*[108] the European Court found a breach of Art.8 where the applicant had been prosecuted and convicted of gross indecency between men under s.13 of the Sexual Offences Act 1956 following a search of his house by police which revealed incriminating video-tapes.[109]

In *R. v Lyons*,[110] the House of Lords considered the duty to reopen proceedings in the context of a pre-2000 criminal trial where the ECtHR had subsequently found a violation of Art.6. It was argued by the appellant that the Court of Appeal had a duty to give effect to the ECtHR's judgments, as applications of a treaty which was binding on the government in international law. Lord Bingham noted that the Court of Appeal's jurisdiction is purely statutory. Further, in determining a criminal appeal against an old conviction, it applies contemporary standards of fairness, but must apply the law applicable at the date of trial. At the date of the appellant's trial, legislation permitted the prosecutor to put in evidence state-ments made by the appellant to investigators exercising compulsory powers of questioning (the issue on which the ECtHR found a breach of Art.6). The Court of Appeal, applying the law which applied at the time of trial, when the HRA was not in force, could not say that the admission of those statements rendered the convictions unsafe, even if the ECtHR had subsequently found a violation. Lord Bingham accepted that:

> "[I]f the question of fairness were at large and the trial judge had been unconstrained by any statutory or common law rule, it would have been open to the Court of Appeal to pay heed and give appropriate weight to the European Court's judgment that the conduct of the appellants' trial was rendered unfair by the admission of the compelled evidence even if the Court of Appeal had previously held the admission of such evidence to be fair."[111]

D. DECLARATIONS OF INCOMPATIBILITY

It is inevitable that in certain cases the Court of Appeal will be confronted with   **17–43** an appellant whose conviction is found to be incompatible with a Convention right as a result of primary legislation which cannot "possibly" be interpreted compatibly, under s.3 of the Human Rights Act. The Court of Appeal has power under s.4 to make a declaration of incompatibility. It has been suggested that the word "may" in s.4 will in practice be interpreted by the court as meaning "shall". It seems unlikely that there will be many cases in which the court would consider it appropriate to exercise its discretion against the making of a declara-tion where the legislation itself was found to be incompatible, and the issue was likely to arise in future cases.

---

[108] (2001) 31 E.H.R.R. 33.
[109] Referred to by the J.C.H.R. in its 13th Report of 2004–05, para.20.
[110] [2003] 1 A.C. 976.
[111] Para.16.

17–44   There might, of course, be cases in which the incompatibility is specific to the particular facts, and is never likely to arise again. But even in that situation the court would presumably have to determine the issue of compatibility as a precondition to the exercise of its discretion under s.4. This would, in itself, come very close to a declaration of incompatibility. One situation in which the court might consider it unnecessary to grant a declaration would be where there was no substantial injustice to the individual and the legislation in question had since been amended or repealed so as to remove the incompatibility.

17–45   Section 5 of the Human Rights Act provides that where the court is considering whether to make a declaration of incompatibility the Crown is entitled to notice and the relevant Minister is entitled to be joined as a party. In criminal proceedings the Crown is of course already a party. However, it is open to doubt whether the presence of prosecuting counsel meets the requirements of s.5. The object of the section is to enable the Minister responsible to make representations to the court. The DPP is not a member of the Executive, and does not act on behalf of any government Minister. It may therefore be appropriate for the Home Office or other relevant body to be notified by the court directly and given an opportunity to intervene, as occurred in *R. v A* in the House of Lords.[112]

17–46   In those cases in which the Court of Appeal does go on to make a declaration under s.4, there is a potentially serious lacuna in the Act. This is because it is for the Minister to determine whether to make a remedial order under s.10 and Sch.2, and if so whether to make it retrospective in effect and whether to grant any incidental relief. The Minister could in principle release an individual from custody pending the making of a remedial order, in the exercise of prerogative powers (although an arrangement under which the Executive—rather than the judiciary—decides on whether an individual should be deprived of their liberty may give rise to other Convention points).

17–47   If a remedial order is made, the Minister can remove all the consequences of the conviction, either by granting a pardon or in the exercise of the powers provided in Sch.2 of the Act. However, a Minister cannot quash a criminal conviction. That can only be done by the Court of Appeal. Thus, if the Court of Appeal is to have power to quash the conviction in these circumstances then it would have to be able to retain jurisdiction over the appeal by adjourning the case after the declaration has been made, so as to enable the Minister to consider his/her response. If that were possible, then the court would also have power to grant bail in a very clear case, where the likely Ministerial response was known.

17–48   However, the terms of the Act appear to preclude this. Under s.10(1) the Minister can only take remedial action following a declaration of incompatibility if all parties to the proceedings in which the declaration was made have abandoned any right of appeal, the time limit for appeal has expired, or any further appeal has been determined. This suggests that the Court of Appeal is *functus officio* once it has made a declaration under s.4. The unfortunate consequence is that the

---

[112] The procedural issue is reported as *R. v A (Joinder of Appropriate Minister)* [2001] 1 W.L.R. 789.

appellant's conviction will have to stand despite any remedial order which the Minister may make in the light of the court's declaration. The appellant's only recourse is to petition the C.C.R.C. for a reference back to the Court of Appeal under s.9 of the Criminal Appeal Act 1995, a result which is cumbersome, expensive and unjust.

E. THE CRIMINAL JUSTICE ACT 2003

I. Prosecution Appeals

Part 9 of the Criminal Justice Act ("the Act") grants the prosecution a right of **17–49** appeal against a judge's rulings in relation to a trial on indictment. Two types of ruling may be appealed: those which have the effect of terminating the proceedings, and those which significantly weaken the prosecution case. It may be that the inevitable delays caused by such appeals will precipitate challenges under the reasonable time guarantee, although it may be noted that the trial judge has a power to order that any appeal be expedited.[113] In *R. v Thompson and another*[114] the Court of Appeal ruled that there is no jurisdiction under s.58 of the 2003 Act to give the prosecution leave to appeal against a dismissal of charges pre-arraignment under para.2 of Sch.3 to the Crime and Disorder Act 1998. A successful application under para.2 of Sch.3 had the effect of dismissing of the charge and, if the indicment had been preferred, quashing the count. It would not lead to an acquittal. Under s.58(8) of the 2003 Act, an acquittal must be the consequence should the prosecution fail in its application for leave to appeal. Accordingly, s.58 could not be used to appeal a successful application by a defendant under para.2 of Sch.3 to the 1998 Act.

Significantly, the prosecution's right does extend to seeking to appeal successful submissions of no case to answer. The Law Commission, which proposed withholding that right, expressed concern that such rulings are analagous to acquittals by a jury, and that it would be unfair to allow further review. It remains to be seen how the appellate courts will approach such submissions, and whether a distinction will be drawn between rulings on issues of law and rulings on sufficiency of evidence.

II. Retrial for Serious Offences

Part 10 of the Act creates an exception to the established common law rule **17–50** against double jeopardy. It applies in cases where new and compelling evidence of guilt comes to light in respect of a qualifying offence, and it is in the interests of justice to quash the acquittal and order a retrial. In determining where the interests of justice lie, s.79 requires *inter alia* the Court of Appeal to consider whether a fair trial would be unlikely in the existing circumstances, and the length of time that has elapsed since the alleged commission of the qualifying offence. This and other issues concerning the Pt 10 powers are considered in more detail in Ch.12.

---

[113] S.59(1).
[114] [2006] EWCA Crim 2849.

CHAPTER 18

THE RIGHTS OF VICTIMS OF CRIME

A. Introduction

The principal purpose of the Convention is the protection of the rights of **18–01** individuals from infringement by states. However, the Court has recognised that, if the rights declared in the Convention are to be protected effectively, certain provisions must be read as imposing positive obligations on the state. This chapter examines those positive obligations that protect victims (and potential victims) of crime, and others (notably witnesses) whose rights may be infringed during the criminal process.[1]

The chapter is divided into six parts. Part B discusses the duty on public **18–02** authorities to take steps to protect individuals from the infringement of their rights under Art.2 and Art.3. Part C examines the state's duty to have in place criminal laws that prohibit certain forms of conduct which infringes Convention rights. Part D concerns the duty to investigate alleged breaches of Arts 2 and 3. Part E examines the related duty to bring a prosecution where there is evidence of such a breach. In Pt F there is discussion of the procedural rights of victims and witnesses in the course of a criminal prosecution. Finally, Pt G examines the rights of victims and their families in relation to the sentencing process.

B. Obligation to Prevent Infringements of Rights under Articles 2 and 3

As its starting point in the judgment in *Osman v United Kingdom*[2] the Court **18–03** made the following general statement:

---

[1] For a general survey, see Mowbray A., *The Development of Positive Obligations under the European Convention on Human Rights by the European Court of Human Rights* (2004), esp. Chs 2, 3 and 8.
[2] (2000) 29 E.H.R.R. 245.

"The Court notes that the first sentence of Article 2(1) enjoins the State not only to refrain from the intentional and unlawful taking of life, but also to take appropriate steps to safeguard the lives of those within its jurisdiction.[3] It is common ground that the State's obligation in this respect extends beyond its primary duty to secure the right to life by putting in place effective criminal law provisions to deter the commission of offences against the person backed up by law enforcement machinery for the prevention, suppression and sanctioning of breaches of such provisions. It is thus accepted by those appearing before the Court that Article 2 of the Convention may also imply in certain well-defined circumstances a positive obligation on the authorities to take preventive operational measures to protect an individual whose life is at risk from the criminal acts of another individual."[4]

18–04 This passage establishes two separate but related obligations. The positive obligation to have "effective criminal law provisions" to protect the Art.2 rights of individuals is a duty that lies on the state as a whole. That obligation extends to enforcement procedures and systems: there must be courts, police, and prosecutors and so forth. But the focus of the present discussion is the related positive obligation to take *operational* measures in order to secure the protection of Art.2 rights in circumstances where particular persons are at risk. The taking of operational measures will usually be a matter for the police, but the state is ultimately responsible for ensuring that Art.2 rights are protected.

18–05 In *Osman*, where the applicant and his family had notified the police about the threatening behaviour of a certain schoolteacher, the government argued before the court that the obligation should not arise unless the failure of the police to perceive the risk to life amounted to gross negligence or wilful disregard of the duty to protect life. However, the Court held that the test is whether "the authorities knew or ought to have known at the time of the existence of a real and immediate risk to the life of an identified individual or individuals from the criminal acts of a third party."[5] Although there will always be difficulties in applying this to the facts,[6] this is a broader standard of liability designed to ensure greater protection for the Art.2 rights of individuals. Mere negligence rather than gross negligence is the ground for liability. Put in terms of the positive obligation, the authorities have a duty to assess the situation as they may reasonably be expected to do.

18–06 The Court acknowledged "the difficulties involved in policing modern societies, the unpredictability of human conduct and the operational choices which must be made in terms of priorities and resources," and it therefore concluded that the scope of the positive obligation must not be such as to "impose an impossible or disproportionate burden on the authorities." However, the Court again rejected the government's argument (summarised at para.107 of the judgment) that gross negligence should be the standard of liability. It held that the test should be whether the authorities "failed to take measures within the scope of their powers

---

[3] The court referred here to its judgment in *LCB v United Kingdom* (1999) 27 E.H.R.R. 212, para.36.

[4] (2000) 29 E.H.R.R. 245 at para.115.

[5] *ibid.*, para.116.

[6] See also *Keenan v United Kingdom*, (2001) 33 E.H.R.R. 38; and *Mastromatteo v Italy*, Judgement, October 24, 2002, ECtHR.

which, judged reasonably, might have been expected to avoid that risk" (i.e. the identified risk to life). Put in terms of the positive obligation, the authorities have a duty to "do all that could be reasonably expected of them to avoid a real and immediate risk to life of which they have or ought to have knowledge."[7]

The Court made it clear that a principal reason for imposing a more demanding   **18–07** standard than that for which the government had contended was the fundamental nature of the right declared by Art.2. Since the right to life is in one sense the most basic of all the Convention rights, it is appropriate to expect the authorities to take seriously any threats to that right, and to give some priority to preventive measures in cases where the risk of an attack on that right is foreseeable. But, as will be seen in s.C below, those preventive measures must be taken with due regard to the rights of others who may be affected. This means not only the right to life of the person who is alleged to pose the threat, but also wider rights of that person and others. Police powers must be exercised

> "in a manner which fully respects the due process and other guarantees which legit-
> imately place restraints on the scope of their action to investigate crime and bring
> offenders to justice, including the guarantees contained in Articles 5 and 8 of the
> Convention."[8]

This last consideration was one of several factors which led the Court to conclude   **18–08** in the *Osman* case that there had been no violation of Art.2 in failing to prevent the incident in which the schoolteacher shot and killed the father of the boy with whom he was infatuated. Although there had been a sequence of incidents, some strange and others potentially dangerous, the Court held that there was no stage at which it could be said that the police knew or ought to have known that the lives of any members of the Osman family "were at real and immediate risk" from the schoolteacher. The police could not be criticised for failing to arrest him, since they have a duty to act in accordance with the rights of freedoms of all individuals, and the required standard of suspicion was not fulfilled.[9]

The decision in *Osman* was followed in the context of an alleged violation of   **18–09** Art.3 in *Z and ors v United Kingdom*.[10] The applicants were four children who suffered appalling neglect at the hands of their parents, over a period of years. The local authority with statutory responsibility for the children were kept fully informed of the conditions, but devoted their resources to keeping them with their parents instead of removing them into care. There was no dispute that the conditions amounted to inhuman and degrading treatment. The more difficult issue was whether the state could be held responsible for the criminal acts of the parents committed in their own home. The Court held that it could:

---

[7] (1998) 29 E.H.R.R. 245 at para.116.
[8] *ibid.*
[9] *Cf.* A different conclusion was reached in a post-Human Rights Act case when the police failed to take reasonable steps to protect a person who had agreed to be a witness in a criminal trial and had sought protection as a result of his fears that he would be the subject of a reprisal attack: *Van Colle v Chief Constable of Hertfordshire Police* [2006] 3 All. E.R. 963, Q.B.D.
[10] (2002) 34 E.H.R.R. 3.

"Article 3 enshrines one of the most fundamental values of a democratic society. It prohibits in absolute terms torture or inhuman or degrading treatment or punishment. [The Convention] requires States to take measures designed to ensure that individuals within their jurisdiction are not subjected to torture or inhuman or degrading treatment, including such ill-treatment administered by private individuals. These measures should provide effective protection, in particular, of children and other vulnerable persons and include reasonable steps to prevent ill-treatment of which the authorities had or ought to have had knowledge ... [The local authority] was under a statutory duty to protect the children and had a range of powers available to them, including removal from their home. The children were however only taken into emergency care, at the insistence of the mother, on 30 April 1992. Over the intervening period of four and a half years, they had been subject in their home to what the consultant child psychiatrist who examined them referred to as horrific experiences. The Criminal Injuries Compensation Board had also found that the children had been subject to appalling neglect over an extended period and suffered physical and psychological injury directly attributable to a crime of violence. The Court acknowledges the difficult and sensitive decisions facing social services and the important countervailing principle of respecting and preserving family life. The present case however leaves no doubt as to the failure of the system to protect these child applicants from serious, long-term neglect and abuse. Accordingly, there has been a violation of Article 3 of the Convention."[11]

18–10 The *Osman* test has also been applied to situations where the authorities have failed to prevent a killing in custody, whether by suicide or third parties. In *Keenan v United Kingdom*,[12] the deceased, who was coming to the end of his sentence, hung himself after he was placed in a segregation unit following an offence against prison discipline. He had a documented history of mental instability and self-harm, and had been perceived as a suicide risk in the recent past. After reiterating the test laid down in *Osman*, the Court proceeded "to consider to what extent this applies where the risk to a person derives from self-harm" (para.89). The Court began by noting that "persons in custody are in a vulnerable position and that the authorities are under a duty to protect them" (para.90). It accepted that the preventive measures taken would have to respect the rights of the detainee. (Thus, for example, there would be limits on the state's duty to force feed a prisoner on hunger strike). But the Court noted that "there are general measures and precautions which will be available to diminish the opportunities for self-harm, without infringing personal autonomy" (para.91). The Court went on to define the applicable test in these terms:

"[W]hether the authorities knew or ought to have known that Mark Keenan posed a real and immediate risk of suicide and, if so, whether they did all that reasonably could have been expected of them to prevent that risk" (para.92).

On the facts of *Keenan*, the Court found that there was sufficient indication of risk to put the authorities on notice (paras 95–6). However, after a detailed examination of the treatment of the deceased, the Court held that it was not apparent that the prison authorities had failed in their duty of care (para.98). The Court went on to hold that the lack of effective monitoring of his condition,

[11] See also *E. v United Kingdom* (2003) 36 E.H.R.R. 31.
[12] (2001) 33 E.H.R.R. 38.

combined with the disciplinary measures which had been taken against him, amounted to a violation of Art.3 (paras 102–115).

In *Edwards v United Kingdom*[13] the Court applied the *Osman* test to the alleged failures of a number of agencies, including medical professionals, the police, the courts and the Crown Prosecution Service. The Court found a violation of Art.2 on the basis of inadequate screening procedures and the failure of the relevant authorities to pass on information about a prisoner who subsequently murdered the applicants' son while they shared a cell together.

In *R. (Amin) v Secretary of State for the Home Department*,[14] the House of Lords **18–11** considered the failure by the authorities to prevent the racist murder of Zahid Mubarek, a 19 year old prisoner serving a sentence in Feltham Young Offenders Institute. As Lord Bingham observed (at para.30), the test for a breach of the positive obligation in Art.2, laid down by the European Court in *Osman*, is essentially the same as the test for a breach of the common law duty of care:

> "A profound respect for the sanctity of human life underpins the common law as it underpins the jurisprudence under articles 1 and 2 of the Convention. This means that a state must not unlawfully take life and must take appropriate legislative and administrative steps to protect it. But the duty does not stop there. The state owes a particular duty to those involuntarily in its custody. As Anand J succinctly put it in *Nilabati Behera v State of Orissa* (1993) 2 SCC 746, 747: 'There is a great responsibility on the police or prison authorities to ensure that the citizen in its custody is not deprived of his right to life.' Such person must be protected against violence or abuse at the hands of state agents. They must be protected against self-harm: *Reeves v Comr of Police for the Metropolis* [2000] 1 AC 360. Reasonable care must be taken to safeguard their lives and persons against the risk of avoidable harm."[15]

The European Court continues to recognise different situations where the appli **18–12** cability of the *Osman* test will arise.[16] Special mention should be given to *Oneryildiz v Turkey*.[17] The applicant and his family lived illegally in a shanty town located on a rubbish tip in Istanbul. As a result of a methane explosion in 1993 nine of his close relatives were killed. The applicant complained that the the the local authority had failed over a number of years to act upon risk assessments that predicted the very disaster that occurred. In addition, he complained that the authorities should have provided the residents with information about the potential risks.[18] The Government argued that the State's responsibility for actions that were not directly attributable to its agents could not extend to all occurrences of accidents or disasters and that in such circumstances the Court's interpretation as

---

[13] (2002) 35 E.H.R.R. 19.

[14] [2004] 1 A.C. 653, HL.

[15] See also *R. (Wright and Bennett) v Secretary of State for the Home Department* [2002] H.R.L.R. 1.

[16] These include the use of army vehicles to control public order disturbances (*McShane v United Kingdom*, (2002) 35 E.H.R.R. 23); the threat posed by prisoners to the local community when released on home leave (*Mastromatteo v Italy*, Judgment, October 24, 2002, ECtHR); and the waste-management of refuge sites that consitute an environmental hazzard (*Oneyildiz v Turkey* (2005) 41 E.H.R.R. 20).

[17] (2005) 41 E.H.R.R. 20.

[18] Para.67.

to the applicability of Art.2 should remain restrictive.[19] Contrary to the Government's submissions, the Grand Chamber held that the positive obligation to protect life under Art.2 "must be construed as applying in the context of any activity, whether public or not, in which the right to life may be at stake", and *a fortiori* in the case of industrial activities, which "by their very nature are dangerous". As to when the positive obligation might be violated, the court gave the following guidance:

> "the harmfulness of the phenomena inherent in the activity in question, the contingency of the risk to which the applicant was exposed by reason of any life-endangering circumstances, the status of those involved in bringing about such circumstances, and whether the acts or omissions attributable to them were deliberate are merely factors among others that must be taken into account in the examination of the merits of a particular case, with a view to determining the responsibility which the State may bear under Article 2".[20]

C. OBLIGATION TO HAVE IN PLACE LAWS WHICH PENALISE INFRINGEMENTS OF BASIC RIGHTS

18–13   Several decisions of the Strasbourg Court confirm that Contracting States have obligations to ensure that their domestic criminal law penalises the infringement of certain basic rights, so as to provide protection for those rights.

I. Protection of Article 3 Rights

18–14   Article 3 has an obvious application in the field of corporal punishment, which may amount to inhuman and degrading treatment. Two separate questions then arise. First, what degree of physical chastisement constitutes "inhuman and degrading treatment" for the purposes of Art.3? And secondly, is the state responsible for what one private individual does to another?

18–15   In the well-known decision in *Tyrer v United Kingdom*[21] the Court held that the use of the birch as a punishment in the Isle of Man was "degrading" and therefore contravened Art.3. By contrast, in *Costello-Roberts v United Kingdom*[22] the Court held that beating a boy three times through his shorts with a rubber-soled gym shoe did not amount to "degrading punishment", the Court referring to the absence of serious long-term physical effects. Two years earlier, in *Y v United Kingdom*,[23] the Commission had found a violation of Art.3 in a case of caning over trousers, where the caning had left the boy with severe bruising and swelling. Neither of the last two cases derived from criminal proceedings, and both of them concerned the use of corporal punishment in schools. Indeed, several applications to Strasbourg have concerned physical discipline at

---

[19] Paras 72.
[20] Para.73.
[21] (1979–80) 2 E.H.R.R. 1.
[22] (1995) 19 E.H.R.R. 112.
[23] (1994) 17 E.H.R.R. 238.

schools,[24] with the Commission particularly ready to find that the treatment or punishment was degrading where it was administered by a male teacher to a teenage girl pupil.[25]

The question of the limits of Art.3 came squarely before the Court in the case of **18–16** *A v United Kingdom*,[26] where the applicant's stepfather had been acquitted of assault occasioning actual bodily harm. It was admitted that the stepfather had caned the boy (then aged nine) on several occasions, but the jury evidently did not believe that the prosecution had proved that the canings were more than "moderate and reasonable chastisement." By the time the case reached the Strasbourg Court the United Kingdom government had accepted that there was a breach of Art.3. The Commission had found that "the strokes were severe enough to leave bruises which ... were visible several days later."[27]

Turning to the issue of state responsibility, the Court held that the United **18–17** Kingdom was responsible for the violation committed by the stepfather because the criminal law afforded too great a degree of latitude to a jury. The obligation laid on states by Art.1 of the Convention, taken together with Art.3:

> "requires States to take measures designed to ensure that individuals within their jurisdiction are not subjected to torture or inhuman or degrading treatment or punishment, including such ill-treatment administered by private individuals. Children and other vulnerable individuals, in particular, are entitled to State protection, in the form of effective deterrence, against such serious breaches of personal integrity."[28]

In principle, therefore, the laws of each state must, at a minimum, be defined in such a way as to ensure that any breach of Art.3 constitutes a criminal offence.

In *A v United Kingdom* the Court held that the breadth of the defence of **18–18** reasonable chastisement in English law is such that it "fails to provide adequate protection to children and should be amended."[29] proper test at common law had been considered by the Court of Appeal *Smith*,[30] where the mother of a six year old boy asked her partner to "smack" the child for disobedience and the man gave the child two strokes with his belt. He was convicted of assault occasioning actual bodily harm, the jury having rejected his defence that he did no more than inflict "moderate and reasonable chastisement". The Court of Appeal dismissed his appeal, on the basis that this was the correct test. Subsequently, in *R. v H.*,[31] the common law defence of lawful chatisement was specifically refined in order to bring it into line with the requirements of Art.3. The Court of Appeal held that

---

[24] See, e.g. *Mrs X v United Kingdom* (1979) 14 D.R. 205, *B and D v United Kingdom* (1986) 49 D.R. 44, and *Family A v United Kingdom* (1987) 52 D.R. 156.
[25] See *Mrs X and Miss Y v United Kingdom* (1984) 36 D.R. 49, and *Warwick v United Kingdom* (1989) 60 D.R. 5 and 22.
[26] (1999) 27 E.H.R.R. 611.
[27] *ibid.*, at 619.
[28] Para.22.
[29] Para.24.
[30] [1985] Crim.L.R. 42.
[31] [2002] 1 Cr.App.R. 7.

pending the Government's plan to reform the law, a judge should direct the jury that, when they were considering the reasonableness or otherwise of the chastisement, they had to consider the nature and context of the defendant's behaviour, its duration, its physical and mental consequences in relation to the child, the age and personal characteristics of the child and the reasons given by the defendant for administering the punishment.

18–19   As a result of s.58 of the Children Act 2004, the defence of reasonable chastisement is no longer available in any proceedings for an offence of assault occasioning actual bodily harm (Offences Against the Person Act 1861, s.47), unlawfully inflicting grievous bodily harm (Offences Against the Person Act 1861, s.20), causing grievous bodily harm with intent (Offences Against the Person Act 1861, ss.18), or cruelty to a child (Offences Against the Person Act 1861, s.16). The law remains unchanged with regard to all other forms of common law assault and battery. In that respect, the new legislation has not dealt with the extent to which chastisement by a parent, which falls short of a violation of Art.3, may nevertheless constitute a violation of Art.8.[32]

18–20   In *R. (Williamson) v Secretary of State for the Home Department*,[33] the House of Lords rejected the submission that the prohibition on any form of corporal punishment under s.548 of the Education Act 1996 amounted to a disproportionate interference with the right of practising Christians to send their children to schools that favoured mild physical correction as part of a biblical education. Lord Nicholls held[34] that the legislature was entitled to take the view that "all corporal punishment of children at school is undesirable and unnecessary and that other, non-violent means of discipline are available and preferable".[35] Lady Hale agreed, relying upon *Pretty v United Kingdom*,[36] that the institution of a universal ban was justified in order to protect a vulnerable class of persons.[37]

II. Protection of Article 2 Rights

18–21   Article 2 declares everyone's right to life, but allows exceptions when deprivation of life "results from the use of force which is no more than absolutely necessary (a) in defence of any person from unlawful violence; (b) in order to

---

[32] See 18–40 to 18–41, below.

[33] [2005] 2 A.C. 246, HL.

[34] at para.50.

[35] at para.80.

[36] (2002) 35 E.H.R.R. 1. at para.74.

[37] The judgment of Lady Hale also provides a detailed description of the obligations of the United Kingdom under the United Nations Convention on the Rights of the Child and the extent to which they impact on the question of corporal punishment both inside the family and in other institutional settings. She concludes (at para.80) that

"[The] state has a positive obligation to protect children from inhuman or degrading punishment which violates their rights under article 3. But prohibiting only such punishment as would violate their rights under article 3 (or possibly article 8) would bring difficult problems of definition, demarcation and enforcement. It would not meet the authoritative international view of what the UNCRC requires".

effect a lawful arrest or to prevent the escape of a person lawfully detained; (c) in action lawfully taken for the purpose of quelling a riot or insurrection."

Justifiable Force

The scope and application of the exceptions in Art.2 were considered in the **18–22** Gibraltar shooting case, *McCann and others v United Kingdom*,[38] where the European Court differed from the Commission's finding and held (by 10 votes to nine) that the United Kingdom had violated Art.2 in the shooting by SAS soldiers of three IRA terrorist suspects. The government's argument had been that the three suspects were believed to have a radio-control detonator which would activate a car bomb, and that it was necessary to kill them to prevent the imminent detonation. In the event, neither a radio-control device nor a car bomb was found. The majority judgment began by stating that the purpose of Art.2 is to secure practical and effective protection of each individual's life, and it went on to make three significant points:

— it emphasised that a person may only be intentionally killed by the state where "absolutely necessary", a "stricter and more compelling test" than that applicable to the phrase "necessary in a democratic society" under para.2 of Arts 8 to 11.

— it stated that its inquiries concerned not only the actions of the law enforcement officers but also the planning of any law enforcement operation, to ascertain whether it was organised so as to "minimise, to the greatest extent possible, recourse to lethal force".

— it held that the actions of the officers should be judged on the facts that they honestly believed, for good reasons, to exist.

The Court found that the soldiers themselves had not violated Art.2 because, on **18–23** the information given to them, they did have good reason for the beliefs that led them to fire the shots. However, the majority of the Court added that the immediate reaction of the soldiers, in shooting the three suspects dead, lacked "the degree of caution in the use of firearms to be expected from law enforcement personnel in a democratic society, even when dealing with dangerous terrorist suspects." The Court went on to hold however that the United Kingdom government had violated Art.2, through its failure to ensure that the operation was planned so as to minimise the risk of death: the killings had not been shown to be "absolutely necessary" for the "defence of any person from unlawful violence."

In the subsequent case of *Andronicou and Constantinou v Cyprus*[39] the Court **18–24** differed from the Commission's finding of a violation of Art.2 and held (by five votes to four) that there had been no breach. The case arose from a siege, in which Andronicou was holding Ms Constantinou hostage. Andronicou was known to be unstable, and to have a gun, and when Ms Constantinou was heard to scream a special police unit went in. They used tear-gas and then, when

---

[38] (1996) 21 E.H.R.R. 97.
[39] (1998) 25 E.H.R.R. 491.

Andronicou fired at them as they entered his house, they replied with several rounds of automatic fire. Andronicou was killed instantly; Ms Constantinou was wounded and died shortly afterwards. The majority of the Court accepted that it had to consider the "planning and control" of the operation, and determine whether the force used was "strictly proportionate" to the purpose, on the facts that the officers honestly believed, for good reasons, to exist. In view of the deployment of machine guns in a confined space the Court regretted that so much fire power had been used, but narrowly concluded that the use of lethal force could not be said to have exceeded what was absolutely necessary for the purpose of defending the lives of Ms Constantinou and of the officers themselves.[40]

18–25　　The application of Art.2 to the facts created great difficulty in these cases: not only did the Commission and the Court take different views, but the Court's decisions were both by the narrowest of majorities and contain some powerful dissenting judgments. Moreover, the Court stated that in interpreting Art.2 it was neither determining the compatibility of a state's laws with the Convention nor determining the criminal liability of any party.[41]

18–26　　However, on a direct analogy with the decision of the Court in *A v United Kingdom*,[42] it can be strongly argued that the rules of English law on self-defence and the justifiable use of force ought to be framed in such a way as to afford greater protection for the right to life of those against whom force is used under colour of justification.[43] The Court in *McCann* considered the Gibraltar law of justifiable force, contained in Art.2 of the Gibraltar Constitution, which provides for a killing to be justified on stated grounds if the force was "reasonably justifiable". The Court observed that "the Convention standard appears on its face to be stricter", but it concluded that the difference was not so great as to justify a finding of a violation of Art.2 on this ground alone.[44] This raises the question whether the even less demanding rules in the United Kingdom, under s.3 of the Criminal Law Act 1967 or at common law, give adequate protection to Art.2 rights.

---

[40] In *Isayeva, Yusupova and Bazayeva v Russia*, Judgment, February 24, 2005, the principles identified in the *McCann* and *Adronicou* judgments were applied by the Court in its assessment that missile attacks on Grozny by the forces of the Russian Federation amounted to a violation of Art.2.

[41] (1996) 21 E.H.R.R. 97 at paras 155 and 173.

[42] Discussed at para.18–08 above.

[43] Since the first edition of this book, the issue has been the subject of academic comment, but has not been litigated in the English courts despite the possibility of doing so under the Human Rights Act. As regards the argument that the common law test for self-defence and s.3 of the Criminal Law Act 1967 may need to be refined in accordance with Art.2 see in particular, Ashworth A., *Principles of Criminal Law* (5th edn 2006), pp.135–149 and Leverick F., *Is English self-defence law incompatible with Article 2 of the ECHR?* [2002] Crim.L.R. 347. For the alternative view, that the English law of self-defence requires no amendment under the *Human Rights Act*, see Buxton R., *The Human Rights Act and Substantive Criminal Law* [2000] Crim.L.R. 331; and Smith J.C., *The Use of Force in Public or Private Defence and Article 2* [2002] Crim.L.R. 958. The latter article by Professor Smith is a response to the above referred to article by Fiona Leverick. She in turn replied in [2002] Crim.L.R. 963. For a thorough analysis, see now Leverick F., *Killing in Self-Defence* (2006), esp. Ch.10.

[44] (1996) 21 E.H.R.R. 97 at paras 154–155.

The jurisprudence starts from the proposition that the right to life of everyone   **18–27** (including suspected or actual offenders) should be protected so far as possible. This emphasis on the right to life is not usually to be found as the starting point in English criminal cases, where the focus is upon whether the court has been left in reasonable doubt over the justifiability of the killing. In the same vein, the term "absolutely necessary" is undoubtedly stronger than the term "necessary" as it is understood in English law. Beyond that, there are at least three issues that warrant further consideration.

First, the Art.2 jurisprudence requires law enforcement officers to plan their   **18–28** operations so as to minimise the risk to life. The requirement of proper planning suggests that the ambit of criminal liability might be spread wider than the law enforcement officers who actually caused the death, and raises the possibility that commanding officers might in some circumstances be prosecuted for aiding and abetting the killing. If it could be established that there had been gross negligence on the part of senior officers which led to deaths, a prosecution for manslaughter might have a realistic prospect of resulting in conviction[45] the Human Rights Act would not be creating a criminal offence,[46] but the Convention would be grounding the duty of the senior police officer which might then be the basis for a manslaughter conviction. This line of argument is strengthened by the decision in *Osman v United Kingdom*.[47] More generally, one implication of s.6 of the Human Rights Act 1998, requiring public authorities to act in accordance with the Convention, is that senior law enforcement officers should train their personnel and plan their operations so as to preserve life to the maximum degree.

Secondly, the Court insisted, in both *McCann*[48] and *Andronicou*,[49] that the beliefs   **18–29** on which officers act should be based on "good reason." This is an objective test which, in effect, places such a high value on the right to life as to require law enforcement officers to make reasonable attempts to ascertain the true facts before using legal force.[50] In that respect it appears to be a more demanding standard than the "honest belief" held sufficient in *Gladstone Williams*[51] and *Beckford v R.*[52] even though the European Court has repeatedly expressed itself as mindful of the need to avoid imposing "an unrealistic burden on the state and its law enforcement officers".

---

[45] *cf.* the facts of the well-known tort case of *Alcock v Chief Constable of South Yorkshire* [1992] 1 A.C. 155, arising out of the Hillsborough football stadium disaster.
[46] S.7(8) of the HRA 1998, discussed at 18–44 below.
[47] (2000) 29 E.H.R.R. 245. See also *Oneryildiz v Turkey* (2005) 41 E.H.R.R. 20.
[48] (1996) 21 E.H.R.R. 97 at para.200.
[49] (1998) 25 E.H.R.R. 491 at para.192.
[50] See also *Ramsahai v Netherlands* (2006) 43 E.H.R.R. 823, re-asserting the strictness of the applicable test at [376–377] and [382].
[51] (1984) 78 Cr.App.R. 276.
[52] [1988] A.C. 130. See also the recent affirmation of the principle of "honest belief" in *Shaw v R.* [2002] 1 Cr.App.R. 10, PC and *R. v Martin (Tony)* [2002] 1 Cr.App.R. 27, CA. See also *R. (Sharman) v H.M. Coroner for Inner North London*, [2005] EWHC 857 (Admin)(police officers shot man carrying a table leg which they believed to be a sawn off shot gun, upheld by the Court of Appeal [2005]).

18–30 In the admissibility decision of *Caraher v United Kingdom*,[53] the Court considered the compatibility of the domestic law of self-defence with Art.2. On its facts, the finding of the court that the application was manifestly ill-founded was relatively straightforward. This was because the trial judge (Hutton C.J., as he then was) had concluded that the defendants had opened fire on a moving vehicle at a time when a fellow soldier was caught on top of its bonnet and the driver of the vehicle had refused to stop. In those circumstances, the judge held that "in the emergency of the moment" there was a reasonable possibility that the two accused fired at the vehicle because "they honestly believed it was necessary to so do in order to save Marine B from serious injury". In assessing the complaint the Court repeated the observations in *McCann*[54] that

> "the use of force may be justified . . . where it is based on an honest belief which is perceived, for good reasons, to be valid at the time but which subsequently turns out to be mistaken. To hold otherwise would be to impose an unrealistic burden on the State and its law-enforcement personnel in the execution of their duty . . . "

In reality, given the findings of fact by the trial judge, this approach would have been sufficient to dispose of the complaint under Art.2. However, the Court then proceded on the assumption that domestic law was not divergent from the "good reasons" test in *McCann*, stating that:

> "the approach taken by the domestic judge in the trial, in having regard to the *honest and reasonable* belief of the two soldiers that one of their collegues was at risk . . . is compatible with the principles established in *McCann*" (emphasis added).

As Fiona Leverick has pointed out,[55] the error of this analysis is that Hutton C.J. was working on the basis of "honest belief" alone, not the "honest and reasonable belief" standard understood by the Court. Thus, although the facts of the complaint might not have required it, the decision of the court means that the question of whether it is compatible to exclude from criminal liability killings that are carried out on the basis of irrational but honest perceptions has been left unanswered.

18–31 In *Brady v United Kingdom*,[56] an officer involved in an operation to thwart a suspected armed raid shot the deceased because he belived that he was pointing a gun at him. It subsequently transpired that the object believed to be a gun was in fact a torch. The Court declared the application inadmissible on the basis that the honest belief of the officer that it was necessary to shoot the deceased in order to protect himself, was nevertheless "derived from good reasons", perceived at the time to be valid, which were later shown to be mistaken.[57] Thus once again, the key issue of principle did not require consideration.

---

[53] Admissibility Decision, January 11, 2000.
[54] Para.200.
[55] See also Leverick, [2002] Crim.L.R. at 356.
[56] Admissibilty Decision, April 3, 2001.
[57] As regards the applicant's complaint about the planning and execution of the arrest operation, the court distinguished *McCann* on the basis that no element of planning or control could have legislated for the individual officer's mistaken belief that the deceased was about to shoot him. Unlike the facts of *McCann*, the superior officers bore no responsibility for the erroneous perception.

A similar approach was taken in *Bubbins v United Kingdom*,[58] where police had   **18–32**
shot dead a man during a siege. The Court stated that a killing could be justified
where based on "an honest belief which is perceived, for good reasons, to be
valid at the time but which turns out to be mistaken", but then emphasised only
the "honest belief" of the police officer who opened fire, and added that the
Court could substitute its own assessment for that of "an officer who was
required to react in the heat of the moment to avert an honestly perceived danger
to his life."[59]

In reality the Court has not yet had to consider a domestic case where the   **18–33**
mistaken belief in question could be properly characterised as irrational. Some
indication of how the court might respond to such a case can be found in the
judgment of *Gul v Turkey*.[60] The applicant's son was shot by police officers firing
through the door of his apartment during a search operation for suspected PKK
terrorists. Prior to the incident information had been received in relation to the
address, but not in relation to the deceased specifically. The police knocked on
the door in the middle of the night and as the deceased was in the process of
opening the door, the officers fired at least fifty shots through the door. In finding
a violation of Art.2, the Court reiterated the *McCann* "good reasons" test.[61] In
applying the test to the facts of the case the court found that:

> "the firing of at least 50–55 shots at the door was not justified by *any reasonable belief*
> of the officers that their lives were at risk from the occupants of the flat. Nor could the
> firing be justified by any consideration of the need to the secure entry to the flat as it
> placed in danger the lives of anyone in close proximity to the door" (emphasis
> added).[62]

The compatibility of domestic law with Art.2 was considered in *R. (Bennett) v*   **18–34**
H.M. Coroner for South London.[63] The submission of the claimant in *Bennett*
was that a direction to a coroner's jury on unlawful killing which allowed them
to consider whether the force used by firearms officers was reasonable was in
itself insufficient to comply with the Art.2 test of absolute necessity. Having
reviewed the case law Collins J. held:

> "It is . . . clear that the European Court of Human Rights has considered what English
> law requires for self-defence, and has not suggested that there is any incompatibility
> with art 2. In truth, if any officer reasonably decides that he must use lethal force, it will
> inevitably be because it is absolutely necessary to do so. To kill when it is not absolutely
> necessary to do so is surely to act unreasonably. Thus, the reasonableness test does not
> in truth differ from the art 2 test as applied in *McCann*. There is no support for the
> submission that the court has with hindsight to decide whether there was in fact absolute
> necessity. That would be to ignore reality and to produce what the court in *McCann*
> indicated was an inappropriate fetter upon the actions of the police which would be
> detrimental not only to their own lives but to the lives of others."[64]

---

[58] (2005) 41 E.H.R.R. 458.
[59] *ibid.*, at para.139.
[60] (2002) 34 E.H.R.R. 28.
[61] Para.78.
[62] Para.82.
[63] (2006) 170 J.P. 109, Q.B.D.
[64] Para.25.

Collins J. had in mind the necessity for any test to incorporate "heat of the moment" reality as perceived by a firearms officer (see para.26 of the judgement where he specifically quotes *Palmer v the Queen* [1971] A.C. 814 at p.832, as "worth bearing in mind".[65]

18–35   Drawing together the points arising from the above case law, the following conclusions can be arrived at. The purpose of the stricter standard in the Strasbourg cases is to provide greater protection of the right to life by requiring law enforcement personnel, where the situation permits it, to make efforts to verify their beliefs. If "good reason" is to be required where a defence of mistaken belief is raised in a case of this kind, the subjective test of mistake may need to be refined where the defence is based on justifiable force. On the other hand the application of Art.2 in *McCann* and *Andronicou* suggests that, even in respect of trained law enforcement officers, some indulgence should be granted to "heat of the moment" reactions, along the lines of *Palmer v R*.[66] The late Professor Smith's solution to this problem was that the law of gross neglisgence manslaughter ought to cater for honestly held but nevertheless grossly unreasonable beliefs that form the foundation for the use of fatal force:

> "This means that where the evidence suggests that the defendant was acting under a mistaken belief, a jury should be directed that, if the force used was reasonable in the circumstances as he honestly believed them to be, then they must acquit him of murder. But, if they do so acquit him, they must go on to consider whether (i) in the actual circumstances, the force used was unreasonable and, if it was, (ii) whether the defendant, in making the mistake, was guilty of gross negligence, so bad as in their judgment to amount to a crime. If they are sure that he was, then they should convict him of manslaughter"[67]

18–36   A third cluster of points relate to the precise wording of the exceptions to Art.2. Although the killing must be "absolutely necessary" for the achievement of one of the three stated purposes, there is no requirement of proportionality on the face of Art.2: that defect in the drafting has, however, been remedied by the case law, and in *Andronicou* the Court stated that the force must be "strictly proportionate."[68] The first exception to Art.2 refers to the "defence of any person from unlawful violence". The reference is to "violence" rather than to "killing", suggesting that it is in conformity to the Convention to deprive a person of their life when that person is inflicting, or about to inflict, serious but non-life-threatening injury on another. The wording also leaves open the question of how imminent the "unlawful violence" must be. This was an issue before the Commission in *Kelly v United Kingdom*,[69] where soldiers in Northern Ireland had

---

[65] [1971] A.C. 814, at 832; see the similar passage in *Bubbins*, cited in 18–32 above.
[66] [1971] A.C. 814.
[67] Smith J.C., *The Use of Force in Public or Private Defence and Article 2* [2002] Crim.L.R. 958 at p.961.
[68] See the Commission's decision in *Stewart v United Kingdom* (1984) 39 D.R. 162, the Court's statement in *Andronicou and Constantinou* (1998) 25 E.H.R.R. 491 at para.171, and the statement and application of the principle in *Gulec v Turkey* (1999) 28 E.H.R.R. 121 at para.71. See also *Gul v Turkey*, (2002) 34 E.H.R.R. 28 at para.82.
[69] (1993) 74 D.R. 139, on which see the valuable discussion by Sir John Smith, "The right to life and the right to kill in law enforcement" (1994) N.L.J. 354.

opened fire on a stolen car containing three youths which was speeding away from a checkpoint, and one of the occupants was killed. In the civil action that followed, the Northern Ireland courts accepted that the soldiers suspected the youths of being terrorists and thought that they would continue terrorist (therefore life-threatening) activities if allowed to drive away. How far into the future might such activities take place, and does this affect the "prevention of crime" justification? These important questions were not resolved by the Commission, which pointed out that the prevention of crime is not mentioned as an exception to Art.2 and could therefore not be relied upon. But the same issue of "imminence" arises in relation to the "unlawful violence" exception in Art.2(2)(a). In *McCann* the point was not tested because it was assumed that the detonation of the alleged bomb was indeed imminent.

In rejecting the application in *Kelly*, the Commission held that the soldiers' use of deadly force was justified according to Art.2(2)(b), as "absolutely necessary . . . in order to effect a lawful arrest." Sir John Smith has pointed out that there was no power of arrest in the circumstances of that case, and that the Commission misunderstood the position.[70] Moreover there is a fundamental question about the drafting of Art.2: how can a killing be necessary to effect an arrest, since by definition there can be no arrest if the person has been killed? Even if this point is regarded as overdone, there are other difficulties. As Trechsel has argued, what is missing from this part of Art.2 "is a reference to the relationship between the force used for the purpose of the arrest on the one hand and the reason for the arrest on the other hand."[71] The force permissible to arrest a speeding motorist, a truanting child or an illegal immigrant ought to be severely limited, as Trechsel argues. It is therefore of some considerable importance that in *Nachova v Bulgaria*,[72] the Court for the first time held as a matter of general principle that

    18–37

> "it can in no circumstances be 'absolutely necessary' within the meaning of Article 2 (2) of the Convention to use such firearms to arrest a person suspected of a non fatal offence who is known not to pose a threat to life or limb, even where a failure to do so may result in the opportunity to arrest the fugitive being lost".[73]

In so finding the Court relied on the United Nations Basic Principles on the Use of Force and Firearms by Law Enforcement Officials,[74] in particular para.9:

> "Law enforcement officials shall not use firearms against persons except in self-defence or defence of others against the imminent threat of death or serious injury, to prevent the perpetration of a particularly serious crime involving grave threat to life, to arrest

---

[70] *ibid.*, at 355.

[71] Trechsel S., "Spotlights on Article 2 ECHR, the Right to Life", in Benedek W., Isak H. and Kicker R. (eds), *Development and Developing International and European Law* (Frankfurt, 1999), p.685.

[72] (2004) 39 E.H.R.R. 37.

[73] Para.105. On the facts of the case, two men of Roma origin were military conscripts who escaped from a construction site and were apprehended by officers that knew that neither of the men were armed. After warning them that they would shoot if they did not surrender, the men refused to give themselves up and were shot.

[74] Adopted on September 7, 1990 by the 8th United Nations Congress on the Prevention of Crime and the Treatment of Offenders.

a person presenting such a danger and resisting their authority, or to prevent his or her escape, and only when less extreme means are insufficient to achieve these objectives. In any event, intentional lethal use of firearms may only be made when strictly unavoidable in order to protect life."[75]

The unequivocal standard recognised by the Court in *Nachova* is in keeping with the approach in other jurisdictions.[76] The Grand Chamber subsequently upheld the Chamber judgment.[77]

18–38   There are also further questions about the scope of the exceptions: Article 2(2)(c) creates an exception for cases of killing in the course of lawful action to quell a riot or insurrection (which must be "strictly proportionate", as for the other exceptions),[78] but the absence of any general "prevention of crime" exception means that killing to protect property is always a breach of the Convention. Only if the term "unlawful violence" in the Convention were to be given an artificially wide meaning could killing in imminent cases of burglary or arson be brought within the exceptions to Art.2, although there might be an argument that robbery (which is defined so as to require an element of force) and rape would satisfy the requirement.[79]

18–39   The Strasbourg case law is of course primarily concerned with killings by law enforcement officers. But the state's positive obligation is to ensure that the law protects the lives of citizens from unjustifiable deprivation by other individuals.[80] Although a private citizen would be unlikely to violate Art.2 rights by failing to plan an "operation" with sufficient care and respect for life,[81] a private citizen might well use force against another without "good reason" and that might lead to an acquittal under current English law whilst violating the Art.2 right of the victim.[82] This may suggest that the relevant rules of English law require adaptation generally, and not just in their application to law enforcement officers.[83]

---

[75] According to other provisions of the Principles, law enforcement officials shall "act in proportion to the seriousness of the offence and the legitimate objective to be achieved" (para.5). Also, "Governments shall ensure that arbitrary or abusive use of force and firearms by law enforcement officials is punished as a criminal offence under their law" (para.7). National rules and regulations on the use of firearms should "ensure that firearms are used only in appropriate circumstances and in a manner likely to decrease the risk of unnecessary harm".

[76] *Tennessee v Garner* (1985) 471 US 1; *Govender v Ministry of Safety and Security* 2001 (4) SA 273; *State v Walters ex p. Ministry of Safety and Security* [2003] 1 L.R.C. 494.

[77] (2006) 42 E.H.R.R. 43.

[78] *Stewart v United Kingdom* (1999) 39 D.R. 162, *Gulec v Turkey* (1999) 28 E.H.R.R. 121.

[79] For comparison, see the extended notion of a "violent offence" for the purpose of s.161(3) of the Powers of Criminal Courts Setencing Act 2000, discussed in *Archbold Criminal Pleading Evidence and Practice 2005*, para.5–9, p.525.

[80] By analogy with the court's decision in *A v United Kingdom* (1998) 27 E.H.R.R. 611. The potential applicability of Art.2 to the content of substantive criminal law as it effects the relationship between private citizens has been recognised by the court in *Vo v France* (2005) 40 E.H.R.R. 12; *Menson v United Kingdom* (2003) 37 E.H.R.R. CD220; *Mastromatteo v Italy*, Judgment, October 24, 2002; and *Cavelli and Ciglio v Italy*, Admissibility Decision, January 17, 2002. In the context of Art.3, see also *X and Y v Netherlands* (1986) 8 E.H.R.R. 235.

[81] There may be rare cases where this is relevant: see Ashworth, "Self-Defence and the Right to Life" [1976] Camb. L.J. 282 at 292–296.

[82] *Cf.* the position of the defence of reasonable.

[83] See Ashworth, p.147.

Finally, any discussion on this issue, must also take account of situations of non-   **18–40**
fatal force and the implications of common law self-defence upon the absolute
right not to be the subject of serious assault under Art.3. Unlike Art.2 (2), Art.3,
on its face, has no exceptions and, indeed, in *Ribitsch v Austria*,[84] the Court
explicitly stated that Art.3 makes "no provision for exceptions".[85] In that same
case, however, the Court in dealing with the *prima facie* degrading practice of
handcuffing prisoners in public, identified, in the context of prison law, exceptions to the prohibition on degrading treatment "made strictly necessary" by the
prisoner's conduct.[86] At least two Strasbourg judgments now recognise that Art.3
must be read subject to the same exceptions as Art.2 in respect of the use of force,
particularly by law enforcement officers.[87] It seems, however, that the "good
reasons" test in *McCann* and *Andronicou* should be equally applicable to non-
fatal force, and so the same questions of compatibility arise with regard to a
defence based on a belief that cannot be justified for good reasons.

Abortion

A second question arising from Art.2 is whether it protects the right to life of a   **18–41**
foetus or unborn child and, therefore, whether the provisions of the Abortion Act
1967 are vulnerable to challenge. The 1967 Act specifies various procedures for
therapeutic abortion, allowing medical termination *inter alia* if the pregnancy is
in the first 24 weeks and "the continuance of the pregnancy would involve risk,
greater than if the pregnancy were terminated, of injury to the physical or mental
health of the pregnant woman or any existing children of her family."

Unlike Art.4 of the American Convention on Human Rights, which provides that   **18–42**
the right to life must be protected "in general, from the moment of the conception", Art.2 of the European Convention is silent as to the temporal limitations
of the right to life and, in particular, does not define "everyone" ("toute
personne") whose "life" is protected by the Convention. Both the Commission
and the Court have avoided definitively determining the issue as regards the
rights of the foetus,[88] although the rights of both the mother and the father have
readily been recognised as being engaged.

In *Paton v United Kingdom*[89] the Commission held that Art.2 does not confer on   **18–43**
unborn children an absolute right to life, and that the abortion of a 10-week old
foetus in order to prevent "injury to the physical or mental health of the pregnant
woman", under the 1967 Act, did not violate Art.2. The Commission stated that,
even assuming that the right to life is secured to a foetus from the beginning of
pregnancy, this right is subject to an implied limitation allowing pregnancy to be

---

[84] (1995) 21 E.H.R.R. 573.
[85] Para.32.
[86] Para.38.
[87] In *Rivas v France* [2005] Crim.L.R. 305, and in *RL and M-J D v France* [2005] Crim.L.R.
307.
[88] *Vo v France* (2005) 40 E.H.R.R. 1, para.75.
[89] (1980) 3 E.H.R.R. 408. Applied in domestic law in *In re F (in utero)* [1988] Fam 122; *In re MB
(Medical Treatment)* [1997] 2 FLR 426; and *Evans v Amicus Health Care Trust* [2005] Fam 1.

terminated in order to protect the mother's life or health.[90] In a subsequent decision, *H. v Norway*,[91] the Commission held that the abortion of a 14-week old foetus on the statutory ground that the "pregnancy, birth or care of the child may place the woman in a difficult situation in life" did not violate Art.2. In a sphere in which the laws of Contracting States vary somewhat, it is normal for the Strasbourg organs to leave a significant margin of appreciation. However, the Commission went on to state that it "will not exclude that in certain circumstances" the right to life of an unborn child might be protected.

18–44   In *Vo v France*,[92] a woman lost her unborn child as a result of negligent medical treatment when she was admitted to hospital, which then necessitated the termination of her pregnancy. The complaint, adjudicated upon by the Grand Chamber, was whether the absence of a criminal penalty in French law for unlawfully causing the death of the foetus amounted to a violation of Art.2. On the critical issue of whether the foetus enjoys independent rights, the Court expressed itself as

> "convinced that it is neither desirable, nor even possible as matters stand, to answer in the abstract the question whether the unborn child is a person for the purposes of Article 2 of the Convention ('*personne*' in the French text)".[93]

However, on the facts of the case, the Court ruled that the unborn child's lack of clear legal status did not necessarily deprive it of all protection under French law because the life of the foetus was intimately connected with the rights of the mother and father who were able to sue in negligence (para.86). As to the absence of a criminal penalty, the Court held that in the sphere of medical negligence it was permissible under Art.2 to afford the victims a remedy in the civil courts, togther with the prospect of claiming damages and invoking appropriate disciplinary measures (para.90).

18–45   There remains a theoretical possibility that the availability of therapeutic abortion up to 24 weeks (under the 1967 Act) might be attacked as affording insufficient protection to the life of the unborn child. This argument is left open by all of the decisions discussed above, although its prospects of success are diminished by the emphasis in the reasoning on the risk to the mother's health and by the considerable margin of appreciation appropriate to this issue. As Trechsel comments, the Commission avoided taking a definite position on the application of Art.2 in this sphere, "by saying that even if a certain protection of the foetus were to be regarded as being covered by the guarantee, the interference was justified in the circumstances."[94] However, it is noteworthy that the German Constitutional Court, in reviewing two successive abortion statutes, has recognised the

---

[90] The applicant in this case was the prospective father, and the Commission considered (and dismissed) various arguments based on Art.8 to the effect that the prospective father's right to respect for his family life was violated if the prospective mother was allowed to have a termination without regard for his wishes.

[91] (1992) 73 D.R. 155.

[92] (2005) 40 E.H.R.R. 12.

[93] Para.85.

[94] Trechsel (n.71, above), p.672.

foetus as having a right to life that should be granted protection under the German constitution—not an absolute right, but one that cannot simply be subordinated to the pregnant woman's interests.[95] By contrast, in South Africa, the High Court has specifically found that a foetus is not a legal persona for the purposes of intepreting s.11 of the Constituion ("everyone has the right to life").[96]

Controversy has also raged on this issue in the United States since the historic **18–46** decision in *Roe v Wade*,[97] where the Supreme Court struck down a Texas statute that prohibited abortion in all cases except where the mother's life was in danger. The rationale for the decision, much debated, was that the pregnant woman's right to privacy was fundamental. The right was not absolute, but states could only place limits on it for compelling reasons. The majority of the court stated, further, that a foetus is not a "person", for constitutional purposes, but that states do have an interest in protecting "potential life", an interest that becomes compelling when the foetus is viable. The decision has generated enormous debate,[98] and subsequent decisions of the Supreme Court have diluted its effect while stopping short of overruling it. There is now recognition that states have an interest in protecting potential human life from the stage of conception,[99] and there is also acceptance that states do not need to find a "compelling" reason for restricting abortion so long as they do not impose an "undue burden on a woman's ability" to make a decision.[100]

A different approach may be found in some of the jurisprudence of the Supreme **18–47** Court of Canada, interpreting Art.7 of the Canadian Charter which guarantees an individual's "right to life, liberty and security of person." In the leading case of *Morgentaler, Smoling and Scott v R*,[101] the court focussed on the bodily security of the pregnant woman. The provisions of the Criminal Code required a pregnant woman who wanted an abortion to submit an application to a local "therapeutic abortion committee", resulting in delays and, in some areas, the virtual unavailability of therapeutic abortions. The Supreme Court found that this procedure infringed the guarantee of security of the person, in both physical and emotional senses, by subjecting pregnant women to psychological stress.[102] It is highly unlikely that existing English procedures would be vulnerable on the *Morgentaler* approach, but if restrictions on the availability of abortions under English law were contemplated, it would be necessary to reckon with the possibility of a challenge under the Convention along these lines.

---

[95] See BVerfGe 39, 1 (1975), and BVerfGe, 203 (1993).
[96] *Christian Lawyers Association of South Africa v Minister of Health* (1998) 50 B.M.L.R. 241.
[97] 410 US 113 (1973).
[98] See, for example, the extensive treatment in Tribe L.A., *American Constitutional Law* (2nd edn 1988), Ch.15, and the same writer's monograph, *Abortion: the Clash of Absolutes* (1990).
[99] *Webster v Reproductive Health Services* 492 US 490 (1989).
[100] *Planned Parenthood v Casey* 505 US 833 (1992). For a recent survey, see Kommers D.P. and Finn J.E., *American Constitutional Law* (1998), pp.450–454 and 460–464.
[101] (1988) 44 D.L.R. (4th) 385.
[102] See also *Winnipeg Child and Family Services (Northwest Area) v G* [1997] 2 S.C.R. 925.

Patients in a Persistent Vegetative State: Withdrawal of Treatment and Euthanasia

18–48   In its well-known decision in *Airedale NHS Trust v Bland*,[103] the House of Lords held that it is lawful to discontinue the life-sustaining treatment of a PVS patient if it is no longer in the patient's best interests for the treatment to continue. The discontinuance of treatment is regarded as an omission, which then raises the question whether there is a duty to continue treatment. If it is not in the patient's best interests, then no such duty exists. Is this reasoning consistent or inconsistent with the right to life declared in Art.2?

18–49   There is no Strasbourg decision on this point. The closest case is *Widmer v Switzerland*,[104] where the applicant alleged a breach of Art.2 when hospital staff had declined to treat his father in an advanced state of Parkinson's disease, who then died. The application was dismissed by the Commission on the ground that the offence of negligent manslaughter in Swiss law was sufficient to discharge the state's positive duty to "take all reasonable steps to protect life" under Art.2. There was no need for the Swiss legislature to go further and to enact a special law penalising passive euthanasia. This ruling suggests that the "negligence" approach is sufficient, and that the question whether there should be a duty to provide life-sustaining treatment where there are unlikely to be any benefits to the patient is crucial.

18–50   The matter becomes more complicated when the patient's will has not been and cannot be expressed. In *NHS Trust A v Mrs M* and *NHS Trust B v Mrs H*,[105] Butler-Sloss P. held that the law as formulated in *Airedale NHS Trust v Bland* is consistent with the Art.2 rights of PVS patients and with the Art.2 obligations of the government. "An omission to provide treatment by the medical team will, in my judgment, only be incompatible with Article 2 where the circumstances are such as to impose a positive obligation on the state to take steps to prolong a patient's life."[106] In *R. (Burke) v General Medical Council*,[107] the claimant, who was suffering from a congenital degenerative brain condition which would inevitably result in his needing to receive nutrition and hydration by artificial means ("ANH"), sought clarification as to the circumstances in which such treatment might lawfully be withdrawn. The court conducted a detailed analysis of the General Medical Council guidelines and held that: (1) if the patient was competent (or, although incompetent, had made a valid and relevant advance directive) his decision as to his best interests and as to what life-prolonging treatment he should or should not have was in principle determinative. (2) Conversely, neither Art.2 nor 3 could entitle anyone to force life-prolonging treatment on a competent patient who refused to accept it. (3) It would (following previous case law) not be a breach of Art.3 for treatment to be withdrawn in circumstances where it was serving absolutely no purpose, other than the very

---

103 [1993] A.C. 789.
104 App. No.20527/92 (unreported).
105 [2001] 2 W.L.R. 942.
106 *ibid.*, para.31.
107 [2005] Q.B. 424.

short prolongation of the life of a dying patient who had slipped into a coma and lacked all awareness of what was happening.[108]

If there is agreement that further treatment will not be in the patient's best   **18–51** interests, there is no duty to continue and the state's obligation does not arise. This reasoning rests on the initial characterisation of the withdrawal of treatment as an omission rather than an action. In a sphere so sensitive as this, it is most unlikely that the Strasbourg Court would adopt an approach which required member states to criminalise withdrawal of treatment, euthanasia, or (probably) even mercy killings.

Prior to *Pretty v United Kingdom*,[109] the Strasbourg courts had never had the   **18–52** occasion to rule definitively on the legality of euthanasia and conversely whether there is *a right to die*. In *R. v United Kingdom*,[110] the Commission found that a prosecution for aiding, abetting, counselling or procuring a suicide was outside the protection of Art.8 since it "tresspased on the public interest of protecting life". On the general issue of euthanasia there is no uniformity among the laws of European states, and van Dijk and van Hoof comment that:

> "even in those situations where it must in reason be assumed that human life still exists, euthanasia does not *per se* conflict with the Convention. In fact, the value of the life to be protected can and must be weighed against other rights of the person in question, particularly his right, laid down in Article 3, to be protected from inhuman and degrading treatment. Whether the will of the person is decisive in such a case depends on whether the right to life is or is not to be regarded as inalienable."[111]

In the *Pretty* case the House of Lords[112] refused to grant a mandatory order   **18–53** requiring the DPP to undertake not to prosecute the husband of Diane Pretty if he assisted her to die. Mrs Pretty was suffering the advanced stages of motor neurone disease and was no longer physically able to take her own life. In the English courts the case was in part decided by the fact that it is only in the most exceptional cases that judicial review can be used to declare a substantive provision of the criminal law unlawful in advance of actual prosecutions. However, both the House of Lords and the European Court considered whether the prohibition on euthanasia in circumstances as those suffered by Mrs Pretty amounted to a breach of Arts 2, 3 and 8. In dealing with the Art.2 claim, the Court refused to accept that "the right to life" can be regarded as involving a negative aspect[113]:

---

[108] See also *W. Healthcare NHS Trust v H.* [2005] 1 W.L.R. 834, CA. As to the approach in other jurisdictions, see *In the Matter of a Ward of a Court* [1995] I.L.R.M. 401 (Irish Supreme Ct.); *Re G* [1997] L.R.C. 146 (Nz High Ct.); *Rodriguez v Att.-Gen. of British Columbia* [1994] 2 L.R.C. 136 (Canadian Supreme Ct.); *Gian Kaur v State of Punjab* [1996] 2 L.R.C. 264 (Indian Supreme Ct.); and *Washington v Glucksberg* 521 US 702 (1997) (US Supreme Ct.).
[109] (2002) 35 E.H.R.R. 1. See also *R. (Pretty) v Director of Public Prosecutions* [2002] 1 A.C. 800, HL.
[110] Application No.20527/92, (unreported).
[111] van Dijk P. and van Hoof G.J.H., *Theory and Practice of the European Convention on Human Rights* (3rd edn 1999), pp.302–303.
[112] [2002] 1 A.C. 800, HL.
[113] (2002) 35 E.H.R.R. 1, para.39.

"While, for example, in the context of art 11 of the Convention, the freedom of association was found to involve not only a right to join an association but a corresponding right not to be forced to join an association, the Court observes that the notion of a freedom implies some measure of choice as to its exercise. Article 2 of the Convention is phrased in different terms. It is unconcerned with issues to do with the quality of living or what a person chooses to do with his or her life. To the extent that these aspects are recognised as so fundamental to the human condition that they require protection from State interference, they may be reflected in the rights guaranteed by other Articles acknowledged in the Convention, or in other international human rights instruments. Article 2 cannot, without a distortion of language, be interpreted as conferring the diametrically opposite right, namely a right to die; nor can it create a right to self-determination in the sense of conferring on an individual the entitlement to choose death rather than life".

18–54   In so finding, the Court held that the regulation of suicidal conduct was a matter of domestic law and could not be considered in the abstract.[114] Given the ongoing pain and suffering that the patient was condemned to in the circumstances, the question arose as to whether it was inhuman and degrading not to allow her to be assisted in ending her own life. Although the Court expressed sympathy for the applicant's situation, it was not prepared to characterise the DPP's refusal to give an undertaking not to prosecute as "treatment" within the meaning of Art.3; neither was the court prepared to accept that the State was under an obligation to permit or facilitate her death.[115] As regards Art.8, the Court held, citing *Rodriguez v Attorney General of Canada*,[116] that Art.8(1) was engaged in circumstances where the applicant was prevented by law from exercising her choice to avoid what she considered to be an an undignified and distressing end to her life.[117] However, in deciding whether the use of a blanket criminal offence for assisted suicides was necessary in a democratic society the Court held, in agreement with the House of Lords and the majority of the Canadian Supreme Court in the *Rodriguez* case, that

"The law in issue in this case, s 2 of the 1961 Act, was designed to safeguard life by protecting the weak and vulnerable and especially those who are not in a condition to take informed decisions against acts intended to end life or to assist in ending life. Doubtless the condition of terminally ill individuals will vary. But many will be vulnerable and it is the vulnerability of the class which provides the rationale for the law in question. It is primarily for States to assess the risk and the likely incidence of abuse if the general prohibition on assisted suicides were relaxed or if exceptions were to be created. Clear risks of abuse do exist, notwithstanding arguments as to the possibility of safeguards and protective procedures".[118]

The Law Commission has now recommended a public consultation on these disputed questions.[119]

---

[114] Para.41.
[115] Para.54.
[116] [1994] 2 L.R.C. 136.
[117] Paras 65–67.
[118] Para.74.
[119] Law Com. No.304, *Murder, Manslaughter and Infanticide* (2006), Pt 7.

Other Surgical Procedures

The Court of Appeal has had to grapple with a question which has not been **18–55** before any of the Strasbourg organs, notably the application of Art.2 to the lawfulness of an operation to separate conjoined twins which is likely to result in the saving of one life and the termination of the other. In *Re A (children)(conjoined twins: surgical separation)*[120] the Court of Appeal held that the operation would be lawful, even though it would result in the death of the weaker twin. The court did not follow the *Bland* decision[121] in characterising the operation as an omission. It accepted that the separation was an intentional act, but held that the intention was to separate the twins so as to give the stronger twin the opportunity of a long and healthy life. This would not breach Art.2 since it would not amount to depriving the weaker twin of her life "intentionally": her death would be "foreseen as an inevitable consequence" of an operation intended to save her sister, and her death would occur because "her body on its own is not and never has been viable."[122] This interpretation restricts the meaning of "intentionally" to "purposively", which Robert Walker L.J. referred to as the "natural and ordinary meaning" of the word,[123] and which is clearly narrower than the meaning adopted for English criminal law by the House of Lords in *Woollin*.[124] However, members of the court felt able to use the doctrine of necessity in order to reach the desired result.

III. Protection of Article 8 Rights

The principal thrust of Art.8(1) is to protect an individual's own private life, and **18–56** therefore an application by a person convicted of aiding and abetting the suicide of others was declared inadmissible.[125]

The concept of "private life" in Art.8 "covers the physical and moral integrity of the person, including his or her sexual life."[126] Whilst the Strasbourg Court has insisted that consensual sexual behaviour between adults in private should not be criminalised,[127] it has also recognised the importance of ensuring that the rights of vulnerable people not to be subjected to sexual abuse should be upheld.[128] Thus in *X and Y v Netherlands*[129] the Court declared that:

---

[120] [2001] Fam 147, CA.

[121] *Airedale NHS Trust v Bland* [1993] A.C. 789.

[122] [2001] Fam 147, CA, *per* Robert Walker L.J. at pp.256G and 259C.

[123] *ibid.*, at p.256H.

[124] [1999] A.C. 92.

[125] *R. v United Kingdom* (1983) 33 D.R. 270—see *Reid* [1982] Crim.L.R. 514. See also *Pretty v United Kingdom*, (2002) 35 E.H.R.R. 1.

[126] *X and Y v Netherlands* (1986) 8 E.H.R.R. 235 at para.22. Increasingly the judgments of the European Court have extended the concept of "private life" to include matters of personal and social development. See *Niemietz v Germany*, (1993) 16 E.H.R.R. 97 at para.29; *Stubbings v United Kingdom*, 23 E.H.R.R. 241 at para.59; *Botta v Italy*, 26 E.H.R.R. 241 at para.32; and *Von Hannover v Germany*, (2005) 40 E.H.R.R. 1 at para.57. The quality and dignity of a person's life is also protected under Art.8: *Pretty v United Kingdom*, (2002) 35 E.H.R.R. 1, at para.65. Thus treatment which does not reach the severity of Art.3 treatment may nonetheless breach Art.8 where there are sufficiently adverse effects on the physical and moral integrity of the individual: *Bensaid v United Kingdom*, (2001) 33 E.H.R.R. 10, at para.46.

[127] *Cf.* the discussion of decisions such as *Dudgeon* and *ADT* in Ch.8 above.

[128] This was recognised by the court in the *Dudgeon* judgment itself: (1982) 4 E.H.R.R. 149.

[129] (1986) 8 E.H.R.R. 235.

"although the object of Article 8 is essentially that of protecting the individual against arbitrary interference by the public authorities, it does not merely compel the State to abstain from such interference; in addition to this primarily negative undertaking, there may be positive obligations inherent in an effective respect for private or family life. These obligations may involve the adoption of measures designed to secure respect for private life even in the sphere of the relations of individuals between themselves."[130]

This statement has particular implications for the sexual abuse of children and the mentally handicapped: States must, in principle, provide protection from sexual molestation in these cases. The difficulty with Netherlands law, which was identified in the *X and Y* case, was that prosecutions for most sexual offences required a complaint by the victim. Where the victim was a child under 16, a parent or guardian could bring the complaint. Where the victim was aged 16 but mentally handicapped, there was no such possibility. Since in this case the victim's mental state was such that she could not make a complaint in the required form, the Netherlands courts had held that her father could not lawfully bring a complaint on her behalf when the prosecution service declined to prosecute. The Court held that "recourse to the criminal law is not necessarily the only" means of ensuring that Art.8 rights are respected, but concluded thus:

"The Court finds that the protection afforded by the civil law in the case of wrongdoing of the kind inflicted on Miss Y is insufficient. This is a case where fundamental values and essential aspects of private life are at stake. Effective deterrence is indispensable in this area and it can only be achieved by criminal provisions; indeed, it is by such provisions that the matter is normally regulated. Moreover ... this is in fact an area in which the Netherlands has generally opted for a system of protection based on the criminal law. The only gap, so far as the Commission and the Court have been made aware, is as regards persons in the situation of Miss Y; in such cases, this system meets a procedural obstacle which the Dutch legislature had apparently not foreseen."[131]

18–57   The Sexual Offences Act 2003 is supposed to take seriously the positive duty to ensure that the Art.8 rights of all persons to sexual autonomy, including the vulnerable. The Act includes many offences specifically to protect the young and the mentally disordered. However, the Act also applies to young defendants involved in sexual acts and experimentation. In *G.*[132] a boy of 15 had sex with a girl of 12, and his plea of guilty was accepted on the basis that she told him she was 15 and that she consented. The charge in this case was rape of a girl under 13, and since consent is not relevant and the law imposes strict liability as to age, the defendant had no choice other than to plead guilty. In the Court of Appeal the question was raised whether conviction of such a serious offence breached G's Art.8 rights, since he ought to have been either cautioned or prosecuted for a lesser offence. Lord Phillips C.J. held:

"We accept the possibility that prosecution of a child under section 5 rather than section 13, or indeed prosecution at all, in relation to consensual sexual intercourse may, on the particular facts, produce consequences that amount to an interference with the child's

---

[130] *ibid.*, at para.23.
[131] *ibid.*, para.27.
[132] [2006] EWCA Crim 821, [2006] Crim.L.R. 930.

Article 8.1 rights that are not justified under Article 8.2. Where, however, as here, no criticism can be made of an initial charge of breach of section 5, we do not consider that it follows that the judge must necessarily substitute an alternative charge of breach of section 13 if it transpires that the sexual activity was, or must be treated as, consensual."

Whether or not one accepts the view that the judge had no obligation to substitute an alternative charge, the duty of every public authority to act in conformity with the Convention (s.6 of the Human Rights Act) would surely ground an obligation by the Crown Prosecution Service to apply to the court to drop the higher charge and substitute a lesser charge. The Court of Appeal gave some weight to the positive obligation under Art.8 by reducing the sentence to a non-custodial one.

IV. The Protection of other Rights

In principle the state has the same duty to ensure the protection of other rights as it has to protect Art.8 rights. The same argument can therefore be mounted in relation to Arts 9, 10 and 11 of the Convention. Thus the State's obligation to ensure protection of the right to practise religion under Art.9 has been recognised in a number of decisions. In *Otto-Preminger-Institut v Austria*[133] the Court held that "the manner in which religious beliefs are opposed or denied is a matter which may engage the responsibility of the State, notably its responsibility to ensure the peaceful enjoyment of the right guaranteed under Article 9 to the holders of those beliefs or doctrines." For this reason the Court held that a prosecution for blasphemy did not violate Art.10. Similar reasoning may be found in *Wingrove v United Kingdom*[134]: Art.10(2) allows for interference with the right to freedom of expression in order to protect the rights of others, and states have a duty to protect the right to freedom of religion. However, the extent of this obligation remains uncertain. The Commission held in *Choudhury v United Kingdom*[135] that the absence of a criminal sanction against publications which offend those of minority faiths was not a violation of Art.9. However, in *Norwood v United Kingdom*,[136] the Court held that the prosecution of a member of the British National Party for religiously aggravated harassment under s.5 of the Public Order Act 1985 for displaying a poster in his shop was not incompatible with Art.10, because the poster in question fell within the meaning of Art.17 of the Convention.[137] Article 17 declares that no person or group has the right to engage in any activity "aimed at the destruction of any of the rights" set forth in the Convention. The Court stated that:

18–58

---

[133] (1995) 19 E.H.R.R. 34 at para.47, citing *Kokkinakis v Greece* (1994) 17 E.H.R.R. 397.

[134] (1997) 24 E.H.R.R. 1 at para.48.

[135] (1991) 12 H.R.L.J. 172.

[136] (2005) 40 E.H.R.R. SE11 affirming *Norwood v DPP* [2003] Crim.L.R. 888, DC. See also *DPP v Hammond* [2004] Crim.L.R. 851, DC. *Cf. Percy v DPP*, (2002) 166 J.P. 93, DC.

[137] The text of Art.17 reads as follows:

"Nothing in this Convention may be interpreted as implying for any State, group or person any right to engage in any activity or perform any act aimed at the destruction of any rights and freedoms set forth herein or at their limitation to a greater extent than is provided for in the Convention".

"The poster . . . in the present case contained a photograph of the Twin Towers in flame, the words 'Islam out of Britain—Protect the British People' and a symbol of a crescent and star in a prohibition sign. The Court notes and agrees with the assessment made by the domestic courts, namely that the words and images on the poster amounted to a public expression of attack on all Muslims in the United Kingdom. Such a general, vehement attack against a religious group, linking the group as a whole with a grave act of terrorism, is incompatible with the values proclaimed and guaranteed by the Convention, notably tolerance, social peace and non-discrimination. The applicant's display of the poster in his window constituted an act within the meaning of Article 17, which did not, therefore, enjoy the protection of Article 10".

Likewise in *WP. v Poland*,[138] the court relied on Art.17 to justify the prohibition of an overtly anti-Semitic organisation on the grounds that its aims were contrary to the text and spirit of the Convention.[139]

18–59   The state's positive obligation to safeguard freedom of assembly under Art.11 has also been recognised explicitly. In *Plattform Artze fur das Leben v Austria*[140] the court acknowledged that the exercise of the right to demonstrate might cause annoyance to other citizens, but maintained the right to demonstrate without fear of attack:

"In a democracy the right to counter-demonstrate cannot extend to inhibiting the right to demonstrate. Genuine, effective freedom of peaceful assembly cannot, therefore, be reduced to a mere duty on the part of the State not to interfere; a purely negative conception would not be compatible with the object and purpose of Article 11. Like Article 8, Article 11 sometimes requires positive measures to be taken, even in the sphere of relations between individuals, if need be."[141]

This passage has significance both for the content of the criminal law and for the practicalities of law enforcement.[142]

V. Section 7(8) of the Human Rights Act

18–60   Section 7(8) of the 1998 Act states that "nothing in this Act creates a criminal offence." Thus, even if an English court were to determine that the state has failed to fulfil one of its positive obligations, the court would be unable to afford a remedy to the victim within the context of the criminal proceedings. The creation of a new offence to meet the requirements of the Convention would require legislation. However, where an English court finds that a particular criminal law defence is too broadly stated to provide adequate protection for the rights of the victim, it would be open to the court to limit the ambit of the defence in accordance with Convention law. This is what the Court of Appeal did in relation to the common law defence of reasonable chastisement in *R. v H*[143] as a

---

[138] (2005) E.H.R.R. SE1.
[139] *Cf. United Communist Party of Turkey v Turkey*, (1998) 26 E.H.R.R. 121.
[140] (1991) 13 E.H.R.R. 204.
[141] *ibid.*, at para.32; note the similarity in the phrasing of the last sentence with the passage cited from *X and Y v Netherlands* at n.103 above.
[142] See the discussion of *Redmond-Bate v DPP* [1999] Crim.L.R. 998 in para.8–62 above.
[143] [2002] 1 Cr.App.R. 7. See now s.58 of the Children Act 2004 and para.18–16 above.

result of the judgment of the European Court in *A v United Kingdom*.[144] Its is also, in effect, what the House of Lords did in *R. v R*,[145] when it removed the marital rape defence on the ground that it reflected an outdated and unacceptable conception of marriage. The effect of such a ruling is undoubtedly to enlarge the scope of the offence, but it is doubtful whether it amounts to the *creation* of an offence for the purposes of s.7(8) of the 1998 Act. If this issue were to arise, the approach of the national courts may well be influenced by the principles applicable under Art.7 of the Convention[146] which have been held to allow "gradual clarification" of the elements of criminal responsibility, providing any resulting development is consistent with the essence of the offence, and could reasonably have been foreseen with appropriate legal advice.[147]

D. DUTY TO INVESTIGATE ALLEGED BREACHES OF ARTICLES 2 AND 3

The state is under a duty to have in place an effective machinery for investigating   **18–61** complaints of violations of Convention rights, especially Arts 2 and 3. Thus in *Ribisch v Austria*[148] the Court held that allegations of ill-treatment in custody, amounting to torture, had not been investigated adequately. The Court stated that "its vigilance must be heightened when dealing with rights such as those set forth in Article 3 of the Convention, which prohibits in absolute terms torture and inhuman or degrading treatment or punishment, irrespective of the victim's conduct."[149] In this case it was held that the Austrian authorities had failed to conduct an investigation which offered a plausible explanation for the injuries sustained by the applicant whilst in custody. There had been a prosecution of one police officer, resulting in an acquittal, but no other inquiry.

In *Aksoy v Turkey*[150] the applicant had been subjected to ill-treatment whilst in   **18–62** police custody which, the court held, amounted to torture. The Turkish prosecutor had a duty to carry out an investigation but, despite the applicant's injuries being brought to his attention, no action was taken. The Court founded its judgment on Art.13 taken together with Art.3:

> "Given the fundamental importance of the prohibition on torture and the especially vulnerable position of torture victims, Article 13 imposes, without prejudice to any other remedy available under the domestic system, an obligation on States to carry out a thorough and effective investigation of incidents of torture."[151]

---

[144] (1998) 27 E.H.R.R. 611.
[145] [1992] A.C. 559.
[146] See Ch.10 above.
[147] *SW and CR v United Kingdom* (1995) 21 E.H.R.R. 363. For criticism of the test adopted in this decision, and its potential application where defences are "narrowed", see paras 10–27 *et seq.* above.
[148] (1995) 21 E.H.R.R. 573.
[149] *ibid.*, at para.32.
[150] (1997) 23 E.H.R.R. 553.
[151] *ibid.*, at para.98. See also *MC. v Bulgaria*, (2005) 40 E.H.R.R. 20.

18–63 In *Aydin v Turkey*[152] the applicant alleged, and the Court found, that she had been subjected by the security forces to rape and prolonged physical and mental violence amounting to torture. The Court adopted the same approach as in *Aksoy*, relying on Art.13 in combination with Art.3:

> "where an individual has an arguable claim that he or she has been tortured by agents of the State, the notion of an 'effective remedy' entails, in addition to the payment of compensation where appropriate, a thorough and effective investigation capable of leading to the identification and punishment of those responsible and including effective access for the complainant to the investigatory procedure."[153]

The Court found that the Turkish prosecutor had conducted an incomplete inquiry with serious shortcomings. It added that in circumstances such as this there must be provision for a sensitive medical examination of the complainant by experts "whose independence is not circumscribed by instructions given by the prosecuting authority as to the scope of the examination."[154]

18–64 The question was raised in relation to Art.2 in *McCann v United Kingdom*,[155] where there had been an inquest into the deaths of the three victims. The applicants alleged that the inquest failed to meet the required standards of thoroughness and impartiality, but the court held otherwise. The Court relied upon Art.1 in combination with Art.2 to ground the right to an official investigation of a death caused by state officials:

> "The obligation to protect the right to life under this provision, read in conjunction with the State's general duty under Article 1 of the Convention to 'secure to everyone within their jurisdiction the rights and freedoms defined in the Convention', requires by implication that there should be some form of effective official investigation when individuals have been killed as a result of the use of force by, *inter alios*, agents of the State."[156]

18–65 In *Jordan v United Kingdom*,[157] the European Court elaborated on the nature and purpose of this procedural obligation under Art.2. First, the Court observed that

---

[152] (1998) 25 E.H.R.R. 251.
[153] *ibid.*, at para.103.
[154] *ibid.*, para.107.
[155] (1996) 21 E.H.R.R. 97, discussed in s.CII above.
[156] *ibid.*, at para.161. The judgment of the court took into account United Nations Principles on the Effective Prevention and Investigations of Extra-Legal, Arbitrary and Summary Execution, adopted 24 May 1989; and the United Nations Manual on the Effective Prevention and Investigations of Extra-Legal, Arbitrary and Summary Execution: Model Protocols for a legal investigation of extra-legal, arbitrary and summary execution (the "Minnesota Protocols"). For the application of these principles in English law, see para.16 of the speech of Lord Bingham in *R. (Middleton) v Secretary of State for the Home Department* [2004] 2 A.C. 182:
> "It seems safe to infer that the state's procedural obligation to investigate is unlikely to be met if it is plausibly alleged that agents of the state have used lethal force without justification, if an effectively unchallengeable decision has been taken not to prosecute and if the fact-finding body cannot express its conclusion on whether unjustifiable force has been used or not, so as to prompt reconsideration of the decision not to prosecute. Where, in such a case, an inquest is the instrument by which the state seeks to discharge its investigative obligation, it seems that an explicit statement, however brief, of the jury's conclusion on the central issue is required".
See also *R. (Stanley) v H.M. Coroner for North London, The Times*, May 12, 2003.
[157] (2003) 37 E.H.R.R. 2.

the obligation to conduct an effective investigation had to be understood in the context of the long-established principle in the Court's caselaw that where a person is injured or dies in custody, the burden of proof is on the state to explain the circumstances to the court's satisfaction, failing which the Court will draw an inference of state responsibility:

> "Where the events in issue lie wholly or in large part within the exclusive knowledge of the authorities, as for example in the case of persons within their control or custody, strong presumptions of fact will arise in respect of injuries or death which occur. Indeed, the burden of proof may be regarded as resting on the authorities to provide a satisfactory and convincing explanation." (para.103)

After reiterating the passage from *McCann* set out in paragraph 18–46 above, the court in *Jordan* held that;

> "The essential purpose of such investigation is to secure the effective implementation of the domestic laws which protect the right to life and, in those cases involving state agents or bodies, to ensure their accountability for deaths occurring under their responsibility." (para.105)

The Court then emphasised that Art.2 imposed an obligation on the state to conduct the investigation *of its own motion*:

> "What form of investigation will achieve those purposes may vary in different circumstances. However, whatever mode is employed, the authorities must act of their own motion, once the matter has come to their attention. They cannot leave it to the initiative of the next of kin either to lodge a formal complaint or to take responsibility for any investigative procedures."

Accordingly, the right to take civil proceedings was to be left out of account in assessing the state's compliance with its obligations under Art.2:

> "As found above, civil proceedings would provide a judicial fact finding forum with the attendant safeguards and the ability to reach findings of unlawfulness, with the possibility of damages. It is however a procedure undertaken on the initiative of the applicant, not the authorities, and it does not involve the identification or punishment of any alleged perpetrator. As such, it cannot be taken into account in the assessment of the state's compliance with its procedural obligations under Article 2 of the Convention." (para.141)

The requirement of effectiveness implied the ability of the procedure in question to reach a determination of state responsibility:

> "The investigation must also be effective in the sense that it is capable of leading to a determination of whether the force used in such cases was or was not justified in the circumstances . . . and to the identification and punishment of those responsible . . . Any deficiency in the investigation which undermines its ability to establish the cause of death or the person responsible will risk falling foul of this standard." (para.107)

The procedure must be transparent, in the sense of permitting public scrutiny of its results:

"For the same reason, there must be a sufficient element of public scrutiny of the investigation or its results to secure accountability in practice as well as in theory." (para.109)

And it must ensure effective participation of the victim or the victim's family:

"In all cases . . . the next of kin of the victim must be involved in the procedure to the extent necessary to safeguard his or her legitimate interests." (para.109)

Finally, the investigation must be "prompt":

"A requirement of promptness and reasonable expedition is implicit in this context . . . .It must be accepted that there may be obstacles or difficulties which prevent progress in an investigation in a particular situation. However, a prompt response by the authorities in investigating a use of lethal force may generally be regarded as essential in maintaining public confidence in their adherence to the rule of law and in preventing any appearance of collusion in or tolerance of unlawful acts." (para.108).

18–66   In *Edwards v United Kingdom*,[158] the European Court went further, and held that the minimum standards identified in *Jordan*, which had hitherto been applied only in cases involving an allegation that death had resulted from the deliberate use of force by agents of the state, ought to apply equally to circumstances where it was alleged that the state was indirectly responsible by failing to discharge its positive obligation to take reasonable care to prevent a foreseeable fatality from occurring. After reiterating the *Jordan* criteria, the Court continued (para.74):

"The Court finds, first of all, that a procedural obligation arose to investigate the circumstances of the death of Christopher Edwards. He was a prisoner under the care and responsibility of the authorities when he died from acts of violence of another prisoner and in this situation it is irrelevant whether state agents were involved by acts or omissions in the events leading to his death. The state was under an obligation to initiate and carry out an investigation which fulfilled the requirements set out [in *Jordan*]. Civil proceedings, assuming that such were available to the applicants, which lie at the initiative of the victim's relatives would not satisfy the state's obligations in this regard.".[159]

18–67   Prior to the coming into force of the Human Rights Act, it was already clear that the mechanism in English law for investigating certain breaches of the Convention, particularly but not limited to Art.2, was inadequate. In two decisions the Strasbourg organs found that the Police Complaints Authority (PCA) was not a satisfactory mechanism for dealing with alleged breaches of Art.8 and, by

---

[158] (2002) 35 E.H.R.R. 19, at paras 69–74.

[159] The Court has subsequently found that the procedural obligation arises in relation to negligent deaths brought about by the acts or omissions of local authorities thereby creating environmental dangers (*Oneryildiz v Turkey* (2005) 41 E.H.R.R. 20); and the management of the 'home leave' system of dangerous prisoners (*Matromatteo v Italy*, Judgment, October 24, 2002). The fact that the death was caused by a private citizen does not absolve the authorities from the requirement to investigate the death towards a prosecution and any insufficiency in that inquiry could found a challenge against a coroner or a HRA action against the police (*Menson v United Kingdom*, (2003) 37 E.H.R.R. CD220; *R. (Hurst) v H.M. Coroner for Northern District of London* [2004] U.K.H.R.R. 139). *Cf. Southall Black Sisters v H.M Coroner for West Coventry* [2002] EWHC 1914 Admin.

implication, other breaches of Convention rights. In *Khan v United Kingdom*[160] the Court found the English system wanting in a number of respects. First, unless the allegation is one of death or serious injury (or certain other specified instances) it is for the local Chief Constable to decide whether to deal with the complaint, and then to appoint a member of his own force to carry out the investigation. Secondly, members of the PCA are appointed and remunerated by the Home Secretary, and the PCA is bound statutorily to have regard to guidance laid down by the Home Secretary. Thus the Court concluded that "the system of investigation of complaints does not meet the requisite standards of independence needed to constitute sufficient protection against the abuse of authority and thus provide an effective remedy within the meaning of Article 13."[161] The Police Act 2002 created the Independent Police Complaints Commission, which does meet the requisite standards of independence.[162]

The more serious area that required reform under the Human Rights Act related **18–68** to conduct of inquiries into deaths in custody (particularly, inquests under the Coroners Act 1988). In *R. (Amin) v Secretary of State for the Home Department*,[163] the House of Lords followed *Edwards*[164] in holding that Art.2 required that the circumstances of the death of a prisoner at the hands of his cellmate had to be the subject of a public inquiry so as to effectively investigate the responsibility of the authorities for placing the deceased in a cell with a dangerous person.[165] In *R. (Middleton) v West Somerset Coroner*,[166] the House of Lords held that in order to be Art.2 compliant it was necessary for the verdict of an inquest to sufficiently identify both the individual and systemic causes of the death and in particular what might have prevented it. The principles derived from *Amin* and *Middleton* have been applied to a failed suicide prisoner who was left brain damaged as a result of his actions.[167] There remains a penumbra of uncertainty as to the extent of the duty to investigate matters of public policy which may have

---

[160] [2000] Crim.L.R. 684.

[161] Judgment, (2001) 34 E.H.R.R. 45, para.47; for a similar stance, see *Ramsahai v. Netherlands* (2006) 43 E.H.R.R. 823.

[162] The requirement for effective involvement of a victim does not extend to an obligation upon the Independent Police Complaints Commission to disclose witness statements and other materials: see *R. (Green) v Police Complaints Authority* [2004] 1 W.L.R. 725 approved in *Green v United Kingdom*, Admissibility Decision, July 27, 2005. The situation is otherwise in relation to an inquest conducted in accordance with the above referred to *Jordan* principles.

[163] [2004] 1 A.C. 653.

[164] See also *R. (Wright and Bennett) v Secretary of State for the Home Department* [2002] H.R.L.R. 1.

[165] The purposes of the investigation required by Art.2 were described by Lord Bingham in *Amin* (at para.31) in these terms:
"[T]o ensure so far as possible that the full facts are brought to light; that culpable and discreditable conduct is exposed and brought to public notice; that suspicion of deliberate wrongdoing (if unjustified) is allayed; that dangerous practices and procedures are rectified; and that those who have lost their relative may at least have the satisfaction of knowing that lessons learned from his death may save the lives of others".

[166] [2004] 2 A.C. 182. See also *R. (Sacker) v West Yorkshire Coroner* [2004] 1 W.L.R. 796, HL.

[167] *R. (D) v Secretary of State for the Home Department (Inquest Intervening)* [2006] 3 All. E.R. 946, CA. This is the first instance where the principles under Art.2 have been held in English law to cross over into Art.3 (see *Aksoy v Turkey* (1996) 23. E.H.R.R. 553 at para.61; and *Assenov v Bulgraia* (1998) 28 E.H.R.R. 652).

caused or contributed to a death.. In the early case of *Taylor, Campton, Gibson v United Kingdom*, the Commission rejected an argument that families of patients murdered by a nurse were entitled to a public inquiry purely to investigate how the NHS could prevent employment of a nurse suffering from Munchausen by proxy syndrome in the future.[168] Given the approach of the House of Lords in *Amin* and *Middleton*, it must be open to serious doubt whether this decision would be followed if the a similar issue were to arise today under the Human Rights Act. On the other hand, it seems clear that the weaker the nexus between the policy issues at stake and the immediate cause of death, the more reluctant the courts will be to impose an investigative obligation under Art.2. Thus, the domestic courts have refused to order public inquiries to investigate the sentencing of young persons[169] or the legality of the decision to go to war.[170]

E. Obligation to Prosecute or Give Reasons

18–69   There is no specific endorsement in the Strasbourg jurisprudence of a duty to bring a prosecution where there is sufficient evidence (howsoever defined) of a breach of Art.2 or Art.3, but there are several statements of the Court which might be said to support that proposition. Thus in *Aydin v Turkey*[171] the Court referred to the need for "a thorough and effective investigation *capable of leading to the identification and punishment of those responsible*". This may be thought to put the matter rather too strongly: all that can reasonably be required is a system designed to ensure that persons against whom there is sufficient evidence are prosecuted.

18–70   The issue arose before the Divisional Court in *R. v DPP ex parte Manning and Melbourne*,[172] where the CPS had decided not to bring a prosecution against a prison officer in respect of the death of a prisoner. There was evidence that the death had been caused by the way in which the prisoner had been restrained by the officer, in response to an incident; the jury at the inquest had returned a verdict of unlawful killing; but the CPS decided that there was not sufficient evidence to raise a realistic prospect of conviction. Lord Bingham C.J. held that such a decision ought to be supported by the disclosure of fairly full reasons:

> "Where such an inquest following a proper direction to the jury culminates in a lawful verdict of unlawful killing implicating a [certain] person ... the ordinary expectation would naturally be that a prosecution would follow. In the absence of compelling grounds for not giving reasons, we would expect the Director to give reasons in such a case: to meet the reasonable expectations of interested parties that either a prosecution would follow or a reasonable explanation for not prosecuting be given, to vindicate the Director's decision by showing that solid grounds exist for what might otherwise appear to be a surprising or even inexplicable decision, and to meet the European Court's

---

[168] (1994) 79-A DR 127.
[169] *R. (Scholes) v Secretary of State for the Home Department* [2006] EWCA Civ 1689.
[170] *R. (Gentle) v Prime Minister* [2006] EWCA Civ 1689.
[171] (1998) 25 E.H.R.R. 251, para.103; see above, n.152 and text; see also *Selmouni v France* (2000) 29 E.H.R.R. 403, para.79.
[172] [2001] Q.B. 330, DC.

expectation that if a prosecution is not to follow a plausible explanation will be given."[173]

This constitutes a significant development of two principles evident in the   **18–71**
Strasbourg jurisprudence—the responsibility of the State for furnishing a plausible explanation of the causes of a death or injury sustained in custody, and the state's duty to provide the machinery for a "thorough and effective investigation" capable of leading to the identification of the probable offender. Lord Bingham's judgment in *Manning* has subsequently been applied to other situations, including deaths in local authority care homes and deaths at work.[174] As a consequence the courts now recognise that any decision as to whether a person should face criminal charges must be revisited in the light of an inquest verdict.[175] In *R. (Armani de Silva) v Director of Public Prosecutions*[176] the Divisional Court considered whether the test set out in the Code for Crown Prosectors requiring a "realistic prospect of conviction" was compatible with the requirements of Art.2 to vindicate the potential breach of rights under Arts 2 and 3 through the bringing of criminal charges. The case concerned the the shooting of Jean Charles De Menezes by officers of the Metropolitan Police and the decision not to prosecute anyone for a homicde offence on the basis that the test for proceeding with such a prosecution was not met, although there was sufficient evidence to justify a prosecution under the Health and Safety at Work Act 1974. The Divisional Court held that the Convention itself did not require a particular evidential test to be applied, and this was not an area where one would expect the Convention to require uniformity of approach:

> "It is certainly relevant to ask whether the evidential test in the Code is compatible with the obligation under article 2 to 'put in place effective criminal law provisions to deter the commission of offences against the person, backed up by law enforcement machinery for the prevention, suppression and punishment of breaches of such provisions' (the formulation in *Osman v United Kingdom* (2000) 29 EHRR 245, as quoted in *Edwards v United Kingdom* (2002) 35 EHHR 19, para 54). In our judgment it is. We do not think that the effectiveness of the system of criminal law in England and Wales or of the machinery for its enforcement would be enhanced by bringing prosecutions that were assessed to be likely to fail even if they could get past a dismissal application and a submission of no case to answer, let alone by differentiating in that respect between cases falling within article 2 and 3 and other cases. On the contrary, such an approach would be liable to undermine public confidence in the system, for the reasons previously discussed"[177]

The court further refused to accept that *Manning* should be revisted in order to require a more intensive form of review than "anxious scrutiny". Anything

---

[173] Para.33.
[174] *R. (Rowley) v Director of Public Prosecutions* [2003] EWHC 693 Admin. (death in a care home); *R. (Dennis) v DPP* [2006] EWHC 3211 Admin (death at work); *R. (Rupert and Sheila Sylvester) v DPP*, (Unreported) May 21, 2001 (use of force in the course of an arrest); *R. (Stanley) v H.M. Coroner for North London, The Times*, May 12, 2003 (fatal shooting by the police). See also *R. (Armani de Silva) v DPP* [2006] EWHC 3204 (shooting of Jean Charles de Menezes).
[175] See *R. (Stanley) v H.M. Coroner for North London, The Times*, May 12, 2003; and *R. (Rupert and Sheila Sylvester) v DPP*, (Unreported) 21st May 2001). See also *R. (Dennis) v DPP* [2006] EWHC 3211 Admin.
[176] [2006] EWCA 3204 Admin.
[177] Para.41.

further "would involve a direct usurpation of the role entrusted by Parliament to the Director and is plainly an untenable position".[178] The principles to be derived from the case law were reviewed by Rix L.J. in *R. (Dennis) v Director of Public Prosecutions* (a case involving the death of a young man during the course of his employment)[179]:

> "First, if it can be demonstrated on an objective appraisal of the case that a serious point or serious points supporting a prosecution have not been considered, that will give a ground for ordering reconsideration of the decision. Second, if it can be demonstrated that in a significant area a conclusion as to what the evidence is to support a prosecution is irrational, that will provide a ground. Third, the points have to be such as to make it seriously arguable that the decision would otherwise be different, but the decision is one for the prosecutor and not for this court. Indeed it is important to bear that fact in mind at all stages. Fourth, where an inquest jury has found unlawful killing the reasons why a prosecution should not follow need to be clearly expressed."

F. Rights of Victims and Witnesses in Criminal Trials

18–72   There is no provision of the Convention which sets out the procedural rights of victims of crime or witnesses. Other international conventions declare certain victims' rights, notably the United Nations Declaration of Basic Principles of Justice for Victims of Crime and Abuse of Power (1985) and the Council of Europe's Recommendations on The Position of the Victim in the Framework of Criminal Law and Procedure (1985).[180] It is possible that the Strasbourg Court will draw upon those declarations, as it has drawn on the United Nations Convention on the Rights of the Child, when interpreting Art.6. However, for the present the Court has begun to construct procedural rights for victims and witnesses out of the Convention itself. Three forms of protection seem to be emerging. First, protection of the identity of a witness who is at risk of reprisal has been recognised as a legitimate ground for implying limitations into Art.6 rights of the accused. Secondly, there are issues about the protection of witnesses from infringements of their rights by questioning during court proceedings. And thirdly, there is the question of access to the medical records of witnesses.

I. Protecting the Identity of Witnesses

18–73   The Court has considered on a number of occasions whether a trial can be fair if witnesses for the prosecution remain anonymous and do not give evidence in open court. Anonymity might be justified as protecting the witness's right to respect for private life and, more seriously, as protecting the witness from the risk of intimidation or physical attack. In *Doorson v Netherlands*[181] the Court held that the trial was not unfair when two prosecution witnesses remained anonymous and were questioned by the judge in the presence of counsel (but not the

---

[178] Para.43.
[179] *R. (Dennis) v DPP* [2006] EWHC 3211 Admin, para.30.
[180] Recommendation R (85) 11 of the Committee of Ministers.
[181] (1996) 22 E.H.R.R. 330.

accused), whereas in *Van Mechelen v Netherlands*[182] the Court held that the trial was unfair when 11 police officers gave evidence for the prosecution, remained anonymous, and were questioned by the judge whilst prosecuting and defence counsel were kept in another room, with only a sound link to the judge's chambers. In both cases there was a fear that the witnesses and their families would be subjected to reprisals if their anonymity was not preserved. In the absence of an express reference in the Convention to the rights of witnesses, the court implied the rights into Art.6:

"It is true that Article 6 does not explicitly require the interests of witnesses in general, and those of victims called upon to testify in particular, to be taken into consideration. However, their life, liberty or security of person may be at stake, as may interests coming generally within the ambit of Article 8 of the Convention ... Contracting States should organise their criminal proceedings in such a way that those interests are not unjustifiably imperilled. Against this background, principles of fair trial also require that in appropriate cases the interests of the defence are balanced against those of witnesses or victims called upon to testify."[183]

These decisions establish the significance of the rights of all witnesses in criminal   **18–74**
proceedings. The rights of the defendant under Art.6 may be curtailed to some extent in order to protect the rights of witnesses, which derive from the right to security of person under Art.5 and the right to respect for private life under Art.8. However, any curtailment of a defendant's rights must be kept to a minimum: "the handicaps under which the defence labours [must] be sufficiently counter-balanced by the procedures followed by the judicial authorities".[184]

The question of informer anonymity has arisen in English law in the context of   **18–75**
disclosure and public interest immunity. One of the grounds on which material used to be classified as "sensitive" under the Attorney-General's 1981 guidelines was that the disclosure of a witness's identity might put him or his family in danger of assault or intimidation. In *Rowe and Davis v United Kingdom*[185] the Strasbourg Court recognised that this could amount to a sufficient reason for withholding evidence from the defence:

"the entitlement to disclosure of relevant evidence is not an absolute right. In any criminal proceedings there may be competing interests, such as national security or the need to protect witnesses at risk of reprisals or keep secret police methods of investigation of crime, which must be weighed against the rights of the accused. In some cases it may be necessary to withhold certain evidence from the defence so as to preserve the fundamental rights of another individual or to safeguard an important public interest."[186]

This judgment follows the approach developed in the *Doorson* and *van Mechelen* judgments. Whilst it approves the risk of intimidation or assault as a justification for withholding evidence, in principle, it also emphasises the need to ensure that

---

[182] (1998) 25 E.H.R.R. 657.
[183] (1996) 22 E.H.R.R. 330 at para.70.
[184] (1998) 25 E.H.R.R. 657 at para.54.
[185] (2000) 30 E.H.R.R. 1.
[186] *ibid.*, at para.61.

the defence is not placed at a greater disadvantage than is strictly necessary to protect the rights of the witness.

18–76   Prior to the coming into force of the Human Rights Act, in circumstances where a tribunal was called upon to exercise a discretion as to whether protection ought to be afforded to a witness whose life was endangered, it was recognised that "when a fundamental right such as the right to life is engaged, the options available to a reasonable decision maker are curtailed" and that it was not open to the decision maker to risk interfering with the right to life "in the absence of compelling justification".[187] As regards the assessment of any such risk to life, the Court of Appeal considering an application for officers to remain anonymous in the Bloody Sunday Inquiry held that the issue was not to be determined by one party discharging a burden of proof on the balance of probabilities, but by "applying, untrammelled by semantics, principles of common sense and humanity".[188] According to Lord Woolf, C.J. (at para.68(5)):

"[The] right approach here once it is accepted that the fears of the soldiers are based on reasonable grounds should be to ask: is there any compelling justification for naming the soldiers, the evidence being that this would increase the risk?"

18–77   Since the coming into force of the Human Rights Act 1998, a court as a public authority for the purposes of s.6 of the Act is under an obligation to inquire into the risk facing a witness, and to consider what steps are available to protect him. On the facts of *R. (A) v Lord Saville of Newdigate*,[189] the Court of Appeal overturned the ruling of the inquiry that the authorities were in a position to provide adequate security for the soldiers to give evidence in Londonderry, rather than taking the evidence in London. In doing so, Lord Phillips M.R. observed that, "The search for a phrase which encapsulates a threshold of risk which engages Article 2 is a search for a chimera". However, the test for responding to a risk created by giving evidence was not as high as the threshold identified in *Osman v United Kingdom*,[190] because in the witness scenario the Court is dealing with a risk which is in part attendant upon its own decision as to how it wishes the evidence to be called (para.28). In approaching the issue, the Court is bound to consider: (1) the subjective fear of the witness; (2) the extent to which the fear can be objectively justified (3) the extent to which the fears can be alleviated by the alternative means of giving evidence and the adverse consequences to the trial if the alternative is adopted: paras 30–31. The approach of the Court of Appeal in the *Saville* cases was recently applied in *R. (A.) v H.M. Coroner for Inner North London*[191] (at para.30) *per* Gage L.J.:

"It seems to me from the observations of Lord Woolf and Lord Phillips that a degree of risk described as 'real and immediate', the *Osman* test, sets the threshold too high. A test based on speculation would clearly set the test too low. Between those two parameters there will be a spectrum of risks of varying seriousness supported by

---

[187] See *R. v Lord Saville of Newdigate Ex. p. A* [2000] 1 W.L.R. 1855.
[188] Applying the dictum of Lord Diplock in *R. v Governor of Pentonville Prison ex parte Fernandez* [1971] 1 W.L.R. 987 at p.994.
[189] *(A) v Lord Saville of Newdigate* [2002] 1 W.L.R. 1249.
[190] (1998) 21 E.H.R.R. 245, paras 115–116 ("real and immediate risk to life").
[191] *R. (A.) v H.M. Coroner for the Inner District of Greater London*, *The Times*, July 12, 2004.

objective evidence of varying degrees of strength. Like Lord Phillips in *Saville (2)* . . . I do not think it is possible or sensible to give any more definitive description than that there must be reasonable grounds which show that the fears of a witness are objectively justified. It will be for a coroner or other decision-maker in each case in which such an application is made to decide whether the evidence is such as to show that the witness' fears are objectively justified. When it comes to the balancing exercise involved in the third [*Saville*] test, obviously, the more serious the risk and the stronger the evidence objectively justifying the fears of the witness, the more likely the balance will favour the grant of anonymity".

II. Protecting Witnesses' Rights during the Trial

There may be situations in which the rights of a witness are put at risk during the **18–78** course of a criminal trial. Some witnesses are vulnerable and therefore require special protection, even in ordinary circumstances. Some witnesses are liable to be questioned in a manner that may be degrading, raising the issue of their Art.3 rights. And on other occasions the nature of the questions may raise the issue of a witness's right under Art.8 to respect for private life. In the key passage in *Doorson v Netherlands*,[192] the Court referred to Arts 5 and 8 as sources of rights for victims and other witnesses; and it is possible that Art.3 would also be invoked if the questioning of the witness was humiliating and debasing, of a certain duration and such as to produce significant adverse physical or mental effects.[193] Article 3 was the basis for the application in *M v United Kingdom*,[194] where a complainant had been subjected to lengthy questioning about sexual details by the defendant in person in a rape trial. The application was withdrawn when the government stated its intention to introduce legislative protection.

There is increasing recognition of the rights of victims and witnesses in English **18–79** law. Thus, in another case where the defendant in person had questioned the complainant in a rape case in an intimidatory and humiliating manner, Lord Bingham C.J. in the Court of Appeal stated that:

"It is the clear duty of the trial judge to do everything he can, consistently with giving the defendant a fair trial, to minimise the trauma suffered by other participants . . . [T]he judge should, if necessary in order to save the complainant from avoidable distress, stop further questioning by the defendant or take over the questioning of the complainant himself. If the defendant seeks by his dress, bearing, manner or questions to dominate, intimidate or humiliate the complainant, or if it is reasonably apprehended that he will seek to do so, the judge should not hesitate to order the erection of a screen, in addition to controlling questioning in the way we have indicated."[195]

Parliament has now stepped in, and s.34 of the Youth Justice and Criminal **18–80** Evidence Act 1999 Parliament attempted to transform the legal playing field. The provision prevents a defendant charged with a sexual offence from cross-examining the complainant in person. Section 35 extends the protection for child

---

[192] See para.18–73 above.
[193] See the definitions of "degrading" in *Costello-Roberts v United Kingdom* (1995) 19 E.H.R.R. 112, para.30, and *A v United Kingdom* (1999) 27 E.H.R.R. 611, para.20.
[194] Unreported (1999).
[195] *Brown (Milton Anthony)* [1998] 2 Cr.App.R. 364 at 371.

witnesses from cross-examination by the defendant. Sections 36 and 37 confer on the courts a power to disallow cross-examination by the defendant in person in other cases which satisfy certain criteria, and s.39 provides a procedure for the appointment of counsel to undertake cross-examination on behalf of the defence if that is necessary.

18–81   It has been suggested that to compel a defendant to have legal representation infringes his rights under Art.6(3)(c), but the Strasbourg caselaw does not support that view. In *Croissant v Germany*[196] the applicant, himself a lawyer, was required by German law to be represented by a court-appointed lawyer during a trial on terrorist charges. The Court held that there was no violation of his rights:

> "It is true that Article 6(3)(c) entitles 'everyone charged with a criminal offence' to be defended by counsel of his own choosing. Nevertheless, and notwithstanding the importance of a relationship of confidence between lawyer and client, this right cannot be considered to be absolute. It is necessarily subject to certain limitations where free legal aid is concerned and also where, as in the present case, it is for the courts to decide whether the interests of justice require that the accused be defended by counsel appointed by them. When appointing defence counsel the national courts must certainly have regard to the defendant's wishes; indeed, German law contemplates such a course. However, they can override those wishes when there are relevant and sufficient grounds for holding that this is necessary in the interests of justice."[197]

18–82   In addition to ss.34–39, there are other provisions in the Youth Justice and Criminal Evidence Act 1999 designed to protect witnesses from unfair treatment. Sections 16–33 provide a statutory framework for the use of screens to protect witnesses, for clearing the court, for the use of video recorded testimony and other measures, all of which go further than the Strasbourg Court's scattered observations would require.[198] Section 41 of the Act places significant constraints on the cross-examination of complainants in sexual cases on their previous sexual behaviour. This is a controversial measure, which makes no separate provision for past sexual experiences which the complainant has had with the accused, treating these in precisely the same way as it treats sexual relations with other men. Where the issue is consent, such evidence could only be introduced where the other sexual act occurred "at or about the same time" as the alleged offence, or there is some similarity about the conduct which cannot be explained on the basis of coincidence. In *R. v A*[199] the House of Lords held that whilst this provision pursued the legitimate object of protecting the complainant against intrusive and irrelevant questioning it had, by extending the restrictions to past sex with the accused, made an excessive inroad into the right to a fair trial. Read according to orthodox cannons of construction it was incompatible with Art.6. In order to achieve compatibility Lord Steyn, with whom the majority agreed, held that the provision should be read subject to an

---

[196] (1993) 16 E.H.R.R. 135.
[197] *ibid.*, at para.29.
[198] The Art.6 compatibility of these provisions was recognised by the House of Lords in *R. (D.) v Camberwell Green Youth Court; R. (DPP) v Same* [2005] 1 W.L.R. 393.
[199] *R. v A. (No.2)* 1 A.C. 45, HL. For a full discussion see para.15–137 above.

implied discretion on the part of the trial judge to ensure that any relevant evidence would be admitted.

III. Victims, Witnesses and Confidential Medical Records

If the medical records of a witness are produced in court by the prosecution, at   **18–83**
a trial of another, it seems clear that this raises questions about the Art.8 rights of the witness. In *Z v Finland*[200] the Court held that there will be an interference with the right to respect for private life under Art.8 where such evidence is adduced without the consent of the witness. However, the Court held that the prosecution may nonetheless be justified in adducing the evidence in certain circumstances. In this case the husband of the witness was being prosecuted for serious sexual offences and for attempted manslaughter, and a key issue was the stage at which he knew he was HIV positive. Both she and her husband had been treated by particular doctors. The Court recognised that the wife's right to the confidentiality of her medical records weighed "heavily in the balance", but held that the prosecution of serious crimes might well give rise to a public interest strong enough to justify the interference with her Art.8 rights. The Court found no breach of Art.8 either in the order for her medical advisers to give evidence or in the seizing of confidential documents for use by the prosecution.

However, the national court had ordered that details of the proceedings should   **18–84**
remain confidential for only 10 years, after which the public interest in publicity should have priority. The Strasbourg Court rejected this, on the ground that it "attached insufficient weigh to the applicant's interests." The Court recalled that, on account of the use of confidential records against her wishes, "she had already been subjected to a serious interference with her right to respect for private and family life."[201] The reasons for removing the ban on publicity after only 10 years were said to be insufficient. Furthermore, the decision of the Finnish court to publish the names of those involved in the case, with the result that the witness could be identified, was a breach of her Art.8 rights without sufficient justification.

To some extent the last point is dealt with in English law by the Sexual Offences   **18–85**
(Amendment) Act 1992, as amended by the Youth Justice and Criminal Evidence Act 1999. However, that legislation is confined to sexual offences, and the general principle in *Z v Finland* applies irrespective of the nature of the proceedings, since the primary concern is to protect the rights of the witness under Art.8.

G. Victims' Rights and the Sentencing Process

In 1985 the Council of Europe agreed a recommendation on The Position of the   **18–86**
Victim in the Framework of Criminal Law and Procedure. Although it declared

---

[200] (1998) 25 E.H.R.R. 371.
[201] *ibid.*, at para.112.

that "the needs and interests of the victim should be taken into account to a greater degree, throughout all stages of the criminal process", it did not recommend a formal role for victims in the sentencing process. It signalled the desirability of a change of emphasis in these terms:

> "Traditionally, criminal legislation and practice have emphasised constitutional guarantees and procedural safeguards for the offender. However, another essential function of a criminal justice system is to do justice to the interests of the victim. This calls for an examination of desirable improvements in national legislation such that the system of criminal justice could take more fully into account the wrongs suffered by the victim. To this end, special account should be taken of the physical, psychological, material (such as damage to property, loss of earnings) or social (such as defamation) damage at every stage in the criminal proceedings."[202]

The emphasis of the report is on the gathering and communication of information, both information *to* the victim about the progress of the case and information *from* the victim to the police, prosecution and the court about the effects of the crime.

18–87   In 2001 the Council of the European Union passed a Framework Decision on the standing of victims in criminal proceedings.[203] It sets out some 18 articles, declaring the right of victims to respect and recognition during criminal proceedings, their right to protection of their safety and privacy, and the right of victims to receive information on a range of matters. Once again, there is no requirement of a specific role for victims at the sentencing stage, but there is a clear requirement to ensure victim compensation. The following Articles are also relevant:

— Article 2: Respect and recognition

> "1. Each Member State shall ensure that victims have a real and appropriate role in its criminal legal system. It shall continue to make every effort to ensure that victims are treated with due respect for the dignity of the individual during proceedings and shall recognise the rights and legitimate interests of victims with particular reference to criminal proceedings.
>   2. Each member State shall ensure that victims who are particularly vulnerable can benefit from specific treatment best suited to their circusmatnces"

— Article 3: Right to be heard and to supply evidence

> "Each Member State shall safeguard the possibility of victims to be heard during criminal proceedings and their right to supply evidence ... "

— Article 6: Right to participate in proceedings and legal aid

— Article 10: Penal mediation in the course of criminal proceedings.

18–88   The terms of this Directive are notable in two respects. First, they constitute evidence of a growing commitment to the recognition of victims' rights in Europe, which is likely to have some influence on the Strasbourg Court in its

---

[202] Council of Europe Recommendation R (85) 11, Explanatory Report, p.15.
[203] Council of the European Union, Framework Decision on the Standing of Victims in criminal proceedings, March 15, 2001 (2001/220/JHA).

interpretation of Convention rights. Secondly, the terms of the document remain relatively flexible. Thus Art.6 merely urges the state to ensure greater victim involvement "to the extent allowed by its legal system," a form of words that allows the diversity of legal responses to be preserved. The qualification "where appropriate" in Art.10 points in the same direction. However, these concessions to national legal traditions leave the broad purposes of the Directive untouched.

The question of victims' rights in the sentencing process has been considered in **18–89** two Strasbourg cases. In *McCourt v United Kingdom*[204] the Commission considered an application by the mother of a woman who had been murdered. She alleged a breach of Art.8 on the ground that she had been accorded no right to participate in the sentencing process, no right to be informed of the date of the murderer's release, and no right to express her views to those deciding on release. The Commission noted that it was the practice of the Home Office to accept submissions from victims' families and to place them before the Parole Board, and also the practice to inform victims' families of the impending release of a murderer. However, the Commission accepted the government's argument that it would be inappropriate to recognise any role for the victim's family in setting the tariff period for the offence, since they would lack the necessary impartiality. The Commission concluded that the application disclosed no interference with the right to respect for family life under Art.8.

In *T and V v United Kingdom*[205] the Court took the exceptional course of **18–90** allowing the parents of James Bulger to intervene in the case brought by the two juveniles convicted of his murder, and permitted the parents' legal representatives to address the court in oral argument. The reasons of the President for taking this course are not set out in the judgment, but they may reflect a more receptive attitude towards hearing representations from victims or their families in matters relating to sentence.

A similar approach is apparent in the *Practice Statement* issued by Lord Woolf **18–91** C.J. which sets out the procedure and considerations for determining the tariff period to be served by young offenders ordered to be detained during Her Majesty's Pleasure.[206] Lord Woolf stated that, before making his recommendation, he would "invite written representations from the detainees' legal advisers and also from the Director of Public Prosecutions who may include representations on behalf of victims' families." Although this procedure preserves the English approach of not allowing victim statements to be submitted directly, and requiring them to be channelled through the prosecution, it gives clear recognition to the relevance of submissions by victims' families.

Although these developments will be welcomed by some, the Strasbourg Court's **18–92** decision to hear submissions from the victim's family in *T and V v United Kingdom* does not deal with the point of principle raised in *McCourt v United*

---

[204] (1993) 15 E.H.R.R. CD 110.
[205] (2000) 30 E.H.R.R. 121.
[206] *Practice Statement (Life Sentences for Murder)* [2000] 2 Cr.App.R. 457.

Kingdom. That point is that every person charged with a criminal offence has the right under Art.6 to a "fair and public hearing ... by an independent and impartial tribunal." The right extends to the sentencing process, and so the question is whether the tribunal's impartiality is compromised by hearing submissions on behalf of the victim's family (or, in non-fatal cases, the victim). The obvious response to this is that the tribunal itself remains impartial, and that its decision-making is no more likely to be prejudiced by representations on behalf of the victim or victim's family than by representations on behalf of the offender. However, it is noteworthy that when the Lord Chief Justice invited representations from the victim's family before setting the tariff period for Thompson and Venables, he: "invited, and received, representations from [Mr Bulger] and his family as to the impact of his son's death on them, but had not invited them to give their views on what they thought was an appropriate tariff."[207]

18–93   This approach draws strength from a line of Court of Appeal decisions in which the court has pointed out why paying heed to representations by victims is not a proper foundation for the administration of criminal justice. The clearest expression of this view is that of Judge L.J.:

> "We mean no disrespect to the mother and sister of the deceased, but the opinions of the victim, or the surviving members of the family, about the appropriate level of sentence do not provide any sound basis for reassessing a sentence. If the victim feels utterly merciful towards the criminal, and some do, the crime has still been committed and must be punished as it deserves. If the victim is obsessed with vengeance, which can in reality only be assuaged by a very long sentence, as also happens, the punishment cannot be made longer by the court than would otherwise be appropriate. Otherwise cases with identical features would be dealt with in widely differing ways, leading to improper and unfair disparity, and even in this particular case ... the views of the members of the family of the deceased are not absolutely identical."[208]

18–94   This was a case in which two members of the victim's family were asking the court to reduce the sentence, but, as Judge L.J. recognises, the argument should be the same whether the submission is for leniency or for severity. Indeed, this is one of the principal difficulties with any acceptance that the views of the victim's family are relevant: that those views may go to one extreme or the other, and a court should not be swayed by those differing reactions, nor should offenders be liable to be sentenced on that basis.[209] The logical consequence of this argument is that the views of the victim or victim's family on sentence are irrelevant, and this points to the conclusion that those views should not be heard. To make provision for them to be heard is either to allow the introduction of irrelevant considerations or to mislead victims' families into thinking that their submissions are relevant when they are not.

---

[207] *Per* Rose L.J. in *R. v Secretary of State for the Home Department and another ex parte Bulger, The Times*, March 7, 2001.

[208] *Nunn* [1996] 2 Cr.App.R.(S) 136 at p.140; see also *Roche* [1999] 2 Cr.App.R.(S) 105 and *Perks* [2001] 1 Cr.App.R.(S). 19.

[209] The last few words of the quotation from *Nunn* also point to a practical difficulty where there are two or more victims, or where a deceased victim's family is making submissions—that there may be different views about what should be done. In *Nunn* two members of the family wanted leniency and two did not.

Arguments of this kind will have to be confronted by the Strasbourg Court   **18–95**
whenever it has to give a reasoned decision on victims' rights in relation to
sentencing. It will be important to distinguish between three different forms of
representation from victims.

First, there are representations about the effects of the offence on the victim and   **18–96**
his or her life and wellbeing. The current scheme of Victim Personal Statementsis
intended to ensure that courts are more fully informed about the effects of crime.
Although there may be procedural issues about victim statements which contain
allegations of a more serious crime than the prosecution has alleged, such
statements are generally consistent with the Convention and with the two European documents outlined above. A victim statement of this kind does not contain
opinions on sentence. This issue is now dealt with *Practice Direction (Criminal
Proceedings: Consolidation)*, para.III. 28,[210] which itself reflects established
Court of Appeal authority which balances the important requirement to ascertain
the subjective impact of an offence upon a victim, against potential unfairness in
raising matters that cannot be realistically investigated by the defence. In May
2006 a Protocol for a voluntary pilot scheme was introduced by Sir Igor Judge
to extend the approach to "family impact statements".

Secondly, there are representations as to the length or type of sentence. It was   **18–97**
argued above that to admit such representations may raise the issue of impartiality under Art.6, as suggested in *McCourt v United Kingdom*, or alternatively may
involve misleading victims and their families as to the significance of their
representations.

Third, there are representations directed solely to issues of compensation. Vic-   **18–98**
tims should have a right to receive compensation from offenders who are in a
position to pay, as the Framework Decision for the European Union recognises
in Art.9:

> "1. Each Member State shall ensure that victims of criminal acts are entitled to
>   obatin a decision within reasonable time limits on compensation by the offender
>   in the course of criminal proceedings, except where, in certain cases, national
>   law provides for comensation to be awarded in another manner,
> 2. Each Member State shall take appropriate measures to encourage the offender to
>   provide adequate compensation to victims.
> 3. Unless urgently required for the purpose of criminal proceedings, recoverable
>   property belonging to victims which is seized in the course of criminal proceed-
>   ings shall be returned to them without delay."[211]

Insofar as victim statements themselves are directed to this purpose, they will
make an important contribution to securing rights that ought to be recognised, but
are not recognised, in the Convention.

Although there is a European Convention on the Compensation of Victims of   **18–99**
Violent Crimes,[212] which the United Kingdom ratified in 1990, the European

---

[210] [2002] 1 W.L.R. 2870.
[211] Above, n.203.
[212] Cmnd.1427, (1988).

Convention on Human Rights does not contain any enforceable right to state compensation for the victims of violent crime. However, the introduction of a statutory system may be held to give rise to a "civil right", which means that Art.6 protections must be in place. It has been argued that some of the procedures of the Criminal Injuries Compensation Appeals Panel may be open to challenge under Art.6.[213]

---

[213] Wadham J. and Arkinstall J., "Rights of Victims of Crime", (2000) *New L.J.* 1023 and 1083, at p.1084.

A: CONVENTION FOR THE PROTECTION OF HUMAN RIGHTS AND FUNDAMENTAL FREEDOMS, AS AMENDED BY PROTOCOL NO. 11

Rome, 4.XI.1950

The governments signatory hereto, being members of the Council of Europe,

Considering the Universal Declaration of Human Rights proclaimed by the General Assembly of the United Nations on 10th December 1948;

Considering that this Declaration aims at securing the universal and effective recognition and observance of the Rights therein declared;

Considering that the aim of the Council of Europe is the achievement of greater unity between its members and that one of the methods by which that aim is to be pursued is the maintenance and further realisation of human rights and fundamental freedoms;

Reaffirming their profound belief in those fundamental freedoms which are the foundation of justice and peace in the world and are best maintained on the one hand by an effective political democracy and on the other by a common understanding and observance of the human rights upon which they depend;

Being resolved, as the governments of European countries which are like-minded and have a common heritage of political traditions, ideals, freedom and the rule of law, to take the first steps for the collective enforcement of certain of the rights stated in the Universal Declaration,

Have agreed as follows:

Article 1—Obligation to respect human rights

The High Contracting Parties shall secure to everyone within their jurisdiction the rights and freedoms defined in Section I of this Convention.

SECTION I—RIGHTS AND FREEDOMS

Article 2—Right to life

1. Everyone's right to life shall be protected by law. No one shall be deprived of his life intentionally save in the execution of a sentence of a court following his conviction of a crime for which this penalty is provided by law.
2. Deprivation of life shall not be regarded as inflicted in contravention of this article when it results from the use of force which is no more than absolutely necessary:

   a. in defence of any person from unlawful violence;

b. in order to effect a lawful arrest or to prevent the escape of a person lawfully detained;

c. in action lawfully taken for the purpose of quelling a riot or insurrection.

Article 3—Prohibition of torture

No one shall be subjected to torture or to inhuman or degrading treatment or punishment.

Article 4—Prohibition of slavery and forced labour

1. No one shall be held in slavery or servitude.
2. No one shall be required to perform forced or compulsory labour.
3. For the purpose of this article the term "forced or compulsory labour" shall not include:

   a. any work required to be done in the ordinary course of detention imposed according to the provisions of Article 5 of this Convention or during conditional release from such detention;

   b. any service of a military character or, in case of conscientious objectors in countries where they are recognised, service exacted instead of compulsory military service;

   c. any service exacted in case of an emergency or calamity threatening the life or well-being of the community;

   d. any work or service which forms part of normal civic obligations.

Article 5—Right to liberty and security

1. Everyone has the right to liberty and security of person. No one shall be deprived of his liberty save in the following cases and in accordance with a procedure prescribed by law:

   a. the lawful detention of a person after conviction by a competent court;

   b. the lawful arrest or detention of a person for non- compliance with the lawful order of a court or in order to secure the fulfilment of any obligation prescribed by law;

   c. the lawful arrest or detention of a person effected for the purpose of bringing him before the competent legal authority on reasonable suspicion of having committed an offence or when it is reasonably considered necessary to prevent his committing an offence or fleeing after having done so;

   d. the detention of a minor by lawful order for the purpose of educational supervision or his lawful detention for the purpose of bringing him before the competent legal authority;

   e. the lawful detention of persons for the prevention of the spreading of infectious diseases, of persons of unsound mind, alcoholics or drug addicts or vagrants;

   f. the lawful arrest or detention of a person to prevent his effecting an unauthorised entry into the country or of a person against whom action is being taken with a view to deportation or extradition.

2. Everyone who is arrested shall be informed promptly, in a language which he understands, of the reasons for his arrest and of any charge against him.

3. Everyone arrested or detained in accordance with the provisions of paragraph 1.c of this article shall be brought promptly before a judge or other officer authorised by law to exercise judicial power and shall be entitled to trial within a reasonable time or to release pending trial. Release may be conditioned by guarantees to appear for trial.

4. Everyone who is deprived of his liberty by arrest or detention shall be entitled to take proceedings by which the lawfulness of his detention shall be decided speedily by a court and his release ordered if the detention is not lawful.

5. Everyone who has been the victim of arrest or detention in contravention of the provisions of this article shall have an enforceable right to compensation.

Article 6—Right to a fair trial

1. In the determination of his civil rights and obligations or of any criminal charge against him, everyone is entitled to a fair and public hearing within a reasonable time by an independent and impartial tribunal established by law. Judgment shall be pronounced publicly but the press and public may be excluded from all or part of the trial in the interests of morals, public order or national security in a democratic society, where the interests of juveniles or the protection of the private life of the parties so require, or to the extent strictly necessary in the opinion of the court in special circumstances where publicity would prejudice the interests of justice.

2. Everyone charged with a criminal offence shall be presumed innocent until proved guilty according to law.

3. Everyone charged with a criminal offence has the following minimum rights:

   a. to be informed promptly, in a language which he understands and in detail, of the nature and cause of the accusation against him;

   b. to have adequate time and facilities for the preparation of his defence;

   c. to defend himself in person or through legal assistance of his own choosing or, if he has not sufficient means to pay for legal assistance, to be given it free when the interests of justice so require;

   d. to examine or have examined witnesses against him and to obtain the attendance and examination of witnesses on his behalf under the same conditions as witnesses against him;

   e. to have the free assistance of an interpreter if he cannot understand or speak the language used in court.

Article 7—No punishment without law

1. No one shall be held guilty of any criminal offence on account of any act or omission which did not constitute a criminal offence under national or international law at the time when it was committed. Nor shall a heavier penalty be imposed than the one that was applicable at the time the criminal offence was committed.

2. This article shall not prejudice the trial and punishment of any person for any act or omission which, at the time when it was committed, was criminal according to the general principles of law recognised by civilised nations.

Article 8—Right to respect for private and family life

1. Everyone has the right to respect for his private and family life, his home and his correspondence.

2. There shall be no interference by a public authority with the exercise of this right except such as is in accordance with the law and is necessary in a democratic society in the interests of national security, public safety or the economic well-being of the

country, for the prevention of disorder or crime, for the protection of health or morals, or for the protection of the rights and freedoms of others.

Article 9—Freedom of thought, conscience and religion

1. Everyone has the right to freedom of thought, conscience and religion; this right includes freedom to change his religion or belief and freedom, either alone or in community with others and in public or private, to manifest his religion or belief, in worship, teaching, practice and observance.
2. Freedom to manifest one's religion or beliefs shall be subject only to such limitations as are prescribed by law and are necessary in a democratic society in the interests of public safety, for the protection of public order, health or morals, or for the protection of the rights and freedoms of others.

Article 10—Freedom of expression

1. Everyone has the right to freedom of expression. This right shall include freedom to hold opinions and to receive and impart information and ideas without interference by public authority and regardless of frontiers. This article shall not prevent States from requiring the licensing of broadcasting, television or cinema enterprises.
2. The exercise of these freedoms, since it carries with it duties and responsibilities, may be subject to such formalities, conditions, restrictions or penalties as are prescribed by law and are necessary in a democratic society, in the interests of national security, territorial integrity or public safety, for the prevention of disorder or crime, for the protection of health or morals, for the protection of the reputation or rights of others, for preventing the disclosure of information received in confidence, or for maintaining the authority and impartiality of the judiciary.

Article 11—Freedom of assembly and association

1. Everyone has the right to freedom of peaceful assembly and to freedom of association with others, including the right to form and to join trade unions for the protection of his interests.
2. No restrictions shall be placed on the exercise of these rights other than such as are prescribed by law and are necessary in a democratic society in the interests of national security or public safety, for the prevention of disorder or crime, for the protection of health or morals or for the protection of the rights and freedoms of others. This article shall not prevent the imposition of lawful restrictions on the exercise of these rights by members of the armed forces, of the police or of the administration of the State.

Article 12—Right to marry

Men and women of marriageable age have the right to marry and to found a family, according to the national laws governing the exercise of this right.

Article 13—Right to an effective remedy

Everyone whose rights and freedoms as set forth in this Convention are violated shall have an effective remedy before a national authority notwithstanding that the violation has been committed by persons acting in an official capacity.

Article 14—Prohibition of discrimination

The enjoyment of the rights and freedoms set forth in this Convention shall be secured without discrimination on any ground such as sex, race, colour, language, religion, political or other opinion, national or social origin, association with a national minority, property, birth or other status.

Article 15—Derogation in time of emergency

1. In time of war or other public emergency threatening the life of the nation any High Contracting Party may take measures derogating from its obligations under this Convention to the extent strictly required by the exigencies of the situation, provided that such measures are not inconsistent with its other obligations under international law.
2. No derogation from Article 2, except in respect of deaths resulting from lawful acts of war, or from Articles 3, 4 (paragraph 1) and 7 shall be made under this provision.
3. Any High Contracting Party availing itself of this right of derogation shall keep the Secretary General of the Council of Europe fully informed of the measures which it has taken and the reasons therefor. It shall also inform the Secretary General of the Council of Europe when such measures have ceased to operate and the provisions of the Convention are again being fully executed.

Article 16—Restrictions on political activity of aliens

Nothing in Articles 10, 11 and 14 shall be regarded as preventing the High Contracting Parties from imposing restrictions on the political activity of aliens.

Article 17—Prohibition of abuse of rights

Nothing in this Convention may be interpreted as implying for any State, group or person any right to engage in any activity or perform any act aimed at the destruction of any of the rights and freedoms set forth herein or at their limitation to a greater extent than is provided for in the Convention.

Article 18—Limitation on use of restrictions on rights

The restrictions permitted under this Convention to the said rights and freedoms shall not be applied for any purpose other than those for which they have been prescribed.

SECTION II—EUROPEAN COURT OF HUMAN RIGHTS

Article 19—Establishment of the Court

To ensure the observance of the engagements undertaken by the High Contracting Parties in the Convention and the Protocols thereto, there shall be set up a European Court of Human Rights, hereinafter referred to as "the Court". It shall function on a permanent basis.

Article 20—Number of judges

The Court shall consist of a number of judges equal to that of the High Contracting Parties.

Article 21—Criteria for office

1. The judges shall be of high moral character and must either possess the qualifications required for appointment to high judicial office or be jurisconsults of recognised competence.
2. The judges shall sit on the Court in their individual capacity.
3. During their term of office the judges shall not engage in any activity which is incompatible with their independence, impartiality or with the demands of a full-time office; all questions arising from the application of this paragraph shall be decided by the Court.

Article 22—Election of judges

1. The judges shall be elected by the Parliamentary Assembly with respect to each High Contracting Party by a majority of votes cast from a list of three candidates nominated by the High Contracting Party.
2. The same procedure shall be followed to complete the Court in the event of the accession of new High Contracting Parties and in filling casual vacancies.

Article 23—Terms of office

1. The judges shall be elected for a period of six years. They may be re-elected. However, the terms of office of one-half of the judges elected at the first election shall expire at the end of three years.
2. The judges whose terms of office are to expire at the end of the initial period of three years shall be chosen by lot by the Secretary General of the Council of Europe immediately after their election.
3. In order to ensure that, as far as possible, the terms of office of one-half of the judges are renewed every three years, the Parliamentary Assembly may decide, before proceeding to any subsequent election, that the term or terms of office of one or more judges to be elected shall be for a period other than six years but not more than nine and not less than three years.
4. In cases where more than one term of office is involved and where the Parliamentary Assembly applies the preceding paragraph, the allocation of the terms of office shall be effected by a drawing of lots by the Secretary General of the Council of Europe immediately after the election.
5. A judge elected to replace a judge whose term of office has not expired shall hold office for the remainder of his predecessor's term.
6. The terms of office of judges shall expire when they reach the age of 70.
7. The judges shall hold office until replaced. They shall, however, continue to deal with such cases as they already have under consideration.

Article 24—Dismissal

No judge may be dismissed from his office unless the other judges decide by a majority of two-thirds that he has ceased to fulfil the required conditions.

Article 25—Registry and legal secretaries

The Court shall have a registry, the functions and organisation of which shall be laid down in the rules of the Court. The Court shall be assisted by legal secretaries.

Article 26—Plenary Court

The plenary Court shall

  a. elect its President and one or two Vice-Presidents for a period of three years; they may be re-elected;

  b. set up Chambers, constituted for a fixed period of time;

  c. elect the Presidents of the Chambers of the Court; they may be re-elected;

  d. adopt the rules of the Court, and

  e. elect the Registrar and one or more Deputy Registrars.

Article 27—Committees, Chambers and Grand Chamber

1. To consider cases brought before it, the Court shall sit in committees of three judges, in Chambers of seven judges and in a Grand Chamber of seventeen judges. The Court's Chambers shall set up committees for a fixed period of time.

2. There shall sit as an *ex officio* member of the Chamber and the Grand Chamber the judge elected in respect of the State Party concerned or, if there is none or if he is unable to sit, a person of its choice who shall sit in the capacity of judge.

3. The Grand Chamber shall also include the President of the Court, the Vice-Presidents, the Presidents of the Chambers and other judges chosen in accordance with the rules of the Court. When a case is referred to the Grand Chamber under Article 43, no judge from the Chamber which rendered the judgment shall sit in the Grand Chamber, with the exception of the President of the Chamber and the judge who sat in respect of the State Party concerned.

Article 28—Declarations of inadmissibility by committees

A committee may, by a unanimous vote, declare inadmissible or strike out of its list of cases an application submitted under Article 34 where such a decision can be taken without further examination. The decision shall be final.

Article 29—Decisions by Chambers on admissibility and merits

1. If no decision is taken under Article 28, a Chamber shall decide on the admissibility and merits of individual applications submitted under Article 34.

2. A Chamber shall decide on the admissibility and merits of inter-State applications submitted under Article 33.

3. The decision on admissibility shall be taken separately unless the Court, in exceptional cases, decides otherwise.

Article 30—Relinquishment of jurisdiction to the Grand Chamber

Where a case pending before a Chamber raises a serious question affecting the interpretation of the Convention or the protocols thereto, or where the resolution of a question before the Chamber might have a result inconsistent with a judgment previously delivered by the Court, the Chamber may, at any time before it has rendered its judgment, relinquish jurisdiction in favour of the Grand Chamber, unless one of the parties to the case objects.

Article 31—Powers of the Grand Chamber

The Grand Chamber shall

1. a. determine applications submitted either under Article 33 or Article 34 when a Chamber has relinquished jurisdiction under Article 30 or when the case has been referred to it under Article 43; and

   b. consider requests for advisory opinions submitted under Article 47.

Article 32—Jurisdiction of the Court

1. The jurisdiction of the Court shall extend to all matters concerning the interpretation and application of the Convention and the protocols thereto which are referred to it as provided in Articles 33, 34 and 47.

2. In the event of dispute as to whether the Court has jurisdiction, the Court shall decide.

Article 33—Inter-State cases

Any High Contracting Party may refer to the Court any alleged breach of the provisions of the Convention and the protocols thereto by another High Contracting Party.

Article 34—Individual applications

The Court may receive applications from any person, non-governmental organisation or group of individuals claiming to be the victim of a violation by one of the High Contracting Parties of the rights set forth in the Convention or the protocols thereto. The High Contracting Parties undertake not to hinder in any way the effective exercise of this right.

Article 35—Admissibility criteria

1. The Court may only deal with the matter after all domestic remedies have been exhausted, according to the generally recognised rules of international law, and within a period of six months from the date on which the final decision was taken.
2. The Court shall not deal with any application submitted under Article 34 that

    a. is anonymous; or

    b. is substantially the same as a matter that has already been examined by the Court or has already been submitted to another procedure of international investigation or settlement and contains no relevant new information.

3. The Court shall declare inadmissible any individual application submitted under Article 34 which it considers incompatible with the provisions of the Convention or the protocols thereto, manifestly ill-founded, or an abuse of the right of application.
4. The Court shall reject any application which it considers inadmissible under this Article. It may do so at any stage of the proceedings.

Article 36—Third party intervention

1. In all cases before a Chamber or the Grand Chamber, a High Contracting Party one of whose nationals is an applicant shall have the right to submit written comments and to take part in hearings.
2. The President of the Court may, in the interest of the proper administration of justice, invite any High Contracting Party which is not a party to the proceedings or any person concerned who is not the applicant to submit written comments or take part in hearings.

Article 37—Striking out applications

1. The Court may at any stage of the proceedings decide to strike an application out of its list of cases where the circumstances lead to the conclusion that

    a. the applicant does not intend to pursue his application; or

    b. the matter has been resolved; or

    c. for any other reason established by the Court, it is no longer justified to continue the examination of the application.

    However, the Court shall continue the examination of the application if respect for human rights as defined in the Convention and the protocols thereto so requires.
2. The Court may decide to restore an application to its list of cases if it considers that the circumstances justify such a course.

Article 38—Examination of the case and friendly settlement proceedings

1. If the Court declares the application admissible, it shall

    a. pursue the examination of the case, together with the representatives of the parties, and if need be, undertake an investigation, for the effective conduct of which the States concerned shall furnish all necessary facilities;

    b. place itself at the disposal of the parties concerned with a view to securing a friendly settlement of the matter on the basis of respect for human rights as defined in the Convention and the protocols thereto.

2. Proceedings conducted under paragraph 1.b shall be confidential.

Article 39—Finding of a friendly settlement

If a friendly settlement is effected, the Court shall strike the case out of its list by means of a decision which shall be confined to a brief statement of the facts and of the solution reached.

Article 40—Public hearings and access to documents

1. Hearings shall be in public unless the Court in exceptional circumstances decides otherwise.
2. Documents deposited with the Registrar shall be accessible to the public unless the President of the Court decides otherwise.

Article 41—Just satisfaction

If the Court finds that there has been a violation of the Convention or the protocols thereto, and if the internal law of the High Contracting Party concerned allows only partial reparation to be made, the Court shall, if necessary, afford just satisfaction to the injured party.

Article 42—Judgments of Chambers

Judgments of Chambers shall become final in accordance with the provisions of Article 44, paragraph 2.

Article 43—Referral to the Grand Chamber

1. Within a period of three months from the date of the judgment of the Chamber, any party to the case may, in exceptional cases, request that the case be referred to the Grand Chamber.
2. A panel of five judges of the Grand Chamber shall accept the request if the case raises a serious question affecting the interpretation or application of the Convention or the protocols thereto, or a serious issue of general importance.
3. If the panel accepts the request, the Grand Chamber shall decide the case by means of a judgment.

Article 44—Final judgments

1. The judgment of the Grand Chamber shall be final.
2. The judgment of a Chamber shall become final

    a. when the parties declare that they will not request that the case be referred to the Grand Chamber; or

    b. three months after the date of the judgment, if reference of the case to the Grand Chamber has not been requested; or

    c. when the panel of the Grand Chamber rejects the request to refer under Article 43.

3. The final judgment shall be published.

Article 45—Reasons for judgments and decisions

1. Reasons shall be given for judgments as well as for decisions declaring applications admissible or inadmissible.
2. If a judgment does not represent, in whole or in part, the unanimous opinion of the judges, any judge shall be entitled to deliver a separate opinion.

Article 46—Binding force and execution of judgments

1. The High Contracting Parties undertake to abide by the final judgment of the Court in any case to which they are parties.
2. The final judgment of the Court shall be transmitted to the Committee of Ministers, which shall supervise its execution.

Article 47—Advisory opinions

1. The Court may, at the request of the Committee of Ministers, give advisory opinions on legal questions concerning the interpretation of the Convention and the protocols thereto.
2. Such opinions shall not deal with any question relating to the content or scope of the rights or freedoms defined in Section I of the Convention and the protocols thereto, or with any other question which the Court or the Committee of Ministers might have to consider in consequence of any such proceedings as could be instituted in accordance with the Convention.
3. Decisions of the Committee of Ministers to request an advisory opinion of the Court shall require a majority vote of the representatives entitled to sit on the Committee.

Article 48—Advisory jurisdiction of the Court

The Court shall decide whether a request for an advisory opinion submitted by the Committee of Ministers is within its competence as defined in Article 47.

Article 49—Reasons for advisory opinions

1. Reasons shall be given for advisory opinions of the Court.
2. If the advisory opinion does not represent, in whole or in part, the unanimous opinion of the judges, any judge shall be entitled to deliver a separate opinion.
3. Advisory opinions of the Court shall be communicated to the Committee of Ministers.

Article 50—Expenditure on the Court

The expenditure on the Court shall be borne by the Council of Europe.

Article 51—Privileges and immunities of judges

The judges shall be entitled, during the exercise of their functions, to the privileges and immunities provided for in Article 40 of the Statute of the Council of Europe and in the agreements made thereunder.

Section III—Miscellaneous provisions

Article 52—Inquiries by the Secretary General

On receipt of a request from the Secretary General of the Council of Europe any High Contracting Party shall furnish an explanation of the manner in which its internal law ensures the effective implementation of any of the provisions of the Convention.

Article 53—Safeguard for existing human rights

Nothing in this Convention shall be construed as limiting or derogating from any of the human rights and fundamental freedoms which may be ensured under the laws of any High Contracting Party or under any other agreement to which it is a Party.

Article 54—Powers of the Committee of Ministers

Nothing in this Convention shall prejudice the powers conferred on the Committee of Ministers by the Statute of the Council of Europe.

Article 55—Exclusion of other means of dispute settlement

The High Contracting Parties agree that, except by special agreement, they will not avail themselves of treaties, conventions or declarations in force between them for the purpose of submitting, by way of petition, a dispute arising out of the interpretation or application of this Convention to a means of settlement other than those provided for in this Convention.

Article 56—Territorial application

1. Any State may at the time of its ratification or at any time thereafter declare by notification addressed to the Secretary General of the Council of Europe that the present Convention shall, subject to paragraph 4 of this Article, extend to all or any of the territories for whose international relations it is responsible.
2. The Convention shall extend to the territory or territories named in the notification as from the thirtieth day after the receipt of this notification by the Secretary General of the Council of Europe.
3. The provisions of this Convention shall be applied in such territories with due regard, however, to local requirements.
4. Any State which has made a declaration in accordance with paragraph 1 of this article may at any time thereafter declare on behalf of one or more of the territories to which the declaration relates that it accepts the competence of the Court to receive applications from individuals, non-governmental organisations or groups of individuals as provided by Article 34 of the Convention.

Article 57—Reservations

1. Any State may, when signing this Convention or when depositing its instrument of ratification, make a reservation in respect of any particular provision of the Convention to the extent that any law then in force in its territory is not in conformity with the provision. Reservations of a general character shall not be permitted under this article.
2. Any reservation made under this article shall contain a brief statement of the law concerned.

Article 58—Denunciation

1. A High Contracting Party may denounce the present Convention only after the expiry of five years from the date on which it became a party to it and after six months'

notice contained in a notification addressed to the Secretary General of the Council of Europe, who shall inform the other High Contracting Parties.

2. Such a denunciation shall not have the effect of releasing the High Contracting Party concerned from its obligations under this Convention in respect of any act which, being capable of constituting a violation of such obligations, may have been performed by it before the date at which the denunciation became effective.

3. Any High Contracting Party which shall cease to be a member of the Council of Europe shall cease to be a Party to this Convention under the same conditions.

4. The Convention may be denounced in accordance with the provisions of the preceding paragraphs in respect of any territory to which it has been declared to extend under the terms of Article 56.

Article 59—Signature and ratification

1. This Convention shall be open to the signature of the members of the Council of Europe. It shall be ratified. Ratifications shall be deposited with the Secretary General of the Council of Europe.

2. The present Convention shall come into force after the deposit of ten instruments of ratification.

3. As regards any signatory ratifying subsequently, the Convention shall come into force at the date of the deposit of its instrument of ratification.

4. The Secretary General of the Council of Europe shall notify all the members of the Council of Europe of the entry into force of the Convention, the names of the High Contracting Parties who have ratified it, and the deposit of all instruments of ratification which may be effected subsequently.

Done at Rome this 4th day of November 1950, in English and French, both texts being equally authentic, in a single copy which shall remain deposited in the archives of the Council of Europe. The Secretary General shall transmit certified copies to each of the signatories.

B: PROTOCOL TO THE CONVENTION FOR THE PROTECTION OF HUMAN RIGHTS AND FUNDAMENTAL FREEDOMS, AS AMENDED BY PROTOCOL NO. 11

Paris, 20.III.1952

The governments signatory hereto, being members of the Council of Europe,

Being resolved to take steps to ensure the collective enforcement of certain rights and freedoms other than those already included in Section I of the Convention for the Protection of Human Rights and Fundamental Freedoms signed at Rome on 4 November 1950 (hereinafter referred to as "the Convention"),

Have agreed as follows:

Article 1—Protection of property

Every natural or legal person is entitled to the peaceful enjoyment of his possessions. No one shall be deprived of his possessions except in the public interest and subject to the conditions provided for by law and by the general principles of international law.

The preceding provisions shall not, however, in any way impair the right of a State to enforce such laws as it deems necessary to control the use of property in accordance with the general interest or to secure the payment of taxes or other contributions or penalties.

Article 2—Right to education

No person shall be denied the right to education. In the exercise of any functions which it assumes in relation to education and to teaching, the State shall respect the right of parents to ensure such education and teaching in conformity with their own religious and philosophical convictions.

Article 3—Right to free elections

The High Contracting Parties undertake to hold free elections at reasonable intervals by secret ballot, under conditions which will ensure the free expression of the opinion of the people in the choice of the legislature.

Article 4—Territorial application

Any High Contracting Party may at the time of signature or ratification or at any time thereafter communicate to the Secretary General of the Council of Europe a declaration stating the extent to which it undertakes that the provisions of the present Protocol shall apply to such of the territories for the international relations of which it is responsible as are named therein.

Any High Contracting Party which has communicated a declaration in virtue of the preceding paragraph may from time to time communicate a further declaration modifying the terms of any former declaration or terminating the application of the provisions of this Protocol in respect of any territory.

A declaration made in accordance with this article shall be deemed to have been made in accordance with paragraph 1 of Article 56 of the Convention.

Article 5—Relationship to the Convention

As between the High Contracting Parties the provisions of Articles 1, 2, 3 and 4 of this Protocol shall be regarded as additional articles to the Convention and all the provisions of the Convention shall apply accordingly.

Article 6—Signature and ratification

This Protocol shall be open for signature by the members of the Council of Europe, who are the signatories of the Convention; it shall be ratified at the same time as or after the ratification of the Convention. It shall enter into force after the deposit of ten instruments of ratification. As regards any signatory ratifying subsequently, the Protocol shall enter into force at the date of the deposit of its instrument of ratification.

The instruments of ratification shall be deposited with the Secretary General of the Council of Europe, who will notify all members of the names of those who have ratified.

Done at Paris on the 20th day of March 1952, in English and French, both texts being equally authentic, in a single copy which shall remain deposited in the archives of the Council of Europe. The Secretary General shall transmit certified copies to each of the signatory governments.

C: PROTOCOL NO. 6 TO THE CONVENTION FOR THE PROTECTION OF HUMAN RIGHTS AND FUNDAMENTAL FREEDOMS CONCERNING THE ABOLITION OF THE DEATH PENALTY, AS AMENDED BY PROTOCOL NO. 11

Strasbourg, 28.IV.1983

The member States of the Council of Europe, signatory to this Protocol to the Convention for the Protection of Human Rights and Fundamental Freedoms, signed at Rome on 4 November 1950 (hereinafter referred to as "the Convention"),

Considering that the evolution that has occurred in several member States of the Council of Europe expresses a general tendency in favour of abolition of the death penalty;

Have agreed as follows:

Article 1—Abolition of the death penalty

The death penalty shall be abolished. No-one shall be condemned to such penalty or executed.

Article 2—Death penalty in time of war

A State may make provision in its law for the death penalty in respect of acts committed in time of war or of imminent threat of war; such penalty shall be applied only in the instances laid down in the law and in accordance with its provisions. The State shall communicate to the Secretary General of the Council of Europe the relevant provisions of that law.

Article 3—Prohibition of derogations

No derogation from the provisions of this Protocol shall be made under Article 15 of the Convention.

Article 4—Prohibition of reservations

No reservation may be made under Article 57 of the Convention in respect of the provisions of this Protocol.

Article 5—Territorial application

1. Any State may at the time of signature or when depositing its instrument of ratification, acceptance or approval, specify the territory or territories to which this Protocol shall apply.

2. Any State may at any later date, by a declaration addressed to the Secretary General of the Council of Europe, extend the application of this Protocol to any other territory specified in the declaration. In respect of such territory the Protocol shall enter into force on the first day of the month following the date of receipt of such declaration by the Secretary General.
3. Any declaration made under the two preceding paragraphs may, in respect of any territory specified in such declaration, be withdrawn by a notification addressed to the Secretary General. The withdrawal shall become effective on the first day of the month following the date of receipt of such notification by the Secretary General.

Article 6—Relationship to the Convention

As between the States Parties the provisions of Articles 1 to 5 of this Protocol shall be regarded as additional articles to the Convention and all the provisions of the Convention shall apply accordingly.

Article 7—Signature and ratification

The Protocol shall be open for signature by the member States of the Council of Europe, signatories to the Convention. It shall be subject to ratification, acceptance or approval. A member State of the Council of Europe may not ratify, accept or approve this Protocol unless it has, simultaneously or previously, ratified the Convention. Instruments of ratification, acceptance or approval shall be deposited with the Secretary General of the Council of Europe.

Article 8—Entry into force

1. This Protocol shall enter into force on the first day of the month following the date on which five member States of the Council of Europe have expressed their consent to be bound by the Protocol in accordance with the provisions of Article 7.
2. In respect of any member State which subsequently expresses its consent to be bound by it, the Protocol shall enter into force on the first day of the month following the date of the deposit of the instrument of ratification, acceptance or approval.

Article 9—Depositary functions

The Secretary General of the Council of Europe shall notify the member States of the Council of:

a. any signature;

b. the deposit of any instrument of ratification, acceptance or approval;

c. any date of entry into force of this Protocol in accordance with Articles 5 and 8;

d. any other act, notification or communication relating to this Protocol.

In witness whereof the undersigned, being duly authorised thereto, have signed this Protocol.

Done at Strasbourg, this 28th day of April 1983, in English and in French, both texts being equally authentic, in a single copy which shall be deposited in the archives of the Council of Europe. The Secretary General of the Council of Europe shall transmit certified copies to each member State of the Council of Europe.

D: PROTOCOL NO. 7 TO THE CONVENTION FOR THE PROTECTION OF HUMAN RIGHTS AND FUNDAMENTAL FREEDOMS CONCERNING THE ABOLITION OF THE DEATH PENALTY, AS AMENDED BY PROTOCOL NO. 11

Strasbourg, 22.XI.1984

The member States of the Council of Europe signatory hereto,

Being resolved to take further steps to ensure the collective enforcement of certain rights and freedoms by means of the Convention for the Protection of Human Rights and Fundamental Freedoms signed at Rome on 4 November 1950 (hereinafter referred to as "the Convention"),

Have agreed as follows :

Article 1—Procedural safeguards relating to expulsion of aliens

1. An alien lawfully resident in the territory of a State shall not be expelled therefrom except in pursuance of a decision reached in accordance with law and shall be allowed:

   a. to submit reasons against his expulsion,

   b. to have his case reviewed, and

   c. to be represented for these purposes before the competent authority or a person or persons designated by that authority.

2. An alien may be expelled before the exercise of his rights under paragraph 1.a, b and c of this Article, when such expulsion is necessary in the interests of public order or is grounded on reasons of national security.

Article 2—Right of appeal in criminal matters

1. Everyone convicted of a criminal offence by a tribunal shall have the right to have his conviction or sentence reviewed by a higher tribunal. The exercise of this right, including the grounds on which it may be exercised, shall be governed by law.
2. This right may be subject to exceptions in regard to offences of a minor character, as prescribed by law, or in cases in which the person concerned was tried in the first instance by the highest tribunal or was convicted following an appeal against acquittal.

Article 3—Compensation for wrongful conviction

When a person has by a final decision been convicted of a criminal offence and when subsequently his conviction has been reversed, or he has been pardoned, on the ground that a new or newly discovered fact shows conclusively that there has been a miscarriage of justice, the person who has suffered punishment as a result of such conviction shall be compensated according to the law or the practice of the State concerned, unless it is proved that the non-disclosure of the unknown fact in time is wholly or partly attributable to him.

Article 4—Right not to be tried or punished twice

1. No one shall be liable to be tried or punished again in criminal proceedings under the jurisdiction of the same State for an offence for which he has already been finally acquitted or convicted in accordance with the law and penal procedure of that State.
2. The provisions of the preceding paragraph shall not prevent the reopening of the case in accordance with the law and penal procedure of the State concerned, if there is evidence of new or newly discovered facts, or if there has been a fundamental defect in the previous proceedings, which could affect the outcome of the case.
3. No derogation from this Article shall be made under Article 15 of the Convention.

Article 5—Equality between spouses

Spouses shall enjoy equality of rights and responsibilities of a private law character between them, and in their relations with their children, as to marriage, during marriage and in the event of its dissolution. This Article shall not prevent States from taking such measures as are necessary in the interests of the children.

Article 6—Territorial application

1. Any State may at the time of signature or when depositing its instrument of ratification, acceptance or approval, specify the territory or territories to which the Protocol shall apply and state the extent to which it undertakes that the provisions of this Protocol shall apply to such territory or territories.
2. Any State may at any later date, by a declaration addressed to the Secretary General of the Council of Europe, extend the application of this Protocol to any other territory specified in the declaration. In respect of such territory the Protocol shall enter into force on the first day of the month following the expiration of a period of two months after the date of receipt by the Secretary General of such declaration.
3. Any declaration made under the two preceding paragraphs may, in respect of any territory specified in such declaration, be withdrawn or modified by a notification addressed to the Secretary General. The withdrawal or modification shall become effective on the first day of the month following the expiration of a period of two months after the date of receipt of such notification by the Secretary General.
4. A declaration made in accordance with this Article shall be deemed to have been made in accordance with paragraph 1 of Article 56 of the Convention.
5. The territory of any State to which this Protocol applies by virtue of ratification, acceptance or approval by that State, and each territory to which this Protocol is applied by virtue of a declaration by that State under this Article, may be treated as separate territories for the purpose of the reference in Article 1 to the territory of a State.
6. Any State which has made a declaration in accordance with paragraph 1 or 2 of this Article may at any time thereafter declare on behalf of one or more of the territories to which the declaration relates that it accepts the competence of the Court to receive applications from individuals, non-governmental organisations or groups of individuals as provided in Article 34 of the Convention in respect of Articles 1 to 5 of this Protocol.

Article 7—Relationship to the Convention

As between the States Parties, the provisions of Article 1 to 6 of this Protocol shall be regarded as additional Articles to the Convention, and all the provisions of the Convention shall apply accordingly.

Article 8—Signature and ratification

This Protocol shall be open for signature by member States of the Council of Europe which have signed the Convention. It is subject to ratification, acceptance or approval. A member State of the Council of Europe may not ratify, accept or approve this Protocol without previously or simultaneously ratifying the Convention. Instruments of ratification, acceptance or approval shall be deposited with the Secretary General of the Council of Europe.

Article 9—Entry into force

1. This Protocol shall enter into force on the first day of the month following the expiration of a period of two months after the date on which seven member States of the Council of Europe have expressed their consent to be bound by the Protocol in accordance with the provisions of Article 8.
2. In respect of any member State which subsequently expresses its consent to be bound by it, the Protocol shall enter into force on the first day of the month following the expiration of a period of two months after the date of the deposit of the instrument of ratification, acceptance or approval.

Article 10—Depositary functions

The Secretary General of the Council of Europe shall notify all the member States of the Council of Europe of:

a. any signature;

b. the deposit of any instrument of ratification, acceptance or approval;

c. any date of entry into force of this Protocol in accordance with Articles 6 and 9;

d. any other act, notification or declaration relating to this Protocol.

In witness whereof the undersigned, being duly authorised thereto, have signed this Protocol.

Done at Strasbourg, this 22nd day of November 1984, in English and French, both texts being equally authentic, in a single copy which shall be deposited in the archives of the Council of Europe. The Secretary General of the Council of Europe shall transmit certified copies to each member State of the Council of Europe.

APPENDIX 5

EUROPEAN COURT OF HUMAN RIGHTS

Rules of Court

(JULY 2006)

REGISTRY OF THE COURT

STRASBOURG

(AS IN FORCE AT 1 JULY 2006)

CONTENTS

TITLE III—TRANSITIONAL RULES

TITLE IV—FINAL CLAUSES

ANNEX TO THE RULES (CONCERNING INVESTIGATIONS)

PRACTICE DIRECTIONS

The European Court of Human Rights,
Having regard to the Convention for the Protection of Human Rights and Fundamental
Freedoms and the Protocols thereto,
Makes the present Rules:

Rule 1[1]

(Definitions)

For the purposes of these Rules unless the context otherwise requires:

(a) the term "Convention" means the Convention for the Protection of Human Rights
and Fundamental Freedoms and the Protocols thereto;

(b) the expression "plenary Court" means the European Court of Human Rights sitting
in plenary session;

(c) the expression "Grand Chamber" means the Grand Chamber of seventeen judges
constituted in pursuance of Article 27 § 1 of the Convention;

(d) the term "Section" means a Chamber set up by the plenary Court for a fixed period
in pursuance of Article 26 (b) of the Convention and the expression "President of
the Section" means the judge elected by the plenary Court in pursuance of Article
26 (c) of the Convention as President of such a Section;

(e) the term "Chamber" means any Chamber of seven judges constituted in pursuance
of Article 27 § 1 of the Convention and the expression "President of the Chamber"
means the judge presiding over such a "Chamber";

(f) the term "Committee" means a Committee of three judges set up in pursuance of
Article 27 § 1 of the Convention;

(g) the term "Court" means either the plenary Court, the Grand Chamber, a Section,
a Chamber, a Committee or the panel of five judges referred to in Article 43 § 2 of
the Convention;

(h) the expression "*ad hoc* judge" means any person, other than an elected judge,
chosen by a Contracting Party in pursuance of Article 27 § 2 of the Convention to
sit as a member of the Grand Chamber or as a member of a Chamber;

(i) the terms "judge" and "judges" mean the judges elected by the Parliamentary
Assembly of the Council of Europe or *ad hoc* judges;

(j) the expression "Judge Rapporteur" means a judge appointed to carry out the tasks
provided for in Rules 48 and 49;

(k) the term "delegate" means a judge who has been appointed to a delegation by the
Chamber and the expression "head of the delegation" means the delegate
appointed by the Chamber to lead its delegation;

(l) the term "delegation" means a body composed of delegates, Registry members and
any other person appointed by the Chamber to assist the delegation;

(m) the term "Registrar" denotes the Registrar of the Court or the Registrar of a Section
according to the context;

(n) the terms "party" and "parties" mean

---

1. As amended by the Court on 7 July 2003.

— the applicant or respondent Contracting Parties;

— the applicant (the person, non-governmental organisation or group of individuals) that lodged a complaint under Article 34 of the Convention;

(o) the expression "third party" means any Contracting Party or any person concerned who, as provided for in Article 36 §§ 1 and 2 of the Convention, has exercised its right or been invited to submit written comments or take part in a hearing;

(p) the terms "hearing" and "hearings" mean oral proceedings held on the admissibility and/or merits of an application or held in connection with a request for revision, interpretation or an advisory opinion;

(q) the expression "Committee of Ministers" means the Committee of Ministers of the Council of Europe;

(r) the terms "former Court" and "Commission" mean respectively the European Court and European Commission of Human Rights set up under former Article 19 of the Convention.

Title I
Organisation and Working of the Court

Chapter I
Judges

Rule 2

(Calculation of term of office)

1. The duration of the term of office of an elected judge shall be calculated as from the date of election. However, when a judge is re-elected on the expiry of the term of office or is elected to replace a judge whose term of office has expired or is about to expire, the duration of the term of office shall, in either case, be calculated as from the date of such expiry.

2. In accordance with Article 23 § 5 of the Convention, a judge elected to replace a judge whose term of office has not expired shall hold office for the remainder of the predecessor's term.

3. In accordance with Article 23 § 7 of the Convention, an elected judge shall hold office until a successor has taken the oath or made the declaration provided for in Rule 3.

Rule 3

(Oath or solemn declaration)

1. Before taking up office, each elected judge shall, at the first sitting of the plenary Court at which the judge is present or, in case of need, before the President of the Court, take the following oath or make the following solemn declaration:

"I swear"—or "I solemnly declare"—"that I will exercise my functions as a judge honourably, independently and impartially and that I will keep secret all deliberations."

2. This act shall be recorded in minutes.

Rule 4

(Incompatible activities)

In accordance with Article 21 § 3 of the Convention, the judges shall not during their term of office engage in any political or administrative activity or any professional activity which is incompatible with their independence or impartiality or with the demands of a full-time office. Each judge shall declare to the President of the Court any additional activity. In the event of a disagreement between the President and the judge concerned, any question arising shall be decided by the plenary Court.

Rule 5

(Precedence)

1. Elected judges shall take precedence after the President and Vice-Presidents of the Court and the Presidents of the Sections, according to the date of their election; in the event of re-election, even if it is not an immediate re-election, the length of time during which the judge concerned previously held office as a judge shall be taken into account.
2. Vice-Presidents of the Court elected to office on the same date shall take precedence according to the length of time they have served as judges. If the length of time they have served as judges is the same, they shall take precedence according to age. The same rule shall apply to Presidents of Sections.
3. Judges who have served the same length of time as judges shall take precedence according to age.
4. *Ad hoc* judges shall take precedence after the elected judges according to age.

Rule 6

(Resignation)

Resignation of a judge shall be notified to the President of the Court, who shall transmit it to the Secretary General of the Council of Europe. Subject to the provisions of Rules 24 § 4 in fine and 26 § 3, resignation shall constitute vacation of office.

Rule 7

(Dismissal from office)

No judge may be dismissed from his or her office unless the other judges, meeting in plenary session, decide by a majority of two-thirds of the elected judges in office that he or she has ceased to fulfil the required conditions. He or she must first be heard by the plenary Court. Any judge may set in motion the procedure for dismissal from office.

Rule 8[2]

(Election of the President and Vice-Presidents of the Court and the Presidents and Vice-Presidents of the Sections)

1. The plenary Court shall elect its President, two Vice-Presidents and the Presidents of the Sections for a period of three years, provided that such period shall not exceed the duration of their terms of office as judges.

2. Each Section shall likewise elect for a period of three years a Vice-President, who shall replace the President of the Section if the latter is unable to carry out his or her duties.

3. A judge elected in accordance with paragraphs 1 or 2 above may be re-elected but only once to the same level of office. This limitation on the number of terms of office shall not prevent a judge holding an office as described above on the date of the entry into force[3] of the present amendment to Rule 8 from being re-elected once to the same level of office.

4. The Presidents and Vice-Presidents shall continue to hold office until the election of their successors.

5. The elections referred to in this Rule shall be by secret ballot. Only the elected judges who are present shall take part. If no candidate receives an absolute majority of the elected judges present, an additional round or rounds shall take place until one candidate has achieved an absolute majority. At each round the candidate who has received the least number of votes shall be eliminated. If more than one candidate has received the least number of votes, only the candidate who is lowest in the order of precedence in accordance with Rule 5 shall be eliminated. In the event of a tie between two candidates in the final round, preference shall be given to the judge having precedence in accordance with Rule 5.

Rule 9

(Functions of the President of the Court)

1. The President of the Court shall direct the work and administration of the Court. The President shall represent the Court and, in particular, be responsible for its relations with the authorities of the Council of Europe.

2. The President shall preside at plenary meetings of the Court, meetings of the Grand Chamber and meetings of the panel of five judges.

3. The President shall not take part in the consideration of cases being heard by Chambers except where he or she is the judge elected in respect of a Contracting Party concerned.

---

1. As amended by the Court on 7 July 2003.
2. As amended by the Court on 7 November 2005.
3. 1 December 2005.

Rule 9A[1]

(Role of the Bureau)

1. (a) The Court shall have a Bureau, composed of the President of the Court, the Vice-Presidents of the Court and the Section Presidents. Where a Vice-President or a Section President is unable to attend a Bureau meeting, he/she shall be replaced by the Section Vice-President or, failing that, by the next most senior member of the Section according to the order of precedence established in Rule 5.

   (b) The Bureau may request the attendance of any other member of the Court or any other person whose presence it considers necessary.

2. The Bureau shall be assisted by the Registrar and the Deputy Registrars.

3. The Bureau's task shall be to assist the President in carrying out his/her function in directing the work and administration of the Court. To this end the President may submit to the Bureau any administrative or extra-judicial matter which falls within his/her competence.

4. The Bureau shall also facilitate co-ordination between the Court's Sections.

5. The President may consult the Bureau before issuing practice directions under Rule 32 and before approving general instructions drawn up by the Registrar under Rule 17 § 4.

6. The Bureau may report on any matter to the Plenary. It may also make proposals to the Plenary.

7. A record shall be kept of the Bureau's meetings and distributed to the Judges in both the Court's official languages. The secretary to the Bureau shall be designated by the Registrar in agreement with the President.

Rule 10

(Functions of the Vice-Presidents of the Court)

The Vice-Presidents of the Court shall assist the President of the Court. They shall take the place of the President if the latter is unable to carry out his or her duties or the office of President is vacant, or at the request of the President. They shall also act as Presidents of Sections.

Rule 11

(Replacement of the President and the Vice-Presidents of the Court)

If the President and the Vice-Presidents of the Court are at the same time unable to carry out their duties or if their offices are at the same time vacant, the office of President of the Court shall be assumed by a President of a Section or, if none is available, by another elected judge, in accordance with the order of precedence provided for in Rule 5.

---

1. Inserted by the Court on 7 July 2003.

Rule 12[1]

(Presidency of Sections and Chambers)

The Presidents of the Sections shall preside at the sittings of the Section and Chambers of which they are members and shall direct the Sections' work. The Vice-Presidents of the Sections shall take their place if they are unable to carry out their duties or if the office of President of the Section concerned is vacant, or at the request of the President of the Section. Failing that, the judges of the Section and the Chambers shall take their place, in the order of precedence provided for in Rule 5.

Rule 13[2]

(Inability to preside)

Judges of the Court may not preside in cases in which the Contracting Party of which they are nationals or in respect of which they were elected is a party, or in cases where they sit as a judge appointed by virtue of Rule 29 § 1(a) or Rule 30 § 1 of these Rules.

Rule 14

(Balanced representation of the sexes)

In relation to the making of appointments governed by this and the following chapter of the present Rules, the Court shall pursue a policy aimed at securing a balanced representation of the sexes.

CHAPTER III
THE REGISTRY

Rule 15

(Election of the Registrar)

1. The plenary Court shall elect its Registrar. The candidates shall be of high moral character and must possess the legal, managerial and linguistic knowledge and experience necessary to carry out the functions attaching to the post.

2. The Registrar shall be elected for a term of five years and may be re-elected. The Registrar may not be dismissed from office, unless the judges, meeting in plenary session, decide by a majority of two-thirds of the elected judges in office that the person concerned has ceased to fulfil the required conditions. He or she must first be heard by the plenary Court. Any judge may set in motion the procedure for dismissal from office.

3. The elections referred to in this Rule shall be by secret ballot; only the elected judges who are present shall take part. If no candidate receives an absolute majority of the elected

---

1. As amended by the Court on 17 June and 8 July 2002.
2. As amended by the Court on 4 July 2005.

judges present, a ballot shall take place between the two candidates who have received most votes. In the event of a tie, preference shall be given, firstly, to the female candidate, if any, and, secondly, to the older candidate.

4. Before taking up office, the Registrar shall take the following oath or make the following solemn declaration before the plenary Court or, if need be, before the President of the Court:

"I swear"—or "I solemnly declare"—"that I will exercise loyally, discreetly and conscientiously the functions conferred upon me as Registrar of the European Court of Human Rights."

This act shall be recorded in minutes.

Rule 16

(Election of the Deputy Registrars)

1. The plenary Court shall also elect two Deputy Registrars on the conditions and in the manner and for the term prescribed in the preceding Rule. The procedure for dismissal from office provided for in respect of the Registrar shall likewise apply. The Court shall first consult the Registrar in both these matters.

2. Before taking up office, a Deputy Registrar shall take an oath or make a solemn declaration before the plenary Court or, if need be, before the President of the Court, in terms similar to those prescribed in respect of the Registrar. This act shall be recorded in minutes.

Rule 17

(Functions of the Registrar)

1. The Registrar shall assist the Court in the performance of its functions and shall be responsible for the organisation and activities of the Registry under the authority of the President of the Court.

2. The Registrar shall have the custody of the archives of the Court and shall be the channel for all communications and notifications made by, or addressed to, the Court in connection with the cases brought or to be brought before it.

3. The Registrar shall, subject to the duty of discretion attaching to this office, reply to requests for information concerning the work of the Court, in particular to enquiries from the press.

4. General instructions drawn up by the Registrar, and approved by the President of the Court, shall regulate the working of the Registry.

Rule 18

(Organisation of the Registry)

1. The Registry shall consist of Section Registries equal to the number of Sections set up by the Court and of the departments necessary to provide the legal and administrative services required by the Court.

2. The Section Registrar shall assist the Section in the performance of its functions and may be assisted by a Deputy Section Registrar.

3. The officials of the Registry, including the legal secretaries but not the Registrar and the Deputy Registrars, shall be appointed by the Secretary General of the Council of Europe with the agreement of the President of the Court or of the Registrar acting on the President's instructions.

CHAPTER IV
THE WORKING OF THE COURT

Rule 19

(Seat of the Court)

1. The seat of the Court shall be at the seat of the Council of Europe at Strasbourg. The Court may, however, if it considers it expedient, perform its functions elsewhere in the territories of the member States of the Council of Europe.
2. The Court may decide, at any stage of the examination of an application, that it is necessary that an investigation or any other function be carried out elsewhere by it or one or more of its members.

Rule 20

(Sessions of the plenary Court)

1. The plenary sessions of the Court shall be convened by the President of the Court whenever the performance of its functions under the Convention and under these Rules so requires. The President of the Court shall convene a plenary session if at least one-third of the members of the Court so request, and in any event once a year to consider administrative matters.
2. The quorum of the plenary Court shall be two-thirds of the elected judges in office.
3. If there is no quorum, the President shall adjourn the sitting.

Rule 21

(Other sessions of the Court)

1. The Grand Chamber, the Chambers and the Committees shall sit full time. On a proposal by the President, however, the Court shall fix session periods each year.
2. Outside those periods the Grand Chamber and the Chambers shall be convened by their Presidents in cases of urgency.

Rule 22

(Deliberations)

1. The Court shall deliberate in private. Its deliberations shall remain secret.
2. Only the judges shall take part in the deliberations. The Registrar or the designated substitute, as well as such other officials of the Registry and interpreters whose assistance

is deemed necessary, shall be present. No other person may be admitted except by special decision of the Court.

3. Before a vote is taken on any matter in the Court, the President may request the judges to state their opinions on it.

Rule 23

(Votes)

1. The decisions of the Court shall be taken by a majority of the judges present. In the event of a tie, a fresh vote shall be taken and, if there is still a tie, the President shall have a casting vote. This paragraph shall apply unless otherwise provided for in these Rules.

2. The decisions and judgments of the Grand Chamber and the Chambers shall be adopted by a majority of the sitting judges. Abstentions shall not be allowed in final votes on the admissibility and merits of cases.

3. As a general rule, votes shall be taken by a show of hands. The President may take a roll-call vote, in reverse order of precedence.

4. Any matter that is to be voted upon shall be formulated in precise terms.

Rule 23A[1]

Decision by tacit agreement

Where it is necessary for the Court to decide a point of procedure or any other question other than at a scheduled meeting of the Court, the President may direct that a draft decision be circulated to the judges and that a deadline be set for their comments on the draft. In the absence of any objection from a judge, the proposal shall be deemed to have been adopted at the expiry of the deadline.

CHAPTER V
THE COMPOSITION OF THE COURT

Rule 24[2]

(Composition of the Grand Chamber)

1. The Grand Chamber shall be composed of seventeen judges and at least three substitute judges.

2. (a) The Grand Chamber shall include the President and the Vice-Presidents of the Court and the Presidents of the Sections. Any Vice-President of the Court or President of a Section who is unable to sit as a member of the Grand Chamber shall be replaced by the Vice-President of the relevant Section.

---

1. Inserted by the Court on 13 December 2004.
2. As amended by the Court on 8 December 2000, 13 December 2004, 4 July 2005, 7 November 2005 and 29 May 2006.

(b) The judge elected in respect of the Contracting Party concerned or, where appropriate, the judge designated by virtue of Rule 29 or Rule 30 shall sit as an *ex officio* member of the Grand Chamber in accordance with Article 27 §§ 2 and 3 of the Convention.

(c) In cases referred to the Grand Chamber under Article 30 of the Convention, the Grand Chamber shall also include the members of the Chamber which relinquished jurisdiction.

(d) In cases referred to it under Article 43 of the Convention, the Grand Chamber shall not include any judge who sat in the Chamber which rendered the judgment in the case so referred, with the exception of the President of that Chamber and the judge who sat in respect of the State Party concerned, or any judge who sat in the Chamber or Chambers which ruled on the admissibility of the application.

(e) The judges and substitute judges who are to complete the Grand Chamber in each case referred to it shall be designated from among the remaining judges by a drawing of lots by the President of the Court in the presence of the Registrar. The modalities for the drawing of lots shall be laid down by the Plenary Court, having due regard to the need for a geographically balanced composition reflecting the different legal systems among the Contracting Parties.

(f) In examining a request for an advisory opinion under Article 47 of the Convention, the Grand Chamber shall be constituted in accordance with the provisions of § 2 (a) and (e) of this Rule

3. If any judges are prevented from sitting, they shall be replaced by the substitute judges in the order in which the latter were selected under paragraph 2(e) of this Rule.

4. The judges and substitute judges designated in accordance with the above provisions shall continue to sit in the Grand Chamber for the consideration of the case until the proceedings have been completed. Even after the end of their terms of office, they shall continue to deal with the case if they have participated in the consideration of the merits. These provisions shall also apply to proceedings relating to advisory opinions.

5. (a) The panel of five judges of the Grand Chamber called upon to consider a request submitted under Article 43 of the Convention shall be composed of

— the President of the Court. If the President of the Court is prevented from sitting, he shall be replaced by the Vice-President of the Court taking precedence;

— two Presidents of Sections designated by rotation. If the Presidents of the Sections so designated are prevented from sitting, they shall be replaced by the Vice-Presidents of their Sections;

— two judges designated by rotation from among the judges elected by the remaining Sections to sit on the panel for a period of six months;

— at least two substitute judges designated in rotation from among the judges elected by the Sections to serve on the panel for a period of six months.

(b) When considering a referral request, the panel shall not include any judge who took part in the consideration of the admissibility or merits of the case in question.

(c) No judge elected in respect of, or who is a national of, a Contracting Party concerned by a referral request may be a member of the panel when it examines that request. An elected judge appointed by the Contracting Party concerned pursuant to Rules 29 or 30 shall likewise be excluded from consideration of any such request.

(d) Any member of the panel unable to sit, for the reasons set out in (b) or (c) shall be replaced by a substitute judge designated in rotation from among the judges elected by the Sections to serve on the panel for a period of six months.

Rule 25

(Setting up of Sections)

1. The Chambers provided for in Article 26 (b) of the Convention (referred to in these Rules as "Sections") shall be set up by the plenary Court, on a proposal by its President, for a period of three years with effect from the election of the presidential office-holders of the Court under Rule 8. There shall be at least four Sections.

2. Each judge shall be a member of a Section. The composition of the Sections shall be geographically and gender balanced and shall reflect the different legal systems among the Contracting Parties.

3. Where a judge ceases to be a member of the Court before the expiry of the period for which the Section has been constituted, the judge's place in the Section shall be taken by his or her successor as a member of the Court.

4. The President of the Court may exceptionally make modifications to the composition of the Sections if circumstances so require.

5. On a proposal by the President, the plenary Court may constitute an additional Section.

Rule 26[1]

(Constitution of Chambers)

1. The Chambers of seven judges provided for in Article 27 § 1 of the Convention for the consideration of cases brought before the Court shall be constituted from the Sections as follows.

(a) Subject to paragraph 2 of this Rule and to Rule 28 § 4, last sentence, the Chamber shall in each case include the President of the Section and the judge elected in respect of any Contracting Party concerned. If the latter judge is not a member of the Section to which the application has been assigned under Rule 51 or 52, he or she shall sit as an *ex officio* member of the Chamber in accordance with Article 27 § 2 of the Convention. Rule 29 shall apply if that judge is unable to sit or withdraws.

(b) The other members of the Chamber shall be designated by the President of the Section in rotation from among the members of the relevant Section.

(c) The members of the Section who are not so designated shall sit in the case as substitute judges.

2. The judge elected in respect of any Contracting Party concerned or, where appropriate, another elected judge or *ad hoc* judge appointed in accordance with Rules 29 and

---

1. As amended by the Court on 17 June and 8 July 2002.

30 may be dispensed by the President of the Chamber from attending meetings devoted to preparatory or procedural matters. For the purposes of such meetings the Contracting Party concerned shall be deemed to have appointed in place of that judge the first substitute judge, in accordance with Rule 29 § 1.

3. Even after the end of their terms of office judges shall continue to deal with cases in which they have participated in the consideration of the merits.

Rule 27

(Committees)

1. Committees composed of three judges belonging to the same Section shall be set up under Article 27 § 1 of the Convention. After consulting the Presidents of the Sections, the President of the Court shall decide on the number of Committees to be set up.

2. The Committees shall be constituted for a period of twelve months by rotation among the members of each Section, excepting the President of the Section.

3. The judges of the Section who are not members of a Committee may be called upon to take the place of members who are unable to sit.

4. Each Committee shall be chaired by the member having precedence in the Section.

Rule 28[1]

(Inability to sit, withdrawal or exemption)

1. Any judge who is prevented from taking part in sittings which he or she has been called upon to attend shall, as soon as possible, give notice to the President of the Chamber.

2. A judge may not take part in the consideration of any case if

(a) he or she has a personal interest in the case, including a spousal, parental or other close family, personal or professional relationship, or a subordinate relationship, with any of the parties;

(b) he or she has previously acted in the case, whether as the Agent, advocate or adviser of a party or of a person having an interest in the case, or as a member of another national or international tribunal or commission of inquiry, or in any other capacity;

(c) he or she, being an ad hoc judge or a former elected judge continuing to sit by virtue of Rule 26 § 3, engages in any political or administrative activity or any professional activity which is incompatible with his or her independence or impartiality;

(d) he or she has expressed opinions publicly, through the communications media, in writing, through his or her public actions or otherwise, that are objectively capable of adversely affecting his or her impartiality;

(e) for any other reason, his or her independence or impartiality may legitimately be called into doubt.

---

1. As amended by the Court on 17 June and 8 July 2002 and 13 December 2004.

3. If a judge withdraws for one of the said reasons he or she shall notify the President of the Chamber, who shall exempt the judge from sitting.

4. In the event of any doubt on the part of the judge concerned or the President as to the existence of one of the grounds referred to in paragraph 2 of this Rule, that issue shall be decided by the Chamber. After hearing the views of the judge concerned, the Chamber shall deliberate and vote, without that judge being present. For the purposes of the Chamber's deliberations and vote on this issue, he or she shall be replaced by the first substitute judge in the Chamber. The same shall apply if the judge sits in respect of any Contracting Party concerned. In that event, the Contracting Party concerned shall be deemed to have appointed the first substitute judge to sit in his or her stead, in accordance with Rule 29 § 1.

5. The provisions above shall apply also to a judge's participation in a Committee, save that the notice required under paragraph 1 or 3 shall be given to the President of the Section.

Rule 29[1]

(*Ad hoc* judges)

1. (a) If the judge elected in respect of a Contracting Party concerned is unable to sit in the Chamber, withdraws, or is exempted, or if there is none, the President of the Chamber shall invite that Party to indicate within thirty days whether it wishes to appoint to sit as judge either another elected judge or an *ad hoc* judge and, if so, to state at the same time the name of the person appointed.

   (b) The same rule shall apply if the person so appointed is unable to sit or withdraws.

   (c) An *ad hoc* judge shall possess the qualifications required by Article 21 § 1 of the Convention, must not be unable to sit in the case on any of the grounds referred to in Rule 28 of these Rules, and must be in a position to meet the demands of availability and attendance provided for in paragraph 5 of this Rule.

2. The Contracting Party concerned shall be presumed to have waived its right of appointment if it does not reply within thirty days or by the end of any extension of that time granted by the President of the Chamber. The Contracting Party concerned shall also be presumed to have waived its right of appointment if it twice appoints as *ad hoc* judge persons who the Chamber finds do not satisfy the conditions laid down in paragraph 1 (c) of this Rule.

3. The President of the Chamber may decide not to invite the Contracting Party concerned to make an appointment under paragraph 1 (a) of this Rule until notice of the application is given to it under Rule 54 § 2 of these Rules. In that event, pending any appointment by it, the Contracting Party concerned shall be deemed to have appointed the first substitute judge to sit in place of the elected judge.

4. An *ad hoc* judge shall, at the beginning of the first sitting held to consider the case after the judge has been appointed, take the oath or make the solemn declaration provided for in Rule 3. This act shall be recorded in minutes.

5. *Ad hoc* judges are required to make themselves available to the Court and, subject to Rule 26 § 2, to attend the meetings of the Chamber.

---

1. As amended by the Court on 17 June and 8 July 2002.

Rule 30[1]

(Common interest)

1. If two or more applicant or respondent Contracting Parties have a common interest, the President of the Chamber may invite them to agree to appoint a single judge elected in respect of one of the Contracting Parties concerned as common-interest judge who will be called upon to sit *ex officio*. If the Parties are unable to agree, the President shall choose the common-interest judge by lot from the judges proposed by the Parties.

2. The President of the Chamber may decide not to invite the Contracting Parties concerned to make an appointment under paragraph 1 of this Rule until notice of the application has been given under Rule 54 § 2 of these Rules.

3. In the event of a dispute as to the existence of a common interest or as to any related matter, the Chamber shall decide, if necessary after obtaining written submissions from the Contracting Parties concerned.

TITLE II
PROCEDURE

CHAPTER I
GENERAL RULES

Rule 31

(Possibility of particular derogations)

The provisions of this Title shall not prevent the Court from derogating from them for the consideration of a particular case after having consulted the parties where appropriate.

Rule 32

(Practice directions)

The President of the Court may issue practice directions, notably in relation to such matters as appearance at hearings and the filing of pleadings and other documents.

Rule 33[2]

(Public character of documents)

1. All documents deposited with the Registry by the parties or by any third party in connection with an application, except those deposited within the framework of friendly-settlement negotiations as provided for in Rule 62, shall be accessible to the public in accordance with arrangements determined by the Registrar, unless the President of the

---

1. As amended by the Court on 7 July 2003.
2. As amended by the Court on 17 June and 8 July 2002, 7 July 2003 and 4 July 2005.

Chamber, for the reasons set out in paragraph 2 of this Rule, decides otherwise, either of his or her own motion or at the request of a party or any other person concerned.

2. Public access to a document or to any part of it may be restricted in the interests of morals, public order or national security in a democratic society, where the interests of juveniles or the protection of the private life of the parties so require, or to the extent strictly necessary in the opinion of the President in special circumstances where publicity would prejudice the interests of justice.

3. Any request for confidentiality made under paragraph 1 of this Rule must include reasons and specify whether it is requested that all or part of the documents be inaccessible to the public.

4. Decisions and judgments given by a Chamber shall be accessible to the public. The Court shall periodically make accessible to the public general information about decisions taken by Committees under Rule 53 § 2.

Rule 34[1]

(Use of languages)

1. The official languages of the Court shall be English and French.

2. In connection with applications lodged under Article 34 of the Convention, and for as long as no Contracting Party has been given notice of such an application in accordance with these Rules, all communications with and oral and written submissions by applicants or their representatives, if not in one of the Court's official languages, shall be in one of the official languages of the Contracting Parties. If a Contracting Party is informed or given notice of an application in accordance with these Rules, the application and any accompanying documents shall be communicated to that State in the language in which they were lodged with the Registry by the applicant.

3. (a) All communications with and oral and written submissions by applicants or their representatives in respect of a hearing, or after notice of an application has been given to a Contracting Party, shall be in one of the Court's official languages, unless the President of the Chamber grants leave for the continued use of the official language of a Contracting Party.

   (b) If such leave is granted, the Registrar shall make the necessary arrangements for the interpretation and translation into English or French of the applicant's oral and written submissions respectively, in full or in part, where the President of the Chamber considers it to be in the interests of the proper conduct of the proceedings.

   (c) Exceptionally the President of the Chamber may make the grant of leave subject to the condition that the applicant bear all or part of the costs of making such arrangements.

   (d) Unless the President of the Chamber decides otherwise, any decision made under the foregoing provisions of this paragraph shall remain valid in all subsequent proceedings in the case, including those in respect of requests for referral of the case to the Grand Chamber and requests for interpretation or revision of a judgment under Rules 73, 79 and 80 respectively.

4. (a) All communications with and oral and written submissions by a Contracting Party which is a party to the case shall be in one of the Court's official

---

1. As amended by the Court on 13 December 2004.

languages. The President of the Chamber may grant the Contracting Party concerned leave to use one of its official languages for its oral and written submissions.

(b) If such leave is granted, it shall be the responsibility of the requesting Party

    (i) to file a translation of its written submissions into one of the official languages of the Court within a time-limit to be fixed by the President of the Chamber. Should that Party not file the translation within that time-limit, the Registrar may make the necessary arrangements for such translation, the expenses to be charged to the requesting Party;

    (ii) to bear the expenses of interpreting its oral submissions into English or French. The Registrar shall be responsible for making the necessary arrangements for such interpretation.

(c) The President of the Chamber may direct that a Contracting Party which is a party to the case shall, within a specified time, provide a translation into, or a summary in, English or French of all or certain annexes to its written submissions or of any other relevant document, or of extracts therefrom.

(d) The preceding sub-paragraphs of this paragraph shall also apply, *mutatis mutandis*, to third-party intervention under Rule 44 of these Rules and to the use of a non-official language by a third party.

5. The President of the Chamber may invite the respondent Contracting Party to provide a translation of its written submissions in the or an official language of that Party in order to facilitate the applicant's understanding of those submissions.

6. Any witness, expert or other person appearing before the Court may use his or her own language if he or she does not have sufficient knowledge of either of the two official languages. In that event the Registrar shall make the necessary arrangements for interpreting or translation.

Rule 35

(Representation of Contracting Parties)

The Contracting Parties shall be represented by Agents, who may have the assistance of advocates or advisers.

Rule 36[1]

(Representation of applicants)

1. Persons, non-governmental organisations or groups of individuals may initially present applications under Article 34 of the Convention themselves or through a representative.

2. Following notification of the application to the respondent Contracting Party under Rule 54 § 2 (b), the applicant should be represented in accordance with paragraph 4 of this Rule, unless the President of the Chamber decides otherwise.

3. The applicant must be so represented at any hearing decided on by the Chamber, unless the President of the Chamber exceptionally grants leave to the applicant to present

---

1. As amended by the Court on 7 July 2003.

his or her own case, subject, if necessary, to being assisted by an advocate or other approved representative.

4. (a) The representative acting on behalf of the applicant pursuant to paragraphs 2 and 3 of this Rule shall be an advocate authorised to practise in any of the Contracting Parties and resident in the territory of one of them, or any other person approved by the President of the Chamber.

(b) In exceptional circumstances and at any stage of the procedure, the President of the Chamber may, where he or she considers that the circumstances or the conduct of the advocate or other person appointed under the preceding sub-paragraph so warrant, direct that the latter may no longer represent or assist the applicant and that the applicant should seek alternative representation.

5. (a) The advocate or other approved representative, or the applicant in person who seeks leave to present his or her own case, must even if leave is granted under the following sub-paragraph, have an adequate understanding of one of the Court's official languages.

(b) If he or she does not have sufficient proficiency to express himself or herself in one of the Court's official languages, leave to use one of the official languages of the Contracting Parties may be given by the President of the Chamber under Rule 34 § 3.

Rule 37[1]

(Communications, notifications and summonses)

1. Communications or notifications addressed to the Agents or advocates of the parties shall be deemed to have been addressed to the parties.

2. If, for any communication, notification or summons addressed to persons other than the Agents or advocates of the parties, the Court considers it necessary to have the assistance of the Government of the State on whose territory such communication, notification or summons is to have effect, the President of the Court shall apply directly to that Government in order to obtain the necessary facilities.

Rule 38

(Written pleadings)

1. No written observations or other documents may be filed after the time-limit set by the President of the Chamber or the Judge Rapporteur, as the case may be, in accordance with these Rules. No written observations or other documents filed outside that time-limit or contrary to any practice direction issued under Rule 32 shall be included in the case file unless the President of the Chamber decides otherwise.

2. For the purposes of observing the time-limit referred to in paragraph 1 of this Rule, the material date is the certified date of dispatch of the document or, if there is none, the actual date of receipt at the Registry.

---

1. As amended by the Court on 7 July 2003.

Rule 38A[1]

(Examination of matters of procedure)

Questions of procedure requiring a decision by the Chamber shall be considered simultaneously with the examination of the case, unless the President of the Chamber decides otherwise.

Rule 39

(Interim measures)

1. The Chamber or, where appropriate, its President may, at the request of a party or of any other person concerned, or of its own motion, indicate to the parties any interim measure which it considers should be adopted in the interests of the parties or of the proper conduct of the proceedings before it.
2. Notice of these measures shall be given to the Committee of Ministers.
3. The Chamber may request information from the parties on any matter connected with the implementation of any interim measure it has indicated.

Rule 40

(Urgent notification of an application)

In any case of urgency the Registrar, with the authorisation of the President of the Chamber, may, without prejudice to the taking of any other procedural steps and by any available means, inform a Contracting Party concerned in an application of the introduction of the application and of a summary of its objects.

Rule 41[2]

(Case priority)

Applications shall be dealt with in the order in which they become ready for examination. The Chamber or its President may, however, decide to give priority to a particular application.

Rule 42 (former 43)

(Joinder and simultaneous examination of applications)

1. The Chamber may, either at the request of the parties or of its own motion, order the joinder of two or more applications.

---

1. Inserted by the Court on 17 June and 8 July 2002.
2. As amended by the Court on 17 June and 8 July 2002.

2. The President of the Chamber may, after consulting the parties, order that the proceedings in applications assigned to the same Chamber be conducted simultaneously, without prejudice to the decision of the Chamber on the joinder of the applications.

Rule 43[1] (former 44)

(Striking out and restoration to the list)

1. The Court may at any stage of the proceedings decide to strike an application out of its list of cases in accordance with Article 37 of the Convention.

2. When an applicant Contracting Party notifies the Registrar of its intention not to proceed with the case, the Chamber may strike the application out of the Court's list under Article 37 of the Convention if the other Contracting Party or Parties concerned in the case agree to such discontinuance.

3. The decision to strike out an application which has been declared admissible shall be given in the form of a judgment. The President of the Chamber shall forward that judgment, once it has become final, to the Committee of Ministers in order to allow the latter to supervise, in accordance with Article 46 § 2 of the Convention, the execution of any undertakings which may have been attached to the discontinuance, friendly settlement or solution of the matter.

4. When an application has been struck out, the costs shall be at the discretion of the Court. If an award of costs is made in a decision striking out an application which has not been declared admissible, the President of the Chamber shall forward the decision to the Committee of Ministers.

5. The Court may restore an application to its list if it considers that exceptional circumstances justify such a course.

Rule 44[2]

(Third-party intervention)

1. (a) When notice of an application lodged under Article 34 of the Convention is given to the respondent Contracting Party under Rule 54 § 2 (b), a copy of the application shall at the same time be transmitted by the Registrar to any other Contracting Party one of whose nationals is an applicant in the case. The Registrar shall similarly notify any such Contracting Party of a decision to hold an oral hearing in the case.

(b) If a Contracting Party wishes to exercise its right under Article 36 § 1 of the Convention to submit written comments or to take part in a hearing, it shall so advise the Registrar in writing not later than twelve weeks after the transmission or notification referred to in the preceding sub-paragraph. Another time limit may be fixed by the President of the Chamber for exceptional reasons.

2. (a) Once notice of an application has been given to the respondent Contracting Party under Rule 51 § 1 or Rule 54 § 2 (b), the President of the Chamber may, in the interests of the proper administration of justice, as provided in Article 36 § 2 of the Convention, invite, or grant leave to, any Contracting Party which

---

1. As amended by the Court on 17 June and 8 July 2002 and on 7 July 2003.
2. As amended by the Court on 7 July 2003.

is not a party to the proceedings, or any person concerned who is not the applicant, to submit written comments or, in exceptional cases, to take part in a hearing.

(b) Requests for leave for this purpose must be duly reasoned and submitted in writing in one of the official languages as provided in Rule 34 § 4 not later than twelve weeks after notice of the application has been given to the respondent Contracting Party. Another time limit may be fixed by the President of the Chamber for exceptional reasons.

3. (a) In cases to be considered by the Grand Chamber the periods of time prescribed in the preceding paragraphs shall run from the notification to the parties of the decision of the Chamber under Rule 72 § 1 to relinquish jurisdiction in favour of the Grand Chamber or of the decision of the panel of the Grand Chamber under Rule 73 § 2 to accept a request by a party for referral of the case to the Grand Chamber.

(b) The time-limits laid down in this Rule may exceptionally be extended by the President of the Chamber if sufficient cause is shown.

4. Any invitation or grant of leave referred to in paragraph 2 (a) of this Rule shall be subject to any conditions, including time-limits, set by the President of the Chamber. Where such conditions are not complied with, the President may decide not to include the comments in the case file or to limit participation in the hearing to the extent that he or she considers appropriate.

5. Written comments submitted under this Rule shall be drafted in one of the official languages as provided in Rule 34 § 4. They shall be forwarded by the Registrar to the parties to the case, who shall be entitled, subject to any conditions, including time-limits, set by the President of the Chamber, to file written observations in reply or, where appropriate, to reply at the hearing.

Rule 44A[1]

(Duty to cooperate with the Court)

The parties have a duty to cooperate fully in the conduct of the proceedings and, in particular, to take such action within their power as the Court considers necessary for the proper administration of justice. This duty shall also apply to a Contracting State not party to the proceedings where such cooperation is necessary.

Rule 44B[1]

(Failure to comply with an order of the Court)

Where a party fails to comply with an order of the Court concerning the conduct of the proceedings, the President of the Chamber may take any steps which he or she considers appropriate.

---

1. Inserted by the Court on 13 December 2004.

Rule 44C[1]

(Failure to participate effectively)

1. Where a party fails to adduce evidence or provide information requested by the Court or to divulge relevant information of its own motion or otherwise fails to participate effectively in the proceedings, the Court may draw such inferences as it deems appropriate.

2. Failure or refusal by a respondent Contracting Party to participate effectively in the proceedings shall not, in itself, be a reason for the Chamber to discontinue the examination of the application.

Rule 44D[1]

(Inappropriate submissions by a party)

If the representative of a party makes abusive, frivolous, vexatious, misleading or prolix submissions, the President of the Chamber may exclude that representative from the proceedings, refuse to accept all or part of the submissions or make any other order which he or she considers it appropriate to make, without prejudice to Article 35 § 3 of the Convention.

Rule 44E[1]

(Failure to pursue an application)

In accordance with Article 37 § 1 (a) of the Convention, if an applicant Contracting Party or an individual applicant fails to pursue the application, the Chamber may strike the application out of the Court's list under Rule 43 of these Rules.

CHAPTER II
INSTITUTION OF PROCEEDINGS

Rule 45

(Signatures)

1. Any application made under Articles 33 or 34 of the Convention shall be submitted in writing and shall be signed by the applicant or by the applicant's representative.

2. Where an application is made by a non-governmental organisation or by a group of individuals, it shall be signed by those persons competent to represent that organisation or group. The Chamber or Committee concerned shall determine any question as to whether the persons who have signed an application are competent to do so.

3. Where applicants are represented in accordance with Rule 36, a power of attorney or written authority to act shall be supplied by their representative or representatives.

---

1. Inserted by the Court on 13 December 2004.

Rule 46

(Contents of an inter-State application)

Any Contracting Party or Parties intending to bring a case before the Court under Article 33 of the Convention shall file with the Registry an application setting out

(a) the name of the Contracting Party against which the application is made;

(b) a statement of the facts;

(c) a statement of the alleged violation(s) of the Convention and the relevant arguments;

(d) a statement on compliance with the admissibility criteria (exhaustion of domestic remedies and the six-month rule) laid down in Article 35 § 1 of the Convention;

(e) the object of the application and a general indication of any claims for just satisfaction made under Article 41 of the Convention on behalf of the alleged injured party or parties; and

(f) the name and address of the person(s) appointed as Agent;

and accompanied by

(g) copies of any relevant documents and in particular the decisions, whether judicial or not, relating to the object of the application.

Rule 47[1]

(Contents of an individual application)

1. Any application under Article 34 of the Convention shall be made on the application form provided by the Registry, unless the President of the Section concerned decides otherwise. It shall set out

(a) the name, date of birth, nationality, sex, occupation and address of the applicant;

(b) the name, occupation and address of the representative, if any;

(c) the name of the Contracting Party or Parties against which the application is made;

(d) a succinct statement of the facts;

(e) a succinct statement of the alleged violation(s) of the Convention and the relevant arguments;

(f) a succinct statement on the applicant's compliance with the admissibility criteria (exhaustion of domestic remedies and the six-month rule) laid down in Article 35 § 1 of the Convention; and

(g) the object of the application;

and be accompanied by

---

1. As amended by the Court on 17 June and 8 July 2002.

(h) copies of any relevant documents and in particular the decisions, whether judicial or not, relating to the object of the application.

2. Applicants shall furthermore

(a) provide information, notably the documents and decisions referred to in paragraph 1 (h) of this Rule, enabling it to be shown that the admissibility criteria (exhaustion of domestic remedies and the six-month rule) laid down in Article 35 § 1 of the Convention have been satisfied; and

(b) indicate whether they have submitted their complaints to any other procedure of international investigation or settlement.

3. Applicants who do not wish their identity to be disclosed to the public shall so indicate and shall submit a statement of the reasons justifying such a departure from the normal rule of public access to information in proceedings before the Court. The President of the Chamber may authorise anonymity in exceptional and duly justified cases.

4. Failure to comply with the requirements set out in paragraphs 1 and 2 of this Rule may result in the application not being examined by the Court.

5. The date of introduction of the application shall as a general rule be considered to be the date of the first communication from the applicant setting out, even summarily, the object of the application. The Court may for good cause nevertheless decide that a different date shall be considered to be the date of introduction.

6. Applicants shall keep the Court informed of any change of address and of all circumstances relevant to the application.

CHAPTER III
JUDGE RAPPORTEURS

Rule 48[1]

(Inter-State applications)

1. Where an application is made under Article 33 of the Convention, the Chamber constituted to consider the case shall designate one or more of its judges as Judge Rapporteur(s), who shall submit a report on admissibility when the written observations of the Contracting Parties concerned have been received.

2. The Judge Rapporteur(s) shall submit such reports, drafts and other documents as may assist the Chamber and its President in carrying out their functions.

Rule 49[2]

(Individual applications)

1. Where the material submitted by the applicant is on its own sufficient to disclose that the application is inadmissible or should be struck out of the list, the application shall be considered by a Committee unless there is some special reason to the contrary.

---

1. As amended by the Court on 17 June and 8 July 2002.
2. As amended by the Court on 4 July 2005.

2. Where an application is made under Article 34 of the Convention and its examination by a Chamber seems justified, the President of the Section to which the case has been assigned shall designate a judge as Judge Rapporteur, who shall examine the application.

3. In their examination of applications Judge Rapporteurs

(a) may request the parties to submit, within a specified time, any factual information, documents or other material which they consider to be relevant;

(b) shall, subject to the President of the Section directing that the case be considered by a Chamber, decide whether the application is to be considered by a Committee or by a Chamber;

(c) shall submit such reports, drafts and other documents as may assist the Chamber or its President in carrying out their functions.

Rule 50

(Grand Chamber proceedings)

Where a case has been submitted to the Grand Chamber either under Article 30 or under Article 43 of the Convention, the President of the Grand Chamber shall designate as Judge Rapporteur(s) one or, in the case of an inter-State application, one or more of its members.

CHAPTER IV
PROCEEDINGS ON ADMISSIBILITY

INTER-STATE APPLICATIONS

Rule 51[1]

(Assignment of applications and subsequent procedure)

1. When an application is made under Article 33 of the Convention, the President of the Court shall immediately give notice of the application to the respondent Contracting Party and shall assign the application to one of the Sections.

2. In accordance with Rule 26 § 1 (a), the judges elected in respect of the applicant and respondent Contracting Parties shall sit as *ex officio* members of the Chamber constituted to consider the case. Rule 30 shall apply if the application has been brought by several Contracting Parties or if applications with the same object brought by several Contracting Parties are being examined jointly under Rule 42.

3. On assignment of the case to a Section, the President of the Section shall constitute the Chamber in accordance with Rule 26 § 1 and shall invite the respondent Contracting Party to submit its observations in writing on the admissibility of the application. The observations so obtained shall be communicated by the Registrar to the applicant Contracting Party, which may submit written observations in reply.

---

1. As amended by the Court on 17 June and 8 July 2002.

4. Before the ruling on the admissibility of the application is given, the Chamber or its President may decide to invite the Parties to submit further observations in writing.

5. A hearing on the admissibility shall be held if one or more of the Contracting Parties concerned so requests or if the Chamber so decides of its own motion.

6. Before fixing the written and, where appropriate, oral procedure, the President of the Chamber shall consult the Parties.

INDIVIDUAL APPLICATIONS

Rule 52[1]

(Assignment of applications to the Sections)

1. Any application made under Article 34 of the Convention shall be assigned to a Section by the President of the Court, who in so doing shall endeavour to ensure a fair distribution of cases between the Sections.

2. The Chamber of seven judges provided for in Article 27 § 1 of the Convention shall be constituted by the President of the Section concerned in accordance with Rule 26 § 1.

3. Pending the constitution of a Chamber in accordance with paragraph 2 of this Rule, the President of the Section shall exercise any powers conferred on the President of the Chamber by these Rules.

Rule 53[2]

(Procedure before a Committee)

1. The judge elected in respect of a respondent Contracting Party, if not a member of the Committee, may be invited to attend the deliberations of the Committee.

2. In accordance with Article 28 of the Convention, the Committee may, by a unanimous vote, declare inadmissible an application or strike it out of the Court's list of cases where such a decision can be taken without further examination. This decision shall be final. The applicant shall be informed of the Committee's decision by letter.

3. If no decision pursuant to paragraph 2 of this Rule is taken, the application shall be forwarded to the Chamber constituted under Rule 52 § 2 to examine the case.

Rule 54[3]

(Procedure before a Chamber)

1. The Chamber may at once declare the application inadmissible or strike it out of the Court's list of cases.

2. Alternatively, the Chamber or its President may decide to

(a) request the parties to submit any factual information, documents or other material considered by the Chamber or its President to be relevant;

---

1. As amended by the Court on 17 June and 8 July 2002.
2. As amended by the Court on 17 June and 8 July 2002 and 4 July 2005.
3. As amended by the Court on 17 June and 8 July 2002.

(b) give notice of the application to the respondent Contracting Party and invite that Party to submit written observations on the application and, upon receipt thereof, invite the applicant to submit observations in reply;

(c) invite the parties to submit further observations in writing.

3. Before taking its decision on the admissibility, the Chamber may decide, either at the request of a party or of its own motion, to hold a hearing if it considers that the discharge of its functions under the Convention so requires. In that event, unless the Chamber shall exceptionally decide otherwise, the parties shall also be invited to address the issues arising in relation to the merits of the application.

Rule 54A[1]

(Joint examination of admissibility and merits)

1. When deciding to give notice of the application to the responding Contracting Party pursuant to Rule 54 § 2 (b), the Chamber may also decide to examine the admissibility and merits at the same time in accordance with Article 29 § 3 of the Convention. In such cases the parties shall be invited to include in their observations any submissions concerning just satisfaction and any proposals for a friendly settlement. The conditions laid down in Rules 60 and 62 shall apply *mutatis mutandis*.

2. If no friendly settlement or other solution is reached and the Chamber is satisfied, in the light of the parties' arguments, that the case is admissible and ready for a determination on the merits, it shall immediately adopt a judgment including the Chamber's decision on admissibility.

3. Where the Chamber considers it appropriate, it may, after informing the parties, proceed to the immediate adoption of a judgment incorporating the decision on admissibility without having previously applied the procedure referred to in § 1 above.

INTER-STATE AND INDIVIDUAL APPLICATIONS

Rule 55

(Pleas of inadmissibility)

Any plea of inadmissibility must, in so far as its character and the circumstances permit, be raised by the respondent Contracting Party in its written or oral observations on the admissibility of the application submitted as provided in Rule 51 or 54, as the case may be.

Rule 56[2]

(Decision of a Chamber)

1. The decision of the Chamber shall state whether it was taken unanimously or by a majority and shall be accompanied or followed by reasons.

---

1. Inserted by the Court on 17 June and 8 July 2002 and amended on 13 December 2004.
2. As amended by the Court on 17 June and 8 July 2002.

2. The decision of the Chamber shall be communicated by the Registrar to the applicant. It shall also be communicated to the Contracting Party or Parties concerned and to any third party where these have previously been informed of the application in accordance with the present Rules.

Rule 57[1]

(Language of the decision)

1. Unless the Court decides that a decision shall be given in both official languages, all decisions of Chambers shall be given either in English or in French.

2. Publication of such decisions in the official reports of the Court, as provided for in Rule 78, shall be in both official languages of the Court.

CHAPTER V

PROCEEDINGS AFTER THE ADMISSION OF AN APPLICATION

Rule 58[1]

(Inter-State applications)

1. Once the Chamber has decided to admit an application made under Article 33 of the Convention, the President of the Chamber shall, after consulting the Contracting Parties concerned, lay down the time-limits for the filing of written observations on the merits and for the production of any further evidence. The President may however, with the agreement of the Contracting Parties concerned, direct that a written procedure is to be dispensed with.

2. A hearing on the merits shall be held if one or more of the Contracting Parties concerned so requests or if the Chamber so decides of its own motion. The President of the Chamber shall fix the oral procedure.

Rule 59[1]

(Individual applications)

1. Once an application made under Article 34 of the Convention has been declared admissible, the Chamber or its President may invite the parties to submit further evidence and written observations.

2. Unless decided otherwise, the parties shall be allowed the same time for submission of their observations.

3. The Chamber may decide, either at the request of a party or of its own motion, to hold a hearing on the merits if it considers that the discharge of its functions under the Convention so requires.

---

1. As amended by the Court on 17 June and 8 July 2002.

4. The President of the Chamber shall, where appropriate, fix the written and oral procedure.

Rule 60[1]

(Claims for just satisfaction)

1. An applicant who wishes to obtain an award of just satisfaction under Article 41 of the Convention in the event of the Court finding a violation of his or her Convention rights must make a specific claim to that effect.

2. The applicant must submit itemised particulars of all claims, together with any relevant supporting documents, within the time-limit fixed for the submission of the applicant's observations on the merits unless the President of the Chamber directs otherwise.

3. If the applicant fails to comply with the requirements set out in the preceding paragraphs the Chamber may reject the claims in whole or in part.

4. The applicant's claims shall be transmitted to the respondent Government for comment.

Rule 61 deleted

Rule 62[2]

(Friendly settlement)

1. Once an application has been declared admissible, the Registrar, acting on the instructions of the Chamber or its President, shall enter into contact with the parties with a view to securing a friendly settlement of the matter in accordance with Article 38 § 1 (b) of the Convention. The Chamber shall take any steps that appear appropriate to facilitate such a settlement.

2. In accordance with Article 38 § 2 of the Convention, the friendly-settlement negotiations shall be confidential and without prejudice to the parties' arguments in the contentious proceedings. No written or oral communication and no offer or concession made in the framework of the attempt to secure a friendly settlement may be referred to or relied on in the contentious proceedings.

3. If the Chamber is informed by the Registrar that the parties have agreed to a friendly settlement, it shall, after verifying that the settlement has been reached on the basis of respect for human rights as defined in the Convention and the Protocols thereto, strike the case out of the Court's list in accordance with Rule 43 § 3.

4. Paragraphs 2 and 3 apply *mutatis mutandis* to the procedure under Rule 54A.

---

1. As amended by the Court on 13 December 2004.
2. As amended by the Court on 17 June and 8 July 2002.

CHAPTER VI
HEARINGS

Rule 63[1]

(Public character of hearings)

1. Hearings shall be public unless, in accordance with paragraph 2 of this Rule, the Chamber in exceptional circumstances decides otherwise, either of its own motion or at the request of a party or any other person concerned.

2. The press and the public may be excluded from all or part of a hearing in the interests of morals, public order or national security in a democratic society, where the interests of juveniles or the protection of the private life of the parties so require, or to the extent strictly necessary in the opinion of the Chamber in special circumstances where publicity would prejudice the interests of justice.

3. Any request for a hearing to be held in camera made under paragraph 1 of this Rule must include reasons and specify whether it concerns all or only part of the hearing.

Rule 64[1]

(Conduct of hearings)

1. The President of the Chamber shall organise and direct hearings and shall prescribe the order in which those appearing before the Chamber shall be called upon to speak.

2. Any Judge may put questions to any person appearing before the Chamber.

Rule 65[1]

(Failure to appear)

Where a party or any other person due to appear fails or declines to do so, the Chamber may, provided that it is satisfied that such a course is consistent with the proper administration of justice, nonetheless proceed with the hearing.

Rules 66 to 69 deleted

Rule 70[2]

(Verbatim record of a hearing)

1. If the President of the Chamber so directs, the Registrar shall be responsible for the making of a verbatim record of the hearing. Any such record shall include:

---

1. As amended by the Court on 7 July 2003.
2. As amended by the Court on 17 June and 8 July 2002.

(a) the composition of the Chamber;

(b) a list of those appearing before the Chamber;

(c) the text of the submissions made, questions put and replies given;

(d) the text of any ruling delivered during the hearing;

2. If all or part of the verbatim record is in non-official language, the Registrar shall arrange for its translation into one of the official languages.

3. The representatives of the parties shall receive a copy of the verbatim record in order that they may, subject to the control of the Registrar or the President of the Chamber, make corrections, but in no case may such corrections affect the sense and bearing of what was said. The Registrar shall lay down, in accordance with the instructions of the President of the Chamber, the time-limits granted for this purpose.

4. The verbatim record, once so corrected, shall be signed by the President of the Chamber and the Registrar and shall then constitute certified matters of record.

CHAPTER VII

PROCEEDINGS BEFORE THE GRAND CHAMBER

Rule 71[1]

(Applicability of procedural provisions)

1. Any provisions governing proceedings before the Chambers shall apply, *mutatis mutandis*, to proceedings before the Grand Chamber.

2. The powers conferred on a Chamber by Rules 54 § 3 and 59 § 3 in relation to the holding of a hearing may, in proceedings before the Grand Chamber, also be exercised by the President of the Grand Chamber.

Rule 72

(Relinquishment of jurisdiction by a Chamber in favour of the Grand Chamber)

1. In accordance with Article 30 of the Convention, where a case pending before a Chamber raises a serious question affecting the interpretation of the Convention or the Protocols thereto or where the resolution of a question before it might have a result inconsistent with a judgment previously delivered by the Court, the Chamber may, at any time before it has rendered its judgment, relinquish jurisdiction in favour of the Grand Chamber, unless one of the parties to the case has objected in accordance with paragraph 2 of this Rule. Reasons need not be given for the decision to relinquish.

2. The Registrar shall notify the parties of the Chamber's intention to relinquish jurisdiction. The parties shall have one month from the date of that notification within which to file at the Registry a duly reasoned objection. An objection which does not fulfil these conditions shall be considered invalid by the Chamber.

---

1. As amended by the Court on 17 June and 8 July 2002.

Rule 73

(Request by a party for referral of a case to the Grand Chamber)

1. In accordance with Article 43 of the Convention, any party to a case may exceptionally, within a period of three months from the date of delivery of the judgment of a Chamber, file in writing at the Registry a request that the case be referred to the Grand Chamber. The party shall specify in its request the serious question affecting the interpretation or application of the Convention or the Protocols thereto, or the serious issue of general importance, which in its view warrants consideration by the Grand Chamber.

2. A panel of five judges of the Grand Chamber constituted in accordance with Rule 24 § 5 shall examine the request solely on the basis of the existing case file. It shall accept the request only if it considers that the case does raise such a question or issue. Reasons need not be given for a refusal of the request.

3. If the panel accepts the request, the Grand Chamber shall decide the case by means of a judgment.

CHAPTER VIII
JUDGMENTS

Rule 74

(Contents of the judgment)

1. A judgment as referred to in Articles 42 and 44 of the Convention shall contain

(a) the names of the President and the other judges constituting the Chamber concerned, and the name of the Registrar or the Deputy Registrar;

(b) the dates on which it was adopted and delivered;

(c) a description of the parties;

(d) the names of the Agents, advocates or advisers of the parties;

(e) an account of the procedure followed;

(f) the facts of the case;

(g) a summary of the submissions of the parties;

(h) the reasons in point of law;

(i) the operative provisions;

(j) the decision, if any, in respect of costs;

(k) the number of judges constituting the majority;

(l) where appropriate, a statement as to which text is authentic.

2. Any judge who has taken part in the consideration of the case shall be entitled to annex to the judgment either a separate opinion, concurring with or dissenting from that judgment, or a bare statement of dissent.

Rule 75[1]

(Ruling on just satisfaction)

1. Where the Chamber finds that there has been a violation of the Convention or the Protocols thereto, it shall give in the same judgment a ruling on the application of Article 41 of the Convention if a specific claim has been submitted in accordance with Rule 60 and the question is ready for decision; if the question is not ready for decision, the Chamber shall reserve it in whole or in part and shall fix the further procedure.

2. For the purposes of ruling on the application of Article 41 of the Convention, the Chamber shall, as far as possible, be composed of those judges who sat to consider the merits of the case. Where it is not possible to constitute the original Chamber, the President of the Court shall complete or compose the Chamber by drawing lots.

3. The Chamber may, when affording just satisfaction under Article 41 of the Convention, direct that if settlement is not made within a specified time, interest is to be payable on any sums awarded.

4. If the Court is informed that an agreement has been reached between the injured party and the Contracting Party liable, it shall verify the equitable nature of the agreement and, where it finds the agreement to be equitable, strike the case out of the list in accordance with Rule 43 § 3.

Rule 76[2]

(Language of the judgment)

1. Unless the Court decides that a judgment shall be given in both official languages, all judgments shall be given either in English or in French.

2. Publication of such judgments in the official reports of the Court, as provided for in Rule 78, shall be in both official languages of the Court.

Rule 77

(Signature, delivery and notification of the judgment)

1. Judgments shall be signed by the President of the Chamber and the Registrar.

2. The judgment may be read out at a public hearing by the President of the Chamber or by another judge delegated by him or her. The Agents and representatives of the parties shall be informed in due time of the date of the hearing. Otherwise the notification provided for in paragraph 3 of this Rule shall constitute delivery of the judgment.

3. The judgment shall be transmitted to the Committee of Ministers. The Registrar shall send certified copies to the parties, to the Secretary General of the Council of Europe, to any third party and to any other person directly concerned. The original copy, duly signed and sealed, shall be placed in the archives of the Court.

---

1. As amended by the Court on 13 December 2004.
2. As amended by the Court on 17 June and 8 July 2002.

Rule 78

(Publication of judgments and other documents)

In accordance with Article 44 § 3 of the Convention, final judgments of the Court shall be published, under the responsibility of the Registrar, in an appropriate form. The Registrar shall in addition be responsible for the publication of official reports of selected judgments and decisions and of any document which the President of the Court considers it useful to publish.

Rule 79

(Request for interpretation of a judgment)

1. A party may request the interpretation of a judgment within a period of one year following the delivery of that judgment.
2. The request shall be filed with the Registry. It shall state precisely the point or points in the operative provisions of the judgment on which interpretation is required.
3. The original Chamber may decide of its own motion to refuse the request on the ground that there is no reason to warrant considering it. Where it is not possible to constitute the original Chamber, the President of the Court shall complete or compose the Chamber by drawing lots.
4. If the Chamber does not refuse the request, the Registrar shall communicate it to the other party or parties and shall invite them to submit any written comments within a time-limit laid down by the President of the Chamber. The President of the Chamber shall also fix the date of the hearing should the Chamber decide to hold one. The Chamber shall decide by means of a judgment.

Rule 80

(Request for revision of a judgment)

1. A party may, in the event of the discovery of a fact which might by its nature have a decisive influence and which, when a judgment was delivered, was unknown to the Court and could not reasonably have been known to that party, request the Court, within a period of six months after that party acquired knowledge of the fact, to revise that judgment.
2. The request shall mention the judgment of which revision is requested and shall contain the information necessary to show that the conditions laid down in paragraph 1 of this Rule have been complied with. It shall be accompanied by a copy of all supporting documents. The request and supporting documents shall be filed with the Registry.
3. The original Chamber may decide of its own motion to refuse the request on the ground that there is no reason to warrant considering it. Where it is not possible to constitute the original Chamber, the President of the Court shall complete or compose the Chamber by drawing lots.
4. If the Chamber does not refuse the request, the Registrar shall communicate it to the other party or parties and shall invite them to submit any written comments within a time-limit laid down by the President of the Chamber. The President of the Chamber shall also fix the date of the hearing should the Chamber decide to hold one. The Chamber shall decide by means of a judgment.

Rule 81

(Rectification of errors in decisions and judgments)

Without prejudice to the provisions on revision of judgments and on restoration to the list of applications, the Court may, of its own motion or at the request of a party made within one month of the delivery of a decision or a judgment, rectify clerical errors, errors in calculation or obvious mistakes.

CHAPTER IX
ADVISORY OPINIONS

Rule 82

In proceedings relating to advisory opinions the Court shall apply, in addition to the provisions of Articles 47, 48 and 49 of the Convention, the provisions which follow. It shall also apply the other provisions of these Rules to the extent to which it considers this to be appropriate.

Rule 83[1]

The request for an advisory opinion shall be filed with the Registrar. It shall state fully and precisely the question on which the opinion of the Court is sought, and also

(a) the date on which the Committee of Ministers adopted the decision referred to in Article 47 § 3 of the Convention;

(b) the names and addresses of the person or persons appointed by the Committee of Ministers to give the Court any explanations which it may require.

The request shall be accompanied by all documents likely to elucidate the question.

Rule 84[1]

1. On receipt of a request, the Registrar shall transmit a copy of it and of the accompanying documents to all members of the Court.
2. The Registrar shall inform the Contracting Parties that they may submit written comments on the request.

Rule 85[1]

1. The President of the Court shall lay down the time-limits for filing written comments or other documents.

---

1. As amended by the Court on 4 July 2005.

2. Written comments or other documents shall be filed with the Registrar. The Registrar shall transmit copies of them to all the members of the Court, to the Committee of Ministers and to each of the Contracting Parties.

Rule 86

After the close of the written procedure, the President of the Court shall decide whether the Contracting Parties which have submitted written comments are to be given an opportunity to develop them at an oral hearing held for the purpose.

Rule 87[1]

1. A Grand Chamber shall be constituted to consider the request for an advisory opinion.
2. If the Grand Chamber considers that the request is not within its competence as defined in Article 47 of the Convention, it shall so declare in a reasoned decision.

Rule 88[1]

1. Reasoned decisions and advisory opinions shall be given by a majority vote of the Grand Chamber. They shall mention the number of judges constituting the majority.
2. Any judge may, if he or she so desires, attach to the reasoned decision or advisory opinion of the Court either a separate opinion, concurring with or dissenting from reasoned decision or advisory opinion, or a bare statement of dissent.

Rule 89[1]

The reasoned decision or advisory opinion may be read out in one of the two official languages by the President of the Grand Chamber, or by another judge delegated by the President, at a public hearing, prior notice having been given to the Committee of Ministers and to each of the Contracting Parties. Otherwise the notification provided for in Rule 90 shall constitute delivery of the opinion or reasoned decision.

Rule 90[1]

The advisory opinion or reasoned decision shall be signed by the President of the Grand Chamber and by the Registrar. The original copy, duly signed and sealed, shall be placed in the archives of the Court. The Registrar shall send certified copies to the Committee of Ministers, to the Contracting Parties and to the Secretary General of the Council of Europe.

---

1. As amended by the Court on 4 July 2005.

CHAPTER X
LEGAL AID

Rule 91

1. The President of the Chamber may, either at the request of an applicant having lodged an application under Article 34 of the Convention or of his or her own motion, grant free legal aid to the applicant in connection with the presentation of the case from the moment when observations in writing on the admissibility of that application are received from the respondent Contracting Party in accordance with Rule 54 § 2 (b), or where the time-limit for their submission has expired.

2. Subject to Rule 96, where the applicant has been granted legal aid in connection with the presentation of his or her case before the Chamber, that grant shall continue in force for the purposes of his or her representation before the Grand Chamber.

Rule 92

Legal aid shall be granted only where the President of the Chamber is satisfied

(a) that it is necessary for the proper conduct of the case before the Chamber;

(b) that the applicant has insufficient means to meet all or part of the costs entailed.

Rule 93[1]

1. In order to determine whether or not applicants have sufficient means to meet all or part of the costs entailed, they shall be required to complete a form of declaration stating their income, capital assets and any financial commitments in respect of dependants, or any other financial obligations. The declaration shall be certified by the appropriate domestic authority or authorities.

2. The President of the Chamber may invite the Contracting Party concerned to submit its comments in writing.

3. After receiving the information mentioned in paragraph 1 of this Rule, the President of the Chamber shall decide whether or not to grant legal aid. The Registrar shall inform the parties accordingly.

Rule 94

1. Fees shall be payable to the advocates or other persons appointed in accordance with Rule 36 § 4. Fees may, where appropriate, be paid to more than one such representative.

2. Legal aid may be granted to cover not only representatives' fees but also travelling and subsistence expenses and other necessary expenses incurred by the applicant or appointed representative.

---

1. As amended by the Court on 29 May 2006.

Rule 95

On a decision to grant legal aid, the Registrar shall fix

(a) the rate of fees to be paid in accordance with the legal-aid scales in force;

(b) the level of expenses to be paid.

Rule 96

The President of the Chamber may, if satisfied that the conditions stated in Rule 92 are no longer fulfilled, revoke or vary a grant of legal aid at any time.

TITLE III
TRANSITIONAL RULES

Rules 97 and 98 deleted

Rule 99

(Relations between the Court and the Commission)

1. In cases brought before the Court under Article 5 §§ 4 and 5 of Protocol No. 11 to the Convention the Court may invite the Commission to delegate one or more of its members to take part in the consideration of the case before the Court.

2. In cases referred to in paragraph 1 of this Rule the Court shall take into consideration the report of the Commission adopted pursuant to former Article 31 of the Convention.

3. Unless the President of the Chamber decides otherwise, the said report shall be made available to the public through the Registrar as soon as possible after the case has been brought before the Court.

4. The remainder of the case file of the Commission, including all pleadings, in cases brought before the Court under Article 5 §§ 2 to 5 of Protocol No. 11 shall remain confidential unless the President of the Chamber decides otherwise.

5. In cases where the Commission has taken evidence but has been unable to adopt a report in accordance with former Article 31 of the Convention, the Court shall take into consideration the verbatim records, documentation and opinion of the Commission's delegations arising from such investigations.

Rule 100

(Chamber and Grand Chamber proceedings)

1. In cases referred to the Court under Article 5 § 4 of Protocol No. 11 to the Convention, a panel of the Grand Chamber constituted in accordance with Rule 24 § 6[1]

---

1. Former version, before 8 December 2000.

shall determine, solely on the basis of the existing case file, whether a Chamber or the Grand Chamber is to decide the case.

2. If the case is decided by a Chamber, the judgment of the Chamber shall, in accordance with Article 5 § 4 of Protocol No. 11, be final and Rule 73 shall be inapplicable.

3. Cases transmitted to the Court under Article 5 § 5 of Protocol No. 11 shall be forwarded by the President of the Court to the Grand Chamber.

4. For each case transmitted to the Grand Chamber under Article 5 § 5 of Protocol No. 11, the Grand Chamber shall be completed by judges designated by rotation within one of the groups mentioned in Rule 24 § 3[1], the cases being allocated to the groups on an alternate basis.

Rule 101

(Grant of legal aid)

Subject to Rule 96, in cases brought before the Court under Article 5 §§ 2 to 5 of Protocol No. 11 to the Convention, a grant of legal aid made to an applicant in the proceedings before the Commission or the former Court shall continue in force for the purposes of his or her representation before the Court.

Rule 102[2]

(Request for revision of a judgment)

1. Where a party requests revision of a judgment delivered by the former Court, the President of the Court shall assign the request to one of the Sections in accordance with the conditions laid down in Rule 51 or 52, as the case may be.

2. The President of the relevant Section shall, notwithstanding Rule 80 § 3, constitute a new Chamber to consider the request.

3. The Chamber to be constituted shall include as *ex officio* members

    (a) the President of the Section;

and, whether or not they are members of the relevant Section,

    (b) the judge elected in respect of any Contracting Party concerned or, if he or she is unable to sit, any judge appointed under Rule 29;

    (c) any judge of the Court who was a member of the original Chamber that delivered the judgment in the former Court.

    4. (a) The other members of the Chamber shall be designated by the President of the Section by means of a drawing of lots from among the members of the relevant Section.

       (b) The members of the Section who are not so designated shall sit in the case as substitute judges.

---

1. As amended by the Court on 12 December 2004.
2. As amended by the Court on 13 December 2004.

Rule 103

(Amendment or suspension of a Rule)

1. Any Rule may be amended upon a motion made after notice where such a motion is carried at the next session of the plenary Court by a majority of all the members of the Court. Notice of such a motion shall be delivered in writing to the Registrar at least one month before the session at which it is to be discussed. On receipt of such a notice of motion, the Registrar shall inform all members of the Court at the earliest possible moment.

2. A Rule relating to the internal working of the Court may be suspended upon a motion made without notice, provided that this decision is taken unanimously by the Chamber concerned. The suspension of a Rule shall in this case be limited in its operation to the particular purpose for which it was sought.

Rule 104[1]

(Entry into force of the Rules)

The present Rules shall enter into force on 1 November 1998.

Annex to the Rules[2]
(concerning investigations)

Rule A1

(Investigative measures)

1. The Chamber may, at the request of a party or of its own motion, adopt any investigative measure which it considers capable of clarifying the facts of the case. The Chamber may, *inter alia*, invite the parties to produce documentary evidence and decide to hear as a witness or expert or in any other capacity any person whose evidence or statements seem likely to assist it in carrying out its tasks.

2. The Chamber may also ask any person or institution of its choice to express an opinion or make a written report on any matter considered by it to be relevant to the case.

3. After a case has been declared admissible or, exceptionally, before the decision on admissibility, the Chamber may appoint one or more of its members or of the other judges

---

1. The amendments adopted on 8 December 2000 entered into force immediately. The amendments adopted on 17 June 2002 and 8 July 2002 entered into force on 1 October 2002. The amendments adopted on 7 July 2003 entered into force on 1 November 2003. The amendments adopted on 13 December 2004 entered into force on 1 March 2005. The amendments adopted on 4 July 2005 entered into force on 3 October 2005. The amendments adopted on 7 November 2005 entered into force on 1 December 2005.

2. Inserted by the Court on 7 July 2003.

of the Court, as its delegate or delegates, to conduct an inquiry, carry out an on-site investigation or take evidence in some other manner. The Chamber may also appoint any person or institution of its choice to assist the delegation in such manner as it sees fit.

4. The provisions of this Chapter concerning investigative measures by a delegation shall apply, *mutatis mutandis*, to any such proceedings conducted by the Chamber itself.

5. Proceedings forming part of any investigation by a Chamber or its delegation shall be held in camera, save in so far as the President of the Chamber or the head of the delegation decides otherwise.

6. The President of the Chamber may, as he or she considers appropriate, invite, or grant leave to, any third party to participate in an investigative measure. The President shall lay down the conditions of any such participation and may limit that participation if those conditions are not complied with.

Rule A2

(Obligations of the parties as regards investigative measures)

1. The applicant and any Contracting Party concerned shall assist the Court as necessary in implementing any investigative measures.

2. The Contracting Party on whose territory on-site proceedings before a delegation take place shall extend to the delegation the facilities and co-operation necessary for the proper conduct of the proceedings. These shall include, to the full extent necessary, freedom of movement within the territory and all adequate security arrangements for the delegation, for the applicant and for all witnesses, experts and others who may be heard by the delegation. It shall be the responsibility of the Contracting Party concerned to take steps to ensure that no adverse consequences are suffered by any person or organisation on account of any evidence given, or of any assistance provided, to the delegation.

Rule A3

(Failure to appear before a delegation)

Where a party or any other person due to appear fails or declines to do so, the delegation may, provided that it is satisfied that such a course is consistent with the proper administration of justice, nonetheless continue with the proceedings.

Rule A4

(Conduct of proceedings before a delegation)

1. The delegates shall exercise any relevant power conferred on the Chamber by the Convention or these Rules and shall have control of the proceedings before them.

2. The head of the delegation may decide to hold a preparatory meeting with the parties or their representatives prior to any proceedings taking place before the delegation.

Rule A5

(Convocation of witnesses, experts and of other persons to proceedings before a delegation)

1. Witnesses, experts and other persons to be heard by the delegation shall be summoned by the Registrar.

2. The summons shall indicate

(a) the case in connection with which it has been issued;

(b) the object of the inquiry, expert opinion or other investigative measure ordered by the Chamber or the President of the Chamber;

(c) any provisions for the payment of sums due to the person summoned.

3. The parties shall provide, in so far as possible, sufficient information to establish the identity and addresses of witnesses, experts or other persons to be summoned.

4. In accordance with Rule 37 § 2, the Contracting Party in whose territory the witness resides shall be responsible for servicing any summons sent to it by the Chamber for service. In the event of such service not being possible, the Contracting Party shall give reasons in writing. The Contracting Party shall further take all reasonable steps to ensure the attendance of persons summoned who are under its authority or control.

5. The head of the delegation may request the attendance of witnesses, experts and other persons during on-site proceedings before a delegation. The Contracting Party on whose territory such proceedings are held shall, if so requested, take all reasonable steps to facilitate that attendance.

6. Where a witness, expert or other person is summoned at the request or on behalf of a Contracting Party, the costs of their appearance shall be borne by that Party unless the Chamber decides otherwise. The costs of the appearance of any such person who is in detention in the Contracting Party on whose territory on-site proceedings before a delegation take place shall be borne by that Party unless the Chamber decides otherwise. In all other cases, the Chamber shall decide whether such costs are to be borne by the Council of Europe or awarded against the applicant or third party at whose request or on whose behalf the person appears. In all cases, such costs shall be taxed by the President of the Chamber.

Rule A6

(Oath or solemn declaration by witnesses and experts heard by a delegation)

1. After the establishment of the identity of a witness and before testifying, each witness shall take the oath or make the following solemn declaration:

"I swear"—or "I solemnly declare upon my honour and conscience"—"that I shall speak the truth, the whole truth and nothing but the truth."

This act shall be recorded in minutes.

2. After the establishment of the identity of the expert and before carrying out his or her task for the delegation, every expert shall take the oath or make the following solemn declaration:

"I swear"—or "I solemnly declare"—"that I will discharge my duty as an expert honourably and conscientiously."

This act shall be recorded in minutes.

Rule A7

(Hearing of witnesses, experts and other persons by a delegation)

1. Any delegate may put questions to the Agents, advocates or advisers of the parties, to the applicant, witnesses and experts, and to any other persons appearing before the delegation.

2. Witnesses, experts and other persons appearing before the delegation may, subject to the control of the head of the delegation, be examined by the Agents and advocates or advisers of the parties. In the event of an objection to a question put, the head of the delegation shall decide.

3. Save in exceptional circumstances and with the consent of the head of the delegation, witnesses, experts and other persons to be heard by a delegation will not be admitted to the hearing room before they give evidence.

4. The head of the delegation may make special arrangements for witnesses, experts or other persons to be heard in the absence of the parties where that is required for the proper administration of justice.

5. The head of the delegation shall decide in the event of any dispute arising from an objection to a witness or expert. The delegation may hear for information purposes a person who is not qualified to be heard as a witness or expert.

Rule A8

(Verbatim record of proceedings before a delegation)

1. A verbatim record shall be prepared by the Registrar of any proceedings concerning an investigative measure by a delegation. The verbatim record shall include:

(a) the composition of the delegation;

(b) a list of those appearing before the delegation, that is to say Agents, advocates and advisers of the parties taking part;

(c) the surname, forenames, description and address of each witness, expert or other person heard;

(d) the text of statements made, questions put and replies given;

(e) the text of any ruling delivered during the proceedings before the delegation or by the head of the delegation.

2. If all or part of the verbatim record is in a non-official language, the Registrar shall arrange for its translation into one of the official languages.

3. The representatives of the parties shall receive a copy of the verbatim record in order that they may, subject to the control of the Registrar or the head of the delegation, make corrections, but in no case may such corrections affect the sense and bearing of what was said. The Registrar shall lay down, in accordance with the instructions of the head of the delegation, the time-limits granted for this purpose.

4. The verbatim record, once so corrected, shall be signed by the head of the delegation and the Registrar and shall then constitute certified matters of record.

PRACTICE DIRECTION[1]
REQUESTS FOR INTERIM MEASURES

(Rule 39 of the Rules of Court)

Applicants or their legal representatives[2] who make a request for an interim measure pursuant to Rule 39 of the Rules of Court, should comply with the requirements set out below.

Failure to do so may mean that the Court will not be in a position to examine such requests properly and in good time.

I. Requests to be made by facsimile, e-mail or courier

Requests for interim measures under Rule 39 in urgent cases, particularly in extradition or deportation cases, should be sent by facsimile or e-mail[3] or by courier. The request should, where possible, be in one of the official languages of the Contracting Parties. All requests should bear the following title which should be written in bold on the face of the request:

"Rule 39—Urgent/Article 39—Urgent"

Requests by facsimile or e-mail should be sent during working hours[4] unless this is absolutely unavoidable. If sent by e-mail, a hard copy of the request should also be sent at the same time. Such requests should not be sent by ordinary post since there is a risk that they will not arrive at the Court in time to permit a proper examination.

If the Court has not responded to an urgent request under Rule 39 within the anticipated period of time, applicants or their representatives should follow up with a telephone call to the Registry during working hours.

II. Making requests in good time

Requests for interim measures should normally be received as soon as possible after the final domestic decision has been taken to enable the Court and its Registry to have sufficient time to examine the matter.

However, in extradition or deportation cases, where immediate steps may be taken to enforce removal soon after the final domestic decision has been given, it is advisable to make submissions and submit any relevant material concerning the request before the final decision is given.

---

1. Issued by the President of the Court in accordance with Rule 32 of the Rules of Court on 5 March 2003.
2. Full contact details should be provided.
3. To the e-mail address of a member of the Registry after having first made contact with that person by telephone. Telephone and facsimile numbers can be found on the Court's website (www.echr.coe.int).
4. Working hours are 8 am–6 pm, Monday–Friday. French time is one hour ahead of GMT.

Applicants and their representatives should be aware that it may not be possible to examine in a timely and proper manner requests which are sent at the last moment.

III. Accompanying information

It is essential that requests be accompanied by all necessary supporting documents, in particular relevant domestic court, tribunal or other decisions together with any other material which is considered to substantiate the applicant's allegations.

Where the case is already pending before the Court, reference should be made to the application number allocated to it.

In cases concerning extradition or deportation, details should be provided of the expected date and time of the removal, the applicant's address or place of detention and his or her official case-reference number.

Practice Direction[1]
Institution of Proceedings[2]

(individual applications under Article 34 of the Convention)

I. General

1. An application under Article 34 of the Convention must be submitted in writing. No application may be made by phone.

2. An application must be sent to the following address:

The Registrar
European Court of Human Rights
Council of Europe
F — 67075 STRASBOURG CEDEX.

3. An application should normally be made on the form[3] referred to in Rule 47 § 1 of the Rules of Court. However, an applicant may introduce his complaints in a letter.

4. If an application has not been submitted on the official form or an introductory letter does not contain all the information referred to in Rule 47, the Registry may ask the applicant to fill in the form. It should as a rule be returned within 6 weeks from the date of the Registry's letter.

5. Applicants may file an application by sending it by facsimile ("fax")[4]. However, they must send the signed original copy by post within 5 days following the dispatch by fax.

6. The date on which an application is received at the Court's Registry will be recorded by a receipt stamp.

---

1. Issued by the President of the Court in accordance with Rule 32 of the Rules of Court on 1 November 2003.
2. This practice direction supplements Rules 45 and 47 of the Rules of Court.
3. The relevant form can be downloaded from the Court's website (www.echr.coe.int).
4. Fax no. +00 33 (0)3 88 41 27 30; other facsimile numbers can be found on the Court's website.

7. An applicant should be aware that the date of the first communication setting out the subject-matter of the application is considered relevant for the purposes of compliance with the six-month rule in Article 35 § 1 of the Convention.

8. On receipt of the first communication setting out the subject-matter of the case, the Registry will open a file, whose number must be mentioned in all subsequent correspondence. Applicants will be informed thereof by letter. They may also be asked for further information or documents.

9. (a) An applicant should be diligent in conducting correspondence with the Court's Registry.

   (b) A delay in replying or failure to reply may be regarded as a sign that the applicant is no longer interested in pursuing his application.

10. Failure to satisfy the requirements laid down in Rule 47 §§ 1 and 2 and to provide further information at the Registry's request (see paragraph 8) may result in the application not being examined by the Court.

11. Where, within a year, an applicant has not returned an application form or has not answered any letter sent to him by the Registry, the file will be destroyed.

II. Form and contents

12. An application must contain all information required under Rule 47 and be accompanied by the documents referred to in paragraph 1 (h) of that Rule.

13. An application should be written legibly and, preferably, typed.

14. Where, exceptionally, an application exceeds 10 pages (excluding annexes listing documents), an applicant must also file a short summary.

15. Where applicants produce documents in support of the application, they should not submit original copies. The documents should be listed in order by date, numbered consecutively and given a concise description (e.g. letter, order, judgment, appeal, etc.).

16. An applicant who already has an application pending before the Court must inform the Registry accordingly, stating the application number.

17. (a) Where an applicant does not wish to have his or her identity disclosed, he or she should state the reasons for his or her request in writing, pursuant to Rule 47 § 3.

   (b) The applicant should also state whether, in the event of anonymity being authorised by the President of the Chamber, he or she wishes to be designated by his or her initials or by a single letter (e.g. "X", "Y", "Z", etc.).

PRACTICE DIRECTION[1]
WRITTEN PLEADINGS

I. Filing of pleadings

General

1. A pleading must be filed with the Registry within the time-limit fixed in accordance with Rule 38 and in the manner described in paragraph 2 of that Rule.

---

1. Issued by the President of the Court in accordance with Rule 32 of the Rules of Court on 1 November 2003.

2. The date on which a pleading or other document is received at the Court's Registry will be recorded on that document by a receipt stamp.

3. All pleadings, as well as all documents annexed thereto, should be submitted to the Court's Registry in 3 copies sent by post with 1 copy sent, if possible, by fax.

4. Secret documents should be filed by registered post.

5. Unsolicited pleadings shall not be admitted to the case file unless the President of the Chamber decides otherwise (see Rule 38 § 1).

Filing by facsimile

6. A party may file pleadings or other documents with the Court by sending them by facsimile ("fax")[1].

7. The name of the person signing a pleading must also be printed on it so that he or she can be identified.

II. Form and contents

Form

8. A pleading should include:

(a) the application number and the name of the case;

(b) a title indicating the nature of the content (e.g. observations on admissibility [and the merits]; reply to the Government's/the applicant's observations on admissibility [and the merits]; observations on the merits; additional observations on admissibility [and the merits]; memorial etc.).

9. A pleading should normally in addition

(a) be on A4 paper having a margin of not less than 3.5 cm wide;

(b) be wholly legible and, preferably, typed;

(c) have all numbers expressed as figures;

(d) have pages numbered consecutively;

(e) be divided into numbered paragraphs;

(f) be divided into chapters and/or headings corresponding to the form and style of the Court's decisions and judgments ("Facts" / "Domestic law [and practice]" / "Complaints" / "Law"; the latter chapter should be followed by headings entitled "Preliminary objection on ... "; "Alleged violation of Article ... ", as the case may be);

(g) place any answer to a question by the Court or to the other party's arguments under a separate heading;

(h) give a reference to every document or piece of evidence mentioned in the pleading and annexed thereto.

10. If a pleading exceeds 30 pages, a short summary should also be filed with it.

---

1. Fax no. +00 33 (0)3 88 41 27 30; other facsimile numbers can be found on the Court's website (www.echr.coe.int).

11. Where a party produces documents and/or other exhibits together with a pleading, every piece of evidence should be listed in a separate annex.

Contents

12. The parties' pleadings following communication of the application should include:

(a) any comments they wish to make on the facts of the case; however,

(i) if a party does not contest the facts as set out in the statement of facts prepared by the Registry, it should limit its observations to a brief statement to that effect;

(ii) if a party contests only part of the facts as set out by the Registry, or wishes to supplement them, it should limit its observations to those specific points;

(iii) if a party objects to the facts or part of the facts as presented by the other party, it should state clearly which facts are uncontested and limit its observations to the points in dispute;

(b) legal arguments relating first to admissibility and, secondly, to the merits of the case; however,

(i) if specific questions on a factual or legal point were put to a party, it should, without prejudice to Rule 55, limit its arguments to such questions;

(ii) if a pleading replies to arguments of the other party, submissions should refer to the specific arguments in the order prescribed above.

13. (a) The parties' pleadings following the admission of the application should include:

(i) a short statement confirming a party's position on the facts of the case as established in the decision on admissibility;

(ii) legal arguments relating to the merits of the case;

(iii) a reply to any specific questions on a factual or legal point put by the Court.

(b) An applicant party submitting claims for just satisfaction at the same time should do so in the manner described in the practice direction on filing just satisfaction claims.[1]

14. In view of the confidentiality of friendly-settlement proceedings (see Article 38 § 2 of the Convention and Rule 62 § 2), all submissions and documents filed within the framework of the attempt to secure a friendly settlement should be submitted separately from the written pleadings.

15. No reference to offers, concessions or other statements submitted in connection with the friendly settlement may be made in the pleadings filed in the contentious proceedings.

---

1. Not yet issued, for the time being see Rule 60.

III. Time-limits

General

16. It is the responsibility of each party to ensure that pleadings and any accompanying documents or evidence are delivered to the Court's Registry in time.

Extension of time-limits

17. A time-limit set under Rule 38 may be extended on request from a party.

18. A party seeking an extension of the time allowed for submission of a pleading must make a request as soon as it has become aware of the circumstances justifying such an extension and, in any event, before the expiry of the time-limit. It should state the reason for the delay.

19. If an extension is granted, it shall apply to all parties for which the relevant time-limit is running, including those which have not asked for it.

IV. Failure to comply with requirements for pleadings

20. Where a pleading has not been filed in accordance with the requirements set out in paragraphs 8–15 of this practice direction, the President of the Chamber may request the party concerned to resubmit the pleading in compliance with those requirements.

21. A failure to satisfy the conditions listed above may result in the pleading being considered not to have been properly lodged (see Rule 38 § 1 of the Rules of Court).

A: HUMAN RIGHTS ACT 1998
1998 CHAPTER 42

Arrangement of Sections

DEROGATIONS AND RESERVATIONS

JUDGES OF THE EUROPEAN COURT OF HUMAN RIGHTS

PARLIAMENTARY PROCEDURE

SUPPLEMENTAL

SCHEDULES

An Act to give further effect to rights and freedoms guaranteed under the European Convention on Human Rights; to make provision with respect to holders of certain judicial offices who become judges of the European Court of Human Rights; and for connected purposes.

[9TH NOVEMBER 1998]

BE IT ENACTED by the Queen's most Excellent Majesty, by and with the advice and consent of the Lords Spiritual and Temporal, and Commons, in this present Parliament assembled, and by the authority of the same, as follows:—

Introduction

The Convention Rights.

1.—(1) In this Act "the Convention rights" means the rights and fundamental freedoms set out in—

(a) Articles 2 to 12 and 14 of the Convention,

(b) Articles 1 to 3 of the First Protocol, and

(c) Articles 1 and 2 of the Sixth Protocol,

as read with Articles 16 to 18 of the Convention.

(2) Those Articles are to have effect for the purposes of this Act subject to any designated derogation or reservation (as to which see sections 14 and 15).

(3) The Articles are set out in Schedule 1.

(4) The Secretary of State may by order make such amendments to this Act as he considers appropriate to reflect the effect, in relation to the United Kingdom, of a protocol.

(5) In subsection (4) "protocol" means a protocol to the Convention—

(a) which the United Kingdom has ratified; or

(b) which the United Kingdom has signed with a view to ratification.

(6) No amendment may be made by an order under subsection (4) so as to come into force before the protocol concerned is in force in relation to the United Kingdom.

Interpretation of Convention rights.

2.—(1) A court or tribunal determining a question which has arisen in connection with a Convention right must take into account any—

(a) judgment, decision, declaration or advisory opinion of the European Court of Human Rights,

(b) opinion of the Commission given in a report adopted under Article 31 of the Convention,

(c) decision of the Commission in connection with Article 26 or 27(2) of the Convention, or

(d) decision of the Committee of Ministers taken under Article 46 of the Convention,

whenever made or given, so far as, in the opinion of the court or tribunal, it is relevant to the proceedings in which that question has arisen.

(2) Evidence of any judgment, decision, declaration or opinion of which account may have to be taken under this section is to be given in proceedings before any court or tribunal in such manner as may be provided by rules.

(3) In this section "rules" means rules of court or, in the case of proceedings before a tribunal, rules made for the purposes of this section—

(a) by the Lord Chancellor or the Secretary of State, in relation to any proceedings outside Scotland;

(b) by the Secretary of State, in relation to proceedings in Scotland; or

(c) by a Northern Ireland department, in relation to proceedings before a tribunal in Northern Ireland—

    (i) which deals with transferred matters; and
    (ii) for which no rules made under paragraph (a) are in force.

Legislation

Interpretation of legislation.

3.—(1) So far as it is possible to do so, primary legislation and subordinate legislation must be read and given effect in a way which is compatible with the Convention rights.

(2) This section—

(a) applies to primary legislation and subordinate legislation whenever enacted;

(b) does not affect the validity, continuing operation or enforcement of any incompatible primary legislation; and

(c) does not affect the validity, continuing operation or enforcement of any incompatible subordinate legislation if (disregarding any possibility of revocation) primary legislation prevents removal of the incompatibility.

Declaration of incompatibility.

4.—(1) Subsection (2) applies in any proceedings in which a court determines whether a provision of primary legislation is compatible with a Convention right.

(2) If the court is satisfied that the provision is incompatible with a Convention right, it may make a declaration of that incompatibility.

(3) Subsection (4) applies in any proceedings in which a court determines whether a provision of subordinate legislation, made in the exercise of a power conferred by primary legislation, is compatible with a Convention right.

(4) If the court is satisfied—

(a) that the provision is incompatible with a Convention right, and

(b) that (disregarding any possibility of revocation) the primary legislation concerned prevents removal of the incompatibility,

it may make a declaration of that incompatibility.

(5) In this section "court" means—

(a) the House of Lords;

(b) the Judicial Committee of the Privy Council;

(c) the Courts-Martial Appeal Court;

(d) in Scotland, the High Court of Justiciary sitting otherwise than as a trial court or the Court of Session;

(e) in England and Wales or Northern Ireland, the High Court or the Court of Appeal.

(6) A declaration under this section ("a declaration of incompatibility")—

(a) does not affect the validity, continuing operation or enforcement of the provision in respect of which it is given; and

(b) is not binding on the parties to the proceedings in which it is made.

Right of Crown to intervene.

5.—(1) Where a court is considering whether to make a declaration of incompatibility, the Crown is entitled to notice in accordance with rules of court.

(2) In any case to which subsection (1) applies—

(a) a Minister of the Crown (or a person nominated by him),

(b) a member of the Scottish Executive,

(c) a Northern Ireland Minister,

(d) a Northern Ireland department,

is entitled, on giving notice in accordance with rules of court, to be joined as a party to the proceedings.

(3) Notice under subsection (2) may be given at any time during the proceedings.

(4) A person who has been made a party to criminal proceedings (other than in Scotland) as the result of a notice under subsection (2) may, with leave, appeal to the House of Lords against any declaration of incompatibility made in the proceedings.

(5) In subsection (4)—

"criminal proceedings" includes all proceedings before the Courts-Martial Appeal Court; and

"leave" means leave granted by the court making the declaration of incompatibility or by the House of Lords.

Public authorities

Acts of public authorities.

6.—(1) It is unlawful for a public authority to act in a way which is incompatible with a Convention right.

(2) Subsection (1) does not apply to an act if—

(a) as the result of one or more provisions of primary legislation, the authority could not have acted differently; or

(b) in the case of one or more provisions of, or made under, primary legislation which cannot be read or given effect in a way which is compatible with the Convention rights, the authority was acting so as to give effect to or enforce those provisions.

(3) In this section "public authority" includes—

(a) a court or tribunal, and

(b) any person certain of whose functions are functions of a public nature,

but does not include either House of Parliament or a person exercising functions in connection with proceedings in Parliament.

(4) In subsection (3) "Parliament" does not include the House of Lords in its judicial capacity.

(5) In relation to a particular act, a person is not a public authority by virtue only of subsection (3)(b) if the nature of the act is private.

(6) "An act" includes a failure to act but does not include a failure to—

(a) introduce in, or lay before, Parliament a proposal for legislation; or

(b) make any primary legislation or remedial order.

Proceedings.

7.—(1) A person who claims that a public authority has acted (or proposes to act) in a way which is made unlawful by section 6(1) may—

(a) bring proceedings against the authority under this Act in the appropriate court or tribunal, or

(b) rely on the Convention right or rights concerned in any legal proceedings,

but only if he is (or would be) a victim of the unlawful act.

(2) In subsection (1)(a) "appropriate court or tribunal" means such court or tribunal as may be determined in accordance with rules; and proceedings against an authority include a counterclaim or similar proceeding.

(3) If the proceedings are brought on an application for judicial review, the applicant is to be taken to have a sufficient interest in relation to the unlawful act only if he is, or would be, a victim of that act.

(4) If the proceedings are made by way of a petition for judicial review in Scotland, the applicant shall be taken to have title and interest to sue in relation to the unlawful act only if he is, or would be, a victim of that act.

(5) Proceedings under subsection (1)(a) must be brought before the end of—

(a) the period of one year beginning with the date on which the act complained of took place; or

(b) such longer period as the court or tribunal considers equitable having regard to all the circumstances,

but that is subject to any rule imposing a stricter time limit in relation to the procedure in question.

(6) In subsection (1)(b) "legal proceedings" includes—

(a) proceedings brought by or at the instigation of a public authority; and

(b) an appeal against the decision of a court or tribunal.

(7) For the purposes of this section, a person is a victim of an unlawful act only if he would be a victim for the purposes of Article 34 of the Convention if proceedings were brought in the European Court of Human Rights in respect of that act.

(8) Nothing in this Act creates a criminal offence.

(9) In this section "rules" means—

(a) in relation to proceedings before a court or tribunal outside Scotland, rules made by the Lord Chancellor or the Secretary of State for the purposes of this section or rules of court,

(b) in relation to proceedings before a court or tribunal in Scotland, rules made by the Secretary of State for those purposes,

(c) in relation to proceedings before a tribunal in Northern Ireland—

(i) which deals with transferred matters; and

(ii) for which no rules made under paragraph (a) are in force,

rules made by a Northern Ireland department for those purposes,

and includes provision made by order under section 1 of the Courts and Legal Services Act 1990.

(10) In making rules, regard must be had to section 9.

(11) The Minister who has power to make rules in relation to a particular tribunal may, to the extent he considers it necessary to ensure that the tribunal can provide an appropriate remedy in relation to an act (or proposed act) of a public authority which is (or would be) unlawful as a result of section 6(1), by order add to—

(a) the relief or remedies which the tribunal may grant; or

(b) the grounds on which it may grant any of them.

(12) An order made under subsection (11) may contain such incidental, supplemental, consequential or transitional provision as the Minister making it considers appropriate.

(13) "The Minister" includes the Northern Ireland department concerned.

Judicial remedies.

8.—(1) In relation to any act (or proposed act) of a public authority which the court finds is (or would be) unlawful, it may grant such relief or remedy, or make such order, within its powers as it considers just and appropriate.

(2) But damages may be awarded only by a court which has power to award damages, or to order the payment of compensation, in civil proceedings.

(3) No award of damages is to be made unless, taking account of all the circumstances of the case, including—

(a) any other relief or remedy granted, or order made, in relation to the act in question (by that or any other court), and

(b) the consequences of any decision (of that or any other court) in respect of that act,

the court is satisfied that the award is necessary to afford just satisfaction to the person in whose favour it is made.

(4) In determining—

(a) whether to award damages, or

(b) the amount of an award,

the court must take into account the principles applied by the European Court of Human Rights in relation to the award of compensation under Article 41 of the Convention.

(5) A public authority against which damages are awarded is to be treated—

(a) in Scotland, for the purposes of section 3 of the Law Reform (Miscellaneous Provisions) (Scotland) Act 1940 as if the award were made in an action of damages in which the authority has been found liable in respect of loss or damage to the person to whom the award is made;

(b) for the purposes of the Civil Liability (Contribution) Act 1978 as liable in respect of damage suffered by the person to whom the award is made.

(6) In this section—

"court" includes a tribunal;
"damages" means damages for an unlawful act of a public authority; and
"unlawful" means unlawful under section 6(1).

Judicial acts.

9.—(1) Proceedings under section 7(1)(a) in respect of a judicial act may be brought only—

(a) by exercising a right of appeal;

(b) on an application (in Scotland a petition) for judicial review; or

(c) in such other forum as may be prescribed by rules.

(2) That does not affect any rule of law which prevents a court from being the subject of judicial review.

(3) In proceedings under this Act in respect of a judicial act done in good faith, damages may not be awarded otherwise than to compensate a person to the extent required by Article 5(5) of the Convention.

(4) An award of damages permitted by subsection (3) is to be made against the Crown; but no award may be made unless the appropriate person, if not a party to the proceedings, is joined.

(5) In this section—

"appropriate person" means the Minister responsible for the court concerned, or a person or government department nominated by him;
"court" includes a tribunal;
"judge" includes a member of a tribunal, a justice of the peace and a clerk or other officer entitled to exercise the jurisdiction of a court;
"judicial act" means a judicial act of a court and includes an act done on the instructions, or on behalf, of a judge; and
"rules" has the same meaning as in section 7(9).

Remedial action

Power to take remedial action.

10.—(1) This section applies if—

(a) a provision of legislation has been declared under section 4 to be incompatible with a Convention right and, if an appeal lies—

(i) all persons who may appeal have stated in writing that they do not intend to do so;

(ii) the time for bringing an appeal has expired and no appeal has been brought within that time; or

(iii) an appeal brought within that time has been determined or abandoned; or

(b) it appears to a Minister of the Crown or Her Majesty in Council that, having regard to a finding of the European Court of Human Rights made after the coming into force of this section in proceedings against the United Kingdom, a provision of legislation is incompatible with an obligation of the United Kingdom arising from the Convention.

(2) If a Minister of the Crown considers that there are compelling reasons for proceeding under this section, he may by order make such amendments to the legislation as he considers necessary to remove the incompatibility.

(3) If, in the case of subordinate legislation, a Minister of the Crown considers—

(a) that it is necessary to amend the primary legislation under which the subordinate legislation in question was made, in order to enable the incompatibility to be removed, and

(b) that there are compelling reasons for proceeding under this section,

he may by order make such amendments to the primary legislation as he considers necessary.

(4) This section also applies where the provision in question is in subordinate legislation and has been quashed, or declared invalid, by reason of incompatibility with a Convention right and the Minister proposes to proceed under paragraph 2(b) of Schedule 2.

(5) If the legislation is an Order in Council, the power conferred by subsection (2) or (3) is exercisable by Her Majesty in Council.

(6) In this section "legislation" does not include a Measure of the Church Assembly or of the General Synod of the Church of England.

(7) Schedule 2 makes further provision about remedial orders.

Other rights and proceedings

Safeguard for existing human rights.

11. A person's reliance on a Convention right does not restrict—

(a) any other right or freedom conferred on him by or under any law having effect in any part of the United Kingdom; or

(b) his right to make any claim or bring any proceedings which he could make or bring apart from sections 7 to 9.

Freedom of expression.

12.—(1) This section applies if a court is considering whether to grant any relief which, if granted, might affect the exercise of the Convention right to freedom of expression.

(2) If the person against whom the application for relief is made ("the respondent") is neither present nor represented, no such relief is to be granted unless the court is satisfied—

(a) that the applicant has taken all practicable steps to notify the respondent; or

(b) that there are compelling reasons why the respondent should not be notified.

(3) No such relief is to be granted so as to restrain publication before trial unless the court is satisfied that the applicant is likely to establish that publication should not be allowed.

(4) The court must have particular regard to the importance of the Convention right to freedom of expression and, where the proceedings relate to material which the respondent claims, or which appears to the court, to be journalistic, literary or artistic material (or to conduct connected with such material), to—

(a) the extent to which—

    (i) the material has, or is about to, become available to the public; or
    (ii) it is, or would be, in the public interest for the material to be published;

(b) any relevant privacy code.

(5) In this section—

"court" includes a tribunal; and
"relief" includes any remedy or order (other than in criminal proceedings).

Freedom of thought, conscience and religion.

13.—(1) If a court's determination of any question arising under this Act might affect the exercise by a religious organisation (itself or its members collectively) of the Convention right to freedom of thought, conscience and religion, it must have particular regard to the importance of that right.

(2) In this section "court" includes a tribunal.

Derogations and reservations

Derogations.

14.—(1) In this Act "designated derogation" means—

(a) the United Kingdom's derogation from Article 5(3) of the Convention; and

(b) any derogation by the United Kingdom from an Article of the Convention, or of any protocol to the Convention, which is designated for the purposes of this Act in an order made by the Secretary of State.

(2) The derogation referred to in subsection (1)(a) is set out in Part I of Schedule 3.

(3) If a designated derogation is amended or replaced it ceases to be a designated derogation.

(4) But subsection (3) does not prevent the Secretary of State from exercising his power under subsection (1)(b) to make a fresh designation order in respect of the Article concerned.

(5) The Secretary of State must by order make such amendments to Schedule 3 as he considers appropriate to reflect—

(a) any designation order; or

(b) the effect of subsection (3).

(6) A designation order may be made in anticipation of the making by the United Kingdom of a proposed derogation.

Reservations.

15.—(1) In this Act "designated reservation" means—

(a) the United Kingdom's reservation to Article 2 of the First Protocol to the Convention; and

(b) any other reservation by the United Kingdom to an Article of the Convention, or of any protocol to the Convention, which is designated for the purposes of this Act in an order made by the Secretary of State.

(2) The text of the reservation referred to in subsection (1)(a) is set out in Part II of Schedule 3.

(3) If a designated reservation is withdrawn wholly or in part it ceases to be a designated reservation.

(4) But subsection (3) does not prevent the Secretary of State from exercising his power under subsection (1)(b) to make a fresh designation order in respect of the Article concerned.

(5) The Secretary of State must by order make such amendments to this Act as he considers appropriate to reflect—

(a) any designation order; or

(b) the effect of subsection (3).

Period for which designated derogations have effect.

16.—(1) If it has not already been withdrawn by the United Kingdom, a designated derogation ceases to have effect for the purposes of this Act—

(a) in the case of the derogation referred to in section 14(1)(a), at the end of the period of five years beginning with the date on which section 1(2) came into force;

(b) in the case of any other derogation, at the end of the period of five years beginning with the date on which the order designating it was made.

(2) At any time before the period—

(a) fixed by subsection (1)(a) or (b), or

(b) extended by an order under this subsection,

comes to an end, the Secretary of State may by order extend it by a further period of five years.

(3) An order under section 14(1)(b) ceases to have effect at the end of the period for consideration, unless a resolution has been passed by each House approving the order.

(4) Subsection (3) does not affect—

(a) anything done in reliance on the order; or

(b) the power to make a fresh order under section 14(1)(b).

(5) In subsection (3) "period for consideration" means the period of forty days beginning with the day on which the order was made.

(6) In calculating the period for consideration, no account is to be taken of any time during which—

(a) Parliament is dissolved or prorogued; or

(b) both Houses are adjourned for more than four days.

(7) If a designated derogation is withdrawn by the United Kingdom, the Secretary of State must by order make such amendments to this Act as he considers are required to reflect that withdrawal.

Periodic review of designated reservations.

17.—(1) The appropriate Minister must review the designated reservation referred to in section 15(1)(a)—

(a) before the end of the period of five years beginning with the date on which section 1(2) came into force; and

(b) if that designation is still in force, before the end of the period of five years beginning with the date on which the last report relating to it was laid under subsection (3).

(2) The appropriate Minister must review each of the other designated reservations (if any)—

(a) before the end of the period of five years beginning with the date on which the order designating the reservation first came into force; and

(b) if the designation is still in force, before the end of the period of five years beginning with the date on which the last report relating to it was laid under subsection (3).

(3) The Minister conducting a review under this section must prepare a report on the result of the review and lay a copy of it before each House of Parliament.

Judges of the European Court of Human Rights

Appointment to European Court of Human Rights.

18.—(1) In this section "judicial office" means the office of—

(a) Lord Justice of Appeal, Justice of the High Court or Circuit judge, in England and Wales;

(b) judge of the Court of Session or sheriff, in Scotland;

(c) Lord Justice of Appeal, judge of the High Court or county court judge, in Northern Ireland.

(2) The holder of a judicial office may become a judge of the European Court of Human Rights ("the Court") without being required to relinquish his office.
(3) But he is not required to perform the duties of his judicial office while he is a judge of the Court.
(4) In respect of any period during which he is a judge of the Court—

(a) a Lord Justice of Appeal or Justice of the High Court is not to count as a judge of the relevant court for the purposes of section 2(1) or 4(1) of the Supreme Court Act 1981 (maximum number of judges) nor as a judge of the Supreme Court for the purposes of section 12(1) to (6) of that Act (salaries etc.);

(b) a judge of the Court of Session is not to count as a judge of that court for the purposes of section 1(1) of the Court of Session Act 1988 (maximum number of judges) or of section 9(1)(c) of the Administration of Justice Act 1973 ("the 1973 Act") (salaries etc.);

(c) a Lord Justice of Appeal or judge of the High Court in Northern Ireland is not to count as a judge of the relevant court for the purposes of section 2(1) or 3(1) of the Judicature (Northern Ireland) Act 1978 (maximum number of judges) nor as a judge of the Supreme Court of Northern Ireland for the purposes of section 9(1)(d) of the 1973 Act (salaries etc.);

(d) a Circuit judge is not to count as such for the purposes of section 18 of the Courts Act 1971 (salaries etc.);

(e) a sheriff is not to count as such for the purposes of section 14 of the Sheriff Courts (Scotland) Act 1907 (salaries etc.);

(f) a county court judge of Northern Ireland is not to count as such for the purposes of section 106 of the County Courts Act Northern Ireland) 1959 (salaries etc.).

(5) If a sheriff principal is appointed a judge of the Court, section 11(1) of the Sheriff Courts (Scotland) Act 1971 (temporary appointment of sheriff principal) applies, while he holds that appointment, as if his office is vacant.

(6) Schedule 4 makes provision about judicial pensions in relation to the holder of a judicial office who serves as a judge of the Court.

(7) The Lord Chancellor or the Secretary of State may by order make such transitional provision (including, in particular, provision for a temporary increase in the maximum number of judges) as he considers appropriate in relation to any holder of a judicial office who has completed his service as a judge of the Court.

Parliamentary procedure

Statements of compatibility.

19.—(1) A Minister of the Crown in charge of a Bill in either House of Parliament must, before Second Reading of the Bill—

(a) make a statement to the effect that in his view the provisions of the Bill are compatible with the Convention rights ("a statement of compatibility"); or

(b) make a statement to the effect that although he is unable to make a statement of compatibility the government nevertheless wishes the House to proceed with the Bill.

(2) The statement must be in writing and be published in such manner as the Minister making it considers appropriate.

Supplemental

Orders etc. under this Act.

20.—(1) Any power of a Minister of the Crown to make an order under this Act is exercisable by statutory instrument.

(2) The power of the Lord Chancellor or the Secretary of State to make rules (other than rules of court) under section 2(3) or 7(9) is exercisable by statutory instrument.

(3) Any statutory instrument made under section 14, 15 or 16(7) must be laid before Parliament.

(4) No order may be made by the Lord Chancellor or the Secretary of State under section 1(4), 7(11) or 16(2) unless a draft of the order has been laid before, and approved by, each House of Parliament.

(5) Any statutory instrument made under section 18(7) or Schedule 4, or to which subsection (2) applies, shall be subject to annulment in pursuance of a resolution of either House of Parliament.

(6) The power of a Northern Ireland department to make—

(a) rules under section 2(3)(c) or 7(9)(c), or

(b) an order under section 7(11),

is exercisable by statutory rule for the purposes of the Statutory Rules (Northern Ireland) Order 1979.

(7) Any rules made under section 2(3)(c) or 7(9)(c) shall be subject to negative resolution; and section 41(6) of the Interpretation Act Northern Ireland) 1954 (meaning of "subject to negative resolution") shall apply as if the power to make the rules were conferred by an Act of the Northern Ireland Assembly.

(8) No order may be made by a Northern Ireland department under section 7(11) unless a draft of the order has been laid before, and approved by, the Northern Ireland Assembly.

Interpretation, etc.

21.—(1) In this Act—

"amend" includes repeal and apply (with or without modifications);
"the appropriate Minister" means the Minister of the Crown having charge of the appropriate authorised government department (within the meaning of the Crown Proceedings Act 1947);
"the Commission" means the European Commission of Human Rights;
"the Convention" means the Convention for the Protection of Human Rights and Fundamental Freedoms, agreed by the Council of Europe at Rome on 4th November 1950 as it has effect for the time being in relation to the United Kingdom;
"declaration of incompatibility" means a declaration under section 4;
"Minister of the Crown" has the same meaning as in the Ministers of the Crown Act 1975;
"Northern Ireland Minister" includes the First Minister and the deputy First Minister in Northern Ireland;
"primary legislation" means any—

(a) public general Act;
(b) local and personal Act;
(c) private Act;
(d) Measure of the Church Assembly;
(e) Measure of the General Synod of the Church of England;
(f) Order in Council—

(i) made in exercise of Her Majesty's Royal Prerogative;
(ii) made under section 38(1)(a) of the Northern Ireland Constitution Act 1973 or the corresponding provision of the Northern Ireland Act 1998; or

(iii) amending an Act of a kind mentioned in paragraph (a), (b) or (c);

and includes an order or other instrument made under primary legislation (otherwise than by the National Assembly for Wales, a member of the Scottish Executive, a Northern Ireland Minister or a Northern Ireland department) to the extent to which it operates to bring one or more provisions of that legislation into force or amends any primary legislation;

"the First Protocol" means the protocol to the Convention agreed at Paris on 20th March 1952;

"the Sixth Protocol" means the protocol to the Convention agreed at Strasbourg on 28th April 1983;

"the Eleventh Protocol" means the protocol to the Convention (restructuring the control machinery established by the Convention) agreed at Strasbourg on 11th May 1994;

"remedial order" means an order under section 10;

"subordinate legislation" means any—

(a) Order in Council other than one—

    (i) made in exercise of Her Majesty's Royal Prerogative;

    (ii) made under section 38(1)(a) of the Northern Ireland Constitution Act 1973 or the corresponding provision of the Northern Ireland Act 1998; or

    (iii) amending an Act of a kind mentioned in the definition of primary legislation;

(b) Act of the Scottish Parliament;

(c) Act of the Parliament of Northern Ireland;

(d) Measure of the Assembly established under section 1 of the Northern Ireland Assembly Act 1973;

(e) Act of the Northern Ireland Assembly;

(f) order, rules, regulations, scheme, warrant, byelaw or other instrument made under primary legislation (except to the extent to which it operates to bring one or more provisions of that legislation into force or amends any primary legislation);

(g) order, rules, regulations, scheme, warrant, byelaw or other instrument made under legislation mentioned in paragraph (b), (c), (d) or (e) or made under an Order in Council applying only to Northern Ireland;

(h) order, rules, regulations, scheme, warrant, byelaw or other instrument made by a member of the Scottish Executive, a Northern Ireland Minister or a Northern Ireland department in exercise of prerogative or other executive functions of Her Majesty which are exercisable by such a person on behalf of Her Majesty;

"transferred matters" has the same meaning as in the Northern Ireland Act 1998; and

"tribunal" means any tribunal in which legal proceedings may be brought.

(2) The references in paragraphs (b) and (c) of section 2(1) to Articles are to Articles of the Convention as they had effect immediately before the coming into force of the Eleventh Protocol.

(3) The reference in paragraph (d) of section 2(1) to Article 46 includes a reference to Articles 32 and 54 of the Convention as they had effect immediately before the coming into force of the Eleventh Protocol.

(4) The references in section 2(1) to a report or decision of the Commission or a decision of the Committee of Ministers include references to a report or decision made as

provided by paragraphs 3, 4 and 6 of Article 5 of the Eleventh Protocol (transitional provisions).

(5) Any liability under the Army Act 1955, the Air Force Act 1955 or the Naval Discipline Act 1957 to suffer death for an offence is replaced by a liability to imprisonment for life or any less punishment authorised by those Acts; and those Acts shall accordingly have effect with the necessary modifications.

Short title, commencement, application and extent.

22.—(1) This Act may be cited as the Human Rights Act 1998.

(2) Sections 18, 20 and 21(5) and this section come into force on the passing of this Act.

(3) The other provisions of this Act come into force on such day as the Secretary of State may by order appoint; and different days may be appointed for different purposes.

(4) Paragraph (b) of subsection (1) of section 7 applies to proceedings brought by or at the instigation of a public authority whenever the act in question took place; but otherwise that subsection does not apply to an act taking place before the coming into force of that section.

(5) This Act binds the Crown.

(6) This Act extends to Northern Ireland.

(7) Section 21(5), so far as it relates to any provision contained in the Army Act 1955, the Air Force Act 1955 or the Naval Discipline Act 1957, extends to any place to which that provision extends

SCHEDULES

SCHEDULE 1

THE ARTICLES

PART I

THE CONVENTION

RIGHTS AND FREEDOMS

ARTICLE 2

Right to Life

1. Everyone's right to life shall be protected by law. No one shall be deprived of his life intentionally save in the execution of a sentence of a court following his conviction of a crime for which this penalty is provided by law.

2. Deprivation of life shall not be regarded as inflicted in contravention of this Article when it results from the use of force which is no more than absolutely necessary:

(a) in defence of any person from unlawful violence;

(b) in order to effect a lawful arrest or to prevent the escape of a person lawfully detained;

(c) in action lawfully taken for the purpose of quelling a riot or insurrection.

Article 3

Prohibition of Torture
No one shall be subjected to torture or to inhuman or degrading treatment or punishment.

Article 4

Prohibition of Slavery and Forced Labour
1. No one shall be held in slavery or servitude.
2. No one shall be required to perform forced or compulsory labour.
3. For the purpose of this Article the term "forced or compulsory labour" shall not include:

(a) any work required to be done in the ordinary course of detention imposed according to the provisions of Article 5 of this Convention or during conditional release from such detention;

(b) any service of a military character or, in case of conscientious objectors in countries where they are recognised, service exacted instead of compulsory military service;

(c) any service exacted in case of an emergency or calamity threatening the life or well-being of the community;

(d) any work or service which forms part of normal civic obligations.

Article 5

Right to Liberty and Security
1. Everyone has the right to liberty and security of person. No one shall be deprived of his liberty save in the following cases and in accordance with a procedure prescribed by law:

(a) the lawful detention of a person after conviction by a competent court;

(b) the lawful arrest or detention of a person for non-compliance with the lawful order of a court or in order to secure the fulfilment of any obligation prescribed by law;

(c) the lawful arrest or detention of a person effected for the purpose of bringing him before the competent legal authority on reasonable suspicion of having committed an offence or when it is reasonably considered necessary to prevent his committing an offence or fleeing after having done so;

(d) the detention of a minor by lawful order for the purpose of educational supervision or his lawful detention for the purpose of bringing him before the competent legal authority;

(e) the lawful detention of persons for the prevention of the spreading of infectious diseases, of persons of unsound mind, alcoholics or drug addicts or vagrants;

(f) the lawful arrest or detention of a person to prevent his effecting an unauthorised entry into the country or of a person against whom action is being taken with a view to deportation or extradition.

2. Everyone who is arrested shall be informed promptly, in a language which he understands, of the reasons for his arrest and of any charge against him.

3. Everyone arrested or detained in accordance with the provisions of paragraph 1(c) of this Article shall be brought promptly before a judge or other officer authorised by law to exercise judicial power and shall be entitled to trial within a reasonable time or to release pending trial. Release may be conditioned by guarantees to appear for trial.

4. Everyone who is deprived of his liberty by arrest or detention shall be entitled to take proceedings by which the lawfulness of his detention shall be decided speedily by a court and his release ordered if the detention is not lawful.

5. Everyone who has been the victim of arrest or detention in contravention of the provisions of this Article shall have an enforceable right to compensation.

ARTICLE 6

Right to a Fair Trial

1. In the determination of his civil rights and obligations or of any criminal charge against him, everyone is entitled to a fair and public hearing within a reasonable time by an independent and impartial tribunal established by law. Judgment shall be pronounced publicly but the press and public may be excluded from all or part of the trial in the interest of morals, public order or national security in a democratic society, where the interests of juveniles or the protection of the private life of the parties so require, or to the extent strictly necessary in the opinion of the court in special circumstances where publicity would prejudice the interests of justice.

2. Everyone charged with a criminal offence shall be presumed innocent until proved guilty according to law.

3. Everyone charged with a criminal offence has the following minimum rights:

(a) to be informed promptly, in a language which he understands and in detail, of the nature and cause of the accusation against him;

(b) to have adequate time and facilities for the preparation of his defence;

(c) to defend himself in person or through legal assistance of his own choosing or, if he has not sufficient means to pay for legal assistance, to be given it free when the interests of justice so require;

(d) to examine or have examined witnesses against him and to obtain the attendance and examination of witnesses on his behalf under the same conditions as witnesses against him;

(e) to have the free assistance of an interpreter if he cannot understand or speak the language used in court.

Article 7

No Punishment without Law
1. No one shall be held guilty of any criminal offence on account of any act or omission which did not constitute a criminal offence under national or international law at the time when it was committed. Nor shall a heavier penalty be imposed than the one that was applicable at the time the criminal offence was committed.
2. This Article shall not prejudice the trial and punishment of any person for any act or omission which, at the time when it was committed, was criminal according to the general principles of law recognised by civilised nations.

Article 8

Right to Respect for Private and Family Life
1. Everyone has the right to respect for his private and family life, his home and his correspondence.
2. There shall be no interference by a public authority with the exercise of this right except such as is in accordance with the law and is necessary in a democratic society in the interests of national security, public safety or the economic well-being of the country, for the prevention of disorder or crime, for the protection of health or morals, or for the protection of the rights and freedoms of others.

Article 9

Freedom of Thought, Conscience and Religion
1. Everyone has the right to freedom of thought, conscience and religion; this right includes freedom to change his religion or belief and freedom, either alone or in community with others and in public or private, to manifest his religion or belief, in worship, teaching, practice and observance.
2. Freedom to manifest one's religion or beliefs shall be subject only to such limitations as are prescribed by law and are necessary in a democratic society in the interests of public safety, for the protection of public order, health or morals, or for the protection of the rights and freedoms of others.

Article 10

Freedom of Expression
1. Everyone has the right to freedom of expression. This right shall include freedom to hold opinions and to receive and impart information and ideas without interference by public authority and regardless of frontiers. This Article shall not prevent States from requiring the licensing of broadcasting, television or cinema enterprises.
2. The exercise of these freedoms, since it carries with it duties and responsibilities, may be subject to such formalities, conditions, restrictions or penalties as are prescribed by law and are necessary in a democratic society, in the interests of national security, territorial integrity or public safety, for the prevention of disorder or crime, for the protection of health or morals, for the protection of the reputation or rights of others, for preventing the disclosure of information received in confidence, or for maintaining the authority and impartiality of the judiciary.

ARTICLE 11

Freedom of Assembly and Association
1. Everyone has the right to freedom of peaceful assembly and to freedom of association with others, including the right to form and to join trade unions for the protection of his interests.
2. No restrictions shall be placed on the exercise of these rights other than such as are prescribed by law and are necessary in a democratic society in the interests of national security or public safety, for the prevention of disorder or crime, for the protection of health or morals or for the protection of the rights and freedoms of others. This Article shall not prevent the imposition of lawful restrictions on the exercise of these rights by members of the armed forces, of the police or of the administration of the State.

ARTICLE 12

Right to Marry
Men and women of marriageable age have the right to marry and to found a family, according to the national laws governing the exercise of this right.

ARTICLE 14

Prohibition of Discrimination
The enjoyment of the rights and freedoms set forth in this Convention shall be secured without discrimination on any ground such as sex, race, colour, language, religion, political or other opinion, national or social origin, association with a national minority, property, birth or other status.

ARTICLE 16

Restrictions on Political Activity of Aliens
Nothing in Articles 10, 11 and 14 shall be regarded as preventing the High Contracting Parties from imposing restrictions on the political activity of aliens.

ARTICLE 17

Prohibition of Abuse of Rights
Nothing in this Convention may be interpreted as implying for any State, group or person any right to engage in any activity or perform any act aimed at the destruction of any of the rights and freedoms set forth herein or at their limitation to a greater extent than is provided for in the Convention.

ARTICLE 18

Limitation on Use of Restrictions on Rights
The restrictions permitted under this Convention to the said rights and freedoms shall not be applied for any purpose other than those for which they have been prescribed.

PART II

THE FIRST PROTOCOL

ARTICLE 1

Protection of Property
Every natural or legal person is entitled to the peaceful enjoyment of his possessions. No one shall be deprived of his possessions except in the public interest and subject to the conditions provided for by law and by the general principles of international law.

The preceding provisions shall not, however, in any way impair the right of a State to enforce such laws as it deems necessary to control the use of property in accordance with the general interest or to secure the payment of taxes or other contributions or penalties.

ARTICLE 2

Right to Education
No person shall be denied the right to education. In the exercise of any functions which it assumes in relation to education and to teaching, the State shall respect the right of parents to ensure such education and teaching in conformity with their own religious and philosophical convictions.

ARTICLE 3

Right to Free Elections
The High Contracting Parties undertake to hold free elections at reasonable intervals by secret ballot, under conditions which will ensure the free expression of the opinion of the people in the choice of the legislature.

PART III

THE SIXTH PROTOCOL

ARTICLE 1

Abolition of the Death Penalty
The death penalty shall be abolished. No one shall be condemned to such penalty or executed.

ARTICLE 2

Death Penalty in Time of War
A State may make provision in its law for the death penalty in respect of acts committed in time of war or of imminent threat of war; such penalty shall be applied only in the

instances laid down in the law and in accordance with its provisions. The State shall communicate to the Secretary General of the Council of Europe the relevant provisions of that law.

SCHEDULE 2

REMEDIAL ORDERS

Orders

1.—(1) A remedial order may—

(a) contain such incidental, supplemental, consequential or transitional provision as the person making it considers appropriate;

(b) be made so as to have effect from a date earlier than that on which it is made;

(c) make provision for the delegation of specific functions;

(d) make different provision for different cases.

(2) The power conferred by sub-paragraph (1)(a) includes—

(a) power to amend primary legislation (including primary legislation other than that which contains the incompatible provision); and

(b) power to amend or revoke subordinate legislation (including subordinate legislation other than that which contains the incompatible provision).

(3) A remedial order may be made so as to have the same extent as the legislation which it affects.

(4) No person is to be guilty of an offence solely as a result of the retrospective effect of a remedial order.

Procedure

2. No remedial order may be made unless—

(a) a draft of the order has been approved by a resolution of each House of Parliament made after the end of the period of 60 days beginning with the day on which the draft was laid; or

(b) it is declared in the order that it appears to the person making it that, because of the urgency of the matter, it is necessary to make the order without a draft being so approved.

Orders laid in draft

3.—(1) No draft may be laid under paragraph 2(a) unless—

(a) the person proposing to make the order has laid before Parliament a document which contains a draft of the proposed order and the required information; and

(b) the period of 60 days, beginning with the day on which the document required by this sub-paragraph was laid, has ended.

(2) If representations have been made during that period, the draft laid under paragraph 2(a) must be accompanied by a statement containing—

(a) a summary of the representations; and

(b) if, as a result of the representations, the proposed order has been changed, details of the changes.

Urgent cases

4.—(1) If a remedial order ("the original order") is made without being approved in draft, the person making it must lay it before Parliament, accompanied by the required information, after it is made.

(2) If representations have been made during the period of 60 days beginning with the day on which the original order was made, the person making it must (after the end of that period) lay before Parliament a statement containing—

(a) a summary of the representations; and

(b) if, as a result of the representations, he considers it appropriate to make changes to the original order, details of the changes.

(3) If sub-paragraph (2)(b) applies, the person making the statement must—

(a) make a further remedial order replacing the original order; and

(b) lay the replacement order before Parliament.

(4) If, at the end of the period of 120 days beginning with the day on which the original order was made, a resolution has not been passed by each House approving the original or replacement order, the order ceases to have effect (but without that affecting anything previously done under either order or the power to make a fresh remedial order).

Definitions

5. In this Schedule—

"representations" means representations about a remedial order (or proposed remedial order) made to the person making (or proposing to make) it and includes any relevant Parliamentary report or resolution; and
"required information" means—

(a) an explanation of the incompatibility which the order (or proposed order) seeks to remove, including particulars of the relevant declaration, finding or order; and

(b) a statement of the reasons for proceeding under section 10 and for making an order in those terms.

Calculating periods

6. In calculating any period for the purposes of this Schedule, no account is to be taken of any time during which—

(a) Parliament is dissolved or prorogued; or

(b) both Houses are adjourned for more than four days.

SCHEDULE 3

DEROGATION AND RESERVATION

PART I

DEROGATION

The 1988 notification

The United Kingdom Permanent Representative to the Council of Europe presents his compliments to the Secretary General of the Council, and has the honour to convey the following information in order to ensure compliance with the obligations of Her Majesty's Government in the United Kingdom under Article 15(3) of the Convention for the Protection of Human Rights and Fundamental Freedoms signed at Rome on 4 November 1950.

There have been in the United Kingdom in recent years campaigns of organised terrorism connected with the affairs of Northern Ireland which have manifested themselves in activities which have included repeated murder, attempted murder, maiming, intimidation and violent civil disturbance and in bombing and fire raising which have resulted in death, injury and widespread destruction of property. As a result, a public emergency within the meaning of Article 15(1) of the Convention exists in the United Kingdom.

The Government found it necessary in 1974 to introduce and since then, in cases concerning persons reasonably suspected of involvement in terrorism connected with the affairs of Northern Ireland, or of certain offences under the legislation, who have been detained for 48 hours, to exercise powers enabling further detention without charge, for periods of up to five days, on the authority of the Secretary of State. These powers are at present to be found in Section 12 of the Prevention of Terrorism (Temporary Provisions) Act 1984, Article 9 of the Prevention of Terrorism (Supplemental Temporary Provisions) Order 1984 and Article 10 of the Prevention of Terrorism (Supplemental Temporary Provisions) (Northern Ireland) Order 1984.

Section 12 of the Prevention of Terrorism (Temporary Provisions) Act 1984 provides for a person whom a constable has arrested on reasonable grounds of suspecting him to be guilty of an offence under Section 1, 9 or 10 of the Act, or to be or to have been involved in terrorism connected with the affairs of Northern Ireland, to be detained in right of the arrest for up to 48 hours and thereafter, where the Secretary of State extends the detention period, for up to a further five days. Section 12 substantially re-enacted Section 12 of the Prevention of Terrorism (Temporary Provisions) Act 1976 which, in turn, substantially re-enacted Section 7 of the Prevention of Terrorism (Temporary Provisions) Act 1974.

Article 10 of the Prevention of Terrorism (Supplemental Temporary Provisions) (Northern Ireland) Order 1984 (SI 1984/417) and Article 9 of the Prevention of Terrorism (Supplemental Temporary Provisions) Order 1984 (SI 1984/418) were both made under Sections 13 and 14 of and Schedule 3 to the 1984 Act and substantially re-enacted powers of detention in Orders made under the 1974 and 1976 Acts. A person who is being examined under Article 4 of either Order on his arrival in, or on seeking to leave, Northern Ireland or Great Britain for the purpose of determining whether he is or has been involved in terrorism connected with the affairs of Northern Ireland, or whether there are grounds for suspecting that he has committed an offence under Section 9 of the 1984 Act, may be detained under Article 9 or 10, as appropriate, pending the conclusion of his examination.

The period of this examination may exceed 12 hours if an examining officer has reasonable grounds for suspecting him to be or to have been involved in acts of terrorism connected with the affairs of Northern Ireland.

Where such a person is detained under the said Article 9 or 10 he may be detained for up to 48 hours on the authority of an examining officer and thereafter, where the Secretary of State extends the detention period, for up to a further five days.

In its judgment of 29 November 1988 in the Case of Brogan and Others, the European Court of Human Rights held that there had been a violation of Article 5(3) in respect of each of the applicants, all of whom had been detained under Section 12 of the 1984 Act. The Court held that even the shortest of the four periods of detention concerned, namely four days and six hours, fell outside the constraints as to time permitted by the first part of Article 5(3). In addition, the Court held that there had been a violation of Article 5(5) in the case of each applicant.

Following this judgment, the Secretary of State for the Home Department informed Parliament on 6 December 1988 that, against the background of the terrorist campaign, and the over-riding need to bring terrorists to justice, the Government did not believe that the maximum period of detention should be reduced. He informed Parliament that the Government were examining the matter with a view to responding to the judgment. On 22 December 1988, the Secretary of State further informed Parliament that it remained the Government's wish, if it could be achieved, to find a judicial process under which extended detention might be reviewed and where appropriate authorised by a judge or other judicial officer. But a further period of reflection and consultation was necessary before the Government could bring forward a firm and final view.

Since the judgment of 29 November 1988 as well as previously, the Government have found it necessary to continue to exercise, in relation to terrorism connected with the affairs of Northern Ireland, the powers described above enabling further detention without charge for periods of up to 5 days, on the authority of the Secretary of State, to the extent strictly required by the exigencies of the situation to enable necessary enquiries and investigations properly to be completed in order to decide whether criminal proceedings should be instituted. To the extent that the exercise of these powers may be inconsistent with the obligations imposed by the Convention the Government has availed itself of the right of derogation conferred by Article 15(1) of the Convention and will continue to do so until further notice.

Dated 23 December 1988.

The 1989 notification

The United Kingdom Permanent Representative to the Council of Europe presents his compliments to the Secretary General of the Council, and has the honour to convey the following information.

In his communication to the Secretary General of 23 December 1988, reference was made to the introduction and exercise of certain powers under section 12 of the Prevention of Terrorism (Temporary Provisions) Act 1984, Article 9 of the Prevention of Terrorism (Supplemental Temporary Provisions) Order 1984 and Article 10 of the Prevention of Terrorism (Supplemental Temporary Provisions) (Northern Ireland) Order 1984.

These provisions have been replaced by section 14 of and paragraph 6 of Schedule 5 to the Prevention of Terrorism (Temporary Provisions) Act 1989, which make comparable provision. They came into force on 22 March 1989. A copy of these provisions is enclosed.

The United Kingdom Permanent Representative avails himself of this opportunity to renew to the Secretary General the assurance of his highest consideration.
23 March 1989.

PART II

RESERVATION

At the time of signing the present (First) Protocol, I declare that, in view of certain provisions of the Education Acts in the United Kingdom, the principle affirmed in the second sentence of Article 2 is accepted by the United Kingdom only so far as it is compatible with the provision of efficient instruction and training, and the avoidance of unreasonable public expenditure.

Dated 20 March 1952
Made by the United Kingdom Permanent Representative to the Council of Europe.

SCHEDULE 4

JUDICIAL PENSIONS

Duty to make orders about pensions

1.—(1) The appropriate Minister must by order make provision with respect to pensions payable to or in respect of any holder of a judicial office who serves as an ECHR judge.

(2) A pensions order must include such provision as the Minister making it considers is necessary to secure that—

(a) an ECHR judge who was, immediately before his appointment as an ECHR judge, a member of a judicial pension scheme is entitled to remain as a member of that scheme;

(b) the terms on which he remains a member of the scheme are those which would have been applicable had he not been appointed as an ECHR judge; and

(c) entitlement to benefits payable in accordance with the scheme continues to be determined as if, while serving as an ECHR judge, his salary was that which would (but for section 18(4)) have been payable to him in respect of his continuing service as the holder of his judicial office.

Contributions

2. A pensions order may, in particular, make provision—

(a) for any contributions which are payable by a person who remains a member of a scheme as a result of the order, and which would otherwise be payable by deduction from his salary, to be made otherwise than by deduction from his salary as an ECHR judge; and

(b) for such contributions to be collected in such manner as may be determined by the administrators of the scheme.

Amendments of other enactments

3. A pensions order may amend any provision of, or made under, a pensions Act in such manner and to such extent as the Minister making the order considers necessary or expedient to ensure the proper administration of any scheme to which it relates.

Definitions

4. In this Schedule—

"appropriate Minister" means—

   (a) in relation to any judicial office whose jurisdiction is exercisable exclusively in relation to Scotland, the Secretary of State; and
   (b) otherwise, the Lord Chancellor;

"ECHR judge" means the holder of a judicial office who is serving as a judge of the Court;

"judicial pension scheme" means a scheme established by and in accordance with a pensions Act;

"pensions Act" means—

   (a) the County Courts Act Northern Ireland) 1959;
   (b) the Sheriffs' Pensions (Scotland) Act 1961;
   (c) the Judicial Pensions Act 1981; or
   (d) the Judicial Pensions and Retirement Act 1993; and

"pensions order" means an order made under paragraph 1.

B: THE CRIMINAL APPEAL (AMENDMENT) RULES 2000

S.I. 2000 No. 2036

Made	*25th July 2000*
Laid before Parliament	*27th July 2000*
Coming into force	*2nd October 2000*

We, the Crown Court Rule Committee, in exercise of the powers conferred on us by sections 84(1), 84(2) and 86 of the Supreme Court Act 1981 and section 5 of the Human Rights Act 1998 hereby makes the following Rules:

Citation and commencement

1. These Rules may be cited as the Criminal Appeal (Amendment) Rules 2000 and shall come into force on 2nd October 2000.

Amendment of Criminal Appeal Rules 1968

2. The Criminal Appeal Rules 1968 shall be amended as follows—

(a) in rule 2, after paragraph (2)(a) there shall be inserted—

"(aa) A notice of the grounds of appeal or application set out in Form 3 shall include notice—

(i) of any application to be made to the court for a declaration of incompatibility under section 4 of the Human Rights Act 1998; or
(ii) of any issue for the court to decide which may lead to the court making such a declaration.

(ab) Where the grounds of appeal or application include notice in accordance with paragraph (aa) above, a copy of the notice shall be served on the prosecutor by the appellant".

(b) after rule 14 there shall be inserted—

"**Human Rights Act**
14A.—(1) The court shall not consider making a declaration of incompatibility under section 4 of the Human Rights Act 1998 unless it has given written notice to the Crown.

(2) Where notice has been given to the Crown, a Minister, or other person entitled under the Human Rights Act 1998 to be joined as a party, shall be so joined on giving written notice to the court.

(3) A notice given under paragraph (1) above shall be given to—

(a) the person named in the list published under section 17(1) of the Crown Proceedings Act 1947; or
(b) in the case of doubt as to whether any and if so which of those departments is appropriate, the Treasury Solicitor.

(4) A notice given under paragraph (1) above, shall provide an outline of the issues in the case and specify—

(a) the prosecutor and appellant;

(b) the date, judge and court of the trial in the proceedings from which the appeal lies;

(c) the provision of primary legislation and the Convention right under question.

(5) Any consideration of whether a declaration of incompatibility should be made, shall be adjourned for—

(a) 21 days from the date of the notice given under paragraph (1) above; or

(b) such other period (specified in the notice), as the court shall allow in order that the relevant Minister or other person, may seek to be joined and prepare his case.

(6) Unless the court otherwise directs, the Minister or other person entitled under the Human Rights Act 1998 to be joined as a party shall, if he is to be joined, give written notice to the court and every other party.

(7) Where a Minister of the Crown has nominated a person to be joined as a party by virtue of section 5(2)(a) of the Human Rights Act 1998, a notice under paragraph (6) above shall be accompanied by a written nomination signed by or on behalf of the Minister.".

(c) in rule 15 after paragraph (1)(d) there shall be inserted—

"(e) in the case of a declaration of incompatibility under section 4 of the Human Rights Act 1998, the declaration shall be served on—

(i) all of the parties to the proceedings; and

(ii) where a Minister of the Crown has not been joined as a party, the Crown (in accordance with rule 14A(3) above)".

Irvine of Lairg,
C.

Harry Woolf,
C. J.

L. Dickinson

Charles Harris

Master Mckenzie

Dated 25th July 2000

INDEX

[889]